Barron's How to Prepare for the College-Level Examination Program

CLEP

General Examinations

Sixth Edition

ENGLISH COMPOSITION
William C. Doster, Editor
Formerly of College of DuPage
Glen Ellyn, Illinois

HUMANITIES
Ruth Ward
Miami-Dade Community College
Miami, Florida

MATHEMATICS
Shirley O. Hockett
Ithaca College
Ithaca, New York

NATURAL SCIENCES
Adrian W. Poitras
Formerly of Miami-Dade Community College
Miami, Florida

SOCIAL SCIENCES—HISTORY
Robert Bjork
Formerly of George Peabody College for Teachers
Nashville, Tennessee

Barron's Educational Series, Inc.
New York / London / Toronto / Sydney

Library of Congress Catalog Card No. 90-31599
International Standard Book No. 0-8120-4348-0

Library of Congress Cataloging-in-Publication Data

Barron's how to prepare for the college-level examination program, CLEP, general examinations/William C. Doster, editor...[et al.]. — 6th ed.
p. cm.
ISBN 0-8120-4348-0
1. College-level examinations—Study guides. I. Doster, William C. II. Title: How to prepare for the college-level examination program, CLEP, general examinations. III. Title: CLEP.
LB2353.68.B37 1990
378′, 1664—dc20 90-31599
CIP

PRINTED IN THE UNITED STATES OF AMERICA

012 100 9 8 7 6 5 4 3 2 1

TABLE OF CONTENTS

ACKNOWLEDGMENTS

CLEP test directions selected from *The College Board Guide to the CLEP Examination,* College Entrance Examinations Board (1987). Reprinted by permission of Educational Testing Service, the copyright owner of the test directions.

Permission to reprint the above material does not constitute review or endorsement by Educational Testing Service or the College Board of this publication as a whole or of any questions or testing information it may contain.

Photographic Credits

Grateful acknowledgment is made to the following photographers, agents, and museums for permission to reprint their materials: British Crown Copyright (reproduced with the permission of the Controller of Her Britannic Majesty's Stationery Office); Hirmer Fotoarchiv Munchen; Jerry Frank; Marlborough Gallery (Estate of David Smith); Metropolitan Museum of Art (Rogers Fund); Metropolitan Museum of Art (Levi Hale Willard Bequest); Metropolitan Museum of Art (Harry G.C. Packard Collection of Asian Art); Metropolitan Museum of Art (Marquand Collection); Metropolitan Museum of Art (bequest of Benjamin Altman); Metropolitan Museum of Art (Michael C. Rockefeller Memorial Collection); Metropolitan Museum of Art (Annenberg Fund, Inc., Gift, and Fletcher, Rogers & Louis V. Bell Funds, and gift of J. Piermont Morgan, by exchange); Metropolitan Museum of Art (Fletcher Fund, Rogers Fund, and bequest of Miss Adelaide Milton de Groot); Mexican-National Tourist Council; Museum of Modern Art (on extended loan from the artist); Museum of Modern Art (acquired through the Lillie P. Bliss Bequest); Museum of Primitive Art; National Gallery of Art (Andrew Mellon Collection); Photo Alinari; Roger Viollet; Solomon R. Guggenheim Museum; Whitney Museum of American Art.

CHAPTER

1

An Introduction to the College-Level Examination Program

The College Entrance Examination Board and Educational Testing Service developed the College-Level Examination Program (CLEP) for a variety of purposes:

1. Many adults were returning to the classroom after a number of years working or in the home rearing a family. During these years, these people continued their educational growth in many ways: reading magazines and other periodicals, watching television, joining discussion groups, reading books, and often just thinking about what had happened to them during these years. On their return to college, these students wanted a valid, standardized examination to demonstrate their self-development; and the colleges wanted an examination in order to be able to advise students properly about possible courses of study and often about the level of difficulty the students might want to attempt.

2. Since 1945, the number of locally controlled two-year colleges has more than tripled, so that in some states over half of all freshmen and sophomores enrolled in college were enrolled in a two-year institution. Since these colleges are, for the most part, autonomous and develop curriculums to suit the needs of their own communities, and since many of their graduates want to transfer to an upper division college or university, there was a problem: how could the receiving institution be sure of the quality of applicants for admission? The CLEP General Examinations battery provides scores which a college might consider in its decision to accept or reject an applicant.

3. For one reason or another, many students attend educational institutions which are not accredited by one of the regional accrediting associations. Often the lack of accreditation is a technical matter which in no way reflects upon the quality of instruction obtainable there; but if the student wants to transfer any or all of his credits to another college, the receiving college needs some instrument to validate that earlier education.

4. Some government agencies have determined that a standardized test covering a variety of subject areas often reveals more about a person applying for a position or for a promotion from one position to another than a transcript of grades or a personal interview. Also, such a required test makes all applicants equal, for their scores are theirs alone and cannot be qualified by prejudices which might influence an interviewer.

5. Many people, interested in self-education, would like to know how

they rate on a comparative scale developed by scoring the CLEP General Examinations of thousands of individuals all over the country. They may never want to attend a college or university, but they are interested in their own growth and development through their own activities.

6. Many students who have come through excellent high schools wish to skip one or more required courses in nearly every college's curriculum: English composition, social sciences, various natural sciences, and basic mathematics. Some colleges now accept certain scores on the CLEP General Examinations sections as demonstration of a student's competence in these areas and do not require him or her to enroll in required courses.

For these reasons, and to aid these individuals and institutions, the CLEP battery was developed by panels of scholars and teachers in five broad subject-matter fields.

The Content of the CLEP General Examinations Battery

The CLEP General Examinations cover the material taught in introductory courses students are often required to take during the first two years of college study. General Examinations are available in the following areas: English Composition, Humanities, Mathematics, Natural Sciences, and Social Sciences and History.

Each examination is in two separately timed sections, according to the following table.

CONTENTS OF GENERAL EXAMINATIONS BATTERY

(NOTE: Percentages are approximate in every instance and may vary from test to test.)

TEST	SECTION	CONTENT OR ITEM TYPES	TIME/NUMBER OF QUESTIONS
English Composition	I	35–40% Usage 35–40% Sentence Correction 25–30% Construction Shift	45 minutes 55 questions
	II (all-multiple-choice version)	60–65% Paragraph redrafting or revising 35–40% Construction Shift	45 minutes 40 questions
	II (essay version)	Written Composition	45 minutes
Humanities	I & II	50% Literature 10% Drama 15–20% Poetry 10–15% Fiction 10% Nonfiction 50% Fine Arts 20% Visual Arts (painting, sculpture, etc.) 15% Music 10% Performing Arts (film, dance, etc.) 5% Architecture	45 minutes each section 75 questions each section
Note: On the Humanities examination, questions from all 8 categories are mixed together.			

TEST	SECTION	CONTENT OR ITEM TYPES	TIME/NUMBER OF QUESTIONS
Mathematics	I (Basic Skills and Concepts)	30% Arithmetic 35% Algebra 15–20% Geometry 15–20% Data Interpretation (graphs and charts)	30 minutes 40 questions
	II (Content)	10% Sets 10% Logic 30% Real Number System 20% Functions and Their Graphs 15% Probability and Statistics 15% Miscellaneous Topics	60 minutes 50 questions
Natural Sciences	I	50% Biological Science 10% Origin and evolution of life, classification of organisms 10% Cell organization, cell division, chemical nature of the gene, bioenergetics, biosynthesis 20% Structure, function, and development in organisms; patterns of heredity 10% Concepts of population biology with emphasis on ecology	45 minutes 60 questions
	II	50% Physical Science 7% Atomic and nuclear structure and properties, elementary particles, nuclear reactions 10% Chemical elements, compounds and reactions; molecular structure and bonding 12% Heat, thermodynamics, and states of matter; classical mechanics; relativity 4% Electricity and magnetism, waves, light and sound 7% The universe: galaxies, stars, the solar system 10% The Earth: atmosphere, hydrosphere, structure, properties, surface features, geological processes, history	45 minutes 60 questions

TEST	SECTION	CONTENT OR ITEM TYPES			TIME/NUMBER OF QUESTIONS
Social Sciences and History	I & II	35%	History		45 minutes each section
			10–15%	United States History	60–65 questions each section
			10–15%	Western Civilization	
			5–10%	African/Asian Civilizations	
		65%	Social Sciences		
			25–30%	Sociology	
			15–20%	Economics	
			15–20%	Political Science	
			3–5%	Social Psychology	
Note: On the Social Sciences and History examination, questions from all 7 categories are mixed together.					

The emphasis of each of the sections of the battery is on the general principles of the subject area being tested, not the mere facts anyone might remember from a specific course. More specific discussion of examination coverage is given in each of the five major parts of this book. In general, however, it is possible to say that the whole battery covers what anyone might be expected to know from the first two years of college work or the equivalent. Most colleges have a required series of courses which provide the type of general information and educational experience that every educated person should have as he or she goes into a specialized area in the third year, and the CLEP General Examinations battery does not go beyond the content of these "general education" courses, as they are so often called. Obviously, not every college provides the same content in each of these courses, and some schools have no such "general education" requirements. Those who have been following their own plans for their own education may find themselves deficient in one area but very good in another, and for most purposes, it is the overall, total score of each test which is meaningful.

Note: NO ONE IS REQUIRED TO TAKE ALL FIVE EXAMINATIONS IN THE CLEP BATTERY UNLESS THE COLLEGE WILL ACCEPT ALL FIVE FOR CREDIT. ANYONE MAY TAKE ONE OR MORE OF THE GENERAL EXAMINATIONS, AND IT IS CERTAINLY NOT ADVISABLE FOR ANYONE TO PLAN TO TAKE MORE THAN TWO ON ANY TESTING DAY.

Organization of the CLEP Examinations

On all of the CLEP General Examinations except the Mathematics each question is a multiple-choice type with five choices given; the questions on the Mathematics Examination have only four answer choices. Only one answer is possible for each question. Often the student's reading comprehension is tested indirectly in all the tests, for he or she must be sure to understand the question before attempting to answer it. There are no "trick" questions, however, for each item has been carefully screened by teachers in the subject field working with test construction experts from Educational Testing Service. An answer sheet will be provided at the time the examination is given, and the examinee should be very careful to follow instructions exactly, or the answers will not be registered by the machine which does the scoring by an optical scanning method. The answer sheet consists of rows of small ovals, and to indicate an answer, the examinee should fill in the appropriate oval completely.

FOR EXAMPLE:

An apple is

(A) a fruit (B) an animal (C) a flower (D) a fish (E) a reptile ● Ⓑ Ⓒ Ⓓ Ⓔ

The obvious answer is A; therefore, A should be filled in completely.

There are separate answer sheets for each examination, and all should be returned to the supervisor of the examination when he or she calls for them.

The Scoring of the Examinations

For each of the examinations in the CLEP General Examination battery (except English Composition), a total score and two sub-scores are provided:

English Composition: a single score
Humanities: sub-scores for Fine Arts and Literature, as well as a total score
Mathematics: sub-scores for Basic Skills and Concepts and for Content, as well as a total score
Natural Sciences: sub-scores for Biological Sciences and Physical Sciences, as well as a total score
Social Sciences–History: sub-scores for Social Sciences and History, as well as a total score

The result sheet that will be sent to the examinee will list these thirteen scores, scaled to a range of (a low of) 200 to (a high of) 800 for the total scores, and a range of 20 to 80 for the sub-scores. Average scores and sub-scores are considered to be 500 and 50, respectively.

Caution: THERE IS NO SUCH THING AS A PASSING OR A FAILING SCORE ON THE CLEP GENERAL EXAMINATIONS BATTERY.

The College Entrance Examination Board merely provides the examinations and the scoring of these examinations; how any school or college interprets these scores is the sole responsibility of the particular institution. Nor does the College Entrance Examination Board offer "credit" for certain scores on the CLEP battery. Before anyone takes the tests, it would be wise to consult the institution which has requested the test to know exactly what will be done with the scores and how that institution will evaluate them for its own purposes.

Penalty for Guessing: The total scores and the sub-scores are derived by subtracting a percentage of the number of incorrect answers from the number of correct answers given on a test; this figure is converted to the scaled score. Thus, there is a penalty for guessing answers if one guesses incorrectly; and pure guessing, that is answering when one has no idea of the correct answer, will probably lower the score on the test. However, if the process of elimination discards one or two of the listed choices, the examinee might consider choosing among the remaining ones. Omitted answers are not counted in this computation.

No one is expected to finish any one of the examinations in the CLEP General Examinations battery within the time limit; therefore if you do not finish, don't worry too much about it. Correct answers to about one-half of the questions on any examination will provide a score above the average score obtained by college sophomores from whose scores the scales were developed.

At the time of the examination, you will be asked to fill out a form which indicates to whom your scores should be sent; if at any time you wish additional transcripts of these scores, they may be obtained by sending $8 for each transcript to the CLEP Transcript Service, P.O. Box 6600, Princeton, New Jersey 08541-6600.

How to Arrange to Take the CLEP Examinations

Educational Testing Service has established test centers at major colleges in all parts of the United States, and information on when and where the CLEP battery is available may be obtained by writing directly to Educational Testing Service, Princeton, New Jersey 08540; by consulting the admissions officer or academic counselling office at any college; or by writing or calling one of the College Entrance Examination Board regional offices listed below:

New England

(Connecticut, Maine, Massachusetts, New Hampshire, Rhode Island, Vermont)
College Board Regional Office
470 Totten Pond Road
Waltham, MA 02154
(617) 890-9150

Middle States

(Delaware, District of Columbia, Maryland, New Jersey, New York, Pennsylvania)
College Board Regional Office
Suite 410, 3440 Market Street
Philadelphia, PA 19104
(215) 387-7600

South

(Alabama, Florida, Georgia, Kentucky, Louisiana, Mississippi, North Carolina, South Carolina, Tennessee, Virginia)
College Board Regional Office
Suite 250, 2970 Clairmont Road
Atlanta, GA 30329
(404) 636-9465

Southwest

(Arkansas, New Mexico, Oklahoma, Texas)
College Board Regional Office
Suite 400, 701 Brazos
Austin, TX 78701
(512) 472-0231

Midwest

(Illinois, Indiana, Iowa, Kansas, Michigan, Minnesota, Missouri, Nebraska, North Dakota, Ohio, South Dakota, West Virginia, Wisconsin)

College Board Regional Office
Suite 401, 1800 Sherman Avenue
Evanston, IL 60201-3715
(708) 866-1700

West

(Alaska, Arizona, California, Colorado, Hawaii, Idaho, Montana, Nevada, Oregon, Utah, Washington, Wyoming)

College Board Regional Office
Suite 480, 2099 Gateway Place
San Jose, CA 95110-1017
(408) 452-1400

or

College Board Regional Office
Suite 900, 4155 East Jewell Avenue
Denver, CO 80222
(303) 759-1800

Subject Examinations

There are a number of special examinations in the College-Level Examinations Program that test the content of specific college courses, such as chemistry, English literature, or world history. Information on these course examinations is also available from College Board Regional Offices or from college admissions officers or college academic advising officers. Many colleges will now permit students to submit scores on these specific course examinations for transcript credit, but these specialized tests are not related to the CLEP General Examinations battery.

Final Caution

Before you plan to take the CLEP battery, consult the person at the institution to which you will direct the scores be sent. You should know exactly how the scores will be interpreted, what uses will be made of the scores, and what specific total scores or sub-scores are required by that institution for admission or for validation of any prior educational experiences. Let us repeat: NEITHER THE COLLEGE ENTRANCE EXAMINATION BOARD NOR EDUCATIONAL TESTING SERVICE EVALUATES THE SCORES YOU RECEIVE; THAT EVALUATION IS THE SOLE PROVINCE OF THE INSTITUTION TO WHICH THE SCORES WILL BE SUBMITTED. Since most institutions have different policies on these matters, important to you, you should have that information before you take the examinations.

Note: The format and content of the CLEP General Examinations Battery are changed periodically, and you should write or call the CEEB regional office nearest you for information about the current content and format.

CHAPTER 2

How to Use This Book in Preparing for the CLEP General Examinations

How to Study for the CLEP General Examinations Battery

The CLEP Examinations represent a survey of five basic subjects. When the test is constructed, each subject is outlined or divided up into a number of main topics. Questions are written which fall under the main headings. In each test, an approximately equal number of questions are drawn from each of the main categories. This is true even though some categories may seem more important than others. For instance, in American History, there are likely to be no more questions on the Civil War than there will be on the Late Nineteenth Century. Because the test has only a limited number of questions, these questions will, for the most part, cover only the main points of any one category. Therefore, in studying for the examination the student should survey the entire subject, draw up an outline of the subject, review the main points in familiar areas, and study those topics with which he or she is less familiar.

This book helps you get used to the actual process of taking multiple-choice tests. At the same time each sample question reveals a topic or subject area that may be on the actual test. Because these questions and those presented on the actual test are not identical, it may be best not to simply memorize answers to the questions in this book. Instead when you run across questions you can't answer, check them off. When you find the answer, try to understand the concept or idea involved. You might keep track of the questions you miss and see if they fall in the same category. In this way you can direct your review toward those areas in which you are least proficient. You may have difficulty with a question because the question contains words you do not know. In this case, write the words down as you confront them and find out what they mean in a dictionary or other reference book.

Because the CLEP General Examinations battery covers a wide area of general knowledge, it would be difficult to start from scratch, learning everything that might be included in the test. However, you should realize that you are not starting from scratch. If you are a recent high school graduate, you will discover that most of the material on the tests is material with which you are already familiar from high school and elementary school courses. If you have been out of school for some time, you will find that much of the material on the actual examination is familiar to you from newspapers, magazines, and your general experience.

In preparing for the test it is best to use books that outline the material to be covered in a brief but concise way. You need to know the main points of a subject. If you do not already have extensive knowledge in a field, it is unreasonable to expect to acquire it now and for the most part it will be unnecessary in terms of this particular examination. Main points you should know include the major persons in a field, the main events, principles involved, and the vocabulary of each field.

The General Examination in Mathematics covers material that is generally taught in a college course for non-mathematics majors. It also tests skills usually acquired in high school: arithmetic, algebra, geometry, and data interpretation. The bibliography given in Chapter 10 will be helpful if you feel the need for a general review of mathematics.

It is important to remember that survey courses for freshmen and sophomores in college, for the most part, repeat a good deal of material that the student should have learned in high school. To be sure, college courses are more compact or concise and may go into the subject in greater depth. Nevertheless, many of the main topics covered are the same as those covered in high school. Do not be overwhelmed by the idea that these are "college" examinations for they are designed for the person who has acquired a basic education on his or her own. Working out the items offered in this book and answering the questions will be one way in which you can review what you have already learned, either in a classroom or on your own.

A Strategy for Taking the CLEP Examination

Different strategies work for different people in taking exams. You should follow whatever procedure seems best for you. Because each test is timed, however, you should not linger too long on any single question. As soon as it becomes obvious to you that you do not know the answer, you should move on to the next question. Many poor test takers get bogged down on one or two questions and don't have time to complete all the questions they could have answered.

A strategy for taking multiple-choice examinations which seems to work for many people is as follows: (1) Read the statement and try to recall the correct answer. (2) See if the answer you recalled is listed among the choices and mark it immediately. (3) If you were not able to *recall* the correct answer, but on the first reading of the choices you *recognize* the correct answer, mark it immediately. (4) If you cannot answer the question on the first reading, immediately go on to the next question. This way you will be spending your time on what you know. The secret of taking this type of test is to decide immediately whether or not you know the answer. If you cannot decide quickly, go on to the next item so that no time is wasted.

After having completed all the questions that you were sure of, you may have time to go back and check some of the questions you did not complete the first time round. When you go back and check the questions that you skipped the first time, you will immediately recognize some of the answers. For the items that still give you difficulty, you might proceed to eliminate the obviously incorrect answers.

FOR EXAMPLE:

The man who invented the first usable electric light was:

(A) Benjamin Franklin (B) George Washington
(C) Thomas Edison (D) Henry Ford (E) Max Planck

You may not know a thing about electricity but certainly you can eliminate the names of George Washington and Henry Ford. You have bettered your odds. Your chances are now one-in-three instead of one-in-five. If you still are not sure which is correct, but have a hunch, then play that hunch. Often, you will have heard or read the correct answer without remembering. You will feel or think a statement is true without knowing why. Play your hunch. If, after having chosen an answer, you still aren't sure, it is best to leave the first answer. Research studies have demonstrated that the first guess is more likely to be correct than a revised guess later on.

The questions on the General Examination in Mathematics can frequently be answered using shortcuts which make pencil and paper unnecessary. These methods will be discussed in detail in Chapter 10. That is, there is often a "trick" by which the answer can be figured out in one's head. The goal is to avoid excessive computation. Since the test places little emphasis on arithmetic calculations, you should not waste time on long computations on any single question. Instead, answer those items that come quickly. Go back to the others if you still have time after you have done the items that come easier.

Some teachers of "cram" courses on test taking allege that someone taking a test can figure out a certain pattern of answers and urge students to mark answers according to that pattern. Thus, these teachers say, if the answer to a question is (A), the answer to the next question will probably be (D), and the correct response to the following question might be (B). YOU SHOULD NOT MARK ANSWERS AT RANDOM ACCORDING TO ANY SYSTEM OF RESPONSES WHICH YOU MIGHT DEDUCE. REMEMBER, THERE IS A PENALTY FOR INCORRECT ANSWERS, AND SUCH GUESSING WILL CERTAINLY INCREASE YOUR NUMBER OF INCORRECT RESPONSES.

Hints for Success:

1. Get plenty of sleep. An important factor in taking an examination is to rest the night before. Fatigue can lower your self-confidence, your ability to concentrate, your speed in taking the examination, and ultimately can lower your score.

2. Arrive early. Arrive at the designated place at least ten or fifteen minutes before the test is scheduled to begin. Be sure you have allowed yourself time to take care of all last minute details. It is important to arrive early so you will not feel rushed and will have time to get adjusted to the surroundings. It is best that whatever shuffling and rearranging you might feel inclined to do be done before the test begins, rather than during the first ten minutes of actual test time. When it is time to start working on the test questions, you should be able to begin immediately with no confusion or warm-up period.

3. Take the following items with you to the test center: (1) personal identification that includes a photograph and your signature, (2) four No. 2 pencils with good erasers, (3) a watch so you can keep track of the time.

4. Wear comfortable clothes. Since you do not know whether the examination room will be warm or cold, wear layers of clothing that can be removed if the room is warm or put on if it is cold.

5. Do not assume anything in regard to test directions. Time will be given to read the test directions before the test begins. Even if you feel completely familiar with the directions from other experiences, you should take time to read them on this particular test so that you know exactly what to expect and don't start out with a false assumption.

6. Relax. Don't let last minute nervousness get the better of you. Almost everyone is a little tense before an examination. If you freeze or clutch during the examination, then forget the questions for a few moments and concentrate on something else. Don't worry about the few minutes you will be losing. You'll waste more time and will be less efficient if you try to struggle through the test with that "locked up" feeling. Relax and be cool. Remind yourself that you're pretty smart and you have what it takes. Then, when you're calmer, pick up your exam and go to it.

7. Pace yourself. To make sure you are not going too slowly, check the time fairly often. You should have finished one quarter of the questions in a section when one quarter of the time is up, half the questions when half the time is up. If you find you have been taking too long, try to speed up your pace a bit for the rest of the test. And remember not to spend too long on any one question.

8. Read all of the answer choices before choosing an answer. The first or second answer choice might seem correct, but the fourth or fifth one might be better—and usually the directions instruct you to pick the *best* answer choice.

9. Record your answer correctly on the answer sheet. Be sure to record your answer next to the question number that corresponds with the number of the question you were answering. If you skip a question, be sure to leave that space blank on your answer sheet and answer the next question in the correct space.

10. Never choose (E) as your answer in the Mathematics examination. The Mathematics test only has four choices (A, B, C, or D) for each question, so (E) can never be the correct answer.

11. Feel free to write in your test booklet. You can draw diagrams, do calculations, make notes, cross out answer choices you know are not correct, circle questions you are not sure of and want to come back to. On the other hand, be very careful not to make marks on your answer sheet, and be sure to erase all stray marks completely.

USING THIS BOOK TO STUDY

When you finish this book with the illustrative and sample test items we have prepared for you, you will have worked through more than 3500 different test items:

English Composition	500
Humanities	680
Mathematics	700
Natural Sciences	750
Social Sciences – History	630

Why so many? We believe that this much practice is necessary for anyone to do well on the CLEP battery, and, of course, we do not expect that anyone will attempt to finish the whole book within a few days. Take your time, and you will be better off.

For example: from the following four statements, several different questions might be written:

1. **William Shakespeare was a playwright of the English Renaissance.**
2. **One of his best and most famous tragedies is *Hamlet*.**

3. "To be or not to be—that is the question" is the first line of one of Hamlet's soliloquies.
4. By definition, a soliloquy is a speech which a character says aloud, alone on stage, and which may represent what he is thinking at the moment.

Now, look at just a few of the different questions which might be derived from these facts:

1. William Shakespeare, author of *Hamlet*, was a playwright during the English
   (A) Renaissance (B) Medieval period (C) Neo-Classic period
   (D) Romantic period (E) Victorian period

2. One of Shakespeare's best and most famous tragedies is
   (A) *All for Love* (B) *Tammarlane the Great* (C) *Dr. Faustus*
   (D) *Hamlet* (E) *Cavalcade*

3. "To be or not to be—that is the question" is the first line of one of Shakespeare's
   (A) dramatic monologues (B) soliloquies (C) sonnets
   (D) epic poems (E) lyric poems

4. One of Shakespeare's famous soliloquies begins
   (A) "What have I got now that I did not have?"
   (B) "To be or not to be—that is the question"
   (C) "A girl's best friend is her mother, not dad."
   (D) "These are the times that sorely try men's souls."
   (E) "Of man's first disobedience, and the fruit"

5. A speech which an actor speaks alone on the stage and which perhaps represents his thoughts at the moment, merely verbalized, is called
   (A) an epic poem (B) an aside (C) a soliloquy
   (D) an interruption (E) a dramatic monologue

We could go on formulating additional questions using the given facts, but you get the idea. If you will note these apparent repetitions, which have been included primarily to reinforce your remembering certain information, you can more easily recall facts if you are confronted with a similar question on an actual examination. Indeed, it is not too much to say that anyone who knows the answer to every question in this book has achieved an educational level which few other people can match, whether they have ever attended college or not.

Review materials for the CLEP battery are primarily of a factual nature, then, except in English Composition and Mathematics. In these two examinations, you will be asked to make applications of certain general principles from the subject area to sentences or problems which you have never seen before—the sentences and problems may be new, but each one incorporates a principle which is illustrated and explained in this book. If you find a question whose answer eludes you, check the answer and answer explanation.

This book is organized into five major parts, one part for each of the five examinations of the CLEP battery. Each part opens with a Trial Examination, which gives you an idea of what the examination is like and lets you determine how you would score on the examination without any specific preparation or practice. Then there is a chapter which provides general information about the examination and a number of items illustrating the basic principles of the subject area as well as the different kinds of information you will need to have or the different responses you might be called upon to make. These sample items you will find in small groups, and we have provided answers and explanations of these answers immediately following each group of questions. We recommend that you work through these groups of items at whatever speed suits you best. We also believe that you can deduce the principles being illustrated from the questions which we have given you to answer.

At the end of each part is a chapter containing three sample examinations, and we suggest, when you do some of these samples, that you follow the time limit that will be imposed during an actual CLEP examination, just to get into the habit of having that limitation as part of the test procedure. An answer key is included at the end of each test so that you can check yourself almost immediately. Answer explanations are also provided; these explanations can help you learn how to read the question carefully and answer exactly what is asked as well as help you recognize your weak spots and plan your studies.

Here are a few other suggestions about using this book:

1. Skip around among parts. For instance, do not work through the whole part on English Composition and then move to the Humanities part. You will find that shifting from part to part will provide some break for you as you work.

2. Do not attempt any of the complete sample examinations at the end of each part until you have worked through all the sample items. As you try the small groups of questions, you will see that each of these groups deals with just one part of the subject area, while in the complete examinations, questions are arranged in an almost random order to cover the whole subject area.

3. Do not despair if you discover that you do not finish each sample examination within the indicated time limit. Test experts tell us that many people do not finish tests for many reasons, but do the best you can, for if you get about 50% of each test correct, your score will be above the average score of all college sophomores in the United States.

4. The vocabulary level of the test items is about Grade 14, which means that the words used are those which any college sophomore should recognize and understand from his or her reading. Sentence structure and syntax are at the same level, and it might be a good idea for you to have a good desk dictionary available in case you find words in the practice groups of questions which you do not know.

5. We have provided answer sheets for the Trial Tests and the Sample Tests. For the practice questions, you can write your answers on a separate sheet of paper as you practice and review.

6. Within each part, there is a brief bibliography of reference works and textbooks that you might want to review if you find that you are weak in one of the subject areas. Most of these books are available in a good public library.

Each of the following five parts of this book opens with a trial test, followed by a description of the CLEP test which that part covers. Read these descriptions carefully and work through each of the sample exercises and examinations just as carefully. When you finish this book, look back through the questions, and check to see just how much factual information you can recall

from your experiences with the sample items. We think that you will be pleasantly surprised.

Good luck!

NOTE: No sample question in this book has ever appeared on an actual CLEP examination. The examinations are security tests, and all material on those tests is protected by copyright in the name of the Educational Testing Service. The test items in this book are meant to be similar in format to an actual CLEP examination, *not* actual items that you might find when you take one or more of the examinations.

Progress Chart

	Total Possible	Trial Test	Exam 1	Exam 2	Exam 3
English Comp 90 minutes	95				
Humanities 90 minutes	150				
Mathematics 90 minutes	90				
Natural Sciences 90 minutes	115–120				
Social Science— History 90 minutes	125				

To calculate your raw score on each sample examination use the following formula:

$$RS = C - \frac{I}{n - 1}$$

in which RS = raw score

C = number of correct answers

I = number of incorrect answers

n = number of answer choices. (Each of the examinations, except the Mathematics examination, has five answer choices; the Mathematics examination has only four choices.)

Note: Omitted items are not counted in the formula.

Example: If you have answered 80 questions correctly and 28 incorrectly on the Natural Sciences Examination, your raw score is

$$RS = C - \frac{I}{n - 1}$$

$$RS = 80 - \frac{28}{4}$$

$$RS = 80 - 7$$

$$RS = 73$$

Only total scores are used to calculate the raw score, not the scores on sections of a single examination.

The raw score on an actual CLEP examination is converted to a three-digit scale score using a complicated statistical formula.

PART ONE

THE ENGLISH COMPOSITION EXAMINATION

ANSWER SHEET — ENGLISH COMPOSITION/TRIAL TEST

Section I

1. Ⓐ Ⓑ Ⓒ Ⓓ Ⓔ
2. Ⓐ Ⓑ Ⓒ Ⓓ Ⓔ
3. Ⓐ Ⓑ Ⓒ Ⓓ Ⓔ
4. Ⓐ Ⓑ Ⓒ Ⓓ Ⓔ
5. Ⓐ Ⓑ Ⓒ Ⓓ Ⓔ
6. Ⓐ Ⓑ Ⓒ Ⓓ Ⓔ
7. Ⓐ Ⓑ Ⓒ Ⓓ Ⓔ
8. Ⓐ Ⓑ Ⓒ Ⓓ Ⓔ
9. Ⓐ Ⓑ Ⓒ Ⓓ Ⓔ
10. Ⓐ Ⓑ Ⓒ Ⓓ Ⓔ
11. Ⓐ Ⓑ Ⓒ Ⓓ Ⓔ
12. Ⓐ Ⓑ Ⓒ Ⓓ Ⓔ
13. Ⓐ Ⓑ Ⓒ Ⓓ Ⓔ
14. Ⓐ Ⓑ Ⓒ Ⓓ Ⓔ
15. Ⓐ Ⓑ Ⓒ Ⓓ Ⓔ
16. Ⓐ Ⓑ Ⓒ Ⓓ Ⓔ
17. Ⓐ Ⓑ Ⓒ Ⓓ Ⓔ
18. Ⓐ Ⓑ Ⓒ Ⓓ Ⓔ
19. Ⓐ Ⓑ Ⓒ Ⓓ Ⓔ
20. Ⓐ Ⓑ Ⓒ Ⓓ Ⓔ
21. Ⓐ Ⓑ Ⓒ Ⓓ Ⓔ
22. Ⓐ Ⓑ Ⓒ Ⓓ Ⓔ
23. Ⓐ Ⓑ Ⓒ Ⓓ Ⓔ
24. Ⓐ Ⓑ Ⓒ Ⓓ Ⓔ
25. Ⓐ Ⓑ Ⓒ Ⓓ Ⓔ
26. Ⓐ Ⓑ Ⓒ Ⓓ Ⓔ
27. Ⓐ Ⓑ Ⓒ Ⓓ Ⓔ
28. Ⓐ Ⓑ Ⓒ Ⓓ Ⓔ
29. Ⓐ Ⓑ Ⓒ Ⓓ Ⓔ
30. Ⓐ Ⓑ Ⓒ Ⓓ Ⓔ
31. Ⓐ Ⓑ Ⓒ Ⓓ Ⓔ
32. Ⓐ Ⓑ Ⓒ Ⓓ Ⓔ
33. Ⓐ Ⓑ Ⓒ Ⓓ Ⓔ
34. Ⓐ Ⓑ Ⓒ Ⓓ Ⓔ
35. Ⓐ Ⓑ Ⓒ Ⓓ Ⓔ
36. Ⓐ Ⓑ Ⓒ Ⓓ Ⓔ
37. Ⓐ Ⓑ Ⓒ Ⓓ Ⓔ
38. Ⓐ Ⓑ Ⓒ Ⓓ Ⓔ
39. Ⓐ Ⓑ Ⓒ Ⓓ Ⓔ
40. Ⓐ Ⓑ Ⓒ Ⓓ Ⓔ
41. Ⓐ Ⓑ Ⓒ Ⓓ Ⓔ
42. Ⓐ Ⓑ Ⓒ Ⓓ Ⓔ
43. Ⓐ Ⓑ Ⓒ Ⓓ Ⓔ
44. Ⓐ Ⓑ Ⓒ Ⓓ Ⓔ
45. Ⓐ Ⓑ Ⓒ Ⓓ Ⓔ
46. Ⓐ Ⓑ Ⓒ Ⓓ Ⓔ
47. Ⓐ Ⓑ Ⓒ Ⓓ Ⓔ
48. Ⓐ Ⓑ Ⓒ Ⓓ Ⓔ
49. Ⓐ Ⓑ Ⓒ Ⓓ Ⓔ
50. Ⓐ Ⓑ Ⓒ Ⓓ Ⓔ
51. Ⓐ Ⓑ Ⓒ Ⓓ Ⓔ
52. Ⓐ Ⓑ Ⓒ Ⓓ Ⓔ
53. Ⓐ Ⓑ Ⓒ Ⓓ Ⓔ
54. Ⓐ Ⓑ Ⓒ Ⓓ Ⓔ
55. Ⓐ Ⓑ Ⓒ Ⓓ Ⓔ

Section II

56. Ⓐ Ⓑ Ⓒ Ⓓ Ⓔ
57. Ⓐ Ⓑ Ⓒ Ⓓ Ⓔ
58. Ⓐ Ⓑ Ⓒ Ⓓ Ⓔ
59. Ⓐ Ⓑ Ⓒ Ⓓ Ⓔ
60. Ⓐ Ⓑ Ⓒ Ⓓ Ⓔ
61. Ⓐ Ⓑ Ⓒ Ⓓ Ⓔ
62. Ⓐ Ⓑ Ⓒ Ⓓ Ⓔ
63. Ⓐ Ⓑ Ⓒ Ⓓ Ⓔ
64. Ⓐ Ⓑ Ⓒ Ⓓ Ⓔ
65. Ⓐ Ⓑ Ⓒ Ⓓ Ⓔ
66. Ⓐ Ⓑ Ⓒ Ⓓ Ⓔ
67. Ⓐ Ⓑ Ⓒ Ⓓ Ⓔ
68. Ⓐ Ⓑ Ⓒ Ⓓ Ⓔ
69. Ⓐ Ⓑ Ⓒ Ⓓ Ⓔ
70. Ⓐ Ⓑ Ⓒ Ⓓ Ⓔ
71. Ⓐ Ⓑ Ⓒ Ⓓ Ⓔ
72. Ⓐ Ⓑ Ⓒ Ⓓ Ⓔ
73. Ⓐ Ⓑ Ⓒ Ⓓ Ⓔ
74. Ⓐ Ⓑ Ⓒ Ⓓ Ⓔ
75. Ⓐ Ⓑ Ⓒ Ⓓ Ⓔ
76. Ⓐ Ⓑ Ⓒ Ⓓ Ⓔ
77. Ⓐ Ⓑ Ⓒ Ⓓ Ⓔ
78. Ⓐ Ⓑ Ⓒ Ⓓ Ⓔ
79. Ⓐ Ⓑ Ⓒ Ⓓ Ⓔ
80. Ⓐ Ⓑ Ⓒ Ⓓ Ⓔ
81. Ⓐ Ⓑ Ⓒ Ⓓ Ⓔ
82. Ⓐ Ⓑ Ⓒ Ⓓ Ⓔ
83. Ⓐ Ⓑ Ⓒ Ⓓ Ⓔ
84. Ⓐ Ⓑ Ⓒ Ⓓ Ⓔ
85. Ⓐ Ⓑ Ⓒ Ⓓ Ⓔ
86. Ⓐ Ⓑ Ⓒ Ⓓ Ⓔ
87. Ⓐ Ⓑ Ⓒ Ⓓ Ⓔ
88. Ⓐ Ⓑ Ⓒ Ⓓ Ⓔ
89. Ⓐ Ⓑ Ⓒ Ⓓ Ⓔ
90. Ⓐ Ⓑ Ⓒ Ⓓ Ⓔ
91. Ⓐ Ⓑ Ⓒ Ⓓ Ⓔ
92. Ⓐ Ⓑ Ⓒ Ⓓ Ⓔ
93. Ⓐ Ⓑ Ⓒ Ⓓ Ⓔ
94. Ⓐ Ⓑ Ⓒ Ⓓ Ⓔ
95. Ⓐ Ⓑ Ⓒ Ⓓ Ⓔ

CHAPTER

3 Trial Test

This chapter contains a trial English Composition test, which you should take to get an idea of what the examination is like and to determine how you would score before any practice or review. The test contains 95 multiple-choice questions, organized into two sections.

Section I

Number of items: 55
Time: 45 minutes

Directions: The following sentences contain problems in grammar, usage, diction (choice of words), and idiom.

Some sentences are correct.
No sentence contains more than one error.

You will find that the error, if there is one, is underlined and lettered. Assume that elements of the sentence that are not underlined are correct and cannot be changed. In choosing answers, follow the requirements of standard written English.

If there is an error, select the one underlined part that must be changed to make the sentence correct.

If there is no error, select answer (E).

1. The greatest poets always imply (A) more in their poetry than they seem to say, for they know how (B) to make use of both denotation (C) and connotation as well as (D) other technical devices of the poem. No error (E)

2. After they had attended the exhibition at the Museum of Modern Art, (A) Jill told Harold that she had just seen (B) the most perfect (C) displays of art works she had ever been delighted by. (D) No error (E)

3. Becoming a resident (A) of Chicago was an experience I shall not soon (B) forget, for I found that I could not understand (C) the city until I had strolled it's (D) interesting streets and admired both the old and new buildings. No error (E)

4. The Boeing 747 having landed safely (A), we greeted the tourists who thronged (B) through the narrow passageway (C) that connected the plane to the terminal. (D) No error (E)

5. Japanese art with its subtle colors and suggestive curving (A) lines symbolizes those (B) characteristics that set them apart (C) from all other people of (D) the world. No error (E)

6. Russia is (A) larger than any country (B) in the world; if you doubt (C) this statement, look at a map of the world, either (D) a globe or a Mecator projection on a flat surface. No error (E)

7. Some of the pie are still (A) left in the plate on the bottom shelf (B) of the refrigerator if you want (C) a small snack before you go (D) to bed. No error (E)

8. In the court (A) of Louis XIV, his closest advisors were (B) nobles of the Catholic church who's loyalty (C) might have been suspected (D) by any impartial observer of the scene. No error (E)

9. All of the evidence (A) the prosecutor had so carefully gathered was ignored by (B) the jury, because the defense attorney made such an emotionally over-whelming (C) speech explaining his client's (D) actions. No error (E)

10. Ted Koppel interviews many celebrities on his daily television (A) program, and many of them seemed confused (B) by his prying questions, the answers to (C) which may reveal some hidden (D) truth. No error (E)

11. In his address, Ronald Reagan made many illusions (A) to the greatness of the United States, its government (B) and its people (C), its great diversity and immensity, its glorious past and future (D) potential. No error (E)

12. All the new cosmetics (A) for men which even the Avon salesperson is bringing to the house notwithstanding, most all men (B) would prefer not to smell like (C) a flower patch in spring or a dirty (D) saddle in a tack room. No error (E)

13. The author of the polemic (A) against radical students indicated (B) that he neither appreciated that some students had legitimate grievances against school administrators or exculpated (C) those on campuses that have not been (D) guilty of violence. No error (E)

14. Current politicians must of been (A) aware that their efforts (B) to spend money foolishly while refusing (C) to raise taxes can only increase (D) budget deficits. No error (E)

15. Chaucer's stories and Dickens's novels seem to have (A) little in common until a perceptive reader (B) enjoys both their ability (C) to keep a story going and their very unique (D) use of language. No error (E)

16. The ill-fated love affair (A) of Tristram and Isolde have (B) inspired such different (C) artists as Richard Wagner and Edward Arlington Robinson to tell the story, each using his (D) own special medium. No error (E)

17. Bob Dylan and the Beatles have (A) had more influence upon (B) contemporary music as any other (C) of the many composers turning out (D) songs by the thousands each week. No error (E)

18. Some users of drugs have (A) justified his addiction (B) to wanting to escape from the many problems (C) that afflict those who are (D) searching for happiness. No error (E)

19. Whoever we elect (A) as our representative (B) to the national convention will have his or her expenses (C) paid from the dues (D) of the local organization. No error (E)

20. Someone invented a better mousetrap (A) that was guaranteed to work every (B) time, but the patent attorney questioned the inventor's use (C) of a nuclear warhead as the agent of destruction (D). No error (E)

Directions: In each of the following sentences, some part or all of the sentence is underlined. Below each sentence you will find five ways of phrasing the underlined part. Select the answer that produces the most effective sentence, one that is clear and exact, without awkwardness or ambiguity. In choosing answers, follow the requirements of standard written English. Choose the answer that best expresses the meaning of the original sentence.

Answer (A) is always the same as the underlined part. Choose answer (A) if you think the original sentence needs no revision.

21. In these times of social change, we can now see that our past was not as great as we thought it was.
(A) was not as great as we thought it was
(B) was not so great as we thought it might have been
(C) was not as positive so that we thought about it
(D) is not what we had hoped it would be
(E) was not as great as they thought it was

22. The minister disappointed his congregation in the course of his initial sermon in which he asked for larger contributions.
(A) in the course of his initial
(B) during his first
(C) during his irritating
(D) in the course of his foremost
(E) in the coarse of his initial

23. It is a sad characteristic of today's modern world that we do not have the precious gift of laughing at ourselves.
(A) of today's modern world
(B) of the world of today
(C) of today's world
(D) with today's modern world
(E) from what I see around me today

24. Americans has the right to change their form of government whenever they are unhappy with it.
(A) Americans has the right to change their form of government whenever they are unhappy with it.
(B) Americans becoming unhappy with their form of government, they have the right to change it.
(C) Americans can change their form of government as often as it fails to satisfy them.
(D) Americans who are unhappy with their form of government has the right to make changes.
(E) Americans have the right to change their form of government; they are unhappy with it.

25. After the confusion in the park was over, the city council passed an ordinance prohibiting rock concerts in any public space.
(A) ordinance prohibiting rock concerts
(B) ordinance which discouraged rock concerts
(C) ordinance which makes it impossible for rock concerts to be held
(D) ordinance for making illegal rock concerts
(E) ordinance permitting rock concerts

26. The candidate campaigned hard for voters, he rushed from place to place in his own airplane.
(A) The candidate campaigned hard for voters, he rushed from place to place in his own airplane.
(B) In his own airplane, the candidate rushed from place to place as they campaigned for election.
(C) Rushing from the place to place, the airplane was campaigning for voters.
(D) The candidate campaigned hard for voters; he rushed from place to place in his own airplane.
(E) The candidate having been campaigning for voters, he rushed from place to place in his own airplane.

27. Suburbanites who are accustomed to commuting into a city by train know not to get upset if schedules cannot be maintained exactly.
(A) Suburbanites who are accustomed to commuting into a city by train know not to get upset if schedules cannot be maintained exactly.
(B) Some of the suburbanites commuting into a city by train is not upset if a train is late once in a while.
(C) A train being late once in a while does not upset those suburbanites whom expect such delays.
(D) Schedules not being maintained as published do not disturb many suburbanites who commuted to a city for a job.
(E) Those suburbanites who commute to the city by train doesn't get upset if the trains are late once in a while.

28. When I think of men traveling to the moon in a spaceship, my mind is filled with respect for the achievement of modern science.
(A) is filled with respect for
(B) is filled up with respect for
(C) fills up with respect for
(D) was filled with respect for
(E) was filled up with respect for

29. John Brown showed his stupidity, for he did not save his money during his prosperous working years.
(A) showed his stupidity, for he
(B) showed his stupidity; for he
(C) showed his stupidity, he
(D) showed his stupidity. For he
(E) showed his stupidity, as a result

30. Jonathan's father was born in Hawaii, the male child of a native princess and a foreign sugarcane worker.
(A) the male child of
(B) being the only male child of
(C) having been sired by
(D) the only male son of
(E) the son of

31. Joe wanted to succeed as a nurse or a teacher, which is one of the highest ambitions any person can have.
(A) Joe wanted to succeed as a nurse or a teacher, which is one of the highest ambitions any person can have.
(B) Joe wanted to succeed as a nurse or to be a teacher, two of the highest ambitions any person can have.
(C) Joe wanted to succeed in nursing or teaching, two professions in which many people with high ambitions have been successful.
(D) Among his other ambitions, Joe wanted to study nurse and teacher.
(E) More than anything else, Joe wished to achieve eminence as a nurse or to be a teacher.

32. Motorists who cross the California dessert is constantly told to take plenty of water for their car radiators.
(A) is constantly told to
(B) cannot but be warned
(C) are always advised to
(D) is told to beware the dangers of dryness
(E) could be constantly advised to

33. The judges of the Miss Universe contest had eliminated all but five of the original candidates, and now their only problem was choosing the winner from among the remaining women.
(A) from among the remaining women
(B) within the finalists
(C) from between the finalists
(D) from the finalists
(E) from the five contestants

34. Because George Washington knew how to submit an expense account was the reason he had so little trouble collecting money due him.
(A) Because George Washington knew how to submit an expense account was the reason he had so little trouble collecting money due him.
(B) George Washington knew how to submit an expense account; therefore, he had little trouble collecting money due him.
(C) The reason that George Washington had so little trouble collecting money due him was because he knew how to submit an expense account.
(D) George Washington had little trouble collecting money due him, he knew how to submit an expense account.
(E) George Washington's expense account, having been so carefully submitted that the cost was paid almost immediately.

35. Since the invitation was addressed to both of us, you should not of been so angry when I opened the letter.
(A) should not of been so angry
(B) could not have been so angry
(C) should of been so angry
(D) would not have been so angry
(E) should not have been so angry

36. Without being invited, the woman has taken a seat at our table and ordered champagne.
(A) woman has taken
(B) woman should have taken
(C) woman took
(D) woman would of taken
(E) woman had took

37. In the South, dogwood and azaleas announce the arrival of spring by bursting into bloom in every garden.
(A) by bursting into bloom in every garden
(B) after they explode into bloom in every garden
(C) when they force their buds into bloom
(D) since they have burst into bloom
(E) while they bloom in every garden

38. A snowplow can clear streets and driveways in a few minutes, but they are troublesome to store in the summer time.
(A) but they are troublesome to store
(B) but it can be troublesome to store
(C) but some people have problems storing
(D) but problems arise when they store them
(E) but they cannot be no trouble to store

39. President Bush has agreed that drugs are a major problem in the world today; he has offered a partial solution to the problem by offering military forces to Colombia.
(A) by offering military forces to Colombia
(B) to offer military forces to Colombia
(C) for offering military forces to Colombia
(D) whoever offered military forces to Colombia
(E) with his offer of armed forces to Colombia

40. Gorbachev and Bush have met several times and seem to agree on a number of things.
(A) Bush have met several times
(B) Bush has met many times
(C) Bush has been meeting
(D) Bush will meet many times
(E) Bush can be meeting several times

Directions: Effective revision requires choosing among the many options available to a writer. The following questions test your ability to use these options effectively.

Revise each of the following sentences according to the directions that follow it. Some directions require you to rephrase only part of the original sentence; others require you to recast the entire sentence. You may need to omit or add certain words in constructing an acceptable revision, but you should keep the meaning of your revised sentence as close to the meaning of the original sentence as the directions permit. Your new sentence should follow the conventions of standard written English and should be clear and concise.

Look through answer choices A–E under each question for the exact word or phrase that is included in your revised sentence. If you have thought of a revision that does not include any of the words or phrases listed, try to revise the sentence again so that it does include the wording in one of the answer choices.

When you take the test, you should feel free to make notes in your test book, but you will need to mark your answers on the separate answer sheet.

41. Americans are dominated by a desire for simple answers to complex questions, perhaps as a result of a national illusion that mere technical proficiency can solve any problem that confronts them.

    Begin with Americans in their search for simple answers.

    (A) elude themselves that
    (B) cause a national delusion
    (C) allude themselves that
    (D) delude themselves that
    (E) result in a national delusion

42. An original painting is much more valuable than a lithograph, especially if the artist is as well known as Picasso.

    Begin with One of.

    (A) Picasso (B) Picasso's (C) Picassos'
    (D) by Picasso (E) as Picasso

43. The peace treaty stated that each country would respect the boundaries of the other, but there was no implication that either nation would defend the other in case of an attack by a third state.

    Begin with The peace treaty, which.

    (A) did not infer (B) drew no implication (C) did not imply
    (D) drew no inference (E) had no reference

44. The residents of the black ghetto resent the whites who are convinced that just more money will solve all the problems of the inner city slums.

    Begin with Whites who are convinced.

    (A) are resented by the residents (B) resent the residents
    (C) create resentment for (D) so resent that
    (E) resent so much

45. The publisher could not accept any reason for the manuscript's being delayed in the mail, for he was not used to such service from the post office.

Substitute unaccustomed for was not used.

(A) mail, unaccustomed to such service
(B) reason, unaccustomed to such service
(C) post office, unaccustomed to such service
(D) The publisher, unaccustomed to such service
(E) delay, unaccustomed to such service

46. Anyone who attempts to read every word in a Sunday edition of *The New York Times* will be busy for several weeks at least.

Begin with If anyone attempts.

(A) they will be (B) one will be (C) a person will be
(D) he or she will be (E) people will be

47. These days it is difficult to distinguish males from females, especially with the unisex clothing styles and the similar coiffures which both young men and women affect.

Eliminate it is.

(A) with the unisex clothing styles and the similar coiffures
(B) unisex clothing styles and the similar coiffures makes
(C) unisex clothing styles and their very similar coiffures make
(D) because unisex clothing styles and the similar coiffures
(E) since unisex clothing styles and the similar coiffures

48. A sedentary individual should not consume as many high calorie foods as someone who engages in heavy physical activity; therefore, a desk-bound clerk should eat less than a ditch digger.

Begin with A ditch digger who engages and eliminate therefore.

(A) who's working sedentary (B) consumes more high calorie foods
(C) who consumes less high calorie foods (D) whose work is sedentary
(E) who eats more

49. Exceeding the speed limit on any street or highway in the country is one sure way of attracting a policeman's attention.

Substitute Anyone exceeding for Exceeding.

(A) he can be sure of (B) can be sure of (C) must be sure of
(D) should be sure of (E) has to be sure of

50. Weeds and insect pests are only two of the banes of a gardener's existence, for he must fight both if he expects any yield for his efforts.

Begin with A gardener must.

(A) either weeds or insect pests
(B) neither weeds nor insect pests
(C) weeds in addition to insect pests
(D) both weeds as well as insect pests
(E) both weeds and insect pests

51. The FBI and local police have warned motorists not to pick up hitch-hikers; in fact, in many states, it is illegal either to solicit or to give a ride on an open highway except in cases of emergency.

Eliminate it.

(A) either to solicit or to give
(B) either soliciting or giving
(C) either for soliciting or for giving
(D) either for solicit or for give
(E) either with soliciting or for giving

52. Most large city police departments maintain a well-equipped crime laboratory where experts can develop evidence that may convict a guilty person or free one who is innocent.

Begin with Evidence to convict the guilty or free the innocent.

(A) may be maintained in
(B) may be developed in
(C) may be equipped in
(D) may be derived from
(E) may be compared in

53. Once the pastor had started his sermon, he was annoyed at being interrupted by late-arriving parishioners.

Begin with Parishioners arriving late.

(A) annoyed the pastor
(B) was annoyed by the pastor
(C) annoyed late-arriving parishioners
(D) annoyed the interruptions
(E) were annoyed by others arriving late

54. The chief along with fifteen Indians attacks the heavily defended fort at least once a day.

Change along with to and.

(A) attacks
(B) is attacking
(C) attack
(D) has attacked
(E) has been attacking

55. The millionaire became cynical because so many people tried to swindle him out of his money with foolish proposals.

Begin with The many attempts.

(A) tried him to become
(B) caused him to become
(C) caused him to try
(D) caused him to make
(E) caused him cynicism

Section II

(of the all-multiple-choice version)

Number of items: 40
Time: 45 minutes

Directions: Each of the following passages consists of a paragraph of numbered sentences. Since the paragraphs appear as they would within a larger piece of writing, they do not necessarily constitute a complete discussion of the issues presented.

Read each paragraph carefully and answer the questions that follow it. The questions test your awareness of characteristics of prose that are important to good writing.

Questions 56–61 are based on the following passage:

[1]For several years, films like *Star Wars*, *Jaws*, *Indiana Jones*, the James Bond series, and *Rain Man* have made millions of dollars for their producers. [2]Other films imitating these highly profitable films have also been made, producers hoping that their efforts will also strike gold at the box office. [3]With all this activity, the stocks of various motion picture companies have risen dramatically in price. [4]When stock market analysts note such a trend, they recommend that their clients purchase these stocks immediately, thus driving the prices even higher. [5]Many small investors have seen dividend increases and are satisfied with the results of their investments, although many of them have not seen the films that created their increased income. [6]Where the whole thing will end, no one knows for sure, but some producers are laughing all the way to the bank.

56. Sentence 2
(A) should be joined with sentence 1 with <u>and</u>
(B) should be the topic sentence of the paragraph
(C) should be placed after sentence 5
(D) should be omitted
(E) be joined to sentence 1 with <u>, however</u>

57. In sentence 4, the last part of the sentence beginning <u>immediately, thus</u> could be rewritten. Which of the following is the best new version of the sentence?
(A) immediately, thus drive the prices higher
(B) immediately, and the prices are driven even higher
(C) immediately; therefore, driving the prices even higher
(D) immediately, and therefore driving the prices even higher
(E) immediately. Thus driving the prices even higher

58. What should be done with sentence 6?
(A) It should be left as it is.
(B) It should be placed after sentence 2.
(C) It should be placed before sentence 4.
(D) It should be placed after sentence 1.
(E) It should be replaced with another sentence that would provide a more logical conclusion for the paragraph.

59. Sentence 1
(A) is the topic sentence of the paragraph
(B) is too long and should be cut in length
(C) is a conclusion that has little to do with the rest of the paragraph
(D) makes a statement that is illogical
(E) merely lists films that have made money over the years

60. Sentence 5
(A) should be divided into two sentences, the second beginning although
(B) introduces a new idea and is, therefore, out of place
(C) is all right and should not be changed
(D) actually is an example of a comma splice (the comma after investments)
(E) is too serious in tone for the rest of the paragraph

61. A logical summary of this paragraph might be this sentence:
(A) Many films over the past ten years have not made much money.
(B) The primary purpose of films these days seems to be to accumulate tremendous profits for producers.
(C) Stock prices are always dependent upon profits in the film industry.
(D) During the past few years, stocks in film companies have risen in value because many films have made tremendous profits.
(E) The profits films make are not related to the quality of those films.

Questions 62–67 are based on the following paragraph:

1The English language is primarily Germanic in structure. 2By this we mean that the order in which words are arranged in a sentence gives meaning to that sentence, in many cases. 3For instance, if the word *bear* appeared on a sheet of paper without any other word to give you a clue to its meaning, you might wonder whether the writer is writing about the animal with that name or about the verb which means *to carry.* 4If someone spoke the word aloud, you might wonder if a third meaning—*nude*—might not be possible. 5Often a word in isolation means nothing or is ambiguous and has one of several possible meanings. 6Thus, it is important to study words within relationships, to see how sentences are put together, and to learn why certain types of words function in certain ways and in those ways only. 7It is important to learn that the meaning and function of a word is frequently determined by its placement in a sentence, and, vice versa—sometimes the placement of a word determines its function in that sentence.

62. Sentence 7 could be combined with sentence 6. The correct form of the combination would be
(A) ways only, it is important
(B) ways only, and therefore, however, it is important
(C) ways only; is important
(D) ways only; it is important
(E) ways only: it is important

63. Sentence 5
(A) should be placed ahead of sentence 3
(B) should be the topic sentence of the paragraph
(C) should be placed after sentence 7
(D) should be eliminated from the paragraph
(E) should be left as it is

64. Sentence 6
(A) should be shortened to eliminate unnecessary words
(B) should be left as it is
(C) should be expanded to provide more examples
(D) should be eliminated
(E) should be moved to the end of the paragraph

65. The paragraph may seem unclear because
(A) *Germanic* is never clearly defined or illustrated
(B) there is only one example *(bear)* to offer evidence of the thesis of the paragraph
(C) the order of the sentences seems confused
(D) the purpose of the paragraph is not stated
(E) all of the above are true

66. The apparent purpose of the paragraph is to
(A) distinguish the English language from German
(B) illustrate how difficult many people find studying English
(C) provide information to someone about the origin of the English language
(D) demonstrate that *bear* has several meanings in English
(E) teach a young person about the English language

67. *For instance* and *Thus* are called
(A) introductory phrases
(B) a transitional word or phrase
(C) concluding words
(D) a summary word or phrase
(E) a function word or phrase

Questions 68–73 are based on the following passage:

[1]A sixth characteristic of language is that it is symbolic in its vocabulary. [2]Sometimes this process of association is conscious, and sometimes it is unconscious. [3]The sound of a word triggers some part of a person's brain and suggests to him/her all kinds of associations and feelings. [4]Take the word *fire,* for example. [5]To one person, the word suggests a blaze on a hearth or out in the open, a sizzling steak, a songfest, a picnic, or the like. [6]In another person, the word might strike terror, because of serious burns received in a burning building. [7]These reactions will differ from person to person, depending upon the context with which the person associates the word. [8]The symbol-making power of words is tremendous, and wars have been fought over the precise meaning of a certain word. [9]Words can also bestow status on an individual: we no longer employ *janitors*—we hire *custodians;* we no longer have *morons*—we have *exceptional children;* we no

longer have *garbage collectors*—we have *sanitary engineers.* [10]The second word or phrase in each of these pairs conveys more *tone* than does the first; the first word lies in the discard pile in connection with the individuals named by the word.

68. What should be done with sentence 2?
(A) It should be placed after sentence 6.
(B) It should be placed before sentence 10.
(C) It should begin the passage.
(D) It should be omitted.
(E) It should be placed after sentence 3.

69. Sentence 9
(A) should begin with some kind of transition phrase
(B) should be left as it is
(C) should be changed so that it is shorter
(D) should be made longer to include more examples
(E) is really a conclusion to the passage

70. A reader can tell that this paragraph is from a longer work
(A) by reading carefully sentence 1
(B) by noting the phrasing of sentence 10
(C) by understanding the transition phrases in sentences 5 and 6
(D) by reading sentence 3 aloud
(E) by having a feeling of incompleteness at the end of sentence 10

71. What is the purpose of the pairs of examples in sentence 9?
(A) They support the point of sentence 2.
(B) They further illustrate the author's idea in the word *fire.*
(C) They are examples of the symbolic quality of language.
(D) They are not important in making clear what the author means.
(E) They display the author's consideration for people with low-status jobs.

72. From the tone of the passage, a reader might well conclude
(A) that it was taken from a sociology textbook
(B) that it was an excerpt from a private letter between friends
(C) that a high school student wrote the paragraph for an impromptu composition
(D) that it was written for a textbook in English or composition
(E) that it is too difficult for anyone but an expert to understand

73. A logical conclusion to the passage would be which of the following?
(A) The science of word meanings, discussed here, is called *semantics,* a word coined by linguists about a century ago.
(B) A student of language does not need to concern herself/himself with the minor points of word meanings.
(C) Many books about semantics have been written, but none of them is very clear.
(D) A dictionary is a very reliable aid to anyone who wishes to know more about language.
(E) Working with language can be a very dull field of activity.

Directions: Effective revision requires choosing among the many options available to a writer. The following questions test your ability to use these options effectively.

Revise each of the following sentences according to the directions that follow it. Some directions require you to rephrase only part of the original sentence; others require you to recast the entire sentence. You may need to omit or add certain words in constructing an acceptable revision, but you should *keep the meaning of your revised sentence as close to the meaning of the original as the directions permit.* Your new sentence should follow the conventions of standard written English and should be clear and concise.

Look through the answer choices A–E under each question for the exact word or phrase that is included in your revised sentence. If you have thought of a revision that does not include any of the words or phrases listed, try to revise the sentence again so that it does include the wording in one of the answer choices.

When you take the test, you should feel free to make notes in your test book, but you will need to mark your answers on the separate answer sheet.

74. Unfortunately, fortunes often cause families to go to court and sue each other, but we live in a litigious age.

Begin with That.

(A) is unfortunate
(B) are the unfortunate results
(C) in an unfortunate age
(D) seem unfortunate
(E) become unfortunate

75. Because many current college students are somewhat spoiled, they do not want to spend too much time in study.

Eliminate Because.

(A) so do not want
(B) but do not want
(C) and do not want
(D) when do not want
(E) for do not want

76. Andrew Lloyd-Webber has many musicals filling theaters all over the world; also, he can buy whatever he wants even after paying tremendous income taxes.

Replace Andrew Lloyd-Webber with his.

(A) such
(B) whenever
(C) that
(D) with
(E) without

77. Many cocaine dealers are being caught, but many more roam the streets freely and create problems.

Eliminate but, and change the compound sentence into a complex one.

(A) because of
(B) even though
(C) so as
(D) inasmuch as
(E) without

78. A large glass of iced tea that frosts from the cold ice is the best refresher one can offer on a hot summer day.

Make the subject of the sentence nothing better.

(A) offer
(B) there are
(C) offers
(D) offered
(E) there is

79. The publisher was astounded by the sales of Bill Jones' first novel; therefore, he offered a much higher royalty arrangement for the second.

Begin with Astounded by.

(A) novel, he
(B) novel, so the publisher
(C) novel, the publisher
(D) novel; so he
(E) novel; the publisher

80. The new electronic ovens which employ high frequency sound waves rather than heat as a means of cooking food use a clock instead of a thermostat as a control device.

Begin with A thermostat is useless in.

(A) because high frequency sound waves employ
(B) because heat employs
(C) because a control device employs
(D) because clocks employ
(E) because they employ

81. Orphans are considered adoptable until they reach the age of seven; if no family has taken them by then, the welfare agency must be willing to keep the children until they finish high school.

Begin with Orphans are not considered adoptable.

(A) after they become seven years old
(B) until they reach the age of seven
(C) since they became seven years old
(D) because they become seven years old
(E) as they reach the age of seven

82. Any success that attends my efforts to write the great American novel will be completely due to the lessons I learned from my tenth grade English teacher.

Substitute If I succeed for Any success.

(A) is completely due
(B) is completely attentive
(C) is completely learned
(D) is completely responsible
(E) is completely effortless

83. Because Amanda Wingfield had a number of gentleman callers in her youth, she assumed that the number of a girl's suitors was a measure of her popularity.

Eliminate because.

(A) youth, therefore,
(B) youth; therefore,
(C) youth, therefore;
(D) youth, so therefore,
(E) youth; so thus

84. Some pain relievers claim to be nonaddictive, no matter how many tablets a user takes, but others warn against anyone's taking more than four every twenty-four hours.

Begin with Users may take an unlimited.

(A) to become addicted
(B) for becoming addicted
(C) from becoming addicted
(D) with becoming addicted
(E) without becoming addicted

85. When a politician prepares a speech for delivery to a woman's organization, he is sure to include some ringing phrases praising motherhood and home cooking.

Change is sure to include to surely includes.

(A) When a politician prepared
(B) Often when a politician prepares
(C) A politician preparing
(D) A politician praising
(E) A politician cooking

86. Many Americans buy foreign-made automobiles like the Volkswagen or the Nissan because these cars have a reputation for high gas mileage.

Begin with The Volkswagen and the Nissan attract.

(A) because of their reputation
(B) because American buyers
(C) because all foreign cars
(D) because American cars
(E) because of lower prices

87. Chefs consider their own recipes more valuable than gold, for a cook's reputation and salary may well depend upon the uniqueness of his sauces.

Begin with Since the uniqueness of a chef's sauces.

(A) may well depend upon
(B) may well be determined by
(C) may well be dependent upon
(D) may well determine
(E) may well constitute a determination of

88. Our scoutmaster called the three of us to the front of the auditorium and announced that each of us had won five merit badges within a month.

Begin with We three boys.

(A) it was announced by our scoutmaster
(B) and announced by our scoutmaster
(C) our scoutmaster announced
(D) announcing by our scoutmaster
(E) our scoutmaster was called

89. In Illinois, the season for locally grown fresh vegetables lasts about two months; frosts in September usually kill the plants that provide us with tomatoes and beans.

Begin with For about two months, we in Illinois.

(A) grow locally produced
(B) locally produced are grown
(C) has locally grown
(D) used to have locally grown
(E) have locally grown

90. Georgia was among the thirteen original colonies as well as one of the states which seceded from the Union in 1861.

Change was among to one of.

(A) was as well as
(B) was both
(C) was also
(D) was and
(E) was therefore

91. Several social psychologists have offered a number of explanations for the rising rate of venereal disease infection among today's teenagers, but none completely satisfies the doctor who must treat these cases.

Begin with No explanation that is completely satisfactory.

(A) has been treated by doctors
(B) has been offered by social psychologists
(C) has been satisfied by statistics
(D) has been offered by doctors
(E) has been provided by today's teenagers

92. Most electric wristwatches are powered by a small battery, which most manufacturers guarantee for one year.

Change are powered to powers.

(A) Most electric wrist watches (B) A guarantee of one year
(C) For one year (D) A small battery
(E) Most manufacturers

93. Researchers know that different kinds of cancer respond to different kinds of treatment; surgical eradication is effective in some cases, but in others, drugs seem to arrest the spread of cancerous cells.

Change different kinds of cancer to either surgery or certain drugs effectively.

(A) eradicate or arrest
(B) eradicating or arresting
(C) the eradication or the arresting
(D) to eradicate or to arrest
(E) having eradicated or having arrested

94. Snowfalls in Chicago average forty inches a year, but in 1979, January alone produced more than that average.

Begin with January 1979.

(A) more snow than
(B) into a forty inch average
(C) no more snow than
(D) no less snow than
(E) a lot less snow

95. The James Bond movies had been very successful at the box office and with critics; the newest in the series, however, did not make money and was condemned by most critics.

Eliminate the semi-colon so that the new sentence begins:

(A) But . . . also (B) Even though (C) Whenever
(D) Because (E) Why

ANSWER KEY—TRIAL TEST

Section I

1. E	12. B	23. C	34. B	45. D
2. C	13. C	24. C	35. E	46. D
3. D	14. A	25. A	36. C	47. C
4. E	15. D	26. D	37. A	48. B
5. C	16. B	27. A	38. B	49. B
6. B	17. C	28. A	39. A	50. E
7. A	18. B	29. A	40. A	51. B
8. C	19. A	30. E	41. D	52. B
9. E	20. E	31. C	42. B	53. A
10. B	21. A	32. C	43. C	54. C
11. A	22. B	33. D	44. A	55. B

Section II

56. D	64. B	72. D	80. E	88. C
57. B	65. E	73. A	81. A	89. E
58. E	66. C	74. A	82. D	90. C
59. A	67. B	75. C	83. B	91. B
60. C	68. E	76. D	84. E	92. D
61. D	69. B	77. B	85. C	93. A
62. D	70. A	78. E	86. A	94. A
63. A	71. C	79. C	87. D	95. B

SCORING CHART—TRIAL TEST

After you have scored your Trial Test, enter the results in the chart below (the Raw Score computation is explained on page 14); then transfer your Raw Score to the Progress Chart on page 14. As you complete the Sample Examinations later in this part, you should be able to achieve increasingly higher Raw Scores.

Total Test	Number Right	Number Wrong	Number Omitted	Raw Score
Section I:				
Section II:				
Total:				

ANSWER EXPLANATIONS—TRIAL TEST

Section I

1. E. The sentence is correct.
2. C. Perfect cannot be logically compared; use most nearly perfect.
3. D. It's should be its, the correct possessive form.
4. E. The sentence is correct.
5. C. Them has no antecedent; use the Japanese.
6. B. Than any country is illogical; use than any other country.
7. A. Are should be is—the singular subject is some.
8. C. Who's should be whose, the correct possessive form.
9. E. The sentence is correct.
10. B. Seemed (past tense) does not match interviews (present tense).
11. A. Illusions should be allusions—incorrect word choice.
12. B. Most should be almost.
13. C. Or should be nor to complete the parallelism correctly.
14. A. Of is not a correct verb form; use have.
15. D. Very unique is an illogical phrase; unique should not be modified in any way.
16. B. Have should be has; affair, subject of the verb, is singular.
17. C. As should be than, the logical comparison word.
18. B. His should be their, the correct agreement of possessive adjective and antecedent.

19. A. Whoever should be Whomever, the correct form for a direct object.
20. E. The sentence is correct.
21. A. (B) contains a poor idiom (so-as). (C) is wordy and the word positive is ambiguous. (D) is is an incorrect shift from past to present time. (E) they is vague and is a shift in pronoun number.
22. B. (A) has too many words. (C) irritating changes the meaning of the sentence too much. (D) foremost implies an idea not in the original sentence. (E) coarse is an incorrect word choice.
23. C. (A) today's modern is redundant. (B) is too wordy. (D) with is an incorrect word choice. (E) changes the meaning of the sentence too much.
24. C. (A) has is an incorrect verb form—the subject is plural. (B) the phrase beginning Americans is a dangling modifier. (D) has is an incorrect verb form. (E) the sentence does not really make sense.
25. A. (B) changes the meaning too much. (C) is wordy. (D) making illegal is ambiguous. (E) permitting changes the meaning of the sentence too much.
26. D. (A) the comma after voters creates a comma splice. (B) they has no specific word as an antecedent. (C) is illogical—the airplane is not campaigning for anything. (E) the introductory phrase beginning the candidate is a dangling modifier.
27. A. (B) is wrong—is is singular and some implies a plural. (C) whom should be who, subject of expect. (D) commuted, a past tense, breaks the sequence of tenses—the other verbs are present tense. (E) doesn't (a singular) does not agree with the plural subject.
28. A. (B) and (C) are too ambiguous with up. (D) and (E) use the past tense.
29. A. (B) is wrong; the semi-colon destroys the meaning of the sentence. (C) the comma creates a comma splice. (D) a sentence fragment follows the period. (E) as a result adds an irrelevant idea.
30. E. (A) is incorrect—male child is redundant. (B) only male child is not supported by the rest of the sentence. (C) having been sired by does not really make sense. (D) male son is repetitious.
31. C. (A) is incorrect—one indicates a single occupation. (B) is an error in parallelism. (D) nurse and teacher are not words that name professions. (E) is an error in parallelism.
32. C. (A) is an error in subject-verb agreement. (B) cannot but be is a double negative. (D) is is also an error in agreement. (E) could be changes the tense sequence.
33. D. (A) among is redundant. (B) within is a poor word choice. (C) between means that there are only two finalists. (E) there were more than five contestants.
34. B. (A) Because . . . the reason is redundant. (C) reason is because is repetitious. (D) the comma creates a comma splice. (E) this possible response is a sentence fragment.
35. E. (A) and (C) of is not a verb form. (B) could changes the tense relationship. (D) also changes the tense relationship.
36. C. (A) has taken is an incorrect verb sequence. (B) should have is also an incorrect verb sequence. (D) would of is an incorrect verb form. (E) had took is an incorrect verb form.
37. A. (B) after is the wrong word because it implies a time sequence that is incorrect. (C) they is a vague pronoun that has no specific antecedent. (D) since also implies a past event. (E) while is an ambiguous word.
38. B. (A) they is a vague pronoun reference. (C) some people changes the meaning too much. (D) they is also a vague pronoun reference. (E) cannot be no is a double negative.
39. A. (B) to offer is a shift in construction. (C) also is a shift in construction. (D) whoever is illogical. (E) is a needless repetition of words.

40. A. (B) has is singular, and the subject is plural. (C) has been meeting is an incorrect tense sequence. (D) will meet is a time sequence error. (E) can be meeting is illogical in this context.
41. D. Americans in their search for simple answers to complex questions delude themselves that mere technical proficiency can solve any problem that confronts them.
42. B. One of Picasso's original paintings is much more valuable than a lithograph.
43. C. The peace treaty, which stated that each nation would respect the boundaries of the other, did not imply that either nation would defend the others in case of an attack by a third state.
44. A. Whites who are convinced that just more money will solve all of their problems are resented by the residents of inner city slums.
45. D. The publisher, unaccustomed to such service from the post office, could not accept any reason for the manuscript's being delayed in the mail.
46. D. If anyone attempts to read every word in a Sunday edition of *The New York Times*, he or she will be busy for weeks.
47. C. These days, unisex clothing styles and their very similar coiffures make distinguishing males from females difficult.
48. B. A ditch digger who engages in heavy physical activity consumes more high calorie foods than a sedentary desk-bound clerk.
49. B. Anyone exceeding the speed limit on any street or highway in the country can be sure of attracting a policeman's attention.
50. E. A gardener must fight both weeds and insect pests if he or she expects any yield from the efforts of gardening.
51. B. The FBI and local police have warned motorists not to pick up hitchhikers, for either soliciting or giving a ride on an open highway is illegal.
52. B. Evidence to convict the guilty or free the innocent may be developed in a well-equipped crime laboratory, maintained by many large police departments.
53. A. Parishioners arriving late annoyed the pastor once he had started his sermon.
54. C. The chief and fifteen Indians attack the heavily defended fort at least once a day.
55. B. The many attempts by so many people to swindle him out of his money with foolish proposals caused him to become cynical.

Section II

56. D. Sentence 2 seems to introduce an idea that does not fit after the thesis statement in sentence 1; therefore, it should be omitted from the paragraph. (B) is wrong; other films would be too vague to be in a thesis statement. (C) is wrong; sentence 2 would be even more out of place after sentence 5. (E) is incorrect; the change with however would distort the meaning of the paragraph.
57. B. (A) is incorrect; drive would have no subject. In (C), the semi-colon is used incorrectly. (D) contains a redundant phrase and therefore. In (E), a sentence fragment follows the period.
58. E. Sentence 6 should be replaced with a more complete conclusion, because the sentence shifts the emphasis from profits to film producers. All of the other choices are incorrect.
59. A. (B) is incorrect; the length of the sentence has no effect upon its meaning. (C) is incorrect; the sentence is not a conclusion and does have some connection to the rest of the paragraph. (D) and (E) are factually incorrect.
60. C. (A) is incorrect; such a division would make what follows although a sentence fragment. (B), (D), and (E) are factually inaccurate.
61. D. (A), (B), (C), and (E) are subordinate ideas in the paragraph and omit much that is relevant to its meaning.

62. D. If such a combination were made, (D) is the only possible correct answer. (A) is factually inaccurate. (B) is wordy and repeats ideas unnecessarily. (C) produces a sentence fragment after the semi-colon. (E) uses the colon incorrectly.

63. A. (B) is not a logical topic sentence for the paragraph. (C) is an illogical placement of the sentence. (D) and (E) are factually inaccurate.

64. B. (A) is inaccurate; any shortening might eliminate an important idea. (C) is incorrect; any additional ideas might complicate the sentence. (D) is incorrect; if it were eliminated, important ideas might also be eliminated. (E) is incorrect; sentence 6 would not be a good conclusion for the paragraph.

65. E. A reader could find all the problems in (A), (B), (C), and (D) true.

66. C. (A) is factually inaccurate. (B) is inaccurate; the paragraph has nothing to say about the difficulty of studying English. (D) is a minor point, an illustration, in the paragraph. The vocabulary and ideas in (E) would make this choice inaccurate.

67. B. All the other choices are factually inaccurate.

68. E. Reversing sentences 2 and 3 provides a more logical development of the idea in the paragraph. (D) is incorrect; sentence 2 expands the idea in sentence 3. (A), (B), and (C) are incorrect; these changes would be even more illogical than the original sentence.

69. B. (A), (C), or (D) would make the whole sentence unclear and the passage too short. (E) sentence 9 is not a conclusion.

70. A. The word sixth implies that the writer has made five other points in the discussion; all the other choices are incorrect.

71. C. (A) asks for no examples to support the meaning. (B) is wrong; fire does not come up until later in the paragraph. (D) and (E) have little or nothing to do with the point of the paragraph.

72. D. All the other choices distort or misstate the audience for the paragraph.

73. A. The paragraph leads logically to the word semantics. (B) is incorrect; it obviously contradicts the implications of the paragraph. (C) is incorrect; it is too vague to be a conclusion. (D) is wrong; there is no discussion of dictionaries in the paragraph. (E) is too vague and general to be a conclusion.

74. A. That families go to court and sue each other over fortunes is unfortunate in this litigious age.

75. C. Many current college students are somewhat spoiled and do not want to spend too much time in study.

76. D. With his many musical hits filling theaters all over the world, Andrew Lloyd-Webber can buy whatever he wants, even after paying tremendous income taxes.

77. B. Even though many cocaine dealers are being caught, many more roam the streets freely and create problems.

78. E. There is nothing better on a hot summer day than a large glass of iced tea that frosts from the cold ice.

79. C. Astounded by the sales of Bill Jones' first novel, the publisher offered a much higher royalty arrangement for the second.

80. E. A thermostat is useless in the new electronic ovens because they employ sound waves rather than heat as a means of cooking and a clock as a control device.

81. A. Orphans are not considered adoptable after they become seven years old; if no family . . .

82. D. If I succeed in my efforts to write the great American novel, my tenth grade English teacher is completely responsible.

83. B. Amanda Wingfield had a number of gentlemen callers in her youth; therefore, she assumed that . . .

84. E. Users may take an unlimited number of tablets of some pain relievers without becoming addicted, but others warn against anyone's . . .

85. C. A politician preparing a speech for delivery to a women's organization surely includes ringing phrases . . .

86. A. The Volkswagen and the Nissan attract many American buyers of foreign-made automobiles because of their reputation for high gas mileage.

87. D. Since the uniqueness of a chef's sauces may well determine his reputation and salary, he considers his recipes more valuable than gold.

88. C. We three boys were called to the front of the auditorium, and our scoutmaster announced that each of us had won three merit badges within a month.

89. E. For about three months, we in Illinois have locally grown fresh vegetables; frosts in September usually . . .

90. C. Georgia was one of the thirteen original colonies and was also one of the states that seceded from the Union in 1861.

91. B. No explanation that is completely satisfactory to doctors, who must treat the venereal disease cases among today's teenagers, has been offered by social psychologists for the rising rate of infection.

92. D. A small battery, which most manufacturers guarantee for one year, powers most electric wristwatches.

93. A. Researchers know that either surgery or certain drugs effectively eradicate or arrest the spread of cancerous cells.

94. A. January 1979 brought Chicago more snow than the annual forty-inch average.

95. B. Even though the James Bond movies had been very successful at the box office, the newest in the series did not make money and was condemned by most critics.

CHAPTER

Background and Practice Questions

4

Note: The College-Level Examination Program (CLEP) has three different examinations that cover the material a student is supposed to master in a college composition course:

1. The English composition examination in the General Examinations battery for which this chapter is a guide.
2. A CLEP subject examination named *College Composition.*
3. A CLEP subject examination named *Freshman English.*

BEFORE YOU TAKE ANY CLEP EXAMINATION, BE SURE YOU KNOW WHICH OF THE THREE EXAMINATIONS WILL BE ACCEPTED BY THE INSTITUTION TO WHICH YOU WILL SEND YOUR SCORES, AND TAKE THE APPROPRIATE EXAMINATION.

DESCRIPTION OF THE ENGLISH COMPOSITION EXAMINATION

The English Composition Examination in the General Examinations battery is offered in two forms:

1. An all-multiple-choice test consisting of about 95 multiple-choice questions divided into two separately timed 45-minute sections. This is the form of the trial test given in Chapter 3 and of the three sample examinations given later.
2. A combination of multiple-choice questions and an essay, consisting of Section I (50–55 items requiring 45 minutes) and Section II (a written essay on an assigned topic, which also requires 45 minutes). This version of the examination is not available each time a CLEP test is administered by a national testing center. Therefore, you will need to check with your college to be sure you are taking the version it accepts and with the test center to be sure when that version is being offered.

As you probably noticed while taking the trial test, the questions deal with logical and structural relationships within sentences, between sentences, between paragraphs, and other matters.

Section I

Section I of both versions of the examination has three types of questions.

1. Identifying wording that is ambiguous or unclear or that violates the standard conventions of written English (35–40 percent of Section I).
2. Choosing the version of a phrase, clause, or sentence that best conveys the intended meaning (35–40 percent of Section I).
3. Choosing the best version of a sentence that has been reworded to change the emphasis in phrasing or to improve clarity (25–30 percent of Section I).

These three question types are used to measure the candidate's awareness of a variety of logical, structural, and grammatical relationships within sentences, including the following:

- Appropriate tense and tense sequence
- Agreement between parts of sentences (subject and verb, pronoun and antecedent)
- Sentence completeness
- Sentence joining (coordination, subordination, modification)
- Shift in focus within sentence structure
- Parallel structures and expressions
- Idiomatic use of language
- Conventions of usage
- Economy and clarity of expression
- Recognition of correctly written sentences

Section II

Since the sample examinations in this book illustrate the all-multiple-choice format, we will concentrate on that one. Later in this chapter, we will provide information about the essay, which is required on the essay version of Section II.

The two kinds of questions you will find on the all-multiple-choice version are these:

1. You are asked to read a short passage or a paragraph and answer questions about its content and organization, using those skills that you would use in writing a composition (60–65 percent of Section II).
2. Some additional items like type 3 of Section I (35–40 percent of Section II).

STUDY SOURCES

For review, you might consult the following books.

Choy, Penelope and James McCormick. *Basic Grammar and Usage*. 3rd ed. Chicago: Harcourt, Brace, Jovanovich, 1990.

Corder, Jim W. and John J. Ruszkiewicz. *Handbook of Current English*. Glenview, IL: Scott, Foresman & Co., 1989.

Flower, Linda. *Problem Solving Strategies for Writing*. 2nd ed. New York: Harcourt, Brace, Jovanovich, 1985.

Fowler, H. Ramsey and Jane E. Aaron. *The Little Brown Handbook*. 4th ed. Glenview, IL: Scott, Foresman & Co., 1989.

Elsbree, Langdon and Gerald P. Mulderig. *The Heath Handbook*. 11th ed. Lexington, MA: D.C. Heath & Co., 1986.

Gefvert, Constance. *The Confident Writer: A Norton Handbook*. 2nd ed. New York: W.W. Norton, 1988.

Hopper, V.F. et. al. *Essentials of English*. 4th ed. Hauppauge, NY: Barron's Educational Series, Inc., 1990.

Leggett, Glenn et. al. *Prentice Hall Handbook for Writers*. Englewood Cliffs, NJ: Prentice Hall, 1988.

McCuen, Jo Ray and Anthony C. Winkler. *Rewriting Writing*. 2nd ed. Chicago: Harcourt, Brace, Jovanovich, 1990.

Troyka, Lynn Quitman. *Simon and Schuster Handbook for Writers*. New York: Prentice Hall, 1987.

Whitten, Mary E, Winfred B. Horner, Suzanne S. Webb. *Harbrace College Handbook*. 11th ed. Chicago: Harcourt, Brace, Jovanovich, 1990.

PRACTICE QUESTIONS FOR SECTION I, QUESTION TYPE 1

The directions and practice questions that follow will give you a good idea of what Type 1 questions are like. The directions, reprinted here by permission of Educational Testing Service, are the actual directions you will find in the test booklet on the day of the exam.

Directions: The following sentences contain problems in grammar, usage, diction (choice of words), and idiom.

Some sentences are correct.
No sentence contains more than one error.

You will find that the error, if there is one, is underlined and lettered. Assume that elements of the sentence that are not underlined are correct and cannot be changed. In choosing answers, follow the requirements of standard written English.

If there is an error, select the one underlined part that must be changed to make the sentence correct.

If there is no error, select answer (E).

To help you review some of the basics of grammar and usage on which you will be tested, the practice questions for Type 1 are grouped by type of grammatical error.

Errors in Case of Pronouns

Example:

1. Between you and I (A), that whole celebration was really (B) an elegant affair (C), I (D) thought. No error (E)

   Explanation: The underlined error is choice (A); I should be me, objective case, object of preposition between.

2. The history teacher, whom (A) I think was the best teacher (B) I ever had, (C) told us (D) that he had served overseas during World War II. No error (E)

   Explanation: The underlined error is choice (A); whom should be who, subjective case, subject of the verb was.

Now, try your hand with the following twelve sentences. You will find the answers and the explanations immediately following the group of sentences:

1. My aunt, whom we admire (A) almost too much, has given we (B) boys ten (C) dollars each to spend at the fair (D) tomorrow. No error (E)

2. When [I showed my] (A) mother the suit [I had selected,] (B) she [objected to me] (C) buying it; [she said it] (D) was too expensive. [No error] (E)

3. [In her note] (A) the teacher [asked the principal] (B) to give some chalk from his supply room to [whomever of] (C) [us boys] (D) would go down to pick it up. [No error] (E)

4. [New York City] (A) [with it's many] (B) suburbs has been called America's fabulous metropolis, [its dirtiest city,] (C) and its most exciting [place for a] (D) brief vacation. [No error] (E)

5. Abraham [Lincolns Gettysburg] (A) Address has been called a [model of brevity,] (B) [the greatest short speech] (C) that [anyone has ever] (D) delivered, and a speech worth more than a longer one would have been. [No error] (E)

6. [Please ask] (A) [whoever you] (B) wish to serve as a fourth member of the [board I am] (C) appointing to study the pollution situation [in your county.] (D) [No error] (E)

7. [The United Nations] (A) has performed many useful tasks [through its various] (B) commissions although there [are representatives on] (C) these commissions [whom everyone] (D) knows are Communists. [No error] (E)

8. The Nobel Prize for Literature [has been awarded] (A) to [John Steinbeck, who's] (B) novels are now [considered among the] (C) greatest that [have] (D) been written in the United States in the twentieth century. [No error] (E)

9. Even though we [know that] (A) we are exercising our rights [under] (B) the United States Constitution, [Gail and myself] (C) are arrested every [time we] (D) picket police headquarters. [No error] (E)

10. When the final [story has been] (A) written for that final newspaper [sometime in] (B) the future, you can be sure [that it's substance] (C) will be some violent act that [has] (D) occurred. [No error] (E)

11. After the bell rang and signaled (A) the end of classes for that day, the teacher told Claire and I (B) that we (C) would have to remain thirty minutes longer for whispering in the back (D) of the room. No error (E)

12. A modern skyscraper is usually constructed (A) with a steel frame which is then covered (B) with concrete slabs, stones (C) of some kind, brick, or any other material that will hide it's metal (D) skeleton. No error (E)

ANSWERS AND EXPLANATIONS

1. B. We should be us; it is the indirect object of the verb has given.
2. C. Me should be my; the possessive case is used with the gerund; the object of the preposition is buying and not me.
3. C. Whomever should be whoever; it is the subject of would go.
4. B. It's should be its; the possessive case of it never has an apostrophe.
5. A. Lincolns should be Lincoln's; this is a possessive, not a plural.
6. B. Whoever should be whomever; objective case needed; object of wish.
7. D. Whom should be who; subject of verb are.
8. B. Who's should be whose; who's is a contraction of who is.
9. C. Myself should be I; I, subject of are arrested; myself is a reflexive pronoun.
10. C. It's should be its; possessive pronoun never has an apostrophe.
11. B. I should be me; object of the verb told.
12. D. It's should be its; it's is a contraction of it is.

Errors in Agreement of Subject and Verb

Example:

1. Washing clothes in an electric washing machine (A) provide (B) the American housewife (C) with something to keep her (D) busy, at least one or twice a week. No error (E)

Explanation: The underlined error is choice (B); provide should be provides; the subject washing clothes is singular.

2. Either John or his two friends is going (A) to find that passing a test (B) on that (C) material is not the easiest thing they (D) have ever done in school. No error (E)

Explanation: The underlined error is choice (A); is going should be are going, to agree with the plural word friends.

► Now, try your hand at the next six items:

1. The committee is deciding (A) now which of the many (B) applicants for the (C) teaching position are going (D) to be hired. No error (E)

2. Despite what each of the experts tell (A) us about how to avoid (B) bankruptcy, some people insist on (C) spending more money each year than they (D) make. No error (E)

3. Each of the critics were (A) assigned a book to read, (B) to discuss within (C) twenty minutes, and to offer (D) his opinion about. No error (E)

4. Although the influence (A) of television on America's buying (B) proclivities have been (C) studied by many psychologists, no one has found exactly what the influence has been. (D) No error (E)

5. No member of a circus troop have (A) the right to play strictly (B) to the audience so that other members (C) of the team do not get their (D) fair share of the applause. No error (E)

6. No matter what statisticians report (A) to the American Automobile Association, accidents just does not (B) happen on today's superhighways (C) unless some driver has been too (D) careless at the wheel of his car. No error (E)

ANSWERS AND EXPLANATIONS

1. D. Are should be is; subject which is singular.
2. A. Tell should be tells; subject each is singular.
3. A. Were should be was; subject each is singular.
4. C. Have should be has; subject influence is singular.
5. A. Have should be has; subject member is singular.
6. B. Does should be do; subject accidents is plural.

Errors in Agreement Between a Pronoun and Its Antecedent

Example:

1. The audience was cheering (A) Laurence Olivier's (B) performance as Hamlet; they refused (C) to leave the theater until he (D) took four curtain calls. No error (E)

Explanation: The underlined error is choice (C); they should be it.

2. No one is able to find their seats (A) in a darkened theater (B) and must ask an (C) usher to bring a flashlight (D). No error (E)

Explanation: The underlined error is choice (A); their seats should be his seat.

Now, try your hand at the following seven items:

1. When anyone expresses his desire (A) to get married (B) as quickly (C) as possible, they always set (D) off gossiping tongues in the community. No error (E)

2. When anyone seeks employment (A) with a large corporation, he should (B) always be sure that his (C) qualifications fit their needs (D). No error (E)

3. Everyone has always wanted their own life-style (A) to be accepted by society (B) as a whole, even though some of these styles (C) are offensive to many in that (D) society. No error (E)

4. When anyone looks up a word (A) in any of the desk dictionaries to check its (B) spelling, you must make (C) sure that the word cannot be spelled in more than (D) one acceptable way. No error (E)

5. The congregation was sitting reverently (A) in their pews (B) when the organ broke the silence (C) with the first chords of a traditional (D) hymn, "The Old Rugged Cross." No error (E)

6. The television industry was (A) jolted when the Federal Communications Commission announced that cigarette advertising would not be permitted (B) on television after January 1, 1971 (C), a move that took away one of their (D) prime sources of revenues. No error (E)

7. When you finally decide upon (A) the career you will follow for the rest of your life, a person should (B) be sure that you have made a choice that (C) will bring you as much personal gratification (D) as possible. No error (E)

ANSWERS AND EXPLANATIONS

1. D. They always set should be he always sets; antecedent anyone is singular.
2. D. Their should be its; antecedent corporation is singular.
3. A. Their should be his or her; antecedent everyone is singular.
4. C. You should be he or she; antecedent anyone is third person.
5. B. Their should be its; antecedent congregation is singular here.
6. D. Their should be its; antecedent industry is singular.
7. B. A person should be you; antecedent you is second person.

Errors in Tense Sequence

Example:

1. Almost every time (A) Jack drives (B) the family car, he has left it (C) completely empty of gasoline (D). No error (E)

Explanation: The underlined error is choice (B); drives should be has driven.

2. If we could only enjoy (A) the pleasures of our youth again (B), we may find (C) that we have not forgotten (D) them after all. No error (E)

Explanation: The underlined error is choice (C); may should be might.

▶ Now, try your hand with these four sentences:

1. This morning (A), all banks in the New York district announce (B) that interest rates (C) for all home loans would be raised to 8% (D). No error (E)

2. The chief strongly opposes the idea of putting a single policeman in cars
A B
that would be cruising at night in high crime districts. No error
C D E

3. According to the schedule posted on the choir's bulletin board, there are
A B
three selections before the offertory but only one after the plates had been
C
passed by the ushers. No error
D E

4. If John Paul Jones had not been victorious in his naval battles, the United
A B
States will have been a second rate power on the seas forever. No error
C D E

ANSWERS AND EXPLANATIONS

1. B. Announce should be announced; correct tense sequence with would be raised.
2. C. Would should be will; correct tense sequence with opposes.
3. B. Are should be were; correct tense sequence with had been passed.
4. C. Will should be would have; correct tense sequence after had not been.

Errors in Word Choices, Diction, and Idioms

An error in diction means that the writer has selected the incorrect word. An error in word choice means that the writer has selected a word that means almost what he or she wanted to say but not quite.

An error in idiom means that the writer has selected the wrong word to complete the idiom that he or she wanted to use.

Example:

1. She looked at both pictures carefully; she could not decide which was the
A B C
most beautiful. No error
D E

Explanation: The underlined error is choice (D); most should be more.

2. While Mary was setting out on the porch, she saw John and Bill walking
A B C
slowly toward her from town. No error
D E

Explanation: The underlined error is choice (A); setting should be sitting.

3. When the baby woke up [A] from his nap [B], he made alot [C] of noise, jumping up [D] and down in his crib. No error [E]

Explanation: The underlined error is choice (C); alot should be a lot.

4. Without no warning [A] at all [B], the policeman fired at the running man [C] and shot him in the back, killing [D] him instantly. No error [E]

Explanation: The underlined error is choice (A); no should be any.

5. The company is having some difficulty of promoting [A] its new [B] detergent; [C] housewives must be sold [D] the idea of switching brands. No error [E]

Explanation: The underlined error is choice (A); of should be in.

6. Every day [A] this summer, all the children [B] in the neighborhood have gone [C] to the village pool where they have swimmed [D] for several hours. No error [E]

Explanation: The underlined error is choice (D); swimmed should be swam or swum.

7. After all the votes have been [A] counted and the winner [B] declared, the new president will be formerly inducted [C] into the office he will occupy [D] for four years. No error [E]

Explanation: The underlined error is choice (C); formerly should be formally.

8. When gold was discovered [A] in California in 1849, there was [B] a mad stampede by people [C] to both buy land in the area or lease claims [D] near Sutter's Mill. No error [E]

Explanation: The underlined error is choice (D); or should be and.

9. No matter how hard the teacher tries to teach [A] her class, her efforts have [B] little affect [C] upon the students who refuse [D] to study the assigned materials. No error [E]

Explanation: The underlined error is choice (C); affect should be effect.

10. With his great strength (A), Samson could of beaten (B) any opponent in the wrestling arena, if he had not (C) allowed his hair to be cut by a conniving (D) woman. No error (E)

Explanation: The underlined error is choice (B); of should be have.

► Now, try your hand at the following twenty-five sentences:

1. After Mother had tucked (A) us into bed and kissed us (B) good night, we continued (C) talking when we should of closed our (D) eyes and gone to sleep. No error (E)

2. No matter how hard (A) I try to finish an assignment, I cannot do (B) it if there is (C) anything laying around (D) that I can play with. No error (E)

3. My Uncle Jack (A), who was setting (B) on the porch and enjoying a cold drink (C), called out and told me (D) to be careful about running into the street without looking. No error (E)

4. I will (A) neither give you money to waste on that junk or (B) offer any further advice if you (C) proceed (D) against my wishes. No error (E)

5. Most all women (A) who support (B) conservative political candidates also support (C) many conservative organizations that (D) have grown in membership within the past decade. No error (E)

6. Because it was (A) the best offer that had been made, the owner decided to except $100,500 (B) for his home although (C) he knew it was worth more on today's (D) market. No error (E)

7. He is tired (A) of picking up all the dirty clothes that (B) his roommate leaves laying (C) on the bathroom floor every morning (D). No error (E)

8. George Gershwin, composer of many of the songs by which American
A
popular music has gained a reputation for greatness, was unhappy and
B C
dissatisfied by his early works and studied to improve his compositions.
D
No error
E

9. Jealousy has been called the more disastrous of all the human emotions
A B
that can wrack the mind, often susceptible to all kinds of fears and
C D
anxieties. No error
E

10. Charles Johnson, one of the smartest lawyers in the United States, has
A B
often told me that most all criminals really want to be kept in jail. No error
C D E

11. Between the several choices on the menu, I can hardly decide whether I
A B C
will order roast beef, fried chicken, broiled fish, or baked ham. No error
D E

12. It is really pitiful to see a small child die without never having lived long
A B C D
enough to accomplish anything. No error
E

13. Ely Culbertson, a famous professional bridge player, said that thirteen
A
spades dealt in one hand is the most unique unusual bridge hand he ever
B C
saw. No error
D E

14. No team ever wants to loose a game, even though it seems that some teams
A B C
make many foolish mistakes and appear to throw a game away. No error
D E

15. When the play had less and less people in its audience as its run grew
A B
longer, the producers began to consider the feasibility of trying to extend its
C D
run beyond six months. No error
E

16. Most historians now agree that the true story about John Smith and
A
Pocahontas has never been told; maybe some of them are even real sorry
B C D
that the facts are still hidden. No error
E

17. While the driver was (A) very carefully moving (B) ahead on the expressway ramp, he did not notice (C) that black Cadillac that was speeding in back (D) of him. No error (E)

18. Your letter in regards to my (A) delinquent bill has been sent (B) to my attorneys for possible suit for slander (C) because it contains several insinuations (D) that are untrue. No error (E)

19. Mother always enjoyed a few quit moments (A) alone in her bedroom (B) before serving dinner (C) so that she could appear at the table calm and relaxed (D). No error (E)

20. There is that bird again, (A) diving at us (B) from her nest in the elm tree, trying to peck (C) us on the head, and then flying off somewheres else (D) to be safe from our retaliation. No error (E)

21. Mother says that we may have (A) no more cookies without we come into (B) the house, clean our rooms thoroughly, (C) and ask politely if there are (D) anymore cookies in the jar. No error (E)

22. In his statement (A) at the press conference, the president inferred that (B) opposition to his foreign policy could be found only among those (C) who had not voted for him in the election (D). No error (E)

23. Now that I have reached the age of eighty-two, (A) I find that I can't hardly do (B) many of the things that were very easy for me (C) when I was sixteen and still (D) vigorous. No error (E)

24. Although I enjoyed the exotic dinner we were served in San Francisco's (A) most famous Chinese (B) restaurant, I felt badly (C) because I knew that I had eaten more than I should have (D). No error (E)

25. With a valid passport, an American citizen can go anywheres in the world, (A) to any country (B) that will give him or her permission to enter except a few (C) nations that the State Department has ruled "out of bounds" (D) for American tourists. No errors (E)

ANSWERS AND EXPLANATIONS

1. D. Of should be have.
2. D. Laying should be lying.
3. B. Setting should be sitting.
4. B. Or should be nor.
5. A. Most should be Almost.
6. B. Except should be accept.
7. C. Laying should be lying.
8. D. Should be with not by his works.
9. B. More should be most.
10. C. Most should be almost.
11. A. Between should be Among.
12. C. Never should be ever.
13. C. Eliminate unique.
14. B. Loose should be lose.
15. A. Less and less should be fewer and fewer.
16. D. Real should be really.
17. D. In back of should be behind.
18. A. Regards should be regard.
19. A. Quit should be quiet.
20. D. Somewheres should be somewhere.
21. B. Without should be unless.
22. B. Inferred should be implied.
23. B. Eliminate hardly.
24. C. Badly should be bad.
25. A. Anywheres should be anywhere.

Errors in Parallelism

Example:

1. As the locomotive (A) left the station, it jerked them so that the passengers (B) were thrown from their seats (C) and who fell (D) on the floor. No error (E)

Explanation: The underlined error is choice (D); the sentence parallels a verb phrase (thrown from their seats) with a dependent clause, beginning who fell.

2. Almost everyone enjoys watching (A) a baseball game on television, having a (B) picnic in a peaceful park, or to visit some (C) strange place abroad (D). No error (E)

Explanation: The underlined error is choice (C); the sentence parallels two verbals (watching and having) with an infinitive to to visit.

▶ Now, try your hand with the following four sentences:

1. Dustin Hoffman, one of Hollywood's great (A) stars, made his reputation playing a confused young man (B), a tubercular panhandler, and he also has (C) enacted other roles (D). No error (E)

2. No one can decide between (A) two alternatives to raise money (B): either the club should sponsor (C) a cookie sale or stage a festival (D) in the town's auditorium. No error (E)

3. During the past five years, many college (A) students have protested by sitting in various (B) campus buildings, by burning campus structures, and they have (C) also intimidated members of the administration (D). No error (E)

4. Joe Namath (A), a professional football player and who (B) has written a book about his experiences on and off (C) the gridiron, is now making a name for (D) himself as an actor in Hollywood. No error (E)

ANSWERS AND EXPLANATIONS

1. C. The sentence parallels two nouns with an independent clause.
2. D. The same construction (a complete clause) should appear after both either and or.
3. C. The sentence parallels two prepositional phrases with an independent clause.
4. B. The sentence parallels a noun with a dependent clause.

Dangling Elements and Misplaced Modifiers

Example:

1. Rising up above (A) the top of a very high mountain (B), we saw the sun make its way (C) slowly (D) to the zenith at noon. No error (E)

   Explanation: The underlined error is choice (A); the participial phrase cannot logically modify the first word after the comma.

2. The young man who was (A) running down the street (B) very rapidly (C) turned the corner and ran into (D) a policeman who was looking for him. No error (E)

   Explanation: The underlined error is choice (C); whether the adverb modifies was running or turned is not clear.

► Now, here are four for practice:

1. After watching plane after plane land (A) without seeing the one he waited for, (B) they left (C) the airport in complete disgust at being so badly fooled (D) by airline schedules. No error (E)

2. Looking ahead as far (A) as the Detroit designers can predict, the automobile will always have (B) four wheels, (C) a steering wheel, two headlights, and four (D) wheel brakes. No error (E)

3. A good definition (A) of a real tragedy is when a fire (B) destroys the home of a man who (C) goes to church, loves his wife and parents, is good to his children, and (D) supports his government by voting in every election. No error (E)

4. The painter broke his hip (A) when the ladder (B) broke, climbing slowly (C) rung by rung until he reached the second floor (D) of the building. No error (E)

ANSWERS AND EXPLANATIONS

1. A. The introductory participial phrase does not modify they.
2. A. The introductory participial phrase does not modify automobile.
3. B. Is when is an illogical construction, usually a misplaced modifying clause.
4. C. The participial phrase has no word in the sentence to modify.

Incorrect Verb Forms

Example:

1. Alcoholics Anonymous exists to rescue (A) those poor souls who have always drank so (B) much that they cannot break (C) away from their addiction alone. (D) No error (E)

Explanation: The underlined error is choice (B); drank should be drunk.

2. When all poverty has been successfully eradicate from (A) the earth and all men live at (B) peace with their neighbors, then one might say that (C) an idyllic condition has finally developed. (D) No error (E)

Explanation: The underlined error is choice (A); eradicate should be eradicated.

▶ Now, try the four sentences which follow:

1. "The Age of Aquarius" is suppose (A) to be an age of youth, an age of great (B) accomplishments by everyone (C), an age in which all of man's hopes and aspirations will be realized (D). No error (E)

2. Just because of (A) the mounting inflation (B) in the United States, many (C) investors have chose (D) to buy stocks in European rather than in American companies. No error (E)

3. Ronald Reagan has probably spoke (A) before larger crowds during his political career than (B) any politician of the seventeenth century ever dreamed would assemble (C) to hear any (D) speaker. No error (E)

4. After many repetitions of the manual of arms (A), a raw recruit becomes use (B) to going through (C) the drill without thinking too hard about what he is doing (D). No error (E)

ANSWERS AND EXPLANATIONS

1. A. Suppose should be supposed.
2. D. Chose should be chosen.
3. A. Spoke should be spoken.
4. B. Use should be used.

Sentence Problems

One of the conventions of writing in English is that sentences should be complete, and you may find that some of the choices among the questions will form a sentence fragment, a comma splice, or a run-together sentence. To help you identify these sentence construction errors, here are three definitions and some illustrations of the errors:

1. A *complete sentence* can be defined as a group of words that has a subject and a verb and that lacks a word that would make the group of words a dependent clause or some other sentence part. For example:

The boy hit the ball.

That collection of words is a complete sentence; it has a subject (boy) and a verb (hit). A complete sentence may be as short as this illustration or much longer, but the definition still holds: there is no word that makes the words a dependent clause as When the boy hit the ball. When makes that example an incomplete sentence.

2. A *sentence fragment* is a group of words that may look like a complete sentence but that lacks a subject or a verb, or that includes a word which makes the group incomplete. Look at the following examples:

Looking up at the airplanes
While the clouds turned darker and darker
A terrible experience for all of us

None of these is a complete sentence, because they each lack one of the characteristics set forth in item 1 above.

3. A *run-together sentence* is defined as two complete sentences that are written as if they were one complete sentence. For example:

The boy worked hard he wanted to succeed.

There are two complete sentences (The boy worked hard and he wanted to succeed), and English convention says that we must have some logical separation of those complete sentences. If you use a comma—The boy worked hard, he wanted to succeed—you will make another error called the comma splice.

Look at some possible questions that might include errors in sentence construction.

Examples:

1. The new Chevrolet Lumina model has captured the admiration of many automobiles critics, they have praised its sleek lines and daring styles.
   (A) critics, they have
   (B) critics; they have
   (C) critics they have
   (D) critics, whom have
   (E) critics, he has
   The correct answer is (B). The semi-colon corrects the comma splice. (C) is incorrect because no punctuation creates a run-together sentence. (D) is incorrect because whom is the objective form of the pronoun. (E) is also incorrect because he (a singular) cannot refer to critics (plural); also the comma splice error has not been changed.

2. Margaret Thatcher, Prime Minister of Great Britain, has changed the course of British history within her first ten years in office.
   (A) Britain, has changed
   (B) Britain, who has changed
   (C) Britain; has changed
   (D) Britain has changed
   (E) Britain, whom has changed
   The correct answer is (A). (B) and (E) are incorrect because the relative pronouns would make the sentence incomplete; whom is also the incorrect case. (C) is incorrect because the semi-colon signals that a comma splice has been corrected, and there is no comma splice in the sentence. (D) is incorrect because there needs to be a comma to set off the appositive phrase.

Now, try several of these types of sentences, illustrating the types of items you will find on an actual CLEP test:

1. A national magazine called president Jimmy Carter "the best ex-president we have ever had" he has worked on many projects to help people.
   (A) have ever had" he has
   (B) have ever had" because he has
   (C) have ever had due to the fact that
   (D) have ever had" being that he has worked
   (E) have ever had", working

2. Dustin Hoffman won an Oscar for his performance as an autistic man, he lived in a sheltered home for many years before being rescued by his brother.
   (A) man, he lived in
   (B) man he lived in
   (C) man who lived
   (D) man whom he had lived in
   (E) man, living in

ANSWERS AND EXPLANATIONS

1. B. Because makes the rest of the sentence a dependent clause. As written, there is a run-together sentence.
2. C. The comma splice is eliminated. (B) is a run-together sentence. (D) and (E) are wrong.

The Dangling Modifier

Another sentence structure problem is called the *dangling modifier*. This error is more accurately called a lapse in logic on the part of the writer, but it can be defined as the use of a modifier—a phrase or clause—that does not have a specific word in the rest of the sentence to modify. For example:

At the age of five, my father died.

If you read that sentence literally, you can only conclude that my father died when he was five years old, a biological impossibility.

Correction: When I was five years old, my father died.

Dangling modifiers do not occur only at the beginning of sentences. For example:

My brother fell and broke his leg in three places, which was too bad.

Which was too bad does not modify a specific word in the rest of the sentence but rather the idea which the rest of the sentence conveys.

Look at a few more examples with corrections:

Looking up, four airplanes were overhead.

Correction: When I looked up, I saw four airplanes overhead.

The robber who was running down the street rapidly turned the corner.

(Does rapidly modify was running or turned? The modifier dangles between the two possibilities, creating an ambiguous sentence.)

Correction: The robber who was running rapidly down the street turned the corner.

or

The robber who was running down the street turned the corner rapidly.

Either makes clear what the writer intended.

While washing clothes, the clock struck three.
Correction: While I was washing clothes, the clock struck three.

My mother won a million dollars in the lottery, which was fortunate.
Correction: It was fortunate that my mother won a million dollars in the lottery.

Correct Sentences

Type 1 questions include some sentences that are correct but that have portions underlined that might contain an error or that are put in to "distract" the test taker.

1. Bill and John (A) started on their hike this morning; (B) we hope they (C) will reach the finish line without having to quit. (D) No error (E)

2. The other night, (A) I was reading Joseph Heller's mad novel about World War II when I decided (B) that all wars are made by (C) insane people who need (D) many sessions on some psychiatrist's couch. No error (E)

3. George Washington, the (A) father of our country, had many problems (B) with the Continental Congress; (C) many times he had to beg for (D) funds to support his starving army. No error (E)

4. Walking up four flights (A) of stairs is not easy (B) for anyone who has (C) any kind of heart trouble or who gets tired very easily. (D) No error (E)

5. Many builders of fine furniture (A) have used designs first created by Adams, (B) Chippendale, Duncan-Phyffe, Morris, as well as other (C) older furniture designers whose work (D) is preserved in museums all over the world. No error (E)

6. Apple pie or ice cream— (A) which has more calories? (B) Even the best (C) diet books published cannot give anyone (D) a clear answer. No error (E)

7. When the final score flashed on the (A) scoreboard, cheers rose from (B) the crowd that had been hoping (C) for that long-awaited victory over the traditional rival. (D) No error (E)

8. According to the code of ethics that all lawyers accept [A], no lawyer should take any [B] action, within or outside [C] the courtroom, that might damage his client's rights [D] to a fair trial. No error [E]

9. In any business, the workers expect [A] to be paid promptly when [B] pay day comes; no one of them can finance his day [C] to day life without such [D] punctuality. No error [E]

10. Jonathan Winters is famous [A] for his expert comedy [B], his ability to assume a number of different roles [C], and his knack of improvising [D] dialogue while the television camera is on. No error [E]

> **Caution:** On the actual CLEP examination, sentences will *not* be isolated by error as these practice pages and items have been organized; therefore, you will have to consider each underlined section carefully and consider the possibility that any one of a number of errors might be present. Also, do not forget that some sentences are correct and contain no error.

PRACTICE QUESTIONS FOR SECTION I, QUESTION TYPE 2

These items test a student's ability to discern what is incorrect about the structure of a sentence, that is, what problems might exist in the sentence as written that would interfere with logical communication.

Directions: In each of the following sentences, some part or all of the sentence is underlined. Below each sentence you will find five ways of phrasing the underlined part. Select the answer that produces the most effective sentence, one that is clear and exact, without awkwardness or ambiguity. In choosing answers, follow the requirements of standard written English. Choose the answer that best expresses the meaning of the original sentence.

Answer (A) is always the same as the underlined part. Choose answer (A) if you think the original sentence needs no revision.

Example:

1. The reason the company failed was because the president spent too much money.
   (A) The reason the company failed was because
   (B) The company failed because
   (C) Because the company failed
   (D) Because the reason was the company failed
   (E) The company failed was because
   The correct answer is (B). The other choices are wordy or create illogical sentences.

2. When four years old, my father died.
(A) When four years old
(B) When four year's old
(C) When he was four years old
(D) When I was four years old
(E) At the age of four
The correct answer is (D). The underlined section in the original sentence is a dangling modifier, and only answer (D) solves that problem.

3. Football teams pay athletes tremendous sums of money each year, the fans pay large sums for seats in the stadium
(A) year, the fans pay large sums
(B) year, the fans paying large sums
(C) year, for the fan pay large sums
(D) year; the fans paying large sums
(E) year, when the fans pay large sums
The correct answer is (C). The original sentence contains a comma splice, and only (C) corrects the problem logically.

4. The lazy old man was lying under his favorite tree, sipping his favorite soft drink, and reading his favorite novel for the fifth time.
(A) man was lying under his favorite tree, sipping
(B) man was laying under his favorite tree, sipping
(C) man was lying under his favorite tree sipping
(D) man laid under his favorite tree, sipping
(E) man lied under his favorite tree, sipping
The correct answer is (A). (B) is incorrect; laying is the wrong word choice. (C) is incorrect; the comma after tree is omitted, distorting the parallelism of the original.
(D) is incorrect; laid is the wrong word choice.
(E) is also incorrect; lied is the wrong word choice.

5. People who attend baseball games often do not know enough about the fine points of offense and defense to enjoy them.
(A) People who attend baseball games often do not know enough about the fine points of offense and defense to enjoy them.
(B) People who attend baseball games do not know a sufficient amount about the fine points of offense and defense to appreciate them.
(C) Some people who attend baseball games do not know enough about the fine points of offense and defense to enjoy the skill of the players.
(D) People who attend baseball games often do not know enough about them to enjoy the fine points of offense and defense.
(E) People who attend baseball games do not understand the fine points of offense and defense.
The correct answer is (C). (A) and (B) has them, which is a vague pronoun.
(D) has the same problem even though them is moved within the sentence.
(E) changes the meaning of the original too much.

Now that you have tried some items of this type, try six more.

1. The wooden house had once been a show piece of antebellum architecture, but time and tide had reduced the structure to wrack and ruin.
   (A) but time and tide had reduced the structure to wrack and ruin
   (B) but time had reduced the structure to wrack and ruin
   (C) but time and tide had reduced the structure to ruin
   (D) but time reduced the structure to a ruin
   (E) but time had reduced the structure to a ruin

2. Bill had to be administered to by a doctor when his admittance to Harvard was refused.
   (A) Bill had to be administered to by a doctor when his admittance to Harvard was refused.
   (B) Bill had to be treated by a doctor when his admission to Harvard was refused.
   (C) Bill had to be treated by a doctor when his admittance to Harvard was refused.
   (D) Bill had to be administered to by a doctor when his admission to Harvard was refused.
   (E) Bill was administered to by a doctor when his admittance to Harvard was refused.

3. Our neighborhood ice cream vendor was refused a license because he sold banana splits to customers that were rotten.
   (A) because he sold banana splits to customers that were rotten
   (B) because he sold banana splits to customers who were rotten
   (C) because he sold banana splits that were rotten to customers
   (D) because he sold banana splits who were rotten to customers
   (E) because he sold rotten banana splits to customers

4. We could only wonder if he were going to attend college this fall, or if he was planning to seek immediate employment.
   (A) this fall, or if he was planning to seek
   (B) fall, or he was planning to seek
   (C) fall, or if he were planning to seek
   (D) fall or was planning to seek
   (E) fall; or he was planning to seek

5. Running the rapids of the Colorado River in a small raft are considered one of the greatest sporting thrills available to anyone.
   (A) the Colorado River in a small raft are considered
   (B) the Colorado River in a small raft is considered
   (C) the Colorado River with a small raft are considered
   (D) the Colorado River in small rafts are considered
   (E) the Colorado's River in a small raft is considered

6. Each of you can do the problem if you will put your mind to work and not give up too easily.
   (A) each of you can do the problem if you will put your
   (B) each of you can do the problem if they will put their
   (C) each and everyone of you can finish the problem if they will put their
   (D) each and everyone one of them can finish the problems if you will put their
   (E) everyone of you can finish the problems if they will put their

ANSWERS AND EXPLANATIONS

1. E. Wrack and ruin and time and tide are clichés. Only choices (D) and (E) eliminate them; choice (D), however, introduces another error, an error in verb tense.
2. B. Administered and admittance are errors in diction. (B) is correct.
3. E. That was rotten (which modifies banana splits) is a misplaced modifier in any position except choice (E).
4. C. Was must be changed to were to make the two parts of the sentence parallel in construction.
5. B. Running . . . raft is the subject of the sentence; therefore, are must be is.
6. A. The sentence is correct as it stands.

PRACTICE QUESTIONS FOR SECTION I, QUESTION TYPE 3

Note: This type of item is also question Type 2 in Section II of the all-multiple-choice version of the exam.

Directions: Effective revision requires choosing among the many options available to a writer. The following questions test your ability to use these options effectively.

Revise each of the following sentences according to the directions that follow it. Some directions require you to rephrase only part of the original sentence; others require you to recast the entire sentence. You may need to omit or add certain words in constructing an acceptable revision, but you should keep the meaning of your revised sentence as close to the meaning of the original as the directions permit. Your new sentence should follow the conventions of standard written English and should be clear and concise.

Look through answer choices A–E under each question for the exact word or phrase that is included in your revised sentence. If you have thought of a revision that does not include any of the words or phrases listed, try to revise the sentence again so that it does include the wording in one of the answer choices.

When you take the test, you should feel free to make notes in your test book, but you will need to mark your answers on the separate answer sheet.

Examples:

1. *Sentence:* Graduates of Harvard's law school are more likely to be hired by large Wall Street firms than graduates of a small midwestern law school.

   Directions: Substitute have fewer chances, for are more likely.

   (A) of being hired (B) by being hired (C) with being hired
   (D) instead of being hired (E) as well as being hired.

   The correct answer is (A). Graduates of a small midwestern law school have fewer chances of being hired by large Wall Street firms than graduates of Harvard's Law School.

2. *Sentence:* Since there were too many books on the weak table, Mary removed two of them and put them on the shelf.

Directions: Begin with Mary removed.

(A) on the weak table (B) by the weak table (C) from the weak table (D) upon the weak table (E) onto the weak table

The correct answer is (C). Mary removed two of the books from the weak table and placed them on the shelf.

3. *Sentence:* The waitress was discharged from her position at the restaurant because she refused to wear the uniform required for anyone serving food.

Directions: Begin with The waitress refused.

(A) food, therefore, she was discharged
(B) food, and was discharged
(C) food, so she was discharged
(D) food and was discharged
(E) food, as a result of which she was discharged

The correct answer is (D). The waitress refused to wear the uniform required of anyone serving food and was discharged from her position in the restaurant.

4. *Sentence:* The old man was tired of listening to his children's complaints; therefore, he disconnected his hearing aid.

Directions: Begin with Tired.

(A) complaints, and he (B) complaints, and the old man
(C) complaints, the old man (D) complaints, he
(E) complaints, so the old man

The correct answer is (C). Tired of listening to his children's complaints, the old man disconnected his hearing aid.

Now try several of this type of question and check the correct answers at the end of the group.

1. **Certain specialized drugs have been used with remarkable success by doctors treating some mental disorders, particularly the manic-depressive syndrome, that thirty years ago would have required the patient to be hospitalized indefinitely.**

Begin with Thirty years ago some mental.

(A) patient, now these disorders
(B) patient, and now these disorders
(C) patient, for these disorders
(D) patient, with these disorders
(E) patient; now these disorders

2. **He was trapped into a loveless marriage by an overly anxious girl; therefore, he was already weary of her chattering before a month had passed.**

Begin with Trapped into.

(A) girl, he (B) girl; he (C) girl, therefore, he
(D) girl, so he (E) girl; therefore, he

3. Members of that loose coalition of groups calling themselves "The New Left" believe that the only solution for the nation's problems is the overthrow, through violence if necessary, of both corrupt capitalism and a corrupt governmental system.

Substitute advocate for believe.

(A) system for the only (B) system through the only
(C) system as well as the only (D) system as the only
(E) system by the only

4. Anyone's first flight is always a unique experience, no matter how many times he has seen pictures of planes flying or heard tales about the first flights of others.

Begin with No matter and substitute anyone for he.

(A) anyone's own (B) a person's own (C) his own
(D) their own (E) theirs

5. The truck driver, tired after forty hours on the highway without rest, took a pep pill; he knew that just one would keep him awake and alert for about three hours.

Begin with The truck driver knew.

(A) hours; so tired (B) hours; therefore, tired
(C) hours; moreover, tired (D) hours, tired
(E) hours, therefore, tired

6. The average laborer with no income except his monthly wages is frequently hard pressed for immediate cash to pay his personal bills.

Substitute whose only for with.

(A) no income except his (B) income except his
(C) income accepts his (D) income is his (E) no income but

7. Radical blacks angrily charge that a corporation which hires minority group workers and then lays them off during a recession is actually intensifying the frustrations of black workers rather than helping them.

Substitute a corporation's for a corporation.

(A) actually intensifying (B) intensifies minority workers
(C) actually intensifies (D) must actually intensify
(E) actually brings on

8. According to an American Medical Association report, psychiatrists should be aware that certain types of female patients will attempt to seduce them.

Begin with An American Medical Association.

(A) bewares psychiatrists (B) arouses psychiatrists
(C) defends psychiatrists (D) declares psychiatrists
(E) warns psychiatrists

9. **No depression in American history has ever lasted as long as the one which began in 1929; it is ironic that only the beginning of World War II in Europe brought prosperity to the United States.**

Begin with It is ironic, and substitute ended for brought.
(A) the lasting depression
(B) the longest depression
(C) the 1929 beginning depression
(D) no prosperity in the United States
(E) no depression in American history

10. **In their support of rising minority group aspirations, large corporations are not only evidencing true altruism in improving the lot of minorities but also producing social changes within the communities in which their plants are located.**

Substitute both for not only.
(A) and (B) but (C) and so (D) as much as (E) for

ANSWERS AND EXPLANATIONS

1. E. Thirty years ago, some mental disorders would have required the indefinite hospitalization of the *patient; now these disorders* respond to treatment by certain specialized drugs.
2. A. Trapped into a loveless marriage by an overly anxious girl, he was already weary of her chattering before a month had passed.
3. D. Members of that loose coalition of groups calling themselves "The New Left" advocate the overthrow, through violence if necessary, of both corrupt capitalism and a corrupt governmental *system as the only* solution for the nation's problems.
4. B. No matter how many times anyone has seen pictures of planes flying or heard tales about the first flights of others, *a person's own* first flight is always a unique experience.
5. B. The truck driver knew that one pep pill would keep him awake and alert for about three *hours, therefore, tired* after forty hours on the highway without rest, he took one.
6. D. The average laborer whose only *income is his* monthly wages is often hard pressed for immediate cash to pay his personal bills.
7. C. Radical blacks angrily charge that a corporation's hiring minority group workers and then laying them off during a recession *actually intensifies* the frustration of black workers rather than helps them.
8. E. An American Medical Association report *warns psychiatrists* that certain types of female patients will attempt to seduce them.
9. B. It is ironic that only the outbreak of World War II ended *the longest depression* in American history and brought prosperity to the United States.
10. A. In their support of rising minority group aspirations, large corporations are both evidencing true altruism in improving the lot of minorities *and* producing social changes within the communities in which their plants are located.

PRACTICE QUESTIONS FOR SECTION II (ALL-MULTIPLE-CHOICE VERSION)

Section II of the all-multiple-choice version uses two types of questions to measure the various skills needed to write an essay. One type of question is based on a brief reading passage in which the sentences are numbered. Candidates are asked to read the passage and then answer questions about it that involve redrafting and revising the passage. The questions ask the candidate about such conceptual and rhetorical considerations as evaluation and organization of evidence, functions and relationships of sentences, and audience and purpose for writing. These questions constitute about 60–65 percent of Section II. The remaining 35–40 percent of Section II contains the same type of questions that were described previously under Section I, Type 3 questions.

The following directions and sample questions will give you an idea of what the passage-based questions in this section are like.

Directions: Each of the following passages consists of a paragraph of numbered sentences. Since the paragraphs appear as they would within a larger piece of writing, they do not necessarily constitute a complete discussion of the issues presented.

Read each paragraph carefully and answer the questions that follow it. The questions test your awareness of characteristics of prose that are important to good writing.

Questions 1–6 are based on the following passage:

[1]My basement is designed to be a family room, although we do not usually use it that way. [2]My desk is down here where it is cool, quiet, and away from the noise of the street outside the house. [3]My living room has three large windows which look out on my neighbors' driveway; thus, I can keep up with their comings and goings all hours of the day. [4]In my basement, I have my typewriter, all the files I need to do my writing, and a radio which I keep tuned to a good FM station. [5]I can get more work done if I have some "white noise" to block out the interference of other noises in the house. [6]When I withdraw to the basement to read papers or write, my wife knows that she is not to disturb me except in case of an extreme emergency like the house catching on fire or something like that. [7]I also have my library stored down here so that I can reach for a book that I might need to refer to when I read or write. [8]There is also a bed; sometimes I get tired of typing and want to stretch out for a few minutes to rest my weary back and fingers.

1. What should be done with sentence 3?
   (A) It should begin the passage.
   (B) It should be omitted.
   (C) It should come after sentence 5.
   (D) It should come after sentence 8.
   (E) It should be combined with sentence 4.

2. Which of the following should be done with sentence 5?
   (A) It should be omitted.
   (B) It should be reduced to a clause, beginning *if*, and joined to sentence 7.
   (C) It should begin with *and* and be joined to sentence 8.
   (D) It should come at the beginning of the passage.
   (E) It should begin with *because* and be joined to sentence 4.

3. A logical concluding sentence for this passage would be which of the following?
(A) My library is the most important thing in my life.
(B) I spend many happy hours in my living room, watching my neighbors.
(C) My basement is the center of my professional life; without it, I would be forced to write less than I do.
(D) My basement is furnished with early American antiques.
(E) My FM radio provides me with many hours of amusement.

4. The paragraph is an example of
(A) descriptive writing
(B) argumentative writing
(C) comparison/contrast writing
(D) writing that is too detailed to be interesting
(E) fiction writing

5. The tone of the paragraph is
(A) very formal
(B) impressionistic
(C) stentorian
(D) relaxed and informal
(E) satiric

6. From the paragraph, a reader might infer that the profession of the writer is
(A) nursing
(B) teaching
(C) radio announcing
(D) preaching
(E) automobile repairman

ANSWERS AND EXPLANATIONS

1. B. (B) shifts from the basement to the living room, and the whole paragraph is about the basement; thus, sentence 3 is irrelevant to the paragraph.
2. E. (A) is incorrect, because sentence 5 adds important information. (B) and (C) would create illogical sentences. (D) is incorrect, because sentence 5 would not be a good topic sentence for the whole paragraph.
3. C. All of the other choices focus on minor points in the paragraph; only (C) summarizes the paragraph effectively.
4. A. The large number of descriptive details about the room lead to no other possible conclusion.
5. D. The tone of a piece of writing is the author's attitude toward the material; the attitude here seems conversational.
6. B. The number of specific references to writing and reading papers, consulting books, and the like force that conclusion.

Section II (essay version)

This section asks you to use forty-five minutes to write an essay on a given topic. You will find below specific directions, one sample topic, and three sample essays written in response to the topic.

In scoring essays, readers look for logical development of the argument, appropriate use of specific examples, unity in the composition, and clarity and effectiveness of expression, as well as use of the conventions of standard written English. They recognize that some errors are the result of haste rather than of ignorance and do not allow such errors to influence their rating of the quality of the total essay.

Directions: You will have 45 minutes to plan and write an essay on the topic specified. Read the topic carefully. You are expected to spend a few minutes considering the topic and organizing your thoughts before you begin writing. *Do not write on a topic other than the one specified. (An essay on a topic of your own choice is not acceptable.)*

The essay is being assigned to give you an opportunity to demonstrate your ability to write effectively. You should, therefore, take care to express your thoughts on a topic clearly and exactly and to make them interesting. Be specific, using supporting examples whenever appropriate. How well you write is much more important than how much you write.

Assignment: Some young people believe that their parents should completely finance a college education for them. These people have the idea that they are owed this financial assistance, because parents have provided such support in the past and because parents want their children to succeed in life.

Write an essay in which you agree or disagree with this argument for parental funding of higher education expenses. Be sure to provide specific evidence to defend your opinion so that what you write has credibility to a reader. If necessary, make up figures to support your position.

Sample Essay

Whether true or false, accurate or inaccurate, many young people today are convinced that their financial success in life can be guaranteed by a college education. They also realize obtaining that education is expensive and going up ten to fifteen percent each year. They ask, "Where is the money coming from?" Many respond, "From my parents."

At the urging of parents, those graduating from high school start in their junior year seeking college scholarships, government grants, privately financed loan funds, and other types of financial aid, but they soon discover that many of these sources offer little hope of financial assistance except to those who are easily identified as disadvantaged in some way or to those in the top two or three percent by grade point average or by extremely high ACT or SAT scores. Many immediately reject the idea of going into debt to finance a college education. Thus, they look to parents for obligatory financial help even though they should realize that parents can not offer much support nor should they, unless they are very wealthy.

Any students who wish to obtain a college education nowadays must be willing to work at least part time to provide some funds. For many students, part-time work is already a part of their life-style, but often the money goes to purchase new cars, new clothes, or expensive stereo sets. Now that expensive college tuition, books, and fees are a reality, these young people must wake up to the fact that parents can not be depended upon any longer for a free ride. These young men and women must accept responsibility for their own education. By the end of high school each child in the family has already used a large amount of family income, and it is unreasonable that more of the family's money should be spent on college. For example, ordinary family expenses (food, shelter, clothing) consume close to seventy-five percent of family financial resources, and college expenses beyond these necessities would be prohibitive for most families.

Thus, children should not consider a college education at family expense a right and must be prepared to help themselves as much as possible through work or through loans. No child should hesitate to mortgage his or her future with a loan if there is no other way to finance college expenses. Moreover, many children could scale down their ambitions to attend expensive private colleges and universities and attend less costly state-supported institutions.

Parents can not be and should not be expected to provide all the necessary education funds. If they did, how could they support themselves?

This sample paper represents the length that readers of your paper (two college English teachers) will expect and find acceptable within the forty-five minute guideline. It contains a clearly organized response to the assignment, uses some specific evidence to support the central idea of the essay (sentence one of paragraph three for example), and seems coherent as the idea is developed. Delaying the statement of the central idea for two paragraphs permits the writer to establish the background for the paper's main point: parents should not be expected to pay all of children's college expenses.

Note that the assignment permits the writer to agree or disagree with the basic statements contained therein. If you decided to support the thesis, obviously you would supply evidence contrary to that which the sample paper presents. Note also that the assigned topic does not require specialized knowledge but relates to a situation familiar to most people.

Other possible topics might include some like the following:

1. You have been offered two positions in a large corporation. One requires you to travel all over the country and often overseas; the other allows you to remain in one place for a few years at least but with the possibility of transfer every few years. The positions pay the same salary with the same fringe benefits, and both offer the same possibilities for promotion.

   In an essay, discuss which position you would choose and provide some specific reasons for your choice.
2. Nowadays, many women are faced with the choice of a home and family or a career that will provide financial rewards. Children have traditionally been the primary responsibility of the woman as care giver, although many enlightened employers now provide day-care facilities for employees' children.

   In an essay, consider the advantages or disadvantages of day-care facilities for the family.
3. Within the past decade, foreign-made automobiles have invaded the United States' market and have become so popular that American-made cars have suffered decreases in sales. Is there anything the federal government can do or should do to reduce competition from these foreign cars?

   In an essay, answer the question with specific reasons for your choice.

ESSAY WRITING HINTS

1. Read the question *very carefully.* Notice the limitations of the topic (e.g., "Choose one side of this question") and any other instructions (e.g., "Give specific details regarding your qualifications and experience").
2. Allow a brief time (perhaps 5 minutes) to think about what you will say, and to decide how you will organize your ideas. Will chronological order be best? Or is a cause-and-effect relationship evident between certain points you want to make? Or would an enumerative order, arranging ideas from the least to the most important, work well?
3. Jot down on the bottom of the instruction sheet important points that you want to include.
4. Begin to write slowly, carefully, and *legibly* on the special answer sheet provided. Bear in mind that there is no requirement as to length. A good essay of reasonable length will be rated higher than a poor one that is twice as long.
5. When you express a generalization, be sure to back it up with examples or other supporting evidence.
6. Before writing a sentence, ask yourself, "Is this idea expressed correctly, concisely, and clearly?"
7. Allow time to read your essay critically. Look for misspellings, grammatical errors, ambiguities, and wordiness. Make necessary corrections and other changes as neatly as you can.

Conclusion

After you have worked through the sample questions in this chapter, you should be prepared for a whole CLEP Examination in English Composition. Three such examinations are given in the next chapter, models of those which you may encounter on an actual CLEP test. Again, we must caution you to ask the college to which your scores will be sent which version of the examination you are required to take—the version *with* the written composition or the version *without* the written composition. Remember, the version *with* the written composition will be given only twice a year, therefore timing is important to you. Good luck on this examination!

ANSWER SHEET — ENGLISH COMPOSITION/SAMPLE EXAMINATION 1

Section I

1. Ⓐ Ⓑ Ⓒ Ⓓ Ⓔ
2. Ⓐ Ⓑ Ⓒ Ⓓ Ⓔ
3. Ⓐ Ⓑ Ⓒ Ⓓ Ⓔ
4. Ⓐ Ⓑ Ⓒ Ⓓ Ⓔ
5. Ⓐ Ⓑ Ⓒ Ⓓ Ⓔ
6. Ⓐ Ⓑ Ⓒ Ⓓ Ⓔ
7. Ⓐ Ⓑ Ⓒ Ⓓ Ⓔ
8. Ⓐ Ⓑ Ⓒ Ⓓ Ⓔ
9. Ⓐ Ⓑ Ⓒ Ⓓ Ⓔ
10. Ⓐ Ⓑ Ⓒ Ⓓ Ⓔ
11. Ⓐ Ⓑ Ⓒ Ⓓ Ⓔ
12. Ⓐ Ⓑ Ⓒ Ⓓ Ⓔ
13. Ⓐ Ⓑ Ⓒ Ⓓ Ⓔ
14. Ⓐ Ⓑ Ⓒ Ⓓ Ⓔ
15. Ⓐ Ⓑ Ⓒ Ⓓ Ⓔ
16. Ⓐ Ⓑ Ⓒ Ⓓ Ⓔ
17. Ⓐ Ⓑ Ⓒ Ⓓ Ⓔ
18. Ⓐ Ⓑ Ⓒ Ⓓ Ⓔ
19. Ⓐ Ⓑ Ⓒ Ⓓ Ⓔ
20. Ⓐ Ⓑ Ⓒ Ⓓ Ⓔ
21. Ⓐ Ⓑ Ⓒ Ⓓ Ⓔ
22. Ⓐ Ⓑ Ⓒ Ⓓ Ⓔ
23. Ⓐ Ⓑ Ⓒ Ⓓ Ⓔ
24. Ⓐ Ⓑ Ⓒ Ⓓ Ⓔ
25. Ⓐ Ⓑ Ⓒ Ⓓ Ⓔ
26. Ⓐ Ⓑ Ⓒ Ⓓ Ⓔ
27. Ⓐ Ⓑ Ⓒ Ⓓ Ⓔ
28. Ⓐ Ⓑ Ⓒ Ⓓ Ⓔ
29. Ⓐ Ⓑ Ⓒ Ⓓ Ⓔ
30. Ⓐ Ⓑ Ⓒ Ⓓ Ⓔ
31. Ⓐ Ⓑ Ⓒ Ⓓ Ⓔ
32. Ⓐ Ⓑ Ⓒ Ⓓ Ⓔ
33. Ⓐ Ⓑ Ⓒ Ⓓ Ⓔ
34. Ⓐ Ⓑ Ⓒ Ⓓ Ⓔ
35. Ⓐ Ⓑ Ⓒ Ⓓ Ⓔ
36. Ⓐ Ⓑ Ⓒ Ⓓ Ⓔ
37. Ⓐ Ⓑ Ⓒ Ⓓ Ⓔ
38. Ⓐ Ⓑ Ⓒ Ⓓ Ⓔ
39. Ⓐ Ⓑ Ⓒ Ⓓ Ⓔ
40. Ⓐ Ⓑ Ⓒ Ⓓ Ⓔ
41. Ⓐ Ⓑ Ⓒ Ⓓ Ⓔ
42. Ⓐ Ⓑ Ⓒ Ⓓ Ⓔ
43. Ⓐ Ⓑ Ⓒ Ⓓ Ⓔ
44. Ⓐ Ⓑ Ⓒ Ⓓ Ⓔ
45. Ⓐ Ⓑ Ⓒ Ⓓ Ⓔ
46. Ⓐ Ⓑ Ⓒ Ⓓ Ⓔ
47. Ⓐ Ⓑ Ⓒ Ⓓ Ⓔ
48. Ⓐ Ⓑ Ⓒ Ⓓ Ⓔ
49. Ⓐ Ⓑ Ⓒ Ⓓ Ⓔ
50. Ⓐ Ⓑ Ⓒ Ⓓ Ⓔ
51. Ⓐ Ⓑ Ⓒ Ⓓ Ⓔ
52. Ⓐ Ⓑ Ⓒ Ⓓ Ⓔ
53. Ⓐ Ⓑ Ⓒ Ⓓ Ⓔ
54. Ⓐ Ⓑ Ⓒ Ⓓ Ⓔ
55. Ⓐ Ⓑ Ⓒ Ⓓ Ⓔ

Section II

56. Ⓐ Ⓑ Ⓒ Ⓓ Ⓔ
57. Ⓐ Ⓑ Ⓒ Ⓓ Ⓔ
58. Ⓐ Ⓑ Ⓒ Ⓓ Ⓔ
59. Ⓐ Ⓑ Ⓒ Ⓓ Ⓔ
60. Ⓐ Ⓑ Ⓒ Ⓓ Ⓔ
61. Ⓐ Ⓑ Ⓒ Ⓓ Ⓔ
62. Ⓐ Ⓑ Ⓒ Ⓓ Ⓔ
63. Ⓐ Ⓑ Ⓒ Ⓓ Ⓔ
64. Ⓐ Ⓑ Ⓒ Ⓓ Ⓔ
65. Ⓐ Ⓑ Ⓒ Ⓓ Ⓔ
66. Ⓐ Ⓑ Ⓒ Ⓓ Ⓔ
67. Ⓐ Ⓑ Ⓒ Ⓓ Ⓔ
68. Ⓐ Ⓑ Ⓒ Ⓓ Ⓔ
69. Ⓐ Ⓑ Ⓒ Ⓓ Ⓔ
70. Ⓐ Ⓑ Ⓒ Ⓓ Ⓔ
71. Ⓐ Ⓑ Ⓒ Ⓓ Ⓔ
72. Ⓐ Ⓑ Ⓒ Ⓓ Ⓔ
73. Ⓐ Ⓑ Ⓒ Ⓓ Ⓔ
74. Ⓐ Ⓑ Ⓒ Ⓓ Ⓔ
75. Ⓐ Ⓑ Ⓒ Ⓓ Ⓔ
76. Ⓐ Ⓑ Ⓒ Ⓓ Ⓔ
77. Ⓐ Ⓑ Ⓒ Ⓓ Ⓔ
78. Ⓐ Ⓑ Ⓒ Ⓓ Ⓔ
79. Ⓐ Ⓑ Ⓒ Ⓓ Ⓔ
80. Ⓐ Ⓑ Ⓒ Ⓓ Ⓔ
81. Ⓐ Ⓑ Ⓒ Ⓓ Ⓔ
82. Ⓐ Ⓑ Ⓒ Ⓓ Ⓔ
83. Ⓐ Ⓑ Ⓒ Ⓓ Ⓔ
84. Ⓐ Ⓑ Ⓒ Ⓓ Ⓔ
85. Ⓐ Ⓑ Ⓒ Ⓓ Ⓔ
86. Ⓐ Ⓑ Ⓒ Ⓓ Ⓔ
87. Ⓐ Ⓑ Ⓒ Ⓓ Ⓔ
88. Ⓐ Ⓑ Ⓒ Ⓓ Ⓔ
89. Ⓐ Ⓑ Ⓒ Ⓓ Ⓔ
90. Ⓐ Ⓑ Ⓒ Ⓓ Ⓔ
91. Ⓐ Ⓑ Ⓒ Ⓓ Ⓔ
92. Ⓐ Ⓑ Ⓒ Ⓓ Ⓔ
93. Ⓐ Ⓑ Ⓒ Ⓓ Ⓔ
94. Ⓐ Ⓑ Ⓒ Ⓓ Ⓔ
95. Ⓐ Ⓑ Ⓒ Ⓓ Ⓔ

CHAPTER

5

Sample Examinations

This chapter includes three sample examinations, each with an answer key, scoring chart, and answer explanations. Take the first exam, check your answers, determine your raw score, and record it on the Progress Chart provided on page 14. Then, as you gain familiarity with the test, take the other two examinations and see your scores climb.

SAMPLE ENGLISH COMPOSITION EXAMINATION 1

Section I

Number of items: 55
Time: 45 minutes

Directions: The following sentences contain problems in grammar, usage, diction (choice of words), and idiom.

Some sentences are correct.
No sentence contains more than one error.

You will find that the error, if there is one, is underlined and lettered. Assume that elements of the sentence that are not underlined are correct and cannot be changed. In choosing answers, follow the requirements of standard written English.

If there is an error, select the one underlined part that must be changed to make the sentence correct.

If there is no error, select answer (E).

1. Because of the cold (A) which seemed to develop quite (B) suddenly, Dorothy woke up feeling badly (C) and decided not to go to work (D) yesterday. No error (E)

2. The Red Cross first aid manual provides the following (A) instructions for an emergency treatment of a heart attack victim: loose his clothing (B), cover him (C) with a blanket, and give no medication (D) until a doctor arrives. No error (E)

3. The trees in the garden (A) have developed (B) their (C) autumn leaf colors (D): red, brown, orange, and yellow. No error (E)

4. After the professor (A) conferred with me about my paper, pointing out to me (B) all the errors I made, I could only (C) agree that my work was not affective (D). No error (E)

5. Assuming that all (A) materials will be delivered (B) by the deadlines the architect has established, we should occupy our new building by the end of October but certainly no later (C) than November 15 (D). No error (E)

6. A perfect umpire should always be disinterested (A) in the game whose rules (B) he is there to interpret for the players; he must (C) maintain complete partiality (D) to avoid being charged with unfair decisions. No error (E)

7. Just above the towering (A) peaks, we saw the glorious sun as it was raising (B), pouring streams of brilliant color over the whole snow-capped mountain (C) range and the verdant valleys (D) below. No error (E)

8. Since 1945, many former colonies (A) of the British Empire has achieved independence from the government (B) in London, and some historians have (C) noted this development with skepticism (D). No error (E)

9. When Willie Mays was a small boy (A), he wanted to play baseball (B) in the major leagues very badly (C), but proving his competence (D) in sandlot and minor leagues was the only route he could take. No error (E)

10. Jack Benny (A), one of the funniest comedians who worked in television, remained thirty-nine years (B) old for more than thirty years; his portrayal (C) of a skinflint and a perpetual worrier have been one of the most successful acts (D) in show business history. No error (E)

11. Few art critics have been able to except the most recent exhibitions
A B
arranged by the curator of the Metropolitan Museum in New York; charges
and countercharges of lack of artistic discrimination have filled the col-
C
umns of the newspapers and magazines. No error
D E

12. Senate investigators have charged that the major weapon systems
A
developed by the Pentagon's research and development sections have cost
B
many billions more than the initial estimates and contracts and that
C
supplemental appropriations must be passed immediately. No error
D E

13. Justification for his allegations came from him and I, as the only two
A B
witnesses to the bizarre crime the old man committed against the attrac-
C
tive woman as she walked by the packing house last night. No error
D E

14. Use any set of criteria you want, but you will never convince me that
A B C
Beethoven is not equally as good a composer as Johann Sebastian Bach.
D
No error
E

15. In San Francisco's North Beach area, there are many transient young
A
people whose weird costumes seem to flaunt conspicuously every moral
B C
code the silent majority accepts as holy. No error
D E

16. In a convoluted style, the novel tells the tragic story of a father's in-
A B
humanity to his daughter, a mother's rejection of her son, and the
C
unnatural affection that developed between the alienated boy and girl.
C D
No error
E

17. Until transmissions were standardized by the automobile industry in the
A
late 1920's, drivers had to learn several different gear positions of the gear
B C
shift lever, which left everyone confused. No error
D E

18. We could only ask ourselves (A) how any sane man could have chosen such (B) an ugly suit to wear when (C), rich as he is, he could have had the pick of any of (D) the suits in the finest men's stores in the community. No error (E)

19. That an artist like Pablo Picasso (A) priced his current paintings at more than (B) \$100,000 each and actually sold as many as he released (C) to the markets seem too (D) fantastic to be believed. No error (E)

20. Whether anyone will do well on (A) an examination has depended (B) upon many factors: whether he knows the material, whether he is feeling good or bad (C), or even whether the seat of the desk is properly adjusted to his height (D). No error (E)

Directions: In each of the following sentences, some part or all of the sentence is underlined. Below each sentence you will find five ways of phrasing the underlined part. Select the answer that produces the most effective sentence, one that is clear and exact, without awkwardness or ambiguity. In choosing answers, follow the requirements of standard written English. Choose the answer that best expresses the meaning of the original sentence.

Answer (A) is always the same as the underlined part. Choose answer (A) if you think the original sentence needs no revision.

21. There were fewer people in the auditorium than we had expected; there were seats for everyone.
(A) There were fewer people in the auditorium than
(B) There were no more people in the auditorium than
(C) In the auditorium, there were a lot more people than
(D) There were not as many people in the auditorium as
(E) A great deal fewer people showed up in the auditorium as

22. During the Renaissance, the Italian peasants could hardly find enough food to keep their families alive and healthy.
(A) the Italian peasants could hardly find enough food
(B) the Italian peasants could hardly locate in the country more food than necessary
(C) the Italian peasants could scarcely find sufficient food
(D) the Italian peasants starved themselves with enough food
(E) the Italian peasants could not have found more than enough food

23. Attending college is a dream which many of today's young people have had for fifteen years, at least.
    (A) which many of today's young people have had
    (B) which many of today's young people has had
    (C) which many of today's young people is having
    (D) which many of today's young people have been having
    (E) which many of today's young people had been having

24. A good plumber can connect one pipe with another so completely that there will be no leak from the joint.
    (A) with another so completely that
    (B) into another with such a high degree of skill as
    (C) with another so that there will be completely
    (D) with another with such little skill that
    (E) with another with such accuracy that

25. My old dog Bruce who is out there lying in the sun has served me well for the past twelve years.
    (A) Bruce who is out there lying in the sun
    (B) Bruce that foolishly is not lying in the sun
    (C) Bruce, on the alert out there in the sun,
    (D) Bruce, working hard for his daily cookie treats,
    (E) Bruce whom we found out in the bright sun of noon

26. Many others who are not so fortunate will lose all the money they have invested in the stock market.
    (A) others who are not so fortunate
    (B) others who have had more fortunes
    (C) others who are not as fortunate
    (D) others whom we find to be among the more unfortunate
    (E) others who have had too many fortunes

27. Marguerite spoke French with a charming accent for she had studied the language with a former Russian countess in Paris.
    (A) Marguerite spoke French with a charming accent for she had
    (B) Marguerite spoke French with a very unique accent because she had
    (C) Marguerite, speaking French with a charming accent, had
    (D) Marguerite had often spoken French with a charming accent so that she had
    (E) Marguerite, speaking French with a charming accent, for she had

28. Frightened by the sound of footsteps, Jane ran upstairs and hide in the closet.
    (A) ran upstairs and hide in the closet
    (B) ran upstairs, having hidden in the closet
    (C) ran upstairs; they went away
    (D) ran upstairs, which was hiding in the closet
    (E) ran upstairs and hid in the closet

29. The more money Mr. Getty accumulated, the more he wanted.
(A) the more he wanted
(B) he increased his desires
(C) the more he accumulated
(D) the greater quantity he desired
(E) the larger in number became his disciples

30. No one doubts Lorraine Hansbury's skill as a dramatist; but there is some critics who believe her plays lack poetic dialogue and skillful exposition.
(A) dramatist; but there is some critics who believe
(B) dramatist; they say
(C) dramatist, although some critics believe
(D) dramatist, believing
(E) dramatist, who some critics believe

31. The bus driver is always pleasant to we riders even though he must become impatient with some of us who never have the correct change.
(A) pleasant to we riders even though
(B) pleasant to us riders although
(C) pleasant to us riders so that
(D) pleasantly to us riders even though
(E) impatient to those riders who

32. The clever orator's presenting a specious argument caused his audience to become restless and inattentive.
(A) The clever orator's presenting a specious argument caused his audience to become restless and inattentive.
(B) When the clever orator presented a specious argument, his audience became restless and inattentive.
(C) The clever orator's presentation of a specious argument, causing his audience to become restless and inattentive.
(D) The clever orator presenting a specious argument was when his audience became restless and inattentive.
(E) The clever orator presented a specious argument because his audience became restless and inattentive.

33. That type of person always strongly resents any attempt by anyone to limit his actions.
(A) That type of person always
(B) That type of person who always
(C) That type person that
(D) He is that type of person who always
(E) He is that type of persons

34. Because he was growing marijuana, Jerry was picked up by the police.
(A) was picked up
(B) was arrested, and they were picked up
(C) was arrested; then held
(D) who was arrested
(E) was arrested without charge

35. While glancing through today's newspaper, I read that the cost of living has risen another four points.
(A) While glancing through today's paper, I read that the cost of living has risen another four points.
(B) Glancing through today's newspaper, the cost of living has risen another four points.
(C) Today's newspaper contained an item that the cost of living has risen another four points.
(D) The cost of living having risen another four points, I read in today's newspaper.
(E) I was glancing through today's newspaper when the cost of living rose another four points.

36. Each time Leonard Bernstein sitting down at the piano, he plays at least one of his own songs.
(A) Leonard Bernstein sitting down
(B) Leonard Bernstein who sits down
(C) Leonard Bernstein while sitting down
(D) Leonard Bernstein, sitting down
(E) Leonard Bernstein sits down

37. While making a pathetic attempt to explain their behavior to the policeman, the young thief and his accomplices was caught in a web of contradictions.
(A) thief and his accomplices was caught
(B) thief and his accomplices who were caught
(C) thief and his accomplices were caught
(D) thief along with his accomplices were caught
(E) thief who had a few accomplices were caught

38. Rudolph acts like a foolish child because he trusts anyone that can tell a story in a believable manner.
(A) he trusts anyone that can tell
(B) he is trusting to anyone who can tell
(C) he can trust anyone that can tell
(D) he trusts anyone who can tell
(E) he is a person who trusts anyone that can tell

39. Shirley remains convinced that she is as young if not younger than her friend Molly.
(A) Shirley remains convinced that she is as young if not younger than her friend Molly.
(B) Shirley remains convinced that she is as young as, if not younger than, her friend Molly.
(C) Shirley is convinced that Molly is much older than she is.
(D) Molly is really much older than Shirley.
(E) Shirley may be younger than her friend Molly.

40. I cannot talk or write in class without the teacher's correcting or embarrassing me.
   (A) I cannot talk or write in class without the teacher's correcting or embarrassing me.
   (B) I cannot hardly talk or write in class without the teacher's correcting and embarrassing me.
   (C) I cannot talk or write in class without the teacher to correct or embarrass me.
   (D) To talk and write in class is a chore, because my teacher always correct and embarrass me.
   (E) Correcting and embarrassing me in class is the result whenever I talk or write.

Directions: Effective revision requires choosing among the many options available to a writer. The following questions test your ability to use these options effectively.

Revise each of the sentences below according to the directions that follow it. Some directions require you to rephrase only part of the original sentence; others require you to recast the entire sentence. You may need to omit or add certain words in constructing an acceptable revision, but you should keep the meaning of your revised sentence as close to the meaning of the original sentence as the directions permit. Your new sentence should follow the conventions of standard written English and should be clear and concise.

Look through the answer choices A–E under each question for the exact word or phrase that is included in your revised sentence. If you have thought of a revision that does not include any of the words or phrases listed, try to revise the sentence again so that it does include the wording in one of the answer choices.

When you take the test, you should feel free to make notes in your test book, but you will need to mark your answers on the separate answer sheet.

41. Ex-convicts who had no opportunity for an education while serving their sentences are more likely to commit another crime than those who were trained for some kind of job.

   Substitute less for more.

   (A) no opportunity for an education
   (B) an opportunity for an education
   (C) were trained for some kind
   (D) little opportunity for an education
   (E) were hardly trained for some kind

42. The old man was tired of listening to his children's complaints; therefore, he disconnected his hearing aid.

   Begin with Tired.

   (A) complaints, and he
   (B) complaints, and the old man
   (C) complaints, the old man
   (D) complaints, he
   (E) complaints, so the old man

43. A frightened man whose anxiety level cannot be controlled is likely to be a treacherous enemy if he is aroused.

Substitute uncontrollable for controlled.

(A) with an (B) with a (C) from an (D) through a
(E) by means of an

44. Population control experts have urged couples to forego having a child of their own in favor of adopting one already born to someone who does not want it.

Substitute adopt for forego.

(A) instead of foregoing (B) instead of bearing
(C) instead of urging (D) instead of adopting
(E) instead of having

45. Within the past few years, the American people have become so conscious of being too fat that some companies have made money selling sugar-free canned fruits and other dietetic products.

Substitute as a result of the American people's for the American people.

(A) becoming so conscious
(B) have become so conscious
(C) are becoming so conscious
(D) becoming almost conscious
(E) has become almost conscious

46. Last night, the old man who had guarded the same school crosswalk for twenty years was honored by his friends with an elaborate farewell banquet.

Eliminate who.

(A) man, having been guarded (B) man, having guarded
(C) man, guarded (D) man, guarding (E) man, guard

47. The writer was distracted from his work by all the noise in the yard; therefore, he covered the typewriter and quit for the day.

Begin with Distracted.

(A) yard; therefore, he (B) yard, so the writer
(C) yard, therefore, he (D) yard and the writer
(E) yard, the writer

48. A constant repression of his feelings and the continued sublimation of his desires can distort a man's real personality, so say psychiatrists.

Begin with If a man constantly represses.

(A) his real personality can be sublimated
(B) his real personality can be continued
(C) his real personality can become distorted
(D) his real personality can be desired
(E) his real personality can be realized

49. The slow evaporation of underground waters has left some beautiful gypsum deposits on the walls of Kentucky's Mammoth Cave.

Begin with Some beautiful gypsum.

(A) have resulted from
(B) have left
(C) has remained from
(D) have left from
(E) has resulted from

50. The advent of new techniques for identifying deafness in babies has completely altered some traditional ideas about the possibility of teaching a deaf child to speak.

Begin with Some traditional ideas.

(A) has been completely altered
(B) has altered completely
(C) have been completely altered
(D) have completely altered
(E) will completely alter

51. The hiker was weary after his twenty-mile walk; he rested for half an hour, then picked up his pack, and walked off into the west again.

Change The hiker was to The hiker.

(A) hour, then (B) hour, and then (C) hour, so then
(D) hour; then he (E) hour; then his pack

52. There are some doctors who attribute about half of their patients' problems to psychosomatic causes rather than to any actual diseases.

Change who attribute to who say that.

(A) are psychosomatic in origin
(B) are caused by actual diseases
(C) are not health problems
(D) are not just imaginary
(E) are attributable to psychosomatic causes

53. On the whole, a literary critic is not likely to praise a novel unless it provides both some new twists on a traditional plot and writing that is free of clichés.

Begin with If an author expects a literary critic.

(A) novel; he must provide
(B) novel, he must provide
(C) novel; then he must provide
(D) novel, they must provide
(E) novel; they must provide

54. The English language is a poor one for a poet who writes only rhyming verse because of the scarcity of rhyming words in its vocabulary.

Begin with Since the vocabulary of English does not.

(A) have a scarcity of rhyming words
(B) have few rhyming words
(C) contain many rhyming words
(D) has few rhyming words
(E) contains many rhyming words

55. Your attempt to justify your actions last night does not convince me that you should be forgiven.

Change your actions to of your actions.

(A) attempted justification
(B) attempt to justify
(C) attempted to justify
(D) attempt to justification
(E) attempted to justification

Section II

Number of items: 40
Time: 45 minutes

Directions: Each of the following passages consists of a paragraph of numbered sentences. Since the paragraphs appear as they would within a larger piece of writing, they do not necessarily constitute a complete discussion of the issues presented.

Read each paragraph carefully and answer the questions that follow it. The questions test your awareness of characteristics of prose that are important to good writing.

Questions 56–61 are based on the following passage:

[1]*Sesame Street* revolutionized the whole idea of television programming for children. [2]Until this program was produced and aired by the Public Broadcasting System, parents had no real options for children's television viewing except *Captain Kangaroo*, violent and crude cartoons on Saturday morning, and a few locally originated programs. [3]But *Sesame Street* is different. [4]Not only does it provide entertainment for viewers but it also provides educational opportunities for children under about ten. [5]The Sesame Street Generation, as some teachers are calling the group of children now in the primary grades, know their numbers and the letters of the alphabet as well as many other facts about life. [6]Perhaps the most important lessons taught by this program derive from its interracial cast, for this program demonstrates that people of all races can live and play together without racially based friction. [7]Whatever this program has cost has been money well spent.

56. Sentences 2 and 3 might be combined. Which of the following is the correct form of the combination?
(A) originated programs, *Sesame Street*
(B) originated programs, however, *Sesame Street*
(C) originated programs, but *Sesame Street*
(D) originated programs, and *Sesame Street*
(E) originated programs with the exception of *Sesame Street*

57. What should be done with sentence 5?
(A) It should be left as it is.
(B) It should be omitted.
(C) It should be placed after sentence 7.
(D) It should be combined with sentence 2.
(E) It should be after sentence 1.

58. Which of the following might better replace sentence 7 as a conclusion to the passage?
(A) *Sesame Street* has revolutionized children's television.
(B) *Sesame Street* is an excellent television program.
(C) The Sesame Street Generation will take over the world when it grows up.
(D) The Public Broadcasting System should be congratulated for providing such an excellent television program as *Sesame Street*.
(E) The money which the Public Broadcasting System has spent on *Sesame Street* may have some questionable returns.

59. Sentence 6 provides
(A) irrelevant information for the reader
(B) a second reason for public acclamation of *Sesame Street*
(C) a plea for funds from the public to support the program
(D) a justification for racial intolerance
(E) praise for the cast's ability to react to children

60. The topic sentence of the paragraph is
(A) 1 (B) 2 (C) 3 (D) 4 (E) 5

61. According to the paragraph, *Sesame Street* is a television program recommended for
(A) adults only
(B) for adolescent boys
(C) for teenage girls
(D) for mature teens
(E) for children up to age ten

Questions 62–67 are based on the following passage.

[1]President Bush says that the United States must win the war against drugs. [2]Urging users to say "no" won't work. [3]Building new jails and hiring more policemen won't work. [4]Telling users the dangers of using drugs won't work. [5]What will? [6]No one can be sure, but there have been many suggestions all the way from a recommendation that all casual users suffer the

same legal penalties as pushers do to the legalization of pot and cocaine with strict controls on the sale of these drugs. [7]Everyone agrees that there is an emergency situation, but no one—not the administration, not Congress, not the American people—seems to want to spend the billions of dollars that may be necessary to halt the widespread use of drugs.

62. One signal that the passage was written in an informal style is
(A) the number of short sentences
(B) the reference to President Bush in sentence 1
(C) the word won't in sentences 2, 3, and 4
(D) the dashes in sentence 7
(E) the two long sentences at the end of the passage

63. Sentences 2, 3, 4, and a part of 7 illustrate which one of the following writing devices?
(A) Effective repetition
(B) Effective piling up of details
(C) Effective double negative
(D) Parallelism
(E) Dangling modifiers

64. Sentence 7
(A) is not a true summary of the passage
(B) is too long and wandering
(C) should be revised and made more concise
(D) should be changed and made a part of sentence 6
(E) follows up the reference to President Bush in sentence 1

65. One valid conclusion a reader might draw from the passage is that the writer
(A) has not studied the drug problem in detail
(B) may be a casual user of cocaine
(C) supports the legalization of certain drugs
(D) uses too many details in his or her writing
(E) offers no solution to the drug problem

66. Sentence 5
(A) is a sentence fragment
(B) is a logical question after sentences 2, 3, and 4
(C) is too short to communicate anything
(D) breaks up the natural rhythm of the passage
(E) should be omitted

67. The purpose of the passage could be
(A) to conclude a longer essay on the drug problem
(B) to express the author's plan to solve the drug problem
(C) to introduce a longer discussion of the drug problem in the United States
(D) to prepare the reader for an appeal for funds in the next paragraph
(E) to express the writer's disagreement with President Bush's war on drugs

Questions 68–73 are based on the following passage:

[1]Language can convey pleasant or unpleasant thoughts; language can be used to speak tender thoughts of love and admiration or to declare unending hostility—the expressed ideas, themselves, are beside the point, however. [2]Can you imagine how handicapped a loving couple would be if they could not exchange outpourings of the affection which they feel? [3]Suzanne Langer, a philosopher, in an essay called "The Language Line" says that it is not a collection of physical characteristics that separate man from the lower animals but very simply the ability to use language as a vehicle of communication. [4]Since almost all language is used in a social context, we must include this characteristic as one of those essential to a definition of language.

68. What is the purpose of sentence 2?
(A) To illustrate the point of sentence 1.
(B) To intrude a new idea into the discussion.
(C) To limit the uses of language to lovers' conversations.
(D) To ask an unanswerable question.
(E) To contradict the idea of sentence 1.

69. The author uses material from a Suzanne Langer essay in which of the following forms?
(A) A direct quotation
(B) A paraphrase
(C) A summary
(D) A qualified quotation
(E) The reader cannot tell because the whole selection is not given.

70. In sentence 4, the phrase social context
(A) should have been more clearly defined
(B) may have several different meanings
(C) is sociological jargon
(D) names the forms of communication implied in earlier sentences
(E) refers to a radical political belief

71. The author identifies Ms. Langer as a philosopher
(A) to explain the use of big words in the sentence
(B) to lend intellectual support to his idea
(C) to appeal to intellectual snobs among the readers
(D) to limit the application of the remark to philosophy
(E) to demonstrate his respect for Ms. Langer as a scholar

72. In sentence 1, the author uses
(A) several positive and negative characteristics of language
(B) an unnecessarily complex system of punctuation—a semi-colon, dashes, commas
(C) techniques of balancing completely opposite notions that language can express
(D) the group of words after the dash to contradict the ideas expressed in the first part of the sentence
(E) too much information for even a long sentence

73. That this passage was taken from a longer essay is shown most clearly in
(A) sentence 1
(B) sentence 4
(C) sentence 2
(D) sentence 3
(E) sentences 1 and 3

Questions 74–79 are based on the following passage.

[1]For over a half century Helen Jackson's romantic story of Spanish and Indian life in California has been widely read and is now an American classic. [2]Originally published in 1884, *Ramona* has been issued in various editions, with a total of 135 printings. [3]*The Atlantic Monthly* has termed the story "one of the most artistic creations of American literature," while the late Charles Dudley Warner called it "one of the most charming creations of modern fiction." [4]Born in 1831, Mrs. Jackson was an ardent champion of the Indians to the end of her useful life, in 1885. [5]*Ramona* has been three times produced as a motion picture, been played on the stage, adapted for a pageant and may eventually be utilized for a grand opera.

Introduction to a 1935 reprint of *Ramona*

74. The function of sentence 1 is
(A) to justify reprinting an 1884 novel in 1935
(B) to define the phrase *American classic*
(C) to identify Helen Jackson
(D) to arouse the readers' interest in buying the book
(E) to introduce the exotic (Spanish and Indian life in California) subject matter of the book.

75. Sentence 2
(A) says that the book is one of the greatest novels ever written
(B) congratulates the author for writing such a best seller
(C) reveals the plot of the book
(D) documents the enormous popularity of the book
(E) shows that the author of the introduction has not done much research

76. The quotations in sentence 3
(A) are so brief as to be meaningless
(B) provide concrete support for the figures in sentence 2
(C) shift the introduction from the quantity of sales to the quality of the novel
(D) play on the sympathy of the reader when Mrs. Jackson's death in 1885 is mentioned
(E) shift the central idea of the passage too quickly

77. The function of sentence 5 is to
(A) add more figures to those of sentence 2
(B) add information that does not mean much to the modern reader
(C) say that popularity is a criterion for quality
(D) imply that any book that has been made into a movie has to be good
(E) provide more evidence of the book's popularity

78. Sentence 4
(A) should be eliminated
(B) gives a brief overview of Mrs. Jackson's life
(C) should have been used as the topic sentence of the passage
(D) should be combined with sentence 1
(E) explains Mrs. Jackson's interest in Indians

79. The passage concentrates
(A) on Mrs. Jackson's life
(B) on *Ramona's* popularity
(C) on critics' opinions of *Ramona*
(D) on Spanish and Indian life in California
(E) on historical facts that are boring

Directions: Effective revision requires choosing among the many options available to a writer. The following questions test your ability to use these options effectively.

Revise each of the sentences below according to the directions that follow it. Some directions require you to rephrase only part of the original sentence; others require you to recast the entire sentence. You may need to omit or add certain words in constructing an acceptable revision, but you should keep the meaning of your revised sentence as close to the meaning of the original sentence as the directions permit. Your new sentence should follow the conventions of standard written English and should be clear and concise.

Look through answer choices A–E under each question for the exact word or phrase that is included in your revised sentence. If you have thought of a revision that does not include any of the words or phrases listed, try to revise the sentence again so that it does include the wording in one of the answer choices.

When you take the test, you should feel free to make notes in your test book, but you will need to mark your answers on the separate answer sheet.

80. In the tenth inning, Ozzie Smith knocked the ball into the left-field stands for a home run.

Change knocked to was knocked.

(A) from (B) at which (C) under (D) with (E) by

81. Looking up, we saw four Boeing 747s, flying in perfect formation.

Begin with While we were.

(A) looking (B) being looked (C) having looked
(D) looked (E) having been looked

82. Unless a criminal charge can be proved in court, a defendant cannot be punished.

Change can to could.

(A) should (B) shall (C) will (D) would (E) must

83. The young man walked to the door; he wanted to see who had rung the bell.

Begin with Because he wanted.

(A) bell so (B) bell; (C) bell and (D) bell for (E) bell,

84. That man is a vertebrate animal has been affirmed by many scientific experiments.

Begin with Many scientific experiments.

(A) has (B) have (C) would (D) been (E) was

85. Some teachers declare vociferously that they are in the classroom to teach students, but their attitude contradicts what they say.

Begin with Some teachers who.

(A) contradicts what they say by (B) contradict what they say for
(C) contradicts what they say from (D) contradict what they say by
(E) contradicts what they say into

86. Insomnia, especially if long standing, is both one of the most troublesome of man's afflictions and one of the most difficult to treat without special medication.

Eliminate both.

(A) so (B) so well as (C) as well as (D) as much as (E) thus

87. Few Americans have been allowed to visit mainland China since 1948 when the Communists caused Chiang to flee to the island of Formosa.

Begin with Communists have permitted.

(A) Chiang fled (B) Communists drove Chiang (C) Chiang allowed
(D) Communists were permitted (E) Chiang was fled

88. No one can possibly comprehend that I can eat and relish fried squid or boiled seaweed, but I am not afraid to sample exotic dishes from strange places.

Change No one can possibly to Everyone finds it.

(A) possible that I can
(B) comprehending that I can
(C) comprehensible that I can
(D) uncomprehending that I can
(E) incomprehensible that I can

89. Some unstable women suffer irreversible traumas when their marriages fail and they are bereft of a husband at a fairly early age.

Begin with Some unstable women whose.

(A) whose husbands are bereft (B) who are bereft
(C) who suffer irreversible traumas (D) whose age is young
(E) they are bereft

90. The doleful sound of the funeral bell reverberated through the village, and we could see the dismal cortege winding its way to the local cemetery.

Begin with With the doleful.

(A) reverberating through the village, so we
(B) reverberating through the village; we
(C) reverberating through the village, we
(D) reverberating through the village, and we
(E) reverberating through the village, thus we

91. A birth rate that continues to increase is no blessing to an island like Java, one of the most densely populated areas in the world with more than twelve hundred people per square mile.

Begin with Java, one of the most.

(A) needs an increasing birth rate
(B) does not increase its birth rate each year
(C) blesses an increasing birth rate
(D) does not need an increasing birth rate
(E) is not overpopulated

92. Old timers say that a job well done is its own reward, but I would rather have my satisfaction in hard cash.

Begin with Hard cash pleases me more.

(A) in spite of what old timers say
(B) by which the old timers worked
(C) under which the old timers worked
(D) and what the old timers say
(E) in spite of what the old timers did

93. When the sun's rays illuminate each small piece of colored glass in that translucent stained glass window and radiate glorious hues throughout the cathedral, a really spectacular effect is created.

Eliminate When, and change illuminate to illuminating.

(A) creates a really spectacular effect
(B) a really spectacular effect is created
(C) a really spectacular sight is effected
(D) create a really spectacular effect
(E) affect a really spectacular sight

94. If the population of the United States ever becomes predominantly submissive and passive, an enemy could quite easily conquer us, for there would be no one willing to fight.

Begin with An enemy could quite easily.

(A) States, if the population of the United States
(B) States with its population
(C) States, unless its population
(D) States, because its population
(E) States, if its population

95. Paul McCartney has had more influence upon contemporary popular music than almost any other composer with the possible exception of Johann Sebastian Bach.

Change more to as much.

(A) if not more than almost
(B) as, if not more than, almost
(C) so, if not more than, almost
(D) also, if not more than, almost
(E) just as, if not more than, almost

ANSWER KEY—SAMPLE EXAMINATION 1

Section I

1. C
2. B
3. E
4. D
5. A
6. D
7. B
8. A
9. E
10. C
11. B
12. E
13. A
14. E
15. E
16. E
17. D
18. B
19. D
20. B
21. D
22. A
23. A
24. E
25. A
26. C
27. A
28. E
29. A
30. C
31. B
32. B
33. D
34. A
35. A
36. E
37. C
38. D
39. B
40. A
41. C
42. C
43. A
44. E
45. A
46. B
47. E
48. C
49. A
50. C
51. D
52. A
53. B
54. D
55. A

Section II

56. C
57. A
58. D
59. B
60. A
61. E
62. C
63. A
64. A
65. E
66. B
67. C
68. A
69. E
70. D
71. B
72. C
73. B
74. D
75. D
76. C
77. E
78. B
79. B
80. E
81. A
82. A
83. E
84. B
85. D
86. C
87. A
88. E
89. B
90. C
91. D
92. A
93. D
94. E
95. B

SCORING CHART—SAMPLE EXAMINATION 1

After you have scored your Sample Examination 1, enter the results in the chart below; then transfer your Raw Score to the Progress Chart on page 14.

Total Test	Number Right	Number Wrong	Number Omitted	Raw Score
Section I: 55				
Section II: 40				
Total: 95				

ANSWER EXPLANATIONS—SAMPLE EXAMINATION 1

Section I

1. C. *Badly* is an adverbial form; *bad* would be correct.
2. B. *Loose* should be *loosen*, the correct form of the verb.
3. E. The sentence is correct.
4. D. *Affective* is an incorrect word—use *effective*.
5. A. A dangling modifier—substitute *Because we assume*.
6. D. *Partiality*—should be *impartiality*.
7. B. *Raising* should be *rising*.
8. A. *Colonies* is plural and the unmarked verb is singular; therefore, the correct version would be *many a colony*.
9. E. The sentence is correct.
10. C. *Portrayal* must be changed to plural to agree with *have*.

11. B. *Except* should be *accept*.
12. E. The sentence is correct.
13. A. *I* should be *me*—the objective case form.
14. E. The sentence is correct.
15. E. The sentence is correct.
16. E. The sentence is correct.
17. D. The clause beginning *which* has no word in the sentence to modify.
18. B. *Choosen* should be *chosen*.
19. D. *Seem* should be *seems*—the subject is the whole clause, therefore singular.
20. B. *Has depended* is an error in sequence of tenses; change to *depends*.
21. D. (A), (B), (C) and (E) are either wordy or change the meaning of the original.
22. A. (B) and (E) are wordy; (C) and (D) are illogical.
23. A. The original sentence is correct; the other choices contain errors in verb forms.
24. E. (A) uses the word "completely," a poor word choice to describe the plumbing ability under discussion; (B) is wordy; (C) is illogical; (D) changes the meaning too much.
25. A. (B) contradicts meaning of original sentence; (C) and (D) change the meaning too much; (E) introduces an irrelevant idea.
26. C. (A) so is an incorrect idiom; (B) confuses fortunate and fortune; (D) is wordy; (E) also confuses fortune and fortunate.
27. A. (B) uses an incorrect phrase—very unique; (C) ignores cause-effect sense of the original; (D) confuses verb time sequences; (E) is a sentence fragment.
28. E. (A) hide should be hid; (B) having hidden is a dangling modifier; (C) and (D) have incorrect clauses.
29. A. The other choices introduce grammatical errors of several kinds.
30. C. (A) has is, an error in subject-verb agreement; (B) they is a vague pronoun; (D) introduces a dangling modifier; (E) who has no verb to complete its meaning.
31. B. (A) we is incorrect case form; (C) is illogical; (D) incorrectly uses the adverb pleasantly instead of the adjective pleasant; (E) changes the meaning of the sentence.
32. B. (A) is illogical; (C) is a sentence fragment; (D) was when is an incorrect idiom; (E) because indicates a false cause-effect relationship.
33. D. (B) and (C) create sentence fragments; (E) persons is an incorrect plural.
34. A. (B) presents information redundantly; (C) the semi-colon is incorrect; (D) forms a sentence fragment; (E) is illogical.
35. A. (B) the introductory phrase is a dangling modifier; (C) is incomplete, for the sense of the original sentence is incomplete; (D) the introductory phrase is a dangling modifier; (E) implies a false sequence of events.
36. E. The other choices are illogical.
37. C. (A) was is an error in subject-verb agreement; (B) would be a sentence fragment; (D) and (E) were is incorrect subject-verb agreement.
38. D. (B) is wordy; the other choices use the incorrect word that.
39. B. (A) as young if is an incorrect idiom, (C), (D) and (E) distort the original meaning.
40. A. (B) contains a double negative; (C) the infinitive seems awkward; (D) correct and embarrass are errors in subject-verb agreement; (E) is both awkward and an incomplete statement of the idea.
41. C. Ex-convicts who *were trained for some kind* of job are less likely to commit another crime than those who had no educational opportunity while they were serving their sentences.
42. C. Tired of listening to his children's *complaints, the old man* disconnected his hearing aid.
43. A. A frightened man *with an* uncontrollable anxiety level is likely to be a treacherous enemy if he is aroused.

44. E. Population control experts have urged couples to adopt a child born to someone who does not want it *instead of having* one of their own.

45. A. Within the past few years as a result of the American people's *becoming so conscious* of being too fat, some companies have made money selling sugar-free canned fruits and other dietetic products.

46. B. Last night, the old *man, having guarded* the same school crosswalk for twenty years, was honored by his friends with an elaborate farewell banquet.

47. E. Distracted from his work by all the noise in the *yard, the writer* covered the typewriter and quit for the day.

48. C. If a man constantly represses his feelings and sublimates his desires, psychiatrists say that *his real personality can become distorted.*

49. A. Some beautiful gypsum deposits on the walls of Kentucky's Mammoth Cave *have resulted from* the slow evaporation of underground waters.

50. C. Some traditional ideas about the possibility of teaching a deaf child to speak *have been completely altered* by the advent of new techniques for identifying deafness in babies.

51. D. The hiker, weary after his twenty-mile walk, rested for half an *hour; then, he* picked up his pack and walked off into the west again.

52. A. There are some doctors who say that about half of their patients' problems *are psychosomatic in origin* rather than caused by any actual diseases.

53. B. If an author expects a literary critic to praise *a novel, he must provide* some new twists on a traditional plot and writing that is free of clichés.

54. D. Since the vocabulary of English does not *contain many rhyming words,* English is a poor language for a poet who writes only rhyming verse.

55. A. Your *attempted justification* of your actions last night does not convince me that you should be forgiven.

Section II

56. C. None of the other choices are grammatically correct.

57. A. Sentence 5 should remain where it is. In sentence 4, the educational benefits of *Sesame Street* are mentioned, making it logical to move to a discussion of schools in sentence 5.

58. D. Since cost was not mentioned elsewhere in the paragraph, it would be better to replace sentence 7 with a concluding sentence that did more to sum up the paragraph.

59. B. The second reason provided in sentence 6 is the advocation of racial harmony.

60. A. Sentence 1 makes the thesis statement the rest of the paragraph goes on to discuss and is, therefore, the topic sentence of the paragraph.

61. E. Sentence 4 states that the program "provides educational opportunities for children under about ten."

62. C. Contractions such as "won't," while permissible in informal writing, are not appropriate in formal writing.

63. A. The repetition in sentences 2, 3, and 4 ("won't work"), and in sentence 5 ("not"), effectively emphasizes the need to move forward in fighting the war against drugs.

64. A. Rather than summing up the passage, sentence 7 brings in a new point, the appropriation of funds.

65. E. The writer points out the problems, but does not offer solutions to them.

66. B. Questions are often used effectively in expository writing to pique the reader's interest.

67. C. Since so much about the topic was left unanswered, it is logical to assume that this paragraph serves as an introduction to a longer discussion of the drug problem.

68. A. Sentence 2 serves as a concrete illustration of the importance of language.

69. E. Since the whole selection is not given, the reader cannot tell whether this is (B) a paraphrase, (C) a summary, or (D) a qualified quotation. The reader can tell, however, that it is not (A) a direct quotation.

70. D. In sentences 1, 2 and 3, language as a means of communication is discussed. In each case, the examples used have to do with language in a social context.

71. B. Writers often support their ideas with confirming statements from an authority in the field.

72. C. The author makes effective use of the technique of balancing opposites in this sentence.

73. B. Sentence 4, the last sentence of the passage, mentions that this is one characteristic of a definition of language. We can assume that other chracteristics will be discussed in following paragraphs.

74. D. The writer has chosen two impressive facts about the book to arouse the reader's interest and has added a little color, as well, by mentioning that it is a romantic story of Spanish and Indian life.

75. D. Sentence 2 offers further proof that the book has continuously been well-received.

76. C. The writer is covering all ground in his or her praise of the book. In sentence 3, the writer uses the quotes to show that the book is not only popular, but that the critics find it to be of substance.

77. E. The writer uses the information in sentence 5 as yet another means of showing the book's popularity.

78. B. Sentence 4 gives a brief overview of Mrs. Jackson's life.

79. B. Throughout the passage, fact after fact is given to show *Ramona*'s popularity.

80. E. In the tenth inning, the ball was knocked into the left-field stands for a home run *by* Ozzie Smith.

81. A. While we were *looking* up, we saw four Boeing 747s, flying in perfect formation.

82. A. Unless a criminal charge could be proved, a defendant *should* not be punished.

83. E. Because he wanted to see who had rung the *bell*, the young man walked to the door.

84. B. Many scientific experiments *have* affirmed that man is a vertebrate animal.

85. D. Some teachers who declare vociferously that they are in the classroom to teach students *contradict what they say by* their attitude.

86. C. Insomnia, especially if long standing, is one of the most troublesome of man's afflictions *as well as* one . . .

87. A. Communists have permitted few Americans to visit mainland China since *Chiang fled* to Formosa in 1948.

88. E. Everyone finds it *incomprehensible that I can* eat . . .

89. B. Some unstable women whose marriages fail and *who are bereft* of husbands at a fairly early age suffer irreversible traumas.

90. C. With the doleful sound of the funeral bell *reverberating through the village, we* could see the dismal cortege winding . . .

91. D. Java, one of the most densely populated areas in the world with more than twelve hundred people per square mile, *does not need an increasing birth rate.*

92. A. Hard cash pleases me more than the mere satisfaction of a job well done, *in spite of what old timers say.*

93. D. The sun's rays illuminating each small piece of colored glass and radiating glorious hues throughout the cathedral *create a really spectacular effect.*

94. E. An enemy could quite easily conquer the United *States, if its population* ever becomes predominantly submissive and passive.

95. B. Paul McCartney has had as much influence upon contemporary popular music *as, if not more than, almost* any other composer with the possible exception of Johann Sebastian Bach.

ANSWER SHEET — ENGLISH COMPOSITION/SAMPLE EXAMINATION 2

Section I

1. Ⓐ Ⓑ Ⓒ Ⓓ Ⓔ
2. Ⓐ Ⓑ Ⓒ Ⓓ Ⓔ
3. Ⓐ Ⓑ Ⓒ Ⓓ Ⓔ
4. Ⓐ Ⓑ Ⓒ Ⓓ Ⓔ
5. Ⓐ Ⓑ Ⓒ Ⓓ Ⓔ
6. Ⓐ Ⓑ Ⓒ Ⓓ Ⓔ
7. Ⓐ Ⓑ Ⓒ Ⓓ Ⓔ
8. Ⓐ Ⓑ Ⓒ Ⓓ Ⓔ
9. Ⓐ Ⓑ Ⓒ Ⓓ Ⓔ
10. Ⓐ Ⓑ Ⓒ Ⓓ Ⓔ
11. Ⓐ Ⓑ Ⓒ Ⓓ Ⓔ
12. Ⓐ Ⓑ Ⓒ Ⓓ Ⓔ
13. Ⓐ Ⓑ Ⓒ Ⓓ Ⓔ
14. Ⓐ Ⓑ Ⓒ Ⓓ Ⓔ
15. Ⓐ Ⓑ Ⓒ Ⓓ Ⓔ
16. Ⓐ Ⓑ Ⓒ Ⓓ Ⓔ
17. Ⓐ Ⓑ Ⓒ Ⓓ Ⓔ
18. Ⓐ Ⓑ Ⓒ Ⓓ Ⓔ
19. Ⓐ Ⓑ Ⓒ Ⓓ Ⓔ
20. Ⓐ Ⓑ Ⓒ Ⓓ Ⓔ
21. Ⓐ Ⓑ Ⓒ Ⓓ Ⓔ
22. Ⓐ Ⓑ Ⓒ Ⓓ Ⓔ
23. Ⓐ Ⓑ Ⓒ Ⓓ Ⓔ
24. Ⓐ Ⓑ Ⓒ Ⓓ Ⓔ
25. Ⓐ Ⓑ Ⓒ Ⓓ Ⓔ
26. Ⓐ Ⓑ Ⓒ Ⓓ Ⓔ
27. Ⓐ Ⓑ Ⓒ Ⓓ Ⓔ
28. Ⓐ Ⓑ Ⓒ Ⓓ Ⓔ
29. Ⓐ Ⓑ Ⓒ Ⓓ Ⓔ
30. Ⓐ Ⓑ Ⓒ Ⓓ Ⓔ
31. Ⓐ Ⓑ Ⓒ Ⓓ Ⓔ
32. Ⓐ Ⓑ Ⓒ Ⓓ Ⓔ
33. Ⓐ Ⓑ Ⓒ Ⓓ Ⓔ
34. Ⓐ Ⓑ Ⓒ Ⓓ Ⓔ
35. Ⓐ Ⓑ Ⓒ Ⓓ Ⓔ
36. Ⓐ Ⓑ Ⓒ Ⓓ Ⓔ
37. Ⓐ Ⓑ Ⓒ Ⓓ Ⓔ
38. Ⓐ Ⓑ Ⓒ Ⓓ Ⓔ
39. Ⓐ Ⓑ Ⓒ Ⓓ Ⓔ
40. Ⓐ Ⓑ Ⓒ Ⓓ Ⓔ
41. Ⓐ Ⓑ Ⓒ Ⓓ Ⓔ
42. Ⓐ Ⓑ Ⓒ Ⓓ Ⓔ
43. Ⓐ Ⓑ Ⓒ Ⓓ Ⓔ
44. Ⓐ Ⓑ Ⓒ Ⓓ Ⓔ
45. Ⓐ Ⓑ Ⓒ Ⓓ Ⓔ
46. Ⓐ Ⓑ Ⓒ Ⓓ Ⓔ
47. Ⓐ Ⓑ Ⓒ Ⓓ Ⓔ
48. Ⓐ Ⓑ Ⓒ Ⓓ Ⓔ
49. Ⓐ Ⓑ Ⓒ Ⓓ Ⓔ
50. Ⓐ Ⓑ Ⓒ Ⓓ Ⓔ
51. Ⓐ Ⓑ Ⓒ Ⓓ Ⓔ
52. Ⓐ Ⓑ Ⓒ Ⓓ Ⓔ
53. Ⓐ Ⓑ Ⓒ Ⓓ Ⓔ
54. Ⓐ Ⓑ Ⓒ Ⓓ Ⓔ
55. Ⓐ Ⓑ Ⓒ Ⓓ Ⓔ

Section II

56. Ⓐ Ⓑ Ⓒ Ⓓ Ⓔ
57. Ⓐ Ⓑ Ⓒ Ⓓ Ⓔ
58. Ⓐ Ⓑ Ⓒ Ⓓ Ⓔ
59. Ⓐ Ⓑ Ⓒ Ⓓ Ⓔ
60. Ⓐ Ⓑ Ⓒ Ⓓ Ⓔ
61. Ⓐ Ⓑ Ⓒ Ⓓ Ⓔ
62. Ⓐ Ⓑ Ⓒ Ⓓ Ⓔ
63. Ⓐ Ⓑ Ⓒ Ⓓ Ⓔ
64. Ⓐ Ⓑ Ⓒ Ⓓ Ⓔ
65. Ⓐ Ⓑ Ⓒ Ⓓ Ⓔ
66. Ⓐ Ⓑ Ⓒ Ⓓ Ⓔ
67. Ⓐ Ⓑ Ⓒ Ⓓ Ⓔ
68. Ⓐ Ⓑ Ⓒ Ⓓ Ⓔ
69. Ⓐ Ⓑ Ⓒ Ⓓ Ⓔ
70. Ⓐ Ⓑ Ⓒ Ⓓ Ⓔ
71. Ⓐ Ⓑ Ⓒ Ⓓ Ⓔ
72. Ⓐ Ⓑ Ⓒ Ⓓ Ⓔ
73. Ⓐ Ⓑ Ⓒ Ⓓ Ⓔ
74. Ⓐ Ⓑ Ⓒ Ⓓ Ⓔ
75. Ⓐ Ⓑ Ⓒ Ⓓ Ⓔ
76. Ⓐ Ⓑ Ⓒ Ⓓ Ⓔ
77. Ⓐ Ⓑ Ⓒ Ⓓ Ⓔ
78. Ⓐ Ⓑ Ⓒ Ⓓ Ⓔ
79. Ⓐ Ⓑ Ⓒ Ⓓ Ⓔ
80. Ⓐ Ⓑ Ⓒ Ⓓ Ⓔ
81. Ⓐ Ⓑ Ⓒ Ⓓ Ⓔ
82. Ⓐ Ⓑ Ⓒ Ⓓ Ⓔ
83. Ⓐ Ⓑ Ⓒ Ⓓ Ⓔ
84. Ⓐ Ⓑ Ⓒ Ⓓ Ⓔ
85. Ⓐ Ⓑ Ⓒ Ⓓ Ⓔ
86. Ⓐ Ⓑ Ⓒ Ⓓ Ⓔ
87. Ⓐ Ⓑ Ⓒ Ⓓ Ⓔ
88. Ⓐ Ⓑ Ⓒ Ⓓ Ⓔ
89. Ⓐ Ⓑ Ⓒ Ⓓ Ⓔ
90. Ⓐ Ⓑ Ⓒ Ⓓ Ⓔ
91. Ⓐ Ⓑ Ⓒ Ⓓ Ⓔ
92. Ⓐ Ⓑ Ⓒ Ⓓ Ⓔ
93. Ⓐ Ⓑ Ⓒ Ⓓ Ⓔ
94. Ⓐ Ⓑ Ⓒ Ⓓ Ⓔ
95. Ⓐ Ⓑ Ⓒ Ⓓ Ⓔ

SAMPLE ENGLISH COMPOSITION EXAMINATION 2

Section I

Number of items: 55
Time: 45 minutes

Directions: The following sentences contain problems in grammar, usage, diction (choice of words), and idiom.

Some sentences are correct.
No sentence contains more than one error.

You will find that the error, if there is one, is underlined and lettered. Assume that elements of the sentence that are not underlined are correct and cannot be changed. In choosing answers, follow the requirements of standard written English.

If there is an error, select the one underlined part that must be changed to make the sentence correct.

If there is no error, select answer (E).

1. When they fought in the field, the armies of Iran and Iraq battled bravely
A B C
until the war is over. No error
D E

2. The young man applied to the welfare department for food stamps to
A
support his family, but they refused his request. No error
B C D E

3. Working both sides of the street, the con man rushed from house to house
A B
briskly making his pitch to home owners. No error
C D E

4. The policeman spoke harshly to he and I about driving too fast on the
A B C
residential street and in a school zone. No error
D E

5. Worrying about what was to happen tomorrow, the decision about the new
A B C
job was upsetting Jim's family routine. No error
D E

6. The chairman of the board of directors announced in Philadelphia today
A
that the company would neither accede to the monetary demands of the
B C
strikers nor accept any further delays by union leaders in accepting a
D
settlement of the dispute. No error
E

7. Listening with rapt attention while the orchestra was performing
A
Beethoven's Fifth Symphony, the concert hall was filled with fashionably
B C
dressed music lovers who followed the conductor's every beat. No error
D E

8. The Pulitzer Prize Committee awarded $1,000 to Bill Mauldin being as
A B
how the group voted his drawings in a Chicago newspaper the best editorial
B C
cartoons published in the nation that year. No error
D E

9. Many expressions that any literate person would not hesitate to use in
A B
everyday conversation he hestitates to write because some English teacher
C
told him such phrases are colloquial. No error
D E

10. The Pat Metheney Group has been playing on the stage for more than an
A
hour without repeating a song and without losing their audience's
B C
attention for even a few seconds. No error
D E

11. Senator Snodgrass must have a very poor speech writer; his inferences are
A B
always so subtle that the listener has to be wary of drawing hasty conclu-
C
sions about what he thinks he heard the senator say. No error
D E

12. Each of the student's individual talents were exercised to their fullest
A B
extent by the long, complicated, and somewhat ambiguous assignment
C
that the professor made last Wednesday. No error
D E

13. When David Brown called the other afternoon, Albert recognized the name
A
immediately, even after all these years, but he could not locate the face
B C
from his memory of the two hundred high school graduates. No error
D E

14. Investigators for the Office of Education spent many months reading
A
reports, collecting information, and interviewing witnesses; their conclu-
B
sion was that about 70% of all schools in the nation were integrated either
C
in whole or in part. No error
D E

15. Our new computer has more memory cells than our old one; therefore, the
A
data that can be recorded and almost instantaneously retreived
B C
is unlimited. No error
D E

16. No privately owned telephone company in the United States can deny its
A B C
employees the right to join whatever union they choose. No error
D E

17. True successful businesspersons may belabor Congress for raising taxes on
A
their profits beyond what they believe they can afford to pay, but they can
B
only admit that high taxes are necessary during a period of increasing
C D
deficits. No error
E

18. If a local arrangements committee can secure suitable hotel accommoda-
A
tions at reasonable rates, the board of directors plan on having its 1990
B C
stockholders' meeting in Cleveland, Ohio. No error
D E

19. Among the luminaries whom the social climbing Washington hostess has
A B
invited to her reception are the secretary of state, the attorney general, the
C
speaker of the house, and even a presidential assistant or two. No error
D E

20. All of the new protein compounds are not to be found in unprocessed foods;
A B
they must be manufactured in an expensive laboratory that few univer-
C D
sities can afford to install. No error
E

Directions: In each of the following sentences, some part or all of the sentence is underlined. Below each sentence you will find five ways of phrasing the underlined part. Select the answer that produces the most effective sentence, one that is clear and exact, without awkwardness or ambiguity. In choosing answers, follow the requirements of standard written English. Choose the answer that best expresses the meaning of the original sentence.

Answer (A) is always the same as the underlined part. Choose answer (A) if you think the original sentence needs no revision.

21. To make their children realize the significance of wise decision making, sometimes parents should let them stew in the juice of their own concoction.
(A) let them stew in the juice of their own concoction
(B) let them suffer the consequences of their actions
(C) let them stew in their own consequences
(D) reduce the penalties for deviant behavior
(E) throw a lifeline to rescue them from the sea of despond

22. The government has passed a law regulating the sale of dangerous drugs to teenagers, therefore, prescriptions from licensed physicians are now required before a druggist can dispense them.
(A) to teenagers, therefore, prescriptions
(B) to teenagers, therefore; prescriptions
(C) to teenagers; therefore, prescriptions
(D) to teenagers, so therefore, prescriptions
(E) to teenagers; and therefore prescriptions

23. If one considers the millions of years during which man has occupied this small space in the vastness of space, they cannot help believing that one man's life is truly insignificant.
(A) space, they cannot help believing
(B) space, but they cannot help but believe
(C) space, he cannot help believing
(D) space, he cannot help but believe
(E) space, they cannot help but believing

24. Andy Warhol was a man of many talents; he painted many strange and unusual pictures, wrote a novel based on the experiences of his coterie, and he produced several experimental films for commercial distribution.
(A) of his coterie, and he produced
(B) of his coterie, and produced
(C) of his coterie; and he has produced
(D) of his coterie and have produced
(E) of his coterie and he has produced

25. Many others who are not so fortunate will lose all the money they have invested in the stock market.
(A) others who are not so fortunate
(B) others who is not so fortunate
(C) others who is not as fortunate
(D) others whom is not so fortunate
(E) others whom are not so fortunate

26. The bus driver was always pleasant to we riders even though he must become impatient with some of us who never have the correct change.
(A) pleasant to we riders even
(B) pleasant to us riders even
(C) pleasant to our riders even
(D) pleasant to no riders
(E) pleasant to their riders

27. Since Old Mother Hubbard hadn't scarcely enough food for herself, her friends wondered how she expected to feed a pet from her meager supply.
(A) Hubbard hadn't scarcely enough
(B) Hubbard had scarcely enough
(C) Hubbard has scarcely enough
(D) Hubbard had scarce enough
(E) Hubbard scarcely have enough

28. While I was looking through the morning newspaper, I read where the cost of living had risen another four points, mainly because food prices had gone up again.
(A) I read where the cost of living
(B) I read when the cost of living
(C) I read that the cost of living
(D) I read because the cost of living
(E) I read after the cost of living

29. That type person always strongly resents any attempt by anyone to inscribe limits around his actions.
(A) That type person always strongly resents
(B) That type person always strongly resent
(C) That type of person always strongly resent
(D) That type person always seldom resents
(E) That type of person always strongly resents

30. Whenever a temptation to engage in an illegal activity arises while you are away from the protection of your parents, remember that they have often informed you that you should not do it.
(A) parents, remember that they have often informed
(B) parents; remember that they have often informed
(C) parents, he should remember that they have often informed
(D) parents, they should remember that they have often been informed
(E) parents, they should remember that they have not informed

31. Reading a good novel can be as great a pleasure as seeing a professional football game on television or catching a four-pound trout in a clear stream in Michigan.
(A) game on television or catching a four-pound trout
(B) game on television or to catch a four-pound trout
(C) game in television or catching a four-pound trout
(D) game on television or caught a four-pound trout
(E) game on television or to caught a four-pound trout

32. In his lecture, the novelist eluded to difficulties with his publisher who insisted that all obscene words be removed from his manuscript.
(A) In his lecture, the novelist eluded to difficulties
(B) In his lecture, the novelist alluded to difficulties
(C) In his lecture, the novelist avoided his difficulties
(D) In his lecture, the novelist inferred to difficulties
(E) In his lecture, the novelist conferred to difficulties

33. The jury found the manager of the office so equally guilty as the clerk of the large establishment.
(A) so equally guilty as the clerk
(B) so much equally guilty as the clerk
(C) as equally guilty just as the clerk
(D) as equally guilty as the clerk
(E) as if equally guilty as the clerk

34. Luckily, the arsonist was arrested before he set any more serious fires by the policeman who took him to jail.
(A) was arrested before he set any more serious fires by the policeman who took him to jail
(B) was arrested by the policeman who took him to jail after he set more serious fires
(C) was arrested by the policeman who took him to jail before he could set any more serious fires
(D) the policeman arrested him before he could set any more serious fires
(E) was taken to jail by the policeman before he could set any more serious fires

35. I shopped in all the stores on Michigan Avenue before I found the exquisite old antique umbrella stand I wanted to give Jim for a Christmas present.
(A) the exquisite old antique umbrella stand I wanted to give
(B) the exquisite antique umbrella stand I wanted to give
(C) the elaborate old antique umbrella stand I wanted to give
(D) the exquisite antique old stand I wanted to give
(E) the exquisite old stand for antique umbrellas I wanted to give

36. A good assistant can relieve an administrator of much of the paperwork, that must be handled within any large organization to expedite its day to day operations.
(A) that must be handled
(B) that should have been handled
(C) that must have been handled
(D) that has got to be handled
(E) that have to be handled

37. The majority political party could not except the conditions of the minority, and the coalition of parties collapsed.
(A) except the conditions of the minority
(B) reciprocate the conditions of the minority
(C) calibrate the conditions of the minority
(D) restrict the conditions of the minority
(E) accept the conditions of the minority

38. That the United States is still suspicious of the U.S.S.R. is why Congress is asked to increase defense spending.
(A) the U.S.S.R. is why Congress
(B) the U.S.S.R. is when Congress
(C) the U.S.S.R. is that Congress
(D) the U.S.S.R. explains why Congress
(E) the U.S.S.R. wants Congress

39. Working hard is not difficult for those people whom are accustomed to getting up early and coming home after dark.
(A) people whom are accustomed to
(B) people whom is accustomed to
(C) people who are accustomed to
(D) people that are accustomed to
(E) people whose are accustomed to

40. In China, the ordinary people are neither permitted to decide things for themselves or allowed to say anything against the government.
(A) things for themselves or allowed
(B) things for themselves or could be allowed
(C) things for themselves nor allowed
(D) things for themselves and allowed
(E) things for themselves therefore allowed

Directions: Effective revision requires choosing among the many options available to a writer. The following questions test your ability to use these options effectively.

Revise each of the sentences below according to the directions that follow it. Some directions require you to rephrase only part of the original sentence; others require you to recast the entire sentence. You may need to omit or add certain words in constructing an acceptable revision, but you should keep the meaning of your revised sentence as close to the meaning of the original sentence as the directions permit. Your new sentence should follow the conventions of standard written English and should be clear and concise.

Look through the answer choices A–E under each question for the exact word or phrase that is included in your revised sentence. If you have thought of a revision that does not include any of the words or phrases listed, try to revise the sentence again so that it does include the wording in one of the answer choices.

When you take the test, you should feel free to make notes in your test book, but you will need to mark your answers on the separate answer sheet.

41. Coney Island, a beach in New York City, is famed for its roller coaster and its many hot dog stands.
Begin with Coney Island, famed.
(A) is **(B) was** **(C) will be**
(D) has been **(E) had been**

42. A woman can seldom force a reluctant husband to attend a concert, an opera, or the opening of a new art gallery unless she resorts to tears or other purely feminine wiles.
Change unless to if.
(A) does **(B) do** **(C) does not**
(D) do not **(E) should not**

43. The proper amount of iron is often just as important in a woman's daily diet as the proper number of units of vitamins A and C.

Substitute more for just as.

(A) only (B) than (C) also (D) both (E) as

44. To eliminate confusion and uncertainty for motorists, Congress should pass a law establishing a nationally uniform code of traffic laws, for, now, every state has its own peculiar rules and regulations.

Begin with Motorists would be spared.

(A) if Congress must pass
(B) if Congress ought to pass
(C) if Congress should not pass
(D) if Congress must establish
(E) if Congress would pass

45. No contemporary man can afford to retreat, as Thoreau did to Walden Pond, unless he has a few benevolent acquaintances who will provide him with the necessities of life.

Begin with When Thoreau retreated to.

(A) just so (B) thus (C) so (D) also (E) too

46. The recent collapse of prices on the New York Stock Exchange has been both a welcome sign that the inflationary spiral is slowing and a signal for large stockholders to begin purchasing large blocks of shares at bargain rates.

Substitute but also for and.

(A) as well as (B) as much as (C) as
(D) too (E) not only

47. Following the ceremony, there will be a small reception in the parish hall only for those who were mailed individual invitations.

Begin with A small reception.

(A) preceding (B) precede (C) follow
(D) following (E) followed

48. Any professional golfer who plays on the tournament circuit year after year may eventually attain his goal of winning the Masters or the National Open.

Delete who.

(A) having played (B) being played (C) having been played
(D) having playing (E) playing

49. After the judge had pronounced sentence upon the convicted bank robber, the spectators in the courtroom applauded because the wretch received ten years in the state penitentiary.

Begin with The convicted bank robber's sentence.

(A) from (B) to (C) into
(D) by means of (E) after

50. A careful reader can often infer a newspaper editor's opinions by noting the amount of space a story is given as well as the page on which the account is printed.

Begin with The amount of space and change as well as to and.

(A) infers (B) indicate (C) inferred
(D) indicated (E) infer

51. Today's newspaper reporters have access to more sources of information within the administration than their predecessors did a century ago.

Begin with More sources of information.

(A) is available
(B) will have been available
(C) having been available
(D) are available
(E) being available

52. The sacrifices which parents make so that their children may enjoy some of life's luxuries are often unappreciated by the ungrateful progeny.

Begin with Ungrateful progeny.

(A) none (B) not (C) no
(D) some (E) any

53. Hester Prynne, the heroine of Hawthorne's *The Scarlet Letter*, was found guilty of adultery and sentenced by colonial magistrates to wear a red A for the rest of her life.

Begin with Colonial magistrates.

(A) finds (B) has found (C) found
(D) has been found (E) was found

54. Mary as well as twenty of her classmates attends the theater every Saturday morning when special matinee prices are in effect at the box office.

Change as well as to and.

(A) attends the theater
(B) has been attending the theater
(C) have been attended at the theater
(D) shall have attended by the theater
(E) attend the theater

55. China and the Soviet Union share a long, almost unprotectable boundary across almost all of Asia, and within recent years disputes over the exact location of that boundary have brought tensions between the two nations.

Begin with Not only.

(A) do (B) does (C) did (D) have shared (E) will share

Section II

Number of items: 40
Time: 45 minutes

Directions: Each of the following passages consists of a paragraph of numbered sentences. Since the paragraphs appear as they would within a larger piece of writing, they do not necessarily constitute a complete discussion of the issues presented.

Read each paragraph carefully and answer the questions that follow it. The questions test your awareness of characteristics of prose that are important to good writing.

Questions 56–61 are based on the following passage.

[1]Many students entering college for the first time are confused by the attitude of many of the faculty members who teach them. [2]Many college professors lecture about their subject, whatever it may be, and assume, sometimes incorrectly, that new students understand the vocabulary which the professor uses, can define the terms from unfamiliar courses, and take notes adequately. [3]The skills are not those which most high school teachers teach or expect. [4]Therefore, both the professors and the students are frustrated because they do not understand each other in the classroom. [5]Too, many students hesitate to ask questions in class or during conferences and continue to be confused when they listen to the professors lecture. [6]One thing colleges could do to alleviate this problem is to offer a preschool seminar in study skills for inexperienced students. [7]Those who take the class would gain valuable knowledge and develop skills that would be helpful to them throughout their college years. [8]Some colleges hesitate to offer such instruction, however, because the colleges seem to say, "Here is the information you need, provided in the way we best provide it; if you students don't get it, that's tough."

56. The function of sentence 1 is primarily to
(A) establish a formal tone for the rest of the paragraph
(B) express a negative attitude toward faculty members
(C) define the phrase *confused student*
(D) express a neutral attitude toward college students
(E) make a generalization that may or may not be universally true

57. Which of the following best describes sentence 2?
(A) It is too long for a reader to understand.
(B) It contains too much internal punctuation.
(C) It uses a series of verbs (*understand, can define, take*) with *students* as the subject.
(D) It provides an example to support sentence 1.
(E) It conveys information through its structure.

58. Sentences 3 and 4 might be logically combined. Which of the following choices contains the correct form?
(A) expect; therefore, (B) expect, therefore,
(C) expect—therefore, (D) expect: therefore,
(E) expect therefore,

59. Sentence 8
(A) uses a direct quotation that restates an idea from sentence 1
(B) logically shifts the central idea of the paragraph from *students* to *colleges*
(C) seems to approve the point of the direct quotation
(D) does not provide a logical conclusion for the paragraph
(E) uses language in the direct quotation that might offend someone

60. Sentence 5
(A) sets up a cause and effect relationship without using signal words such as *because, consequently,* or *hence*
(B) might be eliminated because the idea does not seem related to the rest of the paragraph
(C) contains an ambiguous clause beginning *when*
(D) provides another example of a student
(E) confuses the goal that students and teachers have

61. The central idea of the paragraph seems to be that
(A) college professors seem to lecture too much to their students
(B) colleges could do something to help new students who are confused
(C) new college students are generally unprepared for college work
(D) only students who are super-intellectuals should be in college
(E) even with some help, many college freshmen will probably fail

Questions 62–67 are based on the following passage.

[1]Combine the sugar and flour in a large bowl, and stir well. [2]In a sauce pan, combine the oleo, water, cocoa, and salt; bring to a boil. [3]Stir hot mixture into sugar-flour combination, and beat well. [4]Add eggs, one at a time, beating well after each egg has been added. [5]Dissolve soda in sour milk, and stir well. [6]Stir in vanilla, and beat the batter for one minute. [7]Pour batter into baking pan, and place in oven. [8]Bake for twenty minutes or until a toothpick stuck into cake comes out clean. [9]Remove from oven and cool in baking pan for at least one hour. [10]Frost cake with a favorite icing. [11]Cut into squares and serve cold.

62. The paragraph is
(A) a recipe for preparing a cake
(B) a guide to making a fancy dessert
(C) directions for making a cake
(D) a section of a comparison/contrast composition
(E) obviously from a gourmet's cookbook

63. All of the sentences
(A) are actually sentence fragments because each has no subject
(B) use the imperative mood of the verbs
(C) are too short to be helpful to a cook
(D) use the declarative mood of the verb
(E) use the past tense of the verbs

64. One unique feature of paragraphs of this type is that
(A) sentences can be used in any order
(B) sentences provide several different bits of information
(C) there is a definite sentence of conclusion
(D) there is no expressed topic sentence or central idea
(E) all of the sentences have a different construction

65. Sentences 1 through 6 assume that
(A) the paragraph has been preceded by a list of ingredients with the amount of each one specified
(B) the reader is an experienced cook
(C) only children will use this recipe
(D) the reader can interpret things for himself/herself
(E) cakes are very easy to make

66. Sentence 7 is inadequate for this type of paragraph because
(A) it is broken into two parts with the comma
(B) the oven temperature is not given
(C) the reader is told to do two things
(D) the sentence is too short
(E) the sentence conveys little information

67. One advantage of well-written paragraphs of this type is that the reader
(A) does not have to read every word
(B) does not need to do anything
(C) is not expected to understand what is written
(D) cannot make a serious mistake
(E) is not required to interpret what is written

Questions 68–73 are based on the following passage.

[1]From my study window, I can see a grassy courtyard with some blooming flowers around the sides. [2]Across the courtyard is another apartment with a balcony which is larger than the one I have. [3]Usually, children are playing under the trees, and in the afternoons the noise of their activities is often distractive to my work. [4]From my balcony, I can see seven other balconies of varying sizes as well as seven patios that are attached to the apartments on the first floor. [5]Every Monday or Tuesday, depending upon the weather, several employees of the lawn upkeep service mow the grass, trim the shrubs, rake the clippings, and rake the area under the plants. [6]Just outside my study is a large oak tree that shades the windows from the afternoon sun; further over in the courtyard are two more oak trees that are as tall as the two-story buildings. [7]Some tenants have planted petunias, marigolds, impatiens, and other annuals in flower boxes or at the edges of patios so that we have flowering plants to enjoy until frost comes. [8]One of the trees, a red maple, has already started the annual fall leaf color change so that in a couple of weeks we can hope for reds and browns in the branches to contrast with the green in the grass. [9]Then frost comes . . .

68. Sentence 1 lets the reader assume that
(A) the paragraph will describe the courtyard
(B) the writer will develop some abstract idea about the courtyard
(C) the courtyard has some deep significance to the writer
(D) the paragraph will go from a general statement to something more specific
(E) the courtyard is not very attractive to the viewer

69. Sentence 5
(A) seems a practical statement about the courtyard
(B) demonstrates the apartment manager's concern for the unemployed
(C) changes the subject too abruptly and should be omitted
(D) produces the reason the author should remain in the apartment
(E) praises the services of the lawn upkeep company

70. Sentence 3 implies that
(A) the author does not like children
(B) children enjoy the grassy courtyard
(C) children cannot be trusted in the courtyard
(D) the author has a job that requires peace and quiet
(E) children should be encouraged in their activities

71. In sentence 7, the names of the plants that are in the courtyard illustrate what is said in
(A) sentence 2 (B) sentence 1 (C) sentence 6
(D) sentence 5 (E) sentence 8

72. Sentence 8 relates most closely to what other sentence?
(A) Sentence 3 (B) Sentence 4 (C) Sentence 2
(D) Sentence 9 (E) Sentence 6

73. The effect of sentence 9, incomplete as it is, is
(A) to summarize what the paragraph is all about
(B) to signal the reader that the paragraph is exaggerated
(C) to cast a coat of gloom on the mood of the paragraph
(D) to lighten the whole mood of the paragraph
(E) to show how the author can use an incomplete sentence ineffectively

Questions 74–79 are based on the following passage.

1Who reads poetry any more? 2Why does anyone bother with trying to figure out what someone dead a hundred years or more said about a daffodil, a country church yard, paradise, hell, death, love, a cloud, or whatever? 3What about those who write poetry today? 4Are they spinning their wheels in dry sand, waiting for readers who will never arrive? 5What has poetry to offer a resident of the twentieth century where there are more pressing problems, perhaps, than trying to decide what some stray person has set down to puzzle some stray reader? 6These are difficult questions for anyone to answer, because the twentieth century (for the most part) has been an age of prose, of the essay, of the problem or psychological novel, of the short story, or of other fiction. [7]Still, an examination of what someone calls poetry can lead to delights that can be found in no other medium, *provided* the reader is prepared to accept the poet on her or his own terms and, further *provided*, the reader is willing to ride with the poet wherever the poet travels and on whatever vehicle the poet uses to steer. [8]Poets are like almost no other people in the world—they like to play games with words, with ideas, with forms, with rhythm, with typographical devices. [9]In many cases, the games are just games, but in others, the games have something unique to say to the understanding, sympathetic, and responsive reader.

74. Sentences 1 through 5 are a series of questions. The purpose of these questions is
(A) to leave the reader puzzled and confused
(B) to intrigue the reader to search for answers to the following discussion
(C) to allow the writer to display his arrogance toward the reader
(D) to permit the writer, perhaps a teacher, to ask unanswerable questions
(E) to insult the reader's intelligence

75. Sentence 2 seems to recognize
(A) certain figures of speech
(B) subjects that only modern poets have written about
(C) clichés of poetry because these subjects have been used so often
(D) specific poems and poets who have used these subjects in famous poems
(E) that poems are often about simple subjects

76. What sentence can most logically be called the topic sentence of the paragraph?
(A) Sentence 1 (B) Sentence 3 (C) Sentence 6
(D) Sentence 9 (E) Sentence 7

77. The purpose of sentence 9 is
(A) to justify the means that poets use in their poems
(B) to expand the notion of *games* introduced in sentence 8
(C) to summarize the passage
(D) to define poetry readers
(E) to introduce a sports analogy to poetry reading

78. Sentence 7 uses a metaphor, which is clearly illustrated in the words
(A) *delight, provided, medium*
(B) *poetry, willing, steer*
(C) *rides, travel, vehicle*
(D) *terms, accept, wherever*
(E) *ride, further, whatever*

79. In sentence 4, the phrase *spinning their wheels* might also be expressed by
(A) exploring the unknown
(B) wasting their time
(C) deploring a drought
(D) paying uninterested readers
(E) tilting at windmills

Directions: Effective revision requires choosing among the many options available to a writer. The following questions test your ability to use these options effectively.

Revise each of the sentences below according to the directions that follow it. Some directions require you to rephrase only part of the original sentence; others require you to recast the entire sentence. You may need to omit or add certain words in constructing an acceptable revision, but you should keep the meaning of your revised sentence as close to the meaning of the original sentence as the directions permit. Your new sentence should follow the conventions of standard written English and should be clear and concise.

Look through the answer choices A–E under each question for the exact word or phrase that is included in your revised sentence. If you have thought of a revision that does not include any of the words or phrases listed, try to revise the sentence again so that it does include the wording in one of the answer choices.

When you take the test, you should feel free to make notes in your test book, but you will need to mark your answers on the separate answer sheet.

80. Unfortunately, you have incorrectly inferred from my speech criticizing the college administration that I am unalterably opposed to the regime of President Banks.

Begin with My speech criticizing.

(A) no inference (B) no reference (C) no allegation
(D) no implication (E) no desire

81. In any role Helen Hayes undertakes, she is always sheer magic and plays to the gallery as much as to front row patrons.

Begin with Fans in the gallery as well as.

(A) enjoy the sheer magic of Helen Hayes
(B) undertake the sheer magic of Helen Hayes
(C) plays the sheer magic of Helen Hayes
(D) always radiates sheer magic
(E) act with sheer magic

82. Some historians insist that Columbus did not discover America but that he was preceded on these shores by both Eric the Red and a Mediterranean Semitic people, among others.

Change was preceded to preceded.

(A) Columbus on these shores
(B) Eric the Red on these shores
(C) him on these shores
(D) a Mediterranean Semitic people on these shores
(E) historians on these shores

83. If all species have some innate desire to reproduce, there is evidence that all living things have one thing in common at least.

Change If all species have to All species having.

(A) there was (B) was (C) is there (D) there is (E) is

84. A prudent man should consider all the possibilities before investing money in any plan which seems to promise unlimited profits almost immediately.

Begin with Before a prudent man.

(A) him (B) it (C) his (D) its (E) he

85. Neither the president of the class nor any of its members will be permitted to attend the rally in the park this afternoon.

Substitute Either for Neither.

(A) and any (B) for any (C) or any (D) with any
(E) nor any

86. Won't Christine's parents object if you don't take her home by midnight?

Change the question to a statement.

(A) shall object (B) will object (C) will not object
(D) shall not object (E) had not objected

87. Some people are so immature that they cannot accept any frustration without indulging in violent temper tantrums.

Begin with Some very immature people indulge.

(A) they are frustrated
(B) any frustrations
(C) he is frustrated
(D) they frustrate
(E) he frustrates

88. Without the slightest shred of evidence to support the allegation, the prosecutor charged the hostile witness with perjury and demanded his arrest.

Change the prosecutor charged to the prosecutor demanded.

(A) the hostile witness' allegation for perjury
(B) the hostile witness' charged with perjury
(C) the hostile witness' alleged perjury
(D) the hostile witness' arrested for perjury
(E) the hostile witness' arrest for perjury

89. The undertow was so strong that the lifeguard warned all bathers to return to the beach and not risk being pulled out to sea.

Begin with All bathers.

(A) although (B) how (C) as much as (D) because
(E) where

90. Thoroughly spoiled children are so obnoxious that even their parents become disgusted with their atrocious behavior.

Begin with Thoroughly spoiled children behave so.

(A) atrociously (B) atrocious (C) disgustedly
(D) behaviorally (E) behavioral

91. Conservative bankers do not agree that providing low interest rates for home loans is the best method of fighting inflation.

    Begin with No conservative banker.

    (A) does not agree (B) do agree (C) agrees
    (D) has been agreed (E) will have agreed

92. As head of the copy editing department, Matthew earned a high salary from the nationally distributed news magazine.

    Change earned to was paid.

    (A) from the nationally (B) by the nationally
    (C) with the nationally (D) to the nationally
    (E) at the nationally

93. Since the chairman was not really congenial with other committee members, he did not solicit their opinions before announcing decisions to the press.

    Begin with Not really.

    (A) members, the chairman (B) members, he
    (C) members the chairman (D) members; thus the chairman
    (E) members, and so the chairman

94. Owing to his skill as a football player, John Johns had many offers of athletic scholarships from colleges all over the nation.

    Begin with Colleges all over the nation offered.

    (A) so (B) therefore (C) because
    (D) and (E) while

95. The American Medical Association's canon of ethics declares that no doctor shall participate in a mercy death even if the patient and his family request euthanasia.

    Change declares that no doctor to prohibits a doctor's.

    (A) with participating (B) having any participation
    (C) for participating (D) from participating
    (E) participation

ANSWER KEY—SAMPLE EXAMINATION 2

Section I

1. D	12. A	23. C	34. C	45. C
2. C	13. C	24. B	35. B	46. E
3. C	14. D	25. A	36. A	47. C
4. B	15. D	26. B	37. E	48. E
5. A	16. E	27. B	38. D	49. A
6. E	17. A	28. C	39. C	50. B
7. A	18. C	29. E	40. C	51. D
8. B	19. E	30. A	41. A	52. B
9. E	20. B	31. A	42. C	53. C
10. C	21. B	32. B	43. B	54. E
11. B	22. C	33. D	44. E	55. A

Section II

56. A	64. D	72. E	80. D	88. E
57. C	65. A	73. C	81. A	89. D
58. A	66. B	74. B	82. A	90. A
59. D	67. E	75. D	83. E	91. C
60. A	68. A	76. E	84. E	92. B
61. B	69. C	77. A	85. C	93. A
62. C	70. D	78. C	86. B	94. C
63. B	71. B	79. B	87. A	95. E

SCORING CHART—SAMPLE EXAMINATION 2

After you have scored your Sample Examination 2, enter the results in the chart below; then transfer your Raw Score to the Progress Chart on page 14.

Total Test	Number Right	Number Wrong	Number Omitted	Raw Score
Section I: 55				
Section II: 40				
Total: 95				

ANSWER EXPLANATIONS—SAMPLE EXAMINATION 2

Section I

1. D. Is is present tense and does not logically follow fought and battled, past tense.
2. C. They, a vague reference of pronouns, seems to refer to the welfare department.
3. C. Briskly is an ambiguous modifier.
4. B. He and I are wrong pronoun forms; the objective case should be him and me.
5. A. A dangling modifier.
6. E. Sentence is correct.
7. A. A dangling modifier.
8. B. Incorrect idiom.
9. E. Sentence is correct.
10. C. Change their to its since the Pat Metheney Group is singular (see has).
11. B. Inferences should be implications.
12. A. Each must be changed to a plural to agree with were.
13. C. Locate the face is a poor idiom; use recognize.
14. D. In whole is poor word choice; use wholly.
15. D. Is should be are; data is plural.
16. E. Sentence is correct.
17. A. True should be truly, the adverbial form.
18. C. Plan on having is a poor idiom; use plans to have.
19. E. Sentence is correct.
20. B. Eliminate to be—wordy.
21. B. The original sentence contains a cliché; (B) corrects the problem.
22. C. The comma in the original sentence is a comma splice.
23. C. They is a plural; the antecedent is one, singular. (C) corrects the problem.
24. B. Error in parallelism—the section beginning and he is a complete sentence, and the preceding section is a participle.

25. A. The original sentence is correct.
26. B. We should be us, the objective case.
27. B. Hadn't scarcely is a double negative.
28. C. Where is an incorrect word choice—that is correct.
29. E. That type person is a poor idiom.
30. A. The original sentence is correct.
31. A. The original sentence is correct.
32. B. Incorrect word choice, *eluded* should be *alluded*.
33. D. The correct pair of conjunctions is as . . . as.
34. C. A misplaced and ambiguous modifier—(C) corrects the problem.
35. B. Old and antique are repetitious; (B) solves the problem.
36. A. The original sentence is correct.
37. E. Except has to be accept.
38. D. The is why construction is ambiguous.
39. C. Whom should be who, the correct case form.
40. C. Neither—nor is the correct conjunction form.
41. A. Coney Island, famed for its roller coaster and its many hot dog stands, *is* a beach in New York City.
42. C. A woman . . . art gallery if she *does not* resort to tears . . .
43. B. The proper amount of iron is often more important in a woman's daily diet *than* the proper number . . .
44. E. Motorists would be spared confusion and uncertainty, *if Congress would pass* a law establishing a nationally . . .
45. C. When Thoreau retreated to Walden Pond, he had a few benevolent acquaintances to provide his necessities of life; no contemporary man can *so* retreat without the same kind of help.
46. E. The recent collapse of prices on the New York Stock Exchange has been *not only* a welcome sign that the inflationary spiral is slowing down but also a signal for large stockholders to begin purchasing large blocks of shares at bargain prices.
47. C. A small reception in the parish hall will *follow* the ceremony but only for those who were mailed invitations.
48. E. Any professional golfer *playing* on the tournament circuit year after year may eventually obtain . . .
49. A. The convicted bank robber's sentence of ten years in the state penitentiary, which the wretch received from the judge, brought applause *from* the spectators in the courtroom.
50. B. The amount of space a story is given and the page it is printed on *indicate* to a careful reader a newspaper editor's opinions.
51. D. More sources of information within the administration *are available* to today's newspaper reporters than to their predecessors a century ago.
52. B. Ungrateful progeny do *not* appreciate the sacrifices which parents make so that their children may enjoy some of life's luxuries.
53. C. Colonial magistrates *found* Hester Prynne, the heroine of Hawthorne's *The Scarlet Letter*, guilty of adultery and sentenced her to wear a scarlet A.
54. E. Mary and twenty of her classmates *attend the theater* . . .
55. A. Not only *do* China and the Soviet Union share a long, almost unprotectable border across almost all of Asia, but within recent years disputes over the exact . . .

Section II

56. A. The formal tone of the sentence establishes the tone for the rest of the paragraph.
57. C. (A) and (B) are incorrect; the sentence is neither too long nor does it contain too much punctuation. (D) is inaccurate; this is not an example of why students are confused about their professors' attitudes. (E) is wrong; the information is conveyed through the words, not the structure.

58. A. The punctuation in the other choices is incorrect. (B) and (E) are comma splices; (C) uses dash incorrectly; (D) uses colon incorrectly.

59. D. Rather than providing a conclusion, sentence 8 leaves the discussion up in the air.

60. A. The students' hesitating to ask questions causes them to continue to be confused. This cause and effect relationship is established by the sense of the sentence without the use of traditional cause and effect clue words such as accordingly, because, consequently, for, hence, so...that, etc.

61. B. (A), (D), and (E) are incorrect; nowhere are these suggested. (C) is an inaccurate interpretation; new college students are not unprepared for college work; they simply lack proper college study habits.

62. C. Since the amounts for the ingredients are missing, this is not a complete recipe.

63. B. All of the sentences use the imperative mood, the "you" being understood.

64. D. Because this is a set of directions for baking a cake, there is no need for a topic sentence.

65. A. Without a list specifying the amount of each ingredient, the directions would be meaningless.

66. B. Without instructions about the proper oven temperature, the instructions in sentence 7 are useless.

67. E. The information is straightforward and, therefore, requires no interpretation on the reader's part.

68. A. The narrative tone as well as the sense of the sentence makes the reader expect that a description of the courtyard will follow.

69. C. The change from the mostly tranquil description of the courtyard to the activity of the gardeners disrupts the mood the author is creating.

70. D. The author's statement about the children playing has neither negative nor positive implications. But the author's need for quiet is evident, since the noise of the children distracts the author from his work.

71. B. In sentence 1, the author says he can see "blooming flowers." In sentence 7, he gives specific names of flowers to illustrate his point.

72. E. Sentences 6 and 8 both describe the trees in the courtyard.

73. C. Until this last sentence, the mood of the paragraph has been one of tranquility and joy in the beauty of nature. The mood changes to one of gloom with the mention of frost and the visions that come with it.

74. B. The series of questions is an effective way of getting the reader involved with the discussion that is to follow.

75. D. Most readers will recognize at least a few of the poems alluded to in sentence 2.

76. E. Sentence 7 states the author's position; the rest of the paragraph attempts to persuade the reader to agree with this position.

77. A. To counteract the negative attitude some people have about what they see as the meaningless obtuseness of poets, the author explains why poets use certain "games."

78. C. *Rides, travel,* and *vehicle* clearly illustrate the extended metaphor in sentence 7 that compares studying poetry to taking a trip to new and exciting places.

79. B. The descriptive image of the phrase "spinning their wheels" is used to convey the idea that the poets are going nowhere; they are wasting their time.

80. D. My speech criticizing the college administration contained *no implication* that I am unalterably opposed to the regime of President Banks.

81. A. Fans in the gallery as well as front row patrons *enjoy the sheer magic of Helen Hayes*, playing any role she undertakes.

82. A. Some historians insist that both Eric the Red and a Mediterranean Semitic people preceded *Columbus on these shores;* therefore, the claim that Columbus discovered America may be false.

83. E. All species having some innate desire to reproduce *is* one piece of evidence that all living things have one thing in common at least.

84. E. Before a prudent man invests money in any plan which seems to promise unlimited profits at once, *he* should investigate all the possibilities.

85. C. Either the president of the class *or any* of its members will not be permitted to attend the rally in the park this afternoon.

86. B. Christine's parents *will object* if you don't take her home by midnight.

87. A. Some very immature people indulge in violent temper tantrums whenever *they are frustrated.*

88. E. Without the slightest shred of evidence to support the allegation, the prosecutor demanded *the hostile witness' arrest for perjury.*

89. D. All bathers were warned by the lifeguard to return to the beach *because* of the dangerous undertow that might pull them out to sea.

90. A. Thoroughly spoiled children behave so *atrociously* that even their parents are disgusted by their obnoxious behavior.

91. C. No conservative banker *agrees* that providing low interest rates for home loans is the best method of fighting inflation.

92. B. As head of the copy editing department, Matthew was paid a high salary *by the nationally* distributed news magazine.

93. A. Not really congenial with the other committee *members, the chairman* did not solicit their opinions before announcing decisions to the press.

94. C. Colleges all over the nation offered John Johns athletic scholarships *because* of his skills as a football player.

95. E. The American Medical Association's canon of ethics prohibits a doctor's *participation* in a mercy death even if the patient and his family request euthanasia.

ANSWER SHEET — ENGLISH COMPOSITION/SAMPLE EXAMINATION 3

Section I

1. Ⓐ Ⓑ Ⓒ Ⓓ Ⓔ	15. Ⓐ Ⓑ Ⓒ Ⓓ Ⓔ	29. Ⓐ Ⓑ Ⓒ Ⓓ Ⓔ	43. Ⓐ Ⓑ Ⓒ Ⓓ Ⓔ
2. Ⓐ Ⓑ Ⓒ Ⓓ Ⓔ	16. Ⓐ Ⓑ Ⓒ Ⓓ Ⓔ	30. Ⓐ Ⓑ Ⓒ Ⓓ Ⓔ	44. Ⓐ Ⓑ Ⓒ Ⓓ Ⓔ
3. Ⓐ Ⓑ Ⓒ Ⓓ Ⓔ	17. Ⓐ Ⓑ Ⓒ Ⓓ Ⓔ	31. Ⓐ Ⓑ Ⓒ Ⓓ Ⓔ	45. Ⓐ Ⓑ Ⓒ Ⓓ Ⓔ
4. Ⓐ Ⓑ Ⓒ Ⓓ Ⓔ	18. Ⓐ Ⓑ Ⓒ Ⓓ Ⓔ	32. Ⓐ Ⓑ Ⓒ Ⓓ Ⓔ	46. Ⓐ Ⓑ Ⓒ Ⓓ Ⓔ
5. Ⓐ Ⓑ Ⓒ Ⓓ Ⓔ	19. Ⓐ Ⓑ Ⓒ Ⓓ Ⓔ	33. Ⓐ Ⓑ Ⓒ Ⓓ Ⓔ	47. Ⓐ Ⓑ Ⓒ Ⓓ Ⓔ
6. Ⓐ Ⓑ Ⓒ Ⓓ Ⓔ	20. Ⓐ Ⓑ Ⓒ Ⓓ Ⓔ	34. Ⓐ Ⓑ Ⓒ Ⓓ Ⓔ	48. Ⓐ Ⓑ Ⓒ Ⓓ Ⓔ
7. Ⓐ Ⓑ Ⓒ Ⓓ Ⓔ	21. Ⓐ Ⓑ Ⓒ Ⓓ Ⓔ	35. Ⓐ Ⓑ Ⓒ Ⓓ Ⓔ	49. Ⓐ Ⓑ Ⓒ Ⓓ Ⓔ
8. Ⓐ Ⓑ Ⓒ Ⓓ Ⓔ	22. Ⓐ Ⓑ Ⓒ Ⓓ Ⓔ	36. Ⓐ Ⓑ Ⓒ Ⓓ Ⓔ	50. Ⓐ Ⓑ Ⓒ Ⓓ Ⓔ
9. Ⓐ Ⓑ Ⓒ Ⓓ Ⓔ	23. Ⓐ Ⓑ Ⓒ Ⓓ Ⓔ	37. Ⓐ Ⓑ Ⓒ Ⓓ Ⓔ	51. Ⓐ Ⓑ Ⓒ Ⓓ Ⓔ
10. Ⓐ Ⓑ Ⓒ Ⓓ Ⓔ	24. Ⓐ Ⓑ Ⓒ Ⓓ Ⓔ	38. Ⓐ Ⓑ Ⓒ Ⓓ Ⓔ	52. Ⓐ Ⓑ Ⓒ Ⓓ Ⓔ
11. Ⓐ Ⓑ Ⓒ Ⓓ Ⓔ	25. Ⓐ Ⓑ Ⓒ Ⓓ Ⓔ	39. Ⓐ Ⓑ Ⓒ Ⓓ Ⓔ	53. Ⓐ Ⓑ Ⓒ Ⓓ Ⓔ
12. Ⓐ Ⓑ Ⓒ Ⓓ Ⓔ	26. Ⓐ Ⓑ Ⓒ Ⓓ Ⓔ	40. Ⓐ Ⓑ Ⓒ Ⓓ Ⓔ	54. Ⓐ Ⓑ Ⓒ Ⓓ Ⓔ
13. Ⓐ Ⓑ Ⓒ Ⓓ Ⓔ	27. Ⓐ Ⓑ Ⓒ Ⓓ Ⓔ	41. Ⓐ Ⓑ Ⓒ Ⓓ Ⓔ	55. Ⓐ Ⓑ Ⓒ Ⓓ Ⓔ
14. Ⓐ Ⓑ Ⓒ Ⓓ Ⓔ	28. Ⓐ Ⓑ Ⓒ Ⓓ Ⓔ	42. Ⓐ Ⓑ Ⓒ Ⓓ Ⓔ	

Section II

56. Ⓐ Ⓑ Ⓒ Ⓓ Ⓔ	66. Ⓐ Ⓑ Ⓒ Ⓓ Ⓔ	76. Ⓐ Ⓑ Ⓒ Ⓓ Ⓔ	86. Ⓐ Ⓑ Ⓒ Ⓓ Ⓔ
57. Ⓐ Ⓑ Ⓒ Ⓓ Ⓔ	67. Ⓐ Ⓑ Ⓒ Ⓓ Ⓔ	77. Ⓐ Ⓑ Ⓒ Ⓓ Ⓔ	87. Ⓐ Ⓑ Ⓒ Ⓓ Ⓔ
58. Ⓐ Ⓑ Ⓒ Ⓓ Ⓔ	68. Ⓐ Ⓑ Ⓒ Ⓓ Ⓔ	78. Ⓐ Ⓑ Ⓒ Ⓓ Ⓔ	88. Ⓐ Ⓑ Ⓒ Ⓓ Ⓔ
59. Ⓐ Ⓑ Ⓒ Ⓓ Ⓔ	69. Ⓐ Ⓑ Ⓒ Ⓓ Ⓔ	79. Ⓐ Ⓑ Ⓒ Ⓓ Ⓔ	89. Ⓐ Ⓑ Ⓒ Ⓓ Ⓔ
60. Ⓐ Ⓑ Ⓒ Ⓓ Ⓔ	70. Ⓐ Ⓑ Ⓒ Ⓓ Ⓔ	80. Ⓐ Ⓑ Ⓒ Ⓓ Ⓔ	90. Ⓐ Ⓑ Ⓒ Ⓓ Ⓔ
61. Ⓐ Ⓑ Ⓒ Ⓓ Ⓔ	71. Ⓐ Ⓑ Ⓒ Ⓓ Ⓔ	81. Ⓐ Ⓑ Ⓒ Ⓓ Ⓔ	91. Ⓐ Ⓑ Ⓒ Ⓓ Ⓔ
62. Ⓐ Ⓑ Ⓒ Ⓓ Ⓔ	72. Ⓐ Ⓑ Ⓒ Ⓓ Ⓔ	82. Ⓐ Ⓑ Ⓒ Ⓓ Ⓔ	92. Ⓐ Ⓑ Ⓒ Ⓓ Ⓔ
63. Ⓐ Ⓑ Ⓒ Ⓓ Ⓔ	73. Ⓐ Ⓑ Ⓒ Ⓓ Ⓔ	83. Ⓐ Ⓑ Ⓒ Ⓓ Ⓔ	93. Ⓐ Ⓑ Ⓒ Ⓓ Ⓔ
64. Ⓐ Ⓑ Ⓒ Ⓓ Ⓔ	74. Ⓐ Ⓑ Ⓒ Ⓓ Ⓔ	84. Ⓐ Ⓑ Ⓒ Ⓓ Ⓔ	94. Ⓐ Ⓑ Ⓒ Ⓓ Ⓔ
65. Ⓐ Ⓑ Ⓒ Ⓓ Ⓔ	75. Ⓐ Ⓑ Ⓒ Ⓓ Ⓔ	85. Ⓐ Ⓑ Ⓒ Ⓓ Ⓔ	95. Ⓐ Ⓑ Ⓒ Ⓓ Ⓔ

SAMPLE ENGLISH COMPOSITION EXAMINATION 3

Section I

Number of items: 55
Time: 45 minutes

Directions: The following sentences contain problems in grammar, usage, diction (choice of words), and idiom.

Some sentences are correct.
No sentence contains more than one error.

You will find that the error, if there is one, is underlined and lettered. Assume that elements of the sentence that are not underlined are correct and cannot be changed. In choosing answers, follow the requirements of standard written English.

If there is an error, select the one underlined part that must be changed to make the sentence correct.

If there is no error, select answer (E).

1. Andrew Jackson's quarrel (A) with (B) the socially elite citizens of Washington, D.C., about the manners of some of his supporters (C), demonstrates again that no one can please all of the people (D) all of the time. No error (E)

2. As long as he ruled with an iron hand (A), Joseph Stalin was regarded as a sort (B) of god by the average Soviet citizen; however, after (C) his death, the inevitable degrading of his reputation took place as more facts (D) were revealed about him. No error (E)

3. Running away from home and living in a commune was favorite (A) pastimes (B) for many American young people during the era (C) of the flower children, especially (D) in San Francisco. No error (E)

4. The old author was forgotten by (A) his readers and neglected by his publisher (B) who's more recent (C) best sellers had featured raw (D) sex and violence. No error (E)

5. When we first discovered yogurt (A), we did not like the flavor (B); yet, the more often Mother (C) served it for lunch, the more (D) often we ate it and enjoyed it. No error (E)

6. The credulity (A) of the witness was almost unbelievable; he gave the detective such (B) a complete description of the thief that he was (C) identified almost (D) immediately. No error (E)

7. The Johnsons had been married for more than thirty years (A), and their friends were shocked when the local gazette (B) published the news that he had eloped (C) with his secretary, a girl whom we all thought was (D) too young for him. No error (E)

8. The shock of the sight was so traumatic (A) that the motorist was literally speechless (B); he could only cradle his head (C) in his hands and murmur (D), "I didn't see her! I didn't see her!" No error (E)

9. Like Josephine's letters (A) in which she expressed her love in brilliant phrases (B), the pleasures of reading someone else's (C) intimate correspondence is similar to the slightly illicit joy (D) of eavesdropping. No error (E)

10. She demeaned herself (A) and took a job as hostess in a saloon because (B) she could not afford to remain unemployed (C) and was not qualified by training or experience (D) to seek another position. No error (E)

11. Geography can teach (A) anyone more about the small planet (B) on which they live (C) than just the imaginary boundaries between any two (D) countries. No error (E)

12. Laying on (A) a log worn smooth (B) by the feet of many who had used it as a bridge (C) is my idea of a happy way to spend (D) a lazy summer afternoon. No error (E)

13. The Potomac, once a beautiful river (A) that flows from the Maryland Mountains to (B) Chesapeake Bay, is now so throughly polluted (C) with raw sewage and industrial wastes that citizens of Washington refuse to walk its shores (D). No error (E)

14. An expert candler can package several dozen eggs within a few minutes; it
A
does not take much experience for him to glance at the eggs as they pass the
B C
row of lights and separate out the bad ones. No error
D E

15. If anyone finds a wallet on the street, they should turn it in to the nearest
A B
policeman, who know how to locate the owner even if it contains no
C D
identification papers. No error
E

16. In their canvas covered wagons, many brave pioneers departed from St.
A
Joseph, Missouri for California where gold had been discovered and untold
B
wealth was to be had almost too easily. No error
C D E

17. Despite Richard Nixon's resignation as president of the United States, he
A B C
continues to have the respect of many of his early supporters. No error
D E

18. To our sorrow, we discovered that the street we were seeking was much
A
more further beyond the city limits of Springfield than we had been told by
B C
the service station operator who gave us directions. No error
D E

19. Good writing can frequently be identified by its clarity, its brevity,
A B
its ability to please the reader, and also it is free of grammatical errors.
C D
No error
E

20. President George Bush's proposal to scale down Star Wars planning demonstrates a break with policies of Ronald Reagan, and it may cost him support
A B C
from some ultra-conservative voters. No error
D E

Directions: In each of the following sentences, some part or all of the sentence is underlined. Below each sentence you will find five ways of phrasing the underlined part. Select the answer that produces the most effective sentence, one that is clear and exact, without awkwardness or ambiguity. In choosing answers, follow the requirements of standard written English. Choose the answer that best expresses the meaning of the original sentence.

Answer (A) is always the same as the underlined part. Choose answer (A) if you think the original sentence needs no revision.

21. Your order for our $6.98 rose bushes has been received, and they will be shipped no later than May 15, 1990, as per your instructions.
(A) May 15, 1990, as per your instructions
(B) May fifteenth, 1990, as per your instructions
(C) May 15, 1990, according to your instructions
(D) May 15, Nineteen Ninety, as per your instructions
(E) May Fifteenth, Nineteen Ninety, according to your instructions

22. Among nuclear scientists, Enrico Fermi's name is revered for his research achieved greater results than many other physicists with the Manhattan Project.
(A) greater results than many other physicists with
(B) greater results than those of many other physicists with
(C) greater real results than many other physicists wanted
(D) greatest results than many other physicists with
(E) more greater results than many of the physicists with

23. A guest in those hotels whose reputation is not the best soon learns not to leave loose change lying on the chest; the maid might assume that she is being tipped and put the money in her pocket.
(A) learns not to leave loose change lying on the chest
(B) learns not to leave loose change laying on the chest
(C) learns not to leave lose change lying on the chest
(D) learns not to leave lose change laying on the chest
(E) learns not to leave loose change laid on the chest

24. Modern mathematicians tell we amateurs that children should no longer be told that two plus two equals four; only if the system is base ten is four the correct answer.
(A) mathematicians tell we amateurs
(B) mathematicians tell their amateurs
(C) mathematicians tell them amateurs
(D) mathematicians tell our amateurs
(E) mathematicians tell us amateurs

25. When we rang the bell hanging on the post, the old ferryman sat aside his pipe and started the motor that propelled the creaking ferry across the river.
(A) ferryman sat aside his pipe and started the motor
(B) ferryman sat aside, and started the motor
(C) ferryman sat beside his pipe and started the motor
(D) ferryman set aside his pipe and started the motor
(E) ferryman sits aside his pipe and started the motor

26. John failed Spanish for the third time, and the reason was because he had no facility for languages.
(A) and the reason was because he had
(B) because he had
(C) and he had
(D) unless he had
(E) which he had

27. Hunter is an expert athlete, for he enjoys both swimming, bowling, and tennis.
(A) Hunter is an expert athlete, for he enjoys both swimming, bowling, and tennis.
(B) Hunter is an expert athlete, for he enjoys both swimming, bowling, as well as tennis.
(C) Hunter is an expert athlete, for he enjoys both swimming and bowling and tennis.
(D) Hunter is an expert athlete, for he enjoys swimming, bowling, and tennis.
(E) Hunter is an expert athelete, for he enjoyed swimming, bowling and tennis.

28. Each of you can do the problem if you will put your minds to it.
(A) Each of you can do the problem if you will put your minds to it.
(B) Each of you can do the problem if they will put their minds to it.
(C) Each of you can do the problem if you have put your minds to it.
(D) Each and everyone of you have done the problem if they would only put their minds to it.
(E) Everyone of you can do the problem if you could put your mind to it.

29. I had to leave my car on the dark street which had a broken front axle and a leaking radiator.
(A) the dark street which had a broken front axle
(B) on the dark street; it had a broken front axle
(C) on the dark street, it had a broken front axle
(D) on the dark street as a result of its having a broken front axle
(E) on the dark street, having a broken front axle

30. The principal offered scholarships to only three boys in the senior class—Jack, Jim, and me.
(A) The principal offered scholarships to only three boys in the senior class —Jack, Jim, and me.
(B) The principal had offered scholarships to three boys only in the senior class —Jack, Jim, and me.
(C) The principal offered scholarships to only three boys in the senior class —Jack, Jim, and I.
(D) The principle offered scholarships to only three boys in the senior class —Jack, Jim, and me.
(E) The principal offered only scholarships to three boys in the senior class —Jack, Jim, and me.

31. At six P.M. last night, all television stations broadcast an address by President George Bush.
(A) At six P.M. last night, all television stations broadcast an address by President George Bush.
(B) President Bush addressed the nation via television last night at 6 P.M.
(C) When President George Bush spoke at 6 P.M. last night, all television stations broadcast what he said.
(D) At six last night, all television stations broadcast an address by President George Bush.
(E) President George Bush wanted to make a speech at 6 P.M. last night; all television stations carried the address.

32. We could only wonder if he were going to attend college this fall or if he was planning to seek immediate employment.
(A) fall or if he was planning to seek immediate employment
(B) fall or if he had not been planning to seek immediate employment
(C) fall or if he were planning to seek immediate employment
(D) fall or if he could have been planning to seek immediate employment
(E) fall or if he applied for some jobs

33. Fay Weldon, an outstanding British novelist whose books have created laughter around the world and serious considerations of feminist concern.
(A) Fay Weldon, an outstanding British novelist whose books have created laughter around the world and serious considerations of feminist concern.
(B) Fay Weldon, who is an . . . .
(C) Fay Weldon is . . . .
(D) Fay Weldon, one more . . . .
(E) Fay Weldon, who has been

34. William ate all the roast beef on the plate, but the beans, carrots, and potatoes were untouched by him.
(A) William ate all the roast beef on the plate, but the beans, carrots, and potatoes were untouched by him.
(B) William ate the roast beef on the plate; the beans, carrots, and potatoes were untouched by him.
(C) William ate all the roast beef on his plate along with the beans, carrots, and potatoes.
(D) William ate all the roast beef on the plate; but the beans, carrots, and potatoes were untouched by him.
(E) William ate all the roast beef on the plate, but he left the beans, carrots, and potatoes untouched.

35. For several seasons, Woodbridge and Oakland High Schools have been trying to establish an annual football game which would be played every year in a stadium halfway between the two towns.
(A) which would be played every year in a stadium
(B) which has been played every year in a stadium
(C) which has been played in a stadium
(D) which would be played in a stadium
(E) which had been played in a stadium every year

36. You should have remembered that I was suppose to pick you up at exactly eight o'clock, not eight-fifteen or eight-thirty.
(A) remembered that I was suppose to pick
(B) remembered that I was supposed to pick
(C) remembered that had been able to suppose
(D) remembered that I could have picked
(E) remembered that I should have been suppose

37. Colombian drug lords have been the target of William Bennett's and George Bush's war on drugs in 1989; Congress seems to be reluctant to appropriate the necessary funds.

(A) and George Bush's war on drugs in 1989;
(B) and George Bush's war on drugs in 1989,
(C) and George Bush's war on drugs in 1989
(D) and George Bush's who declared war on drugs in 1989
(E) and George Bush's war on those who use drugs

38. Many cinema buffs who overpraise the films of certain underground directors consider bad acting, poor photography, and sleazy sets the real charm of their esoteric productions.

(A) Many cinema buffs who overpraise the films
(B) Many cinema buffs whom overpraise the films
(C) Many cinema buffs who overpraises the films
(D) Many cinema buff who overpraise the films
(E) Many a cinema buff who overpraise the films

39. That Roseanne Barr and Meryl Streep could co-star in the film *She Devil*, which will be released in 1989, seems amazing, they seem too different to appear together.

(A) seems amazing, they seem too different to appear together
(B) seems amazing they seem too different
(C) seems amazing; they seem too different
(D) seems amazing who seem too different
(E) seems amazing whose acting seems too different

40. The plain truth of the matter is that I am tired of working and can think of nothing better than setting in an easy chair and reading books.

(A) nothing better than setting in an easy chair and reading books
(B) nothing better than to sit in an easy chair and reading books
(C) nothing better than sitting in an easy chair and to read books
(D) nothing better than having an easy chair which would help me read books
(E) nothing better than sitting in an easy chair and reading books

Directions: Effective revision requires choosing among the many options available to a writer. The following questions test your ability to use these options effectively.

Revise each of the sentences below according to the directions that follow it. Some directions require you to rephrase only part of the original sentence; others require you to recast the entire sentence. You may need to omit or add certain words in constructing an acceptable revision, but you should keep the meaning of your revised sentence as close to the meaning of the original sentence as the directions permit. Your new sentence should follow the conventions of standard written English and should be clear and concise.

Look through the answer choices A–E under each question for the exact word or phrase that is included in your revised sentence. If you have thought of a revision that does not include any of the words or phrases listed, try to revise the sentence again so that it does include the wording in one of the answer choices.

When you take the test, you should feel free to make notes in your test book, but you will need to mark your answers on the separate answer sheet.

41. Any teenager receiving an allowance from his parents at least owes them some kind of thanks for the money they provide.

Change receiving to being given.

(A) by his parents (B) from his parents (C) through his parents
(D) like his parents (E) for his parents

42. Hunting for the elusive wild deer and fishing for the fighting mountain trout are two of my favorite sports.

Substitute fish for fishing.

(A) to be hunting (B) to hunting (C) to have hunted
(D) to hunt (E) to be hunted

43. In their conflict with militant demonstrations, hard-hat construction workers are merely defending those social values and attitudes which they learned from their parents and their own work ethic.

Begin with Their parents' and their own work ethic.

(A) within their conflicts with (B) in their conflict with
(C) by their conflicts with (D) from their conflicts with
(E) against their conflicts with

44. The 1989 uprisings against the Communist government in China demonstrates that human beings may refuse to obey orders blindly.

Begin with Human beings may refuse.

(A) had been demonstrated (B) would have demonstrated
(C) was demonstrated (D) could have been demonstrated
(E) is demonstrated

45. Colleges and universities now offer students more than a traditional basic education, for their registrants are demanding that all subjects be more relevant to contemporary life.

Change more than a traditional to not only a traditional.

(A) but also more relevant
(B) but also subjects more relevant
(C) but also contemporary life
(D) but also more life
(E) but also more tradition

46. The autumnal equinox occurs on September 22 and signals the approach of changes in leaf color, temperatures that will be lower, and everyone reaching for warmer clothes.

Begin with When the autumnal equinox.

(A) which signals (B) noboby expects (C) that could signal
(D) everyone rejects (E) it signals

47. Many drivers who are drunk when an accident occurs protest that they can drive safely when they have imbibed several ounces of alcohol.

Begin with Even when they have imbibed.

(A) many drivers who are drunk
(B) when they can drive safely
(C) many drivers who have drunk too much
(D) insofar as an accident occurs
(E) besides which an accident has occurred

48. Mildred Jones is a very meticulous person, for all the spices in her cabinet are arranged alphabetically.

Begin with One can conclude.

(A) because she could only arrange
(B) because she had not arranged
(C) because she refuses to arrange
(D) because she arranges
(E) because Mildred Jones is very peculiar

49. Rudolph acts like a foolish child because he trusts anyone who can tell a story in a believable manner.

Change he trusts to the trust of Rudolph.

(A) who acts like a foolish child
(B) when he acts like a foolish child
(C) when he can tell a story
(D) whenever he believes a wild story
(E) Rudolph, acting like a foolish child

50. About five percent of all American school children exhibit certain learning disabilities, which are due to minimal brain dysfunction.

Begin with Minimal brain dysfunction.

(A) has been due (B) exhibits (C) causes
(D) causing (E) sees that

51. As a young man, James Baldwin fled to Europe because of the bigotry and intolerance which he as an African-American met everywhere he went.

Begin with As an African-American, James Baldwin met.

(A) therefore, he fled (B) so, therefore, he fled
(C) ; fled (D) , he fled (E) ; therefore, he fled

52. The president announced that labor leaders had given him a tacit commitment not to demand exorbitant wage increases when current union contracts expire.

Change when to upon.

(A) which current union contracts expire
(B) the cancellation of current union contracts
(C) the expiration of current union contracts
(D) current union contracts expire
(E) his expiration of current union contracts

53. Researchers drew one startling conclusion from data accumulated during the Head Start program: ghetto children of prekindergarten age learn rapidly in school but soon regress if nothing is done to improve their home situation.

Begin with That ghetto children.

(A) drew one startling conclusion
(B) one startling conclusion was drawn
(C) draw one startling conclusion
(D) was one startling conclusion drawn
(E) were one startling conclusion

54. Because Amanda Wingfield had a number of gentlemen callers in her youth, she assumed that the number of a girl's suitors was a measure of her popularity.

Eliminate because.

(A) youth, therefor (B) youth; therefore, (C) youth, therefore
(D) youth, so therefore (E) youth, so thus

55. When a politician prepares a speech for delivery to a woman's organization, he is sure to include some ringing phrases praising motherhood and home cooking.

Change sure to include to surely includes.

(A) When a politician prepared
(B) Often when a politician prepares
(C) A politician preparing
(D) A politician praising
(E) A politician cooking

Section II

Number of items: 40
Time: 45 minutes

Directions: Each of the following passages consists of a paragraph of numbered sentences. Since the paragraphs appear as they would within a large piece of writing, they do not necessarily constitute a complete discussion of the issues presented.

Read each paragraph carefully and answer the questions that follow it. The questions test your awareness of characteristics of prose that are important to good writing.

Questions 56–58 are based on the following passage.

[1]My daughter's wedding was very inexpensive. [2]We did not have a dinner at the reception. [3]Flowers were few and simple. [4]The bridal gown was on sale for half price. [5]The groom and ushers wore tuxedoes which had been rented, not purchased. [6]There was no champagne for the toast because the church does not permit alcoholic beverages in its parlor. [7]Still, the wedding was beautiful, and the more than one hundred guests seemed to enjoy the festivities. [8]Debbie and Steve are living in Decatur where Steve is selling insurance for one of the large companies which specialize in life and health insurance programs.

56. What should be done with sentence 7?
(A) It should be left as it is.
(B) The word *Still* should be omitted, and the sentence placed before sentence 1.
(C) The words *In the spring* should be added before *Still.*
(D) The word *Still* should be omitted and the sentence joined with sentence 5.
(E) It should be joined to sentence 6: *in its parlor; however, the*

57. What should be done with sentence 8?
(A) It should be moved to the beginning of the passage.
(B) It should begin a second paragraph.
(C) It should be shorter and less detailed.
(D) It should come immediately after sentence 1.
(E) It should be combined with sentence 2.

58. Sentences 1 through 6 could be combined by
(A) substituting commas for all of the periods
(B) subtituting colons for all of the periods
(C) changing the period at the end of sentence 1 to a semicolon and leaving the rest as it is
(D) changing the period at the end of sentence 1 to a colon and the periods at the end of sentences 2, 3, 4, and 5 to semicolons.
(E) eliminating sentence 2 and making sentences 4 and 5 parts of sentence 1

Questions 59–61 are based on the following passage.

[1]In fact, this play has piled up more continuous performances in the same theater than any other play in American theatrical history, and the end of the run is not in sight. [2]*The Fantasticks,* a musical, has been running at a small off-Broadway theater for about thirty years. [3]Many actors and actresses made their debuts in this simple musical comedy and have moved on to starring roles in Broadway productions, on television, and in Hollywood. [4]Why this play, which was ignored by sophisticated critics when it opened, has established such a record is a mystery to many people. [5]The story line is a kind of fairy story, the music is not very distinctive, and the lyrics are full of clichés. [6]But the musical continues to attract an audience, and as long as the producers sell tickets and make money, the play will continue.

59. What should be done with sentence 2?
(A) It should be at the beginning of the passage.
(B) It should be at the end of the passage.
(C) It should be placed after sentence 4.
(D) It should be omitted completely.
(E) It should be left as it is.

60. Sentence 6 should begin
(A) with *The musical continues to, however, attract*
(B) with *Therefore, the musical continues to attract*
(C) with *As a result, the musical continues to attract*
(D) with *On the other hand, the musical continues to attract*
(E) the way it begins now

61. Sentence 4 should
(A) come immediately after sentence 1
(B) come where it is now
(C) be changed so that the first word is *That*
(D) have the word *not* inserted before *established*
(E) come immediately before sentence 6

Questions 62–67 are based on the following passage.

[1]It has become conventional that every president of the United States, once he becomes an ex-president, expects that the taxpayers will build a library or some other building in his honor. [2]These monuments usually cost well into eight figures to construct, and the upkeep (maintenance, employees to serve the institution, etc.) is always a few more million annually. [3]For example, the Jimmy Carter library in Atlanta created some controversy, because architects planned a broad highway leading to the building. [4]The people who lived in the neighborhood protested that traffic would disturb the peace and quiet they had enjoyed before the building was completed. [5]With the protests and threatened lawsuits, we seem to have another example of NIMBY—"Not In My Back Yard," which seems to afflict many people when their health, safety, or convenience is disturbed. [6]A similar protest occurred when a garbage dump for toxic wastes was proposed for a forest preserve area in Illinois. [7]Thus, often we are provided with undesirable options: either to build a building to honor an ex-president with all that follows that decision or to refuse the honor of having a tourist attraction in the neighborhood.

62. Sentence 6
(A) produces a necessary interruption in the paragraph
(B) should be omitted as irrelevant to the paragraph's meaning
(C) provides another example of NIMBY
(D) confuses the tone of the paragraph with the word *garbage*
(E) questions the practice of building libraries to honor ex-presidents

63. Sentence 1
(A) is the basic generalization for the whole paragraph
(B) is too long to be a good topic sentence
(C) contains a grammatical error—*It*
(D) presents a rationale that opposes building presidential libraries
(E) protects the right of anyone to oppose presidential libraries

64. In sentence 2, the word *monuments* suggests that
(A) presidential libraries are a good thing
(B) ex-presidents have not already been honored enough by their former office
(C) libraries are a legitimate means of honoring ex-presidents
(D) ex-presidential libraries provide examples of wasted money and unnecessary expenses
(E) the American people enjoy honoring ex-presidents

65. Sentence 3
(A) moves the development of the generalization in sentence 1 to a specific example
(B) signals the reader too blatantly with *For example*
(C) implies that only Jimmy Carter's memorial was too expensive
(D) begins some harsh criticism of the people of Atlanta
(E) attempts to inspire the reader to protest the situation

66. Sentences 3, 4, and 5
(A) follow logically from what is set out in sentence 2
(B) define the concept of NIMBY not too clearly
(C) provides a unified example to support sentence 1
(D) acts as a contradiction to sentence 1
(E) seem to shift the point from presidential libraries to another subject

67. Sentence 7
(A) is a clear summary of the paragraph
(B) brings up a point completely irrelevant to the sense of the paragraph
(C) presents the reader with a good example of a forceful fallacy
(D) uses an *either-or* construction to demonstrate how poorly the average person thinks
(E) contains a remarkable false conclusion for the paragraph

Questions 68–73 are based on the following passage.

[1]Some critics have said that the short story is dying out as a literary form, that magazines no longer print them or pay as much money for those that do get printed, and that writers would rather not tie themselves down to such a restricted length. [2]But critics have said the same thing recently about poetry, about serious drama, and about novels that concern themselves with subjects other than sexual activities between men and women or two women or two men. [3]The short story has survived for about 250 years as a recognizable literary genre, and there are those who look to the Hebrew books about Esther and Ruth as among the earliest short stories. [4]But as long as *The New Yorker, The Atlantic, Harper's,* and other magazines with limited circulations publish good stories, they will be read. [5]For the past ten years, some of the best short stories could be found in *Playboy* and *Esquire,* and we recommend the printed pages (but not necessarily the *Playboy* centerfold) of these magazines as excellent sources of good short stories.

68. Sentence 1
(A) is a good example of a periodic sentence
(B) violates the principles of good organization by having three negative statements in a row
(C) contains three clauses that function as objects of *have said*
(D) seems to overload the reader's mind with facts
(E) does not attempt to define the short story as a literary genre

69. Sentences 2 and 4
(A) begin with *but,* but do not violate any of the rules of sentence structure
(B) use *but* as a rather weak word for emphasis
(C) use *but* to establish a comparison with what the preceding sentences say
(D) are not effective, and the author should have revised them before publication
(E) probably seem confusing to an average reader

70. The single purpose of sentence 3 in the paragraph is
(A) to demonstrate the author's superior knowledge
(B) to prove that the short story is not dead as a literary genre
(C) to provide the reader with information that he does not need or want
(D) to give a very brief history of the short story
(E) to make a point that any good critic can recognize

71. What should be done with sentence 2?
(A) But should be changed to Needless to say.
(B) But should be changed to Let us, however, keep the following in mind:
(C) It should be broken into two separate sentences.
(D) It should be omitted.
(E) It should be left as it is.

72. Sentences 4 and 5
(A) could be logically combined with some rearrangements of the words
(B) lavish special praise on magazines of limited circulation
(C) single out two magazines for praise; yet, some people have called these magazines obscene
(D) seem too dry and dull for the subject
(E) recommend several sources of good short stories

73. Sentence 5
(A) is a perfect conclusion for the passage
(B) adds a bit of humor to the paragraph
(C) shows that the author wants everyone to read good short stories
(D) may show the author as a dirty old man
(E) presents an author's rather biased attitude

Questions 74–76 are based on the following passage.

[1]When grandparents think of entertaining grandchildren, they should almost automatically consider Santa's Village, located near East Dundee, Illinois, convenient to the Dundee exit from the Northwest Tollway. [2]The playground is almost guaranteed to have something to please all youngsters up to about age twelve, and the inclusive admission is only $6.95 for each person, with a reduction for those under three and over sixty. [3]What will you find? [4]Rides of all kinds—an exciting roller coaster (not too exciting to frighten smaller children), a merry-go-round, bumper cars, a simulated space flight, a ski lift, an antique car ride, and others that will appeal to children of all ages. [5]The smaller ones should not miss the petting zoo with goats, pigs, sheep, cows, chickens, and horses that are all tame

enough for children to play with, nuzzle, and feed. [6]In a separate area, there is a water park, which requires a separate admission fee and which features a long water slide and other attractions for the younger teenager; have children bring bathing suits, for they will get wet. [7]Parking is free, and there are several food areas that serve (at reasonable prices) foods that should appeal to everyone: pizza, hot dogs, bratwurst, french fries, and the like. [8]And, don't forget to let the children visit Santa Claus and have their pictures taken with the venerable gentleman. [9]Allow several hours for each visit, and you might find yourself wanting to return to Santa's Village, route 31 just north of the Northwest Tollway in East Dundee, Illinois—you will enjoy.

74. Sentence 1 tells the location of Santa's Village, information that is repeated in
(A) sentence 9 (B) sentence 6 (C) sentence 4
(D) sentence 8 (E) sentence 2

75. The passage seems to be
(A) a critic's review of the facility, giving both its good and bad features
(B) a letter from doting grandparents to others who may be required to baby-sit
(C) an objective description of the features of Santa's Village
(D) an advertisement for Santa's Village
(E) a child's plea to parents for entertainment

76. The conclusion the publicity person wants everyone to draw about Santa's Village is that
(A) everyone would enjoy a visit to Santa Claus
(B) the visit to Santa's Village isn't too entertaining except for children under five
(C) Santa's Village is little more than a cheaper version of Disneyland
(D) churchgoers should not attend Santa's Village because beer is available
(E) grandparents will enjoy seeing their grandchildren enjoy and react pleasantly to the rides and other features of the park

Directions: Effective revision requires choosing among the many options available to a writer. The following questions test your ability to use these options effectively.

Revise each of the sentences below according to the directions that follow it. Some directions require you to rephrase only part of the original sentence; others require you to recast the entire sentence. You may need to omit or add certain words in constructing an acceptable revision, but you should <u>keep the meaning of your revised sentence as close to the meaning of the original sentence as the directions permit</u>. Your new sentence should follow the conventions of standard written English and should be clear and concise.

Look through the answer choices A–E under each question for the exact word or phrase that is included in your revised sentence. If you have thought of a revision that does not include any of the words or phrases listed, try to revise the sentence again so that it does include the wording in one of the answer choices.

When you take the test, you should feel free to make notes in your test book, but you will need to mark your answers on the separate answer sheet.

77. Walter Mitty coped with the real world through daydreaming; he imagined that he was a pilot, a great surgeon, and a crack pistol shot.

Change imagined, to imagining.

(A) Walter Mitty's
(B) Walter Mittys
(C) Walter Mitty
(D) the day dreaming of Walter Mitty
(E) Walter Mitty in imagining

78. Certain specialized drugs have been used with remarkable success by doctors treating some mental disorders, particularly the manic-depressive syndrome, that forty years ago would have required the patient to be hospitalized indefinitely.

Begin Forty years ago some mental.

(A) patient, now these disorders
(B) patient and now these disorders
(C) patient, for these disorders
(D) patient, with these disorders
(E) patient; now, these disorders

79. He was trapped into a loveless marriage by an overly anxious girl; therefore, he was already weary of her chattering before a month had passed.

Begin with Trapped into.

(A) girl, he (B) girl; he (C) girl, therefore, he
(D) girl, so he (E) girl; therefore, he

80. Members of that loose coalition of groups calling themselves "The New Left" believe that the only solution for the nation's problems is the overthrow, through violence if necessary, of both corrupt capitalism and a corrupt governmental system.

Substitute advocate for believe.

(A) system for the only (B) system through the only
(C) system as well as the only (D) system as the only
(E) system by the only

81. Anyone's first flight is always a unique experience, no matter how many times he has seen pictures of planes flying or heard tales about the first flights of others.

Begin with No matter and substitute anyone for he.

(A) anyone's own (B) a person's own (C) his own
(D) their own (E) theirs

82. The truck driver, tired after forty hours on the highway without rest, took a pep pill; he knew that just one would keep him awake and alert for about three hours.

Begin with The truck driver knew.

(A) hours; so tired (B) hours; therefore, tired
(C) hours; moreover, tired (D) hours, tired
(E) hours, therefore, tired

83. The average laborer with no income except his monthly wages is frequently hard pressed for immediate cash to pay his personal bills.

Substitute whose only for with.

(A) no income except his (B) income except his
(C) income accepts his (D) income is his (E) no income but

84. Radical blacks angrily charge that a corporation which hires minority group workers and then lays them off during a recession is actually intensifying the frustrations of black workers rather than helping them.

Substitute a corporation's for a corporation.

(A) actually intensifying (B) intensifies minority workers
(C) actually intensifies (D) must actually intensify
(E) actually brings on

85. According to an American Medical Association report, psychiatrists should be aware that certain types of female patients will attempt to seduce them.

Begin with An American Medication Association.

(A) bewares psychiatrists (B) arouses psychiatrists
(C) defends psychiatrists (D) declares psychiatrists
(E) warns psychiatrists

86. No depression in American history has ever lasted as long as the one which began in 1929; it is ironic that only the beginning of World War II in Europe brought prosperity to the United States.

Begin with It is ironic, and substitute ended for brought.

(A) the lasting depression
(B) the longest depression
(C) the 1929 beginning depression
(D) no prosperity in the United States
(E) no depression in American history

87. In their support of rising minority group aspirations, large corporations are not only evidencing true altruism in improving the lot of minorities but also producing social changes within the communities in which their plants are located.

Substitute both for not only.

(A) and (B) but (C) and so (D) as much as (E) for

88. While examining the test papers, the teacher found evidence of cheating, which was reported to the principal.

Change examining to examined.

(A) while reporting (B) reported (C) after she reported
(D) when she reported (E) had been reported

89. Speech experts have been working for years on a good definition of language, but no really satisfactory or complete definition has ever been offered.

Change has been offered to have offered.

(A) No speech experts (B) No really satisfactory
(C) No definition of language (D) Work on the problem
(E) Seeing as how no experts

90. Foreign stamps of exotic birds seem to appeal to many collectors, who are pleased by the colors and strange feathers.

Change who to they.

(A) collectors they (B) collectors, they (C) collectors: they
(D) collectors; they (E) collectors—they

91. Nowadays, not many of those voters eligible to cast a ballot bother to exercise their franchise on election day.

Change not many to not one.

(A) their (B) him (C) his (D) himself (E) theirs

92. Among the effects of the deceased railroad president was a solid gold watch which he had been awarded after twenty-five years of faithful service to the company.

Begin with The company awarded.

(A) until his death (B) from his death (C) for his death
(D) after his death (E) with his death

93. Whether the young man is stupid or ignorant is difficult to determine, but we do know that he made a fool of himself at the party last night.

Begin with Whether through and change stupid and ignorant to nouns.

(A) his (B) the young man (C) who (D) he (E) him

94. Marshall McLuhan, a Canadian scholar whose studies of television's effects upon the human personality have revolutionized our thinking about the mass media, has been the target not only of praise but also of severe criticism for his theories.

Begin with Marshall McLuhan was

(A) ; he (B) , but he (C) , for he (D) ; however, he
(E) , although he

95. A good assistant can relieve an administrator of much of the paperwork that must be handled within any large organization to expedite its day-to-day operations.

Substitute generates for must be handled.

(A) within any large organization generates
(B) an administrator generates
(C) its operations generates
(D) a good assistant generates
(E) any large organization generates

ANSWER KEY—SAMPLE EXAMINATION 3

Section I

1. E	12. A	23. A	34. E	45. B
2. B	13. C	24. E	35. D	46. E
3. A	14. D	25. D	36. B	47. A
4. C	15. B	26. B	37. A	48. D
5. E	16. E	27. D	38. A	49. A
6. A	17. E	28. A	39. C	50. C
7. D	18. B	29. B	40. E	51. E
8. B	19. D	30. A	41. A	52. C
9. A	20. C	31. D	42. D	53. D
10. E	21. C	32. C	43. B	54. B
11. C	22. B	33. C	44. C	55. C

Section II

56. A	64. D	72. E	80. D	88. B
57. B	65. A	73. B	81. B	89. A
58. D	66. E	74. A	82. B	90. D
59. A	67. B	75. D	83. D	91. C
60. E	68. C	76. E	84. C	92. D
61. B	69. A	77. A	85. E	93. B
62. C	70. D	78. E	86. B	94. A
63. A	71. E	79. A	87. A	95. E

SCORING CHART—SAMPLE EXAMINATION 3

After you have scored your Sample Examination 3, enter the results in the chart below; then transfer your Raw Score to the Progress Chart on page 14.

Total Test	Number Right	Number Wrong	Number Omitted	Raw Score
Section I: 55				
Section II: 40				
Total: 95				

ANSWER EXPLANATIONS—EXAMINATION 3

Section I

1. E. The sentence is correct.
2. B. Incorrect idiom—a sort of god solves the problem.
3. A. Was should be were—there is a compound subject.
4. C. Who's (which means who is) should be whose, the correct possessive form.
5. E. The sentence is correct.

6. A. Incorrect word choice—credulity should be creditability.
7. D. Whom should be who, subjective case, as subject of was.
8. B. The rest of the sentence contradicts the phrase—lapse of sentence logic.
9. A. The underlined phrase is a dangling modifier.
10. E. The sentence is correct.
11. C. They has to be singular to agree with anyone.
12. A. Laying should be lying—incorrect word choice.
13. C. Throughly should be thoroughly—incorrect word choice.
14. D. Separate out is a poor idiom.
15. B. They must be singular to agree with anyone.
16. E. The sentence is correct.
17. E. The sentence is correct.
18. B. More is redundant and should be eliminated.
19. D. The underlined phrase destroys correct parallelism.
20. C. It has no specific antecedent.
21. C. As per should be eliminated as a poor idiom.
22. B. Research is illogically compared with many other physicists.
23. A. The original sentence is correct.
24. E. We must be us, object of tell.
25. D. Sat is the wrong verb; use set.
26. B. The reason is because is repetitious.
27. D. Both is illogical in (A), (B), and (C); (E) contains an incorrect sequence of tenses.
28. A. The original sentence is correct.
29. B. The underlined section is a misplaced modifier. (C) has a comma splice, (D) is wordy, and (E) has a dangling modifier.
30. A. The original sentence is correct.
31. D. P.M. and last night are redundant—omit one of them.
32. C. Was should be were, proper sequence of tenses.
33. C. The original sentence is a sentence fragment.
34. E. The original has a shift in verb mood; (E) is the only possible correct form.
35. D. Annual and every year are repetitious.
36. B. Supposed is the correct verb form.
37. A. The original sentence is correct.
38. A. The original sentence is correct.
39. C. The original sentence has a comma splice; (C) solves the problem.
40. E. Setting in the original should be sitting.
41. A. Any teenager being given an allowance *by his parents* at least owes them some thanks for the money they provide.
42. D. *To hunt* for the elusive wild deer and to fish for the fighting mountain trout are two of my favorite sports.
43. B. Their parents' and their own work ethic is the source of hard-hat construction workers' defense *in their conflicts with* militant demonstrators.
44. C. Human beings may refuse to obey orders blindly; that fact *was demonstrated* again by the 1989 uprising against the Chinese Communist government.
45. B. Colleges and universities now offer students not only a traditional basic education *but also subjects more relevant* to contemporary life.
46. E. When the autumnal equinox occurs on September 22, *it signals* the approach . . .
47. A. Even when they have imbibed several ounces of alcohol, *many drivers who are drunk* protest that they can drive safely, even though an accident has occurred.
48. D. One can conclude that Mildred Jones is a very meticulous person *because she arranges* her spices on the shelf alphabetically.
49. A. Anyone who can tell a story in a believable manner gains the trust of Rudolph *who acts like a foolish child.*

50. C. Minimal brain dysfunction *causes* about five percent of all American school children to exhibit certain learning disabilities.

51. E. As an African-American, James Baldwin met bigotry and intolerance everywhere he went; *therefore, he fled* to Europe.

52. C. The president announced that labor leaders had given him a tacit commitment not to demand exorbitant wage increases upon *the expiration of current union contracts.*

53. D. That ghetto children of prekindergarten age learn rapidly but soon regress if nothing is done to improve their home situations *was one startling conclusion drawn* during the Head Start program.

54. B. Amanda Wingfield had a number of gentlemen callers in her youth; *therefore,* she assumed . . . .

55. C. *A politician preparing* a speech for delivery to a woman's organization surely includes some ringing phrases . . . .

Section II

56. A. Sentence 7 should be left as it is, as the concluding point. The word *still* is appropriate because it introduces the contrast that follows.

57. B. Sentence 8 has nothing to do with the wedding, which is what the rest of the passage is about; therefore, it should not be included in this paragraph. However, it could logically start a second paragraph, since it continues to discuss the bride and groom.

58. D. This is the only choice that would be grammatically correct.

59. A. Sentence 2 is the logical place to start the paragraph. It introduces the name of the play and states the main point of the passage, that the play has been running for a number of years.

60. E. Sentence 6 should begin the way it begins now. The conjunction *but* is correctly used to show the contrast between the negative assessments of the play in Sentence 5 and the fact that it has been attracting audiences for years.

61. B. The other choices are either illogical or would create an ungrammatical construction.

62. C. Sentence 6 provides another example of NIMBY, only this time a garbage dump rather than a library causes protests.

63. A. Sentence 1 makes the basic generalization that is expanded on in the rest of the paragraph.

64. D. The word *monuments* is used here in a negative sense to suggest that the real reason the libraries are being built is to memorialize ex-presidents.

65. A. Sentence 3 is a good example of moving from a generalization to a specific by the use of concrete examples.

66. E. Sentences 3, 4, and 5 shift the discussion from presidential libraries to NIMBY.

67. B. Sentence 7 is irrelevant to this paragraph.

68. C. Critics "have said" the short story is dying; critics "have said" magazines do not print them anymore; critics "have said" writers do not want to work with a restricted length.

69. A. It is perfectly correct to begin a sentence with *but* as is done here in Sentences 2 and 4.

70. D. Actually, the entire passage is an attempt to prove that the short story is not dead as a literary genre. Sentence 3 helps do this by giving a factual, historical detail to support the thesis.

71. E. The sentence should be left as it is.

72. E. One way the author tries to prove the point that the short story is not dead is to use the fact that several reknown magazines currently publish them. By naming these magazines, the author inadvertently recommends several sources of good short stories.

73. B. Mentioning *Playboy* centerfolds adds a little humor to this otherwise formal passage.
74. A. For emphasis, the location is giving at both the beginning and end of this advertisement.
75. D. The unequivocal praise, as well as all the particulars about Santa's Village, lead to the conclusion that this is an advertisement.
76. E. The publicity person responsible for this advertisement certainly had grandparents in mind as the intended audience. The first sentence of the advertisement suggests this rather directly.
77. A. Imagining that he was a pilot, a great surgeon, and a crack pistol shot was *Walter Mitty's* method of coping with the real world.
78. E. Forty years ago, some mental disorders would have required the indefinite hospitalization of the patients; *now, these disorders* respond to certain specialized drugs.
79. A. Trapped into a loveless marriage by an overly anxious *girl, he* was already weary of her chattering before a month had passed.
80. D. Members of that loose coalition of groups calling themselves "The New Left" advocate the overthrow, through violence if necessary, of both corrupt capitalism and a corrupt government *system as the only* solution for the nation's problems.
81. B. No matter how many times anyone has seen pictures of planes flying or heard tales about the first flights of others, *a person's own* first flight is always a unique experience.
82. B. The truck driver knew that one pep pill would keep him awake and alert for about three *hours; therefore, tired* after forty hours on the highway without rest, he took one.
83. D. The average laborer whose only *income is his* monthly wages is often hard pressed for immediate cash to pay his personal bills.
84. C. Radical blacks angrily charge that a corporation's hiring minority group workers and then laying them off during a recession *actually intensifies* the frustration of black workers rather than helps them.
85. E. An American Medical Association report *warns psychiatrists* that certain types of female patients will attempt to seduce them.
86. B. It is ironic that only the outbreak of World War II ended *the longest depression* in American history and brought prosperity to the United States.
87. A. In their support of rising minority group aspirations, large corporations are both evidencing true altruism in improving the lot of minorities *and* producing social changes within the communities in which their plants are located.
88. B. The teacher examined the test papers, found evidence of cheating, and *reported* the matter to the principal.
89. A. *No speech experts* have offered a good or satisfactory definition of language, despite their working on the problem for years.
90. D. Foreign stamps with pictures of exotic birds seem to appeal to many collectors; *they* are pleased by the colors and strange feathers.
91. C. Nowadays not one of those voters eligible to cast a ballot bothers to exercise *his* franchise on election day.
92. D. The company awarded the railroad president a solid gold watch which was found among his effects *after his death*.
93. B. Whether through stupidity or ignorance is difficult to determine, but we do know that *the young man* made a fool of himself at the party last night.
94. A. Marshall McLuhan was a Canadian scholar whose studies of television's effects upon the human personality have revolutionized our thinking about the mass media*; he* has been the target . . . .
95. E. A good assistant can relieve an administrator of much of the paperwork that *any large organization generates* to expedite its day-to-day operations.

PART TWO

THE HUMANITIES EXAMINATION

ANSWER SHEET — HUMANITIES/TRIAL TEST

Section I

1. Ⓐ Ⓑ Ⓒ Ⓓ Ⓔ
2. Ⓐ Ⓑ Ⓒ Ⓓ Ⓔ
3. Ⓐ Ⓑ Ⓒ Ⓓ Ⓔ
4. Ⓐ Ⓑ Ⓒ Ⓓ Ⓔ
5. Ⓐ Ⓑ Ⓒ Ⓓ Ⓔ
6. Ⓐ Ⓑ Ⓒ Ⓓ Ⓔ
7. Ⓐ Ⓑ Ⓒ Ⓓ Ⓔ
8. Ⓐ Ⓑ Ⓒ Ⓓ Ⓔ
9. Ⓐ Ⓑ Ⓒ Ⓓ Ⓔ
10. Ⓐ Ⓑ Ⓒ Ⓓ Ⓔ
11. Ⓐ Ⓑ Ⓒ Ⓓ Ⓔ
12. Ⓐ Ⓑ Ⓒ Ⓓ Ⓔ
13. Ⓐ Ⓑ Ⓒ Ⓓ Ⓔ
14. Ⓐ Ⓑ Ⓒ Ⓓ Ⓔ
15. Ⓐ Ⓑ Ⓒ Ⓓ Ⓔ
16. Ⓐ Ⓑ Ⓒ Ⓓ Ⓔ
17. Ⓐ Ⓑ Ⓒ Ⓓ Ⓔ
18. Ⓐ Ⓑ Ⓒ Ⓓ Ⓔ
19. Ⓐ Ⓑ Ⓒ Ⓓ Ⓔ
20. Ⓐ Ⓑ Ⓒ Ⓓ Ⓔ
21. Ⓐ Ⓑ Ⓒ Ⓓ Ⓔ
22. Ⓐ Ⓑ Ⓒ Ⓓ Ⓔ
23. Ⓐ Ⓑ Ⓒ Ⓓ Ⓔ
24. Ⓐ Ⓑ Ⓒ Ⓓ Ⓔ
25. Ⓐ Ⓑ Ⓒ Ⓓ Ⓔ
26. Ⓐ Ⓑ Ⓒ Ⓓ Ⓔ
27. Ⓐ Ⓑ Ⓒ Ⓓ Ⓔ
28. Ⓐ Ⓑ Ⓒ Ⓓ Ⓔ
29. Ⓐ Ⓑ Ⓒ Ⓓ Ⓔ
30. Ⓐ Ⓑ Ⓒ Ⓓ Ⓔ
31. Ⓐ Ⓑ Ⓒ Ⓓ Ⓔ
32. Ⓐ Ⓑ Ⓒ Ⓓ Ⓔ
33. Ⓐ Ⓑ Ⓒ Ⓓ Ⓔ
34. Ⓐ Ⓑ Ⓒ Ⓓ Ⓔ
35. Ⓐ Ⓑ Ⓒ Ⓓ Ⓔ
36. Ⓐ Ⓑ Ⓒ Ⓓ Ⓔ
37. Ⓐ Ⓑ Ⓒ Ⓓ Ⓔ
38. Ⓐ Ⓑ Ⓒ Ⓓ Ⓔ
39. Ⓐ Ⓑ Ⓒ Ⓓ Ⓔ
40. Ⓐ Ⓑ Ⓒ Ⓓ Ⓔ
41. Ⓐ Ⓑ Ⓒ Ⓓ Ⓔ
42. Ⓐ Ⓑ Ⓒ Ⓓ Ⓔ
43. Ⓐ Ⓑ Ⓒ Ⓓ Ⓔ
44. Ⓐ Ⓑ Ⓒ Ⓓ Ⓔ
45. Ⓐ Ⓑ Ⓒ Ⓓ Ⓔ
46. Ⓐ Ⓑ Ⓒ Ⓓ Ⓔ
47. Ⓐ Ⓑ Ⓒ Ⓓ Ⓔ
48. Ⓐ Ⓑ Ⓒ Ⓓ Ⓔ
49. Ⓐ Ⓑ Ⓒ Ⓓ Ⓔ
50. Ⓐ Ⓑ Ⓒ Ⓓ Ⓔ
51. Ⓐ Ⓑ Ⓒ Ⓓ Ⓔ
52. Ⓐ Ⓑ Ⓒ Ⓓ Ⓔ
53. Ⓐ Ⓑ Ⓒ Ⓓ Ⓔ
54. Ⓐ Ⓑ Ⓒ Ⓓ Ⓔ
55. Ⓐ Ⓑ Ⓒ Ⓓ Ⓔ
56. Ⓐ Ⓑ Ⓒ Ⓓ Ⓔ
57. Ⓐ Ⓑ Ⓒ Ⓓ Ⓔ
58. Ⓐ Ⓑ Ⓒ Ⓓ Ⓔ
59. Ⓐ Ⓑ Ⓒ Ⓓ Ⓔ
60. Ⓐ Ⓑ Ⓒ Ⓓ Ⓔ
61. Ⓐ Ⓑ Ⓒ Ⓓ Ⓔ
62. Ⓐ Ⓑ Ⓒ Ⓓ Ⓔ
63. Ⓐ Ⓑ Ⓒ Ⓓ Ⓔ
64. Ⓐ Ⓑ Ⓒ Ⓓ Ⓔ
65. Ⓐ Ⓑ Ⓒ Ⓓ Ⓔ
66. Ⓐ Ⓑ Ⓒ Ⓓ Ⓔ
67. Ⓐ Ⓑ Ⓒ Ⓓ Ⓔ
68. Ⓐ Ⓑ Ⓒ Ⓓ Ⓔ
69. Ⓐ Ⓑ Ⓒ Ⓓ Ⓔ
70. Ⓐ Ⓑ Ⓒ Ⓓ Ⓔ
71. Ⓐ Ⓑ Ⓒ Ⓓ Ⓔ
72. Ⓐ Ⓑ Ⓒ Ⓓ Ⓔ
73. Ⓐ Ⓑ Ⓒ Ⓓ Ⓔ
74. Ⓐ Ⓑ Ⓒ Ⓓ Ⓔ
75. Ⓐ Ⓑ Ⓒ Ⓓ Ⓔ

Section II

76. Ⓐ Ⓑ Ⓒ Ⓓ Ⓔ
77. Ⓐ Ⓑ Ⓒ Ⓓ Ⓔ
78. Ⓐ Ⓑ Ⓒ Ⓓ Ⓔ
79. Ⓐ Ⓑ Ⓒ Ⓓ Ⓔ
80. Ⓐ Ⓑ Ⓒ Ⓓ Ⓔ
81. Ⓐ Ⓑ Ⓒ Ⓓ Ⓔ
82. Ⓐ Ⓑ Ⓒ Ⓓ Ⓔ
83. Ⓐ Ⓑ Ⓒ Ⓓ Ⓔ
84. Ⓐ Ⓑ Ⓒ Ⓓ Ⓔ
85. Ⓐ Ⓑ Ⓒ Ⓓ Ⓔ
86. Ⓐ Ⓑ Ⓒ Ⓓ Ⓔ
87. Ⓐ Ⓑ Ⓒ Ⓓ Ⓔ
88. Ⓐ Ⓑ Ⓒ Ⓓ Ⓔ
89. Ⓐ Ⓑ Ⓒ Ⓓ Ⓔ
90. Ⓐ Ⓑ Ⓒ Ⓓ Ⓔ
91. Ⓐ Ⓑ Ⓒ Ⓓ Ⓔ
92. Ⓐ Ⓑ Ⓒ Ⓓ Ⓔ
93. Ⓐ Ⓑ Ⓒ Ⓓ Ⓔ
94. Ⓐ Ⓑ Ⓒ Ⓓ Ⓔ
95. Ⓐ Ⓑ Ⓒ Ⓓ Ⓔ
96. Ⓐ Ⓑ Ⓒ Ⓓ Ⓔ
97. Ⓐ Ⓑ Ⓒ Ⓓ Ⓔ
98. Ⓐ Ⓑ Ⓒ Ⓓ Ⓔ
99. Ⓐ Ⓑ Ⓒ Ⓓ Ⓔ
100. Ⓐ Ⓑ Ⓒ Ⓓ Ⓔ
101. Ⓐ Ⓑ Ⓒ Ⓓ Ⓔ
102. Ⓐ Ⓑ Ⓒ Ⓓ Ⓔ
103. Ⓐ Ⓑ Ⓒ Ⓓ Ⓔ
104. Ⓐ Ⓑ Ⓒ Ⓓ Ⓔ
105. Ⓐ Ⓑ Ⓒ Ⓓ Ⓔ
106. Ⓐ Ⓑ Ⓒ Ⓓ Ⓔ
107. Ⓐ Ⓑ Ⓒ Ⓓ Ⓔ
108. Ⓐ Ⓑ Ⓒ Ⓓ Ⓔ
109. Ⓐ Ⓑ Ⓒ Ⓓ Ⓔ
110. Ⓐ Ⓑ Ⓒ Ⓓ Ⓔ
111. Ⓐ Ⓑ Ⓒ Ⓓ Ⓔ
112. Ⓐ Ⓑ Ⓒ Ⓓ Ⓔ
113. Ⓐ Ⓑ Ⓒ Ⓓ Ⓔ
114. Ⓐ Ⓑ Ⓒ Ⓓ Ⓔ
115. Ⓐ Ⓑ Ⓒ Ⓓ Ⓔ
116. Ⓐ Ⓑ Ⓒ Ⓓ Ⓔ
117. Ⓐ Ⓑ Ⓒ Ⓓ Ⓔ
118. Ⓐ Ⓑ Ⓒ Ⓓ Ⓔ
119. Ⓐ Ⓑ Ⓒ Ⓓ Ⓔ
120. Ⓐ Ⓑ Ⓒ Ⓓ Ⓔ
121. Ⓐ Ⓑ Ⓒ Ⓓ Ⓔ
122. Ⓐ Ⓑ Ⓒ Ⓓ Ⓔ
123. Ⓐ Ⓑ Ⓒ Ⓓ Ⓔ
124. Ⓐ Ⓑ Ⓒ Ⓓ Ⓔ
125. Ⓐ Ⓑ Ⓒ Ⓓ Ⓔ
126. Ⓐ Ⓑ Ⓒ Ⓓ Ⓔ
127. Ⓐ Ⓑ Ⓒ Ⓓ Ⓔ
128. Ⓐ Ⓑ Ⓒ Ⓓ Ⓔ
129. Ⓐ Ⓑ Ⓒ Ⓓ Ⓔ
130. Ⓐ Ⓑ Ⓒ Ⓓ Ⓔ
131. Ⓐ Ⓑ Ⓒ Ⓓ Ⓔ
132. Ⓐ Ⓑ Ⓒ Ⓓ Ⓔ
133. Ⓐ Ⓑ Ⓒ Ⓓ Ⓔ
134. Ⓐ Ⓑ Ⓒ Ⓓ Ⓔ
135. Ⓐ Ⓑ Ⓒ Ⓓ Ⓔ
136. Ⓐ Ⓑ Ⓒ Ⓓ Ⓔ
137. Ⓐ Ⓑ Ⓒ Ⓓ Ⓔ
138. Ⓐ Ⓑ Ⓒ Ⓓ Ⓔ
139. Ⓐ Ⓑ Ⓒ Ⓓ Ⓔ
140. Ⓐ Ⓑ Ⓒ Ⓓ Ⓔ
141. Ⓐ Ⓑ Ⓒ Ⓓ Ⓔ
142. Ⓐ Ⓑ Ⓒ Ⓓ Ⓔ
143. Ⓐ Ⓑ Ⓒ Ⓓ Ⓔ
144. Ⓐ Ⓑ Ⓒ Ⓓ Ⓔ
145. Ⓐ Ⓑ Ⓒ Ⓓ Ⓔ
146. Ⓐ Ⓑ Ⓒ Ⓓ Ⓔ
147. Ⓐ Ⓑ Ⓒ Ⓓ Ⓔ
148. Ⓐ Ⓑ Ⓒ Ⓓ Ⓔ
149. Ⓐ Ⓑ Ⓒ Ⓓ Ⓔ
150. Ⓐ Ⓑ Ⓒ Ⓓ Ⓔ

CHAPTER

6

Trial Test

The Humanities examination measures your knowledge of literature and the fine arts — the visual arts (e.g., painting and sculpture), music, the performing arts (e.g., drama and dance), and architecture. The examination is divided into two parts, each containing 75 questions that cover both literature and the fine arts. On the CLEP examination you are given 45 minutes for each part.

Take the Trial Test and check your answers, thus finding out how you would score before you review any material or practice the type of questions asked.

Section I

Number of Questions: 75
Time: 45 minutes

Directions: Each of the questions or incomplete statements below is followed by five suggested answers or completions. Select the one that is best in each case.

1. Expressionism in art has most to do with
   (A) the intellect (B) the emotions (C) the dream world
   (D) geometric forms (E) decorative line

2. The Impressionists were least concerned with
   (A) the effects of light (B) informal treatment of subject matter
   (C) painting out of doors (D) interpenetration of forms
   (E) broken application of color

3. The length of a vibrating string or a column of air and the pitch either produces constituted the beginning of the science of
   (A) logarithms (B) rhythms (C) acoustics (D) theory (E) fuguery

4. The man who, practically single-handedly, unified the ballet and founded French opera was
   (A) Lully (B) Glinka (C) Gluck (D) Massenet (E) Offenbach

5. An important architect of the Romantic period was
   (A) Walter Gropius (B) Christopher Wren (C) James Wyatt
   (D) Joseph Paxton (E) Henri Labrouste

6. Ibsen did not write
   (A) plays about contemporary people (B) plays with realistic settings
   (C) plays employing well-made structure (D) comedies of manners
   (E) thesis plays

7. **The release of emotions and the attaining of tranquility therefrom in the theater is called**
   (A) pyramidal plot structure
   (B) the author's use of hubris
   (C) the audience escaping dull lives by identifying with kings, aristocrats, and famous people
   (D) empathy
   (E) catharsis

8. **One of the most characteristic types of 18th-century literature was the**
   (A) novella (B) epic (C) nature poem
   (D) periodical essay (E) thesis play

9. Harriet Beecher Stowe unwittingly became a pioneer when she wrote the "propaganda novel"
   (A) *Erewhon* (B) *A Man's Woman* (C) *The Female Quixote*
   (D) *Uncle Tom's Cabin* (E) *The Mysterious Stranger*

10. "Brush my brow with burnished bronze" is an example of
    (A) alliteration (B) consonance (C) dissonance
    (D) onomatopoeia (E) free verse

11. **Stravinsky's "Rite of Spring"**
    (A) is a Baroque-style program piece
    (B) was called the destruction of music
    (C) is representative of the Classical styles
    (D) is in sonata-allegro form
    (E) is a symphony

12. **An instrumental form usually associated with opera is**
    (A) the overture (B) the symphony (C) the suite
    (D) the tone poem (E) the cadenza

13. The type of architecture shown is found in
    (A) India
    (B) Greece
    (C) the United States
    (D) the U.S.S.R.
    (E) Iran

14. Paintings which reflect an interest in the fantastic, dream associations, and the impossible are most likely to have been executed by
    (A) Cezanne, van Gogh, Toulouse-Lautrec
    (B) Gris, Braque, Picasso
    (C) Dali, Miro, de Chirico
    (D) Pollack, Motherwell, Mondrian
    (E) Renoir, Degas, Seurat

15. Confucius, Buddha, and Socrates, all born at the time when "the human mind seems first to have turned over in its sleep," lived in approximately
(A) 1200–1100 B.C. (B) 2500–2400 B.C. (C) 5000–4000 B.C.
(D) 800–700 B.C. (E) 600–400 B.C.

Questions 16 and 17 refer to the following quotation.

"O mother, mother, make my bed,
O make it soft and narrow:
Since my love died for me today,
I'll die for him tomorrow."

16. Which of the following describes these lines?
(A) a couplet (B) a triolet (C) a quatrain (D) a tercet
(E) a sestet

17. The lines are from the ballad
(A) "Sir Patrick Spens" (B) "Barbara Allen" (C) "Lord Randall"
(D) "The Three Ravens" (E) "Robin Hood and the Three Squires"

18. Pop art refers to
(A) musical themes
(B) abstract expressionism
(C) contemporary materialism and commercialism
(D) the religious revival in contemporary art
(E) a return to classicism

19. The first to dedicate their art to the beauty of life were the
(A) Egyptians (B) Renaissance artists (C) Romans
(D) Greeks (E) French impressionists

20. Frank Lloyd Wright's basic role in architecture was
(A) to build a structure that was inexpensive
(B) to use a minimum of materials
(C) to build a structure in harmony with the past
(D) to build a structure that looked as if it grew out of the ground
(E) to build a structure that overpowers man and nature

21. Albert Camus said that capital punishment is
(A) necessary and desirable (B) necessary but undesirable
(C) murder (D) a 20th-century innovation (E) both (A) and (C)

22. One of the greatest of the Middle High German epics is
(A) *The Nibelungenlied* (B) *The Story of Sigurd the Volsung*
(C) *Beowulf* (D) *The Vikings at Helgeland* (E) *The Valkyrie*

23. A famous overture often associated with graduation exercises was written by
(A) Brahms (B) Condon (C) Gluck (D) Palestrina (E) Haydn

24. A famous jazz guitarist of the 1940s was
(A) F. Waller (B) B. Davidson (C) E. Condon
(D) J. Teagarden (E) M. Feld

25. Shakespeare was noted for all but one of the following:
(A) comedies (B) tragedies (C) bourgeois dramas
(D) histories (E) tragi-comedies

26. An outdoor amphitheater seating 20,000 people which has been the scene of ballets and popular concerts directed by world-famous orchestral conductors is the
(A) Rose Bowl (B) Snow Bowl (C) Hollywood Bowl
(D) Musitoreum (E) Sunshine Theater

27. The "father" of Greek tragedy was
(A) Aristotle (B) Sophocles (C) Euripides
(D) Aeschylus (E) Aristophanes

28. All but one of the following are parts of the Greek theater:
(A) eccyclema (B) skene (C) deus ex machina
(D) orchestra (E) movable panels

29. In music, the sign ♯ is called a
(A) flat (B) sharp (C) bass clef
(D) treble clef (E) time signature

30. The term "Western man" or "Western civilization" refers to
(A) the Western hemisphere
(B) our present cultural tradition going back about 4,000 years
(C) a force of history which always moves to the west
(D) Europe
(E) Canada and the United States

31. Richard Strauss is best known for his
(A) fugues (B) motets (C) waltzes (D) madrigals
(E) tone poems

32. Albert Camus, French existentialist writer, believed that the only real philosophical problem was that of suicide. What Shakespearean character expresses this same thought?
(A) Iago (B) Cleopatra (C) Hamlet (D) Caliban
(E) Julius Caesar

33. Cubism is indebted to the pioneering work of
(A) Pollack (B) Cezanne (C) van Gogh (D) Munch (E) Hals

34. Which one of the following is not a stylistic (formal) element of Cubism?
(A) Compressed or "flat" space
(B) Multiple perspective
(C) Atmospheric perspective
(D) Interpenetration of line, color, and shape
(E) An equal stress on negative and positive areas.

35. The term "clerestory" would most likely be used by a(n)
(A) poet (B) architect (C) sculptor (D) painter (E) musician

36. All of the following short stories were written by Edgar Allan Poe *except*
(A) "The Fall of the House of Usher"
(B) "The Murders in the Rue Morgue"
(C) "Rappaccini's Daughter"
(D) "The Purloined Letter"
(E) "The Cask of Amontillado"

37. Sculpture is the art of
(A) making life-like figures (B) making statues of heroes
(C) making memorials to heroes (D) cutting stone and marble
(E) composing in mass and space

38. The philosopher famous for the doctrine that "to be is to be perceived" is
(A) Berkeley (B) Leibniz (C) Hegel
(D) Plato (E) Hume

39. The beginning of the Renaissance may be traced to the city of
(A) Rome (B) San Miniate (C) Venice (D) Florence
(E) Athens

40. The "School of Lyon" was
(A) a 16th-century group of Neo-Platonist and Petrarchan poets
(B) an 18th-century artistic movement
(C) the college attended by Hugo and de Maupassant
(D) a chamber music society founded by Massenet
(E) an attempt to establish a classical spirit in French painting

41. The first most completely American naturalistic novel, *Maggie: A Girl of the Streets*, was written by
(A) Anderson (B) Garland (C) Norris (D) Crane
(E) Robinson

42. The painters Renoir, Monet, and Pissaro were
(A) Expressionists (B) Cubists (C) Mannerists
(D) Impressionists (E) Surrealists

43. The Romans made special use of
(A) post and lintel construction
(B) friezes carved over temple doorways
(C) the rounded arch (D) the pointed arch (E) tempera painting

44. In music, a smooth transition from key to key is known as
(A) modulation (B) constructioning (C) harmony
(D) invention (E) translation

45. All of the following deal with the Trojan War or the men who fought in that war *except*
(A) *The Odyssey* (B) *Agamemnon* (C) *The Iliad*
(D) *Oedipus the King* (E) *The Aeneid*

46. This well-known landmark is to be found in
(A) New York Harbor
(B) Ceylon
(C) India
(D) Australia
(E) Japan

47. The first major American author to be born west of the Mississippi was
(A) William Dean Howells (B) Walt Whitman
(C) Carl Sandburg (D) Mark Twain (E) Ellen Glasgow

48. "Twas brillig, and the slithy toves, Did gyre and gimble in the wabe," is an example of
(A) *vers de société*
(B) nonsense verse
(C) a limerick
(D) shaped verse
(E) Goliardic verse

49. Farcical interludes in dramas
(A) developed during the Middle Ages
(B) dealt with sin
(C) were essentially romantic comedies
(D) developed during the Renaissance
(E) adhered to the unities of time, place, and action

50. *The Decameron,* like *The Canterbury Tales,* has a specific dramatic framework. However, instead of pilgrims journeying to Canterbury, *The Decameron* has seven women and three men withdrawing from their native city for what purpose?
(A) To seek the Holy Grail
(B) To visit the Pope
(C) To see Charles the Great
(D) To make a pilgrimage to the tomb of Abelard
(E) To escape the Black Death

51. "All pigs are equal, but some pigs are more equal than others" is reminiscent of what novel?
(A) *Lassie, Come Home* (B) *The Red Pony*
(C) *Federico and his Falcon* (D) *Animal Farm*
(E) *A Day at the Zoo*

52. An American tap dancer who appeared in musical comedies, revues, and motion pictures is
(A) Mikhail Baryshnikov (B) Ray Jones (C) Adolph Bolm
(D) David Klein (E) Ray Bolger

53. "The Grand Canyon Suite" was composed by
(A) Anton Dvořák (B) George M. Cohan
(C) Edward McDowell (D) Aaron Copland (E) Ferde Grofe

54. The medieval architect symbolized God's presence in the cathedral by
(A) creating great areas of interior space
(B) embellishing the surface with great columns and lacy decorations
(C) creating the choir and high altar areas
(D) combining the arts of painting and free-standing sculpture
(E) placing gargoyles atop the roof to ward off evil spirits

55. "The lost generation" refers to those who lived during the period
(A) 1900-1915 (B) 1920-1940 (C) 1940-1950
(D) 1950-1960 (E) 1960-1970

56. A leader of the "beat generation" was
(A) Ernest Hemingway (B) John Steinbeck
(C) Jack Kerouac (D) Ring Lardner
(E) Flannery O'Connor

57. A short narrative from which a moral can be drawn is
(A) a parable (B) an anecdote (C) an abstraction
(D) an aphorism (E) a frame story

58. Lascaux and Altamira are
(A) two French Gothic cathedrals
(B) two painters working in a surrealistic style
(C) caves in which prehistoric paintings have been found
(D) mythological subjects used by Pierre Cott in "The Tempest"
(E) leaders in the Fauve movement

59. A feeling of unrest and tension in a painting can be achieved by a powerful emphasis upon
(A) horizontal line (B) vertical line (C) parallel line
(D) diagonal line (E) linear grid pattern

60. The way in which we perceive abstractly is largely determined by
(A) cultural conditioning (B) memory learning
(C) individual genes (D) intellectual association
(E) abstract behavior patterns

61. One of the first American "troubadors" and minstrels was
(A) Vachel Lindsay (B) Edward McDowell
(C) John Knowles Pain (D) Aaron Copland
(E) Stephen Foster

62. An early American statesman, writer, inventor, and foreign correspondent, also known as the first American music critic, was
(A) Paul Revere (B) Cotton Mather (C) Benjamin Franklin
(D) Thomas Jefferson (E) Patrick Henry

63. "I have measured out my life with coffee spoons," said
(A) Benjamin Compson (B) Lady Brett Ashley
(C) Scarlet O'Hara (D) Phillip Jordan
(E) J. Alfred Prufrock

64. A " mystery cycle " may best be described as
(A) based upon scriptures
(B) basically religious
(C) short biblical plays produced outside the church
(D) performed by the guilds
(E) all of the above

65. Which of the following has been hailed as a great novel of the women's movement?
(A) *The Golden Notebook* by Doris Lessing
(B) *Emma* by Jane Austen
(C) *Wise Blood* by Flannery O'Connor
(D) *Fluff* by Virginia Woolf
(E) *Swain* by Carolyn Kimball

66. A satire on the medieval chivalric code is
(A) *Don Quixote* (B) *Gulliver's Travels* (C) *Candide*
(D) *Idylls of the King* (E) *Erewhon*

67. One of the most popular English painters of the 18th century, noted for his society portraits, was
(A) John Singleton Copley (B) Sir Edward Burne-Jones
(C) Thomas Gainsborough (D) John Constable
(E) William Blake

68. Included among Johann Sebastian Bach's great works is
(A) "The Well-Tempered Clavier" (B) "The Pathetique Sonata"
(C) *The Student Prince* (D) "The Unfinished Symphony"
(E) *Der Rosenkavalier*

69. Included among Beethoven's great works is
(A) "The Symphonie Espagnole" (B) "The Moonlight Sonata"
(C) "The Mass in B Minor" (D) *The Messiah*
(E) "The Minute Waltz"

70. Nicknamed "Red," the man who became famous for his novels about "main street" America was
(A) Ernest Hemingway (B) John Steinbeck
(C) Sinclair Lewis (D) Upton Sinclair
(E) Booth Tarkington

71. The creative process is
(A) limited to art (B) limited to art and music
(C) limited to the humanities (D) limited to the arts and sciences
(E) not limited

72. Of the Greek playwrights, Euripides is considered the most "modern" because he
(A) usually disregards the unities
(B) concentrates on message rather than moments
(C) does not use women as protagonists
(D) stresses his belief in reform
(E) is most psychological in his treatment of conflict

73. Of which playwright is the following true: Nearly every character in his plays is at one time or another the hero of a tiny "microcosmic" drama that has a beginning, middle, and an end in itself, but does not become the basis for the total plot?
(A) George Bernard Shaw (B) Henrik Ibsen
(C) Arthur Miller (D) Anton Chekhov
(E) Oscar Wilde

74. The opera *I Pagliacci* was written by
(A) Puccini (B) Leoncavallo (C) Mascagni
(D) Verdi (E) Mozart

75. In music, this sign ♭ is called a
(A) flat (B) sharp (C) bass clef
(D) treble clef (E) time signature

Section II

Number of Questions: 75
Time: 45 minutes

Directions: Each of the questions or incomplete statements below is followed by five suggested answers or completions. Select the one that is best in each case.

76. The photograph at the right is
(A) Nike of Samothrace
(B) Venus de Milo
(C) Mercury
(D) Apollo Belvedere
(E) Dionysius

Hirmer Fotoarchiv Munchen

77. The audiences who attended Shakespeare's plays were
(A) aristocrats who enjoyed occasionally letting their hair down
(B) commoners who had aristocratic taste in poetry
(C) primarily drawn from the middle classes
(D) a mixture of all classes
(E) the most tightly knit "in group" in the history of the theater

78. All of the following represent serious barriers to critical perception of plays and films *except*
(A) failing to remember that a drama is not reality
(B) viewing the drama in terms of a particular occupation with which the viewer is familiar
(C) reacting to the characterization of an ethnic type
(D) accepting the drama on its own terms without any bias
(E) entering the theater with the expectation of seeing one's moral values upheld

79. All of the following painters were called by critics "Fauve" or "wild beasts" *except*
(A) Matisse (B) Dufy (C) Vlaminck (D) Rouault
(E) Gauguin

80. The chief exponent of pointillism was
(A) Cezanne (B) Monet (C) de Chirico (D) Courbet
(E) Seurat

81. A leading rock group of the late 1960s took its name from the title of a novel by a German author who died in 1962 and whose works have recently won a new following. The book and the author are
(A) *Steppenwolf* by Herman Hesse
(B) *Death in Venice* by Thomas Mann
(C) *The Weavers* by Gerhart Hauptmann
(D) *Siddhartha* by Herman Hesse
(E) *The Castle* by Franz Kafka

82. A chromatic scale is
(A) all half steps played in order
(B) every other half step played in order
(C) no half steps played
(D) only half steps played
(E) all full steps played in order

Questions 83–85 refer to the following lines.

Come live with me, and be my love,
And we will all the pleasures prove,
That valleys, groves, hills, and fields,
Woods or steepy mountains yields.

83. These lines are from
(A) "The Passionate Shepherd to His Love"
(B) "The Shepherd's Wife's Song"
(C) "A Strange Passion of a Lover"
(D) one of Shakespeare's sonnets
(E) "Troilus and Cressida"

84. The lines were written by
(A) William Shakespeare (B) Christopher Marlowe (C) John Lyly
(D) T.S. Eliot (E) Alexander Pope

85. The verse form is a
(A) couplet (B) sestina (C) sonnet
(D) quatrain (E) cinquaine

86. Most basic to a fundamental appreciation of art are
(A) seeing and feeling
(B) words and descriptions
(C) knowing the life of the artist and understanding his or her ethnic background
(D) understanding the theories of art and their corollaries
(E) courses in art history

87. "Comfort ye, comfort ye, my people," saith your God. "Speak ye comfortably to Jerusalem, and cry unto her, that her warfare is accomplished, that her iniquity is pardoned."

The source of this quotation, which is a portion of the libretto of Handel's *The Messiah* and was taken directly from the Bible, was
(A) Amos (B) Misab (C) Isaiah
(D) Ezekiel (E) Hosea

Questions 88–90 refer to the following groups of people.

(A) John Williams, Burt Bacharach, Henry Mancini
(B) Sir George Solti, Andre Previn, Leonard Bernstein
(C) John Steinbeck, William Faulkner, Sinclair Lewis
(D) Andy Warhol, Joan Miro, Claes Oldenburg
(E) Twyla Tharp, Michael Bennett, Gower Champion

88. Which is a group of contemporary symphony conductors?

89. Which is a group of novelists who won the Nobel Prize for Literature?

90. Which is a group of choreographers for Broadway musicals of the 1970s and 1980s?

91. *The Great Gatsby* was written by
(A) Emerson (B) Lewis (C) Dreiser
(D) Dos Passos (E) Fitzgerald

92. Nietzsche said that the noble man
(A) never notices the unfortunate
(B) always helps the unfortunate out of pity
(C) always seeks to eradicate the unfortunate
(D) helps the unfortunate, not from pity, but rather from an impulse generated out of a superabundance of power
(E) always tries to trick the unfortunate into helping him

93. *Kiss Me Kate* is based upon William Shakespeare's play
(A) *Romeo and Juliet* (B) *The Winter's Tale*
(C) *A Midsummer Night's Dream* (D) *The Tempest*
(E) *The Taming of the Shrew*

94. The artist van Gogh wrote that he
(A) did his best not to put in detail
(B) avoided using black altogether
(C) could only paint when he was nervous
(D) became an artist in order to travel and see the world
(E) became an artist in order to prove he was sane

95. The musical notation 𝄞 indicates
(A) the bass clef (B) crescendo (C) pianissimo
(D) the treble clef (E) 1/2 time

96. A term used to describe choral music without instrumental accompaniment is
(A) cantilena (B) a cappella (C) enharmonic
(D) appoggiatura (E) oratorio

97. All of the following are part of Wagner's cycle of operas *Der Ring des Nibelungen except*
(A) *Das Rheingold*
(B) *Die Walkure*
(C) *Die Meistersinger von Nurnberg*
(D) *Siegfried*
(E) *Die Gotterdammerung*

98. A Southern writer well-known for her short stories, as well as her novels *Wise Blood* and *The Violent Bear It Away*, is
(A) Gwendolyn Brooks (B) Jean Auel (C) Frances Cassidy
(D) Flannery O'Connor (E) Elizabeth James

99. Baroque architecture is characterized by
(A) severe simplicity
(B) ornamentation and curved lines
(C) post and lintel construction
(D) steel and re-enforced concrete
(E) low, heavy domes

100. A good definition of art is
(A) significant form
(B) a production or procession of images expressing the personality of the artist
(C) a reflection in visual form of the philosophy and culture of the period
(D) nature seen through the emotion and intellect of man
(E) all of the above

101. The first spoken line by Hamlet in the play is an aside: "A little more than kin, and less than kind." By this line, he indicates that
(A) he already suspects Claudius of some sort of duplicity
(B) he already knows that Claudius has killed his father
(C) he already has designs on the throne
(D) he is already plotting revenge
(E) he intends to feign madness

102. The Connecticut Wits
(A) were devoted to the modernization of the Yale curriculum and the declaration of independence of American letters from British influences
(B) favored Unitarianism and Transcendentalism
(C) included Timothy Dwight, John Trumbull, and Joel Barlow
(D) all of the above
(E) (A) and (C) above

103. A Latin-American writer, author of *One Hundred Years of Solitude*, is
(A) Isabel Allende (B) Carlos Noriega (C) Gabriel Garcia Marquez
(D) Pablo Neruda (E) Guillermo Gonzalez

104. The creator of Charlie Brown is
(A) Bud Blake (B) Al Capp (C) Charles Schulz
(D) Alex Kotsby (E) Fred Lasswell

105. "Each narrow cell in which we dwell" provides an example of
(A) alliteration (B) internal rhyme (C) sprung rhythm
(D) end rhyme (E) spondaic trimeter

106. A playwright who wrote a modern comic-psychological version of *Antigone* is
(A) Arthur Miller (B) Jean Anouilh (C) Edward Albee
(D) Jean-Paul Sartre (E) Georges Clemenceau

107. This is an example of
(A) Mesopotamian sculpture
(B) Egyptian sculpture
(C) Indian sculpture
(D) prehistoric sculpture
(E) modern sculpture

Estate of David Smith, courtesy of Marlborough Gallery, New York

108. Molière's audiences were predominantly
(A) peasants
(B) a great cross-section of the population
(C) people pretending to a higher station in life
(D) aristocrats
(E) middle class only

109. Edgar Allan Poe believed a short story should
(A) be sufficiently short to permit the reader to finish the work in a single sitting
(B) have a surprise ending
(C) delight and instruct the reader
(D) have complicated characters
(E) be realistic

110. The French word *genre* means
(A) plot (B) category (C) climax (D) story
(E) introduction

111. What Renaissance writer do you associate with the Abbey of Theleme?
(A) Castiglione (B) Shakespeare (C) Ariosto
(D) Rabelais (E) Cervantes

112. Ursula K. LeGuin is regarded primarily as a writer of
(A) poetry (B) romantic fiction (C) mysteries
(D) spy stories (E) science fiction

113. A 19th-century novelist who anticipated many 20th-century discoveries and inventions was
(A) T. H. Huxley (B) Mary Shelley (C) Thomas Hardy
(D) Jules Verne (E) Bram Stoker

114. According to tradition, who wrote *The Odyssey* and *The Iliad?*
(A) Achilles (B) Tacitus (C) Homer (D) Vergil
(E) Thucydides

115. A form of music drama without stage action, of which Handel became a master, is the
(A) oratorio (B) opera (C) cantata (D) castrati
(E) duet

116. To play a musical composition, each musician must have a copy of the notes. The conductor has a similar copy, called the
(A) score (B) libretto (C) manuscript (D) theme
(E) thesis

117. The theme of John Steinbeck's *In Dubious Battle* is
(A) the exodus of the Okies from Oklahoma
(B) the growth of labor unions in America
(C) the frustration of the war in Vietnam
(D) the blacks' fight for freedom
(E) World War II

118. An Aeschylean dramatic pattern made possible the first true plays because it introduced
(A) villainy (B) humanism (C) plausibility
(D) conflict between two characters (E) the family theme

119. The portrait at the right was painted by
(A) da Vinci
(B) Delacroix
(C) van Gogh
(D) Michelangelo
(E) Dali

Roger Viollet

120. In the play *Medea*, what was the name of Jason's ship?
(A) *Tiki* (B) *Pelias* (C) *Dreadnaught* (D) *Medea*
(E) *Argo*

121. Why did Jason set sail on his fateful voyage?
(A) To search for the Golden Fleece
(B) To make war on Sparta
(C) To destroy the port of Colchis
(D) To search for the Holy Grail
(E) To put a stop to pirateering

122. The first permanent stringed orchestra in Europe, introduced during the reign of Louis XIV, was called the
(A) Chapelle (B) Twenty-four Viols (C) Grand Ecurie
(D) Chambre (E) Academy

123. The architect associated with St. Paul's Cathedral is
(A) Inigo Jones (B) Christopher Wren (C) Le Corbusier
(D) Frank Lloyd Wright (E) Walter Gropius

124. The opening scene of Shakespeare's *Henry IV, Part I* establishes for the audience that
(A) all is well in England
(B) a pilgrimage to the Holy Land is in progress
(C) it is raining
(D) the king has two major problems confronting him
(E) the king is dead

125. Byzantine art was a major contribution to the world because of its
(A) sculpture (B) portraits (C) armor (D) mosaics
(E) glassware

126. The variety of styles in modern art is a reflection of
(A) the complexity of modern life
(B) a lack of purpose
(C) a loss of values
(D) foreign influence
(E) our susceptibility to sensationalism and fads

127. In formal science, *all* statements are
(A) intuitively true (B) given meaning by induction
(C) hypothetically true (D) empirically true
(E) given meaning by experiment

128. The poem "Trees" was written by
(A) E. E. Cummings (B) Edna St. Vincent Millay
(C) Joyce Kilmer (D) Lawrence Ferlinghetti
(E) John Frederick Nims

129. Voltaire's Candide journeyed from continent to continent to find his elusive Cunegonde, whose chief virtue was
(A) beauty (B) physical indestructibility (C) piety
(D) faithfulness (E) mental alertness

130. *The Tales of Hoffmann* was written by
(A) De Maistre (B) Bierce (C) Poe (D) Hoffmann
(E) Irving

131. The operatic score for *The Tales of Hoffmann* was written by
(A) Offenbach (B) Adam (C) Rimsky-Korsakov
(D) Schubert (B) Schumann

132. When the Christian Church came into power after the fall of the Roman Empire, it
(A) used professional actors to perform plays
(B) urged the wealthy to sponsor acting groups
(C) emphasized the "here" rather than the "hereafter"
(D) abolished all theatrical activities
(E) began putting on plays in the church itself

133. The death of Seneca in A.D. 65 marks the
(A) end of the Roman Empire
(B) beginning of creative playwrighting
(C) end of creative playwrighting until the Middle Ages
(D) beginning of the Middle Ages
(E) birth of comedy

134. Which of the following, written during the Revolutionary period, is often considered the first American novel?
(A) *McTeague* (B) *Moby Dick* (C) *Huckleberry Finn*
(D) *Golden Wedding* (E) *The Power of Sympathy*

135. The Artful Dodger is a character in the novel
(A) *Oliver Twist* (B) *The Little Prince* (C) *Hard Times*
(D) *David Copperfield* (E) *Vanity Fair*

136. One of the greatest jazz musicians of all time is
(A) "Dizzy" Gillespie (B) Ray Charles (C) Pete Seeger
(D) Arthel Watson (E) David Byrne

137. John Milton in *Paradise Lost* attempted to
(A) justify the ways of men to God
(B) justify the ways of God to men
(C) explain evil
(D) show that Satan and God have equal powers
(E) explain why good and evil are necessary

138. The two great Italian writers of the 14th century were
(A) Petrarch and Pirandello
(B) Petrarch and Boccaccio
(C) Dante and Fellini
(D) Boccaccio and Silone
(E) Machiavelli and Borgia

139. The ghost advises Hamlet, concerning his mother, to
(A) make certain that she does not escape death
(B) bring her to public trial and let the people of Denmark decide her fate
(C) wash her incestuous sheets
(D) allow heaven to decide her fate
(E) deny her Christian burial so that her soul will wander forever, as his is doomed to do

140. A sonata is a musical composition for instrument. A cantata is
(A) a slow symphony (B) an aria (C) a slow madrigal
(D) a choral work (E) a round

141. "But I will start afresh and make dark things plain. In doing right by Laius, I protect myself . . .," said
(A) Phoebus (B) Oedipus (C) Ismene (D) Creon
(E) Jocasta

Jerry Frank

142. The above photograph pictures
(A) an Egyptian temple (B) an Etruscan temple (C) a Mayan temple
(D) a Greek temple (E) a Roman temple

143. A chilling modern novel by Margaret Atwood is
(A) *A Handmaid's Tale* (B) *Fear of Flying* (C) *The House of Sorrows*
(D) *The Eiger Sanction* (E) *As I Lay Dying*

144. The rhyme scheme of Dante's *Divine Comedy* in its original Italian is
(A) sestina (B) terza rima (C) sonnet (D) ballade
(E) rondeau

145. The magnificent achievements of Gothic art are found especially in
(A) the structures of the great cathedrals
(B) the carving of statues on the porches of these cathedrals
(C) the beauty of stained glass
(D) the invention of the flying buttress
(E) all of the above

146. All of the following Americans were awarded the Nobel Prize for Literature *except*
(A) Pearl S. Buck (B) William Faulkner (C) Robert Frost
(D) Ernest Hemingway (E) Eugene O'Neill

147. A *soliloquy* is
(A) a short speech delivered to the audience while other characters are on stage
(B) a few moments of pantomime by the main character in a play
(C) a speech of some length spoken directly to the audience while the character speaking is alone on stage
(D) a verbal exchange between two characters on stage
(E) a short, comic speech by the protagonist

148. Which of the following painters produced a number of canvasses of jungle plants and animals?
(A) Henri Rousseau (B) Paul Cezanne (C) Jackson Pollock
(D) Mary Cassatt (E) Andy Warhol

149. Which of the following conductors began with opera and for many years headed the New York Philharmonic?
(A) George Szell (B) Sir John Barbarolli
(C) Herbert von Karajan (D) Arturo Toscanini
(E) André Previn

150. A handkerchief plays a key role in which of the following tragedies?
(A) *All for Love* (B) *Othello* (C) *King Lear*
(D) *Anthony and Cleopatra* (E) *Macbeth*

ANSWER KEY—TRIAL TEST

Section I

1.	B	14.	C	27.	D	40.	A	52.	E	64.	E
2.	D	15.	E	28.	E	41.	D	53.	E	65.	A
3.	C	16.	C	29.	B	42.	D	54.	A	66.	A
4.	A	17.	B	30.	B	43.	C	55.	B	67.	C
5.	C	18.	C	31.	E	44.	A	56.	C	68.	A
6.	D	19.	D	32.	C	45.	D	57.	A	69.	B
7.	E	20.	D	33.	B	46.	D	58.	C	70.	C
8.	D	21.	C	34.	C	47.	D	59.	D	71.	E
9.	D	22.	A	35.	B	48.	B	60.	A	72.	E
10.	A	23.	A	36.	C	49.	A	61.	E	73.	D
11.	B	24.	E	37.	E	50.	E	62.	C	74.	B
12.	A	25.	C	38.	A	51.	D	63.	E	75.	A
13.	C	26.	C	39.	D						

Section II

76.	A	89.	C	102.	E	115.	A	127.	E	139.	D
77.	D	90.	E	103.	C	116.	A	128.	C	140.	D
78.	D	91.	E	104.	C	117.	B	129.	B	141.	B
79.	E	92.	D	105.	C	118.	D	130.	D	142.	C
80.	E	93.	E	106.	B	119.	A	131.	A	143.	A
81.	A	94.	E	107.	E	120.	E	132.	D	144.	B
82.	A	95.	D	108.	D	121.	A	133.	C	145.	E
83.	A	96.	B	109.	A	122.	B	134.	E	146.	C
84.	B	97.	C	110.	B	123.	B	135.	A	147.	C
85.	D	98.	D	111.	D	124.	D	136.	A	148.	A
86.	A	99.	B	112.	E	125.	D	137.	B	149.	D
87.	C	100.	E	113.	D	126.	A	138.	B	150.	B
88.	B	101.	A	114.	C						

SCORING CHART—TRIAL TEST

After you have scored your Trial Test, enter the results in the chart below (the Raw Score computation is explained on page 14); then transfer your Raw Score to the Progress Chart on page 14. As you complete the Sample Examinations later in this part of the book, you should be able to achieve increasingly higher Raw Scores.

Total Test	Number Right	Number Wrong	Number Omitted	Raw Score
Section I: 75				
Section II: 75				
Total: 150				

ANSWER EXPLANATIONS—TRIAL TEST

Section I

1. B. Expressionism in the arts was a movement during the latter part of the 19th and early part of the 20th centuries that emphasized the objective expression of inner experience through conventional characters and symbols.
2. D. The Impressionists were a group of late 19th century painters who created a general impression of a scene or object by the use of unmixed primary colors and small strokes to simulate actual reflected light.
3. C. Acoustics is the study of sound.
4. A. Jean Baptiste Lully (c. 1633–1687) was an Italian operatic composer who has been called "the father of French opera." In 1653 he was made court composer by Louis XIV, for whom he composed many ballets.
5. C. James Wyatt (1746–1813) restored English Gothic cathedrals at Lincoln and Salisbury and built several buildings at Magdelen College, Oxford.
6. D. A "comedy of manners" is a type of social farce. Ibsen wrote plays of a more serious nature.
7. E. Aristotle stated that the primary purpose of tragedy is to create a catharsis, or purgation, of the emotions.
8. D. The best known essayists of this period were Joseph Addison and Richard Steele, who contributed to both *The Tattler* and *The Spectator*.
9. D. *Uncle Tom's Cabin* ran as a serial in the *National Era*, an abolitionist paper, from June 1851 to April 1852, and was later published as a book.
10. A. Alliteration is the occurrence in a phrase or a line of a speech or writing of two or more words having the same initial sound, as the "b" sound in "brush," "brow," "burnished," and "bronze."
11. B. The ballet "The Rite of Spring" was first produced by Diaghileff's Ballets Russes in Paris in 1913. It raised a storm of protest and was given only six times.
12. A. An overture is an instrumental introduction to an opera.
13. C. The photograph shows a pueblo in Taos, New Mexico.
14. C. Dali, Miro, and de Chirico are three artists noted for their surrealist paintings.
15. E. This is an historical fact.
16. C. A quatrain is a stanza or poem of four lines.
17. B. "Barbara Allen" is an ancient British folk ballad.

18. C. Pop art frequently depicts such things as Campbell's soup cans, flashy cars, and movie stars.
19. D. The Greeks are noted for their graceful statues depicting the human body.
20. D. Wright believed that a building should be built of the materials native to the area and should blend in with its particular surroundings.
21. C. Camus states this in many essays, but no more strongly than in his "Reflections on the Guillotine."
22. A. The *Nibelungenlied*, of unknown origin, was probably composed between the 12th and 14th centuries.
23. A. This is the famous "Pomp and Circumstance" overture.
24. E. None of the others were jazz guitarists.
25. C. Shakespeare never wrote dramas about the middle class.
26. C. The Hollywood Bowl opened in California in 1922.
27. D. Aeschylus, the Athenian tragic poet, was the first of the three great tragedians, the others being Sophocles and Euripides.
28. E. No scenery or props were employed by the Greeks in their open, outdoor theater.
29. B. A sharp is a musical note raised one-half step in pitch.
30. B. This is a standard definition of "Western man" or "Western civilization."
31. E. A tone poem is an elaborate orchestral composition, usually in one movement, having no fixed form and based upon some non-musical, poetic or descriptive theme. Strauss' best known tone poem is "Thus Spake Zarathustra."
32. C. Hamlet's famous "to be or not to be" soliloquy addresses this problem.
33. B. Paul Cezanne (1839–1906) was a French post-impressionist painter. He was noted for the use of very vivid colors, and for a striving for depth in place of flatness, which he achieved by very dark shadows and outlines.
34. C. Cubism is a school of modern art characterized by the use of cubes and other abstract geometric forms rather than by a realistic representation of nature.
35. B. A clerestory is an outside wall of a room or building that is carried above an adjoining roof and pierced with windows.
36. C. "Rappaccini's Daughter" is a short story written by Nathaniel Hawthorne.
37. E. Not all sculpture is a realistic portrayal of the human being; stone and marble can be cut for flooring and may be functional, but not necessarily artistic.
38. A. George Berkeley (1685–1753) denied the independent existence of matter. His was the philosophy of subjective idealism, or immaterialism.
39. D. Florence is a city in Tuscany, Italy. Among those who added luster to its name were the artist Michelangelo and the writers Dante and Boccaccio.
40. A. The principal members of the School of Lyon, headed by Maurice Scève, were Antoine Heroet, Pernette de Guillet, and Louise Labé, all poets.
41. D. Stephen Crane (1871–1900) was an American novelist, poet, and journalist. His *Red Badge of Courage* is a well-known tale of the American Civil War.
42. D. Renoir, Monet, and Pissaro were 19th century painters who attempted to create a general impression of a scene or object by the use of unmixed primary colors and small strokes to simulate actual reflected light.
43. C. This is noticeable in Roman roads and aqueducts as well as in buildings.
44. A. Modulation, in music, is defined as a shifting from one key to another by the transitional use of a chord common to both.
45. D. *Oedipus the King*, a play written by Sophocles, concerns Oedipus, who killed his father and married his mother.
46. D. The photograph is of the Opera House is Sydney, Australia.
47. D. Mark Twain was the pseudonym of Samuel L. Clemens, who was born in Florida, Missouri, in 1835, and spent his childhood in Hannibal, Missouri.
48. B. This example of nonsense verse is from the poem "Jabberwocky," by Lewis Carroll, and is to be found in *Through the Looking Glass*.
49. A. With the fall of the Roman Empire, Christian forces had succeeded in driving the actors out of Rome. Modern drama, including farcical interludes, had its origins in the Middle Ages.

50. E. The Black Death was an epidemic of plague in the 14th century.
51. D. *Animal Farm* is a political satire by George Orwell.
52. E. Bolger, the only tap dancer of the group, appeared in the musical *On Your Toes* and the motion picture *The Wizard of Oz*.
53. E. Ferde Grofé was an American composer and arranger who became famous when he orchestrated Gershwin's *Rhapsody in Blue* in 1924. He also wrote other music describing the American scene, including "The Grand Canyon Suite."
54. A. The great areas of interior space created the feeling of human insignificance and God's infinite and all-powerful presence.
55. B. Some authors pictured the effects of the Great Depression and laborers brutalized by machines.
56. C. Kerouac's novel *On The Road* began a new movement in American literature.
57. A. A parable is sometimes a religious lesson as well.
58. C. Altamira is in northern Spain, and Lascaux is in south-central France.
59. D. This is a basic principle of art.
60. A. Modern psychologists and sociologists have demonstrated that cultural conditioning determines the way we perceive.
61. E. Foster was the composer of "Old Folks at Home," "Oh Susannah," "My Old Kentucky Home," and many other songs.
62. C. Benjamin Franklin (1706–1790) was one of the most versatile of the early American fathers.
63. E. The line comes from T. S. Eliot's poem, "The Love Song of J. Alfred Prufrock."
64. E. The mystery plays were the forerunner of modern drama.
65. A. Lessing's *The Golden Notebook* appeared at the beginning of the Women's Liberation Movement in 1962.
66. A. *Don Quixote*, the best known work of Miguel de Cervantes, is a satire.
67. C. Among Gainsborough's best known works are "Mrs. Siddons" and "The Blue Boy."
68. A. "The Well-Tempered Clavier," sometimes called "The Well-Tempered Clavichord," consists of forty-eight preludes and fugues.
69. B. None of the other works was written by Beethoven.
70. C. Among Lewis' best known novels are *Main Street* and *Babbitt*.
71. E. All people have unlimited abilities.
72. E. Aeschylus and Sophocles were more conservative and traditional in their approach.
73. D. Chekhov is noted for presenting small "slices of life" in his plays.
74. B. Leoncavallo wrote several operas, but only *I Pagliacci* was successful.
75. A. A flat is a musical note one-half step lower than a specified note or tone.

Section II

76. A. This famous Greek statue is presently to be seen in the Louvre in Paris.
77. D. Shakespeare's plays contain elements such as song, dance, and ghostly apparitions because it was necessary for him to appeal to a diverse audience.
78. D. In other words, the viewer must enter the theater with an open mind.
79. E. Paul Gauguin was a French landscape and figure painter best known for his paintings of Tahitian subjects.
80. E. Pointillism is characterized by the application of paint in small dots and brush strokes so as to create an effect of blending and luminosity.
81. A. Hermann Hesse was a Swiss author who wrote *Siddhartha, Demian* and *A Journey to the East*, as well as many other novels.
82. A. This answer is true by definition.
83. A. The poem was first published in *The Passionate Pilgrim* in 1599.
84. B. The poem was published after Marlowe's death.
85. D. A quatrain is a stanza of four lines.

86. A. The appreciation of art is basically an emotional, sensory experience.
87. C. Isaiah was one of the greatest of the Hebrew prophets.
88. B. The other groups consist of those who are not symphony conductors.
89. C. The others are not writers.
90. E. The others are not choreographers.
91. E. F. Scott Fitzgerald is probably the best known writer of the "roaring 20s."
92. D. Nietzsche wrote about the will to power, and the superman who, he believed, is to come.
93. E. Kate is the name of the female lead in Shakespeare's play.
94. E. Van Gogh became an artist, but he did not prove his point.
95. D. This is a traditional musical notation.
96. B. This is a definition of a cappella.
97. C. *Die Meistersinger* is not part of the Germanic myth cycle.
98. D. Mary Flannery O'Connor (1925–1964) lived most of her life in Milledgeville, Georgia.
99. B. This ornate style in art and architecture developed in Europe about 1550 to 1700.
100. E. "Art" is an abstract concept, and therefore may have many definitions.
101. A. Hamlet's mother, Gertrude, is married to Claudius, but Hamlet mistrusts him.
102. E. This group, also called the Hartford Wits, flourished in the late 18th and early 19th centuries.
103. C. Marquez, author of *One Hundred Years of Solitude*, was awarded the Nobel Prize for literature in 1982.
104. C. Shultz is the creator of *Peanuts*.
105. C. Sprung rhythm is a forcefully accentual verse rhythm in which a stressed syllable is followed by an irregular number of unstressed or slack syllables to form a foot having a metrical value equal to that of the other feet in the line.
106. B. Anouilh's play is also entitled *Antigone*.
107. E. Metal is a popular medium for modern sculptors.
108. D. Mólière's attacks on bourgeois morality greatly appealed to his aristocratic audience.
109. A. Poe, one of the first great American short story writers, coined this criterion.
110. B. This is a translation from the French.
111. D. Francois Rabelais (1494–1553) entered a convent but later abandoned monasticism. His best known works are *Gargantua* and *Pantagruel*.
112. E. LeGuin's *The Left Hand of Darkness* is considered a classic in its field.
113. D. Perhaps Verne's best known work is *20,000 Leagues Under the Sea*, in which he anticipated the invention of the submarine.
114. C. There is no proof, but tradition does hold that Homer was the author.
115. A. Handel's most famous oratorios are on biblical subjects, such as *Esther, Deborah*, and *Samson*.
116. A. The score is the written form of a musical composition. The conductor's copy is complete.
117. B. This book shows how labor was oppressed by management in the early days of unionization.
118. D. These characters are termed the protagonist and the antagonist. Without conflict, there can be no drama.
119. A. The painting is of La Gioconda, popularly known as the *Mona Lisa*.
120. E. Jason's men were called Argonauts, after the ship, *Argo*.
121. A. Jason stole the Golden Fleece from Aeetes, with the help of Aeete's daughter, Medea.
122. B. Louis XIV, the "Sun-King," indulged his taste for luxury and elegance to the full. The arts flourished during his reign in France.
123. B. Sir Christopher Wren (1632–1723) was one of the foremost architects of his day. All of his buildings exhibit elegance, vigor, and dignity.
124. D. The king had learned of uprisings in both Scotland and Wales.
125. D. A mosaic is a decorative design or picture made by setting small colored pieces, such as tile, in mortar.

126. A. All the answers to the above are true, but only partial explanations. "A," "the complexity of modern life," encompasses all of them and more.
127. E. Formal science relies heavily upon experimentation for proof of a hypothesis.
128. C. Kilmer's "Trees" is often recited on Arbor Day.
129. B. Cunegonde's many experiences would have killed a weaker individual.
130. D. Ernst Hoffmann (1776–1822) was a German musician, artist, and Romantic writer, who is one of the masters in the field of fantastic prose.
131. A. Jacques Offenbach (1819–1880), a French composer of light operas, is best known for his adaptation of Hoffmann's stories.
132. D. The Roman Church abolished all "immoral activities," theater among them.
133. C. There was no theater under the Roman Church during the Dark Ages in Europe.
134. E. This is the only work mentioned that was written during the Revolutionary period.
135. A. *Oliver Twist* was written by Charles Dickens in 1838.
136. A. John Brinks "Dizzy" Gillespie, along with Charlie Parker, created the style of jazz known as "bop."
137. B. Milton states this in *Paradise Lost*.
138. B. The others are Italian, but not all 14th century writers.
139. D. Hamlet had been contemplating murder, but he listened to the Ghost.
140. D. A cantata is a vocal and instrumental composition comprising choruses, solos, and recitatives.
141. B. Laius, King of Thebes, was the father of Oedipus, who killed him.
142. C. Mayan architecture is to be found in sections of Mexico and Central America.
143. A. Only *A Handmaid's Tale* was written by Atwood.
144. B. Terza rima is composed of tercets which are not separate stanzas, because each is joined to the one preceding and the one following by a common rhyme: aba, bcb, cdc, ded, etc.
145. E. All of the above are to be found in Gothic cathedrals.
146. C. Robert Frost, one of America's most admired poets, never received the Nobel Prize.
147. C. This is the answer by definition of "soliloquy."
148. A. Henri Rousseau was a French primitive painter best known for his "Sleeping Gypsy" and "The Jungle."
149. D. The others either did not begin with opera, did not head the New York Philharmonic, or did neither.
150. B. It is Desdemona's handkerchief that spurs Othello to such jealousy that he kills her.

CHAPTER

7 Background and Practice Questions

The Humanities Examination measures your general knowledge of literature and the fine arts. There are two sections to the examination, each consisting of approximately 75 questions and each requiring 45 minutes to complete. See the following chart for approximate percentages of examination items:

Literature (50%)		Fine Arts (50%)	
5–10%	Drama	25%	Visual arts (painting, sculpture, etc.)
15–20%	Poetry	15%	Music
10–15%	Fiction	5%	Performing arts (film, dance, etc.)
5–10%	Nonfiction	5%	Architecture
5%	Philosophy		

Questions on these topics are interspersed randomly throughout the test. The questions cover all periods from the classical to the contemporary and include aspects of the humanities not necessarily covered in courses in school. In addition to your course work, then, you should have a general interest in the arts. Attending the movies, the theater, and concerts; visiting museums; watching television; and reading widely should provide you with sufficient background. You might also consult any one of a number of excellent histories of the theater, literature, music, the film, and the other fine arts which are available in every public library.

A knowledge of foreign languages is not required. All literary works included are readily available in English translations. It is not necessary to read music to answer any of the questions about music. Though a few questions may appear rather technical, remember that no one is expected to have complete mastery of all fields of the humanities.

KINDS OF QUESTIONS THAT APPEAR ON THE EXAMINATION

Knowledge and Abilities Required

The questions require factual answers, not answers which depend upon your emotional responses or aesthetic tastes. Some questions cover material with which you should be familiar from course work. For other questions, the correct answer can be derived from your ability to analyze artistic creations, to recognize certain basic artistic techniques, and to make analogies between two works of art. You will be expected to identify literary passages and authors. In some cases, you will be presented with pictures of art works which you will be expected to identify by artist, period, or in some other way.

The following questions illustrate the various types.

Knowledge of Factual Information

Questions 1–3 refer to the following groups of people.

(A) John Williams, Burt Bacharach, Henry Mancini
(B) Sir George Solti, Andre Previn, Leonard Bernstein
(C) John Steinbeck, William Faulkner, Sinclair Lewis
(D) Andy Warhol, Joan Miro, Claes Oldenburg
(E) Twyla Tharp, Michael Bennett, Gower Champion

1. Which is a group of contemporary symphony conductors?

2. Which is a group of novelists who won the Nobel Prize for Literature?

3. Which is a group of choreographers for Broadway musicals of the 1970s and 1980s?

Recognition of Techniques and Identification with Artists and Periods

Questions 4–6 refer to the following lines.

Come live with me, and be my love,
And we will all the pleasures prove,
That valleys, groves, hills, and fields,
Woods or steepy mountains yields.

4. These lines are from
(A) "The Passionate Shepherd to His Love"
(B) "The Shepherd's Wife's Song"
(C) "A Strange Passion of a Lover"
(D) one of Shakespeare's sonnets
(E) "Troilus and Cressida"

5. The lines were written by
(A) William Shakespeare (B) Christopher Marlowe
(C) John Lyly (D) T.S. Eliot (E) Alexander Pope

6. The verse form is a
(A) couplet (B) sestina (C) sonnet (D) quatrain
(E) cinquaine

Analysis of Artistic Creations

7. LADY BRACKNELL: "Do you smoke?"
JACK: "Well, yes, I must admit I smoke."
LADY BRACKNELL: "I am glad to hear it. A man should always have an occupation of some sort."

This dialogue from Oscar Wilde's *The Importance of Being Earnest* illustrates

(A) sympathy (B) empathy (C) scorn (D) comic pathos
(E) linguistic wit

Answers

1. B **2.** B **3.** E **4.** A **5.** B **6.** D **7.** E

Format

Most questions are in interrogative or incomplete-sentence form, followed by five answer choices—the standard multiple-choice format. Some of these questions may be based on lines of poetry or prose or on works of art, which are quoted or reproduced above or beside the question. Questions 4–7 in the preceding group illustrate this format.

In a second type of format, the answer choices are given first, followed by a group of numbered items (see questions 1–3 above). You are required to choose for each numbered item the answer choice that best describes or otherwise fits it.

Scoring: Penalty for Guessing

Although each part contains questions on all eight subtopics, a separate subscore is reported for literature and for the fine arts. Each correct answer is worth one point, and there is no penalty for an unanswered question. One fourth of a point is deducted for a wrong answer; therefore random guessing is not likely to improve your score. If, however, you can eliminate one or more answer choices as clearly incorrect, it may be worthwhile to choose from among the remaining choices the one that seems most logical.

STUDY SOURCES

If you would like to review some of the information which you may already have studied or fill in some gaps in your formal education, we recommend the following as excellent sources:

LITERATURE

Abrams, M.H., *The Norton Anthology of English Literature,* 4th ed. New York: W.W. Norton and Co., Inc., 1979.

Baker, Nancy L. *A Research Guide for Undergraduate Students: English and American Literature,* 2nd ed. New York: Modern Language Association of America, 1985.

Brooks, Cleanth, et al., eds. *American Literature: The Makers and the Making,* 4 volumes. New York: St. Martin's Press, Inc., 1974.

Grant, Michael. *Myths of the Greeks and Romans.* New York: New American Library, 1975.

Heiney, D.W. and Downs, L.H. *Contemporary Literature of the Western World,* 4 volumes. Hauppauge, NY: Barron's Educational Series, Inc., 1974.

Perrine, Laurence. *Sound and Sense: An Introduction to Poetry,* 5th ed. New York: Harcourt Brace Jovanovich, Inc., 1977.

FINE ARTS

Apel, Willi. *Harvard Dictionary of Music,* 2nd ed. Cambridge, MA: Harvard University Press, 1969.

Grout, Donald. *A History of Western Music,* 3rd ed. New York: W.W. Norton and Co., Inc., 1980.

Janson, H.W. *History of Art: A Survey of the Major Visual Arts from the Dawn of History to the Present Day,* 2nd ed. New York: Harry N. Abrams, Inc., 1977.

Whiting, Fran M. *An Introduction to the Theatre,* 4th ed. New York: Harper and Row Pubs., Inc., 1978.

In addition to these specific works, you might consult the excellent series of dictionaries for the various art forms published by Oxford University Press in New York. For very recent information, you might consult the music, art and book reviews and film criticisms which appear regularly in such publications as *Playboy, Esquire, Saturday Review, The National Review, The New Republic, The New York Times, The New York Review of Books, The New Yorker, The Film Quarterly,* and other periodicals.

For practice, we will now give you some sample questions in each of the areas which the CLEP Humanities examination will cover; these questions should be considered typical.

PRACTICE QUESTIONS ON THE HUMANITIES

Questions about Literature

Directions: Each of the questions or incomplete statements below is followed by five suggested answers or completions. Select the one that is best in each case.

1. What 17th-century poet attempted to "justify the ways of God to man"?
(A) John Bunyan (B) Samuel Johnson (C) John Dryden (D) John Milton (E) John Donne

2. In poetry, the invention or use of a word whose sound echoes or suggests its meaning is called
(A) amphibrach (B) sprung rhythm (C) onomatopoeia (D) zeugma (E) sententia

3. A Japanese poem of seventeen syllables is the
(A) kyogen (B) haiku (C) sentyu (D) tanka (E) renka

4. The Greek theater contained all but one of the following:
(A) masks (B) boots (C) proscenium
(D) movable props (E) song and dance

5. A well-known 19th-century symbolist poem is "Afternoon of a Faun." This poem was written by
(A) Baudelaire (B) Rimbaud (C) Valéry
(D) Mallarmé (E) Claudel

6. A pastoral elegy, bewailing the death of Edward King, is
(A) "In Memoriam" (B) "Lycidas" (C) "Thyrsis"
(D) "Il Penseroso" (E) "Adonais"

7. An example of an Old English folk epic is
(A) *The Canterbury Tales* (B) *The Iliad* (C) *Beowulf*
(D) *A Midsummer Night's Dream* (E) *Paradise Lost*

8. The essence of comedy is
(A) satire (B) surprise (C) mistaken identity
(D) disguise (E) incongruity

9. The Greek word for "overweening pride" is
(A) hamartia (B) catharsis (C) anagnorisis
(D) peripety (E) hubris

10. The word *utopia* comes from a 16th-century book by
(A) Sir Thomas More (B) Thomas à Becket
(C) Samuel Beckett (D) William Shakespeare
(E) Ben Jonson

11. A famous contemporary of John Dryden was
(A) Alexander Pope (B) Ben Jonson (C) Thomas Macaulay
(D) Leigh Hunt (E) John Milton

12. According to Aristotle, tragedy evokes pity and fear and produces a
(A) catharsis (B) dénouement (C) climax
(D) recognition (E) kothurnos

13. A Japanese play which exists as a harmony of all theatrical elements —poetry, music, dance, costume, mask, setting, and the interaction of performance—is the
(A) kabuki (B) shinto (C) hari kiri
(D) nō (E) joruri

14. The 16th century believed the main purpose of poetry was to
(A) relieve the emotions (B) make science bearable
(C) enliven life (D) delight and instruct (E) philosophize

15. Shakespeare's best known comic character is
(A) Titania (B) Falstaff (C) Henry VIII
(D) Ariel (E) Friar Lawrence

16. A collection of medieval stories concerning a group of people on a pilgrimage is
(A) *The Decameron* (B) *The Canterbury Tales*
(C) *Sir Gawain and the Green Knight* (D) *Morte d'Arthur*
(E) *Idylls of the King*

17. An American poet and novelist, awarded the Pulitzer Prize for her novel *The Color Purple,* is
(A) Zora Neale Hurston (B) Ursula K. LeGuin (C) Barbara Bellows
(D) Cynthia Blake (E) Alice Walker

18. "All are but parts of one stupendous whole,/Whose body Nature is, and God the soul" was written by
(A) Matthew Arnold (B) Alexander Pope
(C) Percy B. Shelley (D) John Milton (E) Robert Browning

19. The author of the novels *My Old Sweetheart* and *The Whiteness of Bones* is
(A) Susanna Moore (B) Margaret Atwood (C) Toni Morrison
(D) Sylvia Plath (E) Frances Jones

20. John Donne and his followers are known to literary historians as the
(A) metaphysical poets (B) Molly Maguires
(C) cavalier poets (D) graveyard school (E) Sons of Ben

21. The "hero" of Milton's *Paradise Lost* is
(A) Satan (B) man (C) God (D) Adam (E) Jesus

22. A convention in drama wherein a character speaks his innermost thoughts aloud while alone on stage is the
(A) aside (B) prologue (C) soliloquy
(D) epilogue (E) proscenium

23. A fire-breathing monster, part lion, part goat, and part serpent, slain by Bellerophon, was the
(A) medusa (B) chimera (C) phoenix
(D) minotaur (E) hydra

24. The French poet Arthur Rimbaud was a forerunner of the
(A) Pre-Raphaelites (B) absurdists (C) realists
(D) naturalists (E) symbolists

25. One of the great Sanskrit epics of Western India is
(A) *The Mahabharata* (B) *Siddhartha* (C) *The Tripitaka*
(D) *The Analects* (E) *The Rubáiyát*

26. A well-known contemporary of William Shakespeare was
(A) John Milton (B) Dante Alighieri (C) Geoffrey Chaucer
(D) Christopher Marlowe (E) John Dryden

27. A 20th-century novel which made the public aware of the plight of migrant laborers is
(A) *East of Eden* (B) *To a God Unknown* (C) *Cannery Row*
(D) *The Grapes of Wrath* (E) *Tortilla Flat*

28. A poet who writes of ordinary people and of nature is considered a
(A) naturalist (B) realist (C) romanticist
(D) medievalist (E) Victorian

29. The "comedy of manners" was most popular during the
(A) 16th century (B) 17th century (C) 18th century
(D) 19th century (E) 20th century

30. One of the first American short story writers was
(A) Washington Irving (B) Edgar Allan Poe
(C) Ambrose Bierce (D) Stephen Crane (E) O. Henry

31. A Greek divinity who punished crimes, particularly those of impiety and hubris, was
(A) Artemis (B) Mercury (C) Clio
(D) Clytaemnestra (E) Nemesis

32. The greatest lyric poet in German before Goethe was the minnesinger
(A) Heinrich Heine (B) Gerhart Hauptmann
(C) Walter von der Vogelweide (D) Gottfried von Strassburg
(E) Friedrich Schiller

33. Restoration comedy, often called "comedy of manners," abounded in "gay remarks and unexpected answers," often referred to as witty
(A) syllogisms (B) doggerel (C) repartee
(D) slapstick (E) cliches

34. Empathy involves which of the following responses on the part of the play-going audience?
(A) alienation (B) projection (C) nostalgia
(D) intensification (E) escape

35. A 20th-century writer who refused the nobel prize for literature was
(A) Faulkner (B) Sartre (C) Camus
(D) Lewis (E) Hemingway

Questions 36–38 refer to the following poem, "The Eagle" by Alfred, Lord Tennyson.

He clasps the crag with crooked hands;
Close to the sun in lonely lands,
Ringed with the azure world, he stands.

The wrinkled sea beneath him crawls;
He watches from his mountain walls,
And like a thunderbolt he falls.

36. Which line contains a metaphor?
(A) line 2 (B) line 4 (C) line 5 (D) line 6
(E) all of these lines

37. Which line contains a simile?
(A) line 1 (B) line 2 (C) line 3 (D) line 5 (E) line 6

38. Which line contains an example of alliteration?
(A) line 1 (B) line 3 (C) line 4 (D) line 5 (E) line 6

ANSWERS TO QUESTIONS ABOUT LITERATURE

1. D	**6.** B	**11.** E	**16.** B	**21.** B	**26.** D	**31.** E	**36.** B
2. C	**7.** C	**12.** A	**17.** E	**22.** C	**27.** D	**32.** C	**37.** E
3. B	**8.** E	**13.** D	**18.** B	**23.** B	**28.** C	**33.** C	**38.** A
4. D	**9.** E	**14.** D	**19.** A	**24.** E	**29.** C	**34.** B	
5. D	**10.** A	**15.** B	**20.** A	**25.** A	**30.** A	**35.** B	

Questions about Music

Directions: Each of the questions or incomplete statements below is followed by five suggested answers or completions. Select the one that is best in each case.

1. The assistant conductor or concertmaster of the orchestra is
   (A) the first chair violinist (B) the second chair violinist
   (C) a pianist (D) a harpist
   (E) standing in the wings ready to take over

2. The instrument with the stablest pitch and therefore the one asked to "sound your A" for all other players is the
   (A) piano (B) first violin (C) first oboe (D) clarinet
   (E) trumpet

3. The tone poem from "Afternoon of a Faun" was composed by
   (A) Debussy (B) Liszt (C) Bizet
   (D) Rimsky-Korsakov (E) Poulenc

4. The first American music comes from the American Indian and, with its emphasis on single rhythms, American Indian music is primarily
   (A) emotional (B) formal (C) heterophonic
   (D) polyphonic (E) choral

5. The difference between the kettle drums and other forms of timpani is that
   (A) they can be used to store small instruments
   (B) they can be tuned (C) they augment strings
   (D) they keep the beat (E) they add a marching effect

6. The "licorice stick" reached the peak of its popularity with band leader Benny Goodman. The "licorice stick" is a
   (A) piccolo (B) flute (C) trombone (D) trumpet
   (E) clarinet

7. The development of early church music and plainsong is attributed to
   (A) Marlow (B) Paul (C) Caniauis (D) Lucifer
   (E) Gregory the Great

8. In music, one tone used against another tone is called
   (A) abstraction (B) a chord (C) a staff
   (D) counterpoint (E) alteration

9. What American choreographer is best known for her "Fall River Legend" and "Rodeo"?
   (A) Agnes deMille (B) Isadora Duncan (C) Martha Graham
   (D) Loie Fuller (E) Doris Humphrey

10. One of America's most popular operas, composed by George and Ira Gershwin, is
    (A) *The Medium* (B) *The Black Crook* (C) *Porgy and Bess*
    (D) *The Little Tycoon* (E) *Amahl and the Night Visitor*

11. Running through music literature is a persistent thread that has affected, positively or negatively, the work of every composer from Bach to our 20th-century modernists. This thread is
(A) melody (B) sonata (C) tone-poem
(D) counterpart (E) atonality

12. The "Unfinished Symphony" was written by
(A) Mendelssohn (B) Schubert (C) Brahms
(D) Tchaikovsky (E) Chopin

13. The opera *The Barber of Seville* has music by
(A) Puccini (B) Verdi (C) Mendelssohn
(D) Rossini (E) Poulenc

14. The opera *The Marriage of Figaro* has music by
(A) Mozart (B) Haydn (C) Verdi (D) Rossini
(E) Puccini

15. A celebrated violinist who made his debut at Carnegie Hall at age eleven and toured the world before his twentieth birthday is
(A) Georges Enesco (B) Aaron Copland (C) Elmer Bernstein
(D) Yehudi Menuhin (D) Andre Previn

16. We get the word *octave* from a Latin word meaning
(A) two (B) four (C) six (D) eight (E) nine

17. The direct ancestor of the symphony is the
(A) concerto (B) sonata (C) motet (D) aria
(E) overture

18. The method of four voices singing different tunes at the same time, yet linked by strict rules, is called a
(A) motet (B) combo (C) chorus (D) fugue
(E) baroque

19. Beethoven is best known for his
(A) tone poems (B) operas (C) symphonies
(D) waltzes (E) fugues

20. Many musicians agree that the greatest choral work ever written is
(A) Beethoven's "Moonlight Sonata"
(B) Bach's "Mass in B Minor"
(C) Schubert's "Second Symphony"
(D) Chopin's "Polonaise Militaire"
(E) Bizet's *Carmen*

ANSWERS TO QUESTIONS ABOUT MUSIC

1. A
2. C
3. A
4. D
5. B
6. E
7. E
8. D
9. A
10. C
11. E
12. B
13. D
14. A
15. D
16. D
17. E
18. A
19. C
20. B

Questions about Fine Arts— Painting, Architecture, Sculpture, Dance

Directions: Each of the questions or incomplete statements below is followed by five suggested answers or completions. Select the one that is best in each case.

1. In painting, *chiaroscuro* refers to
   (A) a light-and-dark technique (B) brilliant colors
   (C) monochromes (D) perspective
   (E) a single stroke technique

2. An abstract Expressionist who was the first modern painter to divorce himself entirely from subject matter is
   (A) Kandinsky (B) Hansen (C) Chagall
   (D) Dali (E) Turner

3. What is the main part of the interior of a church called?
   (A) The nave (B) The transept (C) The altar
   (D) The cruciform (E) The sacristy

4. One of the most famous modern ballet choreographers was
   (A) George Balanchine (B) Nicholas Sergeyev
   (C) Marius Petipa (D) Phillippe Taglioni
   (E) Rudolf von Laban

5. The artist famous for his painting on the ceiling of the Sistine Chapel is
   (A) Raphael (B) da Vinci (C) Michelangelo
   (D) Rembrandt (E) Delacroix

6. A painter noted for his madonnas is
   (A) Botticelli (B) van Gogh (C) Raphael (D) Picasso
   (E) Goya

7. The art of painting on freshly spread moist lime plaster with pigments suspended in a water vehicle is called
   (A) collage (B) pointillism (C) surrealism
   (D) primitivism (E) fresco

8. Ballet, as we know it today, had its origins in
   (A) Italy (B) Germany (C) France (D) Russia
   (E) England

9. An artistic composition of fragments of printed matter and other materials pasted on a picture surface is called
   (A) dadaism (B) a fresco (C) art nouveau
   (D) a collage (E) pop art

10. Perhaps the outstanding master of the engraving and the woodcut was
    (A) Pieter Brueghel (B) Albrecht Dürer (C) William Blake
    (D) Leonardo da Vinci (E) Honoré Daumier

11. An American painter noted for his (her) social realism is
    (A) Ben Shahn (B) Jackson Pollock (C) Mary Cassatt
    (D) John Singer Sargent (E) Benjamin West

12. A "Spanish" painter noted for his thin-faced, elongated individuals was
(A) Goya (B) Velásquez (C) El Greco (D) Picasso
(E) Orozco

13. A mode of sculpture in which forms and figures are distinguished from a surrounding plane surface is called a
(A) frieze (B) collage (C) fresco (D) relief
(E) plaque

14. All of the following are famous male ballet dancers *except*
(A) Andre Eglevsky (B) Feodor Chaliapin
(C) Vaslav Nijinksy (D) Rudolf Nureyev (E) Mikhail Baryshnikov

15. Inigo Jones was a
(A) 17th-century architect and set designer
(B) clarinetist with Bunk Johnson's orchestra
(C) Restoration playwright
(D) leading tenor with the La Scala Opera
(E) 19th-century impressionist painter

16. All of the following painted in the Rococo tradition *except*
(A) Boucher (B) Watteau (C) Fragonard
(D) Chardin (E) Cezanne

17. Perspective, as a unified system for representing space, was brought to perfection during the
(A) Golden Age of Greece (B) Roman Republic
(C) Byzantine period (D) Renaissance
(E) nineteenth century

18. With whom did Ruth St. Denis cofound a dance company?
(A) Michel Fokine (B) George Balanchine (C) Robert Helpmann
(D) Ted Shawn (E) Isadora Duncan

19. A Flemish painter noted for his feeling for the fantastic as well as his manual techniques was
(A) Jan van Eyck (B) Hans Holbein
(C) Rogier van der Weyden (D) Pieter Brueghel
(E) Hugo van der Goes

20. The technique of portraying "a scientifically accurate, detached picture of life, including everything and selecting nothing" is called
(A) Romanticism (B) Realism (C) Naturalism
(D) Primitivism (E) Sentimentalism

ANSWERS TO QUESTIONS ABOUT THE FINE ARTS

1. A	**6.** C	**11.** A	**16.** E
2. A	**7.** E	**12.** C	**17.** D
3. A	**8.** A	**13.** D	**18.** D
4. A	**9.** D	**14.** B	**19.** D
5. C	**10.** B	**15.** A	**20.** C

ANSWER SHEET — HUMANITIES/SAMPLE EXAMINATION 1

Section I

1. Ⓐ Ⓑ Ⓒ Ⓓ Ⓔ
2. Ⓐ Ⓑ Ⓒ Ⓓ Ⓔ
3. Ⓐ Ⓑ Ⓒ Ⓓ Ⓔ
4. Ⓐ Ⓑ Ⓒ Ⓓ Ⓔ
5. Ⓐ Ⓑ Ⓒ Ⓓ Ⓔ
6. Ⓐ Ⓑ Ⓒ Ⓓ Ⓔ
7. Ⓐ Ⓑ Ⓒ Ⓓ Ⓔ
8. Ⓐ Ⓑ Ⓒ Ⓓ Ⓔ
9. Ⓐ Ⓑ Ⓒ Ⓓ Ⓔ
10. Ⓐ Ⓑ Ⓒ Ⓓ Ⓔ
11. Ⓐ Ⓑ Ⓒ Ⓓ Ⓔ
12. Ⓐ Ⓑ Ⓒ Ⓓ Ⓔ
13. Ⓐ Ⓑ Ⓒ Ⓓ Ⓔ
14. Ⓐ Ⓑ Ⓒ Ⓓ Ⓔ
15. Ⓐ Ⓑ Ⓒ Ⓓ Ⓔ
16. Ⓐ Ⓑ Ⓒ Ⓓ Ⓔ
17. Ⓐ Ⓑ Ⓒ Ⓓ Ⓔ
18. Ⓐ Ⓑ Ⓒ Ⓓ Ⓔ
19. Ⓐ Ⓑ Ⓒ Ⓓ Ⓔ
20. Ⓐ Ⓑ Ⓒ Ⓓ Ⓔ
21. Ⓐ Ⓑ Ⓒ Ⓓ Ⓔ
22. Ⓐ Ⓑ Ⓒ Ⓓ Ⓔ
23. Ⓐ Ⓑ Ⓒ Ⓓ Ⓔ
24. Ⓐ Ⓑ Ⓒ Ⓓ Ⓔ
25. Ⓐ Ⓑ Ⓒ Ⓓ Ⓔ
26. Ⓐ Ⓑ Ⓒ Ⓓ Ⓔ
27. Ⓐ Ⓑ Ⓒ Ⓓ Ⓔ
28. Ⓐ Ⓑ Ⓒ Ⓓ Ⓔ
29. Ⓐ Ⓑ Ⓒ Ⓓ Ⓔ
30. Ⓐ Ⓑ Ⓒ Ⓓ Ⓔ
31. Ⓐ Ⓑ Ⓒ Ⓓ Ⓔ
32. Ⓐ Ⓑ Ⓒ Ⓓ Ⓔ
33. Ⓐ Ⓑ Ⓒ Ⓓ Ⓔ
34. Ⓐ Ⓑ Ⓒ Ⓓ Ⓔ
35. Ⓐ Ⓑ Ⓒ Ⓓ Ⓔ
36. Ⓐ Ⓑ Ⓒ Ⓓ Ⓔ
37. Ⓐ Ⓑ Ⓒ Ⓓ Ⓔ
38. Ⓐ Ⓑ Ⓒ Ⓓ Ⓔ
39. Ⓐ Ⓑ Ⓒ Ⓓ Ⓔ
40. Ⓐ Ⓑ Ⓒ Ⓓ Ⓔ
41. Ⓐ Ⓑ Ⓒ Ⓓ Ⓔ
42. Ⓐ Ⓑ Ⓒ Ⓓ Ⓔ
43. Ⓐ Ⓑ Ⓒ Ⓓ Ⓔ
44. Ⓐ Ⓑ Ⓒ Ⓓ Ⓔ
45. Ⓐ Ⓑ Ⓒ Ⓓ Ⓔ
46. Ⓐ Ⓑ Ⓒ Ⓓ Ⓔ
47. Ⓐ Ⓑ Ⓒ Ⓓ Ⓔ
48. Ⓐ Ⓑ Ⓒ Ⓓ Ⓔ
49. Ⓐ Ⓑ Ⓒ Ⓓ Ⓔ
50. Ⓐ Ⓑ Ⓒ Ⓓ Ⓔ
51. Ⓐ Ⓑ Ⓒ Ⓓ Ⓔ
52. Ⓐ Ⓑ Ⓒ Ⓓ Ⓔ
53. Ⓐ Ⓑ Ⓒ Ⓓ Ⓔ
54. Ⓐ Ⓑ Ⓒ Ⓓ Ⓔ
55. Ⓐ Ⓑ Ⓒ Ⓓ Ⓔ
56. Ⓐ Ⓑ Ⓒ Ⓓ Ⓔ
57. Ⓐ Ⓑ Ⓒ Ⓓ Ⓔ
58. Ⓐ Ⓑ Ⓒ Ⓓ Ⓔ
59. Ⓐ Ⓑ Ⓒ Ⓓ Ⓔ
60. Ⓐ Ⓑ Ⓒ Ⓓ Ⓔ
61. Ⓐ Ⓑ Ⓒ Ⓓ Ⓔ
62. Ⓐ Ⓑ Ⓒ Ⓓ Ⓔ
63. Ⓐ Ⓑ Ⓒ Ⓓ Ⓔ
64. Ⓐ Ⓑ Ⓒ Ⓓ Ⓔ
65. Ⓐ Ⓑ Ⓒ Ⓓ Ⓔ
66. Ⓐ Ⓑ Ⓒ Ⓓ Ⓔ
67. Ⓐ Ⓑ Ⓒ Ⓓ Ⓔ
68. Ⓐ Ⓑ Ⓒ Ⓓ Ⓔ
69. Ⓐ Ⓑ Ⓒ Ⓓ Ⓔ
70. Ⓐ Ⓑ Ⓒ Ⓓ Ⓔ
71. Ⓐ Ⓑ Ⓒ Ⓓ Ⓔ
72. Ⓐ Ⓑ Ⓒ Ⓓ Ⓔ
73. Ⓐ Ⓑ Ⓒ Ⓓ Ⓔ
74. Ⓐ Ⓑ Ⓒ Ⓓ Ⓔ
75. Ⓐ Ⓑ Ⓒ Ⓓ Ⓔ

Section II

76. Ⓐ Ⓑ Ⓒ Ⓓ Ⓔ
77. Ⓐ Ⓑ Ⓒ Ⓓ Ⓔ
78. Ⓐ Ⓑ Ⓒ Ⓓ Ⓔ
79. Ⓐ Ⓑ Ⓒ Ⓓ Ⓔ
80. Ⓐ Ⓑ Ⓒ Ⓓ Ⓔ
81. Ⓐ Ⓑ Ⓒ Ⓓ Ⓔ
82. Ⓐ Ⓑ Ⓒ Ⓓ Ⓔ
83. Ⓐ Ⓑ Ⓒ Ⓓ Ⓔ
84. Ⓐ Ⓑ Ⓒ Ⓓ Ⓔ
85. Ⓐ Ⓑ Ⓒ Ⓓ Ⓔ
86. Ⓐ Ⓑ Ⓒ Ⓓ Ⓔ
87. Ⓐ Ⓑ Ⓒ Ⓓ Ⓔ
88. Ⓐ Ⓑ Ⓒ Ⓓ Ⓔ
89. Ⓐ Ⓑ Ⓒ Ⓓ Ⓔ
90. Ⓐ Ⓑ Ⓒ Ⓓ Ⓔ
91. Ⓐ Ⓑ Ⓒ Ⓓ Ⓔ
92. Ⓐ Ⓑ Ⓒ Ⓓ Ⓔ
93. Ⓐ Ⓑ Ⓒ Ⓓ Ⓔ
94. Ⓐ Ⓑ Ⓒ Ⓓ Ⓔ
95. Ⓐ Ⓑ Ⓒ Ⓓ Ⓔ
96. Ⓐ Ⓑ Ⓒ Ⓓ Ⓔ
97. Ⓐ Ⓑ Ⓒ Ⓓ Ⓔ
98. Ⓐ Ⓑ Ⓒ Ⓓ Ⓔ
99. Ⓐ Ⓑ Ⓒ Ⓓ Ⓔ
100. Ⓐ Ⓑ Ⓒ Ⓓ Ⓔ
101. Ⓐ Ⓑ Ⓒ Ⓓ Ⓔ
102. Ⓐ Ⓑ Ⓒ Ⓓ Ⓔ
103. Ⓐ Ⓑ Ⓒ Ⓓ Ⓔ
104. Ⓐ Ⓑ Ⓒ Ⓓ Ⓔ
105. Ⓐ Ⓑ Ⓒ Ⓓ Ⓔ
106. Ⓐ Ⓑ Ⓒ Ⓓ Ⓔ
107. Ⓐ Ⓑ Ⓒ Ⓓ Ⓔ
108. Ⓐ Ⓑ Ⓒ Ⓓ Ⓔ
109. Ⓐ Ⓑ Ⓒ Ⓓ Ⓔ
110. Ⓐ Ⓑ Ⓒ Ⓓ Ⓔ
111. Ⓐ Ⓑ Ⓒ Ⓓ Ⓔ
112. Ⓐ Ⓑ Ⓒ Ⓓ Ⓔ
113. Ⓐ Ⓑ Ⓒ Ⓓ Ⓔ
114. Ⓐ Ⓑ Ⓒ Ⓓ Ⓔ
115. Ⓐ Ⓑ Ⓒ Ⓓ Ⓔ
116. Ⓐ Ⓑ Ⓒ Ⓓ Ⓔ
117. Ⓐ Ⓑ Ⓒ Ⓓ Ⓔ
118. Ⓐ Ⓑ Ⓒ Ⓓ Ⓔ
119. Ⓐ Ⓑ Ⓒ Ⓓ Ⓔ
120. Ⓐ Ⓑ Ⓒ Ⓓ Ⓔ
121. Ⓐ Ⓑ Ⓒ Ⓓ Ⓔ
122. Ⓐ Ⓑ Ⓒ Ⓓ Ⓔ
123. Ⓐ Ⓑ Ⓒ Ⓓ Ⓔ
124. Ⓐ Ⓑ Ⓒ Ⓓ Ⓔ
125. Ⓐ Ⓑ Ⓒ Ⓓ Ⓔ
126. Ⓐ Ⓑ Ⓒ Ⓓ Ⓔ
127. Ⓐ Ⓑ Ⓒ Ⓓ Ⓔ
128. Ⓐ Ⓑ Ⓒ Ⓓ Ⓔ
129. Ⓐ Ⓑ Ⓒ Ⓓ Ⓔ
130. Ⓐ Ⓑ Ⓒ Ⓓ Ⓔ
131. Ⓐ Ⓑ Ⓒ Ⓓ Ⓔ
132. Ⓐ Ⓑ Ⓒ Ⓓ Ⓔ
133. Ⓐ Ⓑ Ⓒ Ⓓ Ⓔ
134. Ⓐ Ⓑ Ⓒ Ⓓ Ⓔ
135. Ⓐ Ⓑ Ⓒ Ⓓ Ⓔ
136. Ⓐ Ⓑ Ⓒ Ⓓ Ⓔ
137. Ⓐ Ⓑ Ⓒ Ⓓ Ⓔ
138. Ⓐ Ⓑ Ⓒ Ⓓ Ⓔ
139. Ⓐ Ⓑ Ⓒ Ⓓ Ⓔ
140. Ⓐ Ⓑ Ⓒ Ⓓ Ⓔ
141. Ⓐ Ⓑ Ⓒ Ⓓ Ⓔ
142. Ⓐ Ⓑ Ⓒ Ⓓ Ⓔ
143. Ⓐ Ⓑ Ⓒ Ⓓ Ⓔ
144. Ⓐ Ⓑ Ⓒ Ⓓ Ⓔ
145. Ⓐ Ⓑ Ⓒ Ⓓ Ⓔ
146. Ⓐ Ⓑ Ⓒ Ⓓ Ⓔ
147. Ⓐ Ⓑ Ⓒ Ⓓ Ⓔ
148. Ⓐ Ⓑ Ⓒ Ⓓ Ⓔ
149. Ⓐ Ⓑ Ⓒ Ⓓ Ⓔ
150. Ⓐ Ⓑ Ⓒ Ⓓ Ⓔ

CHAPTER

8

Sample Examinations

This chapter contains three sample Humanities examinations, each with an answer key, scoring chart, and answer explanations. Calculate and record your scores and see your improvement on the Progress Chart on page 14.

SAMPLE EXAMINATION 1

Section I

Number of Questions: 75
Time: 45 minutes

Directions: Each of the questions or incomplete statements below is followed by five suggested answers or completions. Select the one that is best in each case.

1. Beethoven's only opera is
   (A) *Fidelio* (B) *Eroica* (C) *Peleas and Melisande*
   (D) *Egmont* (E) *Prometheus*

2. Renaissance art is characterized by
   (A) a growing appreciation for the pleasures and satisfaction of this life
   (B) a reflection of the increasing wealth and luxury of the cities of Italy
   (C) an emphasis on human values and the philosophy of Humanism
   (D) the combination of Christian legend with a rediscovery of pagan art and Greek myths
   (E) all of the above

3. *Cacophony* is a "harsh, discordant effect." What is its opposite?
   (A) Consonance (B) Assonance (C) Travesty
   (D) Euphony (E) Apostrophe

4. The meter of a musical composition
   (A) has to do with regularly recurring accents (B) determines tempo
   (C) indicates texture (D) determines dynamics
   (E) is the same as rhythm

5. Spenser intended *The Faerie Queene* to be all of the following *except*
   (A) praise for Queen Elizabeth I (B) a political allegory
   (C) a religious allegory (D) contained within twelve books
   (E) a true picture of Elizabethan England

6. Michelangelo's greatest paintings appear in the
   (A) Brancusi Chapel (B) St. Mark's Cathedral
   (C) Cathedral of Pisa (D) Sistine Chapel
   (E) St. Patrick's Cathedral

7. Structural elements of architecture such as the pointed arch and the flying buttress were extensively used in the period known as
(A) Byzantine (B) Gothic (C) Renaissance
(D) Baroque (E) Victorian

8. **The most intrinsically American and most durable of all motion picture genres is**
(A) romantic comedy (B) black comedy (C) musical comedy
(D) the western (E) tragedy

9. "I have found that all the bronze my furnace contained had been exhausted in the head of this figure [of the statue of Perseus]. . . . It was a miracle . . . I seemed to see in this head the head of God. . . ." This statement was made by
(A) Grangousier (B) Cellini (C) Machiavelli
(D) Michelangelo (E) Praxiteles

10. Which one of the following plays was *not* written by Shakespeare?
(A) ***Titus Andronicus*** (B) *Dr. Faustus*
(C) ***Love's Labour's Lost*** (D) *The Tempest* **(E)** ***Coriolanus***

11. **The monarch known as the "Sun King" was**
(A) Charles II of England (B) Edward I of England
(C) George VI of England (D) Henry IV of France
(E) Louis XIV of France

12. **The difference between sonata and sonata-allegro is**
(A) the sonata is more contrapuntal
(B) the sonata is more homophonic
(C) one is faster than the other
(D) the sonata is a broad form which may contain movements in the sonata-allegro form
(E) the sonata-allegro form preceded the sonata

13. **Impressionism in music originated in France under the leadership of**
(A) Debussy and Ravel (B) Poulenc and Hindemith
(C) Stravinsky and Bartok (D) Debussy and Chopin
(E) Sessions and Varese

14. **Leonardo da Vinci was one of the greatest artists of the period known as**
(A) Baroque (B) the early Renaissance
(C) the high Renaissance (D) Gothic (E) Byzantine

15. The word *philosophy* means literally
(A) love of knowledge (B) knowledge of God (C) love of God
(D) love of wisdom (E) science and progress

16. **The play which shows the downfall of a man as a result of biological urges or his social environment is called**
(A) epic theater (B) neorealism (C) romantic tragedy
(D) deterministic tragedy (E) Ibsenian irony

17. **The unresolved or "open" ending is one of the trademarks of**
(A) Greek tragedy (B) Restoration comedy
(C) Shakespearean comedy (D) Roman tragedy
(E) modern plays and cinema

18. Dante's *Divine Comedy* contains how many cantos?
(A) 3 (B) 4 (C) 33 (D) 99 (E) 100

19. The origins of baroque architecture can be traced to Sansovino, Palladio, and
(A) Bellini (B) Michelangelo (C) Giotto
(D) da Vinci (E) Lorenzo

20. In the theater, a conventional character, a type that recurs in numerous works, is called
(A) a tragic hero (B) a deus ex machina (C) a stock character
(D) a redundant character (E) a supernumerary character

21. The greatest ballet dancer of the beginning of the 20th century and prima ballerina of the Maryinsky Theater was
(A) Tamara Karsavina (B) Galina Ulanova (C) Anna Pavlova
(D) Tamara Toumanova (E) Alexandra Danilova

22. The photo at the right is an example of
(A) 17th century art
(B) 18th century Spanish art
(C) modern Mexican art
(D) medieval art
(E) American primitive art

Collection of Whitney Museum of American Art, New York

23. Polyphonic texture is
(A) chordal texture (B) unaccompanied melody
(C) accompanied melody (D) a combination of melodies
(E) common to all forms

24. *The Tempest* is a play of airy fancy and romantic charm, but it cannot be mistaken for a young man's work because
(A) its comic situations are in reality serious
(B) its conclusion offers no hope for mankind
(C) it contains the kind of crowd-pleasing devices that can come only with experience
(D) it abounds in wise reflections on human nature and human existence
(E) we know that it was the last play that Shakespeare ever wrote

25. A Danish writer, best known for her *Seven Gothic Tales* and *Winter's Tales*, was
(A) Isak Dinesen (B) Karen Petersen (C) Inge Johanssen
(D) Ingeborg Carlsen (E) Gerte Grimm

26. A well-known Spanish court painter of the 18th century was
(A) Velasquez (B) Ribera (C) Pisarro
(D) Goya (E) Pisano

27. The Greek playwright who introduced the third actor into tragedy was
(A) Agamemnon (B) Euripides (C) Socrates
(D) Thespis (E) Clytaemnestra

28. The Romantic Period of literature gave birth to a special kind of horror story, the
(A) pastoral romance (B) epic (C) vignette
(D) Gothic novel (E) dramatic monologue

29. The story of the founding of Rome by the mythical Aeneas was written by
(A) Augustus (B) Vergil (C) Homer (D) Sibyl (E) Romulus

30. Wagner's last opera concerning the search for the Holy Grail is
(A) *Festspielhaus* (B) *Cosima* (C) *Siegfried*
(D) *Parsifal* (E) *Wahnfried*

31. Rome contributed all of the following to architecture *except*
(A) an emphasis on verticality
(B) design of significant interiors
(C) buildings for use
(D) the arch and vault as a building principle
(E) the flying buttress

32. A Post-Impressionist painter best known for his South Seas subjects was
(A) Paul Gauguin (B) Vincent van Gogh
(C) Toulouse-Lautrec (D) Paul Cezanne
(E) Georges Seurat

33. A modern playwright who believes in "aesthetic distancing" is
(A) Arthur Miller (B) Eugene O'Neill (C) Jean Paul Sartre
(D) Stanley Kubrick (E) Bertolt Brecht

34. The central figure in the Bayeux tapestry is
(A) Alexander the Great
(B) William the Conqueror
(C) Edward the Confessor
(D) Gregory the Great
(E) Charlemagne

35. During the Hellenic Period, the great center of Greek culture was located at
(A) Alexandria (B) Antioch (C) Athens (D) Rhodes (E) Pergamon

Questions 36–38 refer to the following groups of people.

(A) Paul Klee, Marc Chagall, Pablo Picasso
(B) Samuel Barber, Alban Berg, George Gershwin
(C) Paul Johnson, Mies van der Rohe, Louis Sullivan
(D) Anne Jackson, Anne Tyler, Anne Bradstreet
(E) Amy Lowell, May Swenson, Nikki Giovanni

36. Which is a group of twentieth century painters?

37. Which is a group of twentieth century American poets?

38. Which is a group of twentieth century composers of opera?

39. All of the following are of the House of Atreus *except*
(A) Agamemnon (B) Menelaus (C) Orestes
(D) Iphigenia (E) Aphrodite

40. Willy Loman is one of the most famous characters in the modern American theater. He appears in
(A) *Cat on a Hot Tin Roof* (B) *Murder in the Cathedral*
(C) *The Sand Box* (D) *Oklahoma!* (E) *Death of a Salesman*

41. Which item does *not* belong in the following group?
(A) *A priori* knowledge (B) Deductive thinking (C) Intuition
(D) Formal science (E) Empirical knowledge

42. Though a Greek slave of Rome, this historian became very interested in the imperial expansion of Rome and wrote much about it. He was
(A) Caesar (B) Polybius (C) Plautus (D) Seneca
(E) Pompey

43. A painter noted for his scenes of the American West was
(A) Thomas Hart Benton (B) Frederick Remington
(C) Grant Wood (D) Edward Hopper (E) John Marin

44. "Capriccio Espagnol" and "Scheherazade" were written by
(A) Glinka (B) Moussorgsky (C) Tchaikovsky
(D) Borodin (E) Rimsky-Korsakov

45. Which of the following composers served as a bridge between the Romantic and Classical periods?
(A) Bruckner (B) Wagner (C) Tchaikovsky
(D) Beethoven (E) Berlioz

46. John Steinbeck traveled America and reported on the people he met, the things he saw. His constant companion on one trip was his dog
(A) Mitzi (B) Rocinante (C) Charlie (D) Joseph
(E) Willie

47. "The Hand of God" and "The Kiss" are sculptures by
(A) Rodin (B) Bertinelli (C) Michelangelo
(D) Brancusi (E) Epstein

48. All of the following operas were written by Mozart *except*
(A) *Don Giovanni* (B) *The Marriage of Figaro*
(C) *Orpheus and Eurydice* (D) *The Magic Flute*
(E) *Cosi fan tutte*

49. The American poet who wrote such works as "Abraham Lincoln Walks at Midnight" and "The Santa Fe Trail" was
(A) Vachel Lindsay (B) William Carlos Williams
(C) Walt Whitman (D) Carl Sandburg (E) Van Wyck Brooks

50. The medieval liturgical drama
(A) was an outgrowth of the Roman theater
(B) was an outgrowth of the Greek theater
(C) sprang up independently of Roman and Greek theaters
(D) was based upon pagan rites and rituals
(E) owed much to such writers as Ben Jonson and William Shakespeare

51. The best known of the medieval morality plays is
(A) *Quem Quaeritis Trope* (B) *The Castell of Perseverance*
(C) *The Life of Christ* (D) *Hamlet* (E) *Everyman*

52. The first collected edition of Shakespeare's plays is known as
(A) *The Collected Works of William Shakespeare*
(B) *The First Quarto*
(C) *The First Folio*
(D) *"Othello" and Other Plays by William Shakespeare*
(E) *Shakespeare's Plays: 1623*

53. An American author who vigorously attacked the "genteel tradition" and who took an active interest in American social problems was
(A) Stephen Crane (B) Edward Arlington Robinson
(C) Edgar Lee Masters (D) Theodore Dreiser
(E) Thomas Wolfe

54. Two composers from the Baroque period are
(A) Brahms and Berlioz (B) Stravinsky and Piston
(C) Bach and Handel (D) Mozart and Haydn
(E) Verdi and Puccini

55. Most jazz has a standard form of
(A) sonata-allegro (B) rondo (C) theme and variation
(D) fugue (E) canon

56. Surrealist art is associated with
(A) frottage, the subconscious, paradox
(B) anxiety, silence, the metaphysical
(C) timelessness, literary origins, loneliness
(D) fantasy, Freud, free association
(E) all of these

57. Unlike most of the later troubadors, the *jongleurs* of the 11th century were
(A) not of noble birth
(B) accompanied by a small orchestra
(C) able to sing the *chanson de geste*
(D) more sophisticated
(E) accompanied by two men

58. According to Plato, the principles of goodness and truth are
(A) purely human conceptions (B) a result of class training
(C) descriptions of the ways our minds work
(D) objective realities that transcend human experience
(E) rationalizations to conceal expediency and laziness

59. Two composers of the Italian Renaissance were
(A) Ockeghem and Paderewski
(B) Monteverdi and Bellini
(C) Palestrina and Josquin
(D) Josquin and Cellini
(E) Parmagianino and Cavalli

60. *Metaphysics* is primarily the study of
(A) morals (B) art (C) being as such
(D) beauty and goodness (E) knowledge

61. The convention by which an actor, "unnoticed" by others on the stage, makes a brief comment to the audience, is the
(A) soliloquy (B) perspective (C) aside
(D) periphery (E) denouement

62. The Globe Theater
(A) was closed on all sides but open on top
(B) had a stage which extended into the audience area
(C) depended upon natural lighting
(D) was built in 1599
(E) all of these

63. "One that lov'd not wisely but too well," describes
(A) Hamlet (B) Romeo (C) Cleopatra (D) Othello (E) Desdemona

64. Chaconne and passacaglia are both
(A) sonata-allegro (B) rondo form (C) scherzo and trio
(D) vocal forms (E) theme and variations

65. Canon and fugue are musical forms characterized by
(A) sonata-allegro form (B) repeated entrance of a theme
(C) augmentation (D) atonality (E) dynamic contrast

66. The above is an example of the architecture of
(A) Christopher Wren (B) Inigo Jones
(C) Frank Lloyd Wright (D) Joseph Paxton
(E) Gustave Eiffel

67. Artists rediscovered man, glorified him as part of the world, and scientists discovered the world around man in the time of
(A) the Roman Empire (B) the Middle Ages
(C) the late 19th century (D) the Greek period
(E) the Renaissance

68. All of the following were written by Ernest Hemingway *except*
(A) *For Whom the Bell Tolls* (B) *The Old Lions*
(C) *The Old Man and the Sea* (D) *Death in the Afternoon*
(E) *The Sun Also Rises*

69. The Renaissance Italian author who, writing in the vernacular, opposed the extension of the Pope's secular power was
(A) Cellini (B) Machiavelli (C) Dante (D) Scotti
(E) Manzoni

70. John Steinbeck once undertook a study of tide pools with Dr. Ed Ricketts, a noted marine biologist. The trip is recorded in Steinbeck's
(A) *Two Years Before the Mast*
(B) *Tide Pools and Sea Urchins*
(C) *Log of the Sea of Cortez*
(D) *The Dory*
(E) *Innocents Abroad*

71. In Shakespeare's plays,
(A) all the female roles were played by boys when the plays were first produced
(B) highly stylized language was a convention of the theater
(C) the "tragic hero" was always of noble birth
(D) the dialogue was written in poetic forms
(E) all of the above

72. A Roman writer of comedy was
(A) Menander (B) Hrosvitha (C) Plautus
(D) Seneca (E) Sodomaeus

73. The American author who gave the English language the word "babbitry" was
(A) Sinclair Lewis (B) Robinson Jeffers (C) Willa Cather
(D) Edward Arlington Robinson (E) John Steinbeck

Questions 74 and 75 refer to the following line of poetry.

"How do I love thee? Let me count the ways."

74. This is the opening line of
(A) *A Midsummer's Night Dream* (B) "Sonnets from the Portugese"
(C) "Burnt Norton" (D) "Sestina Altaforte"
(E) "The Ballade of Dead Ladies"

75. The poem from which the line is taken was written by
(A) William Shakespeare (B) T.S. Eliot (C) Ezra Pound
(D) Robert Browning (E) Elizabeth Barrett Browning

Section II

Number of Questions: 75
Time: 45 minutes

Directions: Each of the questions or incomplete statements below is followed by five suggested answers or completions. Select the one that is best in each case.

76. The photograph above is an example of a style of painting popular during which century?
(A) 15th (B) 17th (C) 18th (D) 19th (E) 20th

77. When the ghost in *Hamlet* appeared, most people in Shakespeare's audience would have
(A) laughed, because the supernatural was considered ridiculous
(B) recognized the figure as a dramatic symbol
(C) been unimpressed, since the device had been over-used
(D) reacted in a manner which we are unable to guess
(E) believed in the actuality of ghosts appearing on stage

78. The architect who designed the Crystal Palace was
(A) Charles Percier (B) P. F. L. Fontaine
(C) Joseph Paxton (D) James Wyatt
(E) Georges-Eugene Haussmann

79. Agamemnon's wife was
(A) Jocasta (B) Clytaemnestra (C) Cassandra
(D) Iphigenia (E) Antigone

80. When we speak of the study of *axiology,* we are talking about the interpretation of
(A) existences (B) essences (C) substances
(D) forms (E) values

81. **The "green ey'd monster which doth mock the meat it feeds on" is**
(A) revenge (B) jealousy (C) pride (D) hatred
(E) lust

82. **Molière wrote during the reign of**
(A) Charles III (B) James II (C) Henry IV
(D) Louis XIV (E) Elizabeth I

83. **The Greek chorus did not**
(A) foretell the future (B) explain past actions
(C) serve as an additional character in the play
(D) philosophize (E) help to move scenery

84. Creon repents and goes to free Antigone, but she has already hanged herself. This is an example of
(A) denouement (B) proscenium (C) deus ex machina
(D) irony (E) *in medias res*

85. The modern meaning of *deus ex machina* in relation to drama is
(A) a wheeled platform used as part of the scenery
(B) a god from a machine
(C) a mechanical device for staging elaborate effects
(D) the catastrophic event at the climax of a play
(E) an unsatisfactory resolution to problems of plot by means of an event for which the audience has not been prepared

86. **Vincent van Gogh**
(A) faithfully followed the Impressionist techniques
(B) felt that Impressionism did not allow the artist enough freedom to express his inner feelings
(C) believed the artist must paint only what he could see, not what appeared in the mind
(D) founded the movement in art called "abstract art"
(E) led seventeenth-century art back to natural forms of realism

87. **A single melody with subordinate harmony demonstrates**
(A) polyphonic texture (B) homophonic texture
(C) monophonic texture (D) bitonality (E) rondo form

88. **The musical terms consonance and dissonance are most properly used in a discussion of**
(A) texture (B) tone color (C) melody (D) rhythm
(E) harmony

89. **Gregorian chants are examples of which textures?**
(A) monophonic (B) contrapuntal (C) polyphonic
(D) homophonic (E) modern

90. **Which of the following is not characteristic of the Gregorian chant?**
(A) meter (B) use of Latin (C) use of eight church modes
(D) male choir (E) a capella

91. A school of art known as *Surrealism* developed in the 1920s. A forerunner of the Surrealist school and the painter of "I and My Village" was
(A) Picasso (B) Chagall (C) Klee (D) Kandinsky
(E) Beckman

92. What author, sometimes called a western realist, wrote many tales of the American West and its mining towns?
(A) A. P. Oakhurst
(B) Ambrose Bierce
(C) Stephen Crane
(D) Bret Harte
(E) M. Shipton

93. A singer, actress, poet, and playwright, perhaps best known for her autobiographical series, which includes *I Know Why the Caged Bird Sings* and *Gather Together in My Name*, is
(A) Alice Walker (B) Linda Reed (C) Maya Angelou
(D) Patricia Goldberg (E) Meryl Brooks

94. "The Rhapsody in Blue" was composed by
(A) Paul Whiteman
(B) Oscar Levant
(C) Leonard Bernstein
(D) Antheil Carpenter
(E) George Gershwin

95. The first "King of Jazz" was a New Orleans barber named
(A) Al Hirt
(B) Bix Beiderbecke
(C) Sidney Bechet
(D) Charles Bolden
(E) Papa Celestine

96. Almost every country in Europe has a national hero who has been enshrined in epic poems and myths. The national hero of Italy is
(A) El Cid (B) Orlando Furioso (C) Beowulf
(D) Roland (E) Giovanni Magnifioso

97. "The Canticle of the Sun" was written by
(A) Dante (B) Chaucer (C) St. Francis of Assisi
(D) Caedmon (E) The Venerable Bede

98. The 20th-century composer who first used the twelve-tone scale was
(A) Arnold Schoenberg (B) Leonard Bernstein
(C) John Cage (D) George Gershwin (E) Richard Rodgers

99. Which of the following statements is *false*?
(A) Satire is a means of showing dissatisfaction with an established institution or principle.
(B) Satire is most easily accepted by an audience holding various beliefs or beliefs different from those of the playwright.
(C) Satire was an early form of comedy.
(D) *Lysistrata* is a classic example of satire.
(E) Modern satire does not run the risk of being offensive.

100. **LADY BRACKNELL:** **"Do you smoke?"**
JACK: **"Well, yes, I must admit I smoke."**
LADY BRACKNELL: **"I am glad to hear it. A man should always have an occupation of some sort."**

The dialogue from Oscar Wilde's *The Importance of Being Earnest* illustrates
(A) sympathy
(B) empathy
(C) scorn
(D) comic pathos
(E) linguistic wit

101. Today's foremost American composer of musicals, noted for *Company, Sweeney Todd,* and *Sunday in the Park with George,* is
(A) Elmer Bernstein
(B) Stephen Sondheim
(C) Richard Rodgers
(D) Frederick Loewe
(E) Ernest Fleischman

102. **Which American author, grandchild of a president, wrote a famous book about his own education?**
(A) Henry Adams **(B) Robert Jackson** **(C) Jonathan Tyler**
(D) Elliot Roosevelt **(E) Howard Taft**

103. Shakespeare did not invent any of his plots, but adapted material from other sources, including a history of the British Isles. Which one of his plays tells of the efforts of a Scots nobleman to become king through murder and blackmail?
(A) *Richard the III*
(B) *Henry the IV, Part 1*
(C) *Macbeth*
(D) *As You Like It*
(E) *A Comedy of Errors*

104. **That Alfred, Lord Tennyson was poet laureate of England's Victorian Age was fitting because he**
(A) pleased his queen only
(B) felt only as the English felt
(C) thought only as Englishmen thought
(D) raised both his feeling and his thought to the realm of the universal
(E) pleased the landed gentry

105. The Mexican painter whose murals can be seen in the Government Palace at Guadalajara is
(A) Rivera
(B) Orozco
(C) Siqueiros
(D) Hernandez
(E) Cinfuentes

106. "I saw the sky descending black and white" is an example of
(A) iambic pentameter
(B) anapestic dimeter
(C) spondaic hexameter
(D) dactylic pentameter
(E) iambic tetrameter

107. Which of the following statements concerning courtly love is *false?*
(A) The idea was born in Provence in the 11th century.
(B) It was limited to the nobility.
(C) True love was considered impossible between husband and wife.
(D) Christian behavior was shunned.
(E) It glorified adultery.

108. The site of Apollo's great oracle was
(A) Parnassus (B) Olympus (C) Athens (D) Crete
(E) Delphi

109. The "Age of Faith" is a term which best applies to the
(A) classical Greek period (B) Baroque period
(C) Gothic period (D) Renaissance (E) 18th century

110. According to the Hedonist philosophers,
(A) actions are right if they tend to promote pleasure
(B) good acts depend primarily upon good intentions
(C) good cannot be separated from work
(D) duty makes an absolute demand upon us
(E) right conduct involves obedience to some established authority

111. Giotto is noted for
(A) writing a poem on a Grecian urn
(B) discovering the principle of the flying buttress
(C) the beginning of realistic painting in Western art, about 1300
(D) impressionistic painting since 1900
(E) inventing a secret process, now lost, for turning jewels into stained glass

Questions 112–114 refer to illustrations (A) through (E).

(A)

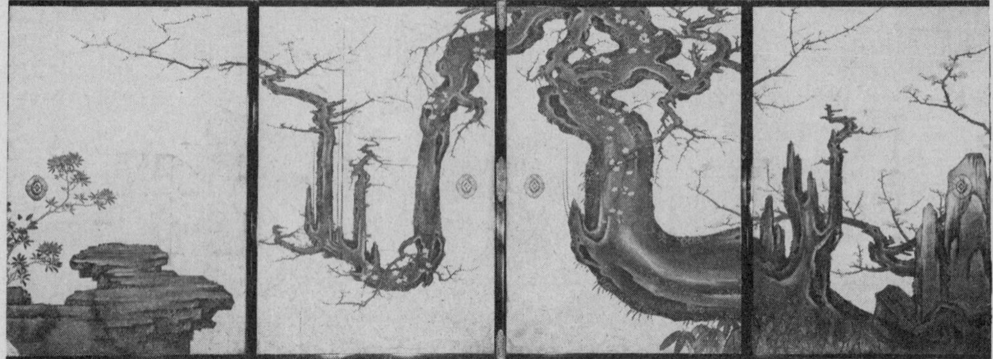

The Metropolitan Museum of Art, The Harry G. C. Packard Collection of Asian Art, Gift of Harry G. C. Packard and Purchase, Fletcher, Rogers, Harris Brisbane Dick and Louis V. Bell Funds, Joseph Pulitzer Bequest and The Annenberg Fund, Inc. Gift, 1975.

(B)

The Metropolitan Museum of Art, Purchased with special contributions and purchase funds given or bequeathed by friends of the Museum, 1967.

(C)

The Metropolitan Museum of Art, Gift of Henry G. Marquand, 1889. Marquand Collection.

(D)

The Metropolitan Museum of Art, Bequest of Benjamin Altman, 1913.

(E)

The Metropolitan Museum of Art, Rogers Fund, 1947.

112. Which is the Rembrandt?

113. Which is Japanese?

114. Which is an example of impressionism?

115. The above is a photograph of
(A) the Parthenon (B) the Coliseum (C) Stonehenge
(D) the Temple at Karnak (E) the Lighthouse at Knossos

116. In ancient and medieval mythology, the griffin is usually represented as a
(A) winged horse
(B) cross between a lion and eagle
(C) creature that is half man-half horse
(D) winged lion with the head of a woman
(E) devil with horns and cloven hooves

117. Deucalion is
(A) the Greek Noah
(B) the 10th book of the Bible
(C) one of the daughters of Danaus
(D) a whirlpool Odysseus encountered on his voyage
(E) the hero of the Trojan War

118. "Ding, dong, bell;
Pussy's in the well.
Who put her in?
Little Johnny Thin."
The lines above are an example of
(A) slant rhyme (B) a run-on line (C) sprung rhythm
(D) hidden alliteration (E) ottava rima

119. A painter noted for his moving portraits, with bright light emerging from a dark canvas, is
(A) Pollack (B) Picasso (C) Rembrandt
(D) Vermeer (E) Van Gogh

120. The musical sign ♭
(A) indicates false notes: falsetto
(B) lowers the pitch of a note by a full step
(C) precedes a note to be raised a full step
(D) precedes a note to be raised by a half step
(E) lowers the pitch of a note by a half step

121. Songs that are not as unreal as operatic arias but are much more sophisticated than folk songs are called
(A) natural (B) erotic (C) lieder
(D) appassionata (E) nova

122. As Candide journeyed from continent to continent, he searched for
(A) Dr. Pangloss (B) the Oreillons (C) Providence
(D) Cacambo (E) Cunegonde

123. The photograph at the right is a bust of
(A) Queen Elizabeth I
(B) Queen Nefertiti
(C) the goddess Athena
(D) Buddha
(E) an unknown African warrior

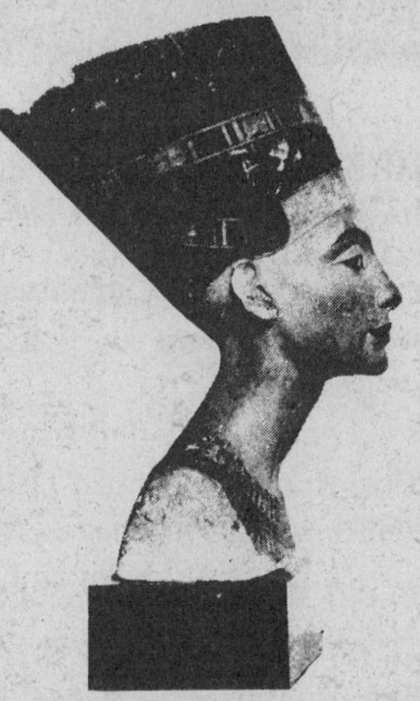

Hirmer Fotoarchiv Munchen

124. "Whereas in silks my Julia goes
Then, then (methinks) how sweetly flows
That liquefaction of her clothes."

The lines above are an example of a
(A) sestet (B) sonnet (C) quatrain (D) triplet (E) couplet

125. Most important to the success of a 19th-century drama was
(A) realism (B) kitchenism (C) contrast
(D) melodrama (E) gentle humor

126. Even though there are relatively few ballads of the American city, perhaps the classic example is "Frankie and Johnny," the main theme of which is
(A) the love of a man for his wife
(B) a woman's love that leads her to destroy her lover
(C) the love of Peddler Frank for his sway-backed horse
(D) the love of a boy for his dog
(E) the love of a man for a woman above his situation in life

127. Two principal forms of irony in tragedy are
(A) Euripidean and Sophoclean (B) Aeschylean and Euripidean
(C) Ibsenian and Shavian (D) Sophoclean and Aeschylean
(E) comic and tragic

128. Leitmotif means
(A) a note that is sung only once
(B) a note or theme that is repeated
(C) the leading motive
(D) an aria
(E) the first violinist is to take over leading the orchestra

129. Which of the following is *not* a convention of the Elizabethan theater?
(A) Women's roles acted by young boys
(B) Setting established by dialogue
(C) A chorus of elders
(D) Poetic language
(E) The soliloquy

130. The basing of knowledge on scientific observation is best illustrated by
(A) empiricists (B) rationalists (C) theologians
(D) both rationalists and theologians (E) existentialists

131. In Greek mythology, the greatest of all musicians was
(A) Dionysius
(B) Musicus
(C) Pan
(D) Apollo
(E) Orpheus

132. Odysseus' old nurse, who recognizes him from a scar on his leg, was named
(A) Argus (B) Euryclea (C) Menelaus
(D) Calliope (E) Nausicaa

133. What Florentine autobiographer, goldsmith, and sculptor was a child of will rather than of reason and the quintessential Renaissance man?
(A) Cellini (B) Lucagnolo (C) Urbrino
(D) Francesco (E) Machiavelli

134. *Libretto* means the
(A) rhythm of a musical composition
(B) words of a musical composition, especially an opera
(C) tempo of a musical composition
(D) directions to the conductor
(E) full orchestra is to play

135. A 20th-century poet who left America, went to England, and became one of England's most famous citizens was
(A) Ezra Pound (B) Robinson Jeffers
(C) Archibald MacLeish (D) Thomas Wolfe (E) T. S. Eliot

136. At the end of Saint-Exupery's fairy tale, *The Little Prince,* the little prince
(A) dies (B) goes home to his planet (C) falls into a deep sleep
(D) decides to remain on earth (E) changes into a star

137. The rebirth of the drama in the Middle Ages can be traced to
(A) the Church (B) strolling players (C) Hroswitha
(D) rich merchants (E) professional acting guilds

138. A versatile artist, the representative sculptor of his period, and immediate artistic ancestor of Michelangelo was
(A) Donatello (B) Cimabue (C) Giotto
(D) da Vinci (E) Ghiberti

139. All of the following operas were written by Puccini *except*
(A) *Norma* (B) *Madama Butterfly* (C) *La Boheme*
(D) *Gianni Schicchi* (E) *Tosca*

140. The Romantic poets were
(A) uninterested in personal liberty
(B) individualistic
(C) conformists
(D) appreciative of formal gardens
(E) all drug addicts

141. The first woman to earn her living as a novelist was
(A) George Eliot (B) Aphra Behn
(C) Harriet Beecher Stowe (D) George Sand
(E) Anna Mowatt Richie

142. Toulouse-Lautrec died from
(A) absinthe poisoning
(B) a fall from a cliff
(C) strychnine, administered by his mistress
(D) a knife wound, administered by a robber
(E) a kick in the head from a horse

143. Coleridge wrote all of the following *except*
(A) poetry (B) novels (C) dramas
(D) criticism (E) essays

144. This art is an example of
(A) expressionism
(B) impressionism
(C) Greek art
(D) Byzantine art
(E) primitive art

145. The author of the one-act plays *The Toilet* and *Dutchman* is
(A) Thomas Wolfe (B) James Baldwin
(C) Lorraine Hansbury (D) LeRoi Jones (Imamu Baraka)
(E) Countee Cullen

146. The modern musical *My Fair Lady* is based upon G.B. Shaw's play
(A) *Man and Superman* (B) *Back to Methusaleh* (C) *Pygmalion*
(D) *Candida* (E) *Arms and the Man*

Questions 147–149 refer to the following lines.

(A) "I have measured out my life in coffee spoons."

(B) "Do not go gentle into that good night,
Old age should burn and rave at close of day;
Rage, rage, against the dying of the light."

(C) "How did they fume, and stamp, and roar, and chafe!
And swear, not Addison himself was safe."

(D) "O Captain! my Captain! our fearful trip is done,
The ship has weather'd every rack, the prize we sought is won,
The port is near, the bells I hear, the people all exulting,
While follow eyes the steady keel, the vessel grim and daring;
But O heart! heart! heart!
O the bleeding drops of red,
Where on the deck my captain lies,
Fallen cold and dead."

(E) "Shall I compare thee to a summer's day?
Though art more lovely and more temperate."

147. Which alludes to the death of Abraham Lincoln?

148. Which is an example of a rhymed couplet?

149. Which is from a Shakesperean sonnet?

150. A cathedral noted for its famous rose windows is located at
(A) Canterbury
(B) Rome
(C) London
(D) Chartres
(E) Istanbul

ANSWER KEY—SAMPLE EXAMINATION 1

Section I

1. A
2. E
3. D
4. A
5. E
6. D
7. B
8. D
9. B
10. B
11. E
12. D
13. A
14. C
15. D
16. D
17. E
18. E
19. B
20. C
21. C
22. E
23. D
24. E
25. A
26. D
27. B
28. D
29. B
30. D
31. E
32. A
33. E
34. B
35. C
36. A
37. E
38. B
39. E
40. E
41. C
42. B
43. B
44. E
45. D
46. C
47. A
48. C
49. A
50. C
51. E
52. C
53. D
54. C
55. C
56. E
57. A
58. D
59. C
60. C
61. C
62. E
63. D
64. E
65. B
66. C*
67. E
68. B
69. C
70. C
71. E
72. C
73. A
74. B
75. E

Section II

76. D**
77. B
78. C
79. B
80. E
81. B
82. D
83. E
84. D
85. E
86. B
87. B
88. E
89. A
90. A
91. B
92. D
93. C
94. E
95. D
96. B
97. C
98. A
99. E
100. E
101. B
102. A
103. C
104. D
105. B
106. A
107. D
108. E
109. C
110. A
111. C
112. D
113. A
114. B
115. C
116. B
117. A
118. C
119. C
120. E
121. C
122. E
123. B
124. D
125. D
126. B
127. A
128. B
129. C
130. A
131. E
132. B
133. A
134. B
135. E
136. B
137. A
138. A
139. A
140. B
141. B
142. A
143. B
144. D***
145. D
146. C
147. D
148. C
149. E
150. D

*The Solomon R. Guggenheim Museum.

**Van Gogh, *The Starry Night*, 1889, Oil on Canvas, 29" x 36¼", Collection, the Museum of Modern Art, New York. Acquired through the Lillie B. Bliss Bequest.

***Enthroned Madonna and Child, Byzantine School, National Gallery of Art, Washington, D.C., Andrew Mellon Collection.

SCORING CHART—SAMPLE EXAMINATION 1

After you have scored your Sample Examination 1, enter the results in the chart below; then transfer your Raw Score to the Progress Chart on page 14.

Total Test	Number Right	Number Wrong	Number Omitted	Raw Score
Section I: 75				
Section II: 75				
Total: 150				

ANSWER EXPLANATIONS—SAMPLE EXAMINATION 1

Section I

1. A. The other works are either not operas or were not written by Beethoven.
2. E. The Renaissance "rediscovered" all of the glories of the Hellenistic world, including its art, literature, and philosophy.
3. D. This is true by definition.
4. A. A meter means a division of music into measures or bars.
5. E. *The Faerie Queene* is a social, political, and religious allegory, and is not to be taken as a factual representation of life.
6. D. The ceiling of the Sistine Chapel is one of Italy's greatest art treasures.
7. B. "Gothic" pertains to an architectural style prevalent in western Europe from the 12th through the 15th centuries.
8. D. Other countries have attempted to make westerns, but none has been successful.
9. B. Benvenuto Cellini (1500–1571) was an Italian sculptor, metal-worker, and author.
10. B. *Dr. Faustus* was written by Christopher Marlowe.
11. E. Louis XIV (1638–1715) was King of France from 1643 to 1715.
12. D. This is true by definition.
13. A. Impressionism was a late 19th century movement. The other composers listed are either not French, not Impressionist composers, or not both.
14. C. The Renaissance originated in Italy in the 14th century, and later spread through Europe. Leonardo da Vinci (1452–1519) lived during the peak of the Italian Renaissance.
15. D. This is true by definition.
16. D. The point is that man is "determined" by heredity and/or environment.
17. E. During other periods in time, all plays had a beginning, a middle, and an end.
18. E. The poem is divided into three canticles, each made up of thirty-three cantos, plus the first canto in "Inferno," which serves as an introduction to the entire poem.
19. B. Michelangelo was the famous painter of the Sistine Chapel.
20. C. Stock characters, such as the braggart soldier, the jealous husband, and the stubborn father, appear as far back as the Greek and Roman comedies.
21. C. Pavlova was promoted to prima ballerina in 1906, after a performance of *Swan Lake*.
22. E. This American primitive work was painted by an unknown artist, circa 1795.
23. D. This is true by definition.
24. E. It is believed *The Tempest* was written between 1611 and 1616. It was first published in the First Folio.
25. A. Isak Dinesen was the pen name of Karen Dinesen von Blixen. She signed her stories "Isak," meaning "he who laughs."
26. D. Goya was the leading painter, etcher, and designer of his day.
27. B. None of the others were Greek playwrights.
28. D. One of the most enduring popular examples of this genre is Mary Shelley's *Frankenstein*.
29. B. The work is *The Aeneid*.
30. D. *Parsifal* was first presented in 1882 in Bayreuth.
31. E. The flying buttress was a development in Gothic architecture.
32. A. Gauguin spent many years in Tahiti, painting native subjects.
33. E. Brecht has even written plays within plays within plays so that the audience is always aware it is attending a play, and not experiencing reality.
34. B. The Bayreux Tapestry depicts the Norman Conquest of England and the events leading up to it.
35. C. Athens was the home of the arts, mathematics, philosophy, etc.
36. A. The others are not 20th century painters.
37. E. The others are not 20th century poets.
38. B. The others are not 20th century composers of opera.

39. E. Aphrodite was the Greek goddess of love.
40. E. The play was written by Arthur Miller, and it ushered in a new concept of tragedy.
41. C. Intuition may be defined as the power or faculty of attaining to direct knowledge or cognition without rational thought. All the other terms imply rational thought.
42. B. Polybius is the only Greek slave in the group.
43. B. Remington is especially noted for his cowboys, Indians, and soldiers.
44. E. Rimsky-Korsakov (1844–1908) was a Russian composer.
45. D. Ludwig van Beethoven (1770–1827) studied with Mozart and Haydn and influenced the later Romantic composers.
46. C. The book Steinbeck wrote was entitled *Travels with Charlie*.
47. A. Auguste Rodin (1840–1917), the great French artist, was perhaps the greatest sculptor of his time.
48. C. *Orpheus and Eurydice* was written by Gluck.
49. A. Vachel Lindsay (1897–1931) was an American poet noted for his individualistic style, characterized by jazz-like rhythm.
50. C. The medieval liturgical drama developed during the celebration of the mass.
51. E. *Everyman* is a 15th century allegorical play. Everyman, the hero, is summoned by Death to appear before God. Of all his friends and virtues, only Good Deeds may accompany him.
52. C. The First Folio was printed in 1623.
53. D. Two of Dreiser's best known novels are *An American Tragedy* and *Sister Carrie*.
54. C. The other composers are not both from the Baroque period.
55. C. Each time a musician plays a jazz work, he or she interprets the piece. Jazz is notoriously individualistic and variable.
56. E. To select but one of the other answers would be to only partially explain surrealism.
57. A. These early medieval minstrels came from the lower classes. They usually accompanied themselves on a simple musical instrument, such as a lute.
58. D. This is one of the basic tenets of Platonism.
59. C. This is the only example of two composers, both Italian and of the Renaissance period.
60. C. Metaphysics may be defined as a branch of philosophy concerned with the nature and relations of being.
61. C. This is true by definition. The aside differs from the soliloquy in that, in the latter, the character reveals his thoughts in the form of a monologue, without addressing a listener.
62. E. To ignore any of the above would be to give an incomplete answer.
63. D. This line is spoken after the death of Othello, and refers to his intense passion for Desdemona, which led to his murdering her in a fit of jealousy.
64. E. This is true by definition.
65. B. This is true by definition.
66. C. Wright was a modern architect who believed in functional buildings, made of materials native to the region.
67. E. The clue is in the word "rediscovered." Renaissance means rebirth or revival of interest in learning.
68. B. Hemingway was a famous 20th century American writer who won the Nobel Prize for literature.
69. C. Dante's best known work is *The Divine Comedy*.
70. C. The Sea of Cortez, located in Mexico, sometimes called the Gulf of California, separates Baja California from Sonora.
71. E. The others are true, but only partial answers.
72. C. Plautus and Terence were the great Roman writers of comedy.
73. A. The word was coined from the title of Lewis' novel, *Babbitt*.
74. B. The sonnet sequence that opens with the line quoted is one of the most famous in English literature.
75. E. Elizabeth Barrett wrote the sonnet sequence for her future husband, Robert Browning.

Section II

76. D. The painting is "The Starry Night," by Van Gogh (1853–1890).

77. B. Ghosts often appeared in Elizabethan plays as dramatic symbols. The audience was accustomed to the dramatic use of the ghost.

78. C. Paxton first designed a similar but larger structure for the London Exhibition of 1851. In 1853 and 1854 he supervised the building of the Crystal Palace at Sydenham, England.

79. B. Agamemnon was the leader of the Greeks in the Trojan War. Upon his return from the war Clytaemnestra and Aegisthus, her lover, murdered Agamemnon in his bath.

80. E. This is true by definition.

81. B. This line is from Shakespeare's *Othello*.

82. D. Louis XIV ruled France from 1643 to 1715.

83. E. The Greeks did not use scenery in their plays.

84. D. Dramatic irony occurs when the audience understands the incongruity between a situation and the accompanying speeches, while the characters in the play remain unaware of the incongruity.

85. E. The modern meaning is that of a contrived or improbable conclusion.

86. B. Van Gogh is generally considered a Post-Impressionist.

87. B. This is true by definition.

88. E. Harmony, in music, refers to the structure of a musical composition from the point of view of its chordal characteristics and relationships.

89. A. Gregorian chants contain a single melodic line.

90. A. Gregorian chant is the monodic liturgical plainsong of the Roman Catholic Church.

91. B. Chagall is also well known for his stained glass windows which adorn churches and synagogues throughout Europe and Israel.

92. D. Two of Harte's best known short stories are "The Outcasts of Poker Flat" and "The Luck of Roaring Camp."

93. C. Angelou, born in Arkansas in 1928, also wrote *Singin' and Swingin' and Gettin' Merry Like Christmas* and *The Heart of a Woman*.

94. E. Gershwin was also the composer of the folk opera Porgy and Bess, as well as many popular songs.

95. D. The others are jazz figures, but none were barbers.

96. B. Ariosto's "Orlando Furioso" is the best known poem on the subject.

97. C. Francis of Assisi was the founder of the Franciscan Order and one of the greatest of Christian saints.

98. A. Schoenberg's twelve-tone system has become perhaps the most controversial musical development of the 20th century.

99. E. Modern satire is often intentionally offensive.

100. E. Wilde was noted for his linguistic wit.

101. B. Sondheim's latest musical is *Into the Woods*. He also wrote the lyrics for *West Side Story*.

102. A. The book is entitled *The Education of Henry Adams*.

103. C. The plots of the other plays mentioned are far different.

104. D. The Victorian Era was one of England's greatest periods. It was an era of artistic achievement, industrialization, and colonization.

105. B. Jose Clemente Orozco (1883–1949) was a painter of revolutionary murals. The imagination and emotional force of the murals in the Government Palace are impressively powerful.

106. A. The iamb is a metrical foot consisting of a short syllable followed by a long or an unstressed syllable followed by a stressed. "Pentameter" means "five meters," or feet, and so iambic pentameter equals five iambs to the line.

107. D. Under the rules of courtly love, the true knight was expected to be the epitome of the Christian man.

108. E. Delphi is located near Mount Parnassus in ancient Greece. The legendary founder of the oracle was the goddess Gaea.

109. C. The Gothic Period approximates the Middle Ages. It was during this period that the Roman Catholic Church had its greatest hold on the populace.

110. A. The Greek doctrine of hedonism states that pleasure is the highest good. In ancient times, hedonism was characteristic of the school of Aristippus.

111. C. Giotto (c.1266–c.1337), Florentine painter and architect, was a perfector of form and movement. His faces and gestures are graceful and lifelike.

112. D. The photograph is of a self-portrait by the 54-year-old Rembrandt whose long series of self-portraits records every stage of his career.

113. A. An ancient plum tree decorates these Japanese sliding screens from the study room of a Zen temple.

114. B. Monet's *Terrace at Sainte-Adresse,* shown in this photograph, is an Impressionist painting.

115. C. Stonehenge, a prehistoric structure, is located on Salisbury Plain, in England.

116. B. The origin of the griffin has been traced to the Hittites. It is also conspicuous in Assyrian and Persian sculpture.

117. A. Deucalion and his wife, Pyrrha, are the principal figures in the Greek flood story.

118. C. Sprung rhythm is a term for a mixed meter in which the foot consists of a stressed syllable which may stand alone, or be combined with from one to three more unstressed syllables.

119. C. Rembrandt van Rijn (1606–1669), Dutch painter and etcher, was the greatest master of the Dutch school.

120. E. This is a standard musical notation, a flat.

121. C. The other words have nothing to do with songs.

122. E. Cunegonde was the woman with whom Candide was in love.

123. B. Nefertiti was an ancient Egyptian queen, wife of Akhenaton, a pharoah who ruled from 1367 to 1350 B.C.

124. D. A triplet is three lines of poetry.

125. D. Melodrama is sometimes said to bear the same relation to tragedy that farce does to comedy. The protagonists are ultra-pure, the antagonists ultra-evil, and the credibility of both character and action is sacrificed for violent effect and emotional opportunism.

126. B. Frankie kills Johnny because he had been unfaithful to her.

127. A. In Sophoclean irony the characters are symbols of tragic human fate. In Euripidean tragedy, the irony lies in the inner psyche of humans, who no longer struggle with fate, but fight with the demons of their own souls; each person is responsible for his or her actions.

128. B. This is true by definition.

129. C. The Elizabethan theater, unlike the Greek, did not make use of a chorus.

130. A. Empiricism may be defined as the practice of relying upon observation and experiment, especially in the natural sciences.

131. E. Orpheus was so skilled in singing and in playing the lyre that he could enchant not only men and animals, but even trees and stones.

132. B. Eurydia appears in the *The Odyssey.*

133. A. None of the others mentioned was as knowledgeable and talented in so many areas as Cellini.

134. B. This is true by definition.

135. E. T.S. Eliot is known as the author of "The Wasteland, " "The Love Song of J. Alfred Prufrock, " the play *Murder in the Cathedral,* and a large number of other works.

136. B. Saint-Exupery tells his reader to look up to the stars, and listen for the laughter of the little prince.

137. A. The beginnings of the modern drama can be traced to the Quem Quaeritis Trope, based on the women's visit to Christ's tomb and acted out by 10th-century ecclesiastics at Easter.

138. A. Donatello (c. 1386–1466) was an Italian sculptor of the Italian Renaissance.

139. A. *Norma* was written by Vincenzo Bellini.

140. B. All of the other answers are completely untrue. The Romantic poets were concerned with individual liberty, were nonconformists, and liked wild, informal gardens, with a hermit ensconced on the property, if possible; only a few were drug addicts.

141. B. Aphra Behn (1640–1689) was an English poet, dramatist, and novelist.

142. A. Absinthe is a green liqueur having a bitter licorice flavor and a high alcohol content.

143. B. Coleridge was a versatile writer of prose and poetry, but he never worked in the genre of the novel.

144. D. Byzantine refers to the style developed in Byzantium from the 5th century A.D. It is characterized by formality of design, frontal, stylized presentation of figures, rich use of color, especially gold, and generally religious subject matter.

145. D. The contemporary American author LeRoi Jones changed his name to Imamu Baraka when he adopted the Muslim faith.

146. C. Shaw's early twentieth century *Pygmalion* is one of his most frequently performed plays. *My Fair Lady* is the musical by Lerner and Loewe.

147. D. The quote is from Walt Whitman's *O Captain! My Captain!*—a poem on Lincoln's death.

148. C. These two lines are an example of a heroic couplet—two rhymed lines of verse of ten syllables each, having the same meter. The example here was writtten by Alexander Pope, a master of the heroic couplet. It is from Pope's "An Epistle to Dr. Arbuthnot."

149. E. These are the first two lines of Shakespeare's Sonnet 18.

150. D. The Gothic cathedral of Chartres is located in northern France.

ANSWER SHEET — HUMANITIES/SAMPLE EXAMINATION 2

Section I

1. Ⓐ Ⓑ Ⓒ Ⓓ Ⓔ
2. Ⓐ Ⓑ Ⓒ Ⓓ Ⓔ
3. Ⓐ Ⓑ Ⓒ Ⓓ Ⓔ
4. Ⓐ Ⓑ Ⓒ Ⓓ Ⓔ
5. Ⓐ Ⓑ Ⓒ Ⓓ Ⓔ
6. Ⓐ Ⓑ Ⓒ Ⓓ Ⓔ
7. Ⓐ Ⓑ Ⓒ Ⓓ Ⓔ
8. Ⓐ Ⓑ Ⓒ Ⓓ Ⓔ
9. Ⓐ Ⓑ Ⓒ Ⓓ Ⓔ
10. Ⓐ Ⓑ Ⓒ Ⓓ Ⓔ
11. Ⓐ Ⓑ Ⓒ Ⓓ Ⓔ
12. Ⓐ Ⓑ Ⓒ Ⓓ Ⓔ
13. Ⓐ Ⓑ Ⓒ Ⓓ Ⓔ
14. Ⓐ Ⓑ Ⓒ Ⓓ Ⓔ
15. Ⓐ Ⓑ Ⓒ Ⓓ Ⓔ
16. Ⓐ Ⓑ Ⓒ Ⓓ Ⓔ
17. Ⓐ Ⓑ Ⓒ Ⓓ Ⓔ
18. Ⓐ Ⓑ Ⓒ Ⓓ Ⓔ
19. Ⓐ Ⓑ Ⓒ Ⓓ Ⓔ
20. Ⓐ Ⓑ Ⓒ Ⓓ Ⓔ
21. Ⓐ Ⓑ Ⓒ Ⓓ Ⓔ
22. Ⓐ Ⓑ Ⓒ Ⓓ Ⓔ
23. Ⓐ Ⓑ Ⓒ Ⓓ Ⓔ
24. Ⓐ Ⓑ Ⓒ Ⓓ Ⓔ
25. Ⓐ Ⓑ Ⓒ Ⓓ Ⓔ
26. Ⓐ Ⓑ Ⓒ Ⓓ Ⓔ
27. Ⓐ Ⓑ Ⓒ Ⓓ Ⓔ
28. Ⓐ Ⓑ Ⓒ Ⓓ Ⓔ
29. Ⓐ Ⓑ Ⓒ Ⓓ Ⓔ
30. Ⓐ Ⓑ Ⓒ Ⓓ Ⓔ
31. Ⓐ Ⓑ Ⓒ Ⓓ Ⓔ
32. Ⓐ Ⓑ Ⓒ Ⓓ Ⓔ
33. Ⓐ Ⓑ Ⓒ Ⓓ Ⓔ
34. Ⓐ Ⓑ Ⓒ Ⓓ Ⓔ
35. Ⓐ Ⓑ Ⓒ Ⓓ Ⓔ
36. Ⓐ Ⓑ Ⓒ Ⓓ Ⓔ
37. Ⓐ Ⓑ Ⓒ Ⓓ Ⓔ
38. Ⓐ Ⓑ Ⓒ Ⓓ Ⓔ
39. Ⓐ Ⓑ Ⓒ Ⓓ Ⓔ
40. Ⓐ Ⓑ Ⓒ Ⓓ Ⓔ
41. Ⓐ Ⓑ Ⓒ Ⓓ Ⓔ
42. Ⓐ Ⓑ Ⓒ Ⓓ Ⓔ
43. Ⓐ Ⓑ Ⓒ Ⓓ Ⓔ
44. Ⓐ Ⓑ Ⓒ Ⓓ Ⓔ
45. Ⓐ Ⓑ Ⓒ Ⓓ Ⓔ
46. Ⓐ Ⓑ Ⓒ Ⓓ Ⓔ
47. Ⓐ Ⓑ Ⓒ Ⓓ Ⓔ
48. Ⓐ Ⓑ Ⓒ Ⓓ Ⓔ
49. Ⓐ Ⓑ Ⓒ Ⓓ Ⓔ
50. Ⓐ Ⓑ Ⓒ Ⓓ Ⓔ
51. Ⓐ Ⓑ Ⓒ Ⓓ Ⓔ
52. Ⓐ Ⓑ Ⓒ Ⓓ Ⓔ
53. Ⓐ Ⓑ Ⓒ Ⓓ Ⓔ
54. Ⓐ Ⓑ Ⓒ Ⓓ Ⓔ
55. Ⓐ Ⓑ Ⓒ Ⓓ Ⓔ
56. Ⓐ Ⓑ Ⓒ Ⓓ Ⓔ
57. Ⓐ Ⓑ Ⓒ Ⓓ Ⓔ
58. Ⓐ Ⓑ Ⓒ Ⓓ Ⓔ
59. Ⓐ Ⓑ Ⓒ Ⓓ Ⓔ
60. Ⓐ Ⓑ Ⓒ Ⓓ Ⓔ
61. Ⓐ Ⓑ Ⓒ Ⓓ Ⓔ
62. Ⓐ Ⓑ Ⓒ Ⓓ Ⓔ
63. Ⓐ Ⓑ Ⓒ Ⓓ Ⓔ
64. Ⓐ Ⓑ Ⓒ Ⓓ Ⓔ
65. Ⓐ Ⓑ Ⓒ Ⓓ Ⓔ
66. Ⓐ Ⓑ Ⓒ Ⓓ Ⓔ
67. Ⓐ Ⓑ Ⓒ Ⓓ Ⓔ
68. Ⓐ Ⓑ Ⓒ Ⓓ Ⓔ
69. Ⓐ Ⓑ Ⓒ Ⓓ Ⓔ
70. Ⓐ Ⓑ Ⓒ Ⓓ Ⓔ
71. Ⓐ Ⓑ Ⓒ Ⓓ Ⓔ
72. Ⓐ Ⓑ Ⓒ Ⓓ Ⓔ
73. Ⓐ Ⓑ Ⓒ Ⓓ Ⓔ
74. Ⓐ Ⓑ Ⓒ Ⓓ Ⓔ
75. Ⓐ Ⓑ Ⓒ Ⓓ Ⓔ

Section II

76. Ⓐ Ⓑ Ⓒ Ⓓ Ⓔ
77. Ⓐ Ⓑ Ⓒ Ⓓ Ⓔ
78. Ⓐ Ⓑ Ⓒ Ⓓ Ⓔ
79. Ⓐ Ⓑ Ⓒ Ⓓ Ⓔ
80. Ⓐ Ⓑ Ⓒ Ⓓ Ⓔ
81. Ⓐ Ⓑ Ⓒ Ⓓ Ⓔ
82. Ⓐ Ⓑ Ⓒ Ⓓ Ⓔ
83. Ⓐ Ⓑ Ⓒ Ⓓ Ⓔ
84. Ⓐ Ⓑ Ⓒ Ⓓ Ⓔ
85. Ⓐ Ⓑ Ⓒ Ⓓ Ⓔ
86. Ⓐ Ⓑ Ⓒ Ⓓ Ⓔ
87. Ⓐ Ⓑ Ⓒ Ⓓ Ⓔ
88. Ⓐ Ⓑ Ⓒ Ⓓ Ⓔ
89. Ⓐ Ⓑ Ⓒ Ⓓ Ⓔ
90. Ⓐ Ⓑ Ⓒ Ⓓ Ⓔ
91. Ⓐ Ⓑ Ⓒ Ⓓ Ⓔ
92. Ⓐ Ⓑ Ⓒ Ⓓ Ⓔ
93. Ⓐ Ⓑ Ⓒ Ⓓ Ⓔ
94. Ⓐ Ⓑ Ⓒ Ⓓ Ⓔ
95. Ⓐ Ⓑ Ⓒ Ⓓ Ⓔ
96. Ⓐ Ⓑ Ⓒ Ⓓ Ⓔ
97. Ⓐ Ⓑ Ⓒ Ⓓ Ⓔ
98. Ⓐ Ⓑ Ⓒ Ⓓ Ⓔ
99. Ⓐ Ⓑ Ⓒ Ⓓ Ⓔ
100. Ⓐ Ⓑ Ⓒ Ⓓ Ⓔ
101. Ⓐ Ⓑ Ⓒ Ⓓ Ⓔ
102. Ⓐ Ⓑ Ⓒ Ⓓ Ⓔ
103. Ⓐ Ⓑ Ⓒ Ⓓ Ⓔ
104. Ⓐ Ⓑ Ⓒ Ⓓ Ⓔ
105. Ⓐ Ⓑ Ⓒ Ⓓ Ⓔ
106. Ⓐ Ⓑ Ⓒ Ⓓ Ⓔ
107. Ⓐ Ⓑ Ⓒ Ⓓ Ⓔ
108. Ⓐ Ⓑ Ⓒ Ⓓ Ⓔ
109. Ⓐ Ⓑ Ⓒ Ⓓ Ⓔ
110. Ⓐ Ⓑ Ⓒ Ⓓ Ⓔ
111. Ⓐ Ⓑ Ⓒ Ⓓ Ⓔ
112. Ⓐ Ⓑ Ⓒ Ⓓ Ⓔ
113. Ⓐ Ⓑ Ⓒ Ⓓ Ⓔ
114. Ⓐ Ⓑ Ⓒ Ⓓ Ⓔ
115. Ⓐ Ⓑ Ⓒ Ⓓ Ⓔ
116. Ⓐ Ⓑ Ⓒ Ⓓ Ⓔ
117. Ⓐ Ⓑ Ⓒ Ⓓ Ⓔ
118. Ⓐ Ⓑ Ⓒ Ⓓ Ⓔ
119. Ⓐ Ⓑ Ⓒ Ⓓ Ⓔ
120. Ⓐ Ⓑ Ⓒ Ⓓ Ⓔ
121. Ⓐ Ⓑ Ⓒ Ⓓ Ⓔ
122. Ⓐ Ⓑ Ⓒ Ⓓ Ⓔ
123. Ⓐ Ⓑ Ⓒ Ⓓ Ⓔ
124. Ⓐ Ⓑ Ⓒ Ⓓ Ⓔ
125. Ⓐ Ⓑ Ⓒ Ⓓ Ⓔ
126. Ⓐ Ⓑ Ⓒ Ⓓ Ⓔ
127. Ⓐ Ⓑ Ⓒ Ⓓ Ⓔ
128. Ⓐ Ⓑ Ⓒ Ⓓ Ⓔ
129. Ⓐ Ⓑ Ⓒ Ⓓ Ⓔ
130. Ⓐ Ⓑ Ⓒ Ⓓ Ⓔ
131. Ⓐ Ⓑ Ⓒ Ⓓ Ⓔ
132. Ⓐ Ⓑ Ⓒ Ⓓ Ⓔ
133. Ⓐ Ⓑ Ⓒ Ⓓ Ⓔ
134. Ⓐ Ⓑ Ⓒ Ⓓ Ⓔ
135. Ⓐ Ⓑ Ⓒ Ⓓ Ⓔ
136. Ⓐ Ⓑ Ⓒ Ⓓ Ⓔ
137. Ⓐ Ⓑ Ⓒ Ⓓ Ⓔ
138. Ⓐ Ⓑ Ⓒ Ⓓ Ⓔ
139. Ⓐ Ⓑ Ⓒ Ⓓ Ⓔ
140. Ⓐ Ⓑ Ⓒ Ⓓ Ⓔ
141. Ⓐ Ⓑ Ⓒ Ⓓ Ⓔ
142. Ⓐ Ⓑ Ⓒ Ⓓ Ⓔ
143. Ⓐ Ⓑ Ⓒ Ⓓ Ⓔ
144. Ⓐ Ⓑ Ⓒ Ⓓ Ⓔ
145. Ⓐ Ⓑ Ⓒ Ⓓ Ⓔ
146. Ⓐ Ⓑ Ⓒ Ⓓ Ⓔ
147. Ⓐ Ⓑ Ⓒ Ⓓ Ⓔ
148. Ⓐ Ⓑ Ⓒ Ⓓ Ⓔ
149. Ⓐ Ⓑ Ⓒ Ⓓ Ⓔ
150. Ⓐ Ⓑ Ⓒ Ⓓ Ⓔ

SAMPLE EXAMINATION 2

Section I

Number of Questions: 75
Time: 45 minutes

Directions: Each of the questions or incomplete statements below is followed by five suggested answers or completions. Select the one that is best in each case.

1. The French legend that dates from the time of Charlemagne is
   (A) *The Song of Ganelon* (B) *The Song of Roland*
   (C) *The Song of Charlemagne* (D) *Heloise and Abelard*
   (E) *The Decameron*

2. A playwright often called the "father of the thesis play" is
   (A) Oscar Wilde (B) Jean Racine (C) William D'Avenant
   (D) Henrik Ibsen (E) Hermann Hesse

3. The Greek tragedies *Oedipus the King* and *Oedipus at Colonnus* were written by
   (A) Aeschylus (B) Aristophanes (C) Sophocles
   (D) Aristotle (E) Euripides

4. The most popular meter in English poetry is
   (A) trochaic trimeter
   (B) anapestic dimeter
   (C) the alexandrine
   (D) iambic hexameter
   (E) iambic pentameter

5. In music, the notation < indicates
   (A) diminuendo
   (B) crescendo
   (C) sharp
   (D) flat
   (E) natural

6. In art, *fresco* is
   (A) a form of sculpture
   (B) diverse materials pasted on a picture surface
   (C) a technique of dotting a surface with color
   (D) a light-and-dark technique
   (E) painting on moist plaster

7. What is commonly called the "song book" of the Bible?
   (A) Proverbs (B) Song of Deborah (C) Ecclesiastes
   (D) The Psalms (E) Daniel

8. *Lysistrata* is considered a great classical satire because
   (A) the protagonist is a good comedian
   (B) it was written about war
   (C) the author has been dead 2,000 years
   (D) it continues to be relevant
   (E) it deals with sex

9. Menotti wrote all of the following *except*
   (A) *The Medium*
   (B) *The Telephone*
   (C) *The Rake's Progress*
   (D) *The Consul*
   (E) *Amahl and the Night Visitor*

10. The photograph (right) is an example of
   (A) neolithic art
   (B) Corinthian art
   (C) Greek art
   (D) Renaissance art
   (E) Egyptian art

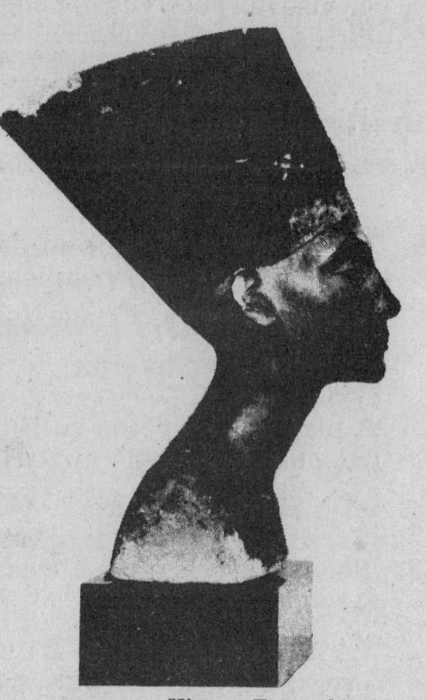

Hirmer Fotoarchiv Munchen

11. *A priori* knowledge is
   (A) knowledge obtained from sensory experience
   (B) knowledge existing in the mind before sensory experience
   (C) a concept stressed particularly by the empiricist
   (D) a concept denied by the objective realist
   (E) knowledge verified by inductive evidence

12. The conclusion of *Candide* is that
   (A) "whatever is, is right"
   (B) "love conquers all"
   (C) "do unto others as you would have others do unto you"
   (D) "we must cultivate our gardens"
   (E) "the end justifies the means"

13. The prefix "ur-" (as in *Ur-Faust, Ur-Hamlet*) means
   (A) early or primitive (B) alternate (C) pirated
   (D) last known (E) composite

14. All of the following are 19th-century Russian writers *except*
   (A) Chekhov (B) Nabokov (C) Tolstoy
   (D) Turgenev (E) Dostoevsky

15. The term *chamber music* can be applied to all of the following *except*
   (A) quartets (B) quintets (C) trios
   (D) symphonies (E) duo sonatas

16. An outside wall of a room or building carried above an adjoining roof and pierced with windows is called a
   (A) transept (B) clerestory (C) pilaster
   (D) transverse arch (E) atrium

17. A contemporary of E. A. Robinson, Edgar Lee Masters, Stephen Crane, and Theodore Dreiser, this poet holds a permanent place in American literature because his poetry is not only highly original, but also stresses the problems of his age. He is
(A) Robert Morse Lovett (B) Walt Whitman
(C) Vachel Lindsay (D) Robinson Jeffers
(E) William Vaughn Moody

18. This female satirist, known especially for her novel *Ethan Frome*, was influenced by Henry James, and her interests were centered mainly in the changing society of New York City. She is
(A) Edith Wharton (B) Lily Bart (C) Zelda Fitzgerald
(D) Dorothy Parker (E) Willa Cather

19. The blind seer who appears in several Greek tragedies is
(A) Tiresias (B) Homer (C) Clytaemnestra
(D) Oedipus (E) Agamemnon

20. A large composition for voices and orchestra, usually based on a religious text, is
(A) an aria (B) an oratorio (C) a capella
(D) a madrigal (E) a mass

21. France's two greatest writers of classical tragedy were
(A) Molière and Rostand
(B) Corneille and Racine
(C) Jarry and Racine
(D) Molière and Corneille
(E) Balzac and Hugo

22. The above painting is
(A) Whistler's "Arrangement in Gray and Black"
(B) Klee's "Around the Fish"
(C) Picasso's "Guernica"
(D) Dürer's "Four Horsemen of the Apocalypse"
(E) Poussin's "Triumph of Neptune and Amphitrite"

23. The author of *The Flies* and *The Clouds* was
(A) Beckett (B) Sartre (C) Menander
(D) Aristophanes (E) Molière

24. Of the following statements concerning a literary work read in translation, which is true?
(A) It cannot escape the linguistic characteristics of the language into which it is turned.
(B) Often one loses the *shade* of meaning when translating from an ancient language.
(C) The translated work reflects the individuality of the age in which it is done.
(D) Both A and B
(E) All of the above

25. The author of "Waltzing Matilda" and "The Man from Snowy River" was the Australian poet
(A) Hart Crane (B) "Banjo" Paterson (C) Lincoln Steffens
(D) T.S. Eliot (E) Allen Ginsberg

26. The musical notation 𝄢 : represents
(A) the bass clef
(B) the treble clef
(C) sharp
(D) flat
(E) diminuendo

27. Which of the following is a multitalented writer of poetry, prose, and children's books, and a guide to Washington, D.C. restaurants?
(A) Judith Viorst (B) Anita Kennedy (C) Nora Ephron
(D) Frances Harmon (E) Rebecca Whitley

28. In the theater, the exploitation of "tender" emotions for their own sake—that is, whether motivated by the action or not—is called
(A) virtue (B) temperamentality (C) melodrama
(D) drama (E) sentimentality

29. If you raise a musical note from G to G sharp, or lower a note from E to E flat, you are practicing
(A) staffing
(B) writing musical shorthand
(C) lengthening the composition
(D) harmonizing
(E) alteration

30. When the fingers of the hand that holds the bow are used to pluck the strings of an instrument, we call this
(A) fortissimo (B) dissonance (C) pizzicato
(D) diminuendo (E) espressivo

31. Perhaps the "perfect courtier" of the Renaissance was
(A) Castiglione (B) Shakespeare (C) Maddox of Leicester
(D) Henry VIII (E) Andrew the Chaplain

32. The beaker in the photograph (right) is
(A) Egyptian
(B) Peruvian
(C) Byzantine
(D) Roman
(E) Greek

The Metropolitan Museum of Art, Rogers Fund, 1917.

Questions 33–35 refer to the following quotation.

"All nature is but Art, unknown to thee;
All Chance, Direction, which thou canst not see;
All Discord, Harmony not understood;
All partial Evil, universal Good:
And, spite of Pride, in erring Reason's spite,
One truth is clear, *Whatever is, is Right.*"

33. The preceding lines are from
(A) Yeats' "Sailing to Byzantium"
(B) Tennyson's "In Memoriam"
(C) Whitman's "Song of Myself"
(D) Wordsworth's "Ode on Intimations of Immortality"
(E) Pope's "Essay on Man"

34. The verse form is the
(A) sestina (B) ballad (C) heroic couplet
(D) sonnet (E) haiku

35. The meter is
(A) iambic pentameter (B) trochaic dimeter
(C) anapestic tetrameter (D) iambic tetrameter
(E) trochaic pentameter

36. The philosopher Nietzsche, from whom the Nazis derived some of their doctrines, taught that the basic human motivation is
(A) intellectual curiosity (B) sensual pleasure
(C) the desire for wealth (D) sex (E) the will to power

37. Two 20th-century composers of atonal music are
(A) Bartok and Schoenberg (B) Stravinsky and Debussy
(C) Ives and Wagner (D) Prokofiev and Poulenc
(E) Rimsky-Korsakov and Rachmaninoff

38. The novels of Honoré de Balzac are known collectively as
(A) *"Pere Goriot" and Other Stories*
(B) *The Collected Works of Honore de Balzac*
(C) *The Human Tragedy*
(D) *The Human Comedy*
(E) *Tales of the Tatras*

39. Which one of the following was a Renaissance painter?
(A) Degas
(B) Picasso
(C) Michelangelo
(D) Goya
(E) Gainsborough

40. "To be, or not to be," is the beginning of a famous soliloquy from
(A) *Dr. Faustus* (B) *Romeo and Juliet* (C) *Tamburlaine*
(D) *Othello* (E) *Hamlet*

41. Just as Aristophanes used satire and humor to attack the existing society in early Athens, so did an American author use these media to express the discrepancy between American expectations and the very disturbing reality of his times. He is
(A) Charles Brockden Brown (B) Augustus Longstreet
(C) Robert Frost (D) Edwin Arlington Robinson
(E) Mark Twain

42. A period of enthusiasm for the classics in art, architecture, literature, drama, etc., is known as
(A) the Age of Enlightenment (B) the Neo-Classic Age
(C) Romantic Age (D) the Classical Age
(E) the Renaissance

43. The painter who became interested in politics and who, under Napoleon, became First Painter of the Empire was:
(A) Goya (B) Gros (C) Géricault (D) Ingres
(E) David

44. Which word comes from the Greek term meaning "unknown" or "without knowledge"?
(A) metaphysics (B) axiology (C) agnosticism
(D) pragmatism (E) skepticism

45. After the Dark Ages, the first professional people to make songs popular were called
(A) troubadors (B) barbershop quartets (C) castrati
(D) church choirs (E) motets

46. In a Greek drama, the protagonist's tragic flaw is frequently pride; in a Greek comedy, it is often
(A) anguish (B) single-mindedness (C) open-mindedness
(D) lust (E) super-intellectualism

47. Stimulated by the Cubist style, the Italian artists who introduced the additional concept of movement in "space-time" were the
(A) Expressionists (B) Impressionists (C) Non-objectivists
(D) Futurists (E) Romanticists

48. Henri Matisse is to Fauvism what Edvard Munch is to
(A) Impressionism (B) Surrealism (C) Cubism
(D) German Expressionism (E) *Die Brucke*

49. Franz Liszt
(A) used classical forms in his music
(B) experimented with atonal music
(C) used romantic forms such as the tone poem
(D) was a virtuoso performer on the violin
(E) rejected the ideals of romanticism

50. In Greek legend, who killed his father, married his mother, and became King of Thebes?
(A) Polynices (B) Agamemnon (C) Laius
(D) Oedipus (E) Jason

51. Johann Strauss is best known for his
(A) waltzes (B) tone poems (C) fugues (D) sonatas
(E) symphonies

52. Often considered the "showpiece of French realism" is
(A) Flaubert's *Madame Bovary* (B) Balzac's *Eugénie Grandet*
(C) Hugo's *Les Misérables* (D) Zola's *Nana*
(E) Voltaire's *The Huron*

53. In an orthodox sense, Arabic literature begins with
(A) *The Rubáiyát* **(B) *The Koran*** (C) *The Book of the Dead*
(D) *The Ramayana* **(E) *The Mahabharata***

Questions 54 and 55 refer to the photograph below.

54. The work pictured is
(A) Michelangelo's "David"
(B) Michelangelo's "Pietá"
(C) "The Nike of Samothrace"
(D) Brancusi's "Father and Son"
(E) Praxiteles' "Hermes"

Hirmer Fotoarchiv Munchen

55. If you wanted to see sculpture of this type in the city where it was created, you would visit
(A) Paris
(B) Washington, D.C.
(C) Rome
(D) Greece
(E) Munich

56. The view that the mind is passive, or a *tabula rasa* upon which experience writes, and that the senses are more reliable than reason, was held by
(A) Hegel (B) Socrates (C) Locke (D) Kant (E) Plato

57. According to legend, what was the cause of the Trojan War?
(A) Argos's need for more land
(B) The sacrifice of Iphigenia
(C) The adultery of Clytaemnestra
(D) The murder of Aegisthus
(E) The kidnapping of Helen by Paris

58. "The Executions of May Third, 1808" was painted by
(A) Goya (B) Canova (C) Vignon (D) Ingres (E) David

59. A writer who exerted a profound influence on the development of the American short story was William Sidney Porter, better known as
(A) Artemus Ward (B) Josh Billings (C) Edgar Allan Poe
(D) Mark Twain (E) O. Henry

60. An American author best known for his depictions of the old French Quarter of New Orleans, ante-bellum plantations, and the survival of the chivalric code in the South is
(A) Rhett Butler (B) George Washington Cable
(C) Joel Chandler Harris (D) William Faulkner
(E) Joseph Lee

61. The most sensitively expressive of all musical instruments made by the family of Stradivari is the
(A) drum (B) violin (C) cymbal (D) oboe (E) piano

62. A contemporary of Johann Sebastian Bach, though not as great an innovator, nevertheless one of the most successful of the world's serious composers, was
(A) Beethoven (B) Mendelssohn (C) Handel
(D) Silbermann (E) Schmidt

63. The one-eyed giant whom Odysseus met on his voyage was named
(A) Dryope (B) Polyphemus (C) Aeolus
(D) Circe (E) Medea

64. The proximity of the audience to the players influenced some of the theatrical devices used by Shakespeare and made feasible
(A) the soliloquy (B) the appearance of boys in feminine roles
(C) the use of special effects (D) music with dance sequences
(E) the use of pantomime

65. The three hideous sisters of Greek mythology, one of whom (Medusa) was killed by Perseus, were called
(A) Gorgons (B) Sphinxes (C) Furies (D) Sirens
(E) Charities

66. The music Beethoven wrote for the theater was all of the following *except*
(A) based on a theme of the quest for individual liberty
(B) based on the cause of popular freedom
(C) reflective of high moral purpose
(D) religious in nature
(E) based on an ideal of human creativity

67. In poetry, the omission of one or more final unstressed syllables is called
(A) anacrusis (B) catalexis (C) feminine rhyme
(D) masculine rhyme (E) caesura

68. Penelope's chief suitor was named
(A) Telemachus (B) Oedipus (C) Creon
(D) Telegonus (E) Antinous

69. Because of his innovations of style, his free hand with form, and his use of extra-musical devices, the man often called the first Romantic composer is
(A) Liszt (B) Beethoven (C) Haydn (D) Mozart
(E) von Weber

70. The great French tragic dramatist of the Neo-Classic period was
(A) Racine (B) Pascal (C) Molière
(D) La Fontaine (E) Sainte-Beuve

71. A stale phrase used where a fresh one is needed is
(A) parallelism (B) a cliché (C) denouement
(D) poetic license (E) a pun

72. Poetry that is not so much read as looked at is called
(A) structured poetry (B) nonsense verse (C) gnomic poetry
(D) euphuistic verse (E) concrete verse

73. Shelley's elegy on the death of John Keats is
(A) "In Memoriam" (B) "Adonais" (C) "Thyrsis"
(D) "Lycidas" (E) "Stanzas Written in Dejection near Naples"

74. Thomas Henry Huxley was
(A) primarily a man of letters
(B) author of *Brave New World*
(C) devoted to the popularization of science
(D) noted for his florid, romantic style
(E) the founder of *The Spectator*

75. A florid, ornate portion of prose or poetry, which stands out by its rhythm, diction, or figurative language, is called
(A) pure poetry (B) a purple passage
(C) quantitative verse (D) prosody (E) hyperbole

Section II

Number of Questions: 75
Time: 45 minutes

Directions: Each of the questions or incomplete statements below is followed by five suggested answers or completions. Select the one that is best in each case.

Photo Alinari

76. The above painting is
(A) Donatello's "Annunciation" (B) Correggio's "Holy Night"
(C) Raphael's "Sistine Madonna" (D) Botticelli's "Birth of Venus"
(E) Rogier van der Weyden's "Nativity"

77. A well-known sonneteer of the 14th century was
(A) Petrarch (B) Dante (C) Shakespeare
(D) Shelley (E) Boccaccio

78. Today's audiences would find strange the theater for which Shakespeare wrote because they
(A) prefer to attend matinees
(B) are not accustomed to intermissions
(C) prefer simple sets and costumes
(D) are not used to listening to such complex language
(E) are less well educated

79. The literal meaning of the word "Renaissance" is
(A) rebirth (B) clarification (C) analysis
(D) enlightenment (E) question

80. Canio is the famous clown from the opera
(A) *I Pagliacci* (B) *Rigoletto* (C) *Cavalleria Rusticana*
(D) *Gianni Schicchi* (E) *Così fan tutte*

81. The English language is most closely related to which of the following in the structure of its sentences?
(A) Latin (B) German (C) French (D) Bulgarian
(E) Italian

82. The period in English literature called the "Restoration" is commonly regarded as running from
(A) 1300 to 1450 (B) 1500 to 1550 (C) 1660 to 1700
(D) 1798 to 1848 (E) 1848 to 1900

83. The above is a photograph of
(A) a Greek temple (B) a Roman temple
(C) an Egyptian temple (D) the University of South Florida
(E) the University of Mexico

84. **Walter Pater believed that one should**
(A) "cultivate one's own garden"
(B) "justify the ways of God to man"
(C) "follow the sun"
(D) "burn with a hard, gem-like flame"
(E) "contemplate the Absolute"

85. **The expressive combination of re-enforced concrete material, cantilevered construction, and a dramatic site are characteristic of the modern architect**
(A) J. J. P. Oud **(B) Walter Gropius** **(C) Louis Sullivan**
(D) Frank Lloyd Wright **(E) Le Corbusier**

86. **The "Theater of the Absurd" is basically**
(A) ridiculous **(B) emotional** **(C) comic** **(D) tragic**
(E) intellectual

87. What daughter of an American president has successfully established herself as a mystery writer?
(A) Amy Carter (B) Margaret Truman (C) Tricia Nixon Cox
(D) Julie Nixon Eisenhower (E) Lynda Johnson Robb

88. **Don Quixote's horse was named**
(A) Escudero **(B) Rocinante** **(C) Sancho Panza**
(D) Dulcinea **(E) Gringolet**

89. A modern folklorist, author of *The Hero with a Thousand Faces,* is
(A) Jacob Grimm (B) Margaret Hunt (C) Padriac Colum
(D) Joseph Stern (E) Joseph Campbell.

90. Sir Arthur Conan Doyle's famous character Sherlock Holmes, the Victorian sleuth, was
(A) based on a character from Edgar Allan Poe
(B) known to be addicted to cocaine
(C) believed to be Jack the Ripper
(D) based on a well-known detective of the time, James Edmunds
(E) killed in an airplane accident

91. **The institution of the villain in drama goes back to**
(A) the Greek epics
(B) the medieval romance
(C) Christianity and the writings of Machiavelli
(D) the Protestant attack on corrupt clergy
(E) an ancient source, probably a ritual

92. **The slogan of the 19th-century Aesthetic Movement was**
(A) "Art is the opiate of the masses"
(B) "Art is life"
(C) "Art for art's sake"
(D) "What is art, that it should have a sake?"
(E) "Burn with a hard, gem-like flame"

93. **The most famous medieval tapestry is the**
(A) Bayeux **(B) Byzantine** **(C) Canterbury**
(D) Hastings **(E) Norman**

94. The main difference between the Pantheon (in Italy) and the Parthenon (in Greece) is that
(A) the Parthenon was constructed of raw concrete
(B) the Pantheon used red bricks and mortar
(C) the Pantheon is topped with a dome, while the roof of the Parthenon is triangular
(D) the Parthenon used plain pillars without any ornamentation, while those in the Pantheon are elaborately decorated
(E) the floor space in the Parthenon is about four times larger

95. The Greek tragedy *Antigone* was written by
(A) Socrates (B) Plato (C) Aristotle
(D) Sophocles (E) Agamemnon

96. The poignant line "But where are the snows of yesteryear?" is from "The Ballade of Dead Ladies" by
(A) Francois Villon (B) Percy Bysshe Shelley (C) John Keats
(D) William Shakespeare (E) Lord Byron

97. Which of the following Hindu holy books especially influenced the so-called "beat generation" of poets and novelists?
(A) *The Bhagavad-Gita*
(B) *Upanishads*
(C) *Carmina Burana*
(D) *Jaina Sutras*
(E) *Mahabharata*

98. When people started to sing different tunes together, which of the following had its beginnings?
(A) Monophony (B) Jazz (C) Polyphony
(D) A capella (E) Homophony

99. During the Renaissance, composers attempting to express a line of poetry in music developed the
(A) madrigal (B) symphony (C) motet
(D) harmony (E) sonata

100. *The Charterhouse of Parma* was written by
(A) Hoffman
(B) Balzac
(C) Dumas
(D) Stendhal
(E) Pushkin

101. *Waverly, Ivanhoe,* and *Quentin Durward* were written by
(A) Sir Thomas Hardy (B) Sir Walter Scott
(C) Henry Makepeace Thackeray (D) Charlotte Brontë
(E) Emily Brontë

102. The medieval poem "Piers Plowman" belongs to the literature of
(A) chivalry (B) social protest (C) mythology
(D) social satire (E) pastoral philosophy

103. The greatest Spanish painter of the 17th century, who worked almost exclusively on portraits of the nobility and court figures, was
(A) Velásquez (B) Murillo (C) Goya (D) Utrillo
(E) El Greco

104. The French novelist George Sand was the mistress of which famous composer?
(A) Verdi (B) Rachmaninoff (C) Prokofiev (D) Chopin
(E) Mahler

105. In music, gradual decrease of tempo is called
(A) retardando (B) accelerando (C) moderato
(D) presto (E) allegro

106. The philosophy best represented by the statement "true ideas are those that work" is
(A) rationalism (B) positivism (C) empiricism
(D) pragmatism (E) Thomism

107. This is an example of
(A) Hindu art
(B) Chinese art
(C) Egyptian art
(D) primitive art
(E) Etruscan art

108. The Russian writer thought to have coined the word "nihilist" was
(A) Chekhov (B) Dostoevsky (C) Pushkin
(D) Tolstoy (E) Turgenev

109. Which one of the following do most critics consider the greatest novel ever written?
(A) *War and Peace*
(B) *The Brothers Karamazov*
(C) *The Forsyte Saga*
(D) *The Sound and the Fury*
(E) *Pride and Prejudice*

110. How many muses were there in Greek mythology?
(A) 3 (B) 4 (C) 7 (D) 9 (E) 11

111. In three novels, called collectively *U.S.A.*, this author employed interludes he dubbed "The Camera Eye" and "Newsreels." The author is
(A) John Dos Passos (B) James Jones (C) John Steinbeck
(D) Truman Capote (E) John P. Marquand

112. The "Father of the Irish Renaissance" was
(A) George Moore (B) George Russell (C) J. M. Synge
(D) W. B. Yeats (E) G. B. Shaw

113. Josiah Wedgwood began making pottery in England during which period?
(A) Medieval (B) Renaissance (C) Neo-Classic
(D) Romantic (E) Victorian

114. A contemporary choreographer whose ballets include "Fancy Free" and the dances in *West Side Story* is
(A) Michael Kidd (B) Agnes de Mille (C) Jerome Robbins
(D) John Cranko (E) Gene Kelly

115. All of the following are Italian film directors who have achieved world-wide fame since 1945 *except*
(A) Roberto Rossellini
(B) Michaelangelo Antonioni
(C) Michelangelo Buonarroti
(D) Federico Fellini
(E) Vittorio de Sica

116. Which one of the following was *not* considered a medieval knightly virtue?
(A) Chastity (B) Honesty (C) Fortitude
(D) Faithfulness (E) Duplicity

117. Chaucer wrote in the dialect of
(A) Mercia (B) Wessex (C) Kent (D) Northumbria
(E) London

Questions 118–120 refer to the following quotation.

"Ring out the old, ring in the new;
Ring, happy bells, across the snow:
The year is going, let him go;
Ring out the false, ring in the true."

118. The lines are quoted from
(A) Tennyson's "In Memoriam"
(B) Milton's "Lycidas"
(C) Browning's "Pippa Passes"
(D) Anonymous: "Christmas Bells"
(E) Poe's "The Bells"

119. The verse form is a
(A) sonnet (B) quatrain (C) couplet (D) tercet
(E) cinquaine

120. The rhyme scheme is
(A) a b a b (B) a b c d (C) a b b c (D) a b b a
(E) a b c b

121. Impressionism found its most frequent expression in painting and music, but there was at least one sculptor who utilized the principles of Impressionism in his work:
(A) Gustave Moreau (B) Odilon Redon
(C) Giovanni Segantini (D) P. W. Steer
(E) Auguste Rodin

122. A contemporary Russian novelist who experienced political difficulties with Soviet authorities because of his criticisms of Stalin and communism is
(A) Ivan Denisovich (B) Konstantin Fedin
(C) Pavel Antokolsky (D) Aleksandr Solzhenitsyn
(E) Alexander Bek

123. Instrumental music which stands on its own merits and has no intrinsic association with extra-musical ideas is called
(A) absolute music (B) national music
(C) extra-musical music (D) liturgical music
(E) program music

124. The first Gothic novel was written in 1764 by Horace Walpole. It was
(A) *The Castle of Otranto* (B) *Frankenstein*
(C) *Caleb Williams* (D) *Northanger Abbey* (E) *Dracula*

125. When an author selects a title for a novel, he may quote another author. When Ernest Hemingway chose *For Whom the Bell Tolls* as the title for his novel about the Spanish Civil War, he was referring to
(A) a poem by Andrew Marvell (B) a satire by Juvenal
(C) a meditation by John Donne (D) a tragedy by John Ford
(E) an essay by William Hazlitt

126. A Gilbert and Sullivan operetta that had a successful revival in London and on Broadway, and even made its way to the movie screen, is
(A) *Iolanthe* (B) *The Mikado* (C) *The Pirates of Penzance*
(D) *H.M.S. Pinafore* (E) *Ruddigore*

127. Samuel Johnson attached the label "Metaphysical Poets" to which of the following groups?
(A) Donne, Marvel, Crashaw, and Herbert
(B) Dryden, Pope, and Young
(C) Greene, Jonson, and Herrick
(D) Shakespeare, Milton, and Pope
(E) Wordsworth, Keats, Shelley, and Byron

128. One of America's best-loved humorists, known for his satiric essays and hilarious cartoons, is
(A) Berke Breathed (B) Walt Kelly (C) Mark Twain
(D) William Zinsser (E) James Thurber

129. Which of the following lists of musical periods is arranged in the correct chronological sequence?
(A) Renaissance, Classical, Baroque
(B) Classical, Medieval, Romantic
(C) Renaissance, Baroque, Romantic
(D) Romantic, Renaissance, Baroque
(E) Medieval, Baroque, Renaissance

130. **The artist usually considered the father of modern abstract sculpture is**
(A) Brancusi (B) Maillol (C) Rodin
(D) Lehmbruck (E) Archipenko

131. **Most readers consider *Frankenstein* only a horror story about a fabricated monster. Few realize it has a social theme of**
(A) racial prejudice
(B) class bigotry
(C) the rejection by society of an individual who differs from the norm
(D) sexual immorality
(E) an individual's dependence upon drugs

132. *Frankenstein* was written in 1817 by
(A) Sir Walter Scott (B) Horace Walpole
(C) William Godwin (D) Mary Godwin
(E) Mary Wollstonecraft Shelley

Questions 133–135 refer to the following quotation.

"It is an ancient Mariner
And he stoppeth one of three.
'By thy long gray beard and glittering eye,
Now wherefore stopp'st thou me?"

133. **The lines were written by**
(A) Keats (B) Eliot (C) Coleridge (D) Tennyson
(E) Shelley

134. **The form is a**
(A) tercet (B) quatrain (C) rondelay (D) haiku
(E) sestina

135. **The form of the whole poem is**
(A) a ballade
(B) a dramatic monologue
(C) a traditional ballad
(D) a literary ballad
(E) an unconventional form which the author invented for this poem and never used again

136. The contemporary American author of *The Fire Next Time* and *Tell Me How Long the Train's Been Gone* is
(A) James Baldwin (B) Margaret Walker
(C) LeRoi Jones (Imamu Baraka) (D) Frederick Douglass
(E) John Williams

137. The immediate intention of the comic theater is to
(A) show the absurdity of life
(B) make us feel better
(C) drive a group of people into hysterical laughter
(D) act as an emotional tranquilizer
(E) convert the audience into giggling optimists

138. In the beginning, conductors performed their task from
(A) a podium
(B) the right side of the stage
(C) the left side of the stage
(D) an instrument, usually a clavier
(E) a pit hidden from the audience

139. "What animal goes in the morning on four feet, at noon on two, and in the evening on three?" is the riddle posed by the
(A) Griffin (B) Jabberwock (C) Sphinx (D) Muses
(E) Furies

140. While David extolled the virtues and nobility of the conqueror Napoleon in his paintings, another artist depicted the sufferings of a subjugated people. He was
(A) Rodin (B) Gros (C) Géricault (D) Goya
(E) Ingres

141. All of the following were essayists of the English Romantic Movement *except*
(A) De Quincey (B) Lamb (C) Addison (D) Hazlitt
(E) Hunt

142. The "vast chain of being" is an important concept of the
(A) 16th century (B) 17th century (C) 18th century
(D) 19th century (E) 20th century

143. The first composer to use hammering repetition as a dramatic device was
(A) Schmoll (B) Beethoven (C) Oberon (D) Offenbach
(E) Stravinsky

144. A 19th-century writer noted for his short stories about life in India and his novels, poems, and children's stories was
(A) George Orwell (B) Thomas Hardy (C) John Masefield
(D) Joseph Conrad (E) Rudyard Kipling

145. In the lines, "Hail to thee, blithe Spirit! Bird thou never wert," the bird referred to is a
(A) sparrow (B) nightingale (C) robin (D) skylark
(E) mockingbird

146. A defector from the Soviet Union and a British Dame formed one of the greatest ballet teams of all time. They are
(A) Mikhail Baryshnikov and Cyd Charisse
(B) Vaslav Nijinsky and Isadora Duncan
(C) Boris Chaliapin and Martha Graham
(D) Rudolf Nureyev and Margot Fonteyn
(E) Jacques d'Amboise and Maria Tallchief

147. Jane Austen's novels *Pride and Prejudice* and *Emma* deal with
(A) the English lower middle-class
(B) the English working class
(C) the problem of getting married
(D) child labor laws
(E) the plight of coal miners in Wales

148. Robert Browning is especially noted for his
(A) short stories **(B)** dramatic monologues **(C)** sonnets
(D) ballads **(E)** dirges

149. The painting of Leda and the swan is associated with which Renaissance artist?
(A) Michelangelo (B) Botticelli (C) daVinci (D) Correggio
(E) Masaccio

150. In scansion of poetry, the symbol / indicates
(A) a slight pause within a line **(B)** a foot
(C) read more slowly **(D)** read faster **(E)** stress the syllable

ANSWER KEY—SAMPLE EXAMINATION 2

Section I

1.	B	14.	B	27.	A	40.	E	52.	A	64.	A
2.	D	15.	D	28.	E	41.	E	53.	B	65.	A
3.	C	16.	B	29.	E	42.	B	54.	E	66.	D
4.	E	17.	E	30.	C	43.	E	55.	D	67.	B
5.	B	18.	A	31.	A	44.	C	56.	C	68.	E
6.	E	19.	A	32.	E	45.	A	57.	E	69.	E
7.	D	20.	B	33.	E	46.	B	58.	A	70.	A
8.	D	21.	B	34.	C	47.	D	59.	E	71.	B
9.	C	22.	C*	35.	A	48.	D	60.	B	72.	E
10.	E	23.	D	36.	E	49.	C	61.	B	73.	B
11.	B	24.	E	37.	A	50.	D	62.	C	74.	C
12.	D	25.	B	38.	D	51.	A	63.	B	75.	B
13.	A	26.	A	39.	C						

Section II

76.	D	89.	E	102.	B	115.	C	127.	A	139.	C
77.	A	90.	B	103.	A	116.	E	128.	E	140.	D
78.	D	91.	C	104.	D	117.	E	129.	B	141.	C
79.	A	92.	C	105.	A	118.	A	130.	A	142.	C
80.	A	93.	A	106.	D	119.	B	131.	C	143.	B
81.	B	94.	C	107.	D***	120.	D	132.	E	144.	E
82.	C	95.	D	108.	E	121.	E	133.	C	145.	D
83.	E**	96.	A	109.	A	122.	D	134.	B	146.	D
84.	D	97.	A	110.	D	123.	A	135.	D	147.	C
85.	D	98.	C	111.	A	124.	A	136.	A	148.	B
86.	E	99.	A	112.	D	125.	C	137.	B	149.	C
87.	B	100.	D	113.	C	126.	C	138.	D	150.	E
88.	B	101.	B	114.	C						

*Picasso, *Guernica*, 1937, Oil on Canvas, 11' 5½" x 25' 5¾". On extended loan to the Museum of Modern Art, New York, from the artist.

**Mexican National Tourist Council.

***Courtesy of the Museum of Primitive Art, New York.

SCORING CHART—SAMPLE EXAMINATION 2

After you have scored your Sample Examination 2, enter the results in the chart below; then transfer your Raw Score to the Progress Chart on page 14.

Total Test		Number Right	Number Wrong	Number Omitted	Raw Score
Section I:	75				
Section II:	75				
Total:	150				

ANSWER EXPLANATIONS—SAMPLE EXAMINATION 2

Section I

1. B. Charlemagne is the hero of "The Song of Roland."

2. D. Ibsen was a Norwegian poet and dramatist. He was noted for his realistic social dramas.

3. C. The others were Greek playwrights, but they did not write *Oedipus the King* and *Oedipus at Colonnus*.

4. E. The iambic foot contains an unstressed followed by a stressed syllable. Pentameter means five meters, or beats. Iambic pentameter, therefore, means five units of unstressed/stressed syllables in a line.

5. B. This is a standard musical notation.

6. E. This is true by definition.

7. D. The Psalms contain 150 hymns. (In the Septuagint canons, 151.)

8. D. *Lysistrata* deals with war, sex, and women's liberation.

9. C. *The Rake's Progress* is a ballet by Gavin-Gordon.

10. E. The statue is of Queen Nefertiti.

11. B. This is true by definition.

12. D. These lines appear in the final chapter of Voltaire's novel.

13. A. This is true by definition.

14. B. Nabokov is a 20th century writer.

15. D. A large symphony orchestra is composed of string, wind, and percussion sections. The other answers refer to two to four instruments.

16. B. This is true by definition.

17. E. None of the other poets has all of the qualifications listed.

18. A. Edith Wharton (1862–1937) was an American poet, short story writer, and novelist.

19. A. Tiresias is important in many of the stories of Thebes. He is consulted also, in the underworld, by Odysseus.

20. B. This is true by definition.

21. B. Pierre Corneille (1606–1684) was the first of the great tragic writers of the era. Jean Racine (1639–1699) is generally described as France's greatest writer of tragedy.

22. C. "Guernica" depicts the ravaging of a small town by that name in Spain during the Revolution.

23. D. Aristophanes was the great Greek writer of comedy.

24. E. To limit the answer to only one of the other statements would be to make an inadequate statement.

25. B. Paterson, whose full name is Andrew Barton "Banjo" Paterson, is the only Australian in the group.

26. A. This is a standard musical notation.
27. A. Viorst, a contributing editor to *Redbook* magazine, has also written for television.
28. E. This is true by definition.
29. E. This answer is true by definition.
30. C. This answer is true by definition.
31. A. Baldassare Castiglione (1478–1529) wrote a handbook of manners, *The Courtier*, which was a guidebook for elegant deportment.
32. E. The artistic style and decorations of the Greeks are far different from any of the others mentioned.
33. E. The philosophy expressed is typical of the Neo-Classic period.
34. C. Couplets are lines of poetry rhyming in pairs. The most widely used couplet form is the iambic pentameter, known as the heroic couplet.
35. A. Iambic pentameter is five feet of unstressed/stressed syllables to the line.
36. E. Nietzsche's *The Will to Power* was published in Germany in 1888. The first English translation appeared in 1909–10.
37. A. The others are either not 20th century composers, not composers of atonal music, or both.
38. D. Honoré de Balzac (1799–1850) wrote *The Human Comedy*. The chief novels in this group are *Père Goriot* and *Eugénie Grandet*.
39. C. Michelangelo (1475–1564) was the most famous artist of the Renaissance period.
40. E. In his famous soliloquy, Hamlet is pondering whether or not to commit suicide.
41. E. Perhaps Twain's most famous satire on contemporary society is *Huckleberry Finn*.
42. B. The late 18th century and early 19th century are known as the Neo-Classic Age.
43. E. Jacques Louis David (1748–1825) was one of the most famous painters of his day.
44. C. This is true by definition.
45. A. The troubadours were lyric poets of the 12th and 13th centuries attached to the courts of Provence and northern Italy.
46. B. A character with one over-riding purpose or opinion is often hilarious.
47. D. Futurism, an artistic movement that originated in Italy about 1910, attempted to depict the dynamic quality of contemporary life influenced by the force and motion of modern machinery.
48. D. Edvard Munch (1863–1944) was a Norwegian painter and printmaker who used intense colors and body attitudes to show love, sickness, anxiety, and death. He greatly influenced the German Expressionist movement of the early 1900s.
49. C. Liszt wrote twelve tone poems, the form of which he invented.
50. D. According to legend, Oedipus killed his father, married his mother, Jocasta, and had four children by her: Polynices, Eteocles, Antigone, and Ismene.
51. A. Johann Strauss was a composer of comic operas, but his reputation rests on some 400 waltzes.
52. A. Flaubert's *Madame Bovary*, published in 1859, was the first of the works which made him a model for later writers of the realistic school.
53. B. *The Koran* is the sacred book of Islam, purportedly revealed by God to the Prophet Mohammed.
54. E. Praxiteles was the most famous of the Attic sculptors.
55. D. Praxiteles was from Athens, Greece.
56. C. John Locke (1632–1704), an English philosopher, is best known for his *Essay Concerning the Human Understanding*, which poses the view of the *tabula rasa*.
57. E. Paris kidnapped Helen, wife of Menelaus, King of Sparta, and brought her back to Troy. The Greek leaders rallied to aid Menelaus, and thus began the Trojan War.
58. A. Goya (1746–1828) was a Spanish painter, etcher, and designer.

59. E. O. Henry is noted for his surprise endings. One of his best known short stories is "The Gift of the Magi." The other writers did not use the pseudonym "O. Henry."

60. B. The others were not writers of ante-bellum New Orleans chivalric literature.

61. B. The Stradivarius is also perhaps the most famous and most expensive violin in the world.

62. C. George Friedrich Handel (1685–1759) is perhaps best known as the composer of "The Messiah."

63. B. Polyphemus is the only cyclops Odysseus met.

64. A. In the soliloquy, the actor could speak his innermost thoughts aloud.

65. A. The others are mythological creatures, but no other fits the description.

66. D. Beethoven was a prolific composer of symphonies, sonatas, opera, but he did not write religious music.

67. B. This is true by definition.

68. E. The other characters were not suitors of Penelope.

69. E. von Weber (1786–1826) was a German who composed his first opera at age thirteen.

70. A. The others were not tragic dramatists of the Neo-Classic period.

71. B. This is true by definition.

72. E. This is true by definition.

73. B. John Keats, English Romantic poet, was a friend of Shelley.

74. C. Huxley was a 19th century evolutionist and social reformer who was instrumental in popularizing science. He was the grandfather of Aldous Huxley, author of *Brave New World*.

75. B. This is true by literary definition.

Section II

76. D. Sandro Botticelli (1444–1510), a Florentine, was one of the great painters of the Renaissance; "The Birth of Venus" is one of his most famous paintings.

77. A. Petrarch's sonnets, mostly inspired by Laura, form one of the most splendid bodies of verse in literature. Petrarch's sonnets were first imitated in England by Sir Thomas Wyatt; the form was later used by Milton, Wordsworth, and other sonneteers.

78. D. The Elizabethan audience insisted upon inflated, poetic language.

79. A. This answer is true by definition.

80. A. *I Pagliacci* is an opera in two acts by Leoncavallo.

81. B. English is considered a Germanic language. Old English and German are similar in many respects.

82. C. In English literature, Restoration generally refers to the period from the accession of Charles II to the throne in 1660 to the death of Dryden in 1770. This period is sometimes called "The Age of Dryden."

83. E. Brilliantly colored mosaics are typical of the art and architecture of the University of Mexico.

84. D. Pater was an important Victorian essayist and literary critic.

85. D. Wright's immensely functional, yet artistic, buildings always blend in with the environment.

86. E. One must be able to intellectualize the absurdity of life in order to enjoy this type of theater.

87. B. Among Ms. Truman's novels are *Murder on Embassy Row, Murder in Georgetown,* and *Murder in the Smithsonian.*

88. B. Rocinante was a run-down nag Don Quixote rode into his famous, or infamous, battles.

89. E. Campbell also authored *The Masks of God* and *Myths to Live By.*

90. B. The novel and movie, *The Seven-Per-Cent Solution,* concerns Holmes's addiction, and his treatment by Dr. Sigmund Freud.

91. C. In Christianity, the Devil is evil incarnate. In Machiavelli's *The Prince*, his greatest work, evil is permissible, if necessary.
92. C. The "art for art's sake" movement was an attempt to break away from all theories and traditions of the past.
93. A. This tapestry depicts scenes of the Norman Conquest of England and the events leading up to it.
94. C. Other than this distinction, the two buildings are architecturally similar in many respects.
95. D. Sophocles is the only playwright in this group.
96. A. Francois Villon (1431–1463?) was a vagabond, a rogue, and the greatest lyric poet of his time.
97. A. Allen Ginsberg, one of the most popular "beat" poets, was greatly influenced by Hindu philosophy and incorporated Hindu chants into some of his poetry.
98. C. Polyphony means the simultaneous combination of two or more independent melodic parts, especially when in close harmonic relationship.
99. A. A madrigal, in Renaissance Italy, was a lyric poem with a pastoral, idyllic, or amatory subject. It may also be further defined as an unaccompanied vocal composition for two or three voices in simple harmony, following a strict poetic form.
100. D. Stendhal, whose real name was Marie Henri Beyle, was a French novelist of the late 18th-early 19th century.
101. B. Sir Walter Scott (1771–1832) was a British novelist and poet.
102. B. "Piers Plowman" is a 14th century English allegorical poem satirizing and attacking the clergy and exalting the simple and truthful life.
103. A. Diego Velázquez (1599–1660) was perhaps the most naturalistic and objective of all the court painters.
104. D. George Sand's liaison with Chopin lasted from 1837 until 1847.
105. A. This is true by definition.
106. D. Another word for pragmatism is practicality.
107. D. One should notice the lack of sophistication in the sculpture.
108. E. *Fathers and Sons* is the most famous nihilist novel by Turgenev.
109. A. This monumental work was written by the Russian writer Tolstoy.
110. D. The Muses, the nine daughters of Zeus and Mnemosyne, were originally the patronesses of literature.
111. A. This trilogy is Dos Passos' most famous work.
112. D. W.B. Yeats (1865–1939) was influenced by Irish folklore and mythology and the French Symbolists. He brought to the Irish literary movement a sophistication of technique it had previously lacked.
113. C. "Neo-Classic" refers to the 17th and 18th centuries in Europe.
114. C. The others are well known figures in the field, but Robbins' dances in *West Side Story* have become classics.
115. C. Michelagnolo Buonarroti is another name for Michelangelo, the famous Italian Renaissance artist.
116. E. Duplicity is not a virtue.
117. E. Most of the educated people in England lived in London, and Chaucer spent most of his life there.
118. A. Tennyson wrote this poem to commemorate the death of his very dear friend, Arthur Hallam.
119. B. Quatrain means four lines of verse.
120. D. The rhyme scheme is determined by listening to the vowel sounds of the last word of each line, and lettering alphabetically; therefore, new = a; snow = b; go (which has the same vowel sound as "snow") = b, and true (which has the same vowel sound as "new") = a.
121. E. Auguste Rodin (1840–1917) was a French sculptor and perhaps the strongest influence on 20th century art.
122. D. Nobel Prize winner Solzhenitsyn has written *Gulag Archipelago*, *Cancer Ward*, and *One Day in the Life of Ivan Denisovich*.
123. A. This is true by definition.
124. A. The others were not written by Walpole.

125. C. John Donne was an English poet and preacher. The meditation referred to is his 17th.

126. C. W.S. Gilbert and Sir Arthur Sullivan collaborated on fourteen operettas.

127. A. The most conspicuous characteristics of this group of 17th century poets are the use of conceits, harshness of versification, and a combination of different types of emotions.

128. E. James Thurber (1894–1961) was well known for his stories and cartoons depicting the battles of the sexes.

129. B. Classic: pertaining to the ancient Greek or Roman period; Medieval: pertaining to the Middle Ages; Romantic: pertaining to the late 18th and early 19th century.

130. A. Constantin Brancusi (1876–1957) was a Rumanian abstract sculptor.

131. C. Mary Shelley intended the monster to arouse the sympathy of her readers.

132. E. Mary Shelley published her novel *Frankenstein* in 1818.

133. C. The poem is "The Ancient Mariner."

134. B. Quatrain means four lines of verse.

135. D. A literary ballad is written in deliberate imitation of the form and spirit of a folk ballad. The ballad stanza is usually a quatrain in alternate 4- and 3-stress lines, rhyming abcb.

136. A. Baldwin is one of America's best known contemporary black writers.

137. B. A good laugh is the best cure for many ills.

138. D. A clavier is a stringed keyboard instrument, such as a harpsichord.

139. C. Oedipus solved the riddle by replying, "It is man."

140. D. Goya (1746–1828) was a Spanish painter, etcher, and designer, and a leading representative of the Spanish school of his day.

141. C. Addison was the leading prose stylist of the early 18th century.

142. C. This is a concept first stated by Aristotle.

143. B. Beethoven's Fifth Symphony is the most obvious example of the use of this technique.

144. E. Kipling is well known for such works as *Gunga Din, Kim*, and *The Jungle Book*.

145. D. The lines are from the poem "To a Skylark, " by Shelley.

146. D. Nureyev is the only one of the group to defect from the Soviet Union; Fonteyn is the only British Dame listed.

147. C. Getting married was of prime consideration to a woman in Victorian England.

148. B. Browning's "My Last Duchess" is perhaps his best known dramatic monologue.

149. C. This painting, to date, has not been found.

150. E. This is a standard accent mark used when scanning poetry.

ANSWER SHEET — HUMANITIES/SAMPLE EXAMINATION 3

Section I

1. Ⓐ Ⓑ Ⓒ Ⓓ Ⓔ
2. Ⓐ Ⓑ Ⓒ Ⓓ Ⓔ
3. Ⓐ Ⓑ Ⓒ Ⓓ Ⓔ
4. Ⓐ Ⓑ Ⓒ Ⓓ Ⓔ
5. Ⓐ Ⓑ Ⓒ Ⓓ Ⓔ
6. Ⓐ Ⓑ Ⓒ Ⓓ Ⓔ
7. Ⓐ Ⓑ Ⓒ Ⓓ Ⓔ
8. Ⓐ Ⓑ Ⓒ Ⓓ Ⓔ
9. Ⓐ Ⓑ Ⓒ Ⓓ Ⓔ
10. Ⓐ Ⓑ Ⓒ Ⓓ Ⓔ
11. Ⓐ Ⓑ Ⓒ Ⓓ Ⓔ
12. Ⓐ Ⓑ Ⓒ Ⓓ Ⓔ
13. Ⓐ Ⓑ Ⓒ Ⓓ Ⓔ
14. Ⓐ Ⓑ Ⓒ Ⓓ Ⓔ
15. Ⓐ Ⓑ Ⓒ Ⓓ Ⓔ
16. Ⓐ Ⓑ Ⓒ Ⓓ Ⓔ
17. Ⓐ Ⓑ Ⓒ Ⓓ Ⓔ
18. Ⓐ Ⓑ Ⓒ Ⓓ Ⓔ
19. Ⓐ Ⓑ Ⓒ Ⓓ Ⓔ
20. Ⓐ Ⓑ Ⓒ Ⓓ Ⓔ
21. Ⓐ Ⓑ Ⓒ Ⓓ Ⓔ
22. Ⓐ Ⓑ Ⓒ Ⓓ Ⓔ
23. Ⓐ Ⓑ Ⓒ Ⓓ Ⓔ
24. Ⓐ Ⓑ Ⓒ Ⓓ Ⓔ
25. Ⓐ Ⓑ Ⓒ Ⓓ Ⓔ
26. Ⓐ Ⓑ Ⓒ Ⓓ Ⓔ
27. Ⓐ Ⓑ Ⓒ Ⓓ Ⓔ
28. Ⓐ Ⓑ Ⓒ Ⓓ Ⓔ
29. Ⓐ Ⓑ Ⓒ Ⓓ Ⓔ
30. Ⓐ Ⓑ Ⓒ Ⓓ Ⓔ
31. Ⓐ Ⓑ Ⓒ Ⓓ Ⓔ
32. Ⓐ Ⓑ Ⓒ Ⓓ Ⓔ
33. Ⓐ Ⓑ Ⓒ Ⓓ Ⓔ
34. Ⓐ Ⓑ Ⓒ Ⓓ Ⓔ
35. Ⓐ Ⓑ Ⓒ Ⓓ Ⓔ
36. Ⓐ Ⓑ Ⓒ Ⓓ Ⓔ
37. Ⓐ Ⓑ Ⓒ Ⓓ Ⓔ
38. Ⓐ Ⓑ Ⓒ Ⓓ Ⓔ
39. Ⓐ Ⓑ Ⓒ Ⓓ Ⓔ
40. Ⓐ Ⓑ Ⓒ Ⓓ Ⓔ
41. Ⓐ Ⓑ Ⓒ Ⓓ Ⓔ
42. Ⓐ Ⓑ Ⓒ Ⓓ Ⓔ
43. Ⓐ Ⓑ Ⓒ Ⓓ Ⓔ
44. Ⓐ Ⓑ Ⓒ Ⓓ Ⓔ
45. Ⓐ Ⓑ Ⓒ Ⓓ Ⓔ
46. Ⓐ Ⓑ Ⓒ Ⓓ Ⓔ
47. Ⓐ Ⓑ Ⓒ Ⓓ Ⓔ
48. Ⓐ Ⓑ Ⓒ Ⓓ Ⓔ
49. Ⓐ Ⓑ Ⓒ Ⓓ Ⓔ
50. Ⓐ Ⓑ Ⓒ Ⓓ Ⓔ
51. Ⓐ Ⓑ Ⓒ Ⓓ Ⓔ
52. Ⓐ Ⓑ Ⓒ Ⓓ Ⓔ
53. Ⓐ Ⓑ Ⓒ Ⓓ Ⓔ
54. Ⓐ Ⓑ Ⓒ Ⓓ Ⓔ
55. Ⓐ Ⓑ Ⓒ Ⓓ Ⓔ
56. Ⓐ Ⓑ Ⓒ Ⓓ Ⓔ
57. Ⓐ Ⓑ Ⓒ Ⓓ Ⓔ
58. Ⓐ Ⓑ Ⓒ Ⓓ Ⓔ
59. Ⓐ Ⓑ Ⓒ Ⓓ Ⓔ
60. Ⓐ Ⓑ Ⓒ Ⓓ Ⓔ
61. Ⓐ Ⓑ Ⓒ Ⓓ Ⓔ
62. Ⓐ Ⓑ Ⓒ Ⓓ Ⓔ
63. Ⓐ Ⓑ Ⓒ Ⓓ Ⓔ
64. Ⓐ Ⓑ Ⓒ Ⓓ Ⓔ
65. Ⓐ Ⓑ Ⓒ Ⓓ Ⓔ
66. Ⓐ Ⓑ Ⓒ Ⓓ Ⓔ
67. Ⓐ Ⓑ Ⓒ Ⓓ Ⓔ
68. Ⓐ Ⓑ Ⓒ Ⓓ Ⓔ
69. Ⓐ Ⓑ Ⓒ Ⓓ Ⓔ
70. Ⓐ Ⓑ Ⓒ Ⓓ Ⓔ
71. Ⓐ Ⓑ Ⓒ Ⓓ Ⓔ
72. Ⓐ Ⓑ Ⓒ Ⓓ Ⓔ
73. Ⓐ Ⓑ Ⓒ Ⓓ Ⓔ
74. Ⓐ Ⓑ Ⓒ Ⓓ Ⓔ
75. Ⓐ Ⓑ Ⓒ Ⓓ Ⓔ

Section II

76. Ⓐ Ⓑ Ⓒ Ⓓ Ⓔ
77. Ⓐ Ⓑ Ⓒ Ⓓ Ⓔ
78. Ⓐ Ⓑ Ⓒ Ⓓ Ⓔ
79. Ⓐ Ⓑ Ⓒ Ⓓ Ⓔ
80. Ⓐ Ⓑ Ⓒ Ⓓ Ⓔ
81. Ⓐ Ⓑ Ⓒ Ⓓ Ⓔ
82. Ⓐ Ⓑ Ⓒ Ⓓ Ⓔ
83. Ⓐ Ⓑ Ⓒ Ⓓ Ⓔ
84. Ⓐ Ⓑ Ⓒ Ⓓ Ⓔ
85. Ⓐ Ⓑ Ⓒ Ⓓ Ⓔ
86. Ⓐ Ⓑ Ⓒ Ⓓ Ⓔ
87. Ⓐ Ⓑ Ⓒ Ⓓ Ⓔ
88. Ⓐ Ⓑ Ⓒ Ⓓ Ⓔ
89. Ⓐ Ⓑ Ⓒ Ⓓ Ⓔ
90. Ⓐ Ⓑ Ⓒ Ⓓ Ⓔ
91. Ⓐ Ⓑ Ⓒ Ⓓ Ⓔ
92. Ⓐ Ⓑ Ⓒ Ⓓ Ⓔ
93. Ⓐ Ⓑ Ⓒ Ⓓ Ⓔ
94. Ⓐ Ⓑ Ⓒ Ⓓ Ⓔ
95. Ⓐ Ⓑ Ⓒ Ⓓ Ⓔ
96. Ⓐ Ⓑ Ⓒ Ⓓ Ⓔ
97. Ⓐ Ⓑ Ⓒ Ⓓ Ⓔ
98. Ⓐ Ⓑ Ⓒ Ⓓ Ⓔ
99. Ⓐ Ⓑ Ⓒ Ⓓ Ⓔ
100. Ⓐ Ⓑ Ⓒ Ⓓ Ⓔ
101. Ⓐ Ⓑ Ⓒ Ⓓ Ⓔ
102. Ⓐ Ⓑ Ⓒ Ⓓ Ⓔ
103. Ⓐ Ⓑ Ⓒ Ⓓ Ⓔ
104. Ⓐ Ⓑ Ⓒ Ⓓ Ⓔ
105. Ⓐ Ⓑ Ⓒ Ⓓ Ⓔ
106. Ⓐ Ⓑ Ⓒ Ⓓ Ⓔ
107. Ⓐ Ⓑ Ⓒ Ⓓ Ⓔ
108. Ⓐ Ⓑ Ⓒ Ⓓ Ⓔ
109. Ⓐ Ⓑ Ⓒ Ⓓ Ⓔ
110. Ⓐ Ⓑ Ⓒ Ⓓ Ⓔ
111. Ⓐ Ⓑ Ⓒ Ⓓ Ⓔ
112. Ⓐ Ⓑ Ⓒ Ⓓ Ⓔ
113. Ⓐ Ⓑ Ⓒ Ⓓ Ⓔ
114. Ⓐ Ⓑ Ⓒ Ⓓ Ⓔ
115. Ⓐ Ⓑ Ⓒ Ⓓ Ⓔ
116. Ⓐ Ⓑ Ⓒ Ⓓ Ⓔ
117. Ⓐ Ⓑ Ⓒ Ⓓ Ⓔ
118. Ⓐ Ⓑ Ⓒ Ⓓ Ⓔ
119. Ⓐ Ⓑ Ⓒ Ⓓ Ⓔ
120. Ⓐ Ⓑ Ⓒ Ⓓ Ⓔ
121. Ⓐ Ⓑ Ⓒ Ⓓ Ⓔ
122. Ⓐ Ⓑ Ⓒ Ⓓ Ⓔ
123. Ⓐ Ⓑ Ⓒ Ⓓ Ⓔ
124. Ⓐ Ⓑ Ⓒ Ⓓ Ⓔ
125. Ⓐ Ⓑ Ⓒ Ⓓ Ⓔ
126. Ⓐ Ⓑ Ⓒ Ⓓ Ⓔ
127. Ⓐ Ⓑ Ⓒ Ⓓ Ⓔ
128. Ⓐ Ⓑ Ⓒ Ⓓ Ⓔ
129. Ⓐ Ⓑ Ⓒ Ⓓ Ⓔ
130. Ⓐ Ⓑ Ⓒ Ⓓ Ⓔ
131. Ⓐ Ⓑ Ⓒ Ⓓ Ⓔ
132. Ⓐ Ⓑ Ⓒ Ⓓ Ⓔ
133. Ⓐ Ⓑ Ⓒ Ⓓ Ⓔ
134. Ⓐ Ⓑ Ⓒ Ⓓ Ⓔ
135. Ⓐ Ⓑ Ⓒ Ⓓ Ⓔ
136. Ⓐ Ⓑ Ⓒ Ⓓ Ⓔ
137. Ⓐ Ⓑ Ⓒ Ⓓ Ⓔ
138. Ⓐ Ⓑ Ⓒ Ⓓ Ⓔ
139. Ⓐ Ⓑ Ⓒ Ⓓ Ⓔ
140. Ⓐ Ⓑ Ⓒ Ⓓ Ⓔ
141. Ⓐ Ⓑ Ⓒ Ⓓ Ⓔ
142. Ⓐ Ⓑ Ⓒ Ⓓ Ⓔ
143. Ⓐ Ⓑ Ⓒ Ⓓ Ⓔ
144. Ⓐ Ⓑ Ⓒ Ⓓ Ⓔ
145. Ⓐ Ⓑ Ⓒ Ⓓ Ⓔ
146. Ⓐ Ⓑ Ⓒ Ⓓ Ⓔ
147. Ⓐ Ⓑ Ⓒ Ⓓ Ⓔ
148. Ⓐ Ⓑ Ⓒ Ⓓ Ⓔ
149. Ⓐ Ⓑ Ⓒ Ⓓ Ⓔ
150. Ⓐ Ⓑ Ⓒ Ⓓ Ⓔ

SAMPLE EXAMINATION 3

Section I

Number of Questions: 75
Time: 45 minutes

Directions: Each of the questions or incomplete statements below is followed by five suggested answers or completions. Select the one that is best in each case.

1. **A study of the development of American literature is not complete** without the reading of *The Leather-Stocking Tales,* a series of novels written by
   (A) Herman Melville (B) Nathaniel Hawthorne (C) Mark Twain (D) James Fenimore Cooper (E) Henry Miller

2. The hero of *The Leather-Stocking Tales* is
   (A) a sado-masochistic pervert in New York
   (B) a brave white man on the American frontier
   (C) a lesbian who holds weird parties in a Chicago penthouse
   (D) a cool black who revolts against Southern intolerance
   (E) a Puritan minister who seduced an innocent young woman

3. All of the following are considered post-Impressionist painters *except*
   (A) van Gogh (B) Gauguin (C) Cezanne (D) Dali (E) Lautrec

4. Paganini is noted for his compositions employing the
   (A) violin (B) piano (C) viola (D) flute (E) trombone

5. The painting at the right is
   (A) primordial
   (B) Etruscan
   (C) Egyptian
   (D) African primitive
   (E) modern

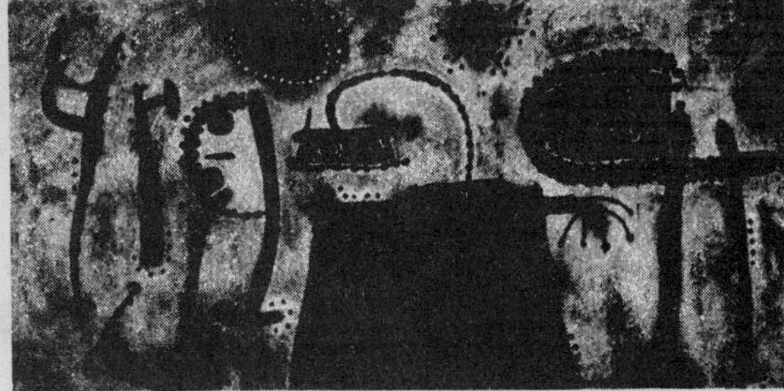

The Solomon R. Guggenheim Museum, New York

6. The Brothers Grimm wrote many fairy tales, among them the story of *Hansel and Gretel,* set to music as an opera by
   (A) Michael Glinka (B) Richard Strauss (C) Giacomo Puccini (D) Engelbert Humperdinck (E) Guiseppe Verdi

7. Rabelais is noted for his
   (A) prodigious vocabulary (B) shifting point of view (C) satire (D) obscenities (E) all of the above

8. The hit musical by Stephen Sondheim and Leonard Bernstein called *West Side Story* was based, loosely, on
   (A) Dryden's *All for Love* (B) Marlowe's *Dr. Faustus*
   (C) Shakespeare's *Romeo and Juliet* (D) Hawthorne's *The Scarlet Letter*
   (E) Whitman's *Leaves of Grass*

9. Perhaps the greatest novel written about American soldiers in World War II is
(A) John Dos Passos' *Three Soldiers*
(B) Erich Maria Remarque's *All Quiet on the Western Front*
(C) E. E. Cummings' *The Enormous Room*
(D) Norman Mailer's *The Naked and the Dead*
(E) James Michener's *The Bridges of Toko-Ri*

Photo Alinari

Questions 10 and 11 refer to the above work of art.

10. The work was painted by
(A) Michelangelo (B) Botticelli (C) da Vinci (D) van Gogh (E) Picasso

11. The work is an example of
(A) an engraving (B) a watercolor on paper (C) oil paint on canvas (D) baked enamel on wood (E) a fresco

12. All of the following are characters in *King Lear except*
(A) Oswald (B) Cordelia (C) Ophelia (D) Goneril (E) Regan

13. Picasso is noted for painting in which of the following styles?
(A) Realist (B) Classic (C) Abstract (D) Cubist (E) All of the above

Questions 14 and 15 refer to the following quotation.

"Fear not, for behold I bring you good tidings of great joy, which shall be to all people. For unto you is born this day in the City of David a Saviour, which is Christ the Lord."

14. The above quotation is from the Book of
(A) Peter (B) Mark (C) John (D) Luke (E) Revelations

15. Many years later, the quotation was used in a great oratorio, composed by
(A) Handel (B) Haydn (C) Bach (D) Mendelssohn (E) Liszt

16. Which of the following would be most characteristic of a naturalistic play?
(A) The belief that the world is moving toward a recognizable goal
(B) The position that nature, including society, is indifferent to human needs
(C) Dialogue as a key to character
(D) Pyramidal or classical structure
(E) A protagonist of noble birth

17. "Tragedy, then, is an imitation of an action that is serious, complete, and of a certain magnitude . . . effecting the proper purgation of the emotions."
These are the words of the first drama critic:
(A) Socrates (B) Thespis (C) Plato (D) Crito (E) Aristotle

18. The life of decadent Europe is contrasted unfavorably with life on an unspoiled, Eden-like island. This is indicative of an Age called
(A) Romantic (B) Neo-Classic (C) Classic
(D) Elizabethan (E) Victorian

19. Robert Louis Stevenson dreamed the plot of one of his most famous works:
(A) *Treasure Island* (B) *Travels With a Donkey*
(C) *Dr. Jekyll and Mr. Hyde* (D) *Kidnapped* (E) *Robinson Crusoe*

20. During the late 1960s, this American playwright had four hit plays running in Broadway theaters simultaneously, a possibly unprecedented feat:
(A) David Merrick (B) Neil Simon (C) Arthur Miller
(D) Joe Orton (E) Jerry Herman

21. What contemporary "pop" artist produced and sold pictures of larger-than-life-size Brillo boxes and Campbell's Soup labels?
(A) Claes Oldenburg (B) Jackson Pollock (C) Andy Warhol
(D) Michael Chaplin (E) Norman Rockwell

22. Byron's great poetic satire is
(A) "Childe Harold's Pilgrimage" (B) "Hours of Idleness"
(C) "Don Juan" (D) "Maid of Athens, Ere We Part"
(E) "The Destruction of Sennacherib"

23. "Beauty is truth, truth beauty,—that is all
Ye know on earth, and all ye need to know."

The above lines are from
(A) Keat's "Ode on a Grecian Urn"
(B) Keat's "Ode to a Nightingale"
(C) Shelley's "To a Skylark"
(D) Shelley's "Ode to the West Wind"
(E) Wordsworth's "My Heart Leaps Up"

24. Odysseus' home was in
(A) Troy (B) Athens (C) Ithaca (D) Ogygia (E) Scheria

25. The architect whom Napoleon commissioned to change the Church of La Madelaine into a Temple of Glory was
(A) Chalgrin (B) Fontaine (C) Vignon (D) Percier
(E) Goya

26. Bertolt Brecht is famous for a theory which asserts that the aim of drama is to entertain by arousing the intellect, not the emotions. The effect sought by this theory is that of
(A) catharsis (B) alienation (C) exposition
(D) symbolism (E) professionalism

27. King Alfred the Great of England (849-901) is noted for all of the following except
(A) translating Boethius' *Consolations of Philosophy*
(B) translating Bede's *Ecclesiastical History of the English People* into English
(C) the consolidation and continuation of *The Anglo-Saxon Chronicles*
(D) establishing English prose literature at a time when most of the other European countries were just producing their first works in verse
(E) establishing English poetic literature at a time when most of the other European countries were just producing their first works in prose

28. The first great composer whose income was derived more often from commissions and the proceeds of his published compositions than from service to the nobility was
(A) Mendelssohn (B) Schumann (C) Mozart
(D) Beethoven (E) Bach

29. *Wuthering Heights* was written by
(A) Aphra Behn (B) Charlotte Brontë (C) Jane Austen
(D) Emily Brontë (E) Mary Wollstonecraft

30. The most famous French Neo-Classic playwright was
(A) Molière (B) Corneille (C) Racine (D) Cocteau
(E) Rostand

31. The Greek playwright noted for his use of "dramatic irony" was
(A) Aristophanes (B) Persephone (C) Antigone
(D) Sophocles (E) Iphigenia

32. What American poet found inspiration in the familiar objects and characters of New England ("The Wood Pile," "Birches," "The Death of the Hired Man")?
(A) Emily Dickinson (B) Carl Sandburg (C) Robert Frost
(D) Edgar Lee Masters (E) Vachel Lindsay

33. The sculptor who utilizes heavy, monumental forms which are perforated or bored through and who said, "A sculptor is interested in the shape of things" is
(A) Hepworth (B) Moore (C) Armitage (D) Butler
(E) Hofman

34. The Greek moralist who wrote biographies of both Greeks and Romans was
(A) Parmenides (B) Epictetus (C) Heraclitus
(D) Plotinus (E) Plutarch

35. The Roman historian who wrote about the customs and manners of the Germans was
(A) Suetonius (B) Caesar (C) Aurelius (D) Tacitus
(E) Quintas

36. The American theater of 1919-1922 saw the development of a new spiritual symbolism. The leading playwright of this period was
(A) Eugene O'Neill (B) Robinson Jeffers
(C) Archibald MacLeish (D) Edward Albee
(E) Tennessee Williams

37. The author of the plays *The Death of Bessie Smith*, *The Zoo Story*, and *The Sand Box* is
(A) Edward Albee (B) Samuel Beckett (C) Eugene O'Neill
(D) Jack Richardson (E) Neil Simon

38. *Aesthetics* is primarily a study of
(A) morals (B) art (C) being as such
(D) beauty and goodness (E) knowledge

39. A 20th-century American author who was interested in Africa and the plight of both the English and Dutch, as well as native tribesmen, was
(A) Donald Wiedner (B) Richard Wright (C) Robert Ruark
(D) Edgar Rice Burroughs (E) Herbert Wendt

Questions 40–42 refer to illustrations (A) through (E).

(A)

The Metropolitan Museum of Art, The Michael C. Rockefeller Memorial Collection Bequest of Nelson A. Rockefeller, 1979.

(B)

The Metropolitan Museum of Art, Rogers Fund, 1933.

(C)

The Metropolitan Museum of Art, The Annenberg Fund, Inc., Gift, and Fletcher, Rogers & Louis V. Bell Funds, and Gift of J. Pierpont Morgan, by exchange, 1976.

(D)

The Metropolitan Museum of Art, Fletcher Fund, Rogers Fund, and Bequest of Miss Adelaide Milton de Groot (1876–1967), by exchange, supplemented by gifts from friends of the Museum, 1971.

(E)

The Metropolitan Museum of Art, Rogers Fund, 1909.

40. Which is Grecian?

41. Which is by Bernini?

42. Which is medieval?

43. Which of the following artists was still alive in 1970?
(A) Picasso (B) Pissaro (D) van Gogh (D) Goya
(E) Manet

44. Who was largely responsible for writing the Declaration of Independence?
(A) Benjamin Franklin (B) Thomas Jefferson
(C) George Washington (D) Samuel Johnson
(E) John Adams

45. The author of *The Mucker* and the Tarzan series was
(A) John Steinbeck (B) Edgar Rice Burroughs
(C) Luke Short (D) Michael Crichton (E) William Burroughs

46. The most famous pupil of Haydn, "that great mogul," was
(A) Beethoven (B) Liszt (C) Chopin (D) Debussy
(E) Moussorgsky

47. A collection of medieval tales, supposedly told by a group of people attempting to escape a plague, is
(A) *Beowulf* (B) *The Decameron* (C) *The Canterbury Tales*
(D) *The Heptameron* (E) *Piers Plowman*

48. A modern artist whose paintings have served as designs for linoleum is
(A) Braque (B) Miro (C) Dali (D) Gris (E) Mondrian

49. A well-known architect and set designer of the 17th century was
(A) Marc Chagall (B) Paul Klee (C) Igor Stravinsky
(D) Inigo Jones (E) Norman bel Geddes

50. Goldsmith's "Deserted Village" is known for its
(A) description of 18th-century funeral customs
(B) musical sound and poetic beauty
(C) minute detail (D) ghoulish overtones (E) slovenly language

51. In his later plays, Shakespeare became interested in
(A) pyramidal plot structure
(B) obeying the unities of time, place, and action
(C) character delineation
(D) flattering Queen Elizabeth I
(E) the hero's struggle with external forces

52. A *leitmotif* is
(A) a short, characteristic musical pattern symbolizing an idea or a person (B) another name for "aria" (C) a tremolo
(D) bel canto (E) a vibrato

53. The term *catharsis*, which Aristotle thought was the main purpose of tragedy, may be defined as
(A) the excitation of the emotions during a performance
(B) the arousal of the killer instinct
(C) the tragic flaw of the classical protagonist
(D) the purging of the emotions leading to a restoration of equilibrium after the tragedy
(E) the point at which the intensification begins

54. Stanislavsky was led away from traditional methods of staging 19th-century plays by his attempt to produce
(A) Ibsen's *Master Builder*
(B) Chekhov's *The Seagull*
(C) Miller's *Death of a Salesman*
(D) Wilde's *The Importance of Being Earnest*
(E) Williams' *The Glass Menagerie*

55. The author of *Portrait of a Lady, Daisy Miller*, and *The Turn of the Screw* was
(A) James Fenimore Cooper (B) Jack London
(C) William Dean Howells (D) Upton Sinclair
(E) Henry James

56. Many of our national airs are considered American in origin; yet the basic melody may come from "the old country," possibly England or Scotland. Which one of the following is truly American?
(A) "Hail, Columbia" (B) "Yankee Doodle"
(C) "The Star-Spangled Banner"
(D) "The Glass Harmonica"
(E) "God Save America"

57. "Phlebas the Phoenician, a fortnight dead,
Forgot the cry of gulls, and the deep sea swell
And the profit and loss."
These lines were written in the
(A) 8th century (B) 15th century (C) 17th century
(D) 18th century (E) 20th century

58. Witty dialogue introduced for its own sake characterized
(A) Neo-Classic tragedy
(B) sentimental drama of the 19th century
(C) comedy of manners (D) theater of cruelty
(E) Elizabethan chronicle plays

59. A surrealist painter whose subjects come from psychoanalytic literature is
(A) Picasso (B) Miro (C) Dali (D) Klee
(E) Duchamp

60. All of the following are 20th-century architects *except*
(A) Alexander Archipenko (B) Frank Lloyd Wright
(C) Le Corbusier (D) Mies van der Rohe (E) Walter Gropius

61. "You don't know about me, without you have read a book by the name of *The Adventures of Tom Sawyer*, but that ain't no matter. That book was made by Mr. Mark Twain, and he told the truth, mainly."
These are the opening sentences to
(A) *The Prince and the Pauper*
(B) *A Connecticut Yankee in King Arthur's Court*
(C) *The Innocents Abroad*
(D) *Huckleberry Finn*
(E) *The Adventures of Tom Sawyer*

62. Prosper Merimée's short story "Carmen" was the subject of an opera by
(A) Puccini (B) Verdi (C) Mozart (D) Bizet
(E) Menotti

63. Virginia Woolf's essay describing the frustrations a talented female writer might have encountered in Elizabethan England is entitled
(A) "Ms. Shakespeare" (B) "If Shakespeare Had Had a Sister"
(C) "Elizabeth the Nearly-Queen" (D) "Sixteenth-century Sinners"
(E) "A Bit of Fluff"

64. Two Roman satiric poets were
(A) Horace and Juvenal (B) Plautus and Terence
(C) Menander and Marcus Aurelius (D) Lucretius and Suetonius
(E) Cicero and Petronius

65. The man who made possible the emergence of the modern ballet as a concrete organization was
(A) Vaslav Nijinsky (B) Serge Diaghileff
(C) Mikhail Mordkin (D) Michel Fokine (E) George Balanchine

66. Painting that has no content in the literal or narrative sense is called
(A) Impressionism (B) Surrealism (C) Non-objective art
(D) Pop art (E) Social Realism

67. Longfellow and Whittier were writers belonging to the
(A) Gilded Age (B) Mauve Decade (C) local-colorist school
(D) Transcendental movement (E) genteel tradition

68. The Romantic Movement in English literature was ushered in by the publication of
(A) "The Seasons" (B) *Lyrical Ballads* (C) "Ode to the West Wind"
(D) *Childe Harold's Pilgrimage* (E) "The Eve of St. Agnes"

69. A Scotch poet who wrote about his own experience and emotions was
(A) Rudyard Kipling (B) John Keats (C) Robert Burns
(D) William Blake (E) Robert Browning

70. The additive method of sculpturing is primarily concerned with
(A) modeling (B) carving (C) mobility
(D) decreasing mass (E) visual qualities

71. A member of the Fauve group who used color in new and daring ways was
(A) Goya (B) Michelangelo (C) da Vinci (D) El Greco (E) Matisse

72. According to *The Iliad*, what great Greek warrior sulked in his tent after a quarrel over a woman and did not rejoin the battle until a friend was killed?
(A) Aeneas (B) Ajax (C) Anchises (D) Achilles
(E) Aphrodite

73. In Greek mythology, the son of Prometheus was
(A) Poseidon (B) Callisto (C) Deucalion (D) Hercules
(E) Odysseus

74. In Elizabeth Barrett Browning's "Sonnets from the Portuguese," she
(A) asks her husband to love her for her beauty
(B) says she shall love him only until her death
(C) says she and her lover are equals
(D) contrasts her poetry with that of her husband
(E) says she feels as young as her husband

Photo Alinari

75. The above is an example of
(A) Byzantine art (B) Greek art (C) Roman art
(D) Egyptian art (E) American primitive art

Section II

Number of Questions: 75
Time: 45 minutes

Directions: Each of the questions or incomplete statements below is followed by five suggested answers or completions. Select the one that is best in each case.

76. Musical tone consists of all of the following except
(A) pitch (B) duration (C) intensity (D) quality (E) tempo

77. The composer of the popular musicals *Evita* and *Cats* is
(A) George M. Cohan (B) Richard Rodgers (C) Stephen Sondheim
(D) Andrew Lloyd Webber (E) Harvey Fierstein

78. All of the following were labors of Hercules except
(A) killing the Nemean lion
(B) killing the Hydra
(C) bringing back the Golden Fleece
(D) cleaning the Augean Stables
(E) bringing the Erymanthian Boar back alive to Eurytheus

79. The mighty Beowulf fought the monster
(A) Hrothgar (B) Hygelac (C) Gringolet
(D) Grendel (E) Wealtheow

80. Go and catch a falling star;
Get with child a mandrake root;
Tell me where all lost years are,
Or who cleft the devil's foot.

The author of these lines was
(A) George Herbert
(B) John Donne
(C) Ben Jonson
(D) The Earl of Rochester
(E) Queen Elizabeth I

81. The vase at the right is
(A) Greek
(B) Roman
(C) Egyptian
(D) Mesopotamian
(E) Mayan

Hirmer Fotoarchiv Munchen

82. Beethoven was known for his
(A) ordered forms of Classicism (B) atonality
(C) humanism (D) sentimentality
(E) thematic development

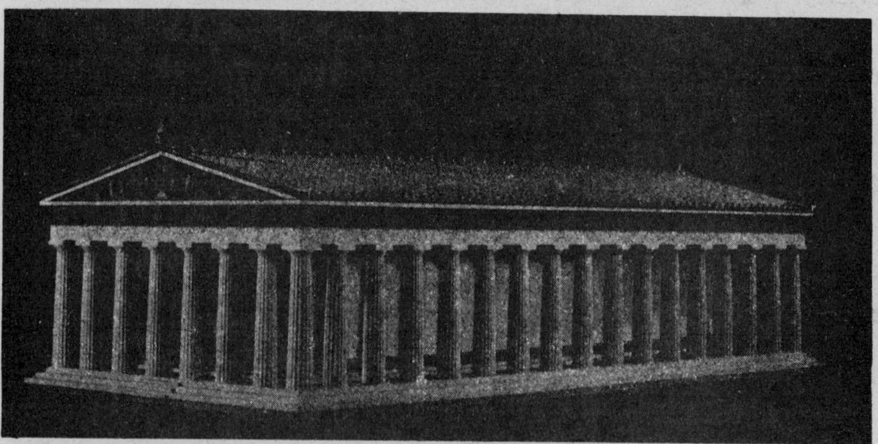

The Metropolitan Museum of Art, Purchase, 1890, Levi Hale Willard Bequest.

83. The above is a photograph of the
(A) Coliseum (B) Forum (C) Parthenon
(D) palace at Knossos (E) Pentagon

84. The Romantic poets were, as a whole,
(A) objective
(B) unemotional
(C) unconcerned with nature
(D) influenced by medieval and classical themes
(E) influenced by the Renaissance

85. A Neo-Classic French writer noted for his fables was
(A) Voltaire (B) Montaigne (C) La Rouchefoucauld
(D) La Fontaine (E) Pascal

86. Odysseus' wife was named
(A) Eumaneus (B) Euryclea (C) Antinous
(D) Penelope (E) Telemachus

87. The musical notation < > means
(A) stop playing after four beats (B) crescendo-diminuendo
(C) play together (D) slow the tempo (E) both B and C

88. All of the following operas were written by Richard Wagner *except*
(A) *Tannhauser* (B) *Salome* (C) *Tristan und Isolde*
(D) *Lohengrin* (E) *Die Meistersinger von Nurnberg*

89. The greatest French satiric dramatist of the Neo-Classic Period was
(A) Pascal (B) Racine (C) Sainte-Beuve
(D) Molière (E) Montaigne

90. *Beowulf* is an example of a
(A) chanson de geste (B) folk epic (C) long short story
(D) medieval metrical romance (E) literary epic

91. Hermann Hesse wrote all but which of the following novels?
(A) *Journey to the West* (B) *Demian* (C) *Steppenwolf*
(D) *Siddhartha* (E) *Magister Ludi or The Glass Bead Game*

92. One of the outstanding science fiction writers of today who also first advanced the theory of communications satellites is
(A) Asimov (B) Clarke (C) Heinlein (D) Pohl
(E) Bradbury

93. The voice of the Beat Generation, author of *On the Road*, was
(A) Ginsberg (B) Kesey (C) Ferlinghetti
(D) Kerouac (E) Wolfe

94. The ontological argument for the existence of a Supreme Being was first fully stated by
(A) Moses (B) St. Anselm (C) St. Thomas (D) St. Paul
(E) Jesus

95. Noted for their civil war stories are
(A) Thoreau and Richardson (B) Crane and Twain
(C) Harte and London (D) Emerson and Hawthorne
(E) Bierce and Crane

96. The attitude of the author, as the reader infers it, in a literary work is referred to as the
(A) plot (B) denouement (C) attitudinem (D) tone
(E) mood

97. The *Bhagavad-Gita* is one of the holy books of which major religion?
(A) Buddhism (B) Hinduism (C) Taoism (D) Islam
(E) Confucianism

98. A *suite* is
(A) a synonym for *symphony*
(B) the second movement of a concerto
(C) a collection of dance tunes
(D) very similar to a fugue
(E) a religious vocal form

99. One of the most noted Americans of the 20th century, composer of "Appalachian Spring," is
(A) Aaron Copland (B) George Gershwin
(C) Tommy Dorsey (D) Vernon Duke (E) Leonard Bernstein

100. A great illustrator and creator of the modern poster was
(A) van Gogh (B) Norman Rockwell (C) Toulouse-Lautrec
(D) Braque (E) Grant Wood

101. A sculptured or richly ornamented band (as on a building) is called a
(A) frieze (B) bartizan (C) fresco (D) flying buttress
(E) batik

102. Plot and character are among the six ingredients of a play, according to Aristotle. So are all of the following *except*
(A) music (B) alienation (C) thought (D) diction
(E) spectacle

103. The Portuguese poet famous for his national epic *The Lusiads* was
(A) Lazarillo de Tormes (B) Miguel de Cervantes
(C) Lope de Vega (D) Luis vaz de Camoens
(E) Guillen de Castro

104. Wolfgang Amadeus Mozart
(A) began composing at four (B) wrote his first oratorio at eleven
(C) wrote forty-one symphonies (D) wrote fifteen masses
(E) did all of the above

105. One of the most famous members of the Fabian Society was
(A) Thomas Carlyle (B) Ezra Pound (C) John Ruskin
(D) William Butler Yeats (E) George Bernard Shaw

106. The time lapse between Sophocles and Shakespeare is about
(A) 500 years (B) 1,000 years (C) 1,500 years
(D) 2,000 years (E) 3,000 years

107. One of the most famous American paintings, "Arrangement in Gray and Black," was painted by
(A) James McNeill Whistler (B) John Singer Sargent
(C) Thomas Eakins (D) Asher B. Durand
(E) Winslow Homer

108. One of the best known Greek sculptors of the 4th century B.C. was
(A) Lysistrata (B) Praxiteles (C) Constantine
(D) Scorpios (E) Euphronius

109. The omission of part of a word, as in "o'er" ("over"), is called
(A) elision **(B) enjambment** **(C) poetic diction**
(D) stichomythia **(E) threnody**

110. **Which of the following is *not* a simile?**
(A) I wandered lonely as a cloud
(B) Busy old fool, unruly Sun
(C) My love is like a red, red rose
(D) Her eyes are lovely as the stars
(E) My heart is like a singing bird

111. Dramatic comedy employing stock characters, performed by professional Italian actors, who improvised while they performed, is called
(A) kabuki **(B) mise en scene** **(C) commedia dell'arte**
(D) deus ex machina **(E) Einfuhlung**

112. A *libretto* is
(A) an instrumental form
(B) a small music library
(C) part of a concerto
(D) an unaccompanied solo passage
(E) the text of an opera

113. Puccini wrote an opera based on Belasco's play
(A) *Madame Butterfly* **(B) *Rigoletto*** **(C) *Manon***
(D) *La Bohème* **(E) *The Consul***

114. Margaret Mitchell won the Pulitzer Prize in 1937 for her novel
(A) *Gone with the Wind* (B) *The Siege of Atlanta*
(C) *Good-bye, Columbia* (D) *The Swan* (E) *Travels with Charlie*

Questions 115–116 refer to the following descriptions of the stage settings of plays.

(A) Torrents of heavy rain. Pedestrians running for shelter into the portico of St. Paul's church in Covent Garden vegetable market.

(B) Orgon's house in Paris.

(C) Central Park, a Sunday afternoon in summer, the present.

(D) The Warfield apartment in the rear of the building. The building is flanked on both sides by dark, narrow alleys which run into murky canyons of tangled clotheslines, garbage cans and the sinister latticework of neighboring fire escapes.

(E) Before the palace of the King of Thebes. A central door and two lateral doors open onto a platform which runs the length of the facade.

115. Which is for a play by Tennessee Williams?

116. Which is for a play by G.B. Shaw?

117. A 14-line poem with the rhyme scheme a b a b c d c d e f e f g g is called a
(A) sestina (B) Petrarchan sonnet (C) rondeau
(D) rondel (E) Shakespearean sonnet

118. In the Middle Ages, art
(A) declined in importance
(B) grew in importance
(C) reflected the prevailing thought
(D) became more realistic
(E) became decadent

119. A dance by two people is called a(n)
(A) pas de quatre (B) entrechat (C) pirouette
(D) pas de deux (E) raccourci

120. A painter famous for his scenes of the American West is
(A) Stuart Davis (B) George Catlin (C) William Gropper
(D) John Marin (E) James McNeill Whistler

121. An undecorated stage which presents actions occurring in both England and France during the course of a single play might be expected by the audience in
(A) the 4th century B.C.
(B) the Elizabethan era
(C) Neo-Classic France
(D) an avant-garde play about two tramps in a park
(E) the early 20th century when verisimilitude was the rage

122. When Jocasta describes her late husband, the former king, as a tall man who resembled Oedipus, we have a good example of
(A) Sophoclean irony (B) exposition
(C) Aristotelian recognition (D) alienation (E) hubris

123. Which of the following can a drama *not* do without?
(A) verisimilitude
(B) denouement
(C) audience empathy
(D) conflict
(E) elaborate sets

124. An example of a strict canon is
(A) "Jailhouse Blues"
(B) "Rock, Rock, Rock Around the Clock"
(C) Beethoven's "Fidelio"
(D) Handel's "Messiah"
(E) "Row, Row, Row Your Boat"

125. Which of the following terms relates to *tempo?*
(A) timbre (B) monophonic (C) crescendo
(D) triad (E) allegro

Questions 126 and 127 refer to the following lines by Alexander Pope.

"Go, wiser thou! and, in thy scale of sense,
Weigh thy opinion against Providence . . .
Snatch from His hand the balance of the rod,
Re-judge His Justice, be the God of God."

126. The above is an example of
(A) satire (B) imagery (C) melodrama (D) euphony
(E) verbal irony

127. The verse form is the
(A) quatrain (B) ballade (C) heroic couplet
(D) rondeau (E) rhyme royal

128. A musical instrument that is tuned with sand paper is
(A) a lute (B) a harpsichord (C) a ukelele (D) a harp
(E) an oboe

129. The Greek drama is said to have developed from
(A) Lenaean rites of spring
(B) city activities during the winter solstice
(C) political action
(D) Dionysian dithyrambs associated with regeneration and spring
(E) Aristotle's *Poetics*

130. Which of the following Greek divinities is *not* correctly identified?
(A) Aphrodite—goddess of love (B) Artemis—goddess of the moon
(C) Apollo—god of the sun (D) Hera—the greatest of the Olympian goddesses (E) Vulcan—god of fire

131. Though his best known work is *The Rise of Silas Lapham,* this author is also known for his biography of the Republican presidential candidate, Abraham Lincoln. He is
(A) Edwin H. Cady (B) Theodore Dreiser
(C) Nathaniel Hawthorne (D) Carl Sandburg
(E) William Dean Howells

132. The practice or technique of applying dots of color to a surface so that from a distance they blend together is called
(A) cubism (B) primitivism (C) chiaroscuro
(D) pointillism (E) rococo

133. All of the following are considered post-Impressionist painters *except*
(A) David (B) Cezanne (C) Gauguin (D) von Gogh
(E) Seurat

134. Egyptian wall painting demonstrates
(A) a fear of death
(B) what the artist knew rather than what he saw
(C) an overriding concern with factual appearances
(D) the style of the individual artist
(E) a knowledge of anatomy

135. All of the following are characteristic of the epic *except*
(A) it is a long narrative poem
(B) the setting is usually the past
(C) it contains figurative language that gives it cosmic significance
(D) there is always a trip to the underworld
(E) it is written, always, in the vernacular of the people

136. Dante's greatest work was called a "comedy" because
(A) it was written in the vulgar language of the people
(B) no one dies during the course of the poem
(C) it begins in misery and ends in happiness
(D) there are many amusing scenes in the poem
(E) the subject matter was not serious enough for the people of his day

137. In Greek tragedy, the "tragic flaw" within a character which precipitates his fall is called
(A) nemesis (B) deus ex machina (C) antistrophe
(D) hubris (E) hamartia

138. A composer noted principally for his piano compositions is
(A) Chopin (B) Haydn
(C) Brahms (D) Tchaikovsky
(E) Mozart

139. *Oratorios* are
(A) large compositions for orchestra
(B) short compositions for solo voice
(C) a part of a religious service
(D) secular compositions for voice and orchestra
(E) large compositions for voice and orchestra usually based on religious texts

140. The founders of Cubism were
(A) Dali and Klee (B) Miro and Gris
(C) Chagall and Cezanne (D) Picasso and Braque
(E) Mondrian and Gauguin

141. A mystic and poet, illustrator and engraver of the Bible, Dante, Milton, and Shakespeare, was
(A) Albrecht Dürer (B) William Blake (C) Hieronymus Bosch
(D) Eugène Delacroix (E) Dante Gabriel Rossetti

142. "The Pleiade" is all of the following *except*
(A) a heavenly constellation
(B) an organized attempt to establish a classical spirit in French writing
(C) a movement begun about 1547 at Paris
(D) a literary group led by Pierre de Ronsard
(E) an opera by Massenet

143. A 19th-century poet famous for his dramatic monologues was
(A) Ruskin (B) Browning (C) Pater (D) Arnold
(E) Tennyson

144. The theory that "this is the best of all possible worlds" was satirized in
(A) Congreve's *Way of the World*
(B) Dostoevsky's *Crime and Punishment*
(C) Zola's *Germinal*
(D) Voltaire's *Candide*
(E) Swift's *Gulliver's Travels*

145. A *motet* is
(A) an instrumental form (B) monophonic
(C) usually secular (D) a choral composition
(E) a 20th-century musical form

146. A *recitative* would most likely be found in
(A) a symphony (B) an opera (C) a sonata
(D) a concerto (E) a quartet

147. All of the following are conventions of the Elizabethan theater *except*
(A) women's roles enacted by young boys
(B) setting established by dialogue
(C) poetic language
(D) a chorus of elders
(E) the soliloquy

148. Literature intended to be enjoyed for its own sake rather than to convey information or serve some immediate practical purpose is called
(A) macaronic (B) belles-lettres (C) paradoxical
(D) georgic (E) Bildungsroman

149. Which of the following lists of vocal registers moves properly from high to low?
(A) bass, baritone, tenor, alto, soprano, mezzo soprano
(B) alto, tenor, mezzo soprano, bass, baritone, soprano
(C) tenor, bass, baritone, soprano, mezzo soprano
(D) soprano, mezzo soprano, alto, tenor, baritone, bass
(E) alto, soprano, mezzo soprano, tenor, baritone, bass

150. The popular modern musical *Cats* is based on *Old Possum's Book of Practical Cats,* written by
(A) Edward Albee (B) Stephen Sondheim (C) Ezra Pound
(D) the Beatles (E) T.S. Eliot

ANSWER KEY—SAMPLE EXAMINATION 3

Section I

1.	D	**14.**	D	**27.**	E	**40.**	E	**52.**	A	**64.**	A
2.	B	**15.**	A	**28.**	E	**41.**	C	**53.**	D	**65.**	B
3.	D	**16.**	B	**29.**	D	**42.**	B	**54.**	B	**66.**	C
4.	A	**17.**	E	**30.**	A	**43.**	A	**55.**	E	**67.**	E
5.	E	**18.**	A	**31.**	D	**44.**	E	**56.**	A	**68.**	B
6.	D	**19.**	C	**32.**	C	**45.**	B	**57.**	E	**69.**	C
7.	E	**20.**	B	**33.**	B	**46.**	A	**58.**	C	**70.**	A
8.	C	**21.**	C	**34.**	E	**47.**	B	**59.**	C	**71.**	E
9.	D	**22.**	C	**35.**	D	**48.**	E	**60.**	A	**72.**	D
10.	C	**23.**	A	**36.**	A	**49.**	D	**61.**	D	**73.**	C
11.	E	**24.**	C	**37.**	A	**50.**	C	**62.**	D	**74.**	D
12.	C	**25.**	C	**38.**	B	**51.**	C	**63.**	B	**75.**	A
13.	E	**26.**	E	**39.**	C						

Section II

76.	E	**89.**	D	**102.**	B	**115.**	D	**127.**	C	**139.**	E
77.	D	**90.**	B	**103.**	D	**116.**	A	**128.**	B	**140.**	D
78.	C	**91.**	A	**104.**	E	**117.**	E	**129.**	D	**141.**	B
79.	D	**92.**	B	**105.**	E	**118.**	C	**130.**	E	**142.**	E
80.	B	**93.**	D	**106.**	D	**119.**	D	**131.**	E	**143.**	B
81.	B	**94.**	B	**107.**	A	**120.**	B	**132.**	D	**144.**	D
82.	E	**95.**	E	**108.**	B	**121.**	B	**133.**	A	**145.**	D
83.	C	**96.**	D	**109.**	A	**122.**	A	**134.**	B	**146.**	B
84.	D	**97.**	B	**110.**	B	**123.**	D	**135.**	E	**147.**	D
85.	D	**98.**	C	**111.**	C	**124.**	E	**136.**	C	**148.**	B
86.	D	**99.**	A	**112.**	E	**125.**	E	**137.**	E	**149.**	D
87.	B	**100.**	C	**113.**	A	**126.**	E	**138.**	A	**150.**	C
88.	B	**101.**	A	**114.**	A						

SCORING CHART—SAMPLE EXAMINATION 3

After you have scored your Sample Examination 3, enter the results in the chart below; then transfer your Raw Score to the Progress Chart on page 14.

Total Test		Number Right	Number Wrong	Number Omitted	Raw Score
Section I:	75				
Section II:	75				
Total:	150				

ANSWER EXPLANATIONS—SAMPLE EXAMINATION 3

Section I

1. D. The best known of the *Leather Stocking Tales* is *The Last of the Mohicans*.
2. B. Leatherstocking is scout, hunter, and trapper.
3. D. Dali is considered the founder of surrealism.
4. A. Nicolo Paganini (1784–1840) was a noted Italian violinist.
5. E. The abstract techniques employed could not be anything but modern.
6. D. Engelbert Humperdinck (1854–1921) was a German operatic composer. His second most famous opera is *Die Königskinder.*
7. E. Any other answer would be incomplete.
8. C. In the modern version, the play takes place in New York's Spanish Harlem.
9. D. The other works were not written about American soldiers in World War II.
10. C. The picture is of the fresco known as "The Last Supper."
11. E. Fresco is the art of painting on fresh plaster.
12. C. Ophelia is a character in Shakespeare's *Hamlet*.
13. E. Picasso was a virtuoso who mastered a variety of styles in painting. He also was a great sculptor.
14. D. Luke was the third of the evangelists, author of the Gospel bearing his name, and of the Book of Acts. "The Gospel According to Luke" is the third book of *The New Testament*.
15. A. Handel's great work was *The Messiah*.
16. B. This is an adequate definition of literary naturalism.
17. E. Aristotle, in "On the Nature of Tragedy," made this statement.
18. A. The Romantic Age originated in Europe toward the end of the 18th century. It asserted the validity of subjective experience.
19. C. Stevenson purportedly wrote the entire book in three days after he had the dream.
20. B. Simon today is one of Broadway's most prolific playwrights.
21. C. The others are not considered "pop" artists.
22. C. The other works are by Byron, but are not satires.
23. A. These are two of the most famous lines of English Romantic poetry.
24. C. Ithaca is one of the Ionian Islands, between Cephalonca and the mainland of Greece.
25. C. Vignon produced the imposing building with its surrounding Corinthian colonnade.
26. E. Brecht believed that theater was contrived. He wanted the audience to examine the work of art as a work of art, not as a game, a childish performance.
27. E. King Alfred's works were in prose.

28. E. Johann Sebastian Bach (1685–1750) was generally unrecognized until the 1800s when Mendelssohn became one of his most zealous champions.
29. D. Emily and her sister Charlotte, author of *Jane Eyre,* originally published their works under assumed names.
30. A. None of the others is a French Neo-Classic playwright.
31. D. The only other person named who was a playwright was Aristophanes, and he was a writer of comedy, not tragedy.
32. C. Frost, one of America's most admired poets, spent much of his adult life in New England and is most noted for his nature poems of the region.
33. B. Henry Moore is perhaps the outstanding contemporary sculptor. His concept of art is to treat space as volume instead of emptiness.
34. E. Plutarch lived from about 46 to 120. Although his history is not always trustworthy, his biographical technique is excellent.
35. D. Tacitus, the celebrated Roman historian, is the only one of this group who wrote about the customs and manners of the Germans.
36. A. O'Neill is the only author mentioned who wrote during the period 1919–1922.
37. A. Albee, an American playwright, deals with ordinary people in commonplace settings. Some plays, like *Who's Afraid of Virginia Woolf ?*, are noted for their realism and grim humor.
38. B. This is true by definition.
39. C. Ruark is perhaps best known for *Uhuru* and *Something of Value*.
40. E. The Old Market Woman is a vivid portrayal of the hardships of life in second century B.C. Greece.
41. C. Bernini's *Faun Teased by Children* is shown in the photograph.
42. B. Shown in the photograph is the Virgin and Child, expressively modeled in medieval times as a loving mother with her playful son.
43. A. Picasso, the only 20th century artist mentioned, has since died.
44. E. John Adams (1735–1826), second President of the United States, was on the committee which drafted the Declaration of Independence, and, in Jefferson's words, "was the pillar of its support on the floor of Congress."
45. B. Edgar Rice Burroughs (1875–1950), an American author, created Tarzan, one of the most famous characters in fiction.
46. A. Beethoven, the great German composer, has been called "the Shakespeare of music."
47. B. Boccaccio's *Decameron* is the only work mentioned that was supposedly told by a group of people attempting to escape a plague.
48. E. Piet Mondrian (1872–1944) was a Dutch Abstractionist.
49. D. Jones, influenced by Italian architecture, erected the royal Banqueting House in Whitehall, London, the earliest portion of Greenwich Hospital, and Covent Garden.
50. C. Goldsmith, who had a degree in medicine, may have been influenced by his medical studies to develop the acute attention to detail found in his works.
51. C. As Shakespeare matured, so did his characters.
52. A. This is true by definition.
53. D. Aristotle discusses this point in his essay *On the Nature of Tragedy.*
54. B. Chekhov's "slice of life" technique was, in itself, an innovation. Stanislavski's method was to force each actor to "feel" the role he was playing.
55. E. Henry James (1843–1916) was a novelist and essayist, and brother of William James, the noted psychologist.
56. A. "Hail, Columbia" is an American patriotic song with words written in 1798 by Joseph Hopkinson. The tune was probably written by Philip Phile, although claims are also made for Johannes Roth.
57. E. These lines are from T.S. Eliot's poem "The Wasteland."
58. C. The comedy of manners is a type of play that satirizes the extremes of fashion and manners of a highly sophisticated society. The English Restoration Period is especially noted for this type of play.
59. C. In drawing on the Freudian theory of psychoanalysis, Dali tried to bring elements of the subconscious to the surface, expressing them in symbolic

forms. In Dali's "Persistence of Memory," he suggests that, by the artist's created work, he defeats time and achieves immortality.

60. A. Archipenko was a sculptor and painter who specialized in female nudes.

61. D. In these lines, Huck mentions that he was a character in an earlier work by Twain, *The Adventures of Tom Sawyer.*

62. D. Georges Bizet's *Carmen,* his greatest success, was first produced in 1875.

63. B. Virginia Woolf (1882–1941) was a member of the "Bloomsbury Group," committed to excellence in art and literature.

64. A. The others are Romans, but not satiric playwrights.

65. B. The Diaghileff ballet played in London, Paris, Berlin, Vienna, and Budapest, as well as Moscow, and was headed by such stars as Michel Fokine, Anna Pavlova, and Vaslav Nijinsky.

66. C. "Non-objective" designates a style of graphic art that does not represent objects.

67. E. Writers of the genteel tradition upheld middle-class manners and morality.

68. B. The joint publication in 1798 of *Lyrical Ballads* by William Wordsworth and Samuel Taylor Coleridge is considered the beginning of the English Romantic Movement.

69. C. Burns is the only Scottish poet in the group.

70. A. In this sense "modeling" means to make by shaping a plastic substance.

71. E. The Fauve or "wild beasts" were organized in 1905 under the leadership of Matisse and included Derain, Vlaminck, Roualt, and Dufy.

72. D. Achilles was famous for his invincibility. The only place he could be injured was in his heel.

73. C. Deucalion and his wife, Pyrrha, were the only survivors of a great flood. An oracle told them to cast behind them the bones of their mother. These bones became human beings.

74. D. Robert Browning, Elizabeth's husband, was one of the major poets of the Victorian Era.

75. A. Byzantine art employed, with true Eastern impulse, materials of opulence and rich coloring, though the plastic forms themselves maintained a general simplicity.

Section II

76. E. Tempo is the relative speed at which a composition is to be played.

77. D. Webber also wrote the hit musical *Phantom of the Opera.*

78. C. Jason was the mythical hero who went in search of the Golden Fleece.

79. D. Grendel is the name of the monster in the Anglo-Saxon epic *Beowulf.*

80. B. The lines are from Donne's poem "Go and Catch a Falling Star," titled after the opening line.

81. B. The border design, plus the physiognomy of the man and the lion, should indicate that the urn is Roman.

82. E. None of the other answers applies to Beethoven's music. He was, however, noted for development, and repetition, of a theme.

83. C. The Parthenon, on the Acropolis at Athens, is the temple sacred to the goddess Athena.

84. D. The Romantic poets were subjective, emotional, and concerned with nature. They were fascinated by the cultures of ancient Greece and Rome and by the chivalric code of the Middle Ages.

85. D. Jean de La Fontaine (1621–1695) was a French poet and fabulist. His fables, written in verse, are models of delicate satire on the society of the period.

86. D. The other characters also appear in *The Odyssey,* but Penelope was Odysseus' faithful wife.

87. B. This is a standard musical notation.

88. B. The music for *Salome* was written by Richard Strauss.

89. D. Mólière was the great French playwright noted for his satiric comedies. None of the others mentioned wrote comedies.

90. B. The epic is a long, narrative poem on a serious subject, centered about a heroic figure on whose actions depends to some degree the fate of a nation or race. The folk epic is traditional in nature, and not written by a sophisticated craftsman, as is the literary epic.

91. A. Hesse's novel is entitled *Journey to the East*, not *Journey to the West*.

92. B. The others are also science-fiction writers, but Arthur C. Clarke is the one credited with first advancing the theory of communications satellites. His short story on the subject, "I Remember Babylon," has become a science-fiction classic.

93. D. Jack Kerouac's *On the Road* began a new era in American literature.

94. B. St. Anselm (1034?–1109) wrote the treatise *Proslogion,* which is an ontological proof of the existence of God.

95. E. Ambrose Bierce's collection of short stories *Tales of Soldiers and Civilians* and Stephen Crane's novel *The Red Badge of Courage* are classics of this period.

96. D. This is true by definition.

97. B. *The Bhagavad-Gita* is a Sanskrit philosophical poem incorporated in the great Hindu epic, the *Mahabharata*.

98. C. This is true by definition.

99. A. Copland won the Pulitzer Prize and the New York Music Critics' Award for "Appalachian Spring."

100. C. Henri de Toulouse-Lautrec (1864–1901) was a French lithographer and illustrator, noted for his lithographs of Montmartre and the music halls of Paris.

101. A. This is true by definition.

102. B. "Alienation" means a state of isolation. Aristotle believed the theater audience, through empathy, would suffer a catharsis of the emotions.

103. D. "The Lusiads," considered one of the great poems of the world, celebrates the adventures of Vasco da Gama and the splendors of Portuguese heroism and history.

104. E. Mozart (1756–1791) also wrote thirty string quartets, many sonatas, and concertos for the violin, piano, and organ, as well as several operas.

105. E. Shaw was one of the greatest playwrights of the English language. Among his best known plays are *Candida, Mrs. Warren's Profession, Pygmalion, Caesar and Cleopatra,* and *Man and Superman*.

106. D. Sophocles, the great Greek tragic poet, was born circa 496 B.C. and died circa 406 B.C. Shakespeare, the great English poet and dramatist, was born in 1564 and died in 1616.

107. A. This painting is more popularly known as "Whistler's Mother."

108. B. None of the others was a sculptor.

109. A. This is true by definition.

110. B. A "simile" is a comparison using "like" or "as."

111. C. "Commedia dell'arte," a type of comedy derived from ancient Greek and Roman models and presented by groups of strolling players in Italy, reached its height in the 16th century and spread through the Continent to England, greatly influencing literature and drama.

112. E. This is true by definition.

113. A. The play was first performed in New York in 1900. Puccini's opera was first performed in 1904.

114. A. *Gone with the Wind* was Mitchell's only great literary success.

115. D. The stage setting described in choice (D) is for Tennessee William's *Glass Menagerie.* The Warfields, the main characters in this play, are mentioned in the description—"the Warfield apartment."

116. A. Mention of Covent Garden, which sets the scene in London, is an important clue to the correct answer. This stage setting is for G. B. Shaw's *Pygmalion.*

117. E. The Shakespearean sonnet contains three quatrains and a concluding couplet.

118. C. Most medieval art centered on legends of great heroes or religion.

119. D. This is a translation from the French meaning "step of two."

120. B. The others are well-known American painters, but they did not paint Western scenes.

121. B. These are characteristics of Shakespeare's era.
122. A. The irony is that Oedipus is in reality the son of Laius, her former husband.
123. D. This is one of the basic tenets of drama.
124. E. This may be defined as a composition or passage in which the same melody is repeated by one or more voices, overlapping in time in the same or a related key.
125. E. Allegro means a rapid tempo.
126. E. In this passage, Pope is telling man to play God, if he dare.
127. C. The heroic couplet consists of two lines of verse, rhyming in pairs, in iambic pentameter.
128. B. None of the other instruments is tuned in this fashion.
129. D. The Greek god Dionysus, god of wine, is the patron of music and the arts.
130. E. Vulcan was the Roman, not Greek, god of fire.
131. E. William Dean Howells (1837–1920) was an American novelist, playwright, editor, and critic.
132. D. This is true by definition.
133. A. Jacques Louis David was a French painter who was born in 1748 and died in 1825. The post-Impressionists were late 19th century painters.
134. B. Egyptian wall paintings are highly stylized and anatomically unrealistic.
135. E. The vernacular, or language of the people, rarely contains figurative language that gives it cosmic significance. The tone of the epic was always lofty, and therefore did not approximate ordinary speech.
136. C. During the Renaissance, a story that ended happily or, at least, did not end miserably, was considered a "comedy."
137. E. This is a translation from the Greek.
138. A. The other composers may have written compositions for the piano, but Chopin is the best known of the group in this area.
139. E. This is true by definition.
140. D. In Cubism, the portrayals of natural forms are geometric. This school was founded circa 1910.
141. B. William Blake (1757–1827) is especially known for his *Songs of Innocence* and *Songs of Experience*.
142. E. Jules Massenet, a French operatic composer, never wrote an opera by this name.
143. B. Robert Browning's best known dramatic monologues are "My Last Duchess," "Fra Lippo Lippi," and "Andrea del Sarto."
144. D. Voltaire's *Candide* satirized the optimistic philosophy of the German Leibnitz.
145. D. This is true by definition.
146. B. A recitative is a musical style in which the text is declaimed in the rhythm of natural speech with slight melodic variation.
147. D. The chorus of elders is a convention of the Greek theater.
148. B. This is true by definition.
149. D. This is the only answer in which the order is correct.
150. C. T.S. Eliot wrote his poems, which were published in 1939 as *Old Possum's Book of Practical Cats,* for his godchildren.

PART THREE

THE MATHEMATICS EXAMINATION

ANSWER SHEET — MATHEMATICS/TRIAL TEST

Section I

1. Ⓐ Ⓑ Ⓒ Ⓓ Ⓔ
2. Ⓐ Ⓑ Ⓒ Ⓓ Ⓔ
3. Ⓐ Ⓑ Ⓒ Ⓓ Ⓔ
4. Ⓐ Ⓑ Ⓒ Ⓓ Ⓔ
5. Ⓐ Ⓑ Ⓒ Ⓓ Ⓔ
6. Ⓐ Ⓑ Ⓒ Ⓓ Ⓔ
7. Ⓐ Ⓑ Ⓒ Ⓓ Ⓔ
8. Ⓐ Ⓑ Ⓒ Ⓓ Ⓔ
9. Ⓐ Ⓑ Ⓒ Ⓓ Ⓔ
10. Ⓐ Ⓑ Ⓒ Ⓓ Ⓔ
11. Ⓐ Ⓑ Ⓒ Ⓓ Ⓔ
12. Ⓐ Ⓑ Ⓒ Ⓓ Ⓔ
13. Ⓐ Ⓑ Ⓒ Ⓓ Ⓔ
14. Ⓐ Ⓑ Ⓒ Ⓓ Ⓔ
15. Ⓐ Ⓑ Ⓒ Ⓓ Ⓔ
16. Ⓐ Ⓑ Ⓒ Ⓓ Ⓔ
17. Ⓐ Ⓑ Ⓒ Ⓓ Ⓔ
18. Ⓐ Ⓑ Ⓒ Ⓓ Ⓔ
19. Ⓐ Ⓑ Ⓒ Ⓓ Ⓔ
20. Ⓐ Ⓑ Ⓒ Ⓓ Ⓔ
21. Ⓐ Ⓑ Ⓒ Ⓓ Ⓔ
22. Ⓐ Ⓑ Ⓒ Ⓓ Ⓔ
23. Ⓐ Ⓑ Ⓒ Ⓓ Ⓔ
24. Ⓐ Ⓑ Ⓒ Ⓓ Ⓔ
25. Ⓐ Ⓑ Ⓒ Ⓓ Ⓔ
26. Ⓐ Ⓑ Ⓒ Ⓓ Ⓔ
27. Ⓐ Ⓑ Ⓒ Ⓓ Ⓔ
28. Ⓐ Ⓑ Ⓒ Ⓓ Ⓔ
29. Ⓐ Ⓑ Ⓒ Ⓓ Ⓔ
30. Ⓐ Ⓑ Ⓒ Ⓓ Ⓔ
31. Ⓐ Ⓑ Ⓒ Ⓓ Ⓔ
32. Ⓐ Ⓑ Ⓒ Ⓓ Ⓔ
33. Ⓐ Ⓑ Ⓒ Ⓓ Ⓔ
34. Ⓐ Ⓑ Ⓒ Ⓓ Ⓔ
35. Ⓐ Ⓑ Ⓒ Ⓓ Ⓔ
36. Ⓐ Ⓑ Ⓒ Ⓓ Ⓔ
37. Ⓐ Ⓑ Ⓒ Ⓓ Ⓔ
38. Ⓐ Ⓑ Ⓒ Ⓓ Ⓔ
39. Ⓐ Ⓑ Ⓒ Ⓓ Ⓔ
40. Ⓐ Ⓑ Ⓒ Ⓓ Ⓔ

Section II

41. Ⓐ Ⓑ Ⓒ Ⓓ Ⓔ
42. Ⓐ Ⓑ Ⓒ Ⓓ Ⓔ
43. Ⓐ Ⓑ Ⓒ Ⓓ Ⓔ
44. Ⓐ Ⓑ Ⓒ Ⓓ Ⓔ
45. Ⓐ Ⓑ Ⓒ Ⓓ Ⓔ
46. Ⓐ Ⓑ Ⓒ Ⓓ Ⓔ
47. Ⓐ Ⓑ Ⓒ Ⓓ Ⓔ
48. Ⓐ Ⓑ Ⓒ Ⓓ Ⓔ
49. Ⓐ Ⓑ Ⓒ Ⓓ Ⓔ
50. Ⓐ Ⓑ Ⓒ Ⓓ Ⓔ
51. Ⓐ Ⓑ Ⓒ Ⓓ Ⓔ
52. Ⓐ Ⓑ Ⓒ Ⓓ Ⓔ
53. Ⓐ Ⓑ Ⓒ Ⓓ Ⓔ
54. Ⓐ Ⓑ Ⓒ Ⓓ Ⓔ
55. Ⓐ Ⓑ Ⓒ Ⓓ Ⓔ
56. Ⓐ Ⓑ Ⓒ Ⓓ Ⓔ
57. Ⓐ Ⓑ Ⓒ Ⓓ Ⓔ
58. Ⓐ Ⓑ Ⓒ Ⓓ Ⓔ
59. Ⓐ Ⓑ Ⓒ Ⓓ Ⓔ
60. Ⓐ Ⓑ Ⓒ Ⓓ Ⓔ
61. Ⓐ Ⓑ Ⓒ Ⓓ Ⓔ
62. Ⓐ Ⓑ Ⓒ Ⓓ Ⓔ
63. Ⓐ Ⓑ Ⓒ Ⓓ Ⓔ
64. Ⓐ Ⓑ Ⓒ Ⓓ Ⓔ
65. Ⓐ Ⓑ Ⓒ Ⓓ Ⓔ
66. Ⓐ Ⓑ Ⓒ Ⓓ Ⓔ
67. Ⓐ Ⓑ Ⓒ Ⓓ Ⓔ
68. Ⓐ Ⓑ Ⓒ Ⓓ Ⓔ
69. Ⓐ Ⓑ Ⓒ Ⓓ Ⓔ
70. Ⓐ Ⓑ Ⓒ Ⓓ Ⓔ
71. Ⓐ Ⓑ Ⓒ Ⓓ Ⓔ
72. Ⓐ Ⓑ Ⓒ Ⓓ Ⓔ
73. Ⓐ Ⓑ Ⓒ Ⓓ Ⓔ
74. Ⓐ Ⓑ Ⓒ Ⓓ Ⓔ
75. Ⓐ Ⓑ Ⓒ Ⓓ Ⓔ
76. Ⓐ Ⓑ Ⓒ Ⓓ Ⓔ
77. Ⓐ Ⓑ Ⓒ Ⓓ Ⓔ
78. Ⓐ Ⓑ Ⓒ Ⓓ Ⓔ
79. Ⓐ Ⓑ Ⓒ Ⓓ Ⓔ
80. Ⓐ Ⓑ Ⓒ Ⓓ Ⓔ
81. Ⓐ Ⓑ Ⓒ Ⓓ Ⓔ
82. Ⓐ Ⓑ Ⓒ Ⓓ Ⓔ
83. Ⓐ Ⓑ Ⓒ Ⓓ Ⓔ
84. Ⓐ Ⓑ Ⓒ Ⓓ Ⓔ
85. Ⓐ Ⓑ Ⓒ Ⓓ Ⓔ
86. Ⓐ Ⓑ Ⓒ Ⓓ Ⓔ
87. Ⓐ Ⓑ Ⓒ Ⓓ Ⓔ
88. Ⓐ Ⓑ Ⓒ Ⓓ Ⓔ
89. Ⓐ Ⓑ Ⓒ Ⓓ Ⓔ
90. Ⓐ Ⓑ Ⓒ Ⓓ Ⓔ

CHAPTER

9 Trial Test

The trial Mathematics test will show you what an actual examination is like and help you decide which areas of mathematics you may need to review.

The examination consists of two separately timed sections. Section I (Basic Skills and Concepts) has 40 questions to be answered in 30 minutes. It tests skills that are generally taught in high school and that are frequently used in college courses other than mathematics—arithmetic, algebra, geometry, and data interpretation. Section II (Content) has 50 questions to be answered in 60 minutes. It covers material that is studied at the college level—sets, logic, the real number system, functions and their graphs, probability and statistics, and miscellaneous topics (for example, complex numbers, logarithms and exponentials).

Section I Basic Skills and Concepts

Directions for questions 1–25: Each of these questions consists of two quantities, one in Column A and one in Column B. You are to compare the two quantities and on the answer sheet blacken space

A if the quantity in Column A is greater;

B if the quantity in Column B is greater;

C if the two quantities are equal;

D if the relationship cannot be determined from the information given.

Notes:

1. In certain questions, information concerning one or both of the quantities to be compared is centered above the two columns.
2. A symbol that appears in both columns represents the same thing in Column A as it does in Column B.
3. Letters such as x, n, and k stand for real numbers.

	COLUMN A	COLUMN B
1.	$3 - 5 + 6 - 8 - 4 + 7$	-2
	Ice cream sells for \$0.55 a pint.	
2.	the cost of $2\frac{1}{2}$ quarts of ice cream	\$2.75
	Everything in a store is marked down 15% in a sale.	
3.	sale price of a \$95 minicomputer	\$80
	The sides of two squares are in the ratio $\sqrt{2} : 1$. Their diagonals are in the ratio $y : \sqrt{2}$	
4.	y	2
	A $2\frac{1}{4}$-lb. package of meat costs \$3.04.	
5.	the cost of one ounce of meat	8¢
6.	one square yard	1600 square inches
7.	the number of cents in d dimes and q quarters	$35q$
8.	$5 - [6 - 2(1 + 3)]$	7
9.	$\frac{\lvert x - y\rvert}{y - x}$	1
	Mike takes 3 hours to mow a lawn; his younger brother Cary takes 4 hours.	
10.	time it takes both boys working together to mow the lawn	$1\frac{1}{2}$ hours
11.	$(1.1)^{-1}$	1

L, M, N: $y°$, $x°$, MN = 2.4"

L′, M′, N′: $y°$, $x°$, L′N′ = 10", M′N′ = 4"

12.	$L'M'$	LN
13.	$\frac{3}{4} \times \frac{10}{7} \div \frac{3}{2}$	$\frac{10}{4} \div \frac{3}{2} \times \frac{3}{7}$

	COLUMN A	COLUMN B

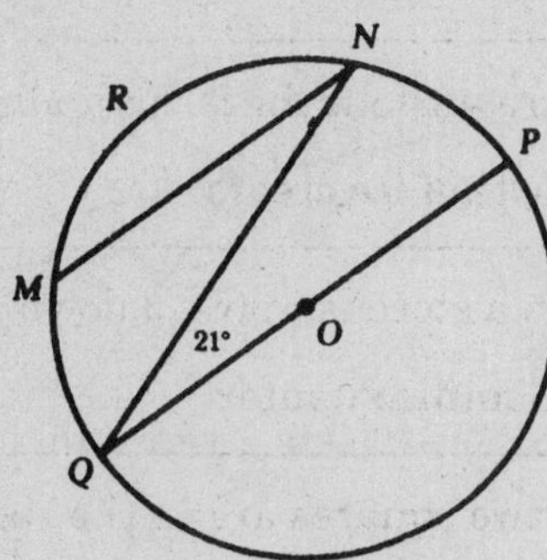

$MN \parallel QP$ in circle O.

14.	measure of $\widehat{MRN}$	96°

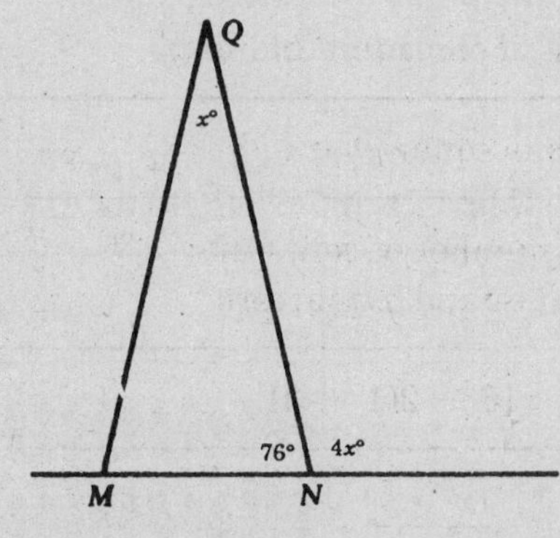

15.	m($\angle M$)	80°

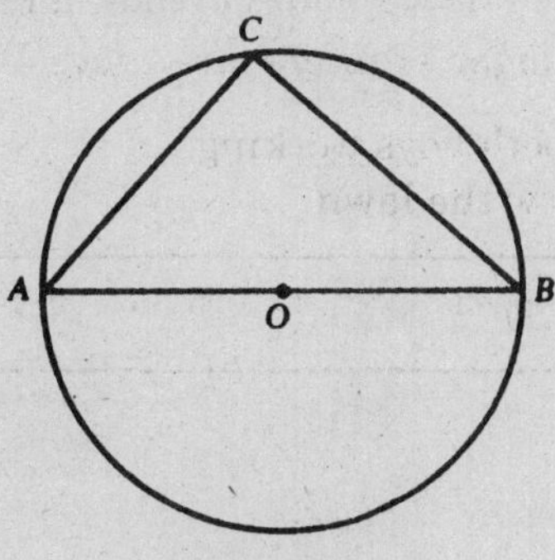

radius $OB = 2''$
$BC = 3''$

16.	AC	OB

The hypotenuse of an isosceles right triangle is 2″.

17.	length of one leg of the triangle	1″

$$2x - y = 2$$
$$x + 2y = 6$$

18.	x	y

	COLUMN A	COLUMN B

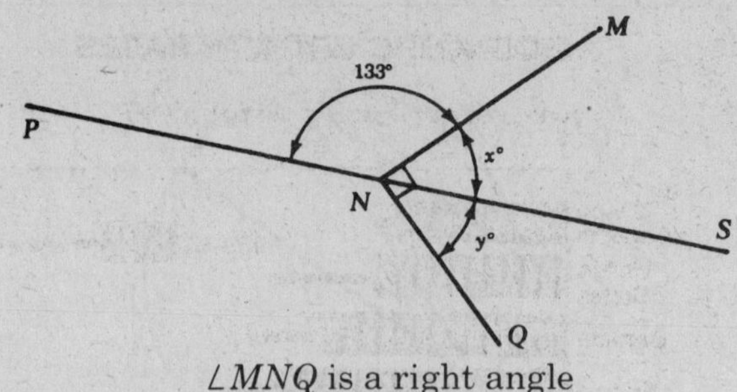

$\angle MNQ$ is a right angle

19.	x	y

A and *B* are 3000 miles apart. A plane travels from *A* to *B* in 5 hours but takes more than 5 hours to fly from *B* to *A*.

20.	The plane's average speed for the round trip	600 mph

Use this figure for questions 21 and 22.

THE TEN MOST POPULOUS COUNTRIES: 1979

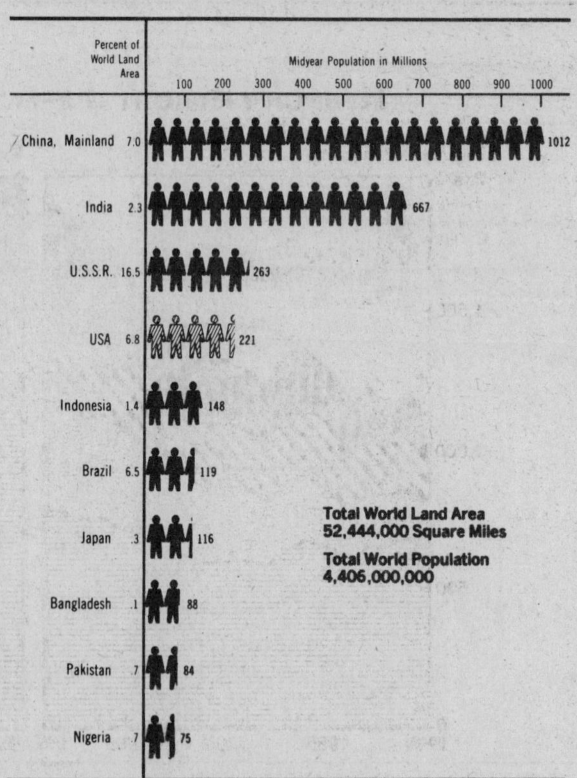

Source: Data, 1979, p. iv.

21.	population, in millions, of Pakistan in 1979	**88**
22.	difference, in millions, between populations of USSR and USA in 1979	**42**

COLUMN A	COLUMN B

Use this bar graph for question 23.

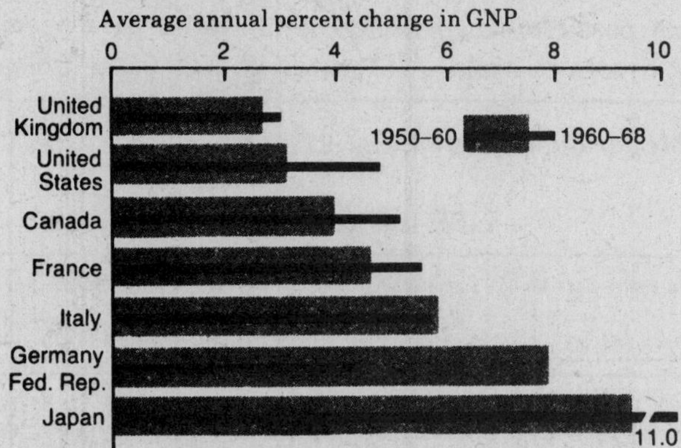

Source: Data, 1971, p. 10.

23. average annual percent change in GNP from 1960 to 1968 in the USA — 4%

Use this figure for questions 24 and 25.

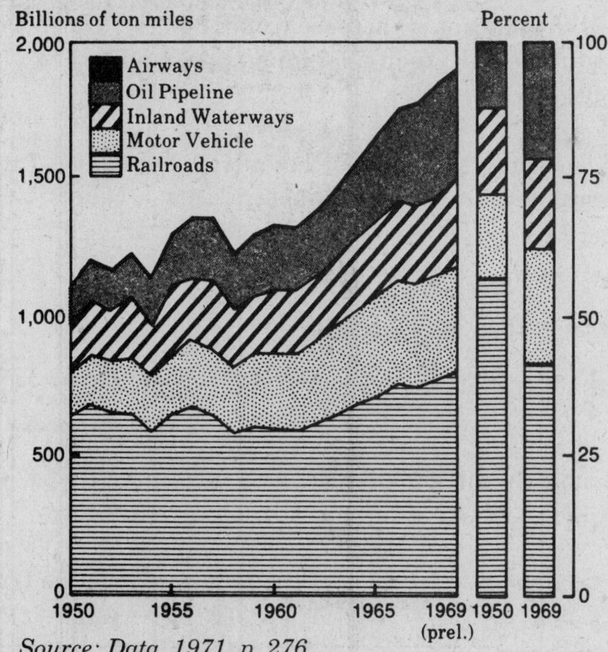

Source: Data, 1971, p. 276.

24. percent of intercity freight traffic carried by motor vehicles in 1969 — 30

Percent of total intercity freight traffic carried by railroads

25. 1950 — 1969

Directions for questions 26–40: For these questions, indicate the correct answer in the appropriate space on the answer sheet.

Note: Figures that accompany the following problems are intended to provide information useful in answering the questions. The figures are drawn as accurately as possible *except* when it is stated in a specific question that the figure is not drawn to scale. All figures lie in a plane unless otherwise stated.

Use this table for questions 26 and 27.

LIFE EXPECTANCY AT BIRTH

In years. Data for 1920 and 1930 for death-registration states only.

Race and sex	1920	1930	1940	1950	1960	1965	1970	1975	1976	1977
Total	54.1	59.7	62.9	68.2	69.7	70.2	70.9	72.5	72.8	73.2
Male	53.6	58.1	60.8	65.6	66.6	66.8	67.1	68.7	69.0	69.3
Female	54.6	61.6	65.2	71.1	73.1	73.7	74.8	76.5	76.7	77.1
White	54.9	61.4	64.2	69.1	70.6	71.0	71.7	73.2	73.5	73.8
Male	54.4	59.7	62.1	66.5	67.4	67.6	68.0	69.4	69.7	70.0
Female	55.6	63.5	66.6	72.2	74.1	74.7	75.6	77.2	77.3	77.7
Black and other	45.3	48.1	53.1	60.8	63.6	64.1	65.3	67.9	68.3	68.8
Male	45.5	47.3	51.5	59.1	61.1	61.1	61.3	63.6	64.1	64.6
Female	45.2	49.2	54.9	62.9	66.3	67.4	69.4	72.3	72.6	73.1

Source: Data, 1979, p. 74, Table No. 61.

26. The life expectancy, in years, of a white male born in 1977 is
(A) 64.6 (B) 69.3 (C) 70.0 (D) 73.2

27. If p is the percent of increase from 1940 to 1977 in the life expectancy of a nonwhite female, then p is equal approximately to
(A) 3% (B) 10% (C) 33% (D) 40%

28. The wavelength of the shortest ultraviolet light is 7.6×10^{-9} meters. If this is written as 7.6×10^{n} centimeters, then n equals
(A) -11 (B) -10 (C) -8 (D) -7

29. If $m \neq 0$, then $\frac{4^0 m^4 n^0}{4m^4} =$
(A) $\frac{1}{4}$ (B) $\frac{n}{4}$ (C) 1 (D) n

30. The smallest integer that satisfies the inequality $5x + 9 > 1$ is
(A) -2 (B) -1 (C) 0 (D) 1

31. If $x > y$ and $x > z$, which of the following must be true for all real x, y, z?
(A) $y > z$ (B) $(x - y)(x - z) > 0$
(C) $x^2 > xy$ (D) $x > 0$

32. $^{13}/_{4} =$
(A) 3.25% (B) $3.33\frac{1}{3}$% (C) 320% (D) 325%

33. If $a:b = 2:3$ and $a = 7$, then $b =$
(A) $^{2}/_{21}$ (B) $4\frac{2}{3}$ (C) 14 (D) $10\frac{1}{2}$

34. Which equation is *not* satisfied by $x = -3$?
(A) $x^2 - 9 = 0$ (B) $x^2 + 3x = 0$
(C) $x^2 + 9 = 0$ (D) $x^2 + x - 6 = 0$

35. 20 is 125% of what number?
(A) 12 (B) 16 (C) 18 (D) 25

36. Which of the following lines is parallel to the line $4x + 3y - 12 = 0$?
(A) $x + 3y - 12 = 0$ (B) $y = {}^4/_3x + 2$
(C) $y = -{}^4/_3x + 4$ (D) $y = -{}^3/_4x + 2$

37. The reciprocal of a real number other than zero is also called its
(A) additive identity (B) additive inverse
(C) multiplicative identity (D) multiplicative inverse

38. If x is different from 0 and 1, then $\frac{x^2 - x}{x(x^2 - 1)} =$
(A) $\frac{1}{x + 1}$ (B) $\frac{1}{x - 1}$ (C) $\frac{1}{x(x + 1)}$ (D) $\frac{1}{x}$

39. What does x equal if the average of x, 5, 8, and 13 is 8?
(A) 6 (B) 7 (C) 8 (D) 10

40. $3^0 + 3^1 + 3^2 =$
(A) 9 (B) 12 (C) 13 (D) 27

Section II Content

Directions: For each the following problems, indicate the correct answer in the appropriate space on the answer sheet.

Note: Figures that accompany problems in this part are intended to provide information useful in solving the problems. They are drawn as accurately as possible *except* when it is stated in a specific problem that the figure is not drawn to scale. All figures lie in a plane unless otherwise stated.

41. If $R = \{a,b\}$, $S = \{a,c,d\}$, and $T = \{b,c\}$, then $R \cap (S \cup T)$ equals
(A) $\{a\}$ (B) $\{b\}$ (C) $\{a,b\}$ (D) $\{a,b,c,d\}$

42. If S has 3 elements, then the number of ordered triples in $S \times S \times S$ is
(A) 3 (B) 9 (C) 27 (D) 81

43. If $R = \{6\}$, $S = \{3,6\}$, $T = \{1,2,3\}$, and $W = \{2,3,6\}$, then it is false that
(A) $R \cup S = W$ (B) $R \cap T = \emptyset$ (C) $R \subset S \subset W$ (D) $(R \cap S) \subset W$

44. $R - S = \{x : x \in R, x \notin S\}$. The Venn diagram for $R - S$ is

(A)

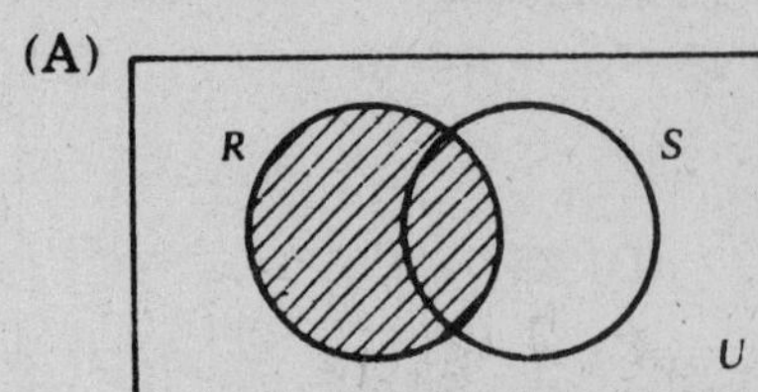

(B)

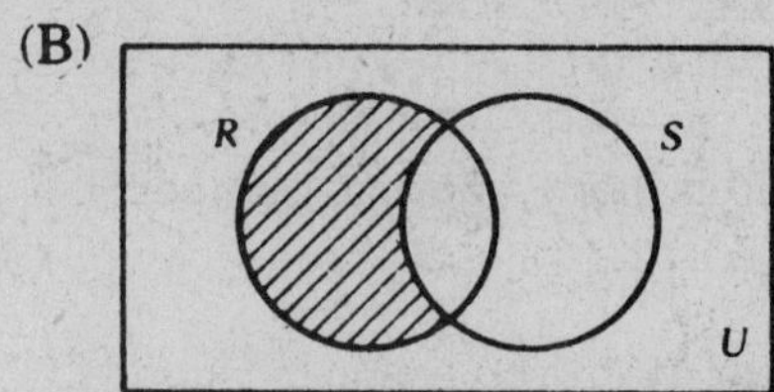

(C)

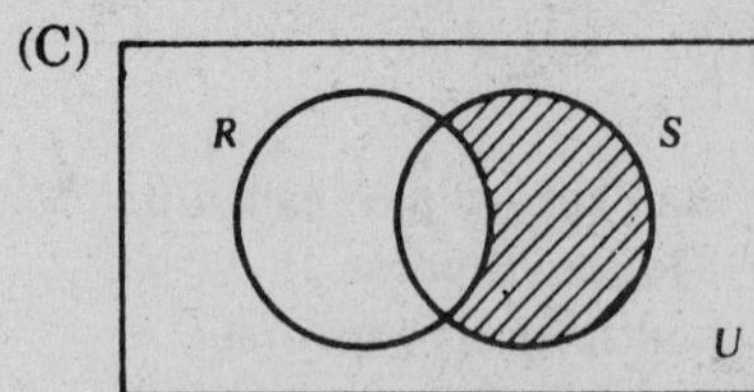

(D)

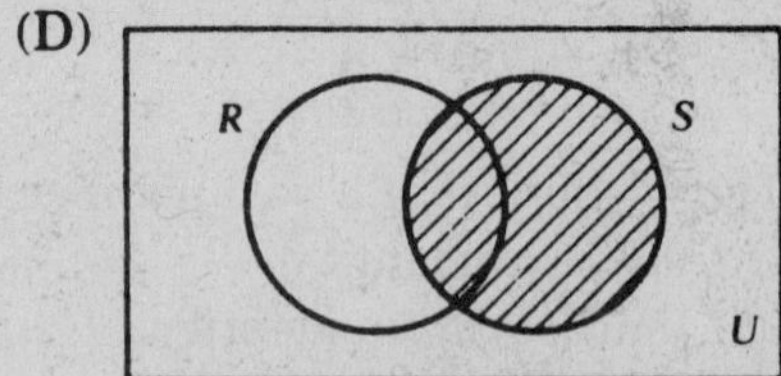

45. If R^+ is the set of positive real numbers and Z is the set of integers, then $R^+ \cap Z$ equals
(A) the set of positive integers (B) $\{x : x \text{ is an integer}, x \geqq 0\}$
(C) Z (D) R^+

46. Which statement is *not* equivalent to "If a korb chools, then it stibbles"?
(A) If a korb does not stibble, then it does not chool.
(B) A necessary condition for a korb to stibble is that it chool.
(C) A korb chools only if it stibbles.
(D) For a korb to stibble it suffices that it chool.

47. If the statements $p \rightarrow q$ and $q \rightarrow \sim r$ are true, then a valid conclusion is
(A) $p \rightarrow r$ (B) $\sim p \rightarrow r$ (C) $r \rightarrow p$ (D) $r \rightarrow \sim p$

48. $\sim(p \vee \sim q)$ is true whenever
(A) p is false and q is true (B) p is true
(C) q is true (D) p and q are both false

49. Let x be an integer. A proof of the claim that "if x^2 is odd, then x is odd" may proceed as follows:
(A) Take an example, say $x = 5$. Note that x^2 is odd and so is x.
(B) Show that if x^2 is even, then so is x.
(C) Show that if x is odd, then so is x^2.
(D) Show that if x is even, then so is x^2.

50. Suppose $a < b$ (a, b real). Then it always follows that
(A) $-a > -b$ (B) $-a < -b$ (C) $-a < b$ (D) none of the preceding

51. $(3^2 + 4^2)^{-1/2} =$
(A) $1/49$ (B) $1/25$ (C) $1/7$ (D) $1/5$

52. Which number is irrational?
(A) 0 (B) x such that $x^2 = 8$ (C) $1/6$ (D) $\sqrt{121}$

53. If a, b, c, d are integers and $bd \neq 0$, then it is false that

(A) $\frac{a}{b} \div \frac{c}{d} = \frac{ad}{bc}$ (B) $\frac{-a}{b} = \frac{a}{-b}$

(C) $\frac{b}{b+d} = \frac{1}{1+d}$ (D) $\frac{b+d}{d} = 1 + \frac{b}{d}$

54. The set of odd integers is closed under

(A) multiplication (B) addition

(C) division (D) subtraction and multiplication

55. The function whose graph is shown is

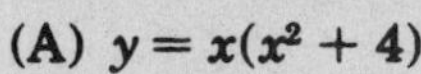

(A) $y = x(x^2 + 4)$

(B) $y = x(4 - x^2)$

(C) $y = x(x^2 - 4)$

(D) $y = x(x^2 + 2)$

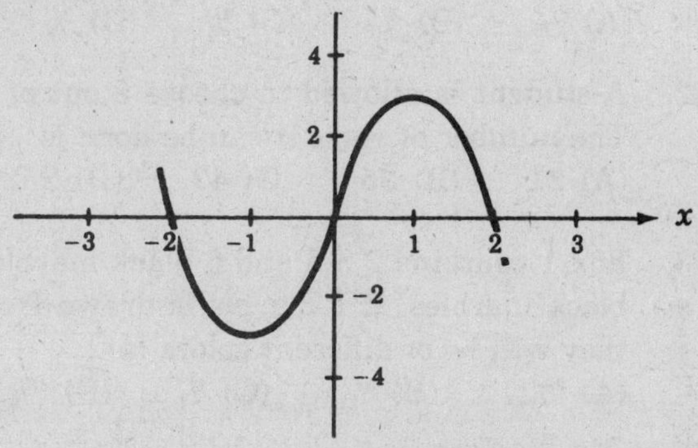

56. If $f(x) = \frac{1}{x+2}$ and $g(x) = \frac{1}{x} - 2$, then $f(g(x)) =$

(A) $\frac{1}{x+2} - 2$ (B) $x + 2$ (C) $\frac{1}{x}$ (D) x

57. Which pair of integers (m,n) does *not* satisfy the inequality $3m - 2n \leq 4$?

(A) $(-4,-9)$ (B) $(-1,2)$ (C) $(2,1)$ (D) $(0,-2)$

58. Which diagram does *not* define a function from $X(x_1,x_2,x_3,x_4)$ into $Y(y_1,y_2,y_3)$?

(A)

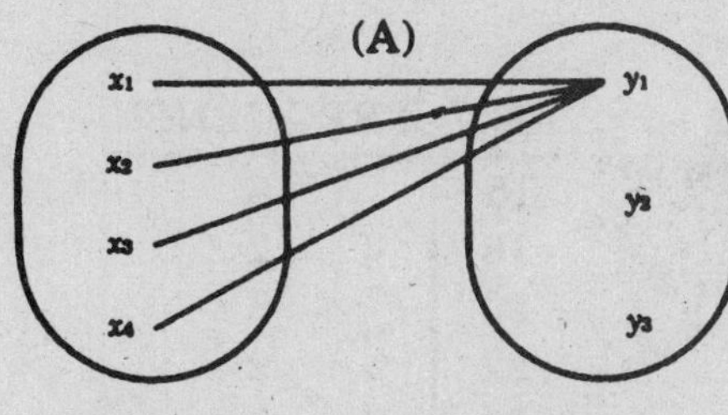

(B)

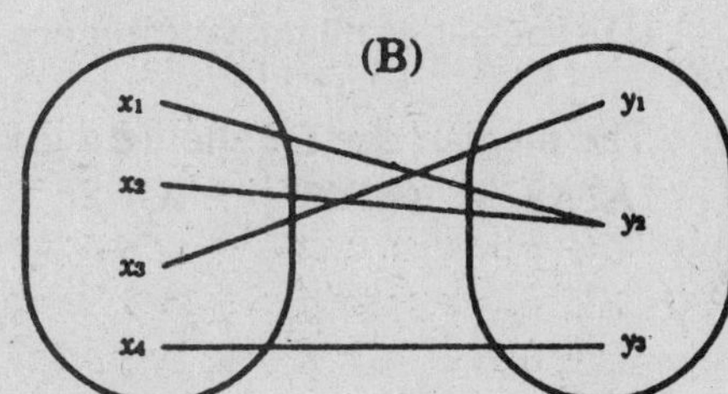

(C)

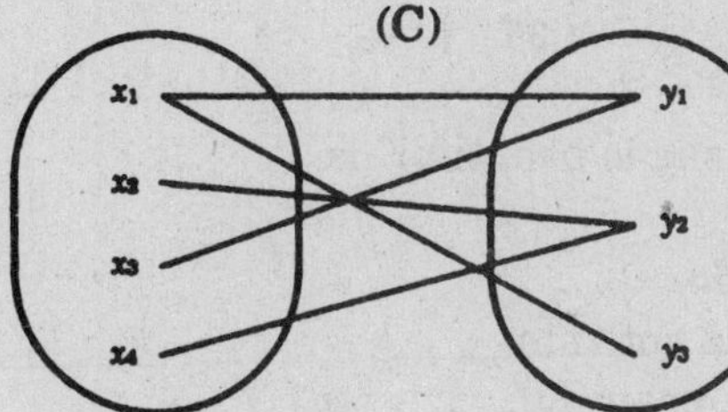

(D)

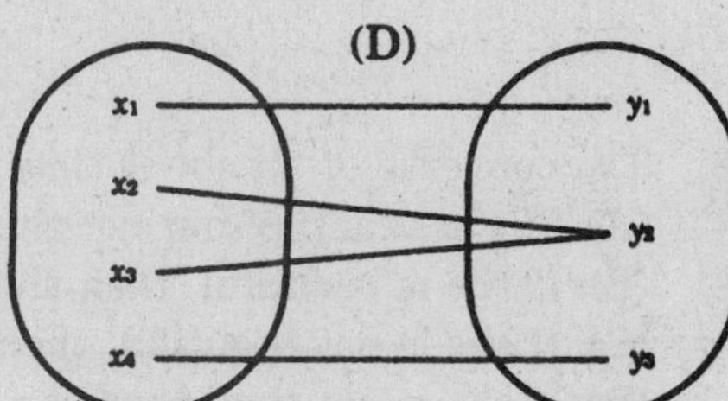

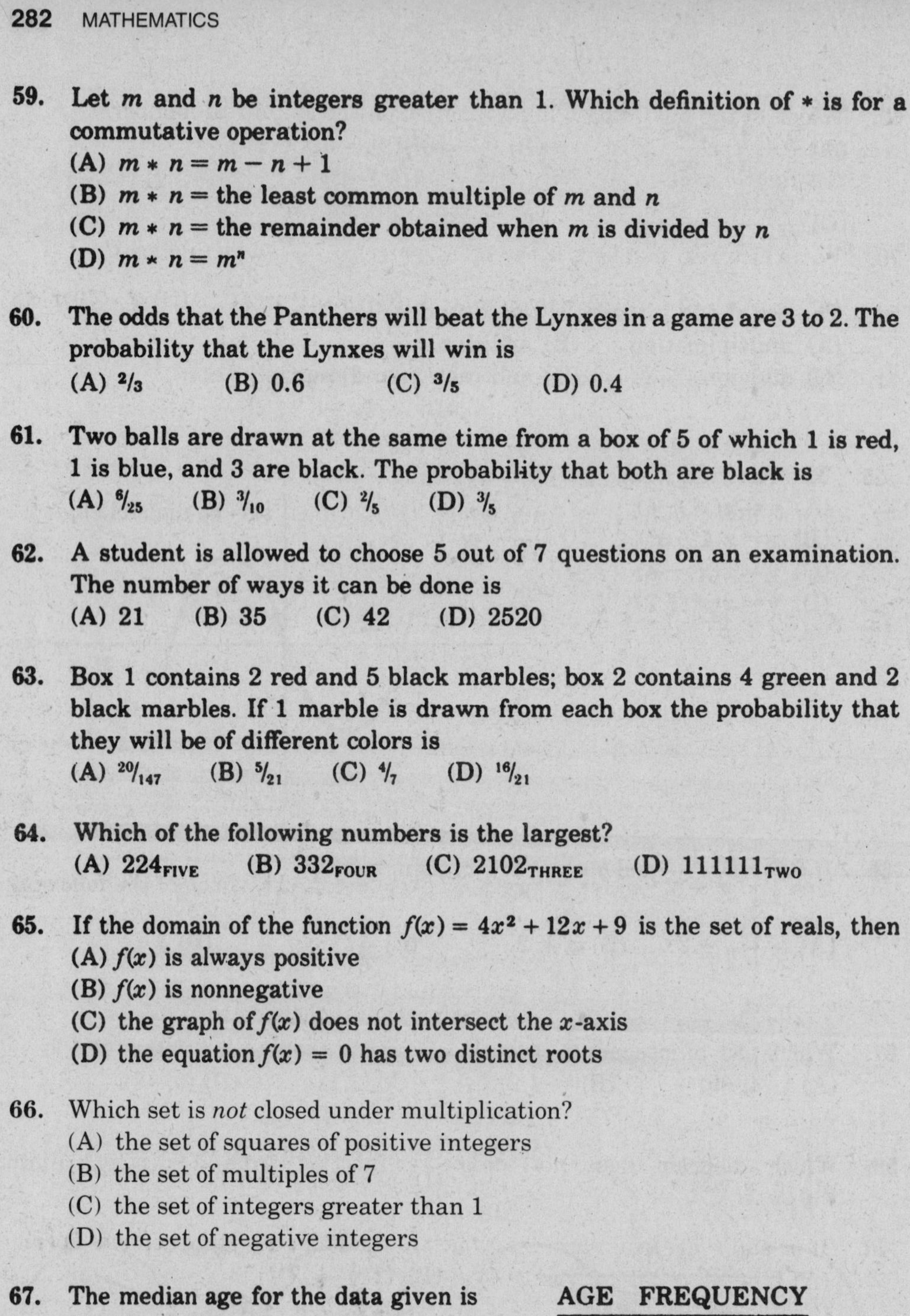

59. Let m and n be integers greater than 1. Which definition of $*$ is for a commutative operation?
(A) $m * n = m - n + 1$
(B) $m * n =$ the least common multiple of m and n
(C) $m * n =$ the remainder obtained when m is divided by n
(D) $m * n = m^n$

60. The odds that the Panthers will beat the Lynxes in a game are 3 to 2. The probability that the Lynxes will win is
(A) $2/3$ (B) 0.6 (C) $3/5$ (D) 0.4

61. Two balls are drawn at the same time from a box of 5 of which 1 is red, 1 is blue, and 3 are black. The probability that both are black is
(A) $6/25$ (B) $3/10$ (C) $2/5$ (D) $3/5$

62. A student is allowed to choose 5 out of 7 questions on an examination. The number of ways it can be done is
(A) 21 (B) 35 (C) 42 (D) 2520

63. Box 1 contains 2 red and 5 black marbles; box 2 contains 4 green and 2 black marbles. If 1 marble is drawn from each box the probability that they will be of different colors is
(A) $20/147$ (B) $5/21$ (C) $4/7$ (D) $16/21$

64. Which of the following numbers is the largest?
(A) 224_{FIVE} (B) 332_{FOUR} (C) 2102_{THREE} (D) 111111_{TWO}

65. If the domain of the function $f(x) = 4x^2 + 12x + 9$ is the set of reals, then
(A) $f(x)$ is always positive
(B) $f(x)$ is nonnegative
(C) the graph of $f(x)$ does not intersect the x-axis
(D) the equation $f(x) = 0$ has two distinct roots

66. Which set is *not* closed under multiplication?
(A) the set of squares of positive integers
(B) the set of multiples of 7
(C) the set of integers greater than 1
(D) the set of negative integers

67. The median age for the data given is
(A) 19 (B) 20 (C) 21 (D) 22

AGE	FREQUENCY
15	6
18	2
20	9
22	2
30	8
31	1

68. The converse of "If she is thin, then she is beautiful" is
(A) She is beautiful but not thin.
(B) If she is beautiful, then she is thin.
(C) If she is not beautiful, then she is not thin.
(D) If she is not thin, then she is not beautiful.

69. Which of the following is *not* a function on the set of real numbers?
(A) $f(x) = x^2$ (B) $f(x) = 3x + 1$
(C) $f(x) = \sqrt{x}$ (D) $f(x) = 1$

70. For which real numbers is the function $f(x) = \dfrac{x}{x^2 - 9}$ *not* defined?
(A) only $x = 0$ (B) only $x = 3$ (C) $x = 0$ or 3 (D) $x = 3$ or -3

71. The set $\{x : x$ is an integer and $|x - 1| < 2\}$ equals
(A) $\{1, 2\}$ (B) $\{-2, -1, 1, 2\}$
(C) $\{-2, -1, 0, 1, 2\}$ (D) $\{0, 1, 2\}$

72. If n is divisible both by 6 and by 10, then it must also be divisible by
(A) 12 (B) 20 (C) 30 (D) 60

73. If $f(x) = x^2 + bx + c$, if $f(0) = 1$ and $f(1) = 2$, then $f(x) =$
(A) $x^2 + 1$ (B) $x^2 + x + 1$
(C) $x^2 - x + 1$ (D) $x^2 + 2x + 1$

74. If a, b, and c are real numbers and $a > b > c$, then which of the following could be false?
(A) $b - a > 0$ (B) $ab > ac$ (C) $-a < -b$ (D) $c - a < 0$

75. If m and n are positive integers, m even and n odd, which of the following numbers is odd?
(A) $mn + 2$ (B) m^n (C) $5n + 1$ (D) n^m

76. If p is false and q is true, then which of the following is false?
(A) $\sim p \rightarrow \sim q$ (B) $p \rightarrow q$ (C) $\sim p \rightarrow q$ (D) $p \rightarrow \sim q$

77. If $f(x) = ax + b$, $f(0) = 2$, and $f(1) = -1$, then
(A) $a = 3, b = 2$ (B) $a = 3, b = -2$
(C) $a = -3, b = 2$ (D) $a = -3, b = -2$

78. If m and n are real numbers, which of the following statements is false?
(A) $2^m \cdot 2^n = 2^{mn}$ (B) $(2^m)^n = 2^{mn}$
(C) $2^m \div 2^n = 2^{m-n}$ (D) $2^m \cdot 2^n = 2^{m+n}$

79. $\log_4 8 =$
(A) $1/2$ (B) $2/3$ (C) $3/2$ (D) 2

80. If $\log_{10} m = 0.1$, then $\log_{10} m^3 =$
(A) 0.001 (B) 0.3 (C) 3.1 (D) 3.3

81. If $m * n = m^2 - 2n$, then $3 * (2 * 1) =$
(A) 23 (B) 9 (C) 7 (D) 5

82. If $i = \sqrt{-1}$, then $i^{19} =$
(A) 1 (B) -1 (C) i (D) $-i$

83. If a die is tossed, what is the probability that the top face will *not* show a 1 or a 2?
(A) $^1/_{36}$ (B) $^1/_6$ (C) $^1/_3$ (D) $^2/_3$

84. If $f(x) = x^3 + k$ and $f(x)$ is divisible by the factor $(x + 2)$, then $k =$
(A) -8 (B) -2 (C) 0 (D) 8

85. The set satisfying the inequality $|x| < 2$ is
(A) $\{x : -2 < x < 2\}$ (B) $\{x : -2 \leq x \leq 2\}$
(C) $\{x : x < -2 \text{ or } x > 2\}$ (D) $\{x : 0 < x < 2\}$

86. For what value of k do the equations
$\begin{cases} 2x - y = 4 \\ 4x + ky = 3 \end{cases}$ have no solution?
(A) -8 (B) -2 (C) 2 (D) 8

87. If $x^2 - x > 0$, then which of the following statements is false?
(A) $x < 0$ (B) $x > 1$ (C) $0 < x < 1$ (D) $x < 0$ or $x > 1$

88. Which function has a graph symmetric to the origin?
(A) $y = x^2$ (B) $y = \frac{1}{x^2}$ (C) $y = x + 3$ (D) $y = \frac{1}{x}$

89. The difference between the mean and the median (mean minus median) for the set {35, 41, 52, 33, 49} is
(A) 0 (B) 1 (C) 2 (D) 3

90. The inverse of the function $y = 2^x$ is
(A) $y = \log_2 x$ (B) $y = -2^x$ (C) $y = 2^{-x}$ (D) $y = x^2$

ANSWER KEY AND REFERENCE CHART—TRIAL TEST

Each answer in the key below is followed by a reference* to the section of the book in which the topic of the question is reviewed. (Explanations of the answers follow the answer key.) The topics covered on the Mathematics examination are listed below with their reference code and the page on which review of the topic begins.

Topic	Reference	Page
Arithmetic	A1	303
Algebra	A2	306
Geometry	A3	310
Data Interpretation	A4	315
Sets	B1	330
Logic	B2	334
Real Number System	B3	337
Functions and Their Graphs	B4	341
Probability and Statistics	B5	346
Miscellaneous Topics	B6	352

*A question in mathematics is often on material from two or more topics. The reference given for each question lists the principal topic covered.

Section I

1.	A (A1)	**11.**	B (A2)	**21.**	B (A4)	**31.**	B (A2)
2.	C (A1)	**12.**	A (A3)	**22.**	C (A4)	**32.**	D (A1)
3.	A (A1)	**13.**	C (A1)	**23.**	A (A4)	**33.**	D (A1)
4.	C (A3)	**14.**	C (A3)	**24.**	B (A4)	**34.**	C (A2)
5.	A (A1)	**15.**	B (A3)	**25.**	A (A4)	**35.**	B (A1)
6.	B (A1)	**16.**	A (A3)	**26.**	C (A4)	**36.**	C (A3)
7.	D (A2)	**17.**	A (A3)	**27.**	C (A4)	**37.**	D (A1)
8.	C (A2)	**18.**	C (A2)	**28.**	D (A1)	**38.**	A (A2)
9.	D (A2)	**19.**	A (A3)	**29.**	A (A2)	**39.**	A (A2)
10.	A (A2)	**20.**	B (A2)	**30.**	B (A2)	**40.**	C (A2)

Section II

41.	C (B1)	**51.**	D (B3)	**61.**	B (B5)	**71.**	D (B3)	**81.**	D (B6)
42.	C (B1)	**52.**	B (B3)	**62.**	A (B5)	**72.**	C (B3)	**82.**	D (B6)
43.	A (B1)	**53.**	C (B3)	**63.**	D (B5)	**73.**	A (B4)	**83.**	D (B5)
44.	B (B1)	**54.**	A (B3)	**64.**	C (B6)	**74.**	B (B3)	**84.**	D (B4)
45.	A (B1)	**55.**	B (B4)	**65.**	B (B4)	**75.**	D (B3)	**85.**	A (B3)
46.	B (B2)	**56.**	D (B4)	**66.**	D (B3)	**76.**	A (B2)	**86.**	B (B3)
47.	D (B2)	**57.**	A (B3)	**67.**	B (B5)	**77.**	C (B4)	**87.**	C (B3)
48.	A (B2)	**58.**	C (B4)	**68.**	B (B2)	**78.**	A (B3)	**88.**	D (B4)
49.	D (B2)	**59.**	B (B6)	**69.**	C (B4)	**79.**	C (B6)	**89.**	B (B5)
50.	A (B3)	**60.**	D (B5)	**70.**	D (B4)	**80.**	B (B6)	**90.**	A (B6)

SCORING CHART—TRIAL TEST

After you have scored your Trial Test, enter the results in the chart below (the Raw Score computation is explained on page 14); then transfer your Raw Score to the Progress Chart on page 14. As you complete the Sample Examinations later in this part of the book, you should be able to achieve increasingly higher Raw Scores.

Total Test	Number Right	Number Wrong	Number Omitted	Raw Score
Section I: 40				
Section II: 50				
Total: 90				

ANSWER EXPLANATIONS—TRIAL TEST

Section I

1. A. $3 - 5 + 6 - 8 - 4 + 7 = 3 + 6 + 7 - (5 + 8 + 4) = 16 - 17 = -1$.
2. C. $2^1/_2$ qts. = 5 pts.; $5(0.55) = 2.75$.
3. A. $0.15(95) < 0.15(100) = 15$; therefore $95 - 0.15(95) > 80$.

4. C. The diagonals are in the ratio $2x : \sqrt{2}x$ or $2 : \sqrt{2}$.

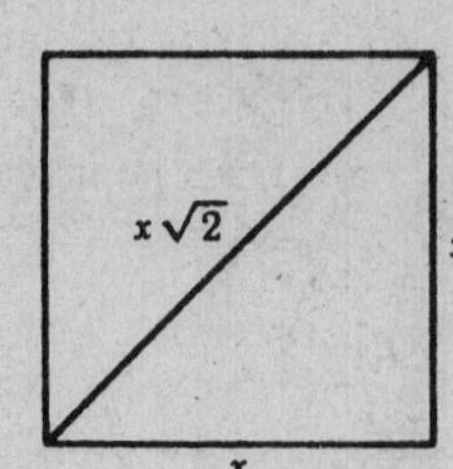

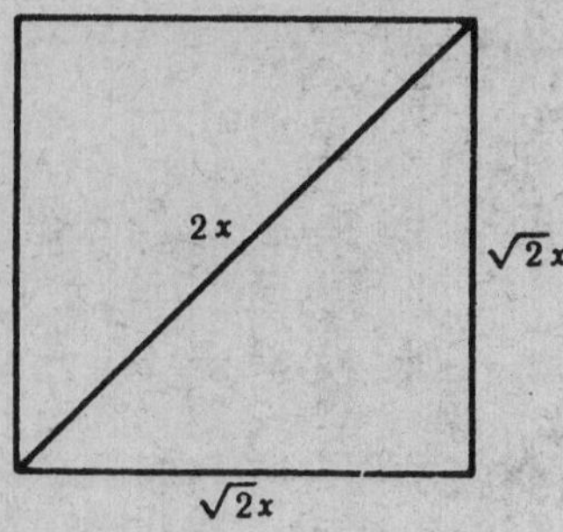

5. A. There are 36 oz. in $2^1/_4$ lbs.; $304 \div 36 > 8$.
6. B. 1 sq. yd. $= 36 \times 36 < 40 \times 40$ sq. in.
7. D. There are $10d + 25q$ cents, but this cannot be compared with $35q$ without information on d and q.
8. C. $5 - [6 - 2(1 + 3)] = 5 - (6 - 8) = 5 - (-2) = 7$.
9. D. If $x = y$, $\frac{|x-y|}{y-x}$ is not defined. If $x - y > 0$, $\frac{|x-y|}{y-x} = -1$; if $y - x > 0$, $\frac{|x-y|}{y-x} = 1$.
10. A. Since Mike takes 3 hours to mow the lawn alone it would have to take Cary only 3 hours alone for them to do it together in $1\frac{1}{2}$ hours. Since Cary takes 4 hrs alone, it takes more than $1\frac{1}{2}$ hours if both boys mow.
11. B. $(1.1)^{-1} = \frac{1}{1.1} < \frac{1}{1} = 1$.
12. A. $\frac{LN}{10} = \frac{2.4}{4}$, so $LN = 6$. But $L'M'$ must be greater than 6 for the sum of the lengths of two sides of the triangle to exceed the third.
13. C. $\frac{3}{4} \times \frac{10}{7} \div \frac{3}{2} = \frac{3}{4} \times \frac{10}{7} \times \frac{2}{3}$; $\frac{10}{4} \div \frac{3}{2} \times \frac{3}{7} = \frac{10}{4} \times \frac{2}{3} \times \frac{3}{7} = \frac{3}{4} \times \frac{10}{7} \times \frac{2}{3}$.
14. C. $\widehat{MQ} = \widehat{NP} = 2(21°) = 42°$. $\widehat{MRN} = 180° - 84° = 96°$.
15. B. $\angle M = 3x°$ and $3x + x = 104$. Therefore $x = 26$ and $3x = 78$.
16. A. $\angle C$ is a right angle; $AC = \sqrt{4^2 - 3^2} = \sqrt{7} > 2$.
17. A. If $x =$ the length of one leg of the isosceles right triangle. then $x^2 + x^2 = 4$ and $x = \sqrt{2}$.
18. C. $2x - y = 2$, $x + 2y = 6$ $\rightarrow$ $4x - 2y = 4$, $x + 2y = 6$; $5x = 10$, $x = 2$.
By substitution in either equation, $y = 2$.
19. A. $x = 47°$ since $\angle MNS$ is supplementary to $\angle PNM$; $y = 43°$.
20. B. The average speed for the round trip is 6000 divided by a number *larger* than 10. This speed is less than 600 mph.
21. B. Pakistan's population in 1979 was 84 million.
22. C. The difference is (263 − 221) million, or 42 million.
23. A. The change for 1960–1968 is the narrower of the two bars. It is almost 5% for the U.S.
24. B. Use the rightmost bar. The percent carried by motor vehicles is just over 20.
25. A. The two vertical bars show that the *percent* of traffic via railroads was greater in 1950 than in 1969.
26. C. The answer is the entry in the rightmost column for White: Male (line 5).
27. C. $p \approx \frac{73 - 55}{55} \approx \frac{18}{55} \approx \frac{1}{3} \approx 33\%$.
28. D. Since 1 m = 100 cm, (7.6×10^{-9})m $= (7.6 \times 10^{-9} \cdot 10^2)$cm $= (7.6 \times 10^{-7})$cm.

29. A. $\frac{4^0m^4n^0}{4m^4} = \frac{1 \cdot m^4 \cdot 1}{4 \cdot m^4} = \frac{1}{4}$ if $m \neq 0$.

30. B. $(5x + 9) > 1 \rightarrow 5x > -8 \rightarrow x > -1^3/_5$. If x is an integer, then x may be $-1, 0, 1, 2, \ldots$.

31. **B. Note that $x \rightarrow y$ and $x \rightarrow z$ are both positive. Find counterexamples for (A), (C), and (D).**

32. D. $\frac{13}{4} = 3\frac{1}{4} = 3.25 = 325\%$.

33. D. $\frac{7}{b} = \frac{2}{3} \rightarrow 2b = 21 \rightarrow b = 10\frac{1}{2}$.

34. C. When $x = -3, x^2 + 9 = (-3)^2 + 9 = 9 + 9 = 18 \neq 0$.

35. B. $20 = (1.25) \times x \rightarrow x = \frac{20}{1.25} = \frac{2000}{125} = 16$.

36. C. Rewriting $4x + 3y - 12 = 0$ in the form

$$y = -\frac{4}{3}x + 4$$

shows that its slope is $-\frac{4}{3}$

37. **D. If x is a nonzero real number, the reciprocal or multiplicative inverse is $\frac{1}{x}$. The product of a number and its multiplicative inverse is equal to 1.**

38. A. $\frac{x^2 - x}{x(x^2 - 1)} = \frac{x(x - 1)}{x(x - 1)(x + 1)} = \frac{1}{x + 1)}$ if $x \neq 0, 1$.

39. A. $\frac{x + 5 + 8 + 13}{4} = 8 \rightarrow \frac{x + 26}{4} = 8 \rightarrow x = 6$.

40. C. $3^0 + 3^1 + 3^2 = 1 + 3 + 9 = 13$.

Section II

41. C. $S \cup T = \{a,b,c,d\}$; $R \cap (S \cup T) = \{a,b\}$.

42. C. $S \times S$ has (3×3) or 9 elements, and $S \times S \times S$ has (9×3) elements.

43. A. If $R = \{6\}$ and $S = \{3,6\}$, then $R \cup S = \{3,6\}$.

44. B. The set $R - S$ contains all the elements of R that are not in S. The shaded region in (B) is $R - S$.

45. A. $R^+ \cap Z$ is the set of elements in both R^+ and Z; that is, the set of positive integers.

46. B. "If p, then q" is equivalent to "if not q, then not p," to "p only if q," to "p is sufficient for q," and to "q is necessary for p."

47. D. $p \rightarrow q$ and $q \rightarrow \sim r$ are equivalent respectively to $\sim q \rightarrow \sim p$ and $r \rightarrow \sim q$, from which it follows that $r \rightarrow \sim p$.

48. **A. Here is the truth table:**

~	(p	∨	~	q)
F	T	T	F	T
F	T	T	T	F
[T]	F	F	F	T
F	F	T	T	F
(5)	(1)	(4)	(3)	(2)

49. **D. This proof uses the contrapositive of the given statement.**

50. **A. $a < b$ implies that $(b - a) > 0$, so $-a > -b$.**

51. D. $(3^2 + 4^2)^{-1/2} = \frac{1}{\sqrt{3^2 + 4^2}} = \frac{1}{5}$.

52. **B. Note that $\sqrt{121} = 11$, a rational number.**

53. **C. Note that although b is a factor of the numerator in (C) it is not a factor of the denominator $b + d$. It therefore cannot be canceled.**

54. **A. A set S is closed under an operation, say $*$, if for every pair of elements a and b in S, $a * b$ is also in S. Note, if a and b are odd integers, that so is $a \times b$.**

55. B. The intercepts can be read from the graph: they are 0, 2, −2. So only (B) and (C) are possible. But from the graph $f(1) > 0$ while for (C) $f(1) < 0$; so (C) is eliminated.

56. D. $f(g(x)) = \dfrac{1}{\frac{1}{x} - 2 + 2} = x.$

57. A. Substitute the first number in the ordered pair for m, the second for n. Only for (A) is $3m - 2n$ *greater* than 4.

58. C. Note, in (C), that x_1 maps into both y_1 and y_2.

59. B. Only in (B) does $m * n = n * m$.

60. D. The probability that the Lynxes will win is $2 \div (3 + 2)$, which equals $\frac{2}{5}$ or 0.4.

61. B. The probability is ${}_3C_2/{}_5C_2$, or $(3 \cdot 2)/(5 \cdot 4)$.

62. A. The answer is the number of combinations of 7 elements taken 5 at a time, or ${}_7C_5$. Since ${}_7C_5 = {}_7C_2$, we get $(7 \cdot 6)/(1 \cdot 2)$, or 21.

63. D. Compute the probability of obtaining two marbles of the same color and subtract from 1. The probability of getting two blacks is $(5/7) \cdot (2/6)$, or $5/21$. The required probability is $1 - 5/21 = 16/21$.

64. C. $224_{\text{FIVE}} = 2(5)^2 + 2(5) + 4 = 64_{\text{TEN}}$
$332_{\text{FOUR}} = 3(4)^2 + 3(4) + 2 = 62_{\text{TEN}}$
$2102_{\text{THREE}} = 2(3)^3 + 1(3)^2 + 2 = 65_{\text{TEN}}$
$111111_{\text{TWO}} = 2^5 + 2^4 + 2^3 + 2^2 + 2^1 + 2^0 = 63_{\text{TEN}}$

65. B. $f(x) = (2x + 3)^2$, which is zero if $x = -3/2$; otherwise $f(x) > 0$.

66. D. The product of two negative integers is positive.

67. B. The total number reported on (that is, the sum of the frequencies) is 28; the middle one (14th or 15th) is age 20.

68. B. The converse of "If p, then q" is "If q, then p."

69. C. $f(x) = \sqrt{x}$ is a function but its domain is the set of nonnegative numbers.

70. D. Division by zero is excluded.

71. D. If $|x - 1| < 2$, then x is within 2 units of 1; that is, $-1 < x < 3$.

72. C. Since $6 = 2 \cdot 3$ and $10 = 2 \cdot 5$, n must be divisible by 2, 3, and 5.

73. A. $f(0) = c = 1$ and $f(1) = 1 + b + c = 1 + b + 1 = 2$, so $b = 0$.

74. B. If $a < 0$, $ab < ac$.

75. D. Let $m = 2$, $n = 3$. Note that (A), (B), (C) are all even.

76. A. $\sim p$ is T, $\sim q$ is F. So $\sim p \rightarrow \sim q$ is F.

77. C. $f(0) = b = 2$; $f(1) = a + b = -1$; so $a + 2 = -1$ and $a = -3$.

78. A. $2^m \cdot 2^n = 2^{m+n}$ as in (D).

79. C. If $\log_4 8 = x$, then $4^x = 8$ or $2^{2x} = 2^3$.

80. B. $\log_{10} m^3 = 3 \log_{10} m = 3(0.1)$.

81. D. $3 * (2 * 1) = 3 * (2^2 - 2 \cdot 1) = 3 * 2 = 3^2 - 2 \cdot 2 = 5$.

82. D. $i^{19} = i^{16} \cdot i^3 = 1 \cdot (-i)$. Note that $i^2 = -1$; $i^3 = i(i^2) = i(-1) = -i$; $i^4 = (i^2)^2 = (-1)^2 = 1$; and so on.

83. D. The die shows 3, 4, 5, or 6 in 4 out of 6 outcomes. So the answer is $1 - 4/6$.

84. D. $f(-2) = 0 = (-2)^3 + k \rightarrow k = 8$.

85. A. $|x| < a$ is equivalent to $-a < x < a$.

86. B. The coefficients of y must be in the same ratio as those of x. Thus k must satisfy the proportion $k : -1 = 4 : 2$. It follows that $2k = -4$ or that $k = -2$.

87. C. $x^2 - x = x(x - 1)$; the product is positive if $x > 1$ or if $x < 0$.

88. D. A graph of $y = f(x)$ is symmetric to the origin if $(-x, -y)$ lies on the graph, that is, if it satisfies the equation. Note that $(-y) = \dfrac{1}{(-x)}$ is equivalent to $y = \dfrac{1}{x}$.

89. B. The mean is the average, or 42; the median is 41.

90. A. To find the inverse of a function, interchange x and y, then solve for y. For $y = 2^x$, we write $x = 2^y$, which yields, after taking the log of each side to base 2, $\log_2 x = y$.

CHAPTER

Background, Review, and Practice Questions

10

The General Examination in Mathematics measures your knowledge of fundamental principles and concepts of mathematics. It covers material that is generally taught in a college course for nonmathematics majors. The examination consists of two separately timed sections. Section I (Basic Skills and Concepts) has approximately 40 questions to be answered in 30 minutes. It tests skills that are generally taught in high school and that are frequently used in college courses besides mathematics—arithmetic, algebra, geometry, and data interpretation. Section II (Content) has approximately 50 questions to be answered in 60 minutes. It covers material that is studied at the college level—sets, logic, the real number system, functions, and probability and statistics.

DESCRIPTION OF THE GENERAL EXAMINATION IN MATHEMATICS

Section I Basic Skills and Concepts

Approximately 40 questions; time allowed 30 minutes.

Subject Area	Approximate percentage of questions	Approximate number of questions
Arithmetic	30%	12
Algebra	35%	14
Geometry	15–20%	6–8
Data Interpretation	15–20%	6–8

Section II Content

Approximately 50 questions; time allowed 60 minutes.

Subject Area	Approximate percentage of questions	Approximate number of questions
Sets	10%	5
Logic	10%	5
Real Number System	30%	15
Functions and Their Graphs	20%	10
Probability and Statistics	15%	7–8
Miscellaneous Topics	15%	7–8

Scoring; Penalty for Guessing

Each correct answer on the mathematics examination earns you one point, but you lose one-third of a point for each incorrect answer. Because of this penalty, we advise against wild or blind guessing, which is likely to lower your score. Educated guesses, however, are recommended. If you can eliminate as wrong one or more of the choices listed for a question, then your chance of guessing the correct answer from among the remaining ones is increased. Omitted answers are not counted in the score.

Both a subscore for each section and a total score are reported. Since Section II is allowed twice as much time as Section I, it counts twice as much as Section I in determining the total score. This reflects the greater emphasis given college-level material, which is tested in Section II.

Calculators Prohibited

According to the CLEP brochure, calculators or other computing devices are *not* permitted on the examination. It is noted that questions were not designed for the use of calculators and that little emphasis is placed on arithmetical computations.

COMMON MATHEMATICAL SYMBOLS AND FORMULAS

Symbols used in arithmetic, algebra, geometry, and so forth:

$a = b$	a equals b
$a \neq b$	a does not equal b
$a \approx b$	a is approximately equal to b
$a > b$	a is greater than b
$a \geqslant b$	a is greater than or equal to b
$a < b$	a is less than b
$a \leqslant b$	a is less than or equal to b
$\|x\|$	the absolute value, or magnitude, of x
$\sqrt{q}$	the square root of q
$\sqrt[3]{q},\ \sqrt[4]{q},\ \sqrt[n]{q}$	the cube root of q, the fourth root of q, the nth root of q
$a : b$	the ratio of a to b, "a is to b"
$A \cong B$	A is congruent to B
$A \sim B$	A is similar to B
$\angle PRQ$	angle PRQ
$\mathrm{m}(\angle A)$	measure or size of angle A
$\triangle ABC$	triangle ABC
$l \perp m$	l is perpendicular to m
$l \parallel m$	l is parallel to m
$\overset{\frown}{AB}$	arc AB (of a circle)
π	the constant pi (the ratio of the circumference of a circle to its diameter; approximately 22/7 or 3.14)

Symbols used in set theory:†

$a \in S$	a is an element of set S
$a \notin S$	a is not an element of set S
$\{a, b, c\}$	the set containing the elements a, b, and c
$\emptyset$	the null or empty set
U	the universal set
$\overline{R}$ (or R' or $\widetilde{R}$)	the complement of set R: the set of all elements that are not in set R
$A \cup B$	the union of sets A and B
$A \cap B$	the intersection of sets A and B
$A \times B$	the Cartesian product of A and B: the set of all ordered pairs whose first element is in A and whose second element is in B
$A \subset B$	A is a subset of B.

(Some authors use "$A \subset B$" to mean A is a proper subset of B and "$A \subseteq B$" to mean A is a subset, proper or improper, of B.)

Symbols used in logic:†

$\sim p$	not p (the negation of p)
$p \wedge q$	p and q (conjunction)
$p \vee q$	p or q (disjunction: p or q or both)
$p \rightarrow q$	if p then q; or p implies q
$p \leftrightarrow q$	p if and only if q, or p is equivalent to q
$\exists_x$	there exists an x; for some x
$\forall_x$	for all x; for each x

Symbols used for functions:†

$f(x)$	A function f of a variable x (see definition of function on page 293).
$f(a)$	The value of the function $f(x)$ when x is equal to a; $f(a)$ is obtained by replacing x wherever it appears in $f(x)$ by a. For example, if $f(x) = x^2 - x + 1$, then $f(-2) = (-2)^2 - (-2) + 1 = 7$.

† Most of these symbols are defined or illustrated when they first occur in the chapter.

$f(g(x))$

The composite of functions f and g; $f(g(x))$ is obtained by replacing x wherever it appears in $f(x)$ by $g(x)$. For example, if $f(x) = 2x^2 - x + 3$ and $g(x) = 4 - x$, then

$$f(g(x)) = 2(4 - x)^2 - (4 - x) + 3$$
$$= 2x^2 - 15x + 31$$

Note that

$$g(f(x)) = 4 - (2x^2 - x + 3)$$
$$= -2x^2 + x + 1.$$

Symbols used in probability and statistics:†

$n!$

n factorial, the product of the first n positive integers:

$$n! = n(n - 1)(n - 2) \cdots 3 \cdot 2 \cdot 1$$

For example, $6! = 6 \cdot 5 \cdot 4 \cdot 3 \cdot 2 \cdot 1 = 720$.

${}_nP_r$ or $P(n,r)$

The number of *permutations* (ordered arrangements) of a set of n objects taken r at a time:

$${}_nP_r = \frac{n!}{(n - r)!}$$

${}_nC_r$ or $C(n,r)$

The number of *combinations* (selections in which order does not matter) of a set of n objects taken r at a time:

$${}_nC_r = \frac{{}_nP_r}{r!} = \frac{n!}{r!\,(n - r)!}$$

$\sum_{k=1}^{n} f(k)$

The sum obtained by letting k vary from 1 through n and adding up the resulting terms:

$$\sum_{k=1}^{n} f(k) = f(1) + f(2) + \ldots + f(n)$$

For example,

$$\sum_{k=1}^{4} 3(k) - 1 = 3(1) - 1 + 3(2) - 1 + 3(3) - 1 + 3(4) - 1$$
$$= 2 + 5 + 8 + 11$$
$$= 26$$

$\overline{x}$

The arithmetic mean (average) of a set of numbers (see definition of mean on page 293). If the set of numbers is $\{x_1, x_2, \ldots, x_n\}$, then

$$\overline{x} = \frac{\sum_{k=1}^{n} x_k}{n}$$

†Most of these symbols are defined or illustrated when they first occur in the chapter.

Other symbols:[†]

i	The imaginary unit in complex numbers; $i = \sqrt{-1}$.
(a,b)	The point in the plane whose abscissa (x-coordinate) is a and whose ordinate (y-coordinate) is b. Also, the ordered pair of elements a and b, where the set containing a and b is specified.
$a * b$	Here "$*$" stands for some algebraic operation; thus $a * b$ is the element obtained by applying this operation to the ordered pair of elements (a,b). For example, if $*$ is ordinary subtraction on the set of integers, then $3 * 7 = 3 - 7 = -4.$
2012_3 or 2012_{THREE}	This is a base-three numeral; its value in our (base-ten) system is $(2 \times 3^3) + (0 \times 3^2) + (1 + 3^1) + (2 \times 3^0) = 54 + 0 + 3 + 2 = 59$

† Most of these symbols are defined or illustrated when they first occur in the chapter.

DEFINITIONS OF SOME COMMON MATHEMATICAL TERMS

prime number	A positive integer other than 1 whose only factors are 1 and itself; for example, 2, 3, 5, ..., 23, 29, ..., 41, 43, ... There are infinitely many primes.
composite number	A positive integer that has a factor other than 1 and itself; for example, 4, 6, 8, 9, 10, 12, ...
function	A correspondence between two sets such that each element of one set, called the *domain,* is associated with one and only one element of the other set, called the *range.*
mean	The arithmetic average of a set of values; the mean of a set is equal to the sum of all the values in the set divided by the number of values in the set.
median	The middle value of a set (or the value halfway between the two middle values) when the values are arranged in order of size. The median of the set [1, 1, 4, 6, 7, 7, 10] is 6; the median of [1, 2, 4, 6, 6, 8] is 5.

mode	The most "popular" or "fashionable" value of a set of values. The mode of [70, 70, 70, 80, 85, 85, 95, 100] is 70.

COMMON GEOMETRIC FORMULAS

Sum of the angles of a triangle. The sum is 180°.

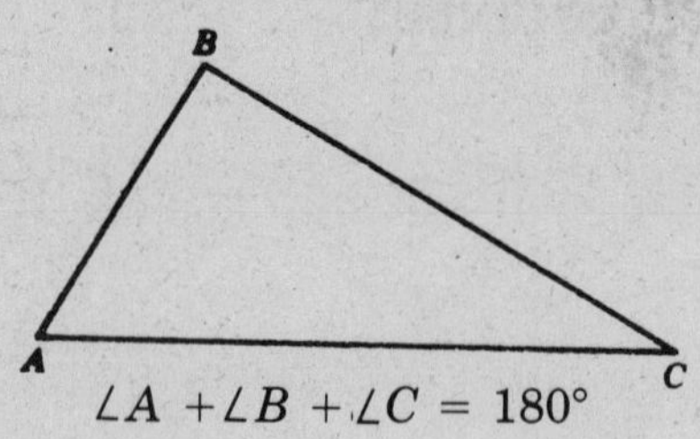

$\angle A + \angle B + \angle C = 180°$

Pythagorean Theorem.
In a right triangle, the square of the length of the hypotenuse equals the sum of the squares of the lengths of the other two sides:

$$c^2 = a^2 + b^2$$

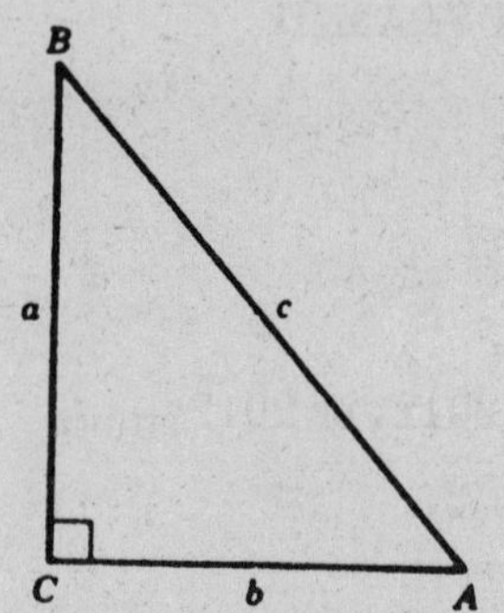

		Areas	Perimeters
RECTANGLE	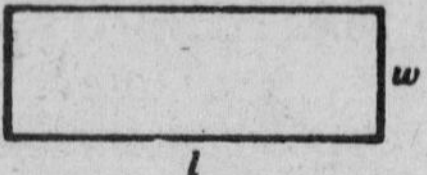	$A = lw$	$P = 2l + 2w$
SQUARE	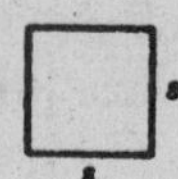	$A = s^2$	$P = 4s$
PARALLELOGRAM	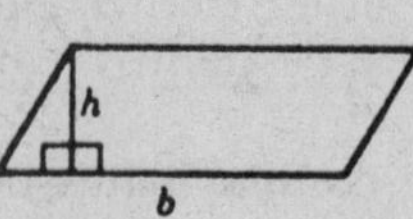	$A = bh$	
TRIANGLE	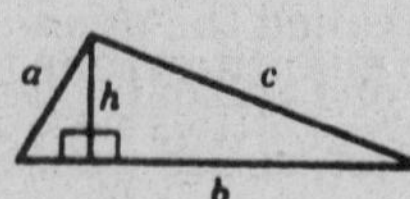	$A = \frac{1}{2}\ bh$	$P = a + b + c$
TRAPEZOID	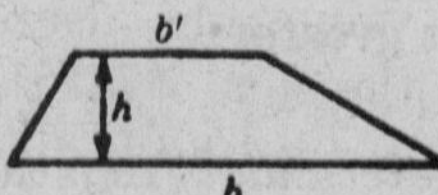	$A = \frac{1}{2}\ (b + b')\, h$	
CIRCLE	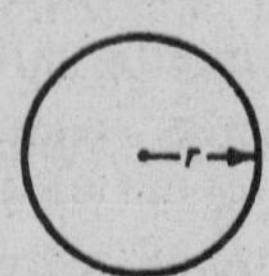	$A = \pi r^2$	

Volumes

PRISM $V = lwh$

CYLINDER $V = \pi r^2 h$

CONE $V = \frac{1}{3} \pi r^2 h$

PYRAMID $V = \frac{1}{3} Bh$

SPHERE $V = \frac{4}{3} \pi r^3$

Surface Areas

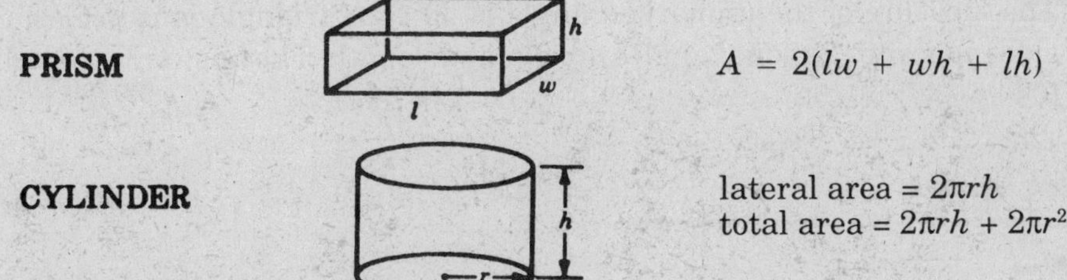

PRISM $A = 2(lw + wh + lh)$

CYLINDER lateral area = $2\pi rh$
total area = $2\pi rh + 2\pi r^2$

TYPES OF QUESTIONS

There are two types of questions in Section I: quantitative comparison and standard multiple-choice. *All* the questions in Section II are of the multiple-choice type.

Here are the directions for **quantitative-comparison questions,** followed by three examples with explained answers.

Directions: Each question consists of two quantities, one in Column A and one in Column B. You are to compare the two quantities and on the answer sheet blacken space

A if the quantity in Column A is greater;
B if the quantity in Column B is greater;
C if the two quantities are equal;
D if the relationship cannot be determined from the information given.

Notes: 1. In certain questions, information concerning one or both of the quantities to be compared is centered above the two columns.
2. A symbol that appears in both columns represents the same thing in Column A as it does in Column B.
3. Letters such as x, n, and k stand for real numbers.

Examples:

	COLUMN A	COLUMN B	ANSWERS
1.	$6 \div 2$	$6 - 2$	**1.** Ⓐ ● Ⓒ Ⓓ Ⓔ
2.	x	-3	**2.** Ⓐ Ⓑ Ⓒ ● Ⓔ
3.	p	q	**3.** Ⓐ Ⓑ ● Ⓓ Ⓔ

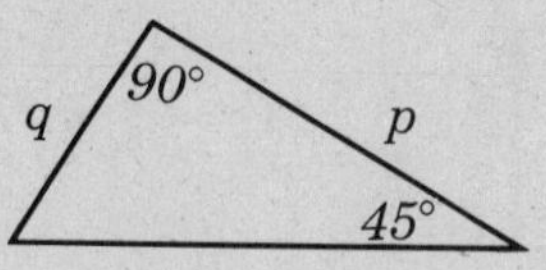

Note: Figure is *not* drawn to scale.

Explanation of Answers to Examples:

1. Since $6 \div 2 = 3$ and $6 - 2 = 4$, the answer is (B), because 4 is greater than 3.
2. The answer is (D) because we cannot determine which quantity, if either, is greater. Note that x may be positive, negative, or zero.
3. The measure of the unmarked angle is 45°; the triangle is isosceles; the sides opposite the equal angles are equal in length. The answer is therefore (C).

Here are the directions for the **multiple-choice questions,** followed by four examples, each with correct answer blackened and an explanation in brackets.

Directions: For each of the following questions, indicate the correct answer in the appropriate space on the answer sheet.

1. If $2x - y = 7$ and $3x + y = 8$, then $x + y$ equals
(A) -4 (B) -2 (C) 0 (D) 2 Ⓐ Ⓑ Ⓒ ● Ⓔ

[Solve the pair of equations simultaneously:

$$\begin{aligned} (1) \quad 2x - y &= 7 \\ (2) \quad 3x + y &= 8 \\ \hline 5x &= 15 \text{ (by adding (1) and (2))} \\ x &= 3 \end{aligned}$$

Then, substituting for x in equation (1), we have

$$\begin{aligned} 2(3) - y &= 7 \\ 6 - y &= 7 \\ y &= -1 \end{aligned}$$

So $x = 3$ and $y = -1$. Then $x + y = 3 + (-1) = 2$.]

2. **Employment and Unemployment**
Persons 16 Years Old and Over

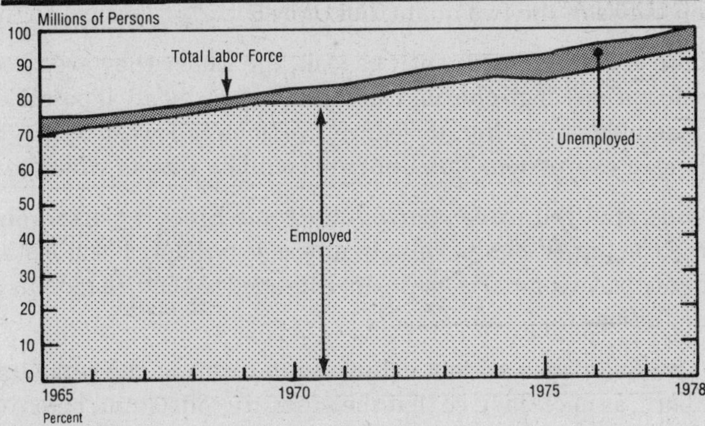

Source: Data, 1979, p. 157

The largest number of unemployed persons occurred in

(A) 1965 (B) 1970 (C) 1975 (D) 1978 Ⓐ Ⓑ ● Ⓓ Ⓔ

[Note that the darker shaded region at the top of the figure represents the number of unemployed. This number is largest when the vertical measurement (from the upper curve of the region for the employed to the heavy, slightly curved line for the total labor force) is greatest.]

3. Suppose $f(x) = \frac{x+1}{x-1}$. Then $f(1)$ equals

(A) −1 (B) 0 (C) 2 (D) none of these Ⓐ Ⓑ Ⓒ ● Ⓔ

[Replacing x by 1, we get

$$f(1) = \frac{1+1}{1-1} = \frac{2}{0}.$$

Since division by zero is excluded, the function is not defined at $x = 1$.]

4. If a is negative, then $|a - 2|$ is equal to

(A) $-(a-2)$ (B) $-a-2$ (C) $a-2$ (D) none of these ● Ⓑ Ⓒ Ⓓ Ⓔ

[The absolute value is defined as follows:

$|x| = x$ if $x \geq 0$ but $|x| = -x$ if $x < 0$.

Since a is given as negative, the quantity $a - 2$ is negative. The absolute value $|a - 2|$ is therefore the opposite or negative of the quantity $a - 2$.]

TIPS ON ANSWERING QUANTITATIVE COMPARISON QUESTIONS

1. Be sure you understand the directions given for deciding which quantity, if either, is greater. Study each illustrative example, and note how the directions are followed to obtain the correct answer.

2. Pay attention to any information that is centered above the two columns, and use it when comparing the quantities.

3. Remember that a symbol appearing in Column A and in Column B represents the same thing in both columns.

4. When comparing the values of two expressions involving only numerals (no variables), choice (D) is *never* correct. You can always determine the relation between the two quantities.

5. The more alike the two quantities look, the easier they are to compare. It may help to rearrange one quantity (just in your head, if possible) so that it most resembles the other, to reduce fractions to lowest terms, to simplify complicated expressions, to eliminate common factors when possible.

6. Remember that you are *comparing* two items. Since it matters only which if either is the larger, don't evaluate unless you must. The questions involving quantitative comparison are not intended to require tedious arithmetical calculations.

7. If the two quantities are not expressed in terms of the same unit, modify one or both, as necessary, so that the units are consistent, before comparing the quantities.

8. Remember that a positive number has *two* square roots. If $x^2 = 4$, then $x = +2$ or $x = -2$.

9. Do not assume that a variable ($x, y, p, q, \ldots$) is a positive number or an integer. It may be a negative number, a fraction, zero—even an irrational number. It may help to visualize the number line and to remind yourself that there is a point on it for every real number.

10. When a figure is drawn, make sure you understand what information is given about it and by it. If a note says that the figure is *not* drawn to scale, as in the example on page 296, do not make false assumptions on the basis of its appearance.

11. In finding a relation between two quantities it may help to substitute simple numbers. For example, to find the ratio of the area of circle B to that of A if the radius of B is twice that of A, let the radius of circle A be, say, 5. Then the radius of circle B is 10, and the ratio of the area of B to the area of A is $\pi \cdot 10^2 : \pi \cdot 5^2 = 100 : 25 = 4 : 1$.

TIPS ON ANSWERING MULTIPLE-CHOICE QUESTIONS

1. Estimate where possible to identify—and to check!—the correct answer. For example, $629.1 \div 38.9$ is equal approximately to $630 \div 40$ or to about 16. You can eliminate answer choices like 162, 1.61, or 0.16.

2. Express all measurements in the same unit: all in feet or all in inches; all in dollars or all in cents; and so on. Make certain the answer you obtain is expressed in the units given in the answer choices.

3. When a question asks which choice satisfies a given condition, mark the first choice you can verify in the answer column, since only one choice is correct. For example:

   Which of the following Venn diagrams is for the set $R \cap S$?

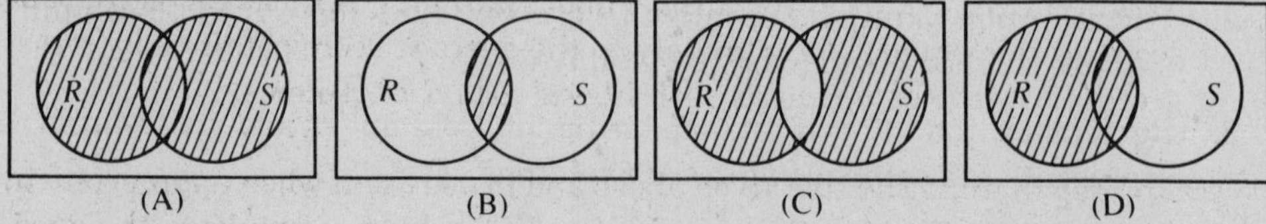

(A) (B) (C) (D)

Choice (A) is incorrect. Since choice (B) is correct, blacken space (B) on the answer sheet immediately without considering the remaining choices. Many multiple-choice questions can be answered using this strategy. Here are four examples: Which of the following statements is true (*or* false *or* impossible)? Which set is *not* empty? Which number is irrational? Which of the following graphs represents a function?

4. We can generalize the strategy of tip 3. As soon as you recognize the correct answer to a multiple-choice question, indicate that choice in the answer column immediately and move on to the next question.

5. Be careful when solving an equation like $x^2 = 3x$. If you divide through by x, you will throw away a root. Instead, rewrite and factor as follows:

$$x^2 - 3x = 0$$
$$x(x - 3) = 0$$
$$x = 0 \text{ or } x = 3$$

6. Draw a sketch, if appropriate, and label the parts with given data or variables. To find a function or express a relation among variables, it may help to replace the variable by simple numbers.

7. Some of the tips on answering quantitative-comparison questions apply to the multiple-choice type too; see tips 8, 9, and 11.

ADDITIONAL TIPS

1. Do not make any marks at all in column E on your answer sheet. Even though the answer sheet has five answer spaces labeled A, B, C, D, and E, you are to choose one correct answer from among the four choices A, B, C, and D only.

2. Avoid excessive computation. Don't use pencil and paper unless you must.

3. Feel free to do any necessary calculations right in your test book. You may also write notes, equations, etc., there. But do not make any stray marks in the answer column.

4 Do not spend too much time on any one question. If you're not sure of the answer, or if your equations or your computations seem unduly complicated, skip the question and return to it later if time permits. If you can eliminate one or two choices, cross them out. When you return to the question, you'll save time by not having to reconsider the crossed-out choices.

5. Keep track of the time. When working on Section I, try to answer about 20 questions during the first 15 minutes. If you answer fewer, work a bit faster on the remaining questions in Section I. On Section II you should answer about 25 questions in the first 30 minutes.

6. You should not be concerned if you do not answer all the questions on the mathematics examination, because no one is expected to do all of them within the time limit. If you answer about half the questions correctly, your score will be equal approximately to the average score obtained by a test group of college sophomores with liberal arts backgrounds.

Try to keep in mind the tips given above and to use them when appropriate in answering the practice questions that follow. When you've completed the questions on quantitative comparison, reread the tips given for answering that type; similarly for the multiple-choice type.

STUDY SOURCES

Throughout this chapter, we will encourage you to develop a systematic approach to problem-solving, suggesting specific techniques and offering further hints on taking the test. You may find it helpful for your review to refer to one or more of the books listed below. These books, or others covering similar material, are available in public and school libraries.

Allendoerfer, C.B., and C.O. Oakley, *Fundamentals of Freshman Mathematics*. Third Edition. New York: McGraw-Hill, 1972.

Benice, Daniel D., *Arithmetic and Algebra*. Englewood Cliffs, NJ: Prentice-Hall, 1985.

Dressler, Isidore, and Edward P. Keenan, *Integrated Mathematics,* Course I. New York: Amsco School Publications, 1980.

Hockett, Shirley O., and Martin Sternstein, *Finite Mathematics*. Malibar, FL: Robert E. Krieger, 1984.

Lipschutz, Seymour, *Finite Mathematics*. New York: Schaum Outline Series, 1966.

Meserve, Bruce E. et al., *Contemporary Mathematics*. Fourth Edition. Englewood Cliffs, NJ: Prentice-Hall, 1987.

Prindle, Anthony, *Math the Easy Way*. Second Edition. Hauppauge, NY: Barron's Educational Series, 1988.

Rising, Gerald et al., *Unified Mathematics,* Books 1, 2, 3. Boston: Houghton Mifflin, 1985.

PRACTICE QUESTIONS

We now present, through practice questions and explanations, a review of the skills and content tested on the CLEP General Examination in Mathematics.

We begin with sets of practice questions, followed by answers and explanations, on each of the topics included in Section I of the Examination: arithmetic, algebra, geometry, and data interpretation.

These are followed by sets of practice questions, with answers and explanations, on each of the topics tested in Section II of the Examination: sets, logic, the real number system, functions and their graphs, probability and statistics, and miscellaneous topics.

Practice Questions for Section I, Basic Skills and Concepts

The 40 questions in Section I of the examination are of two types: quantitative-comparison type and regular multiple-choice type. To provide plenty of practice with the quantitative-comparison type, we will use questions of this type to review the various topics in Section I. We will follow this by a set of supplementary questions on Section I topics, but these will be of the multiple-choice type.

The directions for quantitative comparison are as follows:

Directions: Each question consists of two quantities, one in Column A and one in Column B. You are to compare the two quantities and on the answer sheet blacken space

- A if the quantity in Column A is greater;
- B if the quantity in Column B is greater;
- C if the two quantities are equal;
- D if the relationship cannot be determined from the information given.

Notes:
1. In certain questions, information concerning one or both of the quantities to be compared is centered above the two columns.
2. A symbol that appears in both columns represents the same thing in Column A as it does in Column B.
3. Letters such as x, n, and k stand for real numbers.

We begin with seven examples with answers indicated at the right and explanations given in parentheses.

	COLUMN A	COLUMN B	ANSWERS
1.	$3 + 5$	3×5	1. Ⓐ ● Ⓒ Ⓓ Ⓔ

($3 + 5 = 8$, $3 \times 5 = 15$. Since $15 > 8$, we have marked choice B. Note that you can always immediately eliminate D as the answer to a question such as this which involves only straightforward computation with numbers. The relationship *can* be determined from the information given.)

Example 2 refers to $\triangle ABC$.

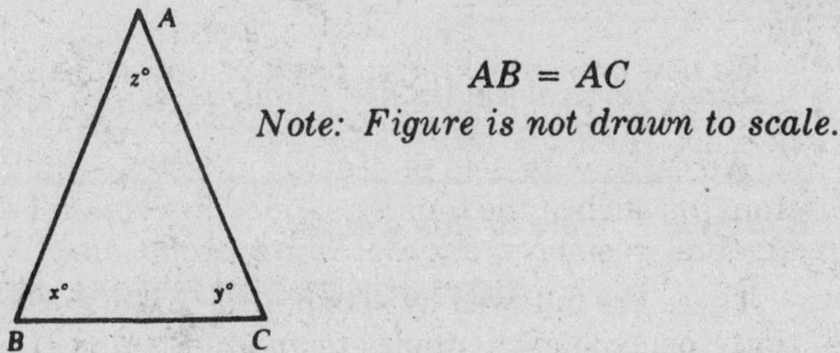

$AB = AC$

Note: Figure is not drawn to scale.

2.	x	z	2. Ⓐ Ⓑ Ⓒ ● Ⓔ

(Since $AB = AC$, the triangle is isosceles and $x = y$; but since the figure is not drawn to scale, we cannot determine how x and z compare.)

3.	an odd number whose square is between 14 and 47	5	3. Ⓐ Ⓑ ● Ⓓ Ⓔ

(The squares between 14 and 47 are $16 = 4^2$, $25 = 5^2$, and $36 = 6^2$. Only 5 is odd.)

	COLUMN A	COLUMN B	ANSWERS
4.	m	$2m$	4. Ⓐ Ⓑ Ⓒ ● Ⓔ

(Be careful! $2m > m$ if m is positive, as for $m = 3$, *but* if $m = 0$ then $2m = m$. Further, if $m = -3$, then $2m < m$ since $2(-3) = -6$ and $-6 < -3$. In a question involving unknowns, try not to overlook zero and the negative numbers. It is often very helpful, also, in comparing signed numbers to visualize the number line:

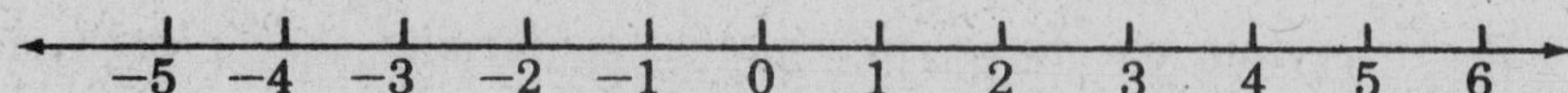

Of two numbers, the one represented by the point to the right is the larger. So, zero is greater than any negative number, $-2 > -5$, $-1 > -2$, every positive number is greater than every negative number, etc.)

5.	$(13)(^1/_7)(^3/_8)$	$(^3/_7)(13)(^1/_{10})$	5. ● Ⓑ Ⓒ Ⓓ Ⓔ

(Instead of computing either of the items we can mentally rearrange the entry in Column B as $(13)(^3/_7)(^1/_{10})$ or $(13)(^1/_7)(^3/_{10})$ so that it most resembles Column A, or vice versa. Then we eliminate the common factors 13, $^1/_7$, and 3. Now we need compare only $^1/_8$ and $^1/_{10}$, and since $^1/_8 > {^1/_{10}}$, the answer is A. Common factors should always be eliminated from the quantities given in the two columns to simplify the comparison. Also, avoid using pencil and paper wherever possible, to save time.)

Example 6 refers to this figure.

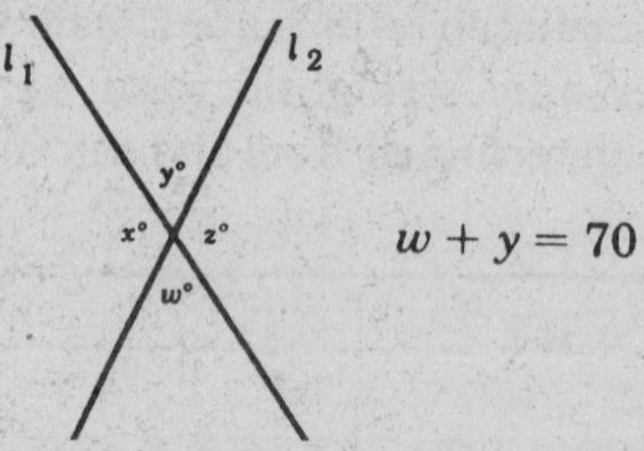

$w + y = 70$

6.	x	150	6. Ⓐ ● Ⓒ Ⓓ Ⓔ

(Since vertical angles are equal, $x = z$ and also $y = w$. Therefore $2w = 70$ and $w = 35$. Then $x = 180 - 35 = 145$.)

Example 7 refers to this chart.

DOW-JONES INDUSTRIAL AVERAGES

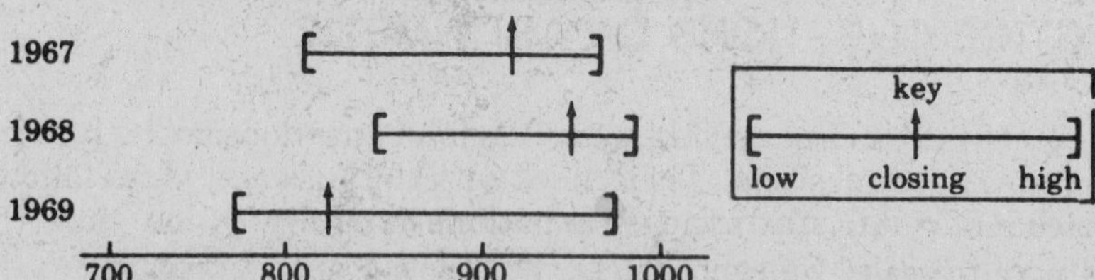

7.	**the high Dow-Jones industrial average for 1967**	the closing Dow-Jones average in 1968	7. ● Ⓑ Ⓒ Ⓓ Ⓔ

(This question is on data interpretation. The key at the right indicates how to use the graph. Since the high for 1967 is to the right of the closing indicator for 1968, A is the correct answer.)

We now give a set of practice questions of the quantitative-comparison type on each topic covered by Section I. Each set begins with a few examples. Reread the test directions for quantitative-comparison questions if necessary.

A1. Arithmetic

The subtopics are whole numbers; fractions; decimals; percent; powers and roots; ratio and proportion.

Here are a few introductory examples, with answers and explanations.

	COLUMN A	COLUMN B	ANSWERS
1.	6 × 1	6 ÷ 1	**1.** Ⓐ Ⓑ ● Ⓓ Ⓔ

(Since 6 × 1 = 6 and 6 ÷ 1 = 6, the quantities are equal. We've therefore marked C.)

2.	price per ounce of detergent if a 40-ounce box costs $0.90	2.1¢	**2.** ● Ⓑ Ⓒ Ⓓ Ⓔ

(90 ÷ 40 = 2.25, which is greater than 2.1. Note, however, that we need carry out the first computation only far enough to see that the answer *exceeds* 2.1.)

3.	8.1 × 0.04	0.32	**3.** ● Ⓑ Ⓒ Ⓓ Ⓔ

(8.1 × 0.04 = 0.324, but even this computation is unnecessary. Since 8.1 × 0.04 > 8 × 0.04 = 0.32, A is obviously the answer.)

4.	**a prime factor of 6**	3	**4.** Ⓐ Ⓑ Ⓒ ● Ⓔ

(6 has two prime factors; 2 and 3. The relationship cannot be determined from the information given.)

PRACTICE QUESTIONS ON ARITHMETIC

Follow the directions on this set of Section I questions on arithmetic. First, try to answer the questions. Then check with the answers, which follow. It will also be beneficial to study the explanations carefully.

	COLUMN A	COLUMN B
1.	8 ÷ 4	8 × $\frac{1}{4}$
2.	0.16	$\frac{1}{6}$

	COLUMN A	COLUMN B
3.	6	$\sqrt{35}$
4.	$\frac{1}{0.004}$	250
5.	$3 + 5 \cdot 2$	$(3 + 5) \cdot 2$
6.	$\frac{1}{2} + \frac{1}{3} + \frac{1}{6}$	$\frac{11}{12}$
7.	$5 - 0.31$	4.7
8.	a number between 0.3 and $\frac{1}{3}$	0.32
	A compact car gets 25 miles to the gallon on the open road.	
9.	number of gallons of gas needed for a 550-mile trip	23
10.	62,364 rounded off to the nearest hundred	62,300
11.	$\frac{100.52}{100}$	1
12.	the simple interest on $350 after 2 years	$42
13.	$\lvert 2 - 4 \rvert$	$\lvert 4 - 2 \rvert$
14.	the average of 20, 29, 35, and 37	the average of 19, 29, 34, and 37
15.	$2900 - 1900.1$	1000.1
16.	$\frac{7}{25}$	0.26
17.	4% of 4805	190
	A TV set can be bought on time for $25 down and twelve monthly payments of $30 each.	
18.	the total cost of the TV set bought on time	$385
	Bruce borrows $960 at $5\frac{1}{2}$% for 3 months.	
19.	the total amount Bruce must repay	$974
20.	the cost of automobile insurance for 15 years if each annual premium is $110	$1600
	Mr. King buys a man-made fur coat marked down 10% in a pre-Christmas sale, and a pair of shoes costing $15. He pays $60 for both items.	
21.	the original price of the coat	$50
22.	$5\frac{1}{3}$ yards	190 inches
23.	the additive inverse of 2	the multiplicative inverse of 2

	COLUMN A	COLUMN B
24.	the time needed to fly 300 miles if the plane covers one mile in ten seconds	50 minutes
25.	the number of ounces in a can of fruit juice	46 oz.
26.	$\lvert 5 - 3 \rvert$	$\lvert (-5) - 3 \rvert$
27.	the fifth term of the sequence 2, 6, 18, 54, . . .	the fourth term of the sequence 21, 42, 84, . . .
28.	the fraction obtained if both the numerator and the denominator of $3/4$ are increased by 1	0.8
29.	the reciprocal of $3/2$	0.6
30.	the least common multiple of 4 and 6	24

ANSWERS AND EXPLANATIONS

to practice Section I questions on arithmetic.

1. C. $8 \div 4 = 2; 8 \times 1/4 = 2$.

2. B. $1/6 = 0.1666\ldots = 0.16\frac{2}{3}$.

3. A. $6^2 = 36 > 35$.

4. C. $\frac{1}{0.004} = \frac{1000}{4} = 250$.

5. B. $3 + 5 \cdot 2 = 3 + 10 = 13; (3 + 5) \cdot 2 = 8 \cdot 2 = 16$.

6. A. $1/2 + 1/3 + 1/6 = 3/6 + 2/6 + 1/6 = 6/6 = 1$.

7. B. $5 - 0.31 = 4.69$.

8. D. There are an infinite number of numbers between 0.3 and 0.333 . . .; some are less than 0.32, some are greater, and exactly one equals 0.32.

9. B. $550 \div 25 = 22$.

10. A. 62,364 rounded off to the nearest hundred equals 62,400, since the digit in the tens place is 5 or more.

11. A. $\frac{100.52}{100} = 1.0052$. To divide by 100 we simply move the decimal point two places to the left.

12. D. The rate of interest is not given.

13. C. $\lvert 2 - 4 \rvert = \lvert -2 \rvert = 2; \lvert 4 - 2 \rvert = \lvert 2 \rvert = 2$.

14. A. The average or arithmetic mean of a set of four numbers is their sum divided by 4. Since 29 and 37 are in both sets, we need only *compare* the other numbers. Since 20 and 35 (in the A column) are greater respectively than 19 and 34 (in the B column), the average in Column A is greater than the average in Column B.

15. B. $2900 - 1900.1 = 999.9$. Since $(2900 - 1900.1) < (2900 - 1900) = 1000$, the correct answer can be selected quickly.

16. A. $7/25 = 28/100 = 0.28$.

17. A. 4% of 4805 = 0.04 × 4805 = 192.20. But note that 0.04 × 4800 = 192, which is greater than 190.
18. C. Cost on time = \$25 + 12(\$30) = \$385.
19. B. The interest equals \$960 × $^{11}/_{200}$ × $^{1}/_{4}$ = \$13.20. The amount equals \$960 + \$13.20 = \$973.20.
20. A. 15 × \$110 = \$1650.
21. C. The sale price of the coat is \$45. 45 = $^{9}/_{10}$ of 50.
22. A. $^{16}/_{3}$ × 36 = 16 × 12 = 192.
23. B. The additive inverse of 2 is −2; the multiplicative inverse of 2 is ½; ½ > −2.
24. C. Since 300 × 10 seconds = 3000 seconds, the number of minutes required is $^{3000}/_{60}$ or 50; or, since one mile in 10 seconds means 6 miles a minute, we can divide 300 by 6, again getting 50 minutes.
25. D. Information is lacking on the size or liquid measure of the can.
26. B. $|5-3| = 2$; $|(-5)-3| = |-8| = 8$.
27. B. The fifth term of the sequence 2, 6, 18, 54, . . . is 162 (each term is 3 times the preceding one). The fourth term of 21, 42, 84, . . . is 168 (the ratio here is 2).
28. C. $\frac{3+1}{4+1} = \frac{4}{5} = 0.8$.
29. A. The reciprocal of $^{3}/_{2}$ is $^{2}/_{3}$ or 0.66 · · ·, which is greater than 0.6.
30. B. The smallest number having both 4 and 6 as factors is 12.

A2. Algebra

The subtopics are signed numbers; algebraic expressions, laws and operations; polynomials; equations; inequalities; special products; factoring; algebraic fractions; and word problems.

Be sure you are familiar with the test directions for quantitative-comparison questions. Here are a few introductory examples, with answers and explanations.

	COLUMN A	COLUMN B	ANSWERS
1.	the solution of the equation $x - 1 = 0$	2	1. Ⓐ ● Ⓒ Ⓓ Ⓔ

(The solution of the equation is $x = 1$.)

$y \geqq 5$

	COLUMN A	COLUMN B	ANSWERS
2.	y	5	2. Ⓐ Ⓑ Ⓒ ● Ⓔ

(Since the solution set of the inequality $y \geqq 5$ is the set of real numbers 5 or larger, the relationship cannot be determined.)

$x = 2, y = 3, z = 1$

	COLUMN A	COLUMN B	ANSWERS
3.	$x - y + z$	$(x - y + z)^2$	3. Ⓐ Ⓑ ● Ⓓ Ⓔ

($x - y + z = 0$; $0^2 = 0 \cdot 0 = 0$.)

Twice a number diminished by 7 equals −1.

	COLUMN A	COLUMN B	ANSWERS
4.	the number	−3	4. ● Ⓑ Ⓒ Ⓓ Ⓔ

(The equation, if x is the number, is $2x - 7 = -1$, yielding $x = 3$; $3 > -3$.)

PRACTICE QUESTIONS ON ELEMENTARY ALGEBRA

Follow the directions given on page 301. First, try to answer the questions. Then check with the answers, which follow, studying the explanations carefully.

	COLUMN A	COLUMN B
	$x = 3$ and $y = -4$	
1.	$x - y$	7
2.	the root of the equation $3x - 1 = 4$	$1\frac{1}{3}$
3.	$x + y$	$x - y$
4.	the number of solutions of the equation $x^2 = 4$	1
	$n > d$	
5.	the number of cents in n nickels	the number of cents in d dimes
6.	the coefficient of xy in the product $(2x + y)(3x - 2y)$	1
	$y \neq 0$	
7.	$3(x + y^2)$	$3x + y^2$
	$y = 3$	
8.	$y^2 + 7y + 12$	$(y + 3)(y + 4)$
	$x^2 - x - 2 = 0$	
9.	the smaller root of the equation	the negative of the larger root of the equation
	$z = -1$	
10.	$(z - 2)(z + 2)$	$z^2 - 4z$
	On a map, 1″ represents 80 miles. Two cities are $2\frac{1}{2}$″ apart on the map.	
11.	the actual distance, in miles, between the two cities	220
	$x < 1$	
12.	x^2	1
13.	the exponent of x in the quotient x^2/x^3	1
14.	$(1 - \sqrt{2})(1 + \sqrt{2})$	1
	$y - z = 2$ $2y + z = 7$	
15.	z	1

	COLUMN A	COLUMN B
16.	**the product of the roots of the equation $x^2 + x + 1 = 0$**	-1
	$x \neq 2$	
17.	$\frac{x^2 - 4}{x - 2}$	$x + 3$
18.	$\|x - 1\|$	$x - 1$
	$\frac{a}{b} = \frac{b}{c} \quad bc \neq 0$	
19.	b^2	ac
20.	**the number of real roots of the equation $x^3 - 4x = 0$**	2
	$u : v = 2 : 3$ **and** $u : u + v = 2 : z$	
21.	z	6
22.	the slope of the line $y = 2x - 1$	the slope of the line $2y = x - 1$
	$a = 2, b = -1$	
23.	$2a + 3b$	$-a - 3b$
	$x = -1$	
24.	**the value of $(4x)^3$**	**the value of $\left(\frac{4}{x}\right)^3$**
25.	**the reciprocal of $(\frac{1}{4} + \frac{1}{5})$**	2.2
26.	the root of the equation $2x - 3 = 3 - x$	3
	Robert walks a distance of 6 miles from *A* to *B* in two hours, but takes 3 hours to return.	
27.	**Robert's average rate, in miles per hour, for the round trip**	2.5
	$y > x + 1$	
28.	x	y
	$\frac{1}{x} = \frac{y}{1}$	
29.	x	y
	Three numbers whose sum is 310 are in the ratio 2 : 3 : 5.	
30.	**the smallest of the three numbers**	62

ANSWERS AND EXPLANATIONS

to practice Section I questions on algebra.

1. C. $3 - (-4) = 7$.
2. A. If $3x - 1 = 4$, $3x = 5$ and $x = 1\frac{2}{3}$.
3. D. The relationship cannot be determined unless values for x and y are given. Note that

$$x + y > x - y \quad \text{if } y > 0$$
$$x + y = x - y \quad \text{if } y = 0$$
$$x + y < x - y \quad \text{if } y < 0.$$

Don't forget zero and negative numbers in a question involving unknowns.

4. A. If $x^2 = 4$, then $x^2 - 4 = 0$ and $(x - 2)(x + 2) = 0$. There are *two* solutions, $x = -2$ and $x = 2$.
5. D. If $n < 2d$, $5n < 10d$; if $n = 2d$, $5n = 10d$; if $n > 2d$, $5n > 10d$.
6. B. $(2x + y)(3x - 2y) = 6x^2 + (3 - 4)xy - 2y^2 = 6x^2 - xy - 2y^2$. The coefficient of xy is -1.
7. A. If $y \neq 0$, $3y^2 > y^2 > 0$. Note that $3(x + y^2) = 3x + 3y^2$.
8. C. $y^2 + 7y + 12 = (y + 3)(y + 4)$ for *all* y.
9. A. $x^2 - x - 2 = 0$ yields $(x - 2)(x + 1) = 0$ with roots $x = 2$, $x = -1$. The smaller root is -1; the negative of the larger root is -2. And $-1 > -2$.
10. B. $(z - 2)(z + 2) = z^2 - 4$. When $z = -1$, this equals -3, while $z^2 - 4z = (-1)^2 - 4(-1) = 1 + 4 = 5$.
11. B. If x = the actual distance, in miles, then

$$\frac{x}{80} = \frac{2\frac{1}{2}}{1} \quad \text{or} \quad x = 80 \times \frac{5}{2} = 200.$$

12. D. If $0 < x < 1$, then $x^2 < 1$, but if $x < -1$, then $-x > 1$ and $x^2 > 1$.
13. B. $x^2 \div x^3 = x^{2-3} = x^{-1}$.
14. B. $(1 - \sqrt{2})(1 + \sqrt{2}) = 1 \cdot 1 - (\sqrt{2})(\sqrt{2}) = 1 - 2 = -1$.
15. C. Add the equations. Then $3y = 9$ and $y = 3$. Substituting in either equation yields $z = 1$.
16. A. For the quadratic equation $ax^2 + bx + c = 0$, the product of the roots is c/a. For the given equation, this is $(+1)/1$ or 1.
17. B. If $x \neq 2$, $\frac{x^2 - 4}{x - 2} = x + 2$. Regardless of the value of x, $x + 3 > x + 2$.
18. D. $|x - 1| = x - 1$ if $x \geqq 1$
    $= 1 - x$ if $x < 1$.
    Information about the value of x is needed.
19. C. The product of the means in a proportion equals the product of the extremes. Multiply both sides of the given equation by bc.
20. A. If $x^3 - 4x = 0$, then $x(x - 2)(x + 2) = 0$ and the roots are 0, 2, and -2.
21. B. $\frac{u}{v} = \frac{2}{3}$ implies that $v = \frac{3}{2}u$. So

$$\frac{u}{u + v} = \frac{u}{u + \frac{3}{2}u} = \frac{u}{\frac{5}{2}u} = \frac{1}{\frac{5}{2}} = \frac{2}{5} = \frac{2}{z}. \text{ So } z = 5.$$

22. A. If the equation of a line is written in the form $y = mx + b$, then its slope is m. So $y = 2x - 1$ has slope 2. Since $2y = x - 2$ can be written $y = \frac{1}{2}x - 1$, its slope is $\frac{1}{2}$.
23. C. $2a + 3b = 2(2) + 3(-1) = 4 - 3 = 1$;
    $-a - 3b = -2 - 3(-1) = -2 + 3 = 1$.
24. C. $(4x)^3 = 4x \cdot 4x \cdot 4x$; here it's $(-4)(-4)(-4) = -64$.

$$\left\{\frac{4}{x}\right\}^3 \text{ here is } \left\{\frac{4}{-1}\right\}^3 = -64.$$

25. A. $\frac{1}{4} + \frac{1}{5} = \frac{5}{20} + \frac{4}{20} = \frac{9}{20}$; the reciprocal is $\frac{20}{9} = 2.22 \ldots$ or $2\frac{2}{9}$; $2.2 = 2\frac{2}{10}$.

26. B. $2x - 3 = 3 - x \rightarrow 3x = 6 \rightarrow x = 2$.

27. B. His average rate is $\frac{6+6}{2+3} = {}^{12}\!/_5 = 2^2\!/_5$, or 2.4 mph.

28. B. Visualize points x and y on the number line such that $y > x + 1$. The point y is to the right of $x + 1$ and therefore to the right of x.

29. D. It follows from the equation that $xy = 1$, but the relative sizes of x and y cannot be determined.

30. C. Let x be the common ratio. Then $2x + 3x + 5x = 310$ and $x = 31$. The smallest number is 2(31) or 62.

A3. Geometry

The subtopics are angles and lines; triangles; polygons and circles; perimeter, area and volume; analytic geometry including the Cartesian plane, distance between points, midpoints, equations, and graphs of lines; and properties of the 30°-60°-90° triangle.

Be sure you are familiar with the test directions for quantitative-comparison questions. Here are a few introductory examples, with answers and explanations.

	COLUMN A	COLUMN B	ANSWERS
	The vertex angle of an isosceles triangle measures 80°.		1. Ⓐ Ⓑ ● Ⓓ Ⓔ
1.	the number of degrees in each base angle of the triangle	50	
	(The sum of the angles of the triangle is 180°.)		
2.	the number of degrees in one angle of a hexagon	the number of degrees in a base angle of an isosceles triangle	2. Ⓐ Ⓑ Ⓒ ● Ⓔ
	(Different isosceles triangles have base angles of different sizes.)		
3.	number of square tiles, one foot on a side, needed to cover a floor 12 feet by $8\frac{1}{2}$ feet	100	3. ● Ⓑ Ⓒ Ⓓ Ⓔ
	(The number of square feet in the floor is $12 \times 8\frac{1}{2} = (12 \times 8) + (12 \times \frac{1}{2}) = 96 + 6 = 102$. Since each tile has area one square foot, 102 tiles are needed.)		
4.	the length of the hypotenuse, in feet, of a right triangle whose legs are 3.09 feet and 4.02 feet in length	5	4. ● Ⓑ Ⓒ Ⓓ Ⓔ
	(By the Pythagorean theorem, the length of the hypotenuse is $\sqrt{(3.09)^2 + (4.02)^2}$ feet; but no computation is necessary if you recall the 3-4-5 right triangle. The length of the hypotenuse of the given triangle must exceed 5.)		

PRACTICE QUESTIONS ON GEOMETRY

Follow the directions given on page 301. First, try to answer the questions. Then check with the answers, which follow, studying the explanations carefully.

	COLUMN A	COLUMN B
1.	the number of degrees in the largest angle of an obtuse triangle	90
2.	the supplement of 55°40′18″	125°

Two angles are complementary and one is 11° larger than twice the other.

3.	number of degrees in the smaller of the two angles	26

50° x°

Note: Figure is not drawn to scale.

4.	x	65

4 ⅘″ 5 ⅓″ 3½″

5.	number of inches in the perimeter of the above triangle	13

This figure is for questions 6-10.

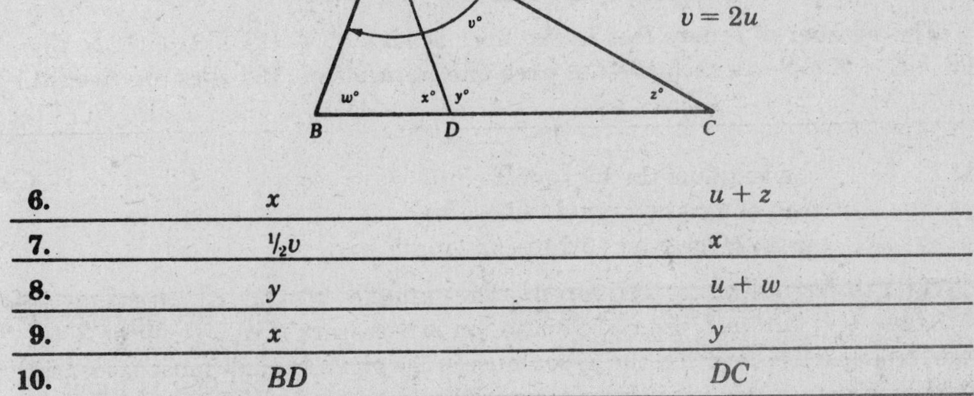

Note: Figure is not drawn to scale.

$v = 2u$

6.	x	$u + z$
7.	$\frac{1}{2}v$	x
8.	y	$u + w$
9.	x	y
10.	BD	DC

	COLUMN A	COLUMN B
	Two angles of a triangle measure 63° and 81°.	
11.	number of degrees in third angle	46

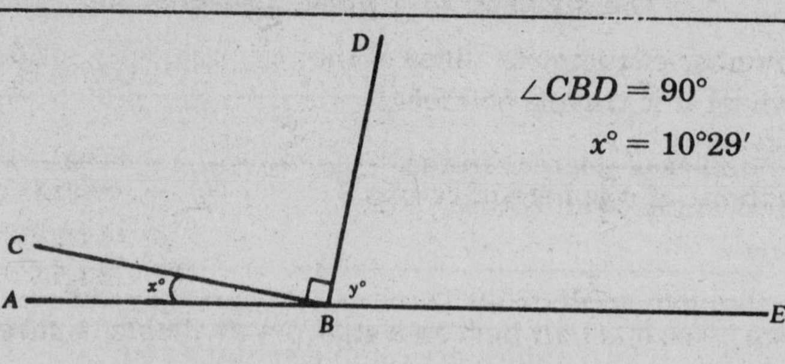

12.	y	$79\frac{1}{2}$

This figure is for questions 13 and 14.

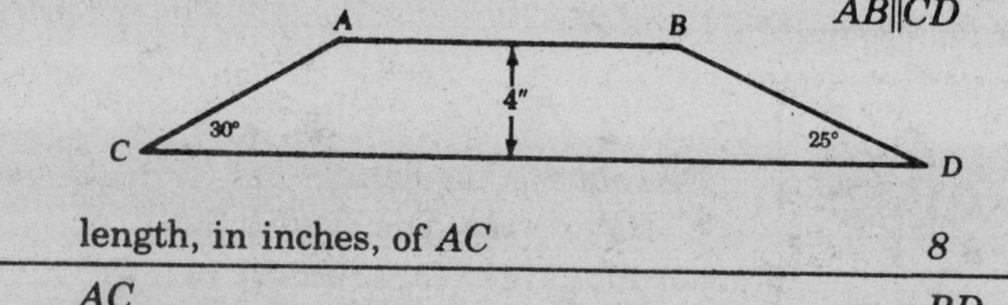

13.	length, in inches, of AC	8
14.	AC	BD
15.	number of degrees in the sum of two angles of an acute triangle	90
16.	circumference, in inches, of a circle whose diameter is 7.1″ (use $\pi = 3.1$)	22
17.	the area, in square inches, of a rectangle 6 inches by 3 feet	218

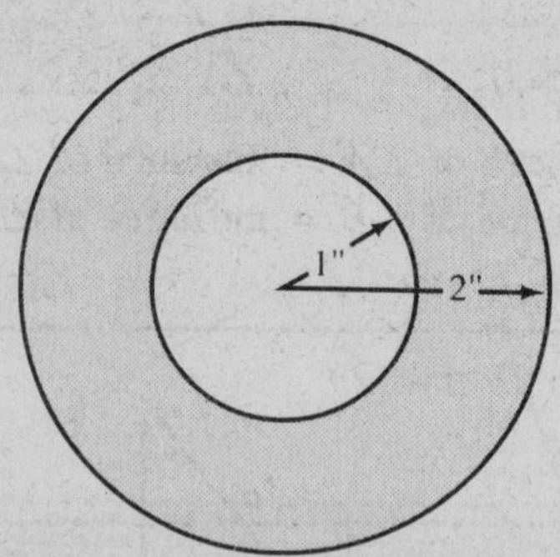

18.	the area of the shaded ring	3π
19.	the perimeter of a square whose edge is 1 unit	the circumference of a circle whose diameter is 1 unit

	COLUMN A	COLUMN B

The sum of the complement and supplement of an angle equals 184°.

20.	**the angle**	**its complement**

The diameter of a wheel measures 35″.

21.	**number of complete turns of the wheel if it travels 550 feet (use $\pi = {}^{22}/_{7}$)**	**55**
22.	**volume of a sphere of radius 3**	**volume of a cylinder of radius 3 and height 4**

Bathroom tiles, one half inch on a side, are available in sheets of 10 by 12 tiles.

23.	**number of sheets needed to cover a wall 5′ × 8′**	**200**

This figure is for questions 24 and 25.

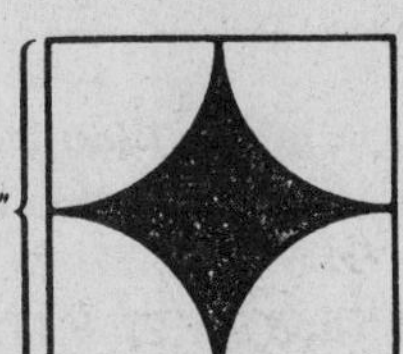

This square has quarter-circles of radius 2″ at each vertex. The shaded part has area (in square inches) $16 - k\pi$

24.	k	**4**
25.	**area of the shaded portion**	**area of one quarter-circle**

A cone and a cylinder of equal volumes have equal heights.

26.	**the radius of the cylinder**	**the radius of the cone**

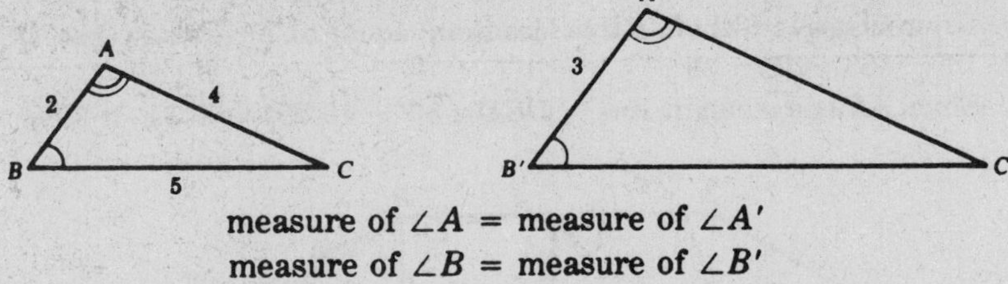

measure of $\angle A$ = measure of $\angle A'$
measure of $\angle B$ = measure of $\angle B'$

27.	$A'C'$	6

This figure is for questions 28 and 29.

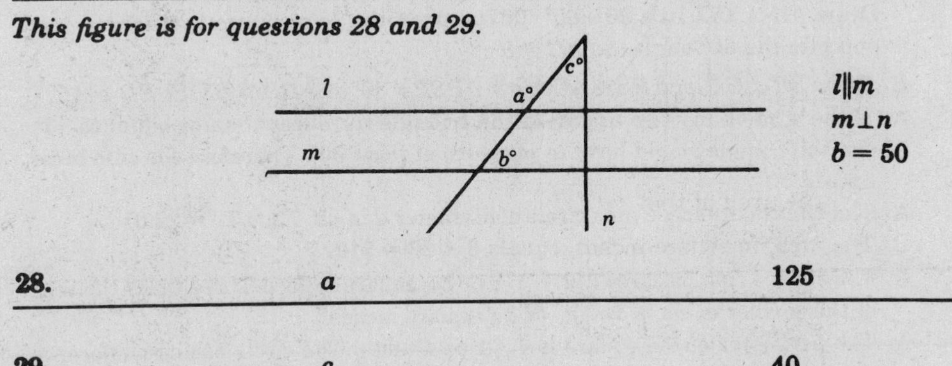

28.	a	**125**
29.	c	**40**

EXAMPLES	COLUMN A	COLUMN B

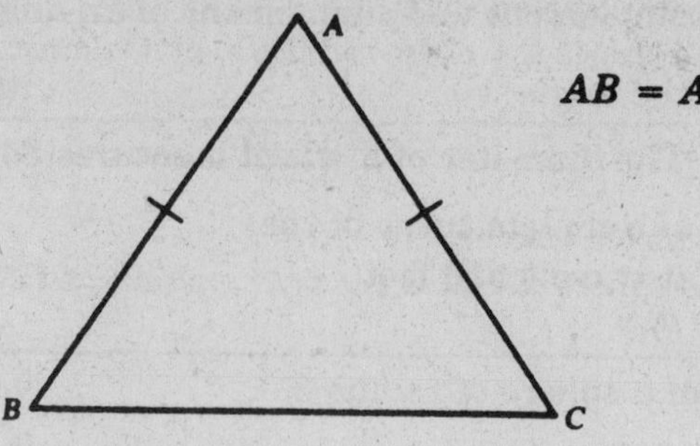

$AB = AC$

30.	measure of $\angle A$	measure of supplement of $2 \times m\angle B$

ANSWERS AND EXPLANATIONS

to practice Section I questions on geometry.

1. A. An obtuse triangle has one obtuse angle—an angle larger than 90°.
2. B. $180° - 55°40'18'' = 179°59'60'' - 55°40'18'' = 124°19'42''$. But this computation is unnecessary, since $180 - 55 = 125 > 180 - 55^{+}$.
3. A. If x is the number of degrees in the smaller angle, then $x + 2x + 11 = 90$ and $x = 26\frac{1}{3}$.
4. D. We cannot assume the triangle is isosceles.
5. A. The perimeter in inches $= 3\frac{1}{2} + 4\frac{1}{5} + 5\frac{1}{3} = 12\frac{31}{30} = 13\frac{1}{30}$.
6. C. $\angle ADB$, the exterior angle of $\triangle ADC$, equals the sum of the two opposite interior angles. So $x = u + z$.
7. B. From question 6, we know that $x > u$. Since $u = \frac{1}{2}v$, $x > \frac{1}{2}v$.
8. C. $y = \frac{1}{2}v + w$ (see answer to 6).
9. D. It appears from the figure that $x < y$, but figures can be drawn with $v = 2u$ where $x > y$ or $x = y$.
10. D. Draw figures in which BD is less than, equal to, or greater than DC.
11. B. $180 - (63 + 81) = 36$.
12. A. Since AE is a straight line, $\angle DBE = 90° - 10°29' = 79°31' > 79\frac{1}{2}°$.
13. C.

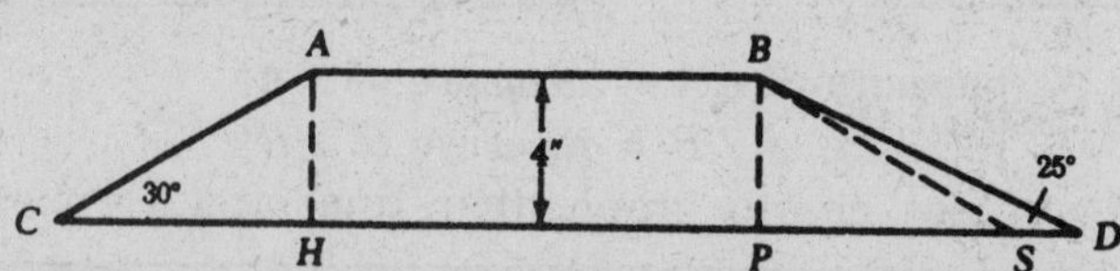

Draw $AH \perp CD$. In a 30°–60°–90° triangle the hypotenuse is twice the leg opposite the 30° angle. So $AC = 8''$.

14. B. Draw $BP \perp CD$, and $BS = AC$. Now $\angle BSP = 30°$ and $BD > BS$. So $BD > AC$.
15. A. If the sum of any two angles of the triangle *were* less than or equal to 90°, the third angle would have to measure at least 90°. Therefore the sum must exceed 90°.
16. A. The circumference, C, of a circle of diameter d is πd. $7.1 \times 3.1 = 22.01$.
17. B. The area, in square inches, equals $6 \times 36 = 216$.
18. C. The shaded ring has area $2^2\pi - 1^2\pi$ or 3π square inches. Three times the area of the smaller circle is $3 \times \pi$, or 3π square inches.
19. A. The perimeter of the square is $4 \cdot 1$ or 4 units. The circle has circumference $2\pi \cdot \frac{1}{2}$ or π units; $\pi \approx 3.1$.

20. B. If x denotes the number of degrees in the angle, then $90 - x + 180 - x = 184$ and $x = 43$. Its complement = 47°.

21. A. Divide the distance travelled, in inches, by the circumference of the wheel in inches:

$$\frac{550 \times 12}{35 \times {}^{22}/_7} = 60.$$

The wheel makes 60 complete turns.

22. C. Volume of a sphere of radius r is ${}^4/_3\pi r^3$; volume of a cylinder of radius r and height h is $\pi r^2 h$.

$$V_{\text{sphere}} = {}^4/_3\pi \cdot 3^3 = 36\pi;$$
$$V_{\text{cylinder}} = \pi \cdot 3^2 \cdot 4 = 36\pi.$$

23. B. We divide the area of the wall, in square inches, by the area of a sheet of tiles, in inches:

$$\frac{5 \times 12 \times 8 \times 12}{10 \times {}^1/_2 \times 12 \times {}^1/_2} = 192 \text{ sheets.}$$

24. C. The area of one quarter-circle is ${}^1/_4 \cdot \pi \cdot 2^2 = \pi$. The shaded part has area $4^2 - 4 \cdot \pi = 16 - 4\pi$.

25. A. $16 - 4\pi = 16 - 4(3.1) \approx 3.6 > \pi$.

26. B. Let the radii of the cylinder and cone be R and r respectively, and let h denote the common height. $V_{cyl} = \pi R^2 h$; $V_{cone} = {}^1/_3\pi r^2 h$. Since $\pi R^2 h = {}^1/_3\pi r^2 h$, therefore $r^2 = 3R^2$ and $r = R\sqrt{3}$. So $r > R$.

27. C. Since the triangles are similar, $A'C':AC = A'B':AB$; so $A'C':4 = 3:2$ and $A'C' = 6$.

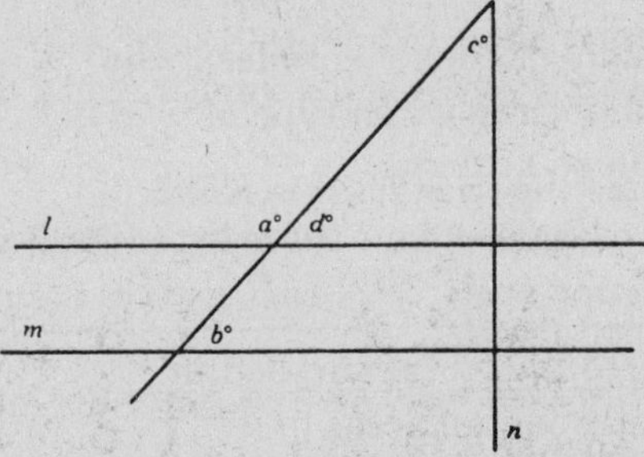

28. A. Since $l \parallel m$, the corresponding angles are equal. Therefore $d = b$ and a and b are supplementary: $a = 130$.

29. C. Since $m \perp n$, $c = 90 - d = 90 - b = 90 - 50 = 40$.

30. C. $\angle B = \angle C$ and $\angle A + \angle B + \angle C = 180°$. Therefore $\angle A = 180° - 2 \times m\angle B$.

A4. Data Interpretation

This topic includes tables, charts, graphs (bar, line, circle, or pie), and pictographs.

In this book the source of a figure or table given as the basis of a question is indicated briefly in italics under the figure or table. The full references are as follows:

Data: Pocket Data Book, USA 1971 and *1979*. Washington, DC: U.S. Department of Commerce, Bureau of the Census.

Developing Skills: Shirley O. Hockett, *Barron's Developing Skills for the High School Equivalency Examination in Mathematics*. Hauppauge, NY: Barron's Educational Series, 1972 and 1978.

Fact: Life Insurance Fact Book 1973. New York: Institute of Life Insurance, 1973.

Social Security Bulletin: issued monthly by the Social Security Administration, Washington, DC.

Be sure you are familiar with the test directions for quantitative-comparison questions. Here are a few introductory examples, with answers and explanations.

Examples 1-4 refer to the following table.

ENROLLMENTS IN COLLEGES IN 1970 (IN THOUSANDS)
BY SEX AND RESIDENCE

	TOTAL ENROLLMENT	2-YR COLLEGES	4-YR COLLEGES 1 and 2 yrs	4-YR COLLEGES 3 and 4 yrs
Sex				
male	3,627	1,001	1,206	1,319
female	2,646	691	1,038	814
total (ages 16-34)	6,274	1,692	2,244	2,133
Residence				
metropolitan areas	4,401	1,220	1,507	1,525
nonmetropolitan areas	1,873	472	737	608

(Figures listed do not add up to total enrollments because some enrolled did not give information requested.)

	COLUMN A	COLUMN B	ANSWERS
1.	number of male enrollees who did not report on type of college attended	100,000	1. ● Ⓑ Ⓒ Ⓓ Ⓔ

(The total enrollment of males minus those listed for 2-year and 4-year colleges equals 101,000.)

2.	percent of total enrolled in metropolitan areas	75%	2. Ⓐ ● Ⓒ Ⓓ Ⓔ

(Since $^3/_4 \times 6274 > 4500 > 4401$, choice B is correct.)

3.	ratio of men in college to men not in college	ratio of women in college to women not in college	3. Ⓐ Ⓑ Ⓒ ● Ⓔ

(Since figures are not given for those *not* enrolled in college, the question cannot be answered.)

4.	number, to the nearest million, of those aged 16 to 34 from metropolitan areas	4,000,000	4. Ⓐ Ⓑ ● Ⓓ Ⓔ

(The numbers given are in thousands; the total enrollment from metropolitan areas is 4,401,000, which rounds to 4,000,000.)

TIPS ON ANSWERING QUESTIONS ON DATA INTERPRETATION

1. Decide what sort of information is given by a graph, chart, or table before trying to answer a question about it.
2. Note the scale on a graph, the key on a chart, or the units (thousands, millions, or the like) in a table.
3. Use a straightedge (your pencil will do) to follow across a row of figures in a table.

4. In using a table or chart, be certain that you correctly locate the entry referred to (that is, that you are in the right row *and* in the right column).
5. To compare distances on a graph, or to estimate a particular distance, use your pencil or other straightedge.
6. To find a percent or to calculate a ratio, it is often convenient to round off numbers that are given. However, be careful about the units and round off similarly in both numerator and denominator to obtain an equivalent answer.

PRACTICE QUESTIONS ON DATA INTERPRETATION

Follow the directions given on page 301. After you answer the questions, check your answers against those that follow immediately. As you read the explanations, note how the above tips are used.

Questions 1–4 refer to the table on enrollments in college in 1970.

	COLUMN A	COLUMN B
1.	**number, to the nearest million, of women enrolled in 4-yr colleges**	2,000,000
2.	percent of total enrolled in **college from nonmetropolitan areas**	40
3.	**ratio of women enrolled in college to men enrolled**	1 : 2
4.	percent of males enrolled who did not report on whether they attended 2-yr. or 4-yr. college	3

Questions 5-7 refer to the pictograph of population given below; each house represents 10,000 people.

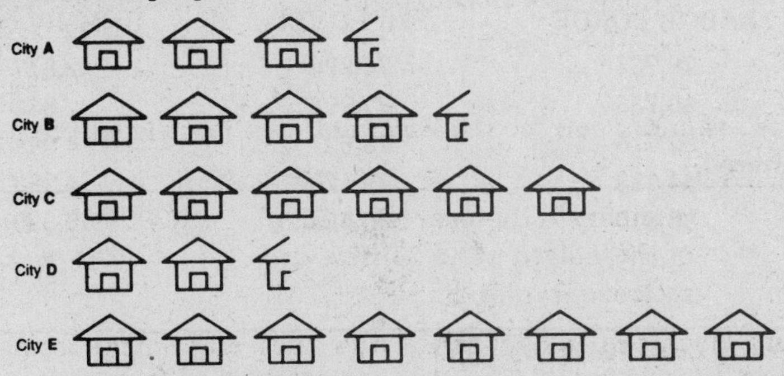

City A

City B

City C

City D

City E

Source: Developing Skills, 1972, p. 212.

	COLUMN A	COLUMN B
5.	difference in population, in thousands, between largest and smallest cities	55
6.	ratio of population of city *C* to that of city *B*	ratio of population of city *B* to that of city *A*
7.	total population, in thousands, of the five cities	245

	COLUMN A	COLUMN B

Questions 8-10 refer to the bar graph given below.

HOW THE COLLINS FAMILY BUDGETED EACH DOLLAR OF INCOME

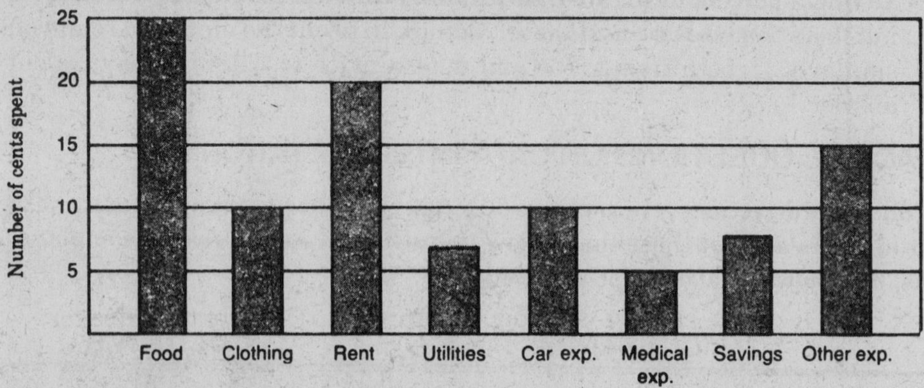

Source: Developing Skills, 1972, p. 214.

	COLUMN A	COLUMN B
8.	percent of dollar budgeted for savings	6

The Collins's income, in 1971, was $14,500.

	COLUMN A	COLUMN B
9.	**amount allowed for food, rent, and medical expenses in 1971**	$7500
10.	**amount budgeted in 1971 for electricity and gas**	**$1000**

Questions 11-13 refer to the following table.

EMPLOYMENT AND UNEMPLOYMENT IN THE UNITED STATES (IN THOUSANDS) CIVILIAN LABOR FORCE, AGED 16 OR OVER

	CIVILIAN LABOR FORCE	EMPLOYED	UNEMPLOYED
1968	78,737	75,920	2,817
1969	80,733	77,902	2,831
1970	82,715	78,627	4,088
1971	84,113	79,120	4,993
(1972 first-half average)	85,615	80,524	5,090)

Source: U.S. Bureau of Labor Statistics.

	COLUMN A	COLUMN B
11.	percent unemployed for the year 1972	percent unemployed for 1971
12.	ratio of employed to unemployed in 1971	15 : 1
13.	percent of civilian labor force unemployed based on the first-half average 1972	$6\frac{1}{2}$

	COLUMN A	COLUMN B

Questions 14-16 refer to the table below.

AVERAGE PRICES RECEIVED BY U.S. FARMERS (DOLLARS PER 100 LBS.)

	hogs	beef cattle	lambs
1968	18.50	23.40	24.40
1969	22.20	26.20	27.20
1970	22.70	27.10	26.40
1971	17.50	29.00	25.90

Source: U.S. Department of Agriculture.

	COLUMN A	COLUMN B
14.	**average price for beef cattle in 1970**	**average price for lambs in 1969**
15.	percent of increase in price of hogs from 1968 to 1970	percent of increase in price of beef cattle from 1968 to 1970
16.	percentage decrease in price of hogs from 1970 to 1971	20

Questions 17-19 refer to the line graph below.

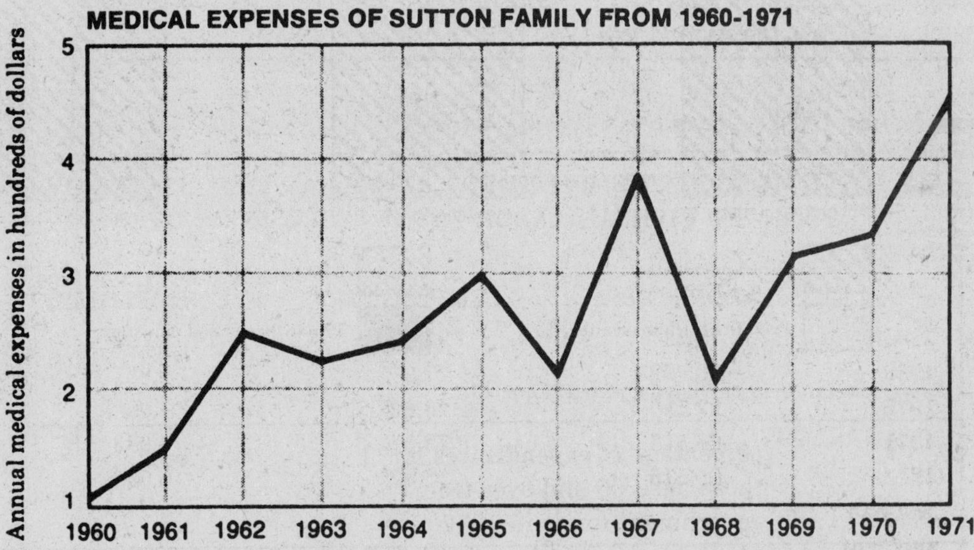

Source: Developing Skills, 1972, p. 215.

	COLUMN A	COLUMN B
17.	the Sutton family's medical expenses in 1963	the Sutton family's medical expenses in 1968
18.	percent of increase in medical expenses from 1961 to 1971	300
19.	difference in medical expenses between 1966 and 1967	difference in medical expenses between 1970 and 1971

COLUMN A	COLUMN B

Use these graphs for questions 20-22.

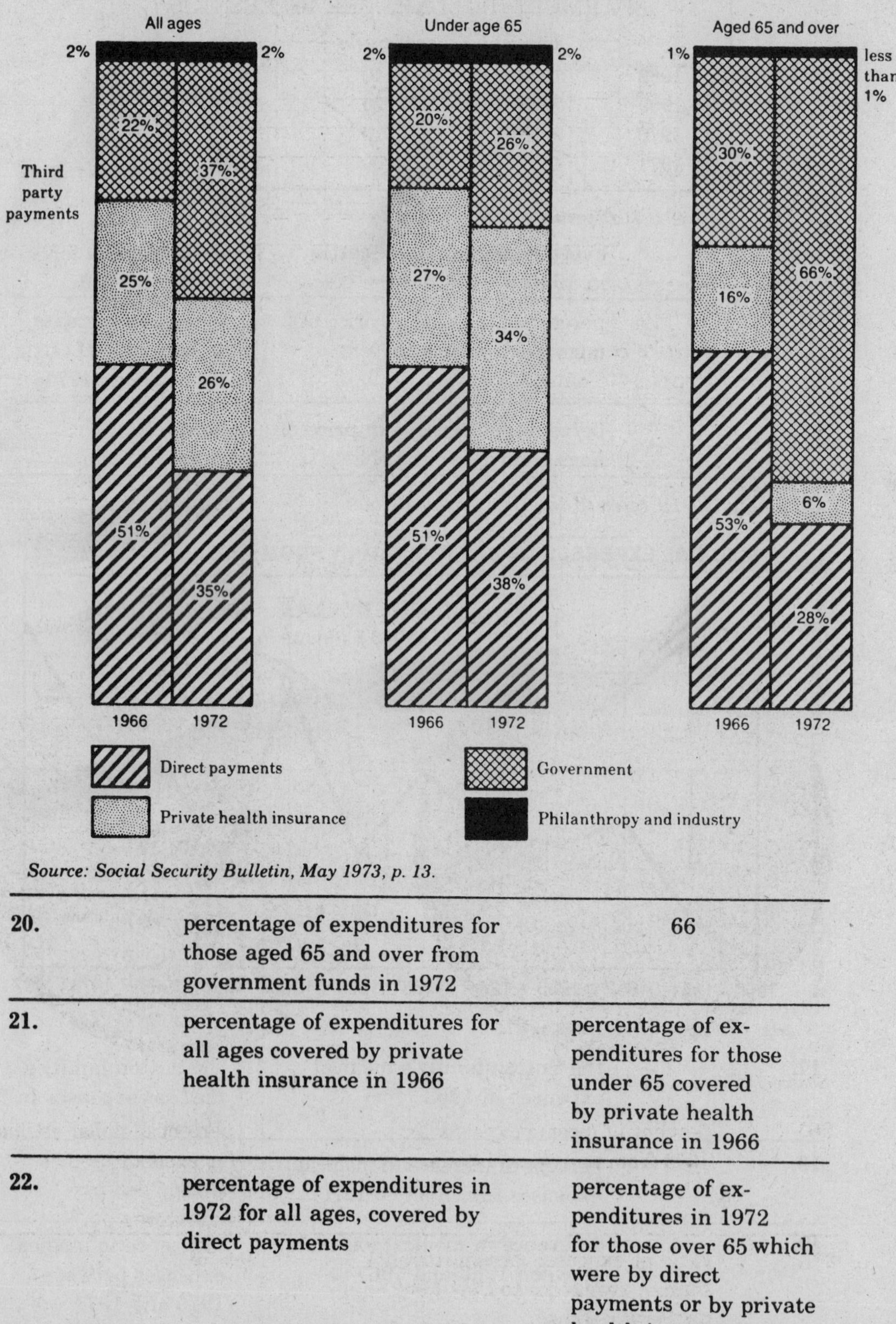

Source: Social Security Bulletin, May 1973, p. 13.

	COLUMN A	COLUMN B
20.	percentage of expenditures for those aged 65 and over from government funds in 1972	66
21.	percentage of expenditures for all ages covered by private health insurance in 1966	percentage of expenditures for those under 65 covered by private health insurance in 1966
22.	percentage of expenditures in 1972 for all ages, covered by direct payments	percentage of expenditures in 1972 for those over 65 which were by direct payments or by private health insurance

	COLUMN A	COLUMN B

Questions 23-25 refer to the figure below.

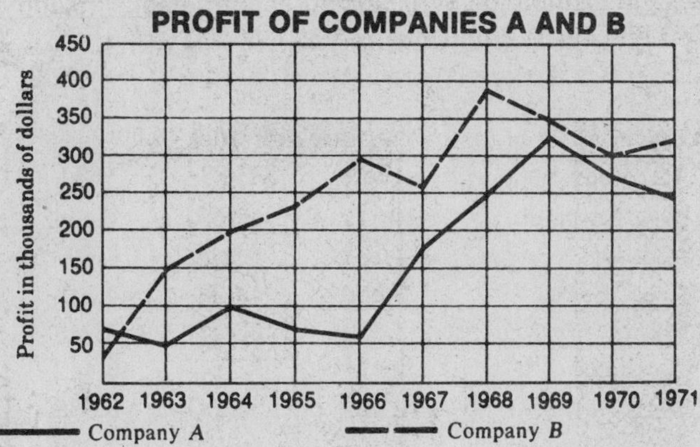

Source: Developing Skills: 1972, p. 224.

	Column A	Column B
23.	**ratio of company *B*'s profits to company *A*'s in 1964**	5 : 2
24.	estimate of company *B*'s profits mid-1970	325,000
25.	difference in profits of the two companies in 1965	difference in their profits in 1968

Questions 26 and 27 refer to the circle graphs below.

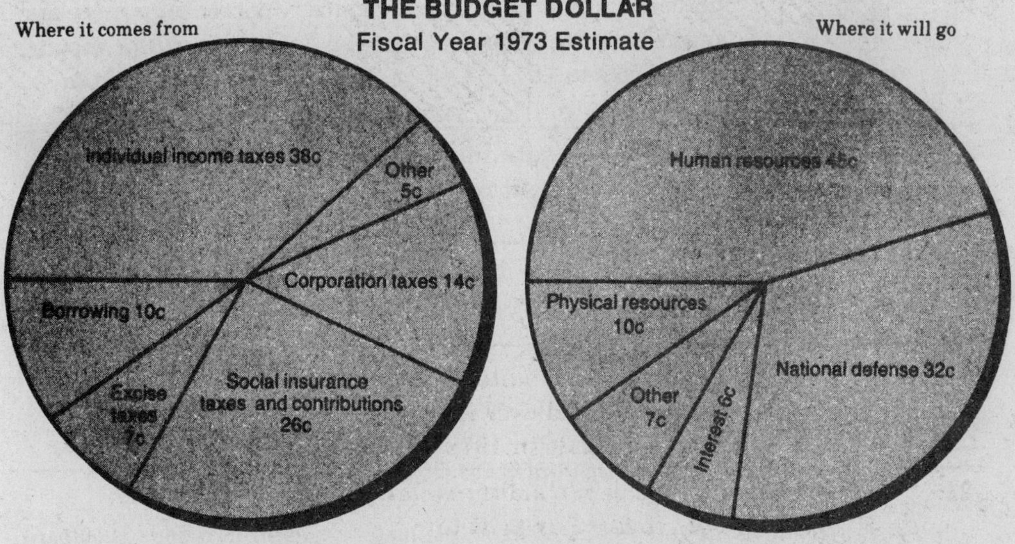

Source: Developing Skills, 1972, p. 217.

	Column A	Column B
26.	percent of income expected in 1973 from individual income taxes	percent of dollar estimated for expenditures on national defense and interest
27.	**ratio of expected expenditure for human resources to that for national defense**	5 : 4

COLUMN A	COLUMN B

Questions 28-30 refer to the following table.

PER CAPITA PERSONAL INCOME,
BY REGIONS OF THE U.S.

Region	Per capita income (in dollars) 1969	1970	1971
New England	4,012	4,259	4,454
Mideast	4,182	4,453	4,697
Great Lakes	3,956	4,098	4,348
Plains	3,509	3,741	3,958
Southeast	2,978	3,214	3,442
Southwest	3,257	3,514	3,688
Rocky Mountain	3,277	3,557	3,809
Far West	4,122	4,327	4,522
United States	3,708	3,933	4,156

Source: U.S. Department of Commerce.

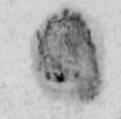

	Column A	Column B
28.	**difference between greatest and least per capita income in 1971**	**difference between greatest and least per capita income in 1969**
29.	**percentage increase in per capita income for New England region from 1969 to 1971**	**percentage increase in per capita income for the U.S. from 1969 to 1971**
30.	**median per capita income in 1971 for the eight regions of the country**	**U.S. per capita income in 1971**

ANSWERS AND EXPLANATIONS

to practice Section I questions on data interpretation.

Note: For many of these questions, only an estimate is needed in order to compare the quantities given in Columns A and B. Valuable time can be saved by avoiding unnecessary computations. This will be demonstrated in the explanations that follow.

1. C. There are (1038 + 814) or 1852 *thousand* women; this rounds up to 2 million. It is sufficient here to note that there are *about* 1,800 thousand women.
2. B. Multiply 6274 by 0.4, or (approximately) 6000 by 0.4. 2400 > 1873.
3. A. Instead of dividing 2646 by 3627, we estimate: 2600 ÷ 3600. It is clearly greater than ½.
4. B. In example 1, we noted that 101 thousand males did not report. 1 divided by 36 (instead of 101 divided by 3627) is less than 0.03.

5. C. $80 - 25 = 55$.

6. A. $6 \div 4\frac{1}{2} = 6 \times \frac{2}{9} = \frac{4}{3} = 1.3^{+}$.
$4\frac{1}{2} \div 3\frac{1}{2} = \frac{9}{2} \times \frac{2}{7} = 1.3^{-}$.
$1.3^{+} > 1.3^{-}$.

7. C. There are 3 half-houses, plus, from top to bottom $(3 + 4 + 6 + 2 + 8)$ whole houses for a total of $24\frac{1}{2}$ houses or 245,000 people.

8. A. The top of the bar above "Savings" is midway between the 5¢ and 10¢ horizontal line; savings, therefore, were allowed about $7\frac{1}{2}$% of the family's dollar.

9. B. Total allowed is $(25 + 20 + 5)$ cents, or 50¢. Half of 14,500 is 7,250.

10. D. Utilities may include more than electricity and gas; e.g., water or telephone.

11. D. It cannot be assumed that the first-half average will apply for the entire year.

12. A. $79 \div 5$ (instead of $79{,}120 \div 4{,}993$) $> 15:1$. (Note that we've rounded both to thousands, and that we've both decreased the numerator *and* increased the denominator; the exact ratio is therefore even greater than $79:5$.)

13. B. Is $0.06\frac{1}{2} \times 80{,}524$ greater than, less than, or equal to 5090? We approximate: $6\frac{1}{2} \times 800 = 5100$.

14. B. The average price for beef cattle in 1970 was \$27.10 (per 100 lbs); the average price for lambs in 1969 was \$27.20.

15. A. $(420 \div 1850) > (370 \div 2340)$ since $(42 \div 19) > 2$ while $(37 \div 23) < 2$.

16. A. Percentage decrease $= \dfrac{22.70 - 17.50}{22.7} > \dfrac{5}{23} > 0.2 = 20\%$.

17. A. The point on the graph above 1963 is higher than that for 1968.

18. B. Percentage increase $\approx \dfrac{450 - 150}{150} \approx 200\%$.

19. A. The difference in medical expenses between 1966 and 1967 > 150; between 1970 and 1971, the difference < 150.

20. C. Use the rightmost bar.

21. B. The Column A percentage is 25; the Column B percentage is 27.

22. A. The answer for Column A is 35%; for Column B $(28 + 6)$%.

23. B. The ratio in 1964 $\approx 2:1$.

24. D. In a graph of this sort, the points representing profits for 2 successive years are connected by a line segment. We cannot interpolate here because we cannot assume that the profits during the year are linear.

25. A. The solid and dotted graphs are farther apart in 1965 than they are in 1968.

26. C. 38%.

27. A. $45:32 > 45:36 = 5:4$.

28. A. $(4697 - 3442) > (4182 - 2978)$.

29. B. For New England, the increase equals $\dfrac{4454 - 4012}{4012} = \dfrac{442}{4012}$; for the U.S. it is $\dfrac{4156 - 3708}{3708} = \dfrac{448}{3708}$. The latter is clearly the greater.

30. B. If an odd set of numbers is arranged in order of size, the middle number is the *median*. If there are an even number of numbers in the set, the average of the two middle numbers is the median. Here the median is $(4348 + 3958) \div 2$, or 4153.

A5. Miscellaneous: Multiple-Choice Questions on Section I Topics

In this subsection we include practice questions on topics that have already been covered above (A1 through A4), as well as on other mathematical topics. Since some of the questions on Section I of the CLEP mathematics examination are of the regular multiple-choice type, the questions that follow are also of this type. Even though the answer column may have five answer boxes, labeled A, B, C, D, and E, you are to choose the *one* correct answer from among A, B, C, and D. Do not make any marks whatever in column E.

Example:

$4 - (6 - 1) =$

(A) −9 (B) −3 (C) −1 (D) 1

Explanation

Since $4 - (6 - 1) = 4 - 5 = -1$, we fill in the oval for choice C.

Answers and explanations follow this set of questions. Note especially the test directions for these questions, which are as follows:

Directions: For each of the following problems, indicate the correct answer in the appropriate space on the answer sheet.

Note: Figures that accompany problems are intended to provide information useful in solving the problems. They are drawn as accurately as possible *except* when it is stated in a specific problem that the figure is not drawn to scale. All figures lie in a plane unless otherwise indicated.

1. $5 - [8 - (3 - 1)] =$

(A) 11 (B) 1 (C) −1 (D) −7

2. $(2x + 3)(x - 1) =$

(A) $2x^2 - x - 3$ (B) $2x^2 + x + 3$

(C) $2x^2 + 2x - 3$ (D) $2x^2 + x - 3$

3. The point with coordinates (−3,2) is in quadrant

(A) I (B) II (C) III (D) IV

4. The value of y that satisfies the pair of equations

$$\left\{\begin{matrix} x + 2y = a \\ x - 2y = a \end{matrix}\right\} \text{ is}$$

(A) 0 (B) $\frac{a}{2}$ (C) $\frac{a}{4}$ (D) $-\frac{a}{4}$

5. If x is 150% of 10, then x equals

(A) 1.5 (B) $6\frac{2}{3}$ (C) 15 (D) 150

6. The number of zeros in $(2 \times 10^3)^2 \times 5$ is

(A) 6 (B) 7 (C) 9 (D) 10

7. It takes 3 men 8 days to build a wall. How long does it take 2 men working at the same rate to build the wall?

(A) $5\frac{1}{3}$ days (B) 10 days

(C) 12 days (D) none of these

8. If an alloy contains 60% silver by weight, how much does the silver in a 270-gram sample weigh?

(A) 16 grams (B) 16.2 grams (C) 162 grams (D) 180 grams

9. If $4x + 3y + 24 = 0$, then when $y = 0$, $x =$

(A) −8 (B) −6 (C) 6 (D) 8

10. The area, in square feet, of a circle is π^2. The length, in feet, of its radius is

(A) π (B) $\sqrt{\pi}$ (C) $\frac{\pi}{2}$ (D) 1

11. $3^2 + 3^0 + 3^{-1} =$

(A) 3 (B) 9 (C) $9\frac{1}{3}$ (D) $10\frac{1}{3}$

12. If a 12-oz. bottle of beer is 3.5% alcohol, then the amount of alcohol in the bottle is about

(A) 0.4 oz. (B) 0.5 oz. (C) 3 oz. (D) 4 oz.

13. In scientific notation 0.12 part of a substance per million is written "1.2×10^k." What does k equal?

(A) −7 (B) −6 (C) 6 (D) 7

14. The area of the shaded region is

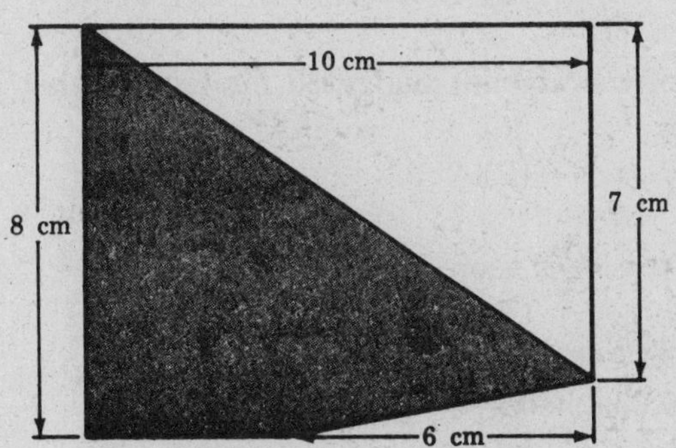

(A) 37 cm² (B) 40 cm² (C) 42 cm² (D) 52 cm²

15. If $x \neq 0$, then $\frac{2x + 4}{2x} =$

(A) 5 (B) $1 + \frac{1}{x}$ (C) $1 + 2x$ (D) $1 + \frac{2}{x}$

16. The linear relationship defined by the table is

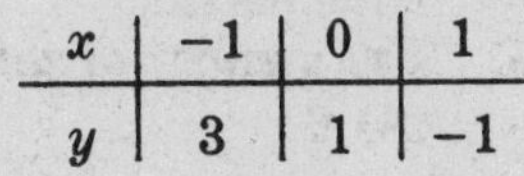

x	−1	0	1
y	3	1	−1

(A) $y = x + 2$ (B) $y = 2x + 1$
(C) $y = 2x + 1$ (D) $y = -2x + 1$

17. The length, to the nearest inch, of the hypotenuse of a right triangle whose legs are 8″ and 10″ is

(A) 11″ (B) 12″ (C) 13″ (D) 14″

18. The slope of the line $3y = x - 3$ is

(A) −1 (B) $\frac{1}{3}$ (C) 1 (D) 3

19. If $0.25x + 0.41 = 0.75x - 2.59$, then $x =$

(A) 6 (B) 3 (C) 0.6 (D) −6

20. Suppose $z = \frac{v^3}{w}$. If v is doubled and w is multiplied by 4, then the ratio of the new value of z to the old is
(A) 1:2 (B) 1:1 (C) 2:1 (D) 4:1

The pie graph is for questions 21 and 22.

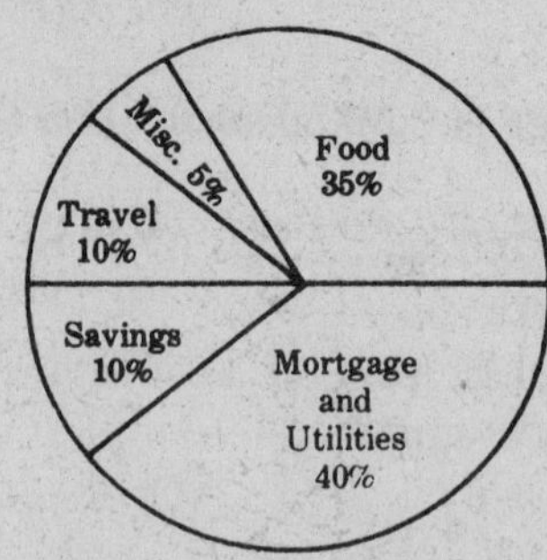

21. When the family's annual income is $22,000, the amount budgeted for mortgage and utilities is
(A) $8800 (B) $8000 (C) $7700 (D) $880

22. The ratio of the amount budgeted for food to that for savings and travel combined is
(A) 7:2 (B) 7:3 (C) 2:1 (D) 7:4

23. If $3x - 4 < x + 2$, then
(A) $x > 3$ (B) $x < 3$ (C) $x < 1$ (D) $x < -3$

24. If $(^1\!/_2)^x = 0.25$, then $x =$
(A) 3 (B) 2 (C) −2 (D) −3

25. If $\frac{1}{z} = \frac{1}{x} + \frac{1}{y}$, then when $x = 15$ and $y = 30$, $z =$
(A) $\frac{1}{45}$ (B) $\frac{1}{10}$ (C) 10 (D) 45

26. The sun is 93 million miles from earth and the speed of light is 186,000 mi./sec. How many minutes, approximately, does it take sunlight to reach the earth?
(A) 1 (B) 8 (C) 10 (D) 12

27. The correct complete factorization of the expression $2t^3 - 8t$ is
(A) $2t(t - 2)(t + 2)$ (B) $2(t - 2)(t^2 + 2t + 4)$
(C) $2t(t^2 + 4)$ (D) $2t(t^2 - 8)$

The figure at the right is for questions 28 and 29; it is NOT drawn to scale.

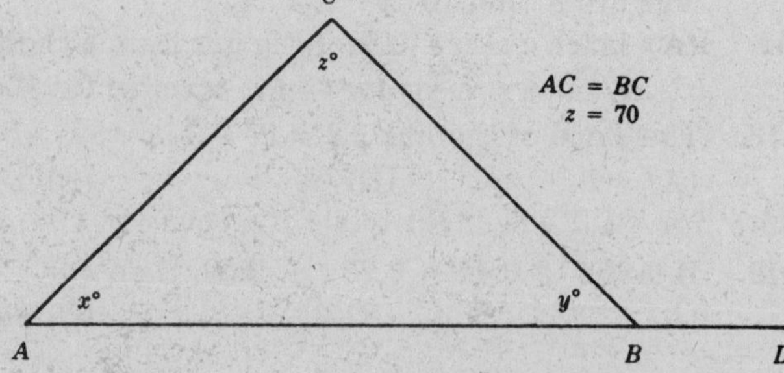

28. The complement of $\angle BAC$ measures
(A) 15° (B) 20° (C) 25° (D) 35°

29. The measure of $\angle DBC$ is
(A) 110° (B) 115° (C) 125° (D) 135°

The graph and table below are for questions 30-32.

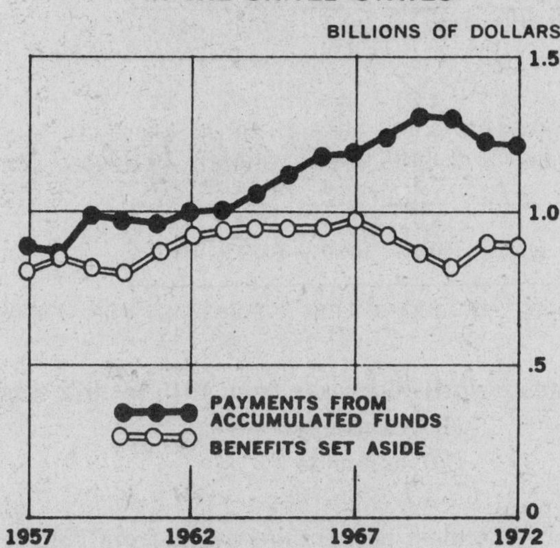

USE OF LIFE INSURANCE BENEFITS UNDER SUPPLEMENTARY CONTRACTS
IN THE UNITED STATES
(000,000 Omitted)

Year	Benefits Set Aside	Payments From Accumulated Funds
1945	$540	$ 295
1950	680	520
1955	780	720
1960	760	970
1965	920	1,110
1966	920	1,180
1967	940	1,190
1968	890	1,240
1969	840	1,310
1970	790	1,290
1971	870	1,220
1972	870	1,210

Source: Fact, p. 52.

30. The difference between payments from accumulated funds and benefits set aside was least in
(A) 1957 (B) 1958 (C) 1970 (D) 1971

31. The difference noted in question 30 was greatest in
(A) 1960 (B) 1969 (C) 1970 (D) 1971

32. The percent of increase in benefits set aside from 1969 to 1972 was approximately
(A) 0.04% (B) 0.4% (C) 4% (D) 40%

33. $\left(\frac{5ab}{2u}\right)\left(\frac{6u^2}{10a^2b}\right) =$
(A) $\frac{3u}{2ab}$ (B) $\frac{6au}{4b}$ (C) $\frac{3u}{2}$ (D) $\frac{3u}{2a}$

34. How much change should you get from a check for $25.58 if your purchases are as follows: meat for $4.67, oranges for 89¢, and eggs for 95¢?
(A) $19.07 (B) $19.17 (C) $19.87 (D) $20.07

35. The solutions of the quadratic equation $x^2 - 5x + 6 = 0$ are
(A) 1 and 6 (B) 1 and −6
(C) −1 and −6 (D) none of these

The table below is for questions 36 and 37.

PERCENTAGE DISTRIBUTION OF ORDINARY POLICYHOLDER DEATHS BY CAUSE

U.S. LIFE INSURANCE COMPANIES

Cause of Death	1945	1950	1955	1960	1965	1971	1972
Natural Causes							
Cardiovascular-renal	49.3%	57.0%	57.2%	55.7%	53.9%	51.7%	51.2%
Cancer	14.8	17.3	18.6	18.7	19.2	20.0	20.4
Pneumonia and Influenza	3.1	1.9	2.0	3.2	3.1	3.0	3.0
Tuberculosis (all forms)	2.8	1.3	.5	.3	.2	.1	.1
Diabetes	1.5	1.3	.9	1.0	1.1	.9	1.0
Other Diseases[2]	18.2	12.0	12.3	13.1	13.6	15.5	15.4
Total	89.7	90.8	91.5	92.0	91.1	91.2	91.1
External Causes							
Motor Vehicle Accidents	2.3	3.1	3.1	2.9	3.6	3.5	3.5
Other Accidents	5.9	3.6	3.2	3.1	3.2	3.0	3.1
Suicide	1.9	2.2	2.0	1.8	1.8	1.7	1.6
Homicide	.2	.3	.2	.2	.3	.6	.7
Total	10.3	9.2	8.5	8.0	8.9	8.8	8.9
Total All Causes	100.0%	100.0%	100.0%	100.0%	100.0%	100.0%	100.0%

Source: Fact, p. 104.

36. The cause of death with the largest *relative* increase from 1945 to 1972 was

(A) cardiovascular-renal (B) cancer
(C) motor vehicle accidents (D) homicide

37. Which cause of death increased by the most percentage points from 1945 to 1972?

(A) cardiovascular-renal (B) cancer
(C) motor vehicle accidents (D) homicide

38. Which of the following statements is incorrect?

(A) $\sqrt{9} + \sqrt{16} = 5$ (B) $\sqrt{4} \cdot \sqrt{9} = 6$
(C) $\dfrac{\sqrt{25} + \sqrt{9}}{\sqrt{4}} = 4$ (D) $\dfrac{\sqrt{9} + \sqrt{4}}{\sqrt{4}} = 1\frac{2}{3}$

39. The product of the roots of the equation $x^2 + 5x - 66 = 0$ is

(A) 66 (B) 5 (C) −5 (D) −66

40. If the average of the set of numbers $\{3,5,6,11,x\}$ is 6, then $x =$

(A) 5 (B) $5\frac{1}{2}$
(C) 6 (D) none of these

ANSWERS AND EXPLANATIONS

to practice Section I questions on miscellaneous topics.

1. C. $5 - [8 - (3 - 1)] = 5 - [8 - 2] = 5 - 6 = -1$.
2. D. $(2x + 3)(x - 1) = (2x)(x) + (2x)(-1) + (3)(x) + (3)(-1) = 2x^2 + x - 3$.
3. B. The signs of a point (x,y) determine the quadrant as follows: $(+,+)$ in quadrant I; $(-,+)$ in II; $(-,-)$ in III; $(+,-)$ in IV.

4. A. Adding the equations yields $2x = 2a$; so $x = a$. Then, using the first equation, we get $a + 2y = a$, $y = 0$.
5. C. Since 150% = 1.5, $x = (1.5)(10) = 15$.
6. B. $(2 \times 10^3)^2 \times 5 = 2^2 \times 10^6 \times 5 = 20 \times 10^6 = 2 \times 10^7$.
7. C. Since 3 men take 8 days, 1 man takes 24 days. So 2 men require 12 days.
8. C. 60% = 0.60; $0.6 \times 270 = 162$.
9. B. $4x + 3(0) + 24 = 0 \rightarrow 4x = -24 \rightarrow x = -6$.
10. B. Since the area of a circle equals πr^2, we have $\pi^2 = \pi r^2$, $\pi = r^2$, and $r = \sqrt{\pi}$.
11. D. $3^2 + 3^0 + 3^{-1} = 9 + 1 + 1/3 = 10 1/3$.
12. A. Since 3.5% = 0.035, we find 0.035×12, which equals 0.42.
13. A. $0.12 \div 1{,}000{,}000 = 0.00000012 = 1.2 \times 10^{-7}$.
14. C. The rectangle has area $(10)(8) = 80$ cm²; the unshaded triangle at the top has area $1/2(10)(7) = 35$ cm²; the unshaded triangle in the right corner has area $1/2(6)(1) = 3$ cm². $80 - (35 + 3) = 42$.
15. D. $\dfrac{2x+4}{2x} = \dfrac{2x}{2x} + \dfrac{4}{2x} = 1 + \dfrac{2}{x}$.
16. D. Perhaps the fastest approach here is to test the points given. In fact, the first one, (−1,3), does not satisfy (A), (B), or (C).
17. C. $\sqrt{8^2 + 10^2} = \sqrt{64 + 100} = \sqrt{164} \approx 13$.
18. B. Rewrite the equation in the form $y = mx + b$, getting
$$y = \frac{1}{3}x - 1.$$
The slope, m, is $\frac{1}{3}$.
19. A. $0.25x + 0.41 = 0.75x - 2.59$
$2.59 + 0.41 = 0.75x - 0.25x$
$$3 = 0.5x \rightarrow x = \frac{3}{0.5} = \frac{30}{5} = 6.$$
20. C. If z' is the new z, then
$$z' = \frac{(2v)^3}{4w} = \frac{8v^3}{4w} = 2\left(\frac{v^3}{w}\right) = 2z.$$
21. A. 40% = 0.4; $0.4 \times 22{,}000 = \$8800$.
22. D. Savings and travel together come to 20%; 35:20 = 7:4.
23. B. $3x - 4 < x + 2 \rightarrow 2x < 6 \rightarrow x < 3$.
24. B. $\left(\frac{1}{2}\right)^x = 0.25 \rightarrow \left(\frac{1}{2}\right)^x = \frac{1}{4} \rightarrow x = 2$.
25. C. $\frac{1}{z} = \frac{1}{x} + \frac{1}{y}$ yields $\frac{1}{z} = \frac{1}{15} + \frac{1}{30} = \frac{2}{30} + \frac{1}{30} = \frac{3}{30} = \frac{1}{10}$ So $z = 10$.
26. B. $\dfrac{93{,}000{,}000}{186{,}000} = 500$ sec. $= \dfrac{500}{60}$ min. $= 8\frac{1}{3}$ min.
27. A. $2t^3 - 8t = 2t(t^2 - 4) = 2t(t - 2)(t + 2)$.
28. D. Since the triangle is isosceles, $x = y$. So $2x + 70 = 180$ and $x = 55$; the complement of $\angle BAC$ measures $90 - 55 = 35$ degrees.
29. C. $\angle DBC$ is the supplement of $\angle ABC$; its measure is $180 - 55 = 125$ degrees.
30. B. The graphs are closest together in 1958.
31. C. The graphs are farthest apart in 1970.
32. C. $(30 \div 840) = (3 \div 84) \approx 0.035 \approx 4\%$.
33. D. $\left(\dfrac{5ab}{2u}\right)\left(\dfrac{6u^2}{10a^2b}\right) = \left(\dfrac{5 \cdot 6}{2 \cdot 10}\right)\left(\dfrac{a}{a^2}\right)\left(\dfrac{b}{b}\right)\left(\dfrac{u^2}{u}\right) = \dfrac{3u}{2a}$.
34. A. $25.58 - (4.67 + 0.89 + 0.95) = 25.58 - 6.51 = \$19.07$.
35. D. $x^2 - 5x + 6 = (x - 2)(x - 3)$, which equals zero if $x = 2$ or 3.
36. D. Note that the percent of increase in homicide deaths from 1945 to 1972 is
$$\frac{0.7 - 0.2}{0.2} = \frac{0.5}{0.2} = 2.5 = 250\%$$
No other cause approaches this in *relative* increase.

37. B. The largest difference between 1945 and 1972 is in cancer (20.4 − 14.8, or 6%).
38. A. $\sqrt{9} + \sqrt{16} = 3 + 4 = 7 \neq 5$.
39. D. The product of the roots of the equation $ax^2 + bx + c = 0$ is c/a. For $x^2 + 5x - 66 = 0$, $a = 1$, $b = 5$, and $c = -66$.
40. A. $(3 + 5 + 6 + 11 + x) \div 5 = 6 \rightarrow (25 + x) \div 5 = 6 \rightarrow 25 + x = 30 \rightarrow x = 5$.

Practice Questions for Section II, Content

Section II of the CLEP mathematics examination is the Content portion. It measures the body of mathematical knowledge that is usually taught in a college course designed for nonmathematics majors. The topics tested are frequently covered in survey courses in mathematics, courses in mathematics offered to meet general education requirements, or courses in the structure of mathematics designed for majors in elementary education.

You will be expected to understand conventional symbols and notation, especially as used for the topics of sets, logic, and functions. Contemporary mathematical terminology and symbolism will generally be used here to familiarize you with it, or afford review of it; as may be necessary.

In the material to follow, practice questions are given separately for each topic covered in Section II: sets, logic, and real number system, functions and graphs, and probability and statistics. The last group of practice questions is on miscellaneous topics.

As noted earlier, you will be allowed 60 minutes for the 50 questions in Section II. All the questions in this section are of the regular multiple-choice type. Even though the answer sheet on the examination may have five answer boxes, labeled A, B, C, D, and E, remember that you are to choose the *one* correct answer from among A, B, C, and D. Do not make any marks whatever in Column E.

The following instructions apply both to the Content part of the CLEP examination and to the practice questions below:

Directions: For each of the following problems, indicate the correct answer in the appropriate space on the answer sheet.

Note: Figures that accompany problems in this part are intended to provide information useful in solving the problems. They are drawn as accurately as possible EXCEPT when it is stated in a specific problem that the figure is not drawn to scale. All figures lie in a plane unless otherwise indicated.

B1. Sets

The subtopics are: union and intersection; subsets; Venn diagrams; and Cartesian product.

We begin with two examples accompanied by answers and explanations.

ANSWERS

1. If $R = \{0,1\}$ and $S = \{2,3,4\}$, then $R \cup S$ equals
(A) $\{0\}$ (B) $\{2,3,4\}$ (C) $\{1,2,3,4\}$ (D) $\{0,1,2,3,4\}$

1. Ⓐ Ⓑ Ⓒ ● Ⓔ

($R \cup S$ denotes the *union* of sets R and S; it consists of *all* the elements in set R or in set S or in both.)

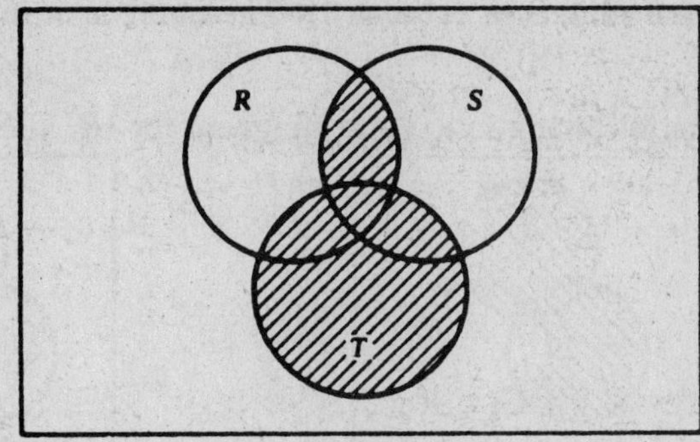

2. The Venn diagram above is for the set

2. Ⓐ ● Ⓒ Ⓓ Ⓔ

(A) $R \cap (S \cup T)$
(B) $(R \cap S) \cup T$
(C) $(R \cup S) \cap T$
(D) $R \cap S \cap T$

(The shaded area consists of elements that are either in both R and S, i.e., in $R \cap S$, or in T.)

PRACTICE QUESTIONS ON SETS

Follow the directions given above for this group of practice questions on sets. If you can eliminate one or more choices, then guess among the remaining ones. The correct answers and explanations will be found following the group of questions.

1. If $R = \{0,2,4\}$ and $S = \{0\}$, then $R \cap S =$
(A) $\{0,2,4\}$ (B) $\{2,4\}$ (C) $\{0\}$ (D) 0

2. If $R = \{a,b\}$, $S = \{b,c\}$, and $T = \{a,c\}$, then $R \cup (S \cap T)$ equals
(A) 0 (B) $\{a,b,c\}$ (C) $\{a,b\}$ (D) $\{c\}$

3. Which of the following is not a subset of $\{p,q,s,v,w\}$?
(A) $\{p,q,s,v,w\}$ (B) $\emptyset$ (C) $\{p\}$ (D) $\{p,q,t\}$

4. If $\overline{P}$ denotes the complement of set P, then the shaded region in the diagram is
(A) $\overline{R \cup S}$
(B) $\overline{R} \cup \overline{S}$
(C) $\overline{R} \cup S$
(D) $R \cap \overline{S}$

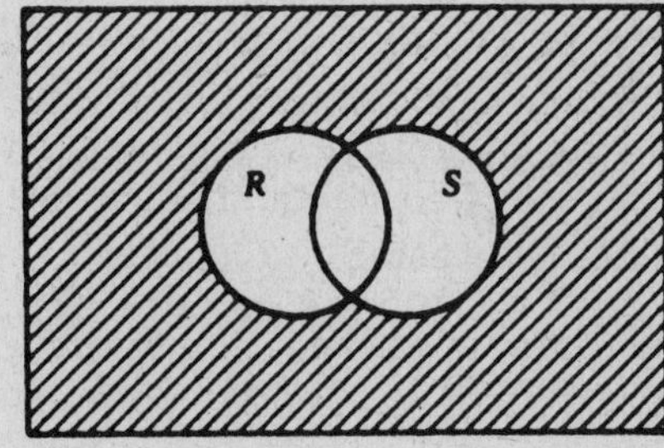

5. If $U = \{a,b,c\}$ and $V = \{d\}$, then $U \times V =$
(A) $\{a,b,c,d\}$ (B) 0
(C) $\{(a,d)(b,d)(c,d)\}$ (D) $\{(d,a)(d,b)(d,c)\}$

6. If $R = \{x : 1 < x < 5\}$, then the number of integers in R is
(A) 2 (B) 3 (C) 4 (D) 5

7. $R = \{x : x \geqslant 0\}$ and $S = \{x : x \leqslant 3\}$. The number of integers in $R \cup S$ is
(A) none (B) 2 (C) 4 (D) infinite

8. **Which of the following is a Venn diagram for $(R \cup S) \cap T$?**

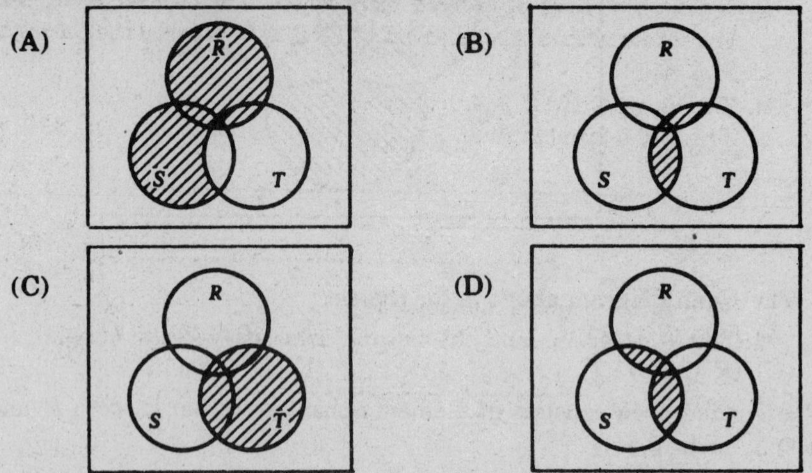

9. $V = \{a,b,c,d\}$ and $W = \{b,d,f\}$. **Which of the following statements is true?**
(A) $W \subset V$ (B) $\{b,f\}$ is a subset of $V \cap W$
(C) $\{a,c\}$ belongs to $V \times W$. (D) $\{a,c,f\}$ is a subset of $V \cup W$.

10. **If $R = \{x : x > 1\}$ and $S = \{x : x \leqq 2\}$, then which of the following is false?**
(A) $R \cap S$ contains two integers (B) $1 \notin R$
(C) $R \cap S = \{x : 1 < x \leqq 2\}$ (D) $1 \in S$

11. **If $R = \{a,b\}$ and $S = \{a,c\}$, then the number of ordered pairs in $R \times S$ is**
(A) 2 (B) 3 (C) 4 (D) 5

12. The number of subsets of $\{a,b,c\}$ is
(A) 8 (B) 6 (C) 5 (D) 3

13. $R \cap (S \cup T)$ equals
(A) $(R \cap S) \cup T$ (B) $(R \cap S) \cup (R \cap T)$
(C) $(R \cup S) \cap (R \cup T)$ (D) $(R \cup S) \cap T$

14. Which of the following is a false statement about the Venn diagram?

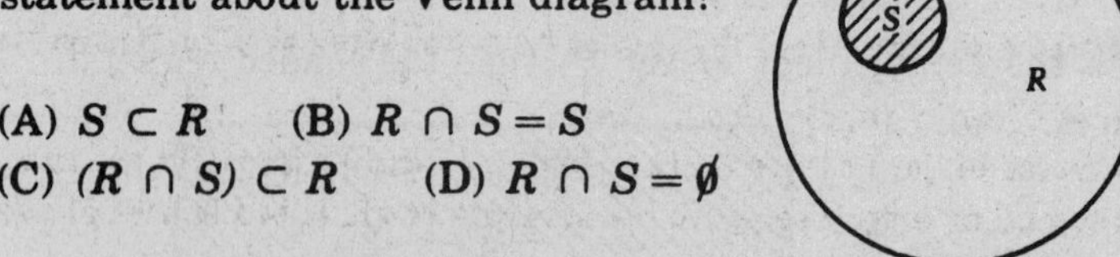

(A) $S \subset R$ (B) $R \cap S = S$
(C) $(R \cap S) \subset R$ (D) $R \cap S = \emptyset$

15. $S - T$ is the set of elements in S but not in T. If S is the set $\{a,b,c,d,e\}$ and $T = \{a,c,f,g\}$, then $S - T$ equals
(A) $\{b,d\}$ (B) $\{b,d,e,f,g\}$ (C) $\{b,d,e\}$ (D) $\{f,g\}$

ANSWERS AND EXPLANATIONS

to practice Section II questions on sets.

1. **C. $R \cap S$ is the *intersection* of sets R and S; it consists of the elements that are in both R and S.**
2. **B. $S \cap T = \{c\}$; $R \cup (S \cap T) = \{a.b.c\}$.**

3. D. Each element in a subset of a set must be an element of the set.

4. A. $\overline{T}$ denotes the complement of T; i.e., the elements not in T. $\overline{R \cup S}$ consists of elements in the universal set which are not in $R \cup S$.

5. C. $U \times V$ is the set of ordered pairs whose first element is an element of U and whose second is an element of V. $U \times V$ is called the *Cartesian product* of U and V.

6. B. The integers are 2, 3, 4.

7. D. Think of a number line:

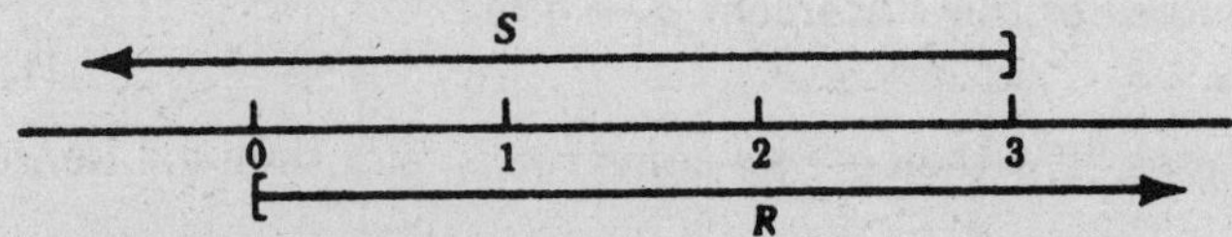

$R \cup S$ is the whole number line.

8. B. Often it helps to label the disjoint, exhaustive sets as shown:

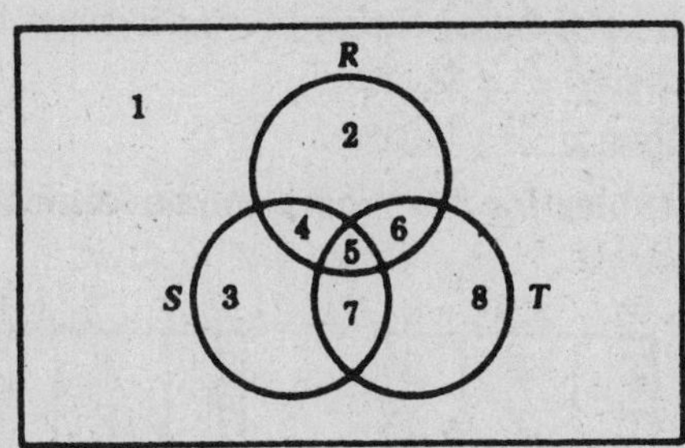

R consists of regions 2, 4, 5, 6
S consists of regions 3, 4, 5, 7
T consists of regions 5, 6, 7, 8
$(R \cup S) \cap T$ consists of (2, 3, 4, 5, 6, 7) $\cap$ (5, 6, 7, 8) = 5, 6, 7.

9. D. Note that $V \cap W = \{b,d\}$, that $\{a,c\} \notin V \times W$, that $V \cup W = \{a,b,c,d,f\}$.

10. A.

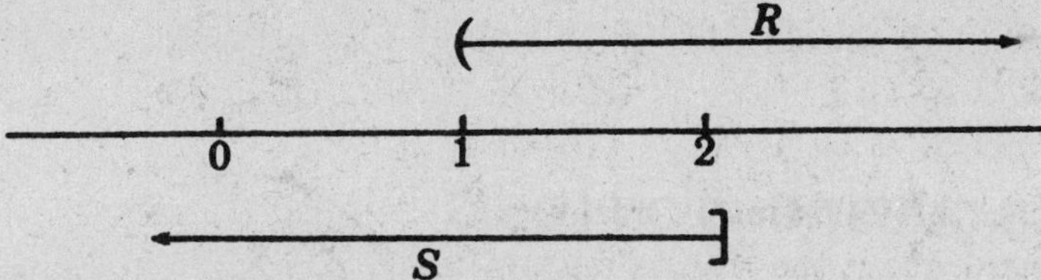

(Note that "$\in$" denotes "is an element of," "$\notin$" denotes "is not an element of," some specified set.)

11. C. $R \times S = \{(a,a), (a,c), (b,a), (b,c)\}$.

12. A. The subsets of $\{a,b,c\}$ are 0, $\{a\}$, $\{b\}$, $\{c\}$, $\{a,b\}$, $\{a,c\}$, $\{b,c\}$, and $\{a,b,c\}$. (0 is the null or empty set with no elements at all; it is a subset of every set.)

13. B. A Venn diagram helps.

The crosshatched region is $R \cap (S \cup T)$ or $(R \cap S) \cup (R \cap T)$. See also the explanation to question 8 above. Note that $R \cap (S \cup T)$ includes regions 4, 5, 6.

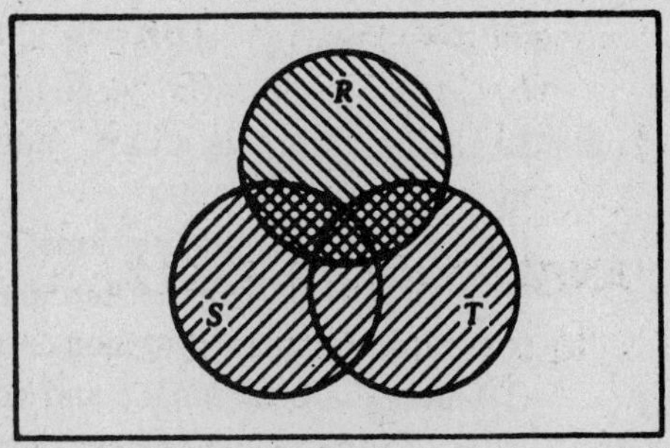

14. D. Note that $R \cap S = S$, and that $S \neq \emptyset$.

15. C. $S - T$ is the set S with all elements in T that are also in S removed from S.

B2. Logic

The subtopics are: truth tables; conjunctions and disjunctions; negations; conditional statements; necessary and sufficient conditions; converse, inverse, and contrapositive; implications, conclusions, and counterexample.

Here are two introductory examples, with answers and explanations.

ANSWERS

1. The converse of the statement $p \rightarrow q$ is — **1.** Ⓐ ● Ⓒ Ⓓ Ⓔ

(A) $p \rightarrow \sim q$ (B) $q \rightarrow p$ (C) $\sim q \rightarrow \sim p$ (D) $\sim p \rightarrow \sim q$

($p \rightarrow q$ denotes "if p then q"; its converse is "if q then p," i.e., $q \rightarrow p$.)

2. Which of the following is false? — **2.** Ⓐ Ⓑ ● Ⓓ Ⓔ

(A) If p is false, then $p \rightarrow q$ is true.
(B) If p and q are both false, then $p \longleftrightarrow q$ is true.
(C) If q is true, then $p \wedge q$ is true.
(D) If p is true, then $p \vee q$ is true.

(Here are the truth tables for the most common logical connectives:

p	$\wedge$	q
T	T	T
T	F	F
F	F	T
F	F	F

p	$\vee$	q
T	T	T
T	T	F
F	T	T
F	F	F

p	$\rightarrow$	q
T	T	T
T	F	F
F	T	T
F	T	F

p	$\leftrightarrow$	q
T	T	T
T	F	F
F	F	T
F	T	F

Use the tables to verify (A), (B), and (D). Note that for $p \wedge q$ to be true, *both* p and q must be true.)

PRACTICE QUESTIONS ON LOGIC

Follow the directions for multiple-choice questions. The correct answers and explanations follow the set of questions.

1. **If p denotes "He is a professor" and q denotes "He is absent-minded," then the statement "It is not true that he is an absent-minded professor"** can be written symbolically as
   (A) $p \wedge \sim q$ (B) $\sim(p \vee q)$. (C) $\sim p \wedge q$ (D) $\sim(p \wedge q)$

2. **Let p be "Mary is smart" and q be "Mary is conscientious." Then $p \rightarrow q$** may be translated as
   (A) If Mary is conscientious, then she is smart.
   (B) If Mary is smart, then she is conscientious.
   (C) Mary is smart but not conscientious.
   (D) Mary is both smart and conscientious.

3. $\sim(p \vee q)$ is equivalent to
   (A) $\sim p \vee \sim q$ (B) $\sim p \wedge q$ (C) $\sim p \wedge \sim q$ (D) $p \wedge \sim q$

4. Given the hypotheses:
   if cats laugh, then $3 < 5$,
   either dogs dance or gas will be rationed,
   select a valid conclusion.
   (A) Cats do not laugh.
   (B) If dogs do not dance, then gas will be rationed.
   (C) Dogs do not dance.
   (D) Gas will be rationed.

5. Which of the following is the truth table for $p \wedge \sim q$?

p	q	(A)	(B)	(C)	(D)
T	T	T	F	F	F
T	F	F	T	F	F
F	T	F	F	F	T
F	F	F	F	T	F

6. The statement $\sim p \vee q$ is false only when
   (A) p is true, q is false
   (B) p and q are both true
   (B) p is false, q is true
   (D) p and q are both false

7. $p \vee (q \wedge r)$ is equivalent to
   (A) $(p \vee q) \wedge r$
   (B) $(p \vee q) \wedge (p \vee r)$
   (C) $(p \wedge q) \vee (p \wedge r)$
   (D) $(p \vee q) \wedge (p \wedge r)$

8. Which of the following statements is not equivalent to "All oriental men are clever"?
   (A) If a man is oriental, then he's clever.
   (B) If a man is not clever, then he's not oriental.
   (C) If a man is clever, then he's an oriental.
   (D) A man is oriental only if he is clever.

9. The negation of the statement "If stock prices are rising, then food prices are high" is
   (A) If stocks are not rising, then food prices are not high.
   (B) If food prices are not high, then stocks are not rising.
   (C) If stocks are falling, then food prices are low.
   (D) Stocks are rising but prices are not high.

10. Let p be "A triangle is isosceles" and q be "A triangle is equilateral." Symbolically, the statement "In order for a triangle to be equilateral it must be isosceles" is
    (A) $p \leftrightarrow q$
    (B) $p \rightarrow q$
    (C) $q \leftrightarrow p$
    (D) $q \rightarrow p$

11. $q \rightarrow p$ may be translated as
    (A) q is sufficient for p
    (B) p only if q
    (C) p implies q
    (D) q is necessary for p

12. Which of the following is false?
    (A) $2 + 1 = 4$ if and only if $(-1)^2 = -1$.
    (B) $3 + 2 = 5$ if and only if $(-x)^2 = x^2$.
    (C) $\sqrt{9} = 3$ if and only if $\sqrt{9} = -3$.
    (D) $x^2 = 4$ if and only if $x = 2$ or $x = -2$.

13. If a statement is true so is its
(A) converse (B) contrapositive
(C) inverse (D) negation

14. Given the statement $p \rightarrow q$, its contrapositive is
(A) $\sim q \rightarrow \sim p$ (B) $q \rightarrow p$
(C) $\sim p \rightarrow \sim q$ (D) $p \rightarrow \sim q$

15. Consider the set of true implications: "If Carl enjoys a subject, then he studies it. If he studies a subject, then he does not fail it." Which of the following is a valid conclusion?
(A) Since Carl failed history he did not enjoy it.
(B) If Carl does not enjoy history, then he fails it.
(C) If Carl does not study a subject, then he does not pass it.
(D) Carl did not fail mathematics; therefore he enjoyed it.

16. The converse of the statement "If dentists have no cavities, then they use Screen toothpaste" is
(A) If dentists have cavities, then they do not use Screen.
(B) If dentists do not use Screen, then they have cavities.
(C) If dentists use Screen, then they have no cavities.
(D) Dentists must use Screen if they are to have no cavities.

17. The negation of the statement "Some students have part-time jobs" is
(A) All students have part-time jobs.
(B) Some students do not have part-time jobs.
(C) Only one student has a part-time job.
(D) No student has a part-time job.

18. To disprove the statement "$x^2>0$ for all real x," which of the following may be offered as a counterexample?
(A) $x=-2$ (B) $x=-1$
(C) $x=0$ (D) $x=1$

19. A statement equivalent to "Some teenagers are poor drivers" is
(A) At least one teenager is a poor driver.
(B) Not all teenagers are poor drivers.
(C) At least one teenager is not a poor driver.
(D) Good drivers are not teenagers.

20. Given the true implications $p \rightarrow q$ and $q \rightarrow r$, which of the following is true?
(A) $r \rightarrow p$ (B) $\sim q \rightarrow \sim r$
(C) $\sim r \rightarrow \sim p$ (D) $\sim p \rightarrow \sim r$

ANSWERS AND EXPLANATIONS

to practice Section II questions on logic.

1. D. $p \wedge q$ denotes "He is an absent-minded professor."
2. B. A translation of $p \rightarrow q$ is "if p then q."
3. C. By one of DeMorgan's laws, $\sim(p \vee q) \equiv \sim p \wedge \sim q$.
4. B. Note that $p \vee q$ is equivalent to $\sim p \rightarrow q$. (Verify with truth tables.)

5. B. The truth table is:

p	q	$\sim q$	$p \wedge \sim q$
T	T	F	F
T	F	T	T
F	T	F	F
F	F	T	F

6. A. Look at the truth table:

p	$\sim p$	$\vee$	q
T	F	T	T
T	F	F	F
F	T	T	T
F	T	T	F

7. B. One of the distributive laws applies here.
8. C. If x is an element of the set of men,
p_x denotes "He is oriental,"
q_x denotes "He is clever,"
then the original statement is $\forall_x(p_x \rightarrow q_x)$. (C) is $\forall_x(q_x \rightarrow p_x)$, which is the (nonequivalent) converse.
9. D. If p denotes "Stock prices are rising" and q denotes "Food prices are high," then we want $\sim(p \rightarrow q)$. This is equivalent to $\sim(\sim p \vee q)$ or $p \wedge \sim q$.
10. D. A restatement is "If a triangle is equilateral, then it is isosceles."
11. A. $q \rightarrow p$ may be translated "If q then p," "p only if q," "q is sufficient for p," "p is necessary for q," or "q implies p."
12. C. The biconditional or equivalence $p \leftrightarrow q$ is true if p and q are both true or both false; $p \leftrightarrow q$ is false if p and q have opposite truth values. $\sqrt{a^2} = |a|$ by definition; i.e., $\sqrt{a^2} \geqq 0$ always.
13. B. A statement and its contrapositive are equivalent.
14. A. The contrapositive of "if r then s" is "if not s then not r."
15. A. Let p be "Carl enjoys a subject,"
q be "Carl studies a subject,"
and r be "Carl fails a subject."
Then it is true that $p \rightarrow q$ and $q \rightarrow \sim r$. (A) can be written symbolically: $r \rightarrow \sim p$. Since $q \rightarrow \sim r$ is equivalent to $r \rightarrow \sim q$ and $p \rightarrow q$ is equivalent to $\sim q \rightarrow \sim p$, it follows that $r \rightarrow \sim p$ (syllogism). None of the others is a valid conclusion.
16. C. The converse of "if r then s" is "if s then r."
17. D. If x denotes "students" and p_x "a student has a part-time job" then we have, symbolically, $\exists_x p_x$. $\sim(\exists_x p_x)$ is equivalent to $\forall_x \sim p_x$, i.e., "no student has a part-time job."
18. C. If $x \neq 0$, then $x^2 > 0$. But if $x = 0$ then $x^2 = 0$.
19. A. "Some" means "at least one."
20. C. $p \rightarrow q$ is equivalent to $\sim q \rightarrow \sim p$. $q \rightarrow r$ is equivalent to $\sim r \rightarrow \sim q$. So $p \rightarrow q \wedge q \rightarrow r$ is equivalent to $\sim r \rightarrow \sim p$ (syllogism).

B3. Real Number System

The subtopics are: prime and composite numbers; odd and even numbers; factors and divisibility; rational and irrational numbers; absolute value and order.

Here are introductory examples, with answers and explanations.

ANSWERS

1. If a and b are real numbers, then $(a)[b + (-b)] = (ab) + (a)(-b)$ because
(A) addition is commutative
(B) multiplication is commutative
(C) the real numbers are closed under multiplication
(D) multiplication is distributive over addition
(This is referred to briefly as the *distributive property*.)

1. Ⓐ Ⓑ Ⓒ ● Ⓔ

2. If $a > b > 0$, then
(A) $\frac{1}{a} > \frac{1}{b}$ (B) $\frac{1}{a} < \frac{1}{b}$
(C) $\frac{1}{a} = \frac{1}{b}$ (D) $-a > -b$
(Since $a - b > 0$ and $ab > 0$, it follows that

$$\frac{a-b}{ab} > 0 \quad \text{or} \quad \frac{1}{b} - \frac{1}{a} > 0.$$

So $\frac{1}{b} > \frac{1}{a}$.)

2. Ⓐ ● Ⓒ Ⓓ Ⓔ

PRACTICE QUESTIONS ON THE REAL NUMBER SYSTEM

Follow the directions for multiple-choice questions. If you can eliminate one or more choices, then guess among the remaining ones. The correct answers and explanations follow the set of questions.

1. Which of the following is *not* a prime number?
(A) 2 (B) 17 (C) 27 (D) 37

2. Which of the following statements is false?
(A) If $ab > 0$, then a and b are both positive.
(B) $a < 0 \rightarrow -a > 0$.
(C) If $a > b$, then $-a < -b$.
(D) If $0 < a < 1$, then $a^2 < a$.

3. Which of the following provides a counterexample to the false statement "If $a > b$, then $a^2 > b^2$"?
(A) $a = 2, b = 1$ (B) $a = 1, b = 0$
(C) $a = -2, b = -1$ (D) $a = 1, b = -1$

4. If $ac < bc$, which of the following is impossible?
(A) $a > b$ (B) $a < b$
(C) $c = 0$ (D) $c < 0$

5. Suppose $a < 0 < b$. Which of the following must hold?
(A) $|a| < |b|$ (B) $|b| < |a|$
(C) $|b - a| = b + a$ (D) $|b - a| = b - a$

6. Which of the following statements about the real number system is false?
(A) The real numbers are closed under addition and multiplication.
(B) Subtraction of reals is commutative.
(C) Every number except 0 has a multiplicative inverse.
(D) The square of every nonzero number is positive.

7. If none of the denominators below is zero, which of the following is true?

(A) $\frac{2p+4q}{p+2q}=2$ (B) $\frac{2m+p}{2q}=\frac{m+p}{q}$

(C) $\frac{q}{q+p}=\frac{1}{p}$ (D) $\frac{3m}{3q+p}=\frac{m}{q+p}$

8. If $|a - 2| = a - 2$, then it is false that
(A) $a > 0$ (B) $a = 2$ (C) $a > 2$ (D) $a < 2$

9. Which of the following numbers is rational?
(A) $\sqrt{2}$ (B) $\sqrt{3}$ (C) $\sqrt{4}$ (D) $\sqrt{5}$

10. The prime factorization of 300 is
(A) $3^2 \cdot 10^2$ (B) $2 \cdot 3^2 \cdot 5^2$ (C) $2 \cdot 3 \cdot 5^2$ (D) $2^2 \cdot 3 \cdot 5^2$

11. Which of the following is meaningless?
(A) $0 \cdot 1$ (B) $0/1$ (C) 1^0 (D) $1/0$

12. Which statement is false?
(A) There is a rational number between every pair of rationals.
(B) There is an irrational between every pair of rationals.
(C) There is a rational number between every pair of irrationals.
(D) The sum of two irrational numbers is always irrational.

13. The repeating decimal 0.444 . . . equals
(A) $4/10$ (B) $3/7$ (C) $4/9$ (D) $5/11$

14. If $R = \{x : x$ is an integer$\}$ and $S = \{x : x$ is a positive real number$\}$, then $R \cap S$ equals
(A) $\{x : x$ is a positive integer$\}$ (B) the empty set (C) R (D) S

15. If $a - b = b - a$, then
(A) $a = b$
(B) $|a - b| = |a + b|$
(C) a and b have opposite signs
(D) a and b must both equal 0

16. If a and b are positive integers with a odd and b even, then which of the following is odd?
(A) $2a + b$ (B) $a^2 + 3b$ (C) $ab + 2a$ (D) b^a

17. The repeating part of the decimal expansion for a rational number whose denominator is 7 has at most
(A) 4 digits (B) 5 digits (C) 6 digits (D) 7 digits

This number line with points q and t as shown is for questions 18 and 19.

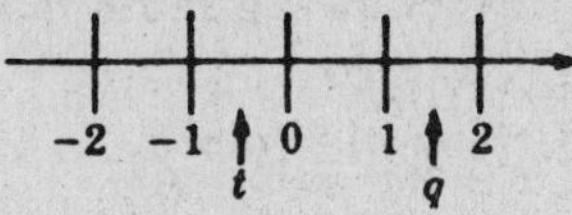

18. Which statement is false?
(A) $q + t > 0$ (B) $q - t > 0$ (C) $q^2 > 1$ (D) $t > -t$

19. Which number is largest?
(A) $q + t$ (B) $q - t$ (C) $t - q$ (D) qt

20. Which set is not empty?
(A) $\{x : x + 2 = 2\}$
(B) $\{x : |x| = -1\}$
(C) $\{x : x$ is real and $x^2 + 1 = 0\}$
(D) $\{x : x \neq x\}$

21. The set of different factors of 135 is
(A) $\{3, 5\}$ (B) $\{3, 7\}$ (C) $\{5, 7\}$ (D) $\{7, 9\}$

22. If $m + n$ is divisible by 6 and m is even, then it is necessarily true that
(A) n is divisible by 3
(B) m is divisible by 3
(C) n is even
(D) m and n are both divisible by 6

23. If p denotes "$x \leq 1$" and q denotes "$x > -2$," then the set that satisfies $p \wedge q$ is
(A) $-2 < x \leq 1$
(B) $1 \leq x$ or $x > -2$
(C) $x < -2$ and $x \geq 1$
(D) $-2 \leq x < 1$

24. To disprove the statement "If x is irrational, then x^2 is rational," choose x to be
(A) $\sqrt{2}$ (B) $3\sqrt{2}$ (C) π (D) $\frac{1}{\sqrt{2}}$

25. If p is divisible by 2 and q is divisible by 5 which of the following must be divisible by 10?
(A) $pq + 15$ (B) $5p + 2q$ (C) $5(p + q)$ (D) $p + q + 10$

ANSWERS AND EXPLANATIONS

to practice Section II questions on the real number system.

1. C. A prime number has only itself and 1 as factors.
2. A. If a and b are both negative, then ab is positive. Verify the truth of (B), (C), and (D).
3. D. $1 > -1$, but $(1)^2 \not> (-1)^2$. (C) is not a counterexample because $-2 \not> -1$.
4. C. Verify that (A), (B), and (D) are possible.
5. D. If $a < 0 < b$, then $b - a$ is a positive number; by definition of absolute value, $|x| = x$ if $x > 0$.
6. B. A counterexample to statement (B): $5 - 3 \neq 3 - 5$.
7. A. $\frac{2p + 4q}{p + 2q} = \frac{2(p + 2q)}{p + 2q} = 2$ if $(p + 2q) \neq 0$.
8. D. $|a - 2| = a - 2$ if $a - 2 \geq 0$, i.e., if $a > 2$ or $a = 2$. If $a \geq 2$, certainly $a > 0$.
9. C. $\sqrt{4} = 2$.
10. D. No other product given even equals 300!
11. D. Division by 0 is impossible.

12. D. $\sqrt{2} + (3 - \sqrt{2}) = 3$ is a counterexample to statement (D). (A), (B), and (C) are true.

13. C. Let $r = 0.444\ldots$ (where the three dots indicate an infinite number of 4's). Then

$$10r = 4.44\ldots$$
$$9r = 4$$

and $r = 4/9$.

14. A. The intersection of two sets contains those elements that are in both sets.

15. A. $a - b = b - a$ yields $2a = 2b$ or $a = b$.

16. B. Convince yourself that the other choices are all even integers.

17. C. When dividing by 7, only one of the remainders 1, 2, 3, 4, 5, or 6 can be obtained. If a particular remainder recurs, the decimal must repeat.

18. D. In (D), note that $t < 0$, so that $-t > 0$.

19. B. The numbers in (C) and (D) are negative. Since $t < 0$, $q - t > q$, whereas $q + t < q$.

20. A. $\{x : x + 2 = 2\} = \{0\}$. None of the other sets contain any elements.

21. A. Note that $135 = 3 \cdot 45 = 3 \cdot 3 \cdot 15 = 3 \cdot 3 \cdot 3 \cdot 5$ or $3^3 \cdot 5$.

22. C. Find examples to show that (A), (B), and (D) may be false.

23. A. $(x \leq 1) \wedge (x > -2)$ is true when both inequalities are satisfied. Thus, x must both exceed -2 and be less than or equal to 1.

24. C. π is irrational, but so is π^2.

25. B. Find p and q that satisfy the given conditions but for which the expressions in (A), (C), and (D) are not divisible by 10.

B4. Functions and Their Graphs

The subtopics are: domain and range; linear, polynomial, composite, and inverse functions.

Here are introductory examples, with answers and explanations.

ANSWERS

1. If $f(x) = x^3 - x - 1$, then $f(-1) =$ **1.** Ⓐ ● Ⓒ Ⓓ Ⓔ

(A) -3 (B) -1 (C) 0 (D) 1

($f(-1) = (-1)^3 - (-1) - 1 = -1 + 1 - 1 = -1$.)

2. If $R = \{1,2,3\}$, which of the following is a function from R into R? **2.** Ⓐ Ⓑ ● Ⓓ Ⓔ

(A) $\{(1,3), (2,1)\}$ (B) $\{(3,1), (2,3), (1,5)\}$
(C) $\{(1,2), (2,2), (3,2)\}$ (D) $\{(1,2), (2,3), (3,1), (3,3)\}$

(A function from R into R may be defined as a set of ordered pairs in which each element of R must be a first element of exactly one pair, and the second element of that pair, its image, must belong to R. (A) is not a function because although $3 \in R$, it has no image; in (B), the image of 1 is 5, which is not in R; and in (D) the element 3 has *two* images.)

3. **Which of the following is the graph of a function $y = f(x)$?** **3.** ● Ⓑ Ⓒ Ⓓ Ⓔ

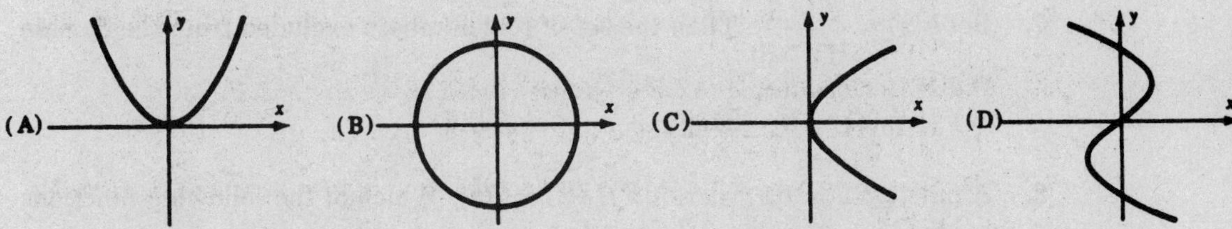

(If $y = f(x)$ is a function, then for each x in the domain there is a *unique* y. A vertical line can cut the graph of a function only once.)

PRACTICE QUESTIONS ON FUNCTIONS AND THEIR GRAPHS

Follow the directions for multiple-choice questions. If you can eliminate one or more choices, then guess among the remaining ones. The correct answers and explanations follow the set of questions.

1. If $g(x) = x^2 - 2x + 1$, then $g(-x) =$
   (A) $x^2 - 2x + 1$ (B) $-x^2 + 2x + 1$
   (C) $x^2 + 2x + 1$ (D) $x^2 + 2x - 1$

2. **Which of the following is the graph of $x + 2y = 2$?**

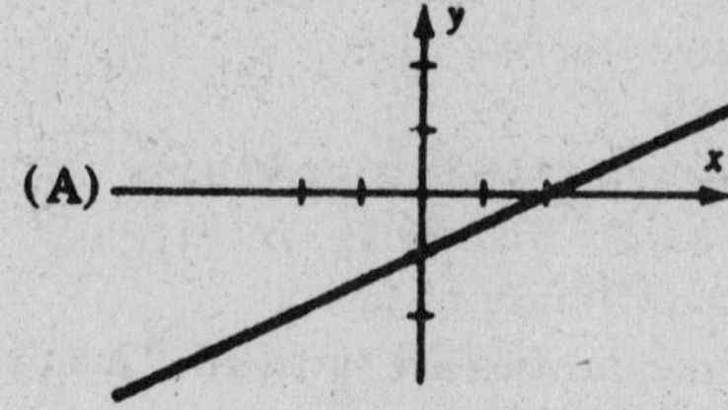

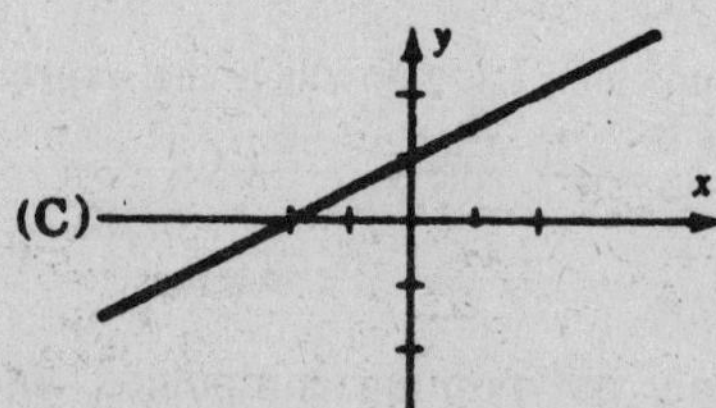

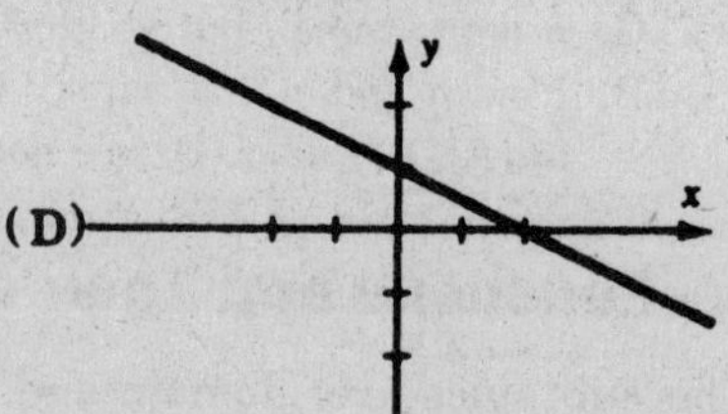

3. If $f(x) = x^2 - x + 3$, then $f(2) =$
   (A) 0 (B) 3 (C) 5 (D) 9

4. If $f(x) = \dfrac{x + 1}{(x - 1)^3}$, then $f(0)$ equals
   (A) -1 (B) 0 (C) 1 (D) none of these

5. If $f(x) = x^2 + 1$, then the domain of f is
   (A) $\{x : x > 0\{$ (B) $\{x : -\infty < x < \infty\}$
   (C) $\{x : x \geq 0\}$ (D) $\{x : x \geq 1\}$

6. The range of the function of question 5 is
   (A) all real numbers
   (B) all positive numbers
   (C) all numbers greater than one
   (D) all numbers y such that $y \geq 1$

7. Let $g(x) = \dfrac{x + 1}{x^2 - x}$. Then the set of real numbers excluded from the domain of g is
   (A) $\{-1,0,1\}$ (B) $\{0,1\}$ (C) $\{1\}$ (D) $\{-1,1\}$

8. A function $y = f(x)$ is *even* if $f(-x) = f(x)$. Which of the following functions is even?
   (A) $f(x) = 2x + 4$ (B) $f(x) = x^2 + 2x$
   (C) $f(x) = 3x^2 + 5$ (D) $f(x) = 4x$

9. **The graph to the right is for the function**

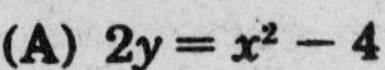

(A) $2y = x^2 - 4$

(B) $y = x^2 - 2$

(C) $2y = x^2$

(D) $y = x^2 - 4$

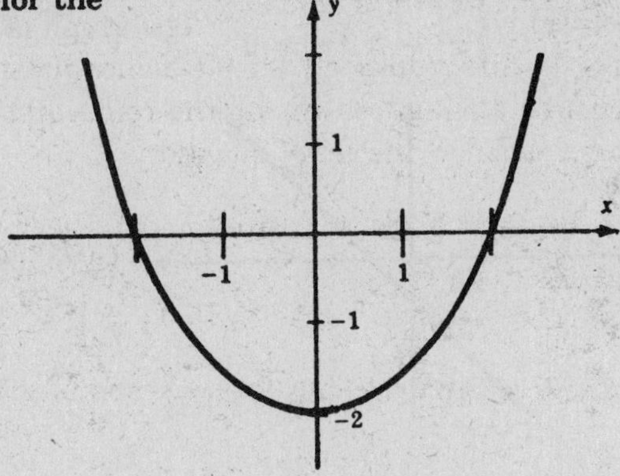

10. **Which of the following points lies on the line $2x - 3y = 6$?**
(A) (3,2) **(B)** (0,2) **(C)** (−3,0) **(D)** (−3,−4)

11. $f(x) = x(x - 2)$ and $g(x) = x + 1$. Then $f(g(0)) =$
(A) 1 (B) 0 (C) −1 (D) −2

12. With f and g defined as in question 5, $g(f(0)) =$
(A) 1 (B) 0 (C) −1 (D) −2

13. If $f(x) = x^2 - 2x + c$ and $f(0) = 1$, then $c =$
(A) −1 (B) 0 (C) 1 (D) 2

14. **The graph of $y = x^2 - 3$ is obtained from that of $y = x^2$ by translating the latter**
(A) to the right 3 units (B) to the left 3 units
(C) up three units (D) down 3 units

15. **Which of the following is a polynomial function?**
(A) $y = 2^x$ (B) $y = \frac{1}{x}$ (C) $y = \log_2 x$ (D) $y = \frac{1}{3}x^2$

16. **Which of the following diagrams does *not* define a function from $\{a,b,c\}$ into $\{d,e,f\}$?**

(A) 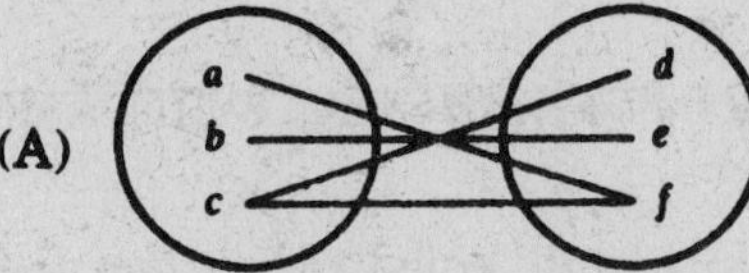

(B) 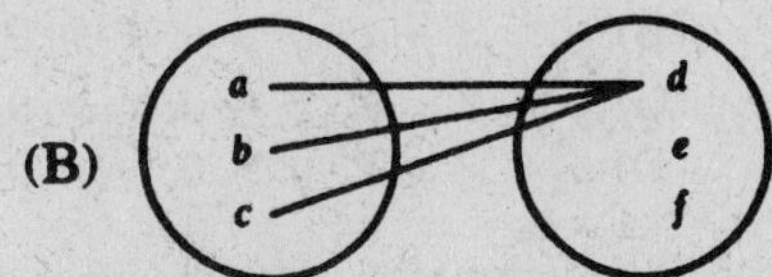

(C) 

(D) 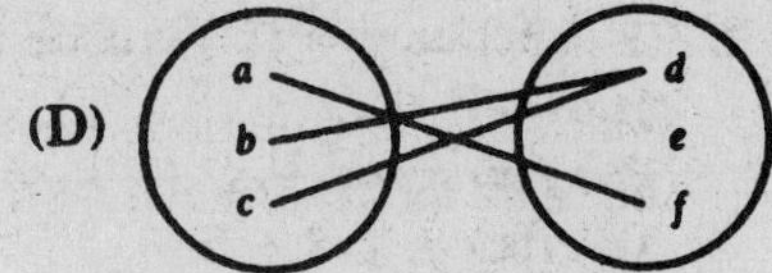

17. Let $f(x) = \begin{cases} x - 1 \text{ if } x < 2 \\ x^2 - 3 \text{ if } x \geq 2 \end{cases}$. The graph of f is

(A) 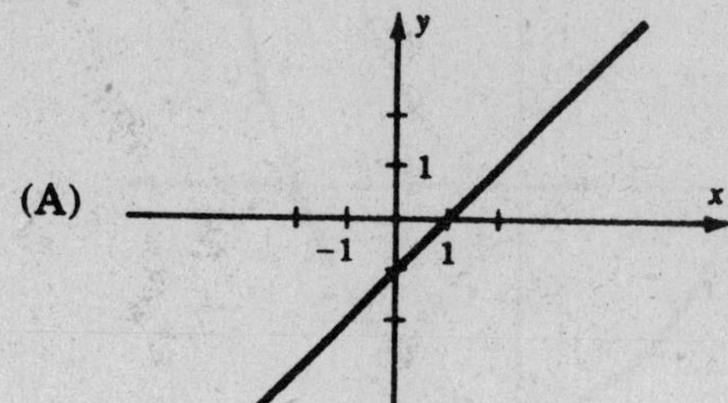

(B) 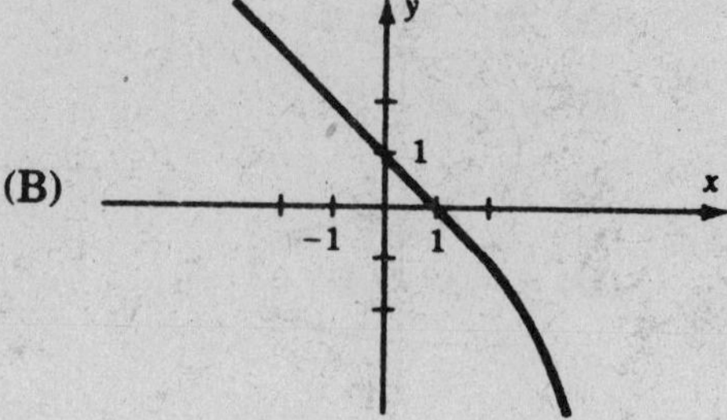

(C) 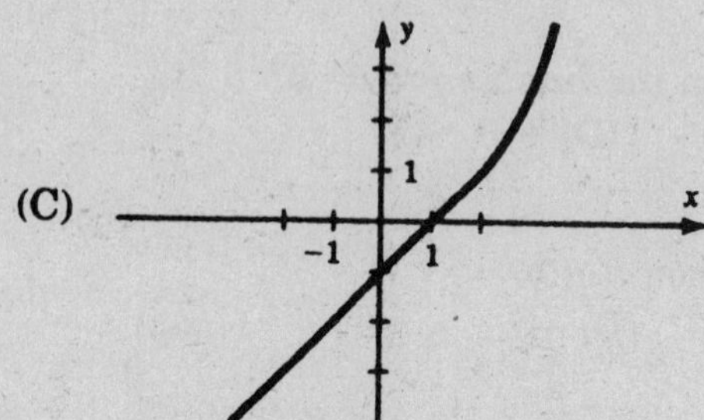

(D) 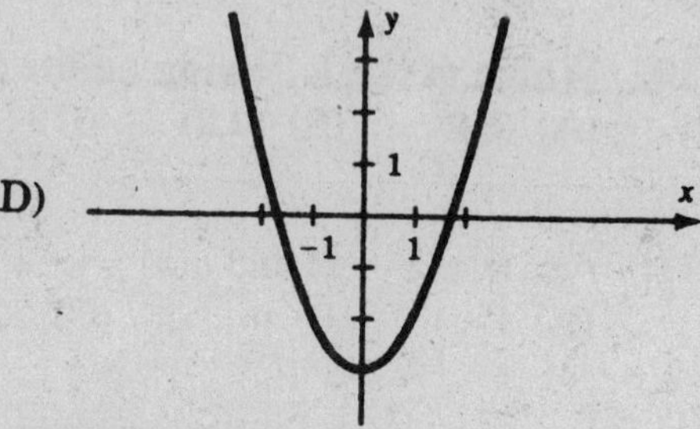

18. If $f(x) = 3x + 2$ and $g(x) = x^2 - 3$, then $f(g(x))$ equals

(A) $9x^2 + 12x + 1$ (B) $3x^2 - 7$
(C) $3x^2 - 1$ (D) $9x^2 + 6x + 1$

19. If $g(x) = 3x + k$ and $g(1) = -2$, then $g(2) =$

(A) -1 (B) 1 (C) 7 (D) 11

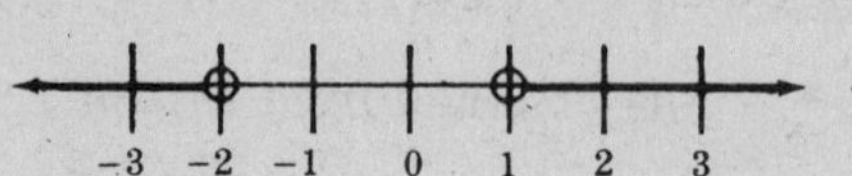

20. The graph above is for the set

(A) $\{x : -2 < x < 1\}$ (B) $\{x : x < -2, x = 1\}$
(C) $\{x : x > 1, x \neq -2\}$ (D) $\{x : x < -2 \text{ or } x > 1\}$

21. The graphs of inverse functions are symmetric

(A) to the x-axis (B) to the y-axis
(C) to the line $y = x$ (D) to the origin

22. The points in the interior, but not on the boundary, of the triangle in the figure satisfy

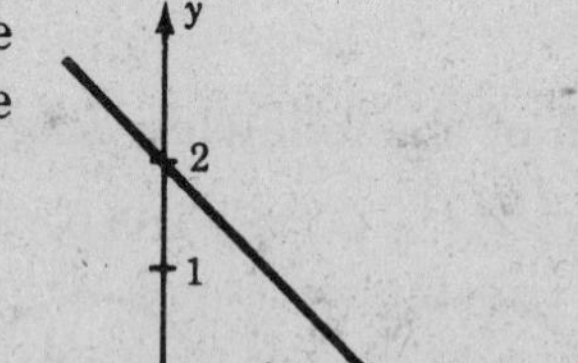

(A) $y < 2 - x, y > 0, x > 0$
(B) $y > 2 - x, y > 0, x > 0$
(C) $y \leq 2 - x, y \geq 0, x \geq 0$
(D) $y < x - 2, y > 0, x > 0$

23. If $[x]$ denotes the greatest integer less than or equal to x, then $[-1.2]$ equals

(A) -2 (B) -1 (C) 0 (D) 1

24. Which of the equations below defines exactly one function $y = f(x)$ from the reals into the reals?

(A) $y^2 = x^2 + 1$ (B) $x^3 - y = 4$
(C) $x - 4y^2 = 2$ (D) $4x^2 + 9y^2 = 36$

25. Which of the following is the graph of a function $y = f(x)$?

(A)

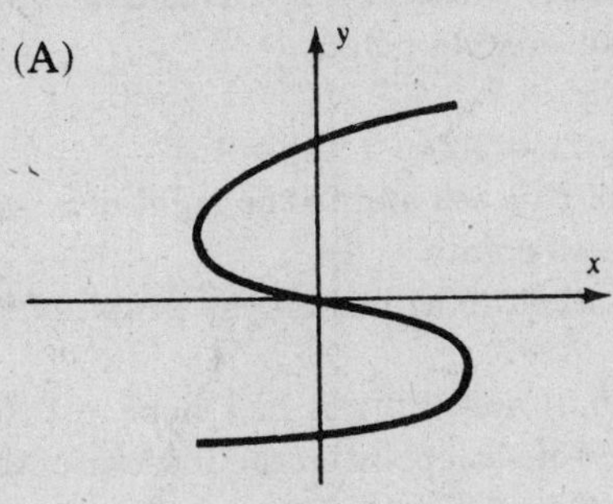

(B)

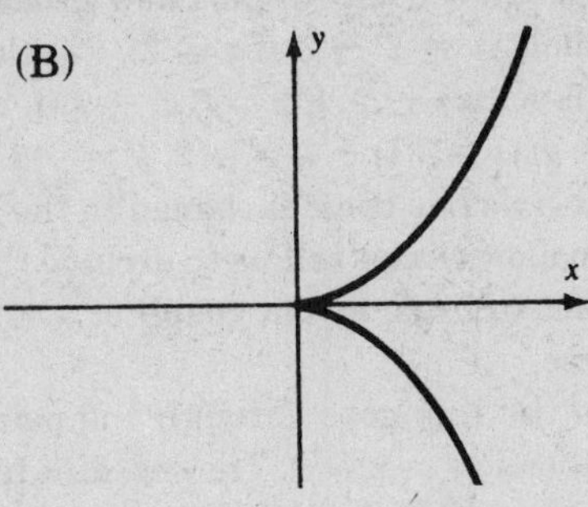

(C)

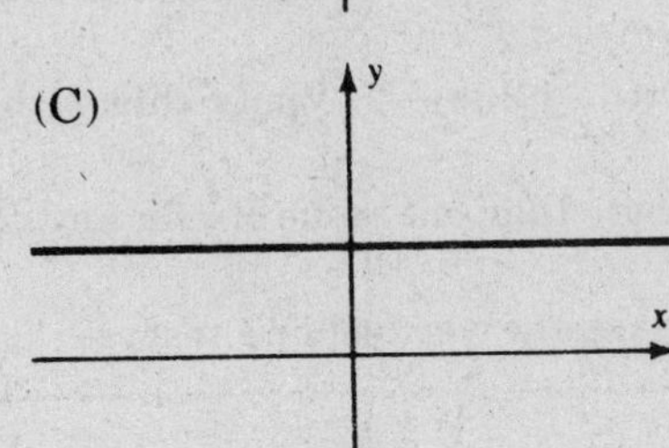

(D)

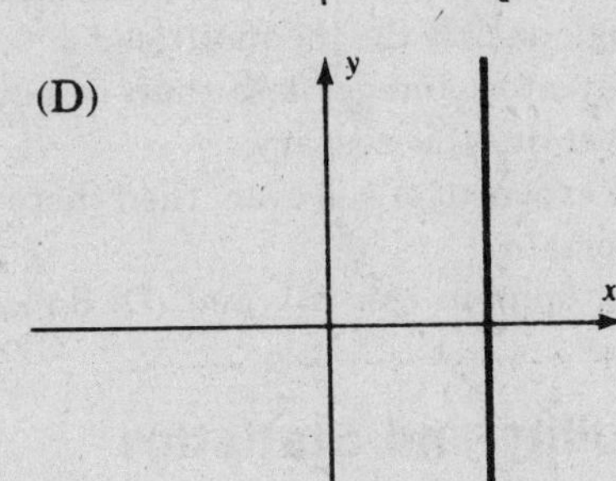

ANSWERS AND EXPLANATIONS

to practice Section II questions on functions and their graphs.

1. **C.** $g(-x) = (-x)^2 - 2(-x) + 1 = x^2 + 2x + 1$.
2. **D. Checking the intercepts of the line is fastest. Here, they are $x = 2$ and $y = 1$. Only (D) qualifies.**
3. **C.** $f(2) = 2^2 - 2 + 3 = 4 - 2 + 3 = 5$.
4. A. $f(0) = \dfrac{0 + 1}{(0 - 1)^3} = \dfrac{1}{-1} = -1$.
5. **B.** } **A sketch of the graph may help**
6. **D.** } **for these two questions.**

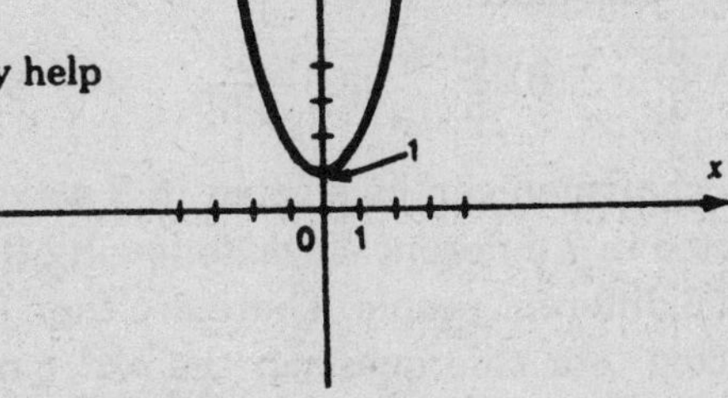

7. **B. Set the denominator of g equal to zero. $x^2 - x = x(x - 1) = 0$ when $x = 0$ or $x = 1$.**
8. **C. Note that (A), (B), and (D) are not even.**
9. **A. Check intercepts first. From the graph we see that $x = \pm 2$ and $y = -2$. Only $2y = x^2 - 4$ has these intercepts.**
10. **D. Substitute 3 for x and 2 for y. The left-hand side must equal 6.**
11. **C.** $g(0) = 0 + 1 = 1$, **and** $f(g(0)) = f(1) = 1(1 - 2) = 1 \cdot -1 = -1$.
12. **A.** $f(0) = 0(0 - 2) = 0 \cdot -2 = 0$, **and** $g(f(0)) = g(0) = 0 + 1 = 1$.
13. **C.** $f(0) = 0^2 - 2(0) + c = 1 \rightarrow c = 1$.
14. **D. For a given x, each y-value of $y = x^2 - 3$ is 3 *less* than that of $y = x^2$.**
15. **D. A polynomial in x is an expression of the form**

$$a_0x^n + a_1x^{n-1} + a_2x^{n-2} + \ldots + a_{n-1}x + a_n$$

where the a's are real numbers and n is a positive integer. The variable never appears in the denominator and the exponents of the variable are always positive integers.

16. A. Note in (A) that the element c has two images, d and f.
17. C. The graph consists of part of a straight line ($y = x - 1$ if $x < 2$) and part of a parabola ($y = x^2 - 3$ if $x \geqq 2$). Checking intercepts helps.
18. B. $f(g(x)) = 3(x^2 + 3) + 2 = 3x^2 - 9 + 2 = 3x^2 - 7$.
19. B. Since $g(1) = 3(1) + k = -2$, $k = -5$. So $g(2) = 3(2) + (-5) = 1$.
20. D. The x-axis has been darkened to the left of $x = -2$ and to the right of $x = 1$. The hollow circles tell us to exclude these two points.
21. C. If point (a,b) is on the graph of $y = f(x)$, then (b,a) lies on the graph of its inverse.
22. A. Since the line goes through the points (0,2) and (2,0), it has slope -1. Its equation is $y = 2 - x$. The coordinates (x,y) of each point in the interior of the triangle satisfy the inequalities $x > 0$, $y > 0$, $y < 2 - x$.
23. A. The greatest integer less than or equal to -1.2 is -2. Verify this with a number line if necessary.
24. B. If the exponent of y is even, then there is more than one value of y for any x in the domain.
25. C. The graphs in (A), (B), and (D) do *not* pass the vertical-line test.

B5. Probability and Statistics

The subtopics are: counting problems, including permutations and combinations; computation of probabilities of simple and compound events; simple conditional probability; the mean and median.

In any question on probability in this book, you may assume that a die or coin is fair; that is, that the outcomes (a particular face showing on the die, or head versus tail on the coin) are equally probable.

Here are introductory examples, with answers and explanations.

ANSWERS

1. How many ways can an 8-member council elect a chairman, a vicechairman, and a secretary if no member may hold more than one office? — 1. Ⓐ ● Ⓒ Ⓓ Ⓔ

(A) $\frac{8!}{3!}$ (B) $\frac{8!}{5!}$ (C) $\frac{8!}{3!5!}$ (D) 8^3

(The chairman can be elected in 8 ways, after which the vice-chairman can be elected in 7 different ways; following this, the secretary can be chosen from among 6 different people. There are then 8 · 7 · 6 different ways the officers can be elected. For this question the *order* matters. An ordered arrangement of n objects taken r at a time is called a *permutation*, and is denoted by ${}_nP_r$ or by $P(n,r)$, $P_{n,r}$, or P^n_r. Note that

$${}_nP_r = \frac{n!}{(n-r)!}$$

If common factors are eliminated from numerator and denominator, a product of exactly r factors remains. Thus

$$\frac{8!}{5!} = \frac{8 \cdot 7 \cdot 6 \cdot 5 \cdot 4 \cdot 3 \cdot 2 \cdot 1}{5 \cdot 4 \cdot 3 \cdot 2 \cdot 1} = 8 \cdot 7 \cdot 6.)$$

2. How many different 3-member committees can be selected from a group of 5 people? — 2. Ⓐ Ⓑ ● Ⓓ Ⓔ

(A) 60 (B) 20 (C) 10 (D) 5

(This question calls for a *combination* of 5 objects taken 3 at a time; i.e., a selection where order does *not* count. A combination of n objects taken r at a time is just the number of different r-element subsets that an n-element set

has. We'll use the notation ${}_nC_r$; others used are $C(n,r)$, $C_{n,r}$, and $\binom{n}{r}$. Since there are $r!$ permutations of each r-element set, we find ${}_nC_r$ by dividing ${}_nP_r$ by $r!$. Here the answer is ${}_5C_3$ or

$$\frac{5!}{2!3!} = \frac{5 \cdot 4 \cdot 3 \cdot 2 \cdot 1}{2 \cdot 1 \cdot 3 \cdot 2 \cdot 1} = 10.$$

For computation, it's easiest to remember ${}_5C_3$ as

$$\frac{5 \cdot 4 \cdot 3}{1 \cdot 2 \cdot 3},$$

where you have the same number of factors in the numerator as in the denominator. Also, ${}_nC_r = {}_nC_{n-r}$. So, for example, to compute ${}_9C_7$ we use instead ${}_9C_2$. Recalling that ${}_9P_2 = 9 \cdot 8$, we have

$${}_9C_2 = \frac{9 \cdot 8}{1 \cdot 2}.)$$

Use the following mortality table to answer questions 3 and 4.

TABLE OF MORTALITY

Commissioners 1958 Standard Ordinary

Age	Number Living	Deaths Each Year	Deaths Per 1,000
0	10,000,000	70,800	7.08
1	9,929,200	17,475	1.76
2	9,911,725	15,066	1.52
3	9,896,659	14,449	1.46
4	9,882,210	13,835	1.40
5	9,368,375	13,322	1.35
6	9,255,053	12,812	1.30
7	9,842,241	12,401	1.26
8	9,829,840	12,091	1.23
9	9,817,749	11,379	1.21
10	9,805,870	11,865	1.21
11	9,794,005	12,047	1.23
12	9,781,958	12,325	1.26
13	9,769,633	12,896	1.32
14	9,756,737	13,562	1.39
15	9,743,175	14,225	1.46
16	9,728,950	14,983	1.54
17	9,713,967	15,737	1.62
18	9,698,230	16,390	1.69
19	9,681,840	16,846	1.74
20	9,664,994	17,300	1.79
21	9,647,694	17,655	1.83
22	9,630,039	17,912	1.86
23	9,612,127	18,167	1.89
24	9,593,960	18,324	1.91
25	9,575,636	18,481	1.93
26	9,557,155	18,732	1.96
27	9,538,423	18,981	1.99
28	9,519,442	19,324	2.03
29	9,500,118	19,760	2.08
30	9,480,358	20,193	2.13
31	9,460,165	20,718	2.19
32	9,439,447	21,239	2.25
33	9,418,288	21,850	2.32
34	9,396,358	22,551	2.40
35	9,373,807	23,528	2.51
36	9,350,279	24,685	2.64
37	9,325,594	26,112	2.80
38	9,299,482	27,991	3.01
39	9,271,491	30,132	3.25
40	9,241,359	32,622	3.53
41	9,208,737	35,362	3.84
42	9,173,375	38,253	4.17
43	9,135,122	41,382	4.53
44	9,093,740	44,741	4.92
45	9,048,999	48,412	5.35
46	9,000,587	52,473	5.83
47	8,948,114	56,910	6.36
48	8,891,204	61,794	6.95
49	8,829,410	67,104	7.60
50	8,762,306	72,902	8.32
51	8,689,404	79,160	9.11
52	8,610,244	85,758	9.96
53	8,524,486	92,832	10.89
54	8,431,654	100,337	11.90
55	8,331,317	108,307	13.00
56	8,223,010	116,849	14.21
57	8,106,161	125,970	15.54
58	7,980,191	135,663	17.00
59	7,844,528	145,830	18.59
60	7,698,698	156,592	20.34
61	7,542,106	167,736	22.24
62	7,374,370	179,271	24.31
63	7,195,099	191,174	26.57
64	7,003,925	203,394	29.04
65	6,800,531	215,917	31.75
66	6,584,614	228,749	34.74
67	6,355,865	241,777	38.04
68	6,114,088	254,835	41.68
69	5,859,253	267,241	45.61
70	5,592,012	278,426	49.79
71	5,313,586	287,731	54.15
72	5,025,855	294,766	58.65
73	4,731,089	299,289	63.26
74	4,431,800	301,894	68.12
75	4,129,906	303,011	73.37
76	3,826,895	303,014	79.18
77	3,523,881	301,997	85.70
78	3,221,884	299,829	95.06
79	2,922,055	295,683	101.19
80	2,626,372	288,848	109.98
81	2,337,524	278,983	119.35
82	2,058,541	265,902	129.17
83	1,792,639	249,858	139.38
84	1,542,781	231,433	150.01
85	1,311,348	211,311	161.14
86	1,100,037	190,108	172.82
87	909,929	168,455	185.13
88	741,474	146,997	198.25
89	594,477	126,303	212.46
90	468,174	106,809	228.14
91	361,365	88,813	245.77
92	272,552	72,480	265.93
93	200,072	57,881	289.30
94	142,191	45,026	316.66
95	97,165	34,128	351.24
96	63,037	25,250	400.56
97	37,787	18,456	488.42
98	19,331	12,916	668.15
99	6,415	6,415	1000.00

Source: Institute of Life Insurance.

3. At age 25, the probability that death will occur within one year is **3.** ● Ⓑ Ⓒ Ⓓ Ⓔ

(A) 0.00193 (B) 0.0193 (C) 0.193 (D) 1.93

(1.93 ÷ 1000 = 0.00193. Note that (D) is impossible since no probability can exceed 1, which implies certainty of occurrence. Life insurance companies usually refer to the *annual death rate* (per thousand) at a certain age rather than to the probability of death.)

4. The probability, to the nearest tenth, that a 65-year-old person will live at least to age 70 is **4.** Ⓐ Ⓑ ● Ⓓ Ⓔ

(A) 0.6 (B) 0.7 (C) 0.8 (D) 0.9

(The answer is $\dfrac{\text{number living at age 70}}{\text{number living at age 65}}$.

It is approximately $^{56}/_{68}$, or about 0.82.)

5. A box contains 4 black and 3 white chips. Two chips are selected at random. The probability that one is black and one is white is **5.** Ⓐ Ⓑ ● Ⓓ Ⓔ

(A) $^2/_7$ (B) $^3/_7$ (C) $^4/_7$ (D) $^7/_{12}$

(The probability of an event is the ratio

$$\frac{\text{number of ways the event can occur}}{\text{total number of possible outcomes}}$$

There are 4 · 3 or 12 ways of selecting 1 black chip and 1 white chip. There are ${}_7C_2$ or (7 · 6) / (1 · 2) ways of choosing 2 chips from 7. The answer is $^{12}/_{21}$ or $^4/_7$.)

PRACTICE QUESTIONS ON PROBABILITY AND STATISTICS

Follow the directions for multiple-choice questions. If you can eliminate one or more choices, then guess among the remaining ones. The correct answers and explanations follow the set of questions.

1. The number of different license plates that start with one letter followed by three different digits selected from the set {0,1,2,3,4,5,6,7,8,9} is
   (A) 26 · 10 · 10 · 10 (B) 26 · 9 · 9 · 9
   (C) 26 · 10 · 9 · 8 (D) 16 · 9 · 8 · 7

2. The number of different license plates beginning with two different letters followed by two digits either of which may be any digit other than zero is
   (A) $26^2 \cdot 8^2$ (B) 26 · 25 · 9 · 9
   (C) $26^2 \cdot 9 \cdot 8$ (D) $26^2 \cdot 9^2$

3. **A box contains 6 green pens and 5 red pens. The number of ways of drawing 4 pens if they must all be green is**
   (A) 5 (B) 6 (C) 10 (D) 15

4. **How many committees consisting of 3 girls and 2 boys may be selected from a club of 5 girls and 4 boys?**
   (A) 6 (B) 20 (C) 60 (D) 72

5. **In how many ways can 2 or more bonus books be selected from a set of 5 offered by a book club?**
   (A) 32 (B) 26 (C) 20 (D) 10

6. **The number of different ways a student can answer a 10-question true-false test is**
   (A) 2 (B) 20 (C) 10^2 (D) 2^{10}

7. **The probability of obtaining a 5 when an ordinary die is cast is** *
   (A) $^1/_3$ (B) $^1/_4$ (C) $^1/_5$ (D) $^1/_6$

8. **If a penny is tossed 3 times, then the number of different possible outcomes is**
   (A) 9 (B) 8 (C) 6 (D) 3

9. If a penny and a die are tossed, then the probability that the penny shows heads and the die an even number is
(A) $\frac{1}{4}$ (B) $\frac{1}{3}$ (C) $\frac{1}{2}$ (D) $\frac{2}{3}$

10. The probability that at least one head shows in a toss of three coins is
(A) $\frac{1}{8}$ (B) $\frac{3}{8}$ (C) $\frac{1}{2}$ (D) $\frac{7}{8}$

11. A college that administered two tests to 100 freshmen got the following results: 14 failed both exams; 28 failed the mathematics exam; 33 failed the English exam. The number of students who passed both exams is
(A) 53 (B) 67 (C) 72 (D) 86

12. If a letter is chosen at random from the word MISSISSIPPI, the probability that it occurs four times in the word is
(A) $\frac{4}{11}$ (B) $\frac{1}{2}$ (C) $\frac{8}{11}$ (D) $\frac{10}{11}$

13. According to polls, candidates X, Y, and Z have a 0.5, 0.3, and 0.2 chance respectively of winning an election. If candidate Z withdraws, then Y's chance of winning is
(A) 0.375 (B) 0.4 (C) 0.475 (D) 0.5

Use this table on the numbers of Americans living at various ages to answer questions 14 and 15.

AGE	NUMBER LIVING	AGE	NUMBER LIVING
0	100,000	45	91,785
1	98,090	50	89,223
5	97,778	55	85,477
10	97,582	60	80,165
15	97,384	65	72,464
20	96,860	70	52,512
25	96,158	75	49,958
30	95,472	80	35,814
35	94,649	85 and up	21,972
40	93,514		

14. The probability, to the nearest tenth, that a person aged 10 will be alive at 65 is
(A) 0.6 (B) 0.7 (C) 0.8 (D) 0.9

15. The probability, to the nearest tenth, that a person aged 40 will die before he is 80 is
(A) 0.4 (B) 0.5 (C) 0.6 (D) 0.7

16. Based on a sample of 500,000 people, the American Cancer Society estimated that 750 persons would die of cancer in 1973. The probability of death from cancer in 1973 for this sample was
(A) 0.17 (B) 0.015 (C) 0.0017 (D) 0.0015

17. If two cards are drawn from an ordinary deck of cards, the probability that they will both be clubs is
(A) $\frac{1}{18}$ (B) $\frac{1}{17}$ (C) $\frac{1}{16}$ (D) $\frac{1}{15}$

18. The number of distinguishable permutations of letters in the word CANAL is
(A) 31 (B) 4! (C) 60 (D) 5!

19. The eye color of students in a class is given by the chart. The probability that a person selected at random is a male or has blue eyes is

	MALES	FEMALES
BROWN EYES	6	4
BLUE EYES	3	7

(A) $3/4$ (B) $4/5$ (C) $9/10$ (D) $19/20$

20. One bag contains 5 black and 3 green marbles. A second bag has 4 black and 2 green marbles. If one marble is chosen from each bag at random, the probability that they are both green is
(A) $1/8$ (B) $1/4$ (C) $1/3$ (D) $5/14$

21. If a pair of dice are cast, then the probability that the sum is greater than 9 is
(A) $1/18$ (B) $1/12$ (C) $1/9$ (D) $1/6$

22. Assume that the probability that it will rain on a day to be selected at random for a picnic is 10%. The probability that a Tuesday will be chosen and that that Tuesday will be dry is
(A) $10/9$ (B) $9/10$ (C) $9/70$ (D) $1/70$

Use the following for questions 23 and 24.

> A college registrar reports the following statistics on 360 students:
> 200 take politics
> 150 take biology
> 75 take mathematics
> 70 take politics and biology
> 50 take biology and mathematics
> 10 take politics and mathematics
> 5 take all three subjects

23. How many students in the report do not take politics, biology, or mathematics?
(A) 0 (B) 30 (C) 60 (D) 100

24. If a student in the report is chosen at random, what is the probability that he studies mathematics but neither politics nor biology?
(A) $1/24$ (B) $1/18$ (C) $1/6$ (D) $5/24$

25. If the average of the set of numbers $\{3, 5, 6, 11, x\}$ is 7, then the median is
(A) 5 (B) $5^1/_2$ (C) 6 (D) 7

ANSWERS AND EXPLANATIONS

to practice Section II questions on probability and statistics.

1. C. We can show how to fill the four "slots" in the license plate schematically by

$$26 \times 10 \times 9 \times 8$$
$$\square \quad \square \quad \square \quad \square$$

where the number above a position indicates how many ways it may be filled. Note that a digit may *not* be repeated.

2. **B. Here we have**

$$26 \times 25 \times 9 \times 9$$

□ □ □ □

The letter may not be repeated, but any of the 9 nonzero digits may be.

3. D. ${}_6C_4$ or its equal, ${}_6C_2$, which is $(6 \cdot 5)/(1 \cdot 2)$.

4. C. ${}_5C_3 \times {}_4C_2$, or $(5 \cdot 4)/(1 \cdot 2) \times (4 \cdot 3)/(1 \cdot 2)$ since ${}_5C_3 = {}_5C_2$.

5. B. ${}_5C_2 + {}_5C_3 + {}_5C_4 + {}_5C_5$.

6. D. The first may be answered in 2 ways, after which the second may be answered in 2 ways, after which the third and so on. This yields $2 \times 2 \times 2 \ldots \times 2$, where there are 10 twos, or 2^{10}. Note for just 3 T-F questions that there are 8 different ways of answering them.

7. **D. There are six possible outcomes, of which obtaining 5 is one outcome.**

8. **B. A tree diagram may be useful:**

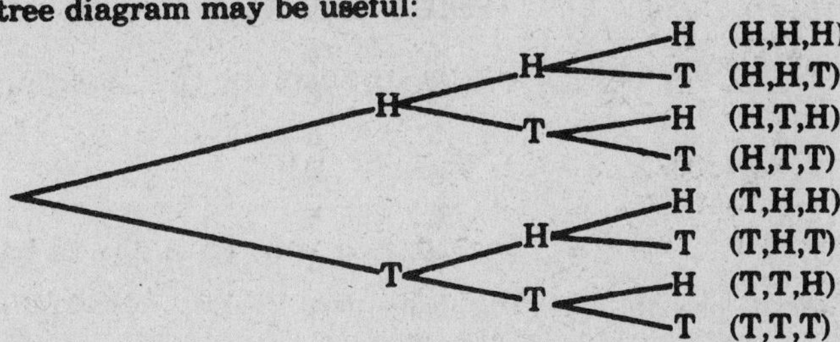

There are 8 possible outcomes. Note that the answer is obtainable immediately from

$$2 \times 2 \times 2$$

□ □ □

where there are 2 outcomes on the first toss, then 2 on the second, then 2 on the third.

9. **A. The probability that the penny shows heads is $\frac{1}{2}$ and that the die shows an even number is $\frac{1}{2}$. The answer is the product since the events are independent.**

10. **D. The tree in the answer to question 8 shows that at least one H occurs in 7 of 8 possible outcomes. Or note that the probability of getting all (3) tails** is $\frac{1}{2} \times \frac{1}{2} \times \frac{1}{2}$, or $\frac{1}{8}$; so the answer is $1 - \frac{1}{8}$.

11. **A. Draw a Venn diagram. Since 14 + 14 + 19, or 47, students failed one or both exams, it follows that 100 − 47 passed both.**

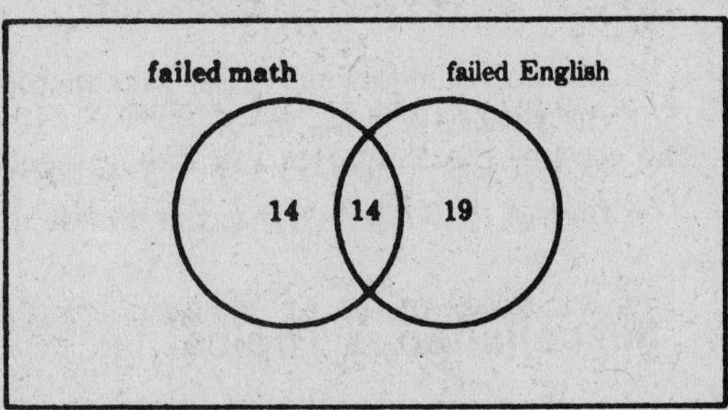

12. **C. There are 11 letters in MISSISSIPPI; 8 of them are I or S.**

13. **A. Assuming that the chances for X and Y are increased proportionately when Z withdraws, then Y's chances become**

$$\frac{0.3}{0.5 + 0.3}$$

14. B. $\dfrac{72{,}464}{97{,}582} \approx \dfrac{72}{98} \approx 0.7.$

15. C. $\dfrac{93{,}514 - 35{,}814}{93{,}514} \approx \dfrac{58}{94} \approx 0.6.$

16. D. $\frac{750}{500{,}000} = 0.0015.$

17. B. $\frac{{}_{13}C_2}{{}_{52}C_2} = \frac{13 \cdot 12}{1 \cdot 2} \div \frac{52 \cdot 51}{1 \cdot 2} = \frac{13 \cdot 12}{52 \cdot 51} = \frac{1}{17}.$

18. C. If the two A's were distinguishable (perhaps subscripted), there would be 5! permutations. We divide by 2 to eliminate identical pairs of permutations.

19. B. If M is the set of males and B the set of blue-eyed people, then we want $\frac{P(M \cup B)}{\text{number in the class}} = \frac{6+3+7}{20} = \frac{4}{5}.$

20. A. $\frac{{}_3C_1}{8} \times \frac{{}_2C_1}{6} = \frac{3}{8} \times \frac{1}{3} = \frac{1}{8}.$

21. D. There are 6 × 6 or 36 possible outcomes when the pair of dice is cast. A sum that exceeds 9 can be obtained in the following six ways:

DIE I	DIE II
4	6
5	6
5	5
6	6
6	5
6	4

Therefore the probability of the event is 6/36.

22. C. The two events, day of the week selected and whether it rains, are independent. The desired product is 1/7 × 9/10.

23. C. A Venn diagram helps.

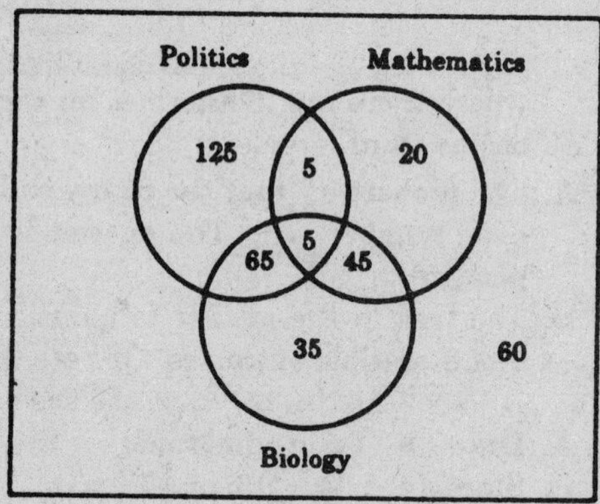

24. B. Since 20 students out of 360 take mathematics but neither politics nor biology, the answer is 20/360, or 1/18.

25. C. $(3 + 5 + 6 + 11 + x) \div 5 = 7 \rightarrow (25 + x) \div 5 = 7 \rightarrow x = 10$. The median of the set {3, 5, 6, 10, 11} is the middle number, 6.

B6. Miscellaneous Topics

The subtopics are: complex numbers; number bases; logarithms and exponentials; newly defined binary operations; identity, and inverse elements.

Here are some introductory examples.

ANSWERS

1. If for all elements p, q, r in a mathematical system, $p(q + r) = pq + pr$, then the system satisfies
(A) the commutative law for addition
(B) the commutative law for multiplication
(C) a distributive law
(D) an associative law

1. Ⓐ Ⓑ ● Ⓓ Ⓔ

2. If $i = \sqrt{-1}$, then $i^7 =$ — 2. Ⓐ Ⓑ Ⓒ ● Ⓔ
(A) 1 (B) −1 (C) i (D) $-i$

(Note that $i^2 = -1$ and $i^4 = (-1)(-1) = 1$; thus $i^7 = i^4 \cdot i^2 \cdot i = (1)(-1)(i) = -i$.)

3. 1001_2 equals what numeral base 10? — 3. Ⓐ ● Ⓒ Ⓓ Ⓔ
(A) 17 (B) 9 (C) 5 (D) 2

($1001_2 = 1 \times 2^3 + 0 \times 2^2 + 0 \times 2^1 + 1 \times 2^0 = 8 + 0 + 0 + 1 = 9$.)

4. If $\log_b 2 = r$ and $\log_b 3 = s$, then $\log_b 18 =$ — 4. ● Ⓑ Ⓒ Ⓓ Ⓔ
(A) $r + 2s$ (B) $2r + s$ (C) $2rs$ (D) r^2s

(Since $18 = 2 \cdot 3^2$, $\log_b 18 = \log_b 2 + \log_b 3^2 = \log_b 2 + 2 \log_b 3 = r + 2s$.)

PRACTICE QUESTIONS ON MISCELLANEOUS TOPICS

Follow the directions for multiple-choice questions. If you can eliminate one or more choices, then guess among the remaining ones. The correct answers and explanations follow the set of questions.

1. If the product of every pair of elements in a set is an element of the set, then
(A) the operation is commutative (B) the set is closed
(C) the set is a group (D) the operation is associative

Use this multiplication table for questions 2 through 4.

+	p	q	r	s
p	p	q	r	s
q	q	r	s	p
r	r	s	p	q
s	s	p	q	r

2. The sum $(r + s)$ equals
(A) p (B) q (C) r (D) s

3. The identity element is
(A) p (B) q (C) r (D) s

4. The additive inverse of q is
(A) p (B) q (C) r (D) s

***Use this multiplication table for questions** 5–8.*

×	0	1	2	3
0	0	0	0	0
1	0	1	2	3
2	0	2	0	2
3	0	3	2	1

5. According to the table, $(2 \times 3) \times 2$ equals
(A) 0 (B) 1 (C) 2 (D) 3

6. The multiplicative identity is
(A) 0 (B) 1 (C) 2 (D) 3

7. The inverse of 3 is
(A) 0 (B) 1 (C) 2 (D) 3

8. Which of the following is false?
(A) The operation is commutative.
(B) The set is closed.
(C) The operation is associative.
(D) Every element has a multiplicative inverse in the set.

9. The roots of the equation $x^2 + 2 = 0$ are
(A) $\pm\sqrt{2}$ (B) $+2i$ (where $i = \sqrt{-1}$)
(C) $\pm i\sqrt{2}$ (D) $\pm\sqrt{2i}$

10. If $\log_a 2 = p$ and $\log_a 3 = s$, then $\log_a \frac{9}{2} =$

(A) $\frac{2s}{p}$ (B) $2s - p$ (C) $\frac{s^2}{p}$ (D) $2s + \frac{1}{p}$

11. $(a^x)^y =$

(A) a^{x+y} (B) $a^x \cdot a^y$ (C) a^{xy} (D) ya^x

12. $(2 + i)(3 - i)$, where $i = \sqrt{-1}$, equals

(A) 7 (B) 5 (C) $5 + i$ (D) $7 + i$

13. If the roots of $x^2 + 2x + d = 0$ are real, then d *cannot* equal

(A) 2 (B) 1 (C) 0 (D) -1

14. If $p * q = p + pq - 1$, then $a * -1$ equals

(A) $a + 1$ (B) $-a + 1$ (C) $-a - 1$ (D) -1

15. If $f(x) = ax^3 + bx^2 + cx + d$ and $f(-1) = 0$, then f must be divisible by

(A) x (B) $x - 1$ (C) $x + 1$ (D) $x^2 - 1$

16. $1001_2 + 11_2 =$

(A) 1010_2 (B) 1100_2 (C) 1110_2 (D) 1111_2

17. $\frac{2^p}{2^{p+q}} =$

(A) 2^q (B) 2^{2p-q} (C) 2^{-q} (D) $\frac{1}{q}$

18. If $\log_3 p = m$ and $\log_3 q = 2m$, then $\log_3 pq =$

(A) $2m$ (B) $3m$ (C) $6m$ (D) $3m^2$

19. Which set is not closed under ordinary multiplication?

(A) {0, 1} (B) {−1, 1} (C) {1, 2} (D) {−1, 0, 1}

20. If $3^{x+1} = 3$, then $x =$

(A) 0 (B) 1 (C) 2 (D) -1

21. Which of the following is the graph of $y = \log_2 x$?

(A)

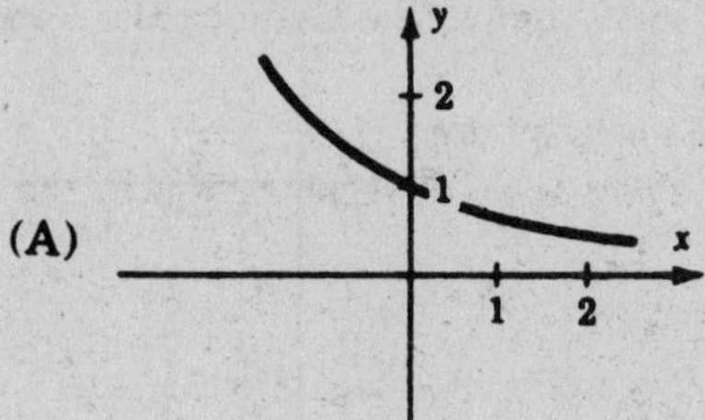

(B)

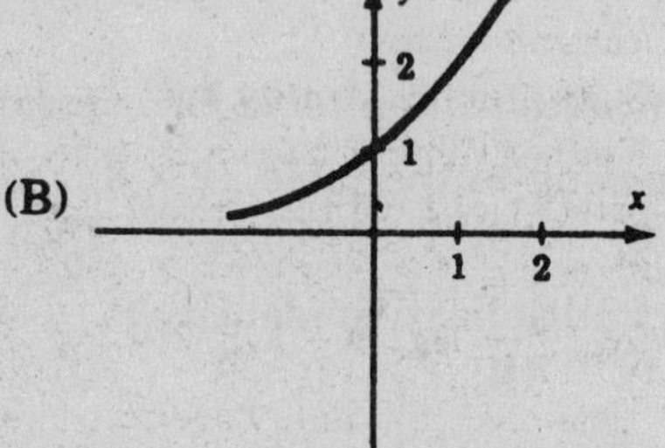

(C)

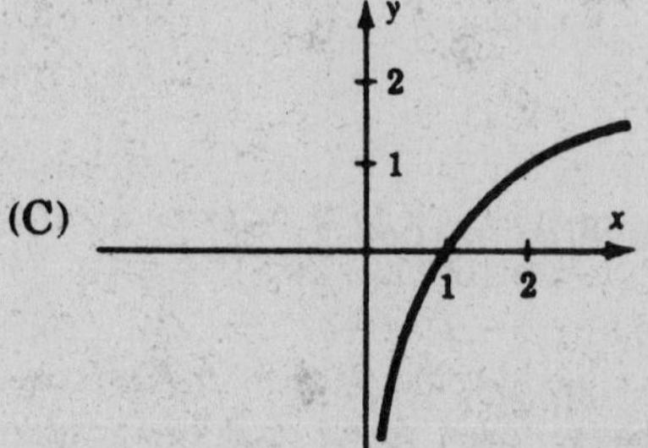

(D)

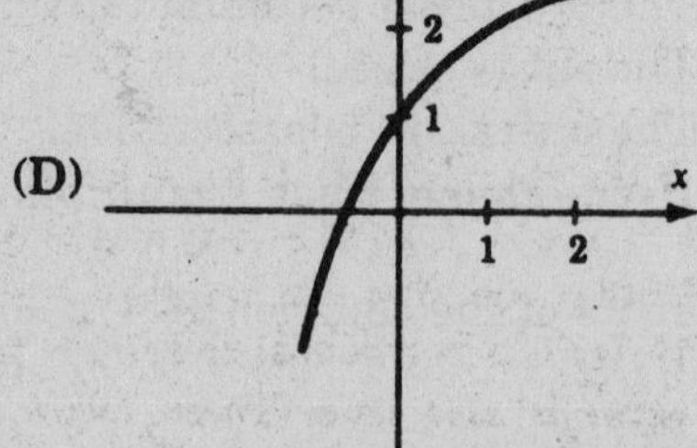

22. 10110_2 corresponds to the base-ten numeral
(A) 14 (B) 20 (C) 22 (D) 28

23. Let $f(x) = x^3 - 2x^2 - x + d$. If $f(1) = 0$, then the roots of $f(x) = 0$ are
(A) 1, 2, and −2 (B) 1, −1, and −2
(C) −1, 2, and −2 (D) 1, −1, and 2

24. $\sqrt{3} \cdot \sqrt{-27} =$
(A) −9 (B) $-9i$ (where $i = \sqrt{-1}$)
(C) $9i$ (D) 9

25. Which equation does *not* have real roots?
(A) $x^2 + 1 = 0$ (B) $x^2 - 2 = 0$
(C) $x^2 + x - 1 = 0$ (D) $x^2 + 4x = 0$

ANSWERS AND EXPLANATIONS

to practice Section II questions on miscellaneous topics.

1. B. A set S is closed under an operation $\times$ if, for every pair of elements a, b in S, the "product" $a \times b$ is in S.
2. B. To find the sum of r and s we move across the r row until we come to the column headed s.
3. A. If e is the identity of a set of elements S under an operation $*$ and x is *any* element of S, then $x * e = e * x = x$. To find e from a table, look for the row which is identical with the row across the top of the table; the element to the left of this row is the identity.
4. D. The inverse element for q is the one such that q "plus" it yields the identity. Since p is the identity for this table, and $q + s = p$, s is the inverse of q. (Note, also, that $s + q = p$.)
5. A. $(2 \times 3) \times 2 = 2 \times 2 = 0$.
6. B. If e denotes the multiplicative identity and a is any element in the set, then $a \times e = e \times a = a$. Look for a column (or row) that is the same as the lead column (or row).
7. D. Since 1 is the identity and $3 \times 3 = 1$, 3 is its own inverse.
8. D. Neither 0 nor 2 has an inverse. Note that there is no element such that the product of 2 with it yields 1.
9. C. $x^2 = -2 \rightarrow x = \pm\sqrt{-2} = \pm\sqrt{2}i$ or $\pm i\sqrt{2}$.
10. B. $\log_a \frac{9}{2} = \log_a 9 - \log_a 2 = \log_a 3^2 - \log_a 2 = 2\log_a 3 - \log_a 2 = 2s - p$.
11. C. Note that, if x and y are integers, $(a^x)^y$ indicates a product of y factors, each equal to a^x:

$$(a^x)^y = \underbrace{a^x \cdot a^x \cdots a^x}_{y \text{ factors}} = a^{\overbrace{(x+x+\cdots+x)}^{y \text{ addends}}} = a^{xy}$$

12. D. $(2 + i)(3 - i) = (2)(3) + (2)(-i) + (i)(3) + (i)(-i)$
$= 6 + i - i^2 = 6 + i - (-1) = 7 + i.$
13. A. If the roots of $ax^2 + bx + c = 0$ are real, then $b^2 - 4ac \geq 0$. Here $a = 1$, $b = 2$, $c = d$, so $b^2 - 4ac = 4 - 4d$, which is greater than zero if $d \leq 1$.
14. D. With $p = a$, $q = -1$, we get $a * -1 = a + a(-1) - 1 = -1$.
15. C. If $f(x)$ is a polynomial and $f(r) = 0$, then $f(x)$ is divisible by $(x - r)$. The converse is also true. These follow from the so-called *factor* and *remainder theorems* of algebra.

16. B. Note how we add in base 2:

eights	fours	twos	units
		1	1
1	0	0	1
+		1	1
1	1	0	0

Here we replaced 1 + 1 (or 2) in the units column by 10, 1 + 1 in the twos column by 100.

17. C. $\frac{2^p}{2^{p+q}} = 2^{p-(p+q)} = 2^{p-p-q} = 2^{-q}$.

18. B. $\log_3 pq = \log_3 p + \log_3 q = m + 2m = 3m$.

19. C. Note for the set {1, 2} that $2 \cdot 2 = 4$, which is not in the set. Verify that the other sets are all closed under ordinary multiplication.

20. A. $3^{x+1} = 3 = 3^1 \rightarrow x + 1 = 1 \rightarrow x = 0$.

21. C. Some of the properties of the graph of $y = \log_2 x$ are: $\log_2 1 = 0$, the domain is $\{x{:}x > 0\}$. Only the graph in (C) satisfies these.

22. C. $10110_2 = 1 \times 2^4 + 0 \times 2^3 + 1 \times 2^2 + 1 \times 2^1 + 0 \times 2^0$
$= 2^4 + 0 + 2^2 + 2^1 + 0$
$= 22$.

23. D. $f(1) = 1^3 - 2(1)^2 - 1 + d = d - 2$.
Since $f(1) = 0$, $d = 2$ and $f(x) = x^3 - 2x^2 - x + 2$.
Since $f(1) = 0$, $x - 1$ is a factor of $f(x)$.
Indeed, $x^3 - 2x^2 - x + 2 = (x - 1)(x + 1)(x - 2)$.

24. C. $\sqrt{3} \cdot \sqrt{-27} = \sqrt{3} \cdot \sqrt{27} \cdot \sqrt{-1} = \sqrt{81} \cdot i = 9i$.

25. A. The roots in (A) are $\pm i$; verify that the roots of the others are all real. Remember, the roots of $ax^2 + bx + c = 0$ are

$$x = \frac{-b \pm \sqrt{b^2 - 4ac}}{2a};$$

the roots are real only if $b^2 - 4ac \geqslant 0$.

CHAPTER

11

Sample Examinations

This chapter has three sample CLEP mathematics examinations. Each examination is followed by an answer key and reference chart, a scoring chart, and answer explanations. The mathematics examination consists both of Section I on Basic Skills and Concepts and Section II on Content. As noted earlier, Section I contains 40 questions, some of the quantitative-comparison type and some of the regular multiple-choice type; Section II has 50 questions, all of the regular multiple-choice type.

Remember that the examination is timed with 90 minutes allowed *altogether* for both parts. However, you will be allowed to *work only on the first part during the first 30 minutes* and *only on the second part during the last 60 minutes*. If you finish Section I before time is called, do *not* go on to Section II; instead, check over your answers in Section I. If you finish Section II before time is called, do *not* go back to Section I; instead, check over Section II. It is recommended that you observe this timing when taking each of the four sample tests in this book.

It is very important that you do not spend too much time on any one question. It is best to answer first those questions that you are pretty sure about, returning after you've gone through the entire examination to those questions that need more thought or work. Keep track of the time so you can pace yourself, remembering that it is not expected that anyone taking the test will answer every question.

For a reminder about the major topics that are covered in each part and the approximate number of questions for each topic, see page 289. The scoring of the examination and whether or not to guess are discussed on page 290.

It will probably be helpful at this point to reread the tips on answering questions involving data interpretation (page 316) and on handling questions of both the quantitative-comparison and multiple-choice types (pages 297–299). Here, again, are some reminders and tips:

1. Read the test directions carefully and study any illustrative examples.
2. Pay attention to any notes about figures. In Section II, figures are intended to provide information useful in answering the questions and are drawn as accurately as possible *except* when specifically noted otherwise.
3. Answer the easy questions first, putting a check by, or encircling, the number of any question you skip. Go back to the latter if you have time.
4. Skip any question on a topic with which you are not familiar.
5. Guess intelligently; avoid wild guessing.

6. When practicing it is often worthwhile to verify that choices not selected are truly incorrect. However, when taking the actual examination it would be needlessly time-consuming (and therefore foolish) to do that. When you decide on the answer to a particular question, mark it in the proper box and move on immediately to the next question.

7. Work steadily, trying not to be careless.

8. Pace yourself but try to take a breather or two in each part.

9. Keep cool. Remember that practically no one answers every question.

10. Even though the answer column may have answer spaces for each question, labeled A, B, C, D, and E, you are to choose the *one* correct answer from among spaces A, B, C, and D. Do not make any marks whatever in space E.

ANSWER SHEET — MATHEMATICS/SAMPLE EXAMINATION 1

Section I

1. Ⓐ Ⓑ Ⓒ Ⓓ Ⓔ
2. Ⓐ Ⓑ Ⓒ Ⓓ Ⓔ
3. Ⓐ Ⓑ Ⓒ Ⓓ Ⓔ
4. Ⓐ Ⓑ Ⓒ Ⓓ Ⓔ
5. Ⓐ Ⓑ Ⓒ Ⓓ Ⓔ
6. Ⓐ Ⓑ Ⓒ Ⓓ Ⓔ
7. Ⓐ Ⓑ Ⓒ Ⓓ Ⓔ
8. Ⓐ Ⓑ Ⓒ Ⓓ Ⓔ
9. Ⓐ Ⓑ Ⓒ Ⓓ Ⓔ
10. Ⓐ Ⓑ Ⓒ Ⓓ Ⓔ
11. Ⓐ Ⓑ Ⓒ Ⓓ Ⓔ
12. Ⓐ Ⓑ Ⓒ Ⓓ Ⓔ
13. Ⓐ Ⓑ Ⓒ Ⓓ Ⓔ
14. Ⓐ Ⓑ Ⓒ Ⓓ Ⓔ
15. Ⓐ Ⓑ Ⓒ Ⓓ Ⓔ
16. Ⓐ Ⓑ Ⓒ Ⓓ Ⓔ
17. Ⓐ Ⓑ Ⓒ Ⓓ Ⓔ
18. Ⓐ Ⓑ Ⓒ Ⓓ Ⓔ
19. Ⓐ Ⓑ Ⓒ Ⓓ Ⓔ
20. Ⓐ Ⓑ Ⓒ Ⓓ Ⓔ
21. Ⓐ Ⓑ Ⓒ Ⓓ Ⓔ
22. Ⓐ Ⓑ Ⓒ Ⓓ Ⓔ
23. Ⓐ Ⓑ Ⓒ Ⓓ Ⓔ
24. Ⓐ Ⓑ Ⓒ Ⓓ Ⓔ
25. Ⓐ Ⓑ Ⓒ Ⓓ Ⓔ
26. Ⓐ Ⓑ Ⓒ Ⓓ Ⓔ
27. Ⓐ Ⓑ Ⓒ Ⓓ Ⓔ
28. Ⓐ Ⓑ Ⓒ Ⓓ Ⓔ
29. Ⓐ Ⓑ Ⓒ Ⓓ Ⓔ
30. Ⓐ Ⓑ Ⓒ Ⓓ Ⓔ
31. Ⓐ Ⓑ Ⓒ Ⓓ Ⓔ
32. Ⓐ Ⓑ Ⓒ Ⓓ Ⓔ
33. Ⓐ Ⓑ Ⓒ Ⓓ Ⓔ
34. Ⓐ Ⓑ Ⓒ Ⓓ Ⓔ
35. Ⓐ Ⓑ Ⓒ Ⓓ Ⓔ
36. Ⓐ Ⓑ Ⓒ Ⓓ Ⓔ
37. Ⓐ Ⓑ Ⓒ Ⓓ Ⓔ
38. Ⓐ Ⓑ Ⓒ Ⓓ Ⓔ
39. Ⓐ Ⓑ Ⓒ Ⓓ Ⓔ
40. Ⓐ Ⓑ Ⓒ Ⓓ Ⓔ

Section II

41. Ⓐ Ⓑ Ⓒ Ⓓ Ⓔ
42. Ⓐ Ⓑ Ⓒ Ⓓ Ⓔ
43. Ⓐ Ⓑ Ⓒ Ⓓ Ⓔ
44. Ⓐ Ⓑ Ⓒ Ⓓ Ⓔ
45. Ⓐ Ⓑ Ⓒ Ⓓ Ⓔ
46. Ⓐ Ⓑ Ⓒ Ⓓ Ⓔ
47. Ⓐ Ⓑ Ⓒ Ⓓ Ⓔ
48. Ⓐ Ⓑ Ⓒ Ⓓ Ⓔ
49. Ⓐ Ⓑ Ⓒ Ⓓ Ⓔ
50. Ⓐ Ⓑ Ⓒ Ⓓ Ⓔ
51. Ⓐ Ⓑ Ⓒ Ⓓ Ⓔ
52. Ⓐ Ⓑ Ⓒ Ⓓ Ⓔ
53. Ⓐ Ⓑ Ⓒ Ⓓ Ⓔ
54. Ⓐ Ⓑ Ⓒ Ⓓ Ⓔ
55. Ⓐ Ⓑ Ⓒ Ⓓ Ⓔ
56. Ⓐ Ⓑ Ⓒ Ⓓ Ⓔ
57. Ⓐ Ⓑ Ⓒ Ⓓ Ⓔ
58. Ⓐ Ⓑ Ⓒ Ⓓ Ⓔ
59. Ⓐ Ⓑ Ⓒ Ⓓ Ⓔ
60. Ⓐ Ⓑ Ⓒ Ⓓ Ⓔ
61. Ⓐ Ⓑ Ⓒ Ⓓ Ⓔ
62. Ⓐ Ⓑ Ⓒ Ⓓ Ⓔ
63. Ⓐ Ⓑ Ⓒ Ⓓ Ⓔ
64. Ⓐ Ⓑ Ⓒ Ⓓ Ⓔ
65. Ⓐ Ⓑ Ⓒ Ⓓ Ⓔ
66. Ⓐ Ⓑ Ⓒ Ⓓ Ⓔ
67. Ⓐ Ⓑ Ⓒ Ⓓ Ⓔ
68. Ⓐ Ⓑ Ⓒ Ⓓ Ⓔ
69. Ⓐ Ⓑ Ⓒ Ⓓ Ⓔ
70. Ⓐ Ⓑ Ⓒ Ⓓ Ⓔ
71. Ⓐ Ⓑ Ⓒ Ⓓ Ⓔ
72. Ⓐ Ⓑ Ⓒ Ⓓ Ⓔ
73. Ⓐ Ⓑ Ⓒ Ⓓ Ⓔ
74. Ⓐ Ⓑ Ⓒ Ⓓ Ⓔ
75. Ⓐ Ⓑ Ⓒ Ⓓ Ⓔ
76. Ⓐ Ⓑ Ⓒ Ⓓ Ⓔ
77. Ⓐ Ⓑ Ⓒ Ⓓ Ⓔ
78. Ⓐ Ⓑ Ⓒ Ⓓ Ⓔ
79. Ⓐ Ⓑ Ⓒ Ⓓ Ⓔ
80. Ⓐ Ⓑ Ⓒ Ⓓ Ⓔ
81. Ⓐ Ⓑ Ⓒ Ⓓ Ⓔ
82. Ⓐ Ⓑ Ⓒ Ⓓ Ⓔ
83. Ⓐ Ⓑ Ⓒ Ⓓ Ⓔ
84. Ⓐ Ⓑ Ⓒ Ⓓ Ⓔ
85. Ⓐ Ⓑ Ⓒ Ⓓ Ⓔ
86. Ⓐ Ⓑ Ⓒ Ⓓ Ⓔ
87. Ⓐ Ⓑ Ⓒ Ⓓ Ⓔ
88. Ⓐ Ⓑ Ⓒ Ⓓ Ⓔ
89. Ⓐ Ⓑ Ⓒ Ⓓ Ⓔ
90. Ⓐ Ⓑ Ⓒ Ⓓ Ⓔ

SAMPLE EXAMINATION 1

Section I: Basic Skills and Concepts

Directions for questions 1–25: Each question consists of two quantities, one in Column A and one in Column B. You are to compare the two quantities and on the answer sheet blacken space

A if the quantity in Column A is greater;
B if the quantity in Column B is greater;
C if the two quantities are equal;
D if the relationship cannot be determined from the information given.

Notes:

1. **In certain questions, information concerning one or both of the quantities to be compared is centered above the two columns.**
2. **A symbol that appears in both columns represents the same thing in Column A as it does in Column B.**
3. **Letters such as x, n, and k stand for real numbers.**

	COLUMN A	COLUMN B
1.	3^2	2^3
2.	$^3/_4 \div 3$	0.25
3.	a fraction between $^1/_3$ and $^1/_5$	$^1/_4$
4.	$(1 - 0.01)(1 + 0.1)(^1/_{10})$	$(0.1)(1.1)(0.99)$

Angles X and Y are supplementary; $m(\angle X) = 109°10'$.

5.	number of degrees in $\angle Y$	70

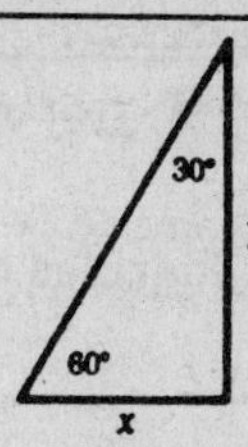

6.	y	$2x$

Use this chart for questions 7 and 8.

DOW-JONES AVERAGE OF 30 INDUSTRIALS: YEARLY RANGES

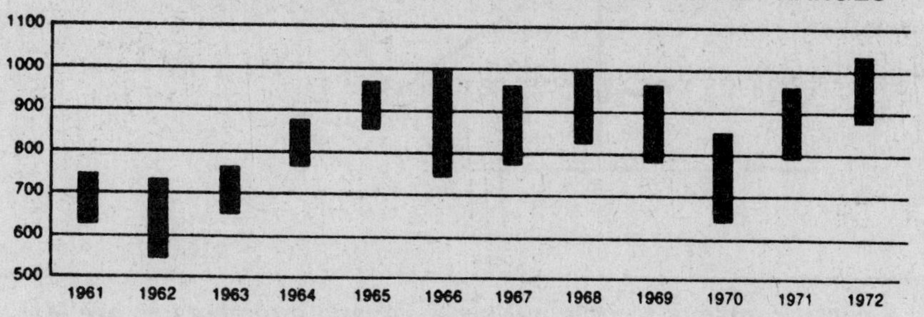

7. the number of points difference in the high and low Dow-Jones averages for the year when that difference was greatest	**225**
8. the low Dow-Jones average in 1972	the high Dow-Jones average for 1970

	COLUMN A	COLUMN B
9.	the cost of 4 candy bars if a dozen bars cost 35¢	14¢
10.	2.9×10^{-4}	0.000029
	The average of Paul's test grades is 76.	
11.	grade Paul must get on next test to average 80	88
12.	$2^3/_{10}$ expressed as a percent	203%
13.	$\sqrt{4} + \sqrt{9}$	$\sqrt{13}$
14.	$r = -1, s = 1, t = 3$	
	$2s - (r + t)$	0
15.	$\lvert x \rvert$	x
16.	the product of the roots of $x^2 + 2x - 3 = 0$	the sum of the roots of $x^2 + 2x - 3 = 0$
17.	$3 \times (2 + 8)$	$3 \times 2 + 8$
	$\frac{x^r}{x^s}$ is written as x^q, and $q = 0$.	
18.	r	s
	$\begin{cases} 5x - y = 11 \\ x = y + 3 \end{cases}$	
19.	y	1
	A bag contains red, green, blue, and white marbles. The ratio of green marbles to red is 1 : 2	
20.	ratio of green marbles to the total number	1 : 2
	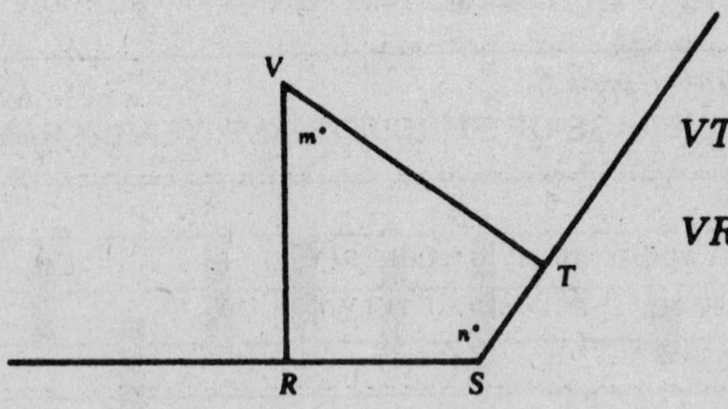 V, R, S, T, m°, n°; $VT \perp ST$; $VR \perp RS$	
21.	$m + n$	180
	A central angle of a circle measures 24° and intercepts an arc MN.	
22.	ratio of arc MN to the circumference of the circle	1 : 16

	COLUMN A	COLUMN B

Use this chart for questions 23, 24, and 25.

AVERAGE ANNUAL PERCENTAGE INCREASE IN THE CONSUMER PRICE INDEX, IN ALL SERVICES, AND IN MEDICAL CARE SERVICES FOR SELECTED PERIODS

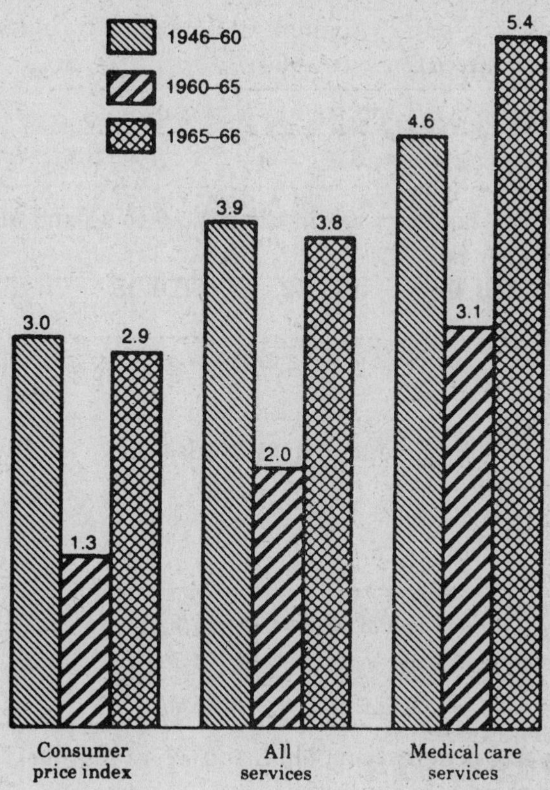

Source: Social Security Bulletin, July 1967, p. 17.

	COLUMN A	COLUMN B
23.	average annual increase in CPI as a whole for the period 1946-1960	average annual increase in CPI as a whole for the period 1965-1966
24.	average annual percentage increase for medical services for the year 1966	5.4
25.	decrease in average annual percentage increase for all services from that for the period 1946–60 to that for the period 1960–65	1.9

Directions for questions 26–40: For these questions, indicate the correct answer in the appropriate space on the answer sheet.

Note: Figures that accompany the following problems are intended to provide information useful in answering the questions. The figures are drawn as accurately as possible *except* when it is stated in a specific question that the figure is not drawn to scale. All figures lie in a plane unless otherwise stated.

26. 4.05 =
(A) $^9/_2$ (B) $^{21}/_5$ (C) $^{81}/_{20}$ (D) $^{81}/_{25}$

27. $(y^2 - 3y + 2) - (2y^2 + 3y - 2) =$
(A) $3y^2$ (B) $-y^2 - 6y + 4$ (C) $-y^2$ (D) $-y^2 + 4$

28. **If two positive numbers are in the ratio 6 to 11 and differ by 15, then the smaller number is**
(A) 3 (B) 6 (C) 12 (D) 18

29. If $0.0328 = 3.28 \times 10^k$, then $k =$
(A) −4 (B) −3 (C) −2 (D) 2

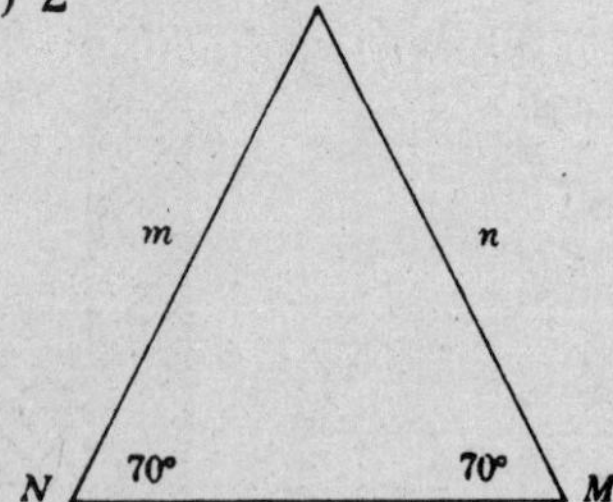

30. Which of the following statements is false?
(A) $m = n$
(B) $q > n$
(C) $m > q$
(D) $n > q$

Note: Figure is not drawn to scale.

Use this figure for questions 31 and 32.

TELEPHONES AND MAIL

Phones (per 1,000 population)
1950 281
1960 408
1965 478
1969 563

Average daily calls (in millions)
1950 176
1960 285
1965 367
1969 462

First Class and Airmail (pieces per capita)

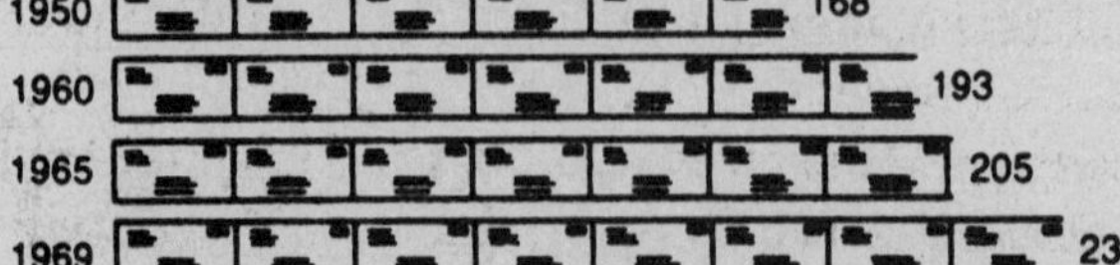

Source: Data, 1971, Figure 65, p. 292

31. Approximately how many million average daily calls does one telephone dial represent?
(A) 25 (B) 35 (C) 50 (D) 176

32. By approximately what percentage did phones (per 1000 population) increase from 1950 to 1969?
(A) 100 (B) 200 (C) 281 (D) 282

33. $(5x + 3)(2x - 3) =$
(A) $10x^2 - 9x$
(B) $10x^2 + 9x - 9$
(C) $10x^2 - 2x - 9$
(D) $10x^2 - 9x - 9$

34. The y-intercept of the line $2x - 3y + 9 = 0$ is
(A) 3 (B) -3 (C) $-4\frac{1}{2}$ (D) -9

35. If the dimensions of a box are all doubled, then the ratio of the volume of the larger to that of the smaller is
(A) 2 : 1 (B) 4 : 1 (C) 6 : 1 (D) 8 : 1

36. The area of a circle is 4π square inches. Its circumference equals
(A) π (B) 2π (C) 4π (D) 8π

37. $3^2 - 3^0 - 3^{-2} =$
(A) -1 (B) $7\frac{1}{9}$ (C) $7\frac{8}{9}$ (D) $8\frac{1}{9}$

38. $(0.02) \times (0.004) =$
(A) 0.000008 (B) 0.00008 (C) 0.0008 (D) 0.008

39.

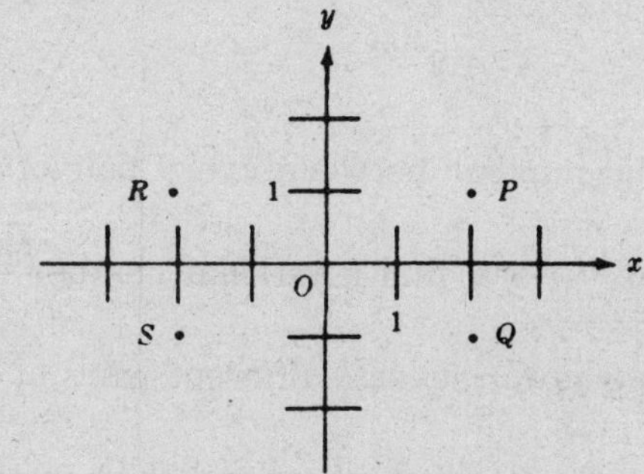

Which point above has coordinates $(2, -1)$?
(A) P (B) Q (C) R (D) S

40. A car travels a scenic route of 15 miles in 30 minutes and the 60-mile balance of a trip in one hour. Its average speed for the trip is
(A) 40 mph (B) 45 mph (C) 50 mph (D) 55 mph

Section II: Content

Directions: For each of the following problems, indicate the correct answer in the appropriate space on the answer sheet.

Note: Figures that accompany problems in this part are intended to provide information useful in solving the problems. They are drawn as accurately as possible *except* when it is stated in a specific problem that the figure is not drawn to scale. All figures lie in a plane unless otherwise indicated.

41. If $R = \{a,b,c,w\}$ and $S = \{a,c,d,w\}$, then $R \cap S$ equals
(A) $\{a,b,c,d,w\}$
(B) $\{a\}$
(C) $\{a,c\}$
(D) $\{a,c,w\}$

42. The solution set of $\{x : x \text{ is a real number and } x^3 - x^2 - 2x = 0\}$ is
(A) $\{0,1,2\}$ (B) $\{0,-1,2\}$
(C) $\{-1,2\}$ (D) $\{0,1,-2\}$

43. Let Z, Q, R denote respectively the sets of integers, of rationals, and of reals. Then it is false that
(A) $(3, 5) \in Z \times Z$ (B) $Z \times Z \subset Q \times Q$
(C) $(1, 1) \in Q \times Q$ (D) $Q \subset R \times R$

44. Which of the following sets is *not* infinite?
(A) the set of multiples of 3
(B) the set of prime numbers
(C) the set of subsets of the set $\{1,2,3, \ldots, 100\}$
(D) the set of integers less than -100

45. Let p denote "Warren wears braces" and let q denote "Warren wears glasses." Then the statement "Warren wears neither braces nor glasses" is written symbolically as
(A) $\sim(p \wedge q)$ (B) $\sim p \vee q$ (C) $\sim p \wedge \sim q$ (D) $\sim p \wedge q$

46. If $\log_2 2^x = 3$, then $x =$
(A) 8 (B) 6 (C) 3 (D) 2

47. To prove that there is a rational number between every pair of rational numbers,
(A) take a pair, such as $1/2$ and $1/3$, and find a rational number between them
(B) show that the statement is true for several different pairs of rational numbers
(C) consider in order every pair of rational numbers and show in each case that there is a rational number between them
(D) let p and q denote any pair of rational numbers, and show that $(p + q)/2$ is a rational number between p and q

48. The negation of "Every college graduate has studied geometry" is
(A) Some college graduates have not studied geometry
(B) No college graduate has studied geometry
(C) Geometry is not necessary for graduation from college
(D) If a person has studied geometry then he is not a college graduate

49. The truth table of $p \rightarrow q$ is

p	q	(A)	(B)	(C)	(D)
T	T	T	T	T	T
T	F	F	F	F	F
F	T	T	F	F	T
F	F	F	F	T	T

50. A counterexample to the claim that $(a^2 > b^2) \rightarrow (a > b)$ is
(A) $a = 3, b = 2$ (B) $a = -2, b = -1$
(C) $a = 1, b = 0$ (D) $a = 1/2, b = 1/3$

51. $|b - 1| =$
(A) $b - 1$ (B) $1 - b$ (C) $b + 1$ (D) none of the preceding

52. Which of the following fractions can*not* be written as a terminating decimal?
(A) $2/7$ (B) $5/16$ (C) $17/40$ (D) $19/25$

53. Which of the laws below holds for real numbers?
(A) division is commutative
(B) subtraction is associative
(C) $(a + b) \div c = (a \div c) + (b \div c)$
(D) $a - b = b - a$

54. Which of the following can*not* be a rational number?
(A) the sum of two irrational numbers
(B) the product of two irrational numbers
(C) the sum of a rational number and an irrational number
(D) the quotient of two irrational numbers

55. If $f(x) = 2x^2 - 3x + 2$, then $f(-x) =$
(A) $2x^2 + 3x + 2$ (B) $-2x^2 + 3x - 2$
(C) $-2x^2 + 3x + 2$ (D) $-f(x)$

56. Which of the following equations has a graph that is symmetric to the x-axis?
(A) $y = x$ (B) $y = x^2 + 3$ (C) $y^2 = x$ (D) $y = x^3 - x$

57. If $f(x) = x + \frac{4}{x}$ and $g(x) = \sqrt{x + 4}$, then $f(g(0))$ is
(A) 2 (B) 3 (C) 4 (D) undefined

58. The graph of $\begin{cases} y \geqq 1 - x \\ x^2 + y^2 \leqq 4 \\ x \geqq 0,\ y \geqq 0 \end{cases}$ is

(A)
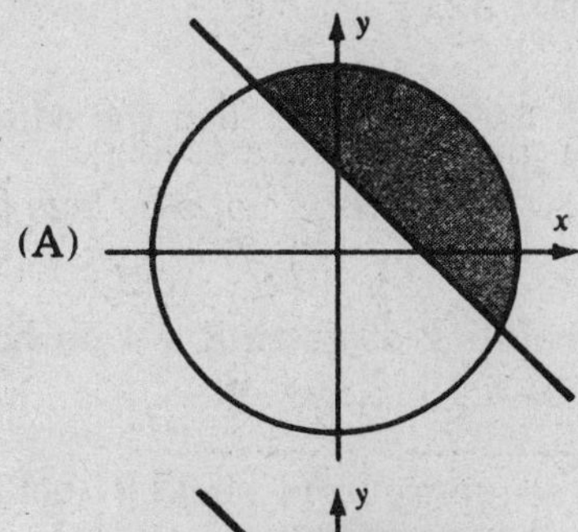

(B)
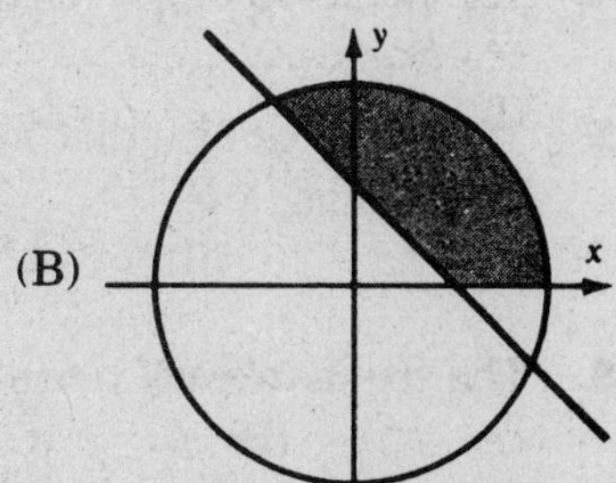

(C)

(D)
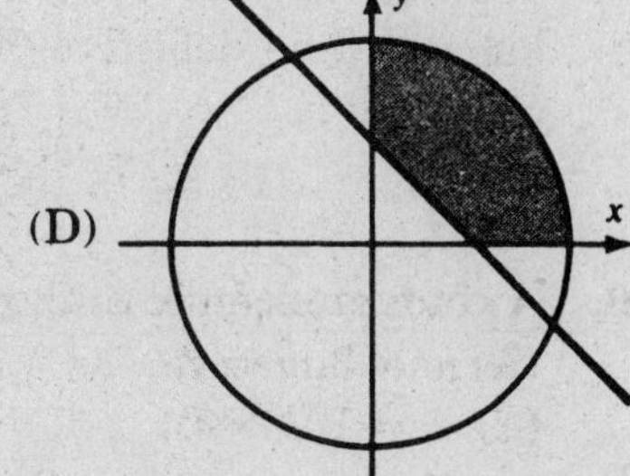

59. Which graph of points, shown below, is *not* that of a function of x?

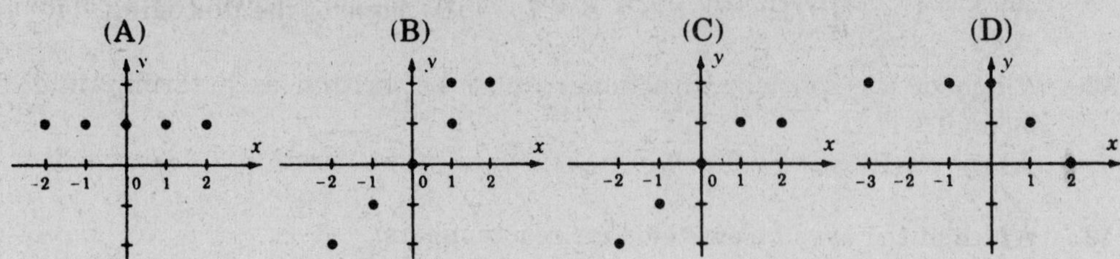

60. If $f(x) = x^2 - 3x - 1$, then $f(1 + h) - f(1)$ equals
(A) $h^2 - h - 3$ (B) $h^2 - h - 6$ (C) $h^2 + 5h$ (D) $h^2 - h$

Use this table for questions 61, 62, and 63.

*	r	s	t	u
r	r	r	r	r
s	r	s	t	u
t	r	t	r	t
u	r	u	t	s

61. $(t * t) * t$ equals
(A) r (B) s (C) t (D) u

62. The inverse of u is
(A) r (B) s (C) t (D) u

63. Which of the statements below is *not* true?
(A) The set has an identity.
(B) The operation is commutative.
(C) Every element has an inverse.
(D) The set is closed under $*$.

64. The number of different 2-digit numerals that can be formed if the digits 2, 4, 6, 7, and 9 are used, and repetitions are permitted, is
(A) 10 (B) 20 (C) 25 (D) 32

65. If the probability that an egg will hatch is 0.20, then the odds in favor of its hatching are
(A) $\frac{1}{5}$ (B) 1 to 5 (C) $\frac{1}{4}$ (D) 1 to 4

66. If a die is tossed twice the probability of getting a 4 on both tosses is
(A) $\frac{1}{36}$ (B) $\frac{1}{12}$ (C) $\frac{1}{6}$ (D) $\frac{1}{4}$

67. Two machine parts are chosen in sequence from a set of 10 of which 3 are known to be defective. The probability that both will be of acceptable quality is
(A) $\frac{21}{50}$ (B) $\frac{7}{15}$ (C) $\frac{4}{15}$ (D) $\frac{1}{15}$

68. A student received quiz grades of 10, 7, 7, 10, 6, 9, 8, 7 in a language class. Her median score was
(A) 7 (B) $7\frac{1}{2}$ (C) 8 (D) $8\frac{1}{2}$

69. A simple closed curve is one that starts and stops at the same point without passing through any point twice. Which of the following is a simple closed curve?

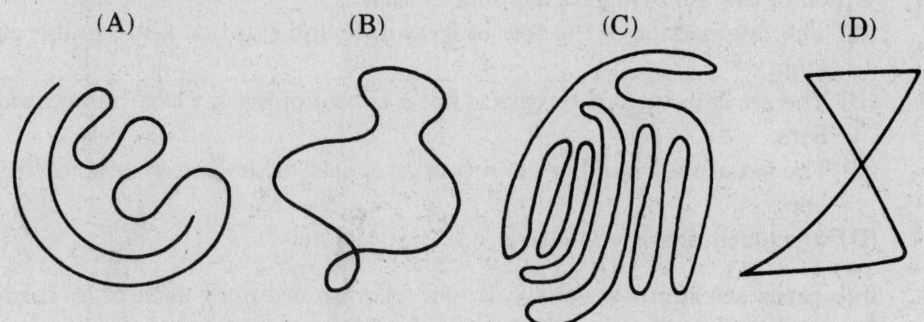

70. Suppose $q < 0$ in the equation $x^2 + px + q = 0$. Then
(A) the equation has no real roots
(B) the equation has one real root
(C) the equation has two real unequal roots
(D) the roots must both be positive

71. Which statement about real numbers is false?
(A) If $\frac{a}{b} = \frac{c}{d}$ $(bd \neq 0)$, then $a = c$ and $b = d$.
(B) If $ab \neq 0$, then neither a nor b can equal 0.
(C) If $\frac{a}{b} = c$ and $b \neq 0$, then $a = bc$.
(D) $1 \div (ab) = (1 \div a)(1 \div b)$ if $ab \neq 0$.

72. The graph is for the function
$y = f(x) =$
(A) 2^x
(B) 2^{-x}
(C) $\log_2 x$
(D) 3^{-x}

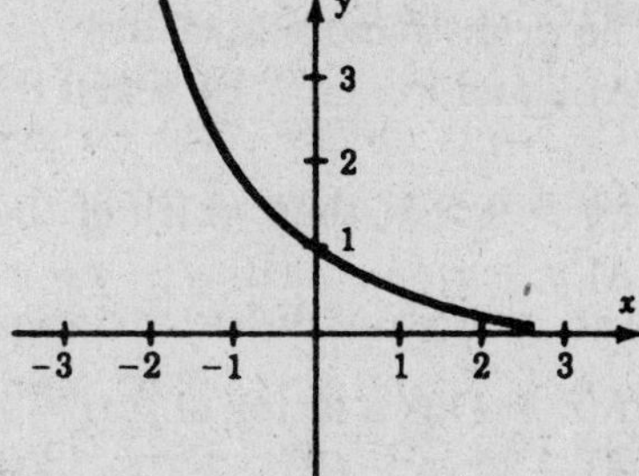

73. A test shows that 10 out of 100 bulbs are defective. If a random sample of 2 bulbs is chosen, then the probability that both are defective is
(A) $1/110$ (B) 0.01 (C) 0.02 (D) $1/10$

74. If the length of one leg of an isosceles right triangle is an integer x, then which statement is false?
(A) The hypotenuse has length $x\sqrt{2}$.
(B) The altitude to the hypotenuse equals one half the hypotenuse.
(C) The length of the hypotenuse is a rational number for appropriate values of x.
(D) The area of the triangle equals $\frac{x^2}{2}$.

75. If $23_{\text{TEN}} = n_{\text{TWO}}$, then n equals
(A) 10101 (B) 10111 (C) 11001 (D) 11011

76. The largest prime factor of 1040 is
(A) 2 (B) 5 (C) 13 (D) 17

77. Which of the following statements is false?
(A) The intersection of the sets of irrational and rational real numbers is empty.
(B) The set of natural numbers is not a subset of the set of rational numbers.
(C) The set of real numbers is a proper subset of the set of complex numbers.
(D) 0 is an integer.

78. Two cards are simultaneously drawn from an ordinary deck of 52 cards. The probability that they are *not* both of the same suit is
(A) $4/17$ (B) $5/17$ (C) $12/17$ (D) $13/17$

79. Which one of the following tables defines a function $y = f(x)$?

(A)

x	1	1	2
y	3	4	5

(B)

x	0	0	1
y	−1	1	2

(C)

x	−1	0	1	1
y	0	1	2	3

(D)

x	1	2	3	4
y	2	2	2	2

80. Which number is prime?
(A) 4 (B) 5 (C) 25 (D) 39

81. The prime factors of 96 are
(A) 2 and 3 (B) 6 and 8 (C) 2, 3, and 4 (D) 8 and 12

82. If $y > 0 > x$, then which of the following is necessarily positive?
(A) $y + x$ (B) $y - x$ (C) $y^2 + x$ (D) $x^2 - 1$

83. If $(x + 1)$ is a factor of $f(x) = x^3 - 2x^2 + 3x + d$, then $d =$
(A) −2 (B) −1 (C) 2 (D) 6

84. Let $f(x) = x + 2$ and $g(x) = x^2$; let p and q be the statements that the point (x,y) lies on the graph of f and on that of g, respectively. If $(x,y) = (1,3)$, which of the following is false?
(A) $\sim q$ (B) $p \vee q$ (C) $p \wedge q$ (D) $p \wedge \sim q$

85. For what value of k is the line $3y - kx = 6$ parallel to the line $y + 3x = 9$?
(A) 9 (B) 3 (C) −3 (D) −9

86. If $\overline{P}$ denotes the complement of Set P, then the shaded set in the Venn diagram is
(A) $\overline{V \cup W}$ (B) $\overline{V \cap W}$
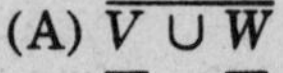
(C) $\overline{V} \cap \overline{W}$ (D) $\overline{V} \cup W$

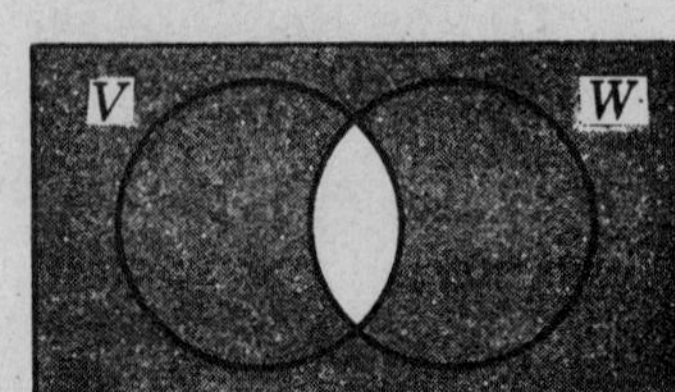

87. There are 5 identical black socks and 5 identical brown ones in a drawer. If you reach in and choose 2 socks without looking, what is the probability that you will get a matching pair?
(A) $4/9$ (B) $1/2$ (C) $2/3$ (D) 1

88. Let the operation ϕ be defined on the real numbers by $m \phi n = mn - n$. Then $1 \phi -1 =$
(A) -2 (B) -1 (C) 0 (D) 1

89. $(4 + i)(4 - i)$, where $i = \sqrt{-1}$, equals
(A) 17 (B) 15 (C) $16 + 8i$ (D) $8i$

90. $(x - 1)(3 - x)^2 > 0$ if and only if
(A) $x > 1$ (B) $1 < x < 3$ (C) $x < 1$ (D) $x > 1, x \neq 3$

ANSWER KEY AND REFERENCE CHART—SAMPLE EXAMINATION 1

Each answer in the key below is followed by a reference to the section of the book in which the topic of the question is reviewed. The topics covered on the examination are listed again below, with their reference codes and the page on which review of the topic begins. Refer to this reference-topic guide when using the answer keys for all of the sample examinations.

Topic	Reference	Page
Arithmetic	A1	303
Algebra	A2	306
Geometry	A3	310
Data Interpretation	A4	315
Sets	B1	330
Logic	B2	334
Real Number System	B3	337
Functions and Their Graphs	B4	341
Probability and Statistics	B5	346
Miscellaneous Topics	B6	352

Section I

1. A (A1)
2. C (A1)
3. D (A1)
4. C (A1)
5. A (A3)
6. B (A3)
7. A (A4)
8. A (A4)
9. B (A1)
10. A (A1)
11. D (A1)
12. A (A1)
13. A (A1)
14. C (A2)
15. D (A2)
16. B (A2)
17. A (A2)
18. C (A2)
19. B (A2)
20. B (A2)
21. C (A3)
22. A (A3)
23. A (A4)
24. D (A4)
25. C (A4)
26. C (A1)
27. B (A2)
28. D (A2)
29. C (A2)
30. B (A3)
31. B (A4)
32. A (A4)
33. D (A2)
34. A (A2)
35. D (A3)
36. C (A3)
37. C (A2)
38. B (A1)
39. B (A3)
40. C (A2)

Section II

41.	D (B1)	**51.**	D (B3)	**61.**	A (B6)	**71.**	A (B3)	**81.**	A (B3)
42.	B (B1)	**52.**	A (B3)	**62.**	D (B6)	**72.**	B (B4)	**82.**	B (B3)
43.	D (B1)	**53.**	C (B3)	**63.**	C (B6)	**73.**	A (B5)	**83.**	D (B3)
44.	C (B1)	**54.**	C (B3)	**64.**	C (B5)	**74.**	C (B3)	**84.**	C (B4)
45.	C (B2)	**55.**	A (B4)	**65.**	D (B5)	**75.**	B (B6)	**85.**	D (B4)
46.	C (B6)	**56.**	C (B4)	**66.**	A (B5)	**76.**	C (B3)	**86.**	B (B1)
47.	D (B2)	**57.**	D (B4)	**67.**	B (B5)	**77.**	B (B3)	**87.**	A (B5)
48.	A (B2)	**58.**	D (B4)	**68.**	B (B5)	**78.**	D (B5)	**88.**	C (B6)
49.	D (B2)	**59.**	B (B4)	**69.**	C (B3)	**79.**	D (B4)	**89.**	A (B6)
50.	B (B2)	**60.**	D (B4)	**70.**	C (B3)	**80.**	B (B3)	**90.**	D (B3)

SCORING CHART—SAMPLE EXAMINATION I

After you have scored your Sample Examination 1, enter the results in the chart below; then transfer your Raw Score to the Progress Chart on page 14.

Total Test	Number Right	Number Wrong	Number Omitted	Raw Score
Section I: 40				
Section II: 50				
Total: 90				

ANSWER EXPLANATIONS—SAMPLE EXAMINATION 1

Section I

1. A. $3^2 = 3 \cdot 3 = 9$; $2^3 = 2 \cdot 2 \cdot 2 = 8$.

2. C. $3/4 \div 3 = 3/4 \times 1/3 = 1/4 = 0.25$.

3. D. There are an infinite number of fractions between $1/3$ and $1/5$; one of them is $1/4$.

4. C. Rewrite the quantity in Column A as $(0.99)(1.1)(0.1)$.

5. A. $m(\angle Y) > 180° - 110°$ (or $70°$).

6. B. $y = x\sqrt{3} \approx 1.7x < 2x$.

7. A. The range was greatest in 1966 and appears to be at least 250 points.

8. A. The low Dow-Jones average was approximately 880 in 1972; the high for 1970 was approximately 850.

9. B. $1/3$ of $35 \approx 12$.

10. A. $2.9 \times 10^{-4} = 0.00029 > 0.000029$. The negative exponent tells us to move the decimal point 4 places to the left.

11. D. Information is needed about the *number* of tests that averaged to 76.

12. A. $2\,3/10 = 2.3 = 230\%$.

13. A. $\sqrt{4} + \sqrt{9} = 2 + 3 = 5$; $\sqrt{13} < \sqrt{16} = 4$.

14. C. $2s - (r + t) = 2(1) - (-1 + 3) = 2 - 2 = 0$.

15. D. If $x \geq 0$, then $|x| = x$; otherwise $|x| = -x$. Test this with $x = 3$, then with $x = -3$.

16. B. $x^2 + 2x - 3 = (x + 3)(x - 1) = 0$ for $x = -3$ and $x = 1$. The sum of the roots is -2; the product is -3.

17. A. $3 \times (2 + 8) = 3 \times 10 = 30$; $3 \times 2 + 8 = (3 \times 2) + 8 = 6 + 8 = 14$.

18. C. $\frac{x^r}{x^s} = x^{r-s}$, which equals x^0 if $r = s$.

19. B. Substitute $x = y + 3$ in the first equation. If $5(y + 3) - y = 11$, then $4y = -4$ and $y = -1$.

20. B. The ratio of green marbles to the total number is $1:n$, where $n > 2$. Therefore $\frac{1}{2} > \frac{1}{n}$.

21. C. The sum of the interior angles is 360°.

22. A. $24:360 = 1:15 > 1:16$.

23. A. For the period 1946-1960, the average annual percentage increase in the CPI was 3.0; for 1965-1966, it was 2.9.

24. D. No information is given about the index for the year 1966.

25. C. The average annual percentage increase for all services decreased from 3.9 for 1946-1960 to 2.0 for 1960-1965.

26. C. $4.05 = 4^5/_{100} = 4^1/_{20} = {}^{81}/_{20}$.

27. B. $(y^2 - 3y + 2) - (2y^2 + 3y - 2) = y^2 - 3y + 2 - 2y^2 - 3y + 2$
$= -y^2 - 6y + 4$.

28. D. Let the numbers be $6x$ and $11x$. Then $11x - 6x$ or $5x = 15$, and $x = 3$. So the smaller number is 6(3), or 18.

29. C. To get 0.0328 from 3.28 we must move the decimal point *two* places to the *left*. So $k = -2$.

30. B. Since the triangle is isosceles, $m = n$. Also, $m(\angle Q) = 180 - 2(70)$, or 40°. Therefore m and n both exceed q.

31. B. $176 \div 5 \approx 35$.

32. A. $\frac{563 - 281}{281} = \frac{282}{281} \approx 1$; the answer is 100%.

33. D. $(5x + 3)(2x - 3) = (5x)(2x) + (5x)(-3) + (3)(2x) + (3)(-3)$
$= 10x^2 - 9x - 9$.

34. A. In the form $y = mx + b$ (where m is the slope and b the y-intercept), we get $y = \frac{2}{3}x + 3$.

35. D. If the dimensions of the original box are l, w, h, then the ratio of the volumes (larger to smaller) is $(2l)(2w)(2h):lwh = 8:1$.

36. C. If r is the radius, the formulas are $A = \pi r^2$ and $C = 2\pi r$. Since $\pi r^2 = 4\pi$, $r = 2$ and $C = 2\pi(2) = 4\pi$.

37. C. $3^2 - 3^0 - 3^{-2} = 9 - 1 - \frac{1}{9} = 8 - \frac{1}{9} = 7\frac{8}{9}$.

38. B. $(0.02) \times (0.004) = 0.00008$, where we counted off as many decimal places in the answer as in the factors combined.

39. B. The point $(2, -1)$ is 2 units to the right of the y-axis and one unit below the x-axis.

40. C. The average speed equals total distance divided by total time.

$$(15 + 60) \div (\frac{1}{2} + 1) = 75 \div \frac{3}{2} = 75 \times \frac{2}{3} = 50 \text{ mph}.$$

Section II

41. D. $R \cap S$ contains elements both in R and in S.

42. B. $x^3 - x^2 - 2x = x(x^2 - x - 2) = x(x + 1)(x - 2)$

43. D. $R \times R$, the Cartesian product, consists only of ordered pairs. Note that (A), (B), (C) are all true.

44. C. $\{1,2,3,\ldots,100\}$ has 2^{100} subsets, a large but finite number.

45. C. A restatement is "He does not wear braces and he does not wear glasses."

46. C. $\log_2 2^x = x \log_2 2 = x \cdot 1 = x$.

47. D. With (A) or (B) we would verify the statement for only some pairs of rational numbers; (D) is impossible to do since the set of rationals is infinite.
48. A. $\sim(\forall_x, p_x) = \exists_x, \sim p_x$.
49. D. The conditional $p \rightarrow q$ is defined as true whenever p is false.
50. B. A counterexample cites values of a and b that satisfy the hypothesis but not the conclusion. Although $(-2)^2 > (-1)^2$, $-2 \not> -1$
51. D. $|b-1| = \begin{cases} b-1 & \text{if } b \geqq 1 \\ 1-b & \text{if } b < 1 \end{cases}$
52. A. Every fraction whose denominator contains only the factors 2 or 5 can be written as a terminating (nonrepeating) decimal.
53. C. (A), (B), and (D) are all false statements.
54. C. If the irrational numbers are $\sqrt{2}$ and $-\sqrt{2}$, for instance, then their sum, product, and quotient are all rational.
55. A. $f(-x) = 2(-x)^2 - 3(-x) + 2 = 2x^2 + 3x + 2$.
56. C. Here are the graphs:

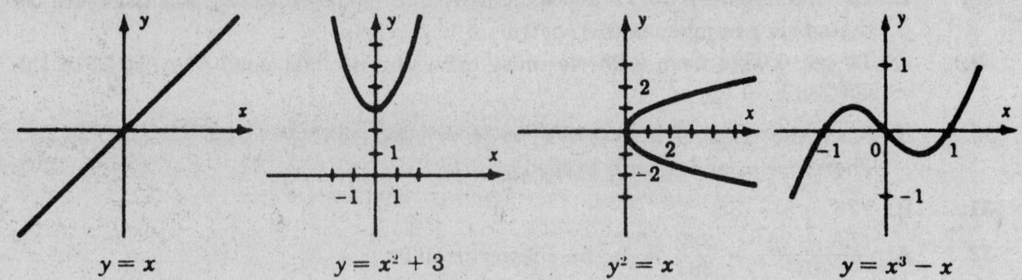

57. D. Since $g(0) = \sqrt{4} = 2$, $f(g(0)) = f(2) = 2 + 4/2 = 4$.
58. D. The inequalities $x \geqslant 0$, $y \geqslant 0$ restrict the graph to the first quadrant.
59. B. For each x in the domain of a function, there must be a *unique* y.
60. D. $f(1) = 1^2 - 3 - 1 = -3$. $f(1+h) - f(1) = (1+h)^2 - 3(1+h) - 1 - (-3)$
$= 1 + 2h + h^2 - 3 - 3h - 1 + 3$
$= h^2 - h$.
61. A. $(t * t) * t = r * t = r$.
62. D. s is the identity element and $u * u = s$.
63. C. t has no inverse under $*$.
64. C. The first digit may be one of five and for each of these so may the second be one of five, yielding $5 \cdot 5$.
65. D. If the probability of an event is p, the odds in its favor are the ratio of p to $(1-p)$. Here it is 0.2 to 0.8, or 1 to 4.
66. A. The probability equals $1/6 \times 1/6$.
67. B. The probability is ${}_7C_2/{}_{10}C_2$ or $\binom{7}{2}/\binom{10}{2}$, or $\frac{7 \cdot 6}{10 \cdot 9}$, which equals $7/15$.
68. B. The median score of the arranged grades 6, 7, 7, 7, 8, 9, 10, 10 is halfway between the two middle grades, 7 and 8.
69. C. (A) starts and stops at different points. Each curve in (B) and (D) goes through one point twice.
70. C. If $q < 0$, then the discriminant $p^2 - 4q > 0$; therefore the roots are real. Note also that $q < 0$ implies that the roots have opposite signs.
71. A. To show that (A) is false, let $\frac{a}{b}$ be $\frac{2}{3}$ and $\frac{c}{d}$ be $\frac{4}{6}$.
72. B. Check out some "easy" points: (0,1), (1,1/2), (−1,2). All three lie only on $y = 2^{-x}$.
73. A. The probability that the first bulb is defective is $10/100$, that the next one is defective is $9/99$. Multiply these.

74. C. Here is a sketch:

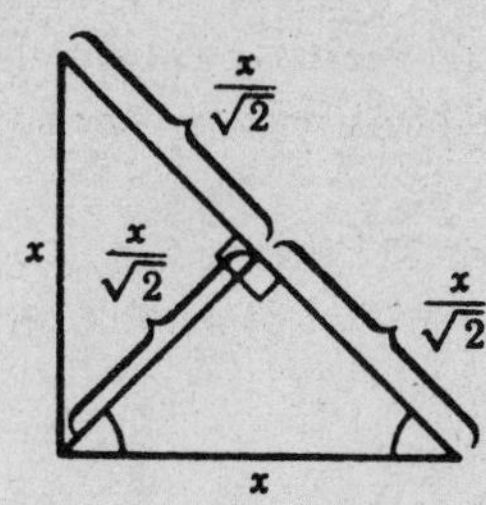

75. B. $23_{TEN} = 16 + 4 + 2 + 1 = 2^4 + 2^2 + 2^1 + 2^0 = 10111_{TWO}$.

76. C. $1040 = 16 \cdot 65 = 2^4 \cdot 5 \cdot 13$.

77. B. (A), (C), and (D) are all true statements.

78. D. One of the cards may be any of 52 (selected from 52 cards); the other (selected from the remaining 51 cards) can be one of 39. The answer is $\frac{52}{52} \cdot \frac{39}{51} = \frac{13}{17}$.

79. D. Remember that if f is a function from a set X into a set Y, each element of X must correspond to a *unique* element in Y. In (A), (B), and (C) there are *two* different images of a single element in the domain.

80. B. A prime number has only 1 and itself as factors. Since $4 = 2 \cdot 2$, $25 = 5 \cdot 5$, and $39 = 3 \cdot 13$, 4, 25, and 39 are composite numbers.

81. A. $96 = 32 \times 3 = 2^5 \cdot 3$; the prime factors are 2 and 3.

82. B. Since $x < 0$, $-x > 0$. Each of the numbers in (A), (B), (D) *can*, for appropriate choices of x and y, be negative or zero.

83. D. Since $(x + 1)$ is a factor of $f(x)$, $f(-1) = 0$. So $(-1)^3 - 2(-1)^2 + 3(-1) + d = 0$ and $d = 6$.

84. C. The point (1,3) lies on the graph of f but not on the graph of g. So p is true, q false. Only $p \wedge q$ is false.

85. D. The slope of $y + 3x = 9$ or $y = -3x + 9$ is -3. Therefore $\frac{k}{3}$ must equal -3.

86. B. The unshaded region is $V \cap W$. The complement is the shaded region.

87. A. You may initially choose any sock from the set of 10, but then, to obtain a matching pair, there are only 4 choices among the remaining 9 socks. The probability is therefore $\frac{10}{10} \cdot \frac{4}{9}$ or $\frac{4}{9}$.

88. C. $1 \phi -1 = 1(-1) - (-1) = -1 + 1 = 0$.

89. A. $(4 + i)(4 - i) = 16 - i^2 = 16 - (-1) = 16 + 1 = 17$.

90. D. $(x - 1)(3 - x)^2 > 0$ if and only if $x - 1 > 0$ and $3 - x \neq 0$; i.e., if and only if $x > 1$, $x \neq 3$.

ANSWER SHEET — MATHEMATICS/SAMPLE EXAMINATION 2

Section I

1. Ⓐ Ⓑ Ⓒ Ⓓ Ⓔ
2. Ⓐ Ⓑ Ⓒ Ⓓ Ⓔ
3. Ⓐ Ⓑ Ⓒ Ⓓ Ⓔ
4. Ⓐ Ⓑ Ⓒ Ⓓ Ⓔ
5. Ⓐ Ⓑ Ⓒ Ⓓ Ⓔ
6. Ⓐ Ⓑ Ⓒ Ⓓ Ⓔ
7. Ⓐ Ⓑ Ⓒ Ⓓ Ⓔ
8. Ⓐ Ⓑ Ⓒ Ⓓ Ⓔ
9. Ⓐ Ⓑ Ⓒ Ⓓ Ⓔ
10. Ⓐ Ⓑ Ⓒ Ⓓ Ⓔ
11. Ⓐ Ⓑ Ⓒ Ⓓ Ⓔ
12. Ⓐ Ⓑ Ⓒ Ⓓ Ⓔ
13. Ⓐ Ⓑ Ⓒ Ⓓ Ⓔ
14. Ⓐ Ⓑ Ⓒ Ⓓ Ⓔ
15. Ⓐ Ⓑ Ⓒ Ⓓ Ⓔ
16. Ⓐ Ⓑ Ⓒ Ⓓ Ⓔ
17. Ⓐ Ⓑ Ⓒ Ⓓ Ⓔ
18. Ⓐ Ⓑ Ⓒ Ⓓ Ⓔ
19. Ⓐ Ⓑ Ⓒ Ⓓ Ⓔ
20. Ⓐ Ⓑ Ⓒ Ⓓ Ⓔ
21. Ⓐ Ⓑ Ⓒ Ⓓ Ⓔ
22. Ⓐ Ⓑ Ⓒ Ⓓ Ⓔ
23. Ⓐ Ⓑ Ⓒ Ⓓ Ⓔ
24. Ⓐ Ⓑ Ⓒ Ⓓ Ⓔ
25. Ⓐ Ⓑ Ⓒ Ⓓ Ⓔ
26. Ⓐ Ⓑ Ⓒ Ⓓ Ⓔ
27. Ⓐ Ⓑ Ⓒ Ⓓ Ⓔ
28. Ⓐ Ⓑ Ⓒ Ⓓ Ⓔ
29. Ⓐ Ⓑ Ⓒ Ⓓ Ⓔ
30. Ⓐ Ⓑ Ⓒ Ⓓ Ⓔ
31. Ⓐ Ⓑ Ⓒ Ⓓ Ⓔ
32. Ⓐ Ⓑ Ⓒ Ⓓ Ⓔ
33. Ⓐ Ⓑ Ⓒ Ⓓ Ⓔ
34. Ⓐ Ⓑ Ⓒ Ⓓ Ⓔ
35. Ⓐ Ⓑ Ⓒ Ⓓ Ⓔ
36. Ⓐ Ⓑ Ⓒ Ⓓ Ⓔ
37. Ⓐ Ⓑ Ⓒ Ⓓ Ⓔ
38. Ⓐ Ⓑ Ⓒ Ⓓ Ⓔ
39. Ⓐ Ⓑ Ⓒ Ⓓ Ⓔ
40. Ⓐ Ⓑ Ⓒ Ⓓ Ⓔ

Section II

41. Ⓐ Ⓑ Ⓒ Ⓓ Ⓔ
42. Ⓐ Ⓑ Ⓒ Ⓓ Ⓔ
43. Ⓐ Ⓑ Ⓒ Ⓓ Ⓔ
44. Ⓐ Ⓑ Ⓒ Ⓓ Ⓔ
45. Ⓐ Ⓑ Ⓒ Ⓓ Ⓔ
46. Ⓐ Ⓑ Ⓒ Ⓓ Ⓔ
47. Ⓐ Ⓑ Ⓒ Ⓓ Ⓔ
48. Ⓐ Ⓑ Ⓒ Ⓓ Ⓔ
49. Ⓐ Ⓑ Ⓒ Ⓓ Ⓔ
50. Ⓐ Ⓑ Ⓒ Ⓓ Ⓔ
51. Ⓐ Ⓑ Ⓒ Ⓓ Ⓔ
52. Ⓐ Ⓑ Ⓒ Ⓓ Ⓔ
53. Ⓐ Ⓑ Ⓒ Ⓓ Ⓔ
54. Ⓐ Ⓑ Ⓒ Ⓓ Ⓔ
55. Ⓐ Ⓑ Ⓒ Ⓓ Ⓔ
56. Ⓐ Ⓑ Ⓒ Ⓓ Ⓔ
57. Ⓐ Ⓑ Ⓒ Ⓓ Ⓔ
58. Ⓐ Ⓑ Ⓒ Ⓓ Ⓔ
59. Ⓐ Ⓑ Ⓒ Ⓓ Ⓔ
60. Ⓐ Ⓑ Ⓒ Ⓓ Ⓔ
61. Ⓐ Ⓑ Ⓒ Ⓓ Ⓔ
62. Ⓐ Ⓑ Ⓒ Ⓓ Ⓔ
63. Ⓐ Ⓑ Ⓒ Ⓓ Ⓔ
64. Ⓐ Ⓑ Ⓒ Ⓓ Ⓔ
65. Ⓐ Ⓑ Ⓒ Ⓓ Ⓔ
66. Ⓐ Ⓑ Ⓒ Ⓓ Ⓔ
67. Ⓐ Ⓑ Ⓒ Ⓓ Ⓔ
68. Ⓐ Ⓑ Ⓒ Ⓓ Ⓔ
69. Ⓐ Ⓑ Ⓒ Ⓓ Ⓔ
70. Ⓐ Ⓑ Ⓒ Ⓓ Ⓔ
71. Ⓐ Ⓑ Ⓒ Ⓓ Ⓔ
72. Ⓐ Ⓑ Ⓒ Ⓓ Ⓔ
73. Ⓐ Ⓑ Ⓒ Ⓓ Ⓔ
74. Ⓐ Ⓑ Ⓒ Ⓓ Ⓔ
75. Ⓐ Ⓑ Ⓒ Ⓓ Ⓔ
76. Ⓐ Ⓑ Ⓒ Ⓓ Ⓔ
77. Ⓐ Ⓑ Ⓒ Ⓓ Ⓔ
78. Ⓐ Ⓑ Ⓒ Ⓓ Ⓔ
79. Ⓐ Ⓑ Ⓒ Ⓓ Ⓔ
80. Ⓐ Ⓑ Ⓒ Ⓓ Ⓔ
81. Ⓐ Ⓑ Ⓒ Ⓓ Ⓔ
82. Ⓐ Ⓑ Ⓒ Ⓓ Ⓔ
83. Ⓐ Ⓑ Ⓒ Ⓓ Ⓔ
84. Ⓐ Ⓑ Ⓒ Ⓓ Ⓔ
85. Ⓐ Ⓑ Ⓒ Ⓓ Ⓔ
86. Ⓐ Ⓑ Ⓒ Ⓓ Ⓔ
87. Ⓐ Ⓑ Ⓒ Ⓓ Ⓔ
88. Ⓐ Ⓑ Ⓒ Ⓓ Ⓔ
89. Ⓐ Ⓑ Ⓒ Ⓓ Ⓔ
90. Ⓐ Ⓑ Ⓒ Ⓓ Ⓔ

SAMPLE EXAMINATION 2

Section I: Basic Skills and Concepts

Directions to questions 1–25: Each of these questions consists of two quantities, one in Column A and one in Column B. You are to compare the two quantities and on the answer sheet blacken space

A if the quantity in Column A is greater;
B if the quantity in Column B is greater;
C if the two quantities are equal;
D if the relationship cannot be determined from the information given

Notes:

1. In certain questions, information concerning one or both of the quantities to be compared is centered above the two columns.
2. A symbol that appears in both columns represents the same thing in Column A as it does in Column B.
3. Letters such as x, n, and k stand for real numbers.

	COLUMN A	COLUMN B
1.	simple interest on \$150 at $4\frac{1}{2}\%$ for 2 years	\$13.50
2.	the reciprocal of $2\frac{1}{3}$	0.5
	An average of 50 on a battery of 5 objective tests, with range 0 to 80, is considered passing. Carly's average on 4 tests is 44.	
3.	score Carly must get on fifth test to pass the battery	72
4.	cost per pound of peaches if 3 pounds cost 55¢	18¢
	An airline allows 44 pounds of luggage. One kilogram (kg) ≈ 2.2 pounds.	
5.	the weight limit	21 kg
	There are three landmarks, A, B, and C, in a big city. A and B are 3 miles apart, and B and C are 4 miles apart.	
6.	distance between A and C	5.1 miles
	A 12-foot board is cut into two pieces in the ratio 7 : 3.	
7.	length of the smaller piece	3 ft. 6 in.
	$m = 3, n = -2$	
8.	$(m + n)^2$	$(2n + m)^2$
	$xy \neq 0$	
9.	$\lvert x + y \rvert$	$\lvert x \rvert + \lvert y \rvert$
10.	y	y^2
11.	$2^0 + 2^{1/2} + 2^{-1}$	3
12.	$(2m - 1)(2m + 1)$	$m^4 - 1$

	COLUMN A	COLUMN B

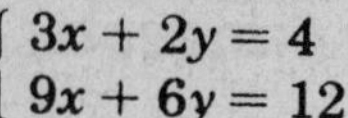

$$\begin{cases} 3x + 2y = 4 \\ 9x + 6y = 12 \end{cases}$$

13. x — y

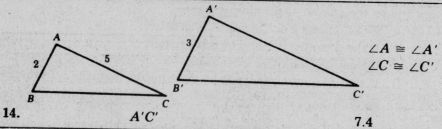

$\angle A \cong \angle A'$
$\angle C \cong \angle C'$

14. $A'C'$ — 7.4

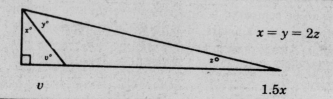

$x = y = 2z$

15. v — $1.5x$

The measures of two complementary angles are in the ratio 5 : 3.

16. the smaller angle — 35°

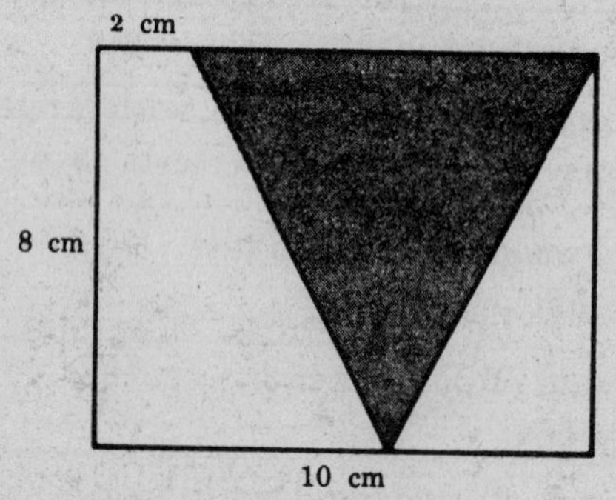

The outer figure is a rectangle.

17. area of unshaded region — 48 cm^2

The radius of a circle is doubled.

18. ratio of circumference of new circle to that of old — 2 : 1

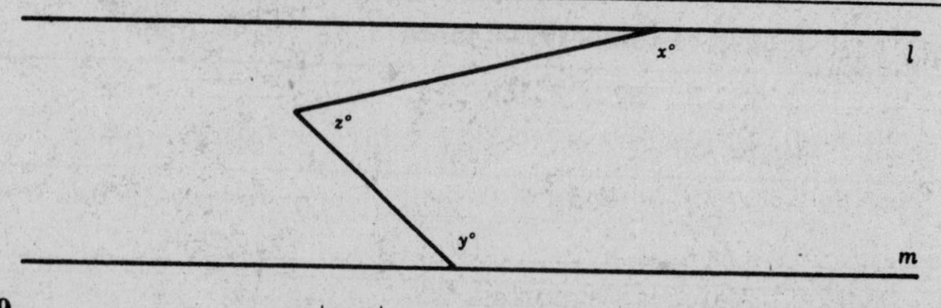

$l \parallel m$

19. $x + y + z$ — 360

$1\frac{1}{4}$ inches on a map = 18 miles; $3\frac{3}{4}$ inches on the map = k miles.

20. k — 54

	COLUMN A	COLUMN B

Use this bar graph for questions 21 and 22.

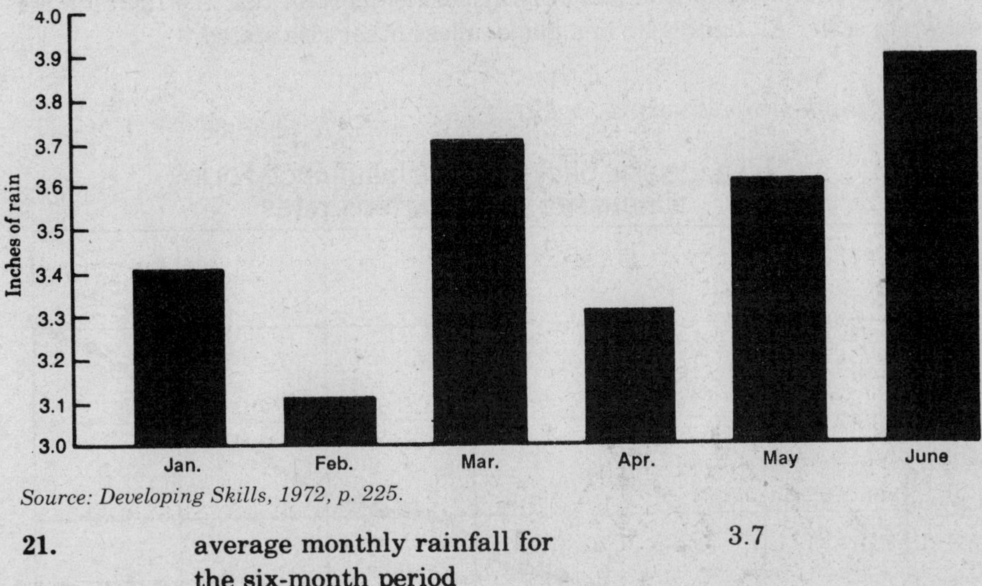

Source: Developing Skills, 1972, p. 225.

	COLUMN A	COLUMN B
21.	average monthly rainfall for the six-month period	3.7
22.	difference, in inches, of average monthly rainfall between least and greatest monthly rainfalls	0.7

Use these circle graphs for questions 23, 24, and 25.

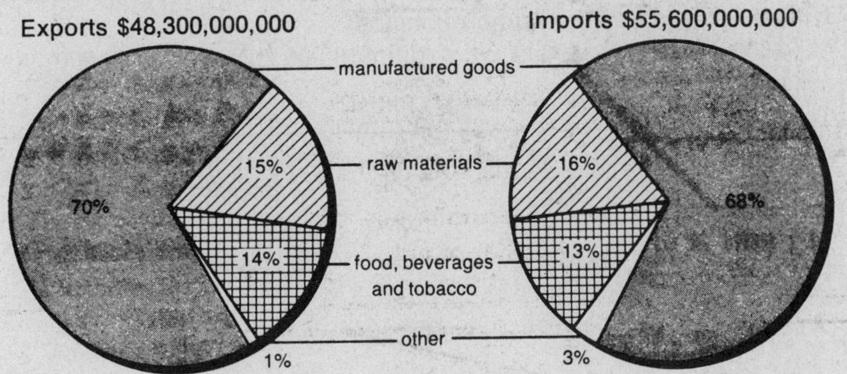

	COLUMN A	COLUMN B
23.	raw materials exported	raw materials imported
24.	manufactured goods exported, in billions of dollars	33
25.	foods, beverages, tobacco imported, in billions of dollars	8

Directions for questions 26–40: For these questions, indicate the correct answer in the appropriate space on the answer sheet.

Note: Figures that accompany the following problems are intended to provide information useful in answering them. The figures are drawn as accurately as possible *except* when it is stated in a specific question that the figure is not drawn to scale. All figures lie in a plane unless otherwise stated.

Use this graph for questions 26 and 27.

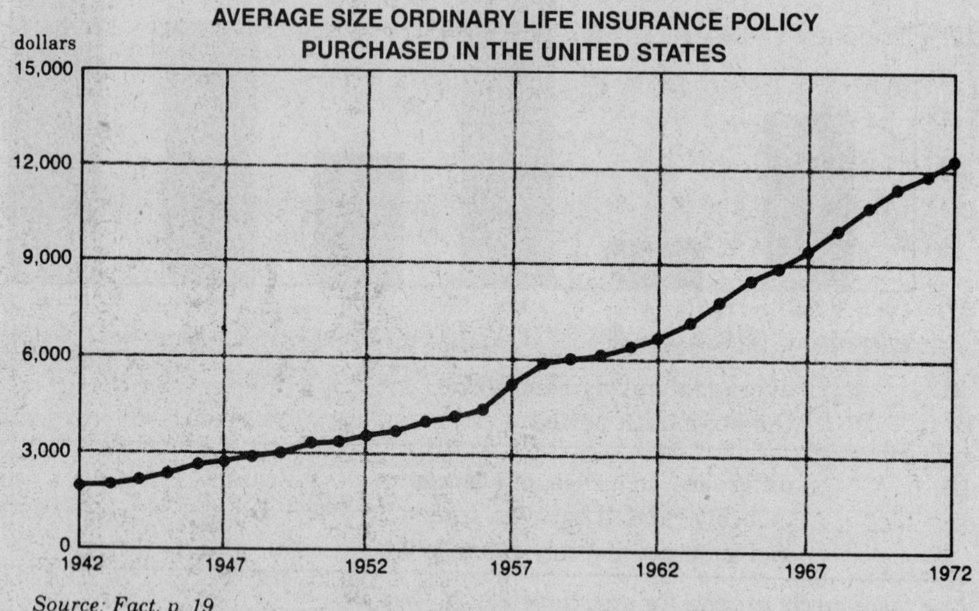

Source: Fact, p. 19.

26. The average size of an ordinary life insurance policy purchased in the United States in 1971 was approximately
(A) \$6000 (B) \$9000 (C) \$10,000 (D) \$12,000

27. The ratio of the average size of an ordinary life insurance policy purchased in the U.S. in 1962 to that purchased in 1972 is approximately equal to
(A) 1 : 3 (B) 1 : 2 (C) 2 : 3 (D) 2 : 1

28. $1\frac{1}{5} =$
(A) 1.2% (B) 102% (C) 120% (D) 125%

29. What percent profit was made on a motorcycle that was bought for \$200 and sold for \$210?
(A) 5 (B) $7\frac{1}{2}$ (C) 10 (D) 20

30. The area of a square is 100. The length of its diagonal is approximately
(A) 10 (B) 12 (C) 14 (D) 20

31. $(3.2) \times (0.01) =$
(A) 0.0032 (B) 0.032 (C) 0.32 (D) 320

32. 8 is what percent of 6?
(A) 1.25 (B) 75 (C) 125 (D) $133\frac{1}{3}$

33. Which number is biggest?
(A) $|3 - 1|$ (B) $|-3| + 1$ (C) $|-3|$ (D) $1 - |3|$

34. $2^{-3} =$
(A) -8 (B) -6 (C) $-\frac{1}{8}$ (D) $\frac{1}{8}$

35. The line $3x + 4y - 6 = 0$ cuts the x-axis at $x =$
(A) -2 (B) $-1\frac{1}{2}$ (C) 2 (D) 3

36. The factors of $3x^2 + 5x - 2$ are
(A) $(3x + 1)$ and $(x + 2)$ (B) $(3x - 1)$ and $(x + 2)$
(C) $(3x + 1)$ and $(x - 2)$ (D) $(3x - 1)$ and $(x - 2)$

37. $(2 + \sqrt{3})(3 - \sqrt{3}) =$
(A) 3 (B) $6 + \sqrt{3}$ (C) $3 - \sqrt{3}$ (D) $3 + \sqrt{3}$

38. If $x + 1 < 3x + 5$, then
(A) $x > -2$ (B) $x < -2$ (C) $x < 2$ (D) $x > 2$

39. If $x \neq -3$, then $\dfrac{1}{x + 3} - \dfrac{1}{3} =$

40. The product of the roots of the equation $x^2 - x - 30 = 0$ is
(A) -1 (B) -30 (C) 1 (D) 30

Section II: Content

Directions: For each of the following problems, indicate the correct answer in the appropriate space on the answer sheet.

Note: Figures that accompany problems in this part are intended to provide information useful in solving the problems. They are drawn as accurately as possible *except* when it is stated in a specific problem that the figure is not drawn to scale. All figures lie in a plane unless otherwise stated.

41. The shaded region in the Venn diagram is for the set
(A) $R \cup (S \cap T)$
(B) $R \cap (S \cup T)$
(C) $(R \cup S) \cap T$
(D) $R \cup (S \cup T)$

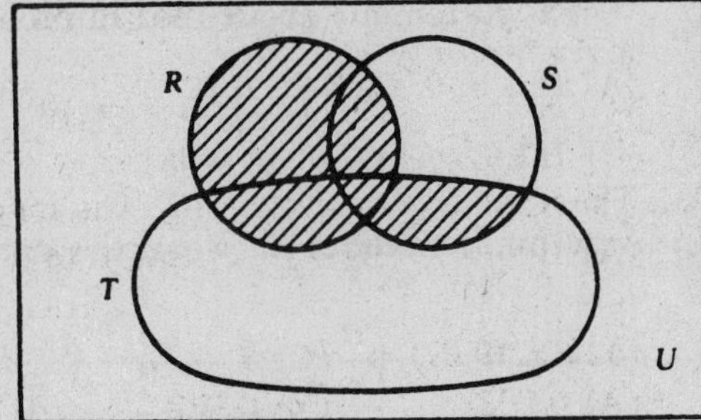

42. If Z, Q, R denote respectively the sets of integers, of rationals, and of reals, then each point of the Cartesian plane corresponds to an element of
(A) $R \times R$ (B) $Q \times Q$ (C) $Z \times Z$ (D) R

43. Which of the sets below is *not* a subset of Q, where $Q = \{x \mid x \text{ is a prime number}\}$?
(A) $\{2\}$ (B) $\{2,3,51\}$ (C) $\{5,7,11,47\}$ (D) $\{2,3,97\}$

44. If $P = \{x : x^2 - 2x - 3 = 0\}$ and $Q = \{x \mid x^2 + x = 0\}$, then $P \cap Q$ equals
(A) $\emptyset$ (B) $\{0,-1,3\}$ (C) $\{1\}$ (D) $\{-1\}$

45. A statement with the truth table shown on the right is
(A) $\sim(p \wedge q)$ (B) $p \vee \sim q$
(C) $\sim q$ (D) $\sim(p \vee q)$

p	q	
T	T	F
T	F	T
F	T	F
F	F	T

46. The negation of $s \rightarrow t$ is
(A) $s \wedge \sim t$ (B) $\sim s \rightarrow t$ (C) $\sim s \wedge \sim t$ (D) $t \rightarrow \sim s$

47. Let s be "Sam is conscientious" and let t be "Sam is bright." Then symbolically the statement "Sam is bright but not conscientious" is
(A) $\sim s \vee t$ (B) $\sim s \wedge t$ (C) $s \vee \sim t$ (D) $\sim(s \wedge t)$

48. A statement equivalent to "If a snuggy is groobly, then it is flissy" is
(A) If a snuggy is not groobly, then it is not flissy
(B) If a snuggy is not flissy, then it is not groobly
(C) If a snuggy is flissy, then it is groobly
(D) A snuggy is groobly if and only if it is flissy

49. If a, b, and c in the equation $ax^2 + bx + c = 0$ are all positive real numbers, then which statement below is true of every such equation?
(A) $b^2 - 4ac$ is negative.
(B) The equation has no real roots.
(C) The equation has no positive root.
(D) $b^2 - 4ac$ equals zero.

50. Consider the sequence of fractions

$$1/2;\ 2/3,\ 3/5,\ 5/8,\ 8/13,\ \ldots$$

If a term in the sequence is denoted by $\frac{p}{q}$, then the next term is
(A) $\frac{p+n}{q+n}$ (B) $\frac{p+3}{q+5}$ (C) $\frac{p+q}{p+2q}$ (D) $\frac{q}{p+q}$

51. Which statement about real numbers is false?
(A) If $a \neq 0$, then $a^2 > 0$. (B) If $a > 0$, then $\frac{1}{a} > 0$.
(C) If $a^2 > b^2$ then $|a| > |b|$. (D) If $a < b$, then $a^2 < b^2$.

52. A rational number between the rational numbers p and q, for all p and q, is
(A) $\frac{p-q}{2}$ (B) $\frac{p+q}{2}$ (C) $\frac{q-p}{2}$ (D) $\frac{p}{2}$

53. Which of the numbers below can*not* be represented by a repeating decimal? decimal?
(A) $^{11}/_{9}$ (B) $^{23}/_{7}$ (C) $\sqrt{3}$ (D) $4^{1}/_{3}$

54. Points in the region enclosed by the parabola and line, shown in the diagram, satisfy the inequalities
(A) $y < 1 + x, y < x^2$
(B) $y > x^2, y < x + 1$
(C) $y > 1 + x, y < x^2$
(D) $y > x^2, y > 1 + x$

[The dotted line segment and dotted curve indicate that the boundaries of the region are excluded.]

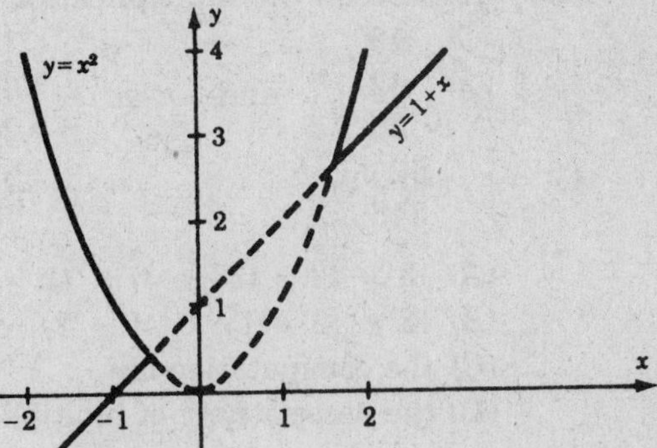

55. Which equation has no real root?
(A) $x^3 + x^2 = 0$ (B) $4x^4 + 1 = 0$
(C) $2x^4 - 1 = 0$ (D) $\frac{1}{x} + 1 = 0$

56. The inverse of the function $y = x + 3$ is
(A) $y = 3 - x$ (B) $y = \frac{1}{x + 3}$
(C) $y = 3x$ (D) $y = x - 3$

57. Which statement about the intersection of a cubic curve and a line is false?
(A) They need have no intersection.
(B) They intersect at least once.
(C) They may intersect twice.
(D) They cannot intersect more than three times.

58. If "$m \equiv n \bmod 5$" means that $(m - n)$ is divisible by 5, which statement below is false?
(A) $19 \equiv 12 \bmod 5$ (B) $13 \equiv 3 \bmod 5$
(C) $17 \equiv 2 \bmod 5$ (D) $3 \equiv 3 \bmod 5$

59. If a die is tossed, the probability that it shows a number greater than or equal to 2 is
(A) $^1/_3$ (B) $^1/_2$ (C) $^2/_3$ (D) $^5/_6$

60. Suppose 3 of a dozen apples are bruised and 2 are chosen at random from the dozen. The probability that both are bruised is
(A) $^1/_{22}$ (B) $^1/_{11}$ (C) $^1/_6$ (D) $^1/_4$

61. For the data 3, 3, 7, 11, 11, 13, 15 the difference (median minus mean) is
(A) 0 (B) 2 (C) 3 (D) 5

62. $\{x : -1 \leqq x \leqq 3\} \cap \{x : 0 \leqq x \leqq 5\}$ equals
(A) $\{x : -1 < x \leqq 5\}$ (B) $\{x : 0 < x \leqq 5\}$
(C) $\{x : 0 \leqq x \leqq 3\}$ (D) the empty set

63. You have randomly drawn 4 cards from a shuffled deck (of 52 cards—no jokers): an ace, a king, a seven, and a three. The probability that the next card you draw will give you a pair is
(A) $^1/_{16}$ (B) $^3/_{13}$ (C) $^1/_4$ (D) $^1/_3$

64. The reason the multiplication 13 × 42 is to be performed

as
$$\begin{array}{r} 13 \\ \underline{42} \\ 26 \\ \underline{52} \\ 546 \end{array}$$
and *not* as
$$\begin{array}{r} 13 \\ \underline{42} \\ 26 \\ \underline{52} \\ 78 \end{array}$$
is

(A) 13 × 42 = (10 + 3) × 42
(B) 13 × 42 = 13 × (40 + 2)
(C) the commutative law
(D) the associativity of multiplication

65. Which set is *not* closed under the binary operation $*$, if $m * n = m^n$?
(A) the set of positive integers
(B) the set of even positive integers
(C) the set of odd positive integers
(D) the set of nonzero integers

66. If $f(x) = 2x + 1$ and $g(x) = x^2 - 3$, then $g(f(x)) =$
(A) $4x^2 + 4x - 2$ (B) $2x^2 - 5$
(C) $4x^2 + 2x - 2$ (D) $2x^2 - 2$

67. The probability of obtaining all heads or tails when three coins are tossed simultaneously is
(A) $^1/_6$ (B) $^1/_8$ (C) $^1/_4$ (D) $^1/_2$

68. Which equation has no rational root?
(A) $x^2 - 1 = 0$ (B) $x^2 - 2 = 0$
(C) $x^2 - 4x + 4 = 0$ (D) $x^2 - x - 2 = 0$

69.

−4 −3 −2 −1 0 1 2 3 4 x

The graph above represents which set?
(A) $\{x : x < 0 \text{ or } x > 3\}$ (B) $\{x : 0 < x < 3\}$
(C) $\{x : x \leq 0 \text{ or } x \geq 3\}$ (D) $\{x : 0 > x > 3\}$

70. If $f(x) = \log_2 x$ and $g(x) = 2^x$, then their graphs are symmetric to the
(A) origin (B) x-axis (C) y-axis (D) line $y = x$

71. The largest value of the function $f(x) = -2(x + 1)^2 + 3$ is
(A) 3 (B) 2 (C) 1 (D) −1

72. If $a > 0$ and $a^x = 0.6$, then $a^{-2x} =$
(A) −1.2 (B) −0.36 (C) $-\frac{1}{0.36}$ (D) $\frac{1}{0.36}$

73. If Z is the set of integers, Q the set of rationals, and R the set of reals, then
(A) $Q \subset Z \subset R$ (B) $R \subset Q \subset Z$
(C) $Z \subset Q \subset R$ (D) $Z \subset R \subset Q$

74. If $i = \sqrt{-1}$, then $5\sqrt{-1} + \sqrt{-4} - \sqrt{-9} =$
(A) 10 (B) $4i$ (C) 0 (D) $-6i$

75. $111_2 + 1_2 =$
(A) 1110_2 (B) 1010_2 (C) 1100_2 (D) 1000_2

76. If $p < 0$ and $q > r$, which statement is false?
(A) $-q < -r$ (B) $pq < pr$
(C) $p(q - r) > 0$ (D) $q + p > r + p$

77. The domain of the function $f(x) = \dfrac{x^2}{x^2 - 4}$ is the set of all reals except
(A) 0 (B) 2 (C) 2 and -2 (D) 0, 2, and -2

78. A counterexample to the statement "If $ax^2 + bx + c = 0$ has two real unequal roots, then $b^2 - 4ac > 3$" is
(A) $x^2 - 3x + 2 = 0$ (B) $x^2 - x + 1 = 0$
(C) $x^2 - 2x + 1 = 0$ (D) $x^2 - 4x + 3 = 0$

79. Which graph below is *not* that of a function $y = f(x)$?

(A)

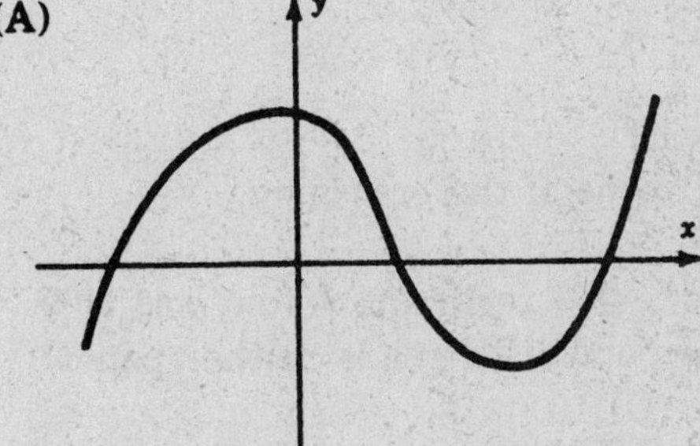

(B)

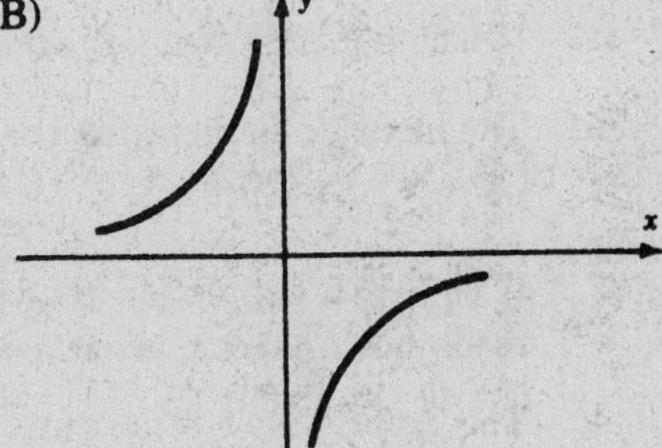

(C)

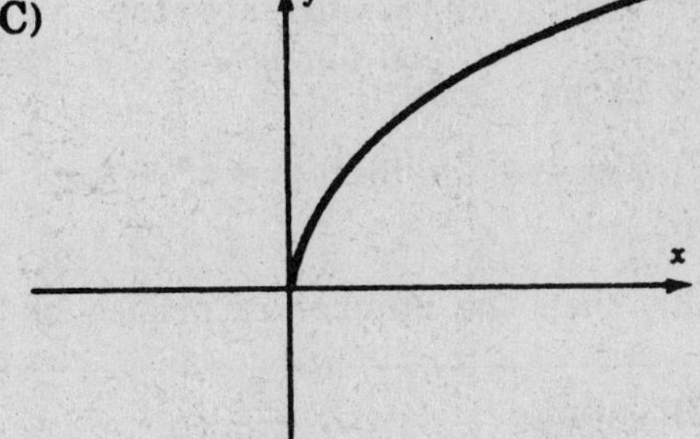

(D)

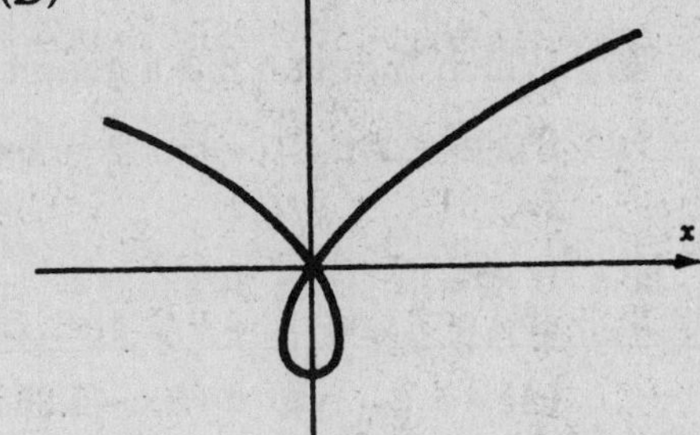

80. Which statement about primes is false?
(A) Every odd prime is of the form $2^n - 1$, where n is an integer.
(B) If a product mn of 2 positive integers is divisible by a prime p, then either m or n is divisible by p.
(C) Every positive integer can be uniquely expressed as a product of primes, except perhaps for the order in which the factors occur.
(D) There are an infinite number of primes.

81. If a divided by 4 leaves a remainder of 2, and b divided by 4 leaves a remainder of 3, then when $a + b$ is divided by 4 the remainder is
(A) 0 (B) 1 (C) 2 (D) 3

82. Which number is *not* a prime factor of 84?
(A) 2 (B) 3 (C) 6 (D) 7

83. If p and q are each divisible by 3, which of the following is *not* necessarily divisible by 3?
(A) $2q + 3$ (B) $4p + q$ (C) $pq + 2$ (D) $p^2 + q$

84. If $g(x) = \frac{\sqrt{x - 3}}{x}$, then $g(4) =$
(A) $\frac{1}{2}$ (B) $\frac{1}{4}$ (C) $-\frac{1}{4}$ (D) $\pm\frac{1}{4}$

Use the table at the right for questions 85 and 86.

*	a	b	c	d
a	a	a	a	a
b	a	b	c	d
c	a	c	a	c
d	a	d	c	b

85. $(b * c) * d =$
(A) a (B) b (C) c (D) d

86. The identity element for the operation $*$ is
(A) a (B) c (C) d (D) none of the preceding

87. If 60% of a population reads the *Journal*, 45% reads the *Moon*, and 30% reads both papers, what percent of the population reads neither paper?
(A) 40 (B) 25 (C) 15 (D) 10

88. How many two-person committees can be formed from a group of 8 volunteers?
(A) 8 (B) 16 (C) 28 (D) 56

89. Which function has a graph symmetric to the y-axis?
(A) $y = |x|$ (B) $y = 2x$ (C) $y = \frac{1}{x}$ (D) $y = x^2 + x$

90. If $R = \{x : x > 2\}$ and $S = \{x : x < 13\}$, then the number of primes in $R \cap S$ is
(A) 3 (B) 4 (C) 5 (D) infinite

ANSWER KEY AND REFERENCE CHART—SAMPLE EXAMINATION 2

See page 371 for an explanation of the reference code given in parentheses after each answer.

Section I

1.	C (A1)	9.	B (A2)	17.	C (A3)	25.	B (A4)	33.	B (A2)
2.	B (A1)	10.	D (A2)	18.	C (A3)	26.	D (A4)	34.	D (A2)
3.	A (A1)	11.	B (A2)	19.	C (A3)	27.	B (A4)	35.	A (A2)
4.	A (A1)	12.	D (A2)	20.	C (A1)	28.	C (A1)	36.	B (A2)
5.	B (A1)	13.	D (A2)	21.	B (A4)	29.	A (A1)	37.	D (A2)
6.	D (A3)	14.	A (A3)	22.	A (A4)	30.	C (A3)	38.	A (A2)
7.	A (A1)	15.	C (A3)	23.	B (A4)	31.	B (A1)	39.	B (A2)
8.	C (A2)	16.	B (A3)	24.	A (A4)	32.	D (A1)	40.	B (A2)

Section II

41.	A (B1)	51.	D (B3)	61.	B (B5)	71.	A (B4)	81.	B (B3)
42.	A (B1)	52.	B (B3)	62.	C (B1)	72.	D (B6)	82.	C (B3)
43.	B (B1)	53.	C (B3)	63.	C (B5)	73.	C (B3)	83.	C (B3)
44.	D (B1)	54.	B (B4)	64.	B (B3)	74.	B (B6)	84.	B (B4)
45.	C (B2)	55.	B (B4)	65.	D (B6)	75.	D (B6)	85.	C (B6)
46.	A (B2)	56.	D (B4)	66.	A (B4)	76.	C (B3)	86.	D (B6)
47.	B (B2)	57.	A (B4)	67.	C (B5)	77.	C (B4)	87.	B (B5)
48.	B (B2)	58.	A (B6)	68.	B (B3)	78.	A (B2)	88.	C (B5)
49.	C (B3)	59.	D (B5)	69.	A (B3)	79.	D (B4)	89.	A (B4)
50.	D (B3)	60.	A (B5)	70.	D (B6)	80.	A (B3)	90.	B (B3)

SCORING CHART—SAMPLE EXAMINATION 2

After you have scored your Sample Examination 2, enter the results in the chart below; then transfer your Raw Score to the Progress Chart on page 14.

Total Test	Number Right	Number Wrong	Number Omitted	Raw Score
Section I: 40				
Section II: 50				
Total: 90				

ANSWER EXPLANATIONS—SAMPLE EXAMINATION 2

Section I

1. **C.** $150 \times 2 = 300$, and $300 \times 4\frac{1}{2} = 300 \times 4 + 300 \times \frac{1}{2} = 1200 + 150$. The answer is \$13.50.
2. **B.** $2\frac{1}{3} = \frac{7}{3}$; its reciprocal is $\frac{3}{7}$, which is less than $\frac{1}{2}$.

3. A. Let x = required score on the fifth test. Then $\frac{4 \cdot 44 + x}{5}$ must equal 50. $176 + x = 250$, and $x = 74$.
4. A. $55 \div 3 > 18$.
5. B. $44 \div 2.2 = 20$.
6. D. Don't assume that $\triangle ABC$ is a right triangle!
7. A. Solving $7x + 3x = 12$ yields $x = 1.2$, and $3x = 3.6$, which is greater than 3.5 (3 ft. 6 in.).
8. C. $(m + n)^2 = (3 - 2)^2 = 1$; $(2n + m)^2 = (-4 + 3)^2 = 1$.
9. D. If x and y have the same sign, then $|x| + |y| = |x + y|$; if they have opposite signs, then $|x| + |y| > |x + y|$.
10. D. Don't forget that y may be negative, zero, or a fraction. If, for example, $y = 0$, then $y = y^2$; if $y = -1$, then $y < y^2$; if, however, $y = \frac{1}{2}$, then $y > y^2$.
11. B. $2^0 + 2^{\frac{1}{2}} + 2^{-1} = 1 + \sqrt{2} + \frac{1}{2} < 1 + 1.42 + 0.5 < 3$.
12. D. $(2m - 1)(2m + 1) = 4m^2 - 1$. The relationship between $4m^2$ and m^4 cannot be determined without information about m.
13. D. $\begin{cases} 3x + 2y = 4 \\ 9x + 6y = 12 \end{cases} \longrightarrow \begin{cases} 9x + 6y = 12 \\ 9x + 6y = 12 \end{cases}$

    There are an infinite number of solutions for this pair of equations.
14. A. If $A'C' = x$, $\frac{2}{3} = \frac{5}{x}$ since the triangles are similar, and $x = 7.5$.
15. C. $v = y + z = x + \frac{1}{2}x = 1.5x$.
16. B. $5x + 3x = 90$ yields $x = 45/4$, and $3x = 135/4$, which is less than 35.
17. C. Area in cm² of unshaded region $= (8 \times 10) - \frac{1}{2}(8 \times 8) = 80 - 32 = 48$.
18. C. $\frac{\text{circumference of new circle}}{\text{circumference of old circle}} = \frac{2\pi(2r)}{2\pi r} = \frac{2}{1}$.
19. C.

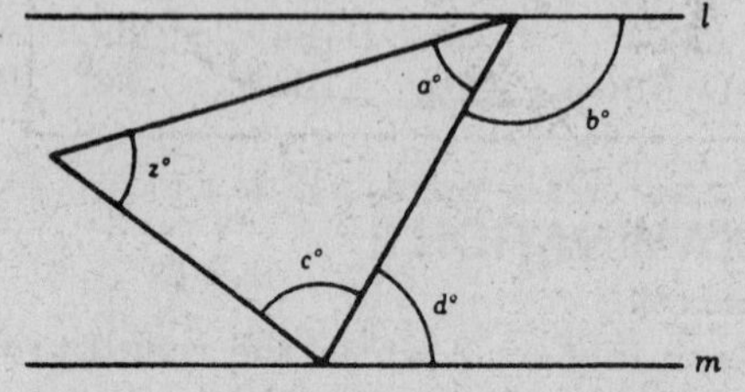

$a + b = x$; $c + d = y$

$a + c + z = 180$

$b + d = 180$ (since $l \parallel m$)

$\therefore x + y + z = 360$.

20. C. Mental arithmetic shows that $54 = 3 \times 18$, and that $(3 \times 1\frac{1}{4}) = 3\frac{3}{4}$.
21. B. Use a straightedge, if necessary, to pinpoint number of inches of rainfall for each month. Here the rainfall is *less* than 3.7 during four of the six months. The six-month average is also less.
22. A. Use a straightedge! It's about 3.9 inches in June, about 3.1 in February. The difference is about 0.8 inches.
23. B. Raw materials are 16% of imports, but only 15% of exports, and total imports exceed exports.
24. A. 70% of 48 = 33.6; this is less than 70% of 48.3 billion.
25. B. 13% of 56 = 7.28, which exceeds the actual amount (13% of 55.6 billion).
26. D. The fourth dot on the graph to the right of the one for 1967 is for 1971. It is just below the horizontal $12,000 line.
27. B. In 1962 the average policy was approximately $6000, in 1972 $12,000.
28. C. $1\frac{1}{5} = 1\frac{20}{100} = 1.20 = 120\%$.
29. A. $(210 - 200) \div 200 = 10 \div 200 = 1 \div 20 = 0.05 = 5\%$.
30. C. If the diagonal has length x, then, since $x^2 = 200$, we see that $x = 10\sqrt{2} \approx 14$.
31. B. Multiply 32 by 1, then mark off 3 decimal places to the left.
32. D. $8 = 6x \rightarrow x = 8 \div 6 = 1\frac{1}{3} = 1.33\frac{1}{3} = 133\frac{1}{3}\%$.

33. B. $|3-1| = |2| = 2$; $|-3| + 1 = 3 + 1 = 4$; $|-3| = 3$;
$1 - |-3| = 1 - 3 = -2$.

34. D. $2^{-3} = \frac{1}{2^3} = \frac{1}{8}$.

35. A. A line cuts the x-axis when $y = 0$: $3x + 4(0) + 6 = 0 \rightarrow x = -2$.

36. B. Consider *only* (B) and (C) since the product of the second terms of their factors is -2. Then check the cross-products; the sum of these must be $+5x$.

37. D. $(2 + \sqrt{3})(3 - \sqrt{3}) = (2)(3) + (2)(-\sqrt{3}) + (3)(\sqrt{3}) + (\sqrt{3})(-\sqrt{3})$
$= 6 + \sqrt{3} - 3 = 3 + \sqrt{3}$.

38. A. $x + 1 < 3x + 5 \rightarrow -4 < 2x \rightarrow -2 < x$.

39. B. $\frac{1}{x+3} - \frac{1}{3} = \frac{3-(x+3)}{3(x+3)} = \frac{-x}{3(x+3)}$.

40. B. Since $x^2 - x - 30 = (x - 6)(x + 5)$, and therefore is zero if $x = 6$ or -5, the product of the roots is $(6)(-5)$, or -30.

Section II

41. A. The shaded region consists of elements in R or in the intersection of S and T. Verification is also possible by assigning numbers to the exhaustive disjoint sets, as indicated:

$R \cup (S \cap T)$
$= (1,2,4,5) \cup (2,3,5,6 \cap 4,5,6,7)$
$= (1,2,4,5) \cup (5,6) = 1,2,4,5,6$
which is the shaded region.

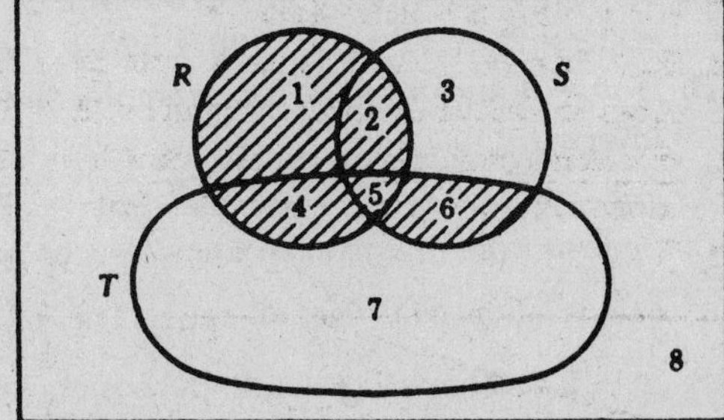

42. A. If R is the set of reals, then each point in the plane is of the form (x,y) where $(x,y) \in R \times R$.

43. B. $51 = 3 \times 17$; therefore 51 is not prime.

44. D. $P = \{3, -1\}$; $Q = \{0, -1\}$.

45. C. Note that the statement is true precisely when q is false.

46. A. $s \rightarrow t$ is equivalent to $\sim s \vee t$. $\sim(\sim s \vee t) = s \wedge \sim t$.

47. B. A translation of $\sim s \wedge t$ is "Sam is not conscientious and Sam is bright."

48. B. (B) is the contrapositive of the given statement.

49. C. If $x > 0$, then $ax^2 + bx + c > 0$. Thus the equation never equals zero for a positive number.

50. D. Note that the numerator of a term is equal to the denominator of the preceding one; a term's denominator equals the sum of the numerator and denominator of the preceding term.

51. D. Note that if $a = -2$, $b = -1$, then $a < b$ but $a^2 > b^2$.

52. B. Let $p = 1$, $q = 2$ to show that the numbers in (A), (C), (D) do not lie between p and q.

53. C. $\sqrt{3}$ is not a rational number; a number can be represented by a repeating or terminating decimal if and only if it is rational.

54. B. The area enclosed by the dotted line segment and dotted arc of the parabola is both above the parabola (that is, $y > x^2$) and below the line (that is, $y < 1 + x$).

55. B. $4x^4 + 1 = 0$ is equivalent to $4x^4 = -1$. No real x satisfies this equation, since $4x^4 \geq 0$ for all real x.

56. D. If $g(x)$ is the inverse of the function $f(x)$, then $g(x)$ is also a function such that $g(f(x)) = f(g(x)) = x$.

57. **A. Every cubic curve and every line intersect at least once and at most three times.**

58. **A. 19 − 12 = 7 and 7 is not divisible by 5.**

59. **D. There are 5 out of 6 ways to get a 2 or more when tossing a die.**

60. **A. The probability is** $\frac{{}_3C_2}{{}_{12}C_2} = \frac{3 \cdot 2}{2 \cdot 1} \div \frac{12 \cdot 11}{2 \cdot 1}$ **or just** $\frac{3 \cdot 2}{12 \cdot 11}$.

61. **B. The median or middle number is 11; the mean is**
$$\frac{3 + 3 + 7 + 11 + 11 + 13 + 15}{7} = \frac{63}{7} = 9.$$

62. **C. The intersection contains elements in both sets. Use a number line:**

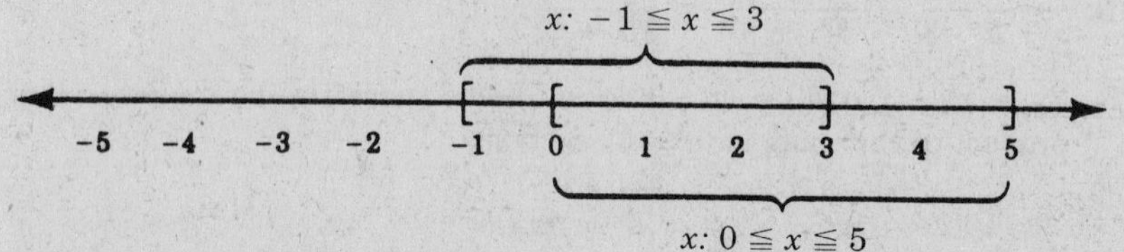

63. **C. You have 48 choices. To get a pair, your card must be an ace, king, seven, or three. There are 12 of these left in the deck; therefore the probability is $^{12}/_{48}$.**

64. **B.** $13 \times 42 = 13 \times (40 + 2) = (13 \times 40) + (13 \times 2)$
$= (13 \times 2) + (13 \times 40) = 26 + 520 = 546.$

65. **D. If $m = 3$ and $n = -2$, for example, then $m * n = 3^{-2} = {}^1/_9$, which is not an integer.**

66. A. $g(f(x)) = (2x + 1)^2 - 3 = 4x^2 + 4x + 1 - 3 = 4x^2 + 4x - 2.$

67. C. See the tree diagram in answer 8 on page 351. Of a total of outcomes, one is all heads, one all tails. The probability of both is the sum $\frac{1}{8} + \frac{1}{8}$.

68. B. $x^2 - 2 = 0$ has roots $\pm\sqrt{2}$. Both roots are irrational.

69. A. The hollow circles at −1 and 3 signify *exclusion* of these points.

70. D. The functions are inverses. Graphs of inverses are symmetric to the line $y = x$.

71. A. Note that the largest value of $-2(x + 1)^2$ is $-2(-1 + 1)^2$, or 0. Any value of x other than −1 yields an f which is less than 3. The graph of $f(x)$ is shown here.

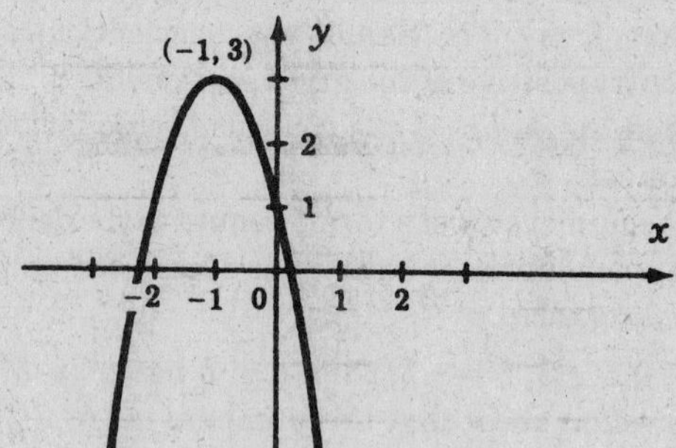

72. D. $a^{-2x} = \frac{1}{a^{2x}} = \frac{1}{(a^x)^2} = \frac{1}{(0.6)^2} = \frac{1}{0.36}$.

73. C. Every integer is a rational number; every rational number is a real number.

74. B. $5\sqrt{-1} + \sqrt{-4} - \sqrt{-9} = 5i + 2i - 3i = 4i.$

75. D. See the answer to question 16 on page 356 for information on adding numbers in base 2.

76. C. Since $p < 0$ and $q - r > 0$, the product $p(q - r)$ is negative.

77. C. Division by zero is prohibited.

78. A. $x^2 - 3x + 2 = (x - 1)(x - 2)$, which is zero for $x = 1, 2$. But $b^2 - 4ac = (-3)^2 - 4(2) = 1$.

79. D. For some x's there are two y's in the graph in (D).

80. A. 5 is a prime, for example, but there is no positive integer n such that $5 = 2^n - 1$.

81. B. Since there are integers p and q such that $a = 4p + 2$ and $b = 4q + 3$, $a + b = 4(p + q) + 5 = 4(p + q + 1) + 1 = 4m + 1$, where m is an integer.

82. C. Since $84 = 4 \cdot 21 = 2^2 \cdot 3 \cdot 7$, the prime factors are 2, 3, and 7; 6 is not a prime number.

83. C. To show this, let $p = q = 3$, for example.

84. B. $g(4) = \frac{\sqrt{4-3}}{4} = \frac{\sqrt{1}}{4} = \frac{1}{4}$. The square root of a positive number is positive, by definition.

85. C. $(b * c) = c$; so $(b * c) * d = c * d = c$.

86. D. The identity element is b.

87. **B. Use a Venn diagram to show the percentages of people who read the papers.**

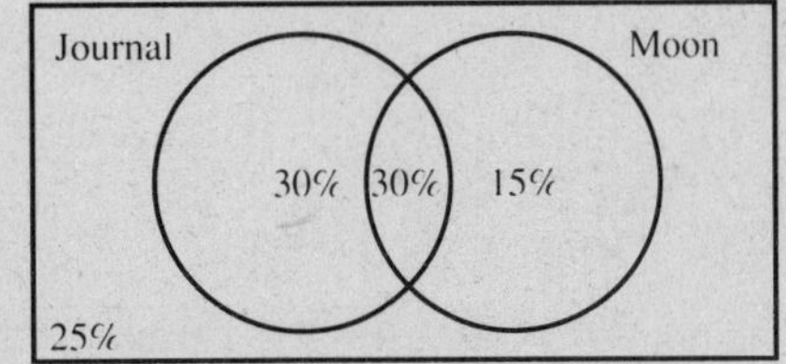

88. C. $C(8,2) = \frac{8 \cdot 7}{1 \cdot 2} = 28$.

89. **A. Remember that $|x|$ is positive or zero for all x. Its graph is at the right.**

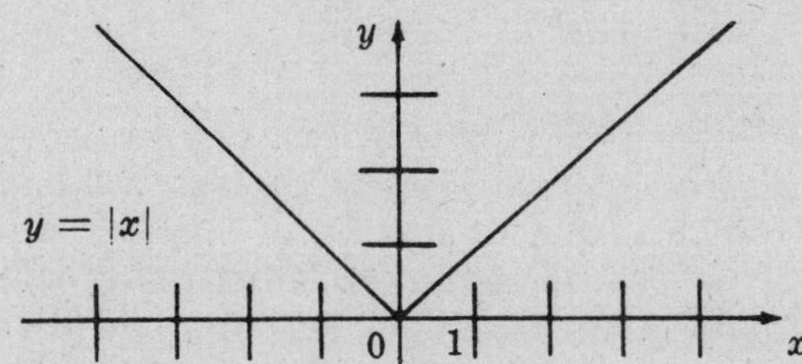

90. **B. $R \cap S = \{x : 2 < x < 13\}$. The primes in this set are 3, 5, 7, 11.**

ANSWER SHEET — MATHEMATICS/SAMPLE EXAMINATION 3

Section I

1. Ⓐ Ⓑ Ⓒ Ⓓ Ⓔ
2. Ⓐ Ⓑ Ⓒ Ⓓ Ⓔ
3. Ⓐ Ⓑ Ⓒ Ⓓ Ⓔ
4. Ⓐ Ⓑ Ⓒ Ⓓ Ⓔ
5. Ⓐ Ⓑ Ⓒ Ⓓ Ⓔ
6. Ⓐ Ⓑ Ⓒ Ⓓ Ⓔ
7. Ⓐ Ⓑ Ⓒ Ⓓ Ⓔ
8. Ⓐ Ⓑ Ⓒ Ⓓ Ⓔ
9. Ⓐ Ⓑ Ⓒ Ⓓ Ⓔ
10. Ⓐ Ⓑ Ⓒ Ⓓ Ⓔ
11. Ⓐ Ⓑ Ⓒ Ⓓ Ⓔ
12. Ⓐ Ⓑ Ⓒ Ⓓ Ⓔ
13. Ⓐ Ⓑ Ⓒ Ⓓ Ⓔ
14. Ⓐ Ⓑ Ⓒ Ⓓ Ⓔ
15. Ⓐ Ⓑ Ⓒ Ⓓ Ⓔ
16. Ⓐ Ⓑ Ⓒ Ⓓ Ⓔ
17. Ⓐ Ⓑ Ⓒ Ⓓ Ⓔ
18. Ⓐ Ⓑ Ⓒ Ⓓ Ⓔ
19. Ⓐ Ⓑ Ⓒ Ⓓ Ⓔ
20. Ⓐ Ⓑ Ⓒ Ⓓ Ⓔ
21. Ⓐ Ⓑ Ⓒ Ⓓ Ⓔ
22. Ⓐ Ⓑ Ⓒ Ⓓ Ⓔ
23. Ⓐ Ⓑ Ⓒ Ⓓ Ⓔ
24. Ⓐ Ⓑ Ⓒ Ⓓ Ⓔ
25. Ⓐ Ⓑ Ⓒ Ⓓ Ⓔ
26. Ⓐ Ⓑ Ⓒ Ⓓ Ⓔ
27. Ⓐ Ⓑ Ⓒ Ⓓ Ⓔ
28. Ⓐ Ⓑ Ⓒ Ⓓ Ⓔ
29. Ⓐ Ⓑ Ⓒ Ⓓ Ⓔ
30. Ⓐ Ⓑ Ⓒ Ⓓ Ⓔ
31. Ⓐ Ⓑ Ⓒ Ⓓ Ⓔ
32. Ⓐ Ⓑ Ⓒ Ⓓ Ⓔ
33. Ⓐ Ⓑ Ⓒ Ⓓ Ⓔ
34. Ⓐ Ⓑ Ⓒ Ⓓ Ⓔ
35. Ⓐ Ⓑ Ⓒ Ⓓ Ⓔ
36. Ⓐ Ⓑ Ⓒ Ⓓ Ⓔ
37. Ⓐ Ⓑ Ⓒ Ⓓ Ⓔ
38. Ⓐ Ⓑ Ⓒ Ⓓ Ⓔ
39. Ⓐ Ⓑ Ⓒ Ⓓ Ⓔ
40. Ⓐ Ⓑ Ⓒ Ⓓ Ⓔ

Section II

41. Ⓐ Ⓑ Ⓒ Ⓓ Ⓔ
42. Ⓐ Ⓑ Ⓒ Ⓓ Ⓔ
43. Ⓐ Ⓑ Ⓒ Ⓓ Ⓔ
44. Ⓐ Ⓑ Ⓒ Ⓓ Ⓔ
45. Ⓐ Ⓑ Ⓒ Ⓓ Ⓔ
46. Ⓐ Ⓑ Ⓒ Ⓓ Ⓔ
47. Ⓐ Ⓑ Ⓒ Ⓓ Ⓔ
48. Ⓐ Ⓑ Ⓒ Ⓓ Ⓔ
49. Ⓐ Ⓑ Ⓒ Ⓓ Ⓔ
50. Ⓐ Ⓑ Ⓒ Ⓓ Ⓔ
51. Ⓐ Ⓑ Ⓒ Ⓓ Ⓔ
52. Ⓐ Ⓑ Ⓒ Ⓓ Ⓔ
53. Ⓐ Ⓑ Ⓒ Ⓓ Ⓔ
54. Ⓐ Ⓑ Ⓒ Ⓓ Ⓔ
55. Ⓐ Ⓑ Ⓒ Ⓓ Ⓔ
56. Ⓐ Ⓑ Ⓒ Ⓓ Ⓔ
57. Ⓐ Ⓑ Ⓒ Ⓓ Ⓔ
58. Ⓐ Ⓑ Ⓒ Ⓓ Ⓔ
59. Ⓐ Ⓑ Ⓒ Ⓓ Ⓔ
60. Ⓐ Ⓑ Ⓒ Ⓓ Ⓔ
61. Ⓐ Ⓑ Ⓒ Ⓓ Ⓔ
62. Ⓐ Ⓑ Ⓒ Ⓓ Ⓔ
63. Ⓐ Ⓑ Ⓒ Ⓓ Ⓔ
64. Ⓐ Ⓑ Ⓒ Ⓓ Ⓔ
65. Ⓐ Ⓑ Ⓒ Ⓓ Ⓔ
66. Ⓐ Ⓑ Ⓒ Ⓓ Ⓔ
67. Ⓐ Ⓑ Ⓒ Ⓓ Ⓔ
68. Ⓐ Ⓑ Ⓒ Ⓓ Ⓔ
69. Ⓐ Ⓑ Ⓒ Ⓓ Ⓔ
70. Ⓐ Ⓑ Ⓒ Ⓓ Ⓔ
71. Ⓐ Ⓑ Ⓒ Ⓓ Ⓔ
72. Ⓐ Ⓑ Ⓒ Ⓓ Ⓔ
73. Ⓐ Ⓑ Ⓒ Ⓓ Ⓔ
74. Ⓐ Ⓑ Ⓒ Ⓓ Ⓔ
75. Ⓐ Ⓑ Ⓒ Ⓓ Ⓔ
76. Ⓐ Ⓑ Ⓒ Ⓓ Ⓔ
77. Ⓐ Ⓑ Ⓒ Ⓓ Ⓔ
78. Ⓐ Ⓑ Ⓒ Ⓓ Ⓔ
79. Ⓐ Ⓑ Ⓒ Ⓓ Ⓔ
80. Ⓐ Ⓑ Ⓒ Ⓓ Ⓔ
81. Ⓐ Ⓑ Ⓒ Ⓓ Ⓔ
82. Ⓐ Ⓑ Ⓒ Ⓓ Ⓔ
83. Ⓐ Ⓑ Ⓒ Ⓓ Ⓔ
84. Ⓐ Ⓑ Ⓒ Ⓓ Ⓔ
85. Ⓐ Ⓑ Ⓒ Ⓓ Ⓔ
86. Ⓐ Ⓑ Ⓒ Ⓓ Ⓔ
87. Ⓐ Ⓑ Ⓒ Ⓓ Ⓔ
88. Ⓐ Ⓑ Ⓒ Ⓓ Ⓔ
89. Ⓐ Ⓑ Ⓒ Ⓓ Ⓔ
90. Ⓐ Ⓑ Ⓒ Ⓓ Ⓔ

SAMPLE EXAMINATION 3

Section I: Basic Skills and Concepts

Directions for questions 1–25: Each question consists of two quantities, one in Column A and one in Column B. You are to compare the two quantities and on the answer sheet blacken space

- A if the quantity in Column A is greater;
- B if the quantity in Column B is greater;
- C if the two quantities are equal;
- D if the relationship cannot be determined from the information given.

Notes:

1. In certain questions, information concerning one or both of the quantities to be compared is centered above the two columns.
2. A symbol that appears in both columns represents the same thing in Column A as it does in Column B.
3. Letters such as x, n, and k stand for real numbers.

	COLUMN A	COLUMN B
1.	$3 \times 5 - 5$	0
2.	$\sqrt{\frac{1}{16}}$	$\frac{0.3}{1.2}$
	The average of seven numbers is 13.	
3.	the sum of the seven numbers	90
	Carpeting costs $9.50 per square yard.	
4.	cost of 122 square yards of carpet	$1220
5.	the cost per ounce of cheese if 12 oz. cost 70¢	the cost per ounce if 1 pound costs 98¢
	The sum of x and a number is zero.	
6.	x	0
7.	$20 \times 6/17 \times 31$	$62 \times 2/17 \times 30$
	An open field, in the shape of a rectangle, is 10 yards by 20 yards.	
8.	**the distance, to the nearest yard, between opposite corners of the field**	25

	COLUMN A	COLUMN B

A one-foot square vinyl tile costs 20¢. A kitchen floor has the shape shown:

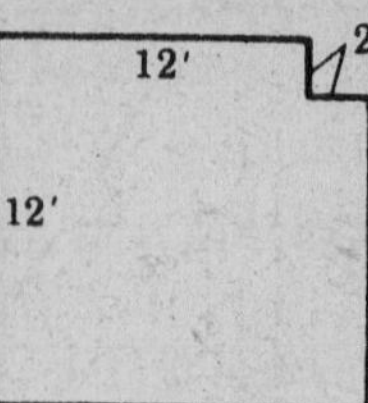

9.	the cost of covering the kitchen floor with vinyl tiles	\$30

Andy takes an hour to bike to his friend's house 8 miles away but takes only 40 minutes to return.

10.	Andy's average speed on the trip	9 mph
11.	the thousands digit in 40,010	the hundreds digit in 3.01×10^3

x is an integer such that $-1 \leqq 2x + 1 < 2$

12.	x	0

$\frac{a}{b} > \frac{c}{d}$, $bd > 0$

13.	ad	bc

$5(3x - 1) - x = 5$

14.	x	$7/5$
15.	the numerical coefficient if $(3x)(8x^{11})(x^{12})$ is simplified	the exponent of x in the final product

$\frac{8}{x} + \frac{1}{2} = \frac{11}{x}$

16.	x	$3/2$

A registry has names of doctors from cities *X*, *Y*, and *Z*. The ratio of the number of doctors from city *Y* to the number from city *Z* is 3 : 1.

17.	**ratio of the total number of doctors to the number from city *Z***	**3 : 1**

	COLUMN A	COLUMN B

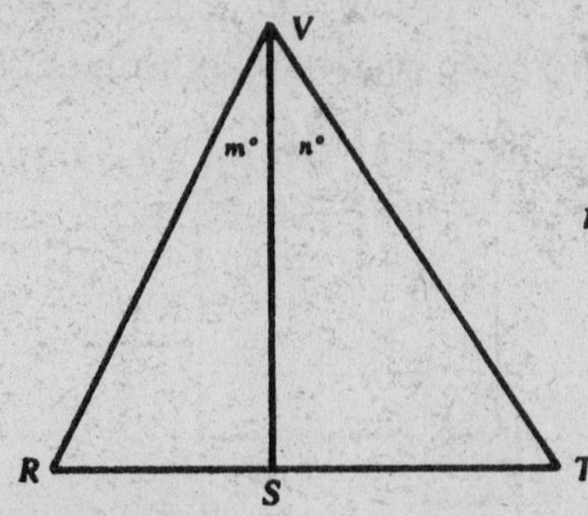

$m = n$

Note: figure is not drawn to scale.

18.	**length of** RS	**length of** ST

A right triangle has sides of lengths 3 in., 4 in., and 5 in.

19.	**the length of the altitude to the 5-inch side**	**2.4 in.**

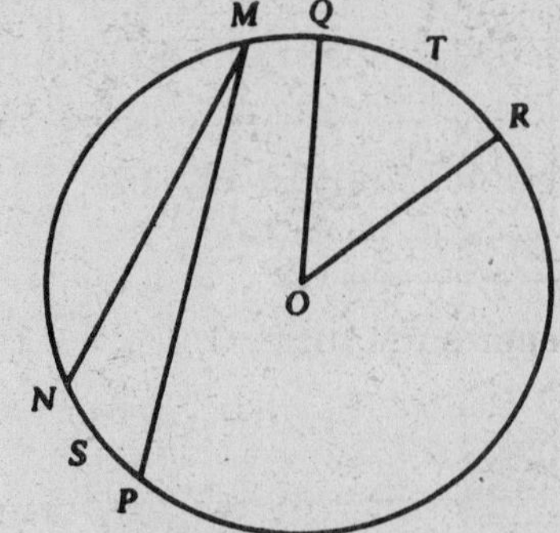

$\frac{m(\overset{\frown}{QTR})}{m(\overset{\frown}{NSP})} = \frac{2}{1}$

O is the center of the circle.

20.	$\frac{m(\angle QOR)}{m(\angle NMP)}$	**4 : 1**

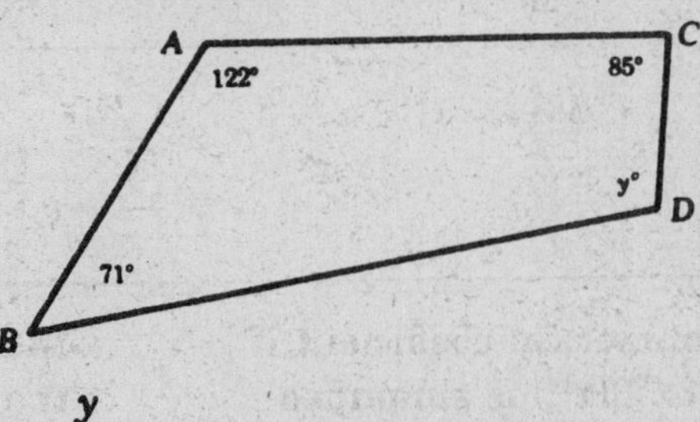

21.	y	72

Area of rectangle $RSTU$ = 8 times area of triangle QRS.

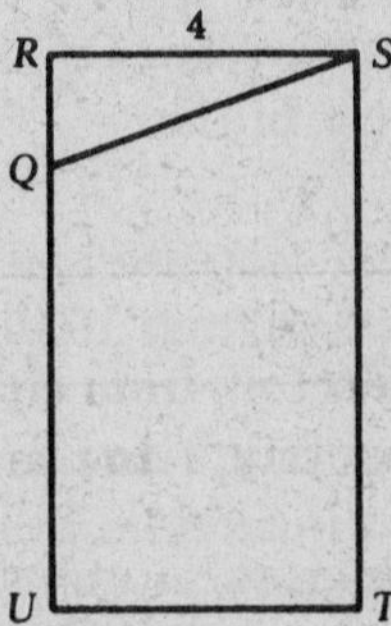

22.	QU	$3RQ$

COLUMN A	COLUMN B

Use this bar graph of employee-benefit plans for questions 23, 24, and 25.

CONTRIBUTIONS AND BENEFITS UNDER EMPLOYEE-BENEFIT PLANS, BY TYPE OF BENEFIT, SELECTED YEARS, 1950–65

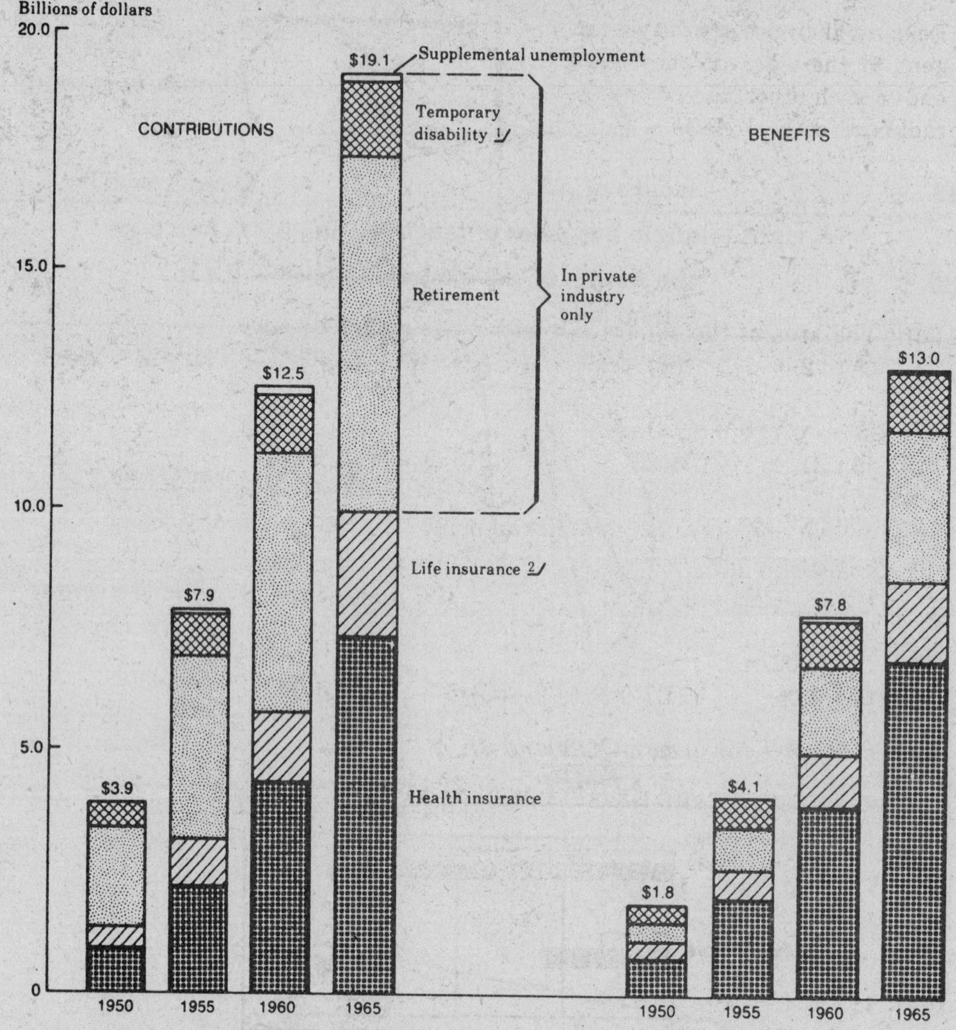

1. Including sick leave. 2. Including accidental death and dismemberment insurance.

Source: ***Social Security Bulletin, April 1967, p. 16.***

	COLUMN A	COLUMN B
23.	**total contributions in 1950 to the nearest billion**	**4 billion**
24.	**percentage increase overall in contributions from 1950 to 1965**	**500**
25.	**ratio of contributions in 1965 for health insurance to total contributions**	**ratio of benefits in 1965 from health insurance to total benefits**

Directions for questions 26–40. For these questions, indicate the correct answer in the appropriate space on the answer sheet.

Note: Figures that accompany the following problems are intended to provide information useful in answering the questions. The figures are drawn as accurately as possible *except* when it is stated in a specific question that the figure is not drawn to scale. All figures lie in a plane unless otherwise stated.

Four equal circles are drawn tangent to the sides of the square and to each other, as shown. The radius of each circle is r.

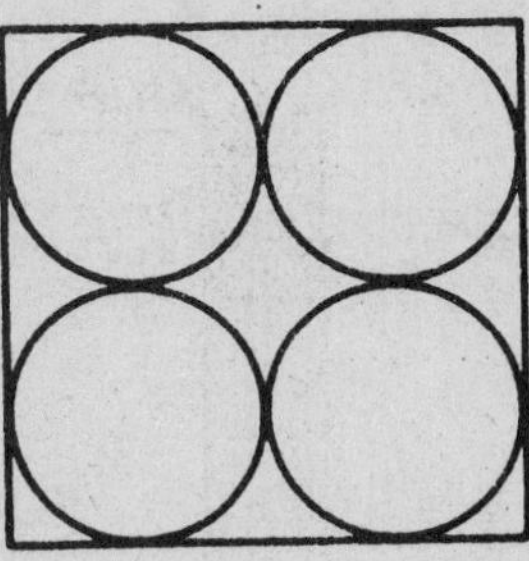

26. The area of the square *not* within the circles equals
(A) $12r^2$ (B) $4\pi r^2$ (C) $(16 - 4\pi)r^2$ (D) $16 - 4\pi r^2$

27. $(5 - \sqrt{2})(5 + \sqrt{2}) =$
(A) 21 (B) 23 (C) 27 (D) 29

28. Which line does *not* contain the point $(3, -1)$?
(A) $x + y = 2$ (B) $x + 3y = 0$
(C) $y - 2x + 5 = 0$ (D) $y = -3x + 8$

29. $1 \div 0.02 =$
(A) 0.05 (B) 0.5 (C) 5 (D) 50

Use this figure for questions 30 and 31.

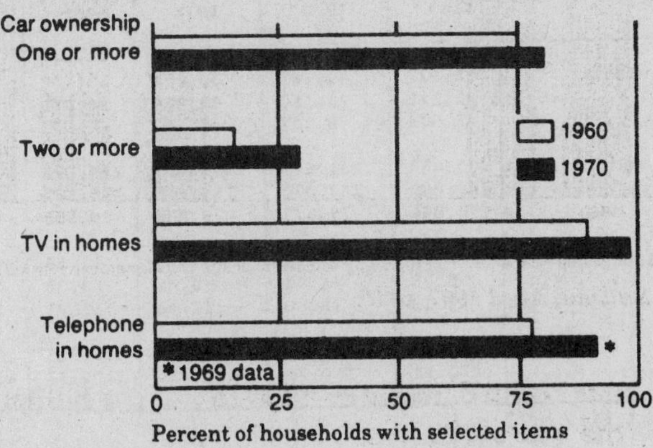

Source: Data, 1971, Figure 13, p. 15

30. The percentage of households with one or more cars in 1960 was approximately
(A) 20 (B) 30 (C) 75 (D) 80

31. The ratio, 1970 to 1960, of households with two or more cars was approximately
(A) 2:1 (B) 3:2 (C) 2:3 (D) 1:2

32. $\sqrt{75} - \sqrt{27} - \sqrt{12} =$
(A) 0 (B) $\sqrt{3}$ (C) $-\sqrt{3}$ (D) $5 - 5\sqrt{3}$

33. How much does 5 yards of material cost at 50¢ a foot if the material is marked down 10%?
(A) $2.25 (B) $6.50 (C) $6.75 (D) $7.00

34. If 3 is to x as 5 is to 8, then $x =$
(A) 4.4 (B) 4.8 (C) 6 (D) 7

35. If $1.06 \times 10^k = 106{,}000$, then $k =$
(A) -5 (B) 3 (C) 4 (D) 5

36. $7/4 =$
(A) 1.75% (B) 17.5% (C) $17\frac{3}{4}$% (D) 175%

37. $\dfrac{x^2 - x}{x(x^2+1)} = \dfrac{x-1}{x^2+1}$ for
(A) all real x (B) $x \neq 0$ (C) $x \neq 1$ (D) $x \neq \pm 1$

38. The solution of the system of equations
$\begin{cases} x + 2y = 1 \\ x - 3y = 6 \end{cases}$ is
(A) $x = 1, y = 0$ (B) $x = -1, y = 1$
(C) $x = 3, y = -1$ (D) $x = -1, y = 2$

Use this table for questions 39 and 40.

Community hospital utilization and expenses, by age group, fiscal years 1969-72

Item	Fiscal year amounts				Percentage change from preceding year		
	1969	1970	1971	1972	1970	1971	1972
Number of admissions (in thousands)	28,027	29,247	30,312	30,706	4.4	3.6	1.3
Under age 65	22,122	23,110	23,966	24,071	4.5	3.7	0.4
Aged 65 and over	5,904	6,137	6,346	6,635	3.9	3.4	4.6
Number of patient days (in thousands)	227,633	231,643	234,413	232,892	1.8	1.2	-0.6
Under age 65	149,585	153,070	155,475	153,587	2.3	1.6	-1.2
Aged 65 and over	78,048	78,573	78,938	79,305	0.7	0.5	0.5
Average length of stay (days)	8.12	7.92	7.73	7.58	-2.4	-2.4	-2.0
Under age 65	6.76	6.62	6.49	6.38	-2.1	-2.0	-1.7
Aged 65 and over	13.22	12.80	12.44	11.95	-3.2	-2.8	-3.9
Total expenses (in millions)	$15,965	$18,693	$21,418	$23,925	17.1	14.6	11.7
Expenses per patient day	$70.13	$80.70	$91.37	$102.73	15.1	13.2	12.4

Source: Social Security Bulletin, May 1973, p. 12.

39. The percentage increase in expenses per patient day from 1970 to 1971 was
(A) over 15% (B) less than 12%
(C) between 13 and 14% (D) between 12 and 13%

40. Of the following, which percentage decrease from the preceding year on the average length of stay was greatest?
(A) aged 65 and over in 1972 (B) aged 65 and over in 1970
(C) under age 65 in 1972 (D) under age 65 in 1970

Section II: Content

Directions: For each of the following questions, indicate the correct answer in the appropriate space on the answer sheet.

Note: Figures that accompany problems in this part are intended to provide information useful in solving the problems. They are drawn as accurately as possible *except* when it is stated in a specific problem that the figure is not drawn to scale. All figures lie in a plane unless otherwise stated.

41. Which set is infinite?
(A) the set of blades of grass in a lawn
(B) the set of grains of sand on Waikiki
(C) the set of points on a 1-inch line segment.
(D) the set of natural numbers less than 10^{10}

42. A Venn diagram for $\overline{R \cup S}$ (where $\overline{T}$ denotes the complement of T) is

(A)

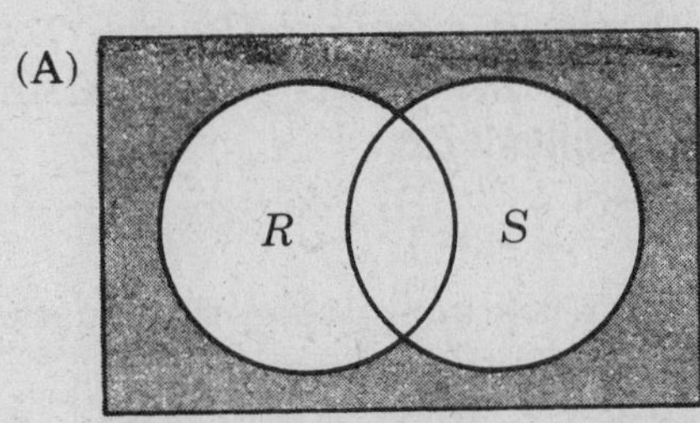

(B)

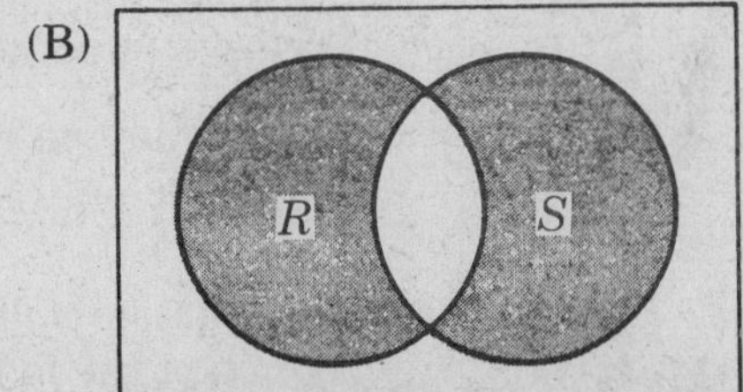

(C)

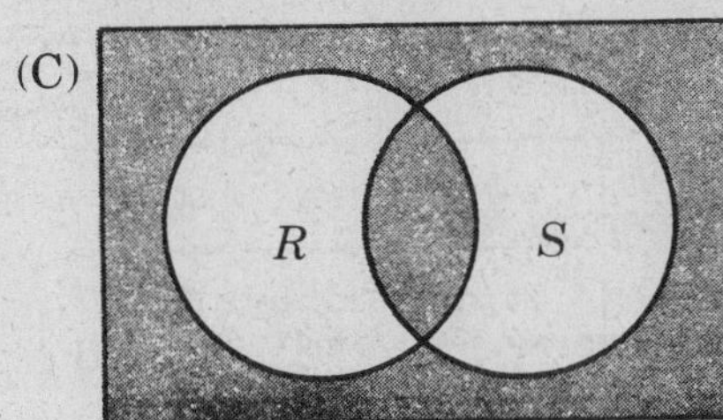

(D)

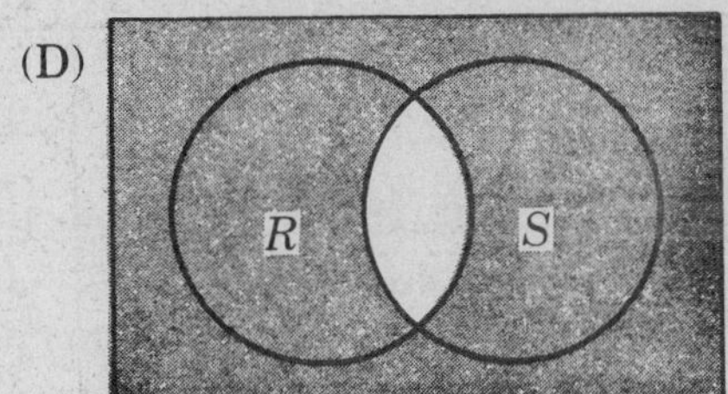

43. If $G = \{x : x \text{ is a prime number}\}$ and $H = \{x : x < 11\}$, then the number of elements in $G \cup H$ is
(A) 4 (B) 5 (C) 6 (D) infinite

44. If $r \rightarrow s$ is true, then so is
(A) $s \rightarrow r$ (B) $\sim s \rightarrow \sim r$ (C) $\sim r \rightarrow \sim s$ (D) $\sim s \rightarrow r$

45. The negation of the statement "Some people cheat on their tax returns" is
(A) Some people do not cheat on their tax returns.
(B) No one cheats on his tax return.
(C) All people cheat on their tax returns.
(D) At least one person cheats on his tax return.

46. The truth table of $p \vee \sim(p \wedge q)$ is

p	q	(A)	(B)	(C)	(D)
T	T	T	T	T	T
T	F	T	T	T	F
F	T	T	F	T	T
F	F	F	F	T	T

47. Assume the truth of the statements: (1) "If women astronauts are used then the space program will be improved"; (2) "If the space program is improved, then it will cost less." A valid conclusion is
(A) If the space program does not cost less, then women astronauts are not being used.
(B) If women astronauts are not used, then the space program will cost more.
(C) If the space program costs less, then women astronauts are used.
(D) If only men are used as astronauts, then the space program will not be improved.

48. Let r be "Tony will pass the CLEP mathematics exam" and let s be "Tony is ill." Then the statement "If Tony is not ill, then he will pass the CLEP mathematics exam" may be written symbolically as
(A) $s \rightarrow \sim r$ (B) $\sim r \rightarrow \sim s$ (C) $r \rightarrow \sim s$ (D) $\sim s \rightarrow r$

49. A Pythagorean triple is a set of 3 numbers (x,y,z) that satisfies the equation $x^2 + y^2 = z^2$. Which of the following is *not* a Pythagorean triple?
(A) (3, 4, 5) (B) $(1, 2, \sqrt{5})$ (C) $(1, 1, \sqrt{2})$ (D) (2, 3, 13)

50. The number of different real values of x for which $x^3 - 4x^2 = 0$ is
(A) 0 (B) 1 (C) 2 (D) 3

51. Which statement below about real numbers is false?
(A) If $a < b$, then $(a + c) < (b + c)$
(B) Every real number has an additive inverse.
(C) Every real number has a multiplicative inverse.
(D) If $a < 0$ and $b > c$, then $ab < ac$.

52. Which of the following is *not* a real number?
(A) $\frac{0}{1/2}$ (B) $\frac{3}{0}$ (C) $\frac{\sqrt{3}}{\sqrt{3}}$ (D) π

53. If $4^{x-2} = 64$, then x equals
(A) 6 (B) 5 (C) 4 (D) 3

54. If the domain of $f(x) = 2x^2 + 1$ is the set of all integers, then the range of f is
(A) all integers
(B) all nonnegative integers
(C) a subset of the positive integers
(D) all integers greater than or equal to 1

55. If $f(x) = 2x + 3$, then $f(f(x)) =$
(A) $4x + 9$ (B) $2x + 6$ (C) $4x + 6$ (D) $4x + 3$

56. If the graph at the right is of the function $y = f(x)$, then the graph of $y = -f(x)$ is

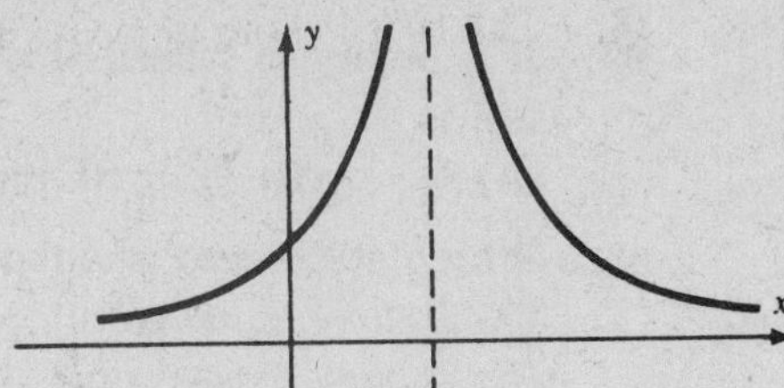

(A)

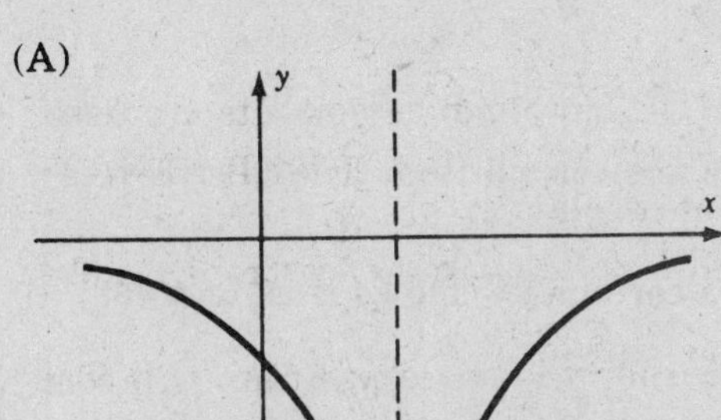

(B)

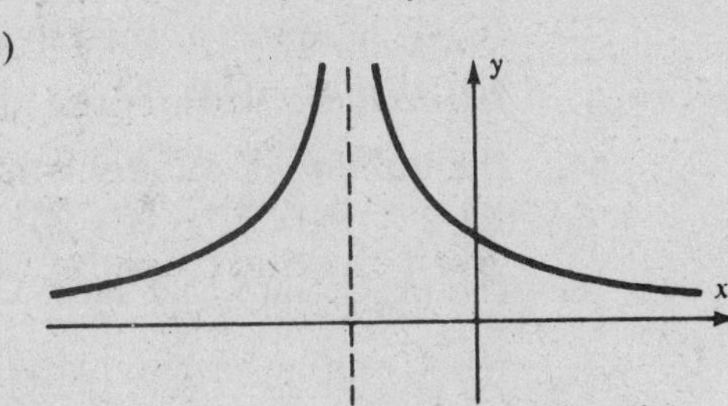

(C)

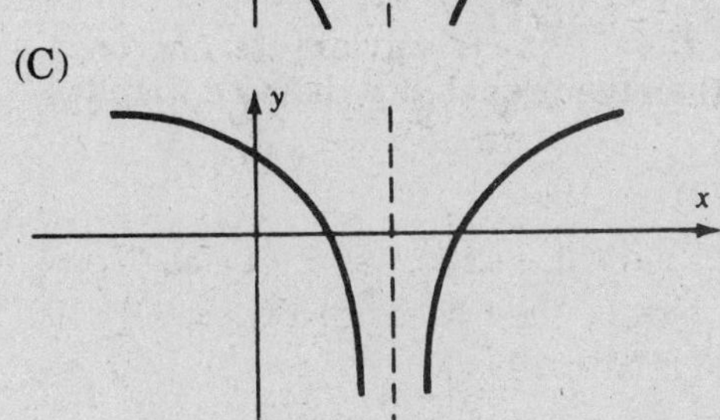

(D)

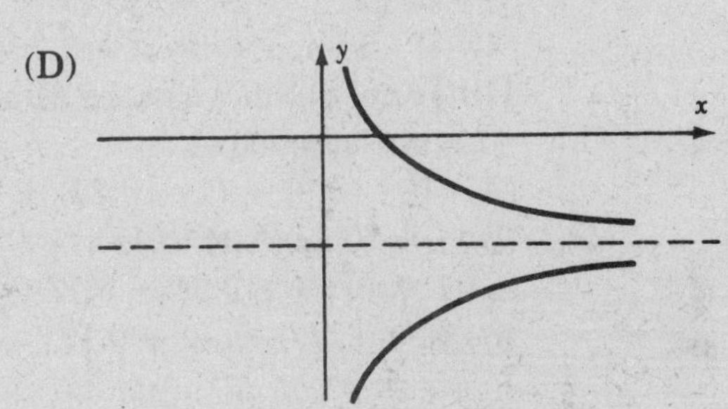

57. Which of the following describes a function with domain the set of real numbers?

(A) $f(x) = \begin{cases} x & \text{if } x \leqq 1 \\ x+1 & \text{if } x \geqq 1 \end{cases}$ **(B)** $f(x) = |x|$ **if** $x \geqq 0$

(C) $f(x) = \dfrac{1}{x}$ **(D)** $f(x) = \begin{cases} 0 & \text{if } x \text{ is rational} \\ 1 & \text{if } x \text{ is irrational} \end{cases}$

58. If for all elements x, y, z in a mathematical system $x \times (y+z) = x \times (z+y)$, then the system satisfies
(A) an associative law
(B) a distributive law
(C) the commutative law for addition
(D) the commutative law for multiplication

59. If the domain of $f(x) = \dfrac{1}{x^2}$ is $\{x : x \text{ is a real number}, x \neq 0\}$, then the range of f is
(A) all real numbers (B) all numbers other than 0
(C) all numbers greater than or equal to 0 (D) all positive numbers

60. Which of the binary operations $*$ defined below on the set of positive integers is *not* commutative?
(A) $m * n = m^n$ **(B)** $m * n = mn + 3$
(C) $m * n = mn + m + n$ **(D)** $m * n = 2^{mn}$

61. If a restaurant offers 5 different fillings for sandwiches on 3 different kinds of bread, with mayonnaise, butter, neither, or both, then the number of different kinds of sandwiches available is
(A) 120 (B) 60 (C) 45 (D) 30

62. If a penny is tossed three times, then the probability of 2 heads and 1 tail is
(A) $\frac{1}{8}$ (B) $\frac{1}{4}$ (C) $\frac{3}{8}$ (D) $\frac{1}{2}$

63. Which statement about the probability of an event is false?
(A) It may equal zero.
(B) It may exceed one.
(C) If it equals p, then $0 \leq p \leq 1$.
(D) It may equal one.

64. The number of different ways one may answer a 5-item true-false test is
(A) 2 (B) 5 (C) 25 (D) 32

65. The probability that Mrs. Corn watches certain TV shows is as follows:

The Lovers	0.29
The Killers	0.34
The Ticklers	0.12

If they are all shown at the same time, then the probability that she watches none of these shows is
(A) $(1 - 0.29) + (1 - 0.34) + (1 - 0.12)$
(B) $1 - (0.29)(0.34)(0.12)$
(C) $1 - (0.29 + 0.34 + 0.12)$
(D) $1 - 0.29 + 0.34 + 0.12$

66. Which pair of points shown is on the parabola $y = x^2 + 2$?
(A) M and N (B) N and Q
(C) M and P (D) P and Q

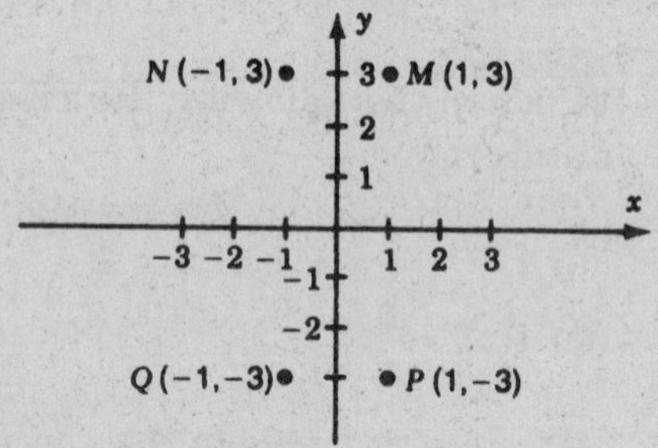

67. Which of the following is a nonnegative integer?
(A) $3 \div 0$ (B) $2 - 4$ (C) $5 \div 2$ (D) $0 \div 1$

68. The number of divisors of 3^{10} which are greater than one but less than 3^{10} is
(A) 8 (B) 9 (C) 10 (D) 36

69. Which line is perpendicular to $5x - y = 1$?
(A) $x + 5y = 9$ (B) $5x - y = 1$
(C) $5x + y = 1$ (D) $5x + y = -1$

70. The largest base-ten number that is a three-digit number base five is
(A) 124 (B) 444 (C) 720 (D) 999

71. If $\log_a x = p$, then $\log_a x^4 =$
(A) 4 (B) $4p$ (C) p^4 (D) $p + 4$

72. If, for real p and q, $p * q = \dfrac{p + q}{p + q - 1}$, then the only pair among the following for which $p * q$ is defined is
(A) $p = 0, q = 0$ (B) $p = 0, q = 1$
(C) $p = 1, q = 0$ (D) $p = -1, q = 2$

73. If $i = \sqrt{-1}$, then $(1 + i)(1 - i) =$
(A) 0 (B) 2 (C) $2i$ (D) $-2i$

74. If $V = \{0, 1, 3\}$, $W = \{1, 2\}$, and $Z = \{0, 1, 4\}$, then $(V \cup W) \cap Z =$
(A) $\{0, 1, 2, 3, 4\}$ (B) $\{0, 1\}$
(C) $\{1\}$ (D) 0

75. Which of the following statements about the set of real numbers is false?
(A) 0 is the additive identity.
(B) 1 is the multiplicative identity.
(C) Multiplication is commutative.
(D) Division is commutative.

76. The roots of the equation $3v^2 + 5v - 1 = 0$ are
(A) not real (B) real, irrational, unequal
(C) real, rational, equal (D) real, rational, unequal

Use this addition table for questions 77 and 78.

+	p	q	r
p	r	p	q
q	p	q	r
r	q	r	p

77. The identity element is
(A) p (B) q (C) r (D) none of the preceding

78. The additive inverse of r is
(A) p (B) q (C) r (D) none of the preceding

79. If $T = \{x : x$ is an integer and $1 < x < 7\}$, then the number of subsets of T is
(A) 6 (B) 12 (C) 16 (D) 32

80. A counterexample to the claim "If n is an odd prime, then so is $n^2 + 4$" is
(A) 11 (B) 7 (C) 2 (D) 1

81. Which of the following is a real number?
(A) $\frac{1}{0}$ (B) $\frac{0}{0}$ (C) $\frac{0}{-2}$ (D) 0^0

82. If $f(x) = x^2 - 5$ and $g(x) = 2^{-x}$, then $f(g(-1)) =$
(A) $-4\frac{1}{4}$ (B) -3 (C) -1 (D) $\frac{1}{16}$

83. Each of the 3-digit numbers that can be formed from the set {2,5,7,9}, allowing repetitions, is written on a piece of paper. One slip is then chosen at random. The probability that the number chosen begins with a 7 is
(A) $\frac{1}{4}$ (B) $\frac{3}{10}$
(C) $\frac{1}{3}$ (D) none of the preceding

84. The median of the set {4,10,7,15,9,10,7,10} is
(A) 8 (B) 9 (C) 9.5 (D) 10

85. If m is odd and n is even, which of the following is even?
(A) $m + n$ (B) $m^2 + n^2$ (C) $m^2 - n^2$ (D) $2m - n$

86. $\log_2 1/2 =$
(A) -1 (B) $1/4$ (C) 1 (D) $\sqrt{2}$

87. The graph of $y = (x - 3)^2$ has a minimum at the point
(A) (0,3) (B) (0,−3) (C) (3,0) (D) (−3,0)

88. The additive inverse of $a - b$ is
(A) $-a - b$ (B) $a + b$ (C) $b - a$ (D) $-(a + b)$

89. A function $f(x)$ is even if $f(-x) = f(x)$. Which of the following functions is *not* even?
(A) $f(x) = x^2 + 3$ (B) $f(x) = (x + 1)^2$
(C) $f(x) = \dfrac{3}{x^2}$ (D) $f(x) = 1 - x^2$

90. For what number a does $a^{-1/2}$ equal 2?
(A) $1/4$ (B) $1/2$ (C) 2 (D) 4

ANSWER KEY AND REFERENCE CHART—SAMPLE EXAMINATION 3

See page 284 for an explanation of the reference code given in parentheses after each answer.

Section I

1.	A (A1)	9.	B (A3)	17.	A (A2)	25.	B (A4)	33.	C (A1)
2.	C (A1)	10.	A (A1)	18.	D (A3)	26.	C (A3)	34.	B (A2)
3.	A (A1)	11.	C (A1)	19.	C (A3)	27.	B (A2)	35.	D (A1)
4.	B (A1)	12.	D (A2)	20.	C (A3)	28.	C (A2)	36.	D (A1)
5.	B (A1)	13.	A (A2)	21.	A (A3)	29.	D (A1)	37.	B (A2)
6.	D (A2)	14.	B (A2)	22.	C (A3)	30.	C (A4)	38.	C (A2)
7.	C (A1)	15.	C (A2)	23.	C (A4)	31.	A (A4)	39.	C (A4)
8.	B (A3)	16.	A (A2)	24.	B (A4)	32.	A (A2)	40.	A (A4)

Section II

41.	C (B1)	51.	C (B3)	61.	B (B5)	71.	B (B6)	81.	C (B3)
42.	A (B1)	52.	B (B3)	62.	C (B5)	72.	A (B3)	82.	C (B4)
43.	D (B1)	53.	B (B3)	63.	B (B5)	73.	B (B6)	83.	A (B5)
44.	B (B2)	54.	C (B4)	64.	D (B5)	74.	B (B1)	84.	C (B5)
45.	B (B2)	55.	A (B4)	65.	C (B5)	75.	D (B3)	85.	D (B3)
46.	C (B2)	56.	A (B4)	66.	A (B4)	76.	B (B3)	86.	A (B6)
47.	A (B2)	57.	D (B4)	67.	D (B3)	77.	B (B6)	87.	C (B4)
48.	D (B2)	58.	C (B3)	68.	B (B3)	78.	A (B6)	88.	C (B3)
49.	D (B3)	59.	D (B4)	69.	A (B4)	79.	D (B1)	89.	B (B4)
50.	C (B3)	60.	A (B6)	70.	A (B6)	80.	A (B3)	90.	A (B3)

SCORING CHART—SAMPLE EXAMINATION 3

After you have scored your Sample Examination 3, enter the results in the chart below; then transfer your Raw Score to the Progress Chart on page 14.

Total Test	Number Right	Number Wrong	Number Omitted	Raw Score
Section I: 40				
Section II: 50				
Total: 90				

ANSWER EXPLANATIONS—SAMPLE EXAMINATION 3

Section I

1. A. $3 \times 5 - 5 = (3 \times 5) - 5 = 15 - 5 = 10$
2. C. $\sqrt{1/16} = 1/4$; $\dfrac{0.3}{1.2} = 3/12 = 1/4$.
3. **A. If the average of 7 numbers is 13, then their sum divided by 7 equals 13; therefore their sum must be 7×13, or 91.**
4. **B. If the carpet costs \$10 a square yard, the total cost of 122 yards would be \$1220.**
5. B. $(70 \div 12) < 6$; $(98 \div 16) > 6$.
6. **D. x may be negative, positive, or even zero.**
7. C. We can rearrange (mentally) the Column B entry, with an eye on Column A, as follows:

$$\begin{aligned} 62 \times 2/17 \times 30 &= (31 \times 2) \times 2/17 \times (3 \times 10) \\ &= 2 \times 10 \times 3 \times 2/17 \times 31 \\ &= 20 \times 6/17 \times 31 \end{aligned}$$

8. B.

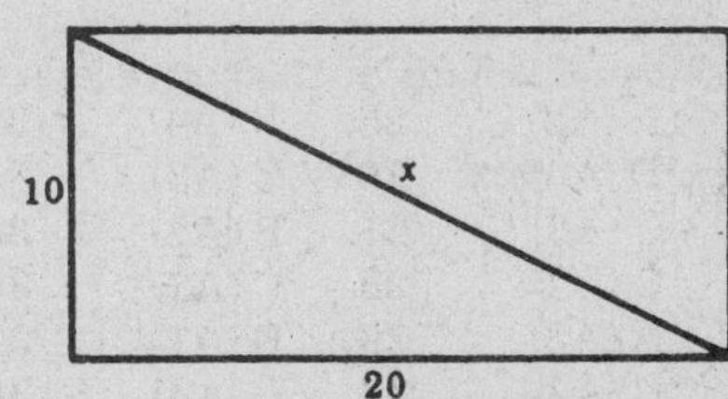

$$x^2 = 100 + 400 = 500$$

$$x = 10\sqrt{5} < 10(2.5) = 25$$

9. **B. The area is $(12 \times 12) - (2 \times 2)$, or 140 square feet; $140 \times 0.20 =$ \$28.**
10. **A. Be careful. The average speed is**

$$\frac{8+8}{1 + 2/3} = \frac{16}{5/3} = 16 \times 3/5 = 48/5 > 9.$$

11. **C. The thousands digit in 40,010, which is underlined, is 0. $3.01 \times 10^3 = 3010$, and the (underlined) hundreds digit is also 0.**
12. D. If $-1 \leq 2x + 1 < 2$, then $-1 - 1 \leq 2x < 2 - 1$, $-2 \leq 2x < 1$, and $-1 \leq x < 1/2$. So if x must be an integer, it may be either -1 or 0.
13. **A. If $bd > 0$, then the inequality is preserved when we multiply by bd. Thus, $ad > bc$.**
14. **B. If $5(3x - 1) - x = 5$, then $15x - 5 - x = 5$, $14x = 10$, and $x = 5/7$.**
15. **C. $(3x)(8x^{11})(x^{12}) = 24x^{24}$.**
16. **A. If $\dfrac{8}{x} + \dfrac{1}{2} = \dfrac{11}{x}$, then $\dfrac{1}{2} = \dfrac{3}{x}$ and $x = 6$.**

17. A. **The ratio of the total number of doctors to the number from city $Z = n : 1$, where $n > 3$.**

18. D. **Don't assume that the segments are of equal length. A counterexample is shown at the right.**

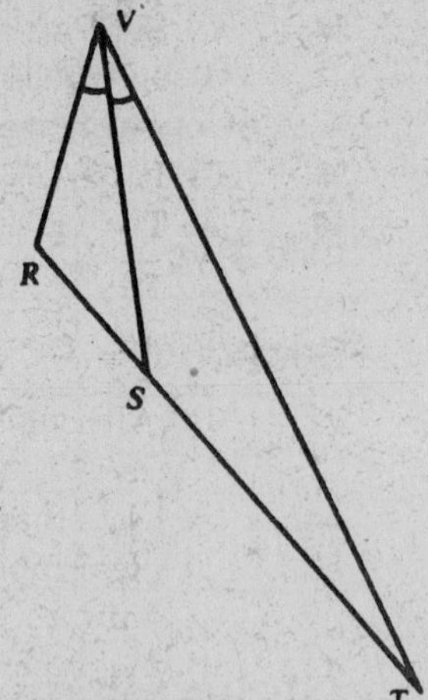

19. 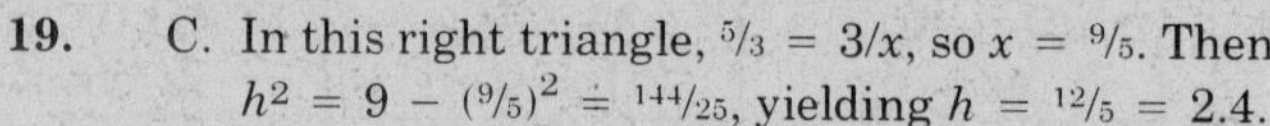
C. In this right triangle, $5/3 = 3/x$, so $x = 9/5$. Then $h^2 = 9 - (9/5)^2 = 144/25$, yielding $h = 12/5 = 2.4$.

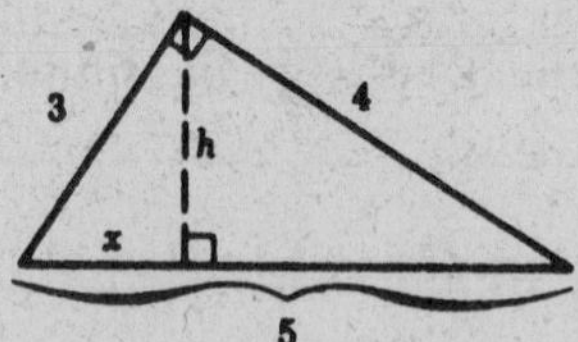

20. C. $m(\angle QOR) = m(QTR)$, since $\angle QOR$ is a central angle; $m(\angle NMP) = \frac{1}{2}m(NSP)$, since $\angle NMP$ is inscribed. Then

$$\frac{m(\angle QOR)}{m(\angle NMP)} = \frac{m(QTR)}{\frac{1}{2}m(NSP)} = \frac{1}{\frac{1}{2}} \cdot \frac{2}{1} = \frac{4}{1} = 4:1.$$

21. A. **The interior angles of the quadrilateral sum to 360°; therefore $y = 82$.**

22. C. Area $RSTU = 4(x + y) =$ $8(\text{area } \triangle QRS) = 8 \cdot \frac{1}{2} \cdot 4x$. $4x + 4y = 16x$; $4y = 12x$, and $y = 3x$.

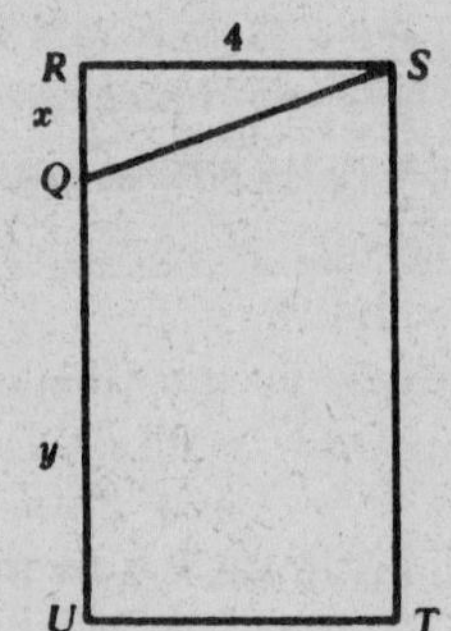

23. C. Contributions under employee-benefit plans in 1950 were $3.9 billion.

24. B. Percentage increase $= \frac{19.1 - 3.9}{3.9} = \frac{15.2}{3.9} < 500\%$

25. B. Ratio described is clearly less for contributions, since the amounts shown for health insurance are roughly equal but total contributions are much greater than total benefits.

26. C. The area of the square is $(4r)^2 = 16r^2$; the area of the four circles is $4\pi r^2$.

27. B. $(5 - \sqrt{2})(5 + \sqrt{2}) = 25 - 2 = 23$.

28. C. Replace x by 3 and y by -1 in each equation. The left side in (C) does not equal the right.

29. D. $\frac{1}{0.02} = \frac{100}{2} = 50$.

30. C. Use the top unshaded bar.

31. A. The black bar is about twice the length of the unshaded one.

32. A. $\sqrt{75} - \sqrt{27} - \sqrt{12} = \sqrt{25 \cdot 3} - \sqrt{9 \cdot 3} - \sqrt{4 \cdot 3}$
$= 5\sqrt{3} - 3\sqrt{3} - 2\sqrt{3} = 0$.

33. C. 5 yd. = 15 ft.; $15 \times 0.50 = 7.50$; $7.50 - \frac{1}{10}(7.50) = 7.50 - 0.75 = \$6.75$.

34. B. $3:x = 5:8 \rightarrow 5x = 24 \rightarrow x = 4.8$.

35. D. The decimal point in 1.06 is moved 5 places to the right to yield 106,000.

36. D. $\frac{7}{4} = 1\frac{3}{4} = 1.75 = 175\%$.

37. B. The fraction at the left is divided by $\frac{x}{x}$. To avoid dividing by zero, x cannot equal zero.
38. C. Subtracting the lower equation from the upper yields $5y = -5$, so $y = -1$; substituting in either equation yields $x = 3$. Or, check the pairs given to see which one satisfies *both* equations.
39. C. It's 13.2%.
40. A. The table tells us that (A) is −3.9%, (B) is −3.2%, (C) is −1.7%, and (D) is −2.1%.

Section II

41. C. Although each set in (A), (B), and (D) is large, it is finite; that is, the elements can (theoretically) be counted.
42. A. Note that $\overline{R \cup S} = \overline{R} \cap \overline{S}$.
43. D. Remember that $G \cup H$ contains elements in G *or* in H and note that G is infinite.
44. B. A statement and its contrapositive are equivalent.
45. B. The negation of $\exists_x, p_x$ is $\forall_x, \sim p_x$.
46. C. Here it is worked out:
The numbers at the bottoms of the columns indicate the order in which the columns were filled.

p	$\vee$	$\sim$	$(p$	$\wedge$	$q)$
T	T	F	T	T	T
T	T	T	T	F	F
F	T	T	F	F	T
F	T	T	F	F	F
(1)	(5)	(4)	(1)	(3)	(2)

47. A. If w denotes "women astronauts are used," s "the space program will be improved," and c "the space program will cost less," then we have $w \rightarrow s$ and $s \rightarrow c$. One valid conclusion is $\sim c \rightarrow \sim s$ and $\sim s \rightarrow \sim w$ or $\sim c \rightarrow \sim w$. No other choice is valid.
48. D. The statement is equivalent to "If not s, then r."
49. D. $2^2 + 3^2 = (\sqrt{13})^2$, *not* 13^2.
50. C. $x^3 - 4x^2 = x^2(x - 4) = 0$ if $x = 0, 4$.
51. C. 0 has no multiplicative inverse.
52. B. Division by zero is not permitted.
53. B. $4^{x-2} = 64 \rightarrow 4^{x-2} = 4^3$; so $x = 5$.
54. C. $f(x) \geq 1$ but the range consists of only some integers, e.g., $f(1) = 3$, $f(2) = 9$, $f(3) = 19$, and so forth.
55. A. $f(f(x)) = 2(2x + 3) + 3 = 4x + 6 + 3 = 4x + 9$.
56. A. $-f(x)$ is the reflection of $f(x)$ in the x-axis.
57. D. In (A), $f(1) = 1$ and 2; (B) is not defined for $x < 0$; and in (C) $f(0)$ is not defined.
58. C. The commutative law for addition specifies for any pair of elements a and b that $a + b = b + a$.
59. D. $\frac{1}{x^2} > 0$ for all x different from 0.
60. A. $m * n = m^n \neq n * m \neq n^m$. If, for example, $m = 3$ and $n = 2$, $m^n \neq n^m$.
61. B. $5 \times 3 \times 4 = 60$.
62. C. **A tree may be most helpful here. There are 3 ways, out of a total of 8 outcomes, of obtaining 2 heads and 1 tail.**

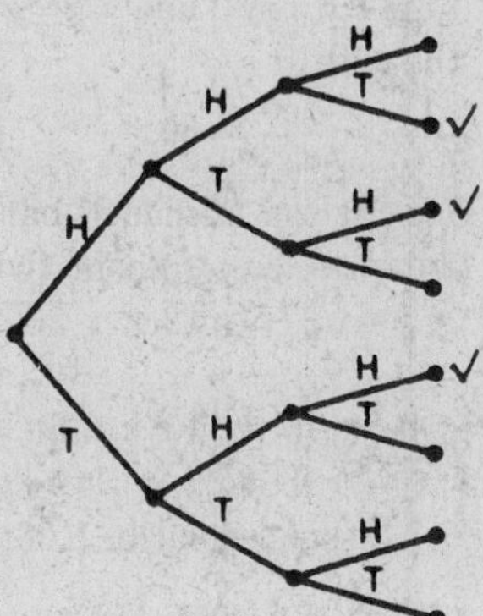

63. B. If p is the probability of an event, then $0 \leq p \leq 1$; p cannot exceed 1.
64. D. Each of the five items may be answered in two ways, yielding 2^5.
65. C. Let L, K, T denote Mrs.Corn's watching *The Lovers, Killers,* or *Ticklers*, respectively. Then $p(L \text{ or } K \text{ or } T) = p(L) + p(K) + p(T) = 0.29 + 0.34 + 0.12$ (since the events are mutually exclusive). The probability that she watches none of these is $1 - [p(L) + p(K) + p(T)]$.
66. A. The graph of $y = x^2 + 2$ is symmetric to the y-axis since $y(-x) = y(x)$.
67. D. $0 \div 1 = 0$. The set of nonnegative integers consists of all the positive integers and zero.
68. B. Since 3 is prime, the divisors of 3^{10} (greater than 1 and less than 3^{10}) are 3^1, $3^2, 3^3, 3^4, 3^5, 3^6, 3^7, 3^8$, and 3^9.
69. A. The slope of $5x - y = 1$ is 5 (write the equation in the form $y = 5x - 1$). The slope of a line perpendicular to it is the negative reciprocal of 5, i.e., $-1/5$.
70. A. The largest three-digit number base 5 is 444_{five}, which equals, base 10, $4 \cdot 5^2 + 4 \cdot 5 + 4$.
71. B. $\log_a x^4 = 4 \log_a x = 4p$.
72. A. The denominator equals 0 except for choice (A).
73. B. $(1 + i)(1 - i) = 1 - i^2 = 1 - (-1) = 2$.
74. B. $V \cup W = \{0,1,2,3\}$. Only the elements 0 and 1 are common to the sets $V \cup W$ and Z.
75. D. It is false that $a \div b = b \div a$ for all real a and b.
76. B. The discriminant equals $5^2 - 4(3)(-1) = 37$.
77. B. Note that if s is any one of the elements in the set, then $s + q = q + s = s$. To find the identity element, look for a column (or a row) identical with the lead column (or row).
78. A. Note that q is the identity and that $r + p = q$.
79. D. Since there are 5 integers in T, T has 2^5 subsets.
80. A. 11 is an odd prime, but $11^2 + 4 = 125$ is not prime.
81. C. Division by zero is prohibited. The numeral "0^0" is not defined.
82. C. $g(-1) = 2^{-(-1)} = 2$, and $f(2) = 2^2 - 5 = -1$.
83. A. There are 4^3 or 64 slips of which 4^2 begin with 7.
84. C. The median is the average of the two "middle" numbers in the arranged set $\{4, 7, 7, 9, 10, 10, 10, 15\}$.
85. D. Since $2m$ and n are both even, so is $2m - n$.
86. A. Since $2^{-1} = 1/2$, $\log_{1/2} 2 = -1$.
87. C. It is the graph of $y = x^2$ translated 3 units to the right.
88. C. The additive inverse of the real number x is $-x$; $-(a - b) = -a + b = b - a$.
89. B. Note that if $f(x) = (x + 1)^2$, $f(-x) = (-x + 1)^2 \neq f(x)$.
90. A. $a^{-1/2} = 2 \rightarrow \frac{1}{a^{1/2}} = 2 \rightarrow \frac{1}{\sqrt{a}} = 2$. So $\frac{1}{a} = 4$ and $a = \frac{1}{4}$.

PART FOUR

THE NATURAL SCIENCES EXAMINATION

ANSWER SHEET — NATURAL SCIENCES/TRIAL TEST

Section I

1. Ⓐ Ⓑ Ⓒ Ⓓ Ⓔ
2. Ⓐ Ⓑ Ⓒ Ⓓ Ⓔ
3. Ⓐ Ⓑ Ⓒ Ⓓ Ⓔ
4. Ⓐ Ⓑ Ⓒ Ⓓ Ⓔ
5. Ⓐ Ⓑ Ⓒ Ⓓ Ⓔ
6. Ⓐ Ⓑ Ⓒ Ⓓ Ⓔ
7. Ⓐ Ⓑ Ⓒ Ⓓ Ⓔ
8. Ⓐ Ⓑ Ⓒ Ⓓ Ⓔ
9. Ⓐ Ⓑ Ⓒ Ⓓ Ⓔ
10. Ⓐ Ⓑ Ⓒ Ⓓ Ⓔ
11. Ⓐ Ⓑ Ⓒ Ⓓ Ⓔ
12. Ⓐ Ⓑ Ⓒ Ⓓ Ⓔ
13. Ⓐ Ⓑ Ⓒ Ⓓ Ⓔ
14. Ⓐ Ⓑ Ⓒ Ⓓ Ⓔ
15. Ⓐ Ⓑ Ⓒ Ⓓ Ⓔ
16. Ⓐ Ⓑ Ⓒ Ⓓ Ⓔ
17. Ⓐ Ⓑ Ⓒ Ⓓ Ⓔ
18. Ⓐ Ⓑ Ⓒ Ⓓ Ⓔ
19. Ⓐ Ⓑ Ⓒ Ⓓ Ⓔ
20. Ⓐ Ⓑ Ⓒ Ⓓ Ⓔ
21. Ⓐ Ⓑ Ⓒ Ⓓ Ⓔ
22. Ⓐ Ⓑ Ⓒ Ⓓ Ⓔ
23. Ⓐ Ⓑ Ⓒ Ⓓ Ⓔ
24. Ⓐ Ⓑ Ⓒ Ⓓ Ⓔ
25. Ⓐ Ⓑ Ⓒ Ⓓ Ⓔ
26. Ⓐ Ⓑ Ⓒ Ⓓ Ⓔ
27. Ⓐ Ⓑ Ⓒ Ⓓ Ⓔ
28. Ⓐ Ⓑ Ⓒ Ⓓ Ⓔ
29. Ⓐ Ⓑ Ⓒ Ⓓ Ⓔ
30. Ⓐ Ⓑ Ⓒ Ⓓ Ⓔ
31. Ⓐ Ⓑ Ⓒ Ⓓ Ⓔ
32. Ⓐ Ⓑ Ⓒ Ⓓ Ⓔ
33. Ⓐ Ⓑ Ⓒ Ⓓ Ⓔ
34. Ⓐ Ⓑ Ⓒ Ⓓ Ⓔ
35. Ⓐ Ⓑ Ⓒ Ⓓ Ⓔ
36. Ⓐ Ⓑ Ⓒ Ⓓ Ⓔ
37. Ⓐ Ⓑ Ⓒ Ⓓ Ⓔ
38. Ⓐ Ⓑ Ⓒ Ⓓ Ⓔ
39. Ⓐ Ⓑ Ⓒ Ⓓ Ⓔ
40. Ⓐ Ⓑ Ⓒ Ⓓ Ⓔ
41. Ⓐ Ⓑ Ⓒ Ⓓ Ⓔ
42. Ⓐ Ⓑ Ⓒ Ⓓ Ⓔ
43. Ⓐ Ⓑ Ⓒ Ⓓ Ⓔ
44. Ⓐ Ⓑ Ⓒ Ⓓ Ⓔ
45. Ⓐ Ⓑ Ⓒ Ⓓ Ⓔ
46. Ⓐ Ⓑ Ⓒ Ⓓ Ⓔ
47. Ⓐ Ⓑ Ⓒ Ⓓ Ⓔ
48. Ⓐ Ⓑ Ⓒ Ⓓ Ⓔ
49. Ⓐ Ⓑ Ⓒ Ⓓ Ⓔ
50. Ⓐ Ⓑ Ⓒ Ⓓ Ⓔ
51. Ⓐ Ⓑ Ⓒ Ⓓ Ⓔ
52. Ⓐ Ⓑ Ⓒ Ⓓ Ⓔ
53. Ⓐ Ⓑ Ⓒ Ⓓ Ⓔ
54. Ⓐ Ⓑ Ⓒ Ⓓ Ⓔ
55. Ⓐ Ⓑ Ⓒ Ⓓ Ⓔ
56. Ⓐ Ⓑ Ⓒ Ⓓ Ⓔ
57. Ⓐ Ⓑ Ⓒ Ⓓ Ⓔ
58. Ⓐ Ⓑ Ⓒ Ⓓ Ⓔ
59. Ⓐ Ⓑ Ⓒ Ⓓ Ⓔ
60. Ⓐ Ⓑ Ⓒ Ⓓ Ⓔ

Section II

1. Ⓐ Ⓑ Ⓒ Ⓓ Ⓔ
2. Ⓐ Ⓑ Ⓒ Ⓓ Ⓔ
3. Ⓐ Ⓑ Ⓒ Ⓓ Ⓔ
4. Ⓐ Ⓑ Ⓒ Ⓓ Ⓔ
5. Ⓐ Ⓑ Ⓒ Ⓓ Ⓔ
6. Ⓐ Ⓑ Ⓒ Ⓓ Ⓔ
7. Ⓐ Ⓑ Ⓒ Ⓓ Ⓔ
8. Ⓐ Ⓑ Ⓒ Ⓓ Ⓔ
9. Ⓐ Ⓑ Ⓒ Ⓓ Ⓔ
10. Ⓐ Ⓑ Ⓒ Ⓓ Ⓔ
11. Ⓐ Ⓑ Ⓒ Ⓓ Ⓔ
12. Ⓐ Ⓑ Ⓒ Ⓓ Ⓔ
13. Ⓐ Ⓑ Ⓒ Ⓓ Ⓔ
14. Ⓐ Ⓑ Ⓒ Ⓓ Ⓔ
15. Ⓐ Ⓑ Ⓒ Ⓓ Ⓔ
16. Ⓐ Ⓑ Ⓒ Ⓓ Ⓔ
17. Ⓐ Ⓑ Ⓒ Ⓓ Ⓔ
18. Ⓐ Ⓑ Ⓒ Ⓓ Ⓔ
19. Ⓐ Ⓑ Ⓒ Ⓓ Ⓔ
20. Ⓐ Ⓑ Ⓒ Ⓓ Ⓔ
21. Ⓐ Ⓑ Ⓒ Ⓓ Ⓔ
22. Ⓐ Ⓑ Ⓒ Ⓓ Ⓔ
23. Ⓐ Ⓑ Ⓒ Ⓓ Ⓔ
24. Ⓐ Ⓑ Ⓒ Ⓓ Ⓔ
25. Ⓐ Ⓑ Ⓒ Ⓓ Ⓔ
26. Ⓐ Ⓑ Ⓒ Ⓓ Ⓔ
27. Ⓐ Ⓑ Ⓒ Ⓓ Ⓔ
28. Ⓐ Ⓑ Ⓒ Ⓓ Ⓔ
29. Ⓐ Ⓑ Ⓒ Ⓓ Ⓔ
30. Ⓐ Ⓑ Ⓒ Ⓓ Ⓔ
31. Ⓐ Ⓑ Ⓒ Ⓓ Ⓔ
32. Ⓐ Ⓑ Ⓒ Ⓓ Ⓔ
33. Ⓐ Ⓑ Ⓒ Ⓓ Ⓔ
34. Ⓐ Ⓑ Ⓒ Ⓓ Ⓔ
35. Ⓐ Ⓑ Ⓒ Ⓓ Ⓔ
36. Ⓐ Ⓑ Ⓒ Ⓓ Ⓔ
37. Ⓐ Ⓑ Ⓒ Ⓓ Ⓔ
38. Ⓐ Ⓑ Ⓒ Ⓓ Ⓔ
39. Ⓐ Ⓑ Ⓒ Ⓓ Ⓔ
40. Ⓐ Ⓑ Ⓒ Ⓓ Ⓔ
41. Ⓐ Ⓑ Ⓒ Ⓓ Ⓔ
42. Ⓐ Ⓑ Ⓒ Ⓓ Ⓔ
43. Ⓐ Ⓑ Ⓒ Ⓓ Ⓔ
44. Ⓐ Ⓑ Ⓒ Ⓓ Ⓔ
45. Ⓐ Ⓑ Ⓒ Ⓓ Ⓔ
46. Ⓐ Ⓑ Ⓒ Ⓓ Ⓔ
47. Ⓐ Ⓑ Ⓒ Ⓓ Ⓔ
48. Ⓐ Ⓑ Ⓒ Ⓓ Ⓔ
49. Ⓐ Ⓑ Ⓒ Ⓓ Ⓔ
50. Ⓐ Ⓑ Ⓒ Ⓓ Ⓔ
51. Ⓐ Ⓑ Ⓒ Ⓓ Ⓔ
52. Ⓐ Ⓑ Ⓒ Ⓓ Ⓔ
53. Ⓐ Ⓑ Ⓒ Ⓓ Ⓔ
54. Ⓐ Ⓑ Ⓒ Ⓓ Ⓔ
55. Ⓐ Ⓑ Ⓒ Ⓓ Ⓔ
56. Ⓐ Ⓑ Ⓒ Ⓓ Ⓔ
57. Ⓐ Ⓑ Ⓒ Ⓓ Ⓔ
58. Ⓐ Ⓑ Ⓒ Ⓓ Ⓔ
59. Ⓐ Ⓑ Ⓒ Ⓓ Ⓔ
60. Ⓐ Ⓑ Ⓒ Ⓓ Ⓔ

CHAPTER

12 Trial Test

The trial Natural Sciences test in this chapter will give you an idea of what the actual exam is like. Take the test, determine your score, and find out which areas of the natural sciences you may need to review.

The test is made up of two parts, one with 60 multiple-choice questions covering the biological sciences, the other with 60 multiple-choice questions covering the physical sciences.

Section I Biological Sciences

Number of Questions: 60
Time: 45 minutes

Directions: Each of the questions or incomplete statements below is followed by five suggested answers or completions. Select the one that is best in each case.

1. What do malaria, amoebic dysentery, and African sleeping sickness have in common?
(A) All are found in Africa only.
(B) All are caused by protozoans.
(C) Each constitutes a serious disease of the central nervous system.
(D) None is of great significance to humans.
(E) All are transmitted by direct contact.

2. Cellular structures responsible for oxidizing food and converting energy to adenosine triphosphate are called
(A) the Golgi apparatus (B) ribosomes (C) chromoplasts
(D) mitochondria (E) the endoplasmic reticulum

3. According to Weismann's theory of the continuity of the germ plasm,
(A) embryos recapitulate embryonic forms of their ancestors
(B) germ plasm remains unaffected by the somaplasm
(C) germ plasm can be influenced only by the somaplasm
(D) genes exist in pairs
(E) genes are in linear order along chromosomes

4. The ribosomes associated with the endoplasmic reticulum consist of
   (A) secretory nodes which control metabolism
   (B) deoxyribose nucleic acid, which synthesizes chromatin
   (C) granular bodies associated with cell division
   (D) ribonucleic acid, which synthesizes protein
   (E) various nucleic acids, each of which is self-perpetuating

5. If a living plant cell is placed in a hypotonic solution,
   (A) turgor pressure decreases
   (B) osmotic pressure increases
   (C) osmotic pressure decreases
   (D) turgor pressure is not affected
   (E) turgor pressure increases

6. In typical ecosystems, the producers are
   (A) heterotrophic (B) parasitic (C) chemotrophic
   (D) photosynthetic (E) saprophytic

7. The light reactions of photosynthesis include those in which
   (A) radiant energy is synthesized into organic materials
   (B) radiant energy is stored
   (C) carbon dioxide is absorbed
   (D) water is split into hydrogen and oxygen
   (E) sugar is formed and oxygen is released

8. The principal water-absorbing structure of a typical root is the
   (A) hair root (B) root cap (C) endodermis
   (D) root hair cell (E) cortex

9. A photosynthetic organism is one which
   (A) obtains energy by the oxidation of inorganic materials
   (B) utilizes solid materials after eating and digesting them
   (C) obtains its nourishment from decaying organic materials
   (D) lives at the expense of other organisms
   (E) uses radiant energy in food synthesis

10. A growth response to the stimulus of light is called
    (A) geotropism (B) phototropism (C) thigmotropism
    (D) photoperiodism (E) hydrotropism

11. The growing of plants under soil-less conditions is called
    (A) aquatics (B) hydrology (C) hydrotropism
    (D) hydroponics (E) hydrotaxis

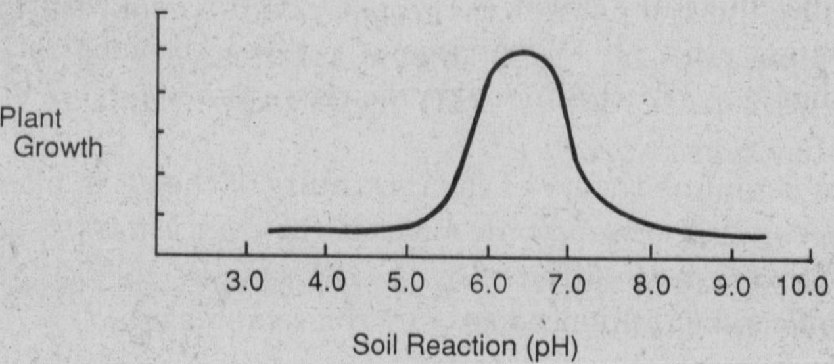

The graph above indicates plant growth in relation to soil reaction or pH. A pH reading below 7.0 is acid; a pH reading above 7.0 is alkaline.

12. On the basis of the information in the graph, one may conclude that
    (A) plant growth causes a shift in soil acidity
    (B) most plants grow best in slightly acid soils
    (C) no plants can survive in alkaline soils
    (D) no plants can survive in acid soils
    (E) soil reaction has little or no effect on plant growth

13. The enzyme-controlled breakdown of carbohydrates under anaerobic conditions is called
    (A) autolysis (B) decomposition (C) bacteriophage
    (D) fermentation (E) interferon

14. In plant reproduction, selected cells of the diploid, spore-producing generation undergo
    (A) diploidization (B) oogenesis (C) spermatogenesis
    (D) meiosis (E) mitosis

15. Structures which are similar because of function are said to be
    (A) analogous (B) homosporous (C) monoecious
    (D) homologous (E) dioecious

16. In blood transfusions, individuals referred to as universal receivers may receive blood from
    (A) group AB (B) groups A, AB (C) groups B, AB
    (D) group O only (E) groups O, A, B, AB

17. Many plants produce an orange pigment called carotene which animals convert to
    (A) ATP (B) hemoglobin (C) vitamin A
    (D) phytol (E) vitamin C

18. Which nerve innervates the semicircular canals?
    (A) Auditory (B) Facial (C) Trochlear
    (D) Spinal accessory (E) Optic

19. The hormone that controls the rate of food conversion to energy is
    (A) insulin (B) thyroxin (C) adrenalin
    (D) cortisone (E) secretin

20. Stimulation by the sympathetic nervous system would result in
    (A) constricted pupils (B) dilated arteries
    (C) accelerated heart beat (D) increased peristalsis
    (E) lower blood pressure

21. Progesterone
    (A) constricts blood vessels
    (B) regulates the menstrual cycle
    (C) stimulates production of thyroxin
    (D) regulates rate of basal metabolism
    (E) regulates sodium metabolism

22. The significance of mitosis is that there is
(A) a quantitative division of the cell
(B) precise distribution of all cell content to the daughter cells
(C) a qualitative division of all cell components
(D) a reduction of chromosome number
(E) precise distribution of DNA to each daughter cell

23. Transfer of genetic information from one generation to the next is accomplished by
(A) RNA (B) messenger RNA (C) codon
(D) translation (E) DNA

24. The inherited variations which are so essential to the concept of natural selection have their source in
(A) acquired characteristics (B) chance variations
(C) mutation (D) the environment (E) special creation

25. Preformationists who were advocates of the theory of embryo development from structures within the sperm were called
(A) ovists (B) animalculists (C) epigenesists
(D) pangenesists (E) phylogenists

26. Permanent wilting is a plant condition caused by the loss of water from which there is no recovery, i.e., no restoration of turgidity. The data below shows the percentages of soil moisture for selected soil types at the time of permanent wilting for the plants indicated.

Soil Moisture % at Time of Permanent Wilting

	Coarse Sand	Fine Sand	Sandy Loam	Loam	Clay Loam
Corn	1.07	3.1	6.5	9.9	15.5
Sorghum	.94	3.6	5.9	10.0	14.1
Oats	1.07	3.5	5.9	11.1	14.8
Pea	1.02	3.3	6.9	12.4	16.6
Tomato	1.11	3.3	6.9	11.7	15.3

On the basis of this information one may conclude that at the time of permanent wilting
(A) sunlight plays a direct role in wilting
(B) water continues to move from particle to particle in the soil
(C) transpiration continues at a reduced rate
(D) soil moisture varies widely for different plants
(E) soil moisture is fairly constant no matter what plant is involved

27. You would expect to observe caribou and lichens in
(A) a tropical rain forest (B) the arctic tundra
(C) a desert (D) a deciduous forest (E) a coniferous forest

28. Plankton includes marine organisms which
(A) exist below low tide and on the continental shelf
(B) exist only in darkness
(C) exist to a depth of 5,000 feet
(D) float on the surface
(E) exist in the deepest ocean trenches

29. Marine organisms characteristic of the abyssal zone would be found
(A) in the inter tidal zone
(B) on the continental shelf to a depth of 500-600 feet
(C) in light
(D) in the deepest ocean trenches
(E) to a depth of 5,000 feet

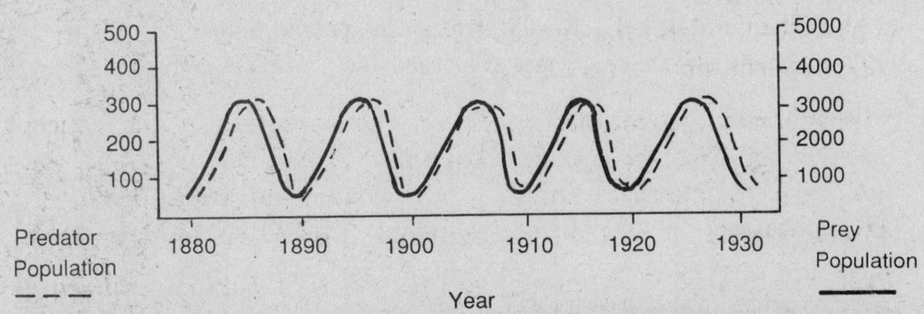

30. In studies of predator-prey populations in a hypothetical situation, the data indicated on the graph above illustrate the cyclical population fluctuations of the predators and the prey.

What conclusion may be drawn from these data?
(A) Predators maintain any population above the capacity of a given environment to support it.
(B) Avoidance of predators has no lasting effect on prey population.
(C) Decreases in populations of prey species are followed by decreases in populations of predator species.
(D) Populations of predators are nourished only by surpluses of prey.
(E) Even when exterminating its prey, a predator never exterminates itself.

31. Interrelationships between organisms are termed commensalism when
(A) both organisms are benefited
(B) mates are defended
(C) one organism benefits at the expense of the other
(D) territories are defended
(E) one organism benefits and the other is not harmed

32. The Cenozoic era is best described as the age of
(A) reptiles (B) seed ferns (C) seed plants and mammals
(D) primitive fishes (E) amphibians

33. In the human circulatory system, blood returns to the heart from the lungs through the
(A) superior vena cava (B) pulmonary veins
(C) inferior vena cava (D) pulmonary artery
(E) descending aorta

34. Blood is supplied to the muscle wall of the heart by the
(A) hepatic portal vein (B) coronary arteries
(C) auricular artery (D) mesenteric artery
(E) coronary veins

35. Hookworm larvae gain access to the body
  (A) by penetrating unbroken skin
  (B) by means of insect bites
  (C) through the mouth in contaminated food
  (D) in improperly cooked pork
  (E) in improperly cooked fish

36. Which of the following diseases of humans is transmitted by the bite of certain ticks?
  (A) Tularemia (B) Rocky Mountain spotted fever
  (C) Sleeping sickness (D) Psittacosis (E) Amebiasis

Questions 37–39

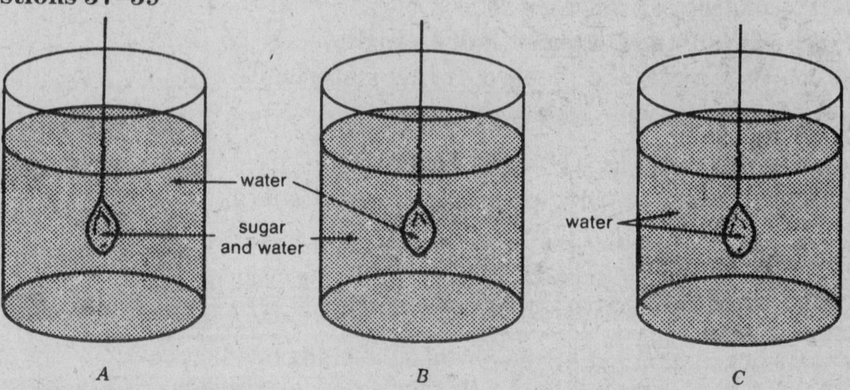

In the diagrams above, water and sugar solutions are separated by cellophane membranes, as indicated. These cellophane membranes are permeable to water molecules and impermeable to sugar molecules. Assume that temperatures are constant and that the cellophane bags are filled equally.

37. In diagram A
  (A) the bag will shrink
  (B) the addition of sugar to the water in the container will cause the turgidity of the bag to increase
  (C) diffusion does not occur
  (D) water molecules diffuse into the bag because there is a greater concentration of water outside than inside the bag
  (E) there is a net movement of water molecules out of the cellophane bag

38. In diagram B
  (A) the bag will shrink
  (B) the bag will swell
  (C) there will be a net movement of water molecules into the bag
  (D) there will be a net movement of sugar molecules into the bag
  (E) sugar draws water out of the bag

39. In diagram C
  (A) water will diffuse into the bag causing it to swell
  (B) water will diffuse out of the bag causing it to shrink
  (C) there is a state of equilibrium in respect to water molecules
  (D) osmosis occurs in the system
  (E) the addition of glass marbles to the container will cause the bag to shrink

40. An organism which obtains energy from the oxidation of inorganic substances is
(A) chemosynthetic (B) photosynthetic (C) parasitic
(D) saprophytic (E) holozoic

41. In a typical lake, the important producers are
(A) commmensals (B) zooplankton (C) nekton
(D) phytoplankton (E) benthos

42. Photosynthesis
(A) results in a decrease in dry weight
(B) is continuous in both light and darkness
(C) produces carbon dioxide and water
(D) results in an increase in dry weight
(E) uses oxygen and glucose as raw materials

43. Photosynthesis
(A) occurs in all living cells
(B) occurs only in the presence of radiant energy
(C) produces carbon dioxide and water
(D) decreases dry weight
(E) occurs in either light or darkness

44. Xylem is the principal constituent of a plant product called
(A) wood (B) bark (C) latex (D) pith (E) resin

45. One side effect that may be produced by the antigen-antibody reaction of the body is
(A) allergy (B) dehydration (C) convulsions
(D) infection (E) pain

46. The body responds to an invasion of viruses by producing
(A) antibodies (B) vaccine (C) antibiotics
(D) antigens (E) immune serum

47. The active substance which appears in a virus-infected cell and which prevents infection by a second virus is called
(A) autolysis (B) interferon (C) lysozyme
(D) bacteriophage (E) rickettsias

48. It is unfortunate for humans that
(A) red blood cells are constantly being formed
(B) blood pressure decreases in the capillaries
(C) the heart beat is a regular rhythmic cycle
(D) the lymphatic system returns fluid to the circulatory system
(E) hemoglobin bonds more firmly to carbon monoxide than to oxygen

49. The Rh factor is fundamentally
(A) a hormonal reaction (B) an antigen-antibody reaction
(C) a form of anemia (D) phagocytosis
(E) a vitamin deficiency

50. A deficiency of vitamin K may result in
(A) soft, weak bones (B) sterility (C) scurvy
(D) beriberi (E) hemorrhage following surgery

51. Roughage is important in the human diet because it
(A) contains vitamins
(B) speeds up digestion
(C) stimulates the walls of the large intestine
(D) slows digestion
(E) stimulates the production of antibodies

52. "Animal starch," a nutrient stored in various types of animal cells, is correctly called
(A) angstrom (B) antigen (C) myosin
(D) glycogen (E) actin

53. When the thyroid gland produces insufficient amounts of thyroxine,
(A) tetany occurs
(B) the basal metabolism rate increases
(C) irregularities in sodium metabolism develop
(D) acromegaly develops
(E) the basal metabolism rate decreases

54. Among the contributions of the ancient Greek scholars
(A) was the law of independent assortment
(B) was the concept of biogenesis
(C) was the concept of recapitulation
(D) were elements of the theory that living organisms have evolved
(E) was the preformation theory

55. The physical basis for heredity was established by T. H. Morgan when he demonstrated his
(A) mutation theory
(B) principle of eugenics
(C) gene theory
(D) theory of recapitulation
(E) chromosome theory of inheritance

56. Paul Ehrlich is best known for his discoveries in
(A) immunization (B) attenuation (C) chemotherapy
(D) antibiosis (E) phytopathology

57. A famous anatomist during the Renaissance was
(A) Bacon (B) Linnaeus (C) Pliny (D) Vesalius
(E) Pasteur

58. In general, short food chains are more efficient than long food chains because in short food chains
(A) there can be no carnivores
(B) there is more energy loss
(C) there are fewer producers
(D) there is less energy loss
(E) there are more producers

59. A population displaying a great number of homologous structures is considered to be
(A) an order (B) a class (C) a family (D) a genus (E) a species

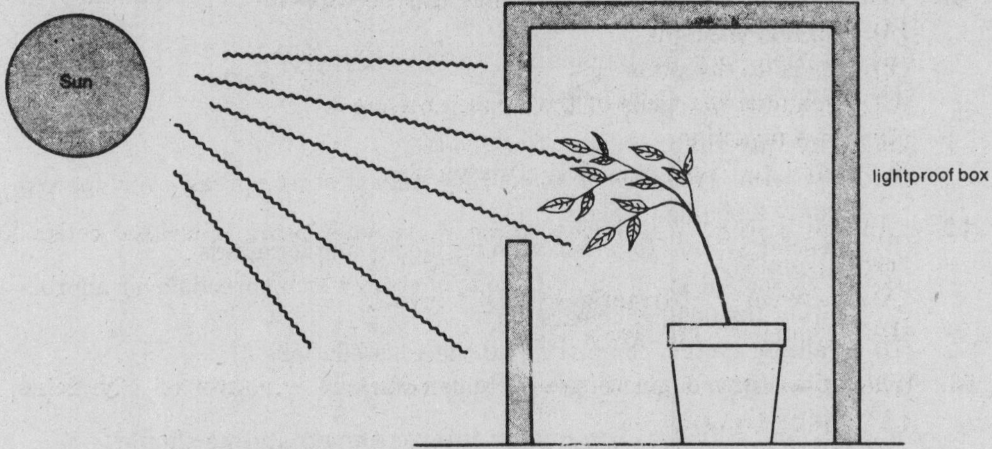

60. Under the conditions of unilateral lighting imposed upon the plant in the diagram above, the plant bends towards the light because
(A) the plant needs more light in order to carry on photosynthesis
(B) the plant grows away from darkness
(C) this is a growth response caused by the unequal distribution of growth-promoting substances in the plant stem
(D) the plant is attracted to light
(E) this is a growth response in an attempt to overcome the growth-repressing effects of darkness

Section II Physical Sciences

Number of Questions: 60
Time: 45 minutes

Directions: Each of the questions or incomplete statements below is followed by five suggested answers or completions. Select the one that is best in each case.

1. If you are standing at 90 degrees north latitude, you will be at the
(A) equator (B) Tropic of Cancer (C) Tropic of Capricorn
(D) North Pole (E) international dateline

2. We credit Pythagoras with the theory which bears his name; but he also discovered
(A) that planets revolve from west to east
(B) that planets revolve from east to west
(C) that big rocks fall faster than little rocks
(D) the nature of eclipses
(E) the cause of earthquakes

3. The basic energy-producing reaction in the sun is the conversion of
(A) mass to energy due to pressure
(B) helium to hydrogen
(C) fuels to heat
(D) heavy elements into lighter elements
(E) hydrogen into helium

4. A term to describe the solar system when the earth is presumably in the center is
   (A) rotation (B) parallax (C) geocentric
   (D) heliocentric (E) ecliptic

5. The Milky Way galaxy is best described as
   (A) a spherical grouping of about fifty million stars spread over approximately 2,000 light-years
   (B) the solar system together with its moons and asteroids
   (C) a disk-shaped grouping of billions of stars which spreads over approximately 100,000 light-years
   (D) a galactic system comprising all the constellations
   (E) a spherical grouping of over a billion stars

6. An eastbound traveler crossing the international dateline should
   (A) set his watch back one hour
   (B) set his watch ahead one hour
   (C) wait until he reaches the midnight meridian
   (D) subtract a day
   (E) add a day

7. When an astronomer detects a shift towards the red end of the spectrum, which of the following may he correctly infer?
   (A) The chemical composition of a star has changed.
   (B) He has discovered a new star.
   (C) A star is stationary.
   (D) The star he is observing has speeded up.
   (E) A star is approaching.

8. One example of geological crosscutting is
   (A) a fault (B) an oxbow (C) a moraine
   (D) a flood plain (E) a stalagmite

9. Fossilized resin from ancient coniferous trees is called
   (A) amber (B) basalt (C) chert (D) dolomite
   (E) halite

10. One outstanding and distinguishing feature of sedimentary rocks is
    (A) their complete lack of fossils
    (B) that they are formed exclusively of precipitates
    (C) that they are formed exclusively of crystals
    (D) the presence of different layers
    (E) that they are formed by the cooling of magma

11. During the radioactive decay of a given element,
    (A) X-rays are emitted
    (B) alpha and beta rays and X-rays are emitted
    (C) alpha and gamma rays and X-rays are emitted
    (D) beta and gamma rays are emitted
    (E) alpha, beta, and gamma rays are emitted

12. As a result of nuclear fission
    (A) there is an increase in mass (B) light atomic nuclei fuse
    (C) X-rays are emitted (D) much energy is consumed
    (E) a chain reaction may occur

13. Color aberrations encountered when using lenses are corrected by
(A) use of convex lenses
(B) use of concave lenses
(C) use of achromatic lenses
(D) reducing the field or the aperture
(E) proper focusing

14. When a body is immersed in a liquid, its weight is determined by
(A) the sum of the external pressures on it
(B) the force per unit area
(C) the depth at which point the weights are equal
(D) the weight of the liquid displaced
(E) the volume of the liquid displaced

15. The three ways by which heat is transferred from a warm to a cold region are
(A) absorption, adsorption and radiation
(B) conduction, convection and infusion
(C) absorption, adsorption and convection
(D) conduction, infusion and vaporization
(E) conduction, convection and radiation

16. One basic function of a transistor is
(A) rectification
(B) to form an electrical connection with any electron-receptive object
(C) to provide high voltage from direct current
(D) to transfer an electric signal across a resistor
(E) to counteract the Edison effect

17. For every known subatomic particle, there is believed to exist
(A) an isotope (B) an ionized equivalent
(C) an antiparticle or antimatter (D) coherent radiation
(E) a thermoelectric effect

18. The science of acoustics is concerned chiefly with
(A) wavelengths (B) loudness (C) frequencies
(D) reverberations (E) amplitude

19. What is an atom that carries an electric charge called?
(A) A catalyst (B) An ion (C) An enzyme
(D) An isotope (E) An ester

20. The continual change in the plane in which a Foucault pendulum swings is evidence that
(A) the earth rotates
(B) the moon revolves around the earth
(C) the earth revolves around the sun
(D) the sun is the center of the solar system
(E) the earth is round

21. When a glass rod is rubbed with a silk cloth
(A) the glass rod gains electrons and becomes negatively charged
(B) the glass rod gains electrons and becomes positively charged
(C) the glass rod remains neutral
(D) the glass rod loses electrons and becomes negatively charged
(E) the glass rod loses electrons and becomes positively charged

22. According to the Second Law of Thermodynamics, ongoing chemical and physical reactions progress from states of high organization to states of low organization unless
(A) a supply of energy is present
(B) a catalyst is added
(C) energy is withdrawn
(D) the reactants are balanced
(E) a buffer is added

23. The speed of molecular activity is dependent upon
(A) sulfonation (B) temperature (C) defloration
(D) concentration (E) saturation

24. Work is accomplished when
(A) direction is imposed upon a moving object
(B) energy output equals energy input
(C) a machine operates without expending energy
(D) force is exerted upon an object, causing it to move
(E) a weight is held stationary at a certain height

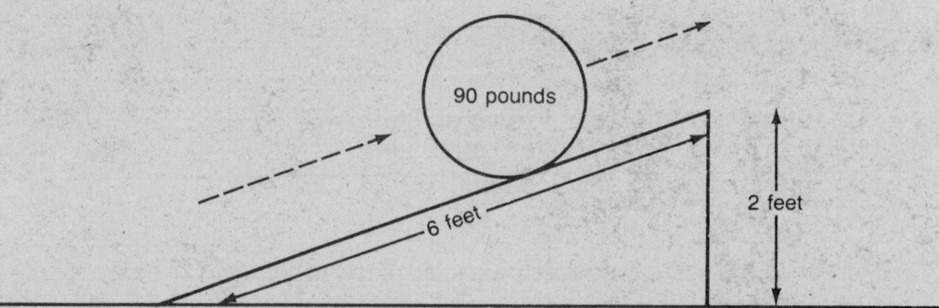

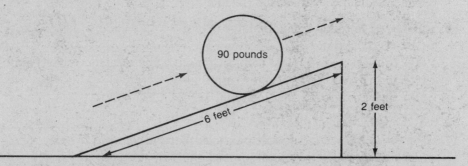

25. In the diagram above, how much effort is required to push the 90-pound barrel up the inclined plane?
(A) 45 pounds effort
(B) 30 pounds effort
(C) 15 pounds effort
(D) 10 pounds effort
(E) 5 pounds effort

26. In a general sense, the measure of the number of atoms or molecules in a solution is called
(A) the atomic number
(B) a mole
(C) its catalytic potential
(D) its coordination number
(E) its electron mass

27. The body of any free-falling object in motion continues to accelerate until until
(A) the law of gravity takes over
(B) its velocity equals the speed of light
(C) air resistance becomes a factor
(D) the law of inertia takes over
(E) it is influenced by the Doppler effect

28. According to Newton's third law, there must be a reaction to the force which propels a bullet from the barrel of a rifle. This force is in the
(A) recoil
(B) friction of the bullet in the barrel
(C) pressure used to squeeze the trigger
(D) shoulder of the person firing the rifle
(E) inertia of the bullet

29. Fusion reactions for the peaceful production of power have been unsuccessful because
(A) they are too powerful
(B) they are too rapid
(C) there is no practical way to control the rate of the fusion reaction
(D) the cost is prohibitively high
(E) radioactive electricity is too dangerous

30. Laser-generated light
(A) is incoherent
(B) is chaotic
(C) is nonchaotic
(D) is disordered
(E) has waves of different frequencies

31. Current kinetic theory in respect to gases is based primarily on
(A) the motion of molecules
(B) the attraction of molecules for each other
(C) the ionization of gas molecules
(D) sublimation
(E) vaporization

32. High-altitude satellites will some day fall to earth because of
(A) drag caused by cosmic radiation
(B) drag caused by infrared radiation
(C) centrifugal force
(D) centrifugal force and the moon's gravity
(E) drag caused by air and particles

33. On which of the following is the pH scale based?
(A) An arithmetic progression of hydrogen ions
(B) An equal balance between hydrogen and hydroxide ions
(C) An estimate of the number of hydrogen ions present
(D) An estimate of the number of hydroxide ions present
(E) The concentration of hydrogen ions in a liter of solution

34. When an object is transferred from the moon to earth, its mass
(A) increases (B) decreases (C) remains constant
(D) and weight increase on earth
(E) and weight decrease on earth

35. The thermodynamic measure of disorder is called
(A) entropy (B) spontaneity (C) momentum
(D) redundancy (E) valence

36. Through a microscope, minute particles are observed to be in an almost constant state of random movement, a phenomenon called
(A) surface tension (B) capillarity (C) osmosis
(D) diffusion (E) Brownian movement

37. The force causing a liquid to rise inside a tube of very small diameter is
(A) surface tension (B) kinetic energy
(C) potential energy (D) adhesion (E) cohesion

38. The atomic number of an element refers to
(A) the total number of electrons and protons it possesses
(B) the number of neutrons it possesses
(C) the number of protons it possesses
(D) its sequential number in the atomic scale
(E) the total number of neutrons and protons it possesses

39. A dispersion in which the particles eventually settle out is an example of
(A) an emulsion (B) a solution (C) a mixture
(D) a colloid (E) a suspension

40. The alkali metal family of chemical elements includes potassium and
(A) calcium (B) iron (C) nickel
(D) sodium (E) aluminum

41. In reduction reactions of organic chemistry
(A) oxygen acts as a catalyst
(B) oxygen is a dephlogisticant
(C) ionic oxygen is consumed
(D) oxygen is removed from a compound
(E) oxygen combines chemically with another substance

42. The primary concern of alchemy was
(A) sublimation (B) vaporization (C) solidification
(D) liquefaction (E) transmutation

43. In any given process
(A) energy may be created
(B) energy may be destroyed
(C) energy may neither be created nor destroyed
(D) the energies of the reactants and products are variable
(E) energy and work are totally unrelated

44. In accordance with Einstein's theory of relativity, as a body gains speed
(A) its mass decreases proportionately
(B) its mass increases proportionately
(C) only electrons in the outer shells of its atoms are affected
(D) mass and energy are not related
(E) only energy is lost

45. Substances which form ions in solution and which can conduct an electric current are called
(A) reactors (B) dispersions (C) substrates
(D) electrolytes (E) conductors

46. When different atoms of an element have different weights, we call them
(A) ions (B) isotopes (C) molecules (D) electrons (E) nuclei

47. Gamma radiation is frequently used successfully to treat tumors and cancer tissue because
(A) such tissues are immune to radiation
(B) such tissues are more sensitive to radiation than are healthy tissues
(C) it acts faster than surgery without the risks of surgery
(D) the induced rate of radioactive decay is indicative of the extent of cure
(E) gamma radiation is low-energy radiation

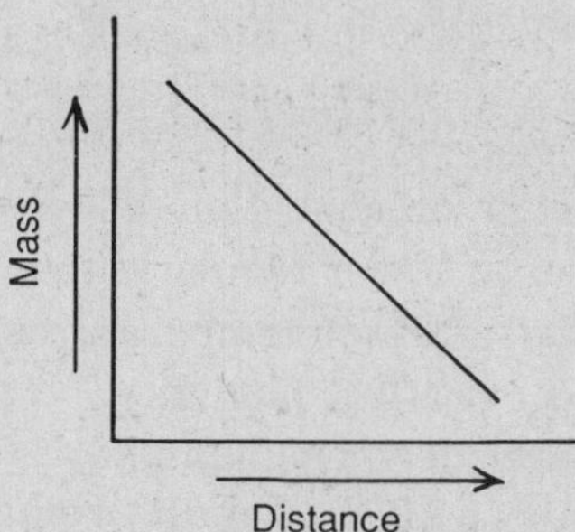

48. The graph above illustrates Newton's Law of Universal Gravitation in respect to the effects of mass and distance.

From this illustration, one may infer that
(A) the strength of gravity increases with the mass of the object exerting the pull and diminishes as the distance from the object being pulled increases
(B) the strength of gravity decreases with the mass of the object exerting the pull and increases as the distance from the object being pulled decreases
(C) the strength of gravity is not affected by mass
(D) the strength of gravity is not affected by distance
(E) the force of gravity is affected by neither mass nor distance

49. Heat is a form of energy existing in matter and is attributed to
(A) the exchange of electrons between atoms
(B) the conversion of matter to energy
(C) the motion of molecules
(D) the conversion of energy to matter
(E) its absorption from the environment

50. By mixing all of the colors of the visible spectrum we produce
(A) infrared light (B) black light (C) purple light
(D) green light (E) white light

51. The change of certain substances from solid to gaseous states without passing through the liquid state is called
(A) sublimation (B) fusion (C) convergence
(D) thermal coefficient (E) reciprocation

Questions 52 and 53

Humidity is a measure of water-holding capacity of the atmosphere and may be expressed in terms of the number of grams of water vapor held per cubic meter of air.

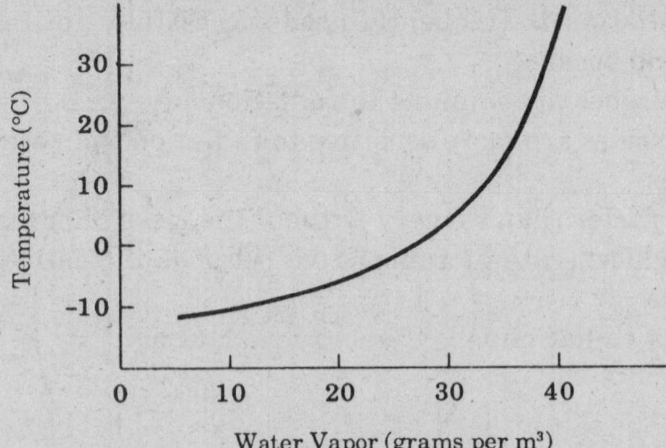

52. According to the illustration above, one may conclude that
   (A) humidity increases at lower temperatures
   (B) humidity decreases at lower temperatures
   (C) temperature does not affect humidity
   (D) higher temperatures decrease humidity
   (E) at temperature above 20°C humidity remains constant

53. From the illustration above, one may also conclude that
   (A) if the humidity increases the temperature will rise
   (B) if the humidity decreases the temperature will rise
   (C) humidity increases uniformly as temperature increases
   (D) saturated air cannot retain its water if the temperature is lowered
   (E) saturated air can hold additional water if the temperature is lowered

54. Although ahead of his time, Roger Bacon contributed to science by stating that intuition or reason is insufficient to justify scientific theory and that, to give certainty to science, there must be
   (A) research (B) data (C) facts (D) observation
   (E) experimentation

55. Electromagnetic waves of extremely high frequency are called
   (A) photons (B) matter waves (C) gamma rays
   (D) X-rays (E) beta rays

Directions: Each group of questions below consists of five lettered choices followed by a list of numbered phrases or sentences. For each numbered phrase or sentence select the one choice that is most closely related to it. Each choice may be used once, more than once, or not at all in each group.

Questions 56–58

(A) Distillation
(B) Evaporation
(C) Radiolysis
(D) Sublimation
(E) Transmutation

56. The conversion of one element to another

57. The radioactive disintegration of radium to radon

58. The direct conversion of a solid to a vapor

Questions 59–60

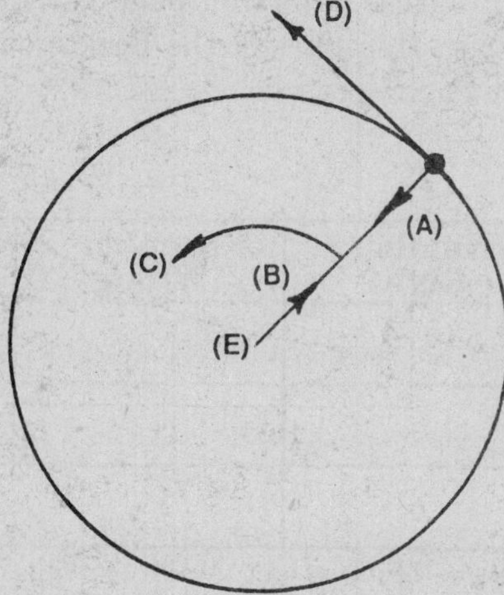

The diagram above represents the circular path of a moving weight tied to the end of a string. The five lettered choices are indicated on the diagram.

59. The velocity of the weight

60. The centrifugal force on the moving weight

ANSWER KEY—TRIAL TEST

Section I Biological Sciences

1. B	11. D	21. B	31. E	41. D	51. C
2. D	12. B	22. E	32. C	42. D	52. D
3. B	13. D	23. E	33. B	43. B	53. E
4. D	14. D	24. C	34. B	44. A	54. D
5. E	15. A	25. B	35. A	45. A	55. C
6. D	16. E	26. E	36. B	46. A	56. C
7. D	17. C	27. B	37. D	47. B	57. D
8. D	18. A	28. D	38. A	48. E	58. D
9. E	19. B	29. D	39. C	49. B	59. E
10. B	20. C	30. C	40. A	50. E	60. C

Section II Physical Sciences

1. D	11. E	21. E	31. A	41. D	51. A
2. A	12. E	22. A	32. E	42. E	52. B
3. E	13. C	23. B	33. E	43. C	53. D
4. C	14. D	24. D	34. C	44. B	54. E
5. C	15. E	25. B	35. A	45. D	55. B
6. D	16. D	26. B	36. E	46. B	56. E
7. D	17. C	27. C	37. D	47. B	57. E
8. A	18. D	28. A	38. C	48. A	58. D
9. A	19. B	29. C	39. E	49. C	59. D
10. D	20. A	30. C	40. D	50. E	60. B

SCORING CHART—TRIAL TEST

After you have scored your Trial Examination, enter the results in the chart below (the Raw Score computation is explained on page 14); then transfer your Raw Score to the Progress Chart on page 14. As you complete the Sample Examinations later in this part of the book, you should be able to achieve increasingly higher Raw Scores.

Total Test	Number Right	Number Wrong	Number Omitted	Raw Score
Section I: 60				
Section II: 60				
Total: 120				

ANSWER EXPLANATIONS—TRIAL TEST

Section I Biological Sciences

1. B. Protozoans include some 30,000 single-celled, usually nongreen organisms, some of which cause these serious human diseases.
2. D. Mitochondria are the sites where energy is transferred from molecules of carbohydrate to those of ATP.
3. B. Reproduction is accomplished, not by somaplasm, but by germ plasm, which is transmitted essentially unchanged from generation to generation.
4. D. Ribosomes are found scattered in the cytoplasms of living cells and in association with the endoplasmic reticulum. They are composed of ribonucleic acid and protein and function in the synthesis of proteins and enzymes.
5. E. A living plant cell placed in a hypotonic solution, i.e., hypotonic to the cell sap, will increase in turgidity.
6. D. Basic food production for most of the biological world is accomplished by photosynthetic producers.
7. D. Photosynthesis is an energy-storing biochemical reaction in which the radiant energy of sunlight is stored in simple sugars in the form of chemical bonds. During its light reactions, water is split into hydrogen and oxygen.
8. D. Root hair cells are hairlike extensions of the epidermal cells of most kinds of plant roots. These provide greatly increased surfaces for water absorption.
9. E. A photosynthetic organism possesses chlorophyll and, in the presence of radiant energy, synthesizes glucose from carbon dioxide and water and stores energy.
10. B. Growth responses of plants are called tropisms. The growth response of plants to light is called phototropism.
11. D. Hydroponics is the growing of plants in a liquid or moist environment (without soil) to which essential mineral nutrients are added.
12. B. Most plants survive and grow best in soils of slightly acid to neutral soil reaction (pH 5.8–7.0).

13. D. Fermentation is the anaerobic breakdown of carbohydrates by the enzymes produced by living microorganisms such as yeasts.

14. D. In plants, diploid spore-mother cells undergo meiosis to produce haploid spores.

15. A. Analogous structures are similar because of functions; the wing of a bird and the wing of a bee are analogous structures.

16. E. Persons with AB type blood are designated as universal receivers. They can receive blood from any other person, regardless of blood type, since they have both antigen A and antigen B.

17. C. Carotene is a precursor of vitamin A.

18. A. The semicircular canals are associated with the inner ear and function to keep the body aware of its position with respect to gravity and motion.

19. B. Thyroxin controls the rate of metabolism by controlling the cellular respiration of food.

20. C. The sympathetic nervous system responds to perceived emotional situations such as anger or fear. One body response to anger or fear is accelerated heart beat.

21. B. The corpus luteum secretes progesterone, which regulates the menstrual cycle and prepares the body for pregnancy.

22. E. Mitosis is both a quantitative and qualitative division of the nucleus of a cell which results in precise and equal distribution of chromatin and, therefore, DNA to each daughter cell.

23. E. Deoxyribonucleic acid (DNA) is the only substance transmitted qualitatively and quantitatively from one generation to the next.

24. C. A mutation is a gene change. Mutations, therefore, are sources of variations and they continue to be handed down to future generations until they mutate again.

25. B. Animalculists were preformationists who believed in a preformation of the individual within the sperm.

26. E. The data indicate that, at the time of permanent wilting, soil moisture is fairly constant, no matter what species of plant is concerned.

27. B. The arctic tundra is treeless and the home of caribou and numerous lichens. It is also the summer breeding ground for numerous migratory birds.

28. D. Plankton consists of free-floating, usually microscopic, plants and animals in a body of water.

29. D. The abyssal zones of the oceans are the deepest ocean trenches.

30. C. The balance between any predator-prey group is delicate; an increase in the population of the prey is typically followed by an increase in the population of the predator, and vice versa.

31. E. Commensalism is a relationship between two species in which one benefits from the other without harming it or giving benefit to it.

32. C. The Cenozoic Era is the last of the great periods of geologic time and is characterized by the advent of mammals and seed plants.

33. B. Pulmonary veins return oxygenated blood from the lungs to the left atrium of the heart.

34. B. Coronary arteries branch from the aorta and carry blood to the heart muscle.

35. A. Hookworm larvae on the ground penetrate unbroken skin, commonly the feet of barefoot children in warm climates.

36. B. Rocky Mountain spotted fever is caused by a rickettsia transmitted to humans through the bite of a tick.

37. D. Sugar molecules inside the bag lower the concentration of water molecules in comparison to the water outside. Therefore, water molecules diffuse into the bag.

38. A. The bag, containing only water, has a higher concentration of water molecules than the surrounding water which also contains sugar molecules. Water will, therefore, diffuse out of the bag and the bag will shrink.

39. C. A state of equilibrium exists and there will be no net diffusion of water either into or out of the bag.

40. A. Some bacteria, such as iron and sulfur bacteria, obtain energy through the oxidation of iron and sulfur compounds respectively.

41. D. Phytoplankton are photosynthetic organisms and because they are so numerous, they are important producers.

42. D. Photosynthesis produces the carbohydrate glucose and therefore increases the dry weight of the plant.

43. B. By definition, photosynthesis means putting together by means of light; hence light is necessary.

44. A. Wood is the tree tissue inside the vascular cambium and is a term synonymous with xylem.

45. A. A single injection of a foreign protein into the body may hyper-sensitize an individual so that future exposure to the same protein results in an allergic reaction.

46. A. A virus invading the body is an antigen. The body's immune system responds by producing antibodies.

47. B. Interferon is produced by body cells into which the foreign nucleic acid of a virus has entered. It renders uninfected cells immune to the virus.

48. E. Carbon monoxide is a major concern since it has a high affinity for hemoglobin.

49. B. Rh-negative individuals develop antibodies to the Rh antigen and these destroy Rh-positive cells.

50. E. Vitamin K is essential for prothrombin synthesis, a step in blood clotting.

51. C. Roughage, such as total grain cereals, is important to the diet because it stimulates the large intestine.

52. D. In humans and other animals, excess glucose is converted into a starch called glycogen, which is stored in muscles and in the liver, where it is readily available.

53. E. Thyroxine deficiency in humans leads to cretinism in early childhood and to a lowered metabolic rate in adults.

54. D. Anaximander, a Greek philosopher (611–547 B.C.), proposed an explanation of evolution based upon observation and reasoning.

55. C. T. H. Morgan first stated the gene theory of inheritance in 1910.

56. C. Ehrlich studied the effects of chemicals upon body tissues and discovered salvarsan, a chemical used to treat syphilis. He was the first to use a systematic approach to treat chemotherapeutic investigations.

57. D. Vesalius was the greatest anatomist of the 16th century and was noted for performing his own dissections.

58. D. At each level in a food chain there is a loss of energy. For this reason, shorter food chains with fewer energy transfers are more efficient.

59. E. One definition identifies a species on the basis of its number of shared homologous structures.

60. C. Unilateral light is responsible for the unequal distribution of growth-promoting substances in the stem, thus causing uneven stem elongation.

Section II Physical Sciences

1. D. Ninety degrees north latitude is as far north as one can travel and is everywhere equidistant from the equator—hence, the North Pole.

2. A. Pythagoras believed that the earth was spherical and that the sun, moon, and planets had movements of their own.

3. E. Hydrogen atoms in the sun undergo fusion. Four atoms of hydrogen fuse to form one atom of helium with a minute quantity of mass left over. This mass is converted into energy.

4. C. Geocentric describes a concept pertaining to the solar system which supposes that the earth is the center of the system.

5. C. The Milky Way is a large spiral galaxy shaped like a disk and is approximately 5,000 light-years thick and 100,000 light-years in diameter.

6. D. When crossing the international dateline in an easterly direction, a traveler loses a day. If, for example, the traveler crosses the international dateline on a Monday, he or she finds that it is now Sunday east of the line.

7. D. The observed frequency of a light wave will decrease (shift) if the source is traveling away from the observer. This is the Doppler effect.
8. A. A fault is a fracture of the earth's crust accompanied by a shift of one side with respect to the other.
9. A. Amber is fossilized resin.
10. D. Probably the most distinguishing feature of sedimentary rock is the fact that it is a layered structure.
11. E. During radioactive decay alpha, beta, and gamma rays are emitted.
12. E. A chain reaction proceeds in a series of steps, each being made possible by the preceeding. If the fission is initiated by neutrons, neutrons are released to continue the reaction.
13. C. Color or chromatic aberration is the failure of the different colors contained in white light to meet in a common point, called the focal point, after they pass through a convex lens. It may be reduced by use of an achromatic lens.
14. D. An object in water displaces an amount of water equal to its own weight.
15. E. Heat may be transferred by conduction, convection, and radiation.
16. D. A transistor is a semiconductor used in modern amplifier and switching circuits.
17. C. In certain situations, such as pair annihilation, an electron and a positron interact and disappear. The positron in this situation is the so-called antiparticle of the electron.
18. D. Sound reverberations are reflections of sound waves, i.e., echoes.
19. B. An ion is defined as an atom bearing an electric charge. Ions are formed whenever atoms gain or lose electrons.
20. A. A Foucault pendulum is so constructed that it always swings in the same plane. The rotation of the earth makes the pendulum appear to change the plane in which it swings.
21. E. Static electricity can be produced by rubbing a glass rod with a piece of silk, during which the silk takes up electrons to become negatively charged. The glass rod gives up electrons to become positively charged.
22. A. According to the Second Law of Thermodynamics, reactions proceed from low to higher entropy, that is, from order to disorder, unless a supply of energy is present.
23. B. The speed of molecules is directly proportional to their temperature.
24. D. Work is defined as the force exerted upon an object multiplied by the distance the object is moved.
25. B. The ratio of the height of the inclined plane to its hypotenuse determines the effort required to move the barrel up the inclined plane.
26. B. A mole is the number of atoms, ions, or molecules in a solution when the molecular formula is known.
27. C. The acceleration of a falling body is expressed as 32.16 feet per second per second, subject to the air resistance on a particular falling body.
28. A. According to Newton's third law, to each and every action, there is an equal and opposite reaction.
29. C. Nuclear fusion promises unlimited supplies of energy with much less environmental danger than from fission reactions. However, to date, no useful fusion reactor has been designed.
30. C. Laser-generated light is coherent, ordered, and nonchaotic, and each wave has the same frequency, phase, and direction.
31. A. The current kinetic-molecular theory is a concept based on studies of the motion of molecules.
32. E. All earth satellites will eventually fall back to earth because of drag which is caused by air molecules (even though sparse) and particulate matter in space.
33. E. The pH scale is based on the concentration of hydrogen ions in a liter of solution and is expressed as a logarithmic progression.
34. C. Mass always remains constant. However, on the moon, due to a lower gravity, an object would appear to be lighter.
35. A. Entropy is the thermodynamic measure of disorder and always increases during any spontaneous process.

36. E. Brownian movement is the result of molecular activity. Under the microscope, visible particles appear to be in a state of erratic motion because they are continually being bombarded (bumped) from all sides by molecules in motion.
37. D. A liquid rises in a tube of small diameter due to the attraction between the liquid and the solid, i.e., adhesion.
38. C. The number of protons in an atomic nucleus is the atomic number.
39. E. Muddy water is a suspension, i.e., it is a dispersion in which the particles eventually settle out.
40. D. The alkali metal family includes sodium, potassium, lithium, cesium, etc.
41. D. In a basic sense, the oxidation/reduction reactions of organic chemistry are concerned with the addition or removal of oxygen.
42. E. In medieval times, alchemy was an endeavor to change base metals into gold, i.e., transmutation.
43. C. The First Law of Thermodynamics states that energy may be neither created nor destroyed.
44. B. Mass and velocity are proportional; as speed approaches the velocity of light, mass approaches infinity.
45. D. Certain molecules ionize (example: NaCl ionizes to Na^+ Cl^- ions) when placed in liquids and are able to conduct an electric current.
46. B. Isotopes are atoms of the same element that have different mass numbers, that is, varying numbers of neutrons in their nuclei.
47. B. Tumor cells are more sensitive to radiation generally than are healthy cells. Therefore, radiation therapy is often a successful tumor therapy.
48. A. The strength of gravity increases with the mass of the object exerting the gravitational pull and decreases the greater the distance from the object being pulled.
49. C. Heat is a form of energy existing in matter resulting from the motion of its molecules. There is no molecular motion at absolute zero.
50. E. Visible light is white and includes wavelengths from red to violet with orange, yellow, green, and blue in between.
51. A. The direct change from the solid state to the gaseous state is called sublimation. An example is the sublimation of ice or snow when air flows over it at below freezing temperatures.
52. B. }
53. D. } The ability of the air to hold moisture in vapor form is inversely proportional to the temperature.
54. E. Roger Bacon is credited with the introduction of the experimental method of science.
55. B. At certain speeds, all matter exhibits wavelengths of extremely high frequency and these have been observed to affect spaces between atoms in crystals.
56. E. Transmutation, in the historic sense, is the conversion of base metals to gold or silver and was a medieval concept that never materialized.
57. E. Radioactive decay of certain elements accounts for one form of transmutation which was unknown before its discovery by Becquerel.
58. D. Under certain conditions, solids may be changed directly into gases or vapors by sublimation.
59. D. }
60. B. } The weight tied to the end of the string tends to move in a straight line but is held in circular orbit by the string. Centrifugal force acts in the direction away from the axis or center.

CHAPTER 13

Background and Practice Questions

DESCRIPTION OF THE NATURAL SCIENCES EXAMINATION

The Natural Sciences Examination tests your knowledge, understanding, and utilization of principles, concepts, and ideas in the biological and physical sciences. Its achievement level is that attained by the *average,* nonscience major after satisfying a distribution or general education requirement in science. Your ability to answer certain questions will depend upon the extent of your reading science articles and science-based materials in magazines, newspapers, and other periodicals, all written for the nonscientist.

The examination consists of 120 multiple-choice questions from the traditional areas of the natural sciences. The examination is given in two separately timed 45-minute sections, one covering biological science and the other covering physical science. The content of the examination and the approximate percent of questions in each of the content areas are as follows:

Biological Science (50%)

- 10% Origin and evolution of life, classification of organisms
- 10% Cell organization, cell division, chemical nature of the gene, bioenergetics, biosynthesis
- 20% Structure, function, and development in organisms; patterns of heredity
- 10% Concepts of population biology with emphasis on ecology

Physical Science (50%)

- 7% Atomic and nuclear structure and properties, elementary particles, nuclear reactions
- 10% Chemical elements, compounds and reactions; molecular structure and bonding
- 12% Heat, thermodynamics, and states of matter; classical mechanics; relativity
- 4% Electricity and magnetism, waves, light and sound
- 7% The universe: galaxies, stars, the solar system
- 10% The Earth: atmosphere, hydrosphere, structure, properties, surface features, geological processes, history

Scoring; Penalty For Guessing

Each of the two parts of the examination is scored separately. Each correct answer is worth one point, and there is no penalty for an unanswered question. One fourth of a point is deducted for an incorrect answer; therefore, random guessing is not likely to improve your score. If, however, you can eliminate one or more answer choices as clearly wrong, it may then be worthwhile to select from the remaining choices the one that seems most logical.

THE KINDS OF QUESTIONS THAT APPEAR ON THE EXAMINATION

There are two important aspects of the examination questions: (1) the knowledge and abilities they test for, and (2) the formats in which they are presented.

What the Questions Test

Some questions require knowledge of basic scientific concepts, facts, and principles, others require application of knowledge, and a third group requires interpretation and understanding of data presented in various forms (graphs, diagrams, tables, lists). The following questions provide examples of each type of question.

Knowledge of Concepts, Facts, and Principles

Directions: Each of the questions or incomplete statements below is followed by five suggested answers or completions. Select the one that is best in each case.

1. A plant tissue whose cells disintegrate, causing leaves to separate from their stems, is called
(A) the annulus (B) a bud scar (C) collenchyma
(D) the abscission layer (E) the cambium

2. When a glowing wood splint introduced into a tube of gas subsequently bursts into flame, what gas is in the tube?
(A) Hydrogen (B) Methane (C) Oxygen (D) Helium
(E) Carbon dioxide

Ability to Apply Knowledge

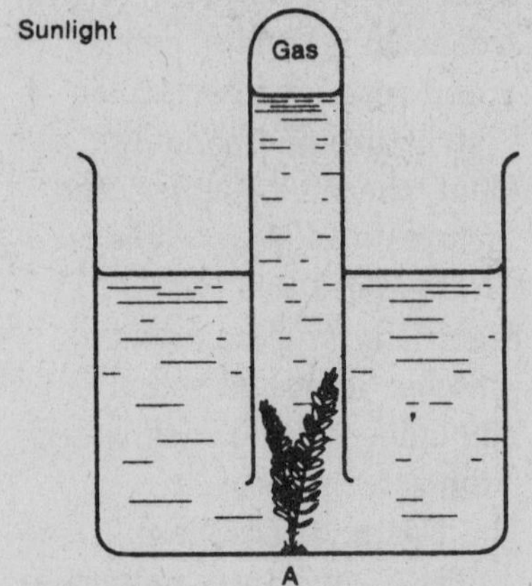

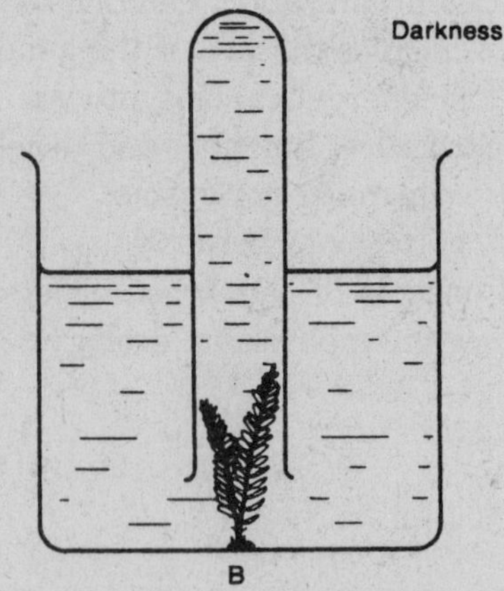

In the diagrams above, aquatic photosynthetic plants are placed under inverted test tubes which are filled with water. Except for light, all environmental and genetic factors are constant and the same for each.

3. After exposing plant A to several hours of sunlight, while plant B is maintained in darkness, it may correctly be concluded that, in respect to gas production,
(A) plant A carried on photosynthesis
(B) plant A carried on both photosynthesis and respiration
(C) darkness inhibits respiration
(D) sunlight is necessary for gas production
(E) sunlight inhibits respiration

Ability to Interpret and Understand Data

Directions: The group of questions below consists of five lettered choices followed by a list of numbered phrases or sentences. For each numbered phrase or sentence select the one choice that is most closely related to it. Each choice may be used once, more than once, or not at all.

(A) Limiting factors of the Environment
(B) High mortality rate
(C) High reproductive rate
(D) Short length of time
(E) Small number of individuals

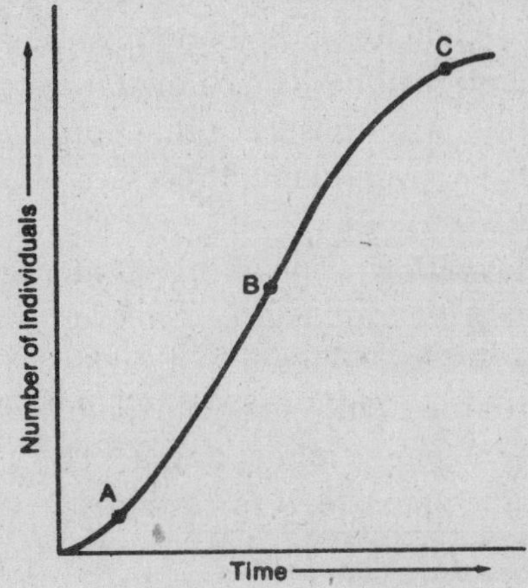

4. A condition limiting the growth rate at position A on the curve

5. A condition limiting the growth rate at position B on the curve

6. A condition limiting the growth rate at position C on the curve

What Formats Are Used

Most questions are in interrogative or sentence-completion form, and require you to select the correct answer from five choices that follow the question. In the preceding group, questions 1–3 are in this format.

A second type lists the answer choices first, and then gives a list of numbered phrases or sentences. You are required to select, for each phrase or sentence, the answer choice that best fits it. Questions 4–6 above, based on a graph, are in this category.

Notice that the directions for the two formats differ.

ANSWERS AND EXPLANATIONS FOR SAMPLE QUESTIONS

1. D. The abscission layer is a layer of plant cells that disintegrates, causing leaves and other structures to separate from the plant.

2. C. A standard laboratory test for oxygen production is that a glowing wood splint bursts into flame in the presence of oxygen.

3. D. Plants A and B are exposed to identical conditions except for sunlight/darkness. There is no evidence that photosynthesis or respiration is occurring. An unidentified gas produced by A is the only observable outcome of this experiment.

4. E.
5. C.
6. A. } The graph represents a standard growth (sigmoid) curve. Over a period of time a small number of individuals existing under normal conditions will increase in number while food, space, etc., are ample, but, as the numbers of individuals increase, competition for food, space, etc., increases and the accumulation of metabolic wastes at the same time slows growth.

GLOSSARY OF SELECTED SCIENTIFIC TERMS AND NAMES

absolute zero The coldest possible temperature, 0 K or −273°C.

abyssal Relating to the oceanic depth zone of 2000 to 6000 meters (about 6000 to 18,000 feet); the bottom waters.

acceleration The change in velocity of an object in relation to time.

acid Any substance that supplies hydrogen ions to another substance.

active transport Processes that use energy to move materials within or between cells.

adaptation The ability of an organism to survive in its environment.

adaptive radiation An evolutionary display in which various descendent species are adapted to a variety of life situations.

adenine One of the purine bases found in nucleic acids (DNA).

adenosine triphosphate (ATP) The substance in cells that stores energy for immediate use. It is used up in every cell activity.

adsorption The depositing of the molecules of a substance on the surface of a solid.

alpha particle The positively charged nucleus of a helium atom, consisting of two protons and two neutrons.

amino acid A chemical compound characterized by an amino ($-NH_2$) group and a carboxyl ($-COOH$) group. Amino acids are the building blocks of proteins.

ampere A unit of measure of electric current equivalent to the flow of one coulomb of current past a given point in a wire in one second.

amplitude The maximum displacement of any particle or field in a wave or vibration from its equilibrium position.

anabolism The constructive processes in living cells in which complex substances are synthesized from simpler ones.

analogous In living things, describing the situation in which structures or other features of organisms are similar because they have similar functions, but different evolutionary and embryonic origins. The wings of birds and the wings of insects are analogous structures; they have similar functions but are completely different in origin, structure, and development.

antibody A protein in the blood of animals that can render a specific antigen inactive.

antigen Any substance (usually a protein or a polysaccharide) that, when introduced into an animal body, stimulates the formation of an antibody.

antitoxin A type of antibody produced in response to a toxin.

aorta The body's main artery, carrying blood from the heart to be distributed throughout the body.

aquifer A rocky or soil substrate through which water moves readily.
Archimedes' Principle The principle of buoyancy, developed by the ancient Greek mathematician and inventor Archimedes; the concept that the loss in weight of a submerged body is equal to the weight of the water it displaces.
Aristotle Ancient Greek philosopher; he pioneered the scientific study of the natural world and developed systems of logic, ethics, politics, etc.
artery A blood vessel with muscular walls that carries blood away from the heart.
assimilation The process of converting digested food into the structural materials of cells and organisms.
asteriod A small planetary body in orbit around the sun.
atom The smallest unit of an element that can combine with other elements.
atomic mass (weight) The atomic mass of any element is the weighted average of the masses of its isotopes as they occur in nature.
atomic nucleus The central portion of the atom, composed of protons and neutrons.
atomic number The number of protons in an atomic nucleus.
autotroph Any organism that obtains its energy from inorganic matter, such as green plants by photosynthesis or certain bacteria by chemosynthesis.
auxin Any plant hormone, such as those restricting cell elongation or promoting root growth.
Avogadro's Law Equal volumes of all gases contain the same number of molecules when the temperatures and pressures are the same.

Bacon, Roger Sixteenth century English philosopher; the first to set forth the goal of experimental investigation by a scientific procedure and to espouse the need for scientific education.
bacteria The smallest microscopic organism, lacking a nucleus.
Banting, Frederick Canadian physician; the first to successfully extract the glucose-regulating hormone, insulin, from the pancreas. This was done in collaboration with J. J. McLeod and Charles Best. Banting and McLeod were awarded the Nobel Prize in physiology in 1923.
base Any substance capable of taking up protons from an acid to form a salt. The acid is neutralized as a result.
bathyal Relating to the oceanic depth zone of 200 to 2000 meters (about 600 to 6000 feet).
benthic Relating to that part of the ocean bottom that is populated by living organisms.
big bang theory The hypothesis that all the matter of the universe was originally concentrated in a tiny, intensely hot mass that exploded.
biomass The total mass of all living organisms in a unit area or volume.
biome A large geographical area having similar climatic and other conditions and characterized by a climax community of plants and animals. An example is the prairie grasslands of central North America.
Boyle's Law The volume of a gas is inversely proportional to its pressure if the temperature is constant.

calorie A unit of energy equal to 4.1805 joules. When spelled with a small "c," it is about the quantity of heat needed to heat one gram of water 1°C. When spelled with a capital "C," it is about the quantity of heat needed to heat 1000 grams of water 1°C.

carbohydrate A compound composed of carbon, hydrogen, and oxygen; sugars, starches, and cellulose.
catabolism Those metabolic processes in which complex organic molecules are converted to simpler ones with the release of energy.
catalyst Any substance that affects the rate of a chemical reaction and can be recovered after the reaction takes place.
cell membrane A thin layer of lipid and protein material that surrounds a cell and controls the passage of materials in and out.
cellulose A complex carbohydrate that forms the major portion of the cell wall of most plant cells.
cell wall The rigid, inert structure that surrounds a plant cell.
chemical bond The linkage that holds the atoms of molecules together.
chromosomes Usually elongated bodies located in the cell nucleus, containing DNA and bearing genes. Chromosome numbers are constant for the members of a given species.
climate For any region, a generalized or average compilation of its weather over a long period of time.
commensalism A close-living relationship between the members of two species in which one benefits from the other without harming or benefiting the other.
condensation The changing of a vapor to a liquid.
conductor Any substance or material that offers little resistance to the flow of an electric current. All metals are conductors.
convergence The evolution of superficially similar traits in different species in response to their living a similar life style.
Copernicus, Nicolaus Polish astronomer; proposed the HELIOCENTRIC THEORY, which considers the sun to be the center of the solar system.
coriolis effect The deflection of the path of a moving substance due to the earth's rotation. It affects the paths of winds, ocean currents, etc.
covalent bond One type of chemical bonding, characterized by bonded atoms sharing electrons.
Crick, Francis English scientist; with James Watson, first suggested the manner in which the various constituents of the deoxyribonucleic acid molecule (DNA) are linked together. Crick and Watson were awarded the Nobel Prize in physiology in 1962.
cytoplasm The part of a cell outside the nucleus.
cytosine A pyrimidine base found in both DNA and RNA.

Dalton, John English chemist; established the scientific basis for the ATOMIC THEORY by relating atoms to chemical changes.
Darwin, Charles English naturalist; proposed the THEORY OF NATURAL SELECTION to explain how the living species of the present changed from prehistoric forms over long periods of time.
decomposers Organisms such as bacteria and fungi that break down dead organic matter.
deoxyribonucleic acid (DNA) The type of nucleic acid found in chromosomes that stores the cell's hereditary information.
differentiation The modification or specialization of a cell from a generalized cell into one capable of performing a specific function or functions.
diffusion The movement of a material in a mixture, such as a solution, toward regions of lower concentration because of the random motion of its molecules.

dominance The relationship between two forms of a gene in which one (the dominant gene) produces its full effect regardless of the properties of the other.
Doppler effect The change in observed frequency of a wave due to the motion of the observer or the source. (It is not relative motion that counts; the effect of a moving source is different from that of a moving observer.)

ecology A field of study concerned with the relationships of living organisms and their environment.
Ehrlich, Paul German bacteriologist; developed the first chemotherapeutic agent synthesized by human effort, Salvarsan, used in the treatment of syphilis.
Einstein, Albert German-born physicist; contributed publications on the special theory of relativity, the quantum theory of light, and the statistical concepts of molecular theory; developed the equation $E = mc^2$; awarded the Nobel Prize for physics in 1921.
electron A subatomic particle, making up the outer part of every atom, having a very small mass and a single unit of negative electric charge.
energy A physical quantity, having the dimensions of work, that takes on many different forms (e.g., kinetic, potential), but whose total value never changes in any interaction.
enzyme In a living system, a protein that acts as a catalyst to accelerate a specific biochemical reaction.
evaporation The changing of a liquid to a vapor at the surface of the liquid.
evolution The process by which genetic differences accumulate over many generations to produce descendants that are very different from their ancestors.

fault A break or a weak point in the earth's surface along which movement has occurred or may occur.
fermentation The anaerobic decomposition of organic compounds by living organisms.
fertilization (a) The union of two gametes, usually a sperm and an egg. (b) The process of supplying needed nutrients to stimulate the growth of plants.
fission (a) The splitting of an atomic nucleus to release energy. (b) The division of a one-celled organism into two equal parts.
food chain The sequence of organisms (producer, consumer, predator) in which each uses the next lower organism as food, and, in turn, is used as food by the next higher organism.
force Any stimulus that may cause a body to accelerate.
fossil Any trace or remains of a former living thing.
front The boundary between two air masses.
fusion The combining of the nuclei of light elements that results in the formation of heavier elements, typically, the combining of hydrogen atoms to produce helium with the release of energy.

Galilei, Galileo (Galileo) Italian renaissance scientist; he supported the Copernican concept of the sun-centered solar system and is best known for his studies on the behavior of moving objects.
gene A section of a DNA molecule, located on a chromosome, that contains the detailed code for the synthesis of a specific protein.
gene pool The total of all the genes in the population of a species.
gravity The force that acts to attract every object to every other; the force that keeps things bound to the earth.

greenhouse effect The general rise in the temperature of the earth produced because atmospheric gases, such as carbon dioxide, absorb infrared radiation from the earth, preventing it from escaping into outer space. (The sun heats the surface of the earth; the hot earth releases infrared radiation, which passes out into space.)

growth The increase in size of an organism. Typically, growth results in an increase in cell number, cell size, and cell specialization.

guanine One of the purine bases found in nucleic acids (DNA).

half-life The amount of time required for half of a radioactive substance to decompose. Radioisotopes have half-lives that range from fractions of a second to many years. The half-life of uranium-238, for example, is 4.5 billion years.

homologous In living things, describing the situation in which structures or other features of different organisms, or parts of the same organism, exhibit similarities because they have evolved from a common ancestor. The arms of a human being, the wings of a bat, and the flippers of a whale are homologous structures; in all of these the bone pattern, derived from a common ancestral species, is the same.

Hooke, Robert English philosopher; the discoverer of the cell and the first to use the term, in 1665.

humidity (relative humidity) The ratio of atmospheric moisture to the total amount of moisture that can be held by the atmosphere at a given temperature.

hybrid The offspring resulting from the mating of genetically different parents.

hypertonic solution An aqueous solution having a higher osmotic pressure (its salinity) than another aqueous solution from which it is separated by a semipermeable membrane. The hypertonic solution will gain water molecules by diffusion.

hypotonic solution An aqueous solution having a lower osmotic pressure (its salinity) than another aqueous solution from which it is separated by a semipermeable membrane. The hypotonic solution will lose water molecules by diffusion.

igneous rock Rock formed from cooling magma.

inbreeding The repeated mating of closely related individuals. Inbreeding is practiced to obtain the homozygous condition for certain traits in plants, but random inbreeding may result in the appearance of undesirable recessive traits.

inertia That property which tends to cause a resting body to remain at rest, or which tends to keep a moving body at a constant velocity, unless an outside force causes change.

interference The combining of the vibrations produced by two waves when they arrive simultaneously at a point. Depending on the phases of the vibrations, they may add together or cancel each other.

ion An atom or group of atoms that has an electric charge due to gain or loss of one or more electrons.

ionic bond A chemical bond formed by the electrical attraction of oppositely charged ions.

isotopes Atoms of the same element in which the nuclei contain different numbers of neutrons, and therefore have different mass numbers. For example, C-12 and C-14 are isotopes of carbon since they have the same atomic number but different mass numbers.

kinetic energy The energy possessed by a moving object as a result of its motion.

laser A device that produces a coherent light all of whose waves are in phase, at the same frequency and in the same direction.
Leeuwenhoek, Anton van Seventeenth-century Dutch lens grinder; the first to see living cells such as protozoa, algae, and bacteria.
Linnaeus, Carolus Eighteenth-century Swedish botanist; the first to devise and use a system of binomial nomenclature in classifying plants and animals.
littoral Relating to the near-shore environment, usually from the high-tide level to 200 meters deep.

magma Molten rock found at a depth, together with dissolved gases and crystals.
mantle The thick layer (1800 miles) of the earth lying below the crust.
mass number The sum of the number of protons and neutrons in an atomic nucleus.
meiosis A type of cell division in both plants and animals whereby the chromosome number is reduced by half. Meiosis occurs before or in the process of forming sex cells or gametes.
Mendel, Gregor Austrian botanist; the founder of modern genetics; he based his ideas on the study of selected characters of garden peas.
messenger RNA (mRNA) The ribonucleic acid involved in the transfer of genetic information from DNA in the nucleus to the ribosomes.
mitosis A qualitative division of the cell nucleus whereby each daughter cell receives the same identical chromosome content as in the parent cell.
molecule The basic particle of a chemical compound consisting of two or more atoms held together by chemical bonds.
mutation An inheritable change in a gene and, therefore, in the traits that it controls.
mutualism A mutually beneficial association between individuals of two different species.

natural selection The process that promotes evolution by providing for the survival and reproduction of the organisms best adapted to their particular environment.
neutron An electrically uncharged particle with large mass that is one of the components of atomic nuclei.
Newton, Sir Isaac Seventeenth-century English scientist and mathematician; he inaugurated the era of modern physics by his mathematical analysis of the forces, including gravity, that control the motions of earthly and heavenly bodies.
nucleotide An organic molecule consisting of either a purine or a pyrimidine, a five-carbon sugar, and a phosphate group.
nucleus (a) The central, positively charged part of an atom, consisting of protons and neutrons. (b) The part of a cell containing the chromosomes and separated from the rest of the cell by a membrane.

ohm The measure of electrical resistance.
osmosis The diffusion of water through a semipermeable (cell) membrane from a high to a lower concentration of water.
oxidation The loss of electrons from an atom or molecule. One common form is the transfer of electrons to an oxygen atom.

pH The measure of the hydrogen-ion concentration of a substance. It is measured on a scale where pure water, which is neutral, has a pH of 7. An acid produces more hydrogen ions than pure water and has a pH of less than 7; an alkaline (basic) substance combines with hydrogen ions and has a pH greater than 7. The pH range extends from 0 (most acidic) to 14 (most basic).
photoelectric effect A situation in which a ray of light is able to produce an electric current.
photon The smallest particle or packet of light energy.
photoperiodism The various behavioral responses by plants to the duration of daylight.
photosynthesis The process by which green plants store the sun's energy by combining carbon dioxide with water to produce sugar.
Planck, Max Twentieth-century German physicist; he initiated the era of quantum mechanics by his study of the energy radiated from hot objects.
plasmolysis In plants, the shrinkage of the cytoplasm away from the cell wall due to the excessive loss of water by osmosis.
plate tectonics The theory that the earth's crust consists of plates which interact in different ways and shift positions.
potential energy The energy possessed by a body because of its position.
Priestley, Joseph Amateur English chemist; the first to describe the production of oxygen as a by-product of photosynthesis, in 1771.
protein The class of chemicals most characteristic of all living things. Protein molecules are enormous, made mainly of long chains of amino acids.
proton A massive, positively charged particle that is one of the components of the atomic nucleus.

recessive gene A gene which, when present along with a dominant version of the same gene, has no effect on development.
reduction The process by which an atom or molecule gains an electron; the opposite of oxidation. Often, the electron comes from an oxygen atom.
retrograde motion Planets of the solar system when viewed from earth move eastward among the stars each day. Periodically, the individual planets appear to stop, reverse direction for a short time, and then resume their eastward motion. This apparent westward movement or drift is called retrograde motion.
ribonucleic acid (RNA) A nucleic acid found in both the nucleus and the cytoplasm; functions in the synthesis of protein.
ribosome A cytoplasmic structure responsible for protein synthesis.

solstice The time when the vertical rays of the sun are striking either the Tropic of Cancer or the Tropic of Capricorn; the longest or shortest days of the year.
specific gravity The ratio of the mass of one gram of a substance to the mass of an equal volume of water at 1°C.
stalactites Iciclelike stone structures hanging from the ceilings of caves.
stalagmites Stone upgrowths from the floors of caves.
sublimation The direct change of a solid to a vapor or vice versa.
succession The changes in the plant population of an area.
superconductor Any material that offers absolutely no resistance to the flow of electric current; this occurs only at very low temperatures (about −270°C).
symbiosis The living together of individuals of two different species, typically, either commensalism, mutualism or parasitism.

taiga A climax biome characterized by a predominance of coniferous trees, moose, etc. The coniferous forest across North America is one example of a taiga.

thermodynamics The study of the relationships between heat and work.

first law of thermodynamics
Energy can be neither created nor destroyed.

second law of thermodynamics
Entropy (disorder) of an undisturbed system always increases, entropy being a measure of disorder.

thymine A pyrimidine base found in DNA.

toxin A product of one organism that is poisonous to another organism. When introduced into the body, it may stimulate the production of an antibody.

transfer RNA (tRNA) The type of RNA that pairs with amino acids, transporting them to the ribosomes, where they are attached to the messenger RNA and then synthesized into proteins.

transformer A device that changes the voltage of alternating-current in an electrical circuit.

transistor A semiconductor used in various amplifier and switching circuits.

translocation (a) The transport of materials from one part of a plant to another. (b) The transfer of a part of one chromosome that becomes attached to another chromosome.

transmutation The changing of one chemical element into another. In radioactive disintegration, for example, radium decomposes by emitting radiation and ultimately becomes lead.

transpiration The evaporation of water from the aerial parts of plants.

tropism Directional growth movements of plants in response to such external stimuli as light, gravity, and water.

tundra A climax biome characterized by its cold climate and flat, treeless terrain. An example is the arctic tundra of northern North America. Alpine tundra has the same characteristics but exists above the tree line on higher mountains.

turgor (turgor pressure) Turgor pressure (turgidity) is a condition of plant cells in which the cytoplasm is held against the cell wall by the water pressure within the vacuole.

uniformitarianism The theory that the various processes that have shaped the earth in the geologic past are the same as the processes that are operating today.

uracil A pyrimidine base found only in RNA.

vaccine A preparation of attenuated pathogens, which, when introduced within the body, stimulates the production of antibodies, that is, immunity.

valence The chemical combining capability of an element.

vein A thin-walled blood vessel with valves, that carries blood toward the heart.

velocity The speed and direction of a body in motion.

viscosity A fluid's resistance to flow.

Watson, James American scientist; together with Francis Crick, first suggested the manner in which the constituents of DNA are attached to one another.

weather The state of the atmosphere at a given time and place.

weight The effect of the force of gravity on a body.

Weismann, August German biologist; proposed the theory of the "continuity of the germplasm," according to which multicellular organisms are made up of gamete-producing cells or germplasm, and cells of the body, the somaplasm. He considered the germplasm to be immortal—an unbroken chain of gametes and embryos reaching back to the dawn of life.

work The force exerted on an object multiplied by the distance it is moved.

zygote The cell formed by the union of two gametes, commonly, a fertilized egg.

STUDY SOURCES

For additional review, you might consult the following books, which present a variety of the types of concepts pertinent to a general understanding of the sciences:

HISTORY AND PHILOSOPHY OF SCIENCE

Asimov, Isaac. *Asimov's Guide to Science*, Rev. Ed. New York: Basic Books, 1972.

Bonner, John T. *The Scale of Nature*. New York: Harper and Row, 1969.

Collis, John Stewart. *The Vision of Glory: The Extraordinary Nature of the Ordinary*. New York: George Braziller, 1973.

Gardner, Eldon J. *History of Biology*, 2nd Ed. Minneapolis: Burgess Publishing Company, 1965.

BIOLOGICAL SCIENCE

Bornstein, Jerry and Sandy. *What is Genetics?* New York: Julian Messner, 1980.

Camp, Pamela S., and Karen Arms. *Exploring Biology*. Philadelphia: Saunders College Publishing Company, 1981.

Keeten, William T., and Carol Hardy McFadden. *Elements of Biological Science*, 3rd Ed. New York: W.W. Norton and Company, 1983.

Luria, Salvador E., Stephen Jay Gould, and Sam Singer. *A View of Life*. Menlo Park, Calif.: Benjamin/Cummings Publishing Company, 1981.

Tippo, Oswald, and William L. Stern. *Humanistic Botany*. New York: W.W. Norton and Company, 1977.

Wallace, Robert A., Jack L. King, and Gerald P. Sanders. *Biosphere*. Scott, Foresman and Company, 1988.

EARTH SCIENCE AND THE ENVIRONMENT

Van Andel, Tjeerd H. *New Views on an Old Planet. Continental Drift and the History of the Earth*. Cambridge University Press, 1985.

Ballard, Robert D. *Exploring Our Living Planet*. Washington, D.C.: National Geographic Society, 1983.

Botkin, David B., and Edward A. Keller. *Environmental Studies*. Columbus, Ohio: Merrill Publishing Company, 1982.

Faul, Henry and Carol. *It Began with a Stone*. New York: John Wiley and Sons, 1983.

Hardy, Ralph, Peter Wright, John Kington, and John Gribbon. *The Weather Book*. Boston: Little, Brown and Company, 1982.

Lounsbury, John F. *Earth Science*, 3rd Ed. New York: Harper and Row, 1979.

Tarbuck, Edward J., and Frederick K. Lutgens. *Earth Science*, 5th Ed. Columbus, Ohio: Merrill Publishing Company, 1988.

PHYSICAL SCIENCE—CHEMISTRY

Allen, Thomas L., and Raymond M. Keefer. *Chemistry, Experiment and Theory*. New York: Harper and Row, 1982.

Staley, Dennis D., Anthony C. Wilbraham, and Michael S. Matta. *Essentials of Chemistry*. Menlo Park, Calif.: Benjamin/Cummings Publishing Company, 1984.

Stine, William R. *Chemistry for the Consumer*. Boston: Allyn and Bacon, 1978.

Young, Jay A. *Chemistry: A Human Concern*. New York: Macmillan Publishing Company, 1978.

PHYSICAL SCIENCE—PHYSICS

Hecht, Eugene. *Physics in Perspective*. Reading, Mass.: Addison-Wesley, 1980.

Krauskopf, Konrad B., and Arthur Beiser. *The Physical Universe*, 5th Ed. New York: McGraw-Hill Book Company, 1986.

Pasachoff, Jay M., and Marc L. Kutner. *Invitation to Physics*. New York: W.W. Norton and Company, 1981.

Taffel, Alexander. *Physics, Its Methods and Meanings*. Reading, Mass.: Allyn and Bacon, 1981.

Turk, Jonathon and Amos. *Physical Science*, 2nd Ed. Philadelphia: Saunders College Publishing Company, 1981.

ASTRONOMY AND THE UNIVERSE

Freidlander, Michael W. *Astronomy, from Stonehenge to Quasers*. Englewood Cliffs, NJ: Prentice-Hall, 1985.

Jastrow, Robert. *Red Giants and White Dwarfs*. New York: Warner Books, 1980.

PRACTICE QUESTIONS ON THE NATURAL SCIENCES

Now, let's look at some of the specific science areas with some sample questions covering each.

Questions about Biology

Directions: Each of the questions or incomplete statements below is followed by five suggested answers or completions. Select the one that is best in each case.

1. At the tissue level of organization
   (A) cells retain their separate functional identity
   (B) dissimilar cells are associated to conduct a variety of functions
   (C) cells are completely independent
   (D) similar cells are associated in the performance of a particular function
   (E) there is no cellular specialization

2. A scientist specializing in the study of the transmission of inherited traits from one generation to another is called a
   (A) physiologist (B) taxonomist (C) parasitologist
   (D) cytologist (E) geneticist

3. All cellular metabolism is controlled by organic catalysts called
   (A) hormones (B) vitamins (C) auxin (D) phlogistons
   (E) enzymes

Questions 4 and 5

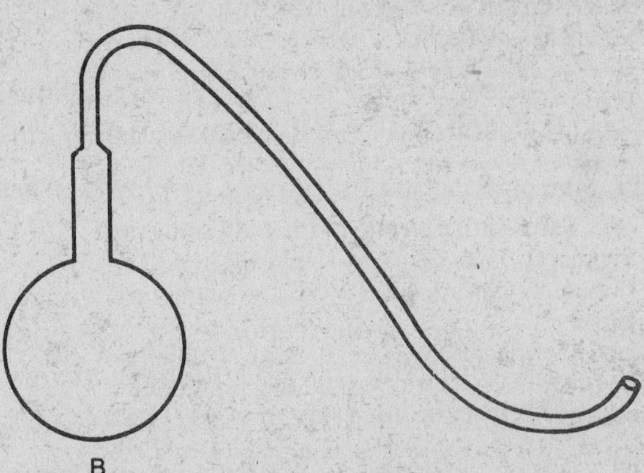

Pasteur placed a nutrient broth in each of two flasks similar to those illustrated above. Both flasks were open to air, but flask B was open only through its curved neck. The broth in both flasks was boiled initially to kill the contained organisms, and then the flasks were left standing. Living organisms soon reappeared in flask A but no life appeared in flask B.

4. Since flask B remained free of life indefinitely, it can be concluded that
   (A) life does not arise spontaneously from the nutrient broth
   (B) flask A permits microorganisms to enter readily
   (C) the curved neck of flask B apparently prevents microorganisms from entering the flask
   (D) none of the above
   (E) all of the above, except D

5. The evidence generated by this experiment supports
   (A) Koch's postulates
   (B) The Hardy-Weinberg Law
   (C) the Germ Theory of disease
   (D) Virchow's theory of biogenesis
   (E) the Cell Theory

6. An organism which utilizes radiant energy in food synthesis is
   (A) holozoic (B) parasitic (C) chemosynthetic
   (D) saprophytic (E) photosynthetic

7. The typical consumers in an ecosystem are
   (A) saprophytic (B) photosynthetic (C) parasitic
   (D) chemosynthetic (E) holozoic

8. In the "dark reactions" of photosynthesis
   (A) chemical energy is changed to radiant energy
   (B) organic synthesis occurs
   (C) carbon dioxide is absorbed
   (D) radiant energy is released
   (E) radiant energy is changed to chemical energy

9. Photosynthesis
   (A) produces oxygen and inorganic compounds
   (B) produces carbon dioxide and water
   (C) produces carbon dioxide and organic compounds
   (D) produces oxygen and organic compounds
   (E) produces oxygen and water

10. A process which results, in part, in the production of carbon dioxide and water is
    (A) respiration (B) photosynthesis (C) secretion
    (D) osmosis (E) phosphorylation

11. An orientation movement by plants in response to an external stimulus is a
    (A) tropism (B) synergism (C) polymorphism
    (D) cyclosis (E) taxis

12. The photoperiodic response for "long-day" plants to short days is
    (A) flowering (B) phototropism (C) flower inhibition
    (D) parthenocarpy (E) photosynthesis

13. Which of the following is an organic compound found in the cell walls of hard wood?
    (A) Lignin (B) Suberin (C) Pectin (D) Cutin
    (E) Resin

14. When you eat a celery "stalk," you are eating
    (A) root tissue (B) stem tissue (C) leaf tissue
    (D) fruit (E) seed

15. Water loss from plants by transpiration would be increased by
    (A) increased air circulation
    (B) darkness
    (C) increased humidity
    (D) lowering the temperature
    (E) decreased air circulation

16. The enzyme-controlled breakdown of carbohydrates, fats, and proteins is called
(A) autolysis (B) putrefaction (C) bacteriophage
(D) fermentation (E) digestion

17. In plants, selected cells of the haploid, gamete-producing generation
(A) become or produce spores
(B) undergo meiosis
(C) undergo cleavage
(D) become or produce eggs or sperm
(E) are polyploid

18. Structures which are similar because of anatomy and development are said to be
(A) analogous (B) dioecious (C) monoecious
(D) homologous (E) homosporous

19. The Rh factor assumes serious proportions when
(A) an Rh-negative mother carries an Rh-positive fetus in a first pregnancy
(B) an Rh-negative mother carries an Rh-negative fetus in a second pregnancy
(C) an Rh-positive mother carries an Rh-negative fetus
(D) an Rh-positive mother carries an Rh-positive fetus
(E) an Rh-negative mother carries an Rh-positive fetus in a second pregnancy

20. Carotene functions in maintaining
(A) night vision (B) normal blood clotting
(C) normal nerves (D) fertility
(E) normal tooth and bone development

21. What is one of the most serious dietary problems in the United States today?
(A) Mineral deficiency (B) Stomach ulcer (C) Obesity
(D) Food allergy (E) Vitamin deficiency

22. Impairment of the spinal accessory nerves would affect
(A) muscles of the shoulder (B) facial muscles
(C) the parotid gland (D) swallowing (E) muscles of the tongue

23. Teeth are innervated by the
(A) oculomotor nerve (B) facial nerve (C) vagus nerve
(D) trochlear nerve (E) trigeminal nerve

24. Stimulation by the parasympathetic nervous system would result in
(A) weaker heart beat (B) erection of hair (C) dilated pupils
(D) higher blood pressure (E) increased sweat secretion

25. Pathologic conditions caused by defects in hormonal action are called
(A) atrophy (B) pheromones (C) infectious diseases
(D) deficiency diseases (E) functional diseases

26. Oxytocin
(A) stimulates basal metabolism
(B) regulates calcium metabolism
(C) constricts blood vessels
(D) regulates phosphorus metabolism
(E) stimulates lactation

27. All of the following may occur during synapsis in meiosis *except*:
(A) crossing over (B) transduction (C) inversion
(D) translocation (E) duplication

28. The appearance of variations in a population may be attributed to either genetic change or
(A) genetic drift (B) changed environmental factors
(C) non-random mating (D) parthenogenesis
(E) adaptive radiation

29. Which one of the following is *not* a type of RNA?
(A) Template RNA (B) Ribosomal RNA (C) Messenger RNA
(D) Gametic RNA (E) Transfer RNA

30. The concept that all eggs have existed since the creation of the world is entailed in the beliefs of
(A) pangenesists (B) animaculists (C) epigenesists
(D) ovists (E) parthenogenesists

31. The ovary of a flower matures into
(A) a seed (B) an embryo (C) a fruit
(D) the endosperm (E) the receptacle

32. You would expect to observe moose and spruce in the
(A) alpine tundra (B) coniferous forest
(C) tropical rain forest (D) grasslands
(E) deciduous forest

33. Nekton includes marine organisms which
(A) exist only in darkness
(B) swim by their own propulsion
(C) exist to a depth of 5,000 feet
(D) exist in the deepest ocean trenches
(E) float on the surface

34. A student of cytogenetics would be concerned with
(A) convergent evolution
(B) the cellular basis of inheritance
(C) prenatal development
(D) the genetic changes in populations
(E) parallel evolution

35. A paleontologist is a biologist concerned primarily with studying
(A) birds (B) snakes (C) rocks (D) insects
(E) fossils

36. An interrelationship between two organisms in which one receives all of the benefits at the expense of the other is called
(A) parasitism (B) commensalism (C) mutualism
(D) symbiosis (E) saprophytism

37. In the human circulatory system, leakage of blood back into the heart is prevented by the
(A) tricuspid valve (B) aortic valve (C) ventricular valves
(D) semilunar valves (E) bicuspid valve

38. Blood leaves the human liver through the hepatic vein and returns to the heart through the
(A) hepatic portal system (B) anterior vena cava (C) azygous vein
(D) inferior mesenteric artery (E) inferior vena cava

39. The Schick test is used to determine whether or not individuals need immunization,or whether or not immunization procedures have been effective,against
(A) smallpox (B) yellow fever (C) polio
(D) scarlet fever (E) diphtheria

40. The greatest significance of sexual reproduction is that it
(A) insures invariable genetic lines
(B) permits new combinations of genes
(C) insures that traits are never lost
(D) eliminates the need for meiosis
(E) stimulates mating

41. What is the probability that any one child will be a boy?
(A) 1/16 (B) 1/8 (C) 1/4 (D) 1/2 (E) 3/4

42. In an individual with genotype "AaBb," the probability of producing gametes with dominant genes ("AB") is
(A) unpredictable (B) 1/16 (C) 1/8 (D) 1/4 (E) 1/2

43. Biochemical analysis of normal and sickle-cell hemoglobin reveals that the difference between the two is based on
(A) sex chromosomes (B) transformation (C) amino acids
(D) different antigens (E) agglutination

44. An ecological niche
(A) is a micro-habitat
(B) is really non-distinguishable
(C) may be occupied by only one species
(D) may be occupied by any number of species
(E) may be occupied by only one individual

45. An organism which exhibits bilateral symmetry
(A) always has a right and left leg
(B) always has a right side and a left side
(C) exhibits universal symmetry internally
(D) could never possess an anterior or posterior end
(E) would give birth to living young

46. The biological speciality called anatomy is concerned with the study of
(A) structure (B) tissues (C) inheritance (D) function
(E) development

47. Amino acids contain a carboxyl group, —COOH, and an amino group,
(A) —HOH (B) $—CH_3$ (C) $—CH_2$ (D) $—H_3C$
(E) $—NH_2$

48. When a living cell is placed in a fluid and there is net movement of water molecules out of the cell, the fluid is said to be
(A) isotonic (B) hypotonic (C) plasmolyzed
(D) hypertonic (E) hydrolyzed

49. An organism capable of synthesizing its own food is described as
(A) holozoic (B) heterotrophic (C) autotrophic
(D) parasitic (E) saprophytic

50. Heterotrophic organisms relying upon decomposing organic materials for nutrition are
(A) parasitic (B) autotrophic (C) holozoic
(D) saprophytic (E) chemotrophic

51. In 1772, Joseph Priestley demonstrated that green plants
(A) carry on photosynthesis (B) absorb water from the soil
(C) give off carbon dioxide (D) absorb minerals from the soil
(E) give off oxygen

52. An enzyme-regulated process in living cells resulting in the transfer of energy to ATP is
(A) reduction (B) assimilation (C) osmosis
(D) absorption (E) respiration

53. Cellular organelles called ribosomes are the sites of
(A) enzyme storage (B) protein synthesis
(C) chromosomal replication (D) cellular respiration
(E) photosynthesis in plants

54. What is the principal absorbing structure of typical roots?
(A) Root cap (B) Root hair cell (C) Endodermis
(D) Hair roots (E) Xylem

55. The loss of water by transpiration is the result of
(A) capillarity (B) diffusion (C) mass movement
(D) cohesive forces (E) adhesive forces

56. The classification of bacteria is determined chiefly by their
(A) cell membranes and capsules (B) movements and environments
(C) morphological characteristics (D) anatomical characteristics
(E) physiological characteristics

57. The union of a sperm and an egg is called
(A) germination (B) homospory (C) fertilization
(D) reduction (E) meiosis

58. The most significant benefit of flowering to humans is
(A) double fertilization (B) the production of fruit and seeds
(C) pollination (D) alternation of generations (E) aesthetic

59. Antigens are foreign proteins which stimulate the production of
(A) fibrin (B) globulins (C) cytochrome
(D) antibodies (E) lymphocytes

60. A deficiency of vitamin D may cause
(A) muscular cramps (B) stunted growth (C) xerophthalmia
(D) retardation of bone and tooth formation (E) paralysis

61. To overcome a thiamine deficiency, you should enrich your diet with
(A) fresh vegetables (B) eggs and dairy products
(C) citrus fruit (D) red meats (E) whole grain cereals

62. Scientific research on the human cerebral cortex reveals that
(A) the parasympathetic system is centered here
(B) it controls smooth muscle
(C) it controls endocrine secretions
(D) it controls subconscious muscle coordination
(E) specific areas control particular functions

63. The phases of mitosis occur in the following sequence:
(A) prophase, anaphase, metaphase, telophase, and interphase
(B) interphase, telophase, prophase, anaphase, and metaphase
(C) interphase, prophase, metaphase, telophase, and anaphase
(D) interphase, telophase, prophase, anaphase, and metaphase
(E) prophase, metaphase, anaphase, telophase, and interphase

64. The constancy of linkage groups may be altered by
(A) transduction (B) crossing over (C) recombination
(D) synapsis (E) assimilation

65. The "dark" reactions of photosynthesis take place in portions of the chloroplast called
(A) grana (B) stomata (C) carotene (D) chlorophyll (E) stroma

66. Cytoplasmic streaming within living cells is called
(A) translocation (B) transpiration (C) helicotropism
(D) helicotaxis (E) cyclosis

67. Cellular respiration in mitochondria may
(A) result in further energy storage
(B) form ATP, an energy-yielding molecule
(C) form ADP, an energy-related substance
(D) release sugar molecules
(E) release a variety of cellular hormones

68. Fibrinogen is
(A) a precursor of certain hormones
(B) formed from fibrin during clotting
(C) involved with blood clotting
(D) a source of globulin
(E) a reservoir of antibodies

69. Systolic pressure is
(A) the lowest pressure of the blood, between heartbeats
(B) the result of a leak in a heart valve
(C) the blood pressure in veins
(D) the pressure on the blood as the ventricles contract
(E) the blood pressure in arteries

70. A toothache involves nerve impulses along the
(A) trochlear nerve (B) facial nerve (C) abducens nerve
(D) trigeminal nerve (E) glossopharyngeal nerve

71. In the prophase of mitosis,
(A) homologous chromosomes become paired
(B) the centriole reappears
(C) chromosomes are doubled and the duplicate chromatids may be observed
(D) tetrads of chromatids appear
(E) synapsis takes place

72. Marine organisms which move by drifting are referred to as
(A) plankton (B) neritic (C) littoral (D) sessile (E) nekton

73. Genes, which control inheritance, are composed of the chemical
(A) adenosine triphosphate (B) ribonucleic acid
(C) adenosine diphosphate (D) deoxyribonucleic acid
(E) acetylcholine

74. Nephrons
(A) are functional units of the pancreas
(B) excrete only water
(C) are functional units of the spleen
(D) regulate body temperature
(E) filter the blood and resorb useful substances

Questions 75 and 76

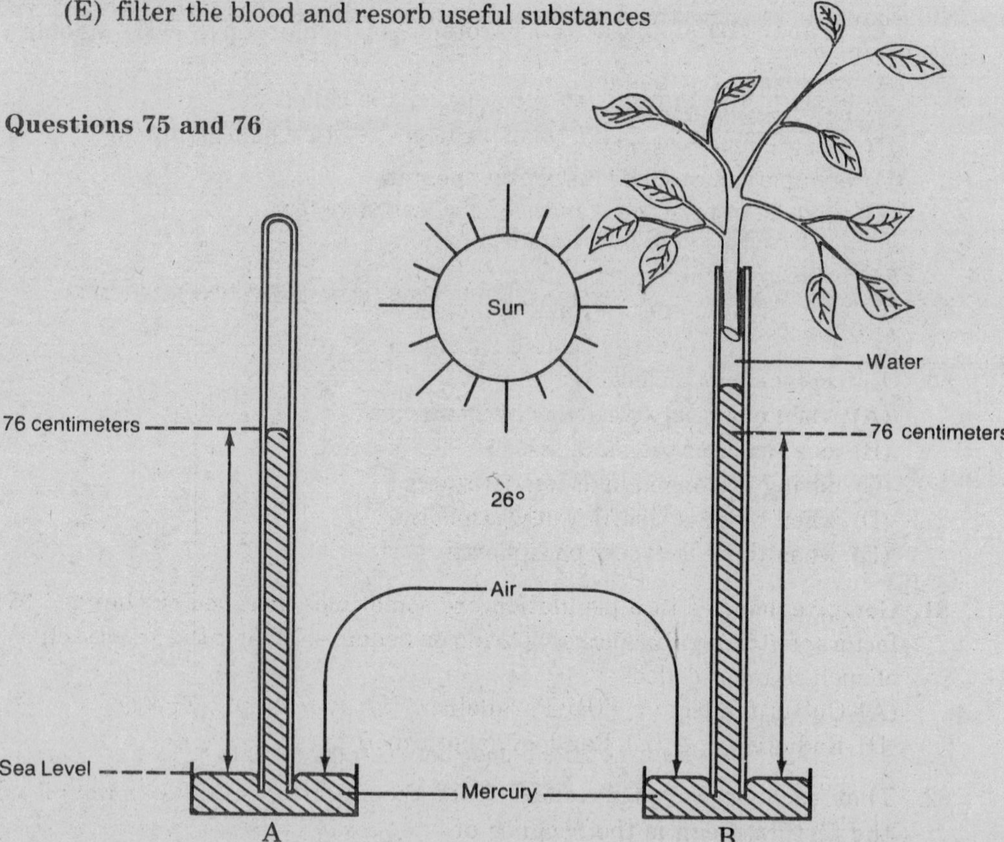

In the diagrams shown above, figure A illustrates a simple mercury barometer, a column of mercury in a sealed glass tube, the open end of which is immersed in a container of mercury which is exposed to atmospheric pressure at sea level. Figure B illustrates a living plant stem, with leaves, sealed in water in the upper end of the glass tubing, which is likewise filled with mercury.

75. What causes the mercury in figure A to rise to a height of 76 centimeters?
(A) Adhesive forces
(B) Cohesive forces
(C) Sunlight heating the mercury, which expands
(D) Atmospheric pressure on the mercury in the dish
(E) The vacuum above the mercury in the glass tube

76. The mercury in figure B rises above 76 centimeters because
(A) the plant stem absorbs mercury, pulling the mercury up the tube
(B) plants grow better at sea level
(C) of external and internal forces, including transpirational pull
(D) the top of the glass tube is not sealed, thus destroying the vacuum
(E) atmospheric pressure is highest at sea level

77. The existence of monotremes, the egg-laying mammals, suggests that
(A) birds and mammals exhibit parallel evolution
(B) mammals evolved before birds
(C) mammals acquired the ability to nurse before any of them substituted live birth for egg-laying
(D) the environment is more favorable to egg-laying
(E) birds and mammals have little in common

78. Experiments using labeled carbon as a tracer have demonstrated that all living cells
(A) require radiant energy
(B) are dependent upon photosynthesis
(C) carry out chemosynthesis
(D) are able to assimilate carbon compounds
(E) produce organic substances and release oxygen

79. Etiolation in plants is the result of
(A) synergism (B) insufficient light (C) photoperiodism
(D) parthenocarpy (E) taxis

80. Eutrophication of a lake may occur
(A) when essential nutrients are insufficient
(B) as a result of too many fish
(C) during prolonged high temperatures
(D) when there is insufficient phosphorus
(E) when there is excess phosphorus

81. Gene frequencies in a population are sometimes modified or changed by factors of little significance or bearing on genetics. What is the genetic effect of such changes called?
(A) Cultural effect (B) Parallelism (C) Morphogenesis
(D) Radiation (E) Random genetic drift

82. That each organism develops from the undifferentiated material of the fertilized egg is the premise of
(A) pangenesis (B) regeneration (C) special creation
(D) fertilization (E) epigenesis

83. Muscles used in chewing are innervated by the
(A) facial nerve (B) glossopharyngeal nerve
(C) abducens nerve (D) trigeminal nerve (E) hypoglossal nerve

84. Blood leaves the right ventricle of the human heart through the
(A) bicuspid valve (B) pulmonary vein
(C) pulmonary artery (D) aorta (E) tricuspid valve

85. When one population cannot survive without the benefits received from another population, the relationship is called
(A) coordination (B) mutualism (C) neutralism
(D) aggregation (E) commensalism

86. Sulfur is important in an ecosystem because it is
(A) important in nerve impulse transmission
(B) important for salt balance in vertebrate blood
(C) essential in photosynthesis
(D) essential for many proteins and certain enzymes
(E) essential in respiration

87. The movement of ions into a living cell against a concentration gradient with the expenditure of energy is called
(A) active transport
(B) osmosis
(C) plasmolysis
(D) phagocytosis
(E) pinocytosis

88. Those viruses which attack and parasitize bacteria are called
(A) interferon (B) synergids (C) rickettsias
(D) lysozymes (E) bacteriophages

89. When no oxygen is available to cells, they may produce ATP by
(A) glycolysis (B) anaerobic respiration (C) use of the TCA cycle
(D) cytochrome interaction (E) the citric acid cycle

90. Niacin functions in maintaining
(A) normal bone formation (B) normal nerve functioning
(C) normal blood clotting (D) normal cellular oxidations
(E) night vision

91. Impairment of the vagus nerves would affect
(A) muscles of the tongue (B) some of the internal organs
(C) facial muscles (D) shoulder muscles (E) swallowing

92. In the farsighted eye,
(A) light rays converge in front of the retina (B) the cornea is defective
(C) light rays converge in the fovea (D) vision is not blurred
(E) light rays converge behind the retina

93. According to the Watson and Crick model of DNA, the bases are paired as follows:
(A) adenine-thymine and cytosine-guanine
(B) adenine-uracil and cytosine-guanine
(C) adenine-cytosine and guanine-thymine
(D) adenine-guanine and cytosine-thymine
(E) adenine-thymine and guanine-uracil

94. Which of the following plants does not produce multicellular embryos?
(A) Clover
(B) Elodea
(C) Tree ferns
(D) Club mosses
(E) Spirogyra

X^RX^r	X^RX^R	X^rX^r	X^RY	X^rY
1	2	3	4	5

95. Which of the genotypes for hemophilia illustrated above would inherit the disease?
(A) 1, 3, and 5
(B) 2 and 4
(C) 4 and 5
(D) 3 and 5
(E) 1, 2, and 4

96. Fats, like carbohydrates, are composed of carbon, hydrogen, and oxygen, but differ from them by having
(A) proportionally more oxygen (B) little stored energy
(C) twice as much hydrogen as oxygen (D) an excess of carbon
(E) proportionally less oxygen

97. Isolation of a population over a long period of time produces
(A) adaptive radiation (B) hybridization (C) inbreeding
(D) interspecific competition (E) parallel evolution

98. As a result of photosynthesis
(A) CO_2 is stored in carbohydrates
(B) light energy is converted into stored chemical energy
(C) entropy is neutralized
(D) energy is released
(E) ATP is energized

99. A deficiency of folic acid could result in
(A) a type of anemia (B) sterility (C) beriberi
(D) gray hair (E) hemorrhage following surgery

100. You would expect to observe buffalo grass and bison in the
(A) desert (B) tropical rain forest (C) deciduous forest
(D) arctic tundra (E) grasslands

101. Blood leaving the left atrium of the human heart enters the
(A) left ventricle (B) pulmonary artery (C) aorta
(D) pulmonary vein (E) superior vena cava

102. An association of species in which neither is able to survive without the other is called
(A) mutualism (B) neutralism (C) competition
(D) amensalism (E) commensalism

103. One of the reasons that Mendel was successful when others before him failed was that
(A) he studied the inheritance of single contrasting characters
(B) he understood mutations
(C) he was able to verify his results by making chromosome studies
(D) he concerned himself with genes, not with how they expressed themselves
(E) he was lucky

104. A cellular activity that results in a decrease in dry weight is
(A) osmosis (B) photosynthesis (C) diffusion
(D) respiration (E) reduction

105. During the blood clotting process, the action of thromboplastin and thrombin is similar to that of
(A) hormones (B) phagocytosis (C) enzymes
(D) antigens (E) vitamins

106. Conversion of molecular nitrogen to ammonia or nitrate is carried out only by
(A) certain bacteria and photosynthesis
(B) bacteria and fungi
(C) earthworms and soil bacteria
(D) lightning, certain bacteria or blue-green algae
(E) lightning, decomposition and fungi

Directions: Each group of questions below consists of five lettered choices followed by a list of numbered phrases or sentences. For each numbered phrase or sentence select the one choice that is most closely related to it. Each choice may be used once, more than once, or not at all.

Questions 107–108

The following list represents factors that affect the growth, reactions, distribution, and reproduction of living organisms.

(A) Genetic
(B) Climatic
(C) Edaphic
(D) Biotic
(E) Fire

107. The factor(s) involved in high soil alkalinity

108. The factor(s) involved in competition between garden beans and weeds

Questions 109–111

(A) Adenosine triphosphate
(B) Deoxyribonucleic acid
(C) Disaccharide
(D) Nucleotide
(E) Phospholipid

109. A chemical compound found in chromosomes that stores hereditary information

110. The immediate source of energy for cellular activities

111. Energy-rich molecules formed in the mitochondrion

ANSWERS AND EXPLANATIONS

1. D. By definition, a tissue is a group of similar cells specialized to perform a particular function or functions.

2. E. Genetics is that branch of biology concerned with the study of heredity and variation in organisms and with the means by which variation takes place.

3. E. Enzymes are proteinaceous materials produced by living cells. Enzymes control cellular metabolism.

4. E. Flask A permits microorganisms to enter readily and the material broth supports their existence and growth. Flask B severely restricts or prevents the entrance of microorganisms and, due to the lack of microorganisms in its broth, one must conclude that microorganisms do not arise spontaneously.

5. D. Biogenesis is the concept that life arises only from preexisting life, a proposal first suggested by Virchow.

6. E. Photosynthesis is the biochemical process which occurs in living cells containing chlorophyll; it occurs only when radiant energy is present and results in the production of the basic food glucose.

7. E. Typical holozoic organisms obtain nourishment by ingesting (eating) their food.

8. B. The dark reactions of photosynthesis include the reduction of CO_2 and its combination into 3-and-6-carbon sugars. This is followed by a series of reactions in which the sugar ribulose is replaced.

9. D. $6CO_2 + 6H_2O$ + Radiant Energy $\rightarrow C_6H_{12}O_6 + 6O_2$

10. A. $C_6H_{12}O_6 + 6O_2 \rightarrow 6CO_2 + 6H_2O$ + *energy* (respiration)

11. A. Tropisms are growth responses of plants to environmental stimuli such as light, water, and gravity.

12. C. "Long day" plants require more than a minimum exposure of 13–14 hours of daylight for flowering. Under conditions of fewer than 13–14 hours of daylight, flowering does not occur.

13. A. Hard woods contain fibers (a type of cell) in addition to tracheids. The cell walls of fibers contain lignin, which resists decay and gives strength.

14. C. Typically, celery has a short, cushiony stem to which the "stalks" are attached. Celery has a compound leaf, i.e., a leaf consists of a petiole, or "stem, " and leaflets.

15. A. Transpiration is the *evaporation* of water from the aerial parts of plants. Any condition which would increase the evaporation of water from an open dish would similarly increase transpiration.

16. E. Digestion is the enzyme-controlled breakdown of organic substances (carbohydrates, fats, and proteins).

17. D. The typical plant life cycle is an "alternation of generations", i.e., the alternation of a diploid, spore-producing generation with a haploid, gamete-producing generation. Following meiosis, haploid spores give rise to the gametophyte generation; haploid gametes, produced by the gametophyte, fuse (fertilization) to produce the zygote, which develops into the diploid sporophyte generation.

18. D. Homologous structures have similarities of structure, embryonic development and relationships.

19. E. An Rh-negative mother carrying an Rh-positive fetus in a first pregnancy develops antibodies to the Rh antigen, which, in turn, destroy the Rh-positive red blood cells of the fetus in a second pregnancy.

20. A. Carotenes are a group of orange to red pigments found in the chromoplastids of certain plant cells. The pigments are converted to vitamin A.

21. C. Overeating and lack of sufficient, appropriate exercise result in a high percentage of the population being overweight.
22. A. Spinal nerves typically innervate muscles and organs of the body while cranial nerves innervate muscles and organs associated with the head.
23. E. Nerve innervations are specific, i.e., the trigeminal nerve innervates the teeth; the optic nerve innervates the eye.
24. A. The sympathetic nervous system typically responds to situations involving anger, fear, etc., with bodily response that provides greater courage, strength, etc. The parasympathetic nervous system tends to counter these by reducing blood pressure, decreasing heart rate, etc.
25. E. Disease may be caused by invading organisms and their products, such as diphtheria or poliomylitis; by deficiencies of minerals and vitamins, such as scurvy or rickets; or by defects in hormonal production and secretion such as goiter. The latter are called functional diseases.
26. E. Endocrine secretions—hormones—are specific in action. Oxytoxin stimulates lactation, or the release of milk.
27. B. Crossing over, inversion, translocation and duplication are events which frequently happen to chromatin materials during meiosis.
28. B. The total development of any individual is determined by its genetic makeup as affected by its environment. Changes in genetic makeup through new gene combinations or by mutation, and/or by changed environmental factors are the only causes of variation in a population.
29. D. No type of RNA is designated "gametic RNA." The RNA of gametes is not so designated.
30. D. Ovists contend that miniature organisms were contained in eggs and that all eggs were created together and have existed since the beginning of the world.
31. C. By definition, a fruit is the matured ovary of a flower.
32. B. The coniferous forest biome, the taiga, is dominated by conifers, especially spruces. It is populated by bears, rodents, birds, and moose.
33. B. Nekton includes large fishes, giant squids, and whales which swim in direct relation to their food supply and independent of wave or current actions.
34. B. Cytogenetics is that branch or division of cytology which emphasizes the behavior of the genetic apparatus, or chromosomes of the cell.
35. E. Paleontology is concerned with a study of life of past geological time periods as revealed by fossil remains.
36. A. A parasite derives its food from the living tissue of other organisms.
37. D. Semilunar valves are found at the entrance of both the pulmonary artery and the aorta.
38. E. The hepatic vein empties into the inferior vena cava.
39. E. The Schick test determines the presence of diphtheria antitoxin in the blood.
40. B. Sexual reproduction is the only reproductive measure which permits new combinations of genes, thus establishing the basis for evolution and adaptation to a constantly changing environment.
41. D. In human sex inheritance, the X and Y chromosome types of sex inheritance are involved. Females are XX. Males are XY and produce sperm carrying either X or Y chromosomes. Eggs carry only an X chromosome. If the fertilized egg contains two X chromosomes, the individual will be female. If it contains an X and a Y chromosome, the individual will be a male.
42. D. The chance of an AB segregation of genes following meiosis in an individual with an "AaBb" genotype is one in four.
43. C. Sickle-cell anemia is due to a mutation and the subsequent substitution of one amino acid for another in the normal hemoglobin protein chain.
44. C. In biotic communities, most populations can be assigned to one of several roles such as a food producer, a first-order consumer, a parasite, a scavenger, etc. Each role is recognized as a niche and only one species occupies a particular and specific niche in a community.
45. B. Animals with bilateral symmetry have right and left sides, a front and back and are usually active movers.

46. A. Anatomy is the study of structure.
47. E. The amino group is represented as —NH_2.
48. D. A hypertonic solution is one with a higher osmotic pressure than the reference (in this case, the living cell) solution.
49. C. An autotrophic organism is able to manufacture its own food, usually by photosynthesis.
50. D. A saprophytic organism derives its food from nonliving organic matter.
51. E. Priestley discovered the opposing natures of photosynthesis and respiration. Respiration uses oxygen and releases carbon dioxide, while photosynthesis uses carbon dioxide and releases oxygen.
52. E. In respiration the energy of foodstuffs is converted through a series of enzyme-regulated reactions into ATP, adenosine triphosphate, the principal energy storage molecule.
53. B. Ribosomes are RNA-containing organelles that are the sites of the synthesis of proteins.
54. B. Root hair cells increase the absorbing surface of roots.
55. B. Transpiration is the evaporation of water from the aerial part of plants. Evaporation is the result of the molecular activity called diffusion.
56. E. There are over 2,000 species of bacteria. Bacteria have few morphological/anatomical characteristics. Bacteria are distinguished by their growth in selected nutrient media and by such tests as the production of acid, gas, etc.—all of which are physiological traits.
57. C. By definition, fertilization is the union or fusion of an egg and sperm which results in the formation of a fertilized egg, or zygote.
58. B. Flowering plants produce the cereal grains in addition to numerous fruits and seeds , all of which are essential to the nutrition of humans and other animals.
59. D. An antigen is any substance which, when introduced into the body, causes the body to produce antibodies against it.
60. D. The physiological function of vitamin D is the regulation of calcium and phosphorus metabolism, hence, bone and tooth formation.
61. E. The chief sources of thiamine are yeast, wheat germ, corn meal and enriched (whole grain) flower products, i.e, the cereals.
62. E. Billions of nerve cell bodies make up the cerebral cortex. By various means (i.e., disease, surgery, electrical stimulation), it has been shown that specific regions of the cerebral cortex control specific functions such as hearing, movement, balance, memory, etc.
63. E. Mitosis is a process consisting of recognized phases which occur in the order prophase, metaphase, anaphase, telophase, and interphase.
64. B. A linkage group consists of a series of inherited traits which are inherited as a "package" because they are in a linear arrangement along a single chromatid. Crossing over, the exchange of segments between the chromatids of a tetrad may disrupt this inheritance package.
65. E. The dark reactions of photosynthesis use the energy of ATP, which is formed in the light, for their essential processes, all of which take place in the clear stroma, which surround the grana of the chloroplast.
66. E. A streaming movement of the cytoplasm (cyclosis) within a cell during periods of photosynthesis apparently presents the contained chloroplastids of each cell to maximum light exposure in sequence.
67. B. Enzymes that control respiration are generally found in the mitochondria and, under suitable conditions, the oxidation of pyruvic acid to carbon dioxide and water with the production of ATP molecules can be demonstrated.
68. C. Under the influence of the enzyme thrombin, fibrinogen is converted into fibrin, which gradually forms a mesh in which blood cells become embedded, thus forming a clot.
69. D. Systole is that phase of the heart's action in which blood is forced out of the ventricles.
70. D. The trigeminal nerve innervates teeth.
71. C. The prophase is recognized as the phase of mitosis in which the chromatids may be observed in the doubled chromosomes.

72. A. Plankton is the myriad of small, microscopic, free-floating aquatic organisms found at or near the surface and subject to tides and currents.

73. D. The genetic material must be able to contain a code and to copy itself exactly. Deoxyribonucleic acid, often abbreviated DNA, has this capability. In addition, it meets the requirements of being able to mutate and undergo crossing-over.

74. E. Nephrons are the functional units of the kidneys that, while secreting quantities of fluid, reabsorb blood sugar and amino acids as well as urea, various ions, and a large amount of water.

75. D. Atmospheric pressure on the surface of the mercury in the sealed tube pushes the mercury to a height of 760 millimeters. This is the basis of the common mercury barometer.

76. C. Atmospheric pressure on the surface of the mercury and the effects of transpirational pull—the evaporation of water from the stem and leaves of the plant—work together in raising the level of the mercury in figure B above 760 millimeters of mercury.

77. C. Monotremes, the most primitive group of mammals, constitute the lowest evolutionary animal group that nurses its young.

78. D. Carbon is an element basic to all organic compounds and is essential to the synthesis of carbohydrates, fats, and proteins.

79. B. Insufficient light stimulates stem elongation, which, when carried to extremes, is known as etiolation.

80. E. Eutrophication occurs when chemical fertilizers containing phosphorus and nitrogen wash into a lake causing photoplankton and bottom vegetation to reach high productivity. This tremendous growth blocks out light, causing deeper plants to die while certain decomposers use all the oxygen, thus suffocating the fish.

81. E. Random genetic drift is one of the ways by which changes in gene frequency are explained when mutation and natural selection do not account for evolution.

82. E. According to epigenesis, the individual arises from the undifferentiated material of the egg.

83. D. The trigeminal nerve innervates the jaw muscles.

84. C. Blood leaving the right ventricle enters the pulmonary artery; blood leaving the left ventricle enters the aorta.

85. B. The distinguishing factor of mutualism is that at least one of the populations cannot survive without the other.

86. D. While carbon, hydrogen and oxygen suffice for all carbohydrates and fats, proteins cannot be synthesized without additional elements including nitrogen and, sometimes, sulfur.

87. A. The transport of ions against a concentration gradient in the direction opposite to that which would occur in osmosis or by diffusion is active transport. The cell expends energy to accomplish this.

88. E. Bacteriophages are viruses that attack and invade bacterial cells converting bacterial DNA to viral DNA.

89. B. Fermentation takes place in yeasts and other cells in the absence of free oxygen and a similar type of reaction takes place in muscle cells. This process produces lactic acid from which the energy-bearing ATP molecule is formed.

90. B. Niacin is usually thought of as the vitamin that prevents pellagra. Persons consuming insufficient niacin may also develop disorders of the digestive system, skin, and the nervous system.

91. B. The vagus nerve innervates the heart, the bronchi, the bladder, and other internal organs, and it is involved with peristaltic movements and secretion.

92. E. In the farsighted eye, the misshapen lens focuses the image behind the retina.

93. A. In the complex DNA molecule, the bases adenine and thymine are always paired as are cytosine and guanine.

94. E. Algae (spirogyra), slime molds, and fungi are the plant groups that do not produce multicellular embryos. All other plants, including mosses and liverworts, and all vascular plants, including club mosses, ferns, gymnosperms, and flowering plants, produce multicellular embryos.

95. D. In human sex-linked inheritance, females, with two X chromosomes, are the "carriers" of the recessive gene for such sex-linked traits as the disease hemophilia. The male Y chromosome lacks a gene for the trait in question. When a male inherits an X chromosome with the recessive gene (X^r), the recessive gene is expressed because no normal gene is present to prevent it.

96. E. In fats, the ratio of hydrogen atoms to oxygen atoms is much higher than 2:1. Tristearin, for example, has the formula $C_{57}H_{110}O_6$.

97. A. Under conditions of isolation, exemplified by Darwin's finches, the production of a number of diverse species from a single ancestral one is referred to as adaptive radiation.

98. B. Photosynthesis results in the conversion of radiant, or light, energy into chemical energy and its storage in the glucose molecule.

99. A. Folic acid is important for normal bone marrow function and a deficiency could result in certain types of anemia.

100. E. Native perennial grasses of the grasslands (prairies) of North America include the so-called buffalo grass, and the predominant animal is the bison.

101. A. In the human heart (and 4-chambered hearts in general), blood goes from the left atrium into the left ventricle and from the right atrium into the right ventricle.

102. A. In a mutualistic relationship, at least one partner is unable to survive without the other.

103. A. Prior to Mendel, most students of inheritance attempted to study inheritance patterns involving all or groups of supposedly inheritable traits. The usual result was confusion and chaos.

104. D. Respiration is a biochemical process that releases energy and carbon dioxide. Dry weight is lost during respiration because organic compounds are used up.

105. C. During blood clotting, thromboplastin acts on prothrombin to produce thrombin, and thrombin, in turn, acts on fibrinogen to produce fibrin. Both reactions are enzymatic.

106. D. Under natural conditions only lightning, certain bacteria and blue-green algae are able to "fix" nitrogen.

107. C. }
108. D. } In their environment, all living things are affected by and respond to various combinations of genetic, climatic, edaphic (soil factors), biotic (living organisms), and fire stimuli.

109. B. Deoxyribonucleic acid, DNA, is found in chromosomes and stores hereditary information in coded form.

110. A. }
111. A. } In the mitochondria, during cellular respiration, energy is transformed from carbohydrate molecules to energy-rich adenosine triphosphate (ATP) for use throughout the cell.

Questions about Astronomy

Directions: Each of the questions or incomplete statements below is followed by five suggested answers or completions. Select the one that is best in each case.

1. Retrograde motion is the
   (A) apparent backward motion of a planet
   (B) apparent backward motion of the moon
   (C) seasonal movement between the vernal equinox and the autumnal equinox
   (D) reciprocal movement of the earth's axis
   (E) retreat of a meteorite

2. Since the same face of the moon is always visible on earth, we must conclude that
   (A) the earth and moon rotate at the same relative rate
   (B) the earth and moon are rotating in opposite directions
   (C) the moon must make one rotation on its axis while revolving once around the earth
   (D) the earth must make one rotation on its axis while revolving around the moon
   (E) their orbits are equal

3. To say that the solar system is heliocentric means that
   (A) the earth is the center of the solar system
   (B) the sun is the center of the solar system
   (C) the sun is highest in the sky
   (D) the sun is lowest in the sky
   (E) the center reflects the perimeter

4. A star that increases to a maximum brightness and does not return to its original condition is known as a
   (A) nova (B) supernova (C) giant
   (D) supergiant (E) binary

5. During a solar eclipse
   (A) the earth's shadow is cast on the moon
   (B) the moon's shadow is cast on the earth
   (C) the earth's shadow falls on the sun
   (D) the earth moves between the sun and moon
   (E) the sun moves between the earth and moon

6. An early Egyptian achievement, based on a knowledge of astronomy, was the
   (A) recording of eclipses
   (B) recording of earthquakes
   (C) invention of time
   (D) development of a 365-day calendar
   (E) development of a decimal system

7. Radio waves of broadcasting frequency are reflected by
   (A) ozone in the stratosphere
   (B) an ionized layer of the troposphere
   (C) a non-ionized layer of the troposphere
   (D) the exosphere
   (E) the ionosphere

8. An eclipse of the moon
   (A) occurs when the earth passes into the shadow of the moon
   (B) occurs when the moon passes between the sun and the earth
   (C) occurs every eight years
   (D) can occur only during a new moon
   (E) can occur only during a full moon

9. The Hawaiian Islands are just east of the international dateline while Wake Island is west. When it is July 4 at Pearl Harbor, what is the date at Wake Island?
(A) July 2 (B) July 3 (C) July 4 (D) July 5
(E) July 6

10. When a space vehicle is at apogee, it is at
(A) maximum speed
(B) minimum speed
(C) the point farthest away from the sun
(D) a point in orbit farthest from the earth
(E) a point in orbit closest to the earth

11. At the time of the summer solstice in the northern hemisphere,
(A) the sun's rays are tangent to the poles
(B) the sun's rays are perpendicular to the equator
(C) days and nights are equal over the entire earth
(D) the sun is directly overhead at the Tropic of Cancer
(E) the sun is directly overhead at the Tropic of Capricorn

12. Small celestial bodies whose orbits generally lie between Mars and Jupiter are called
(A) comets (B) meteoroids (C) asteroids
(D) planets (E) micrometeorites

13. One evidence of the earth's rotation is
(A) the solar eclipse
(B) the lunar eclipse
(C) the changing phases of the moon
(D) the tilt of the earth's axis
(E) the circulation of air as reported on weather maps

14. A lunar eclipse occurs when
(A) the sun, moon, and earth form a triangle
(B) the moon's shadow falls on the earth
(C) the sun moves between the moon and the earth
(D) the moon comes between the earth and the sun
(E) the earth travels between the sun and the moon

ANSWERS AND EXPLANATIONS

1. A. Occasionally planets appear to become stationary and then to drift westward for a short time; then the planet resumes its normal eastward motion. This is known as retrograde motion.
2. C. The direction of the moon's rotation is in the same direction as the earth's rotation, and the moon makes only one rotation on its axis during one revolution around the earth. Therefore, the moon keeps the same side directed towards the earth.
3. B. By definition: having the sun as a center.
4. B. A supernova is a star that has collapsed under intense gravitation and then exploded.

5. B. When the moon lies directly between the earth and the sun we witness a solar eclipse.
6. D. The Egyptians were the first to develop a 365-day calendar.
7. E. A layer of the atmosphere characterized by electrical properties and the presence of ionized particles is called the ionosphere. Radio waves from the earth travel upward to these ionized layers and are reflected back to earth.
8. E. In an eclipse, both the sun and the center of the earth lie in the ecliptic plane and so must the moon lie in the ecliptic plane for, if it is too far from the ecliptic plane, it cannot pass into the shadow of the earth to cause a lunar eclipse. When lying in the ecliptic plane, the moon is, by its location, in the "full moon" phase.
9. D. The International Date Line is designated ± 12 hours based on Greenwich time. Points east and west of this line differ in time by 24 hours.
10. D. In an elliptical orbit, a space vehicle at apogee is at the orbit's farthest distance from earth.
11. D. On June 21, the sun is as far north as it will go and is directly over the Tropic of Cancer, 23° 27′ north of the equator. This date and this position of the sun mark the summer solstice.
12. C. Asteroids include thousands of small planets between Mars and Jupiter with diameters of a fraction of a mile to almost 500 miles.
13. E. Winds are deflected to the right of their paths in the Northern Hemisphere and to the left of their paths in the Southern Hemisphere, deviations which are the result of the earth's rotation. This deviation is called the Coriolis effect. The circulation of air as indicated on weather maps, is, therefore, a direct effect of the earth's rotation.
14. E. In a lunar eclipse, the earth's shadow falls on the moon.

Questions about Earth Science

Directions: Each of the questions or incomplete statements below is followed by five suggested answers or completions. Select the one that is best in each case.

1. A contemporary source of support for the theory of sphericity of the earth is
   (A) the Foucault pendulum (B) photographs taken by astronauts
   (C) computer data (D) Coriolis forces (E) parallax of stars

2. A crystalline calcite column hanging from a cave ceiling is called a
   (A) stalagmite (B) anthracite (C) dolomite
   (D) alabaster (E) stalactite

3. Lava that solidifies in the air and falls to the earth as solid particles is called
   (A) xenoliths (B) laccoliths (C) pyroclastics
   (D) batholiths (E) pahoehoes

4. About 99% of the earth's atmosphere consists of
   (A) nitrogen and oxygen (B) nitrogen (C) oxygen
   (D) oxygen and carbon dioxide (E) nitrogen and carbon dioxide

5. A weathering of rock by a combination of mechanical and chemical forces is
   (A) hydration (B) crosscutting (C) lamination
   (D) intrusion (E) intumescence

6. A surface separating young rocks from older ones is
(A) a moraine (B) a bench (C) a stack
(D) an unconformity (E) a disjunction

7. An earthquake that follows a larger earthquake and originates at or near the same focus is called
(A) the epicenter (B) surface wave (C) an aftershock
(D) seismogram (E) reflected wave

8. A dark-brown residue formed by the partial decomposition of plants that grow in marshes and other wet places is called
(A) coal (B) dolomite (C) peat (D) chert (E) coquins

9. The time period described as the age of the great coal swamps is called the
(A) Oligocene epoch (B) Jurassic period (C) Pennsylvanian period
(D) Pleistocene period (E) Silurian period

10. Rocks formed by solidification of molten material are called
(A) sedimentary (B) igneous (C) fossiliferous
(D) metamorphic (E) monomineralic

11. The gradual dome-like buildup of calcite mounds or columns on the floors of caves results in formations called
(A) stalactites (B) diamonds (C) gypsum
(D) dolomite (E) stalagmites

12. A fracture line of the earth's crust where one portion has shifted vertically in reference to the other is called
(A) a fault (B) a P wave (C) an L wave
(D) an S wave (E) a tremor

13. What are stalagmites?
(A) Graphite columns "growing" down from a cave ceiling
(B) Calcite mounds or columns built up from cave floors
(C) Anthracite deposits in caves
(D) Graphite mounds or columns built up from cave floors
(E) Calcite columns "growing" down from cave ceilings

ANSWERS AND EXPLANATIONS

1. B. Photographs taken from outer space show the earth to be a sphere.
2. E. Crystalline calcite columns called stalactites are formed over long periods of time by dripping water.
3. C. Pyroclastics are particles of solidified lava which have fallen to earth.
4. A. The earth's atmosphere is 78% nitrogen and 21% oxygen. The remaining 1% consists of carbon dioxide, argon, helium, and other gases.
5. A. Mechanical weathering is the breaking of rock into smaller pieces, each retaining the characteristics of the original material. Chemical weathering results when chemical actions alter the rock by either the removal or addition of elements.

6. D. Breaks in the rock record are called uncomformities. One easily recognized unconformity consists of tilted or folded sedimentary rocks that are overlain by other more flat-lying rock strata.
7. C. Aftershocks are earthquakes of less severity that usually follow the primary earthquake.
8. C. As a layer of sphagnum (peat moss) grows over water, older growth is pressed deeper in the water and into darkness where it dies. Initial decay products contain much tannin and this slows down bacterial decay. This becomes the peat of commerce.
9. C. During the Pennsylvanian period, lush vegetation was so profuse that it was buried under successive layers, which in aging under high pressures eventually became coal.
10. B. Rock formed by the cooling of magma is known as igneous rock.
11. E. The calcite mounds built up on cave floors are called stalagmites.
12. A. When portions of the earth's crust fracture as a result of earthquakes, these fracture lines are called faults.
13. B. Stalagmites are calcite mounds built up on cave floors and are the result of dripping water over long periods of time.

Questions about Physics

Directions: Each of the questions or incomplete statements below is followed by five suggested answers or completions. Select the one that is best in each case.

1. During the process called nuclear fission,
   (A) alpha particles are emitted
   (B) light atomic nuclei fuse
   (C) there is an increase in mass
   (D) radioactive fragments are formed
   (E) much energy is consumed

2. Chromatic aberration may be eliminated by the use of
   (A) a convex lens (B) a concave lens
   (C) monochromatic light (D) proper focusing
   (E) a wider lens

3. When a musical note is raised one half step in pitch, it is called
   (A) tremolo (B) syncopation (C) sharp (D) flat
   (E) overtone

4. Pressure in a liquid
   (A) is inversely proportional to depth
   (B) decreases with depth
   (C) is variable at all points at the same level
   (D) is the same at different points at different levels
   (E) is the same at all points at the same level

5. A device in which chemical energy is converted into electrical energy is the
   (A) induction coil (B) rectifier (C) vacuum tube
   (D) amplifier (E) fuel cell

6. The condition created when two wires are connected through such a low resistance that current flow is excessive is called
   (A) a short circuit (B) induction (C) rectification
   (D) a circuit breaker (E) transition

7. Electronics is a field of applied science concerned with
   (A) the flow of electrons along a wire
   (B) the flow of electrons through gases or through a vacuum
   (C) the flow of electrons in liquids
   (D) amplitude modulation
   (E) frequency modulation

8. A prism separates white light because
   (A) parallel rays are reflected
   (B) parallel rays are focused
   (C) the angle of incidence equals the angle of reflection
   (D) the different frequencies are refracted differently
   (E) light rays are absorbed

9. An object traveling at mach 2 is traveling approximately how many miles per hour?
   (A) 750 (B) 1,500 (C) 2,000 (D) 15,000 (E) 20,000

10. A shift in the wave length of light or sound is known as the
    (A) Bernoullian principle (B) Compton effect
    (C) Doppler effect (D) Edison effect (E) Bell effect

11. Heat is the energy represented by
    (A) friction (B) molecular motion (C) thermodynamics
    (D) absolute zero (E) thermostats

12. Magnetic fields
    (A) are indefinite and variable
    (B) cannot exist in a vacuum
    (C) cannot be demonstrated
    (D) can be explained by Gilbert's Theory
    (E) cannot penetrate non-magnetic materials

13. In reference to electrical circuitry, the ohm represents
    (A) the unit of current (B) a force between two electric fields
    (C) the difference of potential (D) the flow of coulombs
    (E) the unit of resistance

14. Work requires that
    (A) direction be changed
    (B) a body be moved by a force
    (C) a definite rate be maintained
    (D) the rate of motion increase
    (E) the rate of motion decrease

15. In using a lever,
    (A) force is gained when the force arm is longer than the weight arm
    (B) force is gained when the force arm is shorter than the weight arm
    (C) force is gained when the force arm and the weight arm are equal
    (D) distance is gained when the force arm is longer than the weight arm
    (E) distance is gained when the fulcrum is central

16. Attics should have provision for ventilation so that hot summer air may be removed by
    (A) conduction (B) expansion (C) convection
    (D) entropy (E) radiation

17. If you swim one kilometer to an island off-shore, how many miles do you swim?
    (A) 0.36 mile (B) 0.5 mile (C) 0.84 mile (D) 0.62 mile
    (E) 1.6 miles

18. Every object remains in its state of rest or in its state of uniform motion unless
    (A) its velocity changes (B) its acceleration varies
    (C) internal forces change (D) internal forces remain constant
    (E) external forces change that state

19. According to Newton's third law of motion,
    (A) force is proportional to mass times acceleration
    (B) momentum equals mass times velocity
    (C) the weight of a body is equal to the gravitational attraction exerted upon it by the earth
    (D) the weight of a body is equal to the gravitational attraction exerted upon it by the sun
    (E) to every action, there is an equal and opposite reaction

Questions 20–22

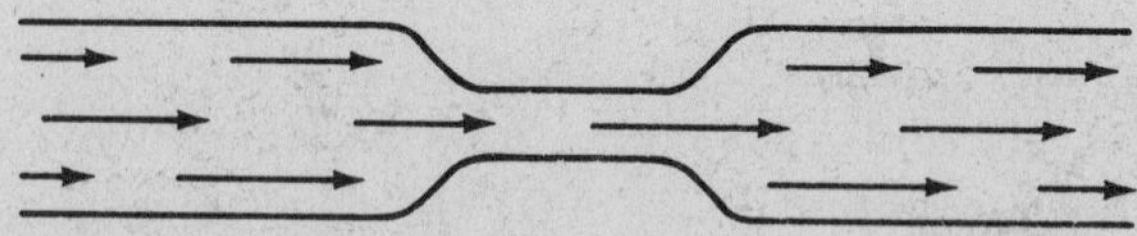

20. A fluid moving through a constriction, as illustrated above, speeds up and at the same time
    (A) its temperature also increases
    (B) its temperature decreases
    (C) its molecules begin to cling together
    (D) the pressure of the fluid within the constriction decreases
    (E) the pressure of the fluid within the constriction increases

21. The phenomenon illustrated is known as
    (A) the Doppler Effect
    (B) Borelli's Constant
    (C) Bernoulli's Principle
    (D) the Mach Effect
    (E) the Schlieren Process

22. One application of the phenomenon illustrated is in the
    (A) calculation of barometric pressure
    (B) verification of translational motion
    (C) design of airplane wings
    (D) determination of wave frequency
    (E) design of internal guidance systems

Questions 23–25

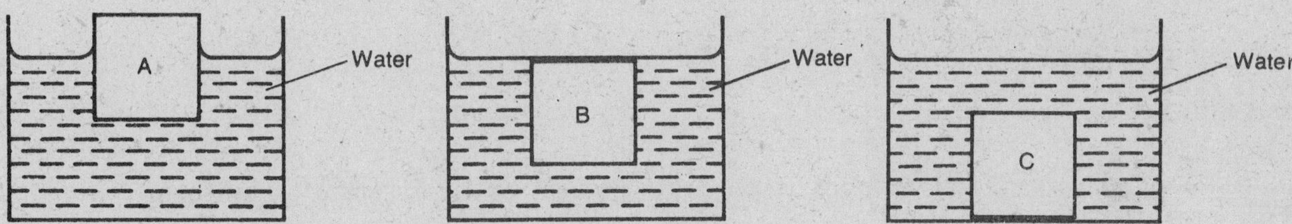

In the figures illustrated above, cubes A, B, and C, which have equal dimensions, are shown in containers of water.

23. In respect to the relative densities of the cubes, it may be concluded that
    (A) cube C has the greatest density
    (B) cube C sinks because its density is equal to the density of water
    (C) cube A has the greatest density
    (D) cube B has the greatest density
    (E) water has less buoyant force than cube A or B

24. Cube C sinks to the bottom because
    (A) cube C has a very low density
    (B) the weight of the displaced water is greater than the weight of cube C
    (C) cube C displaces too much water
    (D) the weight of the displaced water is equal to the weight of cube C
    (E) the weight of the displaced water is less than the weight of cube C

25. The phenomenon illustrated in these figures is best summarized or explained by
    (A) Faraday's Postulates
    (B) Boyle's Law
    (C) Dalton's Theory
    (D) Archimedes' Principle
    (E) Kepler's Laws

26. The energy exerted by a bowling ball as it strikes the pins is
    (A) inertia (B) mass energy (C) kinetic energy
    (D) potential energy (E) transferred energy

27. If a container of ether is unstoppered in a closed room where there are no air currents or air circulation, we soon smell ether because of
(A) osmosis (B) diffusion (C) transpiration
(D) capillarity (E) surface tension

28. When electricity flows through a wire wound in the form of a coil, the coil functions as
(A) a generator (B) a resistor (C) an electromagnet
(D) an electrostatic generator (E) an electroscope

29. When the nucleus of a radium atom emits an alpha particle,
(A) only its atomic number changes
(B) only its mass changes
(C) neither its mass nor atomic number changes
(D) both its mass and atomic number change
(E) it becomes uranium

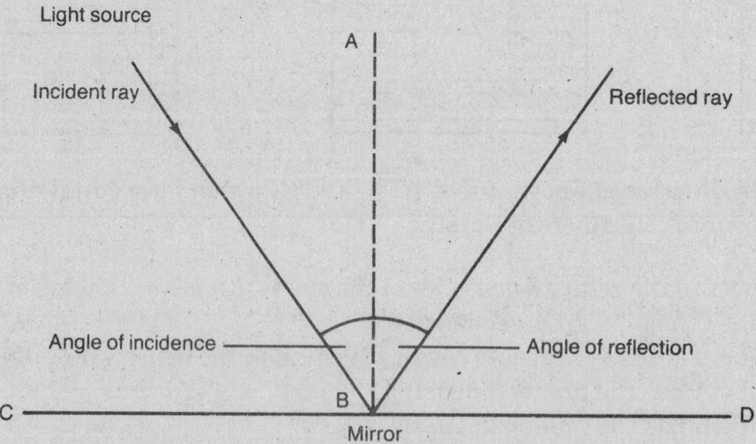

The diagram above illustrates the reflection of a ray of light from a mirror. The imaginary line *AB* is perpendicular to line *CD*.

30. The nature of a reflected ray of light is such that
(A) the angle of incidence is greater than the angle of reflection
(B) the angle of reflection always equals the angle of incidence
(C) the angle of reflection is greater than the angle of incidence
(D) the angle of reflection varies and changes
(E) the sum of the angle of incidence and the angle of reflection is a right angle

31. A vibrating string on a musical instrument will produce a low pitch if it is
(A) short, stretched, and of small diameter
(B) long, stretched, and of small diameter
(C) long, loose, and of small diameter
(D) long, loose, and of large diameter
(E) short, stretched, and of large diameter

Questions 32 and 33

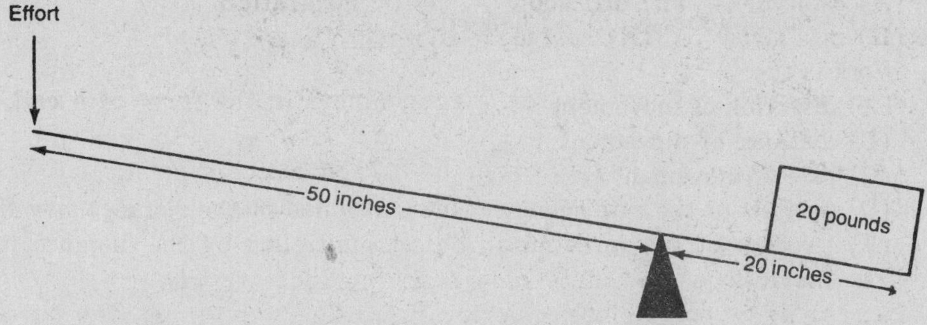

32. The effort required to lift the 20 pound load in the illustration above is
(A) 8 pounds
(B) 10 pounds
(C) 2 pounds
(D) 20 pounds
(E) 40 pounds

33. What is the mechanical advantage of the lever illustrated above?
(A) 1
(B) 10
(C) 7½
(D) 5
(E) 2½

34. In the transmission of electric power, alternating current is used because
(A) its voltage is readily transformed
(B) it is cheaper
(C) it is readily grounded
(D) it is ready to use in household appliances
(E) it has greater resistance

35. Ultraviolet radiation will cause a metal to emit electrons, an activity called
(A) ionization (B) facsimile transmission
(C) electron transformation (D) the Compton effect
(E) the photoelectric effect

36. Materials which transmit no light are referred to as
(A) luminous (B) opaque (C) transparent (D) lucid
(E) translucent

37. Concave lenses cause light rays to diverge by
(A) reflection (B) absorption (C) diffraction
(D) dispersion (E) diffusion

38. The acoustical engineer is chiefly concerned with
(A) amplitude (B) frequencies (C) loudness
(D) reverberations (E) wave length

39. When a bullet is fired upwards vertically, it gains in
(A) momentum (B) speed (C) kinetic energy
(D) potential energy (E) inertia

40. Work is the
(A) direction of movement
(B) distance of movement
(C) rate of movement
(D) product of the rate of movemenτ multiplied by the distance moved
(E) product of the force on an object multiplied by the distance it moves

41. When a hard rubber ball is rubbed by wool, it
(A) gains electrons and becomes positively charged
(B) gains electrons and becomes negatively charged
(C) remains neutral
(D) loses electrons and becomes positively charged
(E) loses electrons and becomes negatively charged

42. Transformers
(A) are coils of wire carrying electric current
(B) change the voltage of alternating current
(C) have the capacity to store electric charges
(D) change the voltage of direct current
(E) are used to break circuits

43. According to Boyle's Law, when the temperature is constant, the volume of a given quantity of gas is inversely proportional to the
(A) viscosity (B) temperature (C) density
(D) surface tension (E) pressure

44. Roger Bacon contributed the
(A) heliocentric theory
(B) idea of the rotation of the earth
(C) experimental approach to science
(D) concept of buoyancy and density
(E) idea of the sphericity of the earth

45. The usual unit of measure used to express the dimensions of living cells is the micron, which is equivalent to
(A) 0.001 kilogram (B) 0.001 meter (C) 0.01 centimeter
(D) 0.000,001 meter (E) 0.000,001 kilometer

46. The inward force that is necessary to keep an object in circular motion is called
(A) centrifugal force (B) inertia (C) centripetal force
(D) net force (E) weightlessness

47. When an object exhibits inertia, it
(A) resists being set in motion
(B) resists friction and slowing down
(C) responds directly to friction forces
(D) exhibits velocity in a specified direction
(E) possesses direction and magnitude

48. The difference between an induced fusion reaction and a thermonuclear reaction is that, in a thermonuclear reaction, nuclei of
(A) heavy atoms are split (B) heavy atoms are fused
(C) light atoms are split (D) light atoms are fused
(E) either heavy or light atoms are split

49. The phenomenon called interference is produced when
(A) light waves are bent
(B) light waves are parallel
(C) two or more waves of the same frequency are superposed
(D) the velocities of sound in air are identical
(E) the frequencies of wave vibrations are equal

50. Which of the following illustrates the phenomenon of "double-bonding"?
(A) H—C≡C—H

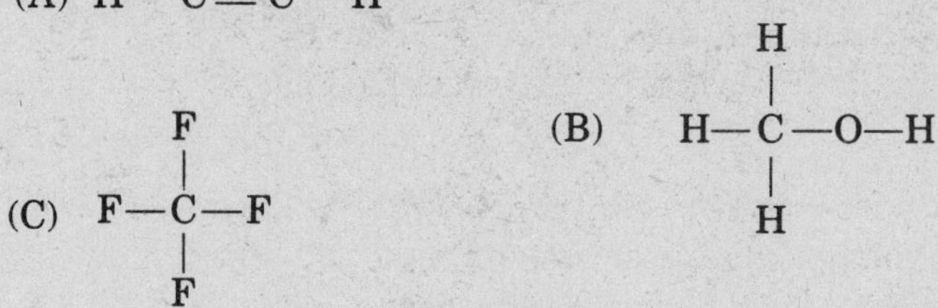

```
       H       H                    H     H
        \     /                     |     |
(E)      C=                (D)  H—C—O—C—H
        /     \                     |     |
       H       H                    H     H
```

51. At the higher altitudes, the existence of a satellite is limited because of drag caused by
(A) cosmic rays from the sun
(B) air and other particles in space
(C) infrared radiation from the sun
(D) centrifugal force
(E) both cosmic rays and centrifugal force

52. According to Einstein's theory of relativity, as the speed of a space ship approaches the speed of light,
(A) metabolism and mass increase
(B) metabolism and mass decrease
(C) metabolism and mass remain constant
(D) aging, relative to earth, would slow down
(E) aging, relative to earth, would speed up

53. When a tractor applies a horizontal force of 400 pounds and pushes an object 20 feet across a loading platform, the work accomplished is equal to
(A) 200 foot-pounds (B) 400 foot-pounds
(C) 2,000 foot-pounds (D) 4,000 foot-pounds
(E) 8,000 foot-pounds

54. When a gas is compressed by pressure,
(A) its component molecules are compressed
(B) space between its molecules decreases
(C) its volume increases
(D) its molecules speed up
(E) its molecules slow down

55. The tendency of all molecules to be in continuous motion and to spread out is a physical phenomenon called
(A) diffusion (B) capillarity (C) surface tension
(D) transpiration (E) osmosis

56. The velocity of an object is a description of
(A) distance and time (D) its mass and weight
(B) its acceleration (E) its speed and direction
(C) its resistance to inertia

57. What is the mechanical advantage of the block and tackle illustrated ?
(A) 1
(B) 2
(C) 3
(D) 6
(E) 9

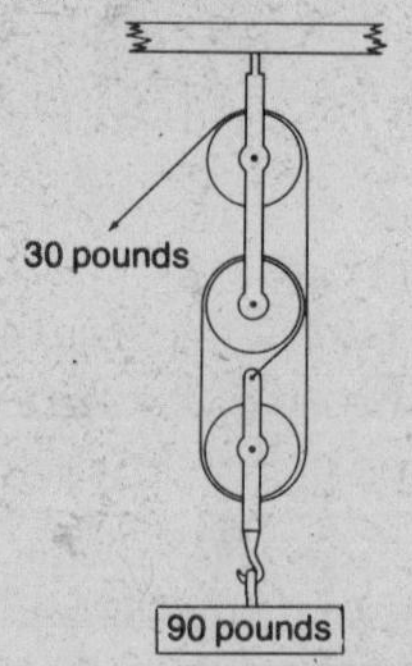

30 pounds

90 pounds

58. The conversion of alternating current to direct current is called
(A) amplification (B) modulation (C) transistorization
(D) induction (E) rectification

59. That property of matter which tends to maintain any motionless body at rest is called
(A) friction (B) mass (C) inertia (D) force
(E) velocity

60. Electric current in which the direction of flow is reversed at regular intervals is called
(A) effective current (B) alternating current
(C) direct current (D) induced current (E) universal current

61. In connection with nuclear reactions, that mass which is just sufficient to make the reaction self-sustaining is called
(A) a fusion reaction (B) a fission reaction
(C) a critical mass (D) deuterium (E) plutonium

62. Echoes are
(A) decibels (B) reflected sound waves
(C) interference (D) reinforcement
(E) diffracted sound waves

63. Heat energy, in today's terminology, is expressed in
(A) calories (B) ergs (C) joules (D) watts (E) kilowatts

Questions 64–67

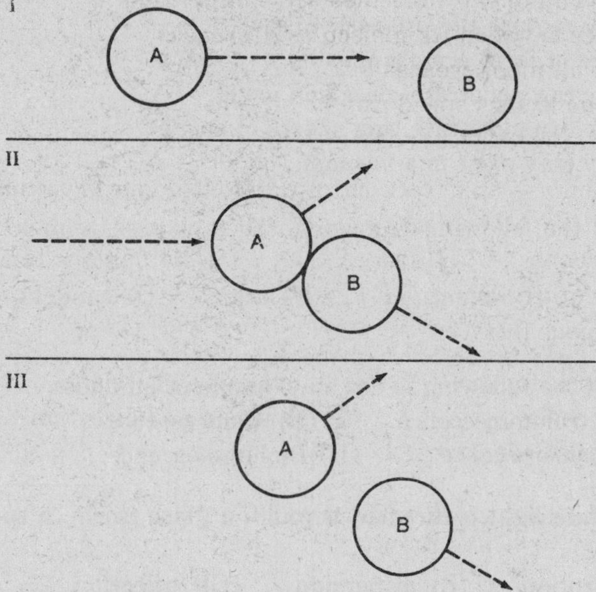

The three diagrams illustrate a sequence in which ball A is moving towards stationary ball B in diagram I; strikes ball B in diagram II; and both balls are moving after ball A strikes ball B in diagram III.

64. In diagram I, the moving ball (ball A)
(A) has a momentum equal to that of ball B
(B) accelerates in direct proportion to its mass
(C) accelerates in indirect proportion to its mass
(D) has zero momentum
(E) has a momentum equal to its mass times its velocity

65. When ball A collides with ball B
(A) ball A's momentum will increase
(B) ball A will retain its initial velocity
(C) ball A's momentum will remain constant
(D) ball A will slow down
(E) the force of the collision represents a gain in momentum

66. After the collision of ball A with ball B
(A) both ball A and ball B will be moving
(B) ball A will have slowed down and changed direction
(C) ball A will have lost momentum; ball B will have gained momentum
(D) the total initial and final velocities of balls A and B will be equal
(E) all of the above

67. Based upon study and observation of the three diagrams, one may conclude that, in accord with Newton's Second Law,
(A) momentum decreases mass
(B) momentum increases mass
(C) velocity is constant
(D) a force is necessary for acceleration
(E) energy is gained following the collision

68. One of the following is not an acceptable statement in respect to magnetic fields:
(A) They require the presence of matter.
(B) Lines of force are changeable.
(C) They can penetrate glass and wood.
(D) They can penetrate thin sheets of copper.
(E) They may exist in a vacuum.

69. Which of the following is a unit used to express a measure of luminous intensity?
(A) volt (B) roentgen (C) erg (D) candela
(E) luminous flux

70. Which of the following is not an example of luminescence?
(A) Electroluminescence (B) Fluorescence
(C) Phosphorescence (D) Bioluminescence (E) Incandescence

71. When white light is directed through a glass prism, a spectrum is formed by its
(A) absorption (B) dispersion (C) reflection
(D) refraction (E) diffusion

72. When light is reflected, the angle of incidence equals the angle of
(A) convergence (B) divergence (C) reflection
(D) refraction (E) dispersion

73. Which of the following represents the rate of flow of luminous energy?
(A) a lumen (B) luminous flux (C) a candela
(D) luminance (E) an erg

Questions 74 and 75 refer to the following diagram, which illustrates the basic characteristics of waves.

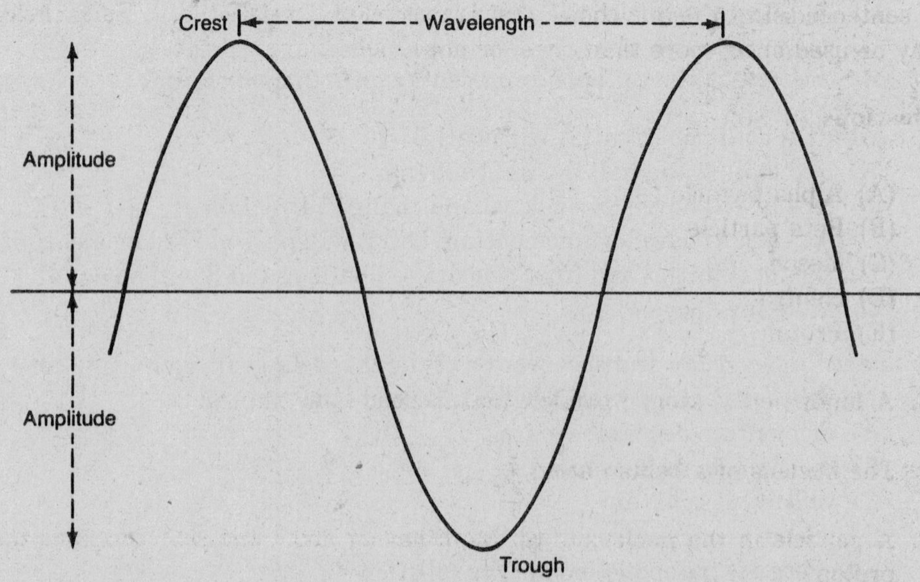

74. Amplitude may be thought of as
(A) an interaction between two different waves
(B) the number of crests passing a given point per second
(C) the distance between two adjacent crests
(D) a complete cycle, from crest to trough
(E) one-half of the vertical distance between crests and troughs

75. Interference is
(A) the simultaneous arrival of two different waves at a single point in space
(B) the combining of two different waves at some point in space
(C) the interaction of two or more waves
(D) "in phase" if two interacting waves are of the same frequency and shape and if they meet crest to crest and trough to trough
(E) all of the above

76. Pressures exerted by the water over a submerged object such as a submarine
(A) are equal to the area divided by the force
(B) are dependent upon direction
(C) are not affected by rate of flow
(D) are lower nearest the bottom
(E) are equal to the weight of a column of water above it

77. In order to accomplish 800 foot-pounds of work, an 80-pound object must be lifted
(A) 1/8 foot (B) 8 feet (C) 10 feet (D) 80 feet
(E) 100 feet

Directions: The group of questions below consists of five lettered choices followed by a list of numbered phrases or sentences. For each numbered phrase or sentence select the one choice that is most closely related to it. Each choice may be used once, more than once, or not at all.

Questions 78–80

(A) Alpha particle
(B) Beta particle
(C) Meson
(D) Neutron
(E) Proton

78. A fundamental atomic particle that is electrically neutral

79. The nucleus of a helium atom

80. A particle in the nucleus of an atom having about the same mass as the proton

ANSWERS AND EXPLANATIONS

1. D. When an atom undergoes fission, it splits into two smaller atoms which are called fission fragments and these are usually radioactive.
2. C. Chromatic aberration is the failure of different colors (wavelengths) of light to meet at the focal point after passing through a convex lens. This can be corrected by combining two or more lenses to ensure that the various colors of light meet at the focal point. The use of monochromatic light (light of one or a few nearly similar wavelengths) also eliminates the condition.
3. C. In music, sharps are notes that are raised one-half step in pitch.
4. E. Pressure is exerted equally in all directions at a given level.
5. E. In a fuel cell, gaseous hydrocarbons are the oxidizable material and air supplies oxygen.
6. A. A "short" is an electrical circuit with a very low resistance.
7. B. Electronics is that branch of physics that studies the emission behavior and effects of electrons in vacuums and in gases.
8. D. When white light passes through a prism it is broken up into an array of colors called a spectrum. The shortest rays of light bend the most and are the violet end of the spectrum. The longest rays bend the least and are the red end of the spectrum. All other colors fall in between, i.e., orange, yellow, green and blue.
9. B. The speed of sound in air at sea level at 0°C is about 741 miles per hour. This rate of speed is rated as Mach 1.
10. C. When the source of a light wave or a sound wave is moving relative to the observer, a change in the observed frequency of light or sound occurs and this change or shift is called the Doppler effect.
11. B. All molecules tend to be in constant motion. The more rapidly molecules move, the more frequent will be their collisions and, therefore, the higher will be the temperature.
12. A. When an alternating current is carried in a wire, a changing magnetic field is produced which, in turn, generates a varying electric field.
13. E. The ohm is the unit of electrical resistance in a given circuit.
14. B. Work is performed when an effort or a force causes a body to move.
15. A. A lever is in balance when the effort and load are in balance, i.e., effort × length of force arm = load × length of weight arm. If other factors remain constant, increasing the length of the force arm gives a gain in force.
16. C. Convection currents transfer heat energy in air by a circulatory motion due to variation in density and the forces of gravity.
17. D. A kilometer is 1000 meters or 0.62 mile.
18. E. Inertia is that property of every object that causes it to remain at rest, or, if in motion, to remain at a constant velocity unless made to change by external forces.
19. E. Whenever something is lifted, pulled, or pushed, it pushes down or resists in return.
20. D. The pressure of a moving fluid (including gases) changes with and is inversely proportional to its speed of motion.
21. C. According to Bernoulli's principle, when a fluid flows through a constriction, it speeds up and its pressure, therefore, decreases.
22. C. An airplane wing is so shaped that air molecules moving over the top surface have farther to travel and, in so doing, they must speed up. This creates a lower air pressure on the top of the wing and the result is lift.
23. A. }
24. E. } All matter consists of atoms. The density of a substance depends on the masses of its atoms and the closeness by which its atoms are packed. A given object, when placed in water, displaces a volume of water equal to its weight.
25. D. According to Archimedes' principle, a floating object displaces an amount of water equal to its own weight.
26. C. Kinetic energy is the energy possessed by a moving object.
27. B. All molecules, except when at absolute zero temperature, tend to remain

in constant motion and to spread out throughout all space available to them. This is diffusion.

28. C. The magnetic field around any long straight wire is circular when an electric current passes through the wire. If an electric current is passed through a coil of wire, the strength of the magnetic field is equal to the number of coils of wire and the amount of current in the coil.

29. D. Radium emits charged helium atoms which are called alpha particles and these are very heavy. This results in a loss of mass. Radium ($_{88}Ra$) has an atomic number of 88, the 88 representing 88 protons or alpha particles. Since helium is $_{2}He$ and comes from the radium atom, the loss of two from the radium to the helium means that the atom is now $_{86}R$, which is another element—radon.

30. B. When a ray of light strikes an object at a specific angle and is reflected, it bounces off the reflecting surface at the same angle at which it approached.

31. D. Small-diametered musical strings produce a high pitch if stretched tightly and large diametered strings produce a low pitch if strung loosely.

32. A. Effort multiplied by the length of the effort arm equals the load multiplied by the length of the load arm.

33. E. Mechanical advantage is calculated either by dividing the load by the effort or by dividing the length of the effort arm by the length of the load arm.

34. A. Electric power transmission is normally transmitted efficiently at higher voltages. Alternating current is easier to transmit and its voltage is readily transformed.

35. E. The outermost electrons of certain metals are not held strongly by the nucleus. Light of certain frequencies can dislodge surface electrons and this movement of electrons constitutes an electric current which is called the photoelectric effect.

36. B. Opaque substances do not permit light penetration.

37. C. Parallel rays of light passing through a concave lens bend outward or spread apart and this is called diffraction.

38. D. Reverberations are sound echoes which distort vocal and musical sounds.

39. D. Potential energy is the energy possessed by a body because of its position. A bullet fired into the air has potential energy because it will fall back to earth due to gravity.

40. E. Work is determined by multiplying the force on an object by the distance it is moved.

41. B. The atoms in the wool lose electrons, becoming positively charged; the atoms in the rubber ball gain electrons, becoming negatively charged.

42. B. Transformers are used to increase or decrease the voltage of alternating current.

43. E. At a constant temperature, the volume of a gas is inversely proportional to the pressure.

44. C. Roger Bacon advocated observation and experimentation as sources of scientific information.

45. D. One meter equals one million microns.

46. C. Centripetal force is the inward force that holds an object, such as a satellite, in circular motion in its orbit.

47. A. Inertia is the tendency of a body in motion to remain in motion or the tendency of a body at rest to remain at rest.

48. D. The light atoms of hydrogen isotopes are fused in a thermonuclear reaction.

49. C. When two different sound waves reach a single point simultaneously they combine in a process called interference.

50. E. The double chemical bond occurs when two electron pairs are shared by bonded atoms.

51. B. Any body anywhere in space is subject to drag caused by the air molecules and other particles found throughout space.

52. D. Speed and time as measured by an observer on a rocket traveling at a speed near the speed of light are different from the speed and time measured by an observer on earth. To the space traveler, light from earth is catching up to the spaceship at one speed; to the observer on earth, light is catching up to the spaceship at a different speed. Both observers are correct.

53. E. Work is defined as weight times distance moved. One foot pound equals a one pound weight being moved one foot.
54. B. In a sense, the same number of molecules occupy less space when a gas is compressed.
55. A. Diffusion is the tendency of molecules to remain in constant motion and to spread throughout all the space available to them.
56. E. Velocity is linear motion in a specific direction.
57. C. Mechanical advantage, in a pulley system, is determined by the number of ropes that support the weight.
58. E. A rectifier is a device used to convert alternating current to direct current.
59. C. That property of any object that keeps it at rest or at a constant velocity unless it is forced to change by external forces is called inertia.
60. B. In alternating current, the direction of current flow is reversed at regular intervals.
61. C. In a nuclear reaction, the minimum mass required to support a self-sustaining chain reaction is called the critical mass.
62. B. Echoes are reflected sound waves.
63. C. The older unit of heat is the calorie; the newer is the joule. One calorie equals 4.184 joules (4.184 J).
64. E. The momentum of any moving body is the product of its mass times its velocity.
65. D.
66. E. When two bodies collide, total momentum after the collision equals total momentum before the collision. Speed and direction may change because the original momentum is redistributed during the collision.
67. D. The acceleration of a body is directly proportional to the force acting on it and inversely proportional to its mass.
68. A. Magnetic fields exist in vacuums and can also penetrate most kinds of matter.
69. D. The power of a light source is called its luminous intensity. A unit of luminous intensity is the candela.
70. E. Incandescence is the emission of radiation by a hot body which makes the body visible.
71. D. When a ray of light moves from one medium to another, such as air through glass, the ray bends. This is refraction. The different wavelengths of white light are, therefore, separated into the visible spectrum since each has its own refractive index.
72. C. When light is reflected from a surface, the angle of reflection equals the angle of incidence.
73. B. Luminous flux is the rate of flow of luminous energy. The lumen is the metric unit for luminous flux.
74. E. Amplitude is measured from a zero point and is one half the vertical distance between the crest of a wave and its trough.
75. E. Interference is the combining of two different waves which meet at a point in space. If they meet crest to crest, trough to trough, they are in phase. If they combine out of phase, they cancel out. If waves of different frequencies combine, they reinforce each other part of the time and cancel each other part of the time.
76. E. Pressures in fluids increase with depth and are higher as depth increases due to the effects of gravity and the weight of the column of water above an object at any given depth.
77. C. Work is the force exerted on an object multiplied by the distance the object is moved.
78. D. Neutrons are fundamental atomic particles that are electrically neutral.
79. A. The nucleus of a helium atom is an alpha particle.
80. D. Neutrons have the same mass as protons.

Questions about Chemistry

Directions: Each of the questions or incomplete statements below is followed by five suggested answers or completions. Select the one that is best in each case.

1. When referring to the half-life of a radioactive element, we mean
   (A) an interval of time during which half of its atoms will undergo radioactive decay
   (B) half of the interval of time during which half of its atoms will undergo radioactive decay
   (C) an interval of time in which a specific atom of the element decays one half
   (D) an interval of time during which a random atom of the element decays one half
   (E) an interval of time during which all atoms of the element undergo one-half radioactive decay

2. In a process called electrolysis,
   (A) there is an interaction between electric currents and magnets
   (B) the motions of electrons in magnetic fields are studied
   (C) chemical compounds are synthesized
   (D) chemical compounds are decomposed by means of electric current
   (E) ionizing radiation may be measured

3. That the volume of a gas is inversely proportional to the pressure is known as
   (A) Kepler's law (B) Boyle's law
   (C) the first law of thermodynamics (D) Charles' law
   (E) Aristotle's theory

4. Elements included in the alkali metal family are unique in that they
   (A) are all heavy metals
   (B) have varying combining qualities
   (C) are difficult to obtain and keep in pure form
   (D) all combine in the same ratio with other elements
   (E) have two valence electrons

Questions 5 and 6

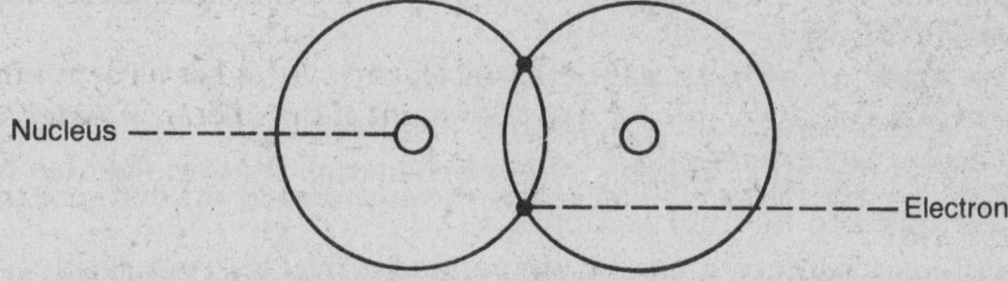

5. The two joined hydrogen atoms shown above illustrate
   (A) surface tension
   (B) ionization
   (C) mass number
   (D) hydrogen bonding
   (E) covalent bonding

6. In the hydrogen molecule, H_2, illustrated
   (A) each atom shares its electron with the other atom
   (B) two hydrogen isotopes are attracted to each other
   (C) positively charged electrons neutralize each other
   (D) the atomic number of each of its hydrogen atoms is four
   (E) hydrogen molecules are held together by surface tension

7. The amino acids in proteins are connected by substances called
   (A) carboxyl groups (B) peptide linkages (C) polymers
   (D) alkyl groups (E) esters

8. When mercuric oxide is heated, it forms metallic mercury and gaseous oxygen, a type of reaction called
   (A) synthesis (B) distillation (C) neutralization
   (D) rearrangement (E) decomposition

9. The chemical property called acidity is always identified with
   (A) turning phenolphthalein pink (B) turning litmus blue
   (C) hydroxide ions (D) bitter or soapy taste
   (E) the hydrogen atom

10. Different forms of a chemical element are called
    (A) anions (B) allotrophs (C) ketones (D) buffers
    (E) cations

11. Which of the following should give you the least concern?
    (A) Carcinogens in soft drinks
    (B) Strontium 90 in dairy products
    (C) DDT in fresh vegetables
    (D) Riboflavin and niacin in bread
    (E) Herbicidal residues in vegetables

12. Atoms having the same atomic number but having different masses
    (A) have the same number of protons and neutrons
    (B) have the same number of electrons and neutrons
    (C) are called isotopes
    (D) are artificially made by man and do not occur naturally
    (E) cannot be made artificially and occur naturally only

13. A solution can be exemplified by
    (A) a scattering of fine particles in water
    (B) a dispersion of sugar molecules in water
    (C) a dispersion of particles which are larger than molecules but too small to be microscopic
    (D) a dispersion in which the suspended particles eventually settle out
    (E) the immiscibility of the dispersed substances

14. The alkali metal family of chemical elements includes sodium and
    (A) aluminum (B) lithium (C) calcium
    (D) phosphorus (E) potassium

15. The energy liberated or consumed in exothermic and endothermic chemical processes is primarily that of
(A) vaporization (B) compression (C) chemical bonds
(D) catalysts (D) enzymes

16. In general, the rate of chemical reactions is directly proportional to
(A) the temperature and concentration of the reacting substances
(B) the exothermic quotient
(C) the endothermic quotient
(D) the availability of ions
(E) the availability of cations

17. A substance consisting of two or more ingredients which are not in chemical combination is called
(A) an ion (B) a mixture (C) a molecule (D) an oxide
(E) a compound

18. The atoms of non-metals tend to gain electrons, resulting in the creacion of negatively charged atoms called
(A) cations (B) acid-base pairs (C) base pairs
(D) anions (E) ions

19. The chemical properties of elements are determined primarily by
(A) electrons (B) ions (C) neutrons (D) mesons
(E) protons

20. Mass number represents
(A) atomic weight expressed in grams
(B) the number of atoms in one gram atomic weight
(C) atomic mass
(D) the sum of the protons and neutrons
(E) atomic weight

21. According to the Celsius scale,
(A) water boils at 212 degrees (B) water boils at 100 degrees
(C) water freezes at 32 degrees (D) ice melts at 32 degrees
(E) water boils at 98.6 degrees

Questions 22 and 23

According to Boyle's law, the pressure and volume of a confined gas are inversely proportional. As a consequence, the product of the pressure and the volume of a gas is constant at a given temperature, i.e., PV = constant.

22. If the pressure of a volume of a gas is halved
(A) its volume is halved
(B) its volume is doubled
(C) its volume remains constant
(D) its volume decreases according to a geometric progression
(E) its volume increases according to a geometric progression

23. Which of the following illustrates the pressure-volume relationship for a gas?
(P = pressure and V = volume)

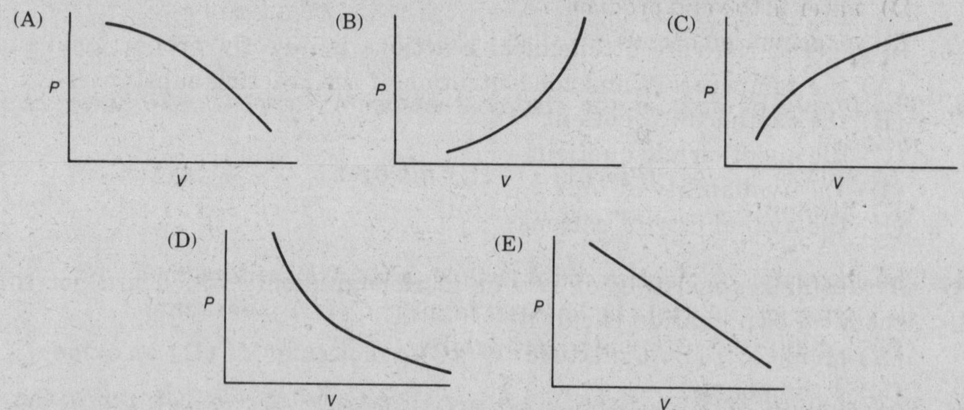

24. The family of chemical elements commonly referred to as the noble gases is characterized chiefly by the fact that its members
(A) form salts when they combine with metals
(B) react violently with water
(C) are not very active chemically
(D) are light, active metals
(E) are heavy, active metals

25. Substances with identical chemical formulas but with various physical and chemical properties are called
(A) ethers (B) ions (C) polymers (D) esters
(E) isomers

26. Which chemical element is found in all proteins?
(A) Sulfur (B) Potassium (C) Phosphorus
(D) Manganese (E) Nitrogen

27. The atomic number of an element means
(A) the number of electrons in its nucleus
(B) the number of neutrons in its nucleus
(C) the sum of its electrons and neutrons
(D) the number of protons in its nucleus
(E) the number of protons in its orbits

28. In the chemical reaction

$$2C_6H_{12}O_6 \rightarrow C_{12}H_{22}O_{11} + H_2O$$

a disaccharide sugar is formed. This kind of reaction is called
(A) condensation
(B) the dark reaction
(C) oxidation
(D) the light reaction
(E) reduction

29. When the disaccharide sugar in the equation above undergoes digestion
(A) water and CO_2 are the end products
(B) energy is stored
(C) water is consumed
(D) water is the end product
(E) condensation occurs

30. The family of nonmetallic chemical elements known as the halogens includes
(A) silicon (B) fluorine (C) nitrogen (D) oxygen
(E) lithium

31. The chemistry of plastics could well be called the chemistry of
(A) synergy (B) the halogen family (C) detergents
(D) polymers (E) biodegradability

32. The smallest existing particle of any chemically pure substance is the
(A) electron (B) proton (C) nucleus (D) ion (E) molecule

33. The changing of one atom into another is called
(A) ionization (B) radiography (C) nuclear fusion
(D) transmutation (E) transduction

34. The chemical bonds which result when two atoms share a pair of electrons are called
(A) double bonds (B) covalent bonds (C) hybridizations
(D) ionic-coordinates (E) double-coordinates

35. Two or more different forms of the same chemical element are called
(A) salts (B) ions (C) esters (D) conformations
(E) allotrophs

36. An element's atomic weight is
(A) the total weight of its electrons
(B) dependent upon uniform temperatures
(C) its weight relative to that of the hydrogen atom
(D) determined by the number of protons in its nucleus
(E) expressed in grams

ANSWERS AND EXPLANATIONS

1. A. Half-life is the time in which half of the atoms of a radioactive material will decay.
2. D. In electrolysis, an electric current is passed through a liquid causing a chemical reaction. In industry, sodium may be produced (purified) by the electrolysis of liquid sodium chloride.
3. B. According to Boyle's law, the volume of a gas is inversely proportional to the pressure.
4. C. Alkali metals are very reactive, readily giving up one electron to form ions.
5. E. } A covalent bond occurs when two atoms share electrons.
6. A. }
7. B. Proteins are composed of amino acids which are united or held together by the C—N—C linkage, commonly called the peptide linkage.

8. E. Heat causes mercuric oxide bonds to break down, thereby permitting the component elements to separate without entering into other compounds—literally, a decomposing of the molecule due to heat.
9. E. Acids are substances whose water solutions contain an excess of hydrogen ions.
10. B. Chemical elements often exist in different forms and these are called allotrophs.
11. D. Riboflavin and niacin are vitamins; all of the other substances listed are hazardous to health.
12. C. Atoms of any element that differ in the number of neutrons in their nucleus are different in mass and are called isotopes.
13. B. Homogenous mixtures have the same composition at the microscopic level throughout. When the dispersed particles are on a molecular scale the mixture is referred to as a solution.
14. E. Sodium and potassium are among the members of the alkali metals family.
15. C. Energy transformations in chemical reactions are concerned with the energy of chemical bonds. Energy loss may be due to the formation of chemical bonds, or energy may be added to break the chemical bonds.
16. A. The rates of chemical reactions are controlled by only a few factors, the most common being the concentrations of the reactants, the temperature, the nature of the reactants, and catalysts.
17. B. A mixture is any portion of matter consisting of two or more substances which can be separated from each other by physical means, i.e., without reacting to form new substances.
18. D. An ion is an atom or a group of atoms functioning as a unit and carrying an electrical charge. Those with positive charges are called cations, those with negative charges anions.
19. A. The chemical properties of elements are an expression of their attraction to or their repulsion from other elements, based primarily on circumstances pertaining to their electrons.
20. D. Mass number is the total number of neutrons and protons in the atom's nucleus.
21. B. The Celsius scale (formerly the Centigrade scale) divides the range of temperatures between the freezing and boiling points of water into 100 units, or degrees, each of which is called 1°C.
22. B.
23. D. According to Boyle's law, the pressure and the volume of a confined gas are inversely proportional.
24. C. Noble gases are extremely stable and undergo reaction only under rigorous conditions. The first noble gas compound was not prepared until 1962, and, prior to this, it was thought that noble gases were chemically inert.
25. E. Isomers are chemical compounds that have the same number of atoms of the same elements, but differ in structural arrangements and properties.
26. E. Nitrogen is found in all amino acids and hence, in all proteins.
27. D. The atomic number of an element is the number of protons in its nucleus.
28. A. Disaccharides form by the joining of two monosaccharide units in a condensation reaction in which a molecule of water is split out.
29. C. Disaccharides can react with water in the presence of a catalyst to form monosaccharides. This is digestion and a water-consuming reaction.
30. B. Halogens include fluorine, chlorine, bromine, etc.
31. D. Polymers are molecules composed of two or more small and repeated units that are chemically bonded together. They may be linear, branched or three-dimensional. Plastic materials are polymers.
32. E. The molecule cannot be further broken down without destroying it and changing its characteristics.
33. D. The concept that atoms (elements) may be changed from one to another is called transmutation.
34. B. A chemical bond represented by a pair of electrons in orbits that are part of both atoms is a covalent bond.
35. E. Allotrophs are the different forms of a given element in the same state of matter.

36. C. An atom's weight is a characteristic of a particular element and the atoms of each element have their own specific atomic weight. Hydrogen has arbitrarily been assigned an atomic weight of 1; the atoms of all the other elements are assigned atomic weights relative to the atomic weight of hydrogen.

Questions about the History of Science

Directions: Each of the questions or incomplete statements below is followed by five suggested answers or completions. Select the one that is best in each case.

1. The philosopher from Thrace famous for his atomic theory was
(A) Aristotle (B) Democritus (C) Thales
(D) Theophrastus (E) Empedocles

2. That living organisms have evolved was first theorized by
(A) Lamarck
(B) ancient Greek philosophers
(C) Darwin and Wallace
(D) Romans in the first century B.C.
(E) the geologist Charles Lyell

3. A famous anatomist during the Renaissance was
(A) Linnaeus (B) Michelangelo (C) Pliny (D) Bacon
(E) Galen

4. A Roman naturalist, literary man, and government worker who composed an encyclopedia called "Historia Naturalis" ("Natural History") was
(A) Lucretius (B) Galen (C) Celsus
(D) Pliny the Elder (E) Dioscorides

5. A pupil of Thales, one of the earliest Greek scholars to be concerned with human evolution, and one who believed in transmutations as a cause of diversity was
(A) Anaximander (B) Galen (C) Heraclitus
(D) Pliny (E) Empedocles

6. A stimulus which influenced the thinking of both Darwin and Wallace was
(A) Lyell's *Principles of Geology*
(B) Malthus' writing on population
(C) Lucretius' poem "De Rerum Natura"
(D) Lamarck's *Philosophie Zooligique*
(E) the writings of Aristotle

7. The ancient Greek scholar who became the "father of medicine" was
(A) Aristotle (B) Theophrastus (C) Alcmaeon
(D) Hippocrates (E) Empedocles

8. The 365-day calendar was first proposed by
(A) Pythagoras (B) Archimedes (C) the Babylonians
(D) the Egyptians (E) the Greeks

9. The field of immunization had its beginning with the work of
(A) Lister (B) Jenner (C) Koch (D) Pasteur (E) Ehrlich

10. According to Ptolemy,
(A) the sun is the center of the solar system
(B) the earth is round, with a circumference of 24,000 miles
(C) the universe is infinite
(D) the earth is a flat, floating disc
(E) the earth is the center of the solar system

11. The concept advocating the particulate or atomic structure of matter was first proposed by
(A) Theophrastus (B) Democritus (C) Pliny
(D) Aristotle (E) Plato

12. The most significant contribution of Isaac Newton was his
(A) heliocentric theory (B) universal law of gravitation
(C) concept of the atom (D) photon theory of light energy
(E) phlogiston theory

13. Who was the earliest Greek scholar to hold that the entire universe is subject to natural law?
(A) Aristotle (B) Thales (C) Anaximander
(D) Theophrastus (E) Empedocles

14. The recording of eclipses was first undertaken by the
(A) Babylonians (B) Egyptians (C) Greeks
(D) Chinese (E) Romans

15. Sterile and antiseptic surgical procedures were introduced by
(A) Fleming (B) Semmelweis (C) Banting
(D) Lister (E) Gorgas

16. First to propose the concept of the atomic structure of matter was
(A) Boyle (B) Kepler (C) Einstein (D) Aristotle
(E) Democritus

17. An early Greek physician whose writings considered medical ethics was
(A) Galen (B) Hippocrates (C) Anaximander
(D) Aristotle (E) Theophrastus

18. The Greek scholar who was the first to relate fossils to living plants and animals was
(A) Anaximander (B) Theophrastus (C) Empedocles
(D) Xenophanes (E) Aristotle

ANSWERS AND EXPLANATIONS

1. B. Democritus was one of the first Greeks to advocate the atomic theory.
2. B. The early Greek philosophers Anaximander and Xerrophanes formulated ideas concerning the origins of life and evolution.
3. B. Michelangelo made dissections of human internal structures so as to represent the features accurately and in proper relation to each other. His statues give evidence of his knowledge of human anatomy.
4. D. Pliny the Elder (A.D. 23–79) compiled a comprehensive encyclopedia called "Natural History."
5. A. Anaximander proposed that humans evolved.
6. B. Malthus' writing on population presented the theme that humans multiply more rapidly than does food supply, thereby creating conditions for the competition for existence.
7. D. The "Hippocratic Oath" honors Hippocrates as the "father of medicine".
8. D. The Egyptians first proposed the 365-day calendar.
9. B. Jenner was not the first to use vaccinations, but he developed the practicality and usefulness of the procedure.
10. E. Ptolemy developed a model of the universe that accounted for the movements of the planets in circular orbits around a motionless earth.
11. B. Democritus' greatest contribution was his atomic theory which held that the universe consists of atoms moving in space with all physical change dependent upon the union and separation of atoms.
12. B. Newton was the first person to recognize gravity as a universal force relative to both "the falling apple" and the orbits of the planets.
13. B. Thales supported both the concept of rational inquiry into nature and the school of thought that presumed that the entire universe is controlled by natural law.
14. A. Earliest written records, found in Babylonia and Mesopotamia, describe eclipses and other astronomical events inscribed in the clay and stone tablets of the time.
15. D. Prior to Lister, most surgical procedures were complicated by infection. Lister devised methods of sterilizing the operating room and its equipment by spraying carbolic acid over the hands of the surgeons and the immediate surroundings while the surgery was in progress.
16. E. Democritus first proposed the atomic structure of matter.
17. B. Hippocrates is called the "father of medicine." His professional writings, entitled "The Law," "The Physician," and "Oath," describe the contemporary attributes and ethics of Greek medicine and of the physicians who practiced it.
18. D. Xenophanes was the first Greek scholar to compare fossils to living organisms.

ANSWER SHEET — NATURAL SCIENCES/SAMPLE EXAMINATION 1

Section I

1. Ⓐ Ⓑ Ⓒ Ⓓ Ⓔ
2. Ⓐ Ⓑ Ⓒ Ⓓ Ⓔ
3. Ⓐ Ⓑ Ⓒ Ⓓ Ⓔ
4. Ⓐ Ⓑ Ⓒ Ⓓ Ⓔ
5. Ⓐ Ⓑ Ⓒ Ⓓ Ⓔ
6. Ⓐ Ⓑ Ⓒ Ⓓ Ⓔ
7. Ⓐ Ⓑ Ⓒ Ⓓ Ⓔ
8. Ⓐ Ⓑ Ⓒ Ⓓ Ⓔ
9. Ⓐ Ⓑ Ⓒ Ⓓ Ⓔ
10. Ⓐ Ⓑ Ⓒ Ⓓ Ⓔ
11. Ⓐ Ⓑ Ⓒ Ⓓ Ⓔ
12. Ⓐ Ⓑ Ⓒ Ⓓ Ⓔ
13. Ⓐ Ⓑ Ⓒ Ⓓ Ⓔ
14. Ⓐ Ⓑ Ⓒ Ⓓ Ⓔ
15. Ⓐ Ⓑ Ⓒ Ⓓ Ⓔ
16. Ⓐ Ⓑ Ⓒ Ⓓ Ⓔ
17. Ⓐ Ⓑ Ⓒ Ⓓ Ⓔ
18. Ⓐ Ⓑ Ⓒ Ⓓ Ⓔ
19. Ⓐ Ⓑ Ⓒ Ⓓ Ⓔ
20. Ⓐ Ⓑ Ⓒ Ⓓ Ⓔ
21. Ⓐ Ⓑ Ⓒ Ⓓ Ⓔ
22. Ⓐ Ⓑ Ⓒ Ⓓ Ⓔ
23. Ⓐ Ⓑ Ⓒ Ⓓ Ⓔ
24. Ⓐ Ⓑ Ⓒ Ⓓ Ⓔ
25. Ⓐ Ⓑ Ⓒ Ⓓ Ⓔ
26. Ⓐ Ⓑ Ⓒ Ⓓ Ⓔ
27. Ⓐ Ⓑ Ⓒ Ⓓ Ⓔ
28. Ⓐ Ⓑ Ⓒ Ⓓ Ⓔ
29. Ⓐ Ⓑ Ⓒ Ⓓ Ⓔ
30. Ⓐ Ⓑ Ⓒ Ⓓ Ⓔ
31. Ⓐ Ⓑ Ⓒ Ⓓ Ⓔ
32. Ⓐ Ⓑ Ⓒ Ⓓ Ⓔ
33. Ⓐ Ⓑ Ⓒ Ⓓ Ⓔ
34. Ⓐ Ⓑ Ⓒ Ⓓ Ⓔ
35. Ⓐ Ⓑ Ⓒ Ⓓ Ⓔ
36. Ⓐ Ⓑ Ⓒ Ⓓ Ⓔ
37. Ⓐ Ⓑ Ⓒ Ⓓ Ⓔ
38. Ⓐ Ⓑ Ⓒ Ⓓ Ⓔ
39. Ⓐ Ⓑ Ⓒ Ⓓ Ⓔ
40. Ⓐ Ⓑ Ⓒ Ⓓ Ⓔ
41. Ⓐ Ⓑ Ⓒ Ⓓ Ⓔ
42. Ⓐ Ⓑ Ⓒ Ⓓ Ⓔ
43. Ⓐ Ⓑ Ⓒ Ⓓ Ⓔ
44. Ⓐ Ⓑ Ⓒ Ⓓ Ⓔ
45. Ⓐ Ⓑ Ⓒ Ⓓ Ⓔ
46. Ⓐ Ⓑ Ⓒ Ⓓ Ⓔ
47. Ⓐ Ⓑ Ⓒ Ⓓ Ⓔ
48. Ⓐ Ⓑ Ⓒ Ⓓ Ⓔ
49. Ⓐ Ⓑ Ⓒ Ⓓ Ⓔ
50. Ⓐ Ⓑ Ⓒ Ⓓ Ⓔ
51. Ⓐ Ⓑ Ⓒ Ⓓ Ⓔ
52. Ⓐ Ⓑ Ⓒ Ⓓ Ⓔ
53. Ⓐ Ⓑ Ⓒ Ⓓ Ⓔ
54. Ⓐ Ⓑ Ⓒ Ⓓ Ⓔ
55. Ⓐ Ⓑ Ⓒ Ⓓ Ⓔ
56. Ⓐ Ⓑ Ⓒ Ⓓ Ⓔ
57. Ⓐ Ⓑ Ⓒ Ⓓ Ⓔ
58. Ⓐ Ⓑ Ⓒ Ⓓ Ⓔ
59. Ⓐ Ⓑ Ⓒ Ⓓ Ⓔ
60. Ⓐ Ⓑ Ⓒ Ⓓ Ⓔ

Section II

1. Ⓐ Ⓑ Ⓒ Ⓓ Ⓔ
2. Ⓐ Ⓑ Ⓒ Ⓓ Ⓔ
3. Ⓐ Ⓑ Ⓒ Ⓓ Ⓔ
4. Ⓐ Ⓑ Ⓒ Ⓓ Ⓔ
5. Ⓐ Ⓑ Ⓒ Ⓓ Ⓔ
6. Ⓐ Ⓑ Ⓒ Ⓓ Ⓔ
7. Ⓐ Ⓑ Ⓒ Ⓓ Ⓔ
8. Ⓐ Ⓑ Ⓒ Ⓓ Ⓔ
9. Ⓐ Ⓑ Ⓒ Ⓓ Ⓔ
10. Ⓐ Ⓑ Ⓒ Ⓓ Ⓔ
11. Ⓐ Ⓑ Ⓒ Ⓓ Ⓔ
12. Ⓐ Ⓑ Ⓒ Ⓓ Ⓔ
13. Ⓐ Ⓑ Ⓒ Ⓓ Ⓔ
14. Ⓐ Ⓑ Ⓒ Ⓓ Ⓔ
15. Ⓐ Ⓑ Ⓒ Ⓓ Ⓔ
16. Ⓐ Ⓑ Ⓒ Ⓓ Ⓔ
17. Ⓐ Ⓑ Ⓒ Ⓓ Ⓔ
18. Ⓐ Ⓑ Ⓒ Ⓓ Ⓔ
19. Ⓐ Ⓑ Ⓒ Ⓓ Ⓔ
20. Ⓐ Ⓑ Ⓒ Ⓓ Ⓔ
21. Ⓐ Ⓑ Ⓒ Ⓓ Ⓔ
22. Ⓐ Ⓑ Ⓒ Ⓓ Ⓔ
23. Ⓐ Ⓑ Ⓒ Ⓓ Ⓔ
24. Ⓐ Ⓑ Ⓒ Ⓓ Ⓔ
25. Ⓐ Ⓑ Ⓒ Ⓓ Ⓔ
26. Ⓐ Ⓑ Ⓒ Ⓓ Ⓔ
27. Ⓐ Ⓑ Ⓒ Ⓓ Ⓔ
28. Ⓐ Ⓑ Ⓒ Ⓓ Ⓔ
29. Ⓐ Ⓑ Ⓒ Ⓓ Ⓔ
30. Ⓐ Ⓑ Ⓒ Ⓓ Ⓔ
31. Ⓐ Ⓑ Ⓒ Ⓓ Ⓔ
32. Ⓐ Ⓑ Ⓒ Ⓓ Ⓔ
33. Ⓐ Ⓑ Ⓒ Ⓓ Ⓔ
34. Ⓐ Ⓑ Ⓒ Ⓓ Ⓔ
35. Ⓐ Ⓑ Ⓒ Ⓓ Ⓔ
36. Ⓐ Ⓑ Ⓒ Ⓓ Ⓔ
37. Ⓐ Ⓑ Ⓒ Ⓓ Ⓔ
38. Ⓐ Ⓑ Ⓒ Ⓓ Ⓔ
39. Ⓐ Ⓑ Ⓒ Ⓓ Ⓔ
40. Ⓐ Ⓑ Ⓒ Ⓓ Ⓔ
41. Ⓐ Ⓑ Ⓒ Ⓓ Ⓔ
42. Ⓐ Ⓑ Ⓒ Ⓓ Ⓔ
43. Ⓐ Ⓑ Ⓒ Ⓓ Ⓔ
44. Ⓐ Ⓑ Ⓒ Ⓓ Ⓔ
45. Ⓐ Ⓑ Ⓒ Ⓓ Ⓔ
46. Ⓐ Ⓑ Ⓒ Ⓓ Ⓔ
47. Ⓐ Ⓑ Ⓒ Ⓓ Ⓔ
48. Ⓐ Ⓑ Ⓒ Ⓓ Ⓔ
49. Ⓐ Ⓑ Ⓒ Ⓓ Ⓔ
50. Ⓐ Ⓑ Ⓒ Ⓓ Ⓔ
51. Ⓐ Ⓑ Ⓒ Ⓓ Ⓔ
52. Ⓐ Ⓑ Ⓒ Ⓓ Ⓔ
53. Ⓐ Ⓑ Ⓒ Ⓓ Ⓔ
54. Ⓐ Ⓑ Ⓒ Ⓓ Ⓔ
55. Ⓐ Ⓑ Ⓒ Ⓓ Ⓔ
56. Ⓐ Ⓑ Ⓒ Ⓓ Ⓔ
57. Ⓐ Ⓑ Ⓒ Ⓓ Ⓔ
58. Ⓐ Ⓑ Ⓒ Ⓓ Ⓔ
59. Ⓐ Ⓑ Ⓒ Ⓓ Ⓔ
60. Ⓐ Ⓑ Ⓒ Ⓓ Ⓔ

CHAPTER

14

Sample Examinations

This chapter has three sample CLEP natural sciences examinations. Each examination is followed by an answer key, scoring chart, and answer explanations.

SAMPLE EXAMINATION 1

Section I Biological Sciences

Number of Questions: 60
Time: 45 minutes

Directions: Each of the questions or incomplete statements below is followed by five suggested answers or completions. Select the one that is best in each case.

1. The smallest and least complex unit of living matter is the
   (A) electron (B) atom (C) ion (D) cell (E) molecule

2. A physiologist is concerned with the
   (A) classification of organisms
   (B) structure of organisms
   (C) functioning of organisms
   (D) interrelationships of organisms
   (E) development of organisms

3. If a living cell is placed in an isotonic fluid, there will be
   (A) a net movement of water molecules into the cell
   (B) an increase in turgidity
   (C) no net movement of water molecules into or out of the cell
   (D) a decrease in cell turgidity
   (E) a net movement of water molecules out of the cell

4. Which one of the following factors does *not* influence enzyme activity?
   (A) Temperature (B) pH (C) Humidity
   (D) Enzyme poisons (E) Concentration

5. Heterotrophs
   (A) utilize radiant energy
   (B) cannot synthesize organic materials from inorganic substances
   (C) are food synthesizers
   (D) oxidize inorganic materials
   (E) synthesize organic materials from inorganic substances

6. A relationship between two organisms in which one is benefited while the second is neither benefited nor harmed is called
   (A) neutralism (B) amensalism (C) mutualism
   (D) competition (E) commensalism

7. A niacin deficiency may best be relieved by enriching the diet with
(A) eggs and dairy products (B) fresh green vegetables
(C) whole grain cereals (D) animal products
(E) citrus fruits

8. Cellular respiration
(A) stores energy
(B) uses oxygen and organic compounds as raw materials
(C) increases dry weight
(D) occurs only in the presence of radiant energy
(E) uses carbon dioxide and water as raw materials

9. A process which increases dry weight is
(A) phosphorylation
(B) osmosis
(C) diffusion
(D) respiration
(E) photosynthesis

10. Plants grown in the dark become
(A) plasmolyzed (B) asphixiated (C) synergistic
(D) etiolated (E) parthenocarpic

11. In plants, water is normally conducted upward by a tissue called the
(A) phloem (B) cortex (C) cuticle (D) pith
(E) xylem

12. The edible part of the sweet potato is
(A) stem tissue (B) root tissue (C) leaf tissue
(D) fruit (E) seed

13. Primitive plants having neither vascular tissues nor multicellular embryos are called
(A) bryophytes (B) thallophytes (C) pteridophytes
(D) spermatophytes (E) xerophytes

14. Plants basic in many food chains are
(A) fungi
(B) bryophytes
(C) gymnosperms
(D) pteridophytes
(E) algae

15. The first step in the formation of a blood clot is the disintegration of platelets and the release of
(A) thrombin (B) fibrinogen (C) fibrin
(D) thromboplastin (E) prothrombin

16. If you have type A blood, agglutination tests will reveal that
(A) type A serum will clump part of the time
(B) type B serum clumps
(C) both type A and B sera will clump
(D) type A serum clumps
(E) neither type A nor type B sera will clump

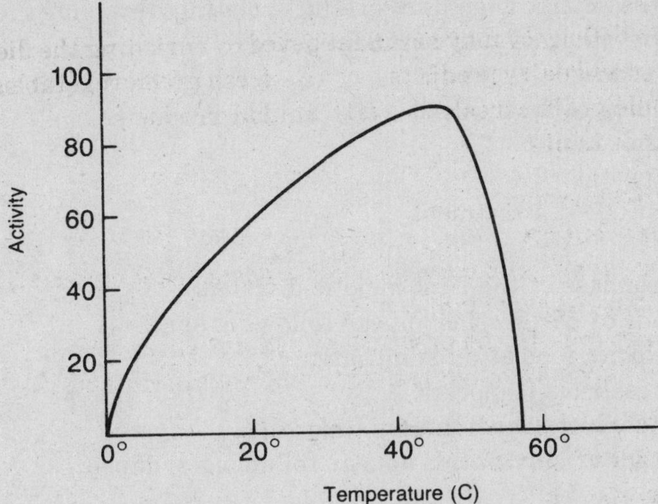

The illustration above represents enzyme activity as a function of temperature.

17. One may conclude, on the basis of the above illustration, that enzymatic activity
(A) is greatest at 60°C
(B) is stopped by temperatures above 60°C
(C) is not affected by temperature
(D) is independent of temperature
(E) is greatest at 20°C

18. The retina of the eye is innervated by the
(A) oculomotor nerve
(B) olfactory nerve
(C) trigeminal nerve
(D) optic nerve
(E) trochlear nerve

19. Nerve impulses from sensory receptors are conducted to the central nervous system
(A) through the ventral root ganglion
(B) along a motor neuron
(C) through the dorsal root ganglion
(D) through a Doric valve
(E) across a synapse between connector and motor neurons

20. Stimulation by the parasympathetic nervous system would result in
(A) slower heart beat
(B) increased blood pressure
(C) erection of hair
(D) accelerated heart beat
(E) slower peristalsis

21. Transpiration benefits plants by
(A) assisting in the upward translocation of dissolved minerals
(B) assisting in the upward translocation of organic substances
(C) assisting in the downward translocation of organic substances
(D) helping the plant to retain heat
(E) maintaining a constant root pressure

22. What is the expected hereditary result of matings involving the interaction of multiple, incompletely dominant genes?
(A) Inbreeding
(B) Blending of the involved traits
(C) Hybridization
(D) Segregation
(E) Independent assortment

23. In the prophase of the first meiotic division,
(A) dyads of chromatids appear following synapsis
(B) cell plate formation is initiated
(C) the centriole reappears
(D) the chromosome number is haploid
(E) tetrads of chromatids appear following synapsis

24. Floods and fires repeatedly destroyed all life on earth, but acts of special creation repopulated the earth: this doctrine was called
(A) catastrophism (B) adaptation
(C) uniformitarianism (D) natural selection
(E) Lamarckianism

25. The adaptation of unrelated species to similar habitats is called
(A) polymorphism (B) divergent evolution
(C) orthogenesis (D) translocation (E) convergent evolution

26. The mutation theory was proposed by De Vries to explain abrupt changes in inheritance patterns which
(A) result from hybridization
(B) breed true
(C) do not breed true in subsequent generations
(D) are environmentally induced
(E) are based on mitotic errors

27. Antiseptic surgery was first performed by
(A) Louis Pasteur (B) John Tyndall (C) Lazaro Spallanzani
(D) John Needham (E) Joseph Lister

28. A Dutch microscope maker who was probably the first to describe bacteria and protozoa was
(A) Harvey (B) van Leeuwenhoek (C) Flemming
(D) Galen (E) Versalius

29. What was Aristotle's greatest contribution to science?
(A) The theory of the four humors (B) The scientific method
(C) The theory of evolution (D) The study of anatomy and medicine
(E) The atomic theory

30. The first to isolate the hormone insulin were
(A) Ascheim and Zondek (B) Banting and Best
(C) Bromer and du Vigneuad (D) Absolam and Grendel
(E) Bayliss and Starling

31. Marine organisms found between the limits of high and low tide exist in the
(A) neritic zone (B) abyssal zone
(C) zone of perpetual darkness (D) bathyal zone
(E) littoral zone

32. An ichthyologist is a specialist in the study of
(A) insects (B) birds
(C) reptiles (D) fossils
(E) fishes

33. When corresponding structures of different species are based on similarities in function only, they are said to be
(A) homologous (B) divergent (C) parallel
(D) convergent (E) analogous

34. An interrelationship between living organisms is called
(A) speciation (B) metamorphosis (C) symbiosis
(D) epigenesis (E) morphogenesis

35. The time period described as the age of reptiles is the
(A) Ordovician period (B) Proterozoic era (C) Mesozoic era
(D) Cenozoic era (E) Miocene epoch

36. In the digestive system of humans, the stomach-produced enzyme rennin splits the
(A) ester bond of fats (B) phosphate esters of DNA
(C) peptide bonds of trypsinogen (D) phosphate esters of RNA
(E) peptide bonds in casein

37. Rodent control is necessary to prevent outbreaks of the following bacterial disease:
(A) psitticosis
(B) amebiasis
(C) plague
(D) typhoid fever
(E) polio

38. If a couple's first child is a boy, what is the probability that the second child will be a girl?
(A) 1/16 (B) 1/8 (C) 1/4 (D) 1/2 (E) 3/4

39. In matings involving individuals that are heterozygous for "A", the genotypes produced would be
(A) 1/8 AA, 3/4 Aa, 1/8 aa
(B) 3/8 AA, 1/4 Aa, 3/8 aa
(C) 1/3 AA, 1/3 Aa, 1/3 aa
(D) 1/4 AA, 1/2 Aa, 1/4 aa
(E) impossible to predict

40. The frequency of crossing over between two linked genes is
(A) controlled by sex chromosomes
(B) controlled by the law of independent assortment
(C) controlled by the Hardy-Weinberg law
(D) inversely proportional to the distance separating them
(E) directly proportional to the distance separating them

41. An antigen stimulates the production of
    (A) blood groups
    (B) platelets
    (C) toxins
    (D) an antibody
    (E) Rh

42. The roots of biology go back to 3000 B.C. in China, where the first principles identified
    (A) were the medicinal values of plants
    (B) related to the theory of the four humors
    (C) reflected early concepts about evolution
    (D) were about atomic theory
    (E) were taxonomy and classification

Questions 43–46

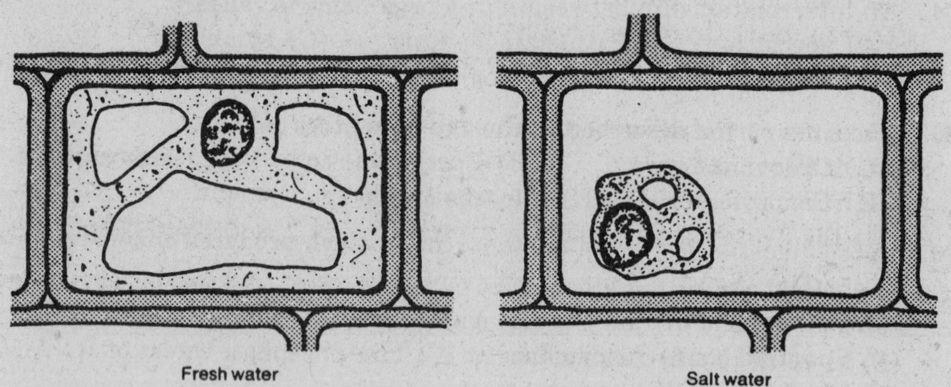

The plant cells diagrammed above are located in fresh water and in salt water, respectively, as indicated.

43. Water has moved out of the cell in salt water by a process called
    (A) diffusion (B) imbibition (C) capillarity
    (D) adhesion (E) plasmolysis

44. The cell in fresh water is "plump" with water, a condition referred to as
    (A) rigid (B) plasmolyzed (C) saturated
    (D) hydrolyzed (E) turgid

45. The condition of the cell in the salt water is a result of
    (A) the flow of water out of the cell
    (B) a net movement of water out of the cell
    (C) salt pulling the water out of the cell
    (D) the forces of imbibition
    (E) the force called cohesion

46. In the case of the cell in fresh water
    (A) nothing is able to move into the cell
    (B) adhesive forces hold water in the vacuoles
    (C) the vacuoles continue to lose and to take in water by diffusion
    (D) the cell walls are impermeable to water
    (E) the cell walls are impermeable to salt

47. The light-sensitive pigment called phytochrome appears to influence
(A) phototropism (B) parthenocarpy (C) photosynthesis
(D) synergistic responses (E) photoperiodism

48. Stems increase in diameter mainly because of cell division by the
(A) cork cambium (B) endodermis (C) medullary rays
(D) cortex (E) vascular cambium

49. The evaporation of water from the aerial surfaces of plants is called
(A) translocation (B) hydrotropism (C) hydroponics
(D) aquaculture (E) transpiration

50. Adrenalin
(A) regulates potassium metabolism
(B) constricts blood vessels
(C) controls bone growth
(D) regulates thyroxine production
(E) regulates the pulse rate and muscle tone

51. The primary significance of mitosis is the fact that
(A) it is quantitative (B) the chromosome number is increased
(C) it results in the production of either eggs or sperm
(D) the chromosome number is reduced (E) it is qualitative

52. The area in the retina of the human eye lacking both rods and cones is called the
(A) alveolus (B) fundibulum (C) fovea
(D) blind spot (E) cornea

53. During the initial stages of blood clot formation, blood platelets require
(A) calcium ions (B) the antihemophilic factor
(C) thrombin (D) prothrombin (E) cytochrome

54. Simple sugars are stored in the liver as
(A) glycerol (B) maltose (C) nucleotides (D) glycogen
(E) casein

Directions: Each group of questions below consists of five lettered choices followed by a list of numbered phrases or sentences. For each numbered phrase or sentence select the one choice that is most closely related to it. Each choice may be used once, more than once, or not at all in each group.

Questions 55–57

(A) Cuvier
(B) Darwin
(C) Lamarck
(D) Lyell
(E) Tyson

55. Proposed the doctrine of catastrophism

56. Suggested that the events in the geologic history of the earth were the product of the same natural forces that are active today

57. Proposed the doctrine of uniformitarianism

Questions 58–60

(A) Cambrian period
(B) Devonian period
(C) Jurassic period
(D) Carboniferous period
(E) Tertiary period

58. A period of psilopsids, lycopsids and seed ferns

59. The period of modern mammals and herbacious angiosperms

60. The age of the great coal swamps

Section II Physical Sciences

Number of Questions: 60
Time: 45 minutes

Directions: Each of the questions or incomplete statements below is followed by five suggested answers or completions. Select the one that is best in each case.

1. Insofar as the earth's atmosphere is concerned, without supplemental oxygen humans are restricted to the
   (A) ionosphere (B) exosphere (C) troposphere
   (D) stratopause (E) stratosphere

2. The same side of the moon is always observed from the earth because the
   (A) moon does not rotate
   (B) moon's orbit is an ellipse
   (C) moon's orbit is inclined
   (D) moon's period of rotation equals its period of revolution
   (E) moon's period of rotation is greater than its period of revolution

3. When a space vehicle is at perigee, it is at
   (A) maximum speed
   (B) minimum speed
   (C) the point farthest from the sun
   (D) a point in orbit farthest from the earth
   (E) a point in orbit closest to the earth

4. There are always two calendar days in effect *except*
   (A) during the summer solstice
   (B) the instant it is noon at Greenwich, England
   (C) the instant it is noon at longitude 180°
   (D) on February 29
   (E) the instant of crossing the International Dateline

5. The accumulated sediment deposited outward from the mouth of a stream forms
(A) a sand bar (B) a flood plain (C) a delta
(D) an alluvial fan (E) an oxbow

6. The theory that land masses wander over the surface of the globe is called
(A) catastrophism (B) plate tectonics (C) sedimentation
(D) fossilization (E) discontinuity

7. Anhydrous chemicals are completely
(A) combustible
(B) without water
(C) hydrated
(D) inactive
(E) pure

8. What are stalactites?
(A) Crystalline calcite columns hanging from cave ceilings
(B) Anthracite deposits in caves
(C) Calcite columns built up from cave floors
(D) Graphite columns hanging from cave ceilings
(E) Graphite columns built up from cave floors

9. According to the quantum theory, if a quantum of energy is absorbed by an electron in orbit around an atom,
(A) the absorbed energy will stimulate the electron and cause it to fluctuate between all of the atom's electron orbits
(B) the kinetic energy of the electron will fluctuate
(C) the electron will "descend" to an orbit closer to the atomic nucleus
(D) the electron will remain in the same orbit
(E) the electron will move to a "higher" orbit

10. In molecules with ionic bonding
(A) electrons are created
(B) electrons are transferred from one atom to another
(C) large energy input is required
(D) attractions exceed repulsions
(E) electrons are destroyed

11. Electron microscopes have a greater resolving power than light microscopes because
(A) there is a laser effect
(B) electrons travel faster than photons
(C) their magnifications are greater
(D) electrons possess less resolving power
(E) electrons possess greater resolving power

12. When light is thrown back from any surface, it is said to be
(A) refracted (B) diffused (C) absorbed
(D) reflected (E) diffracted

13. Interference is a wave phenomenon created when
   (A) there is interaction between two waves which arrive simultaneously at a given point
   (B) waves bend around corners
   (C) wavelength and frequency are equal
   (D) wavelength is greater than frequency
   (E) frequency is greater than wavelength

14. The frequency of sound vibrations is called
   (A) resonance (B) key (C) tone (D) pitch
   (E) overtone

15. Which of the following is an acid?
   (A) NaCl (B) NH_3 (C) $NaNO_3$
   (D) H_3PO_4 (E) NaOH

16. Which of the following is *not* an acceptable statement in respect to magnetic fields?
   (A) Lines of force are unchanging.
   (B) They do not require the presence of matter.
   (C) They can penetrate wood.
   (D) They may exist in a vacuum.
   (E) They can penetrate glass.

17. The unit of measurement of electric current is the
   (A) ohm (B) volt (C) ampere (D) coulomb
   (E) watt

18. A device which produces electricity as a result of rotating a coil between the poles of a magnet is
   (A) an electric motor (B) a commutator (C) a transformer
   (D) an induction coil (E) a generator

19. The part of the atom involved in all instances of radioactive change is the
   (A) orbit (B) electron (C) electrical charge
   (D) half-life (E) nucleus

20. The unusable heat energy "lost" to the environment in converting heat to work is known as
   (A) latent heat of fusion (B) specific heat
   (C) latent heat of vaporization (D) temperature
   (E) entropy

21. If superconductivity is developed for practical use, what will be its primary benefit?
   (A) The loss of magnetic fields around conductors
   (B) The loss of all resistance to the flow of electricity
   (C) The ability to use electric motors of lower power
   (D) The increased use of metallic conductors
   (E) The ease with which contemporary electrical systems could be converted to the use of superconductivity

22. Adoption of which one of the following as standard made the original platinum-iridium standard meter rod useless?
(A) Use of the cesium atom
(B) Substitution of the nickel meter rod
(C) Use of the xenon atom
(D) Orange light emitted by krypton-86
(E) Use of the infrared spectrum

23. In order to apply a force to one object, one must be able to
(A) push against another object
(B) use centrifugal force
(C) use centripetal force
(D) overcome gravity
(E) maintain a constant velocity

24. Energy is defined as the
(A) rate of doing work (B) rate of supply of energy
(C) capacity to accelerate (D) capacity to resist acceleration
(E) capacity to do work

25. A fundamental particle of negative electricity is
(A) a proton (B) an electron (C) a neutron
(D) a meson (E) an ion

26. In reference to light or sound waves, the Doppler effect occurs when
(A) the source and the receiver are in motion relative to one another
(B) waves are of unequal length
(C) waves are parallel
(D) the source and the receiver are stationary
(E) temperature increases

27. A self-sustaining reaction in which the first atoms to react trigger more reactions is called
(A) a photochemical reaction (B) a chain reaction
(C) an accelerator reaction (D) an electrical reaction
(E) a biophysical reaction

28. According to Einstein's theory of relativity, as a spaceship approaches the speed of light,
(A) everything aboard increases in mass
(B) everything aboard decreases in mass
(C) mass remains constant
(D) mass and metabolism decrease
(E) mass and metabolism increase

29. The true weight of an object is defined as the
(A) gravitational attraction of the sun on that object
(B) gravitational attraction of the earth on that object
(C) force of repulsion by the earth on that object
(D) combined gravitational attraction of the sun and moon on that object
(E) total mass of that object

30. For every force there is a force of reaction which is
(A) equal and parallel (B) unequal and transverse
(C) equal and transverse (D) equal and oppositive
(E) unequal and opposite

31. Electricity produced by a nuclear power plant
(A) has higher voltage (B) has lower voltage
(C) is radioactive (D) is the same as any other electricity
(E) is direct current only

32. One degree on the Celsius scale equals how many Fahrenheit degrees?
(A) 5/9° F
(B) 9/5° F
(C) 1° F
(D) −5/9° F
(E) −9/5° F

33. Which of the following is not consistent with Dalton's atomic theory?
(A) All matter consists of minute particles called atoms.
(B) Atoms of a given element are alike.
(C) Atoms are neither created nor destroyed in chemical reactions.
(D) Atoms of different elements have the same weight but different electrical charges.
(E) Typically, atoms combine in small numbers to form chemical compounds.

34. The efficiency of machines is always reduced by
(A) temperature (B) sublimation (C) momentum
(D) friction (E) refraction

35. Valence is
(A) a bundle or quantum of energy
(B) a measure of acidity
(C) a measure of alkalinity
(D) the combining capacity of an element
(E) the energy used in doing work

36. Chemical elements classifield in the halogen family are commonly referred to as
(A) noble gases (B) inert gases (C) alkaline earths
(D) salt formers (E) heavy metals

37. Substances which sometimes change the rate of chemical reactions are called
(A) ions (B) isotopes (C) catalysts (D) neutralizers
(E) bases

38. Of the four known forces in the universe, the strong force
(A) is a force of repulsion
(B) holds the particles inside the atomic nucleus together
(C) causes the sun to shine
(D) holds atoms and molecules together
(E) produces radioactivity

39. Separation of the components in liquid solution by distillation is dependent upon
(A) varying solubilities (B) heat of solidification
(C) adsorption (D) differences in volatility (E) absorption

40. Chemical decomposition accomplished by means of an electric current is called
(A) electrography (B) electromagnetism (C) electrophoresis
(D) electrovalency (E) electrolysis

41. Chemical formulas enable us to determine the kind and number of atoms in a compound, each element's percentage, and
(A) the number and kinds of isotopes (B) its physical properties
(C) its nuclear reactions (D) its half-life
(E) its molecular weight

42. Thermosetting plastics polymerize irreversibly under conditions of
(A) freezing (B) bonding (C) volitilization
(D) heat or pressure (E) crystallization

43. By A.D. 1000, when western Europe was beginning to emerge from the Dark Ages, intellectual development was hindered because
(A) most Arabic and Greek knowledge had been lost
(B) scientists hesitated to experiment
(C) alchemy was supreme
(D) there were formal centers of learning
(E) the Christian Church advocated Aristotle's logic

44. Naturally radioactive elements change to other elements subsequently to their emission of
(A) gamma rays (B) X-rays
(C) alpha particles (D) beta rays (E) gamma rays

45. Parallel light rays are made divergent by
(A) an achromatic lens (B) monochromatic light
(C) a convex lens (D) a plano-concave lens
(E) a concave lens

46. Amplitude and frequency determine
(A) tempo (B) loudness (C) rhythm (D) meter (E) resonance

47. In referring to wave phenomena, the term wavelength means
(A) the bending of the direction of wave motion
(B) the interaction of waves arriving simultaneously at the same point
(C) the distance between crests
(D) one half of the distance in height between a crest and a trough
(E) the number of crests passing a point in a given time

48. The height of transverse sound waves is expressed as
(A) frequency (B) wavelength (C) rarefaction
(D) modulation (E) amplitude

49. Einstein showed that, while energy and matter can be converted into one another,
(A) there is more energy than matter
(B) there is more matter than energy
(C) the total amount of energy and matter remains constant in the universe
(D) the total amount of energy and matter in the universe is unstable
(E) the conversion of matter to energy requires the input of energy, which is lost

50. In medicine, the X rays that enable physicians to photograph the skeleton make use of
(A) radioactive rays
(B) electron beams
(C) kinetic energy
(D) very-high-frequency electromagnetic waves
(E) Brownian movement

51. Electron emission by certain heated metals is
(A) the photoelectric effect (B) electromagnetic induction
(C) commutation (D) the thermionic effect
(E) transformation

52. A lever with a great mechanical advantage for gaining distance would have
(A) a short force arm and a short weight arm
(B) a terminal fulcrum
(C) a long force arm and long weight arm
(D) a long force arm and short weight arm
(E) a short force arm and long weight arm

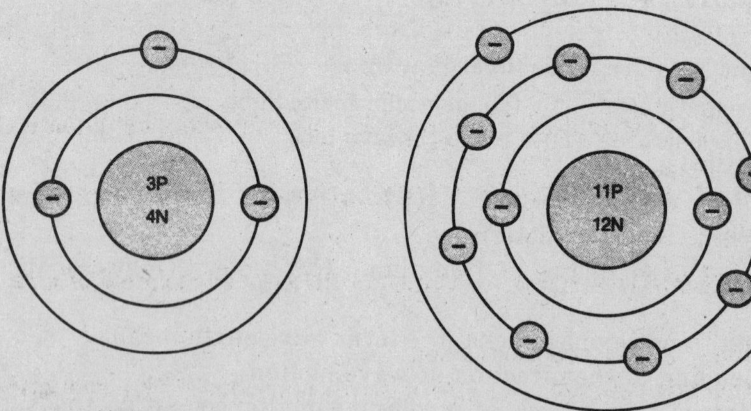

53. The diagrams above show the lithium and sodium atoms. The chemical and physical properties of lithium and sodium are similar because
(A) both possess an uneven number of protons
(B) each has a single electron in its outermost shell
(C) both possess an uneven number of electrons
(D) both have the same atomic number
(E) both are heavy metals

54. Christian theology and Aristotelian philosophy were reconciled in *Summa Theologica,* written by
(A) Francis Bacon (B) Albertus Magnus (C) Roger Bacon
(D) Thomas Aquinas (E) Pope Paul III

55. If the corner of a cube of sugar is placed in contact with iodine solution, the entire cube quickly becomes the color of iodine due to
(A) capillarity (B) surface tension (C) kinetic energy
(D) potential energy (E) convection

56. If one side of a solid is warmer than the other, the faster moving warm molecules collide with the cooler ones, transferring some of their energy to the slower ones. The transfer of heat energy is called
(A) convection (B) radiation (C) adhesion
(D) conduction (E) concussion

57. According to the concept of the conservation of mass, when two or more elements react chemically,
(A) the sum of their masses equals the mass of the compound formed
(B) the sum of their masses is less than the mass of the compound formed
(C) the sum of their masses is greater than the mass of the compound formed
(D) atoms may be created, modified, or destroyed
(E) atoms may be changed from one kind to another

58. The process by which substances are separated by utilization of differences in the degree to which they are absorbed to the surface of any inert material is
(A) fractional distillation
(B) chromatography
(C) filtration
(D) neutralization
(E) isomerism

59. The maintenance of acid-base balance is accomplished by chemical substances called
(A) ionizers (B) polarizers (C) buffers (D) neutralizers
(E) catalysts

60. The equation $Cu(OH)_2 + H_2SO_4 \rightarrow CuSO_4 + 2H_2O$ is an example of a reaction called
(A) oxidation (B) salt formation
(C) an exothermic reaction (D) a chain reaction (E) reduction

ANSWER KEY—SAMPLE EXAMINATION 1

Section I Biological Sciences

1. D	11. E	21. A	31. E	41. D	51. E
2. C	12. B	22. B	32. E	42. A	52. D
3. C	13. B	23. E	33. E	43. A	53. B
4. C	14. E	24. A	34. C	44. E	54. D
5. B	15. D	25. E	35. C	45. B	55. A
6. E	16. B	26. B	36. E	46. C	56. D
7. B	17. B	27. E	37. C	47. E	57. D
8. B	18. D	28. B	38. D	48. E	58. B
9. E	19. C	29. B	39. D	49. E	59. E
10. D	20. A	30. B	40. E	50. E	60. D

Section II Physical Sciences

1. C	11. E	21. B	31. D	41. E	51. D
2. D	12. D	22. D	32. B	42. D	52. E
3. E	13. A	23. A	33. D	43. E	53. B
4. B	14. D	24. E	34. D	44. C	54. D
5. C	15. D	25. B	35. D	45. E	55. A
6. B	16. A	26. A	36. D	46. B	56. D
7. B	17. C	27. B	37. C	47. C	57. A
8. A	18. E	28. A	38. B	48. E	58. B
9. E	19. E	29. B	39. D	49. C	59. C
10. B	20. E	30. D	40. E	50. D	60. B

SCORING CHART—SAMPLE EXAMINATION 1

After you have scored your Sample Examination 1, enter the results in the chart below; then transfer your Raw Score to the Progress Chart on page 14.

Total Test	Number Right	Number Wrong	Number Omitted	Raw Score
Section I: 60				
Section II: 60				
Total: 120				

ANSWER EXPLANATIONS—SAMPLE EXAMINATION 1

Section I Biological Sciences

1. D. Of the choices given, the cell is the smallest and least complex unit of living matter. (If one accepts viruses as units of living matter, then these are smaller and less complex.)

2. C. A physiologist is concerned with the study of function in living organisms.
3. C. An isotonic solution is one with an osmotic pressure equal to the reference solution—in this case, the living cell.
4. C. Humidity has no effect on enzyme activity.
5. B. Heterotrophic organisms require organic compounds as food.
6. E. Commensalism occurs when a smaller, unprotected animal is associated with another, usually for protection.
7. B. Among the chief sources of niacin are yeast, green vegetables, and wheat germ.
8. B. Cellular respiration combines oxygen and organic compounds to release energy, carbon dioxide, and water.
9. E. Photosynthesis produces glucose which increases, or adds to, the dry weight of the plant.
10. D. The absence of light stimulates stem elongation in plants and results in the failure of chlorophyll synthesis. This is etiolation.
11. E. In plants xylem functions chiefly in the upward conduction of water and dissolved minerals and in the support or strengthening of stems.
12. B. The edible portions of the sweet potato plant are the roots which become enlarged due to the accumulation of stored foods.
13. B. Thallophytes, or thallus plants, lack xylem and phloem, the conducting tissues, and they also do not develop multicellular embryos.
14. E. Under normal favorable conditions in the seas and in freshwater lakes and streams, algae are so prolific that they constitute the basic food in many established food chains.
15. D. In blood clotting, in the presence of the antihemophilic factor, blood platelets stick to torn tissue and release thromboplastin and serotonin.
16. B. Type A blood cells contain antigen A and its serum contains antibody B; type B blood cells contain antigen B and its serum contains anitbody A. Type B serum will cause type A blood to clump.
17. B. As indicated on the graph, at temperatures approaching 60°C, enzyme activity stops.
18. D. All nerve impulses initiated in and by the rods and cones of the retina are carried to the brain via the optic nerve.
19. C. All nerve impulses from sensory receptors are conducted to the central nervous system through a dorsal root ganglion.
20. A. The parasympathetic nervous system in a general sense functions to counter the sympathetic nervous system. When the sympathetic nervous system increases the rate of heart beat, the parasympathetic system tends to slow it, etc.
21. A. Transpiration is the evaporation of water from the aerial parts of plants. It has the beneficial effect of transporting dissolved minerals upward from the roots to the stem and leaves.
22. B. The hereditary result of matings involving multiple, incompletely dominant genes is blending of the traits in question. For example, in matings of a wheat homozygous for red grains ($X_1X_1X_2X_2$) with a wheat homozygous for white kernels ($x_1x_1x_2x_2$), the following combinations of genes for color of the grains can be expected: *XXXX, XXXx, XXxx, Xxxx,* and *XXXX,* with varying grain colors from dark red to white as the result.
23. E. During the first meiotic division, chromosome reduction has not yet occurred. Hence, the chromatids of any pair of chromosomes are still in groups of four, or tetrads.
24. A. According to *catastrophism* sudden and violent events changed the earth's surface and destroyed all life and subsequent acts of special creation repopulated the earth.
25. E. Convergent evolution is the development of similar traits, including adaptation to certain habitats, by unrelated or distantly related species.
26. B. Mutations are abrupt and unexpected changes in inheritance patterns that breed true.
27. E. Joseph Lister initiated the era of antiseptic surgery when he began spraying the surgical scene with carbolic acid.

28. B. Anton van Leeuwenhoek made sketches of bacteria and other microorganisms from the plaque around his teeth and from hay infusions.
29. B. Among Aristotle's most noted contributions was the concept of the scientific method.
30. B. In 1920, Banting and Best isolated insulin from pancreatic tissue.
31. E. The littoral zone exists from the high tide level to the area 200 meters deep.
32. E. Ichthyology is the study of fish.
33. E. The key to analogous structures is the word function. The wing of a bird and the wing of a bee are similar in only one category, function. Structurally, they are unrelated.
34. C. The term symbiosis is a general term meaning "living together," often with mutual benefits.
35. C. The giant reptiles flourished in the geologic time period called the Mesozoic era.
36. E. Rennin is a digestive enzyme secreted by the stomach which is partially responsible for casein digestion.
37. C. Plague still exists in certain parts of the world and, since it is associated with rodents and their fleas, rodent control is a necessary control measure.
38. D. In each instance of sex determination in humans, the probability that any one individual will be male or female is one-half at the time of conception.
39. D. When both parents are heterozygous, segregation results in gamete types A and a for both parents. Random fertilization produces three mating types in a ratio of 1:2:1, with one-half being heterozygous for Aa.
40. E. Since the probability of crossing-over between two linked genes on a pair of chromosomes is directly proportional to the distance separating them, crossing-over frequencies are greatest in widely separated genes.
41. D. An antigen is any substance that, when introduced into the body, causes the body to produce antibodies.
42. A. In general, the interest of ancient peoples in biology was limited to the medicinal values of plants.
43. A. Diffusion in this instance is the movement of water molecules from an area of high concentration of water molecules to or towards an area of low or lower concentration of water molecules.
44. E. Turgid or turgor pressure is a positive pressure developed within living plant cells, and therefore in stems and leaves, as a result of internal water pressure.
45. B. The cell in the salt water has lost water by diffusion, the net movement of water molecules out of the cell.
46. C. Diffusion is the movement of water molecules as a result of their molecular activity. In the case of the cell in fresh water, as in the case of the cell in salt water also, water molecules move freely into and out of the cell.
47. E. Phytochrome appears to be necessary for the formation of the hypothetical hormone florigen, which supposedly controls floral initiation.
48. E. Cell division by the vascular cambium produces xylem internally and phloem externally, thus adding to the diameter of the stem.
49. E. Water which moistens the cell walls of leaf mesophyll cells evaporates since these cell walls are exposed to the internal gaseous atmosphere of the leaf. This water loss is called transpiration.
50. E. The effects of adrenalin are body wide, affecting pulse, muscle tone, and the rate of nerve conduction.
51. E. Mitosis is a qualitative distribution of chromatin to each of two different daughter cells. Its primary significance is that each daughter cell receives identical chromatin materials.
52. D. The point where the optic nerve enters the eyeball has neither rods nor cones and, therefore, has no sight capability. It is called the blind spot.
53. B. The antihemophilic factor causes blood platelets to swell into spherical masses and these tend to prevent the loss of other blood components.
54. D. Humans and other animals store simple sugars in the form of glycogen in muscles and in the liver.

55. A. Cuvier suggested that there must have been many floods (catastrophes) that killed most of the organisms living at the time, followed by repeated special creations to repopulate the earth. This idea is called *catastrophism.*

56. D.
57. D. Lyell opposed catastrophism and special creation. He stated that events in the geological history of the earth were the products of the same natural forces active today, i.e., erosion, sedimentation, etc. This doctrine is called *uniformitarianism.*

58. B. The Devonian period was the beginning of true land plants with stomata, vascular tissues and multicellular embryos.

59. E. During the Tertiary, early modern mammals assumed dominance, together with the flowering (seed) plants.

60. D. During the Carboniferous, giant ferns, clubmosses, and horsetails grew in widespread low and swampy regions of the earth. These later formed layers of dead vegetation which did not decompose. This plant material became coal.

Section II Physical Sciences

1. C. The trophosphere is the layer of the earth's atmosphere closest to the earth's surface and only the lower half of the trophosphere will support life without supplemental oxygen.

2. D. The periods of rotation and revolution of the moon are the same, 27⅓ days. Because of this, the same "face" of the moon is always turned towards the earth.

3. E. Perigee is that point in the orbit of a satellite that is nearest to the earth.

4. B. When it is noon at Greenwich, England, it is 12:00 P.M./00:00 A.M. at the International Date Line. At this instant, only one calendar day is in effect, worldwide.

5. C. A delta is a triangle-shaped deposition of sediments at the mouth of a river.

6. B. Plate tectonics is the concept that continents drift in relation to one another on the earth's surface.

7. B. The term anhydrous means free from or without water, especially the water of crystallization.

8. A. Stalactites are calcite columns hanging from cave ceilings. They are formed over long periods of time when water leaking through the cave ceiling evaporates leaving calcite deposits.

9. E. If a quantum of energy is absorbed by an electron of an atom, the electron moves to a "higher" orbit around the atomic nucleus.

10. B. Molecules with ionic bonds are combinations of atoms bound together in predictable ways, either by sharing electrons or by the transfer of electrons from one atom to another.

11. E. The wavelength beam of electrons is very short and, therefore, permits a higher degree of resolution than with a light microscope.

12. D. When electromagnetic waves bounce back from an object, they are said to be reflected.

13. A. Interference is the combining of two or more waves when they reach a given point simultaneously.

14. D. Pitch is a determination of how rapidly an object vibrates; the higher the frequency, the higher the pitch.

15. D. Svante Arrhenius proposed that acids form H^+ ions in water solutions. When H_3PO_4 is added to water, H^+ ions are formed.

16. A. Magnetic fields vary according to their source, the position of their source, and the intensity of their source.

17. C. Electrical current is measured in amperes, one ampere being equal to one coulomb of change past a point in one second.

18. E. When a coil of wire is rotated between the poles of a magnet an electric current is generated.

19. E. In radioactive decomposition as well as in other radioactive changes, the nucleus of the atom is involved exclusively.

20. E. Entropy, or change, is a thermodynamic measure of disorder; entropy, or change which increases disorder, in any undisturbed system always increases. Steam in a closed system can be used to push a piston, but its molecules dissipate after escaping into the atmosphere.

21. B. The primary benefit of superconductors appears to be that they lose all resistance to the flow of electricity. Presently, most superconductors must function at extremely low temperatures, making practical use very difficult.

22. D. The standard meter is based on the wavelength of light emitted by the krypton atom.

23. A. For every force in one direction, there is an equal force in the opposite direction. To move an object in one direction, a stationary base or anchor is required to overcome the force directed in the opposite direction.

24. E. By definition, energy is the capacity to do work.

25. B. By definition, an electron is a fundamental particle of negative electricity.

26. A. The Doppler effect is the apparent change in the pitch of sounds produced by moving objects when an observer is stationary or moving at a different speed than the producer of the sound.

27. B. In a chain nuclear reaction, neutrons strike other atoms which, in turn, release neutrons, which strike additional atoms. When a chain reaction can be sustained, the number or amount of fissionable material is described as a critical mass.

28. A. According to relativity the mass of an object increases with its velocity.

29. B. Weight is the force of gravity acting upon an object.

30. D. For every force in one direction, there is an equal force in the opposite direction.

31. D. The nature of electricity is not affected by the source of its production—hydroelectric power plants, nuclear power plants, or plants that burn fossil fuels.

32. B. Celsius temperatures may be converted to Fahrenheit by multiplying the Celsius temperature by 1.8 and adding 32 degrees.

33. D. Dalton's atomic theory holds that atoms are the unit particles of matter and cannot be subdivided, that atoms of a given element are alike and have the same weight, that atoms of different elements have different weights, that in chemical reactions it is atoms that combine and that the relative weights of the atoms that combine are directly related to the weights of the atoms themselves.

34. D. Friction is a force that opposes motion when two objects in contact with each other attempt to move relative to each other. Friction uses energy and, therefore, reduces mechanical efficiency.

35. D. Valence is the combining capacity of an element—specifically, the number of hydrogen atoms that combine with one atom of that element.

36. D. Elements in the halogen family of chemical elements (e.g., chlorine, iodine) associate readily with other elements and are often referred to as salt formers.

37. C. A catalyst is a substance that initiates or speeds up a chemical reaction without participating in the reaction process.

38. B. The *strong force* holds the particles inside the atomic nucleus together. The *gravitational force* holds objects to the ground. The *electromagnetic force* holds atoms and molecules together and holds electrons to the atomic nucleus. The *weak force* permits some atomic nuclei to break down, producing radioactivity and causing the sun to shine.

39. D. Distillation is a process of boiling a liquid and condensing its vapor. Two or more liquids will usually have different boiling points so they may be separated by first boiling off the vapor of one liquid and condensing it and then boiling off the vapor of the second liquid and condensing it.

40. E. Electrolysis effects chemical change by passing an electrical current through a substance—for example, a salt (NaCl) solution. In the case of a NaCl solution, the result is the separation of the Na^+ and Cl^- ions with the Na^+ ions moving to the cathode and the Cl^- ions moving to the anode.

41. E. A chemical formula is a description, using chemical symbols, of the ratio of atoms in a chemical compound. If the weight ratio and the atomic weight of the elements of a compound are known, the molecular weight of the compound can be calculated.

42. D. The family of plastics referred to as "thermosetting" consists of substances that polymerize irreversibly under heat or pressure forming a hard mass.

43. E. Albertus Magnus and Saint Thomas Aquinas endeavored to harmonize the teachings of Aristotle with church doctrine. Roger Bacon, in opposition, demonstrated the values of observation and experimentation and argued against the age-old scholastic method of education.

44. C. When an atomic nucleus decomposes by emitting alpha or beta particles, it is said to be radioactive. An example would be the loss of an alpha particle by uranium-238 and its subsequent change to thorium-234.

45. E. Parallel light rays passing through a concave lens bend outward so that they spread apart.

46. B. The intensity and loudness of sound are determined by the amplitude of vibration and number of vibrations (frequency) per second.

47. C. Wavelength is the measure of distance between two adjacent crests.

48. E. Amplitude of a sound vibration is the distance that a vibrating object moves as it vibrates.

49. C. Energy and matter can be neither created nor destroyed, but energy and matter can be converted into one another, the total amount in the universe remaining constant.

50. D. X rays, discovered in 1895 by W.C. Roentgen, are very-high-frequency electromagnetic waves that enable one to photograph the skeleton. X rays also have numerous other uses in science and industry.

51. D. When certain metals are heated, they emit electrons, a phenomenon called the thermionic effect.

52. E. Since the effort multiplied by its distance from the fulcrum equals the weight multiplied by its diameter from the fulcrum, a lever with a short force arm and a long weight arm would provide advantage for gaining distance.

53. B. In general, the chemical and physical properties of lithium and sodium are similar because the outer orbit of each atom contains a single electron.

54. D. Thomas Aquinas taught that there is no conflict between faith and reason.

55. A. The force of adhesion between a solid and a liquid based on the relative attraction of the molecules of the liquid in each other and for the solid is called capillarity.

56. D. Conduction is the process whereby heat energy is transmitted directly through materials.

57. A. The law of conservation of mass holds that there is no detectable gain or loss of mass in or as a result of chemical change.

58. B. Various substances may be separated by using the degree to which they are absorbed onto an inert material. If the inert material is paper, the process is called paper chromatography.

59. C. A buffer is any substance capable of neutralizing acids and bases to maintain a given hydrogen ion concentration.

60. B. In a chemical reaction between an acid and a base (in this case, H_2SO_4 and $Cu(OH)_2$, respectively), a salt, $CuSO_4$, is formed.

ANSWER SHEET — NATURAL SCIENCES/SAMPLE EXAMINATION 2

Section I

1. Ⓐ Ⓑ Ⓒ Ⓓ Ⓔ
2. Ⓐ Ⓑ Ⓒ Ⓓ Ⓔ
3. Ⓐ Ⓑ Ⓒ Ⓓ Ⓔ
4. Ⓐ Ⓑ Ⓒ Ⓓ Ⓔ
5. Ⓐ Ⓑ Ⓒ Ⓓ Ⓔ
6. Ⓐ Ⓑ Ⓒ Ⓓ Ⓔ
7. Ⓐ Ⓑ Ⓒ Ⓓ Ⓔ
8. Ⓐ Ⓑ Ⓒ Ⓓ Ⓔ
9. Ⓐ Ⓑ Ⓒ Ⓓ Ⓔ
10. Ⓐ Ⓑ Ⓒ Ⓓ Ⓔ
11. Ⓐ Ⓑ Ⓒ Ⓓ Ⓔ
12. Ⓐ Ⓑ Ⓒ Ⓓ Ⓔ
13. Ⓐ Ⓑ Ⓒ Ⓓ Ⓔ
14. Ⓐ Ⓑ Ⓒ Ⓓ Ⓔ
15. Ⓐ Ⓑ Ⓒ Ⓓ Ⓔ
16. Ⓐ Ⓑ Ⓒ Ⓓ Ⓔ
17. Ⓐ Ⓑ Ⓒ Ⓓ Ⓔ
18. Ⓐ Ⓑ Ⓒ Ⓓ Ⓔ
19. Ⓐ Ⓑ Ⓒ Ⓓ Ⓔ
20. Ⓐ Ⓑ Ⓒ Ⓓ Ⓔ
21. Ⓐ Ⓑ Ⓒ Ⓓ Ⓔ
22. Ⓐ Ⓑ Ⓒ Ⓓ Ⓔ
23. Ⓐ Ⓑ Ⓒ Ⓓ Ⓔ
24. Ⓐ Ⓑ Ⓒ Ⓓ Ⓔ
25. Ⓐ Ⓑ Ⓒ Ⓓ Ⓔ
26. Ⓐ Ⓑ Ⓒ Ⓓ Ⓔ
27. Ⓐ Ⓑ Ⓒ Ⓓ Ⓔ
28. Ⓐ Ⓑ Ⓒ Ⓓ Ⓔ
29. Ⓐ Ⓑ Ⓒ Ⓓ Ⓔ
30. Ⓐ Ⓑ Ⓒ Ⓓ Ⓔ
31. Ⓐ Ⓑ Ⓒ Ⓓ Ⓔ
32. Ⓐ Ⓑ Ⓒ Ⓓ Ⓔ
33. Ⓐ Ⓑ Ⓒ Ⓓ Ⓔ
34. Ⓐ Ⓑ Ⓒ Ⓓ Ⓔ
35. Ⓐ Ⓑ Ⓒ Ⓓ Ⓔ
36. Ⓐ Ⓑ Ⓒ Ⓓ Ⓔ
37. Ⓐ Ⓑ Ⓒ Ⓓ Ⓔ
38. Ⓐ Ⓑ Ⓒ Ⓓ Ⓔ
39. Ⓐ Ⓑ Ⓒ Ⓓ Ⓔ
40. Ⓐ Ⓑ Ⓒ Ⓓ Ⓔ
41. Ⓐ Ⓑ Ⓒ Ⓓ Ⓔ
42. Ⓐ Ⓑ Ⓒ Ⓓ Ⓔ
43. Ⓐ Ⓑ Ⓒ Ⓓ Ⓔ
44. Ⓐ Ⓑ Ⓒ Ⓓ Ⓔ
45. Ⓐ Ⓑ Ⓒ Ⓓ Ⓔ
46. Ⓐ Ⓑ Ⓒ Ⓓ Ⓔ
47. Ⓐ Ⓑ Ⓒ Ⓓ Ⓔ
48. Ⓐ Ⓑ Ⓒ Ⓓ Ⓔ
49. Ⓐ Ⓑ Ⓒ Ⓓ Ⓔ
50. Ⓐ Ⓑ Ⓒ Ⓓ Ⓔ
51. Ⓐ Ⓑ Ⓒ Ⓓ Ⓔ
52. Ⓐ Ⓑ Ⓒ Ⓓ Ⓔ
53. Ⓐ Ⓑ Ⓒ Ⓓ Ⓔ
54. Ⓐ Ⓑ Ⓒ Ⓓ Ⓔ
55. Ⓐ Ⓑ Ⓒ Ⓓ Ⓔ
56. Ⓐ Ⓑ Ⓒ Ⓓ Ⓔ
57. Ⓐ Ⓑ Ⓒ Ⓓ Ⓔ
58. Ⓐ Ⓑ Ⓒ Ⓓ Ⓔ
59. Ⓐ Ⓑ Ⓒ Ⓓ Ⓔ
60. Ⓐ Ⓑ Ⓒ Ⓓ Ⓔ

Section II

1. Ⓐ Ⓑ Ⓒ Ⓓ Ⓔ
2. Ⓐ Ⓑ Ⓒ Ⓓ Ⓔ
3. Ⓐ Ⓑ Ⓒ Ⓓ Ⓔ
4. Ⓐ Ⓑ Ⓒ Ⓓ Ⓔ
5. Ⓐ Ⓑ Ⓒ Ⓓ Ⓔ
6. Ⓐ Ⓑ Ⓒ Ⓓ Ⓔ
7. Ⓐ Ⓑ Ⓒ Ⓓ Ⓔ
8. Ⓐ Ⓑ Ⓒ Ⓓ Ⓔ
9. Ⓐ Ⓑ Ⓒ Ⓓ Ⓔ
10. Ⓐ Ⓑ Ⓒ Ⓓ Ⓔ
11. Ⓐ Ⓑ Ⓒ Ⓓ Ⓔ
12. Ⓐ Ⓑ Ⓒ Ⓓ Ⓔ
13. Ⓐ Ⓑ Ⓒ Ⓓ Ⓔ
14. Ⓐ Ⓑ Ⓒ Ⓓ Ⓔ
15. Ⓐ Ⓑ Ⓒ Ⓓ Ⓔ
16. Ⓐ Ⓑ Ⓒ Ⓓ Ⓔ
17. Ⓐ Ⓑ Ⓒ Ⓓ Ⓔ
18. Ⓐ Ⓑ Ⓒ Ⓓ Ⓔ
19. Ⓐ Ⓑ Ⓒ Ⓓ Ⓔ
20. Ⓐ Ⓑ Ⓒ Ⓓ Ⓔ
21. Ⓐ Ⓑ Ⓒ Ⓓ Ⓔ
22. Ⓐ Ⓑ Ⓒ Ⓓ Ⓔ
23. Ⓐ Ⓑ Ⓒ Ⓓ Ⓔ
24. Ⓐ Ⓑ Ⓒ Ⓓ Ⓔ
25. Ⓐ Ⓑ Ⓒ Ⓓ Ⓔ
26. Ⓐ Ⓑ Ⓒ Ⓓ Ⓔ
27. Ⓐ Ⓑ Ⓒ Ⓓ Ⓔ
28. Ⓐ Ⓑ Ⓒ Ⓓ Ⓔ
29. Ⓐ Ⓑ Ⓒ Ⓓ Ⓔ
30. Ⓐ Ⓑ Ⓒ Ⓓ Ⓔ
31. Ⓐ Ⓑ Ⓒ Ⓓ Ⓔ
32. Ⓐ Ⓑ Ⓒ Ⓓ Ⓔ
33. Ⓐ Ⓑ Ⓒ Ⓓ Ⓔ
34. Ⓐ Ⓑ Ⓒ Ⓓ Ⓔ
35. Ⓐ Ⓑ Ⓒ Ⓓ Ⓔ
36. Ⓐ Ⓑ Ⓒ Ⓓ Ⓔ
37. Ⓐ Ⓑ Ⓒ Ⓓ Ⓔ
38. Ⓐ Ⓑ Ⓒ Ⓓ Ⓔ
39. Ⓐ Ⓑ Ⓒ Ⓓ Ⓔ
40. Ⓐ Ⓑ Ⓒ Ⓓ Ⓔ
41. Ⓐ Ⓑ Ⓒ Ⓓ Ⓔ
42. Ⓐ Ⓑ Ⓒ Ⓓ Ⓔ
43. Ⓐ Ⓑ Ⓒ Ⓓ Ⓔ
44. Ⓐ Ⓑ Ⓒ Ⓓ Ⓔ
45. Ⓐ Ⓑ Ⓒ Ⓓ Ⓔ
46. Ⓐ Ⓑ Ⓒ Ⓓ Ⓔ
47. Ⓐ Ⓑ Ⓒ Ⓓ Ⓔ
48. Ⓐ Ⓑ Ⓒ Ⓓ Ⓔ
49. Ⓐ Ⓑ Ⓒ Ⓓ Ⓔ
50. Ⓐ Ⓑ Ⓒ Ⓓ Ⓔ
51. Ⓐ Ⓑ Ⓒ Ⓓ Ⓔ
52. Ⓐ Ⓑ Ⓒ Ⓓ Ⓔ
53. Ⓐ Ⓑ Ⓒ Ⓓ Ⓔ
54. Ⓐ Ⓑ Ⓒ Ⓓ Ⓔ
55. Ⓐ Ⓑ Ⓒ Ⓓ Ⓔ
56. Ⓐ Ⓑ Ⓒ Ⓓ Ⓔ
57. Ⓐ Ⓑ Ⓒ Ⓓ Ⓔ
58. Ⓐ Ⓑ Ⓒ Ⓓ Ⓔ
59. Ⓐ Ⓑ Ⓒ Ⓓ Ⓔ
60. Ⓐ Ⓑ Ⓒ Ⓓ Ⓔ

SAMPLE EXAMINATION 2

Section I Biological Sciences

Number of Questions: 60
Time: 45 minutes

Directions: Each of the questions or incomplete statements below is followed by five suggested answers or completions. Select the one that is best in each case.

1. The term most appropriate to the passage of molecules across cellular membranes is
   (A) selective permeability (B) porosity
   (C) mass movement (D) capillarity (E) imbibition

2. According to the principle of biogenesis,
   (A) organic evolution is a reality
   (B) life comes from life
   (C) genetics is the study of heredity
   (D) life arose as the result of special creation
   (E) life arises directly from non-living matter

3. The study of cellular and organismal functioning is a biological specialty called
   (A) anatomy (B) physiology (C) genetics
   (D) parasitology (E) cytology

4. When a living cell is placed in a hypertonic fluid, there will be
   (A) a net movement of water molecules into the cell
   (B) no net movement of water molecules into or out of the cell
   (C) an increase in cell turgidity
   (D) an increase in Brownian movement
   (E) a net movement of water molecules out of the cell

5. When an organism is incapable of synthesizing its food from inorganic materials, it is described as
   (A) chemosynthetic (B) autotrophic (C) autophobic
   (D) heterotrophic (E) photosynthetic

6. Carotene of plants can be considered a precursor of
   (A) vitamin C (B) phytol (C) chlorophyll
   (D) hemoglobin (E) vitamin A

7. As a result of the process called cellular respiration,
   (A) dry weight increases
   (B) oxygen and organic compounds are produced
   (C) water and carbon dioxide are consumed
   (D) dry weight decreases
   (E) water and organic compounds are produced

8. An energy-releasing process occurring continuously in all living cells is
   (A) respiration (B) osmosis (C) absorption
   (D) diffusion (E) photosynthesis

9. The chemical compounds called gibberelins
(A) result in chemosynthesis (B) cause unusual cell elongation in plant cells
(C) cause etiolation in plants (D) are inactivated by fungal enzymes
(E) act as intracellular parasites in plants

10. The total amount of organic matter in a population is referred to as
(A) alluvium (B) humus (C) laterite
(D) schist (E) biomass

11. In plants one of the functions of the xylem is to
(A) manufacture organic substances from carbon dioxide and water
(B) reduce transpiration
(C) increase stem diameter by continued cell division
(D) conduct water upwards (E) conduct food substances

12. A grain of wheat is
(A) a fruit (B) a seed (C) an embryo
(D) a cotyledon (E) an hypocotyl

13. Water loss from plants by transpiration is decreased by
(A) light (B) increased air circulation
(C) increased temperature (D) increased humidity
(E) decreased humidity

14. A type of nuclear division in which the chromosome number in the daughter nuclei is reduced is called
(A) karyokinesis (B) mitosis (C) amitosis
(D) meiosis (E) cytokinesis

15. In plants, fertilization
(A) gives rise to the gametophyte
(B) precedes spore formation
(C) precedes gamete formation
(D) restores the diploid condition
(E) may take place between two spores

16. What is the function of genes?
(A) To produce mutations
(B) To produce DNA
(C) To produce transfer RNA
(D) To produce all cellular components
(E) To direct cells to produce specific proteins

17. Within the cytoplasm of living cells, the structures that "read" the genetic code, thereby directing the production of specific enzymes, are the
(A) ribosomes (B) lysosomes (C) Golgi complex
(D) macrosomes (E) mitochondria

18. A relatively new field of research called gene-splicing
(A) permits the creation of entirely new species
(B) permits the transfer of genes between genetically related organisms
(C) can be accomplished between individuals of any species
(D) results in predictable results
(E) creates no environmental hazards

19. Which of the following is a major problem associated with gene-splicing and the release of special strains of microorganisms?
(A) The ultimate cost of development and production
(B) The extremely limited target areas
(C) The fact that expectations, at best, are meager
(D) The fact that all current techniques are uncontrollable
(E) The difficulty of tracing and recalling such released organisms

20. Nerve impulses along motor nerves leave the central nervous system
(A) along a dorsal root axon
(B) along a ventral root axon
(C) after passing through a dorsal root ganglion
(D) along a connector dendrite
(E) along dendrites of sensory neurons

21. The capability of focusing both eyes on the same object is
(A) stigmatism (B) binocular vision (C) glaucoma
(D) hypermetropia (E) myopia

22. Parathormone
(A) dilates blood vessels (B) stimulates lactation
(C) regulates sodium metabolism (D) controls blood sugar
(E) regulates calcium metabolism

23. The mutual exchange of chromosome fragments, which is called crossing over, occurs during
(A) interphase (B) fertilization (C) transduction
(D) synapsis (E) cell plate formation

24. The theory proposing the inheritance of acquired characteristics was proposed by
(A) Alfred R. Wallace (B) Charles Darwin
(C) Jean Baptiste de Lamarck (D) Sir Charles Lyell
(E) Thomas Hunt Morgan

25. The mutation theory was eventually shown to strengthen Darwin's theory of natural selection because it provided
(A) an explanation for genetic coding
(B) for cytoplasmic inheritance
(C) an explanation for pangenesis
(D) a source of inheritable variations
(E) the bridge between biometrics and the Mendelean ratios

26. A disease transmitted by an arthropod vector is
(A) smallpox (B) malaria (C) tuberculosis (D) polio
(E) lockjaw

27. The first to use the word *cell* after studying plant tissue with his microscope was
(A) Brown (B) Leonardo da Vinci (C) Hooke
(D) Grew (E) Schleiden and Schwann

28. The primary characteristic of the disease acquired immune deficiency syndrome (AIDS) is that
(A) it causes a parasitic infection of the digestive tract
(B) it stimulates the development of several types of cancer
(C) it causes a defect in a person's natural immunity against disease
(D) there is no infectious agent
(E) it causes damage to brain tissues

29. Harvey was the first to verify experimentally
(A) chemical oxidation (B) cell reproduction
(C) the biogenetic hypothesis (D) the nerve impulse
(E) circulation of the blood

30. You would expect to encounter numerous epiphytes and a variety of arboreal mammals in
(A) a tropical rain forest (B) a deciduous forest
(C) a coniferous forest (D) an alpine tundra (E) a taiga

31. Marine organisms found on the continental shelf live in the
(A) zone of perpetual darkness (B) neritic zone
(C) littoral zone (D) abyssal zone (E) bathyal zone

32. A diet completely free of cholesterol would include
(A) a balance of all food types, including lean meat
(B) fruits and dairy products
(C) foods of plant origin only
(D) whole grains and dairy products
(E) large doses of supplemental nutrients

33. Homologous structures are indicative of
(A) common ancestry (B) convergence (C) parallel evolution
(D) divergence (E) similar function

34. An organism which obtains its food from non-living organic materials is called a
(A) symbiont (B) saprophyte (C) commensal
(D) parasite (E) buffer

35. The time period described as the age of glaciers is called the
(A) Eocene epoch (B) Late Mesozoic (C) Triassic period
(D) Early Mesozoic (E) Pleistocene epoch

36. Repeated pruning of a row of shrubs commonly results in a dense growth of the shrub branches. The fact that the same shrubs, if not pruned, develop longer main stems with fewer branches is attributed to the action of auxin and is called
(A) phototropism (B) thigmotropism (C) disbudding
(D) apical dominance (E) parthonocarpy

37. Inclusion of sea foods in the human diet normally prevents an insufficiency of thyroxin and the development of
(A) muscular spasms (B) anemia (C) many enzymes
(D) goiter (E) hemoglobin

38. Pasteurization of milk ensures almost complete protection from the bacterial disease called
(A) measles (B) plague (C) smallpox (D) polio
(E) undulant fever

39. In reference to a trait designated as "*A*", the genotypes resulting from a mating between a male parent homozygous for "*A*" and a heterozygous female parent would be
(A) 1/2 *AA*, 1/2 *Aa* (B) 1/4 *AA*, 1/2 *Aa*, 1/4 *aa* (C) 3/4 *Aa*, 1/4 *aa*
(D) 1/4 *Aa*, 3/4 *aa* (E) impossible to predict

40. Enzymes are specific with reference to
(A) the units of energy released
(B) the units of energy absorbed
(C) the high temperatures required for their activation
(D) the low temperatures required for their activation
(E) the raw materials worked on

41. In a single-celled organism such as the amoeba, pinocytic vesicles function by
(A) bringing some solid particles into the cell
(B) discharging needle-like barbs containing poison
(C) propelling the organism
(D) reacting to environmental stimuli
(E) excreting waste substances from the cell

42. Amino acid analysis of proteins has been advanced by
(A) study of hydrolysis reactions
(B) better understanding of anabolic reactions
(C) a technique called paper chromatography
(D) production and study of autoradiographs
(E) study of condensation reactions

43. Saprophytes
(A) utilize radiant energy
(B) rely upon the absorption of nutrients from decomposing organic materials
(C) eat, digest, and assimilate food materials
(D) oxidize inorganic materials
(E) exist at the expense of living organisms

44. As a result of the process called cellular respiration
(A) dry weight increases
(B) oxygen and organic compounds are produced
(C) water and carbon dioxide are consumed
(D) dry weight decreases
(E) water and organic compounds are produced

Questions 45 and 46

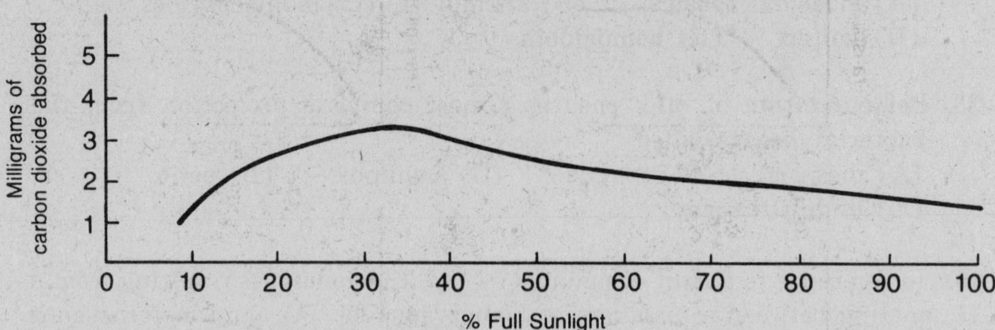

The graph represents the relationship between the rate of photosynthesis (expressed as milligrams of carbon dioxide absorbed per 0.5 square meter of leaf area per hour) and light intensity (expressed as percentages of full sunlight) for woodland ferns.

45. Under the conditions noted above, one may conclude that
(A) ferns use the most sunlight at 100% full sunlight
(B) photosynthesis decreases dry weight
(C) optimum light intensity for ferns is 30-40% full sunlight
(D) photosynthesis increases dry weight
(E) equal increases in light intensity throughout the range of 0-100% of full sunlight bring about equal increases in the rate of photosynthesis for ferns

46. One may also infer that
(A) ferns prefer shade
(B) absorbed carbon dioxide increases to 4 or more milligrams in ferns when exposed to greater than 100% full sunlight
(C) fern leaves are inefficient when it comes to photosynthesis
(D) ferns use more carbon dioxide at 10-50% full sunlight than at 60-100% full sunlight
(E) ferns would grow best in 100% full sunlight

47. Which of the following best describes a nerve impulse?
(A) The transmission of coded signals along a nerve fiber
(B) A wave of depolarization passing along a nerve fiber
(C) A flow of electrons along a nerve fiber
(D) A chemical reaction
(E) A wave of contraction passing along the myelin sheath

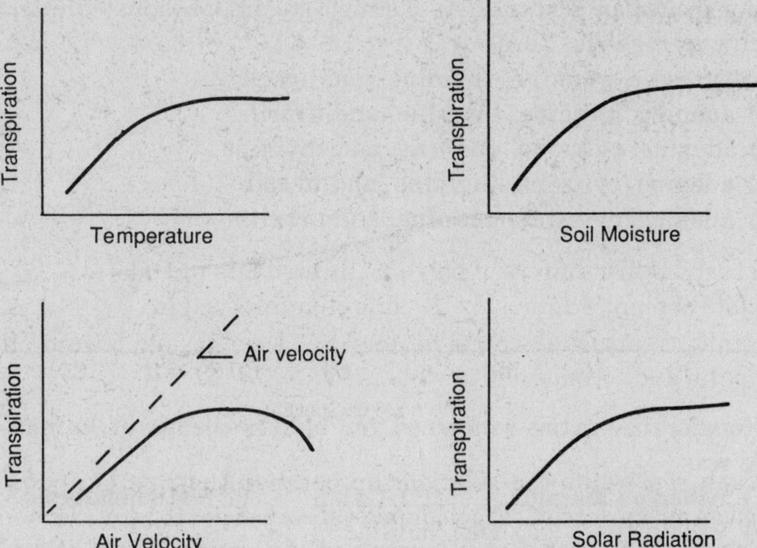

48. The graphs above illustrate the approximate rates of water loss by the aerial parts of plants (transpiration) under varying environmental conditions. On the basis of the information conveyed by the graphs, one may correctly infer that

(A) air velocity is the principal factor affecting transpiration
(B) transpiration is affected by multiple factors
(C) genetic factors exert the primary control over transpiration
(D) the oxygen concentration in soil moisture has no effect on transpiration
(E) plants having high concentrations of anthocyanins have high transpiration rates

49. In the myopic eye, the

(A) light rays converge in front of the retina
(B) light rays converge in the fovea
(C) light rays converge behind the retina
(D) vision is not blurred
(E) cornea is defective

50. Glucose metabolism is regulated by

(A) thyrotropin (B) epinephrine (C) estradiol
(D) progesterone (E) insulin

51. In humans, sex-linked inheritance is concerned with inheritance of

(A) traits whose genes are located on autosomes
(B) traits whose genes are located on the X chromosome
(C) traits whose genes are located on chromosome number 21
(D) traits whose genes are located on the Y chromosome
(E) traits whose genes determine sex

52. The inherited variations commonly referred to in treatises on natural selection and evolution, are, in reality,

(A) merely chance variations (B) induced by the environment
(C) special creations (D) mutations
(E) acquired characteristics

53. Deoxyribonucleic acid consists of simple sugars, phosphate units, and four specific nitrogenous bases:
(A) cytosine, guanine, thymine, and uracil
(B) adenine, guanine, thymine, and uracil
(C) adenine, cytosine, guanine, and thymine
(D) adenine, cytosine, thymine, and uracil
(E) adenine, cytosine, guanine, and uracil

54. The best dietary sources of polyunsaturated fats include
(A) fats of plant origin (B) fats of animal origin
(C) milk, cream, cheese, and butter (D) olive and peanut oils
(E) palm and coconut oils

55. A Renaissance artist renowned for his knowledge of human musculature was
(A) Albertus Magnus (B) Galen (C) Michelangelo
(D) Vesalius (E) De Chauliac

56. The ancient Greek scholar who devoted much study to and wrote much about plant reproduction and seed development, and who is referred to as the "father of botany" is
(A) Aristotle (B) Empedocles (C) Thales
(D) Anaximander (E) Theophrastus

57. Growth responses to external stimuli by actively growing plants are called
(A) plasmolysis (B) synergisms (C) auxins
(D) tropisms (E) parthenocarpy

58. The primary function of root hair cells is
(A) anchorage (B) storage (C) photosynthesis
(D) absorption (E) synergism

59. In respect to dietary fibers, which of the following statements is correct?
(A) A high-fiber diet is high in carbohydrates.
(B) Oat bran lowers cholesterol.
(C) A high-fiber diet may cause colon cancer.
(D) Dry beans and peas are low in dietary fiber.
(E) A high-fiber diet is usually a high-calorie diet.

60. When environmental conditions become unfavorable, certain species of bacteria
(A) develop flagella (B) become aerobic (C) form spores
(D) become anaerobic (E) develop capsules

Section II Physical Sciences

Number of Questions: 60
Time: 45 minutes

Directions: Each of the questions or incomplete statements below is followed by five suggested answers or completions. Select the one that is best in each case.

1. When certain types of atmospheric particles act as nuclei on which water condensation occurs, these fog-forming nuclei are called
(A) hydrologic nuclei (B) condensation nuclei
(C) hydroscopic nuclei (D) hygroscopic nuclei (E) aquifers

2. The earth's orbit is
(A) a parabola (B) a circle (C) an ellipse
(D) a hyperbola (E) a spiral

3. One significant scientific contribution of the Babylonians was the
(A) Pythagorean theorem
(B) combining of mathematics with experimental theory
(C) recording of eclipses
(D) science of alchemy
(E) principle of Archimedes

4. The most accurate timepiece known today is the
(A) atomic clock using the cesium atom (B) electric clock
(C) quartz-crystal clock (D) pendulum clock
(E) solar calendar

5. A star that suddenly increases in brightness and then slowly fades is know as a
(A) supernova (B) nova (C) giant star
(D) visual binary (E) white dwarf

6. When a beam of light passes through a colloidal liquid onto a screen, the beam is diffused on the screen. This scattering of light is known as
(A) the Tyndall effect
(B) a charge-transfer reaction
(C) close packing
(D) destructive interference
(E) the hydrologic effect

7. Deposits of glacial till forming various ridge patterns are called
(A) bergschrunds (B) moraines (C) uplifts
(D) displacements (E) sediments

8. An offshore ridge formed by coral is called
(A) a fjord (B) a continental shelf (C) sediment
(D) a barrier reef (E) an upwelling

9. "Atom-smashing" machines are capable of changing one chemical element into another, a change called
(A) aberration (B) transmutation (C) compression
(D) transduction (E) assimilation

10. Throughout the universe, the force that holds atoms and molecules together is called the
(A) weak force
(B) molality
(C) strong force
(D) electromagnetic force
(E) fifth force

11. Light is made up of tiny particles of packaged energy called
(A) electrons (B) wavelengths (C) refractions (D) photons
(E) mesons

12. Color is primarily the property of those wavelengths of light which are
(A) absorbed (B) reflected (C) produced (D) attracted
(E) adsorbed

13. Why is gravity the dominant force throughout the universe?
(A) The electromagnetic force only holds atoms and molecules together.
(B) The hypothetical "fifth force" is a repulsive force.
(C) The weak force allows some atomic nuclei to break down.
(D) The strong force is vastly stronger than the gravitational force.
(E) Both the strong force and the weak force have very short ranges.

14. The flow of electric current may be measured by
(A) a transistor (B) a galvanometer (C) a rectifier
(D) an induction coil (E) a conductor

15. A device used to switch electricity on and off and to amplify weak electrical currents into strong ones is
(A) the generator (B) the joule (C) the transistor
(D) the moderator (E) the transformer

16. When light is reflected from a surface, the ray striking the surface is
(A) absorbed (B) incident (C) adsorbed (D) refracted
(E) diffused

17. Which of the following statements describing cathode rays is *not* correct?
(A) They are bent by electric fields but not by magnetic fields.
(B) They cast shadows.
(C) They travel in straight lines.
(D) They are bent by both electric and magnetic fields.
(E) They consist of electrons.

18. Radio waves and light waves differ in respect to
(A) amplitude (B) wavelength (C) visibility
(D) velocities (E) diffraction

19. Which one of the following is *not* an acceptable statement in respect to magnetic fields?
(A) They may exist in a vacuum.
(B) Lines of force are indefinite and variable.
(C) They can penetrate glass.
(D) They can penetrate thin sheets of copper.
(E) They do not require the presence of matter.

20. In electrical circuits, the unit of resistance is the
(A) ohm (B) watt (C) volt (D) ampere
(E) coulomb

21. Commercial and home use of alternating current has been made possible by
(A) commutators (B) transformers (C) magnetos
(D) capacitors (E) solenoids

22. Simple machines such as levers enable humans to
(A) gain both force and distance
(B) gain both mechanical advantage and speed
(C) decrease the force arm and increase the weight arm without increasing force
(D) eliminate friction
(E) trade force for distance, or vice versa

23. Heat transfer is accomplished by conduction, radiation, and
(A) vaporization (B) convection (C) expansion
(D) entropy (E) insulation

24. Quantum mechanics is concerned with the
(A) change in velocity of electrons
(B) behavior of the particles inside an atom
(C) transmission of heat energy through gases and liquids
(D) deflection of air flow caused by the earth's rotation
(E) tendencies of materials to fail as a result of repeated stress

25. A property of matter which tends to make it resist any change in motion is called
(A) gravity (B) force (C) mass
(D) acceleration (E) inertia

26. Any physical system is said to possess energy if it
(A) has the capacity to do work (B) has mass
(C) is at absolute zero (D) resists acceleration
(E) resists gravity

27. A fundamental particle with a positive charge found in the nuclei of all heavier atoms is
(A) an ion (B) a meson (C) a proton
(D) an electron (E) a neutron

28. The apparent change in frequency and wavelength of light or sound occurring when the sound and the observer are moving relative to one another is called
(A) the absorption spectrum (B) the band spectrum
(C) the line spectrum (D) the Doppler effect (E) Stefan's law

29. In a chain reaction,
(A) electricity serves as the trigger
(B) light energy stimulates atoms
(C) light energy stimulates molecules
(D) neutrons combine with photons
(E) the first atoms to react trigger additional reactions

30. To state that a football player weighs 220 pounds means that
(A) his body is attracted by the sun with a force equal to 220 pounds
(B) his body is attracted by the sun and the moon with a combined force equal to 220 pounds
(C) his body is attracted by the earth with a force equal to 220 pounds
(D) he has a negative mass equal to 220 pounds
(E) he has a positive mass equal to 220 pounds

31. Water held behind a dam represents what kind of energy?
(A) Kinetic (B) Potential (C) Mass (D) Conserved
(E) Transformed

32. Water will rise inside a glass tube of very small diameter because of
(A) kinetic energy (B) potential energy (C) cohesion
(D) adhesion (E) surface tension

33. In the process called evaporation, the faster molecules of a liquid are able to escape the attractive forces of their slower neighboring molecules. This results in
(A) an increase in temperature (B) a decrease in temperature
(C) adhesion (D) cohesion (E) friction

34. Specific gravity is a measure of the relative density of a liquid in relation to
(A) water (B) air (C) ice
(D) mercury (E) oxygen

35. Which produces hydrogen gas when interacting with metals?
(A) Salts (B) Acids (C) Bases (D) Oxides
(E) Hydroxides

36. The halogen family of chemical elements includes fluorine and
(A) sulfur (B) potassium (C) chromium
(D) bismuth (E) iodine

37. In the photosynthetic process, one role of chlorophyll is that of
(A) an ionizer (B) a polarizer (C) a neutralizer
(D) a catalyst (E) an isotope

38. One class of organic compounds constitutes the building blocks of proteins and is characterized by possessing
(A) a carboxyl group only
(B) an NH_2 group in addition to a carboxyl group
(C) hydrocarbons (D) an alkyl group (E) esters

39. In any physical change,
(A) the reactants disappear
(B) matter does not lose its chemical identity
(C) new substances with different properties appear
(D) energy is released
(E) energy is absorbed

40. In chemical equations, the total molecular weight of the reactants
(A) equals the total molecular weight of the products
(B) is less than the total molecular weight of the products
(C) is greater than the total molecular weight of the products
(D) is not relative to the total molecular weight of the products
(E) is determined by the atomic number of the reactant

41. Alkyd resins are the base of polyesters used in boat construction, fishing rods, and other household items because of their
(A) strength, resistance, and durability (B) thermoplasticity
(C) similarity to foam rubber (D) insulation capability
(E) tensile coefficient

42. Scholasticism was concerned primarily with
(A) literature and language
(B) social reforms
(C) medicine
(D) Aristotle's and St. Augustine's works and teachings
(E) astronomy

43. Proteins are complex compounds containing carbon, hydrogen, oxygen, and nitrogen, and usually
(A) sulfur and potassium (B) sulfur and phosphorus
(C) manganese and phosphorus (D) manganese and potassium
(E) sulfur and manganese

44. Chemical processes in which electrons are taken away from atoms or molecules are referred to as
(A) recombinations (B) tropisms (C) decompositions
(D) oxidations (E) reductions

45. During radioactive decay, a given radioactive element may emit
(A) beta and gamma rays only (B) alpha and gamma rays only
(C) alpha, beta and gamma rays
(D) alpha, beta and gamma, and X-rays (E) X-rays only

Questions 46 and 47

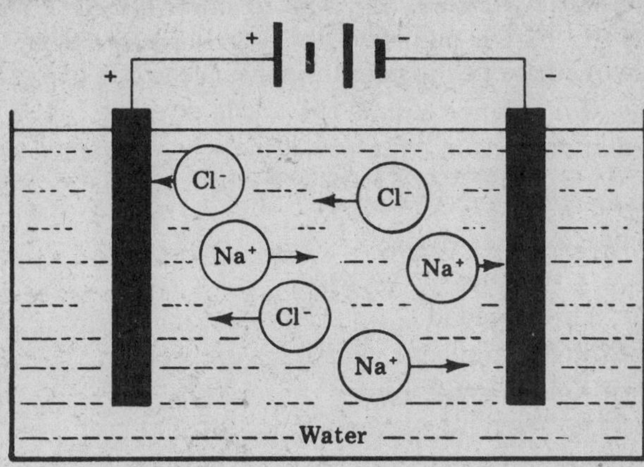

46. After study of the illustration above, one may conclude that
(A) water molecules are attracted by the electrodes
(B) sodium ions are attracted to the positive electrode
(C) sodium chloride dissociates when placed in water
(D) chlorine ions are attracted to the negative electrode
(E) current flow causes an increase in water temperature

47. One may also conclude that
(A) the solution will not conduct current
(B) only sodium ions conduct current
(C) only chlorine ions conduct current
(D) the closed circuit illustrated results in neutrality
(E) when ions are present they are attracted to electrodes having opposite electrical charges

48. Certain metals and alloys, such as nichrome wire, are used in electrical heating devices (toasters , for example) because of their
(A) low melting point (B) high specific resistance
(C) great current flow (D) capacity to discharge electrons
(E) capacity to modify electrons

49. A unique feature of lasers is
(A) the abrupt spreading of their beam of light
(B) their production of coherent radiation
(C) the Peltier effect
(D) the Seebeck effect
(E) the very narrow beam of light produced

50. Ultraviolet light
(A) is more energetic than visual light
(B) is not harmful
(C) has longer wavelengths than visible light
(D) lies in a low energy section of the electromagnetic spectrum
(E) is the light source used in lasers

51. When an electric current is passed through electrodes immersed in an electrolyte, molecules of the electrolyte
(A) precipitate (B) dissociate (C) crystallize
(D) combine (E) neutralize

52. According to the law of reflection,
(A) the angle of incidence is equal to the angle of reflection
(B) the angle of incidence is less than the angle of reflection
(C) the angle of incidence is greater than the angle of reflection
(D) the angle of incidence equals the angle of reflection squared
(E) the angle of reflection equals the angle of incidence squared

53. Whenever an electric current flows,
(A) charged particles combine
(B) no effect is detectable in the wire
(C) a transformer is needed
(D) power obtained equals current times amperage
(E) a magnetic field is generated

54. A coil of wire carrying an electric current behaves as
(A) a stator (B) a commutator (C) a transistor
(D) a bar magnet (E) a capacitor

Directions: Each group of questions below consists of five lettered choices followed by a list of numbered phrases or sentences. For each numbered phrase or sentence select the one choice that is most closely related to it. Each choice may be used once, more than once, or not at all in each group.

Questions 55–57

(A) Binary stars
(B) Black holes
(C) Dwarfs
(D) Neutron stars
(E) Variable stars

55. Stars which fluctuate in brightness

56. Stars appearing to lie in the same line of sight

57. Stars of which supernovae are the most spectacular examples

Questions 58–60

(A) Avogadro's law
(B) Boyle's law
(C) Kinetic-molecular theory
(D) First Law of Thermodynamics
(E) Uncertainty principle

58. States that energy may be neither created nor destroyed

59. Is based on the concept that we cannot know both the position and the energy of an electron at the same time

60. Assumes that gases consist of independently moving molecules

ANSWER KEY—SAMPLE EXAMINATION 2

Section I Biological Sciences

1. A	11. D	21. B	31. B	41. A	51. B
2. B	12. A	22. E	32. C	42. C	52. D
3. B	13. D	23. D	33. A	43. B	53. C
4. E	14. D	24. C	34. B	44. D	54. A
5. D	15. D	25. D	35. E	45. C	55. C
6. E	16. E	26. B	36. D	46. D	56. E
7. D	17. A	27. C	37. D	47. B	57. D
8. A	18. B	28. C	38. E	48. B	58. D
9. B	19. E	29. E	39. A	49. A	59. B
10. E	20. B	30. A	40. E	50. E	60. C

Section II Physical Sciences

1. B	11. D	21. B	31. B	41. A	51. B
2. C	12. B	22. E	32. D	42. D	52. A
3. C	13. E	23. B	33. B	43. B	53. E
4. A	14. B	24. B	34. A	44. D	54. D
5. B	15. C	25. E	35. B	45. C	55. E
6. A	16. B	26. A	36. E	46. C	56. A
7. B	17. A	27. C	37. D	47. E	57. E
8. D	18. B	28. D	38. B	48. B	58. D
9. B	19. B	29. E	39. B	49. E	59. E
10. D	20. A	30. C	40. A	50. A	60. C

SCORING CHART—SAMPLE EXAMINATION 2

After you have scored your Sample Examination 2, enter the results in the chart below; then transfer your Raw Score to the Progress Chart on page 14.

Total Test	Number Right	Number Wrong	Number Omitted	Raw Score
Section I: 60				
Section II: 60				
Total: 120				

ANSWER EXPLANATIONS—SAMPLE EXAMINATION 2

Section I Biological Sciences

1. A. Cellular membranes are selectively permeable since they permit different kinds of molecules to pass at varying rates or not at all and this permeability may constantly change.
2. B. According to biogenesis, all life comes from pre-existing life.
3. B. Physiology is the study of function.
4. E. A hypertonic solution has a higher osmotic pressure than the protoplasm of the cell in question and, therefore, water will diffuse out of the cell with a consequent decrease in turgor pressure.
5. D. Autotrophic organisms have the ability to synthesize their food from inorganic materials; heterotrophic organisms lack this ability.
6. E. Carotenoid pigments (carotenes) of yellow and leafy vegetables are precursors in vitamin A synthesis.
7. D. In cellular respiration organic substances are broken down to release their stored energy. This results in a decrease in dry weight.
8. A. All living cells carry on cellular respiration which is a process that provides energy for the cell's use.
9. B. Like auxins, gibberellins are growth-promoting substances found in plants which cause stem elongation, promote flowering and play a role in seed germination.
10. E. The total weight of protoplasm in a community is referred to as biomass.
11. D. Xylem is the principal water-conducting tissue in vascular plants.
12. A. A fruit is the matured ovary of a flower. A grain of wheat is a matured ovary of the wheat plant.
13. D. Any factor that affects the evaporation of water from an open container will have a similar effect on transpiration by plants. Transpiration is defined as the evaporation of water from the aerial parts of plants.
14. D. In meiosis, the chromosome number is reduced by one half. Actually, chromosomes exist in pairs and in meiosis, the members of each pair are segregated to the daughter cells, resulting in the reduced number of chromosomes.
15. D. The fusion of two haploid (*N*) gametes in plants restores the diploid (2*N*) chromosome number.
16. E. Genes direct cells to produce specific enzymes, all of which are proteins, and these act as the cellular "machines" that control or determine cellular traits.

17. A. All cellular proteins, including enzymes, are produced by ribosomes, which are composed of RNA and proteins and which follow the instructions received from the DNA code of the nucleus.

18. B. The transfer of genes from one organism to another that is genetically related is called gene-splicing and offers possible solutions for selected medical and environmental problems. On the negative side, its results are not readily predictable, may affect food chains, and may upset delicate natural balance.

19. E. Gene-splicing produces new kinds of individuals within species. The interactions of these new kinds of organisms with the environment are not only unpredictable, but also potentially hazardous if something "goes wrong."

20. B. Motor nerve impulses leave the central nervous system along ventral root axons, while sensory impulses move towards the central nervous system along dorsal roots.

21. B. The human visual system is binocular and stereoscopic, i.e., the images of the two eyes fit together to produce roundness and depth.

22. E. Parathormone is necessary for maintaining the proper calcium ion concentration in the blood. Calcium is involved in nerve impulse transmission, blood clotting, bone and teeth formation, and fertilization.

23. D. Synapsis is the pairing of the chromosomes during the prophase and metaphase of the first meiotic division. Since each chromosome consists of two daughter chromatids during this period, a tetrad of four chromatids exists and crossing-over occurs often.

24. C. Lamarck proposed the theory of the inheritance of acquired characteristics, frequently referred to as the theory of "use and disuse."

25. D. The mutation theory proposed by de Vries strengthened Darwin's theory of natural selection because it provided a good explanation for the source of inheritable variations, something Darwin was not able to do.

26. B. The *Anopheles* mosquito is the vector, or carrier, of the protozoan parasite that causes malaria.

27. C. Robert Hooke was the first to use the term "cell" in describing the microscopic units that comprise the tissues and organs of multicellular plants and animals.

28. C. Although AIDS is a very complex disease distinguished by various symptoms, it is primarily characterized by causing major defects in an individual's immunity to disease.

29. E. William Harvey verified experimentally that the blood circulates. He described arteries and veins and predicted the existence of blood capillaries.

30. A. In the tropical rain forest with its excessive rains, the ground level environment is poor. Therefore, many forms of plants and animals are tree dwellers.

31. B. The neritic environment is identified as a region of shallow water adjoining the seacoast and above the continental shelf.

32. C. Cholesterol is not found in foods of plant origin.

33. A. Homologous structures are similar from the standpoint of structure, embryonic development, and relationship and thus indicate common ancestry.

34. B. A saprophyte is an heterotrophic plant that obtains its nourishment from nonliving organic matter.

35. E. In the Pleistocene epoch climates cooled dramatically and there were two glacial periods during which the ice advanced twice.

36. D. Auxin (plant hormone) is produced primarily by terminal buds, and among its induced responses are stem elongation and lateral bud inhibition. Removal of terminal buds by pruning permits lateral buds to grow into branches.

37. D. Seafood contains small quantities of iodine and this element is required for normal thyroid function and the production of thyroxin.

38. E. Protection from undulant fever (brucellosis) can be achieved if all milk is pasteurized and if diseased animals are removed from the herd.

39. A. The male parent produces A-type gametes only, while the female parent produces both A-type and a-type gametes in a 1:1 ratio. During random fertilization, zygotes will be ½ AA and ½ Aa.

40. E. Enzymes are always specific with respect to the substrate (raw material) worked on.

41. A. Solid food particles such as bacterial cells may be brought into the cell by pinocytosis and released into the cytoplasm as a food vacuole.

42. C. Paper chromatography permits the separation of amino acids and relies upon the different solubilities of amino acids and on their differential absorption on paper.

43. B. Saprophytes are heterotrophic plants which obtain their nourishment from non-living organic matter.

44. D. Cellular respiration is the oxidation of carbohydrates which results in the release of energy. The loss of the carbohydrate results in a decrease in dry weight.

45. C.
46. D. } Study of the graph indicates that optimum light intensity for the ferns is 30–40%, since this represents the light intensity at which there is greatest absorption of CO_2. Similarly, ferns use more CO_2 at 10–50% of full sunlight than at 60–100%. On the basis of the information given, no other conclusions are valid.

47. B. The resting nerve fiber is polarized, having its outside positively charged and its inside negatively charged. A stimulus causes a wave of depolarization to pass along the fiber, from which it recovers in about 0.001 second.

48. B. Transpiration is the loss of water from the aerial parts of plants; its rate is affected by several environmental factors, including solar radiation, humidity, air movement, soil moisture, and temperature.

49. A. In myopia, the eyeball is elongated to the extent that the image falls in front of the retina. This is nearsightedness.

50. E. Insulin is produced in the pancreas and is one of the glucose-regulating hormones.

51. B. Sex-linked inheritance in humans is concerned with the inheritance traits whose genes are located on the X chromosome. (The Y chromosome has only a few genes and for different traits.)

52. D. Mutations are the source of the inherited variations and support the theory of evolution by providing the variations needed for natural selection.

53. C. The specific nitrogenous bases of deoxyribonucleic acid are the amino acids adenine, cytosine, guanine, and thymine.

54. A. Polyunsaturated fats are found in largest proportions in plant fats such as sunflower, corn, and soybean oils and in selected fish.

55. C. Michelangelo Buonarroti was a great student of human anatomy who performed many of his own dissections. Evidence of his vast knowledge of anatomy is found in his paintings and sculptures.

56. E. Theophrastus' writings on plants have been preserved and represent the extent of the Greeks' knowledge of science. His greatest work was "Historia Plantarum."

57. D. Plants react to external stimuli by a series of growth responses called tropisms. A growth response in reaction to gravity is geotropism, in reaction to light is phototropism, etc.

58. D. Root hair cells increase the absorbing surface of roots and are the principal water-absorbing structures of typical land plant roots.

59. B. Oat bran has a high proportion of soluble fiber, and it is soluble fiber that lowers cholesterol.

60. C. Spore formation is a response of certain bacteria to an environment which becomes unfavorable. Bacterial spores have thick, resistant spore walls and the living bacterial cell within is in a state of suspended animation. When conditions become favorable, the bacterial cell converts back to its active way of life.

Section II Physical Sciences

1. B. When the atmosphere is saturated with water vapor, minute bits of particulate matter known as condensation nuclei serve as surfaces for the condensation of water vapor.
2. C. Kepler's greatest discovery was the fact that planetary orbits, including that of the earth, are ellipses.
3. C. Ancient civilizations, including the Babylonian, relied on astrology in predicting the future. Astrological events are tied to the behavior of the sun, moon and planets. It is, therefore, not surprising that early Babylonian writings included references to eclipses.
4. A. Since 1964, the international standard for measuring time has been the vibration rate of cesium atoms. According to this standard, one second of time is equal to 9,192,631,770 vibrations of cesium-133.
5. B. Stars that fluctuate in brightness are called variables. In one type, the eruptive variable, a sudden brightening occurs and this is called a nova.
6. A. Colloidal particles scatter light, and this phenomenon is known as the Tyndall effect.
7. B. Glaciers cause the erosion, transportation and deposition of mineral matter and this mass of rock debris deposited as residual matter is referred to as a moraine.
8. D. A barrier reef is a long, narrow coral embankment lying offshore.
9. B. Transmutation is the act of changing one element into another. It occurs naturally in the radioactive elements and may be induced in atom-smashing machines by bombarding elements with high speed protons and other sub-atomic particles.
10. D. The electromagnetic force is the force that holds atoms and molecules together.
11. D. Einstein once reasoned that light travels as streams of energy packets which today are called photons.
12. B. Those wavelengths of the total visible spectrum which are reflected are blended and perceived by the eye as color.
13. E. The strong force and the weak force have very short ranges and are felt only inside the atomic nucleus. The electromagnetic force acts only to hold atoms and molecules together. Gravity, however, is felt throughout the universe.
14. B. A galvanometer is an instrument used to measure electric current.
15. C. The transistor is a small device that requires little power and can switch electricity on and off. It may also be used to amplify weak electric currents.
16. B. The angle of incidence is the angle between the light ray and a line drawn perpendicular to the surface.
17. A. Characteristics of cathode rays include traveling in straight lines, casting shadows, consisting of electrons, and being bent by both electric and magnetic fields.
18. B. Radio waves and light waves are different parts of the electromagnetic spectrum differing primarily in that they have different wavelengths.
19. B. In respect to magnetic fields, lines of force are finite and constant for any condition or set of circumstances.
20. A. The ohm is the unit of electrical resistance in a material.
21. B. A transformer is a device that can be used to increase or decrease the voltage of alternating electrical currents.
22. E. A lever is a machine which can be used to gain force or distance, since the length of the force arm multiplied by the force used equals the length of the weight arm multiplied by the weight.
23. B. Heat energy is transferred within a medium by conduction, radiation and convection.
24. B. Quantum theory identifies the smallest units of energy, the quantum, and quantum mechanics explains their behavior inside the atom.
25. E. Inertia is the tendency of a body at rest to remain at rest or the tendency of a body in motion to remain in motion.

26. A. Energy may be defined as the capacity to perform work.

27. C. Protons are one of the fundamental types of particles found in the nuclei of atoms. Protons have positive charges.

28. D. The Doppler effect is the observed change in the frequency of light or sound waves when the source is moving in relation to the observer.

29. E. If a nuclear fission reaction is initiated by bombardment of atomic nuclei with neutrons and the subsequent fission results in the release of additional neutrons which, in turn, bombard additional atoms, a chain reaction is created.

30. C. Weight is defined as the force of gravity upon an object.

31. B. Potential energy is that energy possessed by an object because of its position.

32. D. Adhesion is the force of attraction between the molecules of two different substances which are in contact.

33. B. The heat of vaporization is the heat energy absorbed by the molecules of an evaporating liquid. The result is cooling or a decrease in temperature.

34. A. The specific gravity of a liquid is the ratio of the density of the liquid to the density of water where both densities are obtained in air.

35. B. Acids are well known for their ability to corrode metals. When an acid solution vigorously attacks a metal, hydrogen gas is evolved.

36. E. The halogen family of chemical elements consists of fluorine, chlorine, bromine, iodine, and astatine.

37. D. In photosynthesis chlorophyll has a dual role, that of absorbing selective wavelengths of radiant energy and as a catalyst by participating in certain chemical reactions which lead to the production of sugar.

38. B. Proteins are polymers consisting of long chains of amino acids, each unit of which is built from an amino group and a carboxyl group.

39. B. In physical changes, the component building blocks of matter, atoms, do not undergo change. They merely combine and separate in different combinations and arrangements.

40. A. In any chemical reaction, the total molecular weight of the reactants always equals the total molecular weight of the products.

41. A. Both thermoplastic and thermosetting plastics made of synthetic resins are used to manufacture thousands of items because of their strength, resistance and durability in various situations.

42. D. Scholasticism was a philosophical movement during the Middle Ages attempting to combine the teachings of Aristotle and St. Augustine with fixed religious dogma.

43. B. Organic compounds always contain carbon, hydrogen and oxygen. Proteins, in addition, have nitrogen and usually sulfur and phosphorus.

44. D. By definition, oxidation is the loss of electrons by atoms, ions or molecules.

45. C. By placing a naturally radioactive substance in a block of lead, a thin radioactive beam may be permitted to come out of the lead through an open hole. When this emitted beam is placed in an electric field, it is split into alpha, beta and gamma particles.

46. C. Dissociation is the breaking up of a chemical substance into its ionic constituents. In this instance NaCl dissociates to form Na^+ ions and Cl^- ions when placed in water.

47. E. Ionic behavior responds to the concept that like (electrical) charges repel each other and unlike charges attract each other.

48. B. Metals possessing high specific resistance to the conduction of electric current heat up since it takes more energy to push current through wires having high resistance and this energy is converted to heat.

49. E. A laser is a device that can focus a beam of light to concentrate a great amount of electromagnetic energy on a very small area.

50. A. Ultraviolet light is more energetic than visual light and can excite electrons in many kinds of molecules causing chemical reactions to occur.

51. B. Molecules of an electrolyte dissociate when it conducts an electric current and simultaneously the newly formed ions migrate with anions moving towards the anode and cations moving towards the cathode.

52. A. When electromagnetic waves strike a surface, they are said to be reflected, and careful measurements will reveal that the angle of incidence is equal to the angle of reflection.

53. E. Whenever an electric current flows, a magnetic field is generated around the wire conducting the current.

54. D. The magnetic field generated in a coil of wire when an electric current passes through it behaves in a manner similar to a bar magnet.

55. E. Stars that fluctuate in brightness are known as variable stars.

56. A. Stars which move about each other and which are attracted by their mutual gravitation are called binary stars.

57. E. When a star increases its brightness several million times it is called a supernova.

58. D. According to the First Law of Thermodynamics, energy may be transformed from one type to another, but may be neither created nor destroyed.

59. E. An electron is displaced by the energy transmitted to it by the photon that strikes it. The electron will then be in a different location. Thus, the energy and the original position of the electron remain unknown, a phenomenon called the uncertainty principle.

60. C. A theory concerning the nature of gases that assumes that gases consist of independently moving molecules is named the kinetic-molecular theory.

ANSWER SHEET — NATURAL SCIENCES/SAMPLE EXAMINATION 3

Section I

1. Ⓐ Ⓑ Ⓒ Ⓓ Ⓔ
2. Ⓐ Ⓑ Ⓒ Ⓓ Ⓔ
3. Ⓐ Ⓑ Ⓒ Ⓓ Ⓔ
4. Ⓐ Ⓑ Ⓒ Ⓓ Ⓔ
5. Ⓐ Ⓑ Ⓒ Ⓓ Ⓔ
6. Ⓐ Ⓑ Ⓒ Ⓓ Ⓔ
7. Ⓐ Ⓑ Ⓒ Ⓓ Ⓔ
8. Ⓐ Ⓑ Ⓒ Ⓓ Ⓔ
9. Ⓐ Ⓑ Ⓒ Ⓓ Ⓔ
10. Ⓐ Ⓑ Ⓒ Ⓓ Ⓔ
11. Ⓐ Ⓑ Ⓒ Ⓓ Ⓔ
12. Ⓐ Ⓑ Ⓒ Ⓓ Ⓔ
13. Ⓐ Ⓑ Ⓒ Ⓓ Ⓔ
14. Ⓐ Ⓑ Ⓒ Ⓓ Ⓔ
15. Ⓐ Ⓑ Ⓒ Ⓓ Ⓔ
16. Ⓐ Ⓑ Ⓒ Ⓓ Ⓔ
17. Ⓐ Ⓑ Ⓒ Ⓓ Ⓔ
18. Ⓐ Ⓑ Ⓒ Ⓓ Ⓔ
19. Ⓐ Ⓑ Ⓒ Ⓓ Ⓔ
20. Ⓐ Ⓑ Ⓒ Ⓓ Ⓔ
21. Ⓐ Ⓑ Ⓒ Ⓓ Ⓔ
22. Ⓐ Ⓑ Ⓒ Ⓓ Ⓔ
23. Ⓐ Ⓑ Ⓒ Ⓓ Ⓔ
24. Ⓐ Ⓑ Ⓒ Ⓓ Ⓔ
25. Ⓐ Ⓑ Ⓒ Ⓓ Ⓔ
26. Ⓐ Ⓑ Ⓒ Ⓓ Ⓔ
27. Ⓐ Ⓑ Ⓒ Ⓓ Ⓔ
28. Ⓐ Ⓑ Ⓒ Ⓓ Ⓔ
29. Ⓐ Ⓑ Ⓒ Ⓓ Ⓔ
30. Ⓐ Ⓑ Ⓒ Ⓓ Ⓔ
31. Ⓐ Ⓑ Ⓒ Ⓓ Ⓔ
32. Ⓐ Ⓑ Ⓒ Ⓓ Ⓔ
33. Ⓐ Ⓑ Ⓒ Ⓓ Ⓔ
34. Ⓐ Ⓑ Ⓒ Ⓓ Ⓔ
35. Ⓐ Ⓑ Ⓒ Ⓓ Ⓔ
36. Ⓐ Ⓑ Ⓒ Ⓓ Ⓔ
37. Ⓐ Ⓑ Ⓒ Ⓓ Ⓔ
38. Ⓐ Ⓑ Ⓒ Ⓓ Ⓔ
39. Ⓐ Ⓑ Ⓒ Ⓓ Ⓔ
40. Ⓐ Ⓑ Ⓒ Ⓓ Ⓔ
41. Ⓐ Ⓑ Ⓒ Ⓓ Ⓔ
42. Ⓐ Ⓑ Ⓒ Ⓓ Ⓔ
43. Ⓐ Ⓑ Ⓒ Ⓓ Ⓔ
44. Ⓐ Ⓑ Ⓒ Ⓓ Ⓔ
45. Ⓐ Ⓑ Ⓒ Ⓓ Ⓔ
46. Ⓐ Ⓑ Ⓒ Ⓓ Ⓔ
47. Ⓐ Ⓑ Ⓒ Ⓓ Ⓔ
48. Ⓐ Ⓑ Ⓒ Ⓓ Ⓔ
49. Ⓐ Ⓑ Ⓒ Ⓓ Ⓔ
50. Ⓐ Ⓑ Ⓒ Ⓓ Ⓔ
51. Ⓐ Ⓑ Ⓒ Ⓓ Ⓔ
52. Ⓐ Ⓑ Ⓒ Ⓓ Ⓔ
53. Ⓐ Ⓑ Ⓒ Ⓓ Ⓔ
54. Ⓐ Ⓑ Ⓒ Ⓓ Ⓔ
55. Ⓐ Ⓑ Ⓒ Ⓓ Ⓔ
56. Ⓐ Ⓑ Ⓒ Ⓓ Ⓔ
57. Ⓐ Ⓑ Ⓒ Ⓓ Ⓔ
58. Ⓐ Ⓑ Ⓒ Ⓓ Ⓔ
59. Ⓐ Ⓑ Ⓒ Ⓓ Ⓔ
60. Ⓐ Ⓑ Ⓒ Ⓓ Ⓔ

Section II

1. Ⓐ Ⓑ Ⓒ Ⓓ Ⓔ
2. Ⓐ Ⓑ Ⓒ Ⓓ Ⓔ
3. Ⓐ Ⓑ Ⓒ Ⓓ Ⓔ
4. Ⓐ Ⓑ Ⓒ Ⓓ Ⓔ
5. Ⓐ Ⓑ Ⓒ Ⓓ Ⓔ
6. Ⓐ Ⓑ Ⓒ Ⓓ Ⓔ
7. Ⓐ Ⓑ Ⓒ Ⓓ Ⓔ
8. Ⓐ Ⓑ Ⓒ Ⓓ Ⓔ
9. Ⓐ Ⓑ Ⓒ Ⓓ Ⓔ
10. Ⓐ Ⓑ Ⓒ Ⓓ Ⓔ
11. Ⓐ Ⓑ Ⓒ Ⓓ Ⓔ
12. Ⓐ Ⓑ Ⓒ Ⓓ Ⓔ
13. Ⓐ Ⓑ Ⓒ Ⓓ Ⓔ
14. Ⓐ Ⓑ Ⓒ Ⓓ Ⓔ
15. Ⓐ Ⓑ Ⓒ Ⓓ Ⓔ
16. Ⓐ Ⓑ Ⓒ Ⓓ Ⓔ
17. Ⓐ Ⓑ Ⓒ Ⓓ Ⓔ
18. Ⓐ Ⓑ Ⓒ Ⓓ Ⓔ
19. Ⓐ Ⓑ Ⓒ Ⓓ Ⓔ
20. Ⓐ Ⓑ Ⓒ Ⓓ Ⓔ
21. Ⓐ Ⓑ Ⓒ Ⓓ Ⓔ
22. Ⓐ Ⓑ Ⓒ Ⓓ Ⓔ
23. Ⓐ Ⓑ Ⓒ Ⓓ Ⓔ
24. Ⓐ Ⓑ Ⓒ Ⓓ Ⓔ
25. Ⓐ Ⓑ Ⓒ Ⓓ Ⓔ
26. Ⓐ Ⓑ Ⓒ Ⓓ Ⓔ
27. Ⓐ Ⓑ Ⓒ Ⓓ Ⓔ
28. Ⓐ Ⓑ Ⓒ Ⓓ Ⓔ
29. Ⓐ Ⓑ Ⓒ Ⓓ Ⓔ
30. Ⓐ Ⓑ Ⓒ Ⓓ Ⓔ
31. Ⓐ Ⓑ Ⓒ Ⓓ Ⓔ
32. Ⓐ Ⓑ Ⓒ Ⓓ Ⓔ
33. Ⓐ Ⓑ Ⓒ Ⓓ Ⓔ
34. Ⓐ Ⓑ Ⓒ Ⓓ Ⓔ
35. Ⓐ Ⓑ Ⓒ Ⓓ Ⓔ
36. Ⓐ Ⓑ Ⓒ Ⓓ Ⓔ
37. Ⓐ Ⓑ Ⓒ Ⓓ Ⓔ
38. Ⓐ Ⓑ Ⓒ Ⓓ Ⓔ
39. Ⓐ Ⓑ Ⓒ Ⓓ Ⓔ
40. Ⓐ Ⓑ Ⓒ Ⓓ Ⓔ
41. Ⓐ Ⓑ Ⓒ Ⓓ Ⓔ
42. Ⓐ Ⓑ Ⓒ Ⓓ Ⓔ
43. Ⓐ Ⓑ Ⓒ Ⓓ Ⓔ
44. Ⓐ Ⓑ Ⓒ Ⓓ Ⓔ
45. Ⓐ Ⓑ Ⓒ Ⓓ Ⓔ
46. Ⓐ Ⓑ Ⓒ Ⓓ Ⓔ
47. Ⓐ Ⓑ Ⓒ Ⓓ Ⓔ
48. Ⓐ Ⓑ Ⓒ Ⓓ Ⓔ
49. Ⓐ Ⓑ Ⓒ Ⓓ Ⓔ
50. Ⓐ Ⓑ Ⓒ Ⓓ Ⓔ
51. Ⓐ Ⓑ Ⓒ Ⓓ Ⓔ
52. Ⓐ Ⓑ Ⓒ Ⓓ Ⓔ
53. Ⓐ Ⓑ Ⓒ Ⓓ Ⓔ
54. Ⓐ Ⓑ Ⓒ Ⓓ Ⓔ
55. Ⓐ Ⓑ Ⓒ Ⓓ Ⓔ
56. Ⓐ Ⓑ Ⓒ Ⓓ Ⓔ
57. Ⓐ Ⓑ Ⓒ Ⓓ Ⓔ
58. Ⓐ Ⓑ Ⓒ Ⓓ Ⓔ
59. Ⓐ Ⓑ Ⓒ Ⓓ Ⓔ
60. Ⓐ Ⓑ Ⓒ Ⓓ Ⓔ

SAMPLE EXAMINATION 3

Section I Biological Sciences

Number of Questions: 60
Time: 45 minutes

Directions: Each of the questions or incomplete statements below is followed by five suggested answers or completions. Select the one that is best in each case.

1. An organism that has a right and a left side exhibits
   (A) asymmetry (B) radial symmetry
   (C) spherical symmetry (D) bilateral symmetry
   (E) universal symmetry

2. Which of the following occurs when water evaporates?
   (A) osmosis (B) simple diffusion (C) capillarity
   (D) mass movement (E) imbibition

3. According to evidence provided by recent and current research, the origin of life on earth is explainable by
   (A) the association of organic molecules in the presence of heat over great expanses of time
   (B) the traveling to earth of living organisms from remote sources in outer space
   (C) numerous instances of spontaneous generation
   (D) the action of radioactivity on inorganic chemicals
   (E) a single instance of spontaneous generation

4. What do physiologists call the first group of chemical reactions in aerobic respiration, in which simple sugars are changed into pyruvic acid under anaerobic conditions?
   (A) Fermentation
   (B) The citric acid cycle
   (C) Chemosynthesis
   (D) Glycolysis
   (E) Heterotrophic nutrition

5. When a living cell is placed in a fluid and there is no net movement of water molecules into or out of the cell, the fluid is said to be
   (A) hypotonic (B) dialyzed (C) diffused (D) isotonic
   (E) hypertonic

6. Autotrophic organisms
   (A) are saprophytic
   (B) are able to synthesize their own food
   (C) always live on decaying organic matter
   (D) exist as parasites
   (E) ingest complex organic foods

7. Organisms which utilize solid food materials after eating them are referred to as
(A) chemosynthetic (B) holozoic (C) photosynthetic
(D) autophobic (E) autotrophic

8. In 1630, van Helmont concluded that green plants
(A) absorb large quantities of minerals from the soil
(B) absorb mainly water from the soil
(C) synthesize their organic materials by photosynthesis
(D) release energy in respiration
(E) use carbon dioxide as the chief source of plant materials

9. Photosynthesis
(A) consumes oxygen and organic materials such as glucose
(B) occurs only in cells containing chlorophyll
(C) gives off carbon dioxide and water
(D) releases energy
(E) occurs in all living cells

10. Cellular respiration
(A) stores energy
(B) increases dry weight
(C) occurs only in plant cells containing chlorophyll
(D) produces oxygen and organic compounds
(E) releases energy

11. Flowering in plants is influenced by the ratio of daylight hours to hours of darkness, a phenomenon called
(A) phototropism (B) photophosphorylation (C) synergism
(D) parthenocarpy (E) photoperiodism

12. One primary function of the phloem in vascular plants is the
(A) reduction of transpiration
(B) conduction of food materials
(C) support of foliage
(D) absorption of water
(E) conduction of water

13. The physical processes responsible for transpiration are
(A) evaporation and capillarity (B) adhesion and cohesion
(C) diffusion and evaporation (D) capillarity and cohesion
(E) capillarity and diffusion

14. Photoperiodism appears to be influenced by
(A) gibberellin (B) phytochrome (C) kinetin
(D) synergistic responses (E) indoleacetic acid

15. The best adjective to describe the occurrence of bacteria is
(A) terrestrial (B) aquatic (C) aerial (D) universal
(E) glacial

16. During mitosis,
(A) the chromosome number remains the same
(B) the chromosome number becomes polyploid
(C) the chromosome number is reduced
(D) either eggs or sperm are produced
(E) one primary and (usually) two secondary polar bodies are formed

17. Double fertilization
(A) occurs when two sperm cells unite with one egg
(B) occurs when asexual spores fuse in pairs
(C) is found in all plants
(D) is found only in flowering plants
(E) occurs when two eggs fuse with one sperm

18. What most significant event that occurred on earth about three billion years ago made possible the proliferation of life forms on earth?
(A) An increase in temperature
(B) A decrease in temperature
(C) The "invention" of an oxygen-releasing process
(D) The emergence of terrestrial life from the sea
(E) The advent of seasons

19. Since the Neolithic Revolution, humans have
(A) increased their dependence on particular biologic communities
(B) become ecologically dependent
(C) altered many chemical cycles of typical biological communities
(D) shifted from hunting and gathering to more efficient systems of food production
(E) applied scientific methods to agricultural problems

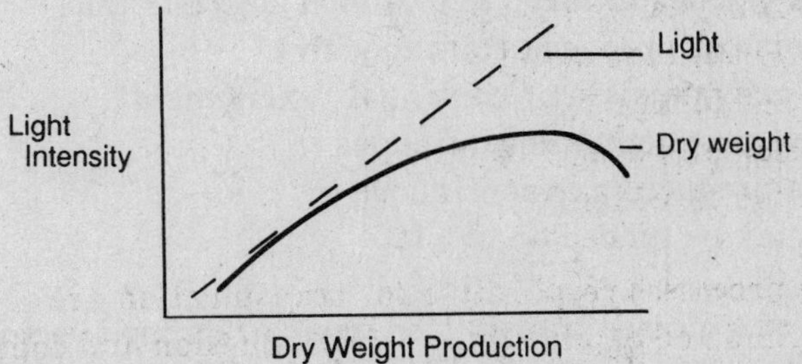

20. The relationship of the intensity of light to the ability of plants to produce dry weight is shown in the graph above. One may infer from the information in the graph that
(A) dry weight production is inversely proportional to light intensity
(B) dry weight production is unlimited in proportion to light intensity
(C) plants grow and produce dry weight best in full sunlight
(D) dry weight production is not affected by light intensity
(E) under natural conditions, plants probably receive greater light intensity than is required for maximum dry weight production

21. Proteins, acting as enzymes, maintain smooth and continuous performance of the numerous chemical activities within living cells and also
    (A) function in intercellular coordination and the conduction of nerve impulses
    (B) serve to maintain a proper osmotic balance in the blood
    (C) act as hydrogen acceptors in respiration
    (D) stimulate the synthesis of thyroxin and other hormones
    (E) function as structural elements in muscle and other tisuses

22. As a result of mitosis,
    (A) each daughter cell receives a randomly selected set of chromosomes
    (B) each daughter cell receives the same kind and number of chromosomes
    (C) four daughter cells are produced
    (D) the chromosome number of the daughter cells is reduced
    (E) the chromosome number remains the same; the number of genes is reduced

23. Experimental evidence obtained in studying crossing-over phenomena indicates that
    (A) the genes of a particular linkage group may lie on two or more chromosomes
    (B) linkage groups are not affected by translocation
    (C) genes are arranged in linear order along chromosomes
    (D) crossing over has no genetic significance
    (E) sex linkage involves the total compliment of chromosomes

24. The proof that the earth is much older than a few thousand years and, therefore, is sufficiently aged to provide time for evolution was demonstrated by
    (A) Lucretius (B) Lyell (C) Thales (D) Wallace (E) Anaximander

25. The "operon" model of Jacob and Monod suggests that
    (A) insulin is not produced continuously
    (B) nerves are in a state of continual "excitement"
    (C) hormone production is continuous
    (D) enzyme production is continuous
    (E) genes may be turned on or off

26. An example of a disease transmitted by an arthropod vector is
    (A) typhoid fever (B) tuberculosis (C) polio
    (D) sleeping sickness (E) smallpox

27. In the ancient world of classical Greek scholars, we find such objective thinkers as Anaximander and Anaximenes, who
    (A) advocated the scientific method
    (B) attempted to explain the physical and living world
    (C) developed medicine and surgery
    (D) produced an encyclopedia
    (E) predicted the existence of atoms

28. Nucleic acids are long-chain molecules made up of substances called
(A) nucleoproteins
(B) cholecystokinin
(C) nucleotides
(D) nucleic bases
(E) polynucleotides

29. You would expect to observe maple trees and black bears in
(A) a tropical rain forest (B) the glasslands
(C) an alpine tundra (D) a deciduous forest
(E) a coniferous forest

30. Bottom-dwelling marine organisms which live along shores in the inter-tidal areas are referred to as inhabiting
(A) the bathyal zone (B) a littoral zone
(C) the brackish zone (D) the neritic zone
(E) the abyssal zone

31. What is one result of photosynthesis in green plants?
(A) The release of molecular oxygen
(B) The release of energy
(C) The production of starch
(D) A decrease in temperature
(E) An increase in temperature

32. Interrelationships between organisms are referred to as mutualism when
(A) one organism benefits and the other is not harmed
(B) territories are defended
(C) both organisms are benefited
(D) mates are defended
(E) one organism benefits at the expense of the other

33. The Archeozoic era is best characterized as an
(A) age of mammals (B) ancient age of unicellular life
(C) age of early land plants (D) age of dinosaurs
(E) age of primitive fishes

34. That gene frequencies remain constant from generation to generation in sexually breeding populations is known as
(A) the principle of selection pressure
(B) convergent evolution
(C) the theory of natural selection
(D) the theory of genetic drift
(E) the Hardy-Weinberg law

35. Blood enters the aorta of the human circulatory system from the
(A) right ventricle (B) superior vena cava (C) left ventricle
(D) inferior vena cava (E) left atrium

36. After drinking contaminated water, you might develop symptoms of
(A) malaria (B) typhoid fever (C) trichinosis
(D) yellow fever (E) schistosomiasis

37. A virus-caused disease which may be prevented by inoculation with a vaccine is
(A) tularemia (B) typhoid fever (C) scarlet fever
(D) septicemia (E) smallpox

38. An energy-storing process occurring in certain kinds of living cells is
(A) respiration (B) phosphorylation (C) oxidation
(D) photosynthesis (E) reduction

39. The shrinkage of the cytoplasm from the cell wall in plant cells subjected to a hypertonic solution is called
(A) plasmolysis (B) turgidity (C) diffusion
(D) secretion (E) osmosis

40. Stringiness in certain otherwise edible plant materials is caused by the
(A) pith (B) cortex (C) vascular bundles (D) endodermis
(E) pericycle

41. Over periods of time, ecosystems undergo patterns of development and change, a process called
(A) mutation (B) succession (C) riffling
(D) inversion (E) foliation

42. Algae are of greatest importance for their role in
(A) feeding mankind directly (B) producing oil deposits
(C) food chains (D) soil building (E) producing oxygen

43. Gamma globulin
(A) contains antibodies (B) is involved with blood clotting
(C) moves by ameboid movement (D) carries on phagocytosis
(E) functions as an anticoagulant

44. An example of an antigen-antibody reaction is
(A) blood clotting (B) anemia (C) phagocytosis
(D) the antihemophilic factor (E) the Rh factor

45. Gregor Mendel
(A) discovered chromosomes and studied the details of mitosis
(B) worked with linkage groups and developed chromosome maps
(C) studied sex-linkage in garden peas
(D) demonstrated that inheritance is governed by laws
(E) was the first to apply the mutation theory of natural selection

46. In the prophase of the first meiotic division
(A) chromatids do not become visible
(B) homologous chromosomes pair in synapsis
(C) the centromeres have already divided
(D) chromosomes remain long and twisted
(E) the chromosome number is haploid

47. Among Aristotle's many contributions was a philosophical treatise concerning
(A) evolution (B) abiogenesis (C) recapitulation
(D) genetics (E) relativity

48. On the basis of evolution and population genetics, each population is characterized by
(A) polyploidy (B) orthogenesis (C) a gene pool
(D) balanced polymorphism (E) translocation

49. Abrupt and unexpected changes in inheritance patterns which seem to have no intermediate forms are called.
(A) chromosonal aberrations (B) variations (C) deletions
(D) mutations (E) hybridizations

50. Francesco Redi appears to have been the first to challenge and disprove the concept of
(A) epigenesis (B) biogenesis (C) spontaneous generation
(D) preformation (E) pangenesis

51. Binomial nomenclature was the basis of the system of classification proposed by
(A) Darwin (B) Cuvier (C) von Linnaeus (D) Lamarck
(E) Dioscorides

52. In genetics, the concept that genes which control two or more pairs of contrasting characteristics are segregated to the gametes independently of each other, and that these gametes then are free to combine randomly at the time of fertilization, is called the
(A) Law of Segregation (B) Law of Dominance
(C) Law of Hybridization (D) Law of Natural Selection
(E) Law of Independent Assortment

53. Proprioceptive senses are concerned with
(A) the repetitive motion that leads to motion sickness
(B) complete relaxation of skeletal muscle
(C) informing the central nervous system of what muscles are doing
(D) maintaining rythmic and uniform heartbeat (E) awareness and the thought process

54. Fungi are of importance to humans for all of the following reasons *except*
(A) they are important decomposers (B) they cause many plant diseases
(C) they may cause diseases of humans and domestic animals
(D) they are important sources of carbohydrates
(E) they produce a variety of antibiotics

Directions: Each group of questions below consists of five lettered choices followed by a list of numbered phrases or sentences. For each numbered phrase or sentence select the one choice that is most closely related to it. Each choice may be used once, more than once, or not at all in each group.

Questions 55–57

(A) Amylase
(B) Lipase
(C) Pepsin
(D) Ribonuclease
(E) Sucrase

55. Breaks bonds between specific amino acids of protein chains

56. Hydrolyzes proteins producing peptid molecules

57. Is involved in the breakdown of disaccharides

Questions 58–60

(A) Adrenalin
(B) Auxin
(C) Colchicine
(D) Thyrotropin
(E) Vassopressin

58. Stimulates secretion of thyroid hormones

59. Causes an increase in blood pressure

60. Causes irritability if hypersecretion occurs

Section II Physical Sciences

Number of Questions: 60
Time: 45 minutes

Directions: Each of the questions or incomplete statements below is followed by five suggested answers or completions. Select the one that is best in each case.

1. Orbital velocities of earth satellites are dependent upon the
   (A) weight of the satellite (B) direction of orbit
   (C) distance from the earth (D) inertia of the satellite
   (E) moon's gravity

2. If you were standing on the equator, as a result of the earth's rotation you would be
   (A) moving westward at about 1,000 mph
   (B) moving eastward at about 1,000 mph
   (C) moving westward at less than 700 mph
   (D) moving eastward at less than 700 mph
   (E) stationary

3. Star temperatures are reliably indicated by color. Which of the following would be the coolest?
   (A) A red star (B) An orange star (C) A yellow star
   (D) A white star (E) A blue-white star

4. An equinox occurs when the
   (A) sun is highest in the sky (B) sun crosses the equator
   (C) sun is lowest in the sky (D) earth and sun are in line
   (E) earth is central in the solar system

5. One of the small number of very large, reddish stars with a diameter of more than 100 times that of the sun would be a
   (A) giant star (B) supergiant star (C) binary star
   (D) nova (E) supernova

6. During a lunar eclipse,
   (A) the earth's shadow is cast on the moon
   (B) the earth's shadow falls on the sun
   (C) the moon's shadow falls on the sun
   (D) the moon comes between the earth and the sun
   (E) the moon's shadow is cast on the earth

7. Wind circulation around a low pressure area is counterclockwise in the northern hemisphere due to
   (A) the revolution of the earth around the sun
   (B) the spheroidal shape of the earth
   (C) the rotation of the earth
   (D) the tidal effects caused by lunar gravity
   (E) the tilting of the earth's axis

8. Igneous or sedimentary rocks which are changed to new forms as the result of interaction with their environment are called
   (A) pyroclastic rocks (B) metamorphic rocks
   (C) batholithic rocks (D) concordant batholiths
   (E) xenolithic rocks

9. Rocks formed by the cooling and solidifying of molten materials are classed as
   (A) igneous rocks (B) metamorphic rocks
   (C) sedimentary rocks (D) monomineralic rocks
   (E) organic limestone

10. Water vapor in the atmosphere
    (A) is the source of all condensation and precipitation
    (B) may vary in concentration from 0.01 to over 12 per cent
    (C) has no effect on air temperature
    (D) has no effect on body temperature
    (E) neither reflects nor scatters solar radiation

11. Study of the moon samples brought back to earth by returning Apollo astronauts reveals that
    (A) organic matter is abundant
    (B) moon rocks have mineral compositions similar to those of igneous rocks on earth
    (C) the age of the moon cannot be more than 1.6 million years
    (D) the moon is 913 million years old
    (E) moon rocks have mineral compositions that are totally different from those of any rocks on earth

12. Einstein's theory of relativity resulted in the thought that mass
    (A) is a distinct and completely independent entity
    (B) remains indestructible
    (C) is another form of energy
    (D) is constant throughout the universe
    (E) is measurable only according to the force necessary to accelerate it

13. Parallel light rays are made convergent by
    (A) monochromatic light (B) an achromatic lens
    (C) a convex lens (D) a concave lens (E) a plano-convex lens

14. The amount of energy in sound wave is known as its
    (A) loudness (B) tempo (C) rhythm (D) amplitude
    (E) intensity

15. That property of water which permits a needle to float and not sink is
    (A) viscosity
    (B) fluidity
    (C) diffusion
    (D) surface tension
    (E) sublimation

16. Polarized light is
    (A) light without shadows (B) incident light
    (C) light that vibrates in one plane only (D) light of low intensity
    (E) light from a "Polaroid" source

17. Early in the era of atomic physics, radioactivity was discovered by
    (A) Bohr (B) Faraday (C) Fermi
    (D) Becquerel (E) Planck

18. When light passes from one medium to another, its direction may be changed, a phenomenon called
    (A) diffusion (B) diffraction (C) refraction
    (D) reflection (E) absorption

19. Air temperature is directly affected by the absorption of large amounts of solar and terrestrial radiation by atmospheric
    (A) dust particles (B) nitrogen (C) water vapor
    (D) oxygen (E) nitrogen and oxygen

20. According to the Bernoullian Principle, as velocity increases
    (A) the pressure increases proportionally (B) mass increases
    (C) mass decreases (D) thrust remains constant
    (E) pressure decreases

21. Interference may result in
    (A) sound waves reinforcing each other
    (B) sound waves compressing each other
    (C) the bending of sound waves
    (D) a decrease in amplitude
    (E) an increase in amplitude

22. In reference to electrical circuitry, the volt represents
    (A) a measure of potential
    (B) the flow of coulombs
    (C) a force between two electrical fields
    (D) the unit of current
    (E) the unit of resistance

23. A lever with a great mechanical advantage for gaining force would have a
    (A) terminal fulcrum
    (B) long force arm and short weight arm
    (C) long force arm and long weight arm
    (D) short force arm and short weight arm
    (E) short force arm and long weight arm

24. Heat transfer is accomplished by convection, radiation, and
    (A) oxidation (B) reduction (C) vaporization
    (D) expansion (E) conduction

25. According to the quantum theory, what is the first step in photosynthesis by green plants?
(A) The change of light energy to chemical energy
(B) The change to longer wavelengths of light
(C) The absorption of photons of light by chlorophyll
(D) The change of light energy to matter
(E) The release of molecular oxygen

26. That property of matter which tends to maintain the uniform movement of a moving body is called
(A) force (B) acceleration (C) velocity (D) deceleration
(E) inertia

27. Which of the following tends to change the state of motion of a body?
(A) Acceleration (B) Equilibrium (C) Velocity
(D) Mass (E) Force

28. An alarming feature of nuclear reactions compared to conventional chemical explosions is their emission of
(A) X-rays (B) fissionable plutonium (C) gamma rays
(D) electrons (E) protons

29. Alternating current is primarily identified by
(A) reversal of direction of flow at regular intervals
(B) reversal of direction of flow at random or chance intervals
(C) a change of magnetic flux
(D) regular fluctuation
(E) its electromagnetic induction

30. The physical damage in a nuclear explosion is caused by
(A) heat and pressure (B) X-rays (C) gamma radiation
(D) intense light (E) radioactive fallout

31. In relation to mass and weight,
(A) weight varies from place to place in the universe
(B) mass varies from place to place in the universe
(C) both weight and mass vary from place to place in the universe
(D) both weight and mass remain constant throughout the universe
(E) weight and mass are affected only by speed

32. Different kinds of atoms may be distinguished from one another by
(A) weighing equal masses and comparing their weights
(B) weighing equal volumes and comparing their weights
(C) determining the sums of the protons and neutrons in their nuclei
(D) determining the number of orbital electrons for each
(E) determining their comparative rates of electron transfer

33. The spreading out of molecules free to do so is called
(A) transpiration (B) transportation (C) diffusion
(D) capillarity (E) osmosis

34. The energy exerted by a golf club as it strikes the ball is
(A) mass energy (B) inertia (C) transferred energy
(D) kinetic energy (E) potential energy

35. The unit of electricity upon which our electric bills are based is the
(A) ampere (B) volt (C) millivolt (D) ohm
(E) kilowatt-hour

36. The name of the process which utilizes an electric current to decompose chemical compounds is
(A) electrophoresis (B) electrolysis (C) electromagnetism
(D) electrotherapy (E) electrodynamics

37. The "venturi effect" in a carburetor is an application of
(A) Avogadro's law (B) Archimedes' principle
(C) Bernoulli's principle (D) Pascal's law
(E) Boyle's law

38. When the positive ions from a base combine with the negative ions from an acid, the resulting substance is called
(A) a buffer (B) a salt (C) a mole (D) an alkane
(E) an ester

39. Forces which hold chemically united atoms together are called
(A) ions (B) chemical bonds (C) magnetism
(D) atomic numbers (E) isotopes

40. Chemical reactions in which oxygen combines with other substances are called
(A) enzymatic reactions (B) catalytic reactions
(C) dephlogistication reactions (D) reduction reactions
(E) oxidation reactions

41. The connecting substance between the amino acids in all proteins is called
(A) a polymer (B) a carboxyl group (C) a fatty acid
(D) the peptide linkage (E) an alkyl group

42. A basic characteristic common to all chemical changes is that
(A) the reactants are stable and persistent
(B) energy is neither released nor absorbed
(C) the initial reactants become parts of the products
(D) the properties of the products are identical to those of the reactants
(E) total mass either increases or decreases

43. In a fundamental sense, chemical reactions are concerned with
(A) periodicity (B) potential energy (C) nuclear energy
(D) interatomic bonds (E) ionic conductivity

44. The major scientific philosopher of the middle ages was Roger Bacon, who
(A) stressed abstract reasoning
(B) accepted reasoning and logic alone as justification for science
(C) advocated deductive instead of inductive reasoning
(D) invented the calendar
(E) advanced mathematics and the experimental method

45. The chemical reaction resulting when an acid solution is combined with a basic solution is called
(A) transformation (B) conservation (C) neutralization
(D) reversal (E) phlogiston

46. The pitch of vibrating musical strings is
(A) directly proportional to the rate of vibration
(B) directly proportional to the length
(C) inversely proportional to the tension
(D) inversely proportional to the rate of vibration
(E) directly proportional to linear density

47. Distinction between colloids, solutions and suspensions is based primarily on
(A) fluidity
(B) saturation
(C) emulsification
(D) particle size
(E) solubility

48. An induction coil will
(A) change alternating to direct current
(B) change direct to alternating current
(C) increase the voltage of an alternating current
(D) increase the voltage of a direct current
(E) decrease the voltage of an alternating current

49. According to the law of conservation of energy, in all energy transformations
(A) the latent heat of vaporization is lost energy
(B) the latent heat of fusion is lost energy
(C) heat energy flows from lower to higher temperature
(D) there is no gain or loss of energy
(E) a certain amount of energy is destroyed

50. In 420 B.C., Democritus introduced the "one-element" theory of matter, which proposed that the indestructable particles of which everything is made should be called
(A) ions (B) atoms (C) electrons
(D) protons (E) molecules

51. The problem of transmitting high-frequency television signals over great distances has been solved by the
(A) coaxial cable
(B) kinescope tube
(C) tuning coil
(D) phototube
(E) iconoscope tube

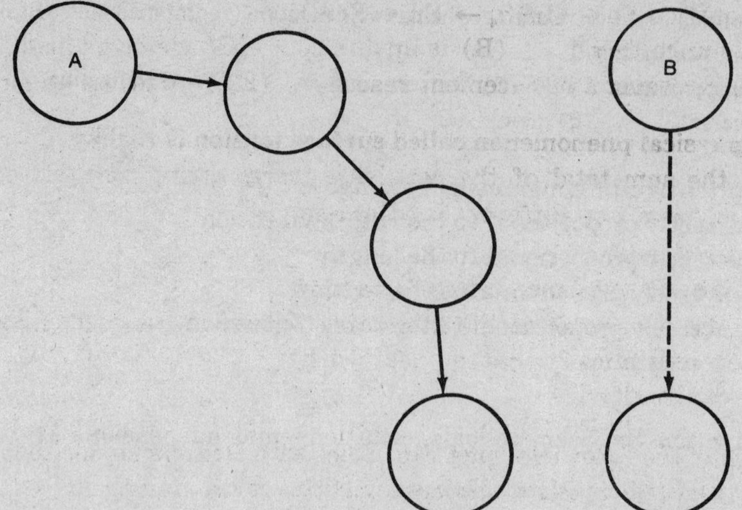

Illustrated above are two falling balls. Ball A is also moving horizontally. The balls are of equal weight.

52. The balls strike the bottom simultaneously because
(A) ball A's speed increases to make up the difference
(B) the horizontal motion of ball A increases the force of gravity
(C) gravity alone is acting on ball B
(D) horizontal motion does not affect the speed of the fall of ball A
(E) the horizontal motion of ball A decreases the force of gravity

53. The velocity of a falling object at the end of the second second of fall would be
(A) about 16 feet per second
(B) about 32 feet per second
(C) about 48 feet per second
(D) about 64 feet per second
(E) about 1036 feet per second

54. Ion rockets are the theoretical future choice for insterstellar space travel because
(A) they are more economical
(B) they are simpler to operate
(C) their fuels add less mass to the rocket
(D) traditional chemical fuels produce insufficient thrust
(E) traditional chemical fuels produce excessive thrust

55. Water rises inside the small-diametered glass tube due to forces called
(A) osmosis (B) gravity
(C) diffusion (D) capillarity
(E) suction

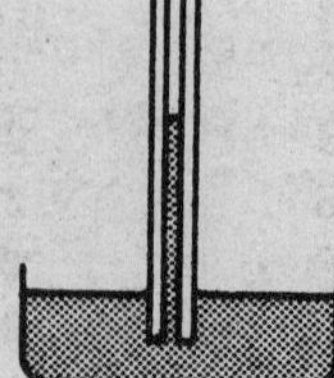

56. The equation Fe + $CuSO_4 \rightarrow$ Cu + $FeSO_4$
(A) is unbalanced (B) is unstable (C) yields an acid
(D) represents a replacement reaction (E) represents an explosion

57. The physical phenomenon called surface tension is really
(A) the sum total of the repulsive forces acting between the molecules of two different substances
(B) an illusion
(C) the result of membrane formation
(D) the sum total of the attractive forces between the molecules of a substance
(E) capillarity

58. Which of the following is not consistent with Dalton's atomic theory?
(A) All matter consists of minute particles called atoms.
(B) Atoms of a given element vary in both weight and electrical charge.
(C) Atoms are neither created nor destroyed in chemical reactions.
(D) Atoms of different elements are of different weights.
(E) Typically, atoms combine in small numbers to form chemical compounds.

59. In forming chemical compounds,
(A) all electrons may be involved
(B) the electrons involved may be from any orbit
(C) the electrons involved are in the outermost orbit only
(D) electrons from inner shells are exceedingly active
(E) electrons may not be shared

60. The two atoms of a sodium chloride (NaCl) molecule are held together by
(A) dissociation (B) an increase in positive valence
(C) the electrical attraction of ions of opposite charges
(D) a decrease in positive valence (E) entropy

ANSWER KEY—SAMPLE EXAMINATION 3

Section I Biological Sciences

1. D	13. C	25. E	37. E	49. D
2. B	14. B	26. D	38. D	50. C
3. A	15. D	27. B	39. A	51. C
4. D	16. A	28. C	40. C	52. E
5. D	17. D	29. D	41. B	53. C
6. B	18. C	30. B	42. C	54. D
7. B	19. D	31. A	43. A	55. C
8. B	20. E	32. C	44. E	56. C
9. B	21. E	33. B	45. D	57. E
10. E	22. B	34. E	46. B	58. D
11. E	23. C	35. C	47. A	59. E
12. B	24. B	36. B	48. C	60. A

Section II Physical Sciences

1. C	13. C	25. C	37. C	49. D
2. B	14. E	26. E	38. B	50. B
3. A	15. D	27. E	39. B	51. A
4. B	16. C	28. C	40. E	52. D
5. B	17. D	29. A	41. D	53. D
6. A	18. C	30. A	42. C	54. C
7. C	19. C	31. A	43. D	55. D
8. B	20. E	32. C	44. E	56. D
9. A	21. A	33. C	45. C	57. D
10. A	22. A	34. D	46. A	58. B
11. B	23. B	35. E	47. D	59. C
12. C	24. E	36. B	48. B	60. C

SCORING CHART—SAMPLE EXAMINATION 3

After you have score your Sample Examination 3, enter the results in the chart below; then transfer your Raw Score to the Progress Chart on page 14.

Total Test	Number Right	Number Wrong	Number Omitted	Raw Score
Section I: 60				
Section II: 60				
Total: 120				

ANSWER EXPLANATIONS—SAMPLE EXAMINATION 3

Section I Biological Sciences

1. D. An organism that exhibits bilateral symmetry has a right and a left side and a front and a back.
2. B. All molecules tend to remain in continuous motion. When water evaporates, some of its faster moving molecules break through the surface layer of molecules and escape into the air. Thus, the basic activity of evaporation is simple diffusion.
3. A. Recent research demonstrates that heated circulating mixtures of water, methane, ammonia, and hydrogen produce amino acids and other organic molecules when passed over two electrodes between which a spark is continually passing.
4. D. Aerobic respiration is a series of chemical processes consisting of two groups of reactions; the first is anaerobic; the second aerobic. Glycolysis is the name given to the anaerobic group of reactions, in which simple sugars are changed into pyruvic acid.
5. D. In an isotonic solution, the osmotic pressure is equal to that of the solution being compared.
6. B. Autotrophic organisms are capable of synthesizing their own food from inorganic substances.
7. B. Holozoic organisms ingest and utilize solid particles of food.

8. B. In experiments with plants growing in containers, van Helmont concluded that plants absorb mainly water from the soil. Increases in dry weight, therefore, were attributed to the production of foods by photosynthesis.

9. B. The presence of chlorophyll is a requirement for photosynthesis since it acts both to absorb radiant energy and as a catalyst for certain of the photosynthetic reactions.

10. E. Cellular respiration is a complex biochemical reaction in which foods (usually glucose) are broken down and their stored energy released.

11. E. Flower initiation appears to be controlled, at least in part, by the number of daylight hours to which plants are exposed. Long-day plants require more than 14 hours of daylight to flower, while short-day plants require less. Still other plants are indeterminate insofar as light requirements are concerned.

12. B. The basic function of phloem tissue in plants is the conduction of food materials.

13. C. Transpiration is defined as the evaporation of water from the aerial parts of plants. Evaporation is basically a simple diffusion phenomenon.

14. B. Photoperiodism in plants is only partially understood, but a pigment called phytochrome seems to be related to the responses of plants to light and darkness.

15. D. Bacteria are universal. They are found in the soil, within and on living organisms, from the bottom of the deepest ocean trenches to the tops of snow-covered mountains, to the polar ice caps, in hot springs, etc.

16. A. Mitosis is both a qualitative and quantitative division of chromatin materials and the resulting chromosome number remains unchanged.

17. D. In double fertilization, typically one sperm nucleus fuses with the egg nucleus and the second sperm nucleus fuses with the endosperm nucleus. This occurs only in flowering plants.

18. C. Initially, the earth's atmosphere was dominated by carbon dioxide. About three billion years ago, certain primitive bacterial forms evolved a type of photosynthesis that released oxygen as a by-product. This enabled life to exist in sunlight, and to proliferate.

19. D. Since the Neolithic Revolution, humans have gradually decreased their dependence on particular biological communities while increasing their ability to replace them with more efficient systems of food production.

20. E. Natural phenomena, such as dry weight production in plants, are controlled by various limiting factors. In this instance, greater light intensity is available, but dry weight production tapers off at a certain intensity of light, indicating that some other factor, possibly temperature or the availability of carbon dioxide, is the limiting factor.

21. E. As elements of structure, proteins function in muscle fibers and supporting tissues, as well as in nails, hair, and skin.

22. B. As a result of mitosis, chromatin materials are qualitatively distributed to the two daughter cells, each of which receives a duplicate of every chromosome.

23. C. Studies involving crossing-over phenomena support the concept that genes are arranged in linear order along chromosomes.

24. B. Lyell's writings support the doctrine of uniformitarianism, the concept that the events in the geologic history of the earth were the product of the same natural forces that are active today—erosion, sedimentation, etc. Lyell's efforts established the foundation for Darwin's theory of Natural Selection.

25. E. The Jacob-Monod hypothesis suggests that the interrelated actions of inducer, repressor, and corepressor molecules control the function of genes. When an inducer molecule is present, the repressor is unable to attach itself, the gene functions, and synthesis takes place. When a corepressor molecule is present, the operon is shut down. In short, it appears that gene action may be turned on or off.

26. D. Sleeping sickness is caused by a trypanosome that is transmitted by the bite of the tsetse fly, an arthropod. The tsetse fly is, therefore, the vector of sleeping sickness.

27. B. Anaximander and Anaximenes attempted to explain the physical phenomena of the universe, including the atmosphere, water, and spontaneous generation of life.
28. C. Nucleic acids consist of long chains of units called nucleotides, each of which consists of a five-carbon sugar, a phosphate group, and one of five nitrogen-containing bases.
29. D. Deciduous trees, including maple, beech, oak and hickory, and such dominant animals as black bears are the primary organisms in the deciduous or temperate forest.
30. B. Littoral species are those living along shorelines between high and low tide marks.
31. A. Photosynthesis is a biochemical process that is carried on by plant cells containing chlorophyll pigments and results in the storage of energy and the release of molecular oxygen.
32. C. Mutualism is an interrelationship between the individuals of two different species in which both are benefited.
33. B. The Archeozoic era is the age during which it is presumed life emerged on earth. It is thought of as the time when only primitive, unicellular life existed.
34. E. Genes generally are not lost from populations. The Hardy-Weinberg law states that, when there is a reservoir of gene variability and no mutations occur, gene frequencies in a sexually breeding population remain constant.
35. C. The left ventricle of the human heart pumps blood into the aorta, which distributes it to arteries that carry it to all parts of the body.
36. B. Typhoid fever is basically a disease of the digestive tract. Sewage-contaminated drinking water is presumed to contain the typhoid bacillus.
37. E. A vaccine is an attenuated form of the causative agent of disease, which, while being incapable of causing the disease, does retain its ability to cause the body to produce antibodies.
38. D. Photosynthesis results in the energy of sunlight being absorbed, converted and stored as the energy of chemical bonds in glucose molecules.
39. A. Plasmolysis is that condition of a plant cell whereby the cytoplasm shrinks away from the cell wall due to a loss of water by the cell. The basic cause of plasmolysis is the fact that a cell is immersed in a hypertonic solution which causes water to diffuse out of the cell.
40. C. Stringiness in certain otherwise edible plant material—green beans, for example—is due to the development of fiber cells and the thickening of cell walls by cells of the xylem and phloem which make up the vascular bundles.
41. B. Ecological succession is the succession of both plants and animal species in a given region which is brought about by species-induced environmental changes.
42. C. Algae are of importance to humans and other parts of the biotic world in many ways, chief among them their role in food chains.
43. A. Gamma globulin is a fraction of the globulin of blood serum with which antibodies are associated.
44. E. The Rh factor is an agglutinogen found in the blood of about 85 percent of Caucasians. The Rh factor is an antigen, stimulating the body to produce antibodies against the Rh factor. It is a concern in both blood transfusions and during pregnancy.
45. D. Gregor Mendel is recognized as the "father of genetics" because his research was the first to demonstrate that inheritance is governed by laws.
46. B. Synapsis is a stage in the first meiotic division in which the homologous chromosomes of each pair come to lie side by side. Since each chromosome at this point consists of two chromatids, it is common to refer to the paired, homologous chromosomes as a tetrad of chromatids.
47. A. While Aristotle recognized no formal system of classification for animals or plants, he did conceive an evolutionary concept to explain their origin.
48. C. A gene pool is the total number of genes in a population.
49. D. A mutation is an unexpected and abrupt heritable change in the offspring of an individual resulting from an alteration of a gene or chromosome or a change in chromosome number.

50. C. Redi was one of the first scientists to question the spontaneous origin of living things. He was able to demonstrate conclusively that flies do not develop spontaneously from putrefying meat, but rather that they come from other flies by means of their eggs.

51. C. Carl von Linnaeus introduced the concept of binomial nomenclature, i.e., the system of naming organisms by giving each species a binomial name, the genus name followed by the species name.

52. E. According to the Law of Independent Assortment, genes that control two or more pairs of contrasting characteristics segregate independently to the gametes, and, subsequently, these gametes combine in fertilization at random.

53. C. Proprioceptive senses inform us about the position of our bodies in relation to the environment that surrounds us by telling us what our muscles are doing.

54. D. Fungi (mushrooms) are of little nutritional value although they may supply certain minerals.

55. C. }
56. C. } In the digestion of proteins, pepsin breaks amino acid bonds in protein chains. Pepsin also hydrolyzes protein.

57. E. In the digestion of carbohydrates, the enzyme sucrase is involved with disaccharide breakdown and digestion.

58. D. Thyrotropin is a hormone secreted by the anterior lobe of the pituitary that controls the secretion of thyroxin.

59. E. Vasopressin is a hormone that causes the muscular walls of the arteries and arterioles to contract. This decreases the diameter of these blood vessels and causes the blood pressure to increase.

60. A. Adrenalin, or epinephrin, is produced by the adrenal medulla. In situations where there is hypersecretion, irritability may result.

Section II Physical Sciences

1. C. Orbital velocity for a spacecraft is dependent upon the spacecraft's distance from the earth since the orbital velocity must overcome the earth's gravity.

2. B. The earth's rotation is in an easterly direction. Since the earth is approximately 25,000 miles in circumference and since it completes one rotation per 24 hour period, a person standing on the equator is moving eastward at about 1,000 mph.

3. A. The colors of stars range from red, the coolest, through orange, yellow, and white to blue, the hottest.

4. B. An equinox occurs at a time when the vertical rays of the sun strike the equator.

5. B. Betelgeuse, a bright red supergiant star, has a radius about 800 times that of the sun. If this star were the center of the solar system, it would reach beyond the orbit of Mars.

6. A. A lunar eclipse occurs when the moon crosses through the earth's shadow.

7. C. Due to the rotation of the earth, the Coriolis force causes winds in the northern hemisphere to be deflected to the right or to rotate clockwise. Winds in the southern hemisphere are deflected to the right also, and therefore, rotate counterclockwise.

8. B. Rocks which have been changed either in physical structure or in chemical composition while in a solid state as a result of the action of heat, pressure, shearing stress, or the infusion of elements, all at great depths, are named metamorphic rocks.

9. A. Rocks solidified from a high-temperature molten state or by the cooling of magma are named igneous rock.

10. A. Whether moisture in the atmosphere condenses on soil or plants directly or whether atmospheric moisture forms droplets while still in the atmosphere as a result of rapid condensation and coalescence which then falls as rain, it is the atmospheric moisture which is the source of the water vapor.

11. B. Chemical analysis of moon rocks revealed that their mineral composition is similar to that of igneous rocks on earth.
12. C. According to the theory of relativity, mass and energy are different forms of the same phenomenon. When hydrogen is converted to helium in a nuclear fusion reaction, about 1 percent of the mass of the hydrogen is converted to energy.
13. C. When parallel light rays pass through a convex lens, they bend inward so that they converge at a point on the other side.
14. E. The intensity of sound is the amount of energy in the sound waves.
15. D. Surface tension is that property of a liquid caused by cohesive forces attracting adjacent molecules of the liquid to each other.
16. C. Polarized light consists of light waves having a simple orderly arrangement that vibrates in one plane or direction only.
17. D. In 1896, the French physicist Becquerel discovered that uranium emits energy in the form of radiation and this emission has come to be called radioactivity.
18. C. Refraction is the bending of a wave when it moves from one medium to another and strikes the second at an angle—for example, the apparent bending of a partially immersed boat oar.
19. C. Water vapor in the atmosphere plays a major role in absorbing heat energy. When water vapor is lacking, air warms rapidly and a high daily temperature results.
20. E. According to the Bernoullian Principle, as a fluid passes through a constriction in a pipe, it speeds up and its pressure decreases.
21. A. If two waves reach a point in space simultaneously, they combine in a process called interference. If the two waves are of the same frequency and shape, and if they meet crest to crest and trough to trough, they will combine and their amplitude will be increased.
22. A. The energy in an electrical circuit is proportional to the electrical potential (volts) × the amount of charge (coulombs).
23. B. Levers work according to the formula: effort times the length of the effort arm (distance from the fulcrum) equals the weight times the length of the weight arm (distance from the fulcrum). A longer effort or force arm or a shorter weight arm will increase mechanical advantage.
24. E. Heat is transferred from one body to another by conduction, convection and radiation.
25. C. The quantum theory considers light to be composed of minute particles called photons or quanta. The absorption of photons of light energy by chlorophyll, therefore, is the first step in photosynthesis.
26. E. According to the concept of inertia, a moving body tends to remain in motion and a resting body tends to remain at rest.
27. E. Force is defined as any influence that causes a body to accelerate.
28. C. The alarming feature in connection with gamma rays is their high energies, high frequencies and short wavelengths.
29. A. Alternating current is an electric current that oscillates in a wire (reverses its direction of flow at regular intervals).
30. A. The physical damage caused by a nuclear explosion is similar to that caused by any other explosion and is due to heat and pressure.
31. A. Mass remains the same throughout the universe, but weight varies from place to place in the universe since it is dependent on gravity.
32. C. An atom may be identified by its atomic number (the number of protons in the atomic nucleus), by its mass number (the sum of the protons and neutrons in the atomic nucleus), and by its atomic mass (weight).
33. C. Diffusion is the tendency of the molecules of a substance to spread out throughout all available space and this is accomplished because all molecules tend to remain in a state of constant motion due to their own inherent energies.
34. D. Kinetic energy is the energy possessed by a moving object.
35. E. The kilowatt-hour is the unit of electricity upon which our electric bills are based.

36. B. Electrolysis is a process whereby an electric current, driven by an external electrical source, brings about chemical change.

37. C. According to Bernoulli's Principle, as the speed of a fluid passing through a constriction increases, the pressure decreases. In a carburetor, this results in the metering of gasoline to the engine.

38. B. In a general sense, a salt is produced when an acid and a base react.

39. B. Chemical bonds are linkages that hold atoms together to form molecules; for example, in a covalent bond, two atoms share electrons.

40. E. Oxidation reactions are chemical reactions in which oxygen combines with other substances. In a more general sense, oxidation is the loss of electrons.

41. D. The peptide linkage is one in which the amino group of one amino acid molecule is united with the carboxyl group of other amino acid molecules.

42. C. In chemical reactions, the initial reactants disappear or are changed to become parts of the products.

43. D. Chemical reactions are concerned with the bonds between atoms in chemical compounds.

44. E. Roger Bacon's major interests were in the physical sciences and he is best remembered for his contributions to mathematics and the development of the scientific method.

45. C. When a solution of an acid is mixed with a solution of a base, neutralization occurs and the end products of the reaction have none of the acid or base properties.

46. A. Pitch is measured by the rate at which an object vibrates. Frequency is the number of vibrations of the object per second.

47. D. When finely divided mud particles are dispersed in water, they eventually settle out because they are much larger than molecules. The dispersed particles of a solution are molecules—sugar dissolved in water, for example. Between these two is the situation in which the dispersed particles are larger than molecules but not so large as to settle out. The latter is the realm of the colloid.

48. B. An induction coil is a coil of wire used to produce alternating current of high voltage by the rapid interruption of a direct current.

49. D. The law of conservation of energy holds that energy may be neither created nor destroyed. Energy may be lost through friction, heat, escape, etc.

50. B. The greatest contribution of Democritus was his atomic theory, which held that the universe is made of atoms and that all physical changes are due to the union and separation of atoms.

51. A. The coaxial cable is a special type of long distance telephone cable used to transmit telephone calls and television programs over long distances.

52. D. Falling bodies are not affected by horizontal motion when their fall is caused by gravity.

53. D. A falling body accelerates at a rate expressed as 32.16 feet per second per second.

54. C. The percentage of total weight of a space vehicle that is occupied by fuel is a major problem. Fuels for ion rockets add much less weight to the rocket.

55. D. The tendency of liquids to rise in small tubes is a phenomenon called capillarity. It is dependent upon the surface tension of the liquid and the diameter of the tube.

56. D. In a replacement type chemical reaction, one element is exchanged or substituted for another.

57. D. Liquids tend to occupy the smallest volume possible by reducing their surface areas to a minimum, the result of the intermolecular forces that exist between the molecules of the liquid at its surface.

58. B. The atoms of an element do not vary in weight or electrical charge.

59. C. The electrons involved in the bonding of the atoms of a chemical compound are those in the outer orbit only.

60. C. The ionic bond is a chemical bond formed by the attraction between oppositely charged ions. In this example, there is attraction between the positively charged sodium (Na^+) ion and negatively charged Cl^- ion.

PART FIVE

THE SOCIAL SCIENCES–HISTORY EXAMINATION

ANSWER SHEET — SOCIAL SCIENCES-HISTORY/TRIAL TEST

Section I

1. Ⓐ Ⓑ Ⓒ Ⓓ Ⓔ
2. Ⓐ Ⓑ Ⓒ Ⓓ Ⓔ
3. Ⓐ Ⓑ Ⓒ Ⓓ Ⓔ
4. Ⓐ Ⓑ Ⓒ Ⓓ Ⓔ
5. Ⓐ Ⓑ Ⓒ Ⓓ Ⓔ
6. Ⓐ Ⓑ Ⓒ Ⓓ Ⓔ
7. Ⓐ Ⓑ Ⓒ Ⓓ Ⓔ
8. Ⓐ Ⓑ Ⓒ Ⓓ Ⓔ
9. Ⓐ Ⓑ Ⓒ Ⓓ Ⓔ
10. Ⓐ Ⓑ Ⓒ Ⓓ Ⓔ
11. Ⓐ Ⓑ Ⓒ Ⓓ Ⓔ
12. Ⓐ Ⓑ Ⓒ Ⓓ Ⓔ
13. Ⓐ Ⓑ Ⓒ Ⓓ Ⓔ
14. Ⓐ Ⓑ Ⓒ Ⓓ Ⓔ
15. Ⓐ Ⓑ Ⓒ Ⓓ Ⓔ
16. Ⓐ Ⓑ Ⓒ Ⓓ Ⓔ
17. Ⓐ Ⓑ Ⓒ Ⓓ Ⓔ
18. Ⓐ Ⓑ Ⓒ Ⓓ Ⓔ
19. Ⓐ Ⓑ Ⓒ Ⓓ Ⓔ
20. Ⓐ Ⓑ Ⓒ Ⓓ Ⓔ
21. Ⓐ Ⓑ Ⓒ Ⓓ Ⓔ
22. Ⓐ Ⓑ Ⓒ Ⓓ Ⓔ
23. Ⓐ Ⓑ Ⓒ Ⓓ Ⓔ
24. Ⓐ Ⓑ Ⓒ Ⓓ Ⓔ
25. Ⓐ Ⓑ Ⓒ Ⓓ Ⓔ
26. Ⓐ Ⓑ Ⓒ Ⓓ Ⓔ
27. Ⓐ Ⓑ Ⓒ Ⓓ Ⓔ
28. Ⓐ Ⓑ Ⓒ Ⓓ Ⓔ
29. Ⓐ Ⓑ Ⓒ Ⓓ Ⓔ
30. Ⓐ Ⓑ Ⓒ Ⓓ Ⓔ
31. Ⓐ Ⓑ Ⓒ Ⓓ Ⓔ
32. Ⓐ Ⓑ Ⓒ Ⓓ Ⓔ
33. Ⓐ Ⓑ Ⓒ Ⓓ Ⓔ
34. Ⓐ Ⓑ Ⓒ Ⓓ Ⓔ
35. Ⓐ Ⓑ Ⓒ Ⓓ Ⓔ
36. Ⓐ Ⓑ Ⓒ Ⓓ Ⓔ
37. Ⓐ Ⓑ Ⓒ Ⓓ Ⓔ
38. Ⓐ Ⓑ Ⓒ Ⓓ Ⓔ
39. Ⓐ Ⓑ Ⓒ Ⓓ Ⓔ
40. Ⓐ Ⓑ Ⓒ Ⓓ Ⓔ
41. Ⓐ Ⓑ Ⓒ Ⓓ Ⓔ
42. Ⓐ Ⓑ Ⓒ Ⓓ Ⓔ
43. Ⓐ Ⓑ Ⓒ Ⓓ Ⓔ
44. Ⓐ Ⓑ Ⓒ Ⓓ Ⓔ
45. Ⓐ Ⓑ Ⓒ Ⓓ Ⓔ
46. Ⓐ Ⓑ Ⓒ Ⓓ Ⓔ
47. Ⓐ Ⓑ Ⓒ Ⓓ Ⓔ
48. Ⓐ Ⓑ Ⓒ Ⓓ Ⓔ
49. Ⓐ Ⓑ Ⓒ Ⓓ Ⓔ
50. Ⓐ Ⓑ Ⓒ Ⓓ Ⓔ
51. Ⓐ Ⓑ Ⓒ Ⓓ Ⓔ
52. Ⓐ Ⓑ Ⓒ Ⓓ Ⓔ
53. Ⓐ Ⓑ Ⓒ Ⓓ Ⓔ
54. Ⓐ Ⓑ Ⓒ Ⓓ Ⓔ
55. Ⓐ Ⓑ Ⓒ Ⓓ Ⓔ
56. Ⓐ Ⓑ Ⓒ Ⓓ Ⓔ
57. Ⓐ Ⓑ Ⓒ Ⓓ Ⓔ
58. Ⓐ Ⓑ Ⓒ Ⓓ Ⓔ
59. Ⓐ Ⓑ Ⓒ Ⓓ Ⓔ
60. Ⓐ Ⓑ Ⓒ Ⓓ Ⓔ
61. Ⓐ Ⓑ Ⓒ Ⓓ Ⓔ
62. Ⓐ Ⓑ Ⓒ Ⓓ Ⓔ
63. Ⓐ Ⓑ Ⓒ Ⓓ Ⓔ

Section II

64. Ⓐ Ⓑ Ⓒ Ⓓ Ⓔ
65. Ⓐ Ⓑ Ⓒ Ⓓ Ⓔ
66. Ⓐ Ⓑ Ⓒ Ⓓ Ⓔ
67. Ⓐ Ⓑ Ⓒ Ⓓ Ⓔ
68. Ⓐ Ⓑ Ⓒ Ⓓ Ⓔ
69. Ⓐ Ⓑ Ⓒ Ⓓ Ⓔ
70. Ⓐ Ⓑ Ⓒ Ⓓ Ⓔ
71. Ⓐ Ⓑ Ⓒ Ⓓ Ⓔ
72. Ⓐ Ⓑ Ⓒ Ⓓ Ⓔ
73. Ⓐ Ⓑ Ⓒ Ⓓ Ⓔ
74. Ⓐ Ⓑ Ⓒ Ⓓ Ⓔ
75. Ⓐ Ⓑ Ⓒ Ⓓ Ⓔ
76. Ⓐ Ⓑ Ⓒ Ⓓ Ⓔ
77. Ⓐ Ⓑ Ⓒ Ⓓ Ⓔ
78. Ⓐ Ⓑ Ⓒ Ⓓ Ⓔ
79. Ⓐ Ⓑ Ⓒ Ⓓ Ⓔ
80. Ⓐ Ⓑ Ⓒ Ⓓ Ⓔ
81. Ⓐ Ⓑ Ⓒ Ⓓ Ⓔ
82. Ⓐ Ⓑ Ⓒ Ⓓ Ⓔ
83. Ⓐ Ⓑ Ⓒ Ⓓ Ⓔ
84. Ⓐ Ⓑ Ⓒ Ⓓ Ⓔ
85. Ⓐ Ⓑ Ⓒ Ⓓ Ⓔ
86. Ⓐ Ⓑ Ⓒ Ⓓ Ⓔ
87. Ⓐ Ⓑ Ⓒ Ⓓ Ⓔ
88. Ⓐ Ⓑ Ⓒ Ⓓ Ⓔ
89. Ⓐ Ⓑ Ⓒ Ⓓ Ⓔ
90. Ⓐ Ⓑ Ⓒ Ⓓ Ⓔ
91. Ⓐ Ⓑ Ⓒ Ⓓ Ⓔ
92. Ⓐ Ⓑ Ⓒ Ⓓ Ⓔ
93. Ⓐ Ⓑ Ⓒ Ⓓ Ⓔ
94. Ⓐ Ⓑ Ⓒ Ⓓ Ⓔ
95. Ⓐ Ⓑ Ⓒ Ⓓ Ⓔ
96. Ⓐ Ⓑ Ⓒ Ⓓ Ⓔ
97. Ⓐ Ⓑ Ⓒ Ⓓ Ⓔ
98. Ⓐ Ⓑ Ⓒ Ⓓ Ⓔ
99. Ⓐ Ⓑ Ⓒ Ⓓ Ⓔ
100. Ⓐ Ⓑ Ⓒ Ⓓ Ⓔ
101. Ⓐ Ⓑ Ⓒ Ⓓ Ⓔ
102. Ⓐ Ⓑ Ⓒ Ⓓ Ⓔ
103. Ⓐ Ⓑ Ⓒ Ⓓ Ⓔ
104. Ⓐ Ⓑ Ⓒ Ⓓ Ⓔ
105. Ⓐ Ⓑ Ⓒ Ⓓ Ⓔ
106. Ⓐ Ⓑ Ⓒ Ⓓ Ⓔ
107. Ⓐ Ⓑ Ⓒ Ⓓ Ⓔ
108. Ⓐ Ⓑ Ⓒ Ⓓ Ⓔ
109. Ⓐ Ⓑ Ⓒ Ⓓ Ⓔ
110. Ⓐ Ⓑ Ⓒ Ⓓ Ⓔ
111. Ⓐ Ⓑ Ⓒ Ⓓ Ⓔ
112. Ⓐ Ⓑ Ⓒ Ⓓ Ⓔ
113. Ⓐ Ⓑ Ⓒ Ⓓ Ⓔ
114. Ⓐ Ⓑ Ⓒ Ⓓ Ⓔ
115. Ⓐ Ⓑ Ⓒ Ⓓ Ⓔ
116. Ⓐ Ⓑ Ⓒ Ⓓ Ⓔ
117. Ⓐ Ⓑ Ⓒ Ⓓ Ⓔ
118. Ⓐ Ⓑ Ⓒ Ⓓ Ⓔ
119. Ⓐ Ⓑ Ⓒ Ⓓ Ⓔ
120. Ⓐ Ⓑ Ⓒ Ⓓ Ⓔ
121. Ⓐ Ⓑ Ⓒ Ⓓ Ⓔ
122. Ⓐ Ⓑ Ⓒ Ⓓ Ⓔ
123. Ⓐ Ⓑ Ⓒ Ⓓ Ⓔ
124. Ⓐ Ⓑ Ⓒ Ⓓ Ⓔ
125. Ⓐ Ⓑ Ⓒ Ⓓ Ⓔ

CHAPTER

15 Trial Test

Take the trial Social Sciences and History examination in this chapter to learn about the examination and determine how you would do on an actual test. Then review those topics you are weak in and prepare to take the sample examinations given later in this part of the book.

Section I

Number of Questions: 63
Time: 45 minutes

Directions: Each of the questions or incomplete statements below is followed by five suggested answers or completions. Select the one that is best in each case.

1. The distribution of members in the House of Representatives by states is determined on the basis of
   (A) population
   (B) population, but subject to a definite maximum number of members from any one state
   (C) the state as a unit regardless of population
   (D) the number of qualified voters of the state
   (E) the number of people who actually vote

2. In the 19th century, United States Senators were elected by
   (A) popular election
   (B) the state legislatures
   (C) the electoral college
   (D) state conventions
   (E) officials selected from each county in the state

3. "Boswash" is a term which is sometimes applied to the
   (A) Irish washerwomen in Boston
   (B) effort to clean up Boston
   (C) "bosh" that goes on in Washington
   (D) WASPs of Boston
   (E) continuous urban area between Boston and Washington

4. Ten men produce 1,000 bushels of tomatoes on ten acres. If ten additional men are hired, the production on the same acreage rises to 1,700 bushels. This phenomenon relates to which one of the following economic concepts?
   (A) Law of diminishing marginal utility
   (B) Supply and demand
   (C) Marginal propensity to consume
   (D) Gross national product
   (E) Law of diminishing returns

5. To the Marxist, profits are
   (A) essential to the health of any economy
   (B) payments to the businessman for his labor
   (C) transitory and characteristic of only one state of history
   (D) the key to a rising standard of living
   (E) constantly increasing in a capitalist society

6. Which of the following can be used to illustrate the cultural impact of China on Japan?
   I. Social and political status of the Samurai class
   II. The Confucian ethical code
   III. Artistic styles in painting, sculpture and ceramics
   IV. Buddhist religious teaching
   V. Characters used in the written language
   (A) I and II only (B) III, IV, and V only (C) I, II, III, and IV only
   (D) II, III, IV, and V only (E) I, II, III, IV, and V

7. Apes and other primates cannot be taught to use highly complex language because
   (A) they are without the biological apparatus of speech
   (B) they are without the ability to learn from communications directed toward them
   (C) they have little mental ability to store or transmit highly abstract ideas
   (D) all of the above
   (E) none of the above

8. The culture concept in social science implies that
   (A) the biological evolution of man is the most important reason for his advances in the past few centuries
   (B) the moral aspects of a thinking, cultured society and people must enlighten its institutions
   (C) the most important lessons for a man are to be found in the cultured societies of Europe
   (D) the reason for differences between our own and other societies is that we, as members of our society, learn different things from those which others learn
   (E) art and music are more important than technology in building cultivated tastes

9. Which of the following doctrines has had the greatest influence on 20th-century American education?
(A) Catholicism (B) Puritanism (C) Socialism
(D) Pragmatism (E) Transcendentalism

10. The census which is commonly considered to indicate the closing of the American frontier was taken in
(A) 1870 (B) 1890 (C) 1910 (D) 1920 (E) 1950

11. Which of the following American political figures was unpopular with the Democratic followers of Jefferson?
(A) Hamilton Fish (B) John Jay (C) John Quincy Adams
(D) James Madison (E) Patrick Henry

12. Which countries became unified in the 19th century?
(A) France and Great Britain (B) France and Spain
(C) Czechoslovakia and Finland (D) Germany and Portugal
(E) Italy and Germany

13. Germany violated the neutrality of which of the following nations in both the First and Second World Wars?
(A) Netherlands (B) Norway (C) Switzerland
(D) Belgium (E) France

14. The United States Senate does not have the power to
(A) approve treaties
(B) approve appointment of federal judges
(C) impeach public officials
(D) approve appointment of Cabinet members
(E) pass legislation already approved by the House of Representatives

15. A man who lived in a certain country from 1860 to 1960 would have lived through absolute monarchy, constitutional monarchy, imperialist expansion, military dictatorship, foreign occupation, extraordinary economic development, and a democratic political order. The above description best fits which country?
(A) Thailand (B) China (C) Japan (D) Egypt (E) Brazil

16. Which of the following professional associations carries the most power and control over training, certification, and entry?
(A) American Association of University Professors
(B) American Medical Association
(C) American Association of American Geographers
(D) National Education Association
(E) American Historical Association

17. A key article of the Leninist communist creed is that, under capitalism,
(A) depressions are inevitable
(B) war over foreign markets is inevitable
(C) class warfare is inevitable
(D) none of the above (E) all of the above

18. A correlation coefficient of minus 0.82 between two phenomena is derived. The relationship between the two phenomena would best be characterized by which of the following?
(A) One thing caused the other.
(B) A third thing caused the two things.
(C) One thing is negative, causing a positive reaction in the other.
(D) It is likely that some relationship exists between the two things.
(E) The two things tend to vary in the same direction.

19. According to decisions handed down by the Supreme Court prior to 1972, one of the following was illegal. Which one?
(A) Refusing for religious reasons to salute the American flag
(B) Using public funds to pay bus transportation for students attending parochial schools
(C) Using public funds to purchase secular textbooks for students attending parochial schools
(D) Sending children to parochial schools
(E) Allowing clergymen to give religious indoctrination in public schools

20. The legal basis for the separation of church and state in the U.S. is found in the
(A) Sixteenth Amendment
(B) Declaration of Independence
(C) Fifth Amendment
(D) First Amendment
(E) Tenth Amendment

21. The American economy is
(A) pure laissez-faire
(B) more planned than laissez-faire
(C) more laissez-faire than planned
(D) centrally directed as under socialism
(E) dominated by traditional custom

22. Which of the following United States government departments and agencies were created after the Second World War?
I. Department of Housing and Urban Development
II. Veterans Administration
III. Environmental Protection Agency
IV. Nuclear Regulatory Agency
V. Social Security Administration
(A) I and III only (B) III and IV only (C) III only
(D) II, III, and IV only (E) I, III, and IV only

23. "The community is a fictitious body . . . the sum of the several members who compose it." This individualist viewpoint is the basic premise of
(A) François Quesnay (B) Thomas Aquinas
(C) William Petty (D) Jeremy Bentham (E) August Comte

24. More characteristic of class than caste is
(A) vertical mobility (B) endogamy (C) distinguishing attire
(D) occupational prohibitions (E) prestige differences

25. Lenin found it necessary to add a corollary to Karl Marx's analysis. This corollary stated that the hour of revolt had been prolonged by
(A) extending suffrage to women and to others
(B) the growth of labor unions
(C) colonial imperialism
(D) the false benefits of capitalism
(E) the graduated income tax and other methods of shifting the tax burden to the rich

26. As people become better off economically, on which of the following do they spend a smaller proportion of their income?
(A) Books (B) Entertainment (C) Transportation
(D) Food (E) Sports

27. Concerning money, it is false to say that money
(A) serves as a standard of deferred payments
(B) is a medium of exchange
(C) may have intrinsic value, that is, be useful in itself
(D) is the difference between a price economy and a planned economy
(E) is a measure of value

28. Which of the following is not a part of our national wealth?
(A) Factories (B) Stored grain (C) Farm land
(D) Corporate stock (E) Post offices

29. According to Karl Marx, "surplus value" arose from the fact that
(A) capitalists sold goods for a profit
(B) labor, unlike other commodities, created more value than it cost to reproduce itself
(C) capitalism was an expanding economy and always needed new markets
(D) each of the four factors of production were entitled to a share of the whole economic product
(E) the state connived with capitalists to consciously rob the workers

30. In the case of Prohibition (of the production and distribution of alcoholic beverages), which of the following most effectively prevented enforcement?
(A) Injunctions
(B) Judicial review
(C) Popular nullification
(D) The refusal of federal officials to enforce the law
(E) Presidential resistance to enforcement

31. Carthage was established as a colony of the
(A) Greeks (B) Phoenicians (C) Romans
(D) Hittites (E) Egyptians

32. In the United States at present, the kinship system
    (A) really does not exist
    (B) is formal, highly elaborated, and closely relevant to all the experiences of the family members
    (C) appears only in times of family crises
    (D) puts strong emphasis on the immediate conjugal family
    (E) emphasizes the role of the patriarch

33. Max Weber pointed out that the bureaucratization of society is usually accompanied by
    (A) raising specific educational standards for office holders
    (B) the decline of the role of "experts"
    (C) greater publicity given to public affairs
    (D) a decline in the role played by intellectuals in public affairs
    (E) a more humane order brought about by efficiency

34. Which of the following developments of the first half of the 20th century seem most clearly to have been forecast in 19th-century Marxian writings?
    (A) The increasing number of persons in advanced societies who consider themselves proletarians
    (B) The spread of ownership through the device of corporate stock
    (C) The spread of Communism among non-industrialized peoples
    (D) The rise of wage standards
    (E) Crises of trade and unemployment

35. The American Federation of Labor, in its first fifty years, was characterized by
    (A) shunning political involvement
    (B) a conservative orientation
    (C) cooperation with the existing economic system
    (D) a "no pie in the sky" ideological orientation
    (E) all of the above

36. The Kentucky and Virginia Resolutions of 1798-9 were invoked in order to prove the
    (A) right of social revolution
    (B) right of a state to secede when it feels wronged
    (C) right of a state to be the judge of constitutionality.
    (D) right to refuse the authority of the Bank of the United States
    (E) right to treat Indians with a strong hand

37. If you were to visit the sites of ancient Mesopotamian culture, to which modern country would you go?
    (A) Egypt (B) Turkey (C) Pakistan (D) Iraq (E) Libya

38. Which of the following ideas would Edmund Burke have rejected?
    (A) The specific is to be preferred over the abstract.
    (B) Society can be safely based on reason alone.
    (C) Lawless action is generally destructive.
    (D) It is often an easy jump from democracy to tyranny.
    (E) Society and government are best when the role of human wisdom and human custom are given due respect.

39. Socrates was condemned to death because he
(A) taught young men to question accepted ideas and practices
(B) was the teacher of Alexander
(C) accepted a bribe from the Persians
(D) denied that there were any fixed standards of good
(E) taught the Greeks that they were inferior

40. The Edict of Nantes
(A) outlawed Roman Catholicism in France
(B) outlawed Protestantism in France
(C) permitted a limited toleration to Protestants in France
(D) established freedom of religion in France
(E) established the doctrine of the trinity in France

41. The patriotic Greek of the 5th century B.C. was primarily loyal to
(A) the Greek nation
(B) his emperor
(C) his religion, which was thought to have no connection with political affairs
(D) his city
(E) his race

42. Which of the following writers hoped that education would engender prudence, late marriage, and smaller families?
(A) Adam Smith
(B) Karl Marx
(C) Thomas Malthus
(D) Walt Rostow
(E) Ragnar Nurske

43. The chief object of Spartan education was to develop
(A) a cultured and artistic citizenry
(B) good soldiers who were obedient citizens
(C) an able body of tradesmen
(D) a select group of priests
(E) expert technicians

44. "People in the same trade seldom meet together but the conversation ends in a conspiracy against the public, or in some diversion to raise prices." This would most likely be found in the writings of
(A) John Law (B) Adam Smith (C) William Petty
(D) Thomas Mun (E) Emile Durkheim

45. "The interest of the landlord is always opposed to the interest of every other class in the community. His situation is never so prosperous, as when food is scarce and dear; whereas, all other persons are greatly benefited by procuring cheap food." You would expect to read this in the writings of
(A) Adam Smith
(B) François Quesnay
(C) David Ricardo
(D) Thomas Jefferson
(E) John Locke

46. Which idea is not included in the theory of Marx?
    (A) Man's religious, ethical, political, and social ideas are determined by economic forces.
    (B) Capitalism cannot reform itself.
    (C) As capitalism matures, much of its greater material wealth will accrue to the workingman.
    (D) Human history is the chronology of the inevitable conflict between two opposing economic classes.
    (E) Capitalists, if they wished, still could not reform conditions in their own particular industries.

47. Physicist is to engineer as sociologist is to
    (A) psychologist (B) theologian (C) social reformer
    (D) historian (E) social philosopher

48. The belief that one's patterns of living are superior to those of other groups is termed
    (A) relativism (B) ostracism (C) ethnocentrism
    (D) all of the above (E) none of the above

49. As a culture becomes more complex it tends to have within it fewer
    (A) alternatives
    (B) specialities
    (C) universals
    (D) exigencies
    (E) institutions

50. Which one of the following arguments did Malthus try to prove?
    (A) Developments in technology are unlikely to relieve, permanently, the pressure of population on the means of subsistence.
    (B) Poverty is primarily the result of employers' greed.
    (C) Population pressure forces national governments into colonization and imperialistic schemes, which is only proper.
    (D) Intelligent government action, such as subsidies to mothers and taxes on bachelors, can alleviate the effects of the laws of population.
    (E) Poverty is particular to capitalism.

51. Which is the most nearly accurate? The 1987 population of the world (in billions) was
    (A) 1.5 (B) 2.0 (C) 4.2 (D) 5.0 (E) 6.2

52. Emile Durkheim described a type of suicide resulting from excessive social integration and called it
    (A) egoistic (B) alienative (C) altruistic (D) anomic (E) rational

53. The development of agriculture was important in that it enabled man to
    (A) settle in one place
    (B) produce more food than required by those producing it
    (C) specialize
    (D) increase his numbers by reducing malnutrition and famine
    (E) all of these

54. Which of the following usually includes all the others?
(A) Institutions (B) Folkways (C) Laws
(D) Social symbols (E) Mores

55. The German Imperial constitution of 1871
(A) gave Prussia a preferred position in the German union
(B) was a generally democratic instrument
(C) declared the equality of all member states
(D) declared the ruler of Austria to be Emperor
(E) was similar to the British constitution

56. William I (the Conqueror) of England was a
(A) Roman (B) Saxon (C) Dane (D) Norman (E) Vandal

57. In 1635, France intervened in the war in Germany in order to
(A) help defeat the Protestants
(B) prevent a Swedish victory
(C) prevent a Hapsburg victory
(D) win the Holy Roman crown for the King of France
(E) weaken the power of the English on the continent

58. The period of the "Roman peace" *(Pax Romana)* was
(A) during the first two hundred years of the Empire
(B) between the reign of Diocletian and 476 A.D.
(C) between the last Punic War and the reign of Diocletian
(D) between the foundation of the Republic and the first Punic War
(E) during the reign of Charlemagne

59. The Punic Wars were between Rome and
(A) Macedonia (B) Carthage (C) Persia
(D) Athens (E) Israel

60. The Caliphs were
(A) the political successors of Mohammed
(B) prophets of Islam through whom further revelation of God's will was made known
(C) peoples from Central Asia who adopted the Islamic faith
(D) a family of Moslem rulers who lived in Spain
(E) foot soldiers in the armies of Islam

61. Both Aristotle and Plato considered that growing numbers of people in a state (if population is already sufficient)
(A) must be handled by increasing technique
(B) must be allowed to grow yet larger in number even if mass poverty result
(C) were not the concern of the state since matters pertaining to reproduction were properly not the business of politics or philosophers
(D) were to be stopped by infanticide or other methods (emigration, if possible) if the stability and well-being of the state were threatened
(E) were always a sign of the increased glory of the state

62. In the latter part of his life Dante became a Ghibelline. This means that he
    (A) was a supporter of the Pope
    (B) hoped the Italian cities would retain their complete independence
    (C) believed that only the Holy Roman Emperor could bring unity and peace to Italy
    (D) hoped for the independence of Sicily from the rest of Italy
    (E) saw that the merchants and banking class meant liberty and progress for the North Italian cities

63. The enlightened despots of the 18th century were so styled because they
    (A) saw how important it was to give important concessions to the common people
    (B) were enlightened enough to maintain the monarchic form of government in an age when the people increasingly demanded representation
    (C) were able to expand their domains
    (D) possessed a high degree of learning and a deep belief in religion
    (E) possessed a desire to improve the lot of their subjects and to improve their own education

Section II

Number of Questions: 62
Time: 45 minutes

Directions: Each of the questions or incomplete statements below is followed by five suggested answers or completions. Select the one that is best in each case.

64. According to Marx and Lenin, the state, in the high stage of communism, will wither away because
    (A) universal coercion will reign over the earth and make national states unnecessary
    (B) the bourgeoisie and proletariat will be able to live in peace without need for the state to mediate between them
    (C) the Communist Party will have consolidated its position to such an extent and rendered the masses so docile that they will no longer need the state
    (D) when there is only one social class, the state, defined as an instrument of class domination, will no longer serve any function and hence will disappear
    (E) the triumphant dialectical process of history will prove statehood to be only a penultimate truth, hence ultimately false in the presence of the final political form, the super-state

65. The Augustinian system of theology held that "Human nature is hopelessly depraved. . . . Only those mortals can be saved whom God for reasons of His own has predestined to inherit eternal life." Which of the following best represents the attitude of the Protestant leaders of the Reformation?
(A) They knew nothing of Augustine and were ignorant of this idea.
(B) They strongly opposed this idea since they believed that it would discourage men from doing good works in the hope of winning salvation.
(C) The idea became very important in the Protestant position.
(D) They refused to consider the idea, since they thought that Roman Catholic Church fathers such as St. Augustine had no claim to authority.
(E) They considered it an idea from pagan Rome and without proper Christian charity.

66. The argument most used to support the congressional committee system is that it
(A) makes sure that minority groups get a fair hearing
(B) increases congressional control of the executive department
(C) reduces the cost of lawmaking
(D) makes possible more careful consideration of bills
(E) makes sure that presidential wishes will prevail

67. The "heroic age," "time of troubles," "stability," and "decline" are historical concepts found in
(A) Marx (B) Sorokin (C) Toynbee (D) Becker (E) Kant

68. "Sire, you can do everything with bayonets but sit on them." This statement made to Napoleon relates to the problem of political
(A) strategy (B) tactics (C) costs (D) legitimacy
(E) formalism

69. Which of the following countries had more of their citizens and soldiers killed in World War II?
(A) The United States
(B) Great Britain
(C) Italy
(D) France
(E) USSR

70. Which of the following countries was not in the League of Nations in 1935?
(A) The United States
(B) USSR
(C) The United Kingdom
(D) France
(E) Yugoslavia

Harding in "Brooklyn Daily Eagle"

"No bathing beyond the ropes"

Questions 71–73 refer to the above cartoon.

71. The cartoon above was drawn in
(A) 1912 (B) 1919 (C) 1925 (D) 1933 (E) 1940

72. The cartoon implies that the U.S. at the time was
(A) still immature
(B) interested in seapower
(C) being treated as immature when it was, in fact, a great world power
(D) not ready to assume world responsibility
(E) afraid to venture into deeper water

73. The President who would have removed the restrictions on U.S. involvement with the League of Nations (represented in the cartoon as "Lodge Reservations") was
(A) Theodore Roosevelt (B) Franklin Roosevelt
(C) Warren Harding (D) Woodrow Wilson
(E) Herbert Hoover

74. "He would have liked to establish a colonial empire, but he knew the British fleet ruled the seas, and so, to prevent this vast region from falling to the British, he sold it to the Americans." What was the region called?
(A) Louisiana (B) Florida (C) Alaska (D) Hawaii (E) California

75. The Erie Canal connected
(A) the Susquehanna and the Potomac
(B) the Hudson and the Delaware
(C) Lake Erie and Niagara
(D) the Hudson and Lake Erie
(E) Lake Huron and the Ohio

76. The political dynasty which began in Louisiana in the 1930s was named after
(A) Long (B) Talmadge (C) Bilbo (D) Crump (E) Wallace

Questions 77–78 relate to GRAPH A.

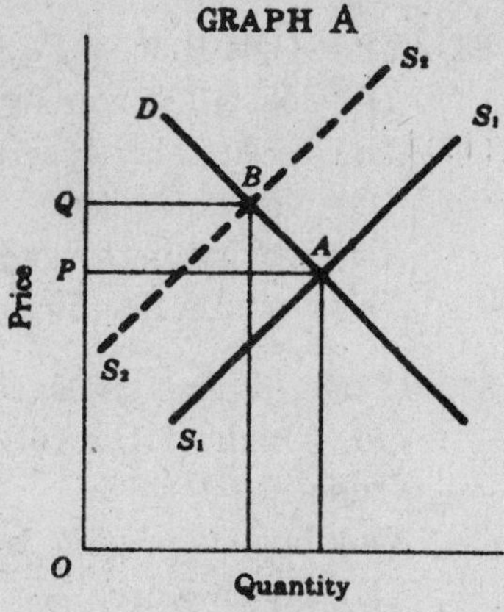

77. The line S_2 S_2 compared to the line S_1 S_1 indicates
   (A) an increase in demand
   (B) an increase in supply
   (C) an increase in monopoly
   (D) a decrease in supply
   (E) a decrease in demand

78. The shift from line S_1 S_1 to S_2 S_2 in Graph A could have occurred because of a
   (A) good year in salt production
   (B) bad year, in that few people desired to purchase "old masters"
   (C) discovery of a new diamond field in Africa
   (D) freeze in the orange groves of Florida
   (E) famine reducing the number of subsistence farmers in a small area of the economy

79. Which of the following statements comes closest to the true Malthusian idea?
   (A) "Population increases rapidly while agriculture lags behind."
   (B) "It is the constant tendency in all animated life to increase beyond the nourishment prepared for it."
   (C) "No progress is possible because of the basic sex drive which increases population at a geometric rate."
   (D) "Nations which are over-populated must be allowed to expand or send their inhabitants abroad."
   (E) "Things can be produced more cheaply if more is produced."

80. Which practice is most compatible with the supposedly rational nature of "the economic man"?
   (A) Installment buying at high interest
   (B) Borrowing from small loan companies
   (C) Reading a consumer research publication
   (D) Asking a salesman's advice
   (E) Buying more than was on your shopping list

81. For many years, until changed by law in 1943, immigrants who had come to the United States from one of the following countries were not allowed to become naturalized citizens. Which one?
   (A) Italy (B) Mexico (C) China (D) Syria (E) Finland

82. In which of the following cities would the proportion of Lutherans in the total population of the city be highest?
   (A) San Francisco, California (B) Nashville, Tennessee
   (C) Atlanta, Georgia (D) Des Moines, Iowa
   (E) Minneapolis, Minnesota

83. Under the British Parliamentary Act of 1911, the House of Lords
   (A) lost all power in legislation
   (B) could delay enactment of an ordinary bill for only two years
   (C) was abolished
   (D) was transformed into a house appointed for life terms
   (E) became finally dominant over the House of Commons

84. If one divides the races of men into Caucasian, Negroid, and Mongoloid, which of the following countries has a head of state who is *not* Caucasian?
   (A) Israel (B) Iran (C) India (D) Egypt
   (E) South Korea

85. *Anthropomorphism* is a religious concept meaning
   (A) belief in animal gods
   (B) belief in a god who died and lived again
   (C) rituals in common usage
   (D) attribution of human characteristics to a god or gods
   (E) holding ancestors worthy of worship

86. The behavior expected of any particular group member is his
   (A) role (B) status (C) performance (D) culture
   (E) ideology

87. "The productive expenditures are employed in agriculture. . . . The sterile expenses are made upon handicraft products . . . commercial expenses . . . etc." This viewpoint is associated with which school of thought?
   (A) Marxism (B) Platonism (C) Physiocracy
   (D) Technocracy (E) Mercantilism

88. About fifty percent of the adult population in America belong to no church. What is their attitude, seemingly toward the organized denominations?
   (A) Anticlerical
   (B) Strongly pro-religious on all controversial issues
   (C) Utterly indifferent
   (D) Mildly friendly
   (E) Militantly atheistic

89. In the 1840s and 1850s a considerable number of the immigrants to the United States came from
   (A) Germany (B) Italy (C) Greece (D) Russia
   (E) Spain

90. After 1815, Germany
   (A) consisted of thirty-eight states loosely joined in the German Confederation
   (B) was established as a unified state
   (C) existed only as the Holy Roman Empire
   (D) was all included within the bounds of Prussia
   (E) formed a part of the Austrian Empire

91. Under the British system of government, the monarch normally selects a prime minister who commands the support of the
(A) retiring prime minister
(B) majority party and with the concurrence of the minority party in the House of Commons
(C) majority party in the House of Commons
(D) majority party in the House of Commons and the House of Lords
(E) commonwealth nations

92. Which country was the moving spirit in organizing the various coalitions against Napoleon?
(A) Russia (B) Austria (C) Britain (D) Prussia (E) Sweden

93. The doctrine of "Manifest Destiny" was most closely associated with which of the following wars involving the U.S.?
(A) Civil War (B) War of 1812 (C) World War I
(D) World War II (E) Spanish-American War

94. "Non-slaveholders of the South: farmers, mechanics and working men, we take this occasion to assure you that the slaveholders, the arrogant demagogues whom you have elected to offices of power and profit, have hoodwinked you, trifled with you, and used you as mere tools for the consummation of their wicked designs." These words reflect the viewpoint of
(A) Henry Clay (B) Stephen A. Douglas
(C) William Lloyd Garrison (D) George Fitzhugh
(E) John C. Calhoun

95. "The great object of Jacobinism, both in its political and moral revolution, is to destroy every trace of civilization in the world and force mankind back into a savage state." These remarks could have been made by
(A) an American Tory during the Revolution of 1776
(B) a follower of Jefferson in 1805
(C) a New England Federalist in 1794
(D) a member of Lincoln's cabinet in 1862
(E) a New Dealer in the 1930s

96. "Men, consciously or unconsciously, derive their moral ideas in the last resort from the practical relations on which their class position is based—from the economic relations in which they carry on production and exchange." Which of the following said this?
(A) Freud (B) Goethe (C) Kant
(D) Engels (E) Hegel

97. The popular election of U.S. Senators was provided for in the
(A) Constitution
(B) Articles of Confederation
(C) Bill of Rights
(D) Declaration of Independence
(E) Seventeenth Amendment

98. The Syllabus of Errors in the 19th century was
   (A) a Marxist attack upon the existing society
   (B) a list of what Pope Pius IX said were errors in modern thinking
   (C) a work by Thomas Huxley setting forth the errors of the old biology
   (D) August Comte's attack upon the errors of traditional social philosophy
   (E) a syllabus which recounted the virtues of British colonial rule

99. William G. Sumner thought the "social question" (existence of social problems) to be the result of the fact that
   (A) all men are not equally equipped for the onerous struggle against nature
   (B) the virtuous are not ordinarily successful
   (C) political equality is absent
   (D) equality before the law is unattainable
   (E) man knows too little about his society

100. It is difficult for an addict to avoid taking drugs after he has been released from treatment because
   (A) he generally returns to his old circle of drug-using friends
   (B) psycho-physiological dependence on drugs, once established, can never be completely eliminated
   (C) people around him generally expect him to become readdicted
   (D) both A and C
   (E) A, B, and C

101. The term "anticlerical" means hostility toward the
   (A) business class (B) government officials
   (C) white collar workers (D) church (E) retail trade

102. The most significant difference between "caste" in the United States and 19th-century India is that in the United States
   (A) there is a great deal of racial intermarriage
   (B) the social inequality of the Negro is sanctioned neither by the dominant religious precepts nor by dominant political ideology
   (C) all occupational fields are equally open to the Negro
   (D) there is no segregation
   (E) the magical notion of pollution is absent

103. The Supreme Court has been referred to as a continuous constitutional convention. The reason for this may be found in the fact that the Supreme Court
   (A) is in session all the time
   (B) changes and enlarges the Constitution by its practice of interpreting the Constitution through its opinions
   (C) is given the right to sit as a constitutional assembly, and to propose, but not ratify or accept, constitutional amendments
   (D) must rule on any proposed amendment regarding its constitutionality
   (E) convokes conventions of high judges which test the Constitution

104. Japan's economy suffered greatly in the late 1920s and early 1930s because of
(A) the decline of population
(B) the decline of foreign trade
(C) industrialization of China
(D) the growing power of the USSR in Asia
(E) the increased competitive power of Britain

105. Confucius and Buddha were contemporaries. In which century of the pre-Christian era did they live?
(A) 20th (B) 12th (C) 6th (D) 1st (E) 3rd

106. There is an inverse relation between fertility and education among most peoples. Among which group has this relation disappeared?
(A) Southern Negroes (U.S.) (B) Puerto Rico
(C) Total U.S. population (D) Taiwan (E) Sweden

107. Modern business
(A) emphasizes teamwork and cooperation
(B) frowns upon "cutthroat" price competition
(C) is an important avenue of social mobility
(D) all of the above
(E) none of the above

108. In 1900, the percentage of people in the United States over twenty years of age with a high school diploma was about
(A) 5% (B) 15% (C) 33% (D) 50% (E) 66%

109. In 1298 A.D., he wrote a book which described Cathay and its people. He mentioned strange customs such as the use of paper money, and, he told of the wars which Kublai Khan fought with the Japanese. His book inspired later explorers such as Christopher Columbus. Who was the author of this travel book?
(A) Dante
(B) Aquinas
(C) Marco Polo
(D) Roger Bacon
(E) Cicero

110. In 1791, the French Constituent Assembly presented France with its first written constitution. This declared France to be
(A) a limited constitutional monarchy
(B) an absolute monarchy
(C) a democracy
(D) a republic
(E) a military dictatorship

111. The modern name for what was formerly referred to as Persia is
(A) Iraq
(B) Kuwait
(C) Yemen
(D) Iran
(E) Pakistan

112. The percent of observations which lie between two standard deviations below and two standard deviations above the mean in a normal distribution is approximately
(A) 30% (B) 40% (C) 55% (D) 75% (E) 95%

113. The increasing proportion of American eighteen to twenty-four year olds in higher education has probably increased most the relative numerical significance of which the following student subcultures?
(A) Collegiate (B) Academic (C) Vocational
(D) Non-conformist (E) Militaristic

114. If a President were to be impeached, the trial would be in the
(A) Supreme Court
(B) Senate
(C) United States Court of Appeals
(D) United States District Court
(E) House of Representatives

115. Which of the following does not always apply to culture?
(A) It is static. (B) It is learned. (C) It is material in part.
(D) It is non-material in part. (E) It includes norms.

116. Today, the tendency of most American families is toward
(A) matriarchy
(B) patriarchy
(C) elaboration in symbolism supporting the authority of extended kin
(D) equality of power of husband and wife
(E) emphasis on the traditional

117. A caste system of social stratification is extremely difficult to maintain in
(A) an urban society
(B) a village or rural society
(C) a highly religious society
(D) an economically poor society
(E) a paternalistic society

118. Which of the following opinions concerning Communism today is *most compatible* with John Stuart Mill's principle of liberty in his essay "On Liberty"? The discussion of Communism in our schools
(A) should not be tolerated; Communism contradicts the American way of life
(B) should be encouraged, for Communists are just as likely to be right as we are
(C) should be tolerated, for no one should ever be inhibited in his beliefs and speech
(D) should be tolerated, for it is highly desirable that we face sincere arguments against our own conventional beliefs
(E) should not be tolerated; Communism is a mistaken belief and therefore should not be represented in public

119. The Japanese rulers suppressed Christianity in the 17th century because they
   (A) thought it would divide their people and bring them under the influence of foreign powers
   (B) feared that the peaceful teaching of Christianity would discourage warlike virtues
   (C) believed that Buddhism was the true faith and all other religions necessarily false
   (D) said that it was a "white man's" religion
   (E) believed that only God was divine and no man could be

120. The evidence against instinct as an explanation of marriage and the family includes all of the following except one. Which one?
   (A) Marriage limits as well as permits sexual expression.
   (B) Women's desires for offspring are not constant.
   (C) Women's physiology is unrelated to their behavior.
   (D) Father and mother do not have the same degree of responsibility toward their children in all societies.
   (E) Men do not inevitably experience emotional conflict when they suppress their sexual urges.

121. Upon which one of the following viewpoints would Alexis de Tocqueville and Karl Marx agree ?
   (A) The tyranny of the majority was the ominous threat of the future.
   (B) Organized religion is an important factor in the preserving of liberty.
   (C) Religion is a good way to calm an oppressed people.
   (D) Most controversy in modern society would be over property rights.
   (E) Societies with conflicting economic interests can, through compromise and proper institutions, achieve a long life.

122. Studies of Western countries show that
   (A) the most secularized and urbanized countries have the highest suicide rates
   (B) the more technologically backward a country is, the higher its suicide rate tends to be
   (C) secularization and urbanization does not seem to account for the relatively low suicide rates of the United States, Canada, England, and Australia
   (D) the larger the proportion of suburban residents in a country, the higher the suicide rate tends to be
   (E) suicide is an excellent indicator of the total worth of a society

123. In the early 19th century (when Great Britain confronted Napoleon), the British position on the rights of neutral countries was nearly the opposite of its position in
   (A) 1837
   (B) 1854
   (C) 1863
   (D) 1915
   (E) 1943

124. In the United States today, which of the following contrasts between middle-class and working-class youths seems most defensible?
   (A) Middle-class youths are usually complacent; working-class youths are usually ambitious.
   (B) Middle-class youths see their problem as deciding what to do; working-class youths see their problem as finding a job.
   (C) Middle-class youths are concerned primarily with income adequate to maintain a given style of life; working-class youths are concerned with achievement that may lead to mobility.
   (D) Middle-class youths are likely to have to depend on their families for guidance; working-class youths are likely to have guidance counselors who will help them with occupational choice.
   (E) Middle-class youths are conservative; working-class youths are radical.

125. All of the following statements concerning banking are true except
   (A) state banks can join the Federal Reserve System
   (B) bank failure is reduced by the influence of F.D.I.C.
   (C) Federal Reserve member banks count their deposits with the Federal Reserve Bank as assets
   (D) When all banks are reducing the cash part of their assets, money supply is increased
   (E) the Federal Reserve is under the authority of the U.S. Treasury

ANSWER KEY—TRIAL TEST

Section I

1. A	12. E	23. D	34. E	44. B	54. A
2. B	13. D	24. A	35. E	45. C	55. A
3. E	14. C	25. C	36. C	46. C	56. D
4. E	15. C	26. D	37. D	47. C	57. C
5. C	16. B	27. D	38. B	48. C	58. A
6. D	17. E	28. D	39. A	49. C	59. B
7. C	18. D	29. B	40. C	50. A	60. A
8. D	19. E	30. C	41. D	51. C	61. D
9. D	20. D	31. B	42. C	52. C	62. C
10. B	21. C	32. D	43. B	53. E	63. E
11. B	22. E	33. A			

Section II

64. D	75. D	86. A	96. D	106. E	116. D
65. C	76. A	87. C	97. E	107. D	117. A
66. D	77. D	88. D	98. B	108. A	118. D
67. C	78. D	89. A	99. A	109. C	119. A
68. D	79. B	90. A	100. D	110. A	120. C
69. E	80. C	91. C	101. C	111. D	121. D
70. A	81. C	92. C	102. B	112. E	122. C
71. B	82. E	93. E	103. B	113. C	123. C
72. C	83. B	94. C	104. B	114. B	124. B
73. D	84. E	95. C	105. C	115. A	125. E
74. A	85. D				

SCORING CHART—TRIAL TEST

After you have scored your Trial Examination, enter the results in the chart below (the Raw Score computation is explained on page 14); then transfer your Raw Score to the Progress Chart on page 14. As you complete the Sample Examinations later in this part of the book, you should be able to achieve increasingly higher Raw Scores.

Total Test	Number Right	Number Wrong	Number Omitted	Raw Score
Section I: 63				
Section II: 62				
Total: 125				

ANSWER EXPLANATIONS—TRIAL TEST

Section I

1. A. The distribution of members in the House of Representatives is determined on the basis of population. The Constitution in Article I Section 2 Clause 3 provides: "Representatives shall be apportioned among the several states which may be included within this Union according to their respective numbers . . . . "
2. B. In the 19th century, United States Senators were elected by the state legislatures. Article I Section 3 Clause 1 of the original Constitution reads: "The Senate of the United States shall be composed of two Senators from each state, chosen by the legislature thereof . . . . " This was changed by the 17th amendment, ratified in 1913.
3. E. "Boswash" is a term which is sometimes applied to the continuous urban area between Boston and Washington. The word consists of a combination of the first syllables of Boston and Washington.
4. E. The law of diminishing returns states that an input of production (such as labor) and the output it helps to produce tend to diminish as more units of the input factor are applied to the same number of the other factors of production (land and capital).
5. C. To the Marxist, profits are transitory and characteristic of only one state of history. Marxism holds that capitalism, the economic system of most of the western world, represents a transitory state of history.
6. D. Japanese culture and values were strongly influenced both by Chinese Confucianism and Buddhism (Ch'an Buddhism, for example, was transmuted into Zen in Japan). Artistic styles, often transmitted through Korea, frequently reflected Japanese adaptations of Chinese sources. Chinese ideographs were adopted as Japan's first written language. However, the exalted social and political status of the Samurai class as warrior scholars had no equivalent in Ancient China where soldiers and warlords were held in low esteem by the mandarin scholar gentry.

7. C. Apes and other primates cannot be taught to use highly complex language because they have little mental ability to store or transmit highly abstract ideas. Some higher primates have been shown to possess potential for learning from communications directed toward them.

8. D. The culture concept in social science implies that the reason for differences between our own and other societies is that we, as members of our society, learn different things from those which others learn. This is the sense in which sociologists use the term "culture."

9. D. Pragmatism, as an educational philosophy, was developed by William James (1842–1910) in the 19th century and, more fully, by John Dewey (1859–1952) in the 20th. It has been the most influential educational philosophy in the United States.

10. B. Frontier "closing" was defined by the Bureau of the Census in its 1890 report: "at present the unsettled area has been so broken into by isolated bodies of settlement (defined elsewhere as 2 or more people per square mile) that there can be hardly said to be a frontier line." By 1890, ownership, if not occupation, of all American land had been established. The census of 1890 counted 63 million Americans of whom 35 percent lived in urban areas.

11. B. John Jay was unpopular with the Democratic followers of Jefferson. In 1794, Jay negotiated a treaty with England. The treaty helped keep America out of the war in Europe between France and England. The Jeffersonians felt that the treaty was favorable to England. They favored France in the European war.

12. E. The unification of Italy, called Risorgimento, was achieved under the leadership of Count Camillo Cavour. Victor Emmanuel II was proclaimed king of a united Italy in 1861. German unification was accomplished mainly through the efforts of Otto von Bismarck. King William I of Prussia was proclaimed Emperor of a united Germany in 1871.

13. D. German armies attacked neutral Belgium in 1914 at the beginning of World War I and again in May 1940, early in World War II. Switzerland remained independent in both wars. The neutrality of the Netherlands and of Norway was not violated in World War I. France was aligned against Germany in both wars.

14. C. The Constitution in Article I Section 2 Clause 5 says: "The House of Representatives . . . shall have the sole power of impeachment." (bringing charges). Article I Section 3 Clause 6 says: "The Senate shall have the sole power to try all impeachments."

15. B. At the beginning of this hundred-year period (1860), China was an absolute monarchy ruled by an emperor. After the Revolution of 1912, China became a republic. In the interim, much of Chinese territory was under foreign occupation. In 1948, Chiang Kai-shek became President under a democratic constitution. One year later, communist forces under Mao Tse-tung drove his armies off the mainland and established the Communist People's Republic of China.

16. B. Each of these is a professional organization, but only the American Medical Association (AMA) exercises dominant control over training of physicians, certification to practice medicine and its various fields of specialization, and entry into the profession of medicine.

17. E. The Leninist communist creed, as one of its key articles, holds that under the capitalist system, depressions are inevitable, war between capitalist countries over markets is inevitable, and war between the capitalist class and the proletariat (working class) is inevitable.

18. D. A coefficient of correlation between two phenomena establishes the relationship between the two in statistical terms. In the situation here described, the relationship is established as minus 0.82.

19. E. Prior to 1972, the Supreme Court had ruled on each of the five issues. Four were declared to be legal. The fifth, allowing clergymen to give religious indoctrination in public schools, was declared unconstitutional in the case of McCollum *v.* Board of Education (1948).

20. D. The First Amendment states: "Congress shall make no law respecting an

establishment of religion, or prohibiting the free exercise thereof. . . . " This is the legal basis for the separation of church and state in the U.S.

21. C. The American economy is described as a "free enterprise" system. This would be completely laissez-faire except that there is planning under such agencies as the Federal Reserve System, as well as in committees of Congress and in the various executive departments.

22. E. The creation of new government departments and executive agencies usually reflects the changing nature (and needs) of American society. The Veterans Administration was created in 1921, for example, to provide for rehabilitation and medical assistance to veterans of the First World War. The Social Security Administration (1935) was part of Franklin D. Roosevelt's "New Deal," designed to combat the economic insecurity of the Great Depression. In the immediate aftermath of the Second World War (August, 1946), President Truman signed the McMahon Act creating the Atomic Energy Commission (now the Nuclear Regulatory Agency) to further the monopoly the United States then held in nuclear arms and possible peaceful uses of atomic energy. The Department of Housing and Urban Development was added to the cabinet in 1965 as part of President Lyndon Johnson's "Great Society" program. During the first Nixon administration, the creation of the Environmental Protection Agency (1971) reflected heightened awareness of threats to the fragile natural environment.

23. D. Jeremy Bentham (1748–1832), English social philosopher, was the leader of a group called the Utilitarians. He held that each person guides his or her conduct entirely by self-interest.

24. A. In a class system, movement from one class to another (vertical mobility) is possible. In a caste system, endogamy (marriage restrictions), distinguishing attire, occupational prohibitions, and prestige differences tend to prevail.

25. C. Marx contended that the Industrial Revolution would bring about the successful revolt of the working class. Lenin noted that the exploitation of colonies under imperialism would ameliorate the plight of the working class and postpone the day of revolt.

26. D. The proportion of one's income spent on food is more restricted by the inherent ability to consume than are books, entertainment, transportation, or sports.

27. D. Price is an aspect of both a planned economy and a free, or laissez-faire, economy. Money is correctly described in each of the other choices.

28. D. Corporate stock may represent each of the other forms of national wealth. But they, in themselves, are not national wealth. Indeed, corporate stock may be worthless if the corporation that issues it is a spurious entity.

29. B. Karl Marx contended that labor produced more of the final product than it received in wages. This excess was described by Marx as "surplus value."

30. C. Prohibition became a national law by the 18th Amendment to the Constitution, adopted in 1919. One of the reasons for its repeal in 1933 by the 21st Amendment was that it was widely flouted by the people.

31. B. Carthage was established as a colony in North Africa by the Phoenicians about 875 B.C. it was situated opposite Sicily near present-day Tunis.

32. D. In the United States at present, the kinship system puts strong emphasis on the immediate conjugal family, that is, the family consisting of husband, wife, and children.

33. A. Max Weber (1864–1920), German sociologist, described the ideal type of bureaucratic structure in his *Essays in Sociology*. He noted that raising specific standards for office holders went hand in hand with the bureaucratization of society. To Weber, the bureaucratic society, despite its faults, represented an advance over its predecessors.

34. E. In his writings, particularly in his major work entitled *Capital*, which was published in 3 volumes between 1867 and 1894, Karl Marx predicted the downfall of capitalism because of its inherent contradictions. This included, in his view, both mass unemployment and wars among the capitalist nations for control of resources and trade.

35. E. The American Federation of Labor was founded in 1881. During its first 43 years, its leader was Samuel Gompers. Under his leadership, skilled workers were organized into craft unions. The AFL did not support any political party. It worked within the system to obtain better pay, better working conditions, and shorter hours for its members.

36. C. The Kentucky and Virginia Resolutions of 1798–9 were drafted by Jefferson and Madison. They were passed by the legislatures of Kentucky and Virginia. They declared the Alien and Sedition Acts, passed by Congress in 1798, to be unconstitutional.

37. D. Mesopotamia (from the Greek, meaning "between the rivers") was the name given to the ancient civilization that was located in the region between the Tigris and Euphrates Rivers. Today this comprises the territory of Iraq, whose chief city and capital is Baghdad.

38. B. Edmund Burke (1729–1797), English statesman and political philosopher, would have rejected the idea that society can be safely based on reason alone. Burke emphasized the need for gradual and orderly change and the significance of historical antecedents in sound social and political development.

39. A. Socrates was condemned to death as a threat to Athens because he taught young men to question accepted ideas. The story of his accusation, trial, and conviction is related by Plato in his dialogue *Apology*. The last hours of Socrates' life are described by Plato in the dialogue *Phaedo*.

40. C. The Edict of Nantes was issued by King Henry IV of France in 1598 after a series of bloody wars between Protestants and Catholics. It allowed Protestantism in towns where it was the chief form of worship but barred it from Paris and its surroundings.

41. D. In the 5th century B.C., Greece consisted of a number of city-states, that is, cities and their surroundings. Each citizen was loyal to his city-state such as Athens, Sparta, and Thebes, not to Greece. The cities often fought against each other.

42. C. Thomas Malthus (1766–1834), English economist, studied population. He concluded that because population grows much faster than food supply, people are doomed to hunger. Hence, he urged education to bring about smaller families.

43. B. Sparta was one of the leading city-states in ancient Greece. It was famous for its army. Sons of the ruling class were trained to be soldiers. Only these warriors, called Spartiates, had legal and civil rights.

44. B. Adam Smith (1723–1790) is best known for his classic work *An Inquiry into the Nature and Causes of the Wealth of Nations* (1776). He showed great insight into the operation of economic forces, including the tendency of tradesmen to seek control of the market.

45. C. David Ricardo (1772–1823), classical economist, defended the new capitalism and the manufacturing class. He noted that landlords profit from a scarcity of food (food is produced on land). But higher rents reduce the profits of the new manufacturing class.

46. C. Karl Marx (1818–1883) predicted increasing tension between the capitalist class and the working class. The other four ideas are included in his description of capitalism in his 3-volume work entitled *Capital*.

47. C. The physicist does research and develops the theoretical basis for the science of physics. The engineer makes practical applications of the physicist's findings. The sociologist does research and develops the theoretical basis for the social science of sociology. The social reformer puts the theories of the sociologist into practice.

48. C. "Ethnocentrism" is the attitude or belief that the way of life of one's own group is superior to that of any other group. "Relativism" is the view that ethical truths depend on the group holding them. "Ostracism" means exclusion from the group.

49. C. Primitive cultures are relatively monolithic. Virtually all behavior is prescribed and universally practiced. More complex cultures accommodate numerous variations in behavior. Hence, they tend to have fewer universals.

50. A. Thomas R. Malthus (1766–1834) wrote a famous *Essay on Population* (1798). He opposed an increase in wages, arguing that it only encouraged larger families. His thesis was that population increased much faster than the food supply. This would not be relieved by developments in technology.

51. D. In 1987, the population of the world was given as 5 billion.

52. C. Emile Durkheim (1858–1917), French sociologist, wrote a book entitled *Suicide* in 1897. He analyzed the psychologic bases of social behavior. He used the term "altruistic" to describe a type of suicide resulting from excessive social integration.

53. E. Prior to the neolithic age, which dates from about 15,000 B.C., man was a nomad who lived by hunting and gathering. When he learned to till the soil and grow food, i.e., with the development of agriculture, the first four choices in this question followed.

54. A. In sociology, each of the following are classified as institutions: folkways, laws, social symbols, and mores.

55. A. The German Imperial constitution of 1871 went into effect after the defeat of France in the Franco-Prussian War. Prussia became the dominant state under the Constitution. The King of Prussia became Emperor Wilhelm I of Germany.

56. D. William I (the Conqueror) of England is also known in history as Duke William II of Normandy. His army crossed the English Channel and defeated the English at the Battle of Hastings in 1066 A.D. He ruled England as William I until his death in 1087.

57. C. In 1635, during the last phase of the Thirty Years' War, France united with Sweden to prevent the Hapsburgs (both Austrian and Spanish) from gaining the victory.

58. A. The period of the "Roman Peace" (*Pax Romana*) was during the first two hundred years of the Roman Empire. The Empire lasted for five hundred years, from about 31 B.C. to 476 A.D. All the lands around the Mediterranean were part of the Empire. The power and efficiency of the Roman legions kept peace throughout the Empire.

59. B. The Punic Wars (264 B.C.–146 B.C.) were fought between Rome and Carthage. Carthage was founded, as a colony, by the Phoenicians. The Latin word for Phoenicia is Punicus.

60. A. In the Islamic religion, the Caliph is the religious head of the government as the agent of God. When Mohammed, the Prophet, died, Abu Bakr was chosen as first calif. Later, Islam split, and different califs claimed to be God's agent.

61. D. both the great Greek philosopher Plato (428 B.C.–348 B.C.) and his most famous pupil, Aristotle (384 B.C.–322 B.C.), justified infanticide (the killing of infants) as a means of keeping population under control.

62. C. Dante (Alighieri), 1265–1321, was perhaps the greatest Italian poet. Guelphs and Ghibellines were opposing political factions during Dante's lifetime. Dante was at first a supporter of the Guelphs but, in later life, joined the Ghibellines because they were the party of the Emperor and, as Dante thought, could bring unity and peace to Italy.

63. E. The enlightened despots of the 18th century—Joseph II of Austria, Catherine II of Russia, and Frederick II of Prussia—wished to improve both the lot of their impoverished subjects and their own education.

Section II

64. D. Marxism sees history in terms of class struggle with the state as an instrument of the dominant class. In the current (final) stage the bourgeoisie is destroyed by the proletariat. With only one class in society, the state will have no function and will disappear.

65. C. Augustine (354–430) taught that divine grace, not human effort, was the source of salvation. This doctrine, called predestination, was a key tenet of the theology of John Calvin (1509–1564) and other leaders of the Protestant Reformation.

66. D. Under the committee system, all bills introduced in the Senate or House of Representatives are referred to the committee in that chamber which is charged with consideration of the particular subject of the bill. Members of each committee specialize in that committee's particular area of legislation so that bills receive special analysis before they are reported to the House or Senate.

67. C. Arnold J. Toynbee, English historian, wrote a scholarly 12-volume *A Study of History* (1933–1961). He described twenty-one historic civilizations. In his study he found that each undergoes a "heroic age," a "time of trouble," "a period of stability," and a final "decline."

68. D. Legitimacy played an important part in European politics in the 18th and 19th centuries. Napoleon was a great general (symbolized by the sword), but he came from a family of commoners in Corsica. After his defeat, he was replaced by King Louis XVIII, the "legitimate" king of France. All the nations he fought—England, Austria, Russia, Prussia, and Sweden—were ruled by "legitimate" kings.

69. E. The USSR suffered more than 7 million military deaths in World War II. Vast areas of the Soviet Union were overrun by the German armies. Leningrad survived a terrible siege. In addition to the military losses, the USSR lost 13 million civilians in the war for a total of 20 million, by far the heaviest losses of all nations in the conflict.

70. A. Even though President Woodrow Wilson was the architect of the League, the Senate of the United States refused to approve U.S. membership. So the United States did not join the League of Nations.

71. B. In 1919, Senator Henry Cabot Lodge of Massachusetts presented, in the U.S. Senate, 14 "reservations" to joining the League of Nations. These reservations are shown as a roped-off area keeping the United States out of the water (the League of Nations). On November 19, 1919, the U.S. Senate rejected the treaty that would have made the U.S.A. a member of the League of Nations.

72. C. The cartoon shows the United States as a big overgrown child (with pail and shovel in the sand). The little U.S. Senate, dominated by Senator Lodge, is making the "child" behave.

73. D. Woodrow Wilson was president of the United States in 1919. Wilson refused to accept any of the Lodge Reservations, fearing they would weaken the League. He could not get two-thirds of the Senate to approve U.S. membership in the League without the reservations.

74. A. The region was called Louisiana. This vast territory between the Mississippi River and the Rocky Mountains was sold to the United States in 1803 by Napoleon for $15,000,000. Thirteen states or parts of states were later carved out of this purchase.

75. D. The Erie Canal extended from Albany on the Hudson River westward to Buffalo on Lake Erie. It was formally opened in October, 1825.

76. A. The political dynasty which began in Louisiana in the 1930's was named after Huey Pierce Long (1893–1935). Long, called "Kingfish," became Governor of Louisiana and U.S. Senator from Louisiana. He ruled the state with an iron hand. He was a candidate for President of the U.S. when he was assassinated in 1935.

77. D. In the graph, the line S_1S_1 moves to S_2S_2 because of an additional cost to the producer. This additional cost causes a decrease in supply represented by movement of the supply curve from S_1S_1 to S_2S_2.

78. D. The shift from S_1S_1 to S_2S_2 which represents a decrease in supply (question #77 above) could have been caused by a freeze in the orange groves in Florida. It could also be caused by a voluntary decrease resulting, for example, from the imposition of a new tax on the producer.

79. B. The concept "It is the constant tendency in all animated life to increase beyond the nourishment prepared for it" is the basic premise of *An Essay on the Principles of Population* (1798). Malthus believed that this tendency would be counteracted by war, famine, disease, or birth control which he called "moral restraint."

80. C. If "economic man" were to act according to supposedly rational nature, he might well subscribe to a consumer research publication, but he would definitely not act as described in any of the other four choices.

81. C. The Chinese Exclusion Act of 1882 was extended and made permanent in 1902. Chinese immigration to the United States was prohibited, and Chinese could not become naturalized citizens. The law was changed in 1943 to allow Chinese in the United States to become naturalized citizens.

82. E. Many Lutherans from Scandinavia migrated to the United States during the 19th century. They tended to settle in places like Minnesota, where the climate and farming conditions were similar to those in Scandinavia (especially Sweden and Norway).

83. B. Prime Minister Herbert Asquith forced the House of Lords to give up its veto power by voting for the Parliament Act of 1911. The House of Lords could still hold up an ordinary bill for two years but no longer.

84. E. The South Korean head of state, President Chun Doo Hwan, is a member of the Mongoloid race. The people of the other four countries are classified as Caucasian.

85. D. The word "anthropomorphic" comes from the Greek, meaning human form. Anthropomorphism as a religious concept means giving human form or characteristics to a god or goddess. This was a key aspect of the religion of the ancient Greeks.

86. A. The term "role" is used in sociology to mean the way a person is expected to behave in a particular group, i.e., family, work group, school, church, or club. Roles are more formalized in primitive societies than they are, for example, in Europe and America.

87. C. The physiocrats were a group of 18th-century French economists whose founder, Francois Quesnay, held that all wealth originated with land. According to the physiocrats, agriculture alone had the potential to increase wealth.

88. D. The attitude of the fifty per cent of Americans who do not belong to a church toward organized denominations seems to be mildly friendly. This is evidenced by charitable contributions, voting patterns, and other public activities relating to church interests.

89. A. More than 17 million Americans trace their ancestry to Germany alone. If partial European ancestry is included, the number of German ancestry becomes 51 million. This is larger than any other national origin of present-day Americans. Heavy German immigration dates from the failure of the liberal movement of 1848 in Germany.

90. A. The Congress of Vienna (1814–15) reorganized Europe after the Napoleonic Wars. The Holy Roman Empire ceased to exist. Thirty-eight states were loosely joined in the German Confederation.

91. C. Under the parliamentary system of government developed by the British, the prime minister is the leader of the majority in the House of Commons. The appointment of the prime minister by the monarch is a mere formality.

92. C. Britain was the moving spirit in organizing the various coalitions against Napoleon. The Quadruple Alliance of 1814, consisting of Russia, Prussia, Austria, and Britain, was organized by Viscount Castlereagh, the British foreign minister. Their combined armies, led by the British Duke of Wellington, defeated Napoleon at the Battle of Waterloo in Belgium (1815).

93. E. "Manifest Destiny" was the belief of American expansionists that it was the obvious fate of the United States to spread its system of democracy. The phrase was used to justify the annexation of Texas, the acquisition of the Oregon territory, the purchase of Alaska, and, finally, the involvement in the Spanish-American War.

94. C. William Lloyd Garrison (1805–1879) was a militant abolitionist. He was publisher of the Boston abolitionist newspaper, *The Liberator.* In the first issue (Jan. 1, 1831), he announced his intention to fight against slavery and said: "I will not retreat a single inch—AND I WILL BE HEARD. "

95. C. The Jacobins were a radical political club in France. They came to power at the height of the French Revolution and conducted a "reign of terror" in

1794. The New England Federalists were opponents of the aims and methods of the revolutionary government of France.

96. D. These were the ideas of Friedrich Engels (1820–1895). He was co-author, with Karl Marx, of the *Communist Manifesto* (1848). He collaborated with Marx in the latter's great work, the three-volume *Capital*.

97. E. The Seventeenth Amendment to the U.S. Constitution, adopted in 1913, reads: "The Senate of the United States shall be composed of two Senators from each state, elected by the people thereof . . . . " The words "elected by the people thereof" replaced the words "chosen by the legislature thereof" in the original Constitution.

98. B. In *The Syllabus of Errors* (1864), Pope Pius IX rejected the liberal ideas of the European Revolutions of 1848. He denounced faith in rationalism and science. The *Syllabus* was in the form of a warning to Catholics, not a matter of dogma incumbent upon them to believe.

99. A. The idea that social problems derive from the fact that all men are not equipped for the onerous struggle against nature was developed by the pioneer American sociologist, William Graham Sumner (1840–1910). His classic work, *Folkways*, was published in 1907.

100. D. Addicts usually return to their old circle of friends who expect them to become readdicted, but psycho-physiological dependence on drugs can be completely eliminated as evidenced by the fact that drug treatment centers have on their staffs former drug addicts who have been cured.

101. D. The term "anticlerical" means hostility toward the church. The word "cleric" is derived from the Latin "clericus," meaning a member of the clergy.

102. B. "Caste" in 19th-century India, a rigid class system, with prescribed rights and privileges, was sanctioned by dominant religious precepts and political ideology. In the United States, the social inequality of blacks is sanctioned by neither.

103. B. The U.S. Supreme Court interprets the Constitution in difficult cases. Its decisions are given in the form of "opinions," both majority and dissenting. These opinions often have the effect of changing or enlarging the Constitution. Hence, the court may be considered a continuous constitutional convention.

104. B. In the late 1920's and early 1930's, Japan's economy suffered because of the decline of foreign trade. Japan has limited natural resources, and its economy, in an industrial world, is dependent on foreign trade. In the late 19th and early 20th centuries, the major industrial powers erected trade barriers and other economic blocks to foreign trade.

105. C. Both Confucius (551 B.C.–479 B.C.) and Buddha (563 B.C.–483 B.C.) lived in the 6th century of the pre-Christian era.

106. E. In Sweden, 75% of the population between 5–19 are in school. The national literacy rate is 99%. The annual natural increase in population is less than one-half of one per cent. The relation between education and fertility has reached an equilibrium.

107. D. Modern business is in sharp contrast to what it was early in this century. Today, teamwork and cooperation feature labor-management relations. "Cutthroat" price competition is avoided. It is not uncommon for children of working-class parents to reach the highest rung of corporate management and control.

108. A. The population of the United States in 1900 was 76,000,000. Of these, some 51 million were over 20 years of age. Of these, 2,100,000, or less than 5%, were high school graduates.

109. C. Marco Polo, 13th-century merchant and traveler, was born in Venice. He traveled overland to China and reached Peiping in 1272. He remained there 20 years. On his return to Venice he wrote an account of his travels and of Kublai Khan, China's ruler.

110. A. The first written constitution, presented in France in 1791 by the Constituent Assembly, vested sovereign power in the Legislative Assembly. The king was given only a suspensive veto power by which legislation desired by the Assembly could be postponed.

111. D. The modern name for what was formerly referred to as Persia is Iran. After World War I, Turkey, and to a lesser extent its neighbor Persia, experienced revolutions. In 1935, to emphasize its break with the past, Persia took the name of Iran.

112. E. The standard deviation is a measure of the spread of a set of numerical values around their mean. In a normal distribution, the per cent of observations falling between two standard deviations above and below the mean would be approximately 95%.

113. C. Higher education has traditionally been academic in character. During the decades since World War II, the vocational, though not entirely absent in the past, has become numerically more significant. Collegiate is an overall term. Non-conformist and militaristic are numerically much less significant.

114. B. If a President were to be impeached, the trial would be in the Senate. Article I, Section 3, Clause 6 provides: "The Senate shall have the sole power to try all impeachments."

115. A. No culture is entirely static. Every culture is learned by its members, is partly material and partly non-material, and includes norms of behavior.

116. D. American culture is in flux and is moving toward equality of power of husband and wife. It is moving away from emphasis on the traditional, away from patriarchy, but not toward matriarchy.

117. A. A caste system of social stratification requires that each individual be easily identified by caste and that he or she remain for life within the caste of birth. In an urban society, individuals tend to become anonymous, intermarry more readily, and thus tend to destroy caste structure.

118. D. In his *On Liberty* (1859), John Stuart Mill, English philosopher, argued for freedom of thought and expression, claiming that exposure to unpopular opposing views was a necessity in a liberal society: "the only purpose for which power can be rightfully exercised over any member of a civilized community, against his will, is to prevent harm to others."

119. A. Christianity had been brought to Japan in 1549 by St. Francis Xavier. For a century, it prospered. Then, in the 17th century, it was violently suppressed. Japan's rulers chose isolation for two centuries. They feared that Christianity, a foreign influence, would be harmful to Japan.

120. C. Items A, B, D, and E are essentially true. They constitute evidence against instinct as an explanation of marriage and the family. Item C is irrelevant to the argument.

121. D. Alexis de Tocqueville (1805–59), French writer, traveled in America during the 1830's. In his *Democracy in America* (1835) he described, with approval, the political and economic growth he saw. He would agree with the economist Karl Marx that most controversy in modern society would be over property rights, a key tenet of Marxian economics.

122. C. Suicide rates in the United States, Canada, England, and Australia are in the middle of brackets, i.e., about 10 to 15 per hundred thousand. Austria, West Germany, Hungary, Japan, Sweden, and Switzerland report rates of over 20 per 100,000, while Italy, the Netherlands, and Spain report under 10 per 100,000. Secularization and urbanization do not seem to be directly related to the incidence of suicide.

123. C. When Great Britain was at war with Napoleon, the British "orders in council" (1807) required that no neutral ship could enter the continent of Europe without first stopping at a British port. In 1863 when Britain was a neutral in the American Civil War, there was strong protest over the removal by the U.S. of two southern agents from the British ship "Trent."

124. B. In the United States today, the contrast between middle-class youth and working-class youth that seems most defensible is: "Middle-class youths see their problem as deciding what to do; working-class youths see their problem as finding a job."

125. E. The Federal Reserve, established by Congress in 1913, is directly responsible to Congress. Its authority and responsibility derive from Congressional legislation and oversight, even though members of its Board of Governors are appointed by the President of the United States for 14-year terms.

CHAPTER 16

Background and Practice Questions

DESCRIPTION OF THE GENERAL EXAMINATION IN SOCIAL SCIENCES AND HISTORY

History and the social sciences are treated together in the CLEP General Examinations. The test consists of 125 questions divided into two forty-five minute parts; each part deals with both history and social sciences. Historical material relating primarily to American, European, and African/Asian history accounts for over one third of the questions. Most of the remainder of the questions relate to concepts and information from sociology, social psychology, economics, political science, and social science methodology. The approximate percent of examination questions for each area covered on the test is as follows:

History (35%)

10–15% United States History
Requires a general understanding of historical issues associated with the following periods in United States history: colonial, revolutionary, late eighteenth and early nineteenth centuries, Civil War and Reconstruction, and late nineteenth and twentieth centuries

10–15% Western Civilization
Requires familiarity with three broad historical periods: ancient, medieval, and modern

Social Sciences (65%)

25–30% Sociology, including topics such as
- Methods and statistics
- Demography
- Ecology
- Social stratification
- Deviance and criminology
- Social organization

15–20% Economics, with emphasis on microeconomics topics such as
- Consumer theory
- Production theory
- Investment function
- Fiscal policy
- Monetary policy
- Money and banking
- Business cycles

5–10% African/Asian Civilizations
Requires knowledge of topics such as colonialism, growth of empire and trade, political developments, the role of Europe in Africa, and independence

15–20% Political Science, including topics such as
- Constitutional government
- Voting and political behavior
- International relations and comparative government

3–5% Social Psychology, including topics such as
- Aggression
- Socialization
- Conformity
- Methodology
- Group formation
- Performance

If you want to do well on this test, you should have a very clear sense of chronological relations in history, as well as an understanding of the issues and ideas which have been current in different historical eras. You should have some idea of the relative significance of various ideologies, scientific concepts, and historical events. If you have, on your own or during the course work, read widely in history and sociology (including the history of economic and sociological theories), you will be able to answer a large number of the questions without difficulty. Technical concepts and terms from contemporary economics, social psychology, and political science are tested in a large number of questions. However, if you have an acquaintance with the material emphasized in introductions to these subjects, you are well prepared to answer the questions.

There are a number of accomplishments which the questions endeavor to test. Some questions require mere factual recall. Others ask you to go beyond factual recall to the deduction of a correct answer from the information given in the question and from your own knowledge. Still others are designed to test your ability to apply conceptual principles or theories to particular problems. Many of the questions will demand much of you. You will be asked to judge, to weigh, to rank, to discriminate, and to compare and contrast facts and ideas.

SCORING; PENALTY FOR GUESSING

Although questions on history and on the social sciences are intermingled in both parts of the examination, a separate subscore is reported for each area. Each correct answer is worth one point. There is no penalty for an unanswered question. One fourth of a point is deducted for a wrong answer; therefore random guessing is not likely to improve your score. If, however, you can eliminate one or more answer choices as clearly incorrect, it may be worthwhile to choose from the remaining choices the one that seems most logical.

THE KINDS OF QUESTIONS THAT APPEAR ON THE EXAMINATION

To give you an idea of the various types of questions you will face, we shall give some examples here and, where necessary, explain the process by which the right answer is derived. Simple recall questions are straightforward and require no explanation. Some examples of simple recall items follow, with the correct square blackened.

When did the British Navy defeat the Spanish Armada? Ⓐ ● Ⓒ Ⓓ Ⓔ
(A) 1066 (B) 1588 (C) 1648 (D) 1688 (E) 1750

What was the name of the treaty ending the Thirty Years' War? Ⓐ Ⓑ Ⓒ ● Ⓔ
(A) Treaty of Ghent (B) Treaty of Paris
(C) Treaty of Burgundy (D) Treaty of Westphalia
(E) Treaty of London

Where did General Grant in 1865 accept the surrender of General Lee? Ⓐ Ⓑ Ⓒ ● Ⓔ
(A) Richmond (B) Vicksburg (C) Gettysburg
(D) Appomattox (E) Atlanta

Who was the Prime Minister of Great Britain during the negotiations leading to the Treaty of Versailles in 1919? Ⓐ Ⓑ Ⓒ ● Ⓔ
(A) Winston Churchill (B) William Pitt (C) Stanley Baldwin
(D) Lloyd George (E) Clement Attlee

A number of questions will test your ability to recall a number of related facts. An example of this type follows:

You are in a small country which now is landlocked. In the 19th century, its major was the capital of an empire with a vast polyglot population. In which of the following countries are you? Ⓐ Ⓑ Ⓒ ● Ⓔ
(A) Bolivia (B) Switzerland (C) Paraguay (D) Austria
(E) France

Explanation: Austria is the answer, but you must know a number of facts to deduce this answer. France's major city was the capital of a vast polyglot empire in the 19th century. But France is not landlocked. Bolivia, Switzerland, and Paraguay are all landlocked, but their major cities were not centers of large empires in the 19th century. Only Austria fits all the conditions. It is now landlocked after losing vast holdings at Versailles. Its capital city, Vienna, was the center of the vast polyglot Austrian Empire during the 19th century.

Another type of question tests your ability to attach major concepts to their original authors. An example follows:

Who held that the division of labor was the key to economic progress and that freedom in trade broadened markets, which in turn led to more division of labor and thus economic progress? Ⓐ Ⓑ ● Ⓓ Ⓔ
(A) Toynbee (B) Marx (C) Adam Smith
(D) Thomas Aquinas (E) Aristotle

Explanation: The interests of all the writers except Adam Smith were centered on issues quite otherwise than the effect of free trade on economic progress. Thus, Adam Smith is the answer.

Another type of question attempts to examine your facility in applying certain social science principles. An example follows:

The marginal propensity to consume in a population is 0.50. Investment expenditures increase by one billion dollars. Everything else being equal, you would expect national income to increase by about how many billion **dollars**? Ⓐ ● Ⓒ Ⓓ Ⓔ
(A) 1 (B) 2 (C) 5 (D) 50 (E) 500

Explanation: The student who is acquainted with the "multiplier" concept and the fact that it is tied to the marginal propensity to consume by the formula $M = \frac{1}{1\text{-}MPC}$ would know that two billion dollars is the answer. He would be applying certain principles from economics to get the answer.

Yet another type of question deals with the central themes which characterize various schools or traditions of thought. An example follows:

History moves in a path which ends only when world-wide stateless communism reigns. The struggle of economic classes is the engine of movement. This viewpoint is characteristic of Ⓐ Ⓑ Ⓒ Ⓓ ●
(A) Transcendentalism (B) Dialectical Idealism
(C) Freudianism (D) Scholasticism (E) Dialectical Materialism

Explanation: The student who knows both that Marxism uses dialectical processes and that Marx thought material conditions the basis of change would see that only the term, Dialectical Materialism, could fit the ideas in the above viewpoint.

HISTORICAL TIME LINE

The time line that follows will give you an overview of important events in history and the sequence in which they occurred. Keep in mind that no list of this sort is exhaustive; do not use the time line alone as the sole source of review for the history portion of the test. Use it as a brief, introductory review, possibly to help you pinpoint the events and historical periods you need to spend most of your study time on. A day or two before the exam, look at the time line again to stimulate your memory and put your mind into the proper historical gear.

HISTORICAL TIME LINE

Ancient World

c. 3500 B.C.	Sumerian civilization (Mesopotamia)
c. 3100 B.C.	Upper and Lower Egypt united under King Menes (First Dynasty)
c. 3000–1550 B.C.	Indus Valley culture
c. 2700–2200 B.C.	Egyptian Old Kingdom
c. 2500–1400 B.C.	Minoan civilization (Crete)
c. 1800 B.C.	Hammurabi's code of laws (Babylonia)
c. 1800–1100 B.C.	Shang (Yin) Dynasty (China)
c. 1375 B.C.	Akhnaton and Egyptian monotheism
c. 1250 B.C.	Moses and Hebrew law
1194–1184 B.C.	Trojan Wars
c. 1122–256 B.C.	Chou Dynasty in China
1025–930 B.C.	Hebrew monarchy
c. 800 B.C.	Homer's epics
c. 753 B.C.	Founding of Rome
745–612 B.C.	Assyrian Empire
c. 630–553 B.C.	Zoroaster (Persia)
c. 604 B.C.	Birth of Lao Tzu (Chinese Taoism)
594–3 B.C.	Solon's laws (Athens)
563–483 B.C.	Buddha (India)
551–479 B.C.	Confucius (China)
509 B.C.	Roman Republic established
490–449 B.C.	Greek (Delian League)—Persian Wars
431–404 B.C.	Peloponnesian Wars
399 B.C.	Death of Socrates
334–323 B.C.	Conquests by Alexander (the Great) of Macedonia
c. 320 B.C.	Gupta Empire founded; India begins a golden age
c. 273–232 B.C.	Reign of Ashoka (India)
264–146 B.C.	Rome's intermittent Punic Wars
221–210 B.C.	Shih Huang-ti (China's "First Emperor"); The Great Wall
202 B.C.	Han Dynasty established (China)
105 B.C.	Chinese invent paper
44 B.C.	Assassination of Julius Caesar
27 B.C.	Augustus Caesar becomes first Roman emperor
c. 6 B.C.	Birth of Jesus
c. 30 A.D.	The Crucifixion
70	Roman forces capture Jerusalem
c. 200	Rise of power of the Papacy
331	Founding of Constantinople
c. 400	Peak of Mayan civilization
400–1240	Ghana controls Niger trade (Africa)
440	Invasion of Europe by the Huns
476	Geramic "barbarians" take Rome

Medieval World

496	King Clovis of the Franks converted to Christianity
527–565	Justinian I rules Byzantine Empire, codifies Roman Law
570	Birth of Mohammed
c. 600	Buddhism reaches Japan
622	The Hejira (Mohammed's flight from Mecca)
711	Arab invasion of Spain from Africa
732	Battle of Tours (Charles Martel leads Franks in victory over invading Arabs)
800	Charlemagne crowned Emperor
936–973	Otto I Holy Roman Emperor
c. 1000	Vikings reach North America
1006	Muslim invasion of India
1066	Norman conquest of England (Battle of Hastings)
1095	Start of the First Crusade
c. 1150	Building of Angkor Wat (Khmers)
1192	Yoritomo becomes first shogun to rule Japan

Medieval World

c.1200–1500	Aztec Empire (Mexico)	1348–50	Black Death (Europe)
1211–23	Conquests of Ghengis Khan	1450	Gutenberg's movable type perfected
1215	Magna Carta (England)	1450	The Renaissance begins in Europe
c. 1279	Kublai Khan leads Mongols in completing conquest of China	1453	Constantinople falls to the Turks
1337–1453	Hundred Years War (Europe)	1469	Birth of Nanak, founder of Sikhism (India)

United States		World	
1492	Columbus's first voyage to America	1492	"Reconquest" of Spain by Christians
		1517	Luther's "95 Theses" (beginning of the Reformation)
		1519–22	Magellan circles the globe
		1519	Cortes conquers the Aztecs (Mexico)
		1533	Pizarro invades Peru
		1536	Henry VIII establishes Anglican Church
		1556–1605	Akbar rules Mughal India
		1571	Turkish fleet defeated at Lepanto
		1588	Defeat of Spanish Armada by Royal Navy of England
		1592	Hideyoshi, Japanese unifier, invades Korea
		1603–1867	Tokugawa Shogunate begins in Japan
1607	Founding of Jamestown, Virginia	1608	French establish Quebec City
		1611	King James version of the Bible
		1618–48	Thirty Years War (Europe)
1619	Virginia establishes House of Burgesses (first legislature)		
1619	First black indentured servants (slaves) arrive in Virginia		
1620	Puritan Separatists (Pilgrims) arrive at Plymouth		
1620	Mayflower Compact		
1636	Harvard founded		
		1642–49	English Civil War ("Great Migration" to America)
1643	New England Confederation organized		
		1644	Manchu dynasty founded (China)

United States		World	
1647	Public schools founded (Massachusetts)		
1651	First English Navigation Act passed	1651	Dutch settlers in South Africa
1676	Bacon's Rebellion (Virginia)		
1676	King Philip's War (New England)		
		1688	Glorious Revolution (England)
		1688	Bill of Rights (England)
1692	Salem witchcraft trials		
1735	John Peter Zenger trial (free press)		
		1751	Diderot's *Encyclopedia* (France)
1754–63	French and Indian War (New France ceded to England)		
		1756–63	Seven Years' War (Europe)
		1759	Watt's steam engine
1765	Stamp Act (repealed in 1766)		
1774	"Intolerable Acts" closed Boston Harbor		
1774	First Continental Congress meets		
1775–83	The American Revolution		
1776	Declaration of Independence	1776	Adam Smith's *Wealth of Nations*
		1776	The Enlightenment period begins in Europe
1778	Alliance with France		
1781	Articles of Confederation ratified		
1783	Treaty of Paris officially ends Revolutionary War		
1787	Shays' Rebellion (Massachusetts)		
1787	Northwest Ordinance		
1787	Constitutional Convention opens		
1789	Washington becomes first president	1789	French Revolution begins
1790	Slater's first textile mill for spinning cotton		
1791	Bill of Rights ratified		
1793	Cotton gin perfected		
1793	Proclamation of Neutrality		
1794	Whiskey Rebellion	1794	Reign of Terror ends in France
		1794	Mackenzie reaches the Pacific (Canada)
1798–99	Undeclared naval war with France		
1798	Alien and Sedition Acts		
1798	Kentucky and Virginia Resolutions		
1803	Louisiana Purchase doubles size of U.S.		

United States		World	
1803	*Marbury v. Madison* (Marshall Supreme Court establishes precedent for judicial review of laws of Congress)		
1804–1806	Lewis and Clark expedition	1804–14	Napoleon is Emperor of France
1807	Embargo Act		
1808	Importation of slaves outlawed		
		1809–26	Wars of Latin-American Independence
1812–15	Second war with England (War of 1812)		
		1815	Battle of Waterloo (Napoleon is defeated)
		1815	Congress of Vienna
1816	Protective tariff		
1816	Second Bank of the U.S. chartered		
1820	Missouri Compromise		
1823	Monroe Doctrine		
1825	Erie Canal opens		
1827	Baltimore and Ohio Railroad chartered		
		1830	Revolutions in Europe
1831	Nat Turner slave rebellion		
1832–33	Nullification crisis (tariff)	1832	English (political) Reform Act
1835	Indian removal ("Trail of Tears")		
1836	Republic of Texas established		
1837	Panic of 1837	1837	Rebellion in Canada
		1839–42	Opium Wars (China)
		1845–47	Potato famine in Ireland
1846–48	Mexican War	1846	Repeal of English Corn Laws
1847	Mormons reach Utah		
1848	Gold discovered in California	1848	Revolutions in Europe
1848	Women's Rights Convention (New York)	1848	Marx's *Communist Manifesto*
1850	Compromise Bills		
1854	Kansas-Nebraska Act (slavery)	1854–56	Crimean War
1854	Republican Party founded	1854	Perry arrives in Japan
		1857–58	"Mutiny" in India
1859	Drake's oil well (first commercially productive oil well)	1859	John Stuart Mill's *On Liberty*
1859	John Brown's raid on Harpers Ferry	1859	Darwin's *The Origin of the Species*
1860	Election of Abraham Lincoln		
1861–65	Civil War	1861	Emancipation of Serfs (Russia)
		1861–66	Maximillian in Mexico
1862	Homestead Act; Landgrant Act		
1863	Emancipation Proclamation		
1865	Lincoln assassinated		

United States

1865–70	Civil War Amendments (13th–15th)
1865–76	Southern "Reconstruction"
1867	U.S. buys Alaska from Russia
1868	Impeachment of Andrew Jackson
1869	First transcontinental railroad
1876	Bell invents telephone
1876	Hayes-Tilden disputed election
1877	Edison invents phonograph
1879	Edison invents electric light
1879	Standard Oil Trust organized
1883	Civil Service reform (Pendleton Act)
1886	Haymarket riot in Chicago (labor)
1886	American Federation of Labor founded
1887	Interstate Commerce Commission
1887	Dawes Act (Native Americans)
1889	First Pan American Conference
1890	Sherman Antitrust Act
1890	Battle of Wounded Knee (last major conflict between Indians and U.S. troops)
1890	"Closing" of the frontier
1896	Marconi's wireless telegraph
1898	Spanish-American War
1898	Philippine "Insurrection"
1899	"Open Door" policy in China
1903	Wright Brothers flight
1908	"Model T" Ford auto
1909	Perry claims to reach North Pole
1914	Panama Canal opened

World

1867	Dominion of Canada established (British North America Act)
1867	Marx's *Das Kapital*
1868	Meiji restoration (Japan)
1869	Suez Canal opened
1870	Italian unification completed
1871	Franco-Prussian War
1871	German unification
1882	British invade and occupy Egypt
1884	Berlin Conference (on partitioning Africa)
1885	Indian Congress Party formed
1889	Japanese Constitution
1894	Sino-Japanese War
1899–1902	Boer War (South Africa)
1899	Boxer Rebellion (China)
1900	Freud's *Interpretation of Dreams*
1904–05	Russo-Japanese War (Japan defeats Russia)
1905	Revolution in Russia
1905	Einstein's theory of relativity
1910	Revolution in Mexico
1911	Chinese Republic (Sun Yat-sen)
1914–18	World War I (The Great War)

United States		World	
1914	Federal Trade Commission created		
1917	U.S. enters the war	1917	Russian Revolution
1919	Senate rejects Treaty of Versailles		
1919–20	"Great Red Scare"		
1920	Woman suffrage amendment (19th)	1920	Founding of League of Nations
1921	Washington Disarmament Conference		
1921 & 24	Restrictive immigration laws		
		1922	Fascist dictatorship in Italy (Mussolini)
		1924	Death of Lenin; Stalin in power
1927	Lindberg's solo flight to Paris		
1929	Stock market crash; Great Depression		
		1930	Gandhi's Salt March (India)
		1931	Japan invades Manchuria
1933	Roosevelt's "100 Days"; New Deal; "Good Neighbor" policy	1933	Hitler in power (Germany)
		1934–35	Long March (China)
1935–37	Neutrality Acts	1935	Italy attacks Ethiopia
		1936–39	Spanish Civil War
		1937	Japan at war with China
		1938	Munich Conference
		1939–45	World War II
		1939–45	The Holocaust
1941	Japanese attack Pearl Harbor	1941	Germany attacks Russia
		1941	Japanese victories in the Pacific
1942	The computer perfected		
		1944	"D Day" landings in France
1945	Atomic bombing of Hiroshima and Nagasaki	1945	United Nations organized
		1946	Nuremberg war crimes trials
		1946–55	Juan Peron (Argentina)
1947	Truman Doctrine ("Cold War" begins)	1947	Independence for India/Pakistan
1947	Marshall Plan for Europe		
1948	Organization of American States created	1948	Assassination of Gandhi (India)
1948	Television mass-marketing begins	1948	Creation of nation of Israel
		1948–49	Berlin blockade and airlift
		1949	NATO established
		1949	Communist victory in China
1950	U.S. enters Korean War		
1953	DNA structure discovered by Watson		
1954	School desegregation decision; integration crises	1954	Battle of Dien Bien Phu (Indo-China)
		1954	Geneva Treaty
		1954	SEATO Alliance formed

United States	
1956	Interstate highway system begun
1961	Bay of Pigs Invasion (Cuba)
1961	Peace Corps; Alliance for Progress
1962	Cuban Missile Crisis
1963	John F. Kennedy assassinated
1964	U.S. military build-up in Vietnam
1964	Johnson's "Great Society" and "War on Poverty"
1967–68	Urban riots
1968	Assassinations of Martin Luther King, Jr. and Robert Kennedy
1969	Men landed on the moon
1969	Anti-Vietnam War demonstrations
1972	Nixon visit to China
1972	SALT Treaty with USSR
1972	Watergate break-in
1973	OPEC oil boycott
1973	U.S. withdrawal in Vietnam
1974	Nixon resigns; pardoned by Ford
1978	Panama Canal retrocession treaty
1979	Three Mile Island, Pennsylvania, nuclear accident
1979–81	Hostages seized in Iran
1980s	AIDS epidemic; rising drug problem
1981	"Supply side" economics; tax cuts; debt increase; trade imbalances
1983	U.S. aid to Nicaraguan contras
1983	Invasion of Grenada
1984	Geraldine Ferraro, first woman vice-presidential candidate

World	
1956	Hungarian Revolution
1956	Suez crisis
1957	Russians launch *Sputnik I,* the first space satellite
1957	Independence for Ghana (Africa)
1957	European Common Market established
1959	Castro victory in Cuba
1961	Berlin Wall constructed
1966–76	Cultural Revolution in China
1967	Arab-Israeli Six Day War
1968	"Prague Spring" (Czechoslovakia)
1973	Yom Kippur War
1973	Coup unseats Allende in Chile
1975	Communist victory in Vietnam
1979	Revolution in Iran topples Shah
1979	USSR invades Afghanistan
1979	Sandinistas oust Somoza (Nicaragua)
1980	Iran-Iraq War begins
1981	Assassination of Egyptian President Anwar Sadat
1981	Solidarity Movement (Poland)
1983	Anti-Apartheid movement (South Africa)
1984	Assassination of Indian Prime Minister Indira Gandhi
1984	Famines in Africa
1985	Gorbachev made Communist Party Secretary (USSR)

United States		World	
1986	Iran-Contra Scandal	1986	Marcos overthrown (Philippines)
		1986	Chernobyl nuclear accident (USSR)
1987	INF Treaty (armaments)	1987	Glasnost and Perestroika (USSR)
		1987	Meech Lake Agreement on French culture in Quebec
		1988	Riots in Israeli-occupied areas
1989	Exxon Valdez oil spill (Alaska) environmental concerns	1989	Student demonstrations in China suppressed
		1989	Nationalist movements in USSR and Eastern Europe

STUDY RESOURCES

For review, you might consult the following books. Note that to prepare for this exam, you will need to use several books since no single book covers all the topics on the test.

GENERAL

Hunt, Elgin F. and David C. Colander. *Social Science: An Introduction to the Study of Society.* 6th ed. New York: Macmillan, 1987.

AMERICAN HISTORY

Bailey, Thomas A. and David M. Kennedy. *The American Pageant: A History of the Republic.* 7th ed. Lexington, MA: D.C. Heath & Co., 1983.

Norton, Mary Beth et al. *A People and a Nation: A History of the U.S.* 2nd ed. Boston: Houghton Mifflin Co., 1986.

WESTERN CIVILIZATION

Langer, William L., ed. *An Encyclopedia of World History.* 5th ed. Boston: Houghton Mifflin Co., 1972/1980.

McNeill, William H. *History of Western Civilization: A Handbook.* 6th ed. Chicago: University of Chicago Press, 1986.

AFRICAN/ASIAN CIVILIZATIONS

Fairbank, John K., Edwin O. Reischauer, and Albert M. Craig. *East Asia: Tradition and Transformation.* Rev. ed. Boston: Houghton Mifflin Co., 1989.

Martin, Phyllis M. and Patrick O'Meara, eds. *Africa.* 2nd ed. Bloomington: Indiana University Press, 1986.

Rosenfeld, E., and H. Geller, *Afro-Asian Culture Studies.* 4th ed. Hauppauge, NY: Barron's Educational Series, 1979.

ECONOMICS

Galbraith, John K. *Economics in Perspective: A Critical History.* Boston: Houghton Mifflin Co., 1987.

Heilbroner, Robert. *The Worldly Philosophers.* 6th ed. New York: Simon & Schuster, 1986.

Heilbroner, Robert and Lester Thurow. *Economics Explained.* New York: Simon & Schuster, 1987.

SOCIOLOGY

Coser, Lewis A. et al. *Introduction to Sociology.* 2nd ed. San Diego: Harcourt Brace Jovanovich, 1987.

Turner, Jonathan H. *Sociology: The Science of Human Organization.* Chicago: Nelson-Hall, 1986.

POLITICAL SCIENCE

Lawson, Kay. *The Human Polity: An Introduction to Political Science.* 2nd ed. Boston: Houghton Mifflin Co., 1989.

Lose, Richard, ed. *Corwin on the Constitution.* 2 vol. Ithaca, NY: Cornell University Press, 1981.

Riemer, Neal. *Political Science: An Introduction to Politics.* San Diego: Harcourt Brace Jovanovich, 1983.

SOCIAL PSYCHOLOGY

Lindesmith, Alfred R. et al. *Social Psychology.* 6th ed. New York: Prentice-Hall, 1988.

ANTHROPO-GEOGRAPHY

De Blij, Harm J. *Human Geography: Culture, Society and Space.* 2nd ed. New York: John Wiley and Sons, 1982.

PRACTICE QUESTIONS ON SOCIAL SCIENCES–HISTORY

Before attempting a whole sample examination over the vast social sciences area, let's look at some other examples, by specific subject. You should become acquainted with the various kinds of information which you will be asked to provide when you take the entire CLEP test. Sometimes it is difficult to decide in which subject area a question belongs, and in some cases we have had to arbitrarily assign a question to a particular discipline.

Questions about American History

Directions: Each of the questions or incomplete statements below is followed by five suggested answers or completions. Select the one that is best in each case.

1. Two churches native to America are
   (A) Mormon and Baptist (B) Salvation Army and Baptist
   (C) Quaker and Mormon (D) Adventist and Mormon
   (E) Methodist and Quaker

2. "He made the American vernacular the medium of a great literary work. The vigor of his prose comes directly from the speech of the great valley of the Far West." This statement refers to which of the following people?
(A) Frederick Jackson Turner (B) James Fenimore Cooper
(C) Thomas Jefferson (D) John Dewey (E) Samuel Clemens

3. Tariffs made up more than 85 percent of the federal government's revenue in which of the following years?
(A) 1800 (B) 1865 (C) 1915 (D) 1937 (E) 1955

MAP A

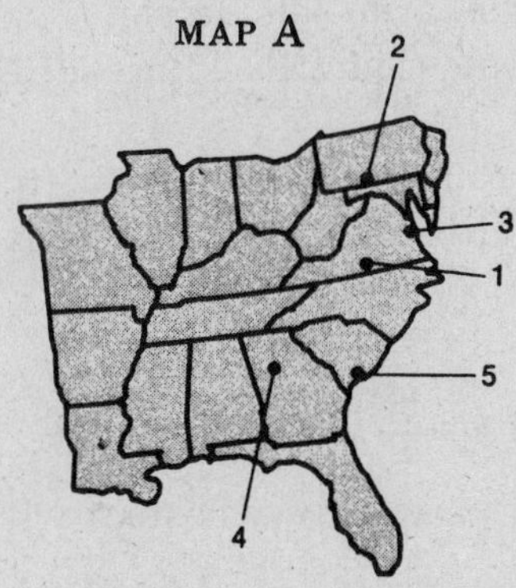

Questions 4–7 pertain to MAP A.

4. Which of the following was the location of the surrender of General Lee to General Grant?
(A) 4 (B) 5 (C) 1 (D) 3 (E) 2

5. Which of the following was the location of a speech by Lincoln after Lee's forces were turned back from their northernmost advance?
(A) 4 (B) 5 (C) 1 (D) 2 (E) 3

6. A fort was fired on in the harbor of this city, and the American Civil War began. Where is it?
(A) 4 (B) 5 (C) 1 (D) 3 (E) 2

7. General Sherman took this city before marching to the sea. Where is it?
(A) 4 (B) 5 (C) 1 (D) 3 (E) 2

8. Which of the following states were formed from the area regulated by the Northwest Ordinance?
(A) Ohio, Indiana, Illinois, Michigan, Wisconsin
(B) Ohio, Kentucky, Illinois, Indiana, Michigan
(C) Ohio, Indiana, Kentucky, Tennessee, Illinois
(D) Ohio, Indiana, Illinois, Iowa, Missouri
(E) Ohio, Indiana, Illinois, Iowa, Nebraska

9. The Jacksonian era was related to
   (A) a reduction in the restrictions regarding suffrage
   (B) the establishment of the Republican party
   (C) legislation creating land grant colleges
   (D) legislation regulating rail transport
   (E) the regular employment of Negroes in government

10. Which of the following sets was not closely associated with the issue of the federal government's sovereignty within the United States?
    (A) Little Rock—Faubus—Eisenhower
    (B) South Carolina—Nullification—Jackson
    (C) Slavery—First Inaugural—Lincoln
    (D) New England—Embargo—Jefferson
    (E) New Deal—Supreme Court Packing—F. D. Roosevelt

11. Each of the following countries is paired with a decade during which large numbers of its citizens migrated to the United States. Which pair is incorrect?
    (A) Sweden—1880s (B) Ireland—1840s (C) Italy—1860s
    (D) Germany—1850s (E) Russia—1890s

12. Which of the following pairs is inconsistent with the rest?
    (A) Lincoln—Douglas
    (B) Jackson—Biddle
    (C) Hamilton—Burr
    (D) Wilson—Lodge
    (E) Jefferson—Madison

13. "How can an industrialized Northeast, a cotton-growing South, and a small farming West now live side by side in peace in our country?" This question about the U.S. might have been asked in
    (A) 1780 (B) 1800 (C) 1815 (D) 1850 (E) 1970

14. The geographical distribution of Negroes in the U.S. changed most in which period?
    (A) 1840-1860 (B) 1860-1880 (C) 1880-1900
    (D) 1920-1940 (E) 1940-1960

15. American politicians talk of the "border" states. Which of the following is one?
    (A) Kansas (B) Indiana (C) Ohio
    (D) Mississippi (E) Tennessee

16. The United States' membership in which of the following organizations is most consistent with the Monroe Doctrine?
    (A) North Atlantic Treaty Organization
    (B) Southeast Asia Treaty Organization
    (C) International Monetary Fund
    (D) Organization of American States
    (E) United Nations Organization

17. "Every state should agree before an action is taken by the federal government." This sentiment is similar to the ideas expressed by
(A) Jackson (B) Webster (C) Hamilton (D) Adams
(E) Calhoun

18. In which presidential election did traditionally Democratic Georgia, Alabama, and Mississippi go Republican?
(A) 1928 (B) 1932 (C) 1956 (D) 1964 (E) 1968

19. In order to avoid involvement in Europe and Asia in the 1930s, the United States relied chiefly upon
(A) collective security
(B) neutrality legislation
(C) the Kellogg-Briand Pact
(D) the League of Nations
(E) the "Good-Neighbor" policy

20. "Things are in the saddle and ride mankind." This statement reflects a revolt against materialism by certain thinkers in 19th-century America. Of which tradition are we speaking?
(A) Liberalism (B) Pragmatism (C) Transcendentalism
(D) Jacksonian Democracy (E) Populism

21. New York became the most populous American city about the time that the
(A) American Revolution ended
(B) Constitution was ratified
(C) Erie Canal was completed
(D) Civil War was fought
(E) link-up of the Union Pacific and the Central Pacific occurred

22. The Supreme Court had ruled that martial law could not legitimately be enforced where civil courts were open. Republicans denounced the decision and talked of "packing" the court. The President at this time in history was
(A) John Kennedy
(B) Abraham Lincoln
(C) Andrew Johnson
(D) Woodrow Wilson
(E) Franklin Roosevelt

ANSWERS TO QUESTIONS ABOUT AMERICAN HISTORY

1. D	**5.** D	**9.** A	**13.** D	**17.** E	**21.** C
2. E	**6.** B	**10.** E	**14.** E	**18.** D	**22.** C
3. A	**7.** A	**11.** C	**15.** E	**19.** B	
4. C	**8.** A	**12.** E	**16.** D	**20.** C	

Questions about Western Civilization

Directions: Each of the questions or incomplete statements below is followed by five suggested answers or completions. Select the one that is best in each case.

1. Which of the following was known to man before the Neolithic period?
   (A) Use of fire
   (B) Domestication of animals
   (C) Making pottery
   (D) Practice of agriculture
   (E) Making glass

2. The center of that civilization which we call Minoan was
   (A) in the islands along the Black Sea
   (B) on the island of Crete
   (C) in the central part of Asia Minor
   (D) on the mainland of Greece
   (E) on the Italian peninsula

3. The decline of power among the Greek city-states can be explained by
   (A) the military power of Persia
   (B) soft living
   (C) rivalry and civil war among the city-states
   (D) the pursuit of philosophy and art to the neglect of political action
   (E) inability to deal with sea power

4. Zoroaster believed that
   (A) the ruler was the living form of a god
   (B) the world was a great struggle between the spirit of good and the spirit of evil
   (C) each part of the world was ruled over by its special spirit
   (D) there was no relation between man's behavior and that of a god
   (E) ancestors should be worshipped

5. As contrasted with English colonial administration, which of the following is true concerning Spanish colonial administration in the 17th and 18th centuries?
   (A) The authority of the Spanish king declined.
   (B) Spain did not maintain or enforce a mercantilist policy.
   (C) Spain permitted religious dissenters in its colonies.
   (D) Spain allowed less autonomy in its provinces in the New World.
   (E) Spain imposed less of a tax burden upon its colonies.

6. Which of the following would have been a member of the bourgeoisie in France prior to 1789?
   (A) Landed noble (B) Peasant (C) Merchant
   (D) Lower-class workman in Paris (E) Bishop

7. In the 4th century B.C., the Greek city-states which had been unable to unite were forcibly brought together under the rule of
(A) Macedon (B) Persia (C) Phoenicia (D) Carthage
(E) Rome

8. The "Donation of Constantine" was a document which supposedly established
(A) Charlemagne's claim to the throne
(B) the Pope's right to political power in the West
(C) Christianity as the legal religion within the Roman Empire
(D) the capital of the Roman Empire at the city of Constantinople
(E) legitimized transfer of power to Byzantium

9. In 1870, a certain nation was among the four or five most populous nations on earth, its language widely used outside its borders. By 1970 it was not among the top ten countries in population, and its influence was much reduced. To what country are we referring?
(A) Netherlands (B) Russia (C) U.S.A. (D) Japan
(E) France

10. What proportion of the USSR's adult citizens are members of the Communist Party?
(A) Over 75% (B) Over 50% (C) Over 33% (D) Over 25%
(E) Under 10%

11. "There are perhaps two nations in this state and great efforts have been made to erase this fact. There is hope these efforts (such as changing the flag design) may succeed." To what country does this statement pertain?
(A) France (B) Sweden (C) Denmark (D) Switzerland
(E) Canada

12. In the 16th century, England was under the rule of which family?
(A) Tudors (B) Stuarts (C) Hapsburgs (D) Valois
(E) Windsors

13. The peace settlement of 1919 divided East Prussia from the rest of Germany by a strip of territory belonging to
(A) Poland (B) Hungary (C) Czechoslovakia
(D) Lithuania (E) Estonia

14. The reign of Marcus Aurelius marked the end of what Edward Gibbon regarded as the great century of the "Roman Peace." Marcus Aurelius lived in which century?
(A) 1st B.C. (B) 1st A.D. (C) 2nd A.D. (D) 4th A.D.
(E) 2nd B.C.

15. Some historians have said that Alexander the Great was "lucky in his death." They mean by this that he
(A) died gloriously in battle amid his troops
(B) died before the beginning of the disastrous retreat from the Indus
(C) died before having to govern the huge empire he conquered
(D) did not live to face defeat at the hands of the conquered peoples who were in revolt
(E) died peacefully of old age

16. Which of these people never invaded the British Isles or established a state there?
(A) Romans (B) Saxons (C) Slavs (D) Danes
(E) Normans

17. Which of these lands was able to remain independent throughout the 19th century?
(A) Burma (B) Java (C) The Philippines (D) Siam
(E) Ceylon

18. In 1904-5, Japan demonstrated its success in modernizing its armed forces by defeating which European power?
(A) Britain (B) France (C) Germany (D) Spain
(E) Russia

19. The Huns were
(A) one of the German tribes
(B) Asian invaders of Europe
(C) Moslem invaders of Europe
(D) the people led by Theodoric who conquered Italy
(E) Vikings who conquered Normandy

20. "If God shows you a way in which you may lawfully get more than in another way (without wrong to your soul or to any other), if you refuse this and choose the less gainful way, you cross one of the ends of your callings, and you refuse to be God's steward." This sentiment was most representative of
(A) Scholasticism (B) 16th-century Anglicanism
(C) 17th-century English Puritanism (D) Monastic thought
(E) Christianity in the 1st century A.D.

21. The Austrian foreign minister who played an important role at the Congress of Vienna was
(A) Talleyrand (B) Metternich (C) Castlereagh
(D) Baron Von Stein (E) Hindenburg

22. Which of the following best describes Alexander the Great?
(A) He dreamed of blending the peoples and cultures of his empire into one.
(B) He so greatly admired Greek culture that he was highly intolerant of all others.
(C) He was interested in nothing but military conquest.
(D) He tried to exterminate the peoples he conquered.
(E) He saw the need to implement Plato's conception of a just republic.

23. "As to the speeches which were made either before or during the Peloponnesian War, it is hard for me, and for others who reported them to me, to recollect the exact words. I have therefore put into the mouth of each speaker the sentiments proper to the occasion, expressed as I thought he would be likely to express them." Who said this?
(A) Homer (B) Herodotus (C) Thucydides
(D) Plato (E) Zeno

ANSWERS TO QUESTIONS ABOUT WESTERN CIVILIZATION

1. A	6. C	11. E	16. C	21. B
2. B	7. A	12. A	17. D	22. A
3. C	8. C	13. A	18. E	23. C
4. B	9. E	14. C	19. B	
5. D	10. E	15. C	20. C	

Questions about African/Asian Civilizations

Directions: Each of the questions or incomplete statements below is followed by five suggested answers or completions. Select the one that is best in each case.

1. Chinese culture and influence were most significant in shaping the institutions of which of the following countries?
(A) India, Japan, and Korea
(B) Indonesia, Thailand, and the Philippines
(C) Burma, Pakistan, and Bangladesh
(D) Japan, Korea, and Vietnam
(E) Japan, Korea, and the Philippines

2. The area of the African continent is approximately
(A) half the area of Western Europe
(B) three times the area of the continental United States
(C) the same as the area of the United States east of the Mississippi River
(D) two times the area of California
(E) four times the area of South America

3. All of the following have been policies of the government of the People's Republic of China EXCEPT
   (A) advocating equality for women in all aspects of Chinese life
   (B) doing away with private ownership of land by collectivizing agriculture
   (C) reemphasizing the importance of marriage and the family as the major socializing institution
   (D) involving all of the people in the political process
   (E) deemphasizing religion, viewing it as merely superstition

4. Between 1965 and 1974, which of the following was true concerning Nigeria, Uganda, and Ethiopia?
   (A) They came under military rule.
   (B) Democratic governments were organized.
   (C) Apartheid became national policy.
   (D) They joined the European Common market.
   (E) They became independent nations.

5. The samurai were
   (A) Japanese scholars
   (B) a people from Central Asia who invaded Japan
   (C) a Buddhist sect in Japan
   (D) a Japanese warrior class
   (E) Japanese industrialists

ANSWERS TO QUESTIONS ABOUT AFRICAN/ASIAN CIVILIZATIONS

1. D 2. B 3. C 4. A 5. D

Questions about Economics

Directions: Each of the questions or incomplete statements below is followed by five suggested answers or completions. Select the one that is best in each case.

1. The most important factor in creating the world "population explosion" has been
   (A) higher fertility (B) more multiple births
   (C) fewer wars (D) more family sentiment
   (E) lower death rates

2. Malthus thought that human population, if unchecked, would tend to grow at
   (A) an arithmetic rate (B) a geometric rate
   (C) a constantly slow rate (D) an undetermined rate
   (E) a rate determined by the sex ratio

3. Scarcity of resources in relation to desires or needs occurs
(A) only under capitalism (B) only under socialism
(C) only during wartime (D) in all societies
(E) in money-using societies

4. The percentage of our work force in agricultural pursuits in 1800 was about
(A) 20% (B) 33% (C) 50% (D) 75% (E) 95%

5. The main reason for organizing the C.I.O. in the 1930s was to
(A) organize Negroes and immigrants who seldom belonged to a labor union
(B) organize mass-production workers
(C) escape the high fees of the A.F. of L.
(D) organize craft workers
(E) organize white-collar workers

6. In what part of the world is the education of women most retarded as to percentage and quality?
(A) North America
(B) Europe
(C) Australia
(D) Moslem Middle East
(E) Japan

7. Which of the following countries raises the most sugar cane?
(A) New Zealand
(B) Canada
(C) Italy
(D) USSR
(E) Cuba

8. One prime weakness in the Ricardian system of economics was thought to be its failure to reconcile interest payment with a labor theory of value. This gap was filled with a new theory in which interest was a payment for abstinence. This theory was supplied by
(A) Say
(B) Sismondi
(C) Senior
(D) Rodbertus
(E) Marx

9. The practice of profitable trade (for monetary ends) was considered by Aristotle to be in the realm of
(A) the admirable
(B) "oikonomik," or useful household management
(C) the sad but necessary pattern of working to resolve economic problems
(D) the unnatural, or "chrematistik"
(E) the inevitable

10. If anyone can be said to profit from a depression, the group favored would likely be
    (A) people with secure sources of fixed income, such as government bonds
    (B) people who borrowed money before the depression and must repay during it
    (C) industrial owners producing consumer goods
    (D) assembly-line workers in automobile plants
    (E) low-level local government workers

11. Statistical evidence shows that the typical American family behaves in which of the following ways with respect to spending out of income?
    (A) An increasing proportion of income is spent on consumption as income increases.
    (B) The same proportion of income is spent on consumption at all except very low income levels.
    (C) The same proportion of income is spent on consumption at all income levels.
    (D) A decreasing proportion of income is spent on consumption as income increases.
    (E) The same proportion of income is spent on consumption at all except very high income levels.

GRAPH A

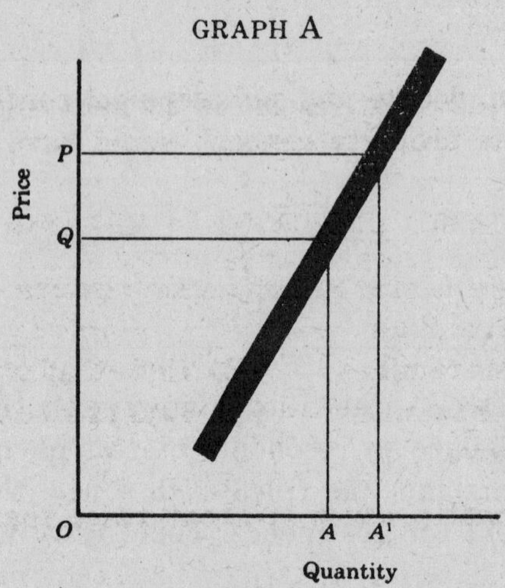

Questions 12–14 refer to GRAPH A.

12. The thick black line in Graph A represents
    (A) supply (B) cost (C) subsidy (D) demand (E) interest

13. Graph A would be most descriptive (because of the attitude of the thick black line) of which one of the following:
    (A) foreign currency (B) aspirin (C) land (D) razor blades
    (E) plastic toys

14. The thick black line in Graph A would be termed
    (A) elastic (B) inelastic (C) in attitudinal (D) formal
    (E) informal

15. The various editions of John Stuart Mill's *Principles of Political Economy* indicate that he
   (A) became increasingly conservative and anti-socialist as he grew older
   (B) made remarkably few changes in the views which he first held as a young Benthamite
   (C) completely abandoned the socialist views he had held as a young man
   (D) increasingly recognized exceptions to a general policy of a laissez-faire society
   (E) became more convinced that economic justice and political monarchy were tied together

16. In Western Europe during the 11th and 12th centuries, the right to coin money was
   (A) reserved to the Holy Roman Emperor
   (B) held only by kings
   (C) a monopoly of the Church
   (D) held by a number of nobles, kings, and cities
   (E) was in the care of the state banks

17. Which of the following countries has the smallest gross national product?
   (A) Sweden (B) France (C) West Germany (D) Japan
   (E) United Kingdom

18. In Western Europe, debate and philosophical conflict over the social value of the private property concept would have been of most concern in
   (A) 1630 (B) 1690 (C) 1750 (D) 1850 (E) 1970

19. In the U.S., if one's family had an annual income of $55,000 in 1978, it had a larger income than
   (A) 25% of all other families (B) 75% of all other families
   (C) 80% of all other families (D) 99% of all other families
   (E) none of the above

20. India's gross national product is about twice that of Sweden. This means
   (A) India is more advanced in technology
   (B) that the average Indian is twice as well-off as the average Swede
   (C) India has sufficient capital
   (D) all of these
   (E) none of these

21. Gross national product in the U.S. in 1987 was about how much greater than the value of all imports into the U.S. in that year?
   (A) 3 times greater
   (B) 5 times greater
   (C) 10 times greater
   (D) 15 times greater
   (E) 100 times greater

22. The transport of goods in the U.S. (in terms of ton-miles) is still primarily by
(A) motor trucks (B) canal barges (C) pipelines
(D) railroads (E) airlines

23. In national income accounting, which of the following is not part of national income but of personal income?
(A) Social Security contributions
(B) Corporate income taxes
(C) Undistributed corporate profits
(D) Personal consumption expenditures
(E) Transfer payments

24. Travel by people between cities in the U.S. is now primarily by
(A) ship (B) railroad (C) motor bus (D) airplane
(E) automobile

25. The flow of money can best be envisaged as
(A) linear
(B) vertical
(C) zigzag
(D) circular
(E) waving

26. All firms, whether competitive or not, will tend to produce to the point where
(A) average revenue equals marginal revenue
(B) fixed costs equal variable costs
(C) marginal costs equal marginal revenue
(D) fixed costs equal marginal revenue
(E) variable costs equal price

27. In 1933 the purpose of the United States government in devaluing the dollar in terms of gold was to
(A) raise domestic prices and make American goods cheaper abroad
(B) lower domestic prices and make American goods more expensive abroad
(C) establish the gold standard
(D) stop excessive exports of American goods
(E) reduce the ability of the gold-producing USSR to exchange gold for industrial and military goods

ANSWERS TO QUESTIONS ABOUT ECONOMICS

1. E	**5.** B	**9.** D	**13.** C	**17.** A	**21.** C	**25.** D
2. B	**6.** D	**10.** A	**14.** B	**18.** D	**22.** D	**26.** C
3. D	**7.** E	**11.** D	**15.** D	**19.** D	**23.** E	**27.** A
4. E	**8.** C	**12.** A	**16.** D	**20.** E	**24.** E	

Questions about Sociology and Social Psychology

Directions: Each of the questions or incomplete statements below is followed by five suggested answers or completions. Select the one that is best in each case.

1. Caste and class are
   (A) different in degree (B) different kinds of social phenomena
   (C) identical concepts (D) not found in America
   (E) capitalist characteristics

2. The marriage of one female to more than one male is called
   (A) monogamy (B) celibacy (C) polyandry
   (D) polygyny (E) endogamy

3. In the original sense, the term civilization meant
   (A) a humane way of living
   (B) citylike ways of life
   (C) a way of living based on food production rather than food gathering
   (D) better ways of living
   (E) a group of tribes with a common king

4. In 1940, American Negroes faced formal segregation in
   (A) the armed forces of the United States
   (B) railroad trains in interstate commerce in the South
   (C) colleges and universities in the South
   (D) all of the above
   (E) none of the above

5. The proportion of people under 15 years of age and over 65 to the number between 15 and 65 is the
   (A) demographic ratio (B) sex ratio (C) population ratio
   (D) natural increase ratio (E) dependency ratio

6. A political role is
   (A) a personality type (B) a position of high prestige
   (C) a sign of success (D) a collection of rights and duties
   (E) independent of reciprocal relations

7. Stratification is most closely related to social
   (A) identification (B) differentiation (C) amalgamation
   (D) disorganization (E) assimilation

8. Which series represents a trend from little to more social mobility?
   (A) Caste, class, estates
   (B) Estates, caste, class
   (C) Caste, estates, class
   (D) Class, caste, estates
   (E) There is an equal amount of social mobility in each.

9. Which of the following statements is incorrect?
   (A) Adherence to the mores is regarded as necessary to the welfare of society.
   (B) In the mores, "right makes might."
   (C) Conviction based on the mores transcends argument and "rational demonstration."
   (D) Mores include taboos and positive injunctions.
   (E) Form and content of mores are universally identical.

10. Folkways might include
   (A) rules of eating
   (B) forms of greeting
   (C) conduct at parties
   (D) all of the above
   (E) none of the above

11. A sociological term for internal migration is
   (A) marginal utility (B) miscegenation
   (C) horizontal mobility (D) vertical mobility
   (E) social dynamics

12. Antagonistic cooperation is another name for
   (A) conflict (B) accommodation (C) competition
   (D) assimilation (E) functionalism

13. The social relationships most prevalent in our society are
   (A) secondary (B) primary (C) migratory
   (D) all of these (E) none of these

14. The Negro fertility rate in the U.S. for the past two decades has been
   (A) the same as the white
   (B) somewhat less than the white
   (C) sometimes less and sometimes more than the white
   (D) about 15% higher than the white
   (E) about 35% higher

15. A caste society is characterized by all but which one of the following?
   (A) Intermarriage is forbidden across caste.
   (B) Most statuses are achieved.
   (C) Taboos define social distance between castes.
   (D) Individual status is hereditary and permanent.
   (E) Occupations are specific to special hereditary groups.

16. A "sect" religion tends to be
   (A) in accord with the values of the society in which it exists
   (B) lenient toward the indifferent
   (C) a reforming element hoping to make the society more livable
   (D) withdrawn from societal norms and extremely pietistic
   (E) the official religion of the state in which it exists

17. A Russian by the name of Pavlov conducted a series of experiments with animals and discovered conditioned reflex. This finding was the basis of which school of thought?
(A) psychoanalysis (B) behaviorism (C) relativism
(D) the new idealism (E) Hegelianism

18. If teaching facts is the *sole* aim of a teacher, she will probably do better if she is
(A) non-directive
(B) permissive and informal
(C) directive and authoritarian
(D) disorganized
(E) group oriented

19. The idea that upper echelon corporate officials develop nervous disorders more frequently than workers down the line is, of course, false. Its persistence is related to the
(A) aesthetic ethic
(B) Puritan ethic
(C) situational ethic
(D) melioristic ethic
(E) pragmatic ethic

20. In *Civilization and its Discontents,* Freud expressed his viewpoint concerning the necessity of controlling the antisocial and aggressive propensities of man. Which of the following authors had the most similar ideas?
(A) Rousseau
(B) Locke
(C) Condorcet
(D) Hobbes
(E) John Dewey

21. Opposition which focuses on the opponent, basically, and only secondarily on the reward is most closely associated with social
(A) accommodation
(B) stratification
(C) competition
(D) conflict
(E) differentiation

22. Cases where infants were subject to prolonged isolation show that
(A) human beings can acquire culture without human contact
(B) human beings cannot become socialized unless they are brought up among human beings
(C) mental-physical development does not depend upon human contacts
(D) people are born with most of the traits they exhibit as adults
(E) language use comes at a certain age, regardless of the social situation

ANSWERS TO QUESTIONS ABOUT SOCIOLOGY AND SOCIAL PSYCHOLOGY

1. A	4. D	7. B	10. D	13. A	16. D	19. B	22. B
2. C	5. E	8. C	11. C	14. E	17. B	20. A	
3. B	6. D	9. E	12. B	15. B	18. C	21. D	

Questions about Political Science

Directions: Each of the questions or incomplete statements below is followed by five suggested answers or completions. Select the one that is best in each case.

1. To which of the following did the U.S. Supreme Court apply the phrase "separate but equal"?
   (A) The formula for racial segregation (1896)
   (B) The nature of federal-state relations (1828)
   (C) The status of Indian tribal governments (1874)
   (D) The relative powers of the Senate and House of Representatives (1810)
   (E) The legal status of men and women (1913)

2. The law that can be considered the most important impetus to trade union organization was the
   (A) Sherman Act of 1890
   (B) Wagner Act of 1935
   (C) Taft-Hartley Act of 1947
   (D) Social Security Act of 1935
   (E) National Recovery Act of 1933

3. The case of *McCulloch* v. *Maryland* is considered one of the most important cases decided by the U.S. Supreme Court. In its decision, the court announced a major Constitutional concept concerning
   (A) separation of church and state (B) judicial review
   (C) segregation (D) anti-trust regulation
   (E) implied powers

4. All of the following features of American government were derived from English government *except*
   (A) the common law (B) bicameralism (C) federalism
   (D) the county as a unit of government
   (E) civil rights such as jury trial and *habeas corpus*

5. One of the following is a judicially recognized limitation of the power of the President to remove civil officers whom he has appointed.
   (A) The Senate has to approve all such removals.
   (B) The President cannot remove individuals belonging to the opposition party.
   (C) The President cannot remove individuals for political reasons.
   (D) Congress can prescribe the reasons for which members of the independent regulatory commissions may be removed from their positions.
   (E) The House must be informed.

6. The position of the Chief Justice of the United States Supreme Court is filled by
   (A) seniority (B) promotion (C) specific appointment
   (D) election (E) rotation among justices

7. The principle of implied powers in the Constitution was established in the case of
   (A) *Marbury* v. *Madison* (B) *McCulloch* v. *Maryland*
   (C) *Fletcher* v. *Peck* (D) *Missouri* v. *Holland*
   (E) *Zorach* v. *Clauson*

8. The body of legal rules based upon reason as applied in past cases going far back in English history is known as
   (A) constitutional law (B) statutory law (C) common law
   (D) administrative law (E) international law

9. Which of the following governmental subdivisions in the state of Louisiana corresponds to the county in other states?
   (A) ward (B) district (C) township (D) parish
   (E) province

10. Ambassadors are appointed by the
    (A) President without the approval of Congress under a special provision of the Constitution
    (B) President from a list chosen by the merit system
    (C) President with the consent of the Senate
    (D) retiring ambassadors, with the approval of the President, from a list of technically trained individuals
    (E) President from a list of graduates of the Foreign Service Academy

11. Puerto Rico is an illustration of
    (A) an unincorporated or partially organized territory
    (B) an incorporated territory
    (C) a protectorate
    (D) a commonwealth
    (E) a dominion

12. In matters of high administration, the armed forces of the U.S. are under the control of
    (A) the Departments of War and of the Navy
    (B) the President (C) Congress (D) the General Staff
    (E) the Secretary of Defense

13. The policy of imperialism in the U.S. from 1890 to 1910 was largely the result of
    (A) the theory of isolation
    (B) a desire to build up a colonial empire
    (C) demands for commercial expansion
    (D) a wide spread desire to become a world power
    (E) missionary zeal

14. In the Constitution, the states were granted the right to
(A) exercise only the powers given to them by the Constitution
(B) settle directly their disputes with Mexico or Canada
(C) establish their own militia without reference to United States Army standards
(D) exercise all powers not denied by the Constitution
(E) refuse to permit women the vote

15. The Senate must ratify or reject all
(A) treaties with other nations, by a two-thirds vote of the Senators present
(B) appointments of the President by a majority vote
(C) treaties or agreements between two states
(D) treaties with other nations by a two-thirds vote of the full membership of the Senate
(E) appointments of minor officials by the President

16. The work of the Department of Labor in the President's cabinet is, in the main,
(A) supporting the American Federation of Labor and other labor organizations in their activities
(B) collecting statistics on labor conditions and making recommendations to the President
(C) regulating labor conditions in industry by issuing orders modifying wages or hours, or both
(D) regulating working conditions of government employees
(E) providing for binding arbitration in industrial disputes

17. The Prohibition Amendment, ratified in 1919, was
(A) repealed by the Twenty-first Amendment
(B) modified but not repealed entirely
(C) repealed by Congress to meet an economic emergency
(D) acted upon by popular conventions in each state
(E) a war measure, not intended to be permanent

18. In some states, voters may originate legislation by
(A) common consent (B) initiative petition
(C) letters to the legislature (D) ordinance (E) church rules

19. When the government (state or national) takes possession and ownership of private property for public use, it is exercising the right of
(A) public ownership (B) eminent domain
(C) state confiscation (D) public domain (E) *ad hoc* rule

20. An American male in 1983 is white, 50 years old, lives in Topeka, Kansas, makes $30,000 a year as an owner of a small business. You would, on the basis of probability, expect him to vote
(A) Democratic
(B) Socialist
(C) States Rights or American Independent
(D) Republican
(E) Socialist Labor

21. Which of the following do most historians agree is most significant for the continuance of democracy?
(A) A written constitution
(B) Control of finances by legislatures
(C) Separation of powers
(D) A large number of political parties
(E) Protection of civil liberties for all citizens

22. Which of the following metropolitan areas gave George Wallace a plurality in 1968?
(A) San Francisco (B) Syracuse (C) Denver
(D) Dallas (E) Nashville

23. "The right of citizens of the United States to vote in any primary or other election for President or Vice-President, for electors for elections for President or Vice-President, or for Senator or Representative in Congress shall not be denied or abridged by the United States or any state by reason of failure to pay any poll tax or other tax." The above statement is taken from which of the following amendments to the United States Constitution?
(A) Fifth (B) Fifteenth (C) Twentieth
(D) Twenty-third (E) Twenty-fourth

24. The largest absolute vote in American history received by a candidate for president *not* of the Republican or Democratic Parties was achieved by
(A) Weaver in 1892 (B) Roosevelt in 1912
(C) LaFollette in 1924 (D) Thomas in 1932
(E) Wallace in 1968

25. The Republican party dominated the presidency from 1860 to 1912. A single Democrat was elected to the presidency in that period. He was
(A) Grover Cleveland (B) Horace Greeley
(C) William Howard Taft (D) William McKinley
(E) Ulysses S. Grant

26. Sovereignty can be defined as
(A) freedom
(B) the power to command and control
(C) government with the consent of the governed
(D) rule by kings
(E) a tyranny of the many over the few

ANSWERS TO QUESTIONS ABOUT POLITICAL SCIENCE

1. A	**6.** C	**11.** D	**16.** B	**21.** E	**26.** B
2. B	**7.** B	**12.** B	**17.** A	**22.** E	
3. E	**8.** C	**13.** C	**18.** B	**23.** E	
4. C	**9.** D	**14.** D	**19.** B	**24.** E	
5. D	**10.** C	**15.** A	**20.** D	**25.** A	

ANSWER SHEET — SOCIAL SCIENCES-HISTORY/SAMPLE EXAMINATION 1

Section I

1. Ⓐ Ⓑ Ⓒ Ⓓ Ⓔ
2. Ⓐ Ⓑ Ⓒ Ⓓ Ⓔ
3. Ⓐ Ⓑ Ⓒ Ⓓ Ⓔ
4. Ⓐ Ⓑ Ⓒ Ⓓ Ⓔ
5. Ⓐ Ⓑ Ⓒ Ⓓ Ⓔ
6. Ⓐ Ⓑ Ⓒ Ⓓ Ⓔ
7. Ⓐ Ⓑ Ⓒ Ⓓ Ⓔ
8. Ⓐ Ⓑ Ⓒ Ⓓ Ⓔ
9. Ⓐ Ⓑ Ⓒ Ⓓ Ⓔ
10. Ⓐ Ⓑ Ⓒ Ⓓ Ⓔ
11. Ⓐ Ⓑ Ⓒ Ⓓ Ⓔ
12. Ⓐ Ⓑ Ⓒ Ⓓ Ⓔ
13. Ⓐ Ⓑ Ⓒ Ⓓ Ⓔ
14. Ⓐ Ⓑ Ⓒ Ⓓ Ⓔ
15. Ⓐ Ⓑ Ⓒ Ⓓ Ⓔ
16. Ⓐ Ⓑ Ⓒ Ⓓ Ⓔ
17. Ⓐ Ⓑ Ⓒ Ⓓ Ⓔ
18. Ⓐ Ⓑ Ⓒ Ⓓ Ⓔ
19. Ⓐ Ⓑ Ⓒ Ⓓ Ⓔ
20. Ⓐ Ⓑ Ⓒ Ⓓ Ⓔ
21. Ⓐ Ⓑ Ⓒ Ⓓ Ⓔ
22. Ⓐ Ⓑ Ⓒ Ⓓ Ⓔ
23. Ⓐ Ⓑ Ⓒ Ⓓ Ⓔ
24. Ⓐ Ⓑ Ⓒ Ⓓ Ⓔ
25. Ⓐ Ⓑ Ⓒ Ⓓ Ⓔ
26. Ⓐ Ⓑ Ⓒ Ⓓ Ⓔ
27. Ⓐ Ⓑ Ⓒ Ⓓ Ⓔ
28. Ⓐ Ⓑ Ⓒ Ⓓ Ⓔ
29. Ⓐ Ⓑ Ⓒ Ⓓ Ⓔ
30. Ⓐ Ⓑ Ⓒ Ⓓ Ⓔ
31. Ⓐ Ⓑ Ⓒ Ⓓ Ⓔ
32. Ⓐ Ⓑ Ⓒ Ⓓ Ⓔ
33. Ⓐ Ⓑ Ⓒ Ⓓ Ⓔ
34. Ⓐ Ⓑ Ⓒ Ⓓ Ⓔ
35. Ⓐ Ⓑ Ⓒ Ⓓ Ⓔ
36. Ⓐ Ⓑ Ⓒ Ⓓ Ⓔ
37. Ⓐ Ⓑ Ⓒ Ⓓ Ⓔ
38. Ⓐ Ⓑ Ⓒ Ⓓ Ⓔ
39. Ⓐ Ⓑ Ⓒ Ⓓ Ⓔ
40. Ⓐ Ⓑ Ⓒ Ⓓ Ⓔ
41. Ⓐ Ⓑ Ⓒ Ⓓ Ⓔ
42. Ⓐ Ⓑ Ⓒ Ⓓ Ⓔ
43. Ⓐ Ⓑ Ⓒ Ⓓ Ⓔ
44. Ⓐ Ⓑ Ⓒ Ⓓ Ⓔ
45. Ⓐ Ⓑ Ⓒ Ⓓ Ⓔ
46. Ⓐ Ⓑ Ⓒ Ⓓ Ⓔ
47. Ⓐ Ⓑ Ⓒ Ⓓ Ⓔ
48. Ⓐ Ⓑ Ⓒ Ⓓ Ⓔ
49. Ⓐ Ⓑ Ⓒ Ⓓ Ⓔ
50. Ⓐ Ⓑ Ⓒ Ⓓ Ⓔ
51. Ⓐ Ⓑ Ⓒ Ⓓ Ⓔ
52. Ⓐ Ⓑ Ⓒ Ⓓ Ⓔ
53. Ⓐ Ⓑ Ⓒ Ⓓ Ⓔ
54. Ⓐ Ⓑ Ⓒ Ⓓ Ⓔ
55. Ⓐ Ⓑ Ⓒ Ⓓ Ⓔ
56. Ⓐ Ⓑ Ⓒ Ⓓ Ⓔ
57. Ⓐ Ⓑ Ⓒ Ⓓ Ⓔ
58. Ⓐ Ⓑ Ⓒ Ⓓ Ⓔ
59. Ⓐ Ⓑ Ⓒ Ⓓ Ⓔ
60. Ⓐ Ⓑ Ⓒ Ⓓ Ⓔ
61. Ⓐ Ⓑ Ⓒ Ⓓ Ⓔ
62. Ⓐ Ⓑ Ⓒ Ⓓ Ⓔ
63. Ⓐ Ⓑ Ⓒ Ⓓ Ⓔ

Section II

64. Ⓐ Ⓑ Ⓒ Ⓓ Ⓔ
65. Ⓐ Ⓑ Ⓒ Ⓓ Ⓔ
66. Ⓐ Ⓑ Ⓒ Ⓓ Ⓔ
67. Ⓐ Ⓑ Ⓒ Ⓓ Ⓔ
68. Ⓐ Ⓑ Ⓒ Ⓓ Ⓔ
69. Ⓐ Ⓑ Ⓒ Ⓓ Ⓔ
70. Ⓐ Ⓑ Ⓒ Ⓓ Ⓔ
71. Ⓐ Ⓑ Ⓒ Ⓓ Ⓔ
72. Ⓐ Ⓑ Ⓒ Ⓓ Ⓔ
73. Ⓐ Ⓑ Ⓒ Ⓓ Ⓔ
74. Ⓐ Ⓑ Ⓒ Ⓓ Ⓔ
75. Ⓐ Ⓑ Ⓒ Ⓓ Ⓔ
76. Ⓐ Ⓑ Ⓒ Ⓓ Ⓔ
77. Ⓐ Ⓑ Ⓒ Ⓓ Ⓔ
78. Ⓐ Ⓑ Ⓒ Ⓓ Ⓔ
79. Ⓐ Ⓑ Ⓒ Ⓓ Ⓔ
80. Ⓐ Ⓑ Ⓒ Ⓓ Ⓔ
81. Ⓐ Ⓑ Ⓒ Ⓓ Ⓔ
82. Ⓐ Ⓑ Ⓒ Ⓓ Ⓔ
83. Ⓐ Ⓑ Ⓒ Ⓓ Ⓔ
84. Ⓐ Ⓑ Ⓒ Ⓓ Ⓔ
85. Ⓐ Ⓑ Ⓒ Ⓓ Ⓔ
86. Ⓐ Ⓑ Ⓒ Ⓓ Ⓔ
87. Ⓐ Ⓑ Ⓒ Ⓓ Ⓔ
88. Ⓐ Ⓑ Ⓒ Ⓓ Ⓔ
89. Ⓐ Ⓑ Ⓒ Ⓓ Ⓔ
90. Ⓐ Ⓑ Ⓒ Ⓓ Ⓔ
91. Ⓐ Ⓑ Ⓒ Ⓓ Ⓔ
92. Ⓐ Ⓑ Ⓒ Ⓓ Ⓔ
93. Ⓐ Ⓑ Ⓒ Ⓓ Ⓔ
94. Ⓐ Ⓑ Ⓒ Ⓓ Ⓔ
95. Ⓐ Ⓑ Ⓒ Ⓓ Ⓔ
96. Ⓐ Ⓑ Ⓒ Ⓓ Ⓔ
97. Ⓐ Ⓑ Ⓒ Ⓓ Ⓔ
98. Ⓐ Ⓑ Ⓒ Ⓓ Ⓔ
99. Ⓐ Ⓑ Ⓒ Ⓓ Ⓔ
100. Ⓐ Ⓑ Ⓒ Ⓓ Ⓔ
101. Ⓐ Ⓑ Ⓒ Ⓓ Ⓔ
102. Ⓐ Ⓑ Ⓒ Ⓓ Ⓔ
103. Ⓐ Ⓑ Ⓒ Ⓓ Ⓔ
104. Ⓐ Ⓑ Ⓒ Ⓓ Ⓔ
105. Ⓐ Ⓑ Ⓒ Ⓓ Ⓔ
106. Ⓐ Ⓑ Ⓒ Ⓓ Ⓔ
107. Ⓐ Ⓑ Ⓒ Ⓓ Ⓔ
108. Ⓐ Ⓑ Ⓒ Ⓓ Ⓔ
109. Ⓐ Ⓑ Ⓒ Ⓓ Ⓔ
110. Ⓐ Ⓑ Ⓒ Ⓓ Ⓔ
111. Ⓐ Ⓑ Ⓒ Ⓓ Ⓔ
112. Ⓐ Ⓑ Ⓒ Ⓓ Ⓔ
113. Ⓐ Ⓑ Ⓒ Ⓓ Ⓔ
114. Ⓐ Ⓑ Ⓒ Ⓓ Ⓔ
115. Ⓐ Ⓑ Ⓒ Ⓓ Ⓔ
116. Ⓐ Ⓑ Ⓒ Ⓓ Ⓔ
117. Ⓐ Ⓑ Ⓒ Ⓓ Ⓔ
118. Ⓐ Ⓑ Ⓒ Ⓓ Ⓔ
119. Ⓐ Ⓑ Ⓒ Ⓓ Ⓔ
120. Ⓐ Ⓑ Ⓒ Ⓓ Ⓔ
121. Ⓐ Ⓑ Ⓒ Ⓓ Ⓔ
122. Ⓐ Ⓑ Ⓒ Ⓓ Ⓔ
123. Ⓐ Ⓑ Ⓒ Ⓓ Ⓔ
124. Ⓐ Ⓑ Ⓒ Ⓓ Ⓔ
125. Ⓐ Ⓑ Ⓒ Ⓓ Ⓔ

CHAPTER

Sample Examinations 17

This chapter contains three sample Social Sciences and History examinations, each followed by an answer key, scoring chart, and answer explanations. After you complete each exam, determine your score and mark it on the Progress Chart on page 14. You will see your score climb as you work through each test and become more familiar with the type of questions asked.

SAMPLE EXAMINATION 1

Section I

Number of Questions: 63
Time: 45 minutes

Directions: Each of the questions or incomplete statements below is followed by five suggested answers or completions. Select the one that is best in each case.

1. Which of the following were periods of inflation in U.S. history?
(A) 1919-21 (B) 1946-48 (C) 1951-52
(D) 1973-78 (E) All of these

2. Which of the following migrations involved most people?
(A) Norsemen into Britain in the 9th and 10th centuries
(B) English into North America in the 17th century
(C) Blacks from Africa into the Western Hemisphere in the 17th and 18th centuries
(D) Spaniards into Mexico in the 16th century
(E) Asiatics into Hawaii in the 19th century

3. Which of the following countries is not a federation in form?
(A) Canada (B) United States (C) Australia
(D) USSR (E) France

4. Governmental control of the air (for aircraft, radio, and television) exists in which of the following countries? I. The Soviet Union, II. The United States, III. Great Britain.
(A) I only (B) II only (C) III only
(D) I and III only (E) I, II, and III

5. Adam Smith contended that
(A) government should run the economy
(B) governments which encourage particular industries with various aids increase real wealth
(C) governments should not interfere in the natural circulation of labor and capital
(D) government must do something direct about labor's poverty
(E) government must redirect the activities of most men

6. If the present rate (1978) of natural increase and net in-migration in America is maintained, the population of the country in the year 2000 A.D. will be approximately
(A) 100,000,000 (B) 180,000,000 (C) 200,000,000
(D) 280,000,000 (E) 500,000,000

7. The proportion of females in the U.S. public school elementary teaching force is about
(A) 95% (B) 70% (C) 60% (D) 50% (E) 30%

8. Which of the following movements has most in common with Calvin's idea of predestination?
(A) Populism (B) Transcendentalism (C) Pragmatism
(D) Puritanism (E) Technocratism

9. "It is a symbol of status. It has altered courting patterns. It has contributed to the increase in obesity and heart disease. It has contributed to a host of services and industries. It has helped the growth of suburbs. It has helped to alter state-federal governmental relations." The problematical "it" in the statement is the
(A) automobile (B) elevator (C) refrigerator
(D) subway (E) railroad

10. The Supreme Court declared state action unconstitutional in all of the following instances *except*
(A) *Dartmouth College* v. *Woodward* (B) *Baker* v. *Carr*
(C) *Lochner* v. *New York* (D) *Gibbons* v. *Ogden*
(E) *Marbury* v. *Madison*

11. The Dred Scott decision, in effect, ruled which of the following unconstitutional?
(A) Agricultural Adjustment Act (B) Sherman Act
(C) Pure Food and Drug Act (D) Missouri Compromise of 1850
(E) The Second Bank of the United States

12. The formula for the investment multiplier in Keynesian macroeconomics is
(A) 1/MPC (B) 1/MPS (C) 1/1-MPS
(D) MPS/1 (E) MPC/1

13. One of the following countries which had been sending large numbers of immigrants to the United States (in the period from 1890 to the mid-1920s) was given a relatively low quota of immigrants by legislation passed in 1924 in the United States. Which one?
(A) Great Britain
(B) China
(C) Japan
(D) Germany
(E) Italy

14. During the nineteenth century, which of the following European countries held no colonies?
(A) France and Switzerland (B) Germany and Finland
(C) Italy and Spain (D) Sweden and Denmark
(E) Sweden and Switzerland

15. Which of the following countries lost territory because of a meeting at Munich in 1938?
(A) Switzerland (B) Poland (C) France
(D) Hungary (E) Czechoslovakia

16. Which of the following assertions influenced Darwin in his formulation of the theory of natural selection?
(A) "Population decreases while agriculture forges ahead."
(B) "It is the constant tendency in all animated life to increase beyond the nourishment prepared for it."
(C) "No progress is possible because of the basic sex drive which increases population at a geometric rate."
(D) "Nations which are over-populated must be allowed to expand their inhabitants abroad."
(E) "Selection of the race which is most military is inevitable."

17. Which best describes the attitude of Mazzini?
(A) He strongly believed in the racial superiority of the Italians since they had given the world so much.
(B) He believed that Italian unity could best be attained under the leadership of a patriotic monarch.
(C) He believed that each nation had a special mission to perform to contribute to the welfare of humanity in general.
(D) He firmly believed in the cosmopolitan ideal of the 18th century, that all men were citizens of the world rather than of a single nation.
(E) He thought that true leadership in Italy would have to come from within the Roman Catholic Church.

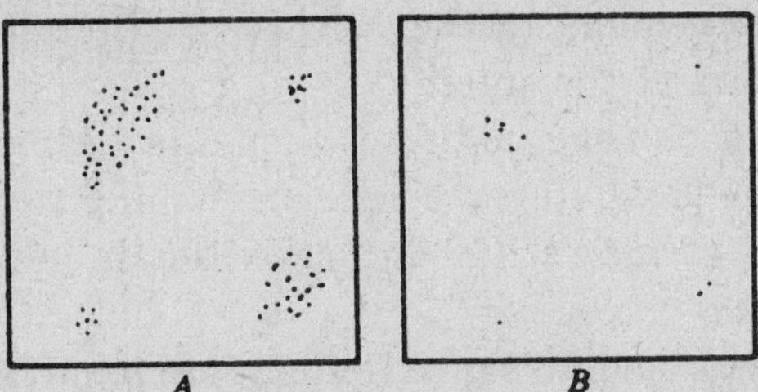

18. If each dot in A represents five hundred refrigerators in a county and each dot in B one drug store in the same county, which of the following statements are likely to be correct? I. There may be a factor underlying the spatial distribution of refrigerators that also underlies the spatial distribution of drug stores. II. Refrigerators and drug stores are similarly distributed in the county, but refrigerators are in greater quantity. III. There are at least four population concentrations in the county. IV. The county is mountainous.
(A) I and III only (B) II and IV only
(C) I, II, and III only (D) II, III, and IV only (E) I only

19. Which of the following belongs in a different category from the others?
(A) Wagner Act (B) Norris-LaGuardia Act (C) Taft-Hartley Act
(D) National Industrial Recovery Act (E) Hawley-Smoot Act

20. To declare a law unconstitutional, the decision of the Supreme Court must be
    (A) unanimous
    (B) by a simple majority
    (C) by a two-thirds majority of the court
    (D) by the vote of seven out of nine justices
    (E) eight out of nine

21. The Hundred Years' War was important in military history because it
    (A) demonstrated that foot troops could not withstand a mounted feudal cavalry
    (B) showed the need for heavily armored troops
    (C) increased the importance of the feudal noble in warfare
    (D) proved the effectiveness of foot soldiers armd with longbows
    (E) showed that seapower was tied to the firepower of ships

22. In year B, total spending was 20% greater than in year A. Given this information alone about the United States economy, we
    (A) know that prices were 20% greater in year B
    (B) know that prices were 10% greater in year B
    (C) know that prices were 15% greater in year A
    (D) can tell little about comparative price levels in the two years
    (E) can be sure that more goods were produced in year B

23. The germ theory of disease was primarily the work of
    (A) Galileo (B) Weismann (C) Pasteur (D) Swann
    (E) Mendel

24. Which of these ideas best represents the position of the Medieval Church upon economic affairs?
    (A) Economics belongs to the world; the Church is concerned only with matters of the spirit.
    (B) Profits on a loan are justified when it is a capital investment.
    (C) A just price is whatever people are willing to pay.
    (D) The whole of man's life and activities is governed by Christian law.
    (E) All Christians should share God's material gifts equally.

25. The production possibility curve indicates
    (A) the maximum output series of any two products
    (B) the minimum output series of any two products
    (C) the gains that can be made by mass production in one product area
    (D) the gains in profit from wider markets
    (E) the gains in profit from controlling prices

26. The best definition of the cost of a resource is
    (A) money spent
    (B) the effort put forth in a given time period
    (C) effort times money
    (D) the amount of labor it takes to create the resource
    (E) the value of alternative uses of the resource

27. Which of the following = NNP?
(A) GNP – direct taxes (B) GNP – depreciation
(C) GNP – indirect taxes (D) GNP – defense costs
(E) GNP – interest

28. The writer to which Malthus most objected (because of what Malthus considered his shallow optimism concerning population) was
(A) Adam Smith (B) David Ricard (C) John Stuart Mill
(D) William Godwin (E) Jeremy Bentham

29. The birth rate in the U.S. over the last 175 years has
(A) remained fairly static
(B) increased greatly
(C) decreased greatly
(D) tended to fluctuate wildly around a stable average
(E) declined in depressed economy periods only

30. The best definition for "nation" is a group of people who
(A) live within the same state
(B) speak the same language
(C) simply feel themselves to be a nation
(D) are of the same racial origin
(E) have the same religious faith

31. Among the following, the best example of a society which used its educational system mainly to train an avocational "gentlemanly" elite was
(A) Ancient Sparta (B) Old China (C) the Soviet Union
(D) the United States today (E) England in the 18th century

32. Which of the following is usually less disapproved of than the others? Illegitimacy resulting from
(A) adultery
(B) incest
(C) cross-caste union
(D) union before marriage (parents marrying at a later date)
(E) union between people sworn to religious celibacy

33. The period of the most massive immigration into the United States was between
(A) 1840 and 1865 (B) 1880 and 1896 (C) 1900 and 1914
(D) 1920 and 1930 (E) 1940 and 1965

34. The American Declaration of Independence states that "men are endowed by their creator with certain inalienable rights." The same idea is also very clearly expressed in the writings of
(A) Bossuet (B) Duke of Sully (C) Machiavelli
(D) John Locke (E) Montaigne

35. Which of the following writers spoke of the potential "despotism of the many" in the United States?
(A) Marx (B) Gaitskell (C) de Tocqueville
(D) Kluckhohn (E) Hook

36. "The value of a commodity is, in itself, of no interest to the capitalist. What alone interests him is the surplus value that dwells in it and is realisable by sale." In which of the following works would this statement occur?
    (A) *Wealth of Nations*
    (B) *Essay on Population*
    (C) *The Protestant Ethic and the Spirit of Capitalism*
    (D) *Theory of the Leisure Class*
    (E) *Capital*

37. The Boers of South Africa were the descendants of settlers who had come to that land from
    (A) England (B) the Netherlands (C) Germany
    (D) Portugal (E) Ireland

38. Which of these English kings was executed by a revolutionary government?
    (A) James I (B) Charles I (C) Charles II (D) James II
    (E) Henry VIII

39. Which of the following held that the qualities of pleasure were roughly equal, or that "push-pin was as good as poetry"?
    (A) John Stuart Mill (B) Wordsworth (C) William Godwin
    (D) Jeremy Bentham (E) William Morris

40. Which of the following peoples were especially influenced by Byzantine civilization and the Byzantine form of Christianity?
    (A) Turks (B) Germans (C) Slavs (D) Celts (E) Iberians

41. In the 18th century scientific thought considered "nature" most commonly in terms of
    (A) growth and development (B) mechanics (C) pure idea
    (D) essence and vital soul (E) categorization

42. The Boxer Rebellion in China was
    (A) an effort to overthrow the rule of the Manchu emperor
    (B) a revolt against the Japanese rule in Korea
    (C) an attack upon foreigners in China
    (D) the revolution which established the Chinese Republic
    (E) a fight to establish Confucianism

43. If you wanted to visit the oldest sites of the civilization of the Incas, you would go to
    (A) Mexico (B) Guatemala (C) Cuba (D) Peru (E) Venezuela

44. Which best describes the following 18th-century rulers: Catherine II of Russia, Frederick II of Prussia, and Joseph II of Austria?
    (A) Made mock of the "divine right" idea of kingship.
    (B) Went to considerable length to avoid war.
    (C) Wished to introduce various reforms which were supposed to contribute to the welfare of their subjects.
    (D) Constitutional monarchs.
    (E) Wished to expand their holdings in South America.

45. The "Great Trek" refers to
(A) the expansion of Canada to the west
(B) the migration of Europeans to New Zealand
(C) the movement of Dutch-speaking Boers out of Cape Colony
(D) the great sheep drives in Australia
(E) General Custer's march into Montana

MAP C

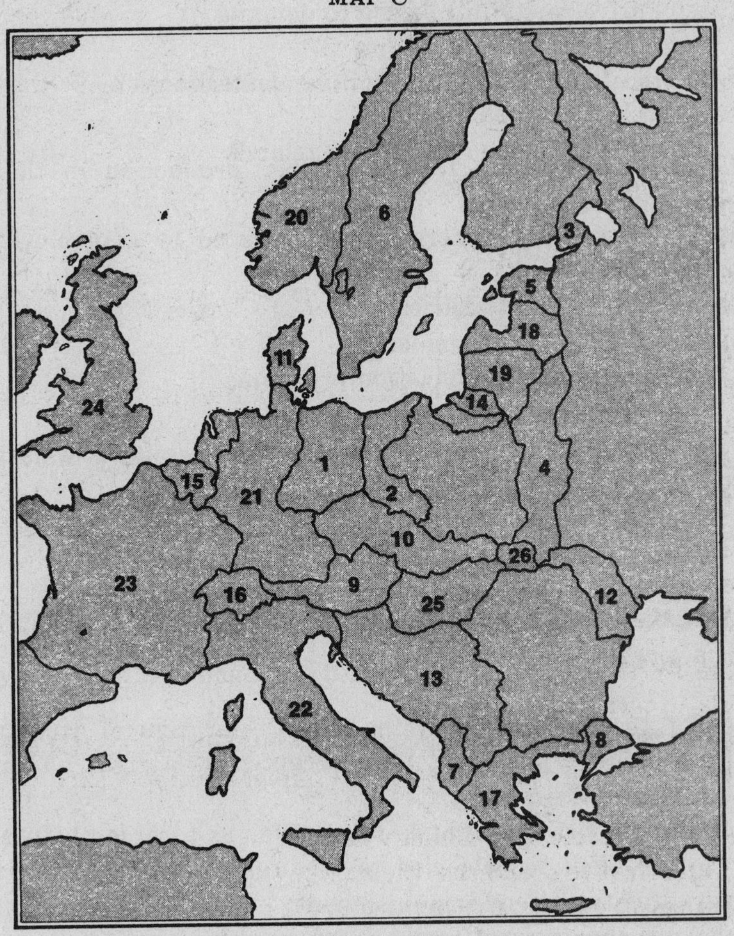

46. Which area, long in Prussian hands, did the USSR annex in 1945?
(A) 2 (B) 10 (C) 4 (D) 5 (E) 14

47. Bonn is the capital of which country?
(A) 2 (B) 1 (C) 10 (D) 16 (E) 21

48. Which area is Turkish, in Europe, and dominates the Dardanelles?
(A) 17 (B) 7 (C) 13 (D) 12 (E) 8

49. The ultimate social aim of all economic activity is to
(A) insure adequate profits to business
(B) give material means to government servants
(C) keep everybody working hard
(D) make private property secure
(E) produce goods for final consumption

50. The best way in economics to define "saving" is to call it
(A) a time deposit (B) an investment
(C) an act of prudence (D) refraining from consumption
(E) the building of national solvency

51. "Marginal utility" is associated with the idea that a high price for a commodity results from
(A) much labor being required to produce it
(B) its relative rarity in relation to demand
(C) its great usefulness to people
(D) its association with an exploitive capitalist system
(E) its not being mass-produced

52. In the U.S., increasing food and fiber production in this century cannot be attributed to
(A) a larger farm work force
(B) more machinery
(C) better seeds and fertilizer
(D) more efficient management
(E) better agricultural education programs

53. Since people interacting take one another into account and modify their behaviors, interaction is
(A) secondary
(B) formal
(C) cohesive
(D) reciprocal
(E) marginal

54. Which of these rights from the UN Declaration of Human Rights would most likely have *not* been accepted as a right by early 19th-century classic liberals?
(A) Everyone has the right to recognition as a person before the law.
(B) No one shall be subjected to torture or to cruel, inhuman, or degrading treatment or punishment.
(C) No one shall be arbitrarily deprived of his property.
(D) Everyone who works has a right to favorable remuneration, which ensures human dignity for his family and provides him with social security.
(E) No one shall be subject to arbitrary arrest.

55. In which state of the U.S. is the rate of college attendance among 18 to 24 year olds the highest?
(A) West Virginia (B) Georgia (C) Pennsylvania
(D) Massachusetts (E) Utah

56. In soliciting funds for volunteer health or community programs, motivational researchers have discovered the most efficient technique is to utilize
(A) sex (B) shame and comparison with others
(C) patriotism (D) charm (E) community welfare

57. The sociologist who was concerned to analyze what he called "mechanical" vs. "organic" solidarity was
(A) Emile Durkheim
(B) C. Wright Mills
(C) Robert Merton
(D) Louis Wirth
(E) Pitirim Sorokin

58. The most common way to secure a wife in most simple patrilocal African societies was by
(A) sororate rules (B) purchase (C) royal dispensation
(D) stealing (E) capture

59. War is utilized in Orwell's *1984* society for all of the following purposes *except*
(A) limiting the relative power of each state through repeated military realignments
(B) assuring the loyalty of party members and the solidarity of the citizenry
(C) gaining permanent control of the uncommitted areas, their resources, and populations
(D) as a means for subjugating the population and destroying the excess products resulting from advanced technology
(E) perpetuating the existent power structure

60. "The young Kaiser William II was jealous of the aged minister who had domineered over Germany so long." Who was the minister?
(A) Tirpitz (B) Dollfuss (C) Stein
(D) Bethman-Hollweg (E) Bismarck

61. In European Medieval agriculture, the three-field system was a
(A) means of dividing agricultural land among the three main social classes
(B) method of rotating crops on the manor
(C) plan in which both the king and the church received part of the product of the land
(D) plan to divide manors among various owners
(E) system of irrigating three or more farms with one canal system

62. When the founding fathers established the electoral college system, they expected that
(A) mass education would improve the electorate and make direct popular election reasonable
(B) partisan conflict over the election of a President could be avoided
(C) a democratic system would evolve whereby the people would select the President according to a weighted formula which equates the popular and electoral votes
(D) a democratic party system would develop, thus making selection of the President a popular decision
(E) Washington would serve two terms, after which an amendment would require the election of a President by the House of Representatives

63. Which of the following is not one of the so-called "Cow Colleges" created under the Morrill Act passed during the Civil War? The University of
(A) Nebraska (B) Tennessee (C) Missouri
(D) Kansas (E) Pennsylvania

Section II

Number of Questions: 62
Time: 45 minutes

Directions: Each of the questions or incomplete statements below is followed by five suggested answers or completions. Select the one that is best in each case.

64. "According to the materialist conception of history the determining element in history is ultimately the production and reproduction in real life. More than this neither Marx nor I have ever asserted." The colleague of Marx who said this was
(A) Lenin (B) Stalin (C) Engels (D) Marshall
(E) Bismarck

65. In the 10th century the ruler of which capital would have called himself "Emperor of the Romans"?
(A) Baghdad (B) Cairo (C) Kiev (D) Constantinople
(E) London

66. Who changed the coins of France so that the old inscription "Liberté, Egalité, Fraternité," was replaced by "Patrie, Travail, Famille"?
(A) DeGaulle
(B) Petain
(C) Mendes-France
(D) Clemenceau
(E) Briand

67. "If an ambitious young man wanted to get into the House of Commons, the quickest way was to pay a large sum to the man whose influence controlled the few votes in some country village that sent members to Parliament." In what year did a reform bill largely end this situation?
(A) 1797 (B) 1832 (C) 1867 (D) 1884 (E) 1929

68. "Forced by the prospect of having to fight both the British and American fleet as well as the Latin American rebels the 'Concert' broke down and Spanish American colonies were allowed to remain republics." This statement refers to the decade starting in
(A) 1790 (B) 1820 (C) 1850 (D) 1870 (E) 1940

69. If greatly diluted amounts of the infection were given in slowly increasing doses, resistance to the disease developed. In 1885, the treatment was tried on a nine-year-old boy bitten by a mad dog. He was cured. Who administered the cure?
(A) Lister (B) Freud (C) Pasteur (D) Spock (E) Koch

70. The animal physiologist whose discovery of the conditioned reflex showed the exclusion of conscious processes from basic behavior patterns was
(A) Darwin (B) Rousseau (C) Freud (D) Pavlov (E) Watson

71. What is the median income of seven families earning the following incomes: (1) $8,000 (2) $10,000 (3) $12,000 (4) $6,000 (5) $15,000 (6) $30,000 (7) $20,000?
(A) $6,000 (B) $12,000 (C) $10,000 (D) $15,000
(E) $16,000

72. Which of the following is not contemporary with the others?
(A) Expansion of U.S. holdings in the Pacific
(B) Heavy immigration into the U.S. from Southern Europe
(C) A tendency to feel that the American frontier had finally vanished
(D) A strong movement to end "Jim Crowism" in the U.S.
(E) Growing sentiment against trusts and monopoly

73. Which of the following is a procedural, rather than a substantive, civil right?
(A) Freedom of religion (B) Freedom of speech
(C) Freedom of assembly (D) The right to vote
(E) The right to trial by jury

74. The political boundaries of states in Africa came about mainly because of
(A) geographic and economic ties between tribes
(B) racial antagonisms
(C) tribal organization and power
(D) 19th century European power politics
(E) nationalist sentiments in African populations at the end of the 19th century

75. The Medieval European intellectual class was drawn almost entirely from
(A) lawyers (B) the clergy
(C) members of the landed aristocracy (D) guildsmen
(E) royalty

76. One attribute of money which is imperative is
(A) gold backing (B) scarcity (C) heavy weight
(D) permanent physical form (E) none of the above

77. If one said that in a certain year the naval strength of the great powers was in the following order: (1) Great Britain, (2) Germany, (3) United States, (4) France, that year would be
(A) 1802 (B) 1840 (C) 1922 (D) 1932 (E) 1913

78. Although religious freedom was granted to all in England by the 18th century, people of which religion could not be members of Parliament?
(A) Anglican (B) Methodist (C) Presbyterian
(D) Quaker (E) Roman Catholic

79. Which prime minister had most to do with a sizeable extension of suffrage in Great Britain in 1867?
(A) Gladstone (B) Pitt (C) Grey (D) Disraeli (E) Baldwin

80. The man responsible for gaining independence for Vietnam from French colonial domination was
(A) Mao Tse-tung (B) Mahatma Gandhi (C) Ho Chi Minh
(D) Bao Dai (E) Richard Nixon

81. "It was a grand time for debtors, especially those in debt for land; they could pay off a mortgage on the farm by selling a single load of apples. But thousands of people on pensions, rigid salaries, or on interest found themselves paupers." This statement would describe
(A) the U.S. in 1873
(B) Germany in 1923
(C) the U.S. in 1925
(D) the U.S. in 1933
(E) Great Britain in 1935

82. The civil liberties guaranteed in the Bill of Rights and the Fourteenth and Fifteenth Amendments to the Constitution were of special concern to the Supreme Court whose Chief Justice was
(A) Charles Evans Hughes (B) William Howard Taft
(C) Roger Taney (D) Earl Warren (E) John Marshall

83. Which of the following books, cited in the 1954 school segregation case, was authored by Gunnar Myrdal?
(A) *The American Commonwealth*
(B) *America as a Civilization*
(C) *An American Dilemma*
(D) *The Promise of American Life*
(E) *America's Sixty Families*

84. President Hoover's statement in the early 1930s, "Prosperity is just around the corner," is most in accord with the thought of
(A) Malthus (B) Ricardo (C) Keynes (D) Marx (E) Veblen

85. American marriage and divorce laws
(A) are outlined in the Constitution
(B) vary from state to state
(C) are uniform for the nation
(D) have no effect on marriage and divorces
(E) all of the above

86. Which group might benefit from inflationary trends?
(A) Old-age pensioners (B) Bondholders
(C) Land speculators (D) Salaried workers
(E) Educators

87. Which of the following is *not* one of the component factors which make possible the flow of production?
(A) Land (B) Labor (C) Capital (D) Capitalism
(E) Organization

88. The federal government's efforts to restrict the growth of monopoly are based on
(A) the Sherman Act (B) the Clayton Act
(C) the Federal Trade Commission Act (D) all of these
(E) none of these

89. The American family is typically
(A) matrilocal (B) patrilocal (C) neolocal
(D) paleolocal (E) rurolocal

90. From a sociological standpoint, the "sacredness" of an object or idea lies in the
(A) object or idea itself
(B) spirit which dwells in the object or idea
(C) type of object or idea
(D) kind of people who believe in it
(E) attitude of the observer

91. Max Weber said that this man's ideas about Christianity contributed in an indirect way to the rise of capitalism. He was
(A) John Calvin (B) Durkheim (C) Thomas Aquinas
(D) Henry VIII (E) Augustine

92. Which can be defined as any formal ceremony prescribed by the group as having symbolic significance?
(A) Mores (B) Folkways (C) Ritual
(D) All of the above (E) None of the above

93. "All persons held as slaves within any State or designated part of a State, the people whereof shall then be in rebellion against the United States shall be then, thenceforward, and forever free." The above statement is taken from the
(A) Abolitionist papers
(B) Fifteenth Amendment to the Constitution
(C) Freedmen's Bureau Act
(D) Thirteenth Amendment to the Constitution
(E) Emancipation Proclamation

94. Dialectical materialism (Marxism) bases a theory of social change on
(A) the struggle of ideas
(B) free will in history
(C) the struggle of economic classes
(D) the cooperation of worker and owner
(E) the religious impulse to communal spirit

95. Traditional French liberalism included all but one of the following:
(A) anti-clericalism
(B) opposition to the aristocracy
(C) anti-Socialism
(D) religious education
(E) protest against big government

96. We sometimes hear a peace described as "Carthaginian." Judging from what you know of the conclusion of the Third Punic War, this term means
(A) a soft and lenient peace
(B) an armistice or temporary cessation of the hostilities
(C) a peace so severe that it means virtual destruction of the enemy
(D) a peace which leaves both sides exhausted
(E) the evolution of a group of allies who stand off a common enemy

97. "I proposed never to accept anything for true which I did not clearly know to be such." Who said this?
(A) Pascal (B) Descartes (C) Bayle (D) Locke (E) Hobbes

98. "The marginal propensity to consume" refers to the
(A) level of income at which consumer spending just equals income
(B) inclination on the part of some to "keep up with the Joneses" in their consumer spending
(C) fraction of extra income that will be spent on consumption
(D) amount a family (or community) will spend on consumption at different levels of income
(E) fact that, at low incomes, families spend more on consumption than the amount of their incomes

99. In the effort to counteract a depression or recession, Federal Reserve Banks might:
(A) increase the reserve requirement
(B) decrease the interest rate charged commercial banks
(C) sell government securities to individuals
(D) raise the interest rate charged commercial banks
(E) raise margin requirements on stock purchases

100. The Mullahs are
(A) a Moslem sect
(B) teachers of Islamic law and dogma
(C) political leaders of the Moslems
(D) a ruling dynasty of Baghdad
(E) followers of Islam who are black

101. A grand jury is
(A) an organization of outstanding civic leaders
(B) a group of citizens whose function is to determine the facts in a civil or criminal trial
(C) the jury used in appellate courts
(D) a group of citizens responsible for bringing formal charges against a person accused of a serious crime
(E) a jury that is called in major cases

102. Justices of the Supreme Court who disagree with a decision may prepare a
(A) concurring opinion (B) advisory opinion
(C) dissenting opinion (D) declaratory judgment
(E) *per curiam* decision

103. Which statement is incorrect about the United States Supreme Court?
(A) The court passes on the constitutionality of all acts of Congress.
(B) The court has jurisdiction in disputes between states.
(C) It may overrule a precedent.
(D) Justices are appointed by the President with the consent of the Senate.
(E) The court makes decisions on the basis of simple majority.

104. The first significant example of colonial unity in America was the
(A) First Continental Congress
(B) Albany Congress
(C) Second Continental Congress
(D) Stamp Act Congress
(E) Articles of Confederation

105. President Roosevelt announced a policy of aid to the opponents of Germany
(A) soon after Hitler became Chancellor of Germany
(B) in a message vetoing the Neutrality Act of 1935
(C) in defining the American attitude toward the Spanish Civil War
(D) after he won the presidential election in November 1940
(E) after a series of German victories had occurred in western and northern Europe

106. Which of the following writers felt that the frontier loosened the bonds of custom, offered new experiences, and had a permanent effect on American institutions?
(A) Henry George (B) Thorstein Veblen
(C) Charles A. Beard (D) Allen Nevins
(E) Frederick Jackson Turner

107. The Meiji Restoration in Japan (1867-68) was
(A) an effort to cut all ties with the West and go back to ancient Japanese ways
(B) the beginning of Japan's modernization
(C) the capture of Formosa by Japan
(D) the overthrow of the Japanese Emperor
(E) the reestablishment of the power of the shogunate

108. "Inconvenience, suffering, and death are the penalties attached by nature to ignorance, as well as to incompetence. . . . It is impossible in any degree to suspend this discipline by stepping in between ignorance and its consequences, without, to a corresponding degree, suspending the progress. If to be ignorant were as safe as to be wise, no one would become wise." This quotation came from
(A) Nikolai Lenin (B) Jean Jacques Rousseau
(C) Cardinal Newman (D) Herbert Spencer (E) John Locke

109. Which of the following pairs are examples of ascribed status?
(A) Age and kinship (B) Sex and kinship (C) Age and sex
(D) All of the above (E) None of the above

110. Those ideas, habits, and conditioned responses common to the members of a society are
(A) alternatives
(B) specialties
(C) individual peculiarities
(D) universals
(E) all of the above

111. In which of the following years has the dependency ratio (proportion of those under fifteen years of age or sixty-five and above to the rest of the population) been highest in the U.S.?
(A) 1900 (B) 1920 (C) 1940 (D) 1950 (E) 1975

112. The concept of anomie refers to
(A) folk society
(B) a highly normative situation
(C) a condition marked by normlessness
(D) a highly dense population
(E) a warring state armed with atomic weapons

113. Ruth Benedict based the landmark anthropological study *Patterns of Culture* (1934) on her study of which of the following groups?
I. Pueblos of New Mexico
II. Dobuans of New Guinea
III. Ainu of Japan
IV. Samoan Islanders of the Pacific
V. Kwakiutl of Vancouver Island
(A) I, II, and V only (B) II and IV only (C) I and V only
(D) II, IV, and V only (E) I, II, IV, and V only

114. The Congo territory was developed and exploited during the last half of the 19th century by a private company which was organized by the king of
(A) Germany (B) Italy (C) Portugal
(D) Belgium (E) Sweden

115. Genghis Khan was the leader of
(A) a nomadic people of Central Asia
(B) the Chinese
(C) a nation of Asian Moslems
(D) a sea-going people of southeast Asia
(E) tribes from northern Japan

116. Thomas Jefferson maintained that
(A) only educated men could know the truth
(B) until the masses were educated aristocratic government was more likely to be just than was republican government
(C) education would make all men equal in ability
(D) by means of education, republican societies should train the ablest minds for leadership
(E) the greatest enemies of liberty were the over-educated

Questions 117–119 relate to the following:

Assume that firm A in a highly competitive industry has the following cost-price situation:

UNITS PRODUCED	PRICE PER UNIT	TOTAL COSTS PER UNIT	MARGINAL COST PER UNIT	TOTAL REVENUE PER UNIT	MARGINAL REVENUE PER UNIT
10,000	$6.00	$17.00	$ 4.00	$6.00	$6.00
30,000	6.00	8.33	4.00	6.00	6.00
50,000	6.00	7.40	6.00	6.00	6.00
60,000	6.00	7.25	6.50	6.00	6.00
70,000	6.00	8.00	12.50	6.00	6.00

117. Firm A will produce a number of units closer to which of the following figures?
(A) 10,000 (B) 30,000 (C) 50,000 (D) 60,000
(E) 70,000

118. Firm A is, at a price of $6.00, in a
(A) slightly profitable situation
(B) highly profitable situation
(C) loss situation
(D) undetermined situation
(E) up and down situation

119. If firm A were in a monopolistic situation, or a partly monopolistic situation, the figures for
(A) marginal costs per unit would change
(B) total costs per unit would change
(C) all columns would stay the same
(D) price per unit would change and thus the revenue figures
(E) the number of units produced would increase

120. Which of the following men would least likely agree with the other four concerning man's basic nature?
(A) Thomas Hobbes (B) Machiavelli (C) Condorcet
(D) Augustine (E) St. Paul

121. Which of the following did not occur during the 1760-1826 period in American history?
(A) A doctrine was formulated concerning American attitudes toward European intervention in the Western Hemisphere.
(B) Political parties appeared in the U.S. for the first time.
(C) The first National Bank was established.
(D) Texas became part of the United States.
(E) Two wars against the British were conducted.

122. "It is difficult to believe in the dreadful but quiet war of organic beings going on in the peaceful woods and smiling fields." Who would have expressed this idea?
(A) Karl Marx (B) John Locke (C) Adam Smith
(D) Charles Darwin (E) Robert Owen

123. If the following historical events were placed in correct chronological order (with the earliest listed first) that order would be:

I. Stamp Act passed by Parliament
II. American-French military alliance agreed to
III. French and Indian War
IV. Meeting of First Continental Congress
V. Declaration of Independence adopted

(A) III, II, IV, I, V (B) I, V, IV, II, III
(C) IV, V, II, III, I (D) III, I, IV, V, II
(E) I, II, III, IV, V

124. You are visiting a rural area. Income per family is less than $1,000 per year; housing is mostly shacks with no electricity or running water; mothers average ten live births during their fertile years. In which of the following states would you probably be?
(A) Delaware (B) Connecticut (C) Ohio
(D) Rhode Island (E) South Carolina

125. Human sexual behavior is expressed and controlled primarily by
(A) instinct (B) drives (C) internalized learning
(D) rational calculation (E) laws

ANSWER KEY—SAMPLE EXAMINATION 1

Section I

1. E	12. B	23. C	34. D	44. C	54. D
2. C	13. E	24. D	35. C	45. C	55. E
3. E	14. E	25. A	36. E	46. E	56. B
4. E	15. E	26. E	37. B	47. E	57. A
5. C	16. B	27. B	38. B	48. E	58. B
6. D	17. C	28. D	39. D	49. E	59. C
7. A	18. C	29. C	40. C	50. D	60. E
8. D	19. E	30. C	41. B	51. B	61. B
9. A	20. B	31. E	42. C	52. A	62. B
10. E	21. D	32. D	43. D	53. D	63. E
11. D	22. D	33. C			

Section II

64. C	75. B	86. C	96. C	106. E	116. D
65. D	76. B	87. D	97. B	107. B	117. C
66. B	77. E	88. D	98. C	108. D	118. C
67. B	78. E	89. C	99. B	109. D	119. D
68. B	79. D	90. E	100. B	110. D	120. C
69. C	80. C	91. A	101. D	111. A	121. D
70. D	81. B	92. C	102. C	112. C	122. D
71. B	82. D	93. E	103. A	113. D	123. D
72. D	83. C	94. C	104. B	114. D	124. E
73. E	84. B	95. D	105. E	115. A	125. C
74. D	85. B				

SCORING CHART—SAMPLE EXAMINATION 1

After you have scored your Sample Examination 1, enter the results in the chart below; then transfer your Raw Score to the Progress Chart on page 14.

Total Test	Number Right	Number Wrong	Number Omitted	Raw Score
Section I: 63				
Section II: 62				
Total: 125				

ANSWER EXPLANATIONS—SAMPLE EXAMINATION 1

Section I

1. E. The following periods in U.S. history were all periods of inflation: 1919–21, 1946–48, 1951–52, and 1973–78. The period 1919–21 followed our participation in World War I; 1946–48 followed World War II: 1951–52 followed the period of major fighting in the Korean War; and 1973–78 followed the Vietnam War.
2. C. During the 17th and 18th centuries a world wide slave trade centered in Africa, where blacks were kidnaped by slavers and shipped to the Western Hemisphere, particularly the United States, where they were sold as slaves. Some 2 million persons were involved in this forced migration.
3. E. France is centrally governed from Paris. The districts (called departments) have relatively little autonomy. The other countries are made up of states (the U.S. and Australia), provinces (Canada), or republics (the U.S.S.R.) which, at least in theory, share power with the central government.
4. E. All the major powers assert control of the air (airspace) over their territory for aircraft, radio, and television.
5. C. Adam Smith (1723–1790), a Scottish economist, wrote *An Inquiry into the Nature and Causes of the Wealth of Nations*, an extremely influential book. In it he developed the theory, usually referred to as "laissez faire" (let do), that economic forces should be allowed to operate without government interference.
6. D. The population of the United States in 1985 is estimated at 235 million. The rate of natural increase (births minus deaths) and net in-migration (immigration minus emigration) is estimated at more than 2½ million annually. This would give us a population of 280,000,000 by the year 2000.
7. A. In the United States, public school elementary teaching has traditionally been a female occupation especially in the elementary schools. About 95% of all teachers in the U.S. public elementary schools are females.
8. D. Calvin believed that the fate of the individual was determined by God before birth. This doctrine is called predestination. The Puritans were followers of Calvin. They left England because they did not accept the doctrines of the Church of England.
9. A. The automobile has altered courting patterns, contributed to obesity and heart disease, produced major industries. helped the growth of suburbs and helped to alter state-federal governmental relations. It is also a status symbol. None of the others fit this description.

10. E. In *Marbury v. Madison* (1803) the Supreme Court declared part of the Judiciary Act, passed by Congress in 1789, unconstitutional. In the other cases the Court declared state action unconstitutional. In the Dartmouth College case it was New Hampshire, in Lochner and Gibbons it was New York, and in Baker *v.* Carr, it was Tennessee.

11. D. The Missouri Compromise of 1850 prohibited slavery in the territories north of 36°30′ except Missouri. Dred Scott, a slave, was taken into free territory and claimed his freedom. The Supreme Court ruled that Dred Scott remained a slave even in free territory. Thus, in effect the Court ruled the Missouri Compromise unconstitutional.

12. B. The formula for the investment multiplier in Keynesian macroeconomics is 1/MPS, MPS being the Marginal Propensity to Save. The MPS is the fraction of each extra dollar that goes to saving instead of consumption.

13. E. The immigration law of 1924 limited immigration to the United States from any country to 2 percent of the persons of that nationality residing in the United States in 1890. This drastically reduced the numbers admitted from Eastern Europe and Southern Europe (Italy).

14. E. Sweden and Switzerland had no colonies during the nineteenth century. France had colonies in Africa and Asia; Germany had colonies in Africa; Denmark ruled Greenland and two of the Virgin Islands; Spain retained control over the Philippines.

15. E. Czechoslovakia was forced to yield to Hitler's claim that the Sudetenland should be ceded to Germany because it contained a majority of ethnic Germans. Neville Chamberlain, Prime Minister of Great Britain, returned from Munich saying "I bring you peace in our time."

16. B. In his formulation of the theory of natural selection, Darwin was influenced by the assertion, "It is the constant tendency in all animated life to increase beyond the nourishment prepared for it. " Darwin's work, *On the Origin of Species*, was published in 1859.

17. C. Mazzini was called "the soul of Italian unification." His belief that each nation had a special mission to perform to contribute to the welfare of humanity in general inspired the Italian people and caused them to fight for Italian unification.

18. C. Statements I, II, and III may reasonably be deduced from the diagram. But there is no way of telling whether the country is mountainous or not.

19. E. The Hawley-Smoot Act of 1930 was a tariff act. The others related to labor.

20. B. Decisions of the United States Supreme Court are by a simple majority. Since 1869, the Court has consisted of nine judges. If all nine judges participate in a decision, a vote of 5 or more for or against the appellant determines the case.

21. D. The Hundred Years War 1337–1453 was fought between England and France. At the Battle of Crecy (1346) the English footsoldiers, armed with longbows, routed the French.

22. D. Many factors account for the level of total spending. These include total income, taxation, people's perception of the future state of the economy, position on the business cycle, war and peace, stock market trends, interest rates and inflation. Hence the level of spending in any two years tells us little about comparative price levels in the two years or the amount of goods produced in the two years.

23. C. Pasteur developed the germ theory of disease and showed that innoculation could prevent anthrax and tetanus.

24. D. The Medieval Church taught that the whole of man's life and activities is governed by Christian law. This, of course, included economic affairs.

25. A. The production possibility curve indicates the maximum output series of any two products. The two products often used as illustrations in economics are guns and butter. The curve shows the maximum output of either.

26. E. The best definition of the cost of a resource is the value of alternative uses of the resource. Of possible alternative uses, the one that has the highest value (in economic terms) determines the cost.

27. B. Net National Product equals Gross National Product minus depreciation.

28. D. William Godwin (1756–1836) English political philosopher wrote *An Enquiry Concerning Political Justice*. His doctrine that man would improve when coercive institutions were removed was naive according to Malthus.

29. C. The factors responsible for the great decrease in the birth rate in the United States during the past 175 years include (1) decrease in the death rate particularly in childhood (2) decline in the farm population and (3) widespread adoption of family planning.

30. C. A nation exists only when people feel themselves to be a nation. People who live within the same state, or who speak the same language, or who are of the same racial origin, or who have the same religious faith are often at war with each other.

31. E. England in the 18th century reserved its educational system mainly for sons of wealthy families who learned to behave as "gentlemen" and to consider themselves better than members of the lower class.

32. D. With the increasing acceptance of cohabitation before marriage, illegitimacy resulting from this union (parents marrying at a later date) has gained a degree of approval. This is partly an outcome of the women's liberation movement.

33. C. During the period 1900–1914 more than 13 million immigrants were admitted into the United States. This was the greatest migration of people in world history. It was sparked by the fear of war, a fear which was realized with the outbreak of World War I in 1914.

34. D. John Locke (1632–1704) English philosopher expressed this idea in his *Two Treatises on Government* (1689). Jefferson had read Locke and may have gotten the idea from him but did not copy it directly when he wrote the Declaration of Independence.

35. C. Alexis de Tocqueville (1805–59) French political scientist traveled in America in 1831 on a mission from his government. When he returned, he described what he had seen in a classic work entitled *Democracy in America*.

36. E. Karl Marx (1818–1883) the father of socialism and communism, developed his ideas fully in his major work, *Das Kapital* (Capital). One of the ideas is that workers receive in wages only part of what they produce. The rest he called "surplus value."

37. B. The first European settlers in South Africa were farmers from the Netherlands. They were called Boers from the Dutch word "boer" which means farmer.

38. B. Charles I was King of England from 1625 to 1649. His army was defeated by the Puritan forces led by Oliver Cromwell. Charles I was beheaded and Cromwell took the titleof Lord Protector.

39. D. Jeremy Bentham (1748–1832) English philosopher, taught that the goal of society is to achieve the greatest good (pleasure) for the greatest number.

40. C. The Byzantine form of Christianity was centered in Byzantium (Constantinople). Here the East Roman Empire continued to exist for 1,000 years (5th to 15th centuries). The Slavs of Southern and Eastern Europe were especially influenced by the culture and religion (Orthodox Christianity) of Byzantium.

41. B. In the 18th century scientific thought considered "nature" most commonly in terms of mechanics. The 18th century is often described as "the age of reason." Scientists concentrated on mechanics. It was the forerunner of the Industrial Revolution.

42. C. In the spring of 1900, a secret society which Westerners called "The Boxers," started a rebellion in China against foreigners who were occupying their country. More than 300 nationals of England, France, the United States and other countries were killed.

43. D. The pre-Columbian Inca empire had a population of 6,000,000 and territory extending over 650,000 square miles. It was centered in Cuzco, Peru.

44. C. The 18th-century rulers Catherine II of Russia, Frederick II of Prussia, and Joseph II of Austria were inspired by the ideas of the 18th-century

Enlightenment. They wished to introduce various reforms, such as liberal land laws, for the welfare of their subjects.

45. C. After the defeat of the Dutch-speaking Boers in South Africa by the British in 1902 the Dutch Boers (farmers) left Cape Colony and made a "Great Trek" north into the interior of the country where they established new settlements and farms.

46. E. After World War II the U.S.S.R. annexed part of East Prussia directly and provided for the annexation of another part of East Prussia to Poland.

47. E. Bonn is the capital of the German Federal Republic (West Germany).

48. E. The area around Instanbul (Constantinople) in Europe is separated from the major part of Turkey in Asia Minor. The Sea of Marmara and the Dardanelles separate European Turkey from Turkey in Asia.

49. E. The ultimate social aim of all economic activity is to produce goods for final consumption. Both capitalism (private enterprise) and Marxism (socialism or communism) agree on this aim. They differ on the means of attaining it.

50. D. The best way in economics to define "saving" is to call it "refraining from consumption. " It is in contrast to consuming all that is produced.

51. B. "Marginal utility" in economics refers to the relation between supply and demand in determining the price of a commodity. High price implies big demand and small supply.

52. A. In the U.S., food and fiber production in the 20th century has increased while the farm work force has steadily declined. This is attributed largely to the other four choices in this question.

53. D. When people interact they tend to take one another into account and modify their behavior accordingly. This interaction is said to be reciprocal. Efforts to achieve behavior modification has attained importance in contemporary psychology.

54. D. The 20th-century goals of favorable remuneration, human dignity and particularly social security as rights would have been rejected by early 19th-century classical liberals.

55. E. The rate of college attendance among 18 to 24 year olds in the United States in 1983 was 32.5 per cent. For Utah the rate was 79.9 per cent.

56. B. In soliciting funds for volunteer health and community programs, motivational researchers have found that potential contributors are most likely to respond to appeals based on shame and comparison to others.

57. A. The French sociologist Emile Durkheim (1858–1917) used statistics to support his theories. He analyzed "mechanical" vs. "organic" solidarity. He held that religion and morality originate in the collective mind of society.

58. B. In most patrilocal African societies, the most simple way to secure a wife was by purchase. This was widely accepted. It had no pejorative aspect.

59. C. In Orwell's *1984* the dominant group uses war primarily as a means of strengthening and perpetuating its absolute control over the citizenry.

60. E. Otto von Bismarck (1815–1898) was premier of Prussia from 1862 to 1890 and Chancellor of Germany from 1871 to 1890. He was called the "Iron Chancellor. " The young Kaiser William II was jealous of him and dismissed him in 1890.

61. B. In European Medieval agriculture, the three field system was a method of rotating crops on the manor. In the absence of artificial fertilizers one of the three fields would lie fallow. The other two would be planted in crops different from the previous year. Exhaustion of the soil was avoided in this way.

62. B. The founding fathers established the electoral college system for choosing a president and vice-president. They provided that the electors be chosen separately in each state and that no Senator or Representative or other United States officer could be an elector. They expected that partisan conflict over the election of a President would thus be avoided.

63. E. The Morrill Act passed in 1862 and signed into law by President Lincoln provided for the establishment of new colleges in the states to promote agriculture. The University of Pennsylvania was chartered as Franklin's Academy in 1754 and became the University of Pennsylvania in 1791.

Section II

64. C. Friedrich Engels (1820–1895) was a colleague and collaborator of Karl Marx. Together they wrote the *Communist Manifesto* (1848).

65. D. The "Roman Empire" in the east continued to exist with its capital in Constantinople for more than ten centuries (5th to 15th centuries) after the decline and fall of Rome.

66. B. Henri Philippe Petain (1856–1951) was placed in charge of the French government at Vichy by the Nazis after the German army conquered France in World War II. The motto of France, "Liberty, Equality, Fraternity" adopted during the French Revolution of 1789, was changed to "Patrie, Travail, Famille" (country, work, family).

67. B. The reform bill of 1832 in England enfranchised a large number of middle class males who had previously been denied the vote. This made it more difficult for any one man to control enough votes to elect a member to the House of Commons.

68. B. In the decade starting in 1820 there was a a movement on the part of the monarchs of continental Europe (the Concert of Europe) to intervene in Latin America against the newly established republics that had broken away from Spain. This failed because of the Monroe Doctrine and the support the U.S. got from Great Britain.

69. C. The cure was administered by Louis Pasteur (1882–1895) the French bacteriologist. He had developed a vaccine which, in accordance with his theory, could conquer the dread disease, hydrophobia (rabies).

70. D. Ivan Petrovich Pavlov (1849–1936), the Russian physiologist, demonstrated the working of the conditioned reflex by an experiment on his dog. He rang a bell just before feeding his dog daily. Soon the dog would salivate when the bell rang and prior to (or regardless of) the feeding.

71. B. The median is determined by arranging the series in order, that is, 6,000, 8,000, etc. to 30,000 and then selecting the middle number, which, in the case of 7 numbers is the fourth (from top or bottom). In this series the median income is $12,000.

72. D. A strong movement to end "Jim Crowism" in the U.S. (unequal treatment of blacks) dates from World War II. The other events occurred during the last decade of the 19th century or first decade of the 20th century.

73. E. The right to trial by jury is a procedure whereby substantive rights (freedom of speech, press, religion, etc.) may be protected.

74. D. During the 19th century, European powers carved out colonies in Africa by asserting their military power against the Africans and against each other. Most of these colonies gained their independence after World War II.

75. B. The clergy of Medieval Europe had to read and interpret the Bible (often available only in Hebrew, Greek and Aramaic). They also read the commentators (Aquinas) in Latin or in the newly emerging national languages. Thus, as students of religion, philosophy, and literature they were the intellectuals of their time.

76. B. If printing presses continue to turn out money in endless quantities, it becomes debased until it loses all value. This happened to German and Russian money toward the end of World War I.

77. E. On the eve of World War I (1913) Great Britain was the greatest naval power in the world. Germany had been building a fleet trying to catch up. The United States was becoming a naval power and had surpassed all but the top two.

78. E. Roman Catholics could not be members of Parliament because it was contrary to their faith to take the required Oath of Supremacy.

79. D. Benjamin Disraeli, leader of the Conservative Party, became Prime Minister of Great Britain in 1867. His Reform Bill of 1867 enfranchised nearly 2,000,000 men.

80. C. Ho Chi Minh led Vietnam in its fight for independence against France. At the Battle of Dien Bien Phu the French army was defeated and driven from Indo China.

81. B. After World War I the German government printed so many marks that by 1923 they were practically worthless. Debtors could easily pay off their debts. People on pensions received money that would buy little or nothing.

82. D. Earl Warren was appointed Chief Justice of the United States Supreme Court in 1953 by President Eisenhower. Under his leadership the Court showed special concern for the civil liberties guaranteed by the Bill of Rights and the Fourteenth Amendment.

83. C. *An American Dilemma*, written by the Swedish sociologist Gunnar Myrdal, was based on a study of the American Negro. It proved that the blacks in America were receiving inferior education and were victims of injustice.

84. B. David Ricardo (1772–1823) British economist wrote *Principles of Political Economy and Taxation*. It said that economic forces would work their way to correct imbalance in the economy.

85. B. American marriage and divorce laws vary from state to state. Under the Constitution, laws about marriage and divorce are left up to the states not to the Federal government.

86. C. Inflationary trends cause land values to rise rapidly. People on pensions or salaries, or holders of bonds with fixed interest rates, find that their income buys less because of inflation.

87. D. Capitalism is the name given to the economic system. Land, labor, capital, and organization are factors of production under capitalism.

88. D. The Sherman Antitrust Act of 1890, the Clayton Antitrust Act of 1914, and the Federal Trade Commission Act of 1914 were all part of the federal government's efforts to restrict the growth of monopoly.

89. C. The American family is regarded by sociologists as a new and developing form. Its distinguishing aspect is neither mother, father, ancient nor rural.

90. E. The attitude of the observer, which is conditioned by the social group to which he or she belongs determines the "sacredness" of an object or idea. This is the sociological approach to "sacredness."

91. A. In his *Protestant Ethic and the Spirit of Capitalism* (1920) Max Weber, the German sociologist, developed the idea that John Calvin's teaching about self-denial as a measure of spiritual discipline is closely related to the rise of capitalism.

92. C. Ritual is a formal ceremony prescribed by a group. The form and content of the ceremony are followed exactly on each occasion. The symbolic significance (whether religious or political) is recognized by all members of the participating group.

93. E. These were the words of the Emancipation Proclamation issued by President Abraham Lincoln September 22, 1862 to take effect January 1, 1863.

94. C. Marxism bases social change on the dialectic (opposing interplay or struggle) of economic classes. Economic materialism is the reality. The final outcome, according to Marx, will be the victory of the proleteriat (working class).

95. D. Traditional French liberalism opposed clericalism (church power), aristocracy, Socialism, and big government. It did not favor religious education.

96. C. At the conclusion of the Third Punic War 146 B.C., Rome defeated the traditional rival, Carthage, in North Africa. The victor razed Carthage to the ground. This gave rise to the term "a Carthaginian peace."

97. B. René Descartes (1596–1650), French philosopher, mathematician, and scientist said: "I proposed never to accept anything for true which I do not clearly know to be such." He is best known for his saying: "I think, therefore I am."

98. C. "The marginal propensity to consume" refers, in economics, to the extra amount that people will want to spend on consumption if given an extra dollar of income.

99. B. In an effort to counteract a depression or recession, Federal Reserve Banks might decrease the interest rate charged commercial banks. This would make it easier for banks to lend money to business. This, in turn, would help business to continue to function.

100. B. The Mullahs are Muslim religious teachers trained in traditional Islamic law and doctrine.

101. D. A grand jury is a group of citizens that examines the evidence against a person accused of a serious crime. If the evidence warrants, the grand jury brings formal charges. Then the accused must stand trial.

102. C. Justices of the Supreme Court who disagree with the majority of the Court may prepare a dissenting opinion. In the dissent, the justice states his reason for disagreement.

103. A. The court passes on the constitutionality of an act of Congress only when a case involving the act is brought before the court. Even then, the court may, if it chooses, refuse to hear the case.

104. B. The Albany Congress met in 1754. The Stamp Act Congress met in 1765, the First Continental Congress in 1774, and the Second Continental Congress in 1775. The Articles of Confederation were drawn up in 1778.

105. E. In the spring of 1940, Nazi Germany occupied Belgium and Holland, prepared the attack on France, and drove the British off the continent at Dunkirk. At this point President Roosevelt announced a policy of aid to the opponents of Germany.

106. E. The American historian Frederick Jackson Turner (1861–1932) published *The Significance of the Frontier in American History* in 1893. He showed that the frontier exercised the greatest influence on American institutions.

107. B. The Meiji Restoration in Japan (1867–68) was the beginning of Japan's modernization. The Emperor regained power after the Shogunate was overthrown. Then Japan proceeded with modernization along western lines.

108. D. Herbert Spencer 1820–1903, British sociologist made this statement. He applied the idea of biological evolution to social institutions.

109. D. Age and kinship, sex and kinship, and age and sex are examples of ascribed status. These pairs are useful in sociological analyses of cultures.

110. D. Those ideas, habits, and conditioned responses common to the members of a society are described as universals. Universals are means of identifying membership in a society and contrasting social groups with respect to universals that apply to one or another.

111. A. The dependency ratio has declined as the size of the nuclear family has declined. Fewer children per family means fewer dependents at one end. Social security has reduced dependency at the other.

112. C. The concept of anomie is used to describe our society where norms of conduct and belief have been weakened or have actually broken down.

113. A. Ruth Benedict's classic social anthropology study examined the Zuni Pueblo Native Americans, the Dobuans of Eastern New Guinea in the Pacific, and the Kwakiutl Indians of the west coast of North America. The equally renowned pioneer study *Coming of Age in Samoa* (1928) was by Margaret Mead. Dr. Benedict's later study *The Chrysanthemum and the Sword* was undertaken in an effort to understand Japanese culture at the time of the Second World War.

114. D. The Congo territory was explored and exploited under the leadership of King Leopold II of Belgium. The Congo, located in south central Africa, was known as the Belgian Congo until it gained its independence in 1960.

115. A. Genghis Khan was the leader of a nomadic people of Central Asia. Under Genghis Khan's leadership, the Mongols invaded Europe during the 13th century and caused havoc in Poland, Hungary, and much of Russia.

116. D. Thomas Jefferson, a strong advocate of education, was the founder of the University of Virginia. He prepared a plan for public elementary and secondary schools also but did not live to see it come to pass. It was part of his plan to train the ablest minds for leadership in the republic.

117. C. Equalizing firm A's marginal cost to marginal revenue gives firm A's maximum profit per units produced. A plotted curve based on the figures in the table shows the number of units produced to be 50,000.

118. C. In the case of firm A, based on the table cited in #117 above, the result is the smallest loss rather than a profit.

119. D. If firm A were in a monopolistic situation, or a partly monopolistic situation, the figures for price per unit would be lowered (because of firm A's more advantageous position) and a profit would result.

120. C. The Marquis de Cordorcet (1743–1794) believed in the indefinite perfectability of man. He was an optimist so far as man's future was concerned.

121. D. Texas became part of the United States in 1845. The other events did occur during the period 1760–1826. The latest of the other four was the Monroe Doctrine issued in 1823.

122. D. Charles Darwin (1809–82), English naturalist could have expressed this idea in his book *The Origin of Species* published in 1859.

123. D. The French and Indian War—the war between England (and the American colonists) and France (and her Indian allies)—began on the Pennsylvania frontier in 1754. Parliament passed the Stamp Act as a revenue measure in 1765, two years after the war ended. Fifty-five delegates to the First Continental Congress met in Philadelphia beginning September 5, 1774. The Declaration of Independence was adopted by the Second Continental Congress on July 4, 1776. In February, 1778, Benjamin Franklin negotiated a treaty of recognition with France and a second treaty creating a formal military alliance.

124. E. In per capita personal income, South Carolina ranks 49th (just above Mississippi) of the 50 states.

125. C. While each of the other four play a part, human sexual behavior is expressed and controlled primarily by internalized learning.

ANSWER SHEET — SOCIAL SCIENCES-HISTORY/SAMPLE EXAMINATION 2

Section I

1. Ⓐ Ⓑ Ⓒ Ⓓ Ⓔ
2. Ⓐ Ⓑ Ⓒ Ⓓ Ⓔ
3. Ⓐ Ⓑ Ⓒ Ⓓ Ⓔ
4. Ⓐ Ⓑ Ⓒ Ⓓ Ⓔ
5. Ⓐ Ⓑ Ⓒ Ⓓ Ⓔ
6. Ⓐ Ⓑ Ⓒ Ⓓ Ⓔ
7. Ⓐ Ⓑ Ⓒ Ⓓ Ⓔ
8. Ⓐ Ⓑ Ⓒ Ⓓ Ⓔ
9. Ⓐ Ⓑ Ⓒ Ⓓ Ⓔ
10. Ⓐ Ⓑ Ⓒ Ⓓ Ⓔ
11. Ⓐ Ⓑ Ⓒ Ⓓ Ⓔ
12. Ⓐ Ⓑ Ⓒ Ⓓ Ⓔ
13. Ⓐ Ⓑ Ⓒ Ⓓ Ⓔ
14. Ⓐ Ⓑ Ⓒ Ⓓ Ⓔ
15. Ⓐ Ⓑ Ⓒ Ⓓ Ⓔ
16. Ⓐ Ⓑ Ⓒ Ⓓ Ⓔ
17. Ⓐ Ⓑ Ⓒ Ⓓ Ⓔ
18. Ⓐ Ⓑ Ⓒ Ⓓ Ⓔ
19. Ⓐ Ⓑ Ⓒ Ⓓ Ⓔ
20. Ⓐ Ⓑ Ⓒ Ⓓ Ⓔ
21. Ⓐ Ⓑ Ⓒ Ⓓ Ⓔ
22. Ⓐ Ⓑ Ⓒ Ⓓ Ⓔ
23. Ⓐ Ⓑ Ⓒ Ⓓ Ⓔ
24. Ⓐ Ⓑ Ⓒ Ⓓ Ⓔ
25. Ⓐ Ⓑ Ⓒ Ⓓ Ⓔ
26. Ⓐ Ⓑ Ⓒ Ⓓ Ⓔ
27. Ⓐ Ⓑ Ⓒ Ⓓ Ⓔ
28. Ⓐ Ⓑ Ⓒ Ⓓ Ⓔ
29. Ⓐ Ⓑ Ⓒ Ⓓ Ⓔ
30. Ⓐ Ⓑ Ⓒ Ⓓ Ⓔ
31. Ⓐ Ⓑ Ⓒ Ⓓ Ⓔ
32. Ⓐ Ⓑ Ⓒ Ⓓ Ⓔ
33. Ⓐ Ⓑ Ⓒ Ⓓ Ⓔ
34. Ⓐ Ⓑ Ⓒ Ⓓ Ⓔ
35. Ⓐ Ⓑ Ⓒ Ⓓ Ⓔ
36. Ⓐ Ⓑ Ⓒ Ⓓ Ⓔ
37. Ⓐ Ⓑ Ⓒ Ⓓ Ⓔ
38. Ⓐ Ⓑ Ⓒ Ⓓ Ⓔ
39. Ⓐ Ⓑ Ⓒ Ⓓ Ⓔ
40. Ⓐ Ⓑ Ⓒ Ⓓ Ⓔ
41. Ⓐ Ⓑ Ⓒ Ⓓ Ⓔ
42. Ⓐ Ⓑ Ⓒ Ⓓ Ⓔ
43. Ⓐ Ⓑ Ⓒ Ⓓ Ⓔ
44. Ⓐ Ⓑ Ⓒ Ⓓ Ⓔ
45. Ⓐ Ⓑ Ⓒ Ⓓ Ⓔ
46. Ⓐ Ⓑ Ⓒ Ⓓ Ⓔ
47. Ⓐ Ⓑ Ⓒ Ⓓ Ⓔ
48. Ⓐ Ⓑ Ⓒ Ⓓ Ⓔ
49. Ⓐ Ⓑ Ⓒ Ⓓ Ⓔ
50. Ⓐ Ⓑ Ⓒ Ⓓ Ⓔ
51. Ⓐ Ⓑ Ⓒ Ⓓ Ⓔ
52. Ⓐ Ⓑ Ⓒ Ⓓ Ⓔ
53. Ⓐ Ⓑ Ⓒ Ⓓ Ⓔ
54. Ⓐ Ⓑ Ⓒ Ⓓ Ⓔ
55. Ⓐ Ⓑ Ⓒ Ⓓ Ⓔ
56. Ⓐ Ⓑ Ⓒ Ⓓ Ⓔ
57. Ⓐ Ⓑ Ⓒ Ⓓ Ⓔ
58. Ⓐ Ⓑ Ⓒ Ⓓ Ⓔ
59. Ⓐ Ⓑ Ⓒ Ⓓ Ⓔ
60. Ⓐ Ⓑ Ⓒ Ⓓ Ⓔ
61. Ⓐ Ⓑ Ⓒ Ⓓ Ⓔ
62. Ⓐ Ⓑ Ⓒ Ⓓ Ⓔ
63. Ⓐ Ⓑ Ⓒ Ⓓ Ⓔ

Section II

64. Ⓐ Ⓑ Ⓒ Ⓓ Ⓔ
65. Ⓐ Ⓑ Ⓒ Ⓓ Ⓔ
66. Ⓐ Ⓑ Ⓒ Ⓓ Ⓔ
67. Ⓐ Ⓑ Ⓒ Ⓓ Ⓔ
68. Ⓐ Ⓑ Ⓒ Ⓓ Ⓔ
69. Ⓐ Ⓑ Ⓒ Ⓓ Ⓔ
70. Ⓐ Ⓑ Ⓒ Ⓓ Ⓔ
71. Ⓐ Ⓑ Ⓒ Ⓓ Ⓔ
72. Ⓐ Ⓑ Ⓒ Ⓓ Ⓔ
73. Ⓐ Ⓑ Ⓒ Ⓓ Ⓔ
74. Ⓐ Ⓑ Ⓒ Ⓓ Ⓔ
75. Ⓐ Ⓑ Ⓒ Ⓓ Ⓔ
76. Ⓐ Ⓑ Ⓒ Ⓓ Ⓔ
77. Ⓐ Ⓑ Ⓒ Ⓓ Ⓔ
78. Ⓐ Ⓑ Ⓒ Ⓓ Ⓔ
79. Ⓐ Ⓑ Ⓒ Ⓓ Ⓔ
80. Ⓐ Ⓑ Ⓒ Ⓓ Ⓔ
81. Ⓐ Ⓑ Ⓒ Ⓓ Ⓔ
82. Ⓐ Ⓑ Ⓒ Ⓓ Ⓔ
83. Ⓐ Ⓑ Ⓒ Ⓓ Ⓔ
84. Ⓐ Ⓑ Ⓒ Ⓓ Ⓔ
85. Ⓐ Ⓑ Ⓒ Ⓓ Ⓔ
86. Ⓐ Ⓑ Ⓒ Ⓓ Ⓔ
87. Ⓐ Ⓑ Ⓒ Ⓓ Ⓔ
88. Ⓐ Ⓑ Ⓒ Ⓓ Ⓔ
89. Ⓐ Ⓑ Ⓒ Ⓓ Ⓔ
90. Ⓐ Ⓑ Ⓒ Ⓓ Ⓔ
91. Ⓐ Ⓑ Ⓒ Ⓓ Ⓔ
92. Ⓐ Ⓑ Ⓒ Ⓓ Ⓔ
93. Ⓐ Ⓑ Ⓒ Ⓓ Ⓔ
94. Ⓐ Ⓑ Ⓒ Ⓓ Ⓔ
95. Ⓐ Ⓑ Ⓒ Ⓓ Ⓔ
96. Ⓐ Ⓑ Ⓒ Ⓓ Ⓔ
97. Ⓐ Ⓑ Ⓒ Ⓓ Ⓔ
98. Ⓐ Ⓑ Ⓒ Ⓓ Ⓔ
99. Ⓐ Ⓑ Ⓒ Ⓓ Ⓔ
100. Ⓐ Ⓑ Ⓒ Ⓓ Ⓔ
101. Ⓐ Ⓑ Ⓒ Ⓓ Ⓔ
102. Ⓐ Ⓑ Ⓒ Ⓓ Ⓔ
103. Ⓐ Ⓑ Ⓒ Ⓓ Ⓔ
104. Ⓐ Ⓑ Ⓒ Ⓓ Ⓔ
105. Ⓐ Ⓑ Ⓒ Ⓓ Ⓔ
106. Ⓐ Ⓑ Ⓒ Ⓓ Ⓔ
107. Ⓐ Ⓑ Ⓒ Ⓓ Ⓔ
108. Ⓐ Ⓑ Ⓒ Ⓓ Ⓔ
109. Ⓐ Ⓑ Ⓒ Ⓓ Ⓔ
110. Ⓐ Ⓑ Ⓒ Ⓓ Ⓔ
111. Ⓐ Ⓑ Ⓒ Ⓓ Ⓔ
112. Ⓐ Ⓑ Ⓒ Ⓓ Ⓔ
113. Ⓐ Ⓑ Ⓒ Ⓓ Ⓔ
114. Ⓐ Ⓑ Ⓒ Ⓓ Ⓔ
115. Ⓐ Ⓑ Ⓒ Ⓓ Ⓔ
116. Ⓐ Ⓑ Ⓒ Ⓓ Ⓔ
117. Ⓐ Ⓑ Ⓒ Ⓓ Ⓔ
118. Ⓐ Ⓑ Ⓒ Ⓓ Ⓔ
119. Ⓐ Ⓑ Ⓒ Ⓓ Ⓔ
120. Ⓐ Ⓑ Ⓒ Ⓓ Ⓔ
121. Ⓐ Ⓑ Ⓒ Ⓓ Ⓔ
122. Ⓐ Ⓑ Ⓒ Ⓓ Ⓔ
123. Ⓐ Ⓑ Ⓒ Ⓓ Ⓔ
124. Ⓐ Ⓑ Ⓒ Ⓓ Ⓔ
125. Ⓐ Ⓑ Ⓒ Ⓓ Ⓔ

SAMPLE EXAMINATION 2

Section I

Number of Questions: 63
Time: 45 minutes

Directions: Each of the questions or incomplete statements below is followed by five suggested answers or completions. Select the one that is best in each case.

MAP A

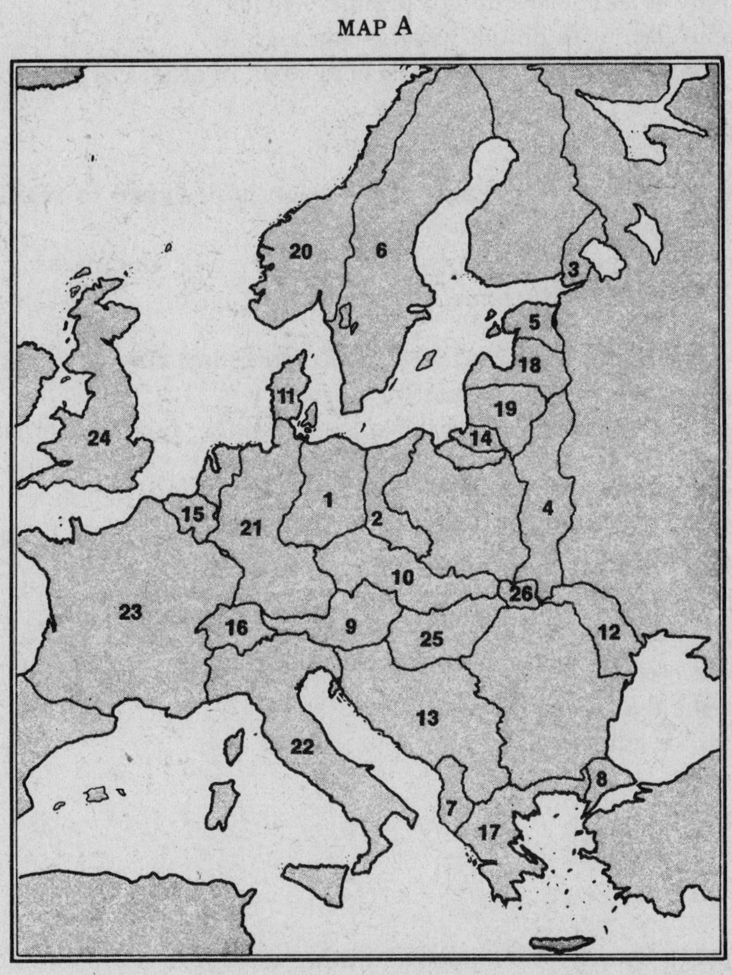

Questions 1–3 refer to MAP A.

1. In which country did the activists of a Nazi sympathizer give the world the term "Quisling"?
   (A) 21 (B) 15 (C) 24 (D) 23 (E) 20

2. Which former area of Rumania was taken by the USSR in 1940?
   (A) 13 (B) 14 (C) 19 (D) 4 (E) 12

3. Which two countries were at war on Albanian soil in 1941?
   (A) 7 and 8 (B) 25 and 9 (C) 13 and 10 (D) 17 and 22
   (E) 17 and 23

4. Malthus' "principle of population" is an instance of the
   (A) law of increasing returns
   (B) law of diminishing returns
   (C) observation that fertility is greater in the tropical than temperate zones
   (D) observation that fertility is greater among the lowest class
   (E) law of diminishing sexual energy

5. The holding company is possible only because
   (A) many stockholders do not permit proxies
   (B) some securities do not have voting rights
   (C) corporations are permitted to hold stock in other corporations
   (D) courts do not enforce the law
   (E) stocks can be bought on margin

6. The Securities and Exchange Commission is designed to regulate the securities business for the benfit of
   (A) small business (B) the consumer (C) the investor
   (D) labor (E) the banking system

7. Youth-parent tensions in American society today may be explained by
   (A) rapid change in our society
   (B) smaller numbers of children per family during the past two decades
   (C) the increasing patriarchal nature of the family
   (D) development of a youth subculture and confusion as to the exact time for attaining "adult" status
   (E) A and D primarily

8. The term "secular power" in Medieval European history would be used to describe the powers of a
   (A) king or emperor
   (B) pope
   (C) bishop
   (D) church council
   (E) cardinal

9. A campaign speech was made containing a reference to "two chickens in every pot." What event occurred shortly after the speech which made this reference seem ironic?
   (A) Pullman transportation strike in 1894
   (B) Defeat of the Populists in 1896
   (C) Election of Alfred E. Smith in 1928
   (D) Stock market crash in 1929
   (E) Rationing of gasoline after 1941

10. The size of the population of the United States in 1790 was about the same as the 1970 population of which of the following states?
   (A) New York (B) California (C) Illinois (D) Nevada
   (E) Tennessee

11. "Now that the Democrats have captured the liberal imagination of the nation, it is forgotten how much of the architecture of America's liberal society was drafted by the Republicans, who are today regarded as the party of the right." To support his point the author might cite all of the following except the
(A) abolition of slavery (B) Pendleton Act
(C) Social Security Act (D) Morrill Act for education
(E) Pure Food and Drug Act

12. Which of these ancient empires was the largest in geographic extent?
(A) Egyptian (B) Persian (C) Assyrian (D) Chaldean
(E) Hittite

13. Which of the following is not an Indo-European language?
(A) Arabic (B) Sanskrit (C) Greek (D) Hittite (E) Latin

14. Monetary policy in the U.S. is administered by
(A) Congress
(B) the President
(C) the Federal Reserve Board of Governors
(D) the Department of Commerce
(E) the Council of Economic Advisors

15. Most of the major rivers in Soviet Asia flow from
(A) west to east
(B) east to west
(C) north to south
(D) south to north
(E) north to southeast

16. The belief in reincarnation is an important part of
(A) Judaism
(B) Confucius' teachings
(C) Hinduism
(D) Zoroastrianism
(E) Islam

17. The total value (in dollars) of goods and services produced in the American economy during the year is called the
(A) net national income
(B) gross private domestic investment
(C) gross national product
(D) net producers domestic gain
(E) net national product

18. In sociology and psychology, "drives" are
(A) behavior that must always be suppressed
(B) factors which incite behavior in the individual
(C) glands which secrete endocrines
(D) mysterious forces which induce people to commit crimes
(E) none of the above

MAP B
SOUTHERN
ASIA

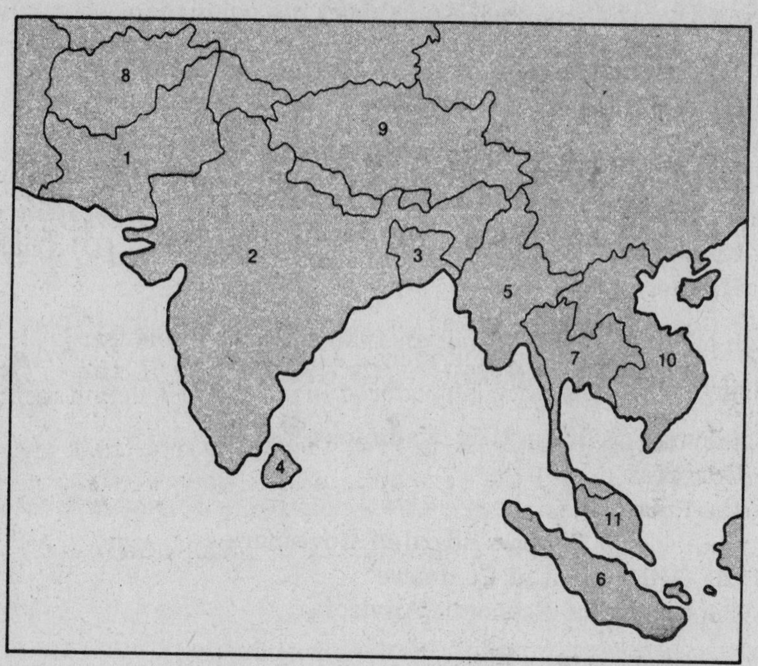

Questions 19–21 pertain to this map.

19. Which area was ruled by the Dutch for a number of centuries?
(A) 2 (B) 3 (C) 5 (D) 7 (E) 6

20. Which country was ruled until 1959 by a Buddhist religious leader called the "Dalai Lama"
(A) 2 (B) 4 (C) 5 (D) 7 (E) 9

21. Which area was split into four states in the 1950s?
(A) 2 (B) 3 (C) 5 (D) 7 (E) 10

22. In the 1950s and '60s the Supreme Court inclined toward "judicial activism" in all of the following areas *except*
(A) civil rights
(B) legislative reapportionment
(C) presidential control over foreign policy
(D) unlawful search and seizure
(E) indigent defendants

23. "The bureaucratization of capitalism . . . carries such examinations all over the world. . . . Today, the certificate of education becomes what the test for ancestors has been in the past." Who said that?
(A) Karl Marx
(B) David Ricardo
(C) Max Weber
(D) Adam Smith
(E) John Maynard Keynes

24. At the time when it achieved recognition as an independent state, in which of the following did a substantial migration in or out of the country take place?
I. Israel, II. India, III. Pakistan, IV. Mexico, V. Yugoslavia.
(A) II only (B) I and IV only (C) I, II, and III only
(D) II, III, and IV only (E) I, II, III, IV, and V

25. In a market economy, price tends to fall whenever
(A) the quantity supplied increases more rapidly than the quantity demanded
(B) the quantity demanded increases more rapidly than the quantity supplied
(C) supply and demand are equal
(D) both supply and demand increase
(E) more of a commodity is produced in a mass production technology

26. The birth rate in country X is 14.0; the death rate, 10.8; the infant mortality rate 9.6; and the per capita income over $8,000.00 per year. The country is
(A) Brazil (B) Egypt (C) Albania (D) Sweden
(E) Union of South Africa

27. The agricultural revolution in the U.S. is related to
(A) the growth of the use of tractors
(B) an increase in the use of electric power
(C) the decline in farm production
(D) all of the above
(E) A and B, but not C

28. The English Reform Bill of 1867 extended the right to vote to
(A) middle-class businessmen
(B) working men in the cities
(C) all adults
(D) all adults living in the cities
(E) the Catholics

29. The increasing number of elderly widows in America is caused by
(A) women marrying at a younger age than in the past
(B) women marrying husbands increasingly older than themselves
(C) women, on the average, having an increasingly longer life span than men
(D) all of the above
(E) B and C, but not A

30. Which of the following reforms was *not* advocated by the Progressive Movement in the United States of the early 20th century?
(A) Referendum
(B) Recall
(C) Primary elections
(D) Nonpartisanship in municipal elections
(E) The removal of restrictions on Negro voting

31. In the history of the presidency until 1974, there had never been an instance of
(A) a Vice-President becoming President
(B) a President failing to be elected by the electoral college
(C) the election of a President by the House of Representatives
(D) the resignation of a President
(E) the assassination of a President

32. Which amendment to the Constitution abolished slavery?
(A) 12th (B) 13th (C) 14th (D) 15th (E) 16th

33. "The American expansionists and imperialists of the 1890s appealed to biological evolution and economic and social history to support their views. We are suffering today because of the hangover from their nonsense." The person saying this would have particularly disliked the
(A) Federal Reserve Act (B) Civil War
(C) Kellogg-Briand Pact (D) Spanish-American War
(E) Russo-Japanese War

34. The interest which Russia historically manifested in the Dardanelles arose from a desire to have an outlet to the
(A) Black Sea (B) Yellow Sea (C) North Sea
(D) Mediterranean Sea (E) Red Sea

35. "L'état, c'est moi." This statement is attributed to
(A) Louis XVI
(B) Louis XV
(C) Louis XIV
(D) Louis XIII
(E) Louis X

36. After the Franco-Prussian War, the German Imperial constitution
(A) made the Prussian king the new emperor
(B) was a generally democratic instrument
(C) declared the equality of all member states
(D) declared the ruler of Austria to be Emperor of the Empire
(E) made Roman Catholicism the state religion

37. In *The Prince*, Machiavelli counsels a ruler that
(A) it is better to be feared than loved
(B) it is better to be loved than feared
(C) he need not worry about arousing the hatred of his subjects
(D) it is best to be both feared and hated
(E) it is better to be truthful with one's subjects

38. "In Hegel's writings, dialectic stands on its head. You must turn it right way up again if you want to discover the rational kernel that is hidden away within the wrappings of mystifications." Who said this?
(A) Charles Darwin (B) Friedrich Nietzsche
(C) Sigmund Freud (D) Karl Marx (E) Max Weber

39. Freud criticized Marxism on the basis that
(A) class struggle encouraged man's aggressive tendencies
(B) it disregarded the evolution of institutions
(C) it was still bound by Hegelian idealism
(D) it left untouched the real causes of human aggressiveness and anxiety
(E) it attacked traditional religion

40. When historians use the title *Augustus* they are referring to
(A) Julius Caesar
(B) Octavian
(C) Marcus Aurelius
(D) Claudius
(E) Trajan

41. In the U.S., the function of the family *least* transferred to outside agencies is the
(A) economic
(B) educational
(C) recreational
(D) religious
(E) emotional

42. The Standard Oil trust was originally organized by
(A) Carnegie
(B) Morgan
(C) Vanderbilt
(D) Rockefeller
(E) Gould

43. What issue or issues in France were significant in the Dreyfus Affair?
(A) Anti-republicanism
(B) Anti-Semitism
(C) Anti-clericalism
(D) A and B, but not C
(E) A, B, and C

44. Bismarck, after 1851, believed that Germany could become strong and united only if
(A) Austria was excluded from German affairs
(B) she became a republic
(C) Austria became the leader
(D) Italy remained divided into small states
(E) colonies could be gained for Germany

45. The Maoris are
(A) Bantus who fought the Boers in South Africa
(B) the aboriginal peoples of Australia
(C) the French Protestant settlers in South Africa
(D) a people who lived in New Zealand before the coming of the British
(E) a group of Irish revolutionaries

46. An increase in the amount of money available
(A) always means an increase in the level of prices
(B) never has an effect on the level of prices
(C) always means a decrease in the level of prices
(D) may cause no change in the level of prices under certain conditions
(E) always acts to expand economic production and activity

47. Which of the following programs of social reform would be, according to the thought of Malthus, based on a correct analysis of the problem of poverty?
(A) Universal education at public expense
(B) Guaranteed minimum wage
(C) Social security
(D) Consumer subsidies
(E) Aid to dependent children

48. If people do not consume all their income, but put the unspent amount into a pillow or buy an old security with it, in national income and product terms they are
(A) saving but not investing
(B) investing but not saving
(C) both saving and investing
(D) neither saving nor investing
(E) saving, but investing only to the extent that they buy old securities

49. Which of the following is *least* common in man's various societies?
(A) Group marriage (B) Divorce (C) Illegitimacy
(D) Intercourse before marriage (E) Homosexuality

50. Compared to 1960, yearly executions of convicted criminals in the U.S. had, by 1976,
(A) doubled (B) stayed about the same (C) increased 25%
(D) decreased slightly (E) dropped to a level of zero

51. When sociologists talk of "social mobility," they usually have in mind
(A) horizontal mobility (B) interracial marriage (C) vertical mobility
(D) rapid social retrogression (E) moral progress

52. The use of the canoe and the moccasin by whites is an example of cultural
(A) invention (B) mobility (C) simplicity (D) diffusion
(E) management

53. Which statement about the corporation is false?
(A) It can secure capital with greater ease than other forms of economic organization.
(B) It can delegate authority and managerial duties to individuals who are experts in their fields.
(C) Since it is an artificial or fictitious person, it is not expected to conform to all laws.
(D) The owners of corporations enjoy limited liability.
(E) It can issue bonds as well as stock.

54. Which of the following was Veblen's attitude toward marginal utility economics? He considered it
(A) analytically proper
(B) overly inductive and oriented to biology
(C) collectivist in its implications
(D) overly deductive, individualistic, and static
(E) too strongly oriented to the labor movement

55. In the eyes of Keynes, the ultimate responsibility for full employment rested with the
(A) natural forces of economic variables
(B) good will of businessmen
(C) central government
(D) divinity
(E) gold-producing countries

Question 56 refers to the following chart.

U.S. PRESIDENTIAL ELECTIONS 1876–1888

Year	Candidates	(Party)	Popular vote	Electoral Vote
1876	Rutherford B. Hayes	(R)*	4,036,572	185
	Samuel J. Tilden	(D)	4,284,020	184
1880	James A. Garfield	(R)*	4,453,295	214
	Winfield S. Hancock	(D)	4,414,082	155
	James B. Weaver (Greenback-Labor)		308,578	0
1884	Grover Cleveland	(D)*	4,879,507	219
	James G. Blaine	(R)	4,850,293	182
	Benjamin F. Butler (Greenback-Labor)		175,370	0
	John P. St. John (Prohibition)		150,369	0
1888	Benjamin Harrison	(R)*	5,477,129	233
	Grover Cleveland	(D)	5,537,857	168
	Clinton B. Fisk (Prohibition)		249,506	0
	Anson J. Streeter (Union-Labor)		146,935	0

56. The information in the above chart illustrates which of the following?
(A) The crucial importance of the popular vote in electing the president
(B) The rapid growth of the American electorate
(C) The incumbent's advantage in an election
(D) How the electoral college system operates
(E) The influence of third parties in election outcomes

57. States with relatively high per capita incomes (by U.S. standards) include
(A) Tennessee, Texas, North Carolina
(B) Texas, Kentucky, North Dakota
(C) Texas, California, Georgia
(D) Connecticut, Virginia, Texas
(E) Connecticut, Delaware, Nevada

58. In 1987, approximately what percent of the American population was residing and working on farms?
(A) 50% (B) 33% (C) 25% (D) 15% (E) 2%

59. In 1980, the states that had the largest representation in the House of Representatives were
(A) Texas, Massachusetts, Virginia
(B) California, Texas, Pennsylvania
(C) New York, Pennsylvania, New Jersey
(D) California, New York, Florida
(E) California, New York, Texas

60. In 1980, the average Congressional district contained the following number of people:
(A) 110,000 (B) 210,000 (C) 520,000 (D) 1,050,000
(E) 3,500,000

61. In which of the following elections was the electoral college vote 523 for the winner (name given first), and 8 for the loser?
(A) Roosevelt, Hoover (B) Johnson, Goldwater
(C) Eisenhower, Stevenson (D) Nixon, Humphrey
(E) Roosevelt, Landon

62. Alexis de Tocqueville's *Democracy in America* had as its basic subject
(A) American political institutions during the presidency of Andrew Johnson
(B) modern democracy and an alleged trend toward equality of conditions
(C) effects of the Industrial Revolution upon America and Europe
(D) amazing prophecies about the future political development of America and France
(E) a contrast between English and American democracy

63. Most countries with high per-capita incomes (above $4,000 per year) have
(A) death rates above 20 per 1000 per year
(B) illiteracy rates of above 50%
(C) more than half their workers in agriculture
(D) birth rates below 20 per 1000 per year
(E) none of the above

Section II

Number of Questions: 62
Time: 45 minutes

Directions: Each of the questions or incomplete statements below is followed by five suggested answers or completions. Select the one that is best in each case.

64. The Huguenots were
(A) a French family which claimed the throne
(B) a party which opposed the king's powers in England
(C) French Protestants
(D) a fleet which Philip II sent to invade England
(E) alchemists

65. Which of these nations came into being as a result of a war for independence during the time of Philip II?
(A) Portugal
(B) Dutch Netherlands
(C) Sweden
(D) Burgundy
(E) Switzerland

66. The peace and unity of the Frankish empire was disturbed in the 9th century by the invasions of the
(A) Vikings (B) Huns (C) Vandals (D) Byzantines
(E) Britons

67. When we measure part of the cost of education by giving a value to the output not produced by students while attending schools, we have taken account of costs termed
(A) direct (B) personal (C) subsidized
(D) opportunity (E) interest

68. Correlations between educational enrollments and GNP per capita in various countries tend to be positive and high. This shows that
(A) rich countries like to spend more resources on education
(B) education acts to help make countries richer
(C) education is a consumer good which rich countries can afford
(D) there is a relation between the two
(E) none of the above is true

69. George Herbert Mead's theory of the origin and functioning of self is best represented by which of the following statements?
(A) The social self is comparable to Freud's id.
(B) We must be others if we are to be ourselves.
(C) The self is unrelated to social control.
(D) All of the above.
(E) None of the above.

70. In an experiment using a control group
(A) change is induced in the control group only
(B) change is induced in the experimental group only
(C) more change is induced in the control group than in the experimental group
(D) less change is induced in the control group than the experimental group
(E) none of these

71. In which of the following job categories in the U.S. has there been an absolute decline over the past thirty years?
(A) Professional (B) Managerial (C) Skilled
(D) Service (E) Farm

72. Norms are sometimes rejected because
(A) they are not considered important (B) they are not understood
(C) some are flexible (D) all of these (E) none of these

73. Louis XIV tried to extend France to its "natural boundaries." Which boundary could be realized only at the cost of a series of wars?
(A) Pyrenees (B) Alps (C) Mediterranean
(D) Rhine (E) English Channel

74. Between 1865 and 1965, Congress admitted fifteen new states, all west of the Mississippi. Which of the following was one of these states?
(A) Nevada
(B) California
(C) Iowa
(D) Missouri
(E) Oklahoma

75. "The government bets you can't live on the land for five years and if you can, you win the land." This statement refers to
(A) the Northwest Ordinance
(B) veterans' preference after World War II
(C) the Homestead Act of 1862
(D) all of the above
(E) none of the above

76. Railway mileage in the U.S. increased most in absolute amount during which of the following decades?
(A) 1840s (B) 1860s (C) 1880s (D) 1950s
(E) 1960s

77. The largest state in area and the smallest in population among the following is
(A) Nevada (B) Texas (C) Montana (D) Maine (E) Alaska

78. "He could no longer draw a north-south line in the continental United States, on one side of which the population was less than two persons per square mile and on the other side it was more." This statement refers to the census director of which year?
(A) 1820 (B) 1860 (C) 1890 (D) 1930 (E) 1940

79. An immigrant arriving in the U.S. in the period 1885-1914 was most likely to be
(A) a young woman (B) an older man (C) a child
(D) a young man (E) an older woman

80. Southern landowners in the decades following the Civil War evolved, as a dominant system for getting work accomplished, the system of
(A) sharecropping (B) migrant labor (C) paid farm labor
(D) A and B, not C (E) none of the above

81. In 1790, the most populous and influential U.S. state was
(A) New York (B) South Carolina (C) Maryland
(D) Virginia (E) Massachusetts

82. The most populous state in the United States in 1860 was
(A) Virginia (B) Massachusetts (C) Illinois
(D) South Carolina (E) New York

83. In the 1960s and 1970s one group which had not previously utilized the strike began to do so. Which one?
(A) Dentists (B) Auto workers (C) Truck drivers
(D) Army officers (E) Teachers

84. The proportion of students in private colleges to all college-going people in the U.S. is
(A) increasing rapidly
(B) increasing slowly
(C) decreasing and increasing in various years
(D) decreasing rapidly
(E) staying the same

85. "We must . . . admit that there is a much wider interval in mental power between one of the lowest fishes . . . and one of the higher apes, than between an ape and a man; yet this interval is filled up by numberless gradations."

The statement above is most characteristic of which of the following?
(A) Pascal (B) Darwin (C) Nietzsche (D) Locke
(E) Bentham

86. In which year would the difference between U.S. gross national product and disposable personal income be the least?
(A) 1929 (B) 1941 (C) 1945 (D) 1965 (E) 1970

87. The opposite of Adam Smith's "invisible hand" would be a "visible hand." Which of the following could be considered the "visible hand"?
(A) God (B) Competition (C) Price warfare
(D) Population increase (E) Government

88. The importance of Thales of Miletus rests in the fact that he
(A) taught a system of morals based on reason
(B) pictured an ideal society in which philosopher-kings would govern
(C) first asked questions about the nature of beauty
(D) advanced a naturalistic explanation for the physical universe
(E) advanced the application of mathematics to practical problems

89. Which of the following is a part of communist theory about capitalist states?
(A) Capitalist states will eventually go to war with one another in an effort to secure control of foreign markets.
(B) In a capitalist state, there must sooner or later occur a class war, with the rich on one side and the poor on the other.
(C) In a capitalist state, a few people will gain control of the economic resources and the great mass of the population will grow steadily poorer.
(D) All of these are parts of communist theory.
(E) None of the above.

90. The increased flow of precious metals from the New World to Europe in the 15th and 16th centuries
(A) caused prices to decrease (B) caused prices to rise
(C) had no effect on price levels (D) discouraged speculation
(E) encouraged small-scale agriculture

91. The term "sociology" (sociologie) was coined by which of the following thinkers?
(A) François Quesnay (B) Saint-Simon
(C) Emile Durkheim (D) Louis Blanc (E) Auguste Comte

92. Which of the following taught the observance of caste rules as a religious obligation?
(A) Islam (B) Buddhism (C) Taoism
(D) Hinduism (E) Judaism

93. "The line of boundary between the territories of the United States and those of Her Britannic Majesty shall be continued westward along the forty-ninth parallel." This provision relates to which of the following?
(A) Gadsden Purchase (B) Louisiana Purchase
(C) Oregon Territory (D) Northwest Ordinance
(E) Mexican War

94. Louis XIV of France was a member of which royal family?
(A) Hapsburgs (B) Bourbons (C) Tudors
(D) Romanovs (E) Orleans

95. In which of the following cities would there be more Baptists in proportion to the population?
(A) Atlanta (B) Minneapolis (C) Salt Lake City
(D) New York City (E) Boston

96. Which of the smaller states of Europe had considerable imperial holdings in Africa before World War I?
(A) Netherlands (B) Belgium (C) Denmark
(D) Norway (E) Switzerland

97. The Roman world suffered shock in the year 410 when the city of Rome was taken by the
(A) Vandals (B) Huns (C) Franks (D) Visigoths
(E) Normans

98. "Implied powers" are the powers of the national government which are necessary to
(A) amend the national Constitution
(B) prevent the state governments from expanding their powers beyond those given to them by the Constitution
(C) allow the national government to do the jobs given to it by the Constitution
(D) allow speedy governmental action in a war
(E) none of these

99. The Supreme Court has upheld certain tax-supported benefits going to parochial school children on the basis of the
(A) "general welfare" clause
(B) First Amendment
(C) Fourteenth Amendment
(D) Fifth Amendment
(E) Tenth Amendment

100. Of the following, all are consumer goods *except*
(A) transport trucks
(B) family automobiles
(C) a performance by the National Symphony Orchestra
(D) a painting by Rembrandt
(E) apples sold at the supermarket

101. Factors which operate to reduce geographical mobility in the labor market include
(A) most pension plans
(B) seniority in labor union contracts with business
(C) government welfare programs
(D) none of these
(E) all of these

102. The typical American corporation of today is likely to be largely controlled by
(A) two or three men, who own most of the stock
(B) a large number of people, each of whom owns a small amount of stock
(C) managers, who are subject to much pressure from the stockholders
(D) managers, who are given a very free hand by the stockholders
(E) a dominant figure who controls the majority of stock

103. Which of these people would have been apt to join one of the unions in the American Federation of Labor?
(A) An automobile assembly line worker in 1937
(B) A brick mason in 1939
(C) A department store clerk in 1950
(D) A nurse in 1965
(E) A school teacher in 1945

104. After he came to power in Turkey, Mustapha Kemal
(A) attempted to restore traditional Turkish ways
(B) introduced many modern reforms
(C) began a war to reconquer the Arab sections of the old Turkish empire
(D) restored the caliph to power
(E) tried to reconquer the Balkan peninsula

105. Henry George's "single tax" was to be applied to
(A) homes (B) income (C) sales (D) land
(E) imports

106. In 1989, the greatest number of American women workers were employed in
(A) social work (B) clerical work (C) accounting
(D) real estate (E) libraries

107. David Ricardo used Malthusian ideas to indicate the basic wage. To him, the reason this wage always tends toward bare subsistence is that
(A) employers are mean
(B) workers dislike ostentation
(C) society is unfair
(D) workers will always reproduce the labor supply to the maximum
(E) unions are prevented by the state from militant action

108. Which of the following did not take part in the 18th-century partition of Poland?
(A) Sweden (B) Austria (C) Prussia (D) Russia
(E) All of the above

109. Which of these peoples were not Germanic?
(A) Visigoths (B) Vandals (C) Huns (D) Lombards
(E) Franks

110. The black proportion of the U.S. population was greatest in
(A) 1870 (B) 1900 (C) 1910 (D) 1930 (E) 1940

111. Emile Durkheim found that suicide was relatively high among all the following people *except* those
(A) in military organizations, where honor is very important
(B) who are rootless and uninvolved
(C) with a highly individualistic success ethic
(D) subject to highly developed ideas of individual responsibility
(E) in extended kinship family structures with religion emphasizing group meaning

112. Which of the following titles carried with it the *least* power in the 17th century?
(A) King of England (B) King of France (C) King of Spain
(D) Holy Roman Emperor (E) King of Sweden

113. A fief was
(A) a person who swore fealty to a lord
(B) a grant, usually of land, made in exchange for promised services
(C) a person bound to the soil
(D) an oath of loyalty
(E) a tariff on trade

114. One of the first things which the Bolsheviks did in Russia when they came into power was to
(A) have the Tsar removed from office
(B) begin negotiations for peace with the Germans
(C) make Stalin the head of the state
(D) drive the Germans completely out of Russian territory
(E) collectivize the land

115. Stress and strain in adolescence are most characteristic of
(A) all known societies (B) preliterate societies
(C) peasant societies (D) modern industrial societies
(E) frontier societies

116. Which of the following methods of social science goes deepest into the motivation and problems of people?
(A) Statistical survey (B) Document research
(C) Interviews (D) Case study (E) Behavioral model

117. In "Federalist #10," James Madison
(A) shows how the American republic is protected against domination by any one faction
(B) shows the merits of democratic government
(C) sets forth an explanation of the contract theory of government
(D) argues the need for a Federal Bill of Rights
(E) indicates the value of the clergy

118. Of the following, which is most clearly an example of reducing the domain of ascribed status?
(A) A young man giving his seat to an older man on a bus that is crowded
(B) Women who devote their time to their homes and church activities
(C) Women serving in the armed forces of the United States
(D) Members of certain racial groups sitting in the back of a bus
(E) Young people beginning compulsory education at an earlier age

119. The Supreme Court
(A) does not allow unconstitutional laws to pass in Congress
(B) reviews all appellate cases brought by citizens
(C) renders advisory opinions on proposed legislation
(D) all of the above
(E) none of the above

120. Karl Marx reacted to the capitalist economic system of his time in a famous tract written in 1848. The title of this work was "The Communist Manifesto." He contended that capitalism was
(A) an artificial conspiracy imposed on society by greedy people
(B) a necessary but temporary stage in the evolution of society
(C) a retrogressive system which had as its main fault the creation of a proletariat
(D) going to improve by reforms instituted through state action
(E) incompatible with Christian morality

121. The election which had most to do with establishing the hold of the Republican and Democratic Parties on the sentiments of their followers for generations was held in
(A) 1824 (B) 1852 (C) 1860 (D) 1880 (E) 1892

122. During the Middle Ages, the history of Spain was part of the story of the war between
(A) the Holy Roman emperors and the Popes
(B) Western Christians and the Byzantines
(C) Christians and Moslems
(D) the Guelphs and the Ghibellines
(E) Protestants and Catholics

123. If, following a reapportionment, a state becomes entitled to additional Representatives, and the legislature fails to redistrict the state, the additional Representatives are
(A) lost to the state until the next decennial census
(B) elected from the state as a whole
(C) lost to the state until the legislature does act
(D) not elected, but the remaining Representatives acting as a group cast the extra votes to which the state is entitled
(E) given observation powers only

124. Judicial self-restraint as applied to the Supreme Court can be described as
(A) a reluctance on the part of the justices to file a dissenting opinion except in rare cases
(B) an awareness of the need for dignity and propriety in courtroom proceedings
(C) a careful consideration of the wisdom and social impact of disputed laws
(D) a careful consideration of the motives of Congress in enacting the disputed laws
(E) a proper concern for the role and judgment of the legislative branch of government

125. Which is not an essential step in making a national law?
(A) A bill is submitted on the floor of either house.
(B) A congressional committee considers it.
(C) The bill passes both houses of Congress.
(D) The bill is presented to the President.
(E) The bill is referred to the United States Supreme Court.

ANSWER KEY—SAMPLE EXAMINATION 2

Section I

1. E	12. B	23. C	34. D	44. A	54. D
2. E	13. A	24. C	35. C	45. D	55. C
3. D	14. C	25. A	36. A	46. D	56. D
4. B	15. D	26. D	37. A	47. A	57. E
5. C	16. C	27. E	38. D	48. A	58. E
6. C	17. C	28. B	39. D	49. A	59. E
7. E	18. B	29. C	40. B	50. E	60. C
8. A	19. E	30. E	41. E	51. C	61. E
9. D	20. E	31. D	42. D	52. D	62. B
10. E	21. E	32. B	43. E	53. C	63. D
11. C	22. C	33. D			

Section II

64. C	75. C	86. A	96. B	106. B	116. D
65. B	76. C	87. E	97. D	107. D	117. A
66. A	77. E	88. D	98. C	108. A	118. C
67. D	78. C	89. D	99. A	109. C	119. E
68. D	79. D	90. C	100. A	110. A	120. B
69. B	80. A	91. E	101. E	111. E	121. C
70. B	81. D	92. D	102. D	112. D	122. C
71. E	82. E	93. D	103. B	113. B	123. B
72. D	83. E	94. B	104. B	114. B	124. E
73. D	84. D	95. A	105. D	115. D	125. E
74. E	85. B				

SCORING CHART—SAMPLE EXAMINATION 2

After you have scored your Sample Examination 2, enter the results in the chart below; then transfer your Raw Score to the Progress Chart on page 14.

Total Test	Number Right	Number Wrong	Number Omitted	Raw Score
Section I: 63				
Section II: 62				
Total: 125				

ANSWER EXPLANATIONS—SAMPLE EXAMINATION 2

Section I

1. E. Vidkun Quisling (1887–1945), Norwegian army officer and founder of the Norwegian Nazi party, collaborated with the German invasion of Norway in 1940. His name has become a synonym for traitor.
2. E. The Rumanian territory of Bessarabia was taken by the USSR in 1940. It had been detached from tsarist Russia at the end of World War I.
3. D. Greece and Italy were at war on Albanian soil in 1941. Albania had gained its independence from the Ottoman Empire in the Balkan Wars of 1912–13. In April 1939, Mussolini took over Albania. Greece sided with Britain against Italy and Germany in World War II.
4. B. Thomas Robert Malthus (1766–1834), English economist, in his *Principles of Population* wrote that population tends to increase in geometric ratio and food supply in arithmetic. The economic law of diminishing returns holds that if one factor in production remains constant, less is produced per unit, by applying other factors. Thus, the relatively constant production from land is outstripped by burgeoning population.
5. C. A holding company is a corporation that holds stock in another company. This is permitted by law, even though a holding company may not produce any goods or services.
6. C. The Securities and Exchange Commission (SEC) was established by Congress in 1934 under the New Deal to protect investors. The SEC prevents illegal stock market dealing such as prevailed prior to the great depression of the 1930's.
7. E. Youth-parent tensions in American society result, in part, from rapid change in our society as well as from the development of a youth subculture which has tended to obliterate the traditional demarcation between youth and adult status.
8. A. The term "secular" means worldly or temporal, in contrast to ecclesiastical. In Medieval European history, the king or emperor exercised "secular power"; the church exercised ecclesiastical authority.
9. D. In the election of 1928, Republican candidate Herbert Hoover promised two chickens in every pot if he were elected. His election to the presidency was soon followed by the great depression of the 1930's when there were no chickens in most pots.
10. E. The population of the United States in 1790 (the first census) was 3,929,214. In 1970, the population of Tennessee was 3,926,018; New York 18,241,391; California 19,971,069; Illinois 11,110,285; Nevada 488,738.
11. C. The Social Security Act was passed in 1935 under the Democratic Administration of Franklin D. Roosevelt. The abolition of slavery came in the Republican administration of Abraham Lincoln; the Pendleton Act in 1883 under Republican President Arthur; the Merrill Act in 1862 under Lincoln; and the Pure Food and Drug Act in 1906 under Republican President Theodore Roosevelt.
12. B. The ancient Persian Empire was the largest. It extended throughout the area we now call the Middle East from Asia Minor in the West to India in the East and from the Caucasus Mountains in the North to the Arabian Sea in the South.
13. A. Arabic is not an Indo-European language. It is one of the Semitic language group. Other languages in the Semitic group are Aramaic, Hebrew, and Ethiopic.
14. C. Monetary policy in the U.S. is administered by the Federal Reserve Board of Governors. The seven-member Board of Governors of the Federal Reserve system in Washington exercises control over the nation's money supply and credit conditions. This is referred to as "monetary policy."
15. D. Most of the major rivers in Soviet Asia flow north from the mountainous regions to the plains and into the seas adjoining the Arctic Ocean.
16. C. Reincarnation, the return of the soul after death in a new living body, is part of the teaching of Hinduism.

17. C. The total value (in dollars) of all goods and services produced in the American economy during a given year is called the gross national product (GNP) for that year. If we subtract depreciation (the using up of capital equipment), we have net national product (NNP).

18. B. In sociology and psychology, "drives" are factors which incite behavior in the individual. The term "drive" indicates an internal force or push which seeks an outlet. In psychoanalysis, "drive" is regarded as an instinct. Examples are thirst, sex, and hunger.

19. E. Indonesia was conquered in 1595 by the Dutch and ruled by the Netherland East India Company until 1798. The Netherland government ruled the colony until 1945 when Indonesia became an independent republic.

20. E. Tibet was ruled until 1959 by a Buddhist religious leader called the "Dalai Lama." In 1959, the Dalai Lama fled from Tibet. The country is under control of Communist China.

21. E. In the 1950's, Indo-China split into Laos, Cambodia, North Vietnam, and South Vietnam.

22. C. In the 1950's and 60's, the Supreme Court did not incline toward "judicial activism" in presidential control over foreign policy. Some felt that it did in civil rights (Brown v. Board of Education, 1954), legislative reapportionment (Baker v. Carr, 1962), unlawful search and seizure (Mapp v. Ohio, 1961), and right of counsel (Gideon v. Wainwright 1963).

23. C. Max Weber (1864–1920), German sociologist, opposed Marxism. He was concerned with the problem of social stratification. He noted that the pre-industrial test of "family" was replaced by "the certificate of education" under capitalism.

24. C. Pakistan, which had previously been governed by Great Britain as a part of India, became a Dominion in the British Commonwealth of Nations, as did India under the provisions of the Indian Independence Act of 1947. There was a mass movement of Moslems from India into Pakistan, and of Hindus from Pakistan into India. After Israel gained its independence (1948), Jews from many countries migrated to Israel.

25. A. In a free market economy, price is determined by an equilibrium between supply and demand. When the quantity supplied increases more rapidly than the quantity demanded, the effect is a decline in price.

26. D. Sweden is the only one of the five countries whose per capita income is anywhere near $8,000 per year in U.S. dollars. Similarly, the birth and death rate in Sweden is much closer to that of the U.S. (birth 15.9 per thousand; death 8.7 per thousand) than any of the others. In infant mortality, the U.S. (14 per thousand) does not do as well as Sweden.

27. E. The agricultural revolution of the 19th and 20th centuries in the U.S. is due to many factors. Among these are the growth of the use of tractors and an increase in the use of electric power. Farm production did not decline; it increased substantially.

28. B. The English Reform Bill of 1867, sponsored by Conservative Prime Minister Benjamin Disraeli, extended the right to vote to working men in the cities. The right to vote had been extended previously to middle-class businessmen by the Reform Bill of 1832.

29. C. Women in America, on the average, have a longer life span than men, though the gap seems to be narrowing as women assume more taxing positions in business and industry. Life expectancy in 1980 was 77.5 years for females and 69.8 for males.

30. E. All of the first four were included in the program of the Progressive Movement in the U.S. in the early 20th century. The removal of restrictions on blacks voting received major impetus after World War II, culminating in the Voting Rights Act of 1965.

31. D. In the history of the presidency until 1974, there had never been an instance of the resignation of a President. When Richard M. Nixon resigned in 1974, impeachment in the House of Representatives was imminent, and there was every indication that he would be removed by the Senate.

32. B. The 13th amendment to the Constitution abolished slavery (1865). It pro-

vided: "Neither slavery nor involuntary servitude . . . shall exist within the United States, or any place subject to their jurisdiction."

33. D. The person making this statement was obviously opposed to the expansionists and imperialists of the 1890's. The latter groups were strong supporters of the Spanish-American War and of American hegemony in Puerto Rico, Cuba, and the Philippines which that war achieved.

34. D. The Dardanelles are part of the passageway between the Black Sea (dominated by Russia) and the Mediterranean Sea, to which Russia does not have direct access. Hence, Russia has had a historic interest in the Dardanelles.

35. C. Louis XIV of France, who inherited the throne at the age of five in 1643, assumed power in 1661 at the age of 23. He ruled until his death in 1775. He was greatly admired and was called "Le Grand Monarque" or Louis the Great. He is supposed to have said, "L'etat, c'est moi" (I am the state).

36. A. The German Imperial Constitution was adopted after the Franco-Prussian War in 1871. By its terms, King William I of Prussia became Emperor William I of the newly created German Empire.

37. A. Niccolo Machiavelli (1469–1527), Italian political philosopher, is best known for his book, *The Prince*. In it, he counsels a ruler on the best way to acquire and hold political power. In a cynical vein, he advises that it is better to be feared than loved.

38. D. Karl Marx (1818–1883) and Friedrich Hegel (1770–1831) were both German philosophers. Hegel contended that Germany was the fruition of a process by which opposing forces produced a new and better civilization. Marx taught that the opposing classes would end in the liquidation of all but the working class. Hence, Marx said Hegel's view of history made dialectic stand on its head.

39. D. For Sigmund Freud (1856–1939), Viennese founder of psychoanalysis, the real causes of human aggressiveness and anxiety were lodged deep in the recesses of the mind. The failure of Marx to take account of psychiatric forces was fatal to his theories, according to Freud.

40. B. When historians use the title *Augustus*, they are referring to Octavian, the first Roman emperor. After he became the ruler of Rome, the Senate gave him titles—"imperator" (general), from which we get "Emperor, " and "Augustus" (revered), by which title he is generally known.

41. E. In the United States, the emotional function of the family, if not satisfactorily performed, devolves on psychological or psychiatric help which, if available, is generally quite costly. Outside agencies, often included in the United Way, may help with economic needs; public schools with educational; parks and playgrounds with recreational; and churches and synagogues with religious.

42. D. The Standard Oil Trust was originally organized in 1882 by John D. Rockefeller. The story is told by Ida Tarbell in *The History of the Standard Oil Company* (1904).

43. E. The Dreyfus affair began in France in 1894 with the charge that Captain Dreyfus, a Jew, had sold military information to the Germans. He was sentenced to life imprisonment on Devil's Island. Dreyfus protested his innocence. Anti-republicans, anti-Semites, and many leaders of the Church lined up against him. His innocence was finally proven, and he was reinstated as a major in the army.

44. A. Otto von Bismarck (1815–1898), leader of German unification, believed Germany could become strong and unified only if Austria were excluded from German affairs. Bismarck was at heart a Prussian. He feared that Austria, if included, would dispute power with Prussia.

45. D. The Maoris are a branch of the Polynesian race. They migrated to New Zealand from the Eastern Pacific before and during the 14th century. The British came to New Zealand during the 18th century. By a treaty in 1840, the Maori chiefs agreed to British sovereignty, and New Zealand became a British colony.

46. D. An increase in the amount of money should, theoretically, bring a corresponding increase in the level of prices. However, when production levels continue to rise rapidly, the level of prices may remain constant despite the increase in the money supply.

47. A. Thomas Malthus (1766–1834), English clergyman and philosopher, was deeply perturbed at the rapid increase in population and the relatively slower increase in the food supply. He foresaw war, plagues, and famine unless population were kept in check. Universal education at public expense offered some hope. The others would only exacerbate the problem.

48. A. If people do not consume all their income, the part not spent is technically saving, no matter what they do with the money. Investing, however, requires that the money be put to work to create new wealth. In national income and product terms, consumption and investment go hand in hand.

49. A. Group marriage, several men and several women living together and cohabiting, is a relatively rare social phenomenon. Each of the other four is far more common in man's various societies.

50. E. During the period 1950–1959, there were 717 executions for crime in the U.S. The number dropped to 181 for the period 1960–64; to 10 for the period 1965–67. There were no executions for crime in the U.S. from 1968–1977 when convicted murderer Gary Gilmore was executed by a Utah firing squad.

51. C. When sociologists talk of "social mobility," they usually have in mind vertical mobility, moving from the socio-economic level into which a person was born into a higher socio-economic level. In an open society, marked by widespread opportunity, this phenomenon is relatively common.

52. D. The use of the canoe and the moccasin, adopted by Europeans from the Indian culture with which they came in contact, is an example of cultural diffusion.

53. C. The corporation is an artificial person and *is* expected to conform to the law. The other statements about the corporation are true.

54. D. Thorstein Veblen (1857–1929), American economist and social philosopher, considered marginal utility economics overly deductive, individualistic, and static. Marginal utility economics teaches that the extra utility added by each last unit of a good will be decreasing, although *total* utility will rise with consumption. In his *Theory of the Leisure Class*, Veblen held that, in an affluent society, most goods are useless except for display to establish status.

55. C. In his *General Theory of Employment, Interest and Money* (1936), the English economist, John Maynard Keynes, stated that the economy could not, of itself, maintain a viable level of employment. This, he said, required and demanded the intervention of the central government.

56. D. The chart illustrates how the electoral college system operates. In all 4 cases, the victor won a majority of the electoral college, but in 2 of the 4 elections, the victor did not win a majority of the popular vote. In the electoral college system, a majority of the popular vote is not necessary to win an election (choice A); only a majority of the electoral vote is necessary. Since no incumbents were running in the elections covered, the chart does not illustrate that incumbent's have an advantage (choice C). Nor does the chart present evidence of how third party candidacies affected the outcome of the elections involved (choice E). Indeed, third party candidates may have pulled more votes from the winners than from the losers. Only in 1988 is a significant increase in popular vote totals evident (choice B).

57. E. According to the census of 1980, Connecticut, with a per capita income of $11,720, was second to Alaska ($12,790), Nevada was 6th, and Delaware was 9th. The other states mentioned finished as follows: California, 3rd; Texas, 18th; Virginia, 22nd; North Dakota, 33rd; Georgia, 36th; North Carolina, 41st; Tennessee, 44th; and Kentucky, 46th.

58. E. In 1987, about 2% of the American population was living and working on farms.

59. E. Representation in the House of Representatives by states is based on population. According to the census of 1980, the "Top 10" states were as follows:

1. California (45), 2. New York (34), 3. Texas (27), 4. Pennsylvania (23), 5. Illinois (22), 6. Ohio (21), 7. Florida (19), 8. New Jersey (14), 9. Massachusetts (11), 10. Virginia (10).

60. C. In 1980, the average congressional district contained 520,000 people. To obtain this figure, divide 226.5 million (the population of the U.S. in 1980) by 435 (the number of members in the House of Representatives).

61. E. In the election of 1936, Franklin D. Roosevelt, Democrat, received 523 electoral votes. The Republican candidate, Governor Alfred M. Landon of Kansas, received 8 electoral votes. He won only the states of Maine and Vermont.

62. B. Alexis de Tocqueville (1805–1859), French writer, traveled throughout the United States in 1831 as an agent of his government. He described his findings in a famous book, *Democracy in America*. In it he wrote: "Nothing struck me more forcibly than the general equality of conditions."

63. D. Most countries with high per-capita income have birth rates below 20 per thousand per year. These include U.S. 15.9, Canada 15.5, Denmark 11.2, France 14.8, Sweden 11.7, Switzerland 11.9. By contrast, the figure for Mexico is 34.0 and for Ethiopia it is 49.9.

Section II

64. C. The Huguenots were French Protestants. They were followers of Calvin and Swiss Protestantism. Persecution in France led many Huguenots to flee to England, Holland, and America.

65. B. During the time of Philip II, the Dutch Netherlands came into being as a result of a war for independence. The Dutch rebelled against Philip II, whom they regarded as a Spanish foreigner attempting to subjugate them. The war for independence which started in 1576 saw the destruction of the Spanish Armada at the hands of British sea-dogs.

66. A. In the 9th century, Scandinavian invaders (Vikings or Norsemen, as they were called on the Continent) overran France and captured London, Cadiz, and Pisa as well.

67. D. Opportunity cost is an economic term which describes the cost represented by the opportunity lost in doing one thing rather than another. Thus, the cost of educating a student includes not only the actual expenditure on the education but the value of what he or she might have produced were they not in school (the opportunity lost).

68. D. In statistical terms, the coefficient of correlation describes the extent of the relationship between two phenomena. When the coefficient is positive and high, as it is between GNP per capita and educational enrollment, it shows there is a strong relationship between the two.

69. B. George Herbert Mead (1863–1931), American philosopher and social psychologist, in his *Mind, Self, and Society* (1934), held that the self arises as a result of social experience and that the individual experiences himself indirectly from the standpoint of others of the same group. In Freud's psychology, the id is completely unconscious, as is the self prior to conscious development.

70. B. In an experiment, change is induced in the experimental group only. The control group is used to determine the amount or effect of the change on the experimental group.

71. E. There has been an absolute decline in farm employment during the past 30 years. In 1955, there were 8,381,000 people employed in farming. Thirty years later (1985), the number was 3,750,000.

72. D. Social norms are guides to appropriate social behavior. Time, place, age, sex, and circumstances are factors in established norms of behavior. A norm may be rejected because it is not considered important or not understood. If a "norm" is flexible, it does not exercise control over acceptable behavior as does a rigid norm.

73. D. Louis XIV (1638–1715) became ruler of France in 1661. He came into conflict with the German states over the Rhine as a "natural boundary." The War of Devolution (1667), the Dutch War (1672), the War of the League of Augsburg (1668), and the War of the Spanish Succession (1702–1713) all involved the eastward expansion of France to the Rhine.

74. E. Oklahoma entered the Union November 16, 1907; Nevada entered October 31, 1864; California September 9, 1850; Iowa December 28, 1864; and Missouri August 10, 1821.

75. C. The Homestead Act of 1862 granted 160 acres of land free to settlers who would live on the land and farm it for a period of five years.

76. C. Railroad mileage in the U.S. increased from 3,000 in 1840 to 190,000 by 1900. The increase by decades was as follows: 1850, 9,000; 1860, 30,000; 1870, 53,000; 1880, 80,000; 1890, 164,000. Thus, the greatest increase in absolute amount was in the 1880's.

77. E. Alaska: area, 589, 757 square miles; population, 400,481
Texas: area, 267,338 square miles; population, 14,228,383
Montana: area, 147, 138 square miles; population, 786,690
Nevada: area, 110,540 square miles; population, 799,184
Maine: area, 33,215 square miles; population, 1,124,660.

78. C. The census of 1890 showed that the population of the least settled area of the United States (the Rocky Mountain area) exceeded 2 persons per square mile. This meant that by 1890 the frontier (fewer than 2 per square mile) had ceased to exist in continental United States.

79. D. During the years 1885–1914, a torrent of 20 million immigrants arrived in the U.S., chiefly from Eastern and Southern Europe. Many were young men fleeing Europe to escape the great war which they knew was coming. Others were young men who hoped to make their fortune and return home.

80. A. The sharecropper worked the land. The owner provided him with credit for seed, tools, living quarters, and food. When the crop was harvested, the owner gave the sharecropper a percentage of the value of the crop minus the amount of the loan and interest. Since little was left for the sharecropper, he was *economically* in a situation not much better than slavery.

81. D. According the the census of 1790, Virginia was the most populous state, with 821,287 people (slaves were counted as 3/5). The next largest state was Pennsylvania, with 434,373. Virginia was most influential, too. Four of our first five presidents—Washington, Jefferson, Madison, and Monroe — were Virginians.

82. E. The most populous state in the United States in 1860 was New York, with 3,880,735. In 1860, the population of Virginia was 1,596,318; Massachusetts 1,231,066; Illinois 1,711,951; and South Carolina 703,708 (slaves in Virginia and South Carolina were counted as 3/5). West Virginia was still part of Virginia in 1860.

83. E. Teachers have two unions, the National Education Association (NEA) and the labor-oriented American Federation of Teachers (AFT). Prior to 1960, there were few teachers' strikes, but, during that decade and increasingly in the 1970s, teachers' strikes, particularly in urban areas, have become commonplace.

84. D. The proportion of students in private colleges to all college-going people in the U.S. is increasing rapidly. In 1965, there were 3,970,000 in public colleges and 1,951,000 in private colleges. By 1980, the relative figures had changed drastically. In that year, there were 9,475,000 in public and only 2,640,000 in private colleges.

85. B. The finding is set forth by Charles Darwin (1809–1882) in his pioneer work *The Origin of Species* (1859), in which he describes his discoveries from biological studies resulting in the theory of evolution.

86. A. The Gross National Product for 1929, the year of the economic collapse ushering in the Great Depression, was $95 billion, Disposable personal income was such as to leave no margin for saving. Hence, the difference, zero, was least of the other years.

87. E. Adam Smith (1723–1790) wrote a classic analysis of economic forces entitled *An Inquiry into the Nature and Causes of the Wealth of Nations* (1776). He referred to the unimpeded force operating in the marketplace as "the invisible hand." Government intervention in the free market would be the "visible hand."

88. D. Thales of Miletus (640 B.C.–546 B.C.) is called the first Greek philosopher. He advanced a naturalistic explanation for the physical universe based on water as the origin of all things. He predicted the total eclipse of the sun in 585 B.C.

89. D. Communist theory about capitalist states, as developed by Marx, holds that modern wars are fought over markets, that an ongoing class war pits the working class against the bourgeoisie, and that, as ownership becomes more concentrated, the masses are steadily ground down.

90. B. The increase in precious metals constituted, in effect, an increase in the money supply. Other things being equal, this steady and substantial increase in coinage was certain to cause an increase in prices.

91. E. The term sociology (sociologie) was coined by the French social philosopher Auguste Comte (1798–1857). Comte's teacher, Saint Simon (1765–1825), believed the industrial revolution necessitated a new science of social progress. Comte named it sociology.

92. D. Hinduism, the chief religion of India, developed prior to the 6th century B.C. The caste system became an integral part of Hinduism. Each individual was born into a caste. Four major castes, with many subdivisions, were Brahmans (priests), military, farmers and merchants, and laborers. A lowest group, pariahs (untouchables), were without caste.

93. C. The dispute between Britain and the U.S. over the Oregon Territory was settled by a treaty in 1846. The forty-ninth parallel of north latitude, constituting the then existing boundary between the U.S. and Canada to the Rockies, was extended to the Pacific.

94. B. Louis XIV of France was a member of the Bourbon family, which ruled France, Spain, and parts of Italy. The family traces its roots to a 9th-century French nobleman whose castle was named Bourbonnais.

95. A. The predominant faith of church members in many parts of the South, particularly in Georgia, is Baptist. In Minneapolis it is Lutheran, in Salt Lake City it is Mormon, in New York City all religions share the spectrum with a large Jewish group, and in Boston there is a large Catholic population.

96. B. Prior to World War I, Belgium was a major imperial power in Africa because of her control of the Congo, a rich territory extending over 331,850 square miles in Central Africa. The other major imperial powers in Africa prior to 1914 were Britain, France, Germany, Italy, Spain, and Portugal.

97. D. The Visigoths (or West Goths), one of the chief groups of the Germans, came into conflict with the Romans. In 395 A.D., Alaric I was proclaimed king of the Visigoths. In 410, his army entered Rome and sacked the city.

98. C. The Constitution, in Article I, Section 8, specifically enumerates 17 of the powers of Congress. Then, in clause 18, it gives Congress power "to make all laws which shall be necessary and proper" to do the job given to it by the Constitution. These are called "implied powers."

99. A. The preamble to the Constitution states the reasons for its establishment. One of the reasons is "to promote the general welfare." The Supreme Court looked to this clause in approving public funds for parochial school children.

100. A. Transport trucks are capital goods used primarily to create new wealth as they are used. The others in the question are consumer goods used primarily for the benefit of the consumer.

101. E. Geographic mobility in the labor market refers to workers' moving to different locations for employment. Workers tend to remain where they are for fear of losing their pensions, or in order to retain their seniority, or if they are receiving government welfare payments.

102. D. In the typical American corporation of today, the managers who control the corporation are given a free hand by the stockholders. Rarely, except for the relatively small corporations, is the majority of the stock held by one or a few individuals.

103. B. The American Federation of Labor was established during the 1880's under the leadership of Samuel Gompers. His purpose was to organize skilled workers into craft unions. Brick masons were organized as one of the constituent unions in the AF of L. The rival union organization, the CIO, organized entire industries such as automotive. It came into being in 1935.

104. B. Mustapha Kemal Ataturk, (1880–1938), Turkish army officer, came into power after World War II. He carried out a revolution in which both the sultanate and the caliphate were abolished and complete separation of church and state instituted in a new Turkish Republic. Universal suffrage, a parliament, a ministry, and a president were established. Women gained a new freedom.

105. D. Henry George (1839–1897), American economist, wrote *Progress and Poverty* (1879). He believed a "single tax" on land would provide for all the necessary costs of government and even leave a surplus.

106. B. In 1989, the greatest number of American women were employed as clerical workers.

107. D. David Ricardo (1772–1823), British economist, wrote *Principles of Political Economy and Taxation* (1817). He maintained that wages cannot rise above the lowest level necessary for subsistence. Workers reproduce to provide a labor supply which keeps wages at this level. Malthus had previously noted the increase of population in geometric ratio.

108. A. There were three partitions of Poland during the 18th century. These occurred in 1772, 1793,and 1795. The nations that participated were Austria, Prussia, and Russia, but not Sweden.

109. C. The Huns were nomadic horsemen from north central Asia. They occupied China for several centuries. During the 4th century, they invaded the Volga valley of Russia, driving the Visigoths before them. The Visigoths, Vandals, Lombards, and Franks were Germanic peoples.

110. A. The black proportion of U.S. population was 12.7% in 1870, 11.6% in 1900, 10.7% in 1910, 9.7 in 1930, and 9.8% in 1940.

111. E. Emile Durkheim (1858–1917), French sociologist, published a study called *Suicide* (1897) and another entitled *The Elementary Forms of Religious Life* (1912). He found a relatively low incidence of suicide in extended kinship family structures in which group meaning is strengthened by religion.

112. D. In the 17th century, the Holy Roman Empire extended from Poland and Hungary to the North Sea. The various countries in the Empire constituted a loose union, but the Emperor exercised little power. It has been said that the Holy Roman Empire, which was finally dissolved by Napoleon in 1806, was neither holy, nor Roman, nor an empire.

113. B. A fief in medieval Europe was an estate over which a nobleman exercised control. The grantor would receive a promise of protection or other service in return for the land.

114. B. In November 1917, the Bolsheviks in Russia, led by V. I. Lenin (1870–1914), overthrew the government and came into power. They immediately began negotiations for peace with the Germans. Lenin regarded the war as an imperialist adventure. He thought both sides—the Germans and the Allies—would destroy each other.

115. D. Anthropologists point to excessive stress and strain in adolescence as a characteristic of modern industrial societies. The anthropologist Margaret Mead studied the non-industrial society of Samoa and reported the relative untroubled adolescence of its members in her *Coming of Age in Samoa* (1928). Her findings have recently been challenged.

116. D. The case study, a method used in the social sciences, delves deeply into the motivation and problems of its subjects.

117. A. In "Federalist #10, " i.e., the tenth of the 85 Federalist Papers published in 1788, which appeared in New York newspapers, signed Publius, Madison shows how the Constitution would protect the American republic against domination by any one faction. The other items are not to be found in the Federalist papers.

118. C. The traditional domain ascribed to women in industrial society is that of homemaker. Women serving in the armed forces of the United States constitute a sharp and symbolic break with this ascribed status.

119. E. The Supreme Court has no authority to dictate or prohibit Congressional legislation. It reviews only those federal cases which it wishes to review. It does not render advisory opinions.

120. B. In *The Communist Manifesto*, Karl Marx (and his co-author Friedrich Engels) contended that capitalism was a necessary step in the evolution of society to communism. Marx thought that the inevitable struggle between the capitalists and the proletariat would end in the victory of the latter (communism). Hence, capitalism was a necessary stage in the evolution of society.

121. C. In the election of 1860, the chief contenders were the Republican, Abraham Lincoln, the northern Democrat, Stephen A. Douglas, and the southern Democrat, John C. Breckenridge. A fourth party nominated John Bell. Lincoln won without carrying a single southern state. He led the North through the Civil War. So the "solid South" remained Democratic and the North Republican for generations after the war.

122. C. The Moors of North Africa converted to Islam in the 8th century and became fanatic Moslems. They crossed into Spain in 711 A.D., overran the country, and spread into France. Christians and Moslems vied for control of Spain from the 11th to the 15th centuries, culminating in 1492 when the Moslems were driven from Spain.

123. B. If, following reapportionment, a state becomes entitled to additional Representatives, and the legislature fails to redistrict the state, the additional Representatives are elected from the state as a whole. It is not unusual to have a Representative-at-large. States with small populations, such as Alaska and Wyoming, have one Representative, elected by all the voters of the state.

124. E. Judicial self-restraint as applied to the Supreme Court can be described as a proper concern for the role and judgment of the legislative branch of government. The Court prefers not to overrule an act of Congress if it can see any way of finding the act compatible with the Constitution.

125. E. The United States Supreme Court plays no part in the making of a national law. The others are essential steps in the national law-making process.

ANSWER SHEET — SOCIAL SCIENCES-HISTORY/SAMPLE EXAMINATION 3

Section I

1. Ⓐ Ⓑ Ⓒ Ⓓ Ⓔ
2. Ⓐ Ⓑ Ⓒ Ⓓ Ⓔ
3. Ⓐ Ⓑ Ⓒ Ⓓ Ⓔ
4. Ⓐ Ⓑ Ⓒ Ⓓ Ⓔ
5. Ⓐ Ⓑ Ⓒ Ⓓ Ⓔ
6. Ⓐ Ⓑ Ⓒ Ⓓ Ⓔ
7. Ⓐ Ⓑ Ⓒ Ⓓ Ⓔ
8. Ⓐ Ⓑ Ⓒ Ⓓ Ⓔ
9. Ⓐ Ⓑ Ⓒ Ⓓ Ⓔ
10. Ⓐ Ⓑ Ⓒ Ⓓ Ⓔ
11. Ⓐ Ⓑ Ⓒ Ⓓ Ⓔ
12. Ⓐ Ⓑ Ⓒ Ⓓ Ⓔ
13. Ⓐ Ⓑ Ⓒ Ⓓ Ⓔ
14. Ⓐ Ⓑ Ⓒ Ⓓ Ⓔ
15. Ⓐ Ⓑ Ⓒ Ⓓ Ⓔ
16. Ⓐ Ⓑ Ⓒ Ⓓ Ⓔ
17. Ⓐ Ⓑ Ⓒ Ⓓ Ⓔ
18. Ⓐ Ⓑ Ⓒ Ⓓ Ⓔ
19. Ⓐ Ⓑ Ⓒ Ⓓ Ⓔ
20. Ⓐ Ⓑ Ⓒ Ⓓ Ⓔ
21. Ⓐ Ⓑ Ⓒ Ⓓ Ⓔ
22. Ⓐ Ⓑ Ⓒ Ⓓ Ⓔ
23. Ⓐ Ⓑ Ⓒ Ⓓ Ⓔ
24. Ⓐ Ⓑ Ⓒ Ⓓ Ⓔ
25. Ⓐ Ⓑ Ⓒ Ⓓ Ⓔ
26. Ⓐ Ⓑ Ⓒ Ⓓ Ⓔ
27. Ⓐ Ⓑ Ⓒ Ⓓ Ⓔ
28. Ⓐ Ⓑ Ⓒ Ⓓ Ⓔ
29. Ⓐ Ⓑ Ⓒ Ⓓ Ⓔ
30. Ⓐ Ⓑ Ⓒ Ⓓ Ⓔ
31. Ⓐ Ⓑ Ⓒ Ⓓ Ⓔ
32. Ⓐ Ⓑ Ⓒ Ⓓ Ⓔ
33. Ⓐ Ⓑ Ⓒ Ⓓ Ⓔ
34. Ⓐ Ⓑ Ⓒ Ⓓ Ⓔ
35. Ⓐ Ⓑ Ⓒ Ⓓ Ⓔ
36. Ⓐ Ⓑ Ⓒ Ⓓ Ⓔ
37. Ⓐ Ⓑ Ⓒ Ⓓ Ⓔ
38. Ⓐ Ⓑ Ⓒ Ⓓ Ⓔ
39. Ⓐ Ⓑ Ⓒ Ⓓ Ⓔ
40. Ⓐ Ⓑ Ⓒ Ⓓ Ⓔ
41. Ⓐ Ⓑ Ⓒ Ⓓ Ⓔ
42. Ⓐ Ⓑ Ⓒ Ⓓ Ⓔ
43. Ⓐ Ⓑ Ⓒ Ⓓ Ⓔ
44. Ⓐ Ⓑ Ⓒ Ⓓ Ⓔ
45. Ⓐ Ⓑ Ⓒ Ⓓ Ⓔ
46. Ⓐ Ⓑ Ⓒ Ⓓ Ⓔ
47. Ⓐ Ⓑ Ⓒ Ⓓ Ⓔ
48. Ⓐ Ⓑ Ⓒ Ⓓ Ⓔ
49. Ⓐ Ⓑ Ⓒ Ⓓ Ⓔ
50. Ⓐ Ⓑ Ⓒ Ⓓ Ⓔ
51. Ⓐ Ⓑ Ⓒ Ⓓ Ⓔ
52. Ⓐ Ⓑ Ⓒ Ⓓ Ⓔ
53. Ⓐ Ⓑ Ⓒ Ⓓ Ⓔ
54. Ⓐ Ⓑ Ⓒ Ⓓ Ⓔ
55. Ⓐ Ⓑ Ⓒ Ⓓ Ⓔ
56. Ⓐ Ⓑ Ⓒ Ⓓ Ⓔ
57. Ⓐ Ⓑ Ⓒ Ⓓ Ⓔ
58. Ⓐ Ⓑ Ⓒ Ⓓ Ⓔ
59. Ⓐ Ⓑ Ⓒ Ⓓ Ⓔ
60. Ⓐ Ⓑ Ⓒ Ⓓ Ⓔ
61. Ⓐ Ⓑ Ⓒ Ⓓ Ⓔ
62. Ⓐ Ⓑ Ⓒ Ⓓ Ⓔ
63. Ⓐ Ⓑ Ⓒ Ⓓ Ⓔ

Section II

64. Ⓐ Ⓑ Ⓒ Ⓓ Ⓔ
65. Ⓐ Ⓑ Ⓒ Ⓓ Ⓔ
66. Ⓐ Ⓑ Ⓒ Ⓓ Ⓔ
67. Ⓐ Ⓑ Ⓒ Ⓓ Ⓔ
68. Ⓐ Ⓑ Ⓒ Ⓓ Ⓔ
69. Ⓐ Ⓑ Ⓒ Ⓓ Ⓔ
70. Ⓐ Ⓑ Ⓒ Ⓓ Ⓔ
71. Ⓐ Ⓑ Ⓒ Ⓓ Ⓔ
72. Ⓐ Ⓑ Ⓒ Ⓓ Ⓔ
73. Ⓐ Ⓑ Ⓒ Ⓓ Ⓔ
74. Ⓐ Ⓑ Ⓒ Ⓓ Ⓔ
75. Ⓐ Ⓑ Ⓒ Ⓓ Ⓔ
76. Ⓐ Ⓑ Ⓒ Ⓓ Ⓔ
77. Ⓐ Ⓑ Ⓒ Ⓓ Ⓔ
78. Ⓐ Ⓑ Ⓒ Ⓓ Ⓔ
79. Ⓐ Ⓑ Ⓒ Ⓓ Ⓔ
80. Ⓐ Ⓑ Ⓒ Ⓓ Ⓔ
81. Ⓐ Ⓑ Ⓒ Ⓓ Ⓔ
82. Ⓐ Ⓑ Ⓒ Ⓓ Ⓔ
83. Ⓐ Ⓑ Ⓒ Ⓓ Ⓔ
84. Ⓐ Ⓑ Ⓒ Ⓓ Ⓔ
85. Ⓐ Ⓑ Ⓒ Ⓓ Ⓔ
86. Ⓐ Ⓑ Ⓒ Ⓓ Ⓔ
87. Ⓐ Ⓑ Ⓒ Ⓓ Ⓔ
88. Ⓐ Ⓑ Ⓒ Ⓓ Ⓔ
89. Ⓐ Ⓑ Ⓒ Ⓓ Ⓔ
90. Ⓐ Ⓑ Ⓒ Ⓓ Ⓔ
91. Ⓐ Ⓑ Ⓒ Ⓓ Ⓔ
92. Ⓐ Ⓑ Ⓒ Ⓓ Ⓔ
93. Ⓐ Ⓑ Ⓒ Ⓓ Ⓔ
94. Ⓐ Ⓑ Ⓒ Ⓓ Ⓔ
95. Ⓐ Ⓑ Ⓒ Ⓓ Ⓔ
96. Ⓐ Ⓑ Ⓒ Ⓓ Ⓔ
97. Ⓐ Ⓑ Ⓒ Ⓓ Ⓔ
98. Ⓐ Ⓑ Ⓒ Ⓓ Ⓔ
99. Ⓐ Ⓑ Ⓒ Ⓓ Ⓔ
100. Ⓐ Ⓑ Ⓒ Ⓓ Ⓔ
101. Ⓐ Ⓑ Ⓒ Ⓓ Ⓔ
102. Ⓐ Ⓑ Ⓒ Ⓓ Ⓔ
103. Ⓐ Ⓑ Ⓒ Ⓓ Ⓔ
104. Ⓐ Ⓑ Ⓒ Ⓓ Ⓔ
105. Ⓐ Ⓑ Ⓒ Ⓓ Ⓔ
106. Ⓐ Ⓑ Ⓒ Ⓓ Ⓔ
107. Ⓐ Ⓑ Ⓒ Ⓓ Ⓔ
108. Ⓐ Ⓑ Ⓒ Ⓓ Ⓔ
109. Ⓐ Ⓑ Ⓒ Ⓓ Ⓔ
110. Ⓐ Ⓑ Ⓒ Ⓓ Ⓔ
111. Ⓐ Ⓑ Ⓒ Ⓓ Ⓔ
112. Ⓐ Ⓑ Ⓒ Ⓓ Ⓔ
113. Ⓐ Ⓑ Ⓒ Ⓓ Ⓔ
114. Ⓐ Ⓑ Ⓒ Ⓓ Ⓔ
115. Ⓐ Ⓑ Ⓒ Ⓓ Ⓔ
116. Ⓐ Ⓑ Ⓒ Ⓓ Ⓔ
117. Ⓐ Ⓑ Ⓒ Ⓓ Ⓔ
118. Ⓐ Ⓑ Ⓒ Ⓓ Ⓔ
119. Ⓐ Ⓑ Ⓒ Ⓓ Ⓔ
120. Ⓐ Ⓑ Ⓒ Ⓓ Ⓔ
121. Ⓐ Ⓑ Ⓒ Ⓓ Ⓔ
122. Ⓐ Ⓑ Ⓒ Ⓓ Ⓔ
123. Ⓐ Ⓑ Ⓒ Ⓓ Ⓔ
124. Ⓐ Ⓑ Ⓒ Ⓓ Ⓔ
125. Ⓐ Ⓑ Ⓒ Ⓓ Ⓔ

SAMPLE EXAMINATION 3

Section I

Number of Questions: 63
Time: 45 minutes

Directions: Each of the questions or incomplete statements below is followed by five suggested answers or completions. Select the one that is best in each case.

1. Which of the following percentages comes closest to describing the proportion of the world's population living in the United States?
   (A) 5% (B) 13% (C) 20% (D) 33% (E) 45%

2. In the case of *McCulloch* v. *Maryland* the Supreme Court held that the
   (A) states could tax the national government
   (B) taxing power of the national government was limited by due process of law
   (C) limitations of the Bill of Rights did not apply to federal regulation of interstate commerce
   (D) powers of Congress might be extended beyond the express grants of power in the Constitution
   (E) national government could not invalidate state action dealing with the internal affairs of a state

3. The Taft-Hartley Act
   (A) outlawed the closed shop
   (B) restricted the union shop
   (C) indicated a determination to regulate labor unions
   (D) all of the above
   (E) none of the above

4. A new employee must belong to the union in order to be hired. This is
   (A) a closed shop (B) an open shop (C) socialism
   (D) a "yellow-dog" contract (E) a union shop

5. Sampling theory is most commonly used in
   (A) historical research (B) monetary theory
   (C) botanical categorization (D) opinion polls
   (E) business accounting

6. A synonym for the word "proletarian" in a capitalist society would be, for the Marxist, which of the following
   (A) union leader
   (B) shopkeeper
   (C) free citizen whose income comes from wages
   (D) wage slave
   (E) serf

7. Economic value is created when
   (A) iron ore is converted to steel
   (B) corn is moved from an Iowa farm to a Milwaukee mill
   (C) strawberries are frozen in summer and stored until winter
   (D) A, B, and C
   (E) A and B, but not C

8. Which of the following status situations suggests a combination of low prestige with high esteem?
   (A) A good doctor
   (B) An inefficient corporation president
   (C) A good street cleaner
   (D) A lawyer who wins few cases
   (E) A ineffective janitor

9. Apes and other primates, in their social organizations, share all but one of the following characteristics with civilized humans. Which one?
   (A) Organization into family groups
   (B) A means of vocal communication
   (C) A high degree of specialization of work
   (D) Some learned behavior
   (E) A system of hierarchy

10. Which of the following German parties lost most votes (as the Nazis grew) between 1928 and 1932?
   (A) (Catholic) Center Party
   (B) Communist Party
   (C) Conservative Party
   (D) Center parties of the middle class
   (E) Royalist Party

11. Since World War II, which American industry has grown at the fastest rate?
   (A) Steel (B) Cigarettes (C) Coal mining
   (D) Railroads (E) Airlines

12. Early in the 5th century B.C., the Greek city-states faced an invasion from the
   (A) Egyptians (B) Assyrians (C) Macedonians
   (D) Persians (E) Romans

13. The Progressive Movement's attitude toward monopoly was one of
   (A) advocating a cooperative economy
   (B) advocating the end of corporate privileges in government and the regulation or destruction of trusts
   (C) encouraging the progressive development of trusts which had a social conscience
   (D) ignoring the subject as of minor importance in comparison with dishonest politics and corrupt morals
   (E) desiring the institution of profit-sharing

14. Eighty percent of her people live within eighty miles of her southern border, an area not more than ten percent of her total area. This country is
(A) Sweden (B) France (C) Japan (D) USSR
(E) Canada

15. A major cause for the decline of Italian commerce in the 16th and 17th centuries was
(A) the lack of national unification
(B) a shift in the spawning ground of herring
(C) the new sea routes to India and America
(D) the religious wars
(E) the Crusades

16. Henry VIII of England took the first steps towards a break between the Church of England and Rome because
(A) he had been an enthusiastic follower of Luther from the very beginning
(B) of a controversy about the respective legal powers of church and state
(C) most Englishmen were becoming Protestants and Henry wanted to keep their loyalty
(D) Christian teaching and practice, he thought, should be purged of error
(E) of Scottish pressure, supported by followers of Knox

17. In the period between 1865 and 1900, Japanese education was greatly affected by all of the following *except*
(A) educational exchange with Europe and America
(B) gifts of private philanthropists
(C) revision of the traditional classical curriculum
(D) compulsory education laws
(E) importation of American school books and equipment

18. Which of the following is not a part of our capital assets?
(A) Virgin grazing land
(B) Shoe machines
(C) Steel bars stored in a warehouse
(D) Office buildings
(E) Corporate research laboratories

19. The Federal Reserve Board is in a position to
(A) influence interest rates
(B) provide public work programs
(C) make payments to the unemployed
(D) balance the federal budget
(E) insure bank deposits

20. Adam Smith believed that tariff restrictions on trade
    (A) decreased a nation's total productivity
    (B) gave a nation more real wealth
    (C) were necessary if any nation were to raise itself above the lowest level of common poverty prevailing in the world
    (D) encouraged high standards of production
    (E) were necessary in infant states

21. "The efficacy of the sentiments in producing social cohesion in no way depends upon the understanding of the function of religion by the members of society. In fact the sentiments prove more effective if they are not scientifically understood by the average person." This statement implies that attachment to religion is probably
    (A) stronger if based on extended reason
    (B) weaker if based on faith
    (C) weaker if exposed to scientific investigation
    (D) essentially an exercise in logic
    (E) unrelated to current matters

22. As Sigmund Freud saw it, there had been three great revolutions which had changed man's view of himself. The last of the three revealed that
    (A) man is part of the animal world and subject to its laws
    (B) there is no object positively true, even in the realm of physics
    (C) men are not wholly masters of their own minds
    (D) men are naturally selfish
    (E) all primeval instincts could be abolished with the advance of rationalism

23. "Men who upset a throne and trample on a race of kings bend more and more obsequiously to the slightest dictate of a clerk." This refers to the growth of
    (A) democracy (B) centralized bureaucracy
    (C) the powers of the clergy (D) popular education
    (E) retail trade

24. According to Max Weber, the "democratization" of society had led to
    (A) the mass of people taking an increasingly active share in government
    (B) the growth of a class of professional administrators and bureaucrats
    (C) administration's falling into the hands of local amateurs
    (D) the decline of bureaucracy
    (E) a rise of "high" culture and art

25. In the case of the American family, the "in-laws" of the husband are usually
(A) given preferential treatment over the "in-laws" of the wife
(B) thought to be of primary importance in decision making
(C) only regarded less than highly favored uncles of the husband
(D) completely ignored
(E) treated equally with the wife's "in-laws" and given as little authority

26. Horace Walpole's statement "that no great country was ever saved by good men because good men will not go the lengths that may be necessary," is most in accord with which of the following works?
(A) *The Prince*
(B) *Candide*
(C) *The Spirit of the Laws*
(D) *Two Treatises of Civil Government*
(E) *Utopia*

27. Which best describes the position concerning priests taken by Luther in *An Appeal to the Ruling Class of German Nationality?*
(A) He declared that Christians should have no priests.
(B) He argued that only nobles should be admitted to the priesthood.
(C) He said that priests differed from other Christians only in that they did different work.
(D) He said that priests were wholly independent of secular power.
(E) He said that Germans were relegated to the lowest of the Roman Church.

28. The Congress of Vienna signalled the end of the
(A) Napoleonic Era
(B) Thirty Years War
(C) Holy Alliance
(D) French Revolution
(E) Austro-Hungarian Empire

29. Herodotus' history deals with the
(A) wars between Athens and Sparta
(B) Persian wars
(C) siege of Troy
(D) legendary wars among the gods
(E) conquests of Alexander

30. The highest of the large castes or orders of Hindu society were the
(A) Brahmans (B) Kshatriyas (C) Vaisyas
(D) Sudras (E) Gurkas

31. Energy in the U.S. derived from falling water makes up about what proportion of all energy sources?
(A) 70% (B) 50% (C) 30% (D) 20% (E) 3%

Questions 32–35 refer to the following map of the territorial expansion of the United States to 1860.

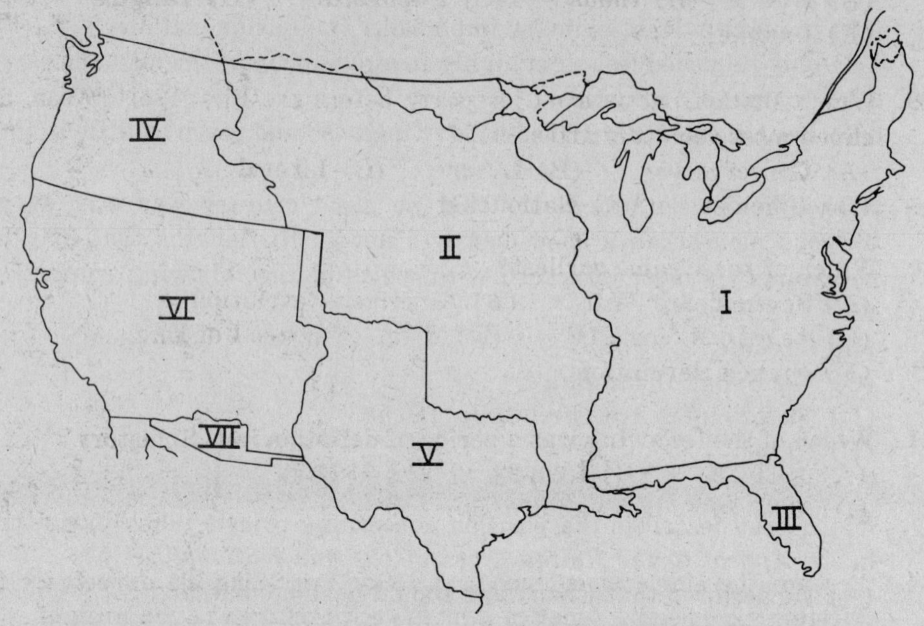

32. Which area(s) was (were) acquired by treaty or purchase?
(A) I and IV (B) IV and VII (C) II and VII (D) VI
(E) II, V, and VI

33. Which area(s) had its borders confirmed by treaty with Great Britain?
(A) I and IV (B) II and IV (C) V (D) I, III, and IV
(E) I, II and IV

34. Which area(s) was (were) an independent republic annexed by the United States?
(A) III (B) II and V (C) IV (D) III and V (E) V

35. Which area(s) was (were) ceded following conquest in a declared war?
(A) II and VI (B) V and VII (C) III (D) VI
(E) III, V, and VI

36. Which of the following Asian nations were able to avoid becoming European or American colonial possessions by 1900?
I. Burma
II. Indonesia
III. Japan
IV. Philippines
V. Siam (Thailand)
(A) I, II, and V only (B) III and V only (C) II and IV only
(D) II, III, and IV only (E) III only

37. Which river served as one of the boundaries of the Roman empire for much of its history?
(A) Rhine (B) Po (C) Seine (D) Rhone (E) Thames

38. Much history is associated with rivers and river valleys. Near which river were the early Sumerian and Mesopotamian cities?
(A) Nile (B) Indus (C) Euphrates (D) Yangtze
(E) Danube

39. Which British party, a major party before the First World War, declined most decidedly after 1919?
(A) Conservative (B) Labor (C) Liberal
(D) Unionist (E) Nationalist

40. Which of these came earliest?
(A) Seven Years' War (B) American Revolution
(C) Reign of Louis XIV (D) Reign of James I of England
(E) French Revolution

41. Which of the following was a period of deflation in U.S. history?
(A) 1930-33 (B) 1893-98 (C) 1873-77
(D) 1837-40 (E) all of these

42. Perhaps the single most important factor increasing life expectancy in Western Europe and America over the last century was the work of
(A) Malthus
(B) DeFoe
(C) Newton
(D) Pasteur
(E) Einstein

43. Which of the following did not occur between 1866 and 1900?
(A) The first federal anti-trust act was passed.
(B) The Sioux Indians were subdued.
(C) The Fourteenth Amendment was used by the courts to protect the rights and privileges of corporations.
(D) The Federal Reserve Banking system was founded.
(E) The forty-fifth state was admitted to the Union.

44. The Kulaks in Russia were
(A) a political party
(B) well-to-do peasants who opposed the collectivization of agriculture
(C) the workers in the cities
(D) intellectuals
(E) agents of the secret police

45. Plato found in Sparta the model for many of his social prescriptions. Which of the following is non-Spartan?
(A) Exposure of unfit infants
(B) Co-educational gymnastic exercises
(C) Common meals among the citizens
(D) Philosopher-kings
(E) Hierarchy

46. Sun Yat-sen was
    (A) a defender of the old imperial rule in China
    (B) a conservative army leader who tried to overthrow the Chinese republic during the First World War
    (C) a leader in the establishment of the Chinese Republic
    (D) the Chinese leader who lost the war against the Chinese Communists
    (E) the man who introduced the federal system to China

47. Which of these countries became a center of Moslem civilization in the Middle Ages?
    (A) Italy (B) Greece (C) Spain
    (D) France (E) England

48. The importance of the Magna Carta rests in the fact that it
    (A) established the principle that the law was above the king
    (B) gave the English trial by jury
    (C) established parliamentary control over the purse
    (D) gave all Englishmen equal rights
    (E) set forth the rights of the lowest orders

49. The characteristics of a caste system include
    (A) unlimited occupational choice
    (B) caste exogamy
    (C) maintenance of ritual avoidance
    (D) normlessness
    (E) all of the above

50. Primogeniture was the
    (A) requirement that a man's first loyalty was to his king
    (B) requirement that a man's first loyalty was to his immediate feudal lord
    (C) rule that the eldest son inherit the entire estate
    (D) primitive means of agriculture still used in the Middle Ages
    (E) idea that the first minister was the prime minister

51. In which of the following legislative bodies is party discipline greatest?
    (A) U.S. Senate
    (B) U.S. House of Representatives
    (C) British House of Lords
    (D) British House of Commons
    (E) New York State Assembly

52. Only one President was elected to office more than twice. Which one?
    (A) Woodrow Wilson (B) Grover Cleveland
    (C) Franklin Roosevelt (D) Dwight Eisenhower
    (E) Abraham Lincoln

53. Between 1824 and 1844 one man was a significant candidate for President three times, yet failed to be elected. Who was he?
(A) Van Buren (B) Webster (C) Fremont
(D) John Quincy Adams (E) Clay

54. If marginal revenue equals price at all levels of production, a firm is operating under
(A) monopolistic conditions
(B) monopolistic competition
(C) oligopoly (D) pure competition
(E) pure oligopoly

55. In the day-to-day life of most societies, the most pervasive feature is
(A) conflict (B) latent conflict (C) complete consensus
(D) cooperation (E) active competition

56. The Soviet Union changed its policies in August 1939 when it
(A) signed a non-agression pact with Germany
(B) announced its hostility toward Hitler
(C) joined an alliance against Hitler
(D) announced demands for Czech territory
(E) invaded Bulgaria

57. The guild system of the Middle Ages
(A) discouraged competition
(B) encouraged the introduction of new ideas and processes
(C) made little effort to regulate standards of work
(D) was always open to any who wished to enter a particular craft
(E) forced non-guild workers into the factories

58. In Utopia, as Thomas More described it, there was no
(A) religion
(B) government
(C) private property
(E) family life
(D) city life

59. Which one of the following functions of the Vice-President is specified by the Constitution?
(A) Serving as president of the United States Senate
(B) Making good-will tours to foreign nations
(C) Relieving the President of a part of his work load
(D) Acting as chairman of cabinet meetings
(E) Acting as party chairman

60. By giving the President authority to be commander-in-chief of the armed forces, the makers of the Constitution tried to make sure that
 (A) there would be civilian control of military forces
 (B) the executive branch of the government would have supreme power over the legislative and judicial branches
 (C) the national government would be able to dominate the states
 (D) only the executive department could declare war
 (E) war would be waged efficiently

61. Justices of the United States Supreme Court are aided in making independent decisions by the fact that they
 (A) have lifetime tenure during good behavior
 (B) are prohibited from belonging to political parties
 (C) achieve their office through winning a nonpartisan election
 (D) cannot be impeached by the United States Congress
 (E) are not allowed to buy stocks

62. In order to operate legally, business corporations must obtain their charters from the
 (A) municipal government
 (B) local Chamber of Commerce
 (C) county government
 (D) National Association of Manufacturers
 (E) state government

63. The famous Eugenic Protection Law which legalized and subsidized abortion in Japan was passed in
 (A) 1925 (B) 1935 (C) 1948 (D) 1968 (E) 1962

Section II

Number of Questions: 62
Time: 45 minutes

Directions: Each of the questions or incomplete statements below is followed by five suggested answers or completions. Select the one that is best in each case.

64. Which of the following describes the appointment and dismissal of a Secretary of State?
 (A) He is appointed by the President with the consent of the Senate but can be dismissed by the President alone.
 (B) He is appointed by the President with the consent of the Senate and can be dismissed by the President if the Senate consents.
 (C) He is both appointed and removed by the President without the consent of the Senate.
 (D) He is appointed by the President and cannot be removed from office once appointed.
 (E) He is both nominated and appointed by the Senate with the consent of the President but can be dismissed by the President alone.

65. When the electoral college fails to choose a President, the President is selected by the
(A) House and Senate sitting jointly, each member having one vote
(B) House only, with each member having one vote
(C) House only, with each state having one vote
(D) Senate only, with each member having one vote
(E) House, which chooses from a list compiled by the Senate

66. The judicial concept of "prior restraint" is most important in relation to
(A) freedom of the press
(B) freedom of religion
(C) double jeopardy
(D) the writ of habeas corpus
(E) self-incrimination

67. Fiscal policy designed to curb inflation might include
(A) raising taxes
(B) drives to sell government bonds to individuals
(C) cutting government spending
(D) all of the above
(E) none of the above

68. Face-to-face social groups in which people treat others as ends and not means are usually referred to as
(A) reference groups
(B) secondary groups
(C) personal groups
(D) categoric groups
(E) primary groups

69. Social scientists, in studying mate selection, have verified that
(A) opposites attract
(B) women will be more successful in finding mates in the East than in the West
(C) "love at first sight" is especially characteristic of the urban lower classes
(D) like tends to marry like
(E) religion is an insignificant factor

70. Which of the following would most clearly be an ascribed status in our society?
(A) The president of a corporation (B) A college professor
(C) A first grade student (D) A salesman (E) A mayor

71. Which of the following writers considered that land speculation was the root cause of economic inequality and poverty?
(A) Henry George (B) Henry Thoreau (C) Jacob Riis
(D) Woodrow Wilson (E) Edward Bellamy

72. All of the following factors contributed to the large increase in the American urban population during the 1920s *except*
   (A) falling farm prices
   (B) cutbacks in federal subsidies to the farmer
   (C) a construction boom in cities
   (D) agricultural mechanization
   (E) improvement in industrial technology

73. The veto power in the UN refers to the
   (A) practice of having each government agree upon any important issue
   (B) power of the Assembly to veto any action of the Security Council
   (C) requirement that all having permanent seats in the Security Council must agree
   (D) power of the Secretary General to veto any Assembly action
   (E) veto power of many small states

74. When the British cabinet loses the support of the majority in the House of Commons on an important bill, it will
   (A) continue in office until the king dismisses it a year later
   (B) ask for a new parliamentary election
   (C) suspend Parliament and govern by decree
   (D) serve out the remaining time of the five year term
   (E) hand the power of government to the loyal opposition

75. During serious economic depressions one of the following things does not occur:
   (A) borrowing declines (B) interest rates rise
   (C) prices fall (D) unemployment increases
   (E) investment declines

76. Which one of the following lived before the others?
   (A) Alexander the Great (B) Hammurabi
   (C) Julius Caesar (D) Marcus Aurelius (E) Hannibal

77. The population of which area is now growing most rapidly?
   (A) Europe (B) USSR (C) North America
   (D) South America (E) Australia

78. In Max Weber's *Protestant Ethic and the Spirit of Capitalism*, the particular type of Protestantism that is especially analyzed is
   (A) Calvinism (B) Anglicanism (C) Unitarianism
   (D) Mormonism (E) Christian Science

79. An ascribed status might be assigned a person because of his
   (A) sex (B) age
   (C) race (D) grades in college
   (E) A, B, and C

80. Which of the following religions may be described as having its followers residing predominantly in one nation state?

I. Christianity
II. Islam
III. Shinto
IV. Buddhism
V. Hinduism

(A) II and IV only (B) III and V only (C) I, II, and III only
(D) I, II, III, and IV only (E) V only

81. Factors keeping unhappy marriages together in the past were
(A) moral and religious convictions of the evils of divorce
(B) social control of the extended family and neighborhood
(C) economic interdependence
(D) all of the above
(E) none of the above

82. The American Constitutional Convention of 1787 was dominated by
(A) backwoods farmers and frontiersmen
(B) men having large property holdings or commercial interests
(C) inflationists and speculators
(D) officers and enlisted men of the Continental Army
(E) artisans and mechanics

83. Lenin's New Economic Policy in 1921 provided for
(A) the re-establishment of limited private ownership of property
(B) the collectivization of agriculture
(C) the immediate socialization of all productive wealth
(D) the building up of heavy industry through the first five-year plan
(E) establishment of the gold standard

84. The samurai were
(A) Japanese scholars
(B) a people from Central Asia which invaded Japan
(C) a Buddhist sect in Japan
(D) a Japanese warrior class
(E) Japanese industrialists

85. Which economist originated the concept "propensity to consume"?
(A) Keynes (B) Veblen (C) Marshall (D) Marx
(E) Malthus

86. Who developed a theory of human development with the three following stages: theological, metaphysical, scientific?
(A) Comte (B) Hegel (C) Marx (D) Saint-Simon (E) Bentham

87. The mercantilists believed
    (A) that the government should not regulate trade or business
    (B) in spite of their name, that trade weakened a country
    (C) that a nation which would be politically powerful should import more than it exports
    (D) that a nation should try to acquire a stock of precious metals through trade
    (E) in laissez-faire

88. A plan for the government of territory east of the Mississippi and north of the Ohio River, drawn up in 1787, was called the
    (A) Great Compromise
    (B) Connecticut Plan
    (C) Treaty of Greenville
    (D) Northwest Ordinance
    (E) National Plan

89. Thomas Jefferson would probably have been *least* likely to have agreed with which of the following statements?
    (A) "The aim of all political association is the conservation of the natural rights of man."
    (B) "The state must grant men liberty and life, in order that they may more fully develop themselves."
    (C) "Nothing then is unchangeable but the inherent . . . rights of man."
    (D) "All men have certain God-given rights and can not justly be denied them."
    (E) "The state is obliged to protect its citizens from disorder and subversive notions."

90. "The President's opposition to the reconstruction policy of Congress led to an effort to impeach him." Who was the President?
    (A) Andrew Jackson (B) Abraham Lincoln (C) U. S. Grant
    (D) Andrew Johnson (E) Franklin D. Roosevelt

91. The main basis of Pakistani nationalism in the 1940s was
    (A) language (B) race (C) religion
    (D) economics (E) geographical attachments

92. The first atomic bomb was exploded in
    (A) Japan (B) Guam (C) Bikini (D) New Mexico
    (E) Russia

93. "Prowess and exploit may still remain the basis of award of the highest popular esteem . . . but for the purposes of a commonplace decent standing in the community these means of repute have been replaced by the acquisition and accumulation of goods." Which of the following writers is well known for his elaboration of these viewpoints expressed above?
    (A) Keynes (B) Ricardo (C) Veblen (D) Bentham
    (E) Quesnay

94. Each of the following Presidents had to deal with challenges made by certain states to the ultimate sovereignty of the federal government *except*
(A) Lincoln
(B) Jackson
(C) Eisenhower
(D) Kennedy
(E) Coolidge

95. A newspaper with a strong laissez-faire principle and very anti-Communist and pro-states-rights posture would have probably reversed its attitudes toward the Supreme Court's power of judicial review between
(A) 1876 and 1900 (B) 1900 and 1927 (C) 1927 and 1937
(D) 1937 and 1965 (E) none of these

96. Unification of Germany and the creation of the German empire occurred under the leadership of
(A) Austria (B) Bavaria (C) Prussia (D) Saxony (E) Hamburg

97. Veblen argued that the price system and double-entry bookkeeping are reflected in
(A) progressive education in the school
(B) the credit and grading system in the school
(C) the attachment of educators to classical subjects
(D) the ideal of the teacher as a servant of higher values
(E) the movement to include entertainment in the school program

98. To Max Weber, bureaucracy necessarily implies all of the following *except*
(A) authoritarian structure
(B) specialization
(C) standardization
(D) formal rules
(E) humane policies

99. The most important source of revenue for local governments is the
(A) personal income tax (B) corporation income tax
(C) general property tax (D) sale of bonds
(E) corporate income tax

100. That the marriage contract is something more than an ordinary contract is shown by the fact that in most countries
(A) it generally cannot be altered by simple mutual consent
(B) often, marriages are recognized which were not contracted according to the law
(C) one becomes a different legal person by contracting marriage
(D) A and B, but not C
(E) A, B, and C

101. Class lines in the U.S. are blurred by
(A) mass communications
(B) geographic mobility
(C) racial, religious, and ethnic heterogeneity
(D) all of the above
(E) none of the above

102. In the Spanish colonies, the *mestizos* were
(A) people of mixed race (Spanish and Indian)
(B) Indians
(C) people of European descent born in the Americas
(D) Europeans who had migrated to the colonies
(E) Negro slaves

103. The term "life chances" refers to
(A) the statistical probability of living the normal life span
(B) the physical hazards normally encountered by all human beings
(C) the process of maturation
(D) the likelihood that given events will happen to a person
(E) none of the above

104. The number of presidential electors coming from each state is determined by
(A) the number of votes cast by the state in the last general election
(B) the number of Senators and Representatives to which the state is entitled in Congress
(C) the population of the state in proportion to total U.S. population
(D) Congressional act
(E) the party elders

105. Most of the members of which of the following groups have voted Democratic in the majority of American presidential elections since 1932? I. Negroes, II. Catholics, III. Protestants, IV. Jews, V. Businessmen.
(A) I and II only (B) II and III only (C) II and IV only
(D) I, II, and IV only (E) I, III, and V only

106. The banking system created by the American government in 1913 is known as the
(A) Federal Intermediate Credits System
(B) Land Bank System
(C) Federal Reserve System
(D) National Banking System
(E) World Bank

107. In waging war against Rome, Hannibal
(A) launched a great fleet against Roman sea power
(B) built up military power in Greece
(C) tried to wear the Romans down by drawing them to fight in North Africa
(D) attacked Rome by land from bases in Spain
(E) used masses of Teutonic mercenaries

108. The assertion that the family is a cultural universal
(A) represents an obsolete anthropological attitude
(B) means that all families everywhere are much the same
(C) means that the family as an institution exists in all cultures
(D) means that all culture is dependent upon the family
(E) means that universal values are embodied in the family

109. Recent sociological studies have usually found that boys in American public high schools admire and give most recognition to
(A) athletic ability (B) religious devotion
(C) scholarly achievement (D) activity leadership
(E) artistic achievement

110. "Relative surplus-population is therefore the pivot upon which the law of supply and demand works." This viewpoint is to be found in the thought of
(A) Malthus (B) Ricardo (C) Marx (D) Veblen
(E) Keynes

111. Quotas based on " national origin" had to do with the
(A) "Gentleman's Agreement" with Japan in 1907
(B) Oriental Exclusion Act of 1882
(C) Immigration Law of 1965
(D) immigration laws passed in the 1920s
(E) Smith Act of 1940 which restricted Communist actions

112. "We hold these truths to be self-evident, that all men are created equal, that they are endowed by their creator with certain inalienable rights, that among these are life, liberty, and the pursuit of happiness. That to secure these rights governments are instituted among men, deriving their just powers from the consent of the governed." This is a quotation from the
(A) Constitution of the United States
(B) Mayflower Compact
(C) Articles of Confederation
(D) Declaration of Independence
(E) United Nations Charter

113. The role played by Cavour in Italy was similar to that of which of the following in his own country?
(A) Napoleon III (B) Bismarck (C) Gladstone
(D) Metternich (E) Lincoln

114. The ruler of the Holy Roman Empire in 962 was
(A) the Pope
(B) a French king
(C) the Emperor at Constantinople
(D) a German king
(E) an Italian king

115. Population growth and economic changes in the United States during the last fifty years have contributed to the growth of all of the following *except*
(A) metropolitan governments (B) county government
(C) special districts (D) regional planning units
(E) quasi-judicial regulatory bodies

116. Which of the following countries did not lose land to the USSR because of World War II?
(A) Germany
(B) Poland
(C) Finland
(D) Czechoslovakia
(E) Austria

117. If one wishes to convert family income (expressed in current dollars) to a figure which takes inflationary trends into account, one looks at the index of
(A) manufacturing
(B) consumer prices
(C) grain production
(D) wholesale prices
(E) car loadings

118. "Why can the deer run so fast? Because the slow deer were eaten, leaving only swift ones to reproduce." This way of thinking is associated with
(A) Plato (B) Aquinas (C) Newton (D) Darwin
(E) Pascal

119. The creative potential of personality is accounted for by
(A) stimulus-response psychology
(B) situational psychology
(C) drive psychology
(D) trait psychology
(E) none of these

120. China was forced to sign treaties opening itself to European nations as a consequence of its defeat in a war in 1839-42 with
(A) Britain (B) Japan (C) Russia (D) Germany
(E) France

121. Which of the following nations was forced out of its colonial holdings in North America in the 17th century?
(A) Netherlands (B) Spain (C) France (D) England
(E) Portugal

122. Regarding exogamy and endogamy, indicate the least valid statement.
(A) In some historical instances, the ban on brother-sister marriage has been lifted.
(B) In many places in the U.S., first cousins may not marry.
(C) In-laws as well as blood relatives have at times been forbidden to marry.
(D) Exogamous practice is more common in feudal society.
(E) Human inbreeding does not inevitably cause physical degeneration of offspring.

Questions 123–125 relate to TABLE X.

TABLE X

U.S. CURRENT AND REAL OUTPUT, 1939-42

	Gross national output measured in current prices	Price index	Gross national output calculated in 1939 prices
1939	$ 90 billions	100	$ 90 billions
1940	100	101	99
1941	125	106	118
1942	160	114	140

Source: U.S. Department of Commerce.

123. In TABLE X, using your knowledge of the period, the increase in gross output between 1939 and 1942 can be attributed mainly to
(A) price increases
(B) the New Deal
(C) an increase in foreign trade
(D) military expenditures which put millions, unemployed in 1939, to work by the end of 1942
(E) the gains in unionism made after 1938

124. Considering only the data in TABLE X, which one of the following characterized the period 1939-42?
(A) Deflation
(B) Decreased government activity
(C) Inflation
(D) Much improved government services, such as education
(E) Increased real investment by business

125. Considering TABLE X, real output increased by well over 50% in only four years. This phenomenon also occurred during what other similar time period?
(A) At the start of World War I
(B) At the end of the Civil War
(C) At the high point years of the 1920s
(D) In the early Kennedy years of the 1960s
(E) Such an increase in four years is unique in American history

ANSWER KEY—SAMPLE EXAMINATION 3

Section I

1. A
2. D
3. D
4. A
5. D
6. D
7. D
8. C
9. C
10. D
11. E
12. D
13. B
14. E
15. C
16. B
17. B
18. A
19. A
20. A
21. C
22. C
23. B
24. B
25. E
26. A
27. C
28. A
29. B
30. A
31. E
32. C
33. A
34. E
35. D
36. B
37. A
38. C
39. C
40. D
41. E
42. D
43. D
44. B
45. D
46. C
47. C
48. A
49. C
50. C
51. D
52. C
53. E
54. D
55. D
56. A
57. A
58. C
59. A
60. A
61. A
62. E
63. C

Section II

64. A
65. C
66. A
67. D
68. E
69. D
70. C
71. A
72. B
73. C
74. B
75. B
76. B
77. D
78. A
79. E
80. B
81. D
82. B
83. A
84. D
85. A
86. A
87. D
88. D
89. E
90. C
91. C
92. D
93. D
94. E
95. D
96. C
97. B
98. E
99. C
100. E
101. D
102. A
103. D
104. B
105. D
106. C
107. D
108. C
109. A
110. C
111. D
112. D
113. B
114. D
115. B
116. E
117. B
118. D
119. B
120. A
121. A
122. D
123. D
124. C
125. E

SCORING CHART—SAMPLE EXAMINATION 3

After you have scored your Sample Examination 3, enter the results in the chart below; then transfer your Raw Score to the Progress Chart on page 14.

Total Test	Number Right	Number Wrong	Number Omitted	Raw Score
Section I: 63				
Section II: 62				
Total: 125				

ANSWER EXPLANATIONS—SAMPLE EXAMINATION 3

Section I

1. A. The world's population is approximately 5 billion; the population of the U.S. is nearly 245 million. The proportion of the world's population living in the United States is 5%.
2. D. In McCulloch *v.* Maryland (1819) the Supreme Court decided that Congress had the power to create a national bank even though the power is not specifically granted to Congress in the Constitution. Said John Marshall, Chief Justice: "Let the end be within the scope of the Constitution . . . all means which are appropriate are constitutional."
3. D. The Taft-Hartley Act (1947) sought to limit the growing power of organized labor. Among other provisions it outlawed the "closed shop" and restricted the union shop. In its general tone and provisions, the Act indicated a determination by Congress to regulate labor unions. The Act was passed over President Truman's veto.
4. A. In a closed shop contract a new employee must belong to the union in order to be hired. A union shop is one in which a recognized union is the bargaining agent but employees are free to join or not. An open shop has no recognized union. A "yellow dog contract, " now outlawed, in one in which an employee agrees not to join a union as a condition of being hired.
5. D. Between World War I and World War II sampling theories based on probability began to be used in opinion polls. The result of each such poll is released with an accompanying probability of error either way, depending on the percentage of the sample relative to the total population studied.
6. D. For the Marxist a "proletarian, " or member of the working class, was nothing but a wage slave. The workers (non-owners) in industry and agriculture were, according to Marx, ineluctably bound to their labor and beholden to their capitalist-employer.
7. D. Economic value is created in each of the examples. Steel has greater economic value than iron before it is processed. When corn is moved from farm to mill its greater economic value is due to place. When strawberries are available in winter, the greater economic value is one of time.
8. C. Esteem means high regard. The street cleaner (but not the corporation president, lawyer, or janitor) would be held in high regard by his colleagues and others. Prestige means status in the community. The occupation "street cleaner" has low status generally. The good doctor would enjoy both prestige and esteem.
9. C. Unlike civilized humans, apes and other primates, in their social organization, do not exhibit a high degree of specialized work. They do, however, exhibit the other four characteristics here described.
10. D. The depression which hit Germany with 6 million unemployed between 1928 and 1932 caused wide discontent in the middle class. Both the National Socialists (Nazis) and the Communists gained following. In 1928 in the Reichstag the Nazis went from 12 seats to 107, the Communists from 54 to 77. This was at the expense of the center parties of the middle class.
11. E. Airlines have shown phenomenal growth since World War II. Revenue rose as follows: 1945, $215 million; 1950, $558 million; 1960, $2.1 billion; 1970, $7.1 billion. Railroads went from $9 billion in 1945 to $12 billion in 1970. Steel has had an even poorer growth rate. Cigarettes too have tailed behind airline growth.
12. D. The Persian invasion of the Green peninsula in the 5th century B.C. is memorialized by the famous Battle of Marathon 490 B.C. There a Persian army of 15,000 sent by Darius was defeated by the Athenians led by Miltiades. News of the victory at Marathon was carried more than 26 miles to Athens by the runner Pheidippides who fell dead after delivering the message.

13. B. The Progressive Movement of the early 20th century advocated the end of corporate privileges in government and the regulation or destruction of trusts. Such books as Ida M. Tarbell's *History of the Standard Oil Company* (1903), Thomas R. Lawson's *Frenzied Finance* (1902) and Gustavus Meyers' *History of the Great American Fortunes* (1910) laid the groundwork for the Progressive program.

14. E. Canada, a land of 3,850,000 square miles has a population of 25 million people, 80% of whom live within eighty miles of her southern border. Canada is the world's second largest country, next to the U.S.S.R. Canada's Northwest Territories, encompassing one-third of her land area, are virtually unsettled.

15. C. Prior to the 16th century, merchants of Genoa and Venice had control of trade with the East by overland routes. In the 16th and 17th centuries, following the discoveries and voyages of Spanish, Portuguese, Dutch, English, and French navigators, sea routes to Asia and Africa diverted this trade from the Italian cities.

16. B. Henry VIII, King of England (1509–1547) had no intention of questioning religious doctrines of the Church. But the refusal of the Pope to annul his marriage led to a controversy which culminated in the 1534 Act of Supremacy declaring the English king to be "Protector and Only Supreme Head of the Church and Clergy of England."

17. B. The Meiji era (1868–1912), when a new emperor (Mutsuhito) ruled, was the great era of Westernization. It was marked by all of the four items here mentioned except gifts of private philanthropists.

18. A. Virgin grazing land is not part of our capital assets because no capital value can be attributed to them until they enter the economy in a productive capacity. The other four choices are capital assets according to this criterion.

19. A. By controlling the amount of lending that member banks can do, the Federal Reserve Board may increase or decrease the money supply and thereby the availability of credit. A tightening of the reins will cause interest rates to rise. A loosening has the reverse effect.

20. A. Adam Smith (1723–1790), Scottish economist, believed that the economic welfare of a nation was best served by a policy of "laissez-faire"; i.e. no government restrictions on the operation of the market. Tariff restrictions, he believed, decreased a nation's productivity because they interfered with the free flow of economic goods.

21. C. The statement makes the point that "the sentiments prove more effective if they are not scientifically understood by the average person." Presumably they would be less effective if understood. If attachment to religion be considered a sentiment, then it probably is weaker if exposed to scientific investigation.

22. C. Sigmund Freud (1856–1939) showed that the events of childhood have lasting effects upon the individual's capacity to adapt to changing circumstances and to learn new ways.

23. B. The term "clerk" in this quotation symbolizes the authority of forms and records in centralized bureaucracy. Form becomes more important than substance and the creative members of society must defer to the keeper of the records.

24. B. Max Weber (1864–1920), German sociologist, called bureaucracy "man's greatest social invention." Essential bureaucratic characteristics, he said, included carefully defined positions or offices, a hierarchical order, technical or professional qualifications, rules and regulations, and security of tenure.

25. E. In the case of the American family, the "in-laws" of the husband are usually treated equally with the wife's "in-laws" and given as little authority.

26. A. In his famous work, *The Prince*, Niccolo Machiavelli (1469–1527), Italian statesman, counsels the young Florentine on the principles of effective government. He cynically advises the ruler to be circumspect rather than good and to do whatever is necessary to attain and retain power.

27. C. In "An Appeal to the Ruling Class of German Nationality" Martin Luther (1483–1546), professor at the University of Wittenberg, declared that the clergy were no different from the laity except in their work. He urged people to find Christian truths in the Bible for themselves.

28. A. The Congress of Vienna (1814–1815) met in September 1814. Napoleon had been defeated and exiled to the island of Elba. The Bourbon monarchy in the person of King Louis XVIII had been restored in France. Now a great congress assembled in Vienna signalizing the end of the Napoleonic Era.

29. B. Herodotus (484 B.C.–425 B.C.), Greek historian, wrote his *History* (449 B.C.) giving a detailed account of the Graeco-Persian War 490 B.C.–479 B.C. ending in victory for the Greeks.

30. A. In traditional Hindu society, the highest of the major castes were the Brahmans, or priests. The Kshatriyas were the military, the Vaisyas the farmers and merchants, the Sudras the laborers. The Gurkas (not a caste) were an ethnic group from Nepal, many of whom served in the British colonial army.

31. E. Energy derived from falling water (hydroelectric) makes up less than 4% of all U.S. energy sources. Major energy sources are coal 32%, natural gas 31%, and crude oil 29%. Nuclear and geothermal make up less than 4%.

32. C. The Louisiana Territory (II) was acquired from France in 1803 for approximately $15 million. The Gadsden Purchase (VII) was secured in 1853 from Mexico for $10 million. (Note that Florida [III] was ceded by Spain in 1819, with the U.S. assuming $5 million in debts owed by Spain to U.S. citizens.)

33. A. The original states and territories of the United States (I) had their borders confirmed by the Treaty of Paris (1783) following the Revolution. The 49th parallel was set as the border of the Oregon Territory (IV) by the Treaty of 1846 with Great Britain.

34. E. The Republic of Texas, which had seceded from Mexico in 1836, was annexed by the U.S. in 1845.

35. D. By the Treaty of Guadalupe Hidalgo following the Mexican War (1848), the United States acquired the New Mexico Territory and California.

36. B. By 1900, Burma, along with neighboring India, was a British colony. Indonesia at that time was the Dutch East Indies. The United States had acquired the Philippine Islands as a result of the War with Spain (1898). Japan had managed to maintain its independence, Siam (now Thailand) benefitted from being regarded as a sovereign, neutral "buffer state" between British Burma and French Indo-China.

37. A. The Rhine River (in today's West Germany) served as one of the boundaries of the Roman Empire for much of its history. It separated the states under Roman control from the Germanic tribes to the East. Ultimately, the Empire collapsed as a result of invasions from the East.

38. C. The early Sumerian civilization c. 3500 B.C. flourished in the valley of the Tigris and Euphrates Rivers. By 2500 B.C. the Mesopotamian civilization was well into the bronze age when Europe was only entering the stone age. Mesopotamia means between the rivers (Tigris and Euphrates).

39. C. During the 19th and early 20th century the Liberal Party in Great Britain alternated with the Conservative Party in governing the country. A new party, the Labour Party, came into being in the early 20th century and replaced the Liberal Party after World War I as one of Britain's two major parties.

40. D. The reign of James I of England (1603–1625) came first. Louis XIV of France (1643–1715), the Seven Years War (1756–1763), the American Revolution (1776–1783) and the French Revolution (1789) followed in that order.

41. E. Each of these periods in U.S. history, 1837–40, 1873–77, 1893–98, and 1930–33 were periods of financial panics and economic collapse. Mass unemployment accompanied by a sharp decline in consumer buying helped cause deflation in each of these periods.

42. D. Louis Pasteur (1822–1895), French bacteriologist, developed the germ theory of disease. Pasteurization of milk, the method of killing harmful microorganisms, a result of Pasteur's research has saved countless lives. He also produced a successful vaccine against the dread disease rabies (hydrophobia).

43. D. The Federal Reserve System was established by Act of Congress in 1913. The Sherman Anti-trust Act was passed in 1890. The Sioux Indians were subdued in 1891. The Supreme Court first used the Fourteenth Amendment to protect corporations in the Slaughterhouse Cases of 1873. The 45th state, Utah, was admitted in 1896.

44. B. The Kulaks in Russia were well-to-do peasants (farmers) who opposed the collectivization of agriculture. During the first Five-Year Plan (1928–32) the Kulaks were liquidated. Hundreds of thousands of Kulaks and their families were killed. Others were sent to labor camps in Siberia.

45. D. Plato (428 B.C.–348 B.C.), Greek philosopher, wrote "dialogues." In *The Republic* he considers the problem of government and concludes that the best form of government is an oligarchy ruled by philosopher-kinds.

46. C. Sun Yat-sen (1866–1925), Chinese hero, led a revolution against the corrupt Ch'ing dynasty. Under his leadership the first Chinese Republic was proclaimed in 1911.

47. C. The Moslem Moors of North Africa entered Spain in the 8th century A.D. and controlled the country until they were evicted by the Christians in 1492. A high degree of civilization including literature, science, and the arts, flourished in Spain when the rest of Europe was in the Dark Ages.

48. A. In 1215, a group of English lords and high churchmen joined by representatives of the City of London, forced King John to sign the Magna Carta. In it he confirmed and guaranteed their historic liberties.

49. C. Membership in a caste system is fixed for life and is hereditary. Caste is closely tied to occupation. Occupational shifts, when tolerated, are between callings at the same level of "ritual purity" or "impurity."

50. C. Primogeniture, the exclusive right of inheritance belonging to the eldest son, was a characteristic of feudal societies. It persisted in England and parts of the American colonies and was abolished in the United States after independence was gained.

51. D. Party discipline is greatest in the British House of Commons. Under the parliamentary system, the majority party must prevail on every important measure that comes before the House of Commons. If the majority (party in power) loses a vote on a major bill, the government falls, and a new election must be held. Hence party discipline is paramount.

52. C. Franklin D. Roosevelt is the only one who was elected president more than twice. He was elected four times—1932, 1936, 1940, and 1944. The 22nd amendment to the Constitution, adopted in 1951, provides that "No person shall be elected to the office of the President more than twice . . ."

53. E. Henry Clay (1777–1852), a leader of the Whig party, was a candidate for President in 1824, 1832, and 1844. Martin Van Buren was elected President in 1836. He ran for President unsuccessfully in 1840 and 1848. Daniel Webster never secured the nomination for President. John C. Fremont ran unsuccessfully in 1856 as the first presidential nominee of the newly organized Republican Party. John Quincy Adams was elected President by the House of Representatives in 1824 but was defeated by Jackson in 1828.

54. D. If marginal revenue equals price at all levels of production a firm is operating under pure competition. In a monopolistic situation, marginal revenue exceeds price because the seller is able to bring about an artificial (contrived) scarcity of the product.

55. D. In the day-to-day life of most societies, a pervasive feature is cooperation. There is rarely complete consensus. We tend to notice conflict and competition which, of course, exist. But voluntary compliance with the laws, customs and traditions, i.e., cooperation pervades our daily life.

56. A. The policy of the Soviet Union, in the decade prior to 1939, was uncompromising opposition to fascism. Hence the world noted a turnabout in Soviet foreign policy when Stalin negotiated a non-agression pact with Hitler in 1939.

57. A. The guild system of industry and business prevailed in Europe during the Middle Ages. The guild comprised a group of members of the same craft (jewelers, tanners, weavers, etc.). By controlling entry into the craft or business, the guilds discouraged competition.

58. C. The name *Utopia*, which has become synonymous with an ideal or visionary society is the title of a book written by Sir Thomas More (1478–1535). In More's *Utopia* there was no private property and no poverty.

59. A. The Constitution (Article I, Section 3, clause 4) reads as follows: The Vice-President of the United States shall be president of the Senate . . ." This is the only function of the Vice-President of the U.S. specified in the Constitution other than succeeding to the Presidency upon removal, death, resignation, or disability of the President.

60. A. The Constitution in Article 2, Section 2, Clause 1 specifies: "The President of the United States shall be Commander in Chief of the Army and Navy of the United States . . . " The Founders were trying to make sure that there would be civilian control of military forces. The above clause made possible President Truman's relieving General MacArthur of command of U.S. troops in Korea in 1951 in a dispute over our China policy.

61. A. The Constitution (Article 3, Section 1) states: "The judges, both of the Supreme and inferior courts, shall hold their offices during good behavior . . . " This lifetime tenure means that the justices may make independent decisions without regard to politics, personal relations or other possible prejudicial factors.

62. E. The power to grant charters to business corporations is impliedly granted to the state government by the 10th amendment. This amendment reads: "The powers not delegated to the United States by the Constitution, nor prohibited by it to the states, are reserved to the states respectively or to the people."

63. C. The Eugenic Protection Law of 1948 in Japan legalized and subsidized abortions and birth control measures including sterilization of women. A phenomenal decline in birth rate occurred between 1947 and 1960—from 33.6 per thousand population to 17.2.

Section II

64. A. All members of the President's cabinet are appointed by the President with the consent of the Senate but can be dismissed by the President alone. The Tenure of Office Act (1867), by which the radicals in Congress attempted to prevent President Johnson from dismissing his Secretary of War was repealed in 1887 during the administration of President Cleveland.

65. C. Amendment 12 (adopted in 1804) provides; "If no person have a majority [in the electoral college], then from the persons having the highest numbers not exceeding three on the list of those voted for as President, the House of Representatives shall choose, by ballot, the President. But in choosing the President, the votes shall be taken by states, the representation from each state having one vote.

66. A. The judicial concept of "prior restraint" is most important in relation to freedom of the press. This is illustrated by the case of the Pentagon Papers, a highly classified 3,000-page report on the Vietnam War. A Federal judge ordered the New York Times to desist from publishing any more of the report (prior restraint). The Supreme Court upheld the right of the New York Times and the Washington Post to continue publication.

67. D. Each of these procedures—raising taxes, selling government bonds to individuals, and cutting government spending would cut down on consumer purchases and thus have the effect of a down pressure on prices.

68. E. Primary groups, as defined in sociology, are groups having an intimate, generally long-lasting relationship. The family is a prime example. Other examples might include close friends or even a closely knit neighborhood. A workplace association does not constitute a primary group.

69. D. It is not really surprising to find, as sociologists have, that like tends to marry like. People associate with those of their class and of their economic and professional levels. Association is also affected by religion, race, and ethnic group.

70. C. An ascribed status is different from an achieved status. An ascribed status results from a person's age, sex, or color—something over which he has no control. A first grade student is an ascribed status. The other examples in this question illustrate achieved status.

71. A. Henry George (1839–1897), American economist and reformer, wrote *Progress and Poverty* (1879). He believed that land speculation was the cause of the inequality and poverty he saw everywhere. He argued that the unearned increment resulting from the increase in land value should be taken by the government. This "single-tax" would make for social justice.

72. B. Causes for the large increase in the U.S. urban population in the 1920s include: falling farm prices, a construction boom in the cities, large scale introduction of machinery in agriculture, and an urban boom in industry. Federal subsidies to farmers were not only not cut back but were extended in several acts, such as the 1922 Capper-Volstead Act.

73. C. There are five permanent members on the Security Council of the U.N.—China, France, United Kingdom, the United States and U.S.S.R. All five must approve any (except purely procedural) acts before they can be implemented. Thus any one of the five has a veto power in this most important of all UN bodies.

74. B. Without the support of the majority in the House of Commons the British prime minister and cabinet cannot govern. Hence if they lose the support of the majority in the Commons on an important bill, they must call for a new election.

75. B. During a serious economic depression unemployment increases, prices fall (no buyers), investment declines (no confidence). Then borrowing declines. When borrowing declines, there is less of a demand for money and interest rates fall.

76. B. The dates are as follows: Hammurabi 1950 B.C.; Alexander the Great 356 B.C.–323 B.C.; Hannibal 247 B.C.–182 B.C.; Julius Caesar 102 B.C. –44 B.C.; Marcus Aurelius 121–180 A.D.

77. D. Annual demographic growth rates for the five areas expressed in percentage figures are as follows: Europe, 0.4; USSR, 0.9; North America 1.1; South American, 2.4; and Australia 1.4

78. A. In his *Protestant Ethic and the Spirit of Capitalism*, Max Weber (1864–1920), German sociologist, identified the rise of capitalism with the strict self denial that characterizes Calvinism.

79. E. An ascribed status, something over which the individual has no control, is illustrated by age, sex, or race. Grades in college, on the other hand, are examples of achieved status.

80. B. Christianity, Islam, and Buddhism have their adherents diffused in many countries of the world. Shinto is a "cultural religion" closely tied to respect for nature and to Japanese nationhood. Over 99% of its practitioners live in Japan. Hinduism, the ancient religion of India, has converted few outside South Asia. The substantial majority of Hindus live in India.

81. D. All of the above were factors keeping unhappy marriages together in the past. The relaxation of moral and religious conviction, the decline in social control formerly exercised by the extended family and neighborhood, and the economic emancipation of women all contribute to the rapid increase in the divorce ratio.

82. B. Of the fifty-five delegates to the American Constitutional Convention of 1787, over half were lawyers. The remainder consisted of well-to-do planters like Washington, prominent merchants like Robert Morris of Pennsylvania, and a few physicians and college professors.

83. A. A severe famine in 1920 in the Soviet Union and a mutiny in the Navy caused Lenin to introduce a New Economic Policy (NEP) in 1921. Private trading for profit was allowed and peasants were permitted to sell farm products for private income.

84. D. The samurai were members of an aristocratic warrior class in Japan. Each wore a long and short sword at his side. This class, established at the beginning of the Tokugawa regime in 1600 was abolished by the new Meiji regime in 1868.

85. A. John Maynard Keynes (1883–1946), English economist, wrote *The General Theory of Employment, Interest, and Money*. He showed the relationship of income to saving and coined the phrase "propensity to consume" to describe the point in income where saving begins.

86. A. Auguste Comte (1798–1857), French philosopher, wrote *Course of Positive Philosophy* (1842) in which he asserted that the mental evolution of the race consisted of three stages: the theological, the metaphysical, and the positive or scientific.

87. D. Mercantilism of the 17th and 18th centuries was a doctrine underlying colonialism. The mother country would import raw material from the colonies and export manufacturers to them. The balance, favoring the imperialist nation, would come to it in the form of gold and silver.

88. D. The Northwest Ordinance of 1787 was adopted by the Congress of the Confederation as a plan of government of the then Northwest Territory. It provided for the admission of 3 to 5 new states (ultimately, Ohio, Indiana, Illinois, Michigan, and Wisconsin), prohibited slavery, and proposed encouragement of public education.

89. E. The germ of the first four statements is contained in the Declaration of Independence. The fifth statement, however, could be used to justify oppression by the state. This danger was allayed by the adoption of the Bill of Rights (1791) which Jefferson strongly supported.

90. D. Andrew Johnson (1808–1875) became president on the death of Lincoln, April 15, 1865. Johnson, a Tennessee Democrat, attempted to carry out Lincoln's more liberal reconstruction policy in defiance of Congress. The House of Representatives impeached him, but the Senate, by 1 vote (May 1868), failed to remove him from office.

91. C. During World War II, the British promised independence (dominion status) to India. The Moslem League demanded separation of predominantly Moslem Pakistan from the rest of India which was chiefly Hindu. In 1947, Pakistan was made a separate dominion. A religious war broke out between Moslems and Hindus in which 1,000,000 people died.

92. D. At dawn on the morning of July 16, 1945, the first atomic bomb was detonated in the desert at Los Alamos, New Mexico. Through their dark glasses, the scientists and military men saw a blinding flash, a fireball, and then "the mushroom" that reached 41,000 feet through the clouds.

93. C. Thorstein Veblen (1857–1929), American economist, emphasized the pecuniary motives of society. In his *Theory of the Leisure Class* (1899), he used the term "conspicuous consumption" to describe the motivating factor behind much economic activity.

94. E. Lincoln met the most serious threat against the sovereignty of the federal government in the secession of the southern states. Jackson contended with the South Carolina Ordinance of Nullification of the Tariff of 1832. Eisenhower confronted the refusal of the southern states to abide by the Supreme Court Decision for the school desegregation in Brown v. Board of Education (1954) and Kennedy faced opposition to his Civil Rights program from southern states.

95. D. During the period between 1937 and 1965 the Supreme Court took an activist position. It interpreted the Fourteenth Amendment to mean that the guarantees of the Bill of Rights applied to the states. It struck down some attempts of the Un-American Activities Committee of Congress to prosecute alleged communists.

96. C. Prussia, under the guidance of premier Otto von Bismarck took the lead in German unification. In a war against Denmark (1864) Prussia took Schleswig and Hollstein. Then in the Austro-Prussian War (1866) Austria was eliminated as a rival. Finally in the Franco-Prussian War (1870–71) Prussia took Alsace and Lorraine and proclaimed the new German Empire.

97. B. In *The Higher Learning in America* (1918) Thorstein Veblen described American education as "a merchantable commodity to be produced on a piece-rate plan, rated, bought and sold by standard units, measured, counted and reduced to staple equivalence by impersonal, mechanical tests. " This comes close to describing the price system and double-entry bookkeeping.

98. E. Max Weber (1864–1920) described the characteristics of bureaucracy in his *Essays in Sociology*. They encompassed an authoritarian structure, specialization, standardization and formal rules. He found humane policies eminently missing.

99. C. The most important source of revenue for local governments is the general property tax. In 1977, for example, all local taxes in the U.S. amounted to $74.8 billion of which $60.3 or 80.6% consisted of property taxes.

100. E. The statements in A, B, and C are true. In the U.S., for example, a court proceeding is necessary for divorce or annulment. Common law marriage is recognized. For some purposes, man and wife become one entity in law.

101. D. Clan lines have never been firm in the U.S. but in the 20th century they have become even more blurred by the mass media, ease of geographic mobility, and dilution of racial, religious and ethnic homogeneity.

102. A. In the Spanish colonies, the mestizos were people of Spanish and Indian mixture. The word "mestizo" in Spanish means mixed.

103. D. The term "life chances" refers to the likelihood that given events will happen to a person. In mathematical terms an event will be realized with relative frequency corresponding to its probability.

104. B. The Constitution (Article 2 Section 1 Clause 2) states: Each state shall appoint, in such manner as the legislature thereof may direct, a number of electors, equal to the whole number of Senators and Representatives, to which the state may be entitled in the Congress.

105. D. Most Negroes, Catholics, and Jews have voted Democratic in the majority of American presidential elections since 1932. Voting pattern of ethnic and religious groups is determined by comparing vote tallies in specific areas with the ethnic and religious groups that predominate as residents in those areas. More recently exit polls have also been used.

106. C. The Federal Reserve System of banking was created by an Act of Congress in 1913. There are 12 Federal Reserve Banks, one in a major city in each part of the country. A Federal Reserve Board, whose members are appointed by the President of the U.S., exercises overall control over the banking system.

107. D. Hannibal commanded the Carthaginian (North African) forces in the Wars against Rome in the 3rd century B.C. He crossed into Spain from Africa and used his bases in Spain to lead a powerful army, with elephants to transport supplies and armaments, across the Alps into Italy.

108. C. The family as an institution is a cultural universal; that is, it is found in all cultures. However, great differences exist with respect to the family among cultures. In the U.S., especially in the traditional middle class family, the kinship group consists of parents and children, whereas in many primitive societies, there is a much more inclusive kinship group.

109. A. Boys in American public high schools admire and give more recognition to athletic ability than they do to academic or other extra curricular excellence. The traditional male role is reinforced by the support of school authorities who provide scholarship, pep rallies, school letters and honoraria for athletes.

110. C. Karl Marx (1818–1883), German social philosopher and economist, maintained that labor received in wages only a portion of what it produced. The excess he described as surplus value. Surplus population would serve to exacerbate this inequity by forcing wages down to bare subsistence according to the law of supply and demand.

111. D. In the 1920's, U.S. immigration laws introduce a quota system. The Act of 1921 limited immigration from any country to 3 percent of that country's nationals residing in the U.S. in 1910; the 1924 act, to 2 percent in 1890.

The act of 1929 shifted the base to 1920 but limited total immigration to 150,000 in any one year.

112. D. This a direct quotation from the Declaration of Independence as written by Thomas Jefferson in June 1776 and approved by the Second Continental Congress, meeting in Philadelphia, July 4.

113. B. Otto von Bismarck (1815–1898) premier of Prussia, was the father of German unification. Count Camillo di Cavour, premier of Sardinia, was the father of Italian unification.

114. D. In 962 A.D. the Saxon (German) Otto I was crowned Holy Roman Emperor by Pope John XII. The Empire was not finally dissolved until 1806 when Napoleon conquered most of Europe.

115. B. There are some 3000 counties (called parishes in Louisiana) in the 50 states. They continue to perform governmental services (legal and educational). However, they have become less important during the past fifty years as population and economic changes have concentrated power in metropolitan areas and in state capitals.

116. E. Austria, farthest from the Soviet Union of the five countries specified, is the only one that did not lose land to the USSR because of World War II. Austria became an independent republic July 22, 1955 by agreement with Britain, France, the United States and the USSR.

117. B. The consumer price index, published monthly by the Bureau of Labor Statistics (BLS), reports the changes in prices paid by a worker's family. Thus, if the index goes up 6.2% over a year and the workers wages go up only 5%, he or she has taken a pay cut in absolute terms. If wages go up faster than the index, the reverse is true.

118. D. Charles Darwin (1809–1882) set forth the theory of evolution in his seminal *On the Origin of Species* (1859). One aspect of evolution is "the survival of the fittest." This is the basis for the statement about the fast deer surviving while the slow deer cease to exist.

119. B. The creative potential of personality, often called personality assessment, may be determined through the use of various techniques and tests over a period of days. This is a doctrine of situational psychology resulting from studies of H. Shartshorne and M. A. May in the late 1920's.

120. A. In the Opium War of 1839–1842, Britain went to war because China attempted to stop British imports of opium from India into China. China was defeated, forced to cede Hong Kong to Britain and open Shanghai, Canton, and other cities, called "treaty ports," to European nations.

121. A. The Dutch colony of New Netherland, extending from New Amsterdam (New York) along the Hudson River to and beyond Albany, and their colony on the Delaware River, were a threat to the English. The latter sent a fleet in 1664 and forced the Dutch to give up their holdings to the British.

122. D. Exogymous practice, marriage outside of a specific group as required by tradition or law, was taboo in feudal society. Nobility married only nobility, commoners only commoners, and clergy were celibate. Endogamy means marriage within a specific group.

123. D. Military expenditures put millions to work during World War II. From 1939 to 1945 the government spent $300 billion to fight the war. In 1940 four million Americans were looking for work (unemployed), while 50,000,000 were at work. By 1945 the number of employed had risen to 64,000,000.

124. C. The figures in Table X apply only to items A (deflation) and C (inflation). The price index rose 14 points between 1939 and 1942 indicating a 14% inflation, since the increase is measured from a base of 100.

125. E. The increase at the start of World War I was about one-fourth of that at the start of World War II. At the end of the Civil War the nation was prostrate and economic recovery was slow. At the high point in the 20s, the output was little more than it had been in World War I and in the Kennedy year of 1963 it was not even that high. The four year increase in World War II is unique in American history.